Poetry
Criticism

Guide to Gale Literary Criticism Series

For criticism on	Consult these Gale series
Authors now living or who died after December 31, 1959	*CONTEMPORARY LITERARY CRITICISM (CLC)*
Authors who died between 1900 and 1959	*TWENTIETH-CENTURY LITERARY CRITICISM (TCLC)*
Authors who died between 1800 and 1899	*NINETEENTH-CENTURY LITERATURE CRITICISM (NCLC)*
Authors who died between 1400 and 1799	*LITERATURE CRITICISM FROM 1400 TO 1800 (LC)* *SHAKESPEAREAN CRITICISM (SC)*
Authors who died before 1400	*CLASSICAL AND MEDIEVAL LITERATURE CRITICISM (CMLC)*
Authors of books for children and young adults	*CHILDREN'S LITERATURE REVIEW (CLR)*
Dramatists	*DRAMA CRITICISM (DC)*
Poets	*POETRY CRITICISM (PC)*
Short story writers	*SHORT STORY CRITICISM (SSC)*
Black writers of the past two hundred years	*BLACK LITERATURE CRITICISM (BLC)*
Hispanic writers of the late nineteenth and twentieth centuries	*HISPANIC LITERATURE CRITICISM (HLC)*
Native North American writers and orators of the eighteenth, nineteenth, and twentieth centuries	*NATIVE NORTH AMERICAN LITERATURE (NNAL)*
Major authors from the Renaissance to the present	*WORLD LITERATURE CRITICISM, 1500 TO THE PRESENT (WLC)*

ISSN 1052-4851

Poetry Criticism

Excerpts from Criticism of the Works of the Most Significant and Widely Studied Poets of World Literature

VOLUME 23

Carol T. Gaffke
Anna J. Sheets
Laura A. Wisner-Broyles
Editors

GALE

DETROIT • LONDON

STAFF

Laura A. Wisner-Broyles, *Editor*

Anna Sheets Nesbitt, Lawrence J. Trudeau, *Associate Editors*

Lynn U. Koch, Susan Salas, Debra A. Wells, *Assistant Editors*

Kimberly F. Smilay, *Permissions Specialist*
Sarah Chesney, *Permissions Associate*
Stephen Cusack, Sandra K. Gore, Kelly Quin, *Permissions Assistants*

Victoria B. Cariappa, *Research Manager*
Michele P. LaMeau, *Research Specialist*
Julie C. Daniel, Tamara C. Nott, Tracie A. Richardson,
Cheryl L. Warnock, *Research Associates*

Mary Beth Trimper, *Production Director*
Carolyn A. Fischer, *Production Assistant*

C. J. Jonik, *Desktop Publisher*
Randy Bassett, *Image Database Supervisor*
Michael Ansari, Robert Duncan, *Scanner Operator*
Pamela Reed, *Photography Coordinator*

Library of Congress Catalog Card Number 91-118494
ISBN 0-7876-2014-9
ISSN 1052-4851

Printed in the United States of America

10 9 8 7 6 5 4 3 2 1

Contents

Preface

A Comprehensive Information Source on World Poetry

Poetry Criticism (PC) provides substantial critical excerpts and biographical information on poets throughout the world who are most frequently studied in high school and undergraduate college courses. Each *PC* entry is supplemented by biographical and bibliographical material to help guide the user to a fuller understanding of the genre and its creators. Although major poets and literary movements are covered in such Gale Literary Criticism Series as *Contemporary Literary Criticism (CLC)*, *Twentieth-Century Literary Criticism (TCLC)*, *Nineteenth-Century Literature Criticism (NCLC)*, *Literature Criticism from 1400 to 1800 (LC)*, and *Classical and Medieval Literature Criticism (CMLC)*, *PC* offers more focused attention on poetry than is possible in the broader, survey-oriented entries on writers in these Gale series. Students, teachers, librarians, and researchers will find that the generous excerpts and supplementary material provided by *PC* supply them with the vital information needed to write a term paper on poetic technique, to examine a poet's most prominent themes, or to lead a poetry discussion group.

Coverage

In order to reflect the influence of tradition as well as innovation, poets of various nationalities, eras, and movements are represented in every volume of *PC*. Each author entry presents a historical survey of the critical response to that author's work; the length of an entry reflects the amount of critical attention that the author has received from critics writing in English and from foreign critics in translation. Since many poets have inspired a prodigious amount of critical explication, *PC* is necessarily selective, and the editors have chosen the most significant published criticism to aid readers and students in their research. In order to provide these important critical pieces, the editors will sometimes reprint essays that have appeared in previous volumes of Gale's Literary Criticism Series. Such duplication, however, never exceeds fifteen percent of a *PC* volume.

Organization

Each *PC* author entry consists of the following components:

- **Author Heading:** the name under which the author wrote appears at the beginning of the entry, followed by birth and death dates. If the author wrote consistently under a pseudonym, the pseudonym will be listed in the author heading and his or her legal name given in parentheses in the lines immediately preceding the Introduction. Uncertainty as to birth or death dates is indicated by question marks.

- **Introduction:** a biographical and critical essay introduces readers to the author and the critical discussions surrounding his or her work.

- **Author Portrait:** a photograph or illustration of the author is included when available.

- **Principal Works:** the author's most important works are identified in a list ordered chronologically by first publication dates. The first section comprises poetry collections and book-length poems. The second section gives information on other major works by the author. For foreign authors, original foreign-language publication information is provided, as well as the best and most complete English-language editions of their works.

- **Criticism:** critical excerpts chronologically arranged in each author entry provide perspective on changes in critical evaluation over the years. All individual titles of poems and poetry collections by the author featured in the entry are printed in boldface type to enable a reader to ascertain without difficulty the works under discussion. For purposes of easy identification, the critic's name and the publication date of the essay are given at the beginning of each piece of criticism. Unsigned criticism is preceded by the title of the journal in which it originally appeared. Publication information (such as publisher names and book prices) and parenthetical numerical references (such as footnotes or page and line references to specific editions of a work) have been deleted at the editor's discretion to enable smoother reading of the text.

- **Explanatory Notes:** introductory comments preface each critical excerpt, providing several types of useful information, including: the reputation of a critic, the importance of a work of criticism, and the specific type of criticism (biographical, psychoanalytic, historical, etc.).

- **Author Commentary:** insightful comments from the authors themselves and excerpts from author interviews are included when available.

- **Bibliographical Citations:** information preceding each piece of criticism guides the interested reader to the original essay or book.

- **Further Reading:** bibliographic references accompanied by descriptive notes at the end of each entry suggest additional materials for study of the author. Boxed material following the Further Reading provides references to other biographical and critical series published by Gale.

Other Features

- **Cumulative Author Index:** comprises all authors who have appeared in Gale's Literary Criticism Series, along with cross-references to such Gale biographical series as *Contemporary Authors* and *Dictionary of Literary Biography*. This cumulated index enables the user to locate an author within the various series.

- **Cumulative Nationality Index:** includes all authors featured in *PC,* arranged alphabetically under their respective nationalities.

- **Cumulative Title Index:** lists in alphabetical order all individual poems, book-length poems, and collection titles contained in the *PC* series. Titles of poetry collections and separately published poems are printed in italics, while titles of individual poems are printed in roman type with quotation marks. Each title is followed by the author's name and the volume and page number corresponding to the location of commentary on specific works. English-language translations of original foreign-language titles are cross-referenced to the foreign titles so that all references to discussion of a work are combined in one listing.

Citing *Poetry Criticism*

When writing papers, students who quote directly from any volume in the Literary Criticism Series may use the following general formats to footnote reprinted criticism. The first example pertains to material drawn from periodicals, the second to material reprinted from books:

[1]David Daiches, "W. H. Auden: The Search for a Public," *Poetry* LIV (June 1939), 148-56; excerpted and reprinted in *Poetry Criticism*, Vol. 1, ed. Robyn V. Young (Detroit: Gale Research, 1990), pp. 7-9.

[2]Pamela J. Annas, *A Disturbance in Mirrors: The Poetry of Sylvia Plath* (Greenwood Press, 1988); excerpted and reprinted in *Poetry Criticism*, Vol. 1, ed. Robyn V. Young (Detroit: Gale Research, 1990), pp. 410-14.

Comments Are Welcome

Readers who wish to suggest authors to appear in future volumes, or who have other suggestions, are cordially invited to contact the editors.

Acknowledgments

The editors wish to thank the copyright holders of the excerpted criticism included in this volume and the permissions managers of many book and magazine publishing companies for assisting us in securing reproduction rights. We are also grateful to the staffs of the Detroit Public Library, the Library of Congress, the University of Detroit Mercy Library, Wayne State University Purdy/Kresge Library Complex, and the University of Michigan Libraries for making their resources available to us. Following is a list of the copyright holders who have granted us permission to reproduce material in this volume of *PC*. Every effort has been made to trace copyright, but if omissions have been made, please let us know.

COPYRIGHTED EXCERPTS IN *PC*, VOLUME 23, WERE REPRODUCED FROM THE FOLLOWING PERIODICALS:

John Clare
1793-1864

English poet and prose writer.

INTRODUCTION

For his vivid and exact descriptions of rural life and scenery, Clare is ranked with the foremost English nature poets. Attempts, however, to place him stylistically within the context of the first half of the nineteenth century have led to critical debate. While some commentators define Clare's importance with reference to the tradition of eighteenth-century descriptive verse, others emphasize the Romantic qualities of his poetry. Most recently, attention has been paid to the works of John Clare as unique poetic expressions in their own right.

Biographical Information

Clare grew up in the Northamptonshire village of Helpston, England, where the rustic countryside was to provide him with inspiration for most of his poetry. As the only son of impoverished field laborers, Clare spent his childhood on the farm working to help support his family. Consequently, his formal education was limited to three months a year, first at a small school in his native village and later at a school in nearby Glinton. Clare's poetic talent was nourished by his parents' knowledge of folk ballads as well as by his own reading of the works of the eighteenth-century poet James Thomson, whose long poem, *The Seasons,* inspired Clare to write verse. At age fourteen, Clare's formal education ended when financial hardship obliged him to obtain permanent employment outside his family. In 1809, while working at the Blue Bell Inn in Helpston, Clare fell in love with Mary Joyce, the daughter of a wealthy farmer. Mary's father quickly broke off the relationship because of Clare's inferior social status. Clare rebounded from this disappointment, eventually meeting, marrying, and having children with Martha ("Patty") Turner. However, the memory of his first love never left him, and Mary Joyce became the subject of many of Clare's poems.

In 1818 Clare tried to publish a volume of poems by subscription. Although the scheme proved unsuccessful, it attracted the attention of the influential London publisher John Taylor, who ultimately published Clare's first volume, *Poems Descriptive of Rural Life and Scenery* (1820). Despite this work's enormous popular success, the contemporary literary reaction to *Poems* was largely patronizing. While Clare's peasant background and minute descriptions of nature were favorably compared with those of Robert Burns and Robert Bloomfield, commentators criticized his grammatical inaccuracies and

provincial expressions. By the time Clare published his second volume of poetry, *The Village Minstrel, and Other Poems* (1821), the vogue for rural verse which had been responsible for the great success of *Poems* had diminished, and *The Village Minstrel, and Other Poems,* sold poorly, as did Clare's third work, *The Shepherd's Calendar; with Village Stories, and Other Poems* (1827).

During these years, Clare struggled to support his growing family on a small annuity from his earlier poems, augmented by seasonal gardening and field work. In 1832 under the auspices of a benevolent patron, Clare and his family moved from their small, crowded home in Helpston to a larger cottage in nearby Northborough. Although grateful to his patron for this new home, Clare profoundly missed the village of his childhood. With the failure in 1835 of his fourth volume, *The Rural Muse,* Clare's mental health collapsed. He began to believe that he was the poet Lord Byron or the famous boxer Jack Randall. He also grew convinced that his first love, Mary Joyce, was in fact his wife and that he lived in bigamy with his real wife, Martha Turner. In 1837 he was confined to a private asylum in High Beech. He escaped four years later and returned to Northborough. His physical health improved but his delusions persisted, and in 1841 he was taken to Northampton General County Lunatic Asylum, where he spent the remaining twenty-three years of his life.

Major Works

Clare's popular first publication, *Poems Descriptive of Rural Life and Scenery,* is a nostalgic lament for the open fields and common meadowlands of his boyhood: This common land, which had been used for centuries by peasants and farmers, was "enclosed," or fenced off, by an 1809 Act of Parliament and subsequently available only to those who owned it. His second volume, *The Village Minstrel, and Other Poems,* was similarly inspired by the countryside where he was born and raised. Clare's most famous work is *The Shepherd's Calendar*—a poem which vividly unfolds the months as they are lived and worked in the villages and farms of rural England. "Don Juan" and "Child Harold" were written after his mental collapse in 1835 and are derivative of Lord Byron's poems of the same names. In fact Clare wrote numerous poems during his asylum years, but only after his death did they receive close attention and serious critical scrutiny.

Critical Reception

The history of Clare criticism is marked by controversy and contention. Several key issues dominate the commentary, including: whether Clare's early or late work is his most distinguished; the influence of the Romantic poetic tradition on his work; and whether he was merely a descriptive poet or was also interested in conveying ideas. To add to the confusion, most of the work published in Clare's lifetime was heavily edited to reflect standard grammar and dialect. What is more, Clare's asylum poems—some of which are deemed his most powerful work—elicited little or no attention during his lifetime. Not until the twentieth century, for example, did poems such as "A Vision" and "Invite to Eternity" receive close study. While scholars continue to disagree over the merits of his early and late poetry and the relationship between his works and those of his predecessors and contemporaries, Clare's reputation as a leading nature poet has been firmly established.

PRINCIPAL WORKS

Poetry

Poems Descriptive of Rural Life and Scenery 1820
The Village Minstrel, and Other Poems 1821
The Shepherd's Calendar; with Village Stories, and Other Poems 1827
The Rural Muse 1835
Poems by John Clare 1908
John Clare: Poems Chiefly from Manuscript 1920
Madrigals and Chronicles: Being Newly Found Poems Written by John Clare 1924

The Poems of John Clare 1935
Poems of John Clare's Madness 1949
The Midsummer Cushion 1979
The Later Poems of John Clare, 1837-1864 1984
The Parish 1985
The Early Poems of John Clare, 1804-1822 1989

Other Major Works

Sketches in the Life of John Clare, Written by Himself (autobiography and sketches) 1931
The Letters of John Clare (letters) 1951
The Prose of John Clare (autobiography, journal, and essays) 1951

CRITICISM

Janet M. Todd (essay date 1974)

SOURCE: "'Very copys of nature': John Clare's Descriptive Poetry", in *Philological Quarterly,* Vol. 53, No. 1, January, 1974, pp. 84-99.

[*In the following excerpt, Todd argues that unlike the Romantic poets, who focused on humanity's spiritual response to nature, Clare described the pure or Edenic qualities of nature and the manner in which it falls victim to humanity's cruelty.*]

In the early nineteenth century, there were two main poetic modes of presenting nature. The first was developed from the Georgic poetry of the eighteenth century and provided close, usually visual descriptions of natural things, without any explicit judgment or emotional response by the poet; this type of poetry can be called descriptive. The second mode is a combination of idealized presentations of natural objects and the poet's response to them. His own judgment and emotion not only affect the natural presentation, but also become the partial or main subject of the poem. This sort of poetry, practised often by Wordsworth, Shelley, and Keats, for example, may be called Romantic.

John Clare's most distinctive pre-asylum verse evidences most of the characteristics associated with the descriptive mode. Although inevitably colored to some extent by the poet's emotions, his descriptions clearly exist for their own sake and not for any insight they might provide into the mental states of the poet. If Clare appears at all in the poem, it is as a perceiver and physical guide rather than as a feeling and imaginative creator.

By the time of Clare's second book of poems in 1821, however, and more obviously by his third in 1827, the descriptive poem was past its heyday, and the Romantic mode of presenting nature was clearly dominant. The descriptive poem thus came to seem anachronistic to the reading public; yet Clare, in spite of the growing evidence of its critical defeat, continued in this mode, which helps to explain the sudden loss of public acclaim he experienced between 1820 and 1827.

The change in taste can be clearly seen in the different poetic fates of Keats and Clare, both published by John Taylor at about the same time. Where Keats, after an initial failure, grew tremendously in popularity, Clare's poetic fate was the reverse. In spite of high regard for each other, Keats and Clare seem to have been aware they were writing in essentially different modes. Of Keats, Clare wrote: "He often described Nature as she appeared to his fancies, and not as he would have described her had he witnessed the things he describes." Clare is, furthermore, clearly doubtful about the "mystical" part of Romantic poetry—by which he would seem to mean the intrusion of the poet's subjective states into his verse—elements of which he found in Keats's work and later in Wordsworth's.

Keats, on the other hand, was criticizing Clare from the Romantic standpoint when he told Taylor that, in Clare's poetry, the "Description too much prevailed over the Sentiment." This criticism is based on an essential tenet of Romantic poetry, but would hardly have been a fault in descriptive verse. A passage from Coleridge will serve to illustrate the Romantic belief, although one could just as easily be found in Wordsworth, Hazlitt, or De Quincey:

> Images, however beautiful, though faithfully copied from nature, and as accurately represented in words, do not of themselves characterize the poet. They become proofs of original genius only as far as they are modified by a predominant passion . . . or lastly, when a human and intellectual life is transferred to them from the poet's own spirit. . . .

In this passage, Coleridge ignores the essential strength of the other type of poetry, the descriptive, which makes the reader see, almost by the naming of what is indeed there but was until then unnoticed. In his pre-asylum poetry it is in this ability that Clare is preeminent, as H. F. Cary noted in his letter to the poet: "What you most excel in is the description of such natural objects as you have yourself had the opportunity of observing, and which none before you have noticed, though every one instantly recognises their truth." In addition to enlarging the reader's visual perception, however, Clare manages in the best of his descriptions without losing any of the appearance of factual truthfulness to convey to the attentive reader a unique view of nature and to suggest the human drama that is related to it. It is this capacity to expand descriptive poetry, without losing the close, truthful copying of nature, that I wish to examine in this essay.

For Clare, nature was primarily an aggregate of plants and small animals. This vital nature became, within a dramatic scheme of innocence and the fall, the unequal antagonist of man. Where man was fallen, nature was innocent; it was in addition eternal through its selflessness and regenerative power, beautiful and sensitive to beauty. Having experienced no fall, it was on earth still Edenic. Man on the other hand was mortal and, through materialism and cruelty, frequently insensitive to beauty and thus to Edenic nature. The human fall Clare regarded more as a process than as a single event; starting from the Biblical expulsion from Eden when death entered the

world and man first tilled the soil to live, it was in Clare's youth still incomplete because selected men, including the poet himself, could to some extent experience Eden through reverent communion with Edenic nature. In Clare's later maturity, however, the human degenerative process quickened and man lost his ability to perceive the Eden of nature; thus he was deprived of any possibility of regeneration through communion with prelapsarian nature. Driven from Eden, he eventually lost sight of it completely, and it is this loss that Clare regards as the ultimate fall.

Although, then, the depravity of man seems the background of Clare's early Edenic nature poems where man's potential destructiveness and his contrast with nature's innocence both indicate he has fallen and been separated from nature, the depravity is not complete, for in the poems the poet at least can perceive the harmony and beauty of nature, even if he cannot see the qualities reflected in himself. In the later pre-asylum poems, it is the loss of this Edenic perception by all men, himself included, that Clare most bitterly laments.

The cause of symptom of this perceptual fall in Clare's view was the enclosure movement, which, through the extension of cultivated land, expanded man's dominion over nature. It expressed and developed the cruelty, selfishness, and materialism of man, and it destroyed the beauty and freedom of nature and thus any possibility of man's appreciation of it. Instead of a state of deferential respect between man and nature, the new relationship consisted of prideful human mastery over the enslaved natural world; man thus lost his vision of Edenic nature and firmly shut the gate against his own return to Eden.

The philosophy of nature and man outlined above is explicitly stated in a few assertive poems of the 1820's and 1830's. [There is as yet no complete text of Clare's poetry. I have in this article used two selections: *Selected Poems and Prose of John Clare,* ed. Eric Robinson and Geoffrey Summerfield (Oxford U. Press, 1967), hereafter cited as *SP*; and *The Poems of John Clare,* ed. J. W. Tibble, 2 vols. (London: Dent, 1933), hereafter cited by volume and page. The former text prints Clare's poems without emendation and additional punctuation.] "The Eternity of Nature" (*SP*, p. 109), for example, ascribes to small natural things, here represented by the daisy, Edenic innocence, eternity, and beauty:

> centurys may come
> And pass away into the silent tomb
> And still the child hid in the womb of time
> Shall smile and pluck them
>
> **(SP, p. 109)**

Formerly, the daisy's beauty might have won

> . . . Eve to stoop adown and show
> Her partner Adam in the silky grass
> This little gem that smiled where pleasure was
> And loving Eve from eden followed ill
> And bloomed with sorrow and lives smiling still
> As once in eden under heavens breath

So now on blighted earth and on the lap of death
It smiles for ever

(*SP,* p. 110)

In a later poem, however, the human perception of this natural Eden is fast disappearing:

The fields grow old and common things
The grass the sky the winds a blowing
And spots where still a beauty clings
Are sighing 'going all a going' . . .
The sky hangs oer a broken dream
The brambles dwindled to a bramble

(*SP,* pp. 182-83)

This same philosophy of nature and man is revealed in two groups of descriptive poems concerning birds and small animals. The two groups are separated by a decade, and the reflection of this separation in the changed perception of the speaker-poet expresses powerfully but implicitly the drama of man's perceptual loss.

In the first group Clare deals with birds in great detail; that is, with the sort of observational exactness he had called for in an essay on the painter De Wint. Here he praised those who allow nature to give them her "own imaging" and so make the "very copys of nature," showing the land as "a Paradise." These are in contradistinction to artists who "imagine" and thus exaggerate aspects of nature, and those who "fancy" and thereby change the whole appearance of their subject according to their own manneristic taste. For the most part, the bird poems are single images, realized by mainly visual description. They work much as Clare had described poetry's functioning in an assertive poem, **"Pastoral Poesy"** (II, 49), by causing the reader to respond with joy as he discovers for himself the joy in the visual image presented; poetry works through "images," not words, and gives to man "the dower / Of self-creating joy." In spite of a general impassiveness before nature, however, the speaker in the poems of bird life and lore does suggest a judgment concerning nature's innocence and immortal beauty. A walk through the woods in **"The Nightingales Nest"** (*SP,* p. 73), detailed as it is, becomes an entrance into the Eden of nature from which men have ejected themselves. It is treated descriptively, but the Edenic associations elaborated in the assertive poems adhere to the details. A specific example from **"The Nightingales Nest"** is the description of the bird's nest:

deep adown
The nest is made an hermits mossy cell
Snug lie her curious eggs in number five
Of deadened green or rather olive brown
And the old prickly thorn bush guards them well
And here well leave them still unknown to wrong
As the old woodlands legacy of song

(*SP,* p. 75)

In this passage, the security, yet vulnerability, of nature is revealed in the adverbs "deep" and "snug," and in the need for a guard. An allusion to nature's immortality is made in the mention of the number five, God's mark on

nature according to **"The Eternity of Nature,"** and the thorn bush and the woodlands are "old." Furthermore, the natural things are described as innocent, "unknown to wrong," and, since the human beings are retreating, nature has still experienced no evil. The effect gained here by the philosophical associations can be seen particularly well when the poem is placed beside Clare's prose description of the same subject:

it is a very deep nest and is generaly placed on the root or stulp of a black or white thorn somtimes a little height up the bush and often on the ground they lay 5 eggs about the size of the woodlarks or larger and of a deep olive brown   (*SP,* p. 76)

In neither passage is there any explicit judgment concerning the significance of the details. In the poetry, however, the adjectives in particular make a pattern that suggests judgment; in the prose no such pattern is revealed.

As well as illustrating the Edenic qualities of nature, the bird poems develop the idea of nature's difference from man and of potential human destructiveness. In **"The Nightingales Nest,"** the poet, through his memory of childhood rapture and his lack of cruelty, can penetrate some way into nature's Eden; he may fancy himself sharing her joy, but the least reminder of his intrusive humanity cuts off the bird's joy and his own:

the happiest part
Of summers fame she shared—for so to me
Did happy fancy shapen her employ
But if I touched a bush or scarcely stirred
All in a moment stopt—I watched in vain
The timid bird had left the hazel bush
And at a distance hid to sing again
Lost in a wilderness of listening leaves

(*SP,* pp. 73-74)

Total participation in nature is then impossible even for the poet, and is but one of his "happy fancys."

In the bird poems, Clare has exploited a poem's need for a reader. Usually the speaker is the perceiver in the poem, and, as in a dramatic monologue, he describes his own actions as they are occurring. His thoughts arise from these actions and are communicated to the reader as if the latter were physically present, not as a reader but as a participant in the poet's activity. That is, Clare imagines an implied reader, who actually accompanies him on his rambles. An actor with a prescribed part, he is led along the paths taken by the poet and is taught to appreciate the scenes chosen for him:

—Hark there she is as usual lets be hush
For in this black thorn clump if rightly guest
Her curious house is hidden—part aside
These hazel branches in a gentle way
And stoop right cautious neath the rustling boughs
For we will have another search to-day
And hunt this fern strown thora clump round and round
And where this seeded wood grass idly bows

Well wade right through—it is a likely nook
In such like spots and often on the ground
Theyll build where rude boys never think to look
Aye as I live her secret nest is here
Upon this white thorn stulp—Ive searched about
For hours in vain—there put that bramble bye
Nay trample on its branches and get near

(SP, p. 74)

This passage from **"The Nightingales Nest"** illustrates the relationship between the poet and the reader. The latter is included in the joint "we," while the poet uses the singular for his own reminiscences and speculations. The reader is told to listen, to move, and to look as the speaker directs. Together with this physical direction, the poet also provides mental guidance. In the dramatic monologue, most obviously in Browning's, the recipient of the speech is often characterized by the speaker; in Clare's poems, the implied reader is developed into the character the poet would wish. He is acquiescent to the speaker and learns to see the birds through his eyes; thus he comes to appreciate the otherness of nature and the secrecy of her ways. In addition, he learns from the speaker's caution that man is potentially destructive, but he learns also to perceive this potential in himself and to restrain it. Ultimately, then, he is persuaded to the poet's pacific actions, as well as to his view of nature, for the poet speaks for both in his joint "we." In **"The Nightingales Nest,"** for example, the reader is led by the speaker as his walking companion to the secret nest of the nightingale, which, unaided, he could not find. In the sequestered spot he must submit to the poet's awe toward nature's sanctity and learn his attitude, in the same way as he learned the path. So he must agree with his guide who says: "We will not plunder music of its dower / Nor turn this spot of happiness to thrall." Again, in **"The Pettichap's Nest"** (II, 219), the reader accompanies the poet on his walk and, with the help of his perceptions, sees the secrecy and security of nature he could not have noticed alone. Here too he must submit to the reverent attitude of his mentor: "We'll let them be, and safety guard them well." The same caution is addressed to the reader in **"The Yellow Hammer's Nest"** (II, 220), where he is warned not to intrude on nature's Eden and so destroy its beauty and happiness: "Let's leave it still / A happy home of sunshine, flowers, and streams."

The relationship of the speaker and reader in the bird poems is unusual in Clare. In the majority of his nature poems, the speaker either relates his observations and actions directly or allows the reader to overhear his ruminations; the imagined involvement and persuasion of the implied reader in the bird poems allow Clare to gain some of the persuasiveness of the assertive poems, while retaining the essentially descriptive nature of his verse. They are, then, like the assertive poems, ultimately didactic in intention, for, while the reader contemplates the described image, he must learn its correct appreciation.

In all these poems, although there are few incidents given of man's cruelty to nature and no explicit statements of his radical difference from it, it is clear that natural things fear man. The existence of that fear is implied in the actions of the birds, as well as in the caution of the speaker. In **"The Yellow Hammer's Nest"** and **"The Pettichap's Nest,"** the birds' fear of man is revealed in the initial circumstances of each poem. In the former, the bird is first seen when it is frightened by a cowboy; in the latter, the fear is of the poet and his companion, whose footsteps alert the bird to the alien presence of man. To enter nature at all, even the reverent poet of **"The Nightingales Nest"** must trample the leaves and branches of trees, and his action indicates his distinction from the creatures he would approach. In **"The Yellow-Hammer's Nest,"** too, the cruelty of man is further hinted at in the similar cruelty of snakes, another kind of creature who is not a part of the Eden of small animals because of his destructiveness, and possibly because of his part in the traditional expulsion of man from Eden.

The potential cruelty of man is a mark of the difference between man and nature, a difference that often prevents man from perceiving nature correctly. Two poems in particular portray the human misunderstanding of nature, and hint at the dangerous result of it. The first is **"Sand Martin"** (*SP*, p. 69), an address to the bird rather than to the reader, which results not in the usual poetic analogy between the poet and the bird but in a partial sharing by the poet of the ineffable feeling of nature, its "lone seclusion and a hermit joy." The innovation in this poem is the speaker's apparent distance from Clare, for, where the speaker of most of the bird poems reveals his assent to Clare's stated philosophy, the speaker here perceives nature correctly at one stage, but apparently not throughout the poem. A measure of this vacillation is the repeated word "lone":

Ive seen thee far away from all thy tribe
Flirting about the unfrequented sky
And felt a feeling that I cant describe
Of lone seclusion and a hermit joy
To see thee circle round nor go beyond
That lone heath and its melancholly pond

(SP, p. 69)

The first time "lone" is used it helps to describe the empathetic feeling the poet has with nature; it is thus an appreciative adjective. The second time it occurs, it aids the process of distancing the speaker, and therefore the reader, from the natural object, so that, as a description of merely human perception at this stage, it has a pejorative association. "Lone" also echoes the opening of the poem, which presents the human view of the sand martin's home;

Thou hermit haunter of the lonely glen
And common wild and heath—the desolate face
Of rude waste landscapes far away from men

(SP, p. 69)

This view is only transformed as the poet comes to feel "the desolate face" of nature as "a hermit joy." At the end, the desolate place is once again "that lone heath and its melancholly pond." Earlier coupled with joy, "lone" is now linked with melancholy; so there seems to be a movement within the speaker of the poem from the solely human regard of nature to the joy-producing human contact with nature and then back to the merely human perception of the wasteland. Nature's reality and man's response to it are therefore contrasted within the changing attitude of the speaker as he moves near to nature and then away from it. The bird's joy in the wasteland is felt for a moment by the poet, and his perception is doubled, but the melancholy loneliness intrudes, and he returns to his single human perception.

In the second poem, **"The Sky Lark"** (*SP,* p. 77), it is not the speaker who is deficient in perception but the school boys. The reader is exhorted to watch as if he were a bystander as the skylark flies up from the nest. The scene of this poem is set not through a broad description of the countryside and sky, but through a selection of small details that suggest the overall scene, almost as if Clare were immediately reminding the reader that nature is a collection of the small details of the earth:

> The rolls and harrows lies at rest beside
> The battered road and spreading far and wide
> Above the russet clods the corn is seen
> Sprouting its spirey points of tender green
> Where squats the hare to terrors wide awake
> Like some brown clod the harrows failed to break
> > (*SP,* p. 77)

The focus moves here through the cornfield to the hare, who has the terror of all small things of nature, as well as their kinship with the earth, the clods of the field. The hare becomes an epitome of all frightened animals, then, and when the skylark is introduced one can assume her characteristics from this description of her fellow creature. After this setting of the scene, the schoolboys enter, the human element coming to raid nature. They surprise the skylark, whose subsequent flight and joy in the sky they see, but not her fall:

> > the sky lark flies
> And oer her half formed nest with happy wings
> Winnows the air till in the clouds she sings
> Then hangs a dust spot in the sunny skies
> And drops and drops till in her nest she lies
> > (*SP,* p. 77)

The rest of the poem concentrates on the typical reaction of the boys to the bird. Not understanding her harelike characteristics, they cannot believe in her earthliness, but consider her "free from danger as the heavens are free / From pain and toil." They imagine her going "about the world to scenes unheard / Of and unseen":

> O where they but a bird
> So think they while they listen to its song
> And smile and fancy and so pass along
> While its low nest moist with the dews of morn
> Lies safely with the leveret in the corn
> > (*SP,* pp. 77-78)

Through his speaker who has seen the hare and the bird and the clods of earth, Clare seems to be contrasting two ways of perceiving nature. With the first, the poet realizes its otherness, its fear of man; and in the "low" nest of the skylark he understands the earthliness and vulnerability of the bird and of all natural things. The second is a purely human, man-centered notion of the animal world, and this the boys show when they unsubstantialize the bird because they do not really see her. In fact they have "unheeding past" the skylark on her nest, and they are thus only seeing the bird partially when they see her in flight. Even then, she becomes not a bird above her nest, but their own aspirations materialized; their "fancy" ignores the real terror and vulnerability of the bird, as well as the careful joy in her nest. This sort of joy, it is implied, they could not understand, for, although they have come merely to pluck the buttercups, it is the same urge that motivates boys in other poems to plunder birds' eggs, and, finally, men to destroy trees and hedges for enclosure.

"The Sky Lark" is very close in its description of the boys' response to Shelley's "To a Skylark," in which the bird becomes an insubstantial symbol of the poet's emotions, and, like the schoolboys' bird in Clare's poem, a creature divorced from earthly fear and pain. By the side of Shelley's poem, then, and many similar examples of Wordsworth's poetry, such as "To the Cuckoo," it is hard to avoid seeing **"The Sky Lark"** as in some way answering the Romantic tendency to regard the human response to, and not the reality of, an object, and, at the same time, to avoid acknowledging in this response man's insensitivity to real nature and his cruelty to it.

In Clare's bird poems it is not our understanding of nature's Eden that is most extended but our realization of man's proper relationship to it. The poems present his correct attitude of joyful contemplation and reverence, and at the same time show his man-centered view and his destructiveness, which are threats to Eden. The potential loss of both nature and man is then one meaning of the bird poems, for not all human intruders into nature will be as cautious and as reverent as Clare's speakers.

During the next decade, Clare's hatred of man's destructiveness became even deeper than it appeared in the bird poems. His sorrow at the uprooting of plants and animals for the enclosure of fields was augmented by his own uprooting from his native village partly owing to the poverty that the enclosure movement brought to many peasants. In addition, as he became convinced of the absolute separation of man and nature, and of the universal human fall from Edenic vision, Clare became most keenly aware of his own loss, and in the 1830's it is this personal loss of Edenic perception that he most frequently laments; the resultant un-Edenic vision, recorded in the descriptive sonnets of 1835 to 1837, implies this perceptual loss.

In the poems concerning the destruction of Eden written before 1835, Clare had conveyed the prelapsarian world through memories and contrasts, for his subject had been mainly the dramatic process of the fall. In the animal sonnets of 1835 to 1837, however, Clare describes only the wintry scene after the fall. Nature's otherness, always stressed as its characteristic, is now its dominant quality for man, and, as a result, the world becomes the scene of the civil war Clare had feared as early as 1821 and had implicitly warned against in the bird poems. The wintry world is conveyed through the speaker who looks at the natural things minutely, neither identifying with them nor personifying them. Here, then, the descriptive method of plain statement without intrusive emotional bias is used to convey a vision that is shocking, but the economy, abruptness, and detail of the poems make it somehow impossible that this vision should be doubted.

"The Badger," "The Marten," "The Hedgehog," and "The Fox" are all similar in form, being groups of sonnets that make up single poems. Throughout the pre-asylum years, the sonnet is one of Clare's most popular forms. A typical sonnet of the 1820's is descriptive, presenting precisely and particularly one or more visual images, rarely with any overt human significance or symbolic connotation. Early in his poetic career, however, Clare seems to have found the form restrictive, and, in a letter of 1820, he scoffs at those who would make "readers believe a Sonnet cannot be a Sonnet unless it be precisely 14 lines." To avoid the brevity of the descriptive sonnet, while keeping its particularity and conciseness, Clare evolved the sonnet group. Each sonnet can to some extent stand alone, but the connection between them remains closer than is usual in a sonnet sequence. In the animal sonnets of the 1830's there is sometimes an incipient narrative line that seems to require their continuous reading, but there is no conclusion in the final sonnet beyond the particulars presented, and each sonnet can be regarded as a whole descriptive incident.

The animals described in the sonnet groups are comparable in their lack of most of the usual Edenic qualities, although a certain bravery and secrecy remain to them. The poems show the invasion of this secrecy by man. "The Badger" (*SP*, p. 84) is a description of badger-baiting, in which the animal is treated with extended human cruelty; the people "bait him all the day with many dogs." He fights fiercely and well, escaping from the crowd of his persecutors. But man's cruelty is persistent; the badger is chased with dogs and men until finally he is overcome:

> He turns agen and drives the noisey crowd
> And beats the many dogs in noises loud
> He drives away and beats them every one
> And then they loose them all and set them on
> He falls as dead and kicked by boys and men
> Then starts and grins and drives the crowd agen
> Till kicked and torn and beaten out he lies
> And leaves his hold and cackles groans and dies
>   (*SP*, p. 86)

There is no explicit moral judgment in **"The Badger,"** although it is implied in the description of the badger as "dimute and small," and in the presentation of man's savage joy in cruelty. In addition, no clear emotional bias emerges; even during the badger's persecution and death

there is no intrusive pity, for the verbs are unadorned, and his death is robbed of our immediate sympathy by the unattractive word "cackles." Again, the energetic bravery of the badger is undercut by the last sonnet which describes a tamed badger who "licks the patting hand and trys to play / And never trys to bite or run away": nature is not only beaten, but humiliated.

In the endless civil war of the fallen world, man, the overall winner, is not always the conqueror in incidental battles. In **"The Marten"** (*SP*, p. 86), the hunters invade the animal's secrecy in a way Clare had warned against in his bird poems. But here the owl wins the contest, and so leaves the marten free for the time being:

> When the grey owl her young ones cloathed in down
> Seizes the boldest boy and drives him down
> They try agen and pelt to start the fray
> The grey owl comes and drives them all away
> And leaves the martin twisting round his den
> Left free from boys and dogs and noise and men
>   (*SP*, p. 87)

So too the fox (*SP*, p. 87), in spite of persistent persecution, "lived to chase the hounds another day." Yet man's defeat never mitigates his cruelty. The fox may win, but the human attitude toward him has already been fully expressed. The ploughman

>   found a weary fox and beat him out
> The ploughman laughed and would have ploughed
>   him in
> But the old shepherd took him for the skin
> He lay upon the furrow stretched and dead
> The old dog lay and licked the wounds that bled
> The ploughman beat him till his ribs would crack
> And then the shepherd slung him at his back
>   (*SP*, p. 87)

If the cruelty of man is pervasive in the poems, so too is nature's strangeness for man, almost its repulsiveness. These qualities are best conveyed in two poems, **Mouse's Nest** (II, 370) and **"The Hedgehog"** (*SP*, p. 88). In the former, a single sonnet, we see through the speaker, who makes no judgments on the natural image he presents and expresses no disgust at it beyond his statement of its grotesqueness. Yet he allows our contemplation of the image through his initial act of petty destruction, when, prodding a ball of grass, he invades the security and privacy of the mouse. In addition, his description allows the mouse to share the alien glitter of her surroundings, and there is none of the joyful lingering over the visual image revealed in the bird poems. The speaker, then, manages to convey the strangeness of his subject; the reader alone, with his memory of the earlier skylark and frightened hare, must see, together with the strangeness, the tenderness and careful secrecy of the mouse:

>   out an old mouse bolted in the wheats
> With all her young ones hanging at her teats . . .
> The young ones squeaked, and as I went away
> She found her nest again among the hay.

The water o'er the pebbles scarce could run
And broad old cesspools glittered in the sun.

(II, 370)

In the second poem, the hedgehog is initially unpleasant, although by the end of the poem he wins a kind of grudging sympathy from the reader. During the first description the hedgehog is referred to as "he," a designation that remains until Clare portrays man's hunting of him. Then "he" becomes "it," a referential method that reflects the human attitude toward the hedgehog, who changes from a little animal filling a nest and hunting for crabs and sloes to "black and bitter and unsavoury meat." The gipsies are the only people who eat the hedgehog meat, and they have something of the animal's strangeness, living on the periphery of humanity. But their position there allows them a better understanding of the hedgehog than the hunters have. They have seen his vulnerability and gentleness, while those who find the meat distasteful and despise the gipsies see the hedgehog only as a victim for their cruelty:

But they who hunt the field for rotten meat
And wash in muddy dyke and call it sweat [sic]
And eat what dogs refuse where ere they dwell
Care little either for the taste or smell
They say they milk the cows and when they lye
Nibble their fleshly teats and make them dry
But they whove seen the small head like a hog
Rolled up to meet the savage of a dog
With mouth scarce big enough to hold a straw
Will neer believe what no one ever saw
But still they hunt the hedges all about
And shepherd dogs are trained to hunt them out
They hurl with savage force the stick and stone
And no one cares and still the strife goes on

(*SP,* pp. 88-89)

The image of vulnerability and gentleness seen only by the gipsies is a typical example of the effect of Clare's animal poems of this time. The image is unpleasant and alien at first; yet by the side of man's familiar ferocity, it becomes, while remaining strange, a positive expression of the hedgehog's tender quality. This strange tenderness and vulnerability of natural things that are grotesque and unpleasant to human sight exactly express the new situation for Clare. Nature might retain some of its Edenic qualities, but for man they are now veiled.

In the animal sonnets, the materialism and cruelty of man that had been a threatening potential in the bird poems becomes a described reality. Man's resulting imperception is implied by the grotesque and alien appearance of nature to him. To this general imperception there are now no exceptions, and the poet's un-Edenic vision is frightening in its stark truthfulness and, compared with the earlier vision, in the extent of the loss it implies.

Clare's bird poems and animal sonnets suggest that inevitably the "very copys of nature" must be the very copies of the poet's perception of his world; when this perception is dramatically changed, the descriptive images themselves will reflect this drama. Yet Clare's descriptive po-

etry never suggests that man's perception creates its objects or that he transfers "a human and intellectual life" to them. Edenic nature for him is not an adjunct of man and its beauty is not the human mind's creation. Eden is an objective reality, which the poet sees in his early innocence, but which he loses sight of in his shared degeneration. The loss of vision is a loss not only of his own faculty, then, but of reality.

The descriptive method is appropriate for a poet who, like Clare, distinguishes so absolutely between the human mind and nature. The human emotional response and judgment of the poet are secondary to the described external world. The reader, on the other hand, is disturbed by the very precision of Clare's descriptive images into his own emotion and thought. Through the details he learns not only to see nature more exactly, but also to understand Clare's Edenic philosophy and to respond to the strangeness and beauty of nature and its verse. Yet his response must be his own creation, for it is suggested, not dictated as in Romantic poetry. Like nature, descriptive poetry gives to the reader "her own imagings," and he in turn must bring to both his own sentiment and judgment.

Timothy Brownlow (essay date 1978)

SOURCE: "A Molehill for Parnassus: John Clare and Prospect Poetry," in *University of Toronto Quarterly,* Vol. XLVIII, No. 1, Fall, 1978, pp. 23-40.

[*In the following excerpt, Brownlow contends that Clare and his detailed view of nature were unique in that he refused to view the landscape with condescension as the "topographical poets" did, nor did he attach human spirituality to nature as did the Romantic poets.*]

I

Topographical poetry in the wide sense is as old as poetry itself, for poets have always felt the need to celebrate their environment, thereby giving their emotions 'a local habitation and a name.' Drayton's *Poly-Olbion* and Jonson's *To Penshurst* are important poems in this tradition. But the publication in 1642 of Sir John Denham's *Cooper's Hill* inaugurated a special type of topographical poem, the hill- or prospect-poem, which had its full flowering in the eighteenth century and which was, in its decline, part of the Romantic poets' inheritance. In this tradition, analogous to the pictorial tradition of the bird's-eye view, the poet climbs a hill, sweeps his eye round the panorama, focuses his attention on the most interesting prospect, and paints a careful word-picture. It did not need much of an effort for eighteenth-century minds to associate the hill in question with Parnassus, but it was also Denham who had domesticated Parnassus for them, as he makes clear in the first eight lines of *Cooper's Hill*:

Sure there are Poets which did never dream
Upon *Parnassus,* nor did tast the stream
Of *Helicon,* we therefore may suppose

Those made not Poets, but the Poets those.
And as Courts make not Kings, but Kings the Court,
So where the Muses & their train resort,
Parnassus stands; if I can be to thee
A Poet, thou *Parnassus* art to me.

The purpose of this article is to show how John Clare
(1793-1864) inherits this tradition, struggles to find his
own voice within it, and eventually creates a unique vision.

Topographical poetry is a branch of landscape poetry and
sets out, in R.A. Aubin's words, to describe *specifically
named actual localities.'* Prospect poetry is a specialized
type of topographical poetry in which an extensive view
is described from one or more points (or 'stations') and
in which the poet draws moral or patriotic lessons from
the scenery. The ambiguity in the word 'prospect' is always present—a 'prospect' is a long view both in space
and in time. While Aubin sees the essential characteristics
of the topographical genre as those which name and describe specific places, John Wilson Foster has attempted
to define the genre more precisely. According to Foster,
topographical poetry is that in which certain structural
devices are employed to describe the landscape; the genre
can be recognized not only by its naming and description
of specific places, but by the way in which description is
controlled by spatial, temporal, and moralistic designs:
'We can say broadly that topographical poetry ceases to
warrant the title when the poet no longer sets up certain
kinds of descriptive patterns to convey corresponding
patterns of moralistic meditation.'

Foster elsewhere stresses the connection between topographical poetry and the sciences of surveying and topography. In discussing *Cooper's Hill,* he writes: 'The
eye-shifts in "Cooper's Hill" bear a close resemblance to
the way sightings were taken with these [surveyors'] instruments.' He explains in another article how enclosure
became a socio-economic spur to the development of surveying. It follows that for Clare the word 'survey' carries
a double threat. On the one hand, scientific surveyors
were enclosing the landscape of his boyhood; on the other,
topographical artists and poets 'overlooked' what made
his life and landscape meaningful. The enclosure of the
land around his Northamptonshire village, Helpston,
began in 1809; later he recorded his reaction to surveyors at work:

> Saw 3 fellows at the end of Royce Wood who I found
> were laying out the plan for an 'Iron railway' from
> Manchester to London it is to cross over Round Oak
> Spring by Royce Wood corner for Woodcroft Castle I
> little thought that fresh intrusions would interrupt &
> spoil my solitudes after the Enclosure they will despoil
> a boggy place that is famous for Orchises at Royce
> Wood end. [J.W. Tibble and Anne Tibble, eds, *The
> Prose of John Clare*, London, 1951, p. 151. Hereafter
> referred to in the text as *Prose*.]

Enclosure, landscape-gardening on a huge scale, and the
railways swept away much of that open nature whose loss
Clare continually laments. The changes were carried out
by a horde of surveyors, representatives of what John

Barrell calls the 'rural professional class,' with little sympathy for or knowledge of Clare's way of life.

Foster's analysis of structural devices is especially applicable to the sub-genre of prospect poetry. If one rests
content with Aubin's definition, the nature of Clare's resistance to the tradition is unclear; but once the connection with scientific surveying is made explicit, Clare's
predicament is highlighted. It is perhaps a sense of threat,
as much as genuine literary influence, which attracted
Clare to landscape poetry before Denham (or outside the
Denham tradition). Clare's affinities with the seventeenth
century are evident from his skilful exercises, 'fathered'
upon Sir Henry Wotton, Sir John Harington, Andrew
Marvell, and others, grouped together by J.W. Tibble under
the heading 'Poems Written in the Manner of the Older
Poets,' and dated between 1824 and 1832. [J.W. Tibble,
ed. *The Poems of John Clare* (London 1935), II, pp.
181-212. Hereafter referred to in the text as *Poems*.]

Clare's approach to eighteenth-century poetry, however,
was necessarily more complex. He would have noticed
how optical and landscape terms had become assimilated
by political and social metaphors—'viewpoint' or 'point
of view' is an intellectual term; one has 'elevated' thoughts
as the result of being in an 'elevated' position; one's life
gains 'perspective' as well as the landscape (painted or
real); one should accept one's 'walk' of life; one ought
not to have ideas above one's 'station'; one's life has
'landmarks' if one 'surveys' it properly; and to 'command' bright 'prospects' is more than just having mental
snapshots of the view, or 'panorama,' from an 'eminence,'
preferably from a 'seat' (garden seat or family seat).
Clare's problem as an artist is how to write descriptive
poetry about his own landscape without recourse to this
alien vocabulary.

II

If Denham's view from Cooper's Hill could be called
telescopic (it is far-ranging but limited to one direction at
a time), Clare's vision could be called kaleidoscopic (it is
not concerned with distancing but with comprehensiveness, a circular all-at-onceness). Apart from juvenilia and
occasional pieces for the Annuals, his vision is never
framed and rarely static, he has no conventional point of
view in either sense, his thoughts are hardly ever elevated, and he eschews perspective. He comes to maturity by
discovering that all things, even the snails which he had
timed with his watch, are in motion, and that objects are
often best seen in close-up, thereby achieving a kind of
fluid crystallization of images.

Clare had read enough as a literary man and suffered
enough as a day-labourer to suspect that the idealization
and the exploitation of a landscape often go together, and
optical instruments are involved in both processes. Something of his vulnerability is revealed in the following passage from 'The Autobiography,' in which he testily dismisses the artificiality of 'an instrument from a shilling
art of painting' (obviously a primitive *camera obscura*)
in favour of the 'instantaneous sketches' of living nature.

It is a dismissal as conscious, radical, and intelligent as Constable's rejection of the academic 'brown tree':

> Sometimes he would be after drawing by perspective & he made an instrument from a shilling art of painting which he had fashiond that was to take landscapes almost by itself it was of a long square shape with a hole at one end to look through & a number of different colourd threads crossd into little squares at the other from each of these squares different portions of the landscape was to be taken one after the other & put down in a facsimile of the square done with a pencil on the paper but his attempts made but poor reflections of the objects & when they were finishd in his best colours they were but poor shadows of the original & the sun with its instantaneous sketches made better figures of the objects in their shadows
>
> (*Prose*, p. 43)

No wonder Clare was nervous when his critics used topographical language. For him it was the language of *dis*integration, *dis*location, *dis*orientation. His publishers, Taylor and Hessey, who vigorously corrected his manuscripts against his will, wrote to him with advice such as: 'if you would raise your views generally & Speak of the Appearances of Nature each Month more philosophically'; and 'What you ought to do is to elevate your Views, and write with the Power that belongs to you under the Influence of true Poetic Excitement—never in a low or familiar Manner'; and 'let [your descriptions] come in incidentally—let them occupy their places in the picture, but they must be subordinate to higher objects.' It is a great honour to Clare as an artist that he ultimately refused to listen to this sort of advice; his refusal made him a poet, but it destroyed his material prospects. His finest book, **The Shepherd's Calendar,** which appeared in 1827 after years of tampering by John Taylor, fell on deaf ears, and an accurate edition did not appear until 1964.

The prospect formula is part of the neo-classical belief in the truth of the generalized, the idealized, the elevated. Dr Johnson, discussing the pastoral genre, writes:

> though nature itself, philosophically considered, be inexhaustible, yet its general effects on the eye and on the ear are uniform, and incapable of much variety of description.

Clare's poetry is a direct challenge to that statement, as it is to Sir Joshua Reynolds' dictum, 'All smaller things, however perfect in their way, are to be sacrificed without mercy to the greater.' Clare's response is in the spirit of his age—botanists, following the pioneering work of Linnaeus, were at this time making a vast number of discoveries, which were then codified and illustrated. Clare himself was a skilful and knowledgeable botanist as well as ornithologist, and his library of about 440 volumes, still in existence at Northampton, contains many books on natural history. Inside the front cover of his copy of Isaac Emmerton's *The Culture & Management of the Auricula, Polyanthus, Carnation, Pink, and the Ranunculus* (1819), Clare has written a list of 22 'Orchis's counted from Privet hedge.' Through his friend Henderson, the butler of his patron Earl Fitzwilliam at Milton House, Clare occasionally got glimpses of finer things. In the following extract from the 'Journal' of 15 December 1824, Clare's instincts run directly counter to Reynolds's generalization, as he carefully checks a personal discovery against the latest scientific codification:

> Went to Milton saw a fine edition of Linnaeus's Botany with beautiful plates & find that my fern which I found in Harrisons close dyke by the wood lane is the thronpointed fern saw also a beautiful book on insects with the plants they feed on by Curtis
>
> (*Prose*, p. 127).

The higher the viewpoint, the more generalized and idealized the view; the lower the viewpoint, the more particular details will crowd out or even obscure the general and ideal and assert their own disturbing independence. It is no accident that Dutch landscape painting, given low priority by Reynolds in his *Discourses,* was admired by English Romantic painters; Clare's favourite painter was De Wint, whereas the favourite landscape painter of the eighteenth century had been Claude Lorraine, whose tradition Clare detests. Nor is it accidental that the first indigenous school of English watercolours emerged in Norwich, in the midst of the great East Anglian plain, where the painter, having few conventional prospects, is forced into a direct contact with the atmospherics of the scene under a huge sky. Gainsborough in his early work such as 'Cornard Wood' and Constable in his most typical work were both inspired by the Suffolk landscape. The link between the Claudean bird's-eye view (used by Dyer and Thomson) and an increasingly lowered viewpoint which demands attention to detail is to be found in the development of the picturesque. At the beginning of the century poets learned to orientate themselves in landscapes by adapting the Claudean view to verse; by 1800 the cult of the visual had led to a complex awareness of stimuli, so that lichens or moss on old stonework could provide not only synaesthetic emotion ('the sight takes so many lessons from the touch' wrote Uvedale Price to Sir George Beaumont) but also could lead the observer into a magically microscopic world, where pictorial rules became irrelevant. Wordsworth writes of the Alps that they abound in 'images which disdain the pencil' and he transcends the picturesque by experiencing the sublime; Clare, as visually acute as Wordsworth, transcends the picturesque by discovering an equally awe-inspiring microcosmos.

The neo-classical theorist maintains that the poet does not number the streaks of the tulip, but Clare's eye-level is often no higher than a tulip, and he numbers meticulously:

> With the odd number five strange natures laws
> Plays many freaks nor once mistakes the cause
> And in the cowslap peeps this very day
> Five spots appear which time neer wears away
> Nor once mistakes the counting—look within
> Each peep and five nor more nor less is seen
> And trailing bindweed with its pinky cup
> Five lines of paler hue goes streaking up

And birds a many keep the rule alive
And lay five eggs nor more nor less than five
  [Eric Robinson and Geoffrey Summerfield, eds,
  Selected Poems and Prose of John Clare, London,
  1967, p. 111. Hereafter referred to in the text as
  SPP. This edition is cited as much as possible, as
  the editors do not tinker with the manuscripts or
  attempt to tidy up Clare's punctuation (or lack of
  it), which all other editors of Clare have done.]

Pope's well-known passage from *An Essay on Man* reads
like an accusation of Clare's passionate botanising:

  Why has not Man a microscopic eye?
  For this plain reason, Man is not a Fly.
  Say what the use, were finer optics giv'n,
  T'inspect a mite, not comprehend the heav'n?

But Clare saw no reason why man should not have such
a vision. His curiosity is scientific as much as poetic;
indeed the modern separation of these two faculties would
have been meaningless to him. He meticulously records
what he calls 'snatches of sunshine and scraps of spring
that I have gathered like an insect while wandering in the
fields.' He would have understood Thoreau's journal entry for 27 July 1840: 'Nature will bear the closest inspection. She invites us to lay our eye level with her smallest
leaf and take an insect view of its plain.' Such a view is
instinctive to a naturalist, but when the father of English
naturalists, Gilbert White, turns to verse, his viewpoint
remains conventional, elevated:

  Romantic spot! from whence in prospect lies
  Whate'er of landscape charms our feasting eyes . . .
  Now climb the steep, drop now your eye below,
  Where round the blooming village orchards grow;
  There, like a picture, lies my lowly seat,
  A rural, shelter'd, unobserv'd retreat.

The 'insect view,' as White the naturalist is aware, is closely allied to that scientific hunger for empirical data which
was to have such momentous results in the nineteenth century. Gray's annotated copy of Linnaeus, Crabbe's botanical studies, Gilbert White's Journals and Garden Kalen-
dar, Coleridge's Notebooks, Clare's Natural History Letters, are pioneering works in the closer study of nature
which preceded Darwin. But as Swift knew when he wrote
Gulliver's Travels, human beings look a lot less beautiful
and important, although vastly more dangerous, when seen
from an 'insect view.' The literary and social establishment ignored Clare's essential achievement for over a
hundred years, and the annuals preferred to publish the
conventional sonnets and ballads which he could churn
out on demand.

The literary expression of the 'insect view' is much rarer
than one might suppose. This is clarified when one thinks
of Clare's lowly predecessors, who without exception were
culturally assimilated, and who adopted linguistic and
spiritual elevation in an attempt to raise themselves above
their station. Perhaps the saddest example is Stephen Duck
(1705-56), whose early poem 'The Thresher's Labour'

contains many realistic descriptions of rustic labouring
conditions. After he had been 'discovered' by Queen
Caroline, presented with a benefice and the custodian-
ship of her strange folly in Richmond Park, Merlin's
Cave, Duck's talent dwindled to a coy mediocrity, as
when he revisits the scenes of his past labours:

  Straight Emulation glows in ev'ry Vein;
  I long to try the curvous Blade again . . .
  Behind 'em close, I rush the sweeping steel;
  The vanquish'd Mowers soon confess my Skill.

Robert Dodsley, the Muse in Livery, wrote in 1731 'An
Epistle from a Footman in London To the Celebrated Stephen
Duck.' He prophesies smiling prospects for them both:

  So you and I, just naked from the Shell,
  In chirping Notes our Future singing tell;
  Unfeather'd yet, in Judgment, Thought, or Skill,
  Hop round the Basis of Parnassus' Hill.

The gods upon Parnassus eventually encouraged the fledg-
ling to higher things, and Dodsley became a successful
publisher. Other poets of lowly birth who wrote topographical verse in the conventional mould were James
Woodhouse, Robert Tatersal, Ann Yearsley, Henry Jones,
and Robert Bloomfield.

In his early years as a writer Clare talks of his own life
and hopes, using the conventional and out-worn metaphors, a terminology derived from his wide reading in
eighteenth-century poetry. (Among poets in the landscape
tradition, Clare was deeply read in Milton, Gray, Collins,
Thomson, Goldsmith, Cowper, and Wordsworth.) The
acquisition of his mature style, which largely dispenses
with trite metaphor, is a hard-earned process. In **'Helpstone,'** written in 1809 when he was sixteen, Clare uses
the analogy of birds which, like Robert Dodsley's, 'Hop
round the Basis of Parnassus' Hill':

  So little birds, in winter's frost and snow,
  Doom'd, like to me, want's keener frost to know,
  Searching for food and 'better life,' in vain
  (Each hopeful track the yielding snows retain),
  First on the ground each fairy dream pursue,
  Though sought in vain; yet bent on higher view,
  Still chirp, and hope, and wipe each glossy bill.
                                                (***Poems,*** I, 3)

Towards the end of another early poem, which describes
a walk around Burghley Park (landscaped extensively by
Capability Brown, 1754-83), Clare climbs Barnack Hill
and gives a prospect, followed, as in Dyer and Bowles, by
an association with time and hope:

  There uncontroll'd I knew no bounds,
    But look'd o'er villages a crowd,
  And cots and spires to farthest rounds,
    While far trees seem'd a misty cloud.

  When tir'd with such far-stretching views,
    I left the green hill's sideling slope,

But oh, so tempting was the muse,
　　She made me wish, she made me hope;
I wish'd and hop'd that future days
　　(For scenes prophetic fill'd my breast)
Would grant to me a crown of bays
　　By singing maids and shepherds drest.

(Poems, I, 34)

Directly in the topographical tradition is **'Elegy on the Ruins of Pickworth, Rutlandshire. Hastily composed, and written with a Pencil on the Spot.'** Clare must have been aware of how he was almost literally making a sketch, in the manner of hundreds of amateur tourists and artists, but his reading to this date (1818) had probably not included William Combe's Dr. Syntax series (1812) with its endless ridicule of such random sketching. The **'Elegy on the Ruins of Pickworth'** is unusual in that Clare very rarely strays outside his own county; his mature verse is marked by its dogged rootedness, or later, a lament over forcible uprootedness. This poem seems all the more in the topographical mode by implying that the author is in transit, that this ruin is just another sought out for comparison by a picturesque tourist, another Dyer with his sketch-book, another Gray with his Claude glass, another Gilpin with his *camera obscura,* or another Bloomfield with his undiscriminating eye. The Pickworth Elegy rings false because Clare is consciously taking up a station, whereas his mature poetry is written by what Gilbert White called a 'stationary' man. In fact, Clare had the opportunity to describe the more varied Rutlandshire landscape intimately, for he obtained a job as a lime-burner for several months near the site of the deserted village of Pickworth. But at this stage his style is heavily imbued with influences, notably of Goldsmith and Gray; indeed, his pen more than once returns an echo of the other more famous elegy:

A time was once, though now the nettle grows
In triumph o'er each heap that swells the ground,
When they, in buildings pil'd, a village rose,
With here a cot, and there a garden crown'd. . . .

The ale-house here might stand, each hamlet's boast;
And here, where elder rich from ruin grows,
The tempting sign—but what was once is lost;
Who would be proud of what this world bestows? . . .

Since first these ruins fell, how chang'd the scene!
What busy, bustling mortals, now unknown,
Have come and gone, as tho' there naught had been,
Since first oblivion call'd the spot her own.

(Poems, I, 53-4)

Clare is never at home with this verse form; if the quatrain suits Gray's 'divine truisms,' it is quite inappropriate to the mature Clare's purpose, which is to catch the animation and detail of nature without imprisoning it in the frame of conventional form or manner, including punctuation. Clare is also uneasy with the visual demands of the perspective, with space used pictorially (the assumption of foreground, middle distance, and background), with time-projections (the retrospective use of a pros-

pect), and with the moral vision controlled by the optical vision. Here he repeats in a laboured way the eighteenth-century device of pointing out landmarks within an ordered design, 'With *here* a cot, and *there* a garden crown'd . . . / The ale-house *here* might stand, each hamlet's boast; / And *here* . . . ' (my italics). This device presupposes that the landscape is seen as a framed picture, and is analogous to the device in painting by means of which a pointing figure draws attention to the focus of the eye.

III

'The Village Minstrel,' the title poem of the 1821 volume, uses 'prospect' in both of its principal senses:

Thus Lubin's early days did rugged roll,
And mixt in timely toil—but e'en as now,
Ambitious prospects fired his little soul,
And fancy soared and sung, 'bove poverty's
　　control.

(Poems, I, 133)

So run the plough-boy's fanciful dreams. Something more imaginative begins to happen later in the poem. Clare has by no means found a voice of his own, but he is beginning to adapt the genre to the harsh facts and often joyous emotions of his life. As time goes on, he realizes that to talk of 'ambitious prospects' is not only trite poetically, but hopelessly unrealistic in terms of his own career. As a poet and as a man, he is more at home on a molehill than on a hill:

Upon a molehill oft he dropt him down,
To take a prospect of the circling scene,
Marking how much the cottage roof's-thatch brown
Did add its beauty to the budding green
Of sheltering trees it humbly peep'd between,
The stone-rock'd wagon with its rumbling sound,
The windmill's sweeping sails at distance seen,
And every form that crowds the circling round,
Where the sky stooping seems to kiss the meeting
　　ground.

(Poems, I, 137)

This verse can be taken as typical of Clare's early work: within it one can see the pull between convention and his own voice taking place. Although he is only on a molehill, he starts out 'to take a prospect'; his problem begins in the very next phrase, 'the circling scene.' His instinctive kaleidoscopic vision runs counter to the demands of the prospect; in order to take a prospect, the viewer must be static and he must look in one direction at a time (he may, of course, like the surveyor, make several sightings from the same spot, but in succession). Clare's enormous ambition seems to be to catch nature's events, pictures, and sequences simultaneously (one remembers the sun making its 'instantaneous sketches'). Furthermore, Clare does not just use the word 'circular'; he uses the active word 'circling.' Nature seems to be in constant motion, flitting past the poet's eye in such kinetic profusion that it threatens to break up the comfortable pictorial framework and the correspondingly strict verse-forms. Clare makes this clearer by repeating the word 'circling' in conjunction with the noun 'round' and hinting at frustration in the verb 'crowds': 'And every form that crowds the circling round.' It is all too much for the eye to take in, and rather than solve it in the easy way by succumbing to the convention (as W.L. Bowles was still doing as late as 1828), Clare senses that a new form of perception will have to be invented.

Clare is consciously committed to the low viewpoint, the 'insect view,' which is part of his problem:

> O'er brook-banks stretching, on the pasture-sward,
> He gaz'd, far distant from the jocund crew;
> 'Twas but their feats that claim'd a slight regard;
> 'Twas his, his pastimes lonely to pursue—
> Wild blossoms creeping in the grass to view,
> Scarce peeping up the tiny bent as high,
> Beting'd with glossy yellow, red, or blue,
> Unnam'd, unnotic'd but by Lubin's eye,
> That like low genius sprang to bloom their day and die.
>
> (***Poems,*** I, 137)

His scientific and his poetic instincts ('Unnam'd, unnotic'd') commit him to 'creeping in the grass.' This position reduces the importance of the purely visual and increases the power of the other senses. The visual, nonetheless, may attain a sort of hallucinatory quality, especially in Clare's later poems, where the 'insect view' in the grasses resembles the disturbing vision of 'The Fairy Feller's Master Stroke' by Richard Dadd.

In *"A Sunday with Shepherds and Herdboys"* Clare begins to describe a prospect which would fit almost unnoticed into dozens of eighteenth-century poems, in the tradition of 'L'Allegro,' or Dyer's 'Grongar Hill,' or Thomas Warton's 'The First of April':

> And oft they sit on rising ground
> To view the landscap spreading round
> Swimming from the following eye
> In greens and stems of every dye
> Oer wood and vale and fens smooth lap
> Like a richly colourd map

But the multiplicity of things, that aspect of life which Louis MacNeice calls 'incorrigibly plural,' crowds in on all Clare's senses, and he becomes sensuously involved with his surroundings, rather than seeing nature at a distance:

> Square platts of clover red and white
> Scented wi summers warm delight
> And sinkfoil of a fresher stain
> And different greens of varied grain
> Wheat spindles bursted into ear
> And browning faintly—grasses sere
> In swathy seed pods dryd by heat
> Rustling when brushd by passing feet
>
> (***SPP,*** p. 94)

'Holywell,' a poem in the topographical tradition, contains another conventional prospect, but Clare then tacks about and rejects the prospect as 'fiction' in favour of the immediacy of 'nearest objects':

> But as we turn to look again
> On nearest objects, wood and plain,
> (So truths than fiction lovelier seem),
> One warms as wak'ning from a dream.
> From covert hedge, on either side,
> The blackbirds flutter'd terrified,
> Mistaking me for pilfering boy
> That doth too oft their nests destroy;
> And 'prink, prink, prink,' they took to wing,
> In snugger shades to build and sing . . .
> I oped each gate with idle swing,
> And stood to listen ploughmen sing;
> While cracking whip and jingling gears
> Recall'd the toils of boyish years,
> When, like to them, I took my rounds
> O'er elting moulds of fallow grounds—
> With feet nigh shoeless, paddling through
> The bitterest blasts that ever blew.
>
> (***Poems,*** I, 164-5)

Clare here brings present and past simultaneously alive with 'cracking whip and jingling gears.' Duck would rather not remember his 'shoeless' feet, and would have thought the following lines, so typical of Clare's later work, beneath his dignity:

> And 'neath the hanging bushes creep
> For violet-bud and primrose-peep,
> And sigh with anxious, eager dream,
> For water-blobs amid the stream;
> And up the hill-side turn anon,
> To pick the daisies one by one
>
> (***Poems,*** I, 166)

'The Woodman' contains another rejection of the conventional view:

> The pleasing prospect does his heart much good,
> Though 'tis not his such beauties to admire;
> He hastes to fill his bags with billet-wood,
> Well-pleas'd from the chill prospect to retire,
> To seek his corner chair, and warm snug cottage fire.
>
> (***Poems,*** I, 202)

The woodman turns from a prospect which is 'pleasing' in terms of fancy, but 'chill' in terms of his own life. There is a gruff, countryman's realism about the line, 'Though 'tis not his such beauties to admire,' and he seeks out the small but vivid comforts of his own experience. If the aristocrat tends to live in the past, and the bourgeois in the future, the countryman lives in the present. The pint of ale in his hand, or his 'snug cottage fire,' is of more interest to him than his ancestors or his prospects.

This uncalculating involvement with the present is well described by W.K. Richmond in his discussion of the poem **'Pleasures of Spring'**: 'It is written as a labourer might hoe a field of turnips, with no eye on the ending, no thought of what is to come next, but with a massive, unquestioning patience which sustains the work and makes it not ignoble.' Clare's prose also has 'no eye on the ending, no thought of what is to come next.' In the following passage from 'The Autobiography,' in spite of the word 'survey' and Clare's position on a 'mossy eminence,' his eye does not pan the view as on a tripod; it zigzags from object to object like a gadfly, it has no resting-place or focal point around which to frame a design, and the writing catches the feeling of breathless excitement:

> I dropt down on the thymy molehill or mossy eminence to survey the summer landscape as full of rapture as now I markd the varied colors in flat spreading fields checkerd with closes of different tinted grain like the colors in a map the copper tinted colors of clover in blossom the sun-tannd green of the ripening hay the lighter hues of wheat & barley intermixd with the sunny glare of the yellow carlock & the sunset imitation of the scarlet headaches with the blue cornbottles crowding their splendid colors in large sheets over the land & troubling the cornfields with destroying beauty the different greens of the woodland trees the dark oak the paler ash the mellow lime the white poplar peeping above the rest like leafy steeples the grey willow shining chilly in the sun as if the morning mist still lingered on its cool green
>
> (*Prose*, p. 25)

That 'survey' would not be of much use to a cartographer. The absence of spacing, design, or perspective is paralleled by the absence of punctuation; one is not given a single comma to draw one's breath, or to feel that this is here, and that is there, or that this impression comes after the previous one. Instead, one is given a kaleidoscopic vision which shares the virtues of Clare's mature poetry—freshness, rhythmical subtlety, euphony, and the crystallization of emotion into haunting images.

IV

The same qualities can be found in the sonnets of Clare's maturity (from about 1821 onwards). If the sonnet is a 'moment's monument,' it is not difficult to understand Clare's success with this form, given his fascination with the ephemeral, the local, and the microscopic. In his use of this form Clare is often at the furthest remove from neoclassical tenets, unconcerned as he is with punctuation and perspective (in the topographical poem the two are connected), and the use of space and time as moral emblems. He extended the range of the sonnet, often in highly irregular ways—seven couplets strung together, for example. But Clare's mature sonnets are never stilted, and they impose upon him the pressure of selection from the endless detail at his disposal. They share Thomas Bewick's intense perception of the minutiae of nature and have Bewick's moral fervour without his moralizing—full of detail and texture, their wholeness is never distorted. They are tail-pieces (or tale-pieces) which catch the multiplicity of the world without imprisoning its bright details:

> Now sallow catkins once all downy white
> Turn like the sunshine into golden light
> The rocking clown leans oer the spinny rail
> In admiration at the sunny sight
> The while the blackcap doth his ears assail
> With a rich and such an early song
> He stops his own and thinks the nightingale
> Hath of her monthly reckoning counted wrong
> 'Sweet jug jug jug' comes loud upon his ear
> Those sounds that unto may by right belong
> Yet on the awthorn scarce a leaf appears
> How can it be—spell struck the wandering boy
> Listens again—again the sound he hears
> And mocks it in his song for very joy
>
> (*SPP*, p. 72)

There is no projection into past and future, no use of space in three dimensions, and no moralizing. Instead, it is the sound of the blackcap which spaces the poem in an arbitrary way, which the eighteenth-century eye might have found disorientating; to the 'rocking clown' it is freedom.

In order to experience the 'instantaneous sketches' of landscape rather than a static view in the single frame, Clare lowers his eye-level until he substitutes a molehill for Parnassus. The observation of the naturalist blends, as always in Clare, with the emotion of the poet:

> Five eggs, pen-scribbled o'er with ink their shells,
> Resembling writing-scrawls, which fancy reads
> As nature's poesy, and pastoral spells—
> They are the yellow-hammer's; and she dwells,
> Most poet-like, where brooks and flowery weeds
> As sweet as Castaly her fancy deems;
> And that old mole-hill is Parnassus Hill,
> On which her partner haply sits and dreams
> O'er all his joys of song. Let's leave it still
> A happy home of sunshine, flowers, and streams.
>
> (*Poems*, II, 221)

The yellow-hammer is 'poet-like,' and 'her partner' is not only the male bird but Clare himself, versed in 'nature's poesy.' This poem is an echo of the earlier, more complex **'Shadows of Taste,'** in which the yellow-hammer is also praised as a poetic model worthy of imitation:

> Taste with as many hues doth hearts engage
> As leaves and flowers do upon natures page
> Not mind alone the instinctive mood declares
> But birds and flowers and insects are its heirs
> Taste is their joyous heritage and they
> All choose for joy in a peculiar way
> Birds own it in the various spots they chuse
> Some live content in low grass gemmed with dews
> The yellow hammer like a tasteful guest
> Neath picturesque green molehills makes a nest
> Where oft the shepherd with unlearned ken
> Finds strange eggs scribbled as with ink and pen
> He looks with wonder on the learned marks
> And calls them in his memory writing larks
>
> (*SPP*, p. 112)

The molehills have not only become Parnassus, they are described as 'picturesque' as well. This adjective crops up frequently in Clare's poetry in the 1820s, but it is rarely used in a derivative way; it is used to create what an art historian has called a 'micro-panorama':

> Rude architect rich instincts natural taste
> Is thine by heritage—thy little mounds
> Bedecking furze clad health & rushy waste
> Betraced with sheeptracks shine like pleasure
>   grounds
> No rude inellegance thy work confounds
> But scenes of picturesque & beautiful
> Lye mid thy little hills of cushioned thyme
> On which the cowboy when his hands are full
> Of wild flowers learns upon his arm at rest
> As though his seat were feathers—when I climb
> Thy little fragrant mounds I feel thy guest
> & hail neglect thy patron who contrives
> Waste spots for thee on natures quiet breast
> & taste loves best where thy still labour thrives

This sonnet, dated by Tibble in the period 1824-1832, is a deliberate inversion of the assumptions and devices of the prospect tradition. The wayward sheeptracks on the heath 'shine like pleasure grounds'; the poet mimics the tradition by pretending to 'climb' the hillocks, and he describes himself as the mole's 'guest,' an admission the topographical poet could not have made, dedicated as he was to creating the illusion that he was monarch of all he surveyed. Both mole and poet now create their own space, and are not passively contained, as objects, by an intellectually and aesthetically imposed order; they both 'choose for joy in a peculiar way.'

The ripening of Clare's vision evidenced by these quotations should be sufficient to refute John Middleton Murry's claim that Clare 'had nothing of the principle of inward growth which gives to Wordsworth's most careless work a place within the unity of a great scheme.' In spite of Eric Robinson's and Geoffrey Summerfield's refutation of this same passage (*SPP*, p xvii), the conscious artifice of Clare's best work is still undervalued. This is the price Clare paid for wanting to be too like nature—a very Romantic dilemma.

Just as Denham had assumed that, given the presence of a poet, Cooper's Hill could be made Parnassus, so Clare assumes that the meanest details of nature are poetic material. The molehills need no reference beyond themselves; they simply have to be loved, and the poet's 'natural taste,' in tune with 'nature's poesy,' will do the rest:

> So where the Muses & their train resort,
> *Parnassus* stands; if I can be to thee
> A Poet, thou *Parnassus* art to me.

If Denham uses his eye like a telescope, Clare, having emancipated himself from the Denham tradition, turns out to be quite unlike those Romantics whose approach to nature might at first seem similar; he feels almost as uneasy with the constant need for elevation of sentiment in Wordsworth and Keats as he does with the ambiguities of the topographical tradition. Clare's reaction to Keats is that 'behind every rose bush he looks for a Venus & under every laurel a thrumming Appollo' (*Prose,* p. 223). The flowers at Clare's feet took all his love, and not those things that they symbolized; he happily ignored Lamb's advice to 'transplant Arcadia to Helpstone.' He also chose to ignore Keats's comment, relayed to him in a letter of 1820 by John Taylor, 'that the Description too much prevailed over the Sentiment.' Sentiment was over-employed by the Victorians until it became sentimentality. Clare's kinetic and microscopic descriptions, devoid of ethical, patriotic, or religious comment, link him rather to twentieth-century sensibilities than to nineteenth. Yet he is rooted in his landscape in a way no modern man can ever be again, which is why his vision is unique, and one for which lovers of poetry should become increasingly grateful.

Anne Williams (essay date 1981)

SOURCE: "Clare's 'Gypsies,'" in *The Explicator,* Vol. 39, No. 3, Spring, 1981, pp. 9-11.

[*In the following essay, Williams demonstrates how Clare uses poetic form, diction, and subject matter to overturn his readers' expectations of the picturesque in his poem "The Gypsies."*]

> The snow falls deep; the forest lies alone;
> The boy goes hasty for his load of brakes,
> Then thinks upon the fire and hurries back;
> The gypsy knocks his hands and tucks them up,
> And seeks his squalid camp, half hid in snow,
> Beneath the oak which breaks away the wind,
> And bushes close in snow like hovel warm;
> There tainted mutton wastes upon the coals,
> And the half-wasted dog squats close and rubs,
> Then feels the heat too strong, and goes aloof;
> He watches well but none a bit can spare,
> And vainly waits the morsel thrown away.
> 'Tis thus they live—a picture to the place,
> A quiet, pilfering, unprotected race.

The subtlety of John Clare's lyric, **"Gypsies,"** may cause the reader to question the critical judgment of him as a poetic primitive, the *douanier* Rousseau of English Romanticism. The poem's grouping of gypsies huddled under winter trees might have won William Gilpin's enthusiasm and approval; but the lyric sets out to deny before it confirms its apparent esthetic context: the picturesque. In all but rhyme it is a sonnet, also, though one almost devoid of the resources common to the lyric—metaphor, symbol, overtly expressive language. And yet, through the poet's apparent esthetic of denial, this anti-lyric, anti-pastoral, anti-sonnet achieves in its spare lines the characteristic aim of most lyrics—the expression of powerful feelings, of empathy, of passion.

By the late eighteenth century, gypsies were a cliché of the picturesque, and of newly popular ballads. The eighteenth-century picturesque was a solidly middle-class, comfortable esthetic, an art of vistas rather than of interiors. The crumbling cottage with ragged children around the door is ideally picturesque from a distance; the filth inside is concealed. One first assumes that Clare's primary impulse is anti-picturesque, for descriptive details are surprisingly frank (the "squalid camp," "tainted mutton," and "half-wasted dog.") And so the conclusion is another jolt: "Tis thus they live—a picture to the place." This statement is at least partly ironic, but **"Gypsies"** is anti-picturesque as Shakespeare's "When icicles hang by the wall" is anti-pastoral. Shivering chickens and chillblains are unexpected in city poetry about country life; yet the touches seem accurate because so keenly observed. Similarly, Clare flouts readers' expectations; these gypsies have no glamor or mystery, and their misery evokes pity rather than fascination.

Clare also teases expectations concerning genre. This poem is a modified sonnet. Its fourteen lines of extremely regular iambic pentameter are divided into a pattern of twelve lines of description closed and judged by a couplet. But Clare depends on substance, not rhyme, to create this shape, for there is only one rhyme in the entire poem. Thus the poem is recognized as a sonnet only in retrospect.

In the first twelve lines, the absence of strong formal outlines permits Clare to create a description that is "picturesque" in the original sense: "suitable for a picture." Compare the reading of this poem to the experience of looking at a painting. The present-tense description creates a sense of suspension and denies the pre-eminence of temporal process. These actors eternally inhabit one time and space. The imagery is almost entirely visual; the poet directs the eye from boy the man to dog, as the eye moves around a painting. Each remains a type, recognized but unknown in a more intimate sense. The characters remain merely figures in a landscape, and the speaker's objectivity suggests a detachment more readily associated with the plastic arts, which are denied the kinds of psychological insights central to literature. The painter can present emotions only through action or concrete symbols. So it is here: we enter a mind only once—the boy "thinks upon the fire and hurries back." Clare illustrates pervasive, unsatisfied hunger not in human thought or action, but by means of the waiting dog; an effective displacement, yet utterly impersonal and objective.

All the speaker's feelings and judgment, suppressed throughout the description, emerge in the final couplet, and with them comes a different kind of poetry: the lines rhyme, the syntax is inverted, the poet allows himself polysyllabic words and tightly organized alliterative patterns. This sudden, extravagant return to poetic resources suggests at first that the speaker has deserted or betrayed his gypsies. It is as if he had stepped back from the picture and flippantly dismissed the world he has created. (Given what is known of Clare, one might identify the motive for this movement as a fear of pain; empathy with outcasts is terrible, and must be avoided. The control and objectivity of the description, it seems, were a sort of repression which he now feels may fail, and so steps back even farther.)

Yet closer examination shows that pity and detachment are equally mixed in the couplet. The last line exemplifies the speaker's balance between sympathy and detachment (characterized in the poem by his tendency to place the gypsies in a "picture.") This final line also removes the poem from any sentimentality or romantic cliché; it is Clare's final surprise for the reader. The alliteration paradoxically emphasizes the understatement. "Pilfering" is petty thievery, and it suggests silent and trivial action (the "tainted mutton" may have a dubious provenance as well as a dubious smell). But the suspicion evoked by thievery is immediately countered by "unprotected." These gypsies are "vagrant dwellers in the houseless woods." Protection—a house—brings legal and social rights and responsibilities. But these gypsies have no shelter; thus their disregard for social conventions is not only understandable but inevitable.

The concluding rhyme gives a strong sense of closure and limitation; it defines the edges of the picture. The figures are set apart, subtly imprisoned. One may see the figures in the landscape painting as immortalized or as frozen, doomed to do the same thing forever; like the "men or gods" on the Grecian urn, Clare's gypsies are cold.

Richard Lessa (essay date 1982)

SOURCE: "Time and John Clare's *Calendar*," in *Critical Quarterly*, Vol. 24, No. 1, Spring, 1982, pp. 59-71.

[*In the following excerpt, Lessa distinguishes between* The Shepherd's Calendar *and other pastoral poems of the era, observing that Clare's* Calendar *relies on precise realism in addition to an understanding of time as cyclical.*]

John Clare's ***The Shepherd's Calendar*** is more descriptively calendar-like than any other pastoral poem that derives its essential structure from the differentiation of days, months or the seasons. The care and precision with which Clare characterises each month according to its weather, customary rural tasks and the typical activities of all living things creates a series of poems unique within the pastoral tradition. Description inevitably had a part in any pastoral, but usually only to provide an appropriate setting for the shepherd-poet whose lyric of love or lament for a lost companion was the poem's real reason for being. And equally remarkable within the pastoral tradition is the fact that never before had the country man been treated quite as he is in Clare's poem. It is true that there are long passages and even whole months where human concerns are the sole subject ('January, a cottage evening', for example, or 'June' or 'December'), but there are many more long passages and whole months where man is seen as nothing more than one kind of living creature doing whatever it is he does to sustain life. Clare has taken his own measure of man. If Wordsworth's *Michael* is remarkable for having given the pastoral genre a shepherd of larger-than-life heroic stature, then ***The Shepherd's Calendar*** is equally remarkable for bringing the country man back into perspective in a world full of life that often has little to do with man. At the same time, rural labour which also achieved a kind of heroic status through the figure of Michael, in Clare's poem becomes once again an endless, often wearisome concomitant of country life. Perhaps more than any other pastoral, *The Shepherd's Calendar* depicts the totality of life in a rural English village as it really did exist.

By refusing to paint a stylised and falsely idealistic picture of rural life, Clare is right on course with the tendency the English pastoral poem had been following since the middle of the eighteenth century. His poem is a calm and reasonable one, free of the strident tones and near hysteria of Crabbe's *The Village* and of a lesser rural poet like Stephen Duck. Clare's controlled and realistic handling of his subject is all the more remarkable when we consider that the plan which finally became *The Shepherd's Calendar* involved for him the facing of more than one dilemma. First, he had to reconcile his inclination, wherein lay his greatest strength as a poet, toward direct, objective representation of a rural world he knew and loved, with the need, encouraged by his publisher, John Taylor, and others, to 'elevate' and thus improve his descriptive poetry with appropriate sentiments. What these no doubt well meaning advisers called for was a kind of poetry more in line with the tradition of Thomson and Cowper, the tradition of nature moralised. It was a type of poetry Clare rarely wrote successfully. And then there was the problem all poets of the countryside faced—the need somehow to come to terms with the notion that the present time seems never to be as satisfactory as past times. A realistic treatment of rural life inevitably must come up against the changing values and the drive for progress that have made the present unlike the past. In Clare's case the fundamental problem was enclosure. It was a problem he had to face both as a poet of real rural life and as a native of the recently enclosed village of Helpston. The effects of enclosure could not be as easily ignored as could the uncongenial advice of publishers and friends.

The pastoral tradition historically offered two basic answers to the questions raised by an unsatisfactory present state of affairs. A poet could paint an idealized picture of life in the countryside and show it to be free of the corruption, exploitation and moral decay that resided of course in the city or court. If the countryside should fall upon hard times, as it does in *The Deserted Village,* one can show that the causes were the city-bred vices of luxury and mercantile greed. The other traditional answer was to devise a means of avoiding bad times by an escape to a safe haven. The barely accessible valley in which Michael lives is just such a means of avoidance, although it is one that does not endure beyond the lifetime of Wordsworth's shepherd-hero. And of course the temptation that besets and overcomes Luke, as well as all Michael's troubles, come from outside Grasmere Vale.

Neither of these alternatives figures significantly in *The Shepherd's Calendar.* There is nothing of the city-country motif in the poem, and its setting is certainly no happy valley, located beyond time and the problems of enclo-

sure. Clare was too honest, perhaps even too limited in his vision, and too much a product of the late eighteenth and early nineteenth-century realistic treatment of the pastoral world to create a false ideal of rural life. But he was also too much distressed by the state of post-enclosure Helpston not to seek relief from his disappointment. The one escape that Clare allows his speaker—and that infrequently—is an escape into childhood and the past of custom and tradition.

The relief that *The Shepherd's Calendar* offers, from a difficult life and ultimately from reality, is an escape not from a place but from time. Clare had no real desire to leave his native village and, in fact, drew upon its sights and sounds as the raw material at least of most of his pre-asylum poetry. So he turned to a time that he could look back on as better than the present. But even to speak of time in regard to a poem that claims an affinity with the pastoral tradition is to suggest that the genre's notion of timelessness had become more complex than early English pastoralism had allowed it to be. And so it had. We normally think of time as a thing of inexorable motion, a thing which, along with the tide, waits for no one. But pastoral time conventionally embodied an eternal present—no time and all time. It assured that the season was always spring and that shepherds and shepherdesses were perpetually young and had fallen in love only a few moments ago. Pastoral time could not be represented as a river or a line, but as a point, a unity, and if divisions were allowed to exist, they were like degrees on the circumference of a circle. Applied to the rural world, the notion of timelessness also had reference to certain values of life, like a simplicity of existence, innocence and a feeling of community, and to the idea that rural but not urban life had retained these values, changing little since the memory of man.

Of course, realistically, rural life was fundamentally concerned with time, much more so than urban life. The merchant, clerk or artisan could ply his trade in the city almost regardless of the time of day or the season of the year. But this was not true of the farmer, the herdsman, or even the farm labourer. What he did and when he did it depended on the time the sun rose and set, on the day of the week ('market day,' for example), but especially on the season. Each of these occurs cyclically—the days, weeks, months and seasons—and represents time as a self-renewing phenomenon, moving through the degrees of a circle and always coming to a new beginning. *The Shepherd's Calendar,* almost by its title alone, suggests such a notion of time. As a pastoral, it evokes a sense of the eternal present that is pastoral time, and as a 'calendar', it represents one round of the cycle that is a year. It is ironic, then, and at the same time a great part of the interest and importance of Clare's poem that both its language and its forays into the remembered past work against the ideas of suspended and cyclical time. My aim is to explore this irony further.

As if to establish early the importance to the country man of the circumstances of each month of the year, and to introduce the whole notion of time which will play so great a role, Clare tells us, thirteen lines into the poem, how a farmer might read bankrupt lists, grain prices,

> Or old moores anual prophecys
> That many a theme for talk supplys
> Whose almanacks thumbd pages swarm
> Wi frost and snow and many a storm
> And wisdom gossipd from the stars
> Of politics and bloody wars
>
> (p. 2)

[All quotations are from Clare's, *The Shepherd's Calendar,* ed. Eric Robinson and Geoffrey Summerfield, London, 1964. In the absence of numbered lines, page numbers follow each quotation.]

In fact, opening in January as it must, the poem plunges immediately into that season of the year when time weighs most heavily on the hands of the country man and makes its presence most keenly felt. Only then can the farmer afford to be idle. Only then can he 'behind the tavern screen / Sit—or wi elbow idly prest / On hob' (p. 1). Nearly all productive labour comes to a halt during this winter season when man and beast alike endure time's slow passage:

> While in the fields the lonly plough
> Enjoys its frozen sabbath now
> And horses too pass time away
> In leisures hungry holiday
> Rubbing and lunging round the yard
> Dreaming no doubt of summers sward
> As near wi idle pace they draw
> To brouze the upheapd cribs of straw
>
> (p. 3)

Except for the necessary feeding of livestock and some indoor tasks like milking and threshing, little rural labour seems to be going forward in 'A Winters Day'. And yet, this first poem shares with *The Shepherd's Calendar* as a whole that quality which immediately strikes readers of Clare's poetry—a sense of perpetual motion. Not only is our attention directed rapidly from object to object and from scene to scene, but also each object, defined briefly and with precision in a line or two, is captured as if it too were in motion. Each living thing that momentarily attracts the speaker's attention is apprehended in the process of doing something:

> The thresher first thro darkness deep
> Awakes the mornings winter sleep
> Scaring the owlet from her prey
> Long before she dreams of day
> That blinks above head on the snow
> Watching the mice that squeaks below
> And foddering boys sojourn again
> By rhyme hung hedge and frozen plain
> Shuffling thro the sinking snows
> Blowing his fingers as he goes
> To where the stock in bellowings hoarse
> Call for their meal in dreary close
> And print full many a hungry track
> Round circling hedge that guards the stack
>
> (pp. 2-3)

The absence of punctuation heightens our sense of rapid motion, but this is only a minor part of the effect of these lines. The key here is the relatively small number of copulative verbs in this verse, and the great number of verbs of action or process. At times the effect is a little like that in the children's verse about the house that Jack built—the thresher *awakes* the morning and *scares* the owl, that *blinks* above and *watches* the mice, that *squeak* below, and so on. Even the hedge, whose function would seem to depend on its remaining stationary, is described as an active doer, when it encircles and guards the hay stack. We leave this first part of 'January' with a sense that even in the frozen dead of winter there is a myriad of live and moving things to be seen and wondered at all around.

'A Winters Day' moves, after a brief look into the village tavern, from the view of a labourer in the pre-dawn darkness to the hurrying home at evening of all who have been abroad. In this chronological movement from morning to evening, the poem is typical of Clare's handling of the days, months and ultimately the whole year that make up *The Shepherd's Calendar.* On the one hand, we have a sense that the spatial pattern of each month's poem is, if not a circle, then at least a multitude of points falling within a circle. The speaker seems to be standing at some point in the centre of a rural village from which he can know what goes on around him. But he never moves out of this village circle to describe any other village or the world at large. And even within his circle, he does not lead us in a linear pattern, down a country road, for example, pointing out objects of interest as he moves along. On the other hand, there is a definite sense of time as a linear phenomenon in *The Shepherd's Calendar.* The poem as a whole moves from January to December, the farmer's labour moves from planting to harvest, and the days move, logically enough, from morning to night. This sense of time's movement is augmented by the overwhelming number of verbs of action which give the verse its sense of perpetual motion. The fact that no object or living thing is viewed as completely static gives each the quality of existing as 'in process'—that is, as something moving or being moved or used through a period of time, however brief. Take, for example, the owlet in the lines quoted earlier. Had Clare spoken of a bird 'That is above head on the snow', we would have been justified in imagining a stop-action photograph, a picture in one frame. But the fact that this is an owlet 'That blinks above head' imparts a sense of process to the line. The blinking of eyes, as instantaneous as the action might be, requires a series of frames, a motion picture, and ultimately the owlet is above and before us for a duration of time.

This quality of Clare's language, creative of a sense of movement through space and through time, and often both, is characteristic of *The Shepherd's Calendar* as a whole, but it is not, alone, what sets this poem apart from others in the pastoral tradition. After all, the characters of any pastoral have always been alive and moving, even if they only move their lips in song. What is unique about Clare's poem is the sense he conveys of life and motion in all things, including the inexorable forward motion of time. *The Shepherd's Calendar* in one respect is closer in character to a poem like *Michael* than to the conventionally timeless pastoral. Like Wordsworth's poem, it deals with the reality of the present time, and also looks back to a better time. The changes that have taken place in the interval between the present time of the speaker standing beside the unfinished sheepfold and the time when that sheep-fold represented a future hope are the essence of Michael's story and the whole poem. This could not be said of *The Shepherd's Calendar.* Change is hardly the poem's primary subject matter, and yet the speaker's glances backward—there are only a few—do point to a better time and in the process drive home the point that the past is indeed the past.

As early as 'A Cottage Evening', the second part of 'January', the poem leaves the present and the forward motion of time. Snug in the cottage before a crackling blaze, the evening meal finished and cleared away, the 'huswife' sits down to tell to her children once again her stock of amazing tales. Yet, as if to say that she is unwilling to lose touch with the present reality, 'Not willing to loose time or toil / She knits or sues and talks the while' (p. 12). Her tales are of mysterious disappearances, 'witches dread powers and fairey feats'—just the sort of things to capture the innocent imaginations of children and child-like adults. With the stories 'half told', the remainder left for 'tomorrows eve', the children creep off to bed while 'faireys like to rising sparks / Swarm twittering round them in the dark' (p. 18). We have been told all of this from the vantage point of an adult, although perhaps one who enjoyed the telling as much as a child might enjoy the listening. But then Clare does something that is unusual in *The Shepherd's Calendar*—he becomes 'philosophical'. Perhaps he acted in response to the urging of his publishers that he should be more 'entertaining'. At any rate, the poem suddenly begins to take on the character of the self-conscious philosophising of a professional versifier, with this apostrophe to the past:

> O spirit of the days gone bye
> Sweet childhoods fearful extacy
> The witching spells of winter nights
> Where are they fled wi their delights
> When listening on the corner seat
> The winter evenings length to cheat
> I heard my mothers memory tell
> Tales superstition loves so well
> Things said or sung a thousand times
> In simple prose or simpler ryhmes
>
> (p. 18)

All of a sudden we are reading a poem in the *ubi sunt* tradition—'Where are they fled . . . Ah where is page of poesy . . . Where are they now . . . To what wild dwelling . . . Where are they gone the joys and fears . . . ' The 'one withering flower' that is left to the adult, for whom reason has taken away 'childhoods visions', is that 'Memory may yet the themes repeat'. Memory is a poor substitute for the 'magic wonders' of childhood, but it is one that seems to be at least temporarily effective for the speaker. For, his poem seems to come to life again as soon as he begins to recall the tales that had once been

sources of wonder to him—the frog 'turned to a king and lover too', 'the tale of Cinderella' and the 'boy that did the jiants slay'. What is more, the speaker betrays his reluctance to give up the feeling of mystery and magic these memories recall when he refuses to leave them in the past. The tales of the 'huswife' are swept aside with the speaker's insistence that the experience of adulthood has destroyed childhood innocence. No doubt, he is right, yet in the telling of what has been lost, he seems to become once again caught up in the magic of these outworn tales. He is so caught up, in fact, that instead of settling for mere titles as a means of describing the stories he remembers from his childhood, he tells us each one almost from beginning to end. He even breaks into the final tale to tell us that in the face of the 'jiants' most awful threats, his heart 'sleeps on thro fear and dread / And terrors that might wake the dead' (p. 21). And then he plunges right back into this description of the giant:

> When like a tiger in the wood
> He snufts and tracks the scent of blood
> And vows if aught falls in his power
> He'll grind their very bones to flower
>
> (p. 21)

While insisting time and again that the past is gone forever, the speaker repeatedly refuses to let go even these momentary illusions of its return.

The old tales have not changed; nor has the child's response to them. It is the speaker himself who has changed. Time and his experience of the world have replaced the delightful fears of childhood imagination with the too real cares of everyday life. The recollection of childhood becomes, then, a nostalgic escape from the reality of the present, just as the pastoral ideal of rural life is an evasion of the reality of life as it is in the country. One might argue that any look backward and toward the simple way of life that is the pastoral ideal is really an attempt to create or recreate, however briefly, the natural feelings of a happy childhood—a lack of care and responsibility, a sense of belonging, and innocence of the complexities of reality. If these feelings are not warranted from an adult point of view, that does not really matter. The choice is finally between the innocence of the childlike mind and the harsh experiences of the adult. Suffering and cares exist whether the child is aware of them or not, just as they implicitly exist (in the city or at court) whether the shepherd of the pastoral tradition is aware of them or not.

Memory, such as that which brings back the speaker's past, reproduces a kind of innocence by simply omitting all that is painful in a child's world. In the present time, in the poem of 'August', a child's day is spent like this:

> The ruddy child nursed in the lap of care
> In toils rude ways to do its little share
> Beside its mother poddles oer the land
> Sun burnt and stooping with a weary hand
> Picking its tiney glean of corn or wheat
> While crackling stubbles wound its legs and feet
>
> (p. 96)

No doubt the speaker himself as a child experienced such days in August, but his memories are only of childhood joys. As he speaks in 'A Cottage Evening' he knows now that the joys and fears he felt as a result of the magic tales of his youth were as fleeting and illusory as the fairies and giants that occasioned them. But he also knows that his brief recapturing of childhood feelings is at least a momentary stay against 'A real world and doubting mind'. Sadly, for the man who would escape the reality of the present, the difference between the joys of childhood and the joys of the pastoral ideal lies in the degree of one's awareness. Childhood cannot see beyond itself, while the creator of an ideal pastoral world (or the poet who attempts to recreate childhood's feelings) must finally come to terms with the fact that he is dealing in illusion.

Nonetheless, the speaker only very reluctantly puts aside his recollection of childhood tales. The same reluctance appears when he has the chance to speak of certain rural customs and traditions of the past. 'May', for example, naturally carries a reminder of old May Day customs, and yet today old glories are 'All fled and left thee every one' (p. 60). But Clare does not leave the subject with just this bald statement. Instead, he tells us all that has fled and left. 'No flowers are pluckt to hail the[e] now' is a line sufficient to convey a simple matter of fact, but it hardly displays the feeling the speaker has for this lost custom. So we have this:

> —May locks new come
> And princifeathers cluttering bloom
> And blue bells from the woodland moss
> And cowslip cucking balls to toss
> Above the garlands swinging hight
> Hang in the soft eves sober light
> These maid and child did yearly pull
> By many a folded apron full
> But all is past
>
> (p. 61)

In the same way that the speaker told us the tales of childhood had lost their magic appeal and then went on to repeat each magic tale, he now tells us that old May Day traditions are no more, and then brings them back into being:

> the merry song
> Of maidens hurrying along
> To crown at eve the earliest cow
> Is gone and dead and silent now
> The laugh raisd at the mocking thorn
> Tyd to the cows tail last that morn
> The kerchief at arms length displayd
> Held up by pairs of swain and maid
> While others bolted underneath
> Bawling loud wi panting breath
> 'Duck under water' as they ran
>
> (p. 61)

This time, however, it is not an individual's inevitable passage from innocence to experience that has taken away some good part of the past. The enemy is called by name:

'And where enclosure has its birth / It spreads a mildew oer her mirth' (p. 61). This couplet is vaguely reminiscent of one in *The Deserted Village*: 'Ill fares the land, to hastening ills a prey, / Where wealth accumulates, and men decay' (ll. 51-2). But as a whole, **The Shepherd's Calendar** contains remarkably few references to enclosure and its effect of Helpston. For the most part, the poem seems simply to accept the present reality, and only in occasional backward glances to hint at a complaint. This is how the speaker leaves 'May':

> Yet summer smiles upon thee still
> Wi natures sweet unalterd will
> And at thy births unworshipd hours
> Fills her green lap wi swarms of flowers
> To crown thee still as thou hast been
> Of spring and summer months the queen
>
> (p. 62)

As it happens, the very next month, with its account of shearing time, again brings up the subject of the changes wrought by enclosure. Old men recall past delights, and we are told of them in loving detail: the great bowl 'of frumity where yearly swum / The streaking sugar and the spotting plumb', the 'stone pitcher' and 'clouded pint horn wi its copper rim' from which 'rude healths was drank' from the 'best broach the cellar would supply' (p. 66). In fact, it is an old man who speaks sadly of a bygone past, and although his reminiscence is momentarily interrupted by the realistic demands of his task, as soon as he can he will 'wipe his brow and start his tale again' (p. 66). Here, he is very much like the poem's speaker, whose recollections of the past are broken off by the intrusions of a present reality, and yet he returns again and again to these memories he cannot easily give up. Not all of the ancient customs, however, have disappeared. There is still the opportunity for a maid 'Giving to every swain tween love and shame / Her "clipping poseys" as their yearly claim' (p. 68). But for those who remember another time, what is left is little compared to what once was, for something more important than 'ale and songs' has been lost:

> And the old freedom that was living then
> When masters made them merry wi their men
> Whose coat was like his neighbors russet brown
> And whose rude speech was vulgar as his clown
> Who in the same horn drank the rest among
> And joined the chorus while a labourer sung
> All this is past—and soon may pass away
> The time torn remnant of the holiday
> As proud distinction makes a wider space
> Between the genteel and the vulgar race
> Then must they fade as pride oer custom showers
> Its blighting mildew on her feeble flowers
>
> (pp. 68-9)

This month's poem does not end with even the mildly positive note of 'May'. The 'proud distinction' that has grown up between the 'genteel and the vulgar race', even in this small village of Helpston, is a much more vicious result of enclosure than the consolidation of some fields and the re-routing of a few country lanes.

Clare makes his point—and it is one worth consideration—but he does not linger over it. There is the present to be lived and work to be done. The poem, from July to November, is again dominated by that sense of perpetual motion I described earlier. In fact, Clare seems to allow his speaker the luxury of pausing to look backward only when he tells of times of relative leisure for the country man or when the memory of strong rural traditions might expectedly be jolted to life. Thus it is that the past is evoked during the frozen months of January and December, during the month of May Day celebrations, and during shearing time when an old clipper has a captive audience of helpers and a host of memories. During the bustle of the harvest, for example, a country man's day is too filled with pressing tasks to permit a look to the past.

'November' is a month of mists and storms, until finally

> winter comes in earnest to fulfill
> Her yearly task at bleak novembers close
> And stops the plough and hides the field in snows
> When frost locks up the streams in chill delay
>
> (p. 123)

Time's inevitable forward movement is also about to be locked in chill delay, for Christmas has come, bringing ancient traditions and memories of childhood. Labour rests from its toil, mirth beguiles care, and old customs are renewed. 'December' is, appropriately, a summing up of the rest of the year, at least with regard to the speaker's earlier thoughts on time's passage and the changes that have come about in time. The opposition of pride to simplicity that we first saw at the end of 'June' reappears to help explain the gradual loss of the old customs. And self-consciously, 'the poets song' is hailed as the preserver of the past. It is a role that is fulfilled by looking in two directions at one time, for it represents both a glance backward to the past and a record for the future. But again, Clare is more concerned to tell of ancient customs than to dwell on the fact of their passing. And so he does tell of singers and village bells, the '"Morrice danse"', the 'prentice boy' and his '"Christmass box"', and the simple mirth of friends gathering.

December is after all just the month to allow Clare to bring together his two principal ideas of the past—the past of each individual, his childhood, and the past of a society, village life before enclosure. 'December' is the natural meeting place for the joys of the child,

> The wooden horse wi arching head
> Drawn upon wheels around the room
> The gilded coach of ginger bread
> And many colord sugar plumb
> Gilt coverd books for pictures sought
> Or storys childhood loves to tell
> Wi many a urgent promise bought
> To get tomorrows lesson well
>
> (p. 129)

and the joys of the adult,

> The shepherd now no more afraid
> Since custom doth the chance bestow
> Starts up to kiss the giggling maid
> Beneath the branch of mizzletoe . . .
> While snows the window panes bedim
> The fire curls up a sunny charm
> Where creaming oer the pitchers rim
> The flowering ale is set to warm
>
> (pp. 126, 127)

The two come together in the realisation that one of the joys of adulthood is the memory of childhood joy at Christmas:

> Tho mankind bids such raptures dye
> And throws such toys away as vain
> Yet memory loves to turn her eye
> And talk such pleasures oer again
>
> (p. 129)

But the joining of these two ideas of the past serves also to suggest that both depend on a state of mind. As in 'A Cottage Evening', the wondrous stories and the Christmas toys have not changed as much as has the man who now perceives them through an adult's eyes. It is an inevitable change that each individual experiences. But village life has also undergone a change from the past to the present time, and the fact that the Christmas season retains at least 'the shadow still of what hath been' makes the loss of other traditions throughout the year that much more poignant. Whether their day to day existence really seemed better to past generations because they had the benefit of the old customs and traditions is not a question that Clare or probably anyone can answer with much assurance. The poet can show us, however, that a man does not regret the loss of the wonder and magic of childhood quite so much when he has the simple traditions of neighbourliness and mutual good cheer to compensate for them.

Enclosure no doubt wrought physical changes in the village of Helpston. Yet it is remarkable that *The Shepherd's Calendar,* a poem almost passionately concerned with accurate description of the physical reality of rural life, does not speak of one such change. When Clare talks of change, it is the intangible changes and losses that he reveals—the new distinction between master and man, and the loss of the feeling for doing things as they had always been done. These changes have not come about in a place, but in time.

Ultimately, perhaps, Clare's poem has more to do with a sense of place than with a sense of time. And yet, to ignore its handling of time is, I think, to deprive the poem of one of its most profound values, both as a pastoral and as an evocation of rural life. From the point of view of time, *The Shepherd's Calendar* piles irony upon irony. The poem is after all a pastoral, so we think of time suspended, and a 'calendar', which sees time as cyclical and ever-renewing. Yet, ironically, its language is the language of a perpetual and forward motion, and it speaks of time's inexorable movement and the pastness of the past.

And finally it is a poem, a work of art that arrests time and holds the past suspended for ever in the present.

> Old customs O I love the sound
> However simple they may be
> What ere wi time has sanction found
> Is welcome and is dear to me
> Pride grows above simplicity
> And spurns it from her haughty mind
> And soon the poets song will be
> The only refuge they can find
>
> (p. 126)

Edward Strickland   (essay date 1982)

SOURCE: "Conventions and Their Subversion in John Clare's 'An Invite to Eternity,'" in *Criticism*, Vol. XXIV, No. 1, Winter, 1982, pp. 1-15.

[In the following excerpt, Strickland demonstrates how Clare subverts the tradition of the poetic 'invitation' in his asylum poem "An Invite to Eternity."]

In recent years several critics have re-examined the nature-poetry of John Clare in relation to the eighteenth-century topographical tradition and its Romantic revisions. This has helped to clarify the context of the better part of the "peasant poet's" corpus. But if Thomson and Cowper ranked among Clare's favorite poets, his favorite play was *Macbeth,* which he claims to have read "about 20 times," and this predilection, along with his years of ballad-collecting, perhaps bears more strongly on the preternatural poems of his twenty-three year confinement in St. Andrew's County Lunatic Asylum. Despite the valuable upsurge of critical interest in the descriptive poetry, the later visionary works remain for many of us Clare's most notable achievements. We may be intrigued by the first but haunted by the second, this reflecting our response to the very different poetic personae of the self-tutored "village minstrel" and the obsessed madman. Ultimately both are perhaps as much literary anomalies as major poets, but the earlier Clare is a curiosity of a cultural sort, the later an archetypal.

Of what precisely does Clare become a living emblem in his confinement? First of all, of the poet martyred to his art. As he informed Agnes Strickland in August 1860 with the poignant directness that characterizes so many of his statements, "Literature has destroyed my head and brought me here." In his confinement "in the land of Sodom where all the peoples brains are turned the wrong way" the retreat of the post-Romantic artist from a progressively brutalized society is raised to the next power, albeit Clare's retreat was involuntary. The otherworldliness of Rossetti's obsession with the image of Beatrice is mirrored, perhaps in a cracked glass, in Clare's monomaniacal reminiscences of Mary Joyce, the "first wife" of his fantasy. Just as his ploughman's experience, and description, of raw nature reveals much landscape poetry, fashionable and greater, as nature glimpsed from between

blinders or through a Claude-glass, so his late poems return us to the High Romantics recalling Lamb's admonition "Dream not, Coleridge, of having tasted all the grandeur and wildness of fancy till you have gone mad!"

But there is more to the almost numinous attraction of the later Clare than his incarnation of literary archetypes. In the terrible delusions about his youthful love, the tormented Clare embodies that element of ourselves which, perhaps accommodating itself functionally to reality while remaining imaginatively disengaged from it, displaces the desire for fulfilment from afterlife (or social millennium) to an equally wish-fulfilling vision of the past. The shallowest form of this is nostalgia; more powerful is a repetition-compulsion of reminiscence; in Clare's obsession, however, we have nothing less than the transformation, the re-writing as it were, of his own past—a process that simultaneously transforms Clare himself. He becomes, ultimately, not only the archetype of the lover unrequited either by his love or reality itself, but of a romantic Adam banished from the Eden of his erotic fancy. Yet if Clare comes to appear a kind of primal victim, a complementary side of his personality, and of human perseverance generally, is displayed in his at once farcical and somehow heroic identification of himself with prizefighters of the day, conflated with one of his literary idols and alter egos in the description of himself as "Boxer Byron" who never backed down from a fight. A complex pathos is evident here, as in Christopher Smart's recounting of his alcohol-inspired public prayer as "I praised the Lord in St. James Park till I routed all the company." For both proclamations, penned in madhouses of different centuries, boast of victory amid quite catastrophic defeat, and if in that defeat we find an image of our own condemnation to the tragic condition of being human, in the boasting we may recognize written large the various forms of vain self-bolstering, public or internal, to which we resort to survive that condition, relatively speaking, intact.

The figure of the later Clare is more imposing than the sum of those poems, letters and utterances in which he gives voice to the various archetypes he personifies. Among the visionary poems, **"I Am"** represents Clare the social and erotic exile longing for his paradise lost. In **"A Vision"** this defeat is qualified—or rather subsumed—by the bizarre and structurally disjointed assertion of apocalyptic triumph in the last six lines. But in **"An Invite to Eternity,"** probably written, like the others, in the mid-1840s, Clare more subtly and cogently unites the sense of utter desolation with the assertion of a singularly desperate will-to-power.

As unique a poem as **"An Invite to Eternity"** is, its generic conventions are venerable. The "invitation" may even be considered a lyric sub-genre, in which the poet traditionally addresses his beloved in an effort of amorous persuasion amid a natural setting. Perhaps the most famous invitations in English are Marvell's "To His Coy Mistress" and Herrick's "Corinna's Going A-Maying," yet proceeding backwards chronologically we find such celebrated lyrics as Jonson's "Come, my Celia, let us prove," Marlowe's "The Passionate Shepherd to his Love" and several songs of John Dowland (e.g., in his *First Booke of Songs* of 1597 numbers XI, "Come away, Come Sweet Love," and XVII, "Come again, Sweet Love doth now Invite)." Wordsworth adapted the convention to non-amorous ends in the early "To My Sister" and "The Tables Turned." Clare himself wrote many conventional invitations, from the early ballad **"Winter's gone, the summer breezes"** to the Northborough poem **"With Garments Flowing"** to the asylum poems **"'Tis April and the morning love"** and that entitled **"The Invitation."** probably composed five years after **"An Invite to Eternity"**:

> Come hither, my dear one, my choice one, and rare one,
> And let us be walking the meadows so fair,
> Where pilewort and daisies in light and gold blazes,
> And the wind plays so sweet in thy bonny brown hair.
> > [In a footnote, the critic states: "I follow the text of *Poems of John Clare's Madness,* ed. Geoffrey Grigson, London, Routledge & Kegan Paul, 1949."]

The first two lines of **"An invite to Eternity"** introduce the poem in a similar vein, and could have served to begin another of the same sort, or a folk-song equivalent like "Wild Mountain Thyme":

> Wilt thou go with me sweet maid
> Say maiden wilt thou go with me.
> > [Text of **"An Invite to Eternity"** from *Clare: Selected Poems and Prose,* pp. 223-24.]

Yet when the itinerary of his voyage is revealed, the convention is transformed.

> Through the valley depths of shade
> Of night and dark obscurity
> Where the path hath lost its way
> Where the sun forgets the day
> Where there's nor life nor light to see
> Sweet maiden wilt thou go with me.

The landscape painted in these lines sends us back to the opening with different ears. The chiastic repetition of the opening, which at first appears delightfully lyrical, now sounds ominous in its insistence, the apostrophe to the "sweet maid" darkly, even diabolically, ironic. Expecting the usual invitation to go a-Maying, we are plunged instead into a bewitched world of darkness visible. In an early poem Clare spoke of his childhood initiation into this realm by the magical folktales told him by his mother, and **"An invite to Eternity"** is on one level a kind of existential version of the "animistic fancy" John and Anne Tibble noted as essential to the "northern fairy-tale" tradition Clare inherited like Burns and others.

It is perhaps because of his exposure to Faerie at so impressionable an age that Clare felt most at home with *Macbeth* of Shakespeare's plays. Another tributary to the witchcraft that flows through **"An invite to Eternity"** is the ballad-tradition, Clare himself having been a post-Percy pre-Child collector of ballads. In this first stanza Clare combines the ontological vacancy of his own con-

finement with the animism of folk-art. The path is not merely lost (cf. *Inferno,* I, 3) but "hath lost its way"; the sun is not merely eclipsed but "forgets the day." This is not an indifferent nature drained of vitality but a vaguely inimical one involved in something like unconscious conspiracy against the poet. This element of nature's antagonism to man continues in the next stanza:

> Where stones will turn to flooding streams
> Where plains will rise like ocean waves
> Where life will fade like visioned dreams
> And mountains darken into caves
> Say maiden wilt thou go with me
> Through this sad non-identity
> Where parents live and are forgot
> And sisters live and know us not.

Analyzing Clare's creative swerve from the panoramic or telescopic technique of the Denham tradition, Timothy Brownlow suggests that Clare's nature poetry adopts a "kinetic and microscopic" viewpoint rather, or "could be called kaleidoscopic (it is not concerned with distancing but with comprehensiveness, a circular all-at-oneness)." In this very achievement are the roots of the pathological intensity achieved later in **"An invite to Eternity"** and to a lesser extent others among the asylum poems. In the hallucinated stanza just quoted kinetic perspective takes on an awesome potency. The volatility of Clare's "all-at-oneness" of viewpoint becomes incorporated by matter itself, the comprehensive effluence of the nature-poet's visionary capability transmuted into, or projected onto, given reality. In Blake's words "the Eye altering alters all." As in the asylum landscapes of Van Gogh, the terrible energy and instability of the artist's psyche divests external reality of its autonomous objectivity and infuses it with its own sense of vertiginous mutability. In this visionary reversal both Van Gogh and Clare invert an impressionistic aesthetic into something proto-expressionist or surrealist. The same process is at work in MS. 110, stanza "2" of the asylum poems, in which valleys are similarly metamorphosed into waves.

Whereas the traditional invitation landscape is a kind of erotic benediction of natural flux—the rebirth of vitality in the animal and vegetative celebrations of the vernal scene—here the progression is not from frozen winter to vibrant spring but from the fixedness of external nature to the frenzy of hallucination. Vision is experienced as an assault. In an awful complementarity with the liquefaction of stones and plains, the dark air undergoes a petrifaction—darkness becomes not only visible but tangible. In this Ultro-like state the ego is paralyzed in face of visionary assault by erstwhile-solid objects become emanations of raw energy. Nature literally rises against the poet as his will contracts in the unchosen cremitism of his "non-identity." The cave is a symbol of Clare's visionary disorientation as much as his physical confinement.

The last quatrain of the stanza modulates into the more personal element of the poet's devastation, the sense of radical solitude of literal unfamiliarity of the inner death he explores in the second half of the poem.

> Say maiden wilt thou go with me
> In this strange death of life to be
> To live in death and be the same
> Without this life or home or name
> At once to be and not to be
> That was and is not—yet to see
> Things pass like shadows—and the sky
> Above, below, around us lie.
>
> The land of shadows wilt thou trace
> And look nor know each others face
> The present mixed with reasons gone
> And past and present all as one
> Say maiden can thy life be led
> To join the living with the dead
> Then trace thy footsteps on with me
> We're wed to one eternity.

What is striking about the third stanza is the relative abnegation of imagery as the poet attempts to describe rather than depict his desolation. This more discursive than imagistic section of the work is disjointed allusively as much as syntactically. Just as the second quatrain opens with the vaguely referential subordinate clause "That was and is not," so the echoes of earlier writers approach in their imprecise citation something like a desperate reliance on remembered snatches of poetry to articulate the ineffable. It is perhaps not indefensible to read that stanza as Clare's premonition of the modernist plight of Eliot attempting to structure the desolation of his later age with the poetry of allusion. These fragments I have shored against my ruin: the echoes of Coleridge's *Rime* and "Epitaph" in "death of life" and "live in death"; of *Hamlet* in "to be and not to be"; and of the last line of Shelley's *Alastor* in the disruptively inserted "That was and is not."

There is another sort of disjunction—i.e., of rhyme scheme—as we enter the third stanza. The first two stanzas follow the model ABABCCDD; the third and fourth shift to AABBCCDD. Apart from this change of course, it seems noteworthy that the first two stanzas are themselves asymmetrical. Rather than octets they are conceived as pairs of quatrains, first ABAB, second AABB. Clare is writing, essentially, in variant ballad stanzas, yoked in pairs somewhat arbitrarily—a situation which becomes particularly evident when syntax breaks down in (double-) stanza three. The tension between invitation address and ballad supernaturalism noted earlier is further reflected structurally in the use of the former's traditional tetrameter and the covert stanzaic form of the latter.

Clare transforms his poem into a darkly parodic epithalamion at the work's conclusion. "Wed to one eternity" culminates a process of physical and chronological breakdown. Just as the marriage ceremony traditionally symbolizes social cohesion and elemental fecundity, so this insane marriage becomes the crowning symbol of a confounding rather than communion of identities. After the loss of all bearings in the nightmarish vertigo depicted at the conclusion of stanza three, matter itself becomes insubstantial. "The land of shadows wilt thou trace"—the verb suggesting not only to measure but to hunt down. In this impossible parody of a quest all distinctions are blurred. The past is as the present. The living are as the dead. Even the loss of the first person in "each others face" suggests the annihilation of identity. It is difficult to share the Tibbles' belief that this eternity is "the eternity of poetry," which "besides being a compensation for his present neglect and isolation, is yet something other than the orthodox 'better world' of happiness beyond the grave." The last clause is self-evident, but is not Clare's eternity in fact the mythic form of his neglect and isolation in the pathological world of his delusions? Alone in his "captivity among the Babylonians," writing letters to his "two wives," one of whom died even before he entered St. Andrew's, he dwells in the a-temporal world of an eternity in which the past has indeed usurped the present and the dead vampirize the living, most of all himself.

II

The precise nature of Clare's invitation is as subject to debate as his eternity. From a very different perspective than the Tibbles', Harold Bloom has found at the end of this "so hopeless" vision "a tone of something like triumph," but is less specific in proposing what that triumph might be. Yet his analysis of the conclusion has the virtue of articulating its central interpretive problems: "What meaning can the poem's last line have if eternity is a state merely of non-identity? Why 'wed' rather than 'bound'? . . . Last, and most crucial, if this *is* an invitation, where is the voluntary element in the vision? What lies in the will of the maiden?"

Perhaps the key to those questions lies in another, namely "Who is the maiden of the invitation?" The biographical answer, identifying her with Mary Joyce, has generally been tacitly assumed, and seems to me both correct and in itself insufficient. For Mary Joyce, the daughter of a Glinton farmer, became many distinct and even contradictory beings, endowed by her absence, like many another beloved, with the protean facility of becoming the embodiment of all the poet had lost and lamented. His deprivation of her became a metonym, in Clare's fantasy, for the various losses of his existence, and even of human existence itself. One critic has suggested that "The phantom of his lost love, Mary Joyce, from being part of the loveliness of Nature became its symbol, till at last in hymning the woman of his dream he is hymning his Nature-love." Eric Robinson and Geoffrey Summerfield concentrate on the archetypal nature of Clare's passion, arguing that after their youthful estrangement Mary remained to Clare "for the rest of his days the symbol of innocence, the Eve of his Eden, the First Love which was to be touchstone for all later experience. In their early *John Clare: A Life* the Tibbles proposed that **"An invite to Eternity"** became an invitation directed "to Love herself perhaps." Mark Storey reflects some of the complexity of the poet's relationship to his lost lady in his evasion of a simple symbolic equation of Mary with a single concept, commenting that "Mary became synonymous with the muse, and with nature" and "is in some sense Clare's prison; he wrote to shackle himself to his ideal, to find a freedom that entails his becoming part of her, his identity lost in hers."

Interpretations of Mary as Eve, Beatrice/Laura, Mary the sister of Lazarus, Nature, Love, the Muse, or the prison house—all find at least sufficient and often explicit support in Clare's writings. One of the most telling lines Clare even penned comes in a song from the ***Child Harold*** cycle: "But Marys absent every where." To a great extent, Clare's identification with Byron's exile-hero is founded on his sense of irreparable divorce from Mary, who in the course of that cycle, the complement to ***The Village Minstrel*** in Clare's own version of the growth of a poet's mind, assumes variously all the symbolic forms explicated by the poet's critics. She as much as Helpstone embodies the exile's lost homeland or harbor and is similarly "abscent" as an image of the idyllism of the poet's childhood.

Beyond this, in her paradoxically omnipresent absence, she symbolizes the insufficiency of reality to human desire and the poet's consequent sense of radical estrangement from his environment. His divorce from reality (here a singularly apt metaphor rather than a clinical cliché) was both the product in part of his separation from Mary and the nurturing soil for his pathological reunion with her in progressively obsessive delusions. If "my dear first love & early wife" helped drive him to the madhouse, it was perhaps only there that he could "wed" himself to her, at least relatively undistracted by the presence of his "real" family. Long since vanished, she becomes almost palpable "every where" by occupying the interstices that exist, for all of us, between the given world and the transcendental thrust of human aspiration. Only a very partial creator of that psychological and spiritual abyss, she becomes its guardian spirit, both a *genius loci* and a censor of the void.

In a sense the blossoming in the 1830s of Clare's delusions concerning his early life with Mary represent the pathology of a convention. Despite his obsession with Mary as the fulfillment of his dreams, we must keep in mind that Clare not only married and raised seven children with his "second wife Patty" (Martha Turner) but addressed many a tender poem to her over the years. Thus a sentimentally indulgent perspective on the earlier relationship merits some of the scorn heaped by D. H. Lawrence on Dante for never mentioning, amid his mystic devotions to Beatrice, the "family of lusty little Dantinos" back home with Signiora Alighieri. And it must also turn a blind eye to the Patty poems, not to mention those lines addressed to **"Sweet Susan," "Bessey of the glen," "My sweet Ann Foot, my bonny Ann," "Sweet Mary Dove," "Miss B—,"** and numerous others.

However intense Clare's first love may have been, it was in fact succeeded if not superseded by others, the absence in some sense filled. Yet the intensity of his feelings of both love and consequent loss grew rather than dimin-

ished with time. Clare's statement "Literature has destroyed my head and brought me here" may be of particular relevance to the Mary Joyce question. For even in the poems of the early 1820s in which Mary appears Clare depicts her as an angelic, elfin, witching form. However sincere his feelings for her, that is to say, her poetic incarnation occurs well within the confines of poetic convention. In the conclusion of **"A Daydream in Summer"** she is the veiled maiden of *Alastor* and the Cynthia of Keats's *Endymion* reincarnate in Northamptonshire: "When her small waist he strove to clasp / She shrunk like water from his grasp." In later poems she assumes a fictive aura that owes as much to Jonson and the Cavaliers as to the *trecento* poets and their descendants.

Mary, as a poetic figure, was from the start conceived as a poetic convention, her absence a prerequisite to her idealization. In her association with the nurturing landscape and imaginative passon of Clare's youth she presents herself as an avatar of the eponymous Rural Muse of Clare's fourth collection. His progressive obsession with her throughout the 1830s was a form of compensation for Clare's painful lack of sympathetic society, the fading of his notoriety, and perhaps his fear of the loss of poetic vision with youthful hopes. Having nowhere to turn for inspiration, and few to turn to for encouragement, he sought both in the resurrection of an adolescent love, the pristine quality of which embodied all the now-shattered hopes delineated in his apologia ***The Village Minstrel.***

As Clare's muse Mary comes to undergo a fearful transformation. Muselike initially in the conventional sense—i.e., as the object of the poet's amorous effusions—she comes to be identified with his imaginative life and poetic capacity itself. Without her, Clare faced an imaginative vacancy inimical to his art. An inspirer of verse and simultaneously a blocking-agent of that vacancy, her image becomes not only the central figure of his imaginative life but its emblem: "Mary the muse of every song I write," "Mary thou ace of hearts thou muse of song". . . . In ***Child Harold*** Clare indulges the curious proclivity to cosmic exaggeration seen in **"A Vision,"** affirming "I loved her in all climes beneath the sun." Here the lunatic, the lover and the poet are truly of imagination all compact—and both the peculiar appeal and clear limitations of Clare's love poetry are founded on their fusion, the inability of the poet to keep distinct the delusions of his fantasy and the exercise of his imagination.

There may be, then, a symbolic truth in Clare's delusions of having committed bigamy. In the isolation of his rural life in the 1830s, finding his diurnal affairs progressively disjunct from his imaginative life, he became torn between the facticity of his life with Martha and the children and the demands of his creativity. The latter came to focus in an ever more exclusive and escapist manner on Mary, only in part as the earlier object of his affections. This conflict of allegiances, which brought about his breakdown finally, was a "bigamous" tension between domestic life and marriage to the Muse-figure who emblematized his imaginative life. The essence of his delusion about Mary is the confluence of woman and archetype, the subsumption of a human memory by a literary convention become a pathological reality.

Clare's poetry progressed from descriptive apostrophe to literal invocation of Mary, as in the ***Child Harold*** song "O Mary sing thy songs to me." Yet his invocation of her went beyond the traditional soliciting of poetic aid. He seems rather to have conjured her habitually as a kind of charm against his desolation. I think we can take Clare quite literally when he describes this almost mantra-like address: "Mary how oft with fondness I repeat / That name alone to give my troubles rest." His imaginative idolatry takes the form of something like a profane rosary.

It is important nonetheless to note that concurrently with his idealizing of woman, Clare indulges in his verse and prose that cynical distrust of her C. S. Lewis has called a twin fruit from the same branch. The conflict of tones is less a matter of complementarity here than simple contradiction, reflecting the extremes of Clare's mental illness, be it cyclothymic or schizophrenic. His ***Don Juan*** is full of bitterness, emulating Byron's, and there are hints of it as early as the ballad "The spring returns, the pewit screams," in which he refers to "woman's [and specifically Mary's] cold perverted will / And soon estrainged opinion." In his letters we find him remarking "a man who possesses a woman possesses losses without gain the worst is the road to ruin & the best is nothing like a good cow—man I never did like & woman has long sickened me." In an asylum letter to the long since dead Mary he turns with pathetically rancorous energy on his "vagrant Muse": "though I have two wives if I got away I should soon have a third & I think I should serve you both right in the bargain by doing so for I dont care a damn about coming home now—so you need not flatter yourself with many expectations of seeing me."

The ambivalence of Clare's feelings of obsessive love and betrayal is articulated in **"An invite to Eternity"** in the sardonic nature of the no-longer conventional invitation. That convention, as remarked, is subverted by the landscape of the work. The terrain of this "eternity" is the demonic obverse of his earlier **"The Eternity of Nature"**—a deracinated world of shifting dimensions akin to the preternature of various folk-ballads. It has the crepuscular aura of "Thomas Rhymer," the protean insubstantiality of "The Young Tamlane." Yet the poem really perhaps recalls most proximately the ballad tradition of the "demon lover," more comprehensively than Coleridge's crucial but passing allusion to the motif in "Kubla Khan."

In the ballad known as "The Carpenter's Wife," for example, a young woman is visited by her seafaring lover who has returned to find her married to another whose child she has borne. After persistent temptation he succeeds in convincing her to run off with him to sea, where at length his diabolic nature (in some versions a "cloven hoof") is revealed before the ship sinks and the runaway wife is drowned. Invited to green foreign hills (in some versions "the banks o' Italie"), she is led to a submarine landscape. Clare's persona in **"An invite to Eternity"** proves similarly diabolical, and in the relationship be-

tween the lovers of the ballad he perhaps found an objective correlative for his own sense of past wrong and ultimate revenge.

But if the biographical roots of the conflict are thus apparent, the explication of its symbolism is nonetheless inseparable from Mary's emblematic nature as a Muse-figure. The poem may be on one level a sardonic and vengeful invitation to a faithless and free lover to join the poet in his physical confinement and mental anguish; on another it is a cry to her, in her function as inspirer, for help.

In the 1860 interview with Agnes Strickland, when asked what he meant by charging "they pick my brains out," Clare replied "Why, they have cut off my head, and picked out all the letters of the alphabet—all the vowels and consonants—and brought them out through my ears; and then they want me to write poetry! I can't do it." Clare's ability to go on creating through two decades of confinement is a singular triumph of the imagination and will over unpropitious conditions, both physical and psychological. **"An invite to Eternity,"** I believe, is concerned more than anything else with articulating his difficulties and his doubts about his ability to go on as a poet.

On this level the opening repeated question is by no means rhetorical. Rather Clare is searching his soul, questioning his own imagination: Muse, wilt thou go with me? Even here—to the disoriented world of madness which he proceeds to delineate, and in depicting which he answers the question finally in the affirmative.

This may be the real triumph of the poem. The "eternity" to which the poet looks is neither solely literary, as in the Tibbles' interpretation of his concern with poetic immortality, nor-extra-literary in any theological sense. Clare's eternity is not the infinite extension of time but its absence—first in the disorientation of his mental state, and secondly in its self-transcendence in the dialectical progress of the poem, which circles back upon itself. The concluding affirmation is nothing less than a hierogamy of poet and Muse, complete with a grimly courageous procession to a visionary altar: "Then trace thy footsteps on with me / We're wed to one eternity." For analogies to this sacred marriage we need not look so far afield as the "chymical wedding" of alchemy or anthropological royal incest, for High Romanticism is full of such unions, from the demonic couplings of Coleridge's mystery triptych to Keats's *Endymion*, "La Belle Dame sans Merci" and *Lamia*. The better part of D. G. Rossetti's poetic corpus consists of variations on this theme.

Yet once again Clare's delineation of the relationship is as subversive as it is conventional. In the poems named, for example, it is the Muse-figure, as the symbol of the creative unconscious, that is at home in the preternature into which she draws the poet or his surrogate. The wailing woman summons the poet of "Kubla Khan" from the fashionable Oriental idyll of the first stanza into a magical realm that was thereafter to become his visionary home, and prison. Cynthia leads Endymion from a native land to which, like the Ancient Mariner after his confrontation with Life-in-Death, he never fully returns. Clare inverts the traditional relationship between Muse and poet, guide and guided. In his madness he is already initiated into a realm to which the Muse is a stranger. She is invited to a landscape that is without substance or stability, which the poet succeeds in traversing and infusing with form by forcing his Muse, the emblem of the transformative imagination, to accompany him. The coerced tracing of rhythmic or metrical footsteps is a Los-like assertion of the imagination's supremacy over chaos in a region as amorphous as the phantasmal forest of Entuthon Benython that surrounds Blake's Golgonooza.

It would be comforting to leave Clare in his moment of complex triumph. But the comfort would be specious since, as I suggested earlier, the figure of the poet confined in "the English Bastile a government Prison where harmless people are trapped and tortured till they die" is greater than the sum of his creations there. Having now spent some time with what is possibly the finest of those works, I will close with a non-poetic utterance, his last letter, in which the aged poet comes to share the mythic aura in which Wordsworth perceived that blind London beggar with the facts of his life pinned to his chest. This letter, written in response to an unknown inquirer Mr. James Hipkin, seems not only a testament to the provisional nature of the redemptive power of poetic form and the ultimate triumph of the ineffable, but almost, like the beggar's label, a symbol "of the utmost we can know, / Both of ourselves and of the universe."

> March 8 1860
>
> Dear Sir,
>
> I am in a Madhouse & quite forget your Name or who you are You must excuse me for I have nothing to communicate or tell of & why I am shut up I dont know I have nothing to say so I conclude
>
> Yours respectfully
>
> John Clare.

Vimala Herman (essay date 1987)

SOURCE: "How to See Things with Words: Language Use and Descriptive Art in John Clare's 'Signs of Winter,'" in *Language and Style,* Vol. 20, No. 2, Spring, 1987, pp. 91-109.

[*In the following excerpt, Herman argues that contrary to popular critical belief, John Clare crafted his poems meticulously with the intention of achieving vivid images and heightened responses.*]

That John Clare was a descriptive poet every reader of his poems would agree. That his descriptive skill was an unalloyed asset to his poetic art is a much more contentious issue. Thus, even the more enthusiastic apprecia-

tions of Clare's descriptive art are tempered with reservations, which echo Keats's observations as conveyed to Clare by John Taylor, that "the Description overlaid and stifled that which ought to be the Prevailing Idea."

John Middleton Murry, while endorsing Clare's "faculty of sheer vision" that he deems to be "unique in English poetry," remarks that "there is an intrinsic impossibility that vision of this kind . . . should ever pass beyond itself. . . . Clare's vision, we might say paradoxically, is too perfect." As John Barrell has reminded us, the assumption behind such statements—the idea that "for a descriptive poem to have content, it must pass beyond itself, into meditation or whatever," that is, that the "Prevailing Idea" must prevail and that the details of description must be subordinated to it—is something we should be wary of. Such assumptions have generated assessments of Clare as a failed Blake or Wordsworth. Until recently, few thought Clare's descriptive art was worth attention in its own right without such distorting external standards being applied to it. That Clare's singularity of vision presented him with artistic problems that needed radical solutions so that his individuality could find expression at all is a fact that has been recognized slowly. His debt to, as well as his distance from, the prevailing aesthetic and poetic conventions of his day are being more fully explored in order that his own artistic practice may be more fairly assessed.

One area that is still underinvestigated is Clare's linguistic art or the stylistic choices used that produce the effect of "purity of vision" in his poetry. This neglect is not surprising. Firstly, Clare's poetry has generally been regarded as a spontaneous overflow of an unmediated vision of nature. Middleton Murry is perhaps typical of this orientation:

> Clare was indeed a singer born. . . . He was either a voice, one of the unending voices of Nature, or he was an eye, an unwearied eye watching the infinite processes of Nature; perhaps never a poet consciously striving by means of art to arouse in men's minds an emotion like his own.

What is missing from such pronouncements is the fact that the poems are crafted language—crafted to communicate the singularity of vision that was Clare's own and that such effects were a product of linguistic and rhetorical choices in Clare as much as they are in the work of any other poet. Secondly, whenever Clare's language has claimed critical attention, it has usually been to his detriment, since the focus has been on elements in his style that were seen as expressions of his social origins—dialect words, "substandard" grammar, lack of punctuation, and the like—which were regarded as offenses against prevailing canons of taste and barriers to artistic achievement. If we accept the modern case that Clare should be judged on his own terms in relation to what he was trying to achieve, then we also accept that his linguistic choices have artistic functions to perform that are worth investigation in their own right, a task that undue concentration on aspects of his biography alone cannot do. As Peter Levi has pointed out,

What was important in John Clare's genuineness was neither the extremity of his madness, nor the sweetness and harshness of his rural youth. They do mark him and limit him and define him. But in his artistry his workshop was the English language, and what is genuine in him could be seen and felt as language. That is the only medium in which we know him.

In attempting to analyze Clare's descriptive art from the linguistic point of view, this study will focus on one poem: **"Signs of Winter."** The aim is to explore the many strategies Clare used to activate a reader's visual sense, for it is in relation to this that the descriptive skill of the poet succeeds or fails.

"Signs Of Winter"

Tis winter plain the images around
Protentious tell us of the closing year
Short grows the stupid day the moping fowl
Go roost at noon—upon the mossy barn
The thatcher hangs and lays the frequent yaum
Nudged close to stop the rain that drizzling falls
With scarce one interval of sunny sky
For weeks still leeking on that sulky gloom
Muggy and close a doubt twixt night and day
The sparrow rarely chirps the thresher pale
Twanks with sharp measured raps the weary frail
Thump and thump right tiresome to the ear
The hedger lonesome brustles at his toil
And shepherds trudge the fields without a song
The cat runs races with her tail—the dog
Leaps oer the orchard hedge and knarls the grass
The swine run round and grunt and play with straw
Snatching out hasty mouthfuls from the stack
Sudden upon the elm tree tops the crows
Unceremonious visit pays and croaks
Then swops away—from mossy barn the owl
Bobs hasty out—wheels round and scared as soon
As hastily retires—the ducks grow wild
And from the muddy pond fly up and wheel
A circle round the village and soon tired
Plunge in the pond again—the maids in haste
Snatch from the orchard hedge the mizled cloaths
And laughing hurry in to keep them dry.

> [Eric Robinson and Geoffrey Summerfield (eds.), **Clare: Selected Poems and Prose** (London: Oxford Univ. Press, 1966), pp. 163-64.]

"Signs of Winter" is a description of a rural village scene. It is written in declaratives, though the lack of stops, graphologically, in the punctuation means that it is a reader's syntactic knowledge that is used to re-organize a continuous passage of twenty-eight metrical lines into accessible syntactic units. The description is in the third person and in the present tense. The overall context of the poem's discourse is that of a viewer who tells us what is going on, of what is being "seen" as it happens. Participating in the discourse of the poem on the part of a reader involves, generally speaking, "sharing the view" of the scene presented—in other words,

the creation, in imagination, of the perceptual context evoked by the poem's language. The persona presents salient details of the scene viewed, and it is open to readers to share the perspective presented, in the act of reading.

The success of such a sharing of perspective depends, we would expect, on the poet's skill in delineating the scene in the first place. But it is here that the first surprise of Clare's technique confronts us. Overall, the language used is remarkably plain and simple. Apart from a few dialect words and the occasional fronting of adverbials and the inversion of the Adj + Noun order, the style is bereft of the usual devices—syntactic deviation, unusual lexical collocations, virtuoso sound patterning, and so forth—that generally gladden an analyst's heart. The language is pared down to the bone, giving the impression of utter simplicity, plainness even, and if foregrounding is to be sought, it is to be found, without doubt, in the sheer ordinariness of the language used, which, in its uncompromising regularity, captures attention.

Out of such seemingly unpropitious materials, Clare has constructed a poem that achieves a vividness of effect that is the more surprising given the odds against it. The techniques used provide the means by which a reader's conceptual and perceptual operations are subtly and surprisingly controlled so as to foreground the act of viewing itself in such a way as to remove the glaze, the film of familiarity through which the habitual and the commonplace are usually perceived.

The poem opens with a simple assertion—"Tis winter plain"—which sets the scene as a wintry one, but the focus on the visual element is introduced in the next clause, when we are further informed that there are "images" around that are indicative of the season. Thus, from the very start there is the promise of a visual experience, the word *images* itself is foregrounded in taking two strong stresses in the opening iambic pentameter line.

Whatever our expectations of descriptions of wintry scenes and of images pertinent to them, Clare's images and the linguistic means of their construction overturn the more comfortable ones. The images chosen are commonplace and the linguistic means of expressing them show little if any originality. The noun phrases are, on the whole, simple—mostly Det + Adj + Noun with the occasional inversion of the Adj + Noun order, or Det + Noun, Adj + Noun, or Noun alone. There is some complex postmodification, as in lines 4, 5, and 6, but this is not usual. The choices of structure can be set out as shown in Table 1.

TABLE 1

Det+Noun	Det+Adj+Noun	Adj+Noun	Noun
the images	the stupid day	sunny sky	noon
the rain	the moping fowl	(plain) winter	night
one interval	the mossy barn	sharp measured raps	day
a doubt	the frequent yaum	sulky gloom	shepherds

the sparrow	the sulky gloom	hasty mouthfuls	straw
the thatcher	the orchard hedge	mossy barn	visit
the ear	the elm tree tops		
the hedger	the muddy pond		
his toil	the mizled cloaths		
the thresher	the (lonesome) hedger		
a song	the weary flail		
the shepherds	the (pale) thresher		
the fields			
the cat			
the dog			
the grass			
the swine			
the stack			
the crows			
the owl			
the barn			
the ducks			
a circle			
the village			
the pond			
the maids			

There is a high preponderance of the definite noun phrase. Most of the head nouns in this list are concrete, though there is some use of abstract and mass nouns as well. In general, the nouns create a lexical field that signify familiar objects in a village scene. They could, in fact, be subdivided into those that have to do with village people and trades *(thatcher, hedger, thresher, shepherd, maids)*, or animals and birds that inhabit the village *(fowl, sparrow, cat, dog, swine, crows, ducks, owl)*, or familiar items of the landscape *(barn, pond, hedge)*. The abstract nouns, on the whole, deal with the season and time of day *(winter, day, noon, night)*, while some nouns deal with the weather *(rain* and *sky)*. The objects denoted are extremely familiar ones, and the "images" that are focused on are those of the known, the familiar, and the everyday in this scene.

The use of adjectives, too, is remarkably simple, giving minimal attention to the quality of things described—thus, *plain, moping, frequent, sulky,* and so forth. Occasionally, nouns are used as adjectives—*orchard* hedge, *elm tree* tops, emphasizing their informational rather than their descriptive use. Clare does not use complex pre- or post-modification in the noun phrase to create intricate conceptual or perceptual configurations. Descriptive detail is kept to a minimum, and the descriptive resources of the language appear to be remarkably underused.

Neither noun nor adjectival usage furthers expectations of descriptive virtuosity. By contrast, verb usage shows variation, mainly stative or lacking in dynamism in the first part of the poem, and much more dynamic in the second part. Thus, up to about line 11 we find verbs like *roost, hangs, lays, falls, leeking, trudge,* which are either long drawn-out actions, or monotonously repetitive ones that inhibit a focus on mobility. After line 15, in the main, dynamic verbs are used: *runs, leaps, knarls, play, snatching, swops, plunge, hurry.* Thus, different qualities of the actions of the participants are focused on, rather than the

actors or objects themselves. The lexis, overall, remains simple.

Such choices are indeed puzzling. As far as the images are concerned, the poem foregrounds concrete, commonplace objects, stereotypes even, with little attempt to make them complex or appealing. Given the expected descriptive goal of the poem, the absence of techniques to exploit the descriptive potential of the language is uncompromising enough to merit attention. On the other hand, the verb usage makes clear that these commonplace images are to be viewed in different aspects of movement. Thus, the fowl is seen about to roost, the thatcher in the actions of hanging and laying the yaum, the hedger hedging, the silent shepherd trudging the field, the cat running around, the dog leaping, the swine knarling grass, the crows and owl and ducks in various kinds of flight—each caught in some natural aspect of movement, making this commonplace scene uncommonly dynamic and mobile.

Even in this informal catalog of events and actions, the bounded and separated nature of the description is obvious. The images appear to have no relation to each other. The syntactic forms used, too, forbid any expansiveness of idea or perception. Although subordination is present, as in lines 5-9, its use seems to be localized. Coordination and parataxis appear to be the predominant forms used, giving the poem a loose, episodic structure. Each image is caught in some aspect of movement and the syntax encourages, in fact, directs, that its individuality and separate identity be respected, which the lack of overt cohesive ties reinforces. This is a crowded scene. Many participants are referred to but few are developed to any great extent. Each subject noun phrase that initiates a new main clause initiates a new topic as well, thus moving our attention to one more object or participant in the scene. Nor are spatial relations among objects themselves given, no hierarchies are established in terms of foreground or background, near or far. Each clause and each piece of information is given equal weight through the mainly paratactic structure—all are equally significant. The syntactic organization is such that we could easily conceive of further clauses being added to the end of the poem without any sense of dislocation. The form appears to be remarkably open-ended.

At first glance, therefore, we appear to be presented with a catalog of objects, a list. But what visual interest could there be in a list? The scene appears to be one of singulars, but how do we order this varied and singular world in order to visualize the objects together as an integrated whole? What we are given is a mode of expression, a style that has eschewed linkages that would give us interpretive directions on interrelating the details—and separate and singular details, do not, in the end, add up to an integrated notion of a whole.

Various ways have been suggested to interpret this aspect of Clare's work. In John Barrell's view, the linear order implicit in the parataxis of the syntax is, in fact, suspended in poems like these, and what is achieved is not linearity but a simultaneity of impressions—not this *and* this *and* this . . . but this *while* this *while*. . . . The images are revealed "as parts not so much of a continuum of successive impressions as one complex manifold of simultaneous impressions." This mode of simultaneous seeing is also used by Barrell to explain the lack of foreground and background in Clare's poetry. The viewpoint is close-up since the observer is not distanced from what is seen, all things are seen in the foreground. Barrell links such a mode of vision—especially the particularity and multiplicity of detail—to Clare's "sense of place," each place existing for Clare as "a manifold of things seen, heard, smelled." The manifold detail is seen as a product of knowledge, knowledge of Helpston, and signifies Clare's sense of Helpston. Thomas Brownlow too emphasizes the particularity of Clare's viewpoint, and awards the viewing persona with an "insect view" of the objects seen—the poems thus providing a "micro-panorama," not a prospect. Brownlow, however, counters the threat of a world of singulars in Clare's style by positing that the sharply delineated singulars "merge" into a whole of a "sharply dynamic picture": "It is as if the individual frames of each single sighted perception *fade* into each other so that nature is seen as a continuum." Thus, Clare's "experience of landscape becomes a continuous series of elements melting into each other."

Both Barrell and Brownlow are primarily engaged in the business of establishing Clare's mode of seeing as valid in its own right, especially when set against the powerful conventions of pictorial viewing promoted by Claude Lorrain and others, from which Clare's own mode of viewing was a radical departure. Clare's interest in the close viewpoint and in the particular was opposed to the principles of pictorial composition established by Claude, Poussin, and others. These principles required, among other things, that the viewpoint be from a height and that the eye be organized by the painting in such a way that it traveled through the painting to a final band of light just below the horizon. Objects in the landscape, too, were subordinated to the general design and awarded no singular interest. The general design predominated, each particular landscape organized, in turn, in terms of the "ideal" landscape, the whole being a triumph of design, of composition, which came to be privileged enough to persuade the ordinary, educated viewer that natural landscape itself was somehow organized in this way. Although these studies establish Clare's differences from the prevailing tradition, it is debatable whether the close-up view of sharply delineated singulars causes them to "fade" or "merge" into each other as suggested by Brownlow, since much in the language used, as we have seen, maintains singularity and respects the boundaries of objects in relation to each other. The notion of the simultaneity of seeing, as proposed by Barrell, is also questionable since it is not clear that we see things in this way, all objects in equally sharp focus, altogether, simultaneously. That the events described are probably happening simultaneously we would agree, but that the description denies order is more contentious. For there *is* an order, but the order is neither in the scene nor imposed upon it by some prior principles of design that the language reflects. It is rather the order of attention and interest of the viewing eye—of

someone implicated in the scene—as it surveys the stuff of its surroundings. The perceptive eye focuses upon each object separately, giving each its due attention and establishes its own rhythm and movement as it gazes on this, glimpses that, or is distracted by something else. Each participant in the scene is focused upon for its own sake, mostly because it is there, as part of a given, habitual world. The interest of the images is the interest invested in them by the perceiver, in the familiar participants of a known scene going about their normal activities regardless of who is viewing them or whether they are being viewed at all.

There is, therefore, no motivation for "composition" in the painterly sense. The activities that occur are those that habitually occur though, perhaps, not in these particular ways each time, nor, we imagine, will the attention focus on identical aspects again. The poem captures an instance in the daily kaleidoscope of activities that occur in a lived locality. We are invited to *see*—to focus on objects with similar attention. It is this seeing, the activity of the gaze, that renders scenic the stuff of the everyday, thereby defamiliarizing the familiar. The moving gaze, in other words, creates the scene out of natural elements that exist outside the conventions of the "painterly" and makes them points of focus through attentiveness in the seeing. The world that emerges is not a mirror image passively recorded by the eye and represented in the language, but one shaped by selectivity and focus from that which has claimed the attention of the observer. The mode of perception presupposed by the poem is, therefore, not the gaze presupposed by a painting, trained and directed by convention and exposure, the preserve of the few, but the "active performance" of any eye turned to the world. That visual perception habitually involves such attentiveness, selectivity, intelligence, and, in its own way, creativity, has been made clear by Rudolf Arnheim:

> As I open my eyes, I find myself surrounded by a given world. . . . It exists by itself without my having done anything noticeable to produce it. But is this awareness of the world all there is to perception? By no means. That given world is only the scene on which the most characteristic aspect of perception takes place. Through that world roams the glance, directed by attention, focussing the narrow range of sharpest vision now on this, now on that spot, following the flight of a distant seagull, scanning a tree to explore its shape. This eminently active performance is what is meant by visual perception. It may refer to a small part of the visual world or to the whole visual framework of space, in which all presently seen objects have their location. The world emerging from this perceptual exploration is not immediately given. Some of its aspects build up fast, some slowly, and all of them are subject to continued confirmation, reappraisal, change, completion, correction, deepening of understanding.

The pleasure of the poem is, in fact, the pleasure to be had by anyone who focuses on the familiar with heightened attention. It is the pleasure one may derive in contemplating the sounds and activities of the street one lives in, or looking again at the objects, lights, and shadows in a familiar or favorite room. Such things are not "composed" (in any sense of the term) for viewing, but seeing them with attentiveness makes them "scenic" for the duration and affords its own satisfaction.

The linguistic choices in the poem heighten the reader's seeing. "Sharing the view" of the persona is primarily to share the rhythm, direction, and intensity of the eye of the viewer as the objects and activities of the scene are focused upon. Most of all, it is the freshness of the familiar that is foregrounded by such perceptual acts. So how is it achieved?

In the first place, certain linguistic choices function as rhetorical strategies to draw the reader into a shared context of habituality and familiarity with the objects and actions described. Thus, the fiction of familiarity with the descriptive context of the poem is created. In particular, definite noun phrases mobilize a reader's sense of involvement in the familiar. The nouns, as we have seen, designate expected objects in a rural scene, but the definite article foregrounds knowledge of the scene described as already in common between, and shared by, the speaking persona and the reader. The reader is drawn into the fiction of a mutually known and shared context, and the surprise is not that such objects and participants are there, since we are supposed to know they are there already, but in seeing them in a particular way, with a particular focus and under certain aspects of their natural existence, patterned into art, which renders the natural, scenic.

The definite article in English has different functions to perform, and Clare brings many of them appropriately into play. It is an identifying and specifying agent; it signals that the item or subclass designated by the noun can be identified, though the direction of identification and referent retrieval can vary with the *phoricity* of the noun phrase in which the definite article functions as determiner; it directs a user to pick out a specific object in a context and reference. The use of the definite article also presupposes prior mention of the item so designated in the discourse. In communication, as Grice has pointed out, the definite article provides an implicature to the effect that the item referred to is known to both speaker and hearer. Thus, an utterance like "I saw the house yesterday" implies that the house in question is known to both speaker and hearer, while an utterance like "I saw a house yesterday" has no such implicature. In processing such utterances, according to Clark and Haviland, the definite article signals old or given information.

Clare's use of the definite article is a consistent feature of his language, and hence, of stylistic value. But his usage is also odd. There is virtually no prior mention of the nouns of the definite noun phrases in his poem, and almost all of them are given first-mentions only. But through its use Clare creates the fiction that the objects referred to are already known and identifiable, and within the mutual knowledge of both persona and reader as participants in the discourse. Selectivity, particularity, and specificity are thus signaled in the language in relation to the objects in this familiar scene.

Another noteworthy aspect of noun-phrase usage in this poem is the way in which such usage creates centers of focus for the viewer's eye. Most of the noun phrases are exophoric in reference. As Halliday and Hasan have pointed out, exophoric reference directs that the information necessary for identifying the referent is to be found in the situational context itself. As an example they give the following: "Don't go; the train's coming," where "the train" is interpreted as "the train we're both expecting." All immediate situational instances of *the* are exophoric in this way. Such types of reference also require satisfaction of the presupposition that the thing or object referred to be identified, and as such provide the cue, the instruction to the reader to satisfy the presupposition. Since this is fictional discourse, imaginative discourse, such acts of identification on the part of the reader involve the *creation* of the required referent—in imagination—so that the referential link with the context may be achieved. The "objects"—images—so created become the visual centers of focus in this familiar scene. The sheer regularity and variety of noun phrases of this kind means also that a whole visual field is created out of such centers of focus as they multiply through the poem. The rhythm established is the rhythm of focus of the seeing eye in relation to objects as it looks at a familiar scene and rests its attentive gaze, now on this, now on that, and heightens interest in the objects so selected by such focus. The creation of such centers of focus serves to frame for seeing the object and activity selected and make them targets of visual attention.

If this is the case, then what of visual interest is there in this selection of details that has been awarded such attention? The nouns signify objects that are exceedingly commonplace. Moreover, elaborate pre- or postmodification in the noun phrase has generally been omitted. Given the simplicity of the structure of the noun phrase, the head nouns become significant and remain the center of focus. This is especially the case in the subject noun phrases of the main clauses since each such noun introduces a new topic of interest. The head nouns so foregrounded refer to expected objects, but there is another dimension to them that functions for visual effect: the level of specificity in categorization specified by such nouns. Roger Brown has noted that, in a language, a referent can have many names—a dime can be a dime, a coin, money, a metal object, a 1952 dime, etc. In each such series consisting of a taxonomic hierarchy, there will be a neutral level of lexicalization, a neutral name, by which a referent is most commonly designated in a speech community and which children first learn. Brown calls this "the level of usual utility" in a community. Thus, a lexical item like *dog* would be at the level of usual utility rather than animal, quadruped, or spaniel, as would apple or orange rather than fruit, and table and chair rather than furniture. D. A. Cruse, developing Brown's arguments, regards such items as exhibiting what he calls "inherently neutral specificity." Contextual factors, however, can influence what passes for the neutral or "unmarked" term. Although *dog* would be the inherently neutral term, in a context that includes two dogs, where referents have to be successfully identified, the more specific term *spaniel* or *Alsatian*, what Cruse calls "contextually neutral terms," would be preferred in response to communicative pressures. Thus, "You take the spaniel for a walk and I'll take the Alsatian" rather than "You take the dog and I'll take the dog." Eleanor Rosch, too, working on the implications of such phenomena for human cognition, states that

> categories within taxonomies of concrete objects are structured such that there is generally one level of abstraction at which the most basic category cut can be made. In general, the basic level of abstraction in a taxonomy is the level at which categories carry the most information, possess the highest cue validity, and are thus most differentiated from each other.

This basic level includes co-occurrence of clusters of attributes believed to be held in common by members of the class named, shared motor movements by humans in relation to them, and "averaged" shape. Pamela Downing, using insights from all three researchers and in relation to narratives elicited from Japanese and American viewers of the "Pear Tree" film, supports Rosch's thesis, since basic-level names outnumber super- and subordinate category names in the narratives analyzed—93 percent of normal mentions being basic-level category names.

The head nouns foregrounded in Clare's poem are, in fact, neutral specificity nouns, lexical items designating this basic level of categorization of objects. Occasionally, we have what could be regarded as context-specificity items, especially in the naming of different birds—fowl, owl, crows, ducks—since more than one kind of bird is mentioned, but these are still "level of usual utility" terms in relation to the classes named. In terms of visual effect, such a stylistic choice has two consequences. Given such neutral specification, emphasized by the absence of pre- or postmodification, readers are free to evoke from memory whichever kind of cat, dog, hedger, etc. they choose. No details of color, physical features, or any other individuating characteristics are given. But what is foregrounded by such usage are shapes—typical shapes of the objects mentioned, or in Rosch's words, "averaged" shapes, of a cat, dog, swine, thatcher, hedger, etc. In the fictional context of viewing a scene, such lexical items direct the focus on outlines of objects rather than on unique visual details about them. The skill of the graphic artist rather than the painter in oils appears to be at work here in the language, providing a purity of line in relation to the objects evoked that creates its own vivid, visual interest.

A tension is set up between the representational and the aesthetic demands of description. On the one hand, the existence of these objects in the visual context is achieved in the naming, which is one of the most obvious functions of the noun phrases used. In context, this function fulfills the expectation of a rural scene and gives the description specificity—*these* identifiable objects known to us, in *this* rural scene—but there are few surprises to be had at this level. On the other hand, the consistency with which a certain type of noun is used for the purpose of designation awards it stylistic value, and given the discoursal goal of visual interest in description, the visually interesting as-

pects of such usage are open to investigation. In the absence of any other cue in such a patterning of noun phrases, to divert the eye, the visual patterns in the objects designated become the centers of exploration for the viewing eye. The natural is thus rendered scenic since the eye is not allowed to pass over objects for information alone, but is made to focus on familiar objects in terms of their visual appeal. The cue is in the patterning, in the consistent choice of a feature—here, a kind of noun in a structurally simple noun phrase—that functions within the visual terms of the discourse, to order disparate natural objects together in relation to a common visual factor for the reader to confront.

This tension between the representational and the aesthetic demands of description is a consistent feature of the poem. In the verb phrases, too, some "true-to-life" aspect of action is delineated in relation to each object named: the hedger hedging, the thatcher about his business, the animals and birds in some familiar aspect of movement. Such actions, like the agents, are unrelated to each other. The lack of cohesive linkages to interrelate clauses ensures that each agent and its action is bounded within the clause in which it is portrayed. The object displayed in action becomes both an informational and a visual unit. In the representational dimension, the existence of such habitual actions reinforces again the sense of being involved in a typical rural scene, with everything going about its normal business. We get a sense, too, of the rich variety of the everyday in the constant flux of movement portrayed. But the patterning of such natural actions, in this normal scene, foregrounds movement and the movements portrayed, natural and unremarkable as they are from the representational point of view, create visual patterns of their own that form a high point of aesthetic interest for the observing eye.

The actions given are rather consistently ordered and pattern contrastively in the poem. This is evident in the types of verbs used: weakly dynamic or stative in the first part of the poem (*roost, hangs, lays, nudged, drizzling, chirps, brustles, to stop, trudge*), where movement, where it exists, is usually monotonous or repetitive, blunting thereby the impact of action. In the second part, by contrast, the verbs are dynamic (*runs, leaps, grunt, play, snatching, pays, swops, flies, bobs, grow, wheel, plunge, snatch, laughing, hurry*). Where the verb portrays less dynamism, the adverbs modify the verbs accordingly: thus *grow wild, pays . . . sudden,* while the word *haste* and its derivations like *hasty* and *hastily* are used often in this part of the poem. The transition from one pattern of movement to the other is sudden.

Action, of course, shows objects in motion, and motion, as Arnheim has reminded us, "is the strongest visual appeal to attention." Action ensures that objects change their relative position in space, and the space traversed by movement is dramatized and highlighted for the eye. Moreover, objects can be related to each other by motion, and this reveals them as belonging to an integrated, individual portion of space. Thus, although spatial relations among objects are not given—there are no interclausal depictions of spatial relations—within each clause, individual objects are linked together into integrated spatial units by the actions described, and thus larger visual units are forged. Spatial units of different sizes are thus bracketed off for attention by the movements that bring them into relation. Thus, the thatcher hanging and laying the yaum brings the height of the barn and the thatcher at work on its roof into relation to form an integrated spatial unit. Similarly, the hedger at work on the hedge forms another unit, as do the shepherds who are located within the expanse of the field. In such units, in this part of the poem, textures are also evoked in the larger and darker masses of barn and hedge, while varying heights can be inferred from such units—the thatcher and the fowl placed higher up than the hedger and the shepherds. Smaller blocks of integrated space are evident in the second half of the poem: the cat chasing its own tail integrates a much smaller amount of space; the dog leaping over the hedge brings the dog in the air, the top of the hedge, and the ground into relation. Similarly, the swine in the vicinity of the haystack close enough to snatch out *hasty* mouthfuls becomes a unit. Height is evoked once again in the crows perching on the elm tree tops, since it is the top of the trees and the crows that are most immediately brought into relation, and although the plural forms are used for both crows and tree tops, it is the action of crows dispersed on branches rather than a massed unit that is evoked. The maids too, in relation to their houses, are scattered rather than massed, as are the ducks in relation of the whole expanse of the village as they fly over it. These create more open spaces. Such integrated spatial units not only provide varied organizations of space in the scene, they also provide different planes of activity, different heights and distances, different textures, but all of them within the visual field of the observer—all, that is, that can naturally be seen in the landscape.

The emphasis on movement produces another effect that is worth noting. Each action mentioned traces its own movements, which animates in highly visual ways the space in which it is performed, since shapes are traced by such movements in space. Shapes thus created provide a high point of interest for the eye. The verbs in the first part of the poem trace repeated movements that either do not occur across space, or occur only very gradually. The repetition of the same movement in this way creates abstract shapes—verticals and horizontals mostly in the first part of the poem. The hanging of the yaum, the incessant drizzle of the rain, the "leeking" of the rain, the up and down sameness of trudging, all of these trace vertical shapes, while the laying and nudging of the yaum, the hedger's toil at his hedge, and even the slow progress of the shepherds create horizontal, linear shapes in the main. The moping fowl remains in a class of its own, the shape given by the noun in focus, the verb holding it in its stillness.

In the second part, the repetition of horizontals and verticals gives way to a whole choreography of dynamic shapes. Thus, circles: the cat running races with its tail, the swine running *round,* the owl that *wheels round.* A parabola is traced in the movement of the dog leaping over the hedge; a circle, or an ellipse, in the movement of the ducks wheeling over the village; zig-zag shapes in the various snatching movements—the swine *snatching out hasty mouthfuls from the stack* and the maids *snatch their cloaths from the orchard hedge;* angles—in the plunge of the ducks into the pond, and their rising, and in the owl that *bobs* out of the barn and bobs back in again. Even a few squiggles are available in the untidy visit of the crows on the treetops, and a horizontal in the linear movement of the maids going indoors.

The patterning of movement in this way provides visual appeal in its own right, but there is another aspect that functions for aesthetic effect. The verbs, as we saw, are patterned in terms of contrast: strongly dynamic in the second part of the poem, weakly so or stative in the first part. In the absence on the whole, of lexis-signifying color in the poem, movement, especially the patterning of contrasting types of movement, is used to "color" the scene. The effect so achieved evokes moods and atmosphere in relation, cumulatively, to a whole cluster of details rather than to distinguish any individual item in terms of its physical appearance. Thus, the first part of the poem is generally leaden and heavy in mood, while the second is light and lively, and the patterning of the verbs into + or - DYNAMIC in the two parts of the poem plays a crucial part in the creation of such an effect.

A heavy film of gray shrouds the first part of the poem, achieved, in particular, by the negative aspect of the verbs. The continuous tense in the description of the rain as *drizzling* and *leeking,* extends these actions of the rain past hope of ceasing, casting a shadow of wetness and gloom over the whole scene. Similarly, the repetitive actions of hanging and laying the yaum, and of trudging, signify monotony and heaviness, the same thing done over and over again, and slowly, laboriously. The threshing, too, foregrounds monotony. The fowl that roosts is both still and about to sleep, and that *at noon,* in which the adverbial reinforces the negative aspects of actions in the verb. Similarly, the positive hint in *grows* is negated by *short,* as is the possibility of dynamism in *brustles,* since the hedger *brustles* only *at his toil,* all of which modify, negatively, the actions signified by the verbs.

These heavy, monotonous, dreary actions are reinforced by the device of using an "insider" perspective, in which the emotional coloring given to events is negative as well. The description of the fowl as *moping* is as it strikes someone who has evaluated its stance. The subordinate clauses, in particular, display such an internally evaluated perspective. Lines 6, 7, and 8 tell us more about the drizzling rain but they are all evaluated observations. "For weeks still leeking on that sulky gloom": the time element has been stretched to "weeks," and hints at a persona who has been present in the scene for a long time, and who is also fed up with the incessant rain. Similarly, *sulky* shows the objective grayness given a subjective rendering, and in the description of the gloom as *a doubt 'twixt night and day,* the doubt is in the persona, not the grayness. The hedger is seen as *lonesome*—again as he appears to an observer, a subjective not an objective detail, while observations like *the shepherds trudge the fields without a song* and *the sparrow rarely chirps* place the observer very firmly *in* the scene, as an insider, someone who is familiar with what to expect and misses the sounds when they are not there. Sounds are also used effectively in the onomatopoeia of *thump after thump* and in *twanks,* since the description is from the point of view of an insider who has heard the sounds to the point of boredom. This perspective on events, similarly, focuses on the negative, the lonely, the monotonous, the dreary aspects of the scene, creating a heaviness and leadenness of mood as a result.

The long vowels used in this part of the poem reinforce this mood of leadenness. Thus, we get lexis with long vowels like *roost, noon, barn, frequent, yaum, falls, weeks, leeking, gloom,* or lexis whose vowels are lengthened by the meter: *hangs, lays,* etc.—that slow down the rhythm and reinforce the general monotony of the actions.

There are long vowels in the second part, but they do not work in tandem with other devices to point in the same interpretive direction, which, in the first part, is mostly negative. Such a mood is radically altered, without warning, in the second part of the poem. The tempo speeds up; dynamic movement, sprightliness, and light enter the scene. The observer has withdrawn from evaluating what occurs, and the dynamism is allowed to speak for itself.

There is little representational motivation for such a contrast of patterning. In fact, in terms of representation and the "realism" expected, this aspect of the poem creates a problem. How do we integrate these two self-contained moods into the same scene? Aesthetically, however, humor is created in this unexpected turn of events. The patterning also enables us to see two otherwise antithetical aspects of the same scene as two differing aspects of life from the persona's perspective. Work is integral to the life of this scene, and by implication, to this community, but the work itself can be laborious, monotonous, and dreary. The humans, apart from the maids, are all seen as restricted and confined both in movement and space by work, and are defined by work. On the other hand, the natural life of the scene is portrayed as free in its natural existence, the rhythms of natural movement, dynamic. Life, therefore, can be hard and gray, but also light and lovely. The patterning foregrounds the distinctiveness of each aspect, but with a gentle humor evident in the co-occurrence. Nor are we allowed to make easy or exclusive conflations of leadenness and humans and lightness and nature. The bedraggled fowl and silent sparrow in the first part and the laughing maids in the second provide cross-connections between the patternings that undercut such exclusions, and integrate these aspects as within the personal experience of the persona.

Such an undercutting has other consequences worth noting. It problematizes the time factor involved in viewing this scene. The persona is located not only as "insider" but as cohabitant in this scene, not a picture-viewer viewing a representation in a gallery, nor a Claudian landscape-viewer, with picture glass in hand. The time presupposed

by the poem is, therefore, the time at the disposal of a cohabitant, someone who has been in the scene and remains within it over a period of time, who has watched the changing aspects of life around him in all weathers, and is responsive to its many facets. The truth to life in this dimension is a truth arising from the stuff of lived experience, through being resident in a place, of being located within it, across real time. It is not the realism derived from the conventions of representational art that we are dealing with here, and its inclusion in the poem, paradoxically, disrupts conventionalized realism. But it is the perspective of such a persona that we share as readers of the poem, whose art of seeing and responding to his familiar world the poem makes available.

And finally, the syntactic structure of the poem, through coordination and subordination, establishes a rhythm as the eye of the observer roams over this scene, linking this world of singulars together, linearly, as the eye encounters and explores the visual events of its world. Thus, the activity of the eye is varied. Coordination generally moves the eye on to different details of the action attended to, while subordination enables the eye to pause, the gaze arrested by some aspect which, in turn, causes some effect on the persona, and a personal, evaluated response is given. Within the main clauses, therefore, spans of attention awarded are ordered differently. A rhythm is established that provides a variety that parallels the different kinds of movement traced.

The activity of the thatcher spans two lines, although the clause itself is constructed of more lines than this. The eye takes in the details of the activity, but as it watches the close laying of the yaum, the persona comments on the unending dreariness of the rain, which the thatcher's work must keep out. While all this is being indulged in, the thatcher and his activity in the incessant rain remains in focus. It is a long pause in relation to the fowl, for instance, or even the hedger or the shepherd. Similarly, the activity of the thresher captures the persona's attention, but here, the time span of the eye is reinforced by the sounds of the activity striking the ear, as the twanking of the *frail* goes on rhythmically, thump after *right tiresome* thump, until the ear is wearied and the eye moves on. In the second part of the poem, we get further instances of complex constructions, but here complexity arises mainly from coordination. The coordinate constructions are generally coordinate verbs. Thus, while the subject remains stable, different actions of the same agent are traced, and this attention to different actions that make up the overall activity is a consistent feature of this part of the poem. The continuity of the agent in the discourse in relation to the actions unifies them, but since they are different actions, the eye remains mobile and particular in its attention to this kind of detail. Smaller rhythms are thus set up in relation to the attention awarded to the overall activity. Thus, the activity of the dog leaping over the hedge and knarling the grass is broken into two time spans for the eye—leaping quicker than the repetition of knarling. The swine *run round, grunt, and play with straw / Snatching out hasty mouthfuls from the stack* similarly creates its own subrhythms of seeing. The stacking of verbs in this way continues: the crows pay an unceremonious visit, croak, then swop away; the owl bobs hasty out, wheels round, scared, hastily retires; the ducks grow wild, fly up, wheel . . plunge. . . . The simple sentences: *Short grows the stupid day, The moping fowl go roost at noon, the cat runs races with her tail* and the like, shorten the time span of attention. In the coordinated units, time is varied—swops, involving less attention than the long sweeping movement of the ducks flying round the village. Subordination, especially in the first part of the poem, appears to provide the longest pauses of all, a long gaze as opposed to the quicker pacing of the eye in the second part. But the eye moves naturally, in relation to the scene. It can glance at something, gaze at something else, or even glimpse a fleeting movement like the laughing of the hurrying maids, contemplate something until it moves into its own thoughts, or is distracted in whatever direction by the sudden movement of some other activity, it can take in a whole wealth of detail as it happens, its rhythms conditioned only by its own responsiveness to whatever is happening around it. This is not the gaze presupposed by eighteenth-century painting—rather the "performance" of active seeing. But the performance, in its rhythms and in its highlighting of its own acts of seeing, foregrounds itself into art.

The performance is not allowed to dull or to go stale on us. The paratactic structure bounds each clause or even a smaller syntactic unit in terms of separateness, but this has its own visual reward. Changes of topic in each of the clauses provide new foci of interest. One is, therefore, not allowed to gaze too long at anything in case the eye is dulled. Arnheim has pointed out that vision is geared more to cope with change than immobility or monotony, and that even primitive animals stop reacting to a given stimulus if it reaches them over and over again. As far as humans are concerned, the eye and brain can be similarly dulled by too much looking on the same thing:

> When a person is forced to stare at a given figure he will use any opportunity to change it by varying it: he may re-organize the grouping of its parts or make a reversible figure switch from one view to the other. A colour looked at steadily tends to bleach, and if the eye is made to fixate a pattern without the small scanning movements that are never absent otherwise, that pattern will disappear from sight after a short while.   [Rudolf Arnheim, *Visual Thinking*]

The changes of topic in the poem ensure that the focus on each of these, in turn, is sharp. Even in the first part of the poem, where repetition of movement and monotony of the work and the weather are portrayed, "scanning movements" are introduced in the repetitions of movement, and the switch is made into the observer's feelings about the scene, thus averting the danger of dulling the eye. Instead, the interest remains on all the other aspects of this part of the scene: its heavier mood, its slower rhythms, the shapes traced by movement and object, the vignettes of daily life portrayed, and the reality of the wintry aspects of the life around. In the second part, of course, changes of topic and movement are car-

ried to a height, so that the exploitation of this aspect of vision achieves a kind of apotheosis. The open-ended nature of the ending holds out the promise of more visual wealth, but wisely refrains from satiating the eye.

John Lucas (essay date 1992)

SOURCE: "England in 1830—Wordsworth, Clare, and the Question of Poetic Authority," in *Critical Survey,* Vol. 4, No. 1, 1992, pp. 62-66.

[*In the following excerpt, Lucas compares a well-known and admired sonnet by Wordsworth with a little-known, radically unconventional sonnet by Clare and argues that it is time that both sonnets and their respective authors be granted the respect or "authority" that each deserve, but that only one has yet received.*]

In November 1830 Wordsworth set out from his home in Grasmere for Cambridge, where he was to stay for a night or two at his old college, Trinity. His route took him across the Pennines and through Derbyshire, and passed close to the Duke of Devonshire's famous house and grounds of Chatsworth. The following sonnet was almost certainly written from the comfort of the poet's former college rooms.

> Chatsworth! thy stately mansion, and the pride
> Of thy domain, strange contrast do present
> To house and home in many a craggy rent
> Of the wild Peak; where new-born waters glide
> Through fields whose thrifty occupants abide
> As in a dear and chosen banishment,
> With every semblance of entire content;
> So kind is simple Nature, fairly tried!
> Yet he whose heart in childhood gave her troth
> To pastoral dales, thin-set with modest farms,
> May learn, if judgement strengthen with his growth,
> That, not for Fancy only, pomp hath charms;
> And, strenuous to protect from lawless harms
> The extremes of favoured life, may honour both.

The Petrarchan form of this sonnet is handled with the neat assurance you would expect of a poet who had had so much practice at it. The break from octave to sestet on the word 'Yet' swings the argument into a new phase, and at the end the issues which have been raised are resolved by a firm closing rhyme. It was Milton who had shifted the Petrarchan sonnet in English from affairs of the heart to public affairs, even to affairs of state; and when at the beginning of the new century Wordsworth set out to write that sequence of poems which became called 'Poems Dedicated to National Independence and Liberty', he took Milton as his model for the sonnets which make up the bulk of the collection. Milton might even be said to act as model for the poem on Chatsworth. Certainly, the opening echoes the rhetorical strategy of 'Lawrence, of virtuous father virtuous son' as of course does Wordsworth's famous sonnet of 1802 which begins, 'Milton, thou shouldst be living at this hour, / England hath need of thee'. And 'strenuous to protect from lawless harms' is in both cadence and diction nothing if not Miltonic. But Milton has been captured for some very dubious motives. Wordsworth's sonnet may have about it a note of authority that suggests a calm impregnability of purpose, but this can't conceal the fact that what is being said is on behalf of the few against the many. November, 1830, was a time when all over the southern half of England the Swing riots were particularly ferocious. Writing from his rooms in Trinity, Wordsworth told those he had left behind at Grasmere that he could see fires started by the rioters reddening the night skies of the surrounding countryside for miles around. Wordsworth's sonnet presents an image of reconciliation between the great house and the small farmsteads and cottages, the 'house and the home', to which at the outset Chatsworth seems to stand in 'strange contrast'. Nature will provide for all, so at least the octave concludes in best Anglican, perhaps Evangelical, fashion. That seems straightforward enough. The sestet isn't so easy to understand. The last lines in particular are a problem. Does Wordsworth mean that now he has seen Chatsworth and its neighbouring houses he can understand that 'pomp'—Chatsworth and all it stands for—doesn't appeal merely to poetic 'Fancy' but has a real practical purpose: to protect 'the extremes of favoured life' from 'lawless harms' and in doing so honour both extremes? This would make a kind of sense: it was what the great house was supposed to do, and certainly this feudalistic reading of social relations was one that Wordsworth had come to hold and on which he was to elaborate in a sonnet sequence dedicated to 'Liberty and Order', as well as in other sonnets of the period, most notably one beginning 'They called thee *Merry England*, in old time'. In these, 'Heaven' or God was called upon to preserve the good relations of the rich man in his castle, the poor man at his gate. But the lines could as well be taken to mean that Wordsworth himself, having learnt the lesson that pomp has to teach, may honour both extremes of favoured life, because he is strenuous to protect them from lawless harms. Either way, we can hardly doubt that the lines amount to a statement in favour of 'pomp', of its use, its being deserving of honour. We are therefore a long way from the spirit of July 1789, which had found Wordsworth ready to believe in the Golden Hours of a new society; and it may well be that the July riots in Paris of 1830, which accompanied the downfall of the Bourbons, brought to the ageing poet's mind uncomfortable memories of his earlier, ecstatic welcome for the revolutionary energies which had swept aside French monarchy and its pomp.

'Pomp' was a word, almost a technical term, which had long been attached to the idea of the great house. And so, in his *Epistle to Burlington,* Pope commends Boyle for showing in his work on Palladian architecture that 'pompous buildings once were things of use'. Any sense of such use has gone from Goldsmith's account of the great houses built during the eighteenth century and which, in imposing themselves on a peopled place, became displays of brutal and strictly useless ostentation (one of Johnson's definitions for 'pomp' was 'A procession of splendour and ostentation'). 'Along the lawn, where scattered ham-

lets rose, / Unwieldy wealth and cumbrous pomp repose.' In that couplet from *The Deserted Village* the vigour of the one rhyme word, 'rose', rebukes the torpor of the answering rhyme, 'repose'. But 'repose' is in the present tense: 'cumbrous pomp' has taken over, has usurped the land, and as a result the hamlets are 'scattered' (the word puns on the idea of them being both 'casually' spread around in true picturesque fashion and actively dispersed—by acts of enclosure, by the depradations of pomp). Well now, few buildings possessed more pomp than Chatsworth, and this extended to its grounds and surroundings. When Wordsworth rode past it in November 1830 the 6th Duke of Devonshire was engaged, as he had been for some years, on enlarging the estate. How much Wordsworth knew about this and about what it involved I don't know; but it seems reasonable to assume that he must have felt pretty guilty about what he feared *might* have been involved. For how else explain those lines in which he refers to the thrifty occupants of fields who, so we are told, 'abide/ As in a dear and chosen banishment, / With every semblance of entire content'? What can this mean if not that Wordsworth guesses that they've been turfed out of their dwellings by the Duke of Devonshire? And what does that do for the man who wishes to honour pomp? Why, it persuades him that the thrifty occupants are so content that it's as though they had chosen of their own accord to get off the Devonshires' land. Perhaps they had, although I doubt it. But that doesn't matter. What does, is Wordsworth's readiness to honour a 'pomp' which had precious little use and which could therefore hardly be offered as a model for that pattern of social relations his deep conservatism led him to endorse. And anyway the uneasy conscience is surely plain in those weasel words '*As in* a dear and chosen banishment, / With *every semblance* of entire content' (my italics). Oh, yes? How does he know? The answer is that he doesn't, that he can't. And if someone—Mary Moorman, perhaps—were to come to his defence by saying 'well, he couldn't be expected to know', the obvious rejoinder is that in that case he shouldn't have pretended he *did* know. But why should he have so pretended? The answer, I am certain, is that Wordsworth deeply believed in the authority of the poet, in the poet's ability to speak to and for the nation; and this betrays him into the Miltonic posture by means of which he can imply another kind of authority for himself: that of divine inspiration. In fact, of course, all he has is a style, a manner in which to honour 'pomp' and so deflect attention away from the question of how far the responsibility for those reddening night skies of the Cambridge countryside might be laid at the door of the 'favoured life' whose apologist he now was. You couldn't in all fairness call this manner one of disdain; but as Goldsmith well knew, disdain and pomp go hand in hand. As he remarked in *The Deserted Village,* 'the rich deride' and 'the proud disdain'.

With this in mind, I want to comment on another sonnet which was written in 1830.

"England 1830"

These vague allusions to a country's wrongs,
  Where one says 'Ay' and others answer 'no'

In contradiction from a thousand tongues,
  Till like to prison-cells her freedoms grow
Becobwebbed with these oft-repeated songs
  Of peace and plenty in the midst of woe—
And is it thus they mock her year by year,
  Telling poor truth unto her face she lies,
Declaiming of her wealth with gibe severe,
  So long as taxes drain their wished supplies?
And will these jailors rivet every chain
  Anew, yet loudest in their mockery be,
To damn her into madness with disdain,
  Forging new bonds and bidding her be free?

We don't know exactly when Clare wrote this sonnet, which was first published over a hundred years later, in 1935. It is, however, quite probable that it was composed in November. The same red skies Wordsworth saw from his favoured window at Trinity College, Cambridge, Clare could have seen from his home village of Helpston, on the Northamptonshire-Cambridgeshire border. And if he had turned in the other direction he would have seen similar skies across the length and breadth of Northamptonshire. The country's wrongs were as visible as they were audibly insisted on—or denied by those who sang of 'peace and plenty in the midst of woe', or who claimed that 'thrifty' occupants of the fields would be looked after by 'kind' Nature. The comparison with Wordsworth is inevitable. His sonnet offers to speak for an England of annealed interests, as the final word shows: 'both'. An argument is rounded out, a firm conclusion provided. This is the voice of poetic authority. Clare's sonnet is very different. It doesn't obey any conventional form of sonnet. The first sentence stops, incomplete, after the first six lines, which compose their own movement. There follow two quatrains (a sort of reversal of the Petrarchan form except that the rhymes don't use the Petrarchan scheme); and the ending is no ending. You can't quite tell whether the final question is intended to be rhetorical or not, and indeed it's easy to imagine a further couplet being tacked on as a way of answering the question: something like, 'Forbid it, Heaven!—and MERRY ENGLAND still / Shall be thy rightful name, in prose and rhyme!' But that of course is Wordsworth. He can come to reassuring conclusions. Clare can't. Hence the radical form of his sonnet. Clare surely means to dislodge the accustomed practice of using the sonnet as a type of authoritative utterance, in the interest of producing a very different voice—*his* voice, or the voice of 'poor truth' which is endlessly mocked by the bland, consoling utterances of those who bid her 'be free'. And here, it is worth noting that by the end of the sonnet the 'country' has become synonymous with 'poor truth'. (The elision occurs at the moment when Clare asks 'And is it thus they mock her year by year, / Telling poor truth unto her face she lies.') In other words, Clare wants to speak for those who are left out of account in the kind of authoritative statement which Wordsworth's sonnet means to make.

The circumstances out of which Clare's sonnet springs can be worked through in some detail. There is neither the space nor the need to do that here, but it is very much to the point to note the remark made by Corrigan and

Sayer in their *The Great Arch: English State Formation as Cultural Revolution* (1985), that during the period leading up to 1830 'the most comprehensive battery of legislative, practical, and other regulatory devices against the emerging working-class is . . . established'. Clare's imagery of prison-cells, of chains and bonds, provides a lived sense of how 'poor truth' understood the reality of what was happening to literally thousands of English people at a time when authority was also insisting on England as a land of freedom. And as the Swing rioters were discovering, the law was hardly likely to act with impartiality, or to look with favour on their activities. State law made possible the taxes which drained money from the poor. In *Captain Swing* (1969) Eric Hobsbawm and George Rudé quote from a radical pamphlet produced in Sussex at the height of the riots there in 1830, in which one Labourer is made to say that all the money collected in taxes 'was given to people who gave nothing in exchange for it, some fine ladies and gentlemen, who like to live without work, and all the time they make the working class pay the present amount of Taxes there will be no better times'. Besides, the law habitually favoured the petitions for enclosure drawn up and presented by those who had much to gain against those who for the most part found it difficult to oppose them, no matter that they were the losers. 'Forging new bonds' is a bitter recognition not only of the making of new chains to bind 'poor truth' but of the fact that the kinds of petitions passing successfully through Parliament were to all intents and purposes acts of forgery. And who made these petitions, and who sanctioned them? Why, those who damned 'poor truth' into 'madness with disdain'. Such disdain implies that bonds would be tightened round the very language that poor truth used. Clare knew all about this kind of bondage, this disdain. By 1830 he had had to suffer endless rewritings of his poems. His publishers had regularly struck out his dialect words, they had altered his syntax, cut lines, stanzas, whole poems (especially the ones that voiced his radical displeasure of 'poor truth' at the rapacity of landlords and at the iniquity of enclosure); and when *The Shepherd's Calendar* was published in 1827 it was subjected to such brutal cutting that Clare's most recent editors are at a loss to explain it other than by assuming that what he wrote 'did not agree with his publisher's sense of poetical fitness'. This is the power disdain can call on.

'England 1830' seems to be at least as authoritative a statement as Wordsworth's. Yet Wordsworth is an accredited 'great' poet, Clare for the best part of a century was virtually unknown. 'England 1830' was never published in his lifetime, a fate it shared with many of his finest poems. And when it eventually saw the light of day it was not as he had intended it. He would neither have indented the lines nor seen any need for the punctuation with which the Tibbles pester the poem. The recovery of Clare is part of a campaign which ought to defeat the coercive claims made for national identity, for homogeneity, for some kind of unifying 'spirit of the people'. What we need is heterogeneity, a denial of that disdain by means of which one kind of voice becomes 'the' voice of authority, claiming to speak for all and in the process denying the voices of most others.

James C. McKusick (essay date 1994)

SOURCE: "John Clare and the Tyranny of Grammar," in *Studies in Romanticism,* Vol. 33, No. 2, Summer, 1994, pp. 255-77.

[*In the following excerpt, McKusick traces the ongoing conflicts between Clare and his editors and patrons, many of whom rejected Clare's use of dialect in his poetry, insisted upon standardized spelling in his publications, and disapproved of his opinions upon landed wealth.*]

John Clare has traditionally been regarded, rather patronizingly, as an uneducated Peasant Poet, exhibiting remarkable talent in minor poetic genres, but remaining something of a *naif* in matters of linguistic scholarship. Certainly it is true that Clare had little formal schooling and was almost completely without knowledge of Latin or Greek, the "learned languages" that still constituted the distinctive badge of an educated gentleman in his day. Even his command of English was distinctly provincial and marked by frequent departures from the normative standard of educated Londoners. Clare's first biographer, Frederick Martin, alleged that "he entirely failed in learning grammar and spelling, remaining ignorant of the sister arts to the end of his days." This traditional view of Clare was first promulgated by John Taylor, the editor and publisher of his first volume of poetry, *Poems Descriptive of Rural Life* (London 1820) "by John Clare, a Northamptonshire Peasant." In his Introduction to this volume, Taylor describes Clare as "a day-labourer in husbandry, who has had no advantages of education beyond others of his class" and draws a somber portrait of Clare's humble living conditions and acute poverty. Although Clare's circumstances were indeed desperate, Taylor's depiction is partly a marketing strategy intended to attract the interest of a sentimental reading public. Primarily, however, Taylor's Introduction serves to justify Clare's abilities as a poet, to account for "his evident ignorance of grammar" and to celebrate his use of dialect, what Taylor calls "*the unwritten language* of England." Taylor concludes that Clare "is most thoroughly the Poet as well as the Child of Nature"; and this view of Clare as an ignorant Peasant Poet, thoughtlessly warbling his woodnotes wild, has conditioned many subsequent critical responses.

Taylor edited Clare's first volume with a heavy hand, correcting grammar and spelling, supplying punctuation, and removing most of Clare's dialect words; the few nonstandard words that remained were defined in a glossary at the end of the book. Taylor's editing of Clare's two subsequent volumes of poetry, *The Village Minstrel* (1821) and *The Shepherd's Calendar* (1827), was even more intrusive, entailing not only the rigorous standardization of Clare's language, but also the ruthless cutting of passages or entire poems deemed tiresome, repetitious, hopelessly ungrammatical, or offensive to good taste. (All modern editions of Clare's poems, until 1964, continued Taylor's policy of normalization, with even less excuse.) Taylor's editorial interventions may perhaps be justified in historical retrospect, since the largely urban readership

of Clare's poetry was unacquainted with his regional dialect and often quite scathing in its criticism of any nonstandard English words or phrases that slipped through the net of Taylor's editing. A contemporary review of *Poems Descriptive* in the *New Monthly Magazine* (March 1820) scornfully describes several of Clare's dialect words, such as *bangs, chaps, eggs on, fex, flops, snifting* and *snufting,* as "mere vulgarisms, and may as well be excluded from the poetical lexicon, as they have long since been banished from the dictionary of polite conversation." An even harsher review of *The Village Minstrel* appeared in the *Monthly Magazine* (November 1821), sneering at

> something more than homeliness, approximating to vulgarity, in many of his themes. . . . We must likewise mark our strong disapprobation of the innovating style introduced in many parts of these volumes, by the employment of unauthorised contractions, and the use of words that have hitherto been strangers alike to our prose and poetry.

This review is unusually explicit in stating the rationale for its objection to Clare's dialect; after citing several "specimens" of nonstandard English, including the contractions *of's, and's, well's,* and the dialect words *soodling, tootling,* and *shool'd,* the review concludes:

> We leave it to the sober judgment of our readers, to decide, whether these, though indisputable, are desirable additions to our language. We may perhaps be told, that a Glossary is annexed to the book; but this does not alter our view of the subject. If the example of Burns, Ramsay, Ferguson, or other Scottish poets be pleaded, we answer, that they employed a dialect in general use through an entire country, and not the mere *patois* of a small district. If the peculiar phraseology of the Northamptonshire rustics is to be licensed in poetry, we see no reason why that of Lancashire, Somersetshire, and other counties should not be allowed an equal currency; and thus our language would be surprisingly enriched, by the legitimization of all the varieties of speech in use among the *canaille* throughout the kingdom.

Faced with such stern criticism of Clare's language, it is hardly surprising, though perhaps regrettable, that Taylor became even more rigorous in his editing of *The Shepherd's Calendar,* excluding dialect words wherever possible and omitting a glossary even for the few dialect words that remained. Evidently the glossaries that were included in *Poems Descriptive* and *The Village Minstrel,* intended to make the volumes more accessible to urban readers, had only attracted hostile criticism by highlighting Clare's nonstandard vocabulary.

These reviews, though unusually explicit in their objections to Clare's language, seem fairly typical of the unfavorable responses occasioned by the prevailing attitudes toward provincial dialect. Clearly there was a distinction, at least in the minds of the London reviewers, between the dialect of Scotland, supposedly characteristic of the entire country, and the dialect of Northamptonshire, local to "a small district." The threat of "legitimization" posed by the publication of Clare's local dialect is stated in overtly political terms: it is threat of the *canaille* (or "rabble") entering the discursive arena hitherto restricted to those who have mastered the standard language of educated gentlemen, the social class that comprises the literary elite of London. By using the French terms *patois* and *canaille,* the reviewer seeks to awaken memories of the French Revolution, when the *canaille* demolished the Bastille, marched on Versailles, and ultimately legitimized a new political *patois* that replaced all honorific forms of address with the simple appellative *citoyen.* Although modern readers may find it ludicrous to suppose that Clare's use of such words as *soodling* and *tootling* could pose any kind of political threat, it is nevertheless apparent that his more conservative contemporaries responded to his poetry in precisely these terms, perceiving a dire threat to the established order in Clare's use of dialect, regardless of Taylor's increasingly cautious editing. It is the *locality* of Clare's dialect that irritates his critics; the Scottish dialect, having a distinct national character, poses no threat to England's national identity. but if the "rustics" of Northamptonshire, Lancashire, and Somersetshire are allowed to publish their local dialects, the cultural and linguistic hegemony of London will be exposed and eventually destabilized. These are some of the latent political issues at stake in Taylor's editing of Clare's poetry.

The politics of publishing were rendered even more exasperating, in Clare's case, by the politics of patronage. Clare received financial support from such wealthy patrons as Lord Milton and Lord Radstock, and he was expected to show due humility and correct political opinions in return. Lord Radstock was appalled to find a denunciation of "accursed Wealth" in the poem **"Helpstone,"** in *Poems Descriptive.* "This is radical slang," retorted Lord Radstock in the margin of this passage, revealing the conflation of political and linguistic criteria in his judgment of Clare's poetry. Incensed by Clare's poignant account of the devastation and misery caused by wealthy landowners through the process of parliamentary enclosure, Radstock issued an ominous warning to Eliza Emmerson, another of Clare's patrons:

> You must tell him—to expunge certain highly objectionable passages in his 1st Volume—before the 3rd Edition appears—passages, wherein, his then depressed state hurried him not only into error, but into the most flagrant acts of injustice; by accusing those of pride, cruelty, vices, and ill-directed passions— who, are the very persons, by whose truly generous and noble exertions he has been raised from misery and despondency.... Tell Clare if he has still a recollection of what I have done, and am still doing for him, he must give me unquestionable *proofs* of being that man I would have him to be—he *must expunge!*

In a letter of May 1820 to John Taylor, Clare responded to this demand by Radstock, as well as to various other complaints by his patrons:

> Being much botherd latley I must trouble you to leave out the 8 lines in 'helpstone' beginning 'Accursed wealth' . . . leave it out & put ***** to fill up the

blank this will let em see I do it as negligent as possible d—n that canting way of being forcd to please I say—I cant abide it & one day I will show my Independance more stron[g]ly than ever

> [*The Letters of John Clare,* ed. Mark Storey, Oxford, Clarendon, 1985, p. 69.]

Being an editor of staunch liberal principles, Taylor initially resisted any political censorship of Clare's poetry; but eventually the required cuts were made in the fourth edition of *Poems Descriptive.* This episode illustrates the pervasiveness of the political constraints exercised by Clare's patrons, and the severe limitations that they imposed upon his expression of controversial opinions, even when these were shared by his publisher. Although Clare never again faced such direct censorship by his patrons, the reason may be that he and Taylor had both learned the harsh necessity of self-censorship, or, more insidiously, had unconsciously internalized the very repression they sought to oppose. Never again would Clare's published poetry express radical political views, and in his manuscript autobiography, "Sketches in the Life of John Clare" (circa 1821), intended for the eyes of his patrons, he voices reassuringly submissive sentiments:

> I believe the reading a small pamphlet on the Murder of the french King many years ago with other inhuman butcheries cured me very early of thinking favourably of radicalism the words 'revolution and reform' so much in fashion with sneering arch infidels thrills me with terror when ever I see them . . . may the foes of my country ever find their hopes blasted by disappointments and the silent prayers of the honest man to a power that governs with justice for their destruction meet always with success [*John Clare's Autobiographical Writings,* ed. Eric Robinson, Oxford, Oxford UP, 1986, p. 26.]

Since Clare elsewhere consistently advocates the necessity of reform (although he often criticizes the reckless violence of reformers), it seems likely that his revulsion against radicalism is exaggerated here in order to present himself as a meek, inoffensive candidate for patronage.

While Clare seemed willing, on occasion, to compromise the expression of his political principles, he was always reluctant to compromise the integrity of his local dialect. In a manuscript note of circa 1819 he boldly defended his use of "vulgar" expressions, seeking at the same time to reappropriate the term "vulgar" to a positive, democratic connotation:

> Bad spelling may be altered by the Amanuensis but no word is to be altered

> "Eggs on" in the **"Address to a Lark"**—whether provincial or not I cannot tell but it is common with the vulgar (I am of that class) & I heartily desire no word of mine to be altered

> The word "twit-a-twit" (if a word it can be called) you will undoubtedly smile at but I wish you to print it as it is for it is the Language of Nature & that can never be disgusting

Clare's fidelity to what he calls the "Language of Nature" and his resistance to substantive editorial alterations frequently recur throughout his editorial correspondence, indicating his enduring allegiance to a defiantly "vulgar" conception of language. In a letter of July 1820 to Taylor's partner, James Hessey, Clare expresses his outrage at deletions made in the third edition of *Poems Descriptive* for the sake of "delicacy":

> I have seen the third Edition & am cursed mad about it the judgment of T[aylor] is a button hole lower in my opinion—it is good—but too subject to be tainted by medlars *false delicasy* damn it I hate it beyond every thing those primpt up misses brought up in those seminaries of mysterious wickedness (Boarding Schools) what will please em? why we well know—but while their heart & soul loves to extravagance (what we dare not mention) false delicasy's seriousness muscles [i.e. muzzles] up the mouth & condemns it . . . I think to please all & offend all we shoud put out 215 pages of blank leaves & call it 'Clare in fashion'
>
> (*Letters* 83-84)

Seeking to justify the earthy expression of sexual matters in such poems as **"Dolly's Mistake,"** Clare denounces the hypocrisy of those squeamish "bluestockings" who attempt to bowdlerize his poems while secretly relishing their salacious language. His most outspoken resistance to grammatical correction occurs in a letter of February 1822, resisting some editorial changes by Taylor:

> I may alter but I cannot mend grammer in learning is like Tyranny in government—confound the bitch Ill never be her slave & have a vast good mind not to alter the verse in question—by g-d Ive tryd an hour & cannot do a syllable so do your best or let it pass
>
> (*Letters* 231)

This stubborn attitude became quite emphatic during the composition of *The Shepherd's Calendar,* when Clare took up a directly adversarial stance toward Taylor. It continued even after Clare's confinement in the Northampton General Lunatic Asylum (in 1841); his keeper, W. F. Knight, testified that Clare "in no instance has ever rewritten a single line—whenever I have wished him to correct a single line he has ever shown the greatest disinclination to take in hand what to him seems a great task."

Despite his overt resistance to Taylor's alterations, Clare recognized their shared responsibility to produce a marketable volume, and in most cases he grudgingly accepted Taylor's revisions, especially in the early part of his career when he was still struggling to master the literary language of his poetic precursors. On several occasions during the composition of his first volume, he instructed Taylor to do whatever he liked with the manuscripts; and he actually invited editorial correction in a letter of 1823: "If there is any bad grammar in the rhymes tell me . . . I shall give my reasons as a critical Bard (not as a critical wolf who mangles to murder) to attempt correction" (*Letters* 267). The extent of Taylor's revisions to Clare's poetry can be determined by comparing the published versions with Clare's original manuscript versions, which have a much higher incidence of dialect words, nonstandard grammar, and idiosyncratic spelling, as well as an almost total absence of punctuation. The necessity of a completely literal transcription of Clare's manuscripts was first recognized by Eric Robinson and Geoffrey Summerfield, and their pioneering editions of Clare's poetry in 1964, 1966, and 1967 still serve as models for the more complete Oxford edition now in progress. Unlike all previous editors of Clare, who found it expedient to tidy up his text, Robinson and Summerfield insisted on an absolute fidelity to Clare's original manuscripts, arguing that "once the business of correction is begun there is no end." It is largely thanks to Robinson and Summerfield that modern readers have gained access to Clare's poems in the full panoply of their jubilantly transgressive individuality.

In these manuscript versions, Clare's unstopped lines provide multiple branching pathways of possible meaning, thereby challenging the tyranny of grammar and its prescriptive requirement of unambiguous expression. Throughout his poetic career, Clare likewise resisted the political process of "inclosure" (as he normally spelled the word, thereby literalizing its etymology), especially its tendency to obliterate the complex network of grassy footpaths that formerly meandered across the landscape, often replacing these with stark, rectilinear turnpikes. As several recent critics have pointed out, Clare's conception of language and his conception of landscape seem closely related; he regards both as ideally constituting an unrestricted communal zone, open to local browsing and free from the linearity, exclusivity, and standardization imposed by outside authorities. Clare's distinct preference for his own regional vernacular, with all of its homely quirks and idiosyncrasies, over the homogenized national standard of discourse, clearly goes beyond a mere inability or refusal to master the conventions of correct expression. If this were the case, all of Clare's poetry would be composed in roughly the same kind of language, with dialect words and grammatical irregularities scattered randomly throughout. But in fact Clare's poetic language falls into several discrete discursive modes, varying from such comic vernacular poems as **"Dolly's Mistake"** to more serious reflective poems, such as **"What is Life?"** or **"The Setting Sun,"** that conform fairly closely to the prevailing standards of lexical and grammatical correctness. Like Burns, a poet whom he admired and occasionally imitated, Clare is not simply a dialect poet, but a poet who employs dialect for deliberate effect. Clare adopts a nonstandard lexicon only when it suits his poetic purpose, and he is fully capable of producing an "educated" sociolect when treating abstract or elevated topics.

Quite early in his career, Clare states a principle of linguistic decorum that reflects his intense awareness of stylistic and lexical norms. In a letter of 1819, discussing William Shenstone's *Pastorals,* Clare complains that "Putting the Correct Language of the Gentleman into the mouth of a Simple Shepherd or Vulgar Ploughman is far from Natural" (*Letters* 12). Rustic speakers must speak like rustics. Yet the following sentence praises Alexander Pope for his "Harmony of Numbers," suggesting that Clare does not object to "the Correct Language of the Gentleman" *per se,* but only when such an idiom is thrust into incongruous contexts. Clare's poetic development consists largely of his learning to manipulate a variety of discursive modes and stylistic models while remaining true to his vernacular roots. Far from being ignorant of grammar and spelling, Clare possessed a fairly good knowledge of the standard authorities and could conform to their prescribed usage when it suited him. Despite his knowledge of these authorities, however, his poetic language actually became *less* conventional over the course of his career, while he became more stubbornly resistant to the attempts of Taylor and others to correct his poems. Far from being a *naif* in matters of grammatical theory, Clare was surprisingly well read in contemporary linguistics, possessing several standard works on the subject. Ultimately, however, he rejected the prevailing linguistic norm, with its emphasis upon the standards of written language, in favor of a more radical tradition of linguistic theory that advocated the expressive potential of local vernacular speech.

Clare evidently encountered the forces of linguistic standardization at an early stage in his career. It is not known precisely how he acquired the rudiments of reading and writing during his elementary education; he had no access to a grammar-book, "nor do I believe my [school]master knew any more about the matter" (*Autobiographical Writings* 28). Presumably he was subjected to a crudely prescriptive approach to grammar, and while he quickly mastered the basic skills involved, he also acquired an enduring hostility to cultural authority figures. The remainder of his education was obtained through desultory reading of whatever books happened to be available, and like many self-educated people, Clare exhibited astonishing gaps in his knowledge, coupled with an equally astonishing wealth of information on particular subjects. In his autobiography, Clare recounts how, at age 13, he purchased his first book of poetry, an edition of James Thomson's *Seasons* (1730), and eagerly devoured its contents (*Autobiographical Writings* 9). He eventually acquired quite a substantial collection of eighteenth-century poets, and he undoubtedly derived a great deal of his literary skill from attentive reading and precise imitation of these favored models. Along with various books and anthologies of poetry, Clare acquired several books on linguistic topics; one of the earliest of these was an elementary spelling-book that gave Clare great annoyance:

> I had hardly hard the name of grammer while at school— but as I had an itch for trying at every thing I got hold of I determined to try grammer, and for that purpose, by the advice of a friend, bought the 'Universal Spelling Book' as the most easy assistant for my starting out, but finding a jumble of words classd under this name and that name and this such a figure of speech and that another hard worded figure I turned from further notice of it in instant disgust

(Autobiographical Writings 15)

Far from undermining his self-confidence, however, Clare's "disgust" with this relentlessly taxonomic spelling-book actually renewed his intuitive sense of literary vocation:

> for as I knew I coud talk to be understood I thought by the same method my writing might be made out as easy and proper, so in the teeth of grammer I pursued my literary journey warm as usual, working hard all day and scribbling at night or any leisure hour in any hole or corner I could shove in unseen

This episode indicates the origin of Clare's skeptical attitude toward prescriptive linguistics and provides a clue to the rationale behind it. Clare's self-confidence derives from a rather sophisticated insight into the nature of language: like the modern generative grammarians, he realizes that the ability to construct well-formed sentences has very little to do with the traditional rules of grammar, and depends much more on early childhood development of linguistic competence through normal conversation. Speech, not writing, provides Clare with a fundamental paradigm of linguistic performance, and despite the exhortations of his genteel friends and patrons he will continue to articulate his local vernacular "in the teeth of grammer."

In April 1820, shortly after the publication of *Poems Descriptive,* Lord Milton presented Clare with a copy of Samuel Johnson's *Dictionary of the English Language . . . Abstracted from the Folio Edition.* This was not the massive folio edition of 1755, but the abridged octavo edition first published in 1756 and frequently reprinted thereafter. This abridged edition omits all of the quotations that lend Johnson's *Dictionary* its unique character; moreover, many of the definitions are shortened, and Johnson states that "many barbarous terms and phrases by which other dictionaries may vitiate the style are rejected from this." This edition includes Johnson's "Grammar of the English Tongue" but omits his history of the English language. Also omitted is Johnson's famous Preface, with its melancholy reflections on the mutability of language; in its place is a shorter and more cheerful preface, also by Johnson, reassuring readers that this abridgement will satisfy their basic reference needs. This brief preface is quite condescending in tone, assuming that readers of "lower characters" are incapable of sustained intellectual engagement with literature:

> Works of that kind [i.e. the folio *Dictionary*] are by no means necessary to the greater number of readers, who, seldom intending to write or presuming to judge, turn over books only to amuse their leisure, and to gain degrees of knowledge suitable to lower characters, or necessary to the common business of life: these know not any other use of a dictionary than that of adjusting orthography, and explaining terms of science or words of infrequent occurrence, or remote derivation.

In thus describing the intended readership for his abridgement, Johnson's preface provides a clue to Lord Milton's intentions in presenting it to Clare: he may have wished that Clare would use it to improve his poetic language by conforming to established standards of spelling and usage. While Johnson certainly was the leading authority in these areas, his abridged dictionary, with its condescending preface and starkly prescriptive definitions, was unlikely to appeal to Clare, and there is no evidence that he ever consulted it. Clare might have enjoyed browsing through the rich trove of quotations in the folio *Dictionary,* but he could hardly be expected to relish the dry bones of the abridgement. Ironically, however, Johnson's *Dictionary* provided the standard by which Taylor measured Clare's departures from normal poetic diction; in his preface to **Poems Descriptive** Taylor states that the glossary includes "all such [words] as are not to be found in Johnson's Dictionary." As we have seen, this glossary provided lethal ammunition to Clare's critics, who used it as a ready-made list of deviations from lexical propriety. Taylor himself sometimes used Johnson's *Dictionary* as a stick to beat Clare; in a pencilled note on the manuscript of **The Village Minstrel** next to the word *swail,* Taylor wrote: "I can find no such word in Dicy / why not Vale?" This evocative dialect word was accordingly deleted from the published version of that poem. [**Early Poems of John Clare** 2: 123n.]

Despite their evident lack of success in reforming Clare's poetic style, his patrons and admirers continued to inundate him with books by the leading linguistic authorities. In about 1820 he received a copy of Hugh Blair's *Lectures on Rhetoric and Belles Lettres* (1783), a compendium of information on stylistic refinement and other aspects of polite literature. In June 1824 he received a copy of William Allen's *Elements of English Grammar* (1813), presented by the author. This was followed in November 1825 by Robert Lowth's *Short Introduction to English Grammar* (1762), presented by Eliza Emmerson. Clare was also familiar with Lindley Murray's *English Grammar* (1795), since he expressed his opinion of it to Charles Lamb during an 1824 visit to London. None of these books would have altered Clare's dim view of prescriptive grammarians. Lowth's work, the first comprehensive English grammar, uses Latin as a model for correct English usage, often at the expense of normal speech. One can imagine Clare's bemusement at such rules as: "Hypothetical, Conditional, Concessive, and Exceptive Conjunctions seem to require properly the Subjunctive Mode after them." Lindley Murray, whose *Grammar* sold millions of copies during Clare's lifetime, was even more rigidly prescriptive and moralistic than Lowth; his grammatical exercises include such obsequious apothegms as: "Patriotism, morality, every public and private consideration, *demand* our submission to lawful government." While Clare may have browsed through these grammar books, there is no evidence that he sought to apply their principles to his own writing. His sardonic response to traditional grammar is reported by Thomas Hood: "[Clare] vehemently denounces all Philology as nothing but a sort of man-trap for authors, and heartily 'dals' [i.e. damns] Lindley Murray for 'inventing it.'"

It would be misleading, however, to suggest that Clare used nothing but his intuitive knowledge of Northamptonshire dialect to withstand the formidable apparatus of the traditional grammarians. In his lifelong resistance to the tyranny of grammar, he possessed the aid and comfort of an alternative tradition of linguistic scholarship, one that emphasized the validity of vernacular speech and sought to uphold local idioms against the encroachment of standardization. Clare became aware of this alternative

tradition quite early in his career, and he continued to explore its ramifications throughout the course of his poetic development. In 1813 he acquired a copy of Nathan Bailey's *Universal Etymological English Dictionary* (thirteenth edition, 1749), a work whose formative influence on Clare's conception of language has not previously been recognized. First published in 1721, this was the most popular eighteenth-century dictionary before Johnson, and it continued to flourish even after the publication of Johnson's *Dictionary,* going through thirty editions by 1802. Johnson consulted Bailey in constructing the wordlist for his own dictionary, but the two works are nevertheless quite dissimilar in their fundamental structure and purpose. Johnson's avowed intention is to establish an enduring standard of English usage, and to that end he excludes most archaic, dialect, and slang expressions from his dictionary. Johnson's classicism is apparent in his etymologies, which systematically ignore native, barbaric, and "vulgar" English and Germanic roots in favor of more remote, yet more refined Latin or Greek analogues. Johnson often imposes class distinctions upon acceptable usage, dismissing the vocabulary of the "laborious and mercantile parts of the people" as mere "fugitive cant" (Preface to folio ed. [1755]). His dictionary enshrines a conservative ideology in its definitions of such words as "equal," "rights," and "liberty." Johnson's political ideology is intimately bound up with his concept of refined usage; both seek to exclude the uneducated masses from participation in the political process.

Bailey's *Universal Etymological English Dictionary,* by contrast, incorporates a great variety of nonstandard words and seems little concerned with the determination of "correct" usage. Bailey's definitions are less precise than those of Johnson, but his etymologies are far more attentive to the native roots of English words, and despite his faulty knowledge of Anglo-Saxon, Bailey seeks to authenticate the legitimacy of local origins. Moreover, Bailey's dictionary is especially rich in English dialect words, proclaiming on its title page that it includes "the Dialects of our different Counties," a feature that doubtless appealed to Clare. De Witt Starnes and Gertrude Noyes have shown that Bailey derived most of his dialect words from previous lexicographers, such as John Kersey (1708), Elisha Coles (1676), and John Ray (1674); his great merit lies not in his originality but in his catholic inclusiveness, drawing upon all available sources to compile the eighteenth century's most comprehensive treatment of English dialect. In addition, Bailey included a large vocabulary of obsolete words, mostly compiled from published glossaries to the works of Chaucer, Spenser, and Shakespeare. Bailey's hoard of archaic and provincial words was a potential goldmine for poets in quest of an alternative to the established Neoclassical poetic diction; Starnes and Noyes point out that "it was mainly from this rich collection of obsolete words that Chatterton constructed his poetic language for the Rowley poems." As we shall see, Bailey's dictionary assumed a similar importance for Clare, not so much as a source of obsolete words (though he may have derived some poetic archaisms from it), but primarily as a means of defending the legitimacy of his "provincialisms" against critical disparagement.

Nathan Bailey was a schoolmaster, lexicographer, and compiler of classical textbooks. He belonged to a marginal sect of Seventh Day Baptists who observed Saturday as the Sabbath, and his own sectarian views are reflected in his dictionary definitions of "Sabbath" and "Sabbatarian." As a Dissenter he was excluded from the elite circles of English society; and his bitter experience of exclusion may have motivated his lexicographic principle of inclusion. The Introduction to his *Universal Etymological English Dictionary* reveals a distinct political agenda: it traces the history of the English language in a way that stresses the survival of local vernaculars despite the repeated invasion of foreign conquerors. Neither the Romans, nor the Danes, nor the Normans were able to suppress the elegance and descriptive intensity of the ancient British tongue. Bailey describes the failed linguistic imperialism of the Romans:

> The *Roman* Legions residing in *Britain* for the Space of above 200 Years, undoubtedly disseminated the *Latin* tongue; and the People being also governed by Laws written in the *Latin,* must necessarily make a Mixture of Languages. This seems to have been the first Mutation the Language of *Britain* suffered: however so tenacious were our Forefathers of their *Native* Language, that it overgrew the *Roman.*

After recounting the incursions of the Saxons and the Danes, Bailey describes the Norman Conquest:

> Then about the Year 1067 *William* Duke of *Normandy,* commonly call'd *William* the *Conqueror,* came over to Britain; and having vanquish'd *Canutus* the *Danish* King, made an intire Conquest of *Britain:* and as a Monument of their Conquest, the *Normans* endeavoured to yoak the *English* under their Tongue, as they had under their Command, by compelling them to teach their Children in their Schools nothing but the *French,* by publishing their Laws in *French,* and by enforcing them most rigorously to plead and be impleaded in that Tongue, for the Space of about 350 Years; by which means the Language of *Britain* became a Dialect of the *English Saxon,* and *Norman French,* which now are the Groundwork or Fundamentals of the Present Language of *Great Britain.*

Bailey laments the linguistic tyranny of the Normans and their wholesale destruction of the Old English language:

> Before I proceed to account for the Alteration of the *English Saxon,* by the two other Causes, I shall mention something relating to the *Saxon* Tongue, of a great Part of which the *Normans* despoil'd us, giving a worse for a better. "Great verily (says *Camden*) was the Glory of our Tongue, before the *Norman* Conquest, in this, that the Old *English* could express most aptly all the Conceptions of the Mind in their own Tongue, without borrowing from any."

Bailey provides several examples of the concision and vividness of the Anglo-Saxon, such as *Inwit* for conscience and *Eoroses-Wele* for fertility. He concludes:

> By these Instances it does appear that the *English Saxon* Language of which the *Normans* despoiled us in great Part, had its Beauties, was Significant and Emphatical, and preferable to what they imposed upon us.

Bailey's predilection for Old English is apparent in his etymologies, which trace Anglo-Saxon roots wherever possible. For Clare, the political implications of Bailey's Introduction would have been quite apparent. If local vernaculars represent the survival of the ancient English language, then any attempt to impose standardization merely reflects the dominance of foreign paradigms. The old words must be cultivated and preserved in order to assure the cultural survival and the political autonomy of England's indigenous people.

Throughout his life, Clare devoted himself wholeheartedly to the preservation of his native language and culture. *The Village Minstrel* is virtually an archive of village customs, games, and stories; he later submitted a prose account of local traditions to William Hone's *Every-Day Book* (1826-1827); and during his asylum period he contributed numerous dialect words to Anne Elizabeth Baker's *Glossary of Northamptonshire Words and Phrases* (1854). Clare's most enduring legacy, however, is the rough-hewn linguistic texture of his poetry; and his resistance to the standardization of his local voice received significant encouragement at a crucial moment from Bailey's dictionary. Taylor, as we have seen, compiled the glossary to *Poems Descriptive* and also presumably to *The Village Minstrel,* as a list of words not authorized by Johnson's dictionary. In some cases the meaning of a dialect word was obvious to Taylor from its context; in other cases he sent queries to Clare, or simply guessed at the meaning. (Sometimes he guessed wrong, as in the definitions for *shool* and *soodles.*) But in several cases Taylor consulted dictionaries other than Johnson's; in the glossary to *Poems Descriptive* he cites Bailey's dictionary for the word *swaliest,* and he cites the 1775 dictionary of John Ash (another reliable authority on regional dialect) for the words *dithering, slive, spinney,* and *witchen.* Taylor possibly derived some other definitions from Bailey; the words *clammed, goss, hob, nappy,* and *siled* do not occur in Johnson, and Taylor's definitions closely resemble those in Bailey. Taylor's public recognition of the authority of Ash and Bailey for Clare's dialect must have bolstered Clare's confidence in the legitimacy of such words and confirmed his allegiance to the vernacular tradition of linguistic scholarship.

Several years later, Clare finally discovered a grammar-book that he could admire; it was by William Cobbett, a self-educated radical pamphleteer whose lower-class origins conditioned his sense of linguistic identity. In a letter of circa 1831-32, Clare asks his friend Marianne Marsh for her opinion of "the best part of Cobbets Gramer," and in a letter of January 1832 to the same correspondent he praises Cobbett as "one of the most powerful prose writers of the age" (*Letters* 556, 560). Clare refers here to Cobbett's *Grammar of the English Language, in a Series of Letters: Intended for the Use of Schools and of Young Persons in general; but more especially for the Use of Soldiers, Sailors, Apprentices, and Plough-boys* (1818). Cobbett regards genteel language as an instrument of fraud and political oppression; he writes with particular vehemence against classical learning, since "a knowledge of the Latin and Greek Languages does not prevent men from writing bad English." Clare shares Cobbett's contempt for classical learning and his linguistic ideology, based on the norms of spoken vernacular and attentive to regional varieties of usage. In a prose fragment of circa 1832, Clare attacks the "pedantic garrison" of the established grammarians while praising Cobbett's theory of grammar:

> Those who have made grammar up into a system and cut it into classes and orders as the student does the animal or vegetable creation may be a recreation for schools but it becomes of no use towards making any one so far acquainted with it as to find it useful—it will only serve to puzzle and mislead to awe and intimidate instead of aiding and encouraging him therefore it pays nothing for the study . . .

> And such a one as Cobbet who has come boldly forward and not only assailed the outworks of such a pedantic garrison but like a skilful general laid open its weakness to all deserves more praise for the use of his labour than all the rest of the castle building grammarians put together for he plainly comes to this conclusion—that what ever is intellig[i]b[l]e to others is grammer and whatever is commonsense is not far from correctness

This is a fairly accurate description of Cobbett's *Grammar,* which seeks to demolish the pretensions of the traditional grammarians, especially Lowth and Murray, by pointing out instances where they break their own rules. Cobbett is delightfully iconoclastic in his choice of quotations to illustrate bad grammar, citing the works of such classically educated authors as Milton, Addison, and Johnson, along with excerpts from parliamentary debates and a speech by the Prince Regent. Grammar for Cobbett is the ultimate leveller, allowing ordinary citizens to penetrate the obscurity and deception of political discourse. Although Cobbett himself does not always avoid the pitfalls of prescriptivism, his advocacy of plain vernacular speech and his satirical exposure of established linguistic authorities evidently appealed to Clare. Indeed, Clare goes much farther than Cobbett in challenging the norms of "educated" language and cultivating his own peculiar modes of expression.

Clare's discovery of his mature poetic voice occurred through a long struggle against the pressures exerted by editors, patrons, and reviewers; he found himself poised unevenly between the fashionable models of his poetic apprenticeship and the rude authenticity of his own native dialect. His earliest poems employ a poetic style that seems at times slavishly derivative of eighteenth-century models, notably the loco-descriptive poetry of Thomson, Cowper, and Gray. This uneasy tension between imitation and originality is especially apparent in his first volume, *Poems Descriptive,* and continues to impede the full range of his poetic voice in his second volume, *The Village Minstrel.* The uneven quality of Clare's early poetry is especially apparent in his sonnets, which present the challenge of innovation within a form constrained by an overbearing weight of historical tradition. His most derivative sonnets are written in fairly standard "educated" language on abstract meditative themes, such as **"On Death," "Peace," "Hope," "Expression,"** and **"To Time"**; he is much more successful when using the sonnet to encapsulate vignettes of life in the Northamptonshire countryside, although even here the temptation to imitation and abstraction tends to vitiate the specificity of his description. Clare's early sonnet **"Winter"** exemplifies this unfortunate tendency to undercut his vivid, earthy dialect by introducing awkward personifications of abstract entities:

> The small wind wispers thro the leafless hedge
> Most sharp & chill while the light snowey flakes
> Rests on each twig & spike of witherd sedge
> Resembling scatterd feathers—vainly breaks
> The pale split sunbeams thro the frowning cloud
> On winters frowns below—from day to day
> Unmelted still he spreads his hoary shroud
> In dithering pride on the pale travellers way
> Who croodling hastens from the storm behind
> Fast gathering deep & black—again to find
> His cottage fire & corners sheltering bounds
> Where haply such uncomfortable days
> Makes muscial the woodsaps fizzling sounds
> & hoarse loud bellows puffing up the blaze
> > (*Early Poems of John Clare* 2: 492)

The personification of Winter as a "frowning" old man spreading his "hoary shroud" across the landscape is certainly a derivative feature of this poem, along with its conventional poetic diction ("haply") and the generic, unspecified loco-descriptive "traveller." But this poem shows considerable promise in its robust regional vocabulary ("dithering," "croodling," "fizzling") and its refusal—typical of Clare—to abide by a standard rhyme-scheme or to follow strict rules of grammar. Thus for no apparent reason except individual eccentricity, Clare introduces a rhyming couplet (behind/find) in the middle of the sonnet, and he follows his own "vulgar" usage in matters of verb agreement, spelling, and punctuation. When this poem was published in *The Village Minstrel,* however, John Taylor normalized its grammar, punctuation, and spelling, reducing its quirky freshness to the prevailing norms of "correct" English.

Taylor's self-appointed role as "Corrector" of Clare's verse was undertaken with Clare's full knowledge and tacit consent, but despite Taylor's good intentions and reasonably competent editing, Clare became increasingly restive under the enforced normalization of his poetic language. As Clare developed a distinctive poetic voice, he became less willing to conform to "correct" linguistic usage and more boldly deviant from lexical and prosodic norms. The poetry of his middle period—including *The Shepherd's Calendar* (1827) and *The Rural Muse* (1835)—explores the rich expressive possibilities of his own regional dialect, using a wide range of dialect terms while returning to the prosodic and rhetorical models of his local culture, especially the folk ballads and lively doggerel verses derived from the oral tradition of his family and neighbors in Helpston. His poetry thus evolves away from what Bakhtin terms a "prim but moribund aristocratic language" toward a vernacular discourse of stubborn locality, synthesizing a variety of repressed or marginalized elements of Northamptonshire dialect.

A characteristic example of Clare's linguistic practice in this middle period may be found in his sonnet, **"Winter Fields,"** which forms part of the manuscript collection assembled by Clare about 1832 under the title *The Midsummer Cushion.* This poem begins with what appears to be another old-fashioned personification of an abstract entity, "rich mirth," but it soon becomes apparent that this abstraction is itself the target of ideological critique. Mirth is the possession of the idle rich who have money and leisure to spend on books, at the expense of the starving underclass described with telling concreteness in the rest of the poem:

> O for a pleasant book to cheat the sway
> Of winter—where rich mirth with hearty laugh
> Listens & rubs his legs on corner seat
> For fields are mire & sludge—& badly off
> Are those who on their pudgy paths delay
> There striding shepherd seeking direst way
> Fearing nights wetshod feet & hacking cough
> That keeps him waken till the peep of day
> Goes shouldering onward & with ready hook
> Progs off to ford the sloughs that nearly meet
> Accross the lands—croodling & thin to view
> His loath dog follows—stops & quakes & looks
> For better roads—till whistled to pursue
> Then on with frequent jumps he hirkles through
>   [*The Midsummer Cushion,* ed. Anne Tibble &
>   R. K. R. Thornton, Northumberland: Mid Northumberland Arts Group, 1979, p. 485.]

The highly conventional, almost parodic opening scene of this poem gives way to a vividly realized description of the shepherd and his dog striding through muddy fields, seeking a home that is never found and maintaining an affectionate loyalty to each other even in the midst of their suffering. Clare implicitly contrasts the narcissistic individualism of the literate class with the communal solidarity of the laboring class, here again expressed in robust dialect words such as "hirkles," which in this context refers to the jerky, uneven motion of the dog as it jumps from side to side. "Hirkles" would also be a good word to describe the rhyme scheme of this sonnet, which follows no traditional pattern but jumps randomly from one rhyme to the next until it reaches the high ground of the final couplet. This innovative use of the sonnet form is triumphant in its very amateurishness, as Clare swerves against the burden of literary tradition to discover an appropriate form to express his stubborn resistance to the ideology of linguistic propriety. Paradoxically, however, this sonnet bears witness to Clare's increasing sense of alienation from his own social class, since the very act of acquiring literacy and publishing books of poetry aligns him with the idle rich, most notably his wealthy patrons, and against the very class whose interests he seeks to advocate.

Clare's struggle to maintain a sense of personal and class identity through a gradually disintegrating literary career, economic hardship, dislocation from his birthplace, and a sense of betrayal and abandonment by friends, patrons, and even his family, cast him into deep depression and eventually resulted in his incarceration in the Northampton General Lunatic Asylum (1841). Despite his imprisonment in what he called the "English Bastille" and his isolation from his former literary mentors, Clare carried on his poetic vocation with enormous strength, dignity, and sense of purpose. His late poems, written in the asylum, go far beyond his published work in their deviation from established norms of linguistic and prosodic form. Critics of Clare's asylum poetry have tended either to patronize "poor Clare" in their sympathy for his sufferings, or to celebrate his visionary power while failing to recognize the latent ideological basis of his formal innovations. The stubbornly unconventional quality of Clare's asylum poetry is apparent in the poem **"Winter,"** written sometime after 1842 and existing only in a transcript prepared by his keeper, W. F. Knight. This poem might be described as the dried, withered husk of a sonnet; it begins with a full-fledged iambic pentameter line, but it dwindles down to shorter and shorter lines, rhyming erratically, and it reaches a final couplet after only eleven lines. In this pared-down, minimal prosodic form, the poem describes a desolate winter scene that suggests an existential analogue to Clare's own sense of isolation and despair:

> How blasted nature is, the scene is winter
> The Autumn withered every branch
> Leaves drop, and turn to colourless soil
> Ice shoots i' splinters at the river Bridge
> And by and bye all stop—
> White shines the snow upon the far hill top
> Nature's all withered to the root, her printer
> To decay that neer comes back
> Winds burst, then drop
> Flowers, leaves and colours, nothing's left to hint her
> Spring, Summer, Autumn's, withered into winter
>   [*The Later Poems of John Clare 1837-1864,* ed.
>   Eric Robinson & David Powell, Oxford: Clarendon, 1984, Vol. 2, p. 813.]

There is a provisional, makeshift quality to the texture of this verse, gesturing in the direction of the sonnet form but reducing it to just a ghost of its former self. The incongruously rich rhymes of "winter/printer/hint her" are counterpointed by the haphazard or nonexistent rhymes of the other lines. This formal innovation hints at the poem's meditation of scarcity, the poverty of language in the presence of a "withered" landscape. The syntactic structure of the poem is remarkably impoverished, lacking essential verbs and conjunctions, so that crucial lines and images remain enigmatic, disconnected. For instance, in the penultimate line, it is unclear whether "Flowers, leaves and colours" are the object of the verb "drop," or an appositive construction to "nothing"—or perhaps both. And in line 7 the phrase "her printer" dangles mysteriously.

As in the earlier sonnets on winter, this poem contains an abstract personification, Nature, who is almost entirely shorn of her traditional attributes. Nature is "blasted" by the unseen force of winter, a force that is emphatically *not* personified, since in this poem "winter" occurs consistently in lowercase while the other seasons are capitalized. Winter is not so much a season as the absence of all season, the passing of all colors into colorlessness, the passing of being itself into sheer nothingness. Like Shelley's West Wind, or Demogorgon in *Prometheus Unbound,* winter is an apocalyptic force that threatens the annihilation of all things, yet it also hints at the possibility that within this desolation are hidden the seeds of future growth. Even though Nature is "withered to the root," this root still abides in the earth, linked paratactically to "her printer." But who is nature's printer? Who can this "printer" be but the poet himself, John Clare, who has striven to publish his poems even beyond the "decay" of his public career? By humbly inscribing himself as Nature's printer, Clare acknowledges that his incarceration has robbed him of a public voice. He can no longer carry on his chosen career as a singer of songs and a teller of tales, but he can still pursue his poetic vocation in the silent medium of print. "Poets love nature," says Clare in another asylum poem, "They are her very scriptures upon earth" (*Later Poems* 1: 313). Clare accentuates the written medium of poetry during his asylum period, and his belated acknowledgment of textuality tends to displace his previous emphasis upon spoken language as a paradigm for poetic discourse.

This conception of Clare's late poetry as essentially *written,* rather than spoken or sung, is likely to raise doubts among those who regard Clare as primarily an oral poet. Certainly it is true that Clare is the beneficiary of a rich folk tradition of oral poetry, and I would not seek to minimize the importance of that tradition to him. Throughout his career, Clare was capable of composing verses modeled upon traditional folksongs and popular ballads with a seemingly effortless grace. But with the gradual loss of his readership, his growing sense of alienation, and his involuntary confinement, Clare seems to have lost the sense of immediacy that is essential to all oral forms of literature. Lacking listeners, his poems must perforce be *written,* either as letters to loved ones or as memoranda to himself. His longest asylum poem, **"Child Harold,"** is subtitled "Prison Amusements," indicating his sense of its self-directedness. Within this sense of language as a textual medium, however, lie the seeds of Clare's astonishing poetic development during the asylum period. Free from constraints imposed by outsiders, he was able to explore the most radical possibilities of poetic language. Clare's linguistic and prosodic experiments during his asylum period represent the final stage of his quest for a mode of poetic discourse free from the tyranny of grammar and adequate to the expression of his tragic struggle for personal and regional identity.

John Wareham (essay date 1994)

SOURCE: "Clare's 'The Awthorn,'" in *The Explicator,* Vol. 53, No. 1, Fall, 1994, pp. 197-200.

[*In the following excerpt, Wareham asserts that with "The Awthorn," Clare strives to unite the "transience" and "perpetuity" of nature within a single poem, thereby presenting his own vision of transcendence.*]

> I love the awthorn well
> The first green thing
> In woods and hedges—black thorn dell
> Dashed with its green first spring
> When sallows shine in golden shene
> These white thorn places in the black how green
>
> How beautifully green
> Though March has but begun
> To tend primroses planted in the sun
> The roots that[s] further in
> Are not begun to bud or may be just begun
>
> I love the white thorn bough
> Hung over the mole hill
> Where the spring feeding cow
> Rubs off the dew drop chill
> When on the cowslip pips and glossy thorn
> The dews hang shining pearls at early morn

The early leafing-out of hawthorn (whitethorn) as harbinger of spring held a special fascination for John Clare. He alluded to it several times, although rarely with the ordered intensity of **"The Awthorn."** [**"The Awthorn,"** Northampton MS 19, 70-71, c. spring 1845. Reproduced in E. Robinson and D. Powell. eds., *The Later Poems of John Clare 1837-1864*, Oxford: Oxford UP, 1984, Vol. 1, pp. 200-201.] Ultimately, the poem transcends landscape. Yet it is an unpeopled spring landscape first, and its poetic resources—among them contrast, repetition, occasionally disjointed syntax, diction, rhyme—strikingly achieve energy, compression, and lyricality. For all its scenery's apparent disorder, the poem's two six-line stanzas symmetrically frame a five-lined center. The sole punctuation—line 3's dash—focuses on the site of interest. The cummings-like "green first spring" (reversing part of "first green thing," so that the particular echoes the opening generality) and "in the black how green" attract attention with their defamiliarizing lyricism. Underpunctuation positively strives to capture the scene before it changes or the feelings that it generates evaporate. "Dashed" vividly conveys the *pointilliste* appearance of incipient foliage. The outer stanzas rhyme on monosyllables to integrate simple things clearly seen and considered, the scene as fresh as when poet, or world, first saw it.

The central section focuses on the hawthorn's precocious greenery. March has hardly begun to foster primroses or roots—the second object of "to tend"—that are "further in" woods, or soil, or dormancy. Those roots, unlike the hawthorn's, have not begun to "bud" or put forth new shoots. "Tend" and "planted," anthropocentric or personifying in the eighteenth-century tradition of nature writing, imply earth's benevolence; but in Clare they are mere counters, for **"The Awthorn"** finds joy in nature despite its indifference. The prominent five rhymes with a consonantal *n* base reflect the way the laggard signs of spring,

outstripped by the hawthorn and signalled by the imped-
ing "Though," are held in abeyance on the same insistent
note. Along with the contemplation of the potentialities of
roots in their subterranean darkness, the repeated "begun"
builds up a head of expectancy at spring's approach.

The final stanza releases, realizes that promise. Opening
like the first, it presents the hawthorn within a web of
connections joining bough to molehill to cow to dewdrop
and back, cyclically, to "thorn." All are organically united
in a whole aesthetically greater than the sum of its parts.
Their particularity achieves an inscape of almost Hopkin-
sian precision: it is a "spring feeding" cow (nourished in
and by the spring, in turn nourishing it), the dewdrop is
"chill," the cowslips yield "pips" (Northamptonshire dialect for the florets in a cluster), and the haw's thorn,
picking up the "shene" of the sallows, is "glossy." Early
sunlight is reflected in dew "pearls," a dead metaphor but
in another poem, **"Twilight,"** "the cowslip pips wi' pearls
untold" are preferred to "crown and scepter": chill dew-
drops are valued more highly than gew-gaw or status symbol. Nevertheless, pearls adorning the objects of veneration are love-tribute and triumphal garland. Dew's connotation of fertility has a vital nexus with the other natural
components of the closure's Bewick-like vignette.

In a sense there are no ideas but in the things of **"The
Awthorn"** and these compose, create, a specific locality.
"The content of Clare's poetry can be said to be his characteristic sense of place," which expresses "*this* is how it
is here." Barrell sees a mature Clare poem as "one complex manifold of simultaneous impressions." **"The Awthorn"** certainly fits this description. Simultaneity is
achieved in the first stanza by "when," indicating the
concurrence of hawthorn's greenery with sallows' sheen,
and by the compressed syntax that puts "woods and hedges" on a level with "blackthorn dell." "Green first spring"
simultaneously conveys color, earliness, and season. The
middle stanza presents the "green" hawthorn at the same
time as primroses and roots. The final stanza establishes
with "where" and "when" the simultaneity of the things
presented in dynamic relationship: bough, molehill, cow,
dewdrop, cowslip, dews, and morn—a simultaneous microcosm of nature. **"The Awthorn"** is consistent with
Barrell's insightful thesis that "This habit of understanding a place as a manifold impressions, not organised by
perspective and thus as it were in the foreground is a habit
formed by an upbringing in an open-field landscape."

"The Awthorn," however, is not pictorially structured
like the earlier landscape poems of Thomson and Dyer
where "each scene is correctly composed . . . to enable
the reader to visualise a picture after the manner of Sal-
vator and Claude." Like Hopkins's "Inversnaid," it neither conjures up a preexisting picture nor sees the landscape itself as a picture. **"The Awthorn"** creates landscape through simultaneous visual impressions, welding
them into a vision of a unified, harmonious, and boundless nature. What holds them is not the forces of New-
tonian rationalism but the poet's loving attention. The
dynamic relationships within this natural order, the interpenetration of entities, the mental pointing, the abne-

gation of self and yet the internalization of things loved,
the veneration of the unremarkable—in such ways Clare
is oriental, Zen-like. Nature's wildness has been drilled
into poetry's discipline. In the Jesuit Hopkins's altogether more watery and turbulent "Inversnaid" too—where
simultaneity is not an organizing principle, for the poem
follows temporally and physically the cascade's course—
the spiritual dimension is implicit. Clare would have
empathized with "Long live . . . the wilderness yet" as
with, elsewhere, the "Sweet especial rural scene."

Although Clare wrote finely of his "daily communings
with God and not a word spoken," **"The Awthorn"** does
not look "thro' Nature up to Nature's God" (Pope, "An
Essay on Man" Ep. iv. 331). It venerates the natural level,
the observable surface of country things exquisitely observed, contemplated. and unified. If Clare was "a primitive poet in the sense that he insisted on writing almost
from the fertility level" that does not preclude a transition
to eternity. He made the transition in

> Leaves from eternity are simple things
> To the world's gaze where to a spirit clings
> Sublime and lasting
>
>   **("The Eternity of Nature")**

and in

> Who ever looks round Sees Eternity there
>   **("Autumn")**

When he made his own heaven he made sure the lowly
hawthorn had a place in it. Clare saw eternity in the hawthorn bough and in the union of other regenerated things
that it protectively "hung over." The poem does not stop
at the simultaneity of open field vision but extends to
perpetuity. **"The Awthorn"** is a poem of becoming as
well as a poem of transience.

FURTHER READING

Criticism

Blackmore, Evan. "John Clare's Psychiatric Disorder and Its
Influence on His Poetry." *Victorian Poetry* 24, No. 3 (Autumn
1986): 209-28.
        Diagnoses Clare's psychiatric malady and examines the
        ways in which it influenced the style and subjects of his
        poems.

Constantine, David. "Outside Eden: John Clare's Descriptive
Poetry." In *An Infinite Complexity: Essays in Romanticism,*
edited by J. R. Watson, pp. 181-201. Edinburgh: Edinburgh
University Press, 1983.
        Explores Clare's relationship to his publishers and public,
        as well as to nature, his poverty, and his own poetry.

Gregory, Horace. "On John Clare, and the Sight of Nature in
His Poetry." In his *The Shield of Achilles: Essays on Beliefs
in Poetry,* pp. 21-32. Westport, Conn.: Greenwood Press, 1944.

Provides a brief biographical sketch and compares Clare's poetry to that of William Blake and William Cowper.

Groves, David. "John Clare and James Hogg: Two Peasant Poets in the *Athenaeum*." *Bulletin of Research in the Humanities* 87, Nos. 2-3 (1986-87): 225-29.

Discusses how the nineteenth-century literary journal *Athenaeum* made a point of publishing new, working-class poets of its day, including John Clare.

Howard, William James. *John Clare*. Boston: Twayne Publishers, 1981, 205 p.

A chronology, a brief biography, and an overview of John Clare's writings, including a selected bibliography.

Jack, Ian. "Poems of John Clare's Sanity." In *Some British Romantics: A Collection of Essays,* edited by James V. Logan, John E. Jordan, and Northrop Frye, pp. 191-232. Columbus: Ohio State University Press, 1966.

Asserts that "it was Clare's misfortune to publish his finest volume [*The Shepherd's Calendar*] at a point when his countrymen were too deeply concerned with political and social reform to have any time to spare for poetry."

Lucas, John. "Prologue: Poetry and Possession." In his *Modern English Poetry from Hardy to Hughes: A Critical Survey,* pp. 9-21. London: B. T. Batsford Ltd., 1986.

Analyzes Clare's poetry with regard to its essential "Englishness," *i.e.* its similarity to that of other writers of Clare's era.

————. "Revising Clare." In *Romantic Revisions,* edited by Robert Brinkley and Keith Hanley, pp. 339-53. Cambridge: Cambridge University Press, 1992.

Examines the conflict that Clare experienced between his role as peasant and as poet and its effect today upon assessing the totality of his poetic works.

MacLennan, George. "John Clare: 'Literature Has Destroyed My Head and Brought Me Here.'" In his *Lucid Interval: Subjective Writing and Madness in History,* pp. 120-52. Leicester: Leicester University Press, 1992.

Looks at Clare's beginnings as a "peasant poet" but focuses in particular on the poems of his insanity and on his obsession with Mary Joyce.

Minor, Mark. "Clare, Byron, and the Bible: Additional Evidence from the Asylum Manuscripts." *Bulletin of Research in the Humanities* 85, No. 1 (Spring 1982): 104-26.

Studies the "Hebrew Melodies" of Clare's asylum years— lesser known poems that are both "scriptural paraphrases and Byronic imitations."

Murry, John Middleton. "The Poetry of John Clare." In his *Countries of the Mind: Essays in Literary Criticism,* pp. 103-19. New York: E. P. Dutton & Company, 1922.

Argues that Clare's poetic gifts are inferior to those of one of his contemporaries, John Keats.

Pearce, Lynn. "John Clare's 'Child Harold': A Polyphonic Reading." *Criticism* XXXI, No. 2 (Spring 1989): 139-57.

Applies formal, deconstructive literary theory to Clare's "Child Harold," a poem which has conventionally been examined primarily for its interest as an asylum poem.

Robinson, Eric. "'To an Oaken Stem': John Clare's Poem Recovered and Reconsidered." *The Review of English Studies* XXXVIII n. s., No. 152 (November 1987): 483-91.

Assesses the poem "To an Oaken Stem" as indicative of "Clare's ability to unite man and nature without the flagrant moralizing of much eighteenth-century poetry."

Storey, Mark, ed. *Clare: The Critical Heritage*. London: Routledge and Kegan Paul, 1973, 453 p.

An anthology of remarks made by Clare as well as criticism and reviews from others, dating from 1818 to 1964.

Strickland, Edward. "John Clare and the Sublime." *Criticism* XXIX, No. 2 (Spring 1987): 141-61.

Maintains that "Clare is poetically more conservative than any of the more famous Romantic poets" and does not often venture beyond descriptive nature poetry and the ballad form into the realm of the sublime.

————. "Boxer Byron: A Clare Obsession." *The Byron Journal,* No. 17 (1989): 57-76.

Investigates Clare's deep admiration for and imitation of the poet George Gordon, Lord Byron.

Swingle, L. J. "Stalking the Essential John Clare: Clare in Relation to His Romantic Contemporaries." *Studies in Romanticism* 14, No. 3 (Summer 1975): 273-84.

Contrasts Clare's early, descriptive poetry with the works of Percy Bysshe Shelley, William Wordsworth, Samuel Taylor Coleridge, and John Keats in order to demonstrate Clare's own poetic characteristics.

Wallace, Anne D. "Farming on Foot: Tracking Georgic in Clare and Wordsworth." *Texas Studies in Literature and Language* 34, No. 4 (Winter 1992): 509-40.

Discusses how Wordsworth and Clare each dealt with the limitations on nature and excursions that the enclosure acts presented to the English countryside and the English poet.

Gunnar Ekelöf
1907-1968

(Full name Gunnar Bengt Ekelöf; also transliterated as Ekeloef) Swedish poet, essayist, and translator.

INTRODUCTION

Ekelöf has often been described as the most important poet of modern Swedish literature. His work, which reflects the influences of the mystical poetry of ancient Persia and the Orient, Taoist and Indian mysticism, and French Symbolism and Surrealism, is complex and enigmatic. Written in the modernist aesthetic tradition, Ekelöf's poetry challenges the reader to abandon conventional perceptions of both poetry and reality. True to the work of the Surrealists, his works also call upon readers to explore the relevance of the subconscious to their thinking. Thus, Ekelöf's work is often filled with fantastic, dreamlike images and symbols which mock rational thought. Against this backdrop, reality and self emerge as Ekelöf's major concerns, while freedom from the dualistic morality of good and evil become his personal and poetic aim.

Biographical Information

Ekelöf was born into a wealthy family in Stockholm, Sweden. He described his mother, with whom he never shared a close relationship, as a member of the "petty nobility." His father, a stockbroker, contracted syphilis while Ekelöf was a child; the disease caused him to lose his sanity, and eventually resulted in his death. The loss of his father led Ekelöf to regard himself as an outsider, and the image of the outcast or loner appears frequently in his poetry. Ekelöf's academic career was widely varied. He studied Asian languages in London, England, as well as in Uppsala, Sweden, and in Paris during the 1920s he studied writing, music, and drawing. Both music and the visual arts surface as important influences in his poetry. Ekelöf was elected to the Swedish Academy in 1958. He died of throat cancer in 1968.

Major Works

Ekelöf's first book of poems, *Sent på jorden* (1932; *Late Arrival on Earth*) proved itself an influential work in its time. Written during a period of the author's deep despair and drawing upon the techniques of French Surrealism, the volume presents a bleak, nihilistic vision of a world hurtling toward destruction. This work, Ekelöf's "suicide book," was written at a time when the bourgeois humanistic culture of Sweden was under fierce criticism by such groups as the Marxists, and is considered revolutionary because it attacked not only the bourgeoisie but also "the conventional structures of language and literature." Full

of nightmarish imagery of death and decay, *Late Arrival on Earth* marks the beginning of Ekelöf's lifelong attack on traditional conceptions of reality as well as of poetry. *Dedikation* (1934; *Dedication*), Ekelöf's second book of poetry, reflects the influence of French Symbolism: here, Ekelöf portrays himself as an interpreter or "seer" whose vision extends beyond the perimeters of superficial reality. More positive than *Late Arrival on Earth*, *Dedication* shows the author groping toward the truth which he believes lies beyond reality and seeking a "oneness" denied by the moralists' artificially constructed poles of good and evil. Transcendence of such boundaries, Ekelöf believed, allows one to become fully "oneself." In *Sorgen och stjärnan* (1935; *Grief and Stars*), Ekelöf denies the existence of reality altogether: concepts, institutions, rules, and boundaries are seen as artificial, the mere inventions of persons struggling to impose order on the chaotic and unending struggle between good and evil. Ekelöf regarded *Färjesång* (1941; *Ferry Song*) as the culmination of his thought. More intellectual than his previous works, *Ferry Song* displays the influence of Symbolism and Romanticism. Attempting to reconcile the ideal and the real, the poet questions the validity of our traditional conceptions of both the self and reality. One of Ekelöf's most frequently discussed works is *En Mölna-elegi* (1960; *A Mölna Elegy*). Reminiscent of James Joyce's novel *Ulysses,* the *Elegy* consists in part of the poet's intricate musings, revolving around a single day he spent on the Mölna jetty outside of Stockholm, and contains an abundance of literary and historical allusions, including obscene lines from ancient Roman poetry. In general, Ekelöf's later poetry pursues themes similar to those of his earlier works, but in a different style and manner. In many of these works, there is an absurd element and an apparent attempt to eliminate all but the most necessary words and images. On numerous occasions, Ekelöf himself denied that these works were even poetry. The most widely-known examples from this phase in Ekelöf's career are *Diwan över Fursten av Emgión* (1965; *Divan about the Prince of Emgión*), *Sagan om Fatumeh* (1966; *The Story of Fatumeh*), and *Vägvisare till underjorden* (1967; *Guide to the Underworld.*)

Critical Reception

Many critics have acclaimed Ekelöf as a profound thinker and have praised his ability to incorporate diverse influences into a coherent pattern of thought. Some commentators have expressed admiration for Ekelöf as a distinctly Swedish poet whose works are permeated by the sentiments and landscapes of his native country. Ekelöf's poetry has been characterized as innovative in form and technique, particularly in its adaptation of musical forms to verse. His poetry, scholars have concluded, is distinguished by its originality and its relevancy to the reader concerned with problems of the modern age.

PRINCIPAL WORKS

Poetry

Sent på jorden [*Late Arrival on Earth*] 1932
Dedikation [*Dedication*] 1934
Sorgen och stjärnan [*Grief and Stars*] 1935
Köp den blindes sång [*Buy the Blind Man's Poem*] 1938
Färjesång [*Ferry Song*] 1941
Non serviam [*I Will Not Serve*] 1945
Dikter (collected poems) 1949
Om hösten [*In Autumn*] 1951
Strountes [*Nonsense* or *Tryflings*] 1955
Opus incertum 1959
En Mölna-elegi [*A Mölna Elegy*] 1960
En natt i Oto ac [*A Night in Oto ac*] 1961
Diwan över Fursten av Emgión [*Divan about the Prince of Emgión*] 1965
Sagan om Fatumeh [*The Story of Fatumeh*] 1966
Vägvisare till underjorden [*Guide to the Underworld*] 1967
Partitur [*Score*] 1969
En röst 1973

Other Major Works

Promenader [*Walks*] (essays) 1941
Utflykter [*Excursions*] (essays) 1947

Blandade kort [*Shuffled Cards*] (essays) 1957
En självbiografi (autobiography) 1971

*Published posthumously and edited by the poet's wife, Ingrid Ekelöf.

CRITICISM

Leif Sjöberg (essay date 1965)

SOURCE: "Allusions in the First Part of *En Mölna-Elegi,*" in *Scandinavian Studies,* Vol. 37, No. 4, November, 1965, pp. 293-323.

[*In the following excerpt, while tracing the literary, mythological, and historical allusions in* A Mölna Elegy, *Sjöberg discusses Ekelöf's fascination with the theme of time and his connections to James Joyce and T. S. Eliot.*]

If there has been a major shift in poetic theory during the past two centuries, it has been *from* an emphasis of the external world (around us) *to* the internal world (within us). Thus, for a long time the consciousness of man has been the primary target for a vast number of writers and poets. The great variety with which these consciousnesses are described may be illustrated by a brief consideration of three outstanding examples. In his *Ulysses* (1922), James Joyce devoted more than a quarter million words to revealing the complexity involved in the passage of a single, ordinary day, and later, in *Finnegans Wake* (1939) used as many words to dramatize a single night of a single character. Eliot, on the other hand, concentrated his discussion of *The Waste Land* to just over four hundred lines. At about the time when Joyce began preparing *Finnegans Wake* for the press, Gunnar Ekelöf (b. 1907) began to write **En Mölna-Elegi,** which was finally published in 1960. In an introductory note in *Bonniers Litterära Magasin* (*BLM*) 1946, Ekelöf described it as a poem concerning itself "with the relativity of time and time experience, perhaps also with a kind of *Lebensstimmung*. It is not a description of a time lapse but is (theoretically) supposed to occur in *one moment* (italics added). In other words: a transverse section of time, instead of a lengthwise section." This moment of *Lebensstimmung,* this second, comprises images from a number of centuries, and from various cultures and religions of the past and the present; it deals with the West as well as the East and with the primitive as well as with the sophisticated. It was a "work in progress" for more than twenty years and can now be read in a book which consists of a little more than sixty pages. . . .

Since Ekelöf's *A Mölna-Elegy* is a meeting place of quotations, allusions, references, and, above all, *identifications,* it is desirable that the reader have a commentary available for a better understanding of the poem. The following essay is an attempt to trace and point out some of these allusions, etc. without propounding interpretations (except in a limited way). In some instances I have managed to get statements authenticated by the poet; in other instances I have quoted what have seemed appropriate passages from his essays.

Ekelöf's relationship to Joyce seems straightforward and generally friendly. For instance, in one of his books of translations in which he preaches a Selective Affinity theory Ekelöf includes four poems from Joyce's *Chamber Music*. The collection of poems that many critics consider his best, **Non Serviam** (1945), may even have derived its title from *Portrait of the Artist as a Young Man*. In **A Mölna-Elegy** Ekelöf has woven in the sentence "when the h, who the hu, how the hue, where the huer?" from *Finnegans Wake* which in a letter he once called "a gigantic cocoon." The telescoping of words that is so characteristic of Joyce is used sparingly in some of Ekelöf's later books.

Ekelöf's relation to Eliot is more involved and not entirely amiable. Ekelöf himself has rather effectively and energetically defended his integrity against some critics' assumption that he was dependent on Eliot:

> Eliot I will undoubtedly have to suffer for all my life. I have (later) studied him by interpreting (= translating) him; I appreciate him as an artist, if not as a cultural critic; I have learned from his free blank verse (but as much from Shakespeare's); yet my poems still do not contain and do not express what his poems express and contain. In regard to the allusion and quotation method particularly in **Non Serviam** and **A Mölna-Elegy,** which I suppose will be especially regarded as inspired by Eliot, it should be noted that it is an age-old method, practised not only by a Petronius, a Dante, even a Rabelais or in our days a Joyce, but in all times by an innumerable host of "hermetic," symbolic, or mystic poets, naturally in such a way that each has sung his song hintingly according to his own turn of mind.

Ekelöf then goes on to say that he does not believe in artistic development by means of "influences," at least not in regard to writers who have something genuinely original to offer; instead he believes in development through a process of identification, i.e., "so that one *recognizes himself* both in what is new and old and furthermore in time, in the changes which the light of time throws onto the picture, which itself is living and changeable."

Nonetheless, on several occasions Ekelöf seems to have been influenced by Eliot. Arne Losman, in his essay "Kring *En Mölna-Elegi*" (1958), has listed a few of these, and makes reference to one of the most important themes of the elegy: a deep mutual connection with the past. This has been expressed in the lines: "Thus I feel / From the depth of my midriff my dead ones." Here Losman thinks he recognizes Eliot's influence, but he fails to be more specific. He goes on:

> It is likely that Ekelöf's understanding of tradition, at least to some extent, has been inspired by Eliot. The **Elegy** is a quite orthodox application of the Englishman's concepts of tradition, which according to his essay "Tradition and the Individual Talent" (1919) involves historic mind, acquired through hard work, coupled with a feeling that all literature of Europe has a

simultaneous existence: the poet becomes part of a living past. According to Eliot the best parts of the poetry are those in which the dead poets make their immortality most strongly felt.

"A few times I have started to read Eliot's essays but never got very far. There didn't seem to be anything there for me to gather. *'The Use of Poetry and the Use of Criticism'* is the only (critical) book I have had a real try at," Ekelöf has stated. Losman notes Ekelöf's introductory remarks to the **Elegy** (*BLM*, 1946), in which "ironically enough Ekelöf made use of the same Baudelaire allusion *hycklande läsare* as Eliot employed in *The Waste Land.* The fact that in the same notes Ekelöf conceded that his quotation method is "only partly a so-called Eliot method, a method which, incidentally, is not only Eliot's but is old as the hills," does not prove anything. The similarities Losman finds between the **Elegy**'s doggerel "It was in the time when". . ." and "Here we go round the prickly pear" in "The Hollow Men" are not very convincing. Is it not more reasonable to assume that Ekelöf has actually *heard* this doggerel rather than *read* it? Losman continues: "But *Four Quartets* are perhaps the poems by Eliot which show the greatest resemblances to the **Elegy** in terms of both form and content. The **Elegy** is 'a poem about the relativity of time and time experience'." Losman is tempted to compare this central theme with the opening lines of *Burnt Norton:* "Time present and time past / Are both perhaps present in time future, / And time future contained in the past." and also with the main theme "In my beginning is my end," from *East Coker,* which Ekelöf translated.

These observations of alleged influence from Eliot could easily be matched with others that are equally facile and unsubstantiated. One such would be from *Burnt Norton* in which Eliot's "three aspects of time have been reduced to the central truth":

> What might have been and what has been
> Point to one end, which is always present.

Ekelöf has written on this:

> One can learn blank verse best from Shakespeare, but there it naturally makes an impression of being old-fashioned. Chiefly, what I have learned from Eliot is perhaps that in our time, too, blank verse works very well when one wants to set poetic prose, or everyday prose, into a kind of verse, thereby giving it a certain higher value. The sentences employing enjambment, with a period in the middle of the line, etc., also give the skillful writer an opportunity to take care of or suppress certain shades of meanings, as the need may be. But this is an artistic device, of which type there are many in existence. It is a part of the handicraft but not a form in itself. Form and contents are something quite different from the art of pounding in a nail, even if the latter may also be very useful. It is odd that such things can satisfy some critics when it is a matter of labeling a poet. But it is convenient, to be sure.

> The sum of my "légitime défense" remains as before that my poems do not contain and do not express the

same as his [Eliot's] poems express or contain, and this goes for both the kind of time experience as well as for the kind of artistic attitude and ultimate goal; it has validity also humanly, religiously or, if you choose, mystically, and in regard to acceptance of history and moral color. If the criteria of contents are insufficient in this case, it means that technical details are considered more significant, which would indeed be absurd.

This is not the occasion to discuss at any length the possible influence Eliot might have exerted on Ekelöf. However, let me report just one bit of evidence to the contrary which has amazed me. In Eliot's opinion, art is an effort "to metamorphose private failures and disappointments." Then should not the subtitle of the *Elegy,* "Metamorphoses," be related to this statement of Eliot's, so that perhaps the whole idea of identity changes in the *Elegy* would have originated from Eliot? The answer to this question is in the negative: From checking the galleys and page proofs of the *Elegy* at Bonnier's, the publisher, I found that the subtitle was added only on the second set of page proofs, marked July 7, 1960, i.e., shortly before publication.

It seems possible that *The Waste Land,* or the existence of such a poem, presented Ekelöf with a kind of warrant to develop the potential poem that was already in his mind. But is it so entirely improbable that Ekelöf with his extraordinary background and aptitude for creative work, would have turned out to be a "learned" poet even without Eliot? At any rate it seems feasible when one considers that Ekelöf had access at school to the same oriental sources as Eliot, and, moreover, that Ekelöf studied them in the original languages (which Eliot did not). Ekelöf also studied the classic authors, even translated Petronius (whom Eliot uses as a motto for *The Waste Land*) long before he had heard of Eliot. The titles of the essays "Vad åskan sade" (*Promenader,* 1941) and "Gerontion" (*Utflykter,* 1947) were probably used polemically. It is hard to determine exactly what part music has played in shaping these "learned" poems with their frequent allusions, repetitions, etc., but it might be pertinent to stress that Ekelöf had a good education in music, certainly better than Eliot's.

"The whole meaning of time itself changed radically as a result of social and technological factors; and this change, in turn, had far-reaching repercussions upon man's thinking about himself and his orientation in the modern world," writes Hans Meyerhoff. As time-saving devices became the symbol for industrial proficiency and progress, and "looking backwards" upon oneself and history was considered a waste of time, because it was a "negation of productivity and value," Ekelöf preoccupied himself with "one moment," which is obviously more than just a framework. However small an entity of "fragmentized" or "meaningless" time, it is nonetheless inseparable from the concept of the self, the identity, which Ekelöf has scrutinized so thoroughly and questioned so effectively in many poems, among them **"Tag och skriv."** "I have always learned from the past and mistrusted those who *teach* the future," Ekelöf has written. In an essay deploring our lack of traditions, Ekelöf has made a plea for a broader kind of

education than our schools provide. It should be *less* divided into compartments, *more* unified, "because culture is one and indivisible." How can a student profit from being taught mere ideas? "Instead give him time, its social tone, its costume among high and low, street-mud and odors, its carriages and horses, music, even the street ballads, painting, even tavern signs, the sex morality, the shape of glasses, the decor on the plates, food recipes, the cries of the chimney sweep lads, the *on dits* and *bon mots* of the day, and give it to him visually."

In another essay, "Modus vivendi," Ekelöf writes:

> I wish to live associatively, want to find out about myself and the world thus: empirically, through memory and its connections, want to experience the world not only in the moment but in many possible moments of what my now is composed. The now has no univocal guide lines to offer me; I return to it when it has become memory, in order laboriously, with the help of other memories, to make a kind of decision, which is hardly more than a confirmed divination. But such confirmed divinations can by and by become a vague conviction which will grow clear. That is my now. Which was then.

The introductory scene of the *Elegy* is set on the Mölna jetty. "I am sitting on a bench of the past / I am writing on a page of the past." The time is at sunset an evening when the transition from September into October is about to take place. Next to the I, the poet, seems to stand a squint-eyed, gaudily dressed Harlequin, or buffoon, who is playing an absurd ditty which is known in numerous variations throughout Europe: "and it was at the time when the legless ran / and the fingerless were playing the guitar till it rang. . . ." With this literal reading the scene sounds more theatrical than it actually is. Not only is it stated that the ditty is "mute," but also that it is sung for someone who is "deaf," which must indicate that the buffoon is a personification for autumn, with its multicolored motley leaves. As further proof of this can perhaps be taken the fact that the buffoon never reappears in the *Elegy* only the musical indication "Sept. Oct."

The poet is experiencing a very special kind of mood, which appears shut off from external reality, only passively acting as a receiving medium of what turns up in his mind, an extraordinary repository of unassorted fragmentary memories, impressions, ideas, and experiences, just like the autumnal leaves, whirling past for a moment, before they quietly fall down and disappear from sight. The time referred to in the absurd ditty is a time of extreme conditions, whether in the past or the present or the future and suggestive of death, ghosts, and, in fact, chaos: more precisely, to the years preceding World War II. But it also has the function of setting the mood for the imagined or experienced metamorphoses occurring in the *Elegy.* The problem of identity, which is such a basic theme in Ekelöf's writing, has in effect been brought up already in these opening lines about the "I" and the personified fall. . . .

A few weeks during "the last summer" the odd-looking buildings at Mölna had been swarming with pitiful crippled children, "incomplete larvae and lemures," (lines 10-14). A common theme in Ekelöf is here reintroduced: incompleteness, captiveness within a higher being, as later on in the sections *Méga Aléxandre* and *Stateíra mo* (lines 369 ff. and 407 ff.). The word *lemures* refers to ancient Roman spirits that moaned at night. This ghostlike, macabre sight conveys a hint of people dressed in institutional garb or soldiers advancing in war-time equipment and at the same time it conveys a hint of peaceful but clumsily manouvered ballet of marionettes. In his *BLM* notes Ekelöf states: "to illustrate the technique of the poem, it can be mentioned that the cripples are a vision with which the main protagonist seeks to disguise the general picture of the Germans invading *the past.* The crippled ones really invaded Mölna a few years earlier."

Now the buildings are deserted again. Perhaps it is the fall of 1937 at Mölna. The external emptiness in the place reflects the internal emptiness or loneliness felt by the main protagonist, the experiencing mind. The relativity of everything is demonstrated in lines 18-20: he feels the same apathy (or perhaps a different one?) as when these wretched beings were about; now they symbolize the advances of Nazi Germany. "What do I care? My life has stopped," he feels. His life is discussed in terms usually reserved for a malfunctioning clock or watch, which fits in with the general theme of time, so often repeated and varied in the *Elegy.* But it may prove more rewarding to read "stannat" (line 20) as "stannat här" or as "blivit instängt," thus emphasizing the physical aspect rather than the psychological. If so, "stopped" would signify the unfeasibility of travelling and also of attempts to change life, which the more alert intellectuals must have felt strongly before the imminent war, as expressed later in the *Elegy:*

> All that never came to be
> All that led to nullity
> Waves that glittered
> Waves of which I used to think:
> You are a way to the world
> As far as desire you bear us
> But it never began

Some indications of time in the beginning of the *Elegy* are: the bench of the past, a page of the past, September, October, November, the time of the "absurd" ballad, last summer, a few weeks' illusion, now and at the end of the poem a slightly modified and improved line from *The Land That Is Not,* by the great Finland-Swedish poet Edith Södergran, in which again an aspect of time is referred to:

> A capricious moment stole from me my future. . . .

In *that* crucial moment the hopes, aspirations, and expectations for the future were destroyed. The recurrence of the line adds to its central thematic significance here.

The beautiful **"Wave Song"** which corresponds to **"Fire Song"** in the latter part of the *Elegy,* repeats the onomatopoetic lines about the wind and the waves which return like echoes from a distant shore. In this "scene" the sun is setting. But note how explicit the image is: "The sun

nailed on *Danviken*'s spire." Danviken was a madhouse, a Bedlam. Ekelöf's essay, "An Outsider's Way," reads in part:

> One of those remarkably strong, early memories was the sunset. That fits a future poet, but I do not know how I happened to become a cloud-watcher. The sunset lay heavy over my childhood and I even saw it in my dreams. The intensely brick-red church outside the windows it was the Johannes Church in Stockholm threw a hectic, sickly and, as it were, magnified reflection of the sunset deep into the rooms. In this red twilight my father wandered about like a shadow, insane for many years, mumbling, and with an absent, dilapidated face, followed by his nurses. When they had managed to place him in an easy chair he could sit for hours and "hear voices," as it was called, i.e., he mumbled monotonously, brooding, incomprehensively, and without end. The apartment had long corridors, and in the twilight there was a strange, ghostly atmosphere in its out-of-the-way spots while the funeral bells rang outside. In my memory red sunsets and bells are always inseparable.

> Later, with the initial boldness of the years of indiscretion, I used to climb up on the roof to see the sunset. The roof was one of the highest on *Johanneshöjden.* I went up through a garret door and scrambled onto it, partly with and partly without the help of the fire ladders, until I could sit straddling the rooftop, where I would smoke forbidden cigarettes and stare at the sun like an anchorite. It was a dizzying height that of the house itself plus that of the ridge, for it stood teetering near the edge of a cliff, the bottom of which was in a backyard on Tegnér Street. The whole city was below me, and now and then the windows way off on *Kungsholmen* would sparkle perhaps they were being washed just then by equally fearless cleaning ladies during the fall housecleanings.

> I didn't do it to show off actually no one knew of it. But I was saturated with a fantastic yearning for beauty that I was completely incapable of expressing. Now I don't understand how I dared. Sometimes I have nightmares about being dizzy.

> These climbs to see the setting sun were related to my musical excesses, etc.

The winds carrying sounds of the ringing church bells across the city of Stockholm have played an immense part in Swedish fiction and poetry, from Almqvist through Strindberg and Söderberg to Siwertz. In his introduction to *Livet i ett svunnet Stockholm* Ekelöf points to the first chapter of Strindberg's *The Red Room,* in which the tolling of bells is particularly pronounced. The great part played by the wide and varied waters in Stockholm should not be forgotten. They seem to amplify further the wanderings of all kinds of sounds, to and fro, even at great distances. In several of Ekelöf's essays the bells of his beloved *and* hated native city resound. A few lines from the essay, "Verklighetsflykt," illustrate this:

> The bells still tolled over the city. He recognized them very easily from church tower to church tower. In the shadow of one of them he was born, and under several

of the others he had lived shorter or longer periods. If he had been able to trace his movements and wanderings on the map of Stockholm, it would be an almost inextricable tangle. A tangle of happiness and unhappiness, successes and failures.

Regarding the word "alfågelklingande" (line 41), it can be mentioned that "alfågeln" even in Latin has a beautiful name *Harelda glacialis* and that it is supposed to have a completely captivating call and is therefore given attention by poets. Karlfeldt thus speaks about "alfågelstoner" in *Flora och Bellona,* and Strindberg in *Hemsöborna* mentions "alfågeln" that used to "alla."

While the sun is setting, **"The Return Trip"** along the canal is undertaken, back to the city from the excursion to Mölna, by way of a ferry service that has long since gone out of business. The trip goes from *Nybroplan,* Stockholm, via various jetties on *Lidingön,* through the narrow *Djurgårds* canal, past *Djurgårdsbrunn,* a route which is said by certain older residents to have been a popular little tour of the Stockholm archipelago. **"The Return Trip"** also represents a return trip in time. We can imagine the lush green of *Djurgården,* its taverns and trees from Bellman's time. It is the scenery which Johan Fredrik Martin (1735-1816) drew so often. When Strindberg was living at *Karlavägen,* in what was then the last building, he says that from his balcony he was able to see the archipelago, which is on the route described. Thus one can again claim an association with Strindberg and his Stockholm world.

In the *Elegy* eighteenth-century notes are struck by a number of words and phrases. The marginal word *Corno,* horn (lines 57-58), occurs frequently in Bellman's *Fredman's Epistles* and *Fredman's Songs* (1790-91). Furthermore, a used contraceptive floating about, mentioned in a somewhat Bellmanesque rococo way, suggests the gaiety of that period. But above all the eighteenth century looms heavily throughout the paraphrasing of the famous Epistle No. 79, "Or Farewell to the Matrons," especially to Mother Maja Myra of Sun-alley at the Big Market. Anno 1785: Charon in his boat is blowing his horn, while in the *Elegy* the ferry is blowing its whistle (line 59). After the blowing of the whistle, the ferry passes under the bridge of *Djurgårdsbrunn* and disappears, as if it had been swallowed up by the powers of Hades.

With the next stanza the first metamorphoses take place. The location could be either this world or Hades, since the identity appears to have dissolved. However, we are probably wise if we remember that in the *Elegy* there hardly exists a "real" identity ("the same or another / I or not I" (lines 67-68)), and that in the poet's opinion, reality is in a constant flux and always has an underlying sub-reality (or an imposed superreality), a reality of expectation, etc. "Time which bolts / years a minute / with a tail of yellow leaves" (lines 70 ff.) vaguely correspond to the cosmic occurrences later in the *Elegy.* The stanza ends with two classical allusions, both from Bellman, on Stockholm (Proud city) and the moira Clotho, one of the three fates in classic mythology. She presided over birth, and drew from her distaff the thread of life, so when Bellman says that

"Fredman sees too soon, alas, / His debt to Nature now must pass, / Clotho just from his garb / Off clipped a button / At Charon's call," it seems that he had Atropos in mind rather than Clotho.

The protagonist is then transformed into an old actor who sits brooding, his chin leaning on the curved handle of his cane and his ring-adorned little finger raised in reminiscence of bygone victories and pleasures. Like Strindberg's Officer in *A Dream Play* he is waiting for his Victoria. The theme of captivity in the opening scene is reiterated (lines 82-83). This as well as the re-intoned beginning of Edith Södergran's line, "A capricious moment. . . ," are among the elements in the musical character of this composition. An even more easily recognized musical pattern is found in the preceding **"Wave Song,"** with its strong onomatopoetical effects, reversals, repetitions, and correspondences. Before the curtain falls, the absurd ditty is heard again, and malformed fairies perform a macabre ballet, the disabled beings from Mölna thus transformed to the world of shadows or the world of the theater. The fact that the fairies as well as human beings are disabled shows an interesting correspondence between the netherworld and what we normally call the "human" world.

In the very moment he is dropping off to sleep, perhaps into that parasleep which is so often described by poets, among them Pierre Reverdy and Tomas Tranströmer, a fantastic, new world reveals itself: an absurd bit of Shakespeare seems to be contained in that instant. Or perhaps a reference to Denmark's Hans Andersen would be more appropriate: the trees in the park begin to talk about his aging since they saw him last. A blind window at the gable of Mölna remembers him as Prospero, the venerable old man and magician from *The Tempest.* Line 106: a falling drop of water and an apple (an erotic symbol?) remind us of the transient, fleeting aspect of time. We might associate these with something general such as the liability of elevated things to fall, to change position, shape, and substantial form; or we may think of something particular, such as Newton's apple and the theory of gravity. The Mill gnome (line 113) belongs to common folklore and ties in with the **"Mill Song"** later in the *Elegy.* The Fairy in the snowberry bushes appears to be Ekelöf's own creation. Ordinarily, a fairy is considered a graceful, diminutive female being, and the fairy of the poem is (we can imagine) as lovely as the traditional image; yet she is also as false as the gaudy finery she wears and as insignificant as a passing moment and not so innocent as her looks imply. Her aim is to prevail over the Mill gnome (line 119) by degrading him, for she suspects he was once "that ugly one," which suggests Caliban, Prospero's brutish servant. Talking to the Mill gnome for a while the Fairy suddenly becomes lyrical at the thought of her past love. But the mood again changes abruptly, when in a self-pitying voice, she contemplates her too small white berries. After the Mill gnome's impudent remark (line 149) about them releases her despair, she hides her face and disappears, saying: "My God, what has become of me!" This familiar refrain appears in many books, among them Miller's *Tropic of Cancer.* The thrush, which has been discussed by the Mill gnome and the Fairy, also disappears on the last pages of the *Elegy,* to be transformed, once more, into a proud (?) heraldic bird. Lines 157 ff. employ a language which seems mockingly humorous in its Desnos or Joycean style. The Biedermeier Lounge and the Front gable clock comment critically on the language that the culprit, the mill gnome, has used, while the Mirror at the window remains unmoved and unconvinced by his attempts to exonerate himself. The Blind window follows up on its earlier thought, as if faced with an insoluble question: "But how can Prospero be alive? And here?" And the poet reminds us that the same Moment is still going on (line 173): the *same* drop continues falling into the barrel, and the *same* apple's fall is re-echoed as before (lines 112 and 177). In the following line, 178, the *same* wind sighs: "Away! Away!" These words of longing for someone or something else are rather typical romantic citations within or preceding a poem, e.g. in Victor Hugo. Among other places, we find them in William Blake's "Mammon." They are, however, more meaningful in Shelley's "The Invitation":

> Away, Away / from men and towns,
> Away, Away!

But the words might well have emanated from yet another source outside of Ekelöf's own mind.

A broken grave plate is the bridge between the past and the next scene. It is adorned with *hederae,* ivy, which is often consecrated to Bacchus, Apollo, and the Muses, but, according to Kaufmann's *Handbuch der altchristlichen Epigraphik* (1917), it is most likely Christian. It contains the Greek name Hesperos, underneath which lies an anchor, the symbol of hope. This is the simplest kind of funerary art, probably more "prospective" than "retrospective" in Erwin Panofsky's terminology, i.e., works of art more in the interest of the deceased than of the survivors. Usually Hesperos stands for the Evening Star, but in Pape-Benseler it is also listed as a name of "ein Milesier, Bewohner des Hesperis." Hesperos, in the first sense, has been often discussed by many poets, among them Ben Jonson in "To Cynthia" and Sappho:

> Hesperos bringing together
> All that the morning star scattered

(XIV)

When the protagonist of the *Elegy* reawakens, he hears, to his amazement, a sound like the screech of a parrot in an old maid's apartment: "How-are-you? Lora, beautiful Lora. . ." This vaguely suggests Strindberg's *Spook Sonata* in the scene in which Hummel imitates a parrot and addresses the Mummy: "Kakadora! Dora!" Ekelöf has, however, made the following statement about it:

> This refers to a completely personal experience. Once long ago I happened to go to the monkey-house at *Skansen* (the Stockholm Zoo), where at that time even some parrots were housed as a bequest to the zoo. One of them, I think it was an Ara parrot, happened to be in a talkative mood and constantly repeated "Lora, beautiful Lora!" or "How are you?" in a sort

of shrill tone which was suggestive of the mistress of her household, I imagine. This vividly presented to my mind a vision of the widows' lodgings or maidens' bowers of which I had seen many in my childhood, filled with souvenirs, costly things mixed with tasteless objects, almost a kind of storehouse for memories of every variety; and of the exaggerated way the ladies greeted visiting friends *(Hur är det meeed dig?),* or took leave. This the parrot told me.

This inquiry is repeated in the poem (lines 186-187) in a more degrading context. The first is the hearty inquiry "How is your health in general?" between old friends, while the second could be the heartless reproach of a casual or a marital (sex) partner. The difference in tone on these two occasions is insignificant, but the significance of the context is crucial. Because the women appearing next seem rather benevolent, fairy-like people, it seems natural to associate Aunts Grey, Green, and Louche with Elsa Beskow's "Tant Brun, Tant Grön, Tant Gredelin," who are so familiar to Swedish children. Ekelöf has indicated, however, that he had two distant relatives and a lady-friend in mind: "One of them was squint-eyed; the others as I have described them." There is reason to speculate that these three ladies represent three different kinds of religions and at the same time three different nationalities: Swedish, German-Jewish, and Finnish-French. Aunt Grey's observation: "How he has grown since last time!" clearly corresponds to the chorus of the trees in the park: "How he has aged since last time!" Like the squint-eyed buffoon at the beginning of the *Elegy* and the Mill gnome, Aunt Louche, as her name indicates, also is squint-eyed, and this adds to our sensation of strangeness in regard to these people. Her echoing of the others ("How are you?") appears to be a meaningless stereotype, and the main protagonist is independent enough to point it out bluntly. Things are completely relative. To him it does not matter any longer whether he says *fine* or *bad.* Mysteriously, time has long ceased to matter to him, and this corresponds to the earlier line: "My life has stopped." With an echo of the haunting Södergran line, "A capricious moment. . ." (line 205) old memories reverberate. It is not immediately clear whom the main protagonist is addressing when he asks: "And do you remember, do you remember / East Indian china with seashells encrusted. . . ." The word "ostindiskt" appears elsewhere in Ekelöf, as in "Den gamle superkargören," and Ekelöf has seen these objects, including the Tula box, at the home of his mother's distant relative, Beda Cygnaeus of Göteborg. He remarks: "Her ancestors seem to have had something to do with the Swedish East India Company, because such exotic porcelain was to be found at her home. It was covered (1) with *havstulpaner* (Balanus), sea acornshells, and (2) with tall sinuous lime serpents (*Kalkormar*) which have been inhabited by I-don't-know-what animal."

The following line: ". . . how long has it waited in the sealed-up hold?" suggests to some readers that the china had been part of a salvaged cargo from the closed section of a hull. This impression is reinforced by line 228: ". . . how long has it lain in the green depth?" However, the poet has made the following note:

These are how matters stand: The proprietor (I think it was) of Fredrikslund, near Uppsala (but I am not entirely sure), had a mistress whom he was unable to marry at the time because of class reasons. She passed away, to his great sorrow. That he loved her greatly is proved by the fact that he had the pavilion where they met closed after her death. Even subsequent generations seem to have honored its "sacredness." The pavilion was opened only sometime in the 1920's, and apart from the ravages of time, it was found in the same condition as it had been when it was closed up, more than one hundred and fifty years earlier.

About the line (213) "under Madame de Mont-Gentil's portrait, a rare avis/at the thé conseilles. . ." we learn a little more from the 1946 version of this passage, published in *Bonniers Litterära Magasin* (p. 366). In that early version, an apposition, "Anna Marias vän," hints even more clearly than the word "Thékonseljerna" that Mme. de Mont-Gentil was a friend of Anna Maria Lennngren, the well-known writer of idylls and satires of the period of the enlightenment. According to letters from Dr. Bo Wennberg, curator of the National Museum in Stockholm, the portrait refers to Anna Catharina Lewin (1760-1814), who was married to Dr. Anders Hedenberg. The portrait of "fru de Mont-Gentil" is not listed in Sixten Strömbom's *Index över svenska porträtt* (Index of Swedish Portraits), since the name is a poet's translation of the name Hedenberg (Ekelöf's mother's maiden name). Ekelöf has left this note concerning her: "Mme. Hedenberg, daughter of the 'court Jew' Adolf Ludwig Lewin and wife of Hedvig Elisabeth Charlotta's resident medical attendant, was an intimate friend of Mrs. Lenngren, Kellgren (the poet), Paykull (the zoologist 1757-1826) and others, and proclaimed the queen of hearts to von Rosenstein, the author of "Försök til en afhandling om uplysningen" (On Enlightenment), which still lies in an ornately dedicated copy on my aunt's bookshelf. She was half Jewish and was considered a beauty." A copy of the actual portrait, done by Carl Gustaf Pilo (?) (1711-1793), can be seen at Ekelöf's cottage. The description of Mme. de Mont-Gentil as a "främmanfågel," a rare avis, has no doubt a relation to the poem "Främmanfåglar" dedicated to Ekelöf by the distinguished Finland Swedish poet Elmer Diktonius.

The memory of 1809, the year of the last revolution in Sweden, is evoked by reworking and shortening a paragraph of *Lefnads-minnen* (Memoirs) of Bernhard von Beskow (1796-1868), the one-time secretary to the Swedish Academy. As we can see from the quotation below, the woman referred to in Ekelöf's version is identical to Mme. de Mont-Gentil. *Castenhof* (line 221), in von Beskow's writing, *Kastenhof,* according to Johan Elers, was a house in Stockholm completed in 1649, which later became a *comme il faut* tavern.

As in a dream, the mood of the poem tends to be simultaneously in the present of the actual moment, and yet provides a certain link with the past. From the emptying of a glass, the association goes back to the beautiful old china covered with dead fossils and items from the East and suddenly leaps to the slaves of the West, and their singing or moaning on the steerage deck.

One characteristic of the dream is also a kind of "rushing" back and forth between the present, the past, and the future, all as independent layers of consciousness. Using this dream-play technique, the poet again makes a retreat, even further back, to 1786. Once again his memory of a relative is revived. He has enlarged on his notes in *BLM,* 1946:

> Gustaf Lewin, brother of Anna Catharina Hedenberg, in order to get merits, took service in a French commercial shipping company, since there was no war at the time. The company happened to consist of slave merchants to the French Caribbean Islands. Since he was not a follower of Rousseau, his conscience did not bother him, although later on, of course, he repented. He did not rise high in the naval hierarchy, but later during the Russian war of Gustavus III he rescued the starving Swedish army in Finland by convoying about one hundred ships with food past Hangö in sight of the Russian chebecks, which could not be rowed like the Swedish ships of Chapman's construction. Later on he took part in the second battle at *Svensksund,* which destroyed the Russian fleet. His sword of honor is in the Marine Museum in Stockholm. His autobiography (Ewa Lewin: *En gustaviansk sjöofficers levnadsberättelse*) is indeed worth reading.

The passage employed for the *Elegy* is a slightly remodeled version from that autobiography, and it is remarkable that this rather crude account could be turned into great poetry (line 234 ff.). The scene is just north of the Equator. From the ship could be seen the light from the myriads of creatures in the sea (238). The concept of *a higher being,* within which myriads of smaller creatures are captive, appears frequently in Ekelöf, e.g., as observed before in the sections *Méga Aléxandre* and *Stateíra mo ,* and it has a very old pre-history, from such Greek writers as Herodotus and Sophocles, and probably also the Swedish mystic Swedenborg.

In line 241 a great star has been spotted "which increased every second in magnitude." This cosmic occurrence at sea a star or a meteor disintegrating close enough to the ship to be vividly seen and experienced causes a dreadful storm and a magnificent spectacle: "rockets / that covered the whole horizon with a shining / so dazzling that you could have seen a hair / if one had been hanging from the masthead!" Afterwards the air clears, stars become visible again, and the moaning of closed-in slaves (line 264, cf. 208 and 228) is again heard in differently syncopated choruses.

Recollecting these dead relatives and their good and bad deeds in times gone by is no necrophilic endeavor (to use a phrase of Unamuno and Erich Fromm), but springs from a synthetic tendency in Ekelöf's philosophy. Like Jan Smuts he feels that all things interact, that every entity (including people), every concept, has a series of complex, interpenetrating relations with its neighbors. None of them can be fully comprehended until they are set in their proper environment, that is, in relation to their past. Everything is dependent on everything else, the lives of the dead are in a way re-lived by the poet, and their lives are his *raison d'être* and also, to some extent, his exculpation. This very idea has been expressed in somewhat similar terms by the poet in **"En dröm (verklig)"** (A dream, real) in *Om hösten* (1951) and also in **"En värld är varje människa"** (A world is every human being) from *Färjesång* (1941).

There is nothing pretentious or peculiar about Ekelöf's quoting some of his ancestors. Like other poets, such as Yeats, Eliot, or Robert Lowell, Ekelöf has a strong sense of the family system. As the critic Åke Janzon has put it:

> The fact that Ekelöf's references in these cases are so personal is irrelevant for the experience of the poem. . . . As pictures of the past these short sections have freshness and significance, and especially the latter gives an enormously concentrated form of vision which in a certain sense could be said to anticipate *Aniara*, Harry Martinson's space poem. . . It is about time; it is with the life of the past in the present and with the lives of the dead in the poet's consciousness that the *Elegy* deals.

The confession of the main protagonist in line 265: "So I feel / in the depth of my midriff these dead: / The air I breathe is clogged with all the dead. . ." shows his extraordinary awareness of the complexity of human consciousness.

From death the line of thought goes to a near-death experience in childhood: a disease which brings on feverish ramblings that made the boy feel completely deserted by everybody. Had they all gone out to the country, or is he just imagining? The open-sided wagon rattling over the cobblestones without ever stopping is a haunting symbol of Time manifesting itself to the feverish child. The feeling of abandonment is clear in the line: "To the suburbs / they all had gone, or to the country," but this makes a neat transition to pleasant memories of the country; of excursions from the manor farm of his father, and of the encouragement to learn by heart his Latin *hic haec hoc*. He recalls memories of games, especially the games of forfeit, where the girl Arrasmiha presided next to Camilla, after having done their farm chores. Arrasmiha appears in Almqvist's "songe" about the strawberry-picking girl, and also in the novel *Drottningens juvelsmycke*. Camilla is, of course, from *Atis och Camilla* (1761) by Gustaf Philip Creutz. In this way Ekelöf has inserted a couple of chords from his beloved eighteenth century.

These co-existing memories seem to pass in review for a while and then develop into a dialogue, but again, as in a dream, they spread somewhat like voices in the wind, and we do not always know who is speaking. "Monsieur Petter" we recognize as Bellman's Ulla Winblad. It is her *nom de guerre*. In his book, *Ulla Winblad*, Gunnar W. Lundberg mentions that her name occurs on a list from the 1780's, "unfortunately under the heading *mademoiselles of an inferior kind*, but here she is nearly first: *Mademoiselle Winblad eller Monsieur Petter*." In lines 296-297 we read about "cousin at the locked gates." "Cousin" presumably refers again to Ulla Winblad, and the high locked gates, according to a note from Ekelöf, to Stockholm's *Kungsträdgården*, which was earlier fenced in with high gates. A soldier kept sentry on *Arsenalsgatan*, which opened only for "people of the higher classes" who wanted to "go for a pleasure stroll." "The corporal in charge here is Bellman's Mollberg."

The little foxes (line 301) may be read about in *The Song of Solomon* (2:15) which again appears in the following two lines (2:6). I have to leave the question open as to the identity of the third person who is alluded to in the quotation. Is it only the lover of *The Song of Solomon*? The transition is from the idyllic exotic groves of the Biblical scene, to the juniper trees and to the stones of *Lövnäs*, in the province of *Södermanland*, Sweden, where Ekelöf grew up and where his interest in natural history, stones, and birds was born.

In the same sequence (lines 310 ff.) the junipers have been transformed to vineyards of time, with its unpredictable harvest periods. We are reminded anew of time, and the relativity of time from a grown man's experience. He vaguely remembers not only the seconds and the moments which have dropped out of memory because of some repressive mechanism, but also the ones that cannot be escaped, some almost intolerable moments, "de fastnaglade," which recur compulsively. It seems likely that there is a correspondence with these "held, riveted" moments, and the riveted figure on the saltire on page 46 in the *Elegy*. Ekelöf may be alluding here to those like Spartacus, Peter, and others, who were nailed head down to some wooden structure, and also possibly to horror stories from the northern part of Sweden about how men used to be nailed to the floor in their clothes, so that they were unable to move and thus perished without visible harm done to their bodies.

The poet claims that he carries time within him, like the pregnant woman in a folk tale who did not want to be delivered and carried her offspring for twenty years, complete, yet unborn. He carries time within himself like a stone child, something produced and ready, though not to be parted with. In the *BLM* version of 1946 there were two additional lines, a beginning of a "Street Ballad":

> Ångest och preventiv
> Ångest och kolokvint. . . .

which associates the stone child with anguish and contraceptives and perhaps, implied, sexual fears. Ekelöf in *BLM* explains that "Street Ballad," the first note of which he has here struck. . . is a counterpart to "Wave Song."

On the following sixteen pages original *graffiti* and Swedish text face each other, like two different parts which join or divide in a bewildering way, sometimes in cacophonous and sometimes in euphonious sounds of the past. In the Swedish text, there is a call for "Great Alexander!" It is obvious from the marginal note about "my Stateria" (on the next page with Swedish text) that the poet is referring to Emperor Alexander and the wife of Darios, King of Persia. In a way the poet is the Emperor. He is the king of the past, a sovereign of myriads of memories of people who were active millennia ago. Time accompanies the poem: "September snows down in red leaves / October flows away in dead leaves." The tick-tock is replaced by "Sept. Oct. / Sept. Oct." This also looks as if it were indicating the relative speed or rate of movement at which a musical composition moves. The Emperor realizes that while he himself is holding sway over hordes of captive ones who have remained in an incomplete, imperfect state, in his turn he himself is incomplete and captive within some other, higher organisation. He may suspect that he is nothing but a toy; that man is a fate, which he is subject to, as the ancient Greeks considered themselves. Nowhere has Ekelöf expressed this clearer than in **"A July Night"** in *Non Serviam.*

Accompanied with the tempo indications, "Sept. Oct." the Emperor "unlocks what is locked," (line 382). This could allude to the oriental saga about the Prince who went from chamber to chamber ("unlatching the latches and unbolting the doors") in search of the last one, where the virgin is waiting for him. However, the following lines, "Thus and for nothing do I step out of mirrors / into mirrors," could perhaps be understood as a continued, feverish self-analysis, yet it is all in vain; he is unable to change the course of his life. The dialogue between Stateira and himself is fragmentary but may at least indicate one similarity of their fates (a captive within a higher being) but also the incompatibility between life and death ("You seek in the eternal the rational? I seek in the temporal the irrational."). "Méga Aléxandre" also touches on "the greatest of all folklore figures over a wider area than any other comparable personages." The *Romance of Alexander,* so full of marvels, miracles, and romantic episodes, as well as other more or less imaginary or historical accounts of Alexander, from Callisthenes, Plutarch, Racine, and E. M. Forster (Pharos and Pharillon) has fascinated the western world, and throughout the Moslem world the legends of Iskander are legion. There could also be a corresponding folklore association in "Gorgo and the cuttlefish" section later on in the *Elegy.*

The punctuation of time, "September snowing down in red leaves, / October thawing away in dead leaves," spills over to become a full scale ballad about the months and numerals and at the same time a daring sexual phantasy. A picture of a winepress or an olive mill from Pompeii (cf. note 40), which suggests a piston, connects with the "dialogue" of some characters from Bellman's writings. Cajsa Stina appears in *Fredman's Epistle* No. 1, and Mother Bobbi takes part in a comedy by Bellman, performed on July 17, 1790, where she innocently sells "nice cherries, red and clear." Here, however, their dialogue with Ensign Morian is nothing but a witch-like conjuration at a violation and abortion scene. Bellman is again reintoned in line 468, "At the far garden-gate, in the woods," which is taken from Fredman's Song, No. 24. The mountain's childbirth (lines 454-455) can be read about in a fable by La Fontaine.

This brings this study to the point where it connects with one published in *Germanic Review* (March, 1965). Occasionally Ekelöf's allusions are so much oriented in his own culture and his own biography that they compound the

difficulty for an interpreter but usually his allusions are of a kind that relate his *Elegy* to mankind's behavior, patterns, and quirks rather than to idiosyncrasies of a private nature. That interest in folklore in general is one proof of his aspiration for broad, "historic" perspectives of mankind. Kierkegaard agreed with philosophers that life had to be understood backwards, but he drew the conclusion that it is impossible to understand existence intellectually, "for the very reason that at no moment of time can I find the perfect repose to take the backwards position." Ekelöf, who is used to starting his investigations from scratch,— *er hat seine Sache auf Nichts gestellt—,* has made a successful attempt at describing one moment and infusing new life into it precisely with the backward position.

"Scholars will have a royal time working out the riddles in this major work of an almost major literature's major poet," wrote George C. Schoolfield when reviewing the *Elegy.* If by the efforts of various scholars and the poet's own notes, some questions about the *Elegy*'s allusion have been answered already, I am afraid it is my experience that they nonetheless just seem to prompt new questions and new speculations. If other questions, such as the musical concept of the *Elegy* barely have been touched on, it is for good reasons. The *Elegy* itself can be looked upon as a musical score which sometimes appears hard to read and sometimes is "illegible" and sometimes is straight, delightful reading. Conclusive interpretations of this score can hardly be achieved, since new readers will continue to read it their own way, without regard for the poet's conscious purpose and the origin of his ideas.

"The musical conception of poetry is not a series of mile posts," says Ekelöf, "but continuous wandering. It is not a monument but a happening. It is not an established memorandum of a moment, not 'I,' but a conglomerate of the me, he, we, you, all the impulses, heredities, memories, associations (meaningful or meaningless ones and without appropriateness), all the polyphonic interplay of the important and less important, the distinct and inseparable detail for which the 'I' is something of an auditive focus. . . . There are many components which live in what I call me. . . ." And Shelley wrote: "A poet is a nightingale, who sits in darkness and sings to cheer its own solitude with sweet sounds; his auditors are as men entranced by the melody of an unseen musician, who feel that they are moved and softened, yet know not whence or why."

Reidar Ekner (essay date 1970)

SOURCE: "Gunnar Ekelöf: The Poet As Trickster," in *Scandinavian Studies,* Vol. 42, No. 4, November, 1970, pp. 410-18.

[*In the following excerpt, Ekner examines the ways in which Ekelöf's shorter poems often seem embedded in an intricate, "larger context," details of which the reader might only discern in the future, when recalling the poem.*]

Gunnar Ekelöf was not a brilliant conversationalist, but when he felt at ease he could be very entertaining. He would talk about his life and his reading, about people he had met, and he would do it laconically and drastically, in short snatches. Eventually, after a long pause, it often happened that he would finish with a sharp and penetrating comment and glance quickly at his listeners to see if they understood. It was not always easy to do so, since he enjoyed being cryptic and making allusions: he took for granted that his listeners were acquainted with many languages and different cultures, and that they had had experiences which anyone would be reluctant to talk about quite openly. He did not like to explain his cryptic remarks, for it would have meant destroying his point, and if he saw that the person with whom he was conversing did not understand, then he preferred to make small talk or to fall silent.

In his poetry he was natural in his own way: he expressed himself exactly, without bothering to explain what in his own eyes was expressed with all desirable clarity. His readers had to submit to him. Nor did he hesitate to provide his poems with ambiguities and trap-doors, to see how many readers would admire the beauty of his language and art before someone stopped to perceive the puzzle-picture beneath the surface.

One example: in **"Absentia animi,"** the long poem that terminates *Non serviam* (1945), Ekelöf, by means of concrete landscape scenes from autumnal Sweden, and with the help of an abstract, intellectual dialectic, tries to enter the *unio mystica* of mysticism. But it was twenty years before someone explained in print the meaning of a crucial word that is repeated throughout the poem, the word "abraxas," which is the name for the highest being of the gnostic creed, a figure found on inscriptions and Hellenistic amulets, showing a human body with the head of a bird and with snakes instead of legs. Five years later another scholar was able to show that the butterfly that is mentioned in the beginning of the poem had fluttered earlier in a poem by Strindberg.

> . . . en trasig fjäril är på väg
> till intet, som är en avblommad ros
> den minsta och fulaste, Och harkrankarna, de
>   dumma djävlarna. . .

In "Indiansommar" Strindberg wrote:

> Då kom en fjäril,
> en brun och otäck fjäril,
> som förr varit kålmask
> men nu kravlat sig upp
> ur en nylagd lövhög
> narrad av solskenet,
> gubevars!

And Strindberg says that the butterfly settled on his flowery blanket, where it "valde bland rosorna / och anilinsyrenerna / den minsta och fulaste." It was still sitting there an hour later:

> Han hade uppfyllt sin bestämmelse
> och var död
> den dumme djäveln!

The realistically depicted autumn scene at the beginning of **"Absentia animi"** insects fluttering towards death and annihilation did not stop Ekelöf from installing a skilful allusion to Strindberg's October poem "Indiansommar." A few lines further on in **"Absentia animi"** we come across a logical intellectual sequence thrown like a spear towards nothingness, which immediately casts it back like the broken reflection of a mirror: "Sats motsats slutsats abraxas abrasax Sats." Abraxas? The supreme being of the gnostics, yes. But also akin to the stupid large white butterfly in Strindberg's poem and the torn one in Ekelöf's: *abraxas,* a genus of the group geometrid moths.

Many of Ekelöf's shorter poems may be read as if they were contributions to some of his own conversations, or short emotive monologues, taken from a larger context. The first words strike a note, some chords follow, and the poem culminates in a sated feeling, the meaning of which the reader does not always find it necessary to analyze. However, knowledge of the large context, or of the secret puzzle-picture if there is one, gives the feeling a consistency that stops it from melting away into associations which threaten to become too private or too vague.

Special attention should be paid to **"Arsinoë"**; as the first poem of *Strountes* (1955) it occupies the key position of that collection. Peter Ortman, by the way, recently devoted a long and interesting, though somewhat meandering commentary to it.

> Jag lindar, jag lindar dessa remsor
> över min älsklings ögon, över dess själ
> Med brunt, nästan utplånat bläck
> skall jag skriva på mina linneremsor
> hemliga tecken
> och jag skall linda dem som en vaggsång
> runt om min älsklings själ
> O aldrig utgjutna salvor
> O smala remsor
> lindade i varv på varv av konstrik flätning!
> Liknar du inte reden en fjärilspuppa
> sådan den hänger i rosenbusken!
> Du med de stora ögonen jag gav dig!
> Du med det obefläckade anletet!

The speaker of the poem compares the action of wrapping linen ribbons round the soul of the beloved to a lullaby, and the poem is in itself a lullaby, lulling somebody who is dead to rest. The song quality of the poem is not stressed but is apparent nonetheless: in the repetitions in the first two lines, in the two exclamatory sentences (lines 8 and 9), and also in the two parallel invocations concluding the poem. The speaker, then, moves from talking *about* to talking *to* somebody: moves from a relatively neutral feeling to an intense and direct outburst of emotion. The information given in the poem is scant but yet sufficient to explain what happens: that a dead child is committed to its last resting-place by one of its parents, probably its mother, and that the scene must be ancient Egypt. The mother wraps the embalmed body of the child with layer upon layer of linen ribbons and promises to write secret signs on them, apparently to protect the soul of the child, now on its way to the realm of the dead. That it is a child we understand from the comparison of the body to the chrysalis of a butterfly, that is, something very small, and from the fact that she mentions the big eyes of the dead and calls its face *obefläckat,* that is, untarnished, immaculate, without sin. Again, she says that she gave the dead one these big eyes, so it is natural to surmise that she is speaking to her child.

During the Hellenistic period of Egypt "Arsinoë" was commonly used as a woman's name. Peter Ortman has found about thirty different "Arsinoës," Egyptian queens or cities and places named after them. All the trails except one seem to be dead ends; the exception leads to the most famous Arsinoë of all, queen of Egypt and wife and joint regent of her brother Ptolemy II. Her story contains some of the most brutal court intrigues of the Hellenistic world. A daughter to Ptolemy I Soter and his queen Berenice, Arsinoë at sixteen was given as a bride to the elderly king Lysimachus of Thrace, whom she bore three children, all of them sons. In order to guarantee access to the throne for her own children, she accused the successor to the throne, Agathocles, who was Lysimachus' son from an earlier marriage, of having plans to murder his father the king. Agathocles was put in jail, where he was murdered by Arsinoë's elder half-brother, Ptolemy Ceraunus. Agathocles' wife, a sister of Arsinoë, then fled to king Seleucus of Syria, who saw his chance and invaded Thrace. In the ensuing battle Lysimachos was killed, and Seleucus proclaimed himself king of Thrace. Shortly afterwards he was killed by the reckless Ptolemy Ceraunus, who put himself on the throne. During these violent events Arsinoë had fled to Ephesus which Lysimachus had renamed Arsinoë in honour of his wife and then to her own royal residence, Chassandreia in Macedonia. With her legitimate claims on the throne, she was a political threat to her half-brother Ptolemy Ceraunus. In order to disarm her in the simplest possible way, he proposed to her. Arsinoë had no choice; possibly the ambitious woman was attracted by the prospect of becoming the queen of three united kingdoms, Thrace, Macedonia, and Syria. However, her acceptance of the proposal proved fatal: shortly afterwards her half-brother, and now also her husband, killed her two youngest sons, only 13 and 16 years old. In vain Arsinoë tried to protect them with her own body. Via the island of Samothrace, where she had erected a temple, Arsinoë now fled to Egypt. In Egypt reigned her full brother Ptolemy II, who was married to a daughter of Lysimachus. (Her name, by the way, was Arsinoë too.) Arsinoë soon managed to lure her brother into casting off her former step-daughter, whose place she took. In spite of her age she was now about forty years old she was apparently still an attractive woman, as well as possessing an able and imposing character. She was raised to joint regent and took active part in the foreign affairs of her country. After her death her brother elevated her to the rank of goddess. Under the name of Arsinoë Aphrodite Philadelphos, the brotherloving love goddess, she was worshipped throughout Egypt.

Three times queen Arsinoë failed to have her deepest wish granted her: unlike her mother Berenice she was not able to secure a throne for any of her four children. Her eldest son died in Egypt, while she was still alive, the son she bore her brother Ptolemy died in infancy. And this brings us back to Ekelöf's poem.

The speaker is an Arsinoë the "brotherloving" Arsinoë, let us assume. Accordingly we may surmise that she now bids farewell to the hope she cherished throughout her turbulent life. The words the poet lets her speak make us feel how deeply she mourns the dead child, and we see how she tries to beseech Osiris, the god of the dead. The Egyptians believed in resurrection, hence they embalmed their dead and gave them food and wooden servants to help them on the long journey into their next life, and Arsinoë is careful not to use the word "body." She wraps the *soul* of her beloved child in winding cloths. Her belief that the child will enter a new life is revealed when she compares it to the chrysalis in the rosebush. (Here the butterfly and the rose are not a symbol of extinction, as in **"Absentia animi,"** but of resurrection.) She sings a lullaby for the dead child, death is a sleep from which the child, as a result of the mother's care, will wake to a new life. From the insignificant chrysalis a new, sparkling creature will emerge.

The poem is a variation of the theme of **"Galla Placidia,"** a poem that is also found in **Strountes**. In the latter poem Ekelöf describes the mosaics that surround the dead queen Galla Placidia in her chapel, and speaks to her about the beautiful scenes she will meet after her resurrection. Arsinoë also reminds the reader of Niobe cruelly punished and weeping, in Ekelöf's collection **Sagan om Fatumeh**: "Niobe begråter sina barn. . . ."

In Ekelöf's short poem Arsinoë is a mother figure; her adventurous life, her intrigues and incestuous marriages are not mentioned. There is even reason to doubt that Ekelöf, when the poem was originally written, was thinking of Arsinoë. Possibly he later found that her fate was compatible with the poem, that it could be put in her mouth without doing violence to historical truth.

The fact that the poem originally was called "Vaxmåleri" (*Dagens Nyheter,* March 23, 1952) indicates that this might be the case. Even the original title has Egyptian associations, if not with Arsinoë. The oldest known canvas paintings are Hellenistic portraits excavated from Egyptian tombs, where they had been placed over the heads of the dead. The ancient painters mixed the pigment with wax, which they then burned into the canvas (or wood) at hand. This method is called wax-painting, or encaustic painting. It is reasonable to believe that Ekelöf had seen many examples of such encaustic paintings in museums he visited, and there are many reproductions of such paintings in art books. A characteristic trait of these burial portraits is the big dark eyes, eyes that also seem to look at us in Ekelöf's poem. A seeming inconsistency in the poem makes such a provenience likely. As Ortman has pointed out, Arsinoë cannot possibly write with an ink that has already become almost extinguished. It must be the poet who from his own time looks backwards through the centuries at her faded signs. In *En outsiders väg* Ekelöf mentions the mummies wrapped in linen ribbons which he has seen in the museums of Uppsala, Paris and Rome; in these museums numerous papyrus fragments with a sepia and faded writing are also exhibited.

The line "O aldrig utgjutna salvor" still lacks an explanation, however. Why are the ointments never used? Have they something to do with the process of embalming? Or is the dead child a little girl, and does her mother regret that she has not been allowed to become a woman, that she has not been given the chance to use the perfumes and ointments belonging to the cosmetics of a distinguished Egyptian lady? Both alternatives are possible, and the latter brings us away from Arsinoë, who never bore a daughter. Her name in the title therefore ought not to be regarded as a key, but as a hint and a direction. It points to a certain time and culture, and nothing more.

In his paper Peter Ortman has succumbed to an understandable temptation to speculate on Ekelöf's interest in alchemy and embalming, and his yielding has resulted in many entertaining digressions. But the text of the poem gives only frail support to far-reaching speculations, and I will here content myself with the question: why did Ekelöf choose to open **Strountes** with "**Arsinoë**"? I find it difficult to answer the question in any way save one: that Ekelöf, while editing his poems, saw a similarity between those secret signs Arsinoë writes on her linen ribbons, and those signs, letters, words and meanings, he had written in his own poems. A similarity, nothing more. His poems *are* not these secret signs, ribbons, big eyes, this immaculate face. But they can be *compared to* chrysalises, which in the consciousness of future readers will change into living butterflies.

Since the poem "**Arsinoë**" has led us to the Orient, let us consider another **Strountes**-poem, published in *Opus incertum*:

> Ur det förflutna steg flodens ande som en dimma
> svävade av och an och samlade sig framför de
>   undrande träden
> frågade med sin mumlande röst: Var är jag? Vem
>   väckte mig?
> Ingen skräckslagen fiskare svarade, ingen
> bjöd den åter stänga sig inne i flaskan
> men när den såg Salomos insegel växa på strand
> skyggade den i virveln av ett kallt luftdrag
> Sedan spridde den sig över ängarna, sökande
> tusen förlorade år.

The poem is immediately pathetic but obscurely contradictory. Almost every line puts unanswered questions. The impressive melody arouses sympathy for the spirit of the river which hovers uneasily back and forth until, startled by "a cold draught," it spreads through the fields, in a landscape that itself seems cold and desolate, and where no one but the wondering trees pays attention to the river's re-awakened soul. The spirit, I believe, is to be regarded as the soul of the river. Passing by other points of comparison, one makes a ready association with Stagnelius' poem, "Näcken," about the nixy, who, with tears running down his face, plunges into his silver brook when the boy on the bank tells him that he shall never behold

"Edens blomsterkrönta slätter." Nor has the river-spirit in Ekelöf's poem any chance to see its wishes come true. But the nixy's longing is directed forwards, to the impossible religious deliverance, while the longing of the river-spirit is directed backwards, to the past that has swallowed up its lost years. But what does the river sigh in Ekelöf's poem?

There is an element of Arabic wonderland in the poem, of *The Arabian Nights* with its djinns confined in bottles friendly spirits with the power to fulfill any wish, or evil spirits with the power to destroy, if they are let loose. (In Swedish the *Arabian Nights* is called *Tusen och en natt*, a number that is reflected in the last line of the poem.) The spirit of the river rises out of the past, but the world that confronts it is completely different from the one that bore it and that it remembers. Here there are no terrorstricken fishermen, no one who is afraid of it or bids it welcome, no one with the power to command it. The wonderland is dead and gone, the spirit is the sole survivor, a powerless ghost of the past. But when it sees "Salomos insegel" on the river bank, it shudders "in the swirl of a cold draught" and spreads over the fields, seeking its lost years. Why is it frightened just then?

Solomon (Salomo) is a hero not only in the Old Testament and Hebrew legend, but also in the Arabic realm, where he appears as a wise man and sorcerer with a power over demons. By means of a seal, signet, or magic ring Solomon seals bottles where he keeps the demons, and the river spirit shies in fear of becoming confined again, a baseless feeling in the poem's world, since Solomon's seal has lost its magic power long ago. However, Salomo's seal *is growing* on the bank, which it does because it only indirectly has anything to do with the past. The expression "Solomon's seal" has consciously been given a double meaning in the poem, and the primary meaning is not likely to enter the reader's mind at first, that is, Salomo's signet ring, but a meaning that is derived from it. The seal growing on the bank is a plant, a sealwort, or any plant belonging to the genus *polygonatum*. Plants of this genus are distinguished by a characteristic rootstock, and it is this peculiarity that Ekelöf, in a clever way, has made literary use of. The rootstock of the sealwort seems to consist of joints; on the upper side it has a series of rounded scars, which have given rise to many superstitions. The scars look like the impressions of a seal hence the common name. The scars are the marks of last year's flower-stalks, which formed the tip of the root-stock. The stock then continued to grow through a side bud that was formed at the base of the flowering shoot; the root-stock may live many years, and by counting the scars one can determine the "age" of the plant. The reader must imagine that this is exactly what the river spirit does, with its penetrating eyes. It counts the scars, and so it understands that it has been confined in the bottle for no less than a thousand years. In the cold swirl of this insight it disperses like a haze over the fields of the desolate landscape, in an unquenchable desire to recover the lost years of its life.

A closely related motif is to be found in two other poems by Ekelöf: "**Emigranten**," first published in 1941, and "**Den**

61

förtrollade ön," in *Vägvisare till underjorden.* With an interval of many years, the emigrant has twice been conveyed to the cellar of a temple, perhaps a Mayan temple, situated near a beach, the first time after a shipwreck, the second time after having lost consciousness while staying in a large city. The emigrant now appeals to the "honorable judge" for another investigation concerning his case. When he assembles all the facts, a whole year of his life is missing, and he realizes that a crime must have been committed. A similar discrepancy between experienced and chronological time is revealed in **"Den förtrollade ön,"** another branch of the tree called the Arabian Nights. A prince, on an excursion to an island, drinks from a magic well, and when he returns to the beach he finds the whitened bones of his companions. On his return to his town he is told his own story, as a legend from the distant past. The poem is a virtuoso-piece of comparison, where different time levels cancel out one another.

Fascinated by the concept of time and the experience of time, Ekelöf tried to catch the time experience in a single moment that annihilates the flux of time: he does it in *En Mölna-Elegi,* while in the word sonata of his youth, **"En natt vid horssonten,"** he tried to force time to stop like an unborn fetus with its head pointing downward at the exit of the world.

Leif Sjöberg (essay date 1970)

SOURCE: "The Later Poems of Gunnar Ekelöf: *Diwan* and *Fatumeh,"* in *Mosaic,* Vol. IV, No. 2, Winter, 1970, pp. 101-15.

[*In the following excerpt, Sjöberg explores Ekelöf's blending of Eastern mysticism with the Christian figure of the Virgin Mary in two of his later poems.*]

In his prose works, the Swedish writer Gunnar Ekelöf (1907-1968) often returned to memories and dreams, somewhat as Proust did. What triggered Ekelöf's memory might be a fragrance, a tone, or a certain light. He described childhood experiences, his observations from travels in the Mediterranean area or in Lapland, his fascination with people, books, and pictures. Certain of these themes appear quite frequently in his poems. In the essay "En outsiders väg" ("An Outsider's Way," 1947) he gives part of his lyrical autobiography. When he calls himself an autodidact, he does not mean it in the proletarian sense. "My childhood environment was well-to-do but so far beyond the normal and so alien to life, that there was plenty of room for a peculiar kind of want." And it is on this lack, in the midst of abundance, he says that he has lived.

"Music has given me the most and the best," he stated. It was Oriental mysticism, however, that engrossed him during his years of awakening. "I learned to hate Europe and Christianity and during morning prayers at school I began to mumble my "Om mani padme hum" ("The innermost secret is in the lotus flower") as a protest. His favorite book for a long time was *Tarjumàn al Ashwáq* by Ibn al-Arabi. Ekelöf also in the same way tells of his dreaming

about emigrating to India, his preparation for studying at the School of Oriental Languages in London, his having to abandon his dreams, and his ending up at the University of Uppsala studying Persian and Sanskrit. A long illness, combined with restlessness and new dreams, made him leave the university.

From mysticism he turned to music which always remained vital to him. Although he went to Paris to study music, he became involved in literary and art circles, and became a poet. What he was looking for was "the hidden meaning a kind of *Alchimie du Verbe."* In an early essay he notes: "Poetry is this very tension-filled relationship *between* the words, *between* the lines, *between* the meanings. I have actually learned to write as a child learns to read: B A becomes, strangely enough, BA. You must of course also have something to say, but it is well if you begin by learning how to say it and begin at the beginning. Many authors have neglected the ABC-book that is published in only one copy and that they carry within themselves." In the essay "Verklighetsflykt" ("Flight from Reality,") he said he could envision peace only when people have learned to live "with the great, simple things: the sea, the forest, music, i.e., the music which is based on silence. And by travelling and being homeless. And how does that wisdom manifest itself? In one's ability to wish for things for oneself without becoming hysterical and wanting one's wishes at any price."

In 1932 he published *Sent på jorden* (*Late on Earth*), the first significant attempt at lyrical modernism in Sweden. An original achievement, it was nonetheless overlooked and misunderstood by all Swedish critics except one. The book had been written in the midst of a personal crisis. In "An Outsider's Way" Ekelöf called *Sent på jorden* "a suicide book." He also stated that he literally used to walk about with a revolver in his pocket. "In my general despair I did everything possible to remain in my dream-world or to be quickly removed from it," he wrote. "Crush the alphabitch between your teeth," "Cut open your stomach and don't think of tomorrow," "Give me poison to die or dreams to live" were some of the lines in these poems. In the last one there is an implied appeal: Either the world will perish, or it shall listen to my poetry! His feeling of doom was coupled with a strong healthy streak, so he decided for a while to rely on dreams.

In the 1940's he gained recognition as *the* pioneer in Swedish modernism. This was achieved through *Färjesång* (*Ferry Song,* 1941), which Ekelöf himself considered his personal breakthrough. It is a volume permeated with paradoxes and Oriental philosophy. In a key poem **"Open It, Write"** (alluding to St. Augustine) he sets out to solve the problem of dualism by finding a "third position" beyond good and evil, the totally unconnected point of view, which is symbolized in the virgin. The poet discusses the nature of the "self", and gives an analysis of the mechanism of life as seen from man's tragic predicament. His "third-position philosophy" (with no metaphysical overtones) has never entered the political sphere, but on many occasions Ekelöf has successfully engaged in polemics against society, church, and authoritarians.

Non Serviam (1945), with obvious references to Satan, and Stephen Dedalus in Joyce, gave Ekelöf his breakthrough with critics and the public. The long 'musical' poem **"Absentia Animi"** is outstanding:

Thesis anthithesis synthesis which again becomes thesis
          Meaningless
Unreal. Meaningless.
And spiders spin their webs across the silent night
Cicadas scrape
        In autumn

In the poem **"The Gymnosophist"** Ekelöf again returned to mystic concepts: "some one else" or "something else." He contended that "beyond reason and experience begins something else," as he had stated in an early aphorism. In other words: Whatever the vision (or experience), there is always something else, beyond that vision, which can only vaguely be divined.

Strountes (1955, *Tryflings*), as Muriel Rukeyser translates the title, [or *Nonsense,*] contained whims, often with puns, but as Carl Fehrman puts it, "The implication of the word and the concept *strunt* for Ekelöf becomes almost metaphysical: from reality he wants to 'squeeze out its meaninglessness' and at the same time to seek an ironical redemption." Even in much of *Opus incertum* (1959) and *En natt i Oto ac* (*A Night in Oto ac* 1961) Ekelöf has an antipoetic approach. A work of "metamorphoses" begun in the late thirties and considered "work in progress" until publication in 1960, *En Mölna-elegi* (*A Mölna Elegy*, [1973]) was an elaborate composition, with witty or personal elements and a number of "learned" allusions and references. Its main theme concerns time and the relativity of the experience of time, and it was an experiment in recapturing the "mood" of one given moment. The "action" takes place at Mölna, just outside of Stockholm, Ekelöf's birthplace and the city he loved *and* hated.

Ekelöf displayed a continuity of development in which his solid, personal reliance on the living part of the Swedish, European, and Oriental cultural traditions was a striking feature. Reality, self, identity, birth, death, love, and nature were some of the most common themes in his poetry. As to what was *materia poetica* he undoubtedly concurred with Wallace Stevens' dictum, "Consider (a) that the whole world is material for poetry; (b) that there is not a specific poetic material."

If Ekelöf's sources of inspiration varied greatly, from art to nature, he was somewhat ambivalent about inspiration itself. His first poem, from 1927, came over him as a kind of ecstasy. "It was like a shower of shooting stars and I remember that I staggered a bit on my way home." Some forty years later Ekelöf completed the last volume of his "Byzantine" trilogy, which to a large extent consisted of mystical or ecstatic poems. Yet, in 1951, he said he thought that inspiration as a standard concept ought to be abolished, since it has as many variations as there are poets. There was a kind of inspiration of the type that Mallarmé had that Ekelöf recognized: the slow, laborious composing of word upon word, work that could take years. As for himself, he said he had all sorts of inspiration. Sometimes it came quickly, sometimes it took years. Occasionally he dreamed poems so completely, that as he said in one essay, he was able to take down hastily the dream that had awakened him.

During his last few years, when he was suffering from cancer of the throat, he was often in great pain; but even greater was his urge to compose new poems, sometimes as if in a trance. During four weeks in the spring of 1965, beginning in Constantinople, he wrote "a mystical ode of some fifty or sixty poems," later called *Diwan över fursten av Emgión* (*Diwan upon the Prince of Emgion*) "It is my greatest poem of love and Passion. I cannot touch it nor see it because I grow ill when I see this blind and tortured man . . . As far as I can understand someone has written [i.e. the poems] using me as a medium . . . Really, I have never before had such an experience, or not one as complete," Ekelöf wrote to a friend.

This Prince of Emgión about whom Ekelöf wrote his *Diwan* had put in an appearance in Ekelöf's collection, of poems *Non Serviam* (1945) and *Opus incertum* (1959). Ekelöf has related how he first came across the word "Emgión." It was in the 1930's, when with friends in an Östermalm apartment in the Östermalm district of Stockholm he asked at a gay spiritualist session where his spiritual "I" was to be found. The answer was, "In Persia," in the guise of "The Prince of Emghionn" (as the oracle, an upside-down drinking glass, indicated). In his *Diwan* Ekelöf included a melancholy, yet defiant, portrait of himself, starting with the lines:

In the calm mirror I saw mirrored
Myself, my soul:
Many wrinkles
The beginnings of a turkey-cock neck
Two sad eyes
Insatiable curiosity
Incorrigible pride
Unrepentant humility
A harsh voice
A belly slit open
And sewn up again
A face scarred by torturers
A maimed foot
A palate for fish and wine
One who longs to die
Who has lain with some
In casual beds but for few
Has felt love and for him
Necessary love
One who longs to die
With someone's hand in his
Thus I see myself in the water
With my soiled linen left behind me when I am
    gone
A Kurdic Prince called a dog
By both Roumaians and Seldjuks
In the water my bald forehead:
All the mangled tongues
Which have convinced me

That I am mute
And those stains on my shirt
Which water will never wash out
Indelible like blood, like poison
The stains of the heretic
Shall strike them like the plague
With still blacker stains.

When the Prince of Emgión returned in *Diwan* the fictitious and historic ground had been effectively prepared by Ekelöf, who for several years had steeped himself in Byzantine art and history. His intuition led him to combine the fictitious Prince of Emgión with elements from the Byzantine eleventh century epic romance about Digenis Acritas, a hero who was the son of a Byzantine mother and an Arab father (hence he had the name Digenis, of two races, and Acritas, margrave as one who defends the borders). Because of his unusual, and not very happy, home conditions as a child (the father was a wealthy broker who caught syphilis and became insane, the mother a self-centered, unloving lady of the lower nobility whose interest was travelling) Gunnar Ekelöf could easily identify with Digenis.

The Prince had been involved in war activities (we are told) and it turned out that he had supported the loser. He was taken captive and was kept as a prisoner of war and jailed in the Vlacherne prison. His treatment in jail, his experiences, and his visions of the Madonna are described in (*Diwan,*) a poem called **"Ayíasma"** (Hagiasma, holy, purifying well). The image of the Madonna is black from the smoke of the thousands of votive candles lighted in her honor. Since the believers threatened the very existence of this Madonna with their devotional kisses, a silver *basma,* a shield had been installed to cover everything except her face and hands. There are obviously several strands of interest in Ekelöf's poem, which to me in a most palpable way suggests the passage of time, *and* the passion of those prayings; while the prolonged passion "liberates" them, it "destroys" the exterior of the object of prayer:

The black image worn to shreds by kisses
The Darkness, O the darkness
Worn to shreds by kisses
The Darkness in our eyes
Worn to shreds by kisses
All we wished for
Worn to shreds by kisses

Darkness in our eyes is of special significance since, as we learn, the Prince is not only tortured but also blinded. To sustain himself in this time of terror, he resorts to contemplation of the Madonna, to whom he (as well as the poet) directs passionate hymns. But there also appears another female, one who may be his wife, daughter, or sister and who is unselfish and generous like a *real* mother. He has fantasies of a surgeon-barber fastening a silver thread with his own image between the madonna's breasts (in the poem beginning "You who came upon me / In the day of my affliction"). The Virgin, whom the blinded and mutilated Prince celebrates in song, while he is being led

towards Van, is a common theme in Ekelöf's poetry. She usually stands for the independent, unconnected party, the balance point, between two forces (like in **"Open it, Write"**). She can be called virgin, because she is in no way yoked with the sterotype opposites that we always are dealing with, i.e. light-darkness, death-life, east-west, good-evil. "The devil is god / and God is the devil," both of them equally demanding, "Until I became aware of / Love, a chink / Between the two locked in combat," it says in one poem here. His love for this virgin is also love for the Panayía, (Panhagía, the high-holy one, the holy virgin,) who also has features of the Cosmic Mother:

Mysterious you shall stand
Aloft in the sky
Your eyes like stars
Shall beam upon the flocks
Of us who are shepherds

. . . . .

But you shall remain unattainable
You shall remain the one.

While Gunnar Ekelöf was still only a child, his father died from syphilis. With a mother who gave him no love, what would be more natural for the boy than to resort to dreaming? One of his dreams as an adolescent must have been about the pure and undefiled virgin. The theme of the virgin, that recurs many times in Ekelöf's poetry, can barely be touched upon here, for a number of reasons. Often the poet managed to see her as the balance, the resting point between conflicting forces, the most central of all. Perhaps this central position reveals that he actually had a *real* mother foremost in his mind. Why else would he take pains to make her into a distant, unattainable Cosmic Mother, if not in an attempt to displace the rejection he had met in his most formative years?

"Together the poems of the *Diwan* constitute one great creedless religious poem, in intensity and purity without counterpart in Swedish literature after the Romantic period" says Reidar Ekner, one of Sweden's leading contemporary critics and scholars. Ekelöf in a lengthy Postscript revealed he had reason to believe that the Prince of Emgión, his fictional I, had been of Armenian-Kurdish (i.e., North Persian) stock, half-Christian and Gnostic. He gave explanations of the following words:

Ayíasma (Hagiasma), purifying well. "The water cult is still alive in Greece and the Near East. A glass of cold water is the holy welcoming drink among the people."

Átokos (nullipara), the one who has not borne any child or any son; here in contrast to Theotókos, the one who has borne a god, or a holy virgin. It seems as if the Prince called not on the latter but on a considerably older type of goddess, the great Near Eastern virgin mother who has all human beings as her children and no one in particular. She was worshiped under different forms. To us she is above all known, through St. Paul, as the "Diana of the Ephesians."

The Blacherne Madonna, the most celebrated of all the miracle-working icons.

Enípnion (Enýpnion), roughly a dreamlike slumber, things that one sees in his dream.

Logothétis (Logothétes), the Emperor's minister, counsellor. *He* is supposed to have made the annotation about the Prince of Emgión. The punishment of blinding was in Greece as old as the myth of Oedipus.

Sagan om Fatumeh (*The Tale of Fatumeh,* 1966) which followed next can be considered a counterpart by contrast to the *Diwan.* While the *Diwan* dealt with a Prince who prayed to a cosmic virgin, *The Tale of Fatumeh* deals with a tellurian woman who became a whore. Fatumeh's fate, as the poet saw it, was to be transformed from an overgenerous loving girl into a young courtesan; later she becomes the beloved of a prince, whose child she bears; and finally, left alone, perhaps deserted by him, she is brought to the Harem at the Erechtheion. Eventually thrown out of the harem, she leads a miserable life as she ages, selling her favors to keep alive. Summarized in this direct way the theme may seem less than promising for poetic treatment and not very appealing. But Ekelöf was a master who knew how to handle words and their relationships, his touch was light, his contours were vague yet firm enough to stir his readers. The themes of love and death are intertwined.

In *The Tale of Fatumeh* the visible and the invisible, light and shadow, the pale and the spectacularly colored, are more pronounced than in most other books by Ekelöf. One poem is entitled "Karagöz," referring to a well-known Turkish shadow-play, a popular amusement in many places before the introduction of motion pictures. Shadows, different angles of light, changes of situation in connection with symbolic light effects, are frequently employed in these poems. There is, for instance, "a peep-show of darkness" in one poem; in another "a shadow / Which lives without Sun and Moon"; in a third poem is the line "does my shadow melt into your shadow." In one of the last poems Fatumeh is identified with physical and psychological suffering, and united with the one who suffers:

Sleep is far away
Pain lies here
I am lying here with you, Fatumeh
Whose paralyzed body is pressed against mine
in an embrace without end.

This mysterious everpresent shadow is not death. It is rather the process of dying. In a note on Fatumeh Ekelöf wrote: "The shadow is the consumption (the wear and tear) that we are all exposed to in the course of life; it devours us little by little. Do not think that the first time you encounter it will be the last!" The "market-place which is called the Square of the Wall" may be read as the place of your death, and "the pillar of Shadow, / Which can be seen from all sides, / A round Shadow" is clearly death itself.

The swarm of flat shadows you see
On these streets which are walls are people
But the Square of the Wall is already empty
Except for the pillar of Shadow in the middle.

Here it is said: Death reigns supreme! Even a seemingly unimportant poem at the beginning of *The Tale of Fatumeh* is infused with significance:

As if the sea followed me
And flung its arms around me
In my room, in the night
  As if the sea wrapped around me
Its arms of sounds
The sea grips me
The sea embraces me.

Reidar Ekner has suggested that Ekelöf here was making a reference to prenatal life. He also has pointed out correctly that for Ekelöf woman represented "birth and death, life and mystical extinction."

It is typical that Ekelöf endowed the pillar (or statue) of the Square with a round shadow, which was supposed to convey a female. The progression after the prenatal state is then an increased awareness in the course of life:

Five times I saw the Shadow
And greeted her as we passed
But the sixth time
In a narrow alley of the lower city
Suddenly she stood before me
Barring my way
And began to revile me
In the coarsest language
Then she asked me:
"Why have you rejected me?
Why have you not lain with your Shadow?
Am I so repulsive?"
To which I answered:
"How can a man lie with his Shadow?
It is customary
To let it walk two paces behind one
Until the evening"
She smiled scornfully
And pulled her black shawl tighter about her face:
"And after sunset?"
"Then the wanderer has two shadows,
One from the lantern he has just left behind him
And one from the lantern he is just approaching:
They keep changing places"
She smiled scornfully and laid her hand on the
    neighbouring wall:
"Then I am not your Shadow?"
I said: "I do not know whose shadow you are"
And meant to walk on
But, lifting her hand, she showed its black
    impression
In the moonlight on the white wall
And said again:
"Then I am not your Shadow?"
To which I answered:

"I see who you are.
It is for you to take me
Not for me to take you"
She smiled scornfully. "Beloved", she said
"At your place? Or at mine?"
"At yours", I answered.

It has to end with obliteration. Dying is seen as an act of love. Man is intimately wedded to suffering. Darkness, the shadow, which is related to the concept of nothingness, is also an *obscurum per obscurius,* "a path leading back to the profound mystery of the Origin," according to J. E. Cirlot. It devours him bit by bit. Ekelöf's sober observation is simple: just as light has its shadow, life is endowed with suffering. The "Outside" must have its "Inside," the body its soul. It is logical that the shadow in "End of the Tale of Fatumeh" should be entirely black, which indicates disappearance:

"Beloved, shall we meet at your place or at mine?"
So echoed her mocking question in the Night
"At yours!" So echoed his mocking answer
Once more they wandered through the Night
Far out of the City, far beyond the suburbs
Over the oasis gardens, up out of the Night
The red dawn rose. Further on the road
Lost itself in the sand, in the Sun
That climbed higher out of the Night
The Moon turned pale. The Sun cast darker
    shadows
As it set they came to her place. In the Night
All roads had vanished. They lay down beside each
    other
Beneath him nothing was to be seen of her Shadow
But when they shifted positions as lovers will
Nothing was to be seen under his Shadow
Thus the Night became a Day and the Day again a
    Night.

Ekelöf had a special philosophy of oddness, calling life an odd number, and death an even number:

I saw a coffin, draped in green, being borne from Eyub
By ten, by a hundred, by a thousand relatives and friends
How is it possible, you may ask, for such a multitude
To act as bearers for one coffin of average human length?
Oh, that's easy, that lightens the burden:
The pair at the tail of the procession keep hurrying
    forward
To relieve the pair at its head
Who shift their hold and become the second pair
Then the third, then the fourth, as a new pair come to
    the front
After ranking as chief mourners, they take second place
    and so on
Until, by and by, they rank as cousins twice removed
And so on until they come to the rear and the process
    begins again
In this way the last shall always be first.
Death's number is even, life's is odd.
That is why the one they bear is the thousand-and-First.

His numerological fantasies are expressed in his division of his book into a *nazm,* a string of beads, and *tesbih,* a rosary, each consisting of twenty-nine numbered poems.

A 1962 reprint of Ekelöf's first published book of poetry, *Late on Earth,* on its back cover had the thin contours of the poet's diminished hand, in a raised position. There was no shadow in that hand. It is fitting and logical that the small version of his hand on the back cover of the original *Tale of Fatumeh* should be filled with a dark blue shadow. The poet's life was fast approaching even darker shadows. The raised hand, incidentally, does not have to be seen either as a warning or as a protecting sign. It could be the symbol of song: in the earlier instance meaning "Listen to my song!" in the later instance suggesting, "My song is coming to an end, listen to it!"

Frequently among his works a number of poems have been inspired by fairly easily recognized art works. A case in point is **"The Harem at Erechtheion"**:

Those knowing eyes look at me
Steadfastly without blinking
They give me their glances
Before they vanish
At every moment
They look at me with their look

You put your hand under her veil
Under her mantle
And touch the dagger
The hilt of the dagger under her left breast
A little to one side
In the crease just under the breast
You see and, seeing, you know
That everything is turning to ashes
That your look is changing
And soon will cease to be
Yet there remains
The golden light of evening through the open door
And the evening's ashes

Reidar Ekner has conclusively shown, I believe, that the poem is related to an early art work of Ekelöf's own making, an early short story, "Fallet Skönheten," ("The Case of Beauty," 1934). Through his vivid imagination a young writer on a cruise is connected "with all the dreams of the world, in the dim and distant past, and in the future." He mysteriously appears to be put to death by "the greatest and mildest criminal of all, Beauty, which, without taking the lives of its victims, nonetheless relieves them of a forced existence with their own unsatisfied longing as dagger." In the poem Beauty has been replaced by a feeling of relief, "almost melancholy after a burdensome life," says Ekner, who also points out that the poem can be read as a love poem. "Those knowing eyes" looking "steadfastly without blinking" (in **"The Harem at Erechtheion"**), however, surely must belong to another art work, a marble statue, on the outside of the

Erechtheion on the Acropolis, which Ekelöf visited. It should perhaps also be noted that the poem has a relationship with the poem **"Xoanon"**: "I remove the arms / The brown hand with its rose, and the brown breasts / The right breast first, then the left, but gently / To ease the pain," (*de bruna brösten / det högra först, det vänstra sist / med smärtorna*). Ekelöf's intense study of the constantly changing light on the sculpture at sunset, explains, of course, only part of the poem. Concerning the line "That everything is turning to ashes": in the manuscript Ekelöf had toyed with different ideas "how everything is changing into its opposite," "and ends in its opposite, / and at the same time is. Now, here."

There are also references to other art works, such as films and music, but above all to icons.

> It is true, as you said, that I am dark
> But the veil has a hem of silver
> I said: "I am your mirror, your mirror."
> And now I say:
> These Turkmenian eyes
> Are narrow as knives
> Quivering in the wood at which they have been
>   flung
> Close to the temples, under the arm-pits
> So that a man stands nailed to the wall
>
> These eyes looking downwards
> Cheek bent towards cheek
> Pouring tenderness over a child
> Like a hive of wild honey
>
> I am your child, nailed to the wall
> And resting in your lap
> I am your child and I shine
> Close around me, rays
> Stand quivering like knives
> I shine because your eyes are dark
> And because you are so dark.

In a letter of January, 1967, Ekelöf explained that his most immediate model was a Russian icon, "Glykophilousa," from the Russian Museum in Leningrad. "These Turkmenian eyes" referred to a film he had seen in Berlin in 1933, "perhaps one of the last decent films before the *Machtübernahme*. It dealt with some little Herr Schmidt or other, who unexpectedly had received a legacy and, quite dazed, got involved in a round of night club visits. During one of these visits, with a band of Circassians executing a dance with knife-throwing, he happened to enter on the wrong side of the stage ramp, which excited these daredevils to the extent that they exposed him to knife-throwing in the highest degree, until he was unable to move. . . . I was glad once more to find the same glance of cruelty and tenderness in enigmatic union. . . . *Re* those people in Berlin, I don't know of what kind they were, Caucasian or beyond, but the knife-eyes lodged in me. So did the Russian madonna of folk mixture."

The poem **"Joasaph and Fatumeh"** clearly has some emblematic features. Above all **"Xoanon"** describes an icon

in great detail. The Panayía, the Madonna, wears a crown on her head (Ekelöf had a liking for crowns), and the icon, a favorite of the poet's, was acquired by the Ekelöfs when visiting Athens in 1961. In a hastily jotted down note Ekelöf had written:

> With the madonna one cautiously lifts and uncovers
> The last coating of color, and the very base color
> A piece of olive tree wood, holy, let it be
> That is the simple tree
> Which patiently has carried your wishes
> Has endured . . .

One poem opens with

> Your face covered
> With blood and dirt
> You lay in the street
> And the richly dressed
> Who passed you by
> These rich in garments
> Of silver, of gold
>
> Their eyes looking straight ahead
> In the right direction
> Composed the gold ground for your face
> As you lay in the Street
> Covered with blood and dirt.

The gold ground is, of course, the same as often can be found on an icon. And the face is a counterpart to that of an icon. The function of the others is limited to providing background, emphasizing the woman's central, human significance. Here she is one wronged in life who never *per se* will be debased. She continued to depend on her visions, just as the main protagonist in **Diwan** sustained his life on *his* visions.

Why all these gory, unpleasant elements? Do they belong less to our time than to classical times? In Ekelöf's vision of Near Eastern life, which he knew from his travels, from what he termed "many years of unsystematic Byzantine studies," of eclectic affinities, he felt obliged to include a considerable amount of the debased, ugly, and frightful, which certainly had little to do with the emblems. Take as an example the rape of the dwarf woman in one poem, or the "used up whaura," Fatumeh, describing her grotesque bodily advantages! The reason for his employing these elements is clearly to strike a balance with all the previous devotion. When Fatumeh admits to having been "selfish but faithful / On occasion you found me obstinate / And could not bear it / Now I am a skeleton / But a beautiful one / with joints well set in their sockets" etc., it is not necessary for us to visualize a beautiful skeleton, but rather to see a Fatumeh who has a certain beauty even in her used up state.

A lighter erotic touch can be found in several poems, one of which signals sexual distress:

> You whose body is in such dire want
> How can you endure?

Doubly tormented
By a want within and a want from without
Love and Friendship walked by
Arm in arm and said:
Truly
Her life is a thin membrane
Stretched taut like a drum-skin
Between this and That
The mere touch of a finger
The mere flick of a nail
Sets her vibrating
As if she were alive

Thus with over-tones I accompany
The rhythm of your voice, its choked wailing
And the strum of your fingers
On that single string.

Ekelöf was a great fan of Boris Christoff's interpretations of Moussorgsky's song cycles and played some of his records over and over again. On the day when I happened to have an appointment with Ekelöf at his home, he was tired and tense. Almost the only subject he could talk about with any enthusiasm at all was music, and whatever way the conversation turned it always came back to Moussorgsky. When the topic was exhausted, it started all over again with this marvellous bass, Boris Christoff, (Ekelöf had seen and heard Chaliapin in the 1930's in Paris.) The session ended with Ekelöf's playing of records of Moussorgsky's children's songs. Deeply moved, gesticulating and humming, he finally sat back on his bed when the music became less emotional. Peace came over his face, and he fell asleep, while the music of Moussorgsky continued. One of his favorites was a lullaby with a recurring "Báju! Báju!" (lullay lullay), which the Ekelöfs heard as "Avgó! Avgó!" associating with the Greek word for egg. This song "Avgó!" Ekelöf telescoped with a reproduction of a fresco from a Serbian church, in which an angel before an old shepherd points up towards the sky, while placing his arm around the shepherd's shoulders. The old man looks up with reverence and awe. In the picture there is neither egg nor moon. But the poet had made Russian "Báju" into "Avgo," then made his egg into a moon; moved by the shepherd's simple piety and profound experience, before the sublimity of the scene Ekelöf sang "Avgó! Avgó!" Later he made the old shepherd into an old woman, thereby further underscoring the female dominance, if not to say the almost frenzied devotion to female beings, in *The Tale of Fatumeh.*

Georg Otter (review date 1972)

SOURCE: "East Meets West—Gunnar Ekelöf in English," in *Moderna språk,* Vol. LXVI, No. 2, 1972, pp. 124-30.

[*In the following excerpt, Otter offers a mixed review of* Selected Poems *as translated by W.H. Auden and Leif Sjöberg, arguing that while some of the translation decisions made in the volume are imprecise and misleading and indicate "a certain lack of feeling for Ekelöf's mys-* ticism and his style," *it is useful to have an English translation of Ekelöf's later poems which has the potential to "reach a very wide public."*]

One of Gunnar Ekelöf's earliest attempts at revolt against society and Christianity took the form of muttering to himself during school prayers "Om mani padme hum". This youthful protest, blended with mysticism, is evidence already of his interest in the East, which he later fed to the full at the Royal Library in Stockholm. Here, through Heidenstam's *Endymion,* he was led to a book which for a time was to become his favourite, and which was to remain a recurrent source of inspiration to the end of his life: the *Tarjúmàn al-Ashwáq* ("Translator of the Desires") of Ibn al-'Arabi, called Muhyi al-Din, a 12 13th century Sufi mystical poet. This book, a collection of mystical odes of platonic love expressed in erotic terms, first taught him, he said, what symbolism and surrealism really were.

Three attempts to leave Sweden "for good" in pursuit of his dream sent him first, with the idea of emigrating to India, to the London School of Oriental Studies. The "childish" methods of language instruction employed there drove him back to study Persian at Uppsala. His restlessness next took him to Genoa, where he seems to have missed the boat that was to take him to a coffee-planter's life in Kenya (one thinks of Rimbaud, another youthful mystic, leaving behind his poetry and his visions to live the reality in action), and finally to Paris to study music, but where he was caught and held by poetry, and whence poverty sent him back to Sweden.

Ekelöf's interest in the Orient centred at length around the Near East and Greece. He was particularly fascinated by the Byzantine Empire, with its compound of races and beliefs from East and West, of refinement and barbarity. Yet he hated it. The translators of the selection under review [Gunnar Ekelöf, *Selected Poems.* Translated by W. H. Auden & Leif Sjöberg. With an Introduction by Göran Printz-Påhlson. Penguin Modern European Poets. Penguin Books Ltd. 1971. 141 pp. This collection is referred to in this essay by the editors' initials, AS.] quote a letter in which he claims that ". . . Byzantine life, traditionally and according to deep-rooted custom, is like the political life in *our* cities and states. I am intensely interested in it because I hate it. I hate what is Greek. I hate what is Byzantine. . . . *Diwan* is a symbol of the political decadence we see around us. *Fatumeh* is a symbol of the degradation, the coldness between persons, which is equally obvious." (p. 10).

This passion for the Byzantine seems to have boiled up again in his last years, during a journey to Turkey in 1965. The importance of this experience and the richness of inspiration that dominated his last three years produced three volumes of poetry: *Diwan över fursten av Emgión,* 1965 (written in the space of 4-5 weeks, according to the translators), *Sagan om Fatumeh,* 1966, and *Vägvisare till underjorden,* 1967, while a good deal of the posthumous collection of the surviving material from those years published by Ekelöf's wife in *Partitur,* 1969, is devoted to the same themes.

The present translation of the first two of these volumes is preceded by a Foreword by Auden & Sjöberg containing brief biographical details about Ekelöf, taken mainly from his essay "En outsider's väg" (*Utflykter,* 1947), and a note about the *Diwan* and *Fatumeh.* A short bibliography is followed by a very perceptive Introduction by Göran Printz-Påhlson, who discusses Ekelöf's poetic development and method and the peculiar quality of his vision.

A more primitive level of existence is Ekelöf's real subject man between a life that holds little and a death that holds nothing, the thin thread of being that survives mutilation of the body and returns to the universal on its death, that which is common to beggar and prince.

The main figure in the *Diwan* is the Prince of Emgión, a Kurdish-Armenian border prince of mixed Christian, Gnostic, Greek, Arabian and Persian ideas. Captured in battle, he suffered the same fate as his Emperor, Romanós Diogénes, being tortured, blinded and imprisoned. In the *Diwan* he is later freed and makes his way back on foot to his own country, led by a mysterious female figure, who appears in a number of the poems as his daughter, sister, wife, mother, and perhaps also the Virgin Goddess whose image pervades the whole of the trilogy. Curiously enough, in their foreword the translators appear to have confused the Prince of Emgión with Digenís Akrítas, the hero of a medieval Greek epic, to whom they attribute the same fate. It seems clear from Ekelöf's poems and notes, however, that the "I" of the *Diwan* is this probably imaginary prince, who feels that Digenís has betrayed him; in **"Legender"** (the second part of the book) he says that Digenís is dead.

The Fatumeh of the second book is, in the *nazm* (the first section), a young girl sold by her mother to become a courtesan, then the mistress of a prince by whom she has a child; she is then to be found in the harem at Erechteion. In the *tesbih* (the second section), she has apparently left the harem and is a prostitute; later we see her as a "bleareyed hag", an old worn-out street-walker.

Both the Prince and Fatumeh, through all their tortures and suffering, hold on to the thin thread of existence, borne up by their vision of the Virgin, whose presence haunts many of the poems. Although she is described from time to time in ikons, she is not the Christian Virgin Mary but that other 'more ancient' "barnlösa moder åt oss alla", the "mångbröstade" Panayía (Panhagía), "Medelhavets gudinna", who appears in earlier poems of Ekelöf's (cf. **"Minnesbilder"**, *En natt i Oto ac*), the Diana of the Ephesians of St. Paul.

In a way, Ekelöf is much nearer to our metaphysical poets in his sense of the continual presence of death; the vision is too consistent to be merely surrealist. Behind his apparent stoicism ("Jag är litet tapprare idag än igår", he would say during his last illness) lies an Indian belief in the fundamental unity of all forms of life, and a feeling that Life and Death are one at the most primitive level. Often in these last books, through the eyes of princess and housewife, prostitute and beggar-woman, even through

the eyes of the Virgin Mary, there looks out the grave compassion of the Great Earth Mother, she who has milk for us all. Often through crowded streets stalks the Shadow, of death perhaps, of husband, lover, mistress, child, of someone vaguely apprehended who is a mirror image of oneself. Ekelöf's explanation of the name "Fatumeh" is significant. The original meanng, he says, is "woman who is weaning her child," but he prefers to see in it also an allusion to the Latin word "fatum" (*Sagan om Fatumeh* notes, p. 109).

In *Fatumeh, tesbih* 24 (AS 134), Ekelöf says that death is an even number, life an odd one. One aspect of his mysticism is his preoccupation with symbol and number, shown in the arrangement of the poems in the three last books. Thus *Sagan om Fatumeh* consists of two groups of poems called *nazm* a necklace, or collection of poems, representing the young Fatumeh, and *tesbih* a rosary, representing the aged Fatumeh together with 3 single poems. In the East, according to Ekelöf, these rosaries (a pre-Christian device) usually consist of groups of 33 beads separated by a larger bead. In more elaborate rosaries these larger beads are often carved in the form of a python's head. Instead of groups of 33 poems, the poet has chosen groups of 29 (a prime number), "som när det hela är färdigt ger en bättre siffersumma". The arrangement in *Diwan* is similar, but with only one single poem separating the two groups. This single poem, or "paustecken", is also an "ormhuvud", and its use "antyder också att jag tänkt mig en fortsättning, att Diwanen blivit en art 'work in progress'" (See *Sagan om Fatumeh,* notes, pp. 109-110).

The total number of poems in the *Diwan* is 59 (a prime number), in *Fatumeh* 61 (again a prime number). *Vägvisare till underjorden* ("tänkt som mittvalvet av ruinen Diwan", i.e. as the second book of the trilogy) contains 43 poems (another prime number) arranged in a slightly different fashion (3 groups of 13 separated by 2 groups consisting of 1 "ormhuvud" and 1 other poem). The total number of poems in the three books is 163, once more a prime number; and no doubt Ekelöf, had he lived, would have continued with this scheme in succeeding books on the Byzantine/Greek theme. Is it a mere coincidence that the posthumous *Partitur,* although not overlooked by the poet himself, also contains 2 groups, each of 23 items (still another prime number)?

Auden & Sjöberg regret having had to abandon Ekelöf's plan in their version of *Fatumeh,* but do not explain that the plan applied to the *Diwan* also. They further obscure the plan by not numbering the poems and by omitting the title of the *Diwan*'s second necklace or rosary: **"Legends and Dirges"** (*Legender och Mirolóyier*, ett urval). In any case, it is rather a pity that even if they had no space for the 8 poems omitted from the *Diwan* they could not include the 4 they left out of *Fatumeh.* These "collections of poems" are, in fact, strings of matching pearls, with shifting lights and colours, themes and allusions repeated along the rows.

The translation is reasonably direct, with few departures from the text, and only occasional changes of construction. Numerous small felicities and the general flow of the lines ensure that the version does not read too often like a translation. One difficulty in comparing the translation with Ekelöf's published texts is that the translators have incorporated into their version emendations derived from the manuscripts, so that it is often impossible without research to know whether a change or omission is inadvertent, or based on a misconception, or the result of a correction in Ekelöf's manuscript. Although this is only a popular edition, a note of which poems had been emended would have been useful.

I mention here a few other points in the translation which are worth notice.

The title **Diwan över fursten av Emgión** means a "collection of poems about the Prince of Emgión". It has been translated literally, however, ". . . over the Prince of Emgión", as if Diwan meant "funeral oration" or "dirge". The dirges (mirolóyier) form only part of the second half of the book, in fact.

The dedicatory lines of this book, taken from *Tarjúmàn al-Ashwáq,* read:

> Denna min dikt är utan rim: jag
> ägnar den endast Henne.
> Ordet "Henne" är mitt mål, och för Hennes
> skull vill jag inte gå med på annan
> byteshandel än "Ge" och "Ta".

The translators' version is: "This poem of mine is without rhyme: I intend by it / only Her. / The word 'Her' is my aim, and for Her sake I am / not fond of bartering except with 'Give' and 'Take'." Are "sake" and "take" not rhymes? They echo strongly in the reader's mind and make nonsense of the first line. This could easily have been avoided by a less literal rendering of "för Hennes skull" as "because of Her".

In D21 (AS p. 35), a bird's feather floats through the grating of the Prince's prison cell: "Vinden förde den hit / eller någon annan förde den / Den fick ligga på golvet, länge / innan jag tog den i handen / en vanlig duvofjäder . . ." The translation here gives: ". . . or else somebody carried it" and "Before I cradled it in my hands". Ekelöf's text gives a gentle hint that the wind, too, is a being, not a mere object. His "jag tog den i handen" (I took it in my hand) does not express in words the sentiment introduced by "cradled" and "hands"; the sentimental picture is evidently not part of Ekelöf's plan or poem.

In D24, *Hayíasma* (Hagíasms a purification well) (AS p. 38) "två dunkla ögon" are not "sad" eyes but enigmatic ones.

In D25 (AS p. 40), "ett hemligt ansikte / såg meningsfullt på mig" is translated as "an enigmatic face / looked intently at you". Apart from the translation of "mig" by "you", which does not seem justifiable here, "intently" does not render "meningsfullt"; the line should rather be: "looked at me meaningly", "gave me a meaning look".

D27, another *ayíasma* (AS p. 42), is devoted to an ikon: "Den svarta bilden / under silver sönderkysst /" . . . Runt

kring bilden / det vita silvret sönderkysst / Runt kring bilden / själva metallen sönderkysst / Under metallen / den svarta bilden sönderkysst" etc. Some ikons were credited with wonderful cures and other miracles, and were carried round from place to place to be presented to the faithful. To protect the picture of the Virgin from the lips of the multitudes, a thin silver plate (the *basmá*) covering the Virgin and Child completely except for faces and hands was sometimes attached to the ikon, as were other details, such as jewels. (An ikon of this sort is described in **Fatumeh,** *nazm* 25, **"Xoanon"**, AS p. 107.) The ikon was also occasionally set in a frame of silver. The translators do not seem to have fully realised this, for they render "Den svarta bilden / under silver sönderkysst" and its repetitions by "The black image (here, perhaps, "blackened" would be better) / Framed in silver worn to shreds by kisses". Here Ekelöf is referring to the *basmá,* and "under silver" should be "beneath silver". "Runt kring bilden / det vita silvret . . .", then, refers to the frame, and the version given, "All round the image", is acceptable.

The other poem about an ikon which I have mentioned, **"Xoanon"** (**Fatumeh,** *nazm* 25), is discussed by Printz-Påhlson in his Introduction (AS pp. 13-14), where he argues that the slow stripping of the ikon, first of its *basmá* and its removable attributes, then of the paint and ground right down to the wood it is painted on, represents Ekelöf's view of the poetic process, his method of arriving at what is common to man, the universal. There are one or two differences in the version given of this difficult poem, some of which may be due to Ekelöf's manuscript corrections. Ekelöf's punctuation is generally very scanty and often rather obscure, but it ought to be respected. Some guidance is given by his use of capital letters only for names and at the beginning of a sentence, not at the beginning of each line as in English verse. **"Xoanon"** begins. "Jag äger, i dig, en undergörande Ikon / om detta att äga är att ingenting äga / så som hon äger mig. Så äger jag henne." The translated version is: "In you I possess a miracle-working Icon / If to possess is to possess nothing: / As she possesses me, so I possess her". This version seems to me to misrepresent Ekelöf's thought.

In this ikon, "ett vuxet lindebarn" "står på en omvänt perspektivisk pall". This is translated by "On a footstool in receding perspective", an odd expression. Reference to almost any early ikon containing a stool or a throne, however, will show that the perspective is *reversed,* as Ekelöf says it is, that is the stool is depicted as growing *wider* towards the back, instead of narrower.

When removing the painted dress and body from the figure of the Virgin, Ekelöf writes: "Jag löser vecken över hennes högra bröst / och varligt vecken över hennes vänstra / med smärtorna. . . . / . . . Jag lösgör armarna / . . . de bruna brösten / det högra först, det vänstra varligt sist / med smärtorna, . . .". The translation given is: "I relax the creases . . . / . . . over the left / Gently, to ease the pain. . . / . . . I remove . . . / The right breast first, then the left, but gently / To ease the pain, . . .". This "gently, to ease the pain" does not satisfy. The word "smärtorna" is an allusion to St. Luke 2, xxxv, where the aged Simeon says to the mother of the child Jesus: "(Yea, a sword shall pierce through thy own soul also), that the thoughts of many hearts may be revealed." Ekelöf's meaning is rather that the left breast is the one with the heart, the one with the pains, the pain of the sword and the suffering of the eternal mother before the fate of her child, who is to suffer for many in Israel. These pains are an inseparable part of the Virgin's heart, they cannot be eased but reverence is due to the bosom that bears them.

"The Logothete's Annotation" (AS p. 45), the *Diwan*'s "paustecken", gives an example of a play on words that the translators have ignored. When the Prince of Emgión is imprisoned for four or five years, "Hans hustru eller måhända dotter bad för honom / med kropp och själ". "With heart and soul", which the translators have employed for "kropp och själ", is a common expression in English, but in the circumstances it is more than probable that the princess's body would have been employed as an additional means of supplication. The translation could well have been "with body and soul", though the suggestion is slightly cruder in English.

In Diwan **"Legender"** 12 (AS p. 58), a hasty mistranslation has confused Ekelöf's image. After shameful torture to make him betray his friends, the Prince says: "Men mitt kön, bödel / är inte mellan mina ben / Mitt förstånd, bödel / som förrådde inbillade namn / är inte i mitt förstånd, bödel / Det är i mitt hjärta, bödel / Stick i det, bödel". "Förstånd" has been rendered as "senses" (pl.) and "Det är i mitt hjärta" as "It is in my heart", which here therefore means "my *sex* is in my heart". But "förstånd" means sense, understanding, and it is the understanding that is in his heart.

Fatumeh, nazm 29 (AS pp. 112-113) is a poem which obviously describes a picture of a young prince embracing an urn about which is wrapped a veil. From a reference in *nazm* 23 (AS p. 105), the young man is the son Fatumeh had by her princely lover when she was young (according to *nazm* 22, pp. 103-4, Prince Joasaph). But the young prince is also to be nameless. Now Ekelöf, among other explanations of the name Emgión (*Diwan,* notes, pp. 106-7), also suggests that it is merely a description of the Prince's state as a hostage, and that therefore "har min furste inget namn utan han är en Namnlös". Thus the reference to the young prince as one "vars namn bör vara onämnt" is a small example of the many cryptic allusions that link together all the poems of this last period and give them such a strong sense of unity.

However, the picture in the poem is built up partly by a series of questions which strongly recall Keats's *Ode to a Grecian Urn;* for instance:

> Varför välsignar honom trädens grenar
> och varför är de evigt vårliga? Och fåglarna
> gömda i buskarna, säg varför de klagar
> som om de frågade: Vem är därinne?

Whether the translators have realised that this poem is directly inspired by a particular painting is not certain. They have rendered ". . . allt i denna bild är redan ut-

plånat" by ". . . everything in this *image* has faded already". Throughout the book, "bild" is translated as "image", a word which may be appropriate when applied to an ikon depicting the Virgin, but is out of place here. The painting which has evidently inspired the poem is an 18th century Persian miniature that is reproduced on the front cover of *Sagan om Eatumeh.* If the translators had observed this, they could have added a note.

To sum up, although it betrays a certain lack of feeling for Ekelöf's mysticism and his style, this translation of a large part of his last work ought to reach a very wide public. It would be interesting to speculate on its effect on English-speaking poets, with their very different attitudes and preoccupations. Auden's name should at least ensure that the book will not be ignored.

Ross Shideler (essay date 1973)

SOURCE: "Listening to the Voices," in *Voices Under the Ground: Themes and Images in the Early Poetry of Gunnar Ekelöf,* University of California Press, 1973, pp. 1-34.

[*In the following excerpt, Shideler asserts that the poem "Voices Under the Ground" serves as a commentary on the absurdity of death and as a reflection of the dialogues which occur within one's own consciousness.*]

Gunnar Ekelöf's poem **"Voices Under the Ground,"** published in **In Autumn** (1951) has been only casually touched upon by Swedish critics, yet it is one of Ekelöf's major poems. In it many of the crucial themes and images of the first twenty years of his poetry reach full fruition, for, with complete technical mastery, he draws upon the unconscious to symbolize and to identify his concern with dreams and with man's alienated and mortal consciousness. At first this poem seems like an incomprehensible dialogue between voices under the ground, with some unidentified observer above the ground. Upon further analysis, however, the poem has the unified structure of a dream and the dialogue represents a dialogue within the narrator's own consciousness.

This seemingly unstructured poem has a rather clear framework that can be outlined in musical terms, but the full depth of the poem is illuminated only when we see how Ekelöf uses symbols such as the bird and the stone within the structure of a dream. Ultimately, the poem deals in archetypal imagery with the narrator's lack of a space that he can comfortably inhabit and with his ambivalence toward death.". . .

The title **"Voices Under the Ground"** gives some idea of what is to be expected. The most probable "voices" one might hear, or imagine hearing, under the ground are those of the dead. The image in the title also creates a concept of planes or levels. To suggest an "under" is to imply an "over" or above. Assuming the voices are coming from the dead, and given the title, the reader's first assumption is probably just that, the possibility is set up for a listener, for someone hearing the voices, presumably someone on the earth's surface.

Within the first stanza of the poem, there are two different styles, one that seems rather objective, and another that is subjective. The difference between the styles is emphasized by the identing dash, often performing the function of quotation marks. The first style is that of the opening lines.

Common and simple sentence structure is used in the first three lines as typified by the use of the definite article in the first line and followed by the "It is. . ." of the next two lines. The lines, I suggest, are spoken from the most uninvolved level, by a narrator or the poet if one wishes to personify that level.

The next line, idented, is difficult to separate from the preceding lines, although it does seem less objective and the sentence structure is not as plain. The words imply someone who sees and evaluates, but someone other than the first person speakers of the following two lines. One theory could be that the first three lines represent thoughts of the narrator, while the next sentence may be spoken aloud by the same person.

With the two "I long from. . ." lines the first-person statement and vocabulary is almost colloquial. These two lines, it is presumed, represent the voices referred to in the title.

Basically, the two styles or tones within the poem are differentiated by third and first person speakers. Occasional passages are difficult to place, but these become clearer as our reading of the poem progresses. The first plane is that of the objective narrator or the stage-setter. It is this objective narration that may be considered upon or above the earth's surface, whereas the voices are beneath. This analogy will break down later, but it allows the reader to follow the poem somewhat more easily on a first reading.

Studying the poem from the viewpoint of levels or planes, decreases the importance of determining the identity and the number of the speakers. I find it easiest to read it as simply two voices in a dialogue, but since there is no clear way of verifying this, it may be read as a series of voices listening to one another and chiming in with comments. After the stage is set by the narrator, the two voices continue in a dialectical question and answer method. For purposes of convenience, I shall label the first speaker, voice A, and the second, voice B.

If a generalization could be made from this point, the poem would be called essentially "associative" with a major portion forming a dialogue of the type presentday readers know as "absurd." It is distinctly a twentieth-century poem in that it lacks a traditional beginning and ending and presents a slice, rather than a complete picture, of a universe that lacks light, center, or surface.

A close reading of the poem is helpful to establish a basic foundation of agreement and to lead into a more precise idea than the generalizations above. After the two lines of longing at the conclusion of the first stanza, there is a

long stanza that returns to the third person narrative and repeats in its final lines a resumé of the opening lines. It can be assumed, therefore, that we are back to the observing level of the narrator.

The contents of the lines reinforce this assumption, since they continue to fill the visual stage of the poem. The opening lines were abstract and not localized apart from the morning light and the floors of drugstores. In these lines the poem becomes populated. A young man, a pale girl, and additional details are added, such as the flowers in the window.

These concrete phenomena are left open to the reader's imagination and he is invited to use it: "she exists only in connection with her hand which exists only in connection with. . ." This invitation to the reader's imagination is extended by means of the bird. The association lies in the movement of the girl's hands and the bird's flight, and in posing the question of the relation or connection between one thing and another. The old woman and the man at the desk seem to be further details on what I refer to as the stage as well as examples of the problem of relationship.

No reason is given to connect these various singular entities, but the child at the blackboard reintroduces the question of relationship. Once again the association and the question are posed in terms of a hand apparently in motion, then of things related to the scene. The entire passage is summarized with "Where is the hand?" and with the references to the flowers, time, morning light and, finally, the black-white checkered floors.

The summary of this scene reminds the reader that a group of characters have been seen, almost as if they were on stage, but no plot, no reason to connect them have been given. Instead, the reader has been asked to consider what it is that unites them on this particular black and white stage.

Before we are given a chance to consider that scene, however, we are drawn into a converstion. The objectivity and narrative quality of the first section is dropped. "What a lovely name!" is a colloquial and evaluative phrase and the first person "My" of "My bird" verifies that we are overhearing a conversation. The two voices, who are familiar with each other, are discussing the extinct primeval bird the archaeopteryx. The discussion at first has no apparent connection with the opening passage, but the references to flying and to light remind us of it.

A conversation about an extinct bird that is alive need not be illogical, if it is agreed that the voices actually are under the earth. Then an ageless sense of petrification, of time's progression in thousand-year beats is quite comprehensible. The voices identify with the stone of the earth and seem to feel an interchangeability between themselves and everything else that is within the stone. The dominant theme of the passage is the osmotic quality given to stone, envisioned possibly as a thick doughy substance or liquid, with the voice, lizards, birds, and presumably an infinity of dead life existing in it.

There is, however, a subtheme reminiscent of the opening passage. The concept of "connection" of "relation" continues by the absence-presence of the bird, and the same verb, flight, is used to pose the question. This theme of relation is further developed by creating a tension between the voice that is forced to remain "bound to the stone" and the bird "with its flight." Once it is created, this picture of voice, bird, stone, and their union, is broken.

One of the voices wanted to know something from the bird. We do not know what. The bird has the capacity to influence the speakers. "The bird took my wings and gave them to another light. The light went out." Although we do not know what the relation is between the bird and the speakers, we can see that the dialectical method of the poem is worked out more clearly here. The lines are reduced in length, and we can see a questioner and an answerer. Speaker A, the one who longs for the bird and who asked it for something, fears the emptiness and darkness of the pitlike abyss. Speaker B apparently delights in telling A of the confusing chaos that we begin to suspect is the universe. The description extends out to "the house of the stars," then back to the original area, "Birds and shellfish sleep there like you. . ."

The image of the stone is given even greater range. It becomes like a pulsing heart.

> With thousand-year beats beat the'r hearts of stone
> in veins of stone.
> For yearbillions of stone time swirls them with itself
> in raging storms of stone through seas of stone
> to heavens of stone. . .

The intensity of this experience becomes comparable to the pounding of one's heart during a nightmare. The imagery extends itself to the limits of the universe and then abruptly returns, apparently illogically to the speakers. A asks, almost as if he were awaking, "Where am I? Where are you?" B tells him to "Wake up!" The complexity of A's awakening is that there seems to be no difference between reality and nightmare. He repeats his earlier question, "Is there no forgetfulness in the house of the abyss?"
This question leads into a scene suggestive of a hospital and again is extended to a terrifying point of chaos. "Everything lies on its back, everything turns again and again on its back." Darkness is again a crucial aspect, and here, in the form of night, it becomes a frightening element climbing floor after floor of some unspecified building, possibly the hospital suggested earlier.

Speaker A abruptly takes us back to the black and white floors of the opening scene. The heart is now mentioned in the simile of the radiator, and the black and white floors are connected with the underlying "loneliness" theme of the absurd dialogue. With one more image filled with movement and implying chaos, "darkness rushes around the gables of the house," the opening scene is reestablished, with basically one character on stage: death.

Almost as a refrain the entire poem is summarized in the last four lines which give both the objective narrator and the two voices.

> Hours pass. Time passes by.
> Slowly the morning light pulverizes the drug of sleep.
> I long from the black square to the white.
> I long from the red thread to the blue.

Having completed a general summary of the poem, one remains somewhat vague and confused about the poem as a whole. Certain scenes are easily visualized, but to put the opening and closing sections into some kind of meaningful relationship with the central dialogue is difficult.". . .

In **"Voices,"** after the image of the morning light and the black and white checkered floors, there is the bitter but perhaps also pensive "tired as never years and days to death . . ." This line is immediately followed by a speaker, "I long from the black square to the white," who refers to the floors that resemble a chessboard. "I long from the red thread to the blue" is spoken by a second speaker. I suggest that it is the author's imaginary second self.

Let me refer to my initial introduction of these lines. I noted that the objectivity, traditional grammatical structure, and lack of colloquial language suggested a narrator, someone we might call an uninvolved perceiver. Now read this as the objective author whose thoughts appear in the next lines, "Silently, the morning light shrugs away the drug of sleep. Then he begins to play an intellectual game with himself.". . .

A review of the poem along the above lines is useful at this point. It is easier to follow the poem if it is thought of as divided into levels or planes as I first suggested. A personification of those levels, however, would put the poet describing and thinking on one level, the outer or objective, and the two imaginary opponents on the second or inner level. Dividing the poem this way may seem a dubious method, but it can provide a fruitful way of looking at the themes and methods employed in the poem. The poet-narrator opens the poem. He describes, then thinks to himself, but as he sees the floor, he imagines his chess game, imagines he can hear the two speakers.

The poet pensively returns to an objective scene, but he keeps demanding of its elements some coherence or cogency that, apart from the passage of time, they do not have. The grammatical and syntactical differences, as I have noted, support this interpretation. The third person emphasis of "That young man" down to "with the black-white checkered floors" contrasts with the more human first person passages that precede and follow it. The observations of the third person are either critical, "there is something wrong with his face," unresolved, "which exists only in connection with. . . ," or questioning, such as the hand and the chalk.

If the two voices are in fact part of a fictitious inner dialogue, we should expect some carryover between the objective world of the poet and the conversation. This connection may be seen in the bird that flies "With its flight" in the observed passage, yet is extinct, made of stone, in the dialogue passage. There are other obvious similarities such as the verb "come back" and the essential questioning in both passages of the relation between things: what does the hand "exist in connection with," and what is the relation between the archaeopteryx and the speakers?

After this initial transition into the world below the black and white floors, the dialectic of the conversation becomes clearer. The transition itself must be seen as establishing the concept of time as a predominant theme. It was obvious in the objective world of the narrator, "Hours pass," and it is in the dialogue with its themes of extinction and petrification.

This "time" theme has ramifications that can be extended from my opening discussion of the poem. I suggested that the title automatically inferred an above and a below and quite possibly the living and the dead. This assumption is not necessarily discredited by interpreting the poem as occurring within the poet's consciousness. As he begins playing chess within his thoughts, he allows the central concerns of his mind to develop the patterns of the game.

The narrator begins with "time" and "connection" but allows his image, the black-white checkered floors, to influence him. He imagines a dialogue among the dead and continues his concern with the relation between meaning and time. If a bird above the earth is the symbol of freedom, as implied in the objective stage of the poem, then it is possible a bird would be the same symbol to the dead. An extinct bird makes the contrast explicit.

Through the image of the bird we are led into the debate of the two speakers. Their central problem is their inability to move, a fact more painful to them because "the bird is free." It can fly. Speaker A says, "I myself am bound to the stone, the primal stone." Oddly enough, from the earlier chirping of the bird and the fact that it cannot sleep, it is difficult for us to determine whether the bird can actually fly or simply represents flight. The clearest point is that the speaker identifies with stone, but would rather identify with the bird. The reason for this preference becomes clear in the next section beginning with "Is there no forgetfulness in the house of the abyss?"

The value of my suggestion that the voices are opposing voices within the poet himself becomes clearer in reference to this passage. Dialogues about the absurdity of the world and the universe are hardly original to this century, but this century has certainly overworked them. If the poem is simply an imagined conversation of the dead about the absurdity of the universe, it lacks originality and is somewhat confusing. If, however, it can be read not only at the above level, but at the level of the individual and his conscious and unconscious conflicts, the meaning of the poem is greatly expanded. The possibility of a "collective unconscious" becomes a major addition through such an interpretation.

The reason this extension occurs is that the narrator, that is, the individual human, becomes a sphere containing voices, dead and alive, just as the earth is such a sphere, and possibly the universe. Discussion of this sphere is the basis of the dialogue between the two speakers. Most of this dialogue can be studied as occurring either within the narrator or, in a more abstract fashion, simply in the universe. The quality of the dialogue is reminiscent of what we find in absurd theater, yet it preceded *Waiting for Godot* (1952). Initially, A and B establish a surfaceless abyss in which lamps hold useless watch over stone. "This is hell! No, it is emptiness. And the house of the stars is empty. . ." represents a transition outward and away from the downward thrust of the previous part of the poem.

Previously, the bird was an ideal and the context of the poem was the earth or beneath. As the dialogue progresses, however, stone is retained but extended outward in a spiral of endless time. The emptiness of the universe is compared to stone, "For yearbillions of stone time swirls them with itself in raging storms of stone through seas of stone to heavens of stone." With these explicit lines the universe itself is envisioned as a petrified substance, an earth of rock rippling outward like circles in a pool. The effect of this image upon A is to put him to sleep, in a sense to hypnotize him into the spiral of stone. He is dazed and asks, "Where am I? Where are you?"

Speaker B wakes up A but their conversation immediately returns to the same subject, "the house of the abyss." Now, however, the imagery is centered upon scenes familiar to the average man. No longer is it beneath the earth nor in the sky, but almost at the level of the opening passage, a city building, where the two speakers discuss their world. The implied characters may have something to do with the opening characters. "And all these invalids who drift homeless around the rooms." The use of repetition and the apparent chaos of the scene combine qualities from the previous passages.

Light or its absence is once again crucial. "Is it night or day?" This night image is added to the city building and is seen flooding upward, again a motion reminiscent of the spiral. The passage openly poses the battle of light against dark.

> It throbs in the radiators like a strained heart.
> the lamps blink dead when they offer opposition
> and try to hold back the darkness.
> A white loneliness against a black loneliness.

The black and white lonelinesses refer to the floors and to the concept of a game or battle. The final lines of this section possibly represent the returning integration of the narrator's consciousness and the two players or voices he has imagined. The opening stage is once again present, but now only the man at the desk is there and we are told who he is: death.

The closing refrain concludes the cycle by beginning it again: the neutral passage of time, a sense of awakening, and from that awakening the admission or discovery of desire.

> Slowly the morning light pulverizes the drug of sleep.
> I long from the black square to the white.
> I long from the red thread to the blue.

My digression of tying the voices to the narrator and his vision of the black and white checks may be used now as an effective tool. The splitting of consciousness or, phrased in a different way, the process of listening to the voices within one's self, is not only a technical point but allows consideration of the themes of human consciousness and human existence in relation to time.

The narrator is listening to the voices of the past within himself. This means that just as time is a stonelike structure rippling eternally outward and enclosing layers of existence within it, so man too contains time within himself. The voices of the past argue inside of him. The substance of their argument concerns the meaning and quality of life. What is the relationship, if any, among things? Why is life chaotic and apparently homeless and futile? Is there any chance of escape by the flight of the bird, or by exchanging one location or one ideal for another?

The depth of these questions is strengthened by the technical quality of the device of the multiple self. As used in this poem, it is not unlike a Greek play with the narrator functioning as the probing and repeating Greek chorus. This repetition, association, and contrast may be studied to gain further insight into the poem. Ekelöf has stated some theories about poetry which are useful in looking at the structure of **"Voices."**

> Poetry to me is mysticism and music. Mysticism to me is not to nail together abstruse themes; it is the deep experience of life itself, the apprehension of the eternally elusive, shifting, returning in everything which is related to picture, tone, thought, feeling, and life.

"Voices" seems to correspond to this theory of a shifting and elusive poetry. The two voices are preoccupied in some metaphorical or allegorical way with the continually changing yet related images of life. Ekelöf's mention of music provides a basis for further analysis.

> Thus poetry is for me an art form which has much to do with music because it occurs both for the poet and the reader, with words as notes, with the relations of word contents, with the nuances one word gives the next and the following throws back on the previous, like tone color, or harmony. . . . It is a form which among other things works with repetitions, motive repetitions, and development, allusion to what has been or will come, parallelisms, likenesses, all of those devices in the power of which man seeks to "enjoy" existence. . .

There is an underlying theme in ["**Voices**"] of the need or the wish to provide one's own light. "The harsh stare" of external lamps may show us reality, but they provide no internal illumination. One cannot renounce life, but if one wishes to create, the dream must be preserved, even at the expense of external life. "A white loneliness against a black loneliness" applies to the dilemma of a poet of dreams. Ekelöf is such a poet and he fought the dilemma throughout much of his life.". . .

Irene Scobbie (essay date 1978)

SOURCE: "Swedish Poetry of the Twentieth Century," in *Essays on Swedish Literature from 1880 to the Present Day*, edited by Irene Scobbie, University of Aberdeen, 1978, pp. 125-72.

[*In the following excerpt, Scobbie traces the development of Ekelöf's poetic career, focusing on its complexity and allusiveness, and noting the poet's interest in mysticism, Asian culture, and music.*]

[Ekelöf's] first published collection of poetry, entitled *sent på jorden* (1932), was advertised as Sweden's first Surrealistic poetry. Reluctant as ever to be categorised, Ekelöf declined to accept the label "Surrealist"; nevertheless, in spite of his claim that 'jag arbetade aldrig surrealistiskt', the description seems accurate to most readers. Images are linked in striking but unexpected combinations and create a dream-like atmosphere reminiscent of paintings by Salvador Dali; it is as if the poet's subconscious were addressing the reader direct, missing out the normal, conventional logic of speech:

> *hjälp mig att söka min egen snäcka som försvunnit i*
> *oändlighetens hav och det stora obestämda som jag*
> *älskar blint som ett barn för hoppet om livets pärla*
> [. . .]
> *trädena klär av sig stjärnorna börjar falla*
> *det är sent på jorden*
>
> *("kosmisk sömngångare")*

Ekelöf indicated that *sent på jorden* was influenced greatly by Stravinsky he would play records of *The Rite of Spring* repeatedly while writing and called the collection 'en självmordsbok'. The final poem, **"apoteos"**, opens with the much-quoted line 'ge mig gift att dö eller drömmar att leva' and ends with a wish to dissolve into the absolute, the last line 'till intet' being followed by the symbol for infinity. The suicide reference seems to hark back to the Nirvana wish of Oriental mysticism, although there are also illustrations in the book of the Surrealistic trend of wishing to destroy violently all established conventions. One of the best examples is **"sonatform denaturerad prosa"** in which Ekelöf vents his desire to smash the conventions of language:

> *krossa bokstävlarna mellan tänderna gäspa vokaler,*
> *elden brinner i helvete kräkas och spotta nu eller aldrig*
> *jag och svindel du eller aldrig svindel nu eller aldrig*
> *vi börjar om*

As the title suggests, the poem is constructed in accordance with the rules of sonata form in music although individual "notes" are disjointed and linked polyphonically, even discordantly, rather than harmoniously; the rhythms also create a persistent, drumming effect which tends to benumb the senses and combines with the words to eradicate the distinction between "jag" and "han hon det".

Dedikation (1934) is prefaced by a quotation from the French Surrealist Rimbaud: 'Jag säger: man måste vara siare, man måste göra sig till siare'. The desire to annihilate reality in the previous book is now replaced by a positive hope for the future: 'En lång, regnig afton kände jag inom mig hur den nya människan längtade att födas' (**"Betraktelse"**). The links with Swedish Romanticism are affirmed in a series of elegies dedicated to and in the spirit of Stagnelius, and a favourite theme of Ekelöf's is frequently sounded, the continuing connection between past and present. *Dedikation* was followed two years later by *Sorgen och stjärnan,* in which the Romantic trends are even more pronounced (cf. **"Sommarnatten"**). Many of the poems are descriptions of nature in calm and controlled verse, the mood generally being wistful, even melancholic. The poet is isolated, lonely and contemplative.

Ekelöf continued with his "outsider" stance in the title poem of his next book, *Köp den blindes sång* (1938). The poet symbolically adopts the yellow and black armband worn on the Continent by blind persons, thus renouncing the political insignia of the activists preparing for the imminent World War II: "De seende, som svindlas / och svindlar och luras och litar, / må pryda sin arm med vita, / svarta och bruna bindlar. . . / Köp den blindes sång!" The trend towards simpler language and simpler poetic style is continued and there are several nature poems that could easily have appeared in the previous book. However, the theme of blindness and darkness running through *Köp den blindes sång* refers to the gloomy state of world events. 'Här är det mörkt och tomt / i framtidens land' he writes in **"Elegier I"**; but the opening of the final poem, **"Coda"**, indicates Ekelöf's faith in the future: 'Allt har sin tid, så även detta mörker'. He may not be sure about the nature of reality, but he can assert that 'den allena / som tjänar livets sak, skall överleva'.

Färjesång (1941) is a powerful book, full of animated argument culminating in what appears to be the attainment of a philosophical standpoint which satisfies the poet: 'allt som var outsägligt och fjärran är outsägligt och nära' (**"Eufori"**). A succession of paradoxes runs through the poems, a key motif being variations on the dialectic theme of thesis-antithesis-synthesis. Ekelöf's answer to the question 'what is reality, what is truth?' is the individualistic outsider's solution:

> Liv är kontrasternas möte,
> liv är ingendera parten.
> Liv är varken dag eller natt
> men gryning och skymning.
> Liv är varken ett ont eller ett gott,
> det är mälden mellan stenarna.
> Liv är inte drakens och riddarens kamp,
> det är jungfrun.

> (**"Tag och skriv"**-4)

It is also the solution of a poet steeped in Oriental mysticism: 'En människa är aldrig homogen: / Hon är sitt första och sitt andra, / på en gång! Inte i tur och ordning'.

Ekelöf considered *Färjesång* to be a break-through as far as his own attitudes and achievements were concerned, but his break-through with the reading public and critics came with his next work, *Non serviam* (1945). The title echoes Satan's refusal to serve and hence his expulsion from heaven, also the attitude of James Joyce's Stephen Dedalus (first referred to specifically in Chapter 3 of *Portrait of the Artist as a Young Man*); it is an affirmation of Ekelöf's individualistic, anarchistic stance. His impatience with the paternalistic, over-organised side of modern Swedish society is expressed in the title poem ('Jag är en främling i detta land / (. . .) / Här, i de långa, välfödda stundernas / trånga ombonade Sverige / där allting är stängt för drag". . . är det mig kallt'), and he demonstrates his cynicism at the expense of "Folkhemmet" in the satirical poem **"Till de folkhemske"**. The horrors of war are evocatively expressed in **"Jarrama"** and were also the starting point for the deeply disturbing poem **"Samothrake"**, a haunting vision concerning death and the meaning of human life. The finest poem in the book is probably **"Absentia animi"** in which Ekelöf continues the metaphysical and mystical meditations characteristic of his previous work. In his search for Abraxas (or Abrasax), an ancient name for the highest being, the poet delves into his own self to find something beyond time and space which is the essence of all existence which, in line with mystical tradition, he calls simply 'någonting annat':

> O långt långt bort
> i det som är bortom
> finns någonting nära!
> O djupt nere i mig
> i det som är nära
> finns någonting bortom
> någonting bortomnära
> i det som är hitomfjärran
> någonting varken eller
> i det som är antingen eller

The plays on words and rhythmical repetitions create a trance-like atmosphere, suggesting parallels with Indian music, until the words fall into an apparently meaningless jumble; and the poem ends by returning to its beginning, closing with the words 'om hösten'. Ekelöf took that line as the title of his next book, *Om hösten* (1951), which contains poems written over a number of years, including sketches of earlier poems and preliminary workings of themes to be treated again later. The collection begins and ends with poems about dreams called **"En verklighet (drömd)"** and **"En dröm (verklig)"** to stress the motif of contrasts and paradoxes that runs through the book. In **"Röster under jorden"** the poet investigates the nature of life and death, of individual existence and the passage of time, using as a key image the fossilised remains of prehistoric birds.

Strountes (1955) refers to an Almqvist quotation stressing the almost insuperable difficulty of writing whimsical trifles ('strunt'). The poems abound in wit, plays on words and cross-references to other literature: as the poet declares in **"När man kommit så långt"**: 'När man kommit så långt som jag i meningslösher / är vart ord åter intressant'. Frequently the playfulness is not as nonsensical as it seems, as is hinted in **"Ex Ponto"**: 'Det är inte konstverket man gör / Det är sig själv / Och man måste alltid börja från grunden / åter och åter börja från grunden'. *Opus incertum* (1957) and *En natt i Oto ac* (1961) are similar in kind to *Strountes* in the afterword to *En natt i Oto ac* Ekelöf commented: 'Jag skulle ha kunnat kalla denna bok *Opus incertum II* (eller rent av *Strountes* n:r 2) eftersom den tillhör samma antiestetiska, bitvis antipoetiska linje'. In "Poetik" he claims that formal perfection is:

> . . . sökandet efter ett meningslöst
> i det meningsfulla
> och omvänt
> och allt vad jag så konstfullt söker dikta
> är kontrastvis någonting konstlöst
> och hela fyllnaden tom.
> Vad jag jar skrivit
> är skrivet mellan raderna.

Oto ac is a town in Yugoslavia, but in the afterword referred to above Ekelöf indicated that it can be interpreted as Hell; in the paradoxical fashion typical of him, he seeks Heaven in Hell. What he has written is 'written between the lines': similarly the elusive *helheten* he is searching for may be found among disparate, chaotic things. He is too much of an anarchist ever to believe he will find it, but it is essential to conduct the search even so. 'De som lever för *en* stor sak är lyckliga', he writes in **"Poesi i sak"**, 'De som soker denna enda stora sak i ett otal saker / i mångfalden / han blir utnött och trött som jag'.

In 1960 Ekelöf had published a remarkable long poem on which he had been working for more than twenty years: *En Mölna-Elegi.* Several excerpts of the Elegy had been published previously, notably the first third of the finished poem in *BLM* in 1946: a note explained that it was 'en dikt om tidens och tidsupplevelsens relativitet, kanske också en art av "levnadsstämning"'. A figure is standing on Mölna jetty (a place on Lidingö near Stockholm) in late September or early October watching the sun set over the water. An apple and a drop of water fall to the ground and the lake respectively, and the poem refers to the noise they make: the sounds are heard both near the beginning and near the end of the poem, and it is stressed that they are the same sounds we hear; in other words, the whole work takes place in a very short space of time. By employing a complicated technique of allusion and quotation, however, Ekelöf is able to compress into that very short space of time the cultural experience of centuries.

Nevertheless, the starting point of the poem is personal. The figure on the jetty is Ekelöf himself, and the chain of memories which flash through his consciousness includes several of the poet's relatives and ancestors. A key quotation is a line from Edith Södergran, one of Ekelöf's favourite poets: 'Ett flyktigt ögonblick stal min framtid' (Södergran actually wrote 'ett nyckfullt ögonblick'), and many other quotations illustrate Ekelöf's preference James Joyce, for instance, Rimbaud, Swedenborg, Ibn el-Arabi, and a number of references to Bellman (Ekelöf was particularly fond of the eighteenth century). Most startling, however, is the middle section of the poem where the left-hand page is taken up by vulgar Latin and Greek quotations, most of them authentic graffiti from the walls of ancient Italy and many of them unashamedly obscence. The right-hand page is in Swedish and, broadly speaking, the verse echoes the spirit of the

Latin with a "dirty ditty" and descriptions of rape and abortion. Some authentic drawings, chosen by Ekelöf himself, illustrate the text, which is sometimes in dramatic form and has marginal comments, usually a key-word setting the tone of the section.

By stressing the parallels and connections, Ekelöf is trying to show the essential similarity of people and events at different periods of time as well as pursuing his mystical search for the unifying factor of life, the familiar theme from earlier works. The stress on sex in *En Mölna-Elegi* seems to be an acknowledgement of Freud's psychoanalytical theories and the poet's assessment of his own nature. Another motif is that of the four elements, earth, air, fire and water, especially the last two; many memories are triggered off by a section marked "Böljesång" which some critics see as a high-point of lyricism in Ekelöf's poetry:

> Vindsus och vågstänk
> Vågsus och vindstänk
> Vågor och dessa skiftande
> klockklangsviftande
> vindar närmare, fjärmare . . .

In the last section of the poem, after the sexual violence, the water-poetry is echoed in terms of fire before reverting back to water to signify the return of the poem to its starting point.

Generally speaking, critics were impressed by *En Mölna-Elegi* although there was a feeling of disappointment with the final section which, it was considered, did not measure up to the promise of the earlier parts. Moreover, it was felt that the Latin and Greek graffiti did not merge with the Swedish poem as easily and naturally as they might: they tend to be adornments rather than constituent parts of the poem as a whole. Understandably, there was complete agreement about the difficulty of interpreting the work: no doubt it will be many years before light is thrown on all its obscurities and the full extent of its treasures revealed.

In 1962 Ekelöf published a revised edition of *sent på jorden* in a volume which also contained *En natt på horisonten* (the latter collection having the explanatory parenthesis "1930-1932"). In both cases, the poet was returning to his beginnings, wrestling once more with the problems that had concerned him in the early 1930s and solving them with the wisdom acquired in thirty years of writing poetry. There were some alterations and additions, but many of the poems were left in their original and hence definitive state.

Having completed that circle, Ekelöf was ready to proceed to his last and what is generally considered to be his greatest work, a trilogy consisting of *Diwan över Fursten av Emgion* (1965), *Sagan om Fatumeh* (1966) and *Vägvisare till underjorden* (1967). Like all Ekelöf's works the *Diwan* trilogy is carefully composed as a whole. In his notes to *Vägvisare till underjorden,* the poet explains that although this part was published last, it was conceived as what he calls *mittvalvet* of the trilogy his choice of words stresses the architectural construction, and a drawing at the end of

Vägvisaren shows how that book itself was planned architecturally. The middle work is symmetrically balanced, and the first and third parts of the trilogy can be seen as counterbalancing each other: the basic components of the "outer" books are two series of 29 poems, and in connection with *Sagan om Fatumeh* Ekelöf explained that they correspond to a "nazm", a string of beads, and a "tesbih", a rosary. Ekelöf's preoccupation with Oriental mysticism is clear in the form as well as the content of his *Diwan* trilogy.

The material for each of the three books is based on authentic myths and historical happenings pertaining to the Byzantine Empire in the Middle Ages: *Diwan över Fursten av Emgión* refers to an eleventh-century epic romance describing the capture and sufferings of Digenís Acrítas, *Sagan om Fatumeh* tells the tale of an Arab girl in the fourteenth century who deteriorates from a position as a courtesan and the beloved of a prince to wretched existence as a whore, while *Vägvisare till underjorden* contains a less unified selection of thoughts and dreams and features a meeting between a Novice nun and Satan in a Byzantine palace situated in Yugoslavia. It will be obvious that to understand the trilogy properly, the average reader needs a battery of notes and explanations; Ekelöf provides some at the end of each volume, but in addition to the historical, mythological and linguistic complications there is also the fact that the poet refers to or quotes from a large number of other literary works indeed, he frequently quotes from his own earlier poems.

Nevertheless, one can read the *Diwan* trilogy in ignorance of many of the subtleties and be fascinated by the love poems, the sufferings and erotic adventures of Fatumeh (whose name incorporates the Latin word for Fate), the torture and religious search of the Prince. Familiar Ekelöf themes and symbols recur, notably the *jungfru* (cf. the quotation from **"Tag och skriv"** above), whose symbolic significance hovers between an erotic ideal, the Virgin Mary, a cosmic mother-figure and the mystical 'någonting annat' which formed the core of Ekelöf's creed. The other great theme is that of time which, as was shown by *En Mölna-Elegi,* the poet did not see as a mere linear process. The symmetrical form of the trilogy and the network of references to different epochs illustrate the concept; some of its implications are perhaps best expressed in the concluding poem of *Vägvisare till underjorden,* the last part of the trilogy to be written:

> *Ensam i tysta natten trivs jag bäst*
> *Ensam med vägguret, denna maskin för icke-tid*
> *Vad vet väl en metronom om musik, om takt*
> *om den är konstruerad att mäta. Dess ansikte*
> *är blankt och uttryckslöst som en främmande gudabilds*
> *Det gör mig medveten om relativiteternas oförenlighet*
> *Liv kan inte mätas med död, musik inte med taktslag*

Gunnar Ekelöf received many prizes and honorary awards in the last ten years of his life, and was elected a member of the Swedish Academy in 1958. He died in 1968 after a long and painful illness, suffering from cancer of the throat:

Partitur. Efterlämnade dikter (1969) contains some moving poems from this last period. Perhaps the most appropriate epitaph is a quotation from *Strountes*:

> *Mot helheten, ständigt mot helheten*
> *går min väg*
> *O mina kringkastade lemmar!*
> *Hur längtar ni inte till era fästen*
> *till helheten, till en annan helhet!*

Leif Sjöberg (essay date 1979)

SOURCE: "Gunnar Ekelöf's *A Mölna Elegy*: The Attempted Reconstruction of a Moment," in *Comparative Criticism: A Yearbook,* Vol. 1, 1979, pp. 199-214.

[*In the following excerpt, Sjöberg analyzes literary allusions modern as well as Classical in* The Mölna Elegy *and discusses the poem's predominant theme of time.*]

Muriel Rukeyser's translation marks the first English publication of Gunnar Ekelöf's *En Mölna-elegi* (Stockholm, 1960). Classified as 'work in progress' for more than twenty years prior to its publication, the *Elegy* demanded nearly a decade for the location and identification of its learned allusions and borrowings and nearly two decades for its publication in entirety in the English language.

Ekelöf's poem 'concerns itself with the relativity of time and time-experience, perhaps also with a kind of *Lebensstimmung*. It is not a description of a time lapse but (theoretically) is supposed to occur in one moment. In other words: it is a cross-section of time instead of a section lengthwise', wrote Ekelöf in a note in *BLM* in 1946. Later he warned against attempts to overemphasize the 'one moment'. He added:

> Time and time, What is it? It is supposed to occur not in a lapse of time but outside [of] time, in a mood of passivity and receptivity towards one's self, when everything and anything is possible and nearby. *The ideal psychoanalytical moment* [my italics]. What matter if the hand of your watch has moved one minute or ten from the point when you started summarizing (or memorizing) your situation, your dreams, etc.? It is a moment all the same.

> I sit on a bench of the past;
> I write on a page of the past.

(lines 1-2)

The place is the jetty at Mölna, consisting of a few strange-looking old buildings on the island of Lidingö, close to Stockholm, which, a couple of years earlier, had functioned as a summer camp for crippled children. (Ekelöf used to walk to Mölna in the early 1930s). 'Mölna is a symbol of something *cut off,* something posthumous', he commented, adding, 'but the past is alive in you'. The year is that of the beginning of World War II, presumably 1939-40, and the season is the autumn. It should be noticed that the 'I' is not set in a social context: on the contrary, it is relegated to itself, isolated independent and unattached. It functions as a passive, experiencing medium.

> There are many 'personalities' which live in that which I call me. The 'I' functions as a practical spokesperson, however, and each 'personality' must speak in turn. But what the spokesperson, the 'I', ought to say is not: I want it to be this way. He or she ought to summarize and make distinctly audible what is said in me so 'distinct' that even the obscure uncertainty experienced may remain mysterious, uncertain as it is, as long as it remains that way.

It is obvious from this that Ekelöf's central concern is the problem of *identity,* even in this initial scene. A problem Ekelöf touches on is thus the lack of constancy, on the one hand, and the abundance of change in reality, on the other, His view of identity is evident in one manuscript of *A Mölna Elegy*: 'Each person's contents of people and worlds. He who has experienced experiences and re-experiences; this is one, not one, but many in one. He calls himself I; *that* is merely a psychical-geographical attribute.'

While most people prefer not to discuss their sudden and abrupt shifts in identity, for fear that they may be considered unsteady or lacking in character as Strindberg points out Ekelöf more than once expressed the opinion that he himself (or humans in general) had the ability to change identity, that he virtually could *be* the person he was not. The transformations begin early in the *Elegy*:

> Windrush and wavespray
> waverush and windspray
> spray of the roller's blow
> cool upon cheeks and brow
> isolation and I:
> the selfsame or another
> I or not I?
> The future now the past
> time running wild
> years last for minutes
> with a tail of yellow leaves
> or time held
> stockstill in the elms'
> wetblack branches held
> Clotho cuts off the button. . .
> Proud city
>
>   (lines 62-77)

A Mölna Elegy has a subtitle, *Metamorphoses,* which links it to a certain kind of literature. It is the task of the reader to attempt to sense where and how the changes occur. Promptly, in the stanza following the one just quoted, the protagonist appears as the 'Old actor' who speaks of his 'appointment with the past'. He is waiting for his Victoria, thus suggesting Strindberg's Officer in *A Dream Play,* written in Stockholm in 1901.

> That was another season, when the legless sprang
> and the fingerless played their guitars till they rang. . .
>
>   (lines 8-9)

are lines from the 'absurd' ditty, perhaps suggesting the times of war as well as absurdity in general. The section ends with the structurally important line, 'A flying moment . . . ', which is re-intoned just before the '1809' episode and echoed in the 'Marche funèbre' section, and which was given *in extenso* in the opening scene:

> A flying moment robbed me of my future. . .

The proper interpretation of this central line (*Ett flyktigt / nyckfullt ögonblick*: a flying/flighty moment) is open to question. Suffice it to say that it is taken in slightly modified form from one of Ekelöf's favourites, the Finnish-Swedish poet, Edith Södergran (1892-1923). Her poem, 'Min framtid' ('My Future') reads as follows:

> A capricious moment
> stole from me my future,
> the casually constructed.
>
> I shall build it up much more handsomely
> as I had intended it from the beginning.
> I shall build it upon the firm ground
> that is called my will.
>
>   . . . . .
>
> I shall build it with a high tower
> called solitude.

It is worth pursuing the theme of time, if only for 'a moment'. *A Mölna Elegy* begins with the greeting *Ave viator!* ('Hail to thee, wanderer!') and, appropriately, it ends with *Vale viator!* ('Farewell, wanderer!'). Such inscriptions are traditional greetings to be found on gravestones along the Appian Way, the famous Roman highway from Rome to Greece and the East, built in 312 B.C. There is something symbolic in this: the 'wanderings' in *A Mölna Elegy* may originate in Ekelöf's beloved and hated Stockholm, and its surroundings, such as Mölna, and they end there, too, via a reference to the mystic, Emanuel Swedenborg, taken from *Drömboken* (*Journal of Dreams,* written in 1743-5 but not published until the middle of the nineteenth century):

> I left Oehlreick
> and there was deep water in the road. . .

There are numerous allusions to the past, especially to Ekelöf's favourite period and place, eighteenth-century Sweden, and references to the poet's own ancestors (the sections marked '1809', the year of revolution in Sweden, and '1786'); but the main 'action' in the *Elegy* is set in the Mediterranean area and some of it even in the East. The reader, in the person of a wanderer examining the *Ave!* and the *Vale!* is greeted by the dead, almost literally in the moment between putting one foot down and putting the other down. If the completion of the wanderer's step takes but a moment, it is in this compressed or extended moment that the *Elegy* is in imagination contained. This idea of a *frame* some kind of 'moment' was not merely a casual whim of the poet's, as is shown in 'The Return Journey' (at the beginning of the **Elegy**):

> The sun setting
> glows through fading
> greens . . . clucking of jetties
>
> (lines 44-6)

and towards the end just before the 'March funèbre' section:

> The sun in perpetual sunset
> Fire-clouds shifting flaunting
> Beyond reach burning images
> O holy clouds!
>
> (lines 605-8)

from which it is evident that, while Ekelöf's 'moment' passes, the sun proceeds to set.

When the 'Old actor' drops off that is, *in the very moment* he drops off to sleep for a while we hear a version of Shakespeare in reverse: the trees of Mölna speak about his ageing since last they saw him. A blind window at the gable of Mölna remembers him as Prospero, the magician, the genius loci, from *The Tempest*. A drop of water and an apple, falling, remind us of the 'momentary' aspect of 'time'. While the mill-gnome is from an old tale, the elf in the snowberry bush, representing one kind of woman, appears to be Ekelöf's invention. She wishes to prevail over him by degrading him, since she refers to him as 'the punk', literally 'the ugly one', thereby meaning Caliban. In mockingly humourous language, referring us to Joyce and Desnos, the Biedermeier sofa and the front gable clock comment on some kind of transgression, while the blind window contemplatively wonders: 'But how can Prospero be alive? And here?' The drop falling into the barrel indicates that the 'moment' is still going on. That is why it is emphasized (in line 174) that the 'same' apple thuds dully, bumps, lies dumb. The 'same' wind in the trees sighs, in a longing, romantic fashion: 'Away! Away!'

Then starts a round of recollections of the past in which the poet's ancestors appear: in the '1809' section, Anna Catharina Hedenberg (Madame Mont-Gentil), peripherally involved in a revolutionary episode in Sweden in the year 1809; and in the '1786' section, her brother (Gustaf Lewin), a naval officer who in that year experienced a cosmic occurrence near the equator, while on a slave trade mission.

> So I feel
> in the depth of my midriff these dead:
> The air I breathe is clogged with all the dead,
> the thirst I drink is mixed with all the dead
>
> (lines 262-5)

The recollection of these dead relatives, and their bad and good deeds in times gone by, can be seen as an effort at synthesis on the part of the poet: all things people, objects, concepts interact, and all of them have series of complex relations with their neighbours or surroundings. None of them can be fully understood until they have been placed in their proper context, i.e., in relation to their past.

If everyone and everything is dependent on everything else, the past lives of the dead are part of the present life of the poet and are relived by him. This idea was expressed in Ekelöf's **'A Dream (Real)'** (1951) and in his poem **'A World Is Everyone'** (1941). Like other poets, such as Yeats, Eliot, Robert Lowell, or James Wright, Ekelöf had a strong sense of family tradition, of what has been handed down and entrusted to the next generation. But the poet also rebels against tradition when it grows stale. The very fact that his *persona* is a complete outsider in *A Mölna Elegy* can be seen as an act of rebellion.

From an experience of being near death when as a child he is in bed with fever, in acute pain and distressed for want of breath, an episode which exemplifies two aspects of psychological 'time': 'in one moment / of intolerable speed and in the next unendurably slow' (lines 276-7), there is a neat transition to pleasant memories of country excursions and 'rewards' for diligent learning at school.

> And then I remember the hours clocked, the long
>   hours clocked,
> the ticked minutes, minute minutes tocked,
> slowly lockstepping, slowly
> shoulder-borne
> I remember the seconds, the dropped moments
> or the held, riveted ones. I remember
> Time,
> I carry it in me
> I bear it in me like a rock, a child of stone,
> complete and unborn
>
> (lines 311-20)

Moments that have dropped out of memory because of some repressive mechanism, but also those almost intolerable moments, 'the riveted ones', obsessive thoughts that recur incessantly all is remembered, but by whom? By the one who carries time, literally, like a stone-child, 'like a rock, a child of stone, / complete and unborn'. The concept 'stone-child' is a clinical reality, although rare. *Lithopedion* is a dead fetus that has become petrified. In a note to Muriel Rukeyser on 'stone-child', Ekelöf stated: 'Taken out of an Elzevier *De renum et vesicae* in my father's bookcase.'

If it is not too far-fetched to look for a mythological carrier of the 'stone-child', perhaps Chronos himself, or more correctly, Cronus, would fit. Cronus is 'primarily a harvest-god' and just before the quoted passage, 'harvest-times' appears. Cronus, being afraid of an oracle's prediction that his sceptre would be struck out of his hand by his own offspring, swallowed his children, until Rhea outwitted him and gave him a 'black stone wrapped in swaddling clothes, and he swallowed the stone', after which Poseidon was born. Marianne Moore refers to this at the end of 'Four Quartz Crystal Clocks':

> hearing Jupiter or jour pater, the day god
>   the salvaged son of Father Time
> telling the cannibal Chronos
>   (eater of his proxime
> newborn progeny) that punctuality
>   is not a crime.

Whatever the correct interpretation is, it is striking that the Mediterranean material, especially the use of myth, increases from now on, i.e., in the latter part of the *Elegy,* which is introduced by a graffito from Pompeii, actually from the coition chamber of the Villa dei Misteri. The text is very difficult to decipher, but a scholar claims she has identified five or six words, 'sufficient for her to divine the character of the text', Ekelöf noted, and thus the graffito has more than a decorative, or even 'timely' purpose.

Almost all these Latin inscriptions are documented in Diehl's anthology of inscriptions, *Pompeianische Wandinschriften* (1910). Readers with no more than school Latin are likely to find it strenuous work to decipher the vulgar wall inscriptions that Ekelöf perhaps as an antidote to the many 'respectable' quotations and references found worthy of inclusion in his *Elegy* (all on the left-hand pages). What is the general content of these mscriptions from Pompeii? Some are friendly or hostile greetings, others deal with business matters, but by far the greatest number are concerned with love or lovemaking of one kind or another. The incantation beginning with 'Atracatetracatigallara', allegedly spoken by the witch, the Saga, actually consists of three authentic *defixiones,* nailings, which Jan Stolpe located in Audollent's *Defixionum tabellae* (1904). We can easily recognize the phrase in the second nailing:

dii iferi
vobis comedo
si quicqua sanctitates habetes

(You gods of the underworld!
I commend you,
if you have something holy.)

This *defixio* is from Latium. The third *defixio* is from Nomentum, north of Rome: 'On this leaden tablet I rivet Malchio, Nico's son's eyes, hands, fingers, arms, nails, hair, head, feet, thighs, stomach, buttocks, navel, chest, nipples, neck, mouth, cheeks, teeth, lips, chin, eyes, forehead, eyebrows, shoulderblades, shoulders, muscles, bones, marrow, stomach, phallus, shins, his proceeds [?] and profit.' The *defixio* continues: 'Rufa, Pulica's daughter, her hands, teeth, eyes, arms, stomach, breasts, chest, bones, marrow, stomach, shins, legs, feet, forehead, nails, fingers, stomach, navel, womb, vulva, abdomen, Rufa, Pulica's daughter, I rivet on this tablet.' Finally the magical incantation from the beginning is repeated.

The *Carmen faeculare,* 'Excrement song', alludes to Horace's *Carmen saeculare.* Ekelöf has arranged the graffiti into an alternating song, 'a dramatically composed dialogue between [heterosexual] boys, girls, and homosexual adults, as well as the old industrious couple Philemon and Baucis'. Ekelöf has occasionally made small changes. A case in point is Baucis ('recocta vino / trementibus labellis'), which is to be found in Petronius's *Fragmenta 21 v.* What Baucis (old wino, lips shaking) says is, roughly, 'An experienced woman is better than a girl who has not yet got any pubic hair.' Among all those 'Voces repercussae' (Reverberating voices), Ekelöf has again included a refrain: *'Mádeia perimádeia'* ('Well done, by Zeus, Oh

yea by Zeus!'). In the final greetings by the boys, which is a counterpart of their initial greeting to Victoria, Ekelöf has changed the authentic name, Noëte, to Sabina. The section ends, as it began, with the part of Saga, a *defixio,* only now the Latin text is written in the Greek alphabet.

Why did Ekelöf employ these Pompeian graffiti in his *Elegy*? Whatever the answer may be, the voices of the past were important to him in various ways. He may often have wanted to listen to the voices 'down below' more than to the loud voices of his own time, in which he did not feel at home. The informal tone, the spontaneous quality in these scribblings, appealed to him. What then, was his motive in including a large number of grave-inscriptions in the remaining Latin part of the *Elegy*?

These grave-inscriptions originate in different social groups and different provinces of the Roman Empire. It is obvious from Ekelöf's manuscripts that his inclusion of this vast number of quotations was not a whim: he copied or studied about two thousand grave-inscriptions and then selected some to fit together as he wanted them to appear in his *Elegy.* The 'parts' have been added by Ekelöf: 'Conservi, Conservae / Pueri, Puellae et Infantes' (Slaves, bondwomen, boys, girls and children), who all cry:

Tene me ne fugia
Tene me ne fugia

Hold me or I shall escape
Hold me or I shall escape

Ekelöf was fascinated by the strong pessimism expressed in lines like:

Nunc mors perpetua(m)
libertatem dedit

Now death
gave eternal freedom

In Latin, this statement is as eloquent as if it had been composed by a Lucretius, Ekelöf said. All those formulaic 'Dis Manibus. Hic iaceo', to the good gods, 'the gods under the world' as Muriel Rukeyser translated with their mention of the year, month, day, even hour of the departed one's life all this seems to have touched the poet, in its naivety. He empathized with the simple ancient people who considered death a prelude to a happier life, a *dies natalis,* a kind of birthday to a new existence. Ekelöf's concern with death is as intense as is his concern with life. If his assimilated quotations, in general, are anything to go by, he relied much more heavily on sayings of the dead than those of the living. One can perhaps infer that he had more use for their 'voices' than for living voices. The 'outsider' Ekelöf, the individualist, more often than not sought his support among the 'greater majority' (to quote Petronius) than among the living.

The section ends with a reminder:

Vos superi
bene facite

diu vivite
et venite!

which Ekelöf read as:

You who live on earth
after me
do good deeds
and live a long life
and come
i.e., down to us dead.

It is a rare occasion indeed when he employs such a blatantly moral statement as that! On the next left page, he placed his own drawing of a strange-looking creature nailed upside-down to the saltire. It is hard to determine whether he is alluding to Spartacus or Peter.

The Latin part is concluded by another *defixio* which is from Carthage. It consists of the riveting of race horses in *quadrigas,* teams of four horses each. The original, as Stolpe observed, has a picture of a circus with the *meta,* the conical column with signal flags serving as a turning post at each end of the Roman Circus; four horses circle the *meta* clockwise. As we can see, the names have been selected in such a way that they suggest the four elements. To some extent they correspond to the four elements in the Brinvilliers section on the facing page of the *Elegy.* By employing the *quadriga* Ekelöf introduced a new aspect of time into his poem, and by building the theme of the *quadriga* into four, he added great complexity by simple graphic design.

Clearly, Ekelöf did not support the Romantic view of Pompeii, as embodied in Shelley's *Arria Marcellina,* Madame de Staël's *Corinne,* or Bulwer Lytton's *The Last Days of Pompeii;* nor does he reflect Wilhelm Jensen's *Gradiva* in the presentation of snapshots from Pompeii. The destruction (metamorphosis) of the city and its people can be seen as a parallel to the permanent petrifaction that Archaeopteryx met in its flight.

Parallel to the Latin runs the English. The call of . . . (Méga Aléxandre) and . . . (State ra mo), makes it clear that the transformations have led to Alexander the Great, with a suggestive mirror-motif. The 'sexy ditty' and the 'violation and abortion scene' (with minor characters from the eighteenth-century Swedish poet, Carl Michael Bellman's world) are linked together by a picture of an olive press from Pompeii. The marginal note, 'A fourth a fifth!' repeats frequent musical concepts or terms in the *Elegy.* It indicates, roughly, where the most hermetic part of the *Elegy* begins.

Never step
upon a crack
or you'll break
your mother's back

(lines 441-4)

are taboo-like admonitions, perhaps obsessions of a child. They are followed by a playful promise of

tales
broad as doorways
long as flails

(lines 445-7)

the ensuing fulfilment of which is provided by seven summarized memorable dreams that the Swedish scientist, philosopher, and theologian Emanuel Swedenborg (1688-1772) took down for his *Dream Journal.* 'The naturalist suddenly realizes the irrational in his own intellectual life', commented Ekelöf. 'Dreams like ringing from the deeps' (line 461) suggests common European folk tales in the ringing of bells, or bells that have sunk into the sea. Bells ringing from the deeps corresponds to the earlier ringing of bells from heights, i.e., from belfries. 'Oarfish inland-driven' (line 638) is a deep-sea fish, presumably symbolizing deeply hidden forces in the personality. 'Sea-creatures that gape over the ships' (line 468) are to be seen in maps and drawings, such as in *Carta Marina* by Olaus Magnus (1555). The scene then moves from Nordic waters to the Mediterranean, to Southern shores, where 'Lestrygonians' introduce the well-known myth in the *Odyssey.* It reminds us of the monster Cyclops whose father was Poseidon, who makes an appearance in the *Elegy* and the Lestrygonians, the gigantic cannibals (Book x) whose king feasted on one of the three men Odysseus had sent inland. While the two men fled, the Lestrygonians destroyed all ships except the one on which Odysseus sailed. Ekelöf's reference is primarily neither to Book x of the *Odyssey* nor to chapter 8 of Joyce's *Ulysses;* he alludes to 'the famous antique fresco fragments in the Vatican'. There are eight scenes in this unique fresco of the episode. Alinari's superb photograph no. 38029, *Distruzione della flotta di Ulisse,* is the best reproduction, but occasional reproductions of separate parts of the fresco can be found in, for example, B. Nogara's *Art Treasures of the Vatican.* The reader should be able to perceive echoes of Homer's wallowing waves and sense something of the dangers and excitement of seafaring life.

pigs that cry and try to speak:
'Have we not conquered?'

(lines 474-5)

suggests the sailing to the island of Aeaea, where Circe tapped half of Odysseus's crew with her magic wand, transforming them into talking swine. There follows the visit to Hades, the cremation of Elpenor, and a necessary sacrifice to Poseidon before 'The Man of Grief' (Odysseus) can return home.

If, indeed, in the previous lines, the question was whether to 'eat or be eaten', as Bloom speculates, in the next, it is not giants eating men, but *lithophages,* 'stone-eaters', eating away at a god Poseidon making if not 'holes and swellings' at least 'holes' in his limbs. As a result of a shipwreck at sea, the statute of Poseidon was seen by the eyes of fish rather than humans until finally it was recovered from the Bay of Baia (the 'old china' just before the '1809' episode was recovered from a shipwreck in the harbor of Gothenburg, incidentally). It can now be seen at Pozzuoli (Puteoli). This drowned god has thus been created and salvaged by humans and brought not to a temple but to a museum where he can be looked at. In a sense this is creation in reverse. Even if the god somewhat resembles almighty Zeus, Amedeo Maiuri is fully convinced that it is a Poseidon-Neptune statue:

> Lithophages in the deeps:
> Holes and swellings on the limbs of the god
>
> (lines 476-7)

'The coral red tree of aerated blood' suggests that the pattern of the circulation of blood in anatomy might remind us of a silhouetted image of a tree with branches and roots, or perhaps of corals, the trees of the sea. The pyre on the beach could be an allusion to 'Shelley's funeral pyre', of which Trelawny wrote several accounts.

'Quick! Have you other lives?' (line 486) is a line that, in Ekelöf's own translation of Rimbaud's 'Mauvais sang', had been taken from *Une saison en enfer* ('Vite! est-il d'autres vies'?). 'Can we reach across the sea to another reality via dream?' suggested A. Losman. Others might want to interpret the line as a question of whether or not there is an after-life.

The voice crying from the tree's bark is that of the Dryad, the tree-nymph, who lost her life when the tree in which she lived was being cut down. Eurydice, the wife of Orpheus the poet, was the most renowned of the dryads; with his lyre he visited the underworld and nearly recovered her, a queen of the dead. The kid sucking the breast of a *panisca,* an inferior woodland deity representing Pan, can be seen in the Villa dei Misteri in Pompeii.

'The unicorn seeking refuge' (line 491) alludes above all to the first of the famous 'La dame à licorne' tapestries in the Musée de Cluny, Paris, and also to the equally famous Unicorn Tapestries in the Cloisters, New York City. The unicorn, according to legend, was the shyest of all animals and could be captured only by an innocent maid. If and when it encountered such a virgin, it would go to her of its own accord and piously settle itself on her lap, as it does in this poem.

The line 'O purity, purity!' (line 493) has a double meaning in Swedish where *'O'* can stand both for the exclamation 'O!' and a negating prefix 'im-', making it refer to 'impurity' as well as to the principle meaning, 'purity'. The line is another echo from *Une saison en enfer,* in which the last line of the poem 'L'Impossible' reads 'O pureté! pureté! The virgin motif has been explored extensively in Ekelöf's poetry.

The 'Fire Song' is partly a description and interpretation of the 'Garden of Delights' triptych (Prado, Madrid) by Hieronymus Bosch:

> Flames and these dancing
> fire-mills shifting
> obscure signals
> significant glances
>
> (lines 496-9)

which are to be seen on the upper part of the right panel.

> Devils that fly on ladders
> high above the onlookers
>
> (lines 510-11)

These lines also refers to Bosch. When the hellish visions recede, the concern of the 'I'-persona is with the ceremonies after his death. A connection is established with the funeral pyre (earlier) and the infernal fire by the afterthought:

> No, just be burnt to ashes.
>
> (line 541)

The quotation that follows reiterates the cremation theme:

> Enfin c'en est fait,
> La Brinvilliers est en l'air
> de sorte que nous la respirerons!
>
> (lines 551-3)

is from Mme de Sévigné's letter of 17 July 1676, and refers to an episode typical of the widespread belief in witchcraft and epidemic of poisonings prevalent in Europe and New England in the latter half of the seventeenth century. In the next scene, with the Greek Gorgon, water is again the chief element. When Perseus had composed himself, and had, with the help of gods (Hermes and Athena), fulfilled his pledge, the presentation of the Gorgon Medusa's head, he had mastered her petrifying stare and thus overcome death and at the same time become an overlord of death. Many strands are woven together in this central poem of the Gorgon: as an octopus and a sea monster; the Gorgon as Alexander's cursed sister; the Gorgon as a form of the Great Goddess 'in her aspect as goddess of death' and the octopus as a human, because it carries on a philosophical monologue!

The 'Eleo sa' in the Gorgon section is the Mother of God, depicted on a variety of Greek and Russian icons, in which the position of the child God differs considerably, but generally shown as the merciful one, i.e., the Eleo sa, with her head lovingly titled towards that of the child God. The entire scene is again a double exposure; 'reeds hardly grow by the Mediterranean shores, but rather at Mölna', thus establishes a return to the opening of the *Elegy* in 'The return journey': 'The reeds bowing'. . .

In spite of the fact that *A Mölna Elegy* was partially written during the World War II, there are only a few references to the war, one of them being,

> all of us floating here
> floating along
> O these carcasses that float
> that head into the reeds
> but rock uncertainly outside.
>
> (lines 582-6)

Another is found in 'Marche funèbre':

> A flighty moment
> and now the devil is in the belfry

he who robbed us of our future

(lines 617-19)

Here 'the devil' stands for Hitler, according to the manuscripts. It is a slightly revised line from Rimbaud's 'Nuit de l'enfer' in *Une saison en enfer.* If the citation of Chopin's Funeral March suggests the banality of *sorrow,* the reference to Hitler can possibly hint at the banality of *violence* and its impermanence. The red fever-ball a childhood experience corresponds to the slightly revised line from Desnos's 'Définition de la Poésie pour' (*sic!*), attributed to Max Ernst: 'la boule rouge qui bouge et roule', which is to be found in Rrose Sélavy (1922-3) in *Corps et Biens* (no. 125). 'O saisons, ô châteaux!' is from Rimbaud's *Une saison en enfer* and deals with happiness. Ekelöf had translated the poem in his volume of French poetry, *From Baudelaire to Surrealism* (1934).

'Leavetaking', which is less than the coda to be expected, re-introduces the 'same apple', thus reminding us of the continuing moment, while 'the front gable clock' speaks a line from *Finnegans Wake.* The preceding line of that book, 'Gunnar's gustspells', apostrophizes the poet's own name and includes several references to theater (Schouwburg; Uplouderamain; Curtain drops), which may give us the associations to the 'Old Actor' (from the beginning of the *Elegy*).

One can read about 'ragas and raginis' in A. H. Fox-Strangways' *The Music of Hindustan,* a book which had accompanied Ekelöf since his youth. These melodies are personified as fairies, mostly female, in Mogul miniatures, samples of which are to be found in the British Museum, where Ekelöf first saw them. 'A genius' introduces himself now as le Roquefort, now as le Brie, which are both, as Göran Printz-Påhlson has noted, to be found in Rimbaud's poem 'Rêve', from about 1874. The jocular genius in the *Elegy* (and in 'Rêve') constantly seems to change identity and therefore fits the theme of metamorphoses. The genius may have a counterpart in one of the many spirits who earlier filed past in the *Elegy.* 'The disabled emanations (dancing)' parallel the lame elves' dance before the 'Park Scene'.

Ibn el-Arabi was one of Ekelöf's favorite authors, who speaks a single word in the *Elegy:* 'Labbayka!' which means 'At thy service!' This word is part of the Mohammedan pilgrimage rituals, the essential sign of the consecrated state. The Thrush a symbol for the poet himself now silent with an upthrust beak, has found a place on the family heraldic armorial. The silent heraldic thrush could have served as a dignified emblem to end the *Elegy,* but in his remarkable mosaic of quotations, allusions, and reminiscences, Ekelöf apparently wanted to apostrophize Edith Södergran and Emanuel Swedenborg. We are fortunate enough to have Ekelöf's comments on these two quotations. He intimated that the mother (in the Södergran poem) soothes the child while they are waiting at the station. War is raging and along the roadbed are dead soldiers. The situation is not as yet dangerous, but it is precarious.

The Swedenborg quotation is the last one in the *Elegy.* Here a mystic concerned with dreams had the final say.

The word 'water' is mentioned twice and suggests other analogies and parallels in the *Elegy,* indeed, it begins with a water image and it ends with water. In the rhymed final lines, *time* is again the central theme. On the very last page of the *Elegy* the reader is saluted: *Vale viator!,* just as he was greeted with *Ave viator!* at the beginning of the long 'moment'. In a note Ekelöf wrote: 'a moment becomes timeless when the itinerant wanderer passes the gravestone and sees its *Vale!* and *Ave!* or the reverse . . . Such a fugue should be read both ways, [but] I have not reached as far as that in perseverance.' Below the salutation *vale viator!* is a picture of Archaeopteryx, the primitive bird whose fossil remains were discovered in the nineteenth century, in Bavaria.

It seems clear, then, that there are several kinds of unity in this complex poem. At one level, there is a unity akin to that of Strindberg's *A Dream Play:* there is an auditive focus, a 'dreamer', who is the centre of all the metamorphoses. The theme of 'Time' as transformation links all the sections, and, in a brilliant and original way, the notion of the moment as a simultaneity of transformations provides a solution to the problem explored by T. S. Eliot of striking a line for our own times through the past while maintaining and displaying the belief that 'the whole of the literature of Europe . . . composes a simultaneous order'.

Sven Birkerts (review date 1984)

SOURCE: "A Cull of Trance-Roamers," in *Parnassus: Poetry in Review,* Vol. 11, No. 2, Fall/Winter, 1984, pp. 192-212.

[*In the following excerpt, Birkerts reviews* Songs of Something Else: Selected Poems, *and analyzes three poetic styles—surreal, mystical but conflicted, and lyrically spiritual—represented in Ekelöf's work.*]

"Poetry is something which is only done by the whole man."

Gunnar Ekelöf

Gunnar Ekelöf came to poetry by a circuitous route. He first studied music in Paris, and when he abandoned that, it was to move to London to pursue Oriental Studies. It was not until illness forced him to drop his plan of travelling to Asia that he finally turned to poetry. He did not relinquish either interest and the poetry of his later years has often been characterized as a kind of Eastern music but many years had to pass before such a synthesis could be effected. First there came a surrealist phase, and then, for decades, lyrical and metaphysical impulses merged to shape a unique and constantly changing idiom. This "middle phase" forms the bulk of Ekelöf's production and is crucial to any tracing of his full trajectory. Leonard Nathan and James Larson have made a judicious selection and a careful translation of poems from these decades (1938-1959). In *Songs of Something Else* we now have for the first time a full sense of Ekelöf's poetic dynamic. After reading this volume sequentially we are better prepared to follow his ultimate mystical undertaking, the Byzantine triptych comprising the ***Diwan over the Prince of Emigon, The Tale of Fatumeh,*** and ***Guide to the Underworld.*** No previous selection has managed to impose perspective upon the spiritual growing pains of this most volatile poet.

Ekelöf's first collection, ***Late Arrival on Earth*** which he referred to as his "suicide book," was published in Sweden in 1932. That mordant epithet may allude to some felt impulse; it may on the other hand signal a belief that one has to die to all competing aspirations in order to be reborn as a poet. Ekelöf never treated his calling as anything but sacred.

Late Arrival on Earth reflected the strong influence of the French Surrealists, even though Ekelöf repudiated the undisciplined working methods of Breton and his followers. But a more profound influence was Rimbaud, whom he translated, and in whom he found the appealing vision of poet as scientist:

> The poet makes himself a *seer* by a long, gigantic and rational *derangement* of *all the senses.* All forms of love, suffering, and madness. He searches himself. He exhausts all poisons in himself and keeps only their quintessences . . . he becomes among all men the great patient, the great criminal, the one accursed and the supreme Scholar!

> (Rimbaud letter to Paul Demeny, 1871, tr. Wallace Fowlie)

And, truly, Ekelöf's early poetry was a strenuous Rimbaldian assault upon poetic respectability, its tendencies both gnomic:

> Hair and fingernails grow slowly into the silence
> The door's lips are closed to reversed values

>   (from **"At Night,"** tr. Robert Bly)

and frenzied:

> crush the alphabet between your teeth yawn vowels
> the fire is burning in hell vomit and spit now or
> never I and dizziness you or dizziness now or
>   never.

(from **"Sonata for Methylated Prose,"** tr. Robert Bly)

Late Arrival on Earth may have been shocking in its day, and it did bring the stream of surrealism northward, but one could not really say that Ekelöf had found his voice. These lines have little in common with the unique, haunted sonorities of the later lyrics. I would speculate that the transition from early to middle phase was prompted by Ekelöf's discovery of his own unique vocal instrument. Most likely there were transitional poems for few poets step unerringly into mature style but these are not represented in *Songs of Something Else.* Here, right from the start, we hear the clear, unconcealed speech of a man.

In their Introduction, Nathan and Leonard discuss the phenomenon of Ekelöf's voice:

> As our familiarity with and affinity for the poet grew, Ekelöf's poetic voice came to seem to us the most important formal element in these poems. This voice is impossible to describe in general terms inward, remote, reflective, formal, severe, yet somehow colloquial but we became convinced that if we could convey something of the quality of this voice in English, our problems would be solved.

It is a measure of their success that, for all the diversity and tonal variation of these lyrics, a clear print of identity is struck on the page. To speak of a "voice" in this way is not just to speak of sound or characteristic diction, either. Voice, in this higher sense, is realized inner speech; it is the all-but-intangible quality that marks off greatness from high competence in a writer. For there is no voice without the daring of self-exposure. In Ekelöf this self-exposure is critically linked to a vision of self-transformation: he was, by his own avowal, a mystic in pursuit of enlightenment. Poetry was for him the agency of soul-making.

The spiritual aspiration was present from the start the early study of Oriental religions was already purposeful. And the subsequent transformations comprise a continual movement toward the "something else" that he apostrophizes in his poems. The mystic, by definition, cannot believe in the sufficiency of the material world. He believes in the soul and the possibility of its communion with a universal force. For some mystics that force manifests itself as a pervasive moral order, a *logos* deriving directly from a deity. For others and Ekelöf was of this stamp it is sheer being, a potency pervading all, a *tao* (though he never names it as such) bearing no moral imperative, requiring only submission. Ekelöf's poetry, from the middle period on, is a path toward submission. The convolutions of that path indicate just how much of a struggle with contrary tendencies was involved.

In **"Elegy,"** the very first poem in this collection from the section dated 1938 Ekelöf writes:

> And fall will return again
> however much of spring there was!
> What does it matter to life
> that someone calls himself "I"
> and pleads for his wishes!
> What does it matter to earth
> which slowly turns itself around
> from season to season
> that someone struggles against its turning!
>
> We humans lack patience,
> we have no time to wait,
> but darkness is all around us
> and darkness has ample time:
> Suns and stars are wheels
> that move the eternal clock
> —slowly, infinitely slowly
> everything is altered
> to eternally the same.

Both Eastern and Western mysticism call for the over-throw of the "I" it is illusion, obstacle, sin, maya. Here, though Ekelöf is declaring the frailness and inconsequentiality of the "I," he opposes nothing to it but infinite magnitude and endless time. No sense of higher animate being is given. Implacable, mechanistic law is implicit, but the "I" has no connection to it. It "pleads" and "struggles," while the earth, active but indifferent, "slowly turns itself around." What tension there is in the poem derives from the simple contrast between the finite and the infinite orders. We find simplicity, plainness of utterance, and, in spite of the exclamation points, calm the calm of the stoic's sidereal perspective. But a familiarity with Ekelöf's later torments suggests that it is an unearned, mentally-grounded calm. The Ekelöf who speaks here, or in the lovely short poem **"Coda,"** also from this period, has not yet passed through the purging fire. The grip of intellect has not yet been shattered.

> Everything has its time, even this darkness
> and these catacombs finally
> life needs those who want a meaning.
>
> What would the weave of events be without
> the red thread, the thread of Ariadne,
> vanished now and then but always woven in!
>
> And even now in these deadly times,
> something still holds fast: that he alone
> who serves life shall survive.
>
> **("Coda")**

There is a striking difference between these two poems. Life, in **"Elegy,"** is rendered as utterly neutral ("What does it matter to life / that someone calls himself 'I'"). In **"Coda"** Ekelöf establishes some ground of interdependence ("finally / life needs those who want a meaning"). A slight red thread makes all the difference; the scale is completely different. The closing lines discover a wisdom entirely free of moral suggestion.

The well-known Zen parable relates that before initiation mountains are mountains, that during initiation mountains are no longer mountains, that initiation is past when mountains are once again mountains. Ekelöf's development embodies something of this movement. From the relative serenity of these early poems, he moves into a phase of disruptive intensity: the straight way has been lost. And the change in style is immediately obvious. We find a dialectical velocity, the goal of which, it seems, is to uproot the dialectical process, to destroy all categories of thought, to get rid of the *ratio*.

> You say "I" and "it concerns me"
> but it concerns a what:
> in reality you are no one.
> Reality is so without I, naked and shapeless!
>
> (from **"Write It Down"**)

Lines like these, though they recall those of **"Elegy,"** already carry an acceleration of breath, a greater urgency. And this soon intensifies:

> What is it I want? What is it I mean?
> I know what it is and I don't know what it is!
> It has no name, no place, no kind
> I can't call it, I can't explain it
> It is what gets a name when I call
> It is what gets a meaning when I explain
> It is this but before I have yet called
> It is this but before I have yet explained
> It is this which still has no name
> What has got a name is not something else
>
> (from **"The Gymnosophist"**)

Or:

> O deep down in me
> from the surface of the eye of black pearl
> is reflected in happy half-awareness
> a picture of a cloud!
> It is not this that is
> It is something else
> It exists in what is
> but is not this that is
> It is something else
> O far far away
> in what is distant
> there is something close!
>
> (from **"Absentia animi"**)

In these poems Ekelöf is hunting the paradox; he negates his negations, tries to point by way of a stream of cancellations at that "something else" that cannot be named, but that exists, essential, in spite of every mental operation. From a philosophical perspective it appears that he is trying to break through from the phenomenal to the noumenal reality which, according to Kant, is impossible. The problem is, of course, the "I," that net of deceptions. Ekelöf tries to repudiate the "I" in **"Write It Down,"** but he cannot. At best he can frame its indeterminate status. As we see in **"The Gymnosophist,"** he requires an "I" as a provisional pivot. Without it, he cannot hurl himself at the surrounding flux. These epistemological assaults are not, perhaps, the most successful poems in the Ekelöf canon their single-mindedness limits them but they demonstrate an energy and commitment that are not to be denied. Ekelöf, so obviously not interested in being innovative or "different," is forcing his poetry to accommodate and act upon a crisis of the soul.

This period of struggle roughly the decade between 1941 and 1951 also brings forth a sequence of sarcastic, mocking poems that logically accompany the involuted interrogations, and they signal that Ekelöf is by no means unaware of the larger social panorama. He certainly knows what an absurd figure the tormented poet cuts in the public eye. The poem **"Interview"** makes clever play with this and is a good example of his cutting style. Ekelöf makes a strong case for the immediate expulsion of the poet from the Republic:

> What do you think your task is in life?
> I am an utterly useless person.
> What is your political creed?

The old order is O.K. Opposition
to the old order is O.K. You could also
imagine a third but what?
Your view of religion, if you have one?
The same as my view of music: That only
the truly unmusical can be musical.
What do you look for in people? My relations
sorry to say have little or no steadiness.
What do you look for in books? Philosophical
    depth?
Breadth or height? Epic? Lyric?
I'm seeking the perfect sphere.
What's the most beautiful thing you know?
Birds in cemetaries, butterflies on a battlefield,
somewhere in between. I don't know.
Your favorite hobby? I have no hobbies.
Your favorite little vice? Masturbating.
And finally (as briefly as possible):
Why do you write?
For want of anything better to do. *Vade retro.*
Being witty, eh?
Yes! I'm being witty.

                                        (**"Interview"**)

If the tensions of the poet's struggle are manifest in the poems of this period, the process of inner reconciliation remains opaque. We feel a change as we read through the last poems of the 1941-1951 section. Sarcasm, negation, and argumentation, the armature of the earlier poems, are gradually replaced by lyricism. The tone becomes less and less strident. Acceptance ousts opposition. We can only guess at the sources of this reconciliation: did Ekelöf succeed in destroying his dialectical bent, was he granted some transfiguring insight? Whatever the explanation, Ekelöf is no longer at war with the premises of his being. The "something else" is not some impossible antagonist or unattainable *fata morgana,* but a fount of inner replenishment. As Ekelöf writes in the closing lines of **"I Heard Wild Geese,"** closely recalling Hopkins:

> Deep in me abides a freshness
> that no one can take from me
>   not even I myself

The poem **"Raga Malkos,"** which also dates from this time, gives us one kind of clue about Ekelöf's turn-around. Not only does it show his imagination repossessing the East, but it also suggests that Ekelöf is looking in that direction for spiritual resources. His invocation of the Hindu god Krishna combines languorous rhythms with a vision of immersion in experience that is far removed from the dialectical to and fro of the earlier poems:

> Beautiful-eyed one, you walk
> with the sway of your loins
> to bathe yourself in us
> the dark reeds and obscure waters
> which hide the struggle
> the struggle through beauty to joy
> childhood through fortune
> flailing fortune

> wisdom and eternal life
> Night and good cheer!

                                        (from **"Raga Malkos"**)

The final section 1955-1959 marks a completion of the cycle. The lyrical note returns but now it is very different from that in the earlier poems. There the lyricism depended upon a vision of transience. What Ekelöf stated directly in **"Elegy"** also emerged in more crepuscular fashion in **"To Remember"**:

> Voices near
> and voices in the distance
> the sadness of spring twilight. . .
> We used to stand on the bridge.
> We stood there a long time
> in the deepening blue nights
> when the pike leaped
>   saw the rings spread,
> saw the moon path become
> a winding serpent
> in last year's reeds. . .

But in the poems from the late 1950s it is clear that Ekelöf has changed the whole basis of his perception. The "I" has been vanquished, and what was formerly suffered as transience is now celebrated as the truth of eternal movement. Eastern spirituality is everywhere evident. Poem after poem is now imbued with the idea of the Void the Nothing that is the plenum through which all creation passes:

> This music is like ankle-rings
> if nothing is the ankle and nothing the rhythm
> in which the foot stirs itself and slowly stamps
> round round a rounded carpet.

                            (from **"Like Ankle-rings"**)

And:

> That's why you sing for me bird, that's why the raw
>   chill feels fresh
> Seductive tones, seductive tones, o hunger that can
>   be satisfied only
> when you have caught in your beak the insect of nothing
> that every moment vanishes in the empty air.

                            (from **"Why do you sing my bird"**)

The "insect of nothing" is quite compatible with the lyric mode. If we read **"Why do you sing my bird"** right after **"Elegy,"** we can see that a complete transformation of vision has been effected, with no sacrifice of delicacy or poetic power.

Ekelöf is, I have stressed, a poet for whom creation and self-discovery are a single process. He is not being rhetorical when he writes: "Poetry is something which is only done by the whole man." This identification cannot but raise the stakes: each finished poem is there for itself *and* as a moment, or step, in a sustained search. We do not know the eventual issue of that search any more than the poet does. The *oeuvre* reminds us, more than any single poem, that identity is not a gift passively received, but a determined creative action in the midst of a vast unknown. Ekelöf's evolution from Western skepticism to Eastern mysticism is a fascinating *pas de deux* of mind and spirit, all the more fascinating in the way that it bypasses Christianity entirely. His path is eccentric but no more so than that of Yeats or Merrill. Complex souls have complex expedients. For our part, we must hope that *Songs of Something Else* will prompt the publication of all three parts of Ekelöf's triptych. Then we will be able to start assessing the full meaning of these expedients. . . .

Aris Fioretos (essay date 1990)

SOURCE: "Now and Absence in the Early Ekelöf," in *Scandinavian Studies* Vol. 62, No. 3, Summer, 1990, pp. 319-30.

[*In the following excerpt, Fioretos focuses on "osynlig närvaro" ("invisible presence"), a poem which appears in* Late Arrival on Earth, *as a pioneering example of Swedish modernism.*]

Gunnar Ekelöf's poem **"osynlig närvaro" ("invisible presence"**), first published as the fourth entry in *sent på jorden* (1932; *late on earth*), bears upon questions of poetic articulation. As such, it must be understood to express concerns that generate the texts of Ekelöf's debut collection in general. Demonstrating a paradoxical relationship between visibility and invisibility, the poem conveys a disturbingly impenetrable presence. The lack of a substantial core in this presence, intimated by the title and recurring in other *late on earth* poems, permits a rotating motion of polarities, such as those of sight and sound, interior and exterior, presence and absence. The vacillating between these polarities will be the concern of this paper.

The poem reads:

> gryningen kom med brusten blick,
> fönstret stirrade länge
> i ögonblicket som föll bort
> då väckarklockan ringde . . .
>
> en gäspning släpade sig över golvet
> och drunknade i lavoaren,
> vinden öppnade badrumsfönstret,
> gardinen dansade på tvären . . .
>
> därute drack vattendropparna ljus i dimman
> som speglade gatuförsäljarnas osynliga rop
> och de stora svarta trädena liknade
> ljudlösa rop med armarna i luften . . .

Frederic Fleisher, thus far the only English translator of the poem, renders it in the following way:

> dawn came with a shattered gaze,
> the window stared at length

> at the moment that fell away
> when the alarm clock rang . . .
>
> a yawn dragged itself across the floor
> and drowned in the washstand,
> the wind opened the bathroom window,
> the curtain danced sideways . . .
>
> outside the water-drops drank light in the mist
> that mirrored the invisible cries of the street
>   peddlers
> and the large black trees resembled
> soundless cries with their arms in the air . . .

The semantics of Ekelöf's text refuse any easy crystallization into understanding. As has been well documented in Ekelöf scholarship, this refusal was one of the capital reasons for the abundant criticism his debut received at the dawn of Swedish modernism. The way of writing poetry revealed by *late on earth* was seen to upset the usually unquestioned rules governing the transmission of belief, emotion, and perception from text to reader, hitherto taken for granted by an audience raised on Mascoll Silfverstolpe or the young Gullberg. Georg Svensson's pejorative comments on the incomprehensibility of Ekelöf's "uttrycksform" ("form of expression"), is instructive in this respect, since it was precisely Ekelöf's reluctance to administrate his poetic practice in accordance with established usage of poetic discourse that caused the irritation. Svensson calls it a "förödelse" ("disaster") in his review in *Bonniers litterära magasin,* adding that,

> . . . naturligtvis kan det ligga något patetiskt och fantasieggande över ett skönt fragment, som slitits ur sitt sammanhang, men att basera en hel uttrycksform på desorganisation och intellektuell och emotionell viljelöshet är estetism av osundaste sort.

> (. . . in a beautiful fragment torn from its context, there may of course be something pathetic and stimulating to the imagination, but to found a whole form of expression on disorganization and intellectual and emotional lack of will is an aestheticism of the most unhealthy kind.)

Falling back on cumbersome value criteria such as hygiene or health, Svensson's opinion about *late on earth* is indeed supremely deaf to the importance of Ekelöf's early work. It may nevertheless be worth tracing some of these aspects of Ekelöf's disastrous "form of expression" as they occur in **"invisible presence,"** in order to read the way in which the poem performs its disorganization of traditional poetry in favor of a different manner of articulation. This articulation may indicate the originality of Ekelöf's writing in the early thirties, as well as the poetical novelties that forced its readers to trail behind.

The poem displays a number of stylistic features we know from Ekelöf's inventory of poetic techniques at the time. Some already documented observations on the style in *late on earth* may also characterize "invisible presence" and point to its exemplarity. The poem reveals an attenuating abstraction and an attempt "att applicera ett s. k. non-figurativt bildseende [Ulf Thomas Moberg]" ("to apply a so-called nonfigurative imagination"); one also notices "de syntaktiska och grammatiska destruktionerna [Bengt Landgren]" ("the syntactical and grammatical destructions") characteristic of Ekelöf's poetry at the time, and a "reducering av den poetiska vokabulären [Anders Olsson]" ("reduction of poetic vocabulary"); lastly, the "utstrykande av all subjektivitet och erfarenhet [Olsson]" ("erasure of all subjectivity and experience"), and "tanken på döden i livet, likgiltigheten [och] tröttheten [Landgren]" ("the thought of death in life, the apathy [and] the fatigue") can be singled out as typical features. Indeed, the "radikalt normbrytande och brutalt provokativa draget" ("radically norm-breaking and brutally provocative feature"), to use Bengt Landgren's description of *late on earth,* bears that Mallarméan imprint we have learned to expect from the author of *En natt vid horisonten.* The language of the poem appears as a self-sufficient entity, positing an anonymous world where the enigmatically bleak reality is meticulously deprived of expressions of subjective intent. The impersonal tonality not only gives voice to a fragmented and mechanical set of events but also performs a withdrawal from the realm of sensory perception that inversely, *ex negativo,* introduces a positive element in that very void it leaves behind by privileging the intrinsic attributes of language. The text that asserts the erasure of the I or self is not affected by this deprivation, however, since it must be thought of as the nucleus that engenders the assertion. It may seem, therefore, as if the rhetoric of "invisible presence" promotes a paradoxical presence in the very absence of thematically anchored subjectivity.

The poem performs a verbal furnishing of Mallarmé's Nothing or Absence, though sparsely. The hollow markers of this furnishing a "yawn" and an open "bathroom window," mirrored "invisible cries" and "black trees" "with their arms in the air" are inscribed in the text through a rhetorical figuration that includes the repetition of aposiopeses at the end of each stanza and, more importantly, anthropomorphisms and a catachresis. Thus the invisibility thematized by the text is made present through rhetorical devices that fill out the vacuum surrounding a consciousness devoid of activity and participation. By disorganizing the usual perception of the physical world, the poem by the same token establishes an autonomous poetic reality from which conventional comprehension is excluded. This is a movement that can be seen to recur throughout the poems of Ekelöf's debut, though it may require a certain misapprehension to view it with that feeling one has, according to Svensson, "när man ser ett vackert föremål, som tappats i golvet och slagits i tusen spillror ("when one sees a beautiful object dropped on the floor and shattered into a thousand pieces"). In fact, if the dismembered parts of Ekelöf's poetic world are governed by a unifying principle but that may be doubted this precept may well reside in the homology of the rhetorical structure of each individual text, rather than in the grammatical or descriptive consolidation of their arrangement. Readings not aware of this possibility are bound to repeat Svensson's essentially aestheticizing evaluation, based as it

is on unquestioned notions of the poetic text as an organic whole, harmonious and excelling in euphonic beauty.

In **"invisible presence,"** a principle of equality distributes an equal portion of thematic dignity to each perceptual fragment, image, and stanza. This equalization occurs through a series of short sequences that more often than not consist in nominal phrases. Throughout the poem, the temporal mode is phrased in the preterit: "came," "stared," "rang," "dragged," "drowned," "drank," and so forth a catalogue of verbs that, in its repetitive unfolding of a temporality that is precisely not present, underscores a disorganization of conventional reality through which the imaginary world of the poem, in its turn, gains in corresponding actuality. The independent thematic sequences of the text, nearly synonymous with the three stanzas of the poem, depict a room at dawn. A gradual centering takes place, from the approaching morning to a considerably more narrow perspective to a *punctum,* in fact, being the very moment when the sudden ringing of the alarm clock punctuates the poem, and sets its narrative chronology in motion. This ringing moment initiates a curious activity: a yawn drags "itself across the floor" and drowns "in the washstand." Near the washstand, the wind opens a bathroom window, and passing by way of the poetically rewarding transit of an aposiopesis we are once again introduced to the early morning, the bleak light penetrating the mist, the street peddlers, and the black trees that resemble "soundless cries with their arms in the air."

The break with normal rules of perception in **"invisible presence"** corresponds to a privileging of deliberately fragmented iconic qualities. Ekelöf's contact with contemporary nonfigurative painting predominantly various forms of post-Cubism, such as *Art concret* and Purism has rightly been stressed by several scholars, including Ulf Thomas Moberg and Anders Olsson. In the case of "invisible presence," it is evident that its Mallarméan diction is permeated by a manner of elocution whose technique is imported from that kind of painting. The poem reveals an attempt to capture objects or emotions through a dense diversity of perspectives, thus reflecting and transforming an inherent multi-dimensionality in a way that does linguistic justice to its motif. On the typographical level, for example, one finds a consistent use of small letters, recurring throughout *late on earth,* that accentuates an uninterrupted linking together of seemingly arbitrary events. On the lexical level, words are usually excerpted from the vocabulary of a "denaturerad prosa" ("denatured prose"), to use a term provided by the title of another poem in the collection. At the level of syntax, the sequentiality is underscored by a paratactic omission of conjunctions condensing the poetic texture. As for sonority, the use of alliterations and assonances further emphasizes the very absence created by the poem. In addition, finally, various expressions that recur in the text endow the inarticulate with an onomatopoetically twisted articulation: the *ä*-sound of "*gä*spningen *slä*pade sig" in the second stanza, for example, or the *o*-sound of "*o*synliga r*o*p" in the third.

The poem is one of the few Ekelöf commented on himself (**"osynlig närvaro"**). Yet Ekelöf's considerations in the autobiographical margin of his text seem to trouble the reading of it in a particularly instructive manner. Under the vignette **"Diktaren om dikten" ("The Poet on the Poem")**, the title of a series of essayistic reflections first published in the periodical *Samtid och framtid* (4 [1951]), Ekelöf commented on two poems from his first volume. One of them is **"invisible presence."** The scenario of the text, he then tells us,

är square de Châtillon, Paris, i fjortonde arrondissementet där jag en tid bebodde en liten våning. Stämningen är dagen efter. I "ögonblicket som föll bort" torde den för läsaren osynlige lägenhetsinnehavaren ha begrundat vad det var han inte kom ihåg. . . . [F]ramför allt minns jag en tiggare, en osynlig närvaro eftersom jag på grund av stängda persienner aldrig sett, bara hört honom. . . . Men dikten är också någonting annat. Kubismen hade denna tid (20-talet) ingått i en fridsammare och på sätt och vis "lycklig" period. Det var framför allt Picasso och Braque som inaugurerade fönsterbilden med det karakteristiska järngallret. Detta är ett försök i ord till en sådan bild: fönsterdöbattanger öppna, gardin, spjäljalusiner, träd därute och i förgrunden en i olika attityder komponerad "närvaro."

(is the Square de Châtillon, Paris, in the fourteenth arrondissement, where for a time I occupied a small flat. The mood is the morning after. In "the moment that fell away," the inhabitant of the flat, invisible to the reader, should have established what it was he did not remember. . . . [F]irst of all I remember the beggar, an invisible presence, since I, owing to closed blinds, never saw him, only heard him. . . . But the poem is also something else. At this time [the 1920s], Cubism had entered a more peaceful, in some ways "happier" period. It was primarily Picasso and Braque who inaugurated the window image, with the characteristic iron grille. This is an attempt in words at such a picture: shutters open, curtain, Venetian blind, trees beyond, and in the foreground a "presence" composed in various attitudes.)

Ekelöf stayed in Paris from the end of September 1929 to June 1930. He originally planned to study music. In a fictional letter to a friend, written some five years later and printed in the fragmentary attempt at an autobiography, *En självbiografi* (1971), the Parisian stay is discussed (88-91). While cautioning that "[m]innet bedrar" ("[m]emory betrays"), Ekelöf writes:

Först minns jag den ofantliga, ohyggliga ensamheten. . . . I det ena rummet var fönsterluckorna alltid stängda. . . . [E]nsamheten . . . spann sina spindeltrådar över fönstren och slog sin klo i min själ. På bordet låg en anteckningsbok öppen. Där skrev jag en tanke då och då. . . . Det avlövade trädet utanför mitt fönster kunde inte växa mer övergivet och mer undergivet än jag själv." . . . Ibland kom en gatusångare in i den lilla gränden och ställde sig där för att sjunga. Klagande gammalmansröster, slitna och färglösa som det mulna ljuset en höstdag. oändligt långsamma, släpande melodier och tiggande tonfall. Gatuförsäljarnas rop trängde också in dit, men man kunde aldrig höra vad det var de sålde, det lät bara som spridda lockrop utan någon mening.

. . . För övrigt nådde mig bullret av världen utanför endast som obestämda ljud man hör i sömnen.

(First I remember the immense and frightful loneliness. . . . In one of the rooms, the window shutters were always closed. . . . [T]he loneliness [spun] its spider web over the windows and [dug] its claw into my soul. On the table, a notebook lay open. Now and then I wrote down a thought in it. . . . The defoliated tree outside my window could not grow more abandoned and more resigned than I myself. . . . Sometimes a street singer came into the small alley and stood there to sing. Complaining old-mens' voices, worn and colorless as the clouded light on a fall day, infinitely slow, dragging melodies and begging tones. The cries of the street peddlers also intruded, but one could never hear what it was they were selling; it sounded only like dispersed cries without any meaning. . . . Besides that, the noise of the world outside reached me only as the undefined sounds one hears in sleep.)

The setting is familiar: an interior, invaded by ennui and voided of affirmative action, is juxtaposed with an exterior, a noisily intrusive apparition, but one deprived of the signification that usually goes along with sound. The "dispersed cries without meaning," mentioned in this autobiographical account and belonging to the realm of exteriority, only reach the passive subject "as the undefined sounds one hears in sleep." This perforation of the bar that separates inner actuality from outer reality, silence from sonority, consciousness from corporeality, is paralleled in Ekelöf's late account by the intrusion of undetermined sound into sleeping. Impossible to block out and yet bereft of any meaning, the vacillating of such an intrusion is the principle governing the rotating motion of polarities in "invisible presence." The image of the window, borrowed from Cubist paintings, establishes the vacillation and may be read as its emblem.

Ekelöf's fictive letter suggests one way of interpreting the title of the poem. It proffers the street singer outside the window, but invisible to the inhabitant of the flat and singing "infinitely slow, dragging melodies and begging tones." The interpretation in *Samtid och framtid*, on the other hand, leaves the matter more open. There, Ekelöf speaks about remembering the beggar an "invisible presence," as he puts it but also mentions the "inhabitant of the flat, invisible to the reader," who "'in the moment that fell away'. . . should have established what it was he did not remember." This may be worth noticing, since the former character the beggar, or the street singer singing "begging tones" belongs to the realm of exteriority, whereas the latter the inhabitant of the flat is part of the interior world. Ekelöf himself, reminiscent of the situation and yet warning that "[m]emory betrays," thus prolongs the question of the invisible presence, rather than puts it to rest.

The strange and impenetrable presence of which the poem speaks indeed cannot be seen. It may even seem undecidable, given the mutually exclusive suggestions proffered by Ekelöf's two accounts. The presence is devoid of that materiality which would make its identity ascertainable.

One commentator, Rabbe Enckell, noticing the general lack of subjectivity in *late on earth,* writes that,

> . . . jaget förlorar sin naturgivna kapacitet till självidentitet och man väntar detonationen efter en självsprängning i det själsliga landskapets förtunnade atmosfär.

> (. . . the I loses its naturally inherent capacity for self-identity, and one awaits the detonation after a self-explosion in the attenuating atmosphere of the spiritual landscape.)

The observation is cogent, though not free from apocalyptic inclination. The spiritual setting of Ekelöf's poem surely harbors a reified world where objects do not disclose any order that is graspable or, for that matter, possible to utter in harmony with preestablished categories of meaning. "Korrespondensen mellan jaget och sinnevärlden är störd" ("The correspondence between the self and the material world is disturbed"), Enckell rightly infers. There may be perception in Ekelöf's poem, visual as well as auditive, but what is perceived seems deprived of further signification. The text weaves the pattern of a perceptual disturbance. The record of this perception, though no longer interpretable according to traditional doctrines of poetic validity, is eminently textual, thus still readable. In the poem, it may therefore be worth paying attention to the way in which the text performs that absence of perceptual normality-which it in fact is about.

"[O]synlig närvaro" opens *in medias res.* A dawn comes with a shattered gaze. This anthropomorphism allows for a reversal of attributes, yet it likewise assumes in the words of Paul de Man "an identification on the level of substance" (241). The spiritless morning hour of "invisible presence" is animated, in other words, and given sight. The giving of vision, however, does not stop at this. It continues in "the window [that] stared," and is thereafter temporalized: the window stared "at length," the text has it, "at the moment that fell away." The original has *ögonblick,* "moment" or "blink," which is an idiomatically economic coagulation of time and momentary sight, temporality and vision. After this curious opening, follows a yawn that drags itself across the floor and drowns in the washstand. The synecdoche here standing in for a tired subject who is denied more qualified presence is then left in the bathroom, while the narrative of the poem takes us out through the window, to the trees and the soundless cries. These latter anthropomorphisms "water-drops" that drink light and "large black trees" with arms may be read as attempts at figuratively manifesting a presence that cannot be seen.

The setting pictured in the poem is spelled out mainly through this confusion of essentially different realms of existence: on the one hand, the realm of objects, deprived of soul and intention; on the other, the realm of consciousness, burdened by languid desolation. Anthropomorphism is the principal conceit of this confusion, by which human properties are projected into the natural world. By taking the natural world as human, it simulta-neously takes the human as something already given (cf. de Man). This entwinement of different orders of being thus implies creating a naturalness of man which, in its turn, suggests that man and nature vanish as categories, as their difference from each other is eliminated. Ekelöf's text demonstrates such an elimination of the distinction between the order of man and the order of nature, between consciousness and reality, and the image of the window may be read as the emblem of its possibility, since it is that phenomenon establishing the interior and exterior worlds of the poem which permits Ekelöf to turn normal perception inside out. But if anthropomorphism still allows us to identify something on the level of substance, there is another, more violent figure in Ekelöf's poem that radicalizes the perceptual ambiguities put forth by the text.

In Ekelöf's 1951 interpretation of **"invisible presence,"** he largely characterized the method by which elimination is brought into poetic play, when he stated that the poem was "an attempt in words at such a picture [i.e., a Cubist "window image"]: shutters open, curtain, Venetian blind, trees beyond and in the foreground a 'presence' composed in various attitudes." The mention of Venetian blinds makes it easier to picture the morning light that arrives with a "shattered gaze." The curtain that dances "sideways" underscores this arrival, as do the drops of water that prismatically reflect the light they drink in the mist, with the invisible cries from the street peddlers contained therein. The physical world here comes to speak through a transaction of human properties, which then grants natural elements the poetic license of assuming perception and articulation. The window renders possible the exchange between interior and exterior. This essentially rhetorical movement indicates, in the text, the proximity of anthropomorphism to another and more disruptive figure of speech, catachresis that arbitrary imposition of trope which gives name to a yet unnamed entity by the "misuse" of figural speech. Catachresis is the misapplication of a word that gives face to the faceless "the eye of a hurricane," say, or "the leg of a chair" as is the case with the very moment at which the "dawn came" and "the window stared." This "moment" is an *ögonblick,* which is a misuse of figural speech, since it gives face and sight to an entity that most certainly has neither. Through the peculiar twists of the Swedish idiom, temporality is here given eyes to see even if only for a short while. Prior to any perception, this is the catachrestic moment that inaugurates Ekelöf's poem, marking the instant that initiates the text's process of signification. What makes this more than a random occurrence of trope, however, is that the vision of the catachresis is conferred at the very instant that the text shifts from the figuration of visibility to audibility, "at the moment that fell away / when the alarm clock rang." The rhetorical movement by which the moment of the arriving dawn is made visible occurs at the same instant as the language of the poem speaks of the power of sound. Thus the literal report of this transition also marked syntactically, by the temporal conjunction "when" in the fourth line is not so much a denomination of property as the indication of a rhetorical movement. The catachresis of *ögonblick* coincides, simultaneously, with the ringing of the alarm clock. Hence it grounds an invisibility, since sound cannot be seen, as the poem rightly points out later, mentioning the *"invisible* cries" from outside. This is an invisibility that is nonetheless made present all the more so, inasmuch as sound can be seen to be a feature of language that is necessarily immanent to it.

Rather than being the passive reflection of a very empty reality, Ekelöf's poem reveals a conception of language as act, as a making-present. Reading a reading devoted to the figurative fragmentation displayed by Ekelöf's early poetry is the only practice in which such a movement may become present. The "presence" of **"invisible presence"** is therefore not so much an *a priori* presence as it is "made" present through catachresis. This difference generates the conflict between perception and trope articulated by Ekelöf's poem. It is the initial imposition of catachresis that renders possible the poetic process of comparison and identification, organized in various figurative patterns with anthropomorphism as dominating trope. The moment in which **"invisible presence"** inaugurates its presence, however, is said to be a moment "that fell away." What the text thus actually makes present can preside only *in absentia.* As in the case of Mallarméan poetics, figural language fills out a voided center, allowing it to circulate linguistically by being phenomenalized as time and ringing, temporality and sound, the two inherent features of speech. The text engenders a presence bound to be invisible. It is a presence that can occur only in that Now which always, necessarily, coincides with the act of reading. Yet the poem tells us that this Now is a moment that simultaneously falls away, thereby depriving us of the scene of action that Svensson apostrophized, derogatorily speaking about an "intellectual and emotional lack of will" in *late on earth.* This lack which now turns out to be rigorously linguistic, but hardly aesthetic is what Ekelöf's text renders present. The invisibility must occur by a process of signification, a process that reading only unravels. Nothing substantial remains after its having taken place, however, so there may be a sort of "disaster." Yet in that case, it is a "disaster" proper to all language.

That this seems to be what Ekelöf's poem speaks about only underscores the acuity of his debut collection and the understandable momentum it formulated at the dawn of Swedish modernism. From the reader's or critic's view point (*pace* Svensson), it may be comforting, though decidedly more unsettling, that Ekelöf's poem thereby also points to that other disaster Novalis touched upon when stating that it would be "Unglück, wenn die Poësie auf die Theorie wartete."

FURTHER READING

Criticism

Benedikt, Michael. "Critic of the Month: IV." *Poetry* 113, No. 3 (December 1968): 188-215.
    Brief discussion of Robert Bly's English translation of Ekelöf's poetry, entitled *I Do Best Alone at Night.*

Harvey, Steven. "The Changed Name of God." *The Iowa Review* 25, No. 2 (Spring/Summer 1995): 40-6.
    Compares Ekelöf with poet John Logan.

Lesser, Rika. "Gunnar Ekelöf and Hjalmar Gullberg: 'But in Another Language . . . '". *The American Poetry Review* 10, No. 5 (September/October 1981): 42-7.
    A positive assessment of Muriel Rukeyser and Leif Sjöberg's 1979 English translation of *A Mölna Elegy.*

Mattsson, Margareta. Review of *Songs of Something Else,* by Gunnar Ekelöf, translated by Leonard Nathan and James Larson. *World Literature Today* 57, No. 1 (Winter 1983): 122.
    A generally favorable review of *Songs of Something Else.*

Merwin, W. S. "Into English." *The New York Times Book Review* (March 17, 1968): 6.
    A largely negative review of *Selected Poems of Gunnar Ekelöf,* as translated by Muriel Rukeyser and Leif Sjöberg.

Printz-Påhlson, Göran. Introduction to *Selected Poems*, by Gunnar Ekelöf, translated by W. H. Auden and Leif Sjöberg, pp. 13-18. Pantheon Books, 1971.
    Surveys the development of Ekelöf's poetry, and describes Ekelöf himself as "a guardian of the border regions of the mind."

Shideler, Ross. "A Functional Theory of Literature Applied to Poems by Paul Valéry and Gunnar Ekelöf." *Psychocultural Review* 2, No. 3 (Summer 1978): 181-201.
    Includes a close reading of Ekelöf's "En prins var namn bör vara onämnt" ("A Prince Whose Name Must Not Be Known") that examines how the poem acts upon the reader's "emotive and cognitive" perceptions.

Sjöberg, Leif. "Gunnar Ekelöf's 'Tag och skriv': A Reader's Commentary." *Scandinavian Studies* 35, No. 4 (November 1963): 307-24.
    Provides a close reading of a poem from *Ferry Song,* and stresses the differences between Ekelöf and poet T. S. Eliot.

———. "Allusions in the Last Part of Gunnar Ekelöf's *En Mölna-Elegi.*" *The Germanic Review* XL, No. 2 (March 1965): 132-49.
    Offers "a preparatory study" of a part of Ekelöf's complex poem that had not been completed at the time this essay was published.

———. "Gunnar Ekelöf: Poet and Outsider." *The American Scandinavian Review* LIII, No. 2 (June 1965): 140-6.
    An interview with Ekelöf at his home, a visit to which, Sjöberg observes, is treated almost as a pilgrimage by poets and readers alike.

———. "Note: Two Poems by Ekelöf." *Scandinavica* 5, No. 1 (May 1966): 126-30.
    Compares two short poems by Ekelöf with the two paintings that inspired them.

————. "A Note on Poems by Ekelöf." *Scandinavian Studies* 39, No. 2 (May 1967): 147-52.

>   Discusses the inspiration from the visual arts upon which Ekelöf relied for many of his poems.

"Two Quotations in Ekelöf's 'Absentia Animi.'" *The Germanic Review,* XLIV (January 1969): 45-60.

>   Focuses on the imagery of a butterfly and on some lines inspired by Rimbaud, whom Ekelöf admired, in "Absentia Animi."

Stendahl, Brita. Review of *Guide to the Underworld,* by Gunnar Ekelöf, translated by Rika Lesser. *World Literature Today* 55, No. 3 (Summer 1981): 488-89.

>   Positive review of *Guide to the Underworld.*

Thygesen, Erik. Review of *Skrifter,* Vols. 1-7, by Gunnar Ekelöf, edited by Reidar Ekner. *World Literature Today* 68, No. 1 (Winter 1994): 149-50.

>   Largely positive review of Ekner's stated attempt to offer the reader "the whole Ekelöf" in this Swedish-language collection of Ekelöf's poetry and prose.

Young, Vernon. "Nature and Vision: Or Dubious Antithesis." *The Hudson Review* XXV, No. 4 (Winter 1972-73): 659-74.

>   Young describes Ekelöf's later poems as Eastern in philosophy and "quite unlike any Western poems [he] can remember."

Additional coverage of Ekelöf's life and career is contained in the following sources published by The Gale Group: *Contemporary Authors,* **Vols. 25-28 (rev. ed.), 123;** *Contemporary Literary Criticism,* **Vol. 27; and** *DISCovering Authors: Poets Module.*

Nicolás Guillén
1902-1989

(Full name Nicolás Cristobal Guillén y Batista) Cuban poet, journalist, and editor.

INTRODUCTION

Guillén is known as one of Cuba's finest poets and as an important figure in contemporary West Indian literature. Named National Poet of Cuba by Cuban dictator Fidel Castro in 1961, Guillén, who was committed to Marxist ideology and the Cuban Revolution, chronicled the turbulent social and political history of his native land. He is also credited as one of the first poets to affirm and celebrate the black Cuban experience and is noted for introducing the *son,* an African-Cuban dance rhythm, to literary audiences. Guillén's poetry has been translated into more than thirty languages, and he has been nominated numerous times for the Nobel Prize for literature.

Biographical Information

Guillén, a mulatto from the Cuban provincial middle class, was born in Camagüey to Nicolás Guillén y Urra and Argelia Batista y Arrieta, both of whom were descendants of Africans and Spaniards. Guillén's father, a journalist and Liberal senator, was assassinated in a political skirmish in 1917. According to Vera M. Kutzinski, after his father's death, "the young Guillén became increasingly interested in poetry and journalism," and his poems were first published in the journal *Camagüey Gráfico* in 1919. Guillén graduated from high school in 1920 and then attended the University of Havana, where he planned to study law. Guillén left school after a year, however, and founded the literary magazine *Lis* with his brother Francisco while also writing for various Cuban newspapers and magazines. In 1937, Guillén joined the Communist Party, campaigning for various political offices throughout the 1940s. He became president of the Cuban National Union of Writers and Artists in 1961, a position he held for twenty-five years. His honors include the Lenin Peace Prize from the Soviet Union in 1954 and the Cuban Order of José Martí in 1981. Guillén died after a long illness in 1989. He was given a state funeral with military honors.

Major Works of Poetry

The majority of Guillén's poems are informed by his African and Spanish heritage, often combining the colloquialisms and rhythms of Havana's black districts with the formal structure and language of traditional Spanish verse to address the injustices of imperialism, capitalism, and

racism. In his first acclaimed volume of poetry, *Motivos de son* (1930), Guillén utilized the rhythmic patterns of the *son* to evoke the energetic flavor of black life in and around Havana. Guillén expanded his focus in his next volume, *Sóngoro cosongo* (1931), to include poems depicting the lives of all Cubans, with emphasis on the importance of mulatto culture in Cuban history. Following the demise of the corrupt government headed by Gerardo Machado in 1933 and the increasing industrial and political presence of the United States in Cuba, Guillén began to write poetry with overtly political implications. In *West Indies, Ltd.* (1934), a collection of somber poems imbued with anxiety and frustration, he decried the social and economic conditions of the Caribbean poor. Guillén attacked imperialism through his recurring description of the region as a vast, profitable factory exploited by foreign nations. The poet's commitment to social change grew when he traveled to Spain in 1937 to cover the Spanish Civil War for *Mediodía* magazine and subsequently participated in the antifascist Second International Congress of Writers for the Defense of Culture. That year he joined the Cuban Communist Party and produced an extended narrative poem chronicling the Spanish Civil War, *España: Poema en cuatro angustias y una esperanza* (1937). In 1937, Guillén also published *Cantos para soldados y sones para turistas,* a volume of poetry denouncing the escalating military presence in Cuban society. He employed biting satire in poems that contrast the darkness and squalor of Cuba's ghettos with the garish atmosphere of downtown tourist establishments. Guillén spent much of the 1940s and 1950s in exile in Europe and South America during the height of the Fulgencio Batista y Zaldivar regime in Cuba. His works of this period reflect his opposition to Batista's repressive politics and denounce racial segregation in the United States. The poems in *La paloma de vuelo popular* (1958), favor revolution, praising the activities of such political figures as Castro and Che Guevara. Guillén returned to Cuba following the Cuban Revolution and Batista's expulsion in 1959, and in 1964 he published *Tengo [Tengo]*. In this volume, Guillén celebrated the triumph of the revolution and the abolition of racial and economic discrimination. In *El gran zoo* (1967; *(¡Patria o Muerte! The Great Zoo and Other Poems*), Guillén drew from the bestiary tradition of such writers as Aesop, Guillaume Apollinaire, and Pablo Neruda to present people, places, and institutions as animals in order to metaphorically address social issues. *La rueda dentada* (1972), in which Guillén created new forms and adapted old ones to the changing social and political situation in Cuba, emphasizes social responsibility and addresses subjects not treated in the years before the revolution. *El diario que a diario* (1972) combines poetry and journalism to ironically and satirically examine what Guillén considered the injustice, immorality, and absurdity of Cuban colonial society before the Cuban Revolution.

Critical Reception

Many commentators have distinguished between Guillén's early *poesía negroide,* or Afro-Cuban influenced poems, and the political poems he produced after converting to communism. However, because of Guillén's broad range of subject matter and his use of various poetic forms throughout his career, critics have found his work difficult to classify. As Richard Jackson noted, "Some critics have focused on Guillén as an exponent of Afro-Cuban poetry while others have viewed him as a poet having little to do with Africa. Some perceive a black aesthetic in his poetry; others say he is the most Spanish of Cuban poets. Some see him as a poet who stopped writing black poetry; others declare that he never wrote black poetry at all." Although early critics tended to label Guillén a black or political poet and related his poetry almost exclusively to political life in Cuba, contemporary scholars have begun to focus on Guillén's artistry and aesthetic concerns, commenting on a wide range of folkloric, satirical, elegiac, and lyrical elements in his poetry. Despite controversy concerning Guillén's treatment of racial themes and his status as a political poet, many scholars have found coherence in his oeuvre, consistently praising his focus on oppression and injustice, his mastery of diverse poetic forms, his celebration of black Cuban culture and identity, and his belief that poetry has the power to influence society and lead to constructive change.

PRINCIPAL WORKS

Poetry

Motivos de son 1930
Sóngoro cosongo: Poemas mulatos 1931
West Indies, Ltd. 1934
Cantos para soldados y sones para turistas 1937
Eligías 1937
España: Poema en cuatro angustias y una esperanza 1937
Cuba Libre: Poems by Nicolás Guillén 1948
Elegía a Jacques Roumain en el cielo de Haití 1948
Versos negros 1950
Elegía a Jesús Menéndez 1951
Elegía cubana 1952
La paloma de vuelo popular: Elegías 1958
Buenos días, Fidel 1959
¿Puedos? 1960
Antología Mayor 1964
Poemas de amor 1964
Tengo [Tengo] 1964
Che Comandante 1967
El gran zoo [¡Patria o Muerte! The Great Zoo and Other Poems by Nicolás Guillén] 1967
Cuatro canciones para el Che 1969
El diario que a diario 1972
La rueda dentada 1972
Man-Making Words: Selected Poems of Nicolás Guillén 1972
Obra Poética, 1920-1972 1974
El corazón con que vivo 1975
Poemas manuables 1975
Summa poética 1976
Por el mar de las Antillas anda un barco de papel 1977
Música de cámara 1979
Páginas veultas: Memorias 1982
Sol de domingo 1982

Other Major Works

Prosa de prisa: crónicas (prose) 1962
Prosa de prisa: 1929-1972 (prose) 1975-76
El libro de las décimas (prose) 1980

CRITICISM

Nicolás Guillén with Ciro Bianchi Ross (interview date 1972)

SOURCE: "Nicolás Guillén's 70th Birthday Conversation with Ciro Bianchi Ross," in *The Poetry of Nicolás Guillén,* New Beacon Books, 1976, pp. 58-80.

[In the following excerpt from a 1972 interview, originally published in Cuba Internacional, *Guillén discusses his Cuban childhood, his thoughts on negritude, Cuban politics, and major themes in his work.]*

[Ciro Bianchi Ross]: *How do you judge the literary formation that you received in your childhood? Which things in that childhood are you interested in highlighting now?*

[Nicolás Guillén]: No, I couldn't speak about a literary formation in the more or less strict sense of the word; and naturally neither from the academic point of view. What happened is that I found so much in my father's house as in my godfather's—both learned and scholarly—books of Spanish and world literature which awoke a great artistic concern in me. My father was a man well informed about the politics and literature of his time, and he was the one to whom I submitted for his opinion my first literary efforts; but I repeat, I had neither a systematic nor strict formation. Furthermore my father was a Liberal leader with a very active life, and a professional journalist of high standing. Having just returned from the War of Independence, in which he achieved the rank of second lieutenant, he founded, with a confederate of his named Pedro Mendoza—an orator who sometimes wrote poetry—a newspaper which they called *The Two Republics*. It seems to me that both my father and his friend succumbed to a political mirage, the same one which deceived many Cubans when the Republic was established. There is little doubt in my mind that those "two republics" were Cuba and the United States, since as is well known the Yankees disguised their imperialist penetration in our country, directed towards the exploitation of our resources, under the cloak of a "protection" which never existed.

When I was born, then, *The Two Republics* was a familiar newspaper in my home, and later, for ten or twelve years more was the only important Liberal newspaper in the city. When I was six or eight years old I used to go to the presses and the news office of that paper. I do not remember if already then there was on the door of the house where *The Two Republics* was edited, the sign which I saw later when the newspaper office and the presses changed location when I was older. That sign displayed in the centre the title of the newspaper, on one hand the coat of arms of the USA and on the other the Cuban. The Yankee coat of arms naturally had an eagle with wings spread open wide, fierce of eye, very strong claws and very hooked beak.

I remember clearly from those days when the Liberals rose up against the Conservative President Estrada Palma. I, having been born in 1902, was then about six or seven years of age. The streets of Camagüey, muddy, full of horsemen wearing huge hats woven of palm, my father going to the "Circle" (that was the popular name of the place where the Liberal Party authorities had their office) and from the "Circle" to our home, left a deep mark on my memory. As is known, in the elections which the Americans held, having almost been called in by the Conservative government, the Liberals were triumphant, which brought about the election of my father as Senator for what they then called a "short" period, that is, for four years, as opposed to the "long" period which was for eight.

In spite of the fact that my father was obliged for reasons of his position to spend a lot of time in Havana, none of our family saw the capital, and I, who was the first to do so, had to wait until 1920. Those long absences of my father had as compensation the joy of his return. In those days motor cars were not frequently seen in Camagüey, so that the public made use of hired cars. My father, surrounded by parcels and a huge suitcase with presents for my mother, would always arrive in one of those. And it was on one of these trips that he brought the gramophone, already without that enormous horn which on the publicity brochures appeared with a little dog "listening to his master's voice". Along with the gramophone my father brought a series of records, whose names I still remember, since they had a deep effect on my childish imagination: a big one with the Sextet from Lucia, another with Schubert's Serenade, another with the duet from La Africana, others, finally, with passages from La Traviata, "El Rey que rabió", "El año pasado por agua", etc. Of course, both Caruso and Tita Rufo were included, both very famous at that time. There were also national records with numbers by Regino López, Hortensia Valerón, Floro y Cruz, the "danzón" of the Bombin (Bowler Hat) of Barreto, another "danzón" which I did not hear again, called "Las Botellas", and others.

Certainly, from hearing the Sextet from Lucia so often I learnt it by heart and I used to whistle it much to my father's delight.

I do not know who thought he discovered in me an aptitude for music; but the truth is that, without knowing how or when, I found myself in the hands of a maestro in this art, whom everyone called Señor Pérez, and who never managed to get me to come down from the roof of my house where I used to wait for him flying kites.

Coming back to my godfather . . . his name was don Sixto Vasconcelos, and I remember him from when he was President of the High Court in Camagüey. He was a man with a very pleasant face, clear discerning eyes, a thick moustache, and bald. I heard him say more than once that in Madrid he had been a literary companion of Emilio Bobadilla. In spite of the fact that at that time it was not necessary because my father was a Senator, he committed himself to the responsibility for my classes in a school which was almost in the basement of the house where he lived. It was an old one-storey house, with two wooden windows facing the street and a big garden encircled by a series of rooms where the classrooms were. The proprietor of this establishment was a Spaniard, whose surname was Rodríguez. I remember, I don't know why, in the clearest way, details of that environment, not that of the school but that of the street and the neighbours. For example, the little greengrocery belonging to a Spanish woman called Rosita who had a most beautiful daughter; the washday linen of some boys who were sons of a Spaniard named Villanueva; a house where the Escoto family lived, and whose head was a great friend of my father; Augustín Vasconcelos, slightly older than I, who taught me to make kites; the Baptist Church in the same row as my godfather's house and the school and as the only free side of the Provincial government building, and some others. Along Cisneros Street and in that neighbourhood also could be found the house in which a Conservative politician called Aurelio Alvarez had installed a journalistic organ of his party, called *The Word*. In the same way, the High Court building, where I have already mentioned that my godfather was president; in the opposite row, was the Spanish Colony building; Marrero's printing shop; the office of a family friend called Amado López, whose index finger on one hand had been mutilated by a revolver shot; Pancho Bueno's bookstore, where, as time went by, I would buy my school requirements; the Town Hall; the Casualty Hospital, and, finally, Agramonte Park where Negroes and mulattoes were forbidden to stroll. Opposite this park was the El Liceo Club, which with the passage of time had moved away from the goal pursued by its founders in the 19th century, among them the Marquis of Santa Lucia, Salvador Cisneros. The El Liceo was a centre for provincial aristocrats, dealers in cattle and sugar, and idle and imbecile young men. On the feast days of St. John, or on our Carnival days, which occurred under the blazing June sun, the members of the El Liceo would sit on large leather stools at their clubhouse gates and throw at the strollers little cartridges of red ochre and other colouring substances, when they were not throwing damaging objects.

This savagery reached the extreme if any "coloured" family had the temerity to pass in front of that club, for besides the cartridges mentioned insults referring to skin colour were added. They would sing, for example

"The Negro who rides in a car
will never get very far"

and other refrains of a similar nature. Generally, the El Liceo became a hateful society hated by the people of Camagüey. Opposite it, exactly in Agramonte Park, when I was a boy, there was a terrific clash when a group of negroes and mulattoes dared to stroll past that spot one night during a band concert, as a result of which a girl by the name of Rita Digna Varona was wounded.

What did you study in Camagüey?

I graduated with my bachillerato in Arts and Science. But I was never able to attend classes at the High School or Lyceum because of my job. I had to work as a typographer (along with my brother Francisco, who is a lawyer today) in a printing shop called El Nacional, owned by some friends of my father, who was dead by then. The timetable was not like nowadays. You began at seven a.m. and left at noon; you returned at one p.m. and left at six. At eight p.m. I went to my classes until ten. At that time the official teachers not only used to give private lessons, paid for in advance, of course, but also gave them in accordance with a text book published by them and which the student had to buy: grammar, literatures (preceptive and historical), and mathematics.

Something shameful used to occur in the English class, and it was that the teacher of the course had devised a scale of prices for passing the students: 25 pesos, pass; 50, good; 75, excellent. On the eve of the examinations, students would go to his house and a little rehearsal would be conducted on how and what was the answer to questions arranged with him. His name was Bernardo Junco. A tall, stout old man, with an apopletic face. Today's young Cubans do not have the faintest idea of this, and I understand quite well that they cannot conceive of it. When I graduated with my degree I entered the University of Havana, the only one in existence then, as a Law student. I studied for only one year, which I passed. I abandoned the study of Law, and as I did that I published a poem in three sonnets, entitled **"Al margen de mis libros de estudios"**. It was published in the first number of the University journal *Alma Mater*, where Julio Antonio Mella appeared as "administrator". Later I returned to Camagüey, where I remained for several years working as a journalist, until in December 1927 I returned to Havana . . .

And what did you do here then?

It was the third time that I came, and it was third time lucky, since I obtained a post in the Government Secretariat through the efforts of friends of my father. Four years later I published the **Motivos de Son**, which caused a great commotion, largely the responsibility of José Antonio Fernández de Castro. However I never collaborated on the famous Sunday magazine which he used to edit in the **Diario de la Marina**. The confusion stems from what I did on another page in the same newspaper, the Ideales de una Raza (Ideals of a Race) of Urrutia. Neither did I ever publish a line in the *Revista de Avance* where one has to recognise its merit of having "ventilated" to no little extent the Cuban cultural ambit.

What valid contributions did those poems make to the black movement? And which were not so valid?

I believe that they made the eyes of public criticism turn to a phenomenon up to then considered not important or even non-existent—the rôle of the Negro in our national culture, and the proof was in those poems whose rhythms indicated the possibility of *injecting a mulatto element* into the Spanish romance, that is, to Cubanise it, returning it to its pristine state as in the times of the Ma Teodora. Look . . . one thing is certain, and it is that when concern for things Negro (la moda de lo negro) came to Cuba, not directly from Africa, but by way of Montparnasse and the Latin Quarter, it was converted into a way of seeing (modo) determined by the historical formation of our people, product of the African cultures coming to our country for more than three centuries, mixed with the Spanish culture. For we all are acquainted with the examples of Góngora and Lope; but in the Cuban environment, with Afro-Hispanic roots, it was not a matter of an adventure, or of an endeavour, as in those men of talent, but of establishing the serious contribution of one culture to another, in an incessant and vital interchange.

I believe that the youn gpoets should linger a bit to study the good models— and I am not referring to the "older" poets, but to the classics. At times I think that it would be necessary for some poets of undoubted talent to study seriously the means of expression, that is, grammar, metric forms, literary genres, some language—and of course , Spanish.

—Nicolás Guillén

From being the guitar of the people, the "son" passed on to the salons of the aristocracy, and influenced not only the nature of our music, but also the literature. . . . Forgive me; but this intermingling is not very hard to see throughout my work, from the **Motivos**—forty-two years ago—to today.

Do you consider yourself a poet of Negritude?

You ask me whether I consider myself a poet of Negritude, and I answer you in the negative. The same thing happens with Negritude as with Socialist Realism, of which everyone gives a different explanation, and perhaps they are all right. Sometimes I remember how Voltaire defined metaphysics as the search, in a dark room, for a black cat which is not in the room. All right then, I believe that Negritude can be explained in the struggle, among oppressed, alienated, denied black people against imperialism personified by the Americans, French, English and Dutch, that is to say by white men who oppress, alienate and deny them. For example, in Africa. The same thing happens in the Lesser Antilles, especially Guadeloupe and Martinique, islands which to the French are "les Antilles", and when they say "Antilles" they never think of an Antillean island the size of Cuba, which is the largest of them all. In Cuba itself, before the Revolution, Negritude or "negrismo" could be explained, because it revindicated the artistic, political, cultural, in short, the human values of the Negro in the face of discrimination or slavery, and his rôle in the national culture. It was one of the manifestations of the class struggle. But when a revolution wipes out that struggle and gives power to the working class without regard to skin colour, then that concept of racial superiority ceases to exist. There are moments—historical moments—when Negritude is bound to the national freedom movements; but it is impossible to maintain it as an attitude *a outrance* (excessively), because then it would be converted into another form of racism.

What books did you read when you were writing **Sóngoro Cosongo?**

You may laugh, but I was reading a book which had nothing to do with my position at that time; nothing less than Spengler's *Decline of the West,* very much in fashion at the time. I also read Ortega.

Although in **Sóngoro Cosongo** *there is no direct confrontation with reality, it can already be noticed in it some evidence of social preoccupations. How had reality acted on you?*

This book was written in the climate created by Ideales de una raza, and all that it produced. Because in spite of not being a revolutionary publication, but rather a reformist one, one must recognise in that page its great merit as a generator of social awareness. On the other hand, there was great latitude as regards publication and public treatment of the problems pertaining to black and white coexistence.

From the musical or rhythmic point of view, I was greatly influenced by the "Sexteto Habanero", which had spread the western "son" throughout the Island and especially in Havana. It would be an exaggeration to say that **Sóngoro Cosongo** expressed a great social concern, yet it is not lacking, above all considering certain poems like **"Caña"**, **"La pequeña oda a un negro boxeador cubano"**, etc. Some of my critics of the time, themselves Negroes, could not or would not see that in the very *Motivos* there were signs of an affirmation that was aesthetic and Negro—not racist—but not devoid of what has since been called Negritude. Read, for example, a poem like **"Negro Bembón"**, which has an attitude of smiling protest against the predominance of the canons of white beauty, whose archetypes belong to the European culture brought by the conqueror and imposed on the slaves, as I said a moment ago. In **Sóngoro Cosongo** you have to consider the fit of non-conformity in me, in the face of racial discrimination, especially in my native province, so deeply reactionary.

Between **Sóngoro Cosongo** *and* **West Indies Ltd.** *there is a lapse of three years. From one book to another there is a development of your poetry and your thinking. From black poetry it has gone on to Cuban poetry (color cubano), from poetry with social outlines it has gone on to full social poetry. Could you trace for us the reason for that evolution?*

The fall of Machado had a great influence on the course of my poetry and my life. I used to live on the fringe of Cuban politics, in spite of the fact that many of my articles—as can be seen in the majority of those which I published from 1928 on in *Ideales de una raza*, Urrutia's page—had an open and even violent revolutionary content. In truth, I was a non-conformist young man, deluded by that kind of activity, which reminded me negatively of the death of my father, an event which left a deep mark on me. Besides the fact that he was a mentor as regards my intelligence, I always felt lovingly bound to him. After his death, I had the clear knowledge that I had lost him in a stupid war, the civil war called "La Chambelona", in which conservatives and liberals confronted each other, groups which between them were no different except in name, since both were an expression of the electoral juggling in which the national bourgeosie, under Yankee imperialism, enjoyed power, by means of two great partisan elements, which were really only one, in the Yankee pattern. Therefore, my attitude was one of rebuke against national politics, to the extent that I never voted. When Machado fell, the picture of Cuban politics changed markedly. Different young groups sprouted, all calling themselves revolutionaries, among which the most prominent was the ABC, clearly fascist, from its ideology to its green shirts, its racism, its contempt for the masses, etc. I did not feel inclined to join any of those parties because, as Martínez Villena showed in those days, they were markedly reactionary in character. From 1934 I joined as a "fellow traveller" the ranks of the Cuban Communist Party, which was not even ten years old. So for example I worked with the Brotherhood of Young Cubans, the Pro-Abyssinian Committee, and with the Committee for Aiding the Spanish people.

I got together with friends of similar persuasion, and we founded the journal *Mediodía,* which soon changed its predominantly literary character to become a political and Communist organ, called upon to play a great rôle in the revolution. My activities, however insignificant, created an uncomfortable situation for me in Cuba. At that time I received an invitation, through Marinello—who was then in Mexico—to the conference organised by the League of Revolutionary Writers and Artists in that country; and I travelled to it by sea to Veracruz passing by Yucatán and then by train to Mexico City. Those were the days of the worthy general Lázaro Cárdenas, and under the protection of the democratic climate which characterised his government, I participated in revolutionary work over there, which helped one tremendously.

And from Mexico on to Spain, right?

Right. While I was in Mexico there occurred another great event in my life, again of fundamental importance, and it was my trip to Spain accompanied by Juan Marinello, Octavio Paz, José Mancisidor, Juan de la Cabada, Silvestre Revueltas and others to take part in the Second World Conference for the Defence of Culture, which took place in Valencia, Madrid, Barcelona and finally in Paris, where it was wound up. It was then that I met great names in world literature: Vallejo, Aragon, Ludwig Renn, Alberti, Spender, Anna Seghers, Ehrenburg, Huidobro, Neruda, Miguel Hernández, Bergamin and so many, many others that it would make the list endless. In Valencia I joined the Communist Party in 1938. In short, I'd say that it was those two events, the fall of Machado and the struggle of the Spanish people against Franco, that gave maturity and impetus to my revolutionary and political vocation, which I have served for about forty years with my poetry and which I shall continue serving to the end of my days. Of the people mentioned before, I had already met some in Cuba, such as Rafael Alberti and his wife María Teresa León, who were in Havana in 1935.

When did you begin to perceive that soldiers were of the people?

When I wrote the poem *West Indies Ltd.,* or rather when I happened to be writing it. Remember the part in which I refer to soldiers in the service of the bourgeosie:

!Dramática ceguedad de la tropa,
que siempre tiene presto el rifle

para disparar contra el que proteste o chifle,
porque el pan está duro o está clara la sopa!

Dramatic blindness of the soldiers,
With rifles always at the ready
to shoot a protester or a complainer
that the bread is hard or the soup watery!

And also:

los que ante el máuser exclaman "¡hermanos
    soldados!"
y ruedan heridos
con un hilo rojo en los labios morados.

Those who in the face of the mauser exclaim:
    "Brother soldiers!"
And roll wounded
with a red line on their violet lips.

Do you remember?

When I finished writing *West Indies Ltd.* I already had the material for the next book: *Cantos para soldados y sones para turistas.*

As we know, "Guadalupe W.I." included in subsequent editions did not appear in the first one of West Indies Ltd. *Discounting this, your preoccupation with the Americas began to reveal itself in* El Son Entero, *and your concern for the world at large in* La Paloma de vuelo popular. *Did your journeys abroad contribute to the grounds for those concerns? Were they the same before the trips?*

First, the poem about Guadeloupe does not appear in the first edition of *West Indies Ltd.* because it was written after a trip which at that time I had not yet made; specifically, the return journey from Spain, where I had spent about a year, at the height of the Civil War. In a previous poem, **"La pequeña oda a un negro boxeador cubano"**—which first appeared dedicated to Kid Chocolate—there was mention of the cane plantation, and imperialism, and even long before that the seed of the same idea could be found in the poem **"Futuro"**, which was in 1927, or rather, it was published in that year, in the journal *Orto,* by Manzanillo, and I don't remember whether I composed it before, though I assume I did, yes, it was before. Remember also the poem **"Llegada"**, from *Sóngoro Cosongo,* also of undoubted universal force. Of course, all that served as a propitious mould for establishing an ecumenical preoccupation and occupation. So that my journeys widened more and more the framework within which my poetry was inserted.

All your work is a struggle against prejudices. In your opinion, how has it contributed to their breakdown?

From a very early age I became accustomed to the struggle against racial prejudice. In Camagüey, my home town, there was always a dominant élite of cattlemen as ignorant as they were vain. I don't remember if I already told you that it was a group called El Liceo, centre and cradle of the most culturally narrow people in the province, perhaps in the whole Island. From my childhood, then, I saw the spectacle of discrimination against Negroes because of the colour of their skin, and against quite a few whites too because of their social extraction. This turned me into a rebel against a society like that, and from that rebellion sprang my non-conformity not only as regards racial prejudice, but also against all the others; that can be seen in my poetry. As far as my work contributing to the breakdown of certain prejudices, I say that it is possible, along with the work of other writers who were on the same level. Nevertheless, I am convinced that the collapse of those prejudices came about as a result of the triumph of our Revolution.

You have written two theatrical poems. In many of your poems dialogue plays a main rôle. Have you never planned to write a theatrical work of great spirit?

I ask myself that, I mean, why haven't I written a play. Rivas Cherif is amazed that with so many characters in my poetry—Papá Montero, Antonio's wife, Quirino with his "tres", el Negro Bembón, el Chévere, Cantaliso, Sargeant José Inés, Miguel Paz the soldier and many others—I haven't put them on the stage, moving them in the national ambit. At these levels it is now impossible, even if I were to consider that.

How was the "Elegía a Jesús Menéndez" conceived? And how was it written?

One afternoon in 1948, after lunch, I left the house where I was living, which belonged to the famous painter Cándido Portinari on Cosme Velho Street in Río de Janeiro, to go downtown. I returned some time later, and as I reached home, Portinari told me—"A leader among the workers in your country has been killed," and handed me a newspaper. It was the paper *O Globo,* and on the front page I learnt of the death of Jesús Menéndez, with not many details. Reading that news was a real shock. Menéndez and I were very close friends, so much so that when he sought nomination as representative of the People's Socialist Party in La Villas province, I was selected to accompany him on a tour of different places throughout that region. He gave talks and speeches, and I read poems, making up between the two of us a kind of political-cultural evening in every spot we visited. These activities further reaffirmed our friendship, which had many brotherly characteristics. On that very evening that I learnt of the death of Jesús, I began to write a poem for him.

Since I was at the time writing the Elegies which appear in *La paloma de vuelo popular,* I proposed writing an elegy for Menéndez. Well, I had only managed to write some verses, since I left Brazil for Cuba, and it was here, in Havana, where the poem took shape and was finally completed, after three years of labour. It was published at the height of dictatorship. It was a very complicated poem, as you know, and it took me many hours of hard work every day. Besides I came across certain technical difficulties which I think I was able to overcome, such as the one caused by the "romance" verse structure which forms part

III of the "Elegía". It was first written in octosyllabic lines which definitely seemed to me to be too weak for what I wanted. I then undertook the transformation of the "romance" from eight syllables to one of nine, and I don't think it has turned out too badly.

Along with irony and satire there is in your poetry a capacity for extraordinary tenderness. Yet still, the universal theme of love does not appear in your work until **El Son entero,** *and is later fully manifested in* **Poemas de amor.** *Why this absence of love until so late?*

I do not think that the expression "absence of love" is appropriate. Rather, it is a question of shyness, the shyness of expressing love in public. Amorous verses interest a small number of readers, among whom must be included the protagonists of the poems, and very few more.

> **I do all my writing on the typewriter, since I am not capable of writing even a couplet by hand. Furthermore, I indefatigably seek perfection, always unattainable. I ceaselessly correct what I write and I am never satisfied with what emerges out of my writings.**
>
> **— Nicolás Guillén**

Well, as far as I am concerned it cannot be said that love in my poetry came too late. A poem which I consider anthological, a romantic poem, was written in 1919 or 1920: that is, **"La Balada azul"**. From that same period there is a composition in four sonnets, **"Rosas de elegía"**. There are also some more not only of that time, but also of the period immediately following. So that today's poems which you consider late in reality have a very luxuriant origin. On the other hand, I believe that those who sing loudest about love or speak the most about it, are those who *practise* it least.

In the prologue to **Sóngoro Cosongo** *you spoke of color cubano (the Cuban colour). In your judgement, in which of your books is this best represented?*

I believe that it is in all of my work.

What opinion do you have of the works which the composers have made out of your poems?

I cannot give an opinion on this from a technical point of view, since as you know I cannot differentiate between a sharp and a flat. The only thing I have noticed is that some composers let themselves be carried along by the verbal rhythm of the poem and make a simple translation from the literary field to the musical. Others, on the contrary, turn away from that path and construct their own rhythm without formally adhering to that of the poem, although of course they keep it in mind.

For the rest, apart from the technical reasons which I mentioned at the beginning, I would not be able to revise all the musical texts written about my poems, since both within Cuba and outside they exceed one hundred.

In **El Gran Zoo** *you again refer to—"Avio-mamut", "Reloj"—themes which recall your "vanguardista" stage. Furthermore, the brevity of your poems reminds us of those in the* **Odas Mínimas**. *Why the return to the beginnings?*

Throughout my practice of poetry, some quarries remained unexploited, as I saw myself spurred on by revolutionary tasks, and if you allow me to say so, also by a somewhat sectarian criterion of my poetic office. So that as soon as circumstances permitted, I returned to those quarries to extract from them materials which I did not believe that I had sufficiently worked on when I handled them for the first time.

Many foreign editions of **El Gran Zoo** *have been made. My attention has been drawn to the Spanish one mutilated by censorship. How did you receive this?*

There are many. In none of them was I led to intervene, and naturally I do not know what they contain. Therefore I do not really care what Spanish censorship did. Besides, don't you think that historically it is a curious edition and that it is amusing to compare it with the editions from Cuba and from other countries?

Notice that the censor carried his zeal to the point of suppressing lines such as, e.g.:

. . . los generales con su sable de cola . . .
(generals with their tail-like sabres)

and also:

en su caballo estatua el héroe mono
(the monkey-hero in his equestrian statue).

To whom must he have thought, more daring than I, was I referring? Furthermore, the allusion to San Isidro Street in Havana disappeared from my poem **"El Chulo"**, I suppose it was because San Isidro is the patron saint of Madrid, and the street which bears his name in our city was a meeting place for prostitutes in times now gone. Of course, the poem **"Policía"** was dynamited, and not even a spark remained of it as a memory. Anyhow, no problem, for I have a copy . . .

About **El Gran Zoo** *a young poet manifested that it was a book which ought to have been written by a member of his generation. And you answered him: "It would have been magnificent. The only thing that the young man who might have written that book needed was fifty years of poetic experience". Using this as an entrée what do you think of the poetry which young people are writing at present in Cuba?*

In fact, it did happen the way you relate it. With reference to the young poets I think that at times they are in too much of a hurry. I sympathise with them all, in spite of the fact that it does not occur often, that is, there are not many poets of my age who in their pride, or worse, in their vanity gives the "alternativa" [a ceremony in which a senior matador authorises a novice matador to kill the bull, thus making the novice a full-fledged matador]—as they say in bullfighting—to young colleagues. Perhaps there are not many young people desirous of being together with the older ones, or letting the latter participate with them in the same work, which is the practice of poetry—well, I believe that the young poets should linger a bit to study the good models—and I am not referring to the "older" poets, but to the classics. At times I think that it would be necessary for some poets of undoubted talent to study seriously the means of expression, that is, grammar, metric forms, literary genres, some language—and of course, Spanish. I do not mean that I am asking, especially at these levels, that young poets should write like the poets of the Golden Age; but I really do believe that the latter are sound examples for a good literary formation. For the present I usually ask young poets when they do me the honour of submitting some poem for my judgement, if they have written at least a sonnet. I do not feel comfortable when I realise that they are unacquainted with even the most elementary strophic forms. In my opinion, to revolutionise an art, no matter what it may be, it is indispensable that it be first completely grasped. . . .

How do you work?

I work when I have the inclination. As soon as I realise that my inclination has disappeared, I do not touch the typewriter again. In that connection I'll tell you that I do all my writing on the typewriter, since I am not capable of writing even a couplet by hand. Furthermore, I indefatigably seek perfection, always unattainable. I ceaselessly correct what I write and I am never satisfied with what emerges out of my writings. I don't know if I told you that the **"Elegía a Jesús Menéndez"** took me three years.

In times that were difficult for the creative process and sometimes for living, how did you reconcile your work of creation with that of subsistence?

I always lived somewhat oppressed by circumstances, as much political as economic. Nevertheless, I never lacked time for writing—verse at night-time, or on days that I had more or less free, and prose when pressed by my journalistic occupation. When my prose works are published, you will see that they comprise mainly articles and chronicles. . . .

What historical events—national or international—which have occurred during your lifetime, have had the greatest effect on you?

The event which has influenced my life most profoundly has been our Revolution. May the reader, and you too, forgive me this slight immodesty; but the true fact is the Cuban Revolution is foreshadowed in my book ***Cantos para soldados y sones para turistas*** thirty-five years ago; and I alone do not say so, but also someone who has greater authority than I . . . I am very proud of that.

What is your opinion of the revolutionary policy of confronting cultural colonisation?

I believe that if in Cuba everything has changed, if everything is changing under the sway of the Revolution, it is inconceivable that there can be a literature or an art in disagreement with that process, that is to say, which denies or contradicts it in order to serve our enemies. In the same way that we are politically and economically free, we want to be that way in the cultural sphere. It isn't that we are attacking or rejecting world culture; and we agree with the theory that, as Lenin said, the conqueror receives from the conquered a cultural heritage which criticises and purifies, incorporating it into the national fund, adjusting it to its necessities. But we believe that we must express our own selves, and that we cannot invent types nor conflicts which do not belong to our idiosyncrasy, to our character, to our temperament. There is no Cuban Proust, no Cuban Joyce, no Cuban Gide. On the other hand, there is present everywhere that multiple and grandiose character of ours which is the Revolution. In Cuba imperialism has availed itself of innumerable agents to colonise our spirit, to transform us into imitators of their life style: that happened with the cinema, with music and—more serious still—with the language. The Congress of Education and Culture attached responsibility to our artists and writers, calling upon them to struggle openly against all spiritual colonisation.

In your work many references are found to sport. Can we consider you a sports fanatic? Since your poetry is eminently of the people, are the references to sport an expression of the interest of the Cuban in it?

From childhood—like every Cuban—I was crazy about baseball, and later as a young man I played it with friends of my age and from the district. I always wanted to be a pitcher; but I never succeeded in striking out a single batter. I do not like boxing, and I understand very well the repugnance it aroused in Martí. Nevertheless, I am not unaware of nor do I despise the credit brought to Cuba by men such as Kid Chocolate or Kid Charol. I speak about them in a poem. On the other hand I believe that sport is a wonderful instrument for understanding and fellowship among people, so that sometimes more is done in this sense by a good baseball club, a good stable of boxers, a good tennis team and even one of ping-pong players, than a minister or an ambassador. Turning back to baseball, I can say that I shall always remember ballplayers and clubs famous sixty years ago: el Almendares (I was always a fan of theirs), el Habana, el Fe . . . and men like Marsans, Almeida, whom Victor Muñoz nicknamed "el Marqués", Romañach, el Gran Méndez, Pedroso, the Calvo brothers, Cueto, Palmero, Violá, el Pájaro Cabrera, Hungo Strike González, Joséito y Merito Acosta, Jabuco and many more. This was baseball, and in general the sport was converted into business or industry, in which the players were sold and bought like horses, and which depended on what happened in the so-called American Major Leagues, where on the other hand Negro players were not admitted, not even important ones such as el Diamante Negro, José de la Caridad Méndez, already mentioned, who achieved the useless glory of pitching a no-hitter against the Philadel-

phia team managed by Connie Mack. The boom in baseball, the fact that in this and in all the other sports Cuba has attained extraordinary heights, is due precisely to the fact that the Cuban Revolution dynamited the colour bar, so that great athletes, formerly discriminated against, now had the opportunity to put their extraordinary qualities at the service of the sport which they practised and therefore of Cuba . . . You don't know how pleased I was to see, in the first days of the Revolution, a Negro boy playing golf in one of the old aristocratic clubs in Cuba, I do not know whether it was in the Biltmore Yacht Club, the Miramar Yacht Club, the Vedado Tennis Club or what. The fact is that I approached the little fellow and asked him if he liked that sport. The boy looked at me, his face lit up with joy and he replied: —"Do I like it? I have become an Eisenhower!"

Helene J. Farber de Aguilar (review date 1973)

SOURCE: "Poetry from Latin America: 'The Most Important Harvest of the Times,'" in *Parnassus: Poetry in Review,* Vol. 1, No. 2, Spring/Summer, 1973, pp. 175-86.

[*In the following excerpt, Farber de Aguilar favorably reviews* Guillén: Man-making Words, *praising the artistry and intelligence of Guillén's political poems.*]

It is unfortunate that [in *Guillén: Man-making Words,* Guillén's translators, Robert Márquez and David Arthur McMurray], have chosen to label him so quickly as "implacably anti-bourgeois." He *is* implacably anti-bourgeois; but the epithet is misleading, since about ninety percent of his colleagues, most of them lesser artists, would consider themselves marketable under the same sticker. Radical poets do not generally work in mysterious ways, and books prefaced with these *a priori* allegations of leftist commitment make me nervous. I always suspect that such political posturings are going to precede some very mediocre verse which I will then not feel free to dislike: nobody, after all, wants to knock the good guys. The wonderful thing about Guillén is that nobody has to. Cuba's national poet, the grand old man of the downtrodden and the insurgent, is as implacably artistic, as implacably meaningful and as implacably just as he is antibourgeois.

Nicolás Guillén is seventy years old. He is not widely read in the United States and even in Spanish-language anthologies tends to be treated as the leader of a specialized "Afro-Cuban" or "Black" movement in poetry (a kind of separate-but-equal division of poets) characterized principally by much rhythmic innovation, a certain casual folksiness and a sentimental, anecdotal strain of social commentary. Márquez and McMurray avoid fomenting this limited image. They have included only one "son," a few love lyrics—**"Ovenstone"** and **"Ana Maria"**—and one dedicatory poem, a delicate homage to Guillén's friend, Paul Eluard. For the rest, they have concentrated on the most significant feature of the poet's work: its political integrity.

Perhaps the highest compliment one can pay Guillén is to say that it is in just this sphere that his artistry is perfectly fulfilled. This is unusual. I can think of only one other modern poet in Spanish America—Cardenál—whose best and truest voice is heard in his poetry of protest. Sociopolitical themes often vitiate the literary quality of even great poems: Neruda's love poems excel his propaganda in those passages where his politics become explicit.

Most radical poetry follows one of two main routes to third-world realities. The first is a rhapsodic, mystical transfiguration of *el pueblo;* the second is a belligerent and oddly deadpan indictment of the folks on top. Revolutionary verse, until quite recently, oscillated between the incorrigibly mystical and the incorrigibly blunt, producing a general impression of pure incorrigibility and thoughtlessness. Nicolás Guillén's steady intelligence, the conspicuous thoughtfulness of his work, distinguishes him among the numerous poets of the left.

Guillén is always reasoning with the world around him, seeking agreement. He is rarely a prey to the amorphic, apocalyptic visions typical of so much radical art. His apostrophes are specific, making necessary the excellent glossary appended by the editors for the benefit of people like me who didn't even know who Capablanca was. (José Raul Capablanca, 1888-1942, Cuban chess grandmaster, held the title of World Champion from 1922 to 1927.) His questions are not rhetorical. Guillén does not want us to cheer: he wants us to *think:*

> Now then, ladies,
> gentlemen, girls,
> old men, rich men, poor men,
> Indians, Mulattoes, Negroes, Zambos,
> think what it would be:
> a world all South,
> a world all blood and lash,
> a world of white schools for whites,
> a world all Rock and all Little,
> a world all Yankee and all Faubus . . .

>   Consider that a moment.
> Imagine for just one instant!

                                        ("Little Rock")

A real person always stands at the other end of his dialogues, as in the **"Pequeña oda a un negro boxeador cubano"**—a poem, incidentally, not flawlessly translated: why "vital blood" for "toda la sangre"? And, "Let the envy of the whites / know proud, authentic black" is an unhappy rendering of the unpretentious "Y frente a la envidia de los blancos / hablar en negro de verdad." Blackness is not, in Guillén, a superior state of being: it is, as in this particular line, a language; and like other languages, a means to an end—communication with the rest of humanity. Even his overt calls to revolt display this gentle empathy. One of his most effective poems, **"Sabás,"** which is not included in this anthology, ends like this:

> For Heaven's sake, Sabás, stop being so crazy!
> Sabás, don't be so stupid
> nor so good!

Guillén is full of this painful, conversational rationality; he is never enthralled with the necessity of hate; rather, he seems sorry to find it necessary. The rhyme and rhythm of many poems accentuates this regret about the condition of the world:

> In the winter in *Paris*
> the *sans-abris*
> fair badly;
> the *sans-logis*
> fair badly;
> the *sans-nourrix*
> fair badly
> in the winter in *Paris.*

>   . . . . .

> In the winter in *Paris*
> the bourgeois comes
> (who loves *la vie*)

>   . . . . .

                              ("In the winter in Paris")

There is never the slightest hint that Guillén enjoys rage, however justified.

Elsewhere his poetry gives little shrugs of vivacity and black (in both senses) humor: "A great Alliance of Standard and United is arranged; / The Progress of those two is nothing strange." He can alternate six-line quips—barely poems at all—with works of deep racial sorrow. Yet an all-embracing *caritas* seems to be present at the back (at least) of the poet's mind; the **"Ballad of the Two Grandfathers"** reconciles enemies:

> I bring them together.
>   'Federico!
> Facundo!' They embrace. They sigh,
> they raise their sturdy heads;
> both of equal size,
> beneath the high stars;
> both of equal size,
> a Black longing, a White longing,
> both of equal size,
> they scream, dream, weep, sing.
> They dream, weep, sing.
> They weep, sing.
> Sing!

Through the gradual elimination of verbs of strife, mankind reaches song. Guillén's works are indeed "man-making." There is no grandiloquence in them, only grandeur.

The Márquez-McMurray book includes all Guillén's "Elegies." I should like to remark, also, on the magnificent rhyme of the English translations. Guillén is one of the very few poets who suffers less from rhymed translations than from unrhymed and this anthology appears to prove that it *is* possible, with minimal distortion, to approximate the original text via analogous rhyme.

Guillén: Man-making Words is a dignified introduction
to a major political poet. Readers indifferent to "radical
poetry" may find themselves converted. Even the overtly
hostile, especially those whose objections hinge primarily
on the supposed lack of aesthetic worth in most "political" art, will be surprised by Guillén's warmth and intelligent, human compassion. A word of caution to the skeptical: skip the editors' introduction, a masterpiece of col-
legiate pomposity. Read the notes and the poems.

Richard L. Jackson (essay date 1979)

SOURCE: "The Turning Point: The Blackening of Nicolás
Guillén and the Impact of his *Motivos de son*," in *Black
Writers in Latin America,* University of New Mexico Press,
1979, pp. 80-92.

[*In the following essay, Jackson discusses Guillén's rejection of the white literary aesthetic and his development of a black sensibility in his works of the late 1920s
and early 1930s, focusing on the volumes* Motivos de
son, Sóngoro cosongo, *and* West Indies, Ltd. *Jackson
maintains that Guillén "represents the major turning point
for literary blackness in Latin America."*]

Nicolás Guillén, . . . had his "white" stage, but . . . has
lived long enough to pass through it and to go on to
become the premier black poet writing in Spanish. Guillén's
earlier poetry was definitely non-black and largely incon-
sequential, of interest to contemporary readers only as
illustrations of his early expertise and technical domination of traditional Spanish verse forms, particularly those
in vogue during and just after the literary reign of Rubén
Darío, and as contrast they illustrate, as well, how far he
has come in the blackening process he underwent from
Cerebro y corazón (1922) to ***Motivos de son*** (1930). Before this metamorphosis, Guillén's literary output in the
twenties, with only a very few exceptions, followed European models. Literary historians who want to "deblacken"
him or turn him into a nonblack poet can find ample
evidence in these adolescent poems to support their view
which, as best expressed by Luis Iñiguez Madrigal [in his
introduction to Guillén's ***Summa poética,*** 1976], is that
Nicolás Guillén is not—nor has he ever been—a black
poet in language, style, or theme. Madrigal has another
view, namely, that Nicolás Guillén is not even a predominantly social poet, but one who writes primarily on "other" themes. Madrigal can find some evidence in these
early poems to support both his views, as Guillén's pre-
Motivos de son work is dominated by such universal or
colorless themes as love, death, nature, religion, and other
abstract head and heart ("cerebro y corazón") subjects.

But a turning point came early in Guillén's literary career
when he decided to focus his attention on the true black
experience in the New World, starting with his native
Cuba, where he saw the black as the one most affected by
imperialist exploitation and other evils. Refusing to continue to go the way of [Panama poet] Gaspar Octavio Hernández, Guillén abandoned the white muse he had followed in
his youth and infused his literature with a black sensibility
which has permeated his work for more than forty years.
A similar black sensibility, . . . characterized the originality
of the black Colombian poet, Candelario Obeso, who had
set his sights in the same direction. But Nicolás Guillén
represents the major turning point for literary blackness in
Latin America. The appearance of his ***Motivos de son*** in
1930, an authentic literary happening, was upsetting, unsettling and controversial, partly because they broke
momentarily with traditional Spanish verse expression and
partly because they dealt with authentic black characters,
but largely because they brought to literature a new and
genuine black concern, perspective, and poetic voice, which
even some blacks misunderstood.

The ***Motivos de son*** had a strong impact on black and
white Cubans alike. White readers, after getting over the
initial shock of seeing authentic blacks in literature, were
pleased to see them appear because, on the surface, Guillén
in ***Motivos de son*** seemed to highlight the comic and
picturesque side of the black locked into an uneducated
happy-go-lucky lower class image. Black readers were quick
to react negatively against the ***Motivos de son*** largely for
the same reason. They were not pleased to see the *negro
bembón* given center stage in literature nor were they
pleased to see what appeared to be the perpetuation of
stereotyped images of the black. Both groups, however,
soon came to realize that Guillén's ***Motivos de son*** went
far deeper than racial insult and superficial entertainment.
For one thing, both groups began to see in them the
unmistakable call to black pride. It was soon recognized
that the ***Motivos de son*** incorporated into formal poetic
structure distinctive oral forms from the musical heritage
of black people, but popular song and dance forms (the
son) that were familiar to all Cubans. Black and white
Cubans came to understand that Nicolás Guillén was using black talk and black rhythms to set escape motifs like
wine, women, and song against a harsh background of
unemployment, poverty, prejudice, and misery while making, in effect, a subtle plea for black pride and racial
identity as well as for more awareness of social inequities,
and of the growing presence of the United States in Cuba.

Although many critics prefer to hasten through this black
period in the poet's development, moving on to what they
think are his less racial stages, we cannot overestimate the
importance of Guillén's work in the late twenties and early
thirties. In these years Guillén laid the groundwork that
gave his later work meaning and direction, rejecting the
white aesthetic whether adhered to by whites, mulattoes,
or blacks. It is also during this period that he first declared
the black to be as Cuban as anyone else. Guillén attacked
in particular during this period the black's own propensity
to abrogate his rights by forfeiting them to white Cubans
who, though not always backed by law, were willing to
take advantage. To Guillén the black's own black phobia,
that is his own fear of being black and of identifying with
his *son,* his *rumba,* and his *bongó,* was the first obstacle
to overcome as he sought ways to restore value to a
people long denied it. Rejection of the white aesthetic and
a plea for black recognition are really the keys, paradoxically, to his theory of *mulatez,* of a mulatto Cuba. In

essence this theory represents the elevation of the black to the level already occupied by whites. Guillén's desire to write Cuban poetry, and not black poetry, is really the culmination of that elevation since Cuban poetry after Guillén can never again mean solely white or European poetry. Moreover, Guillén's subsequent rejection of the term Afro-Cuban paradoxically is the most problack statement he could make. To him the term "Cuban" already includes the "Afro," for the term has come of age and been elevated to the highest degree. Without the black, in other words, there would be no theory of *mulatez;* instead, there would only be white poetry in Cuba. Guillén, then, forces the black man into social recognition, and the white Cuban's acceptance of that theory is in effect a compromise.

Guillén's blackening process, his metamorphosis from a white escapist poet to a black poet, represents a rejection of the white aesthetic in general. More specifically, though, his defiant turnabout can be seen as a black reaction to poetic Negrism, which was a local movement staffed by white intellectuals largely in the Caribbean whose interest in things black in the late twenties and early thirties coincided with the black as *nouvelle vogue* in Europe and America. Rather than associate Guillén with poetic Negrism, we should see his dramatic conversion to blackness in the late twenties and early thirties as a reaction against this white literary fad that was sweeping the world, one Guillén himself defined [in his *Prosa de prisa: 1929-1972,* 1975-76] as

> circumstantial tourism which never penetrated deeply into the human tragedy of race, being more like excursions organized for photographing coconut trees, drums and naked Negroes, whilst there existed the seething drama of the flesh and blood Negro bearing the scars of whiplashes, a Negro now fused with the whites to produce an indelible mulatto imprint on the Cuban social scene.

Guillén writes with characteristic sarcasm in **"Pequeña oda a un negro boxeador cubano,"** the white man

> se desnuda
> para tostar su carne al sol
> y busca en Harlem y en La Habana
> jazz y son.
>
> undresses
> to toast his body in the sun
> and seeks in Harlem and Havana
> jazz and *son.*

By drawing directly from the black experience and by giving black reaction to that experience in the *Motivos de son,* Guillén pits the black as speaker from his own environment against the superficial interest in blacks, thus revealing a closeness to the subject, scene, or emotion depicted in each *poema-son* not found in poetic Negrism. It is this closeness, together with Guillén's understanding of his subject, that gives the *Motivos de son* their startling authenticity and Nicolás Guillén the title of authentic black poet.

Guillén lost little time in reaffirming that his conversion to blackness was not a passing fancy. One year later, in *Sóngoro cosongo* (1931), his second volume of black verse, he again set himself apart from the *negrista* craze. In the Prologue to this volume Guillén formulates in unequivocal terms a black credo justifying his new ethnic orientation. He writes, "I am not unaware of the fact that these verses will be repugnant to many persons, because they deal with issues concerning Negroes and the people, but that does not matter to me. Rather, I am happy." Although in this same prologue Guillén talks about "Cuban color" and calls his poems "mulatto verses," we should again remember that this is his way of forcing acceptance of the black as this prologue repeatedly makes reference to the "African shot-in-the-arm" the black presence represents in Cuba. The poems in this volume almost without exception continue to deal with the black experience in Cuba. Just as the semblance of self-mockery and black insult had helped gain respectability among the white *literati* for the *Motivos de son,* so too does his use of the term mulatto (which gives the white a share in blackness) for his black verse, help protect *Sóngoro cosongo* against white backlash.

If anything, the black racial nature of Guillén's poetry intensifies in *Sóngoro cosongo.* The language changes a bit, becoming less colloquial, and the form moves closer to recognizable Spanish verse. The emphasis, though, is the same: black pride, the black experience, and black types continue to dominate his poetry. Guillén continues to introduce the Cuban reader to the black world. But unlike the *Motivos de son* where the black is largely the speaker and singer, in *Songoro cosongo* the black, for the most part, is spoken about. The *Motivos de son,* in other words, is closer to black speech and black song (*son*) in poetic form, while *Sóngoro cosongo* is closer in several poems to the Spanish *romance* or ballad form, but with *son* elements. *Sóngoro cosongo* represents growth as Guillén includes variations on the *son* form while enlarging the black world he is introducing by bringing in black folklore, superstitions, even negative types. The black world of the time he represents was not always a pleasant one, but his point is clear: the black has arrived and literature must recognize this fact.

Perhaps the best illustration of this point can be seen in **"Llegada"** (**"The Arrival"**), the poem that, significantly, opens this volume. In this lead-off statement which ostensibly describes the arrival of the black as slave to the Island, Guillén repeatedly writes as refrain "¡Aquí estamos!" ("Here we are!") as the poem develops into yet another expression of black racial affirmation. **"Pequeña oda a un negro boxeador cubano,"** which Guillén first published in 1929, one year before the *Motivos de son,* has the same turning-point impact. This poem, like **"Mujer nueva"** whose black woman figure "trae la palabra inédita" ("brings new knowledge"), is a strong call for racial pride and black identity. To be sure, **"Pequeña oda a un negro boxeador cubano"** can be read on several levels: (1) as a poem about a black boxer; (2) as a poem where the black boxer acts as symbol for all blacks in struggle; and (3) as a poem about a struggle between nations, more specifically, about impending conflict between Cuba and the United

States. But it is the final verse of that poem, where the poet exhorts the black to "hablar en negro de verdad" ("speak in real black talk")—a phrase that certainly refers to more than just black dialect—that underscores the authentic blackening of the poet in this early period. From the black fist of the boxer in **"Pequeña oda a un negro boxeador cubano"** to the black fist of the slave rower in **"Llegada,"** who has now exchanged his oar for a knife, "apto para las pieles bárbaras" ("appropriate for foreign skins"), there is really very little distance. These three poems, **"Pequeña oda a un negro boxeador cubano," "Llegada,"** and **"Mujer nueva,"** and others in *Sóngoro cosongo* are very black indeed even though they do not contain any of the phonetic speech characteristic of his *Motivos de son*.

In 1934 Guillén published *West Indies Ltd.,* a volume widely hailed as his first volume of social (as opposed to racial) protest poetry. But it is in this volume in which Guillén widens his perspective or attack that he, at the same time, deepens the blackening process begun in the late twenties, crystallized with *Motivos de son* in 1930, and continued in 1931 with *Sóngoro cosongo*. It is evident that Nicolás Guillén focuses as well on the dispossessed white, "Dos niños: uno negro, otro blanco . . . ramos de un mismo árbol de miseria" ("Two children: one black, one white . . . two branches from the same tree of misery"), to illustrate yet another victim, like the black, of United States imperialism in the Antilles, but it would be a mistake to accept that Guillén's concern for the black in this volume is only a symbolic one. The poet continues to depict specific black figures and black folklore, and he also continues his program of instilling black pride in those blacks like Sabás—in a poem of the same name—who continue to go about with their hands out begging rather than shaking the strong black fist, the "puño fuerte elemental y puro" ("fists, pure, unadorned and strong"), of **"Nocturno en los muelles,"** and the "puños los que me das / para rajar los cocos tal como un pequeño dios colérico" ("fists that you give me to slice open coconuts like a small angry god") of **"Palabras en el trópico,"** the lead-off poem in the *West Indies Ltd.* collection. Guillén perhaps more insistently than in his two previous volumes of black verse makes himself the focal character in many of the poems as time and again he emphasizes his own black identity. In **"Palabras en el trópico,"** the poet speaks of his "dark body," his "curly hair." In **"Adivinanzas"** "the black" becomes "I." Either he or other blacks like "I, Simón Caraballo the black" in **"Balada de Simón Caraballo"** or "The blacks, working" in **"Guadalupe W.I."** are the stars. Most importantly in **"West Indies Ltd.,"** the long poem that gives the collection its title, it is clear that Guillén's concerns have moved beyond Cuba, but it is equally clear that the poet of black pride admonishing Sabás is the same poetic voice speaking at times in the sarcastic tone of an intelligent observer and at other times through the *son* sung at intervals throughout the poem by Juan el Barbero. This is a point the poet does not want the reader to miss, as he closes this poem with the words, "This was written by Nicolás Guillén, *antillano,* in the year nineteen hundred and thirty-four."

Despite Guillén's ever-widening circle of concerns that he has pursued throughout his long career, he has never left the black man behind or out of his poetry. In one of the few published studies of its kind, Constance Sparrow de García Barrio [in *Blacks in Hispanic Literature,* 1977] recently traced Guillén's creation of new black characters through his later poetry that includes poems, for example, on such contemporary black figures as Martin Luther King and Angela Davis. In *Tengo* (1964), Guillén, significantly, speaks specifically as a black man in praise of Castro's Cuba where some allege, including Guillén himself, racial identity is no longer important. Throughout his career it has been his insistence on elevating the black that has given his poetry the extra dimension and excitement that makes him a "classic poet" who "has a clear understanding of his art and an absolute control of his technique, as well as something to say" [Arturo Torres Rioseco, in *The Epic of Latin American Literature,* 1959]. It is this "something to say" that distinguishes his *Motivos de son* and his later poetry from his earlier nonblack work and that sets his verse off from the *negrista* poetry of his white contemporaries. It is also this "something to say" that had a profound effect on Fernando Ortiz, the white Cuban specialist on things black, whose racist research had provided source material and orientation to white *negrista* poets *prior* to Guillén's appearance and domination of the Cuban literary scene in the late twenties and early thirties.

Guillén not only turned himself and *negrista* poetry around but his theory of *mulatez* seems to have been instrumental in turning Ortiz away from a rather clinical examination of the black largely as isolated criminal and slave and more toward the integration of blacks and whites in Cuba, the essence of Ortiz's well-known concept of *cubanidad,* which he developed in the forties. Rather than saying, as G. R. Coulthard has done [in *Race and Color in Caribbean Literature,* 1962], that "Guillén's work in many respects appears as an artistic transposition of the ideas of Ortiz," we should be saying that Ortiz's later work reflects Guillén's ideas on matters of race. Before Guillén's conversion to and insistence on blackness in Cuba, Ortiz was known in part for his *Glosario de Afronegrismos* (1923), a collection of African words and words that sound African that, because of their rhythmic quality, proved useful to the *negrista* poets. He was known also for what can be called his "unholy trinity," a series of works on "el hampa afro-cubano": *Los negros brujos* (1906), *Los negros esclavos* (1916), and "Los negros curros," a lecture he gave in 1911 whose title he had planned to give to a third volume in the trilogy. This third volume that, according to Alberto Pamies [in *Los negros brujos,* 1973] was one of the studies Ortiz was working on at the time of his death in 1959, would have completed the trilogy, but judging from its emphasis on "certain ruffians that *infest* [italics mine] Cuban life"—the definition Ortiz gives for *negros curros*—its publication would have been a retrograde step for Ortiz. The unilateral negativity of that view had been superseded in his work in the *Revista de estudios Afro-Cubanos* (1937-40), in his essay "Por la integración cubana de blancos y negros," in his *Engaño de la raza* (1947), and especially in his "Los factores humanos de la cubanidad," where the antiracist and prointegration stance of Nicolás Guillén's are best reflected. Ortiz even co-opts the word *ajiaco* from Guillén's poem **"La canción del bongó,"** the only real "mulatto verse" in *Sóngoro cosongo.* Ortiz uses this word as the central metaphor for Cuba in his essay, "Los factores humanos de la cubanidad." After the blackening of Nicolás Guillén, Ortiz intensifies his view that "Cuba is an *ajiaco* (stew)." It is also after Guillén that words like *creación mulata* and *música blanquinegra* become a part of Ortiz's repertoire. Before Guillén, in short, Ortiz's emphasis was on the Cuban black, not on the black Cuban or the mulatto Cuban, and on the "Afro" part of the term "Afro-Cuban"—an isolated, negative part at best.

Guillén's decision, then, during the late twenties and early thirties to write as a black about blacks and to blacks, and to whites and mulattoes, too, was an influential one that represented a new departure for himself and for his contemporaries. But what was the immediate impulse that brought him to that new commitment? Literary historians and Nicolás Guillén, too, usually point to a moment in 1930 when the words and rhythm of *negro bembón* came to the poet in a dreamlike trance after which the ***Motivos de son*** were written, dashed off, as it were, in white hot heat. But what put him in that trance in the first place? Angel Augier in his well-documented background study to Guillén up to 1947 [*Nicolás Guillén, notos para un estudio biográfico crítico,* 1962] sees the collective unconsciousness at work here. This may well be true, but Guillén's new *racial* plan of attack was more than involuntary. We know that his turning point was inspired in part by his own personal experiences of racism, by his awareness of worsening economic conditions for blacks in Cuba, and by the control of the black literary and cultural image that was being taken over by white intellectuals like Fernando Ortiz and the *negrista* poets. We know also that Guillén had many local black models to emulate, including his father, Lino Dou, Juan Gualberto Gómez, and Gustavo E. Urrutia, the Director of Ideales de la Raza, the black section of the *Diario de la Marina* where Guillen published much of his first work. But most of all, I believe, the black model or example set by Langston Hughes provided one of the most immediate sparks.

Langston Hughes, the dean of black poets in the United States, was already famous when he made his second trip to Cuba in February 1930. Guillén met Hughes on this trip, showed him around, and as a journalist published an interview he had with him that he called "Conversation with Langston Hughes" on 9 March 1930, in the *Diario de la Marina.* The very next month, on 20 April 1930, Guillén published his ***Motivos de son.*** For a black writer who had already begun to see that the black problem was really a white problem, the black pride and racial flavor of Langston Hughes' verse and manner had to have an impact on any black, certainly on one who writes. I think what moved Guillén deeper into his blackening process was Langston Hughes' physical or somatic appearance. In Guillén's words [in the interview], Hughes "looked just like a little Cuban mulatto. One of those dandies who spends all his time organizing little family parties for two dollars a ticket." This description, of course, is negative, but Guillén's appraisal of "this great Black poet," "one of the souls most interested in the black race," is overwhelmingly positive. The impact for Guillén, I believe, comes with the realization that Hughes, a mulatto like himself, could gen-

uinely identify with blacks with a dedication so intense that his only concern "is to study his people, to translate their experience into poetry, to make it known and loved." When Guillén says that Langston Hughes is unique, we have to understand this statement to mean both Hughes' total concern "with everything related to blacks" and the fact that this concern can come from a mulatto.

In this same interview, Guillén says that the Hughes poem containing the words, "I am a Negro / Black as the night is black / Black like the depths of my Africa," makes him feel as though it "springs from the depths of my own soul." Guillén decided shortly after Hughes' departure to inject some authentic blackness into Cuban letters, from the bottom up. He decided, quite simply, that it was time for "The New Negro" to make his appearance in Cuba as well. We should not forget that the twenties had been the decade of the world famous Harlem Renaissance, which influenced just about everybody who adopted a black perspective from that decade on, and Langston Hughes was at the center of that movement from its very beginning. Guillén himself writes about Harlem in an article, "Camino de Harlem," published in 1929, that can be seen as the starting point of his determination to bring to his country a corrective vision regarding Cuba's ethnic composition. It is this new vision that his poetry celebrates with himself at the center as a symbol of the mulatto nature of that ethnic composition. Guillén also was concerned that Cuba avoid taking the negative direction to which "going the way of Harlem" could lead. He did not want black Havana to become as black Harlem had become, a city within a city. He wanted the black recognized but at the same time fully integrated. Nor did he want the black to be a passing fancy, a danger he saw inherent in *negrismo* and perhaps in The Harlem Renaissance, which despite the authentic blackness of Langston Hughes and others, did contain some of the superficiality that white interest and involvement in the movement had fostered. Perhaps more interesting than Guillén's portrait of blacks is his self-portrait as one who resolves in his *son* all the racial and cultural contradictions of a black and white society. His own *mulatez* certainly resolves that conflict. He extends that personal identity through his mulatto verses to his country. That is why I think Langston Hughes' identification with blacks could not go unnoticed by Guillén, especially since the tendency in the Antilles was for mulattoes to identify or to align with whites. Guillén decided, in short, that in Cuba he would bring all the people together-black, white, and mulatto-through his concept of *mulatez.* This is the face Cuba has put on to the world ever since.

It is not surprising, then, that Guillén's conversion to blackness becomes complete shortly after Hughes' departure from the Island. Guillén even deleted an unfavorable reference to Langston Hughes that had appeared in the original 1929 version of his **"Pequeña oda a un negro boxeador cubano,"** one accusing Hughes of being unconcerned about the black boxer. Nor is it surprising to see the *Ltd.* of Hughes' *Scottsboro Ltd.* (1932) reappear in Guillén's title ***West Indies Ltd.*** (1934), or to see Guillén try the *son*-form, which sometimes has a blues effect, considering Hughes' earlier success with blues and jazz forms in poetry. One also can see the striking similarity between Guillén's black credo in the prologue to his *Sóngoro cosongo* (1932), especially the part where Guillén says that it does not matter if people are not pleased with what he is doing, and Hughes' own well-known declaration of artistic and racial commitment published five years earlier. He wrote in that piece ["The Negro Artist and the Racial Mountain," *The Nation,* 23 June, 1926], "If white people are pleased we are glad. If they are not it doesn't matter . . . If colored people are pleased we are glad. If they are not their displeasure doesn't matter either." Were it not for such credos firmly rooted in black ethnic identity, it is possible that the later revolutionary vision these two poets developed might not have been so intense. Guillén realized, as did Hughes, that "the very root of Fascism grows out of terrain fertilized by racial hatred and the division of men into inferior and superior beings and that he, the Negro, has been assigned the lowest place." It was that indirect vested racial interest that carried them both to Spain to oppose fascism during the Spanish Civil War. The same concern prompts Guillén to care about the dispossessed of whatever color and to oppose what he sees as racist tinged United States imperialism. It is but a small step, then, from Guillén's early black poetry of his *Motivos de son* days . . . to his current revolutionary poetry. The two are not as mutually exclusive as some would have us think.

I see a compatibility between Guillén poet of negritude and Guillén poet of revolutionary Cuba. Guillén need not have continued with the black talk of the *Motivos de son* to be considered a poet of negritude as Gordon Brotherston [*Latin American Poetry,* 1975] and others seem to think. Nor was it necessary for him to abandon the black man to be considered a universal poet. Although Guillén now rejects the term negritude that he insists on seeing in its strictest sense, there can be little doubt that he was just as much a forerunner of the term in its strictest racial sense as he is now a leading exponent of what I have called elsewhere [*The Black Image in Latin American Literature,* 1976] the negritude of synthesis, which is negritude understood in a broader sense that does not reject "a quest for an antiracist, possibly universal culture, 'the culminating point of the dream of every serious advocate of Negritude,' a universal brotherhood in which the black man will establish solidarity with all mankind." The organization of this section on the Major Period reflects the central role Guillén played in the development of black consciousness and black literature in Latin America in the thirties and forties, when—under his influence—the black as author became just as visible as the black as subject. This period is major because of the high visibility given the black as author through the appearance of works like Pilar Barrios' *Piel negra* (1947) and Virginia Brindis de Salas' *Pregón de Marimorena* (1947) in Uruguay, Juan Pablo Sojo's *Nochebuena negra* (1943) in Venezuela. Adalberto Ortiz's *Juyungo* (1943) in Ecuador, and Jorge Artel's *Tambores en la noche* (1940) and Arnoldo Palacios' *Las estrellas son negras* (1949) in Colombia. These works and others such as Guillén's *El son entero* (1947) that follow his initiative of the thirties, made the forties especially a fertile decade for black writers in Latin America.

Keith Ellis on Guillén's place in history:

Guillén's wide span of interests has been channelled, by an ideological outlook that has grown in firmness with time, into a powerful current of poetry. Always a conscientious artist, he mastered early the conventional forms of Hispanic poetry and soon contributed innovations and variations, some of which derived from his discernment of the artistic possibilities of popular Cuban culture. This innovative virtuosity has constantly permitted him to find forms appropriate to expressing, first, advanced insights into the conditions of his country—for Cuba is the trunk of the tree of his poetry—and the universal ramifications of these insights. The lucidity and impeccable gracefulness with which his social perceptions emerge from his poems and the mature coherence of his total work make this Cuban, West Indian, and Spanish-American poet an outstanding international figure who occupies a high and secure place in the history of poetry.

Keith Ellis, in Cuba's Nicolás Guillén: Poetry and Ideology, *University of Toronto Press, 1983.*

Stephanie Davis-Lett (essay date 1980)

SOURCE: "Literary Games in the Works of Nicolás Guillén," in *Perspectives on Contemporary Literature,* Vol. 6, 1980, pp. 135-42.

[*In the essay below, Davis-Lett examines Guillén's use of literary games, specifically, mockery of traditional poetry in his works.*]

Nicolás Guillén is most recognized for his Afro-Cuban poetry written during the 1930's and for his social poetry written since then. But while he has achieved fame as a black social poet, he unfortunately has not been recognized as one of the greatest humorists in Latin American literature. Since much of his humor results from a sense of play or poetic games, no true appreciation of Guillén the humorist can overlook the aspect of play or game in his poetry. The purpose of the present study is to examine these poetic games so frequent in Guillén's works.

Games and play take many forms in Guillén's poetry; indeed, far too many for me to examine here. For this reason, I would like to consider only one of the most outstanding manifestations of play in Guillén's poetry—literary games. In general, we can reduce Guillén's literary games to one broad category—a mockery of traditional poetry (especially Modernist verse) and all that this type of poetry implies: a certain tone and rhetoric, traditional images, an appropriate subject matter, and even a specific form or structure, such as stanzaic arrangement.

Guillén's literary games date back to one of his earliest collections, the *Poemas de transición* or *Transitional Poems,* written between 1927 and 1931. As we know, this is the period of Charlie Chaplin, of the famous Cuban literary journal *Revista de Avance,* and of *avant garde* literary movements throughout the Hispanic world which demonstrated, according to Dámasco Alonso [in *Poetas españoles contemporáneos,* 1958], an "ennoblement of humor, or perhaps better expressed, of a certain sportive and frivolous happiness." Thus, it should come as no surprise to us that a young Guillén beginning to write poetry during this period should consider fundamental a sense of play or game.

More than anything else, Guillén and his Hispanic contemporaries sought to strike out against or rather laugh in the face of Modernist poetry. It must be remembered that the *modernismo* prevalent in Cuba during the first two decades of the twentieth century was not the elegant, silken verse of Rubén Darío or even the energetic poetry of José Martí (who, incidentally, was virtually unknown in Cuba until the vanguardist period). Rather it was the weaker, lifeless verses of their imitators which circulated in Cuban literary circles of the day. The literary critic Ángel Augier commented [in *Nicolás Guillén: Obra poetica,* Vol. 1, 1972] that Guillén began to write when "the agonizing death-song of the Modernist swan had exhausted its last lyrical force and conserved only a distant echo of its once beautiful harmony," and that Modernist poetry had degenerated to little more than a combination of "hand-worn images," "hackneyed constructions," and "simple formulas of commonplaces." It was against this moribund *modernismo* that Guillén rebelled with his first literary games.

In one of these games Guillén makes fun of the notion of the poetic muse traditionally invoked by poets for inspiration. The muse is generally considered to be an abstract entity to whom the poet speaks in a most serious, almost reverent tone. But not so with Guillén, who in his **"Elegía moderna del motivo cursi"** ("Modern Elegy on an Affected Motif") insists that his muse is a real woman:

No sé lo que tú piensas, hermano, pero creo
que hay que educar la Musa desde pequeña en una
fobia sincera contra las cosas de la Luna,
satélite cornudo, desprestigiado y feo.

Edúcala en los parques, respirando aire libre,
mojándose en los ríos y secándose al sol;
que sude, que boxee, que se exalte, que vibre,
que apueste, en las carreras y que juegue hand ball.

Tú dirás que el consejo es pura "pose", ¿no es
    eso?
Pues no, señor, hermano. Lo que ocurre es que
    aspiro
a eliminar el tipo de la mujer-suspiro,
que está dentro del mundo como un párajo preso.

Por lo pronto, mi musa ya está hecha a mi modo.
Fuma. Baila. Se ríe. Sabe algo de derecho,
es múltiple en la triste comunidad del lecho
y dulce cuando grito, blasfemo o me incomodo.
Por otra parte, cierro mi jardín de tal suerte
que no hay allí manera de extasiarse en la Luna.

(Por la noche, el teatro, el cabaret, o alguna
recepción . . .) Y así vivo considerado y fuerte.

Not only is Guillén's muse real, she is scandalous as well, engaging in activities "unbecoming a lady" during that epoch: smoking, boxing, and playing handball. (We note, incidentally, the many references to games or sports mentioned among the muse's activities: horse racing, boxing, and handball.) Thus, in no way does this poet's muse correspond to the traditional idea of the poetic muse.

Also, if we examine Guillén's references here to the moon, another cliché in traditional poetry, we find that his tone is equally as disrespectful since he considers this celestial body to be nothing but a "cuckolded satellite" who is "ugly and without prestige," and capable of "intoxicating" the young muse. Perhaps inspired by Jules Laforgue and Leopoldo Lugones, earlier poets who had also poked fun at the traditional image of the moon, Guillén ridicules the image of the beautiful, romantic moon because it represents the kind of imagery that was stagnant in pre-vanguardist poetry. Guillén's preference for startling imagery was quite common among *avant garde* writers because they inevitably sought to shock their readers. What interets us, however, is that the use of such images was not a passing phase with Guillén but rather a stylistic constant. What was a broken rule in the game of traditional or late Modernist poetry (i.e., the replacement of worn-out images with shocking metaphors) became a basic rule to be followed in the poetic world which Nicolás Guillén would establish for himself and his readers.

In **"Nieve"** [Snow] from the **Rueda dentada** collection [*The Serrated Wheel*; 1974], Guillén's target is traditional love poetry. In this poem we immediately recognize a parody of the famous "Il pleure dans mon coeur" by Verlaine. But in Guillén's version, the poet-lover speaks of snow instead of rain.

Como la nieve cae aquí,
nieva también dentro de mí.
(Verlaine con nieve¿ no es así?)
De ti me acuerdo-ya sin ti.

¿A qué llorar, me digo yo,
por quien no llora ni lloró?
Si estuve escrito, me borró,
si ardí un instante, me apagó.

Caiga la nieve, está muy bien.
Mas no por eso va Guillén
a entristecerse si no hay quien
del mismo mal muera también.

Literatura, en realidad,
nimia de toda nimiedad.
¿Que está nevando en la ciudad?
Al fin y al cabo es la verdad.

Any successful parody employs imitation and variation on two levels: formal and thematic. Guillén's imitation of the Verlaine poem on a formal level can be seen in his copying the very regular meter of the original French poem (a meter which was itself an imitation of falling rain), his altering only slightly Verlaine's rhyme pattern, and his faithfully following the stanzaic grouping of the French original. But in his treatment of the theme, Guillén has perverted the "spirit" of the French poem since his poem is not a mournful complaint, but rather a witty, light-hearted piece in which the rejected lover pragmatically accepts his plight. That Guillén is playing a game is witnessed not only by the conversion of rain into snow, but by his intra-textual references to Verlaine and himself. Also, his use of opposites ("De ti me acuerdo—ya sin ti," "Si estuve escrito, me borró," "Si ardí, me apagó") represents another element of play in the poem. And finally, the last stanza contains a succinct statement of Guillén's feelings about traditional love poetry: "Literatura, en realidad, nimia de toda nimiedad" ("Literature is the most trivial of all triviality"). Thus once again, flippancy reigns supreme, and the Cuban poet has played the love-poetry game according to his own rules.

With regard to imagery, we have already seen Guillén's playful spirit at work in his depiction of the moon in the **"Elegía moderna."** But the height of his mockery of traditional imagery appears in his collection **El Gran Zoo (The Great Zoo)**, published in 1967. The use of unusual imagery is crucial to this collection because each "animal" in the zoo is developed through a series of fleeting metaphors. Because of such metaphoric language, as well as the brevity of the poems (they all represent signs or placards in the zoo), the total effect of the collection is impressionistic.

What immediately shocks the reader about **El Gran Zoo** is the fact that many of the "animals" in the zoo are not really animals. Guillén has populated his zoo with such "beasts" as: mountains, rivers, moneylenders, gangsters, speechmakers, musicians, diseases (cancer), clouds, and the moon. This celestial body, which had appeared in the **"Elegía moderna"** as a "satélite cornudo y feo", is now presented as:

> Mamífero metálico. Nocturno
> Se le ve
> el rostro comido por un acné.
>
> Sputniks y sonetos.

Likewise, Guillén's image of the tiger is interesting: an animal "trapped in his cage of tough, black stripes." The great rivers of the world are depicted as "powerful springs of gigantic trucks," while thirst is a "sponge of sweet water which devours a river and strangles with a thin, red ribbon." Moneylenders are presented as "monstrous bird-like creatures" and the guitar is "svelte and refined, with the eyes of a fertile *mulata*." These unusual images, the formal appearance of the poems, plus the over-all idea of a zoo with animals which aren't really animals, indicate that Guillén in this collection has set up an entirely different poetic game in which he alone makes up the rules.

The poems we have examined thus far have considered the poet's mockery of traditional poetic rhetoric or imagery. But in what is perhaps Guillén's most famous collection, the **Motivos de son** or *"Son" Motifs* (1930), the poet mocks poetic form as well. The eight poems in this

collection, all of whose protagonists are poor blacks from Havana's slums, are designed to capture in verse a popular song and dance form of the 1930's—the Cuban *son*. The *son* was a song whose melody came from Spain, but whose rhythmical flourishment was African in origin. The structure of the *son* consisted of two parts: (1) a *largo* or *motivo* in which the theme of the song was introduced and (2) the *montuno* in which the theme is expanded and a chorus or refrain is introduced. Guillén's attempt to imitate this song form resulted in a highly rhythmical poetry, based largely on octo-syllabic verses and verses with a strong final beat (*versos agudos*). He called these poems *poemas-sones*.

That there is much play at hand in the **Motivos de son** can be seen in the analysis of a typical poema-son, **"Mulata"**:

> Ya yo me enteré, mulata,
> mulata, ya sé que dise
> que yo tengo la narise
> como nudo de cobbata.
>
> Y fíjate bien que tú
> no ere tan adelantá,
> poqque tu boca e bien grande,
> y tu pasa, colorá.
>
> Tanto tren con tu cuerpo,
> tanto tren;
> tanto tren con tu boca,
> tanto tren;
> tanto tren con tu sojo,
> tanto tren.
>
> Si tú supiera, mulata,
> la veddá;
> ¡quo yo con mi negra tengo,
> y no te quiero pa na!

The theme of the poem is obvious: a black suitor has been rejected by a mulatto woman because she feels he is too dark-complexioned. The lover retorts by pointing out to her that she, too, despite her light skin ("ser adelantada") has African blood, as witnessed by her overly-curly hair ("pasa colorá") and her big mouth ("tu boca e bien grande"). Throughout the poem there exists an element of teasing (a technique whose very roots lie in the notion of play), and this teasing reaches its climax in the *montuno* of the poem with the refrain "tanto tren." "Tanto tren," a Cuban expression meaning "such a fuss over," is employed by Guillén not only to point out the *mulata*'s vanity, but also to suggest the very rhythmical movement of her body. (This sense of rhythm is produced by the constant alternation of seven-syllable verses with *agudo* verses of four syllables.)

To Guillén, poetry should be no stagnant reservoir of cliché ideas or rhetoric, but rather a vibrant form of expression always open to change.

—Stephanie Davis-Lett

Other violations of traditional poetry in **"Mulata"** include: (1) the presentation of poor black characters as subject matter, since this was taboo in Cuban poetry of the era, (2) the use of black Cuban dialect (as exhibited by Guillén's strange orthography in the poem), (3) the presence of a popular lexicon (as witnessed in such expressions as "ser adelantada," "pasa," "tanto tren"), and a mockery of cliché imagery (when the poet refers to the black man's nose as a "knot of a necktie" or "nudo de cobbata"). In **"Mulata"** we see that Guillén, by form, rhetoric, and even characterization, has gone beyond what was typical in Cuban poetry up until that time; he has once again created a new game.

In **"Si tú supiera"** ("If You but Knew"), another *poema-son,* the type of play at hand is a play on sounds. This poem makes use of the *jitanjáfora,* a meaningless word or phrase used only for a sonorous effect. The *jitanjáfora* "sóngoro cosongo" and its variations appear in the *montuno* of the poem as an expression of the narrator-lover's anguish:

> ¡Ay, negra
> si tú supiera!
> Anoche te bi pasá
> y no quise que me biera.
> A é tú le hará como a mí,
> que cuando no tube plata
> te corrite de bachata,
> sin accodadte de mí.
> Sóngoro cosongo,
> songo be;
> Sóngoro cosongo
> de mamey.
> sóngoro, la negra
> baila bien;
> sóngoro de uno
> sóngoro de tre.
> Aé,
> bengan a be;
> aé,
> bamo pa be;
> bengan, sóngoro cosongo,
> sóngoro cosongo de mamey!

The ultimate step in Guillén's game of mocking traditional poetic form can be seen in his collection *El diario que a diario* (*The Daily Daily*), published in 1974. In this collection the Cuban poet goes one step further when he challenges the traditional stanzaic format and spatial arrangement of poetry. If the poems in *El Gran Zoo* are supposed to represent signs, those in *El diario* imitate articles or advertisements in a newspaper that recounts the history of Cuba. Thus, many of the poems bear a close resemblance to prose. Examples of this type of poetic game are the advertisements or announcements about slaves, announcements which would have been typical in colonial Cuban newspapers:

"Ventas"

Una pareja de blanquitos, hermanos de 8 y 10 años, macho y hembra, propios para distraer niños de su

edad. También una blanquita (virgen) de 16. En la calle del Cuervo, al 430, darán razón y precio.

In addition to the play on poetic form in this poem, the reader immediately becomes aware of another type of play, a play on history, since the slaves presented in **"Ventas"** are not black but white.

But the best example of Guillén's mockery of a traditional poetic format is the poem **"Grenouille"** ("Frog"), also from *El diario que a diario.* In this poem the poet resorts to expressive typography as he imitates a neon sign:

"La Rana Restaurant"

La Rana Restaurant
La Rana Restaurant
La Rana Restaurant   Anuncio luminiscente
La Rana Restaurant   intermitente
La Rana Restaurant
La Rana Restaurant

LA RANA RESTAURANT

Besides the use of expressive typography, Guillén's sense of play can also be seen in his conversion of the elegant-sounding French word *"grenouille"* into the commonplace Spanish *"rana."* Hence, this brief poem, through the spatial arrangement of the verses, as well as the play on words, represents a masterpiece in poetic games by Guillén.

In conclusion, the presence of play or game in the poetry of Nicolás Guillén is no mere coincidence but rather a constant which performs a vital function in this poet's works. To Guillén, poetry should be no stagnant reservoir of cliché ideas or rhetoric, but rather a vibrant form of expression always open to change. Thus, the poet, who as a youth was fascinated by the flippancy of *avant garde* literary movements, today continues steadfastly in this attitude of play. The result is poetry which at first glance may seem overly simple, but which upon further examination reveals masterpieces of literary skill.

Dellita L. Martin (essay date 1980)

SOURCE: "West African and Hispanic Elements in Nicolás Guillén's 'La canción del bongó'," in *SAB: South Atlantic Bulletin,* Vol. XLV, No. 1, January, 1980, pp. 47-53.

[*In the following essay, Martin examines elements of West African and Hispanic folk music forms in the poem "La canción del bongó."*]

"La canción del bongó," originally published in Guillén's *Sóngoro Cosongo* (1931), is a poem that succinctly illustrates the fusion of the West African and Hispanic oral traditions. This is so because it is a *romance* which functions like a *son.* Moreover, the image of the *son,* which infuses this *poema mulato,* is projected as a symbol of Cuba's cultural essence, which Guillén defines as *mulatismo* in his prologue to *Sóngoro Cosongo:*

Diré finalmente, que ésos son unos versos mulatos.
Participan acaso de los mismos elementos que entran
en la composición étnica de Cuba, donde todos somos
un poco níspero. ¿Duel? No lo creo. En todo caso,
precisa decirlo antes de que lo vayamos a olividar. La
inyección africana en esta tierra es tan profunda, y se
cruzan y entrecruzan en nuestra bien regada hidrografia
social tantas corrientes capilares, que sería trabajo de
miniaturistas desenredar el jeroglifico. Opino, por tanto,
que una poesía criolla entre nosotros no lo será de un
modo cabal con olvido del negro. El negro—a mi juicio—
aporta esencias muy firmes a muestro *cotel*.

Because the raw material for **"La canción del bongó"** involves folk music forms, my approach is to adopt a method of analysis devised by the folklorists Abrahams, Ben-
Amos, and Dundes, who have studied folklore as a triadic
formula that includes text, texture, and context. According
to Dundes, "the text of an item of folklore is essentially a
version or a single telling of a tale, a recitation of a proverb,
a singing of a folksong" "Texture, Text, and Context," in
Southern Folklore Quarterly, 28 (1964)]. Texture refers to the
actual language used in folklore and includes elements like
stress, pitch, juncture, tone, and onomatopoeia. And Dundes
continues, "the context of an item of folklore is the specific
social situation in which that particular item is actually
employed." Context also includes function, which refers to
the use or purpose of a given folklore event. In fact, the
event itself is the context. In relation to **"La canción del
bongó,"** the triadic approach enables one to understand the
nature of the *son,* the oral genre which informs this poem.

The text of **"La canción del bongó"** (quoted in part here)
is a *romance* in "o" assonance produced by the conscious, imaginative skills of a poet. Although it assumes
a literary form, the poem is constructed around the dynamic structure of the *son* and, as such, captures the aura of
the latter, especially when read aloud:

Ésta es la canción del bongó:

—Aquí el que más fino sea,
responde, si llamo yo.
Unos dicen: ahora mismo,
otros dicen: allá voy.
Pero mi profunda voz,
convoca al negro y al blanco,
que bailan el mismo son,
cueripardos o almiprietos
más de sangre que de sol,
pues quien por fuera no es noche,
por dentro ya oscureció.

Aquí el que más fino sea,

. . . . .

En esta tierra, mulata
de africano y español
(Santa Bárbara de un lado,
del etro lado, Changó),
siempre falta algún abuelo,
cuando no sobra algún don

y hay títulos de Castilla
con parientes en Bondó:
vale más callarse, amigos,
y no menear la cuestión,
porque venimos de lejos
y andamos de dos en dos.
Aquí el que más fino sea,

. . . . .

Habrá quien Hegue a insultarme,
pero no de corazón;
habrá quien me escupa en público,
cuando a solas me besó . . .

A ése, le digo:

—Compadre,

ya me pedirás perdón,
ya comerás de mi ajiaco,
ya me darás la razón,

. . . .

ya bailarás a mi voz,

. . . .

ya estarás donde yo estoy:
ya vendrás de abajo arriba,
ique aquí el más alto soy yo?

As a musical form the structure of the *son* consists of
what Durán defines [in *Recordings of Latin American
Songs and Dances,* 1942] as ". . . an exposition of undetermined length for solo voice and a four measure contrasting refrain called 'montuno' sung twice by the chorus." Carpentier adds [in *La musica en Cuba,* 1946] that
the initial exposition, known as the *largo* in Spanish, uses
the *romance* form. Thus, it is the interplay of *largo* and
montuno that illustrates the antiphonal nature of the West
African music which produced the *son* in Cuba. Furthermore, antiphony assumes two basic forms: (1) a call-and-
response dialogue in which the response element serves
as a commentary on the solo verses; (2) a call-and-re-
sponse pattern in which the refrain (again the response
element) is repeated as an *estribillo.*

The antiphonal arrangement of the traditional *son* is evident in **"La canción del bongó"** in that the poem contains
three *largo* stanzas of 10, 12, and 14 lines, respectively,
that are interlaced with the repeated *estribillo,* "Aquí el
que más fino sea, / responde, si llamo yo." In addition, the
bongó, a Cuban instrument of West African origin, functions as soloist and chorus in a kind of ironic dialogue
with itself. One can even postulate that the *bongó* conveys in drum language the tale of miscegenation which is
the history of Cuban society in particular and New World
cultures in general. Nevertheless, unlike the text of an oral
son, that of the poem is fixed in written form. Consequently, one is reminded of its literary nature.

The texture of **"La canción del bongó"** includes the actual language of the poem as well as certain musical qualities like percussive attack and rhythmic versification, which I shall discuss beginning with the last element first. With respect to the rhythmic-metric complexity of the *son*-poem, rhythmic patterns do not depend so much on the alternation or counting of syllables as they do on the marking of stressed and unstressed syllables, on strong and weak beats. In **"La canción del bongó"** the main stress contour falls around the first, third, fifth, and seventh syllables, with a secondary stress contour around the second, fourth, and seventh syllables:

    Examples

  1   3   5   7
Unos dicen: ahora mismo,

  1   3   6 7
otros dicen: allá voy.

    · · · · ·

    2   4   7
convoca al negro y al blanco,

    2   5   7
que bailan el mismo son,

In explaining rhythmic versification, Jahn states [in *Munto,* 1901] that "the accented syllables are emphasized by rhyme or position and are sharply scanned but the unstressed syllables in between—one, two, or often three in number—are so articulated that a tension arises between the basic rhythm, and the accents frequently fall in the syncope." In short, the verse accommodates itself to the musical form in that its measure is precise, short, and has well-marked accents on tones that are usually the length of a syllable.

The second textural element of this *son*-poem is percussive attack, which is achieved by the onomatopoetic repetition of the "o" rhyme in conjunction with occlusive, dental, and silibant consonants (for example, *voy, voz, son, sol, Bondó, perdón, dos,* etc.). Repetition of the adverb "ya" in the final stanza also conveys the force of the *bongó*'s drum language, a technique that moves the poem towards its *crescendo.*

The third textural element in **"La canción del bongó"** is its language, a colloquial Spanish through which the theme of cultural miscegenation emerges. Although *mulatismo* is represented by the image of the *son,* Guillén employs several specific techniques to underscore this theme. The first is to contrast phrases, images, and metaphors. For example, in the first stanza, "Unos dicen: ahora mismo" is opposed to "otros dicen: allá voy."; "repique bronco" stands opposite "profunda voz"; and "negro-blanco," "cueripardos-almiprietos," "sangresol," and "por fuera-por dentro" all are juxtaposed with one another. The second device involves the use of parallel structures to give a sense of the binary rhythmic beat, illustrated by the phras-

es "Pero mi repique bronco, / pero mi profunda voz," "cueripardos-almiprietos / más de sangre que de sol," and "noche-oscureció." The introduction of neologisms is a third method utilized by Guillén. "Cueripardos" and "almiprietos" refer to the "dark skin" and "dark soul" of the Cuban people, respectively. There is a play on words in that "cuero" literally means the leather skin of the *bongó;* but with the addition of the adjective "pardo," it figuratively suggests the brown tones of the mulatto skin color. In the neologism "almiprietos," the adjectival qualifier "prietos," meaning "dark-colored," concretizes an intangible entity, the "alma" (soul). This relationship between appearance and essence is reiterated in the contrast of "sangre" and "sol." In addition, the latter metaphor is inverted in terms of the first half of this four-part association because "sangre" has "almiprietos" as its referent, while "sol" points back to "cueripardos." The external-internal contrast is completed in the final two lines of stanza one with the use of the "fuera-no noche" metaphor as a foil for "dentro-ya oscureció." In essence, the *son* has moved beyond its original point of reference and is no longer just a dance but the symbol of cultural syncretism.

The second stanza focuses on the historical milieu of the *son,* expressed in the phrase, "tierra, mulata." Again the poet uses the devices of contrast and parallelism to highlight the bicultural heritage of Cuba. The "africano-español" metaphor is the essential one here because all the other elements constitute reiterations of this generic expression. The first specific instance of the mingling of the two bloodlines is religious syncretism, represented by the juxtaposition of *Santa Bárbara,* the Roman Catholic saint who protects soldiers and controls the thunder of *Changó,* the West African god of war and thunder. In fact, in the practice of *Santeria,* the two gods are often employed interchangeably, for *Changó* is androgenous. As a powerful warrior-god, "he" is *Changó;* as a strong protectress from thunder, "she" is *Santa Bárbara*—two aspects of the same deity.

The social implications of miscegenation are exemplified in the parallel contrasts of certain conventions of the Cuban people. For instance, the expression "falta algún abuelo" is opposite in meaning to "sobra algún don," and this whole idea stands analogous to "hay tititítulos de Castilla" versus "con parientes en Bondó." All of this refers to the custom of denying the existence of an African ancestor, while simultaneously producing a Spanish progenitor for whose origins no one can account. The title "don" was reserved for those of the upper class and used exclusively by the *criollo* (white) Cubans in Guillén's day. However, those *criollos* who had grown materially successful could quietly buy titles from their local parish church. This discrepancy is conveyed through irony, for Guillén switches the terms of the relationship so that "falta algún abuelo" corresponds structurally with "hay titulos de Castilla" and "sobra algún don" with "con parientes en Bondó:." In short, the continuous interlacing of African and Spanish elements has resulted in an intricate cultural tapestry whose threads are not easily unraveled. The phrases "venimos de lejos" and "andamos de dos en dos" synthesize this idea, which is really a poetic restatement of the one offered in the prologue to **Sóngoro Cosongo**—that Cuba is a mulatto nation.

The poet's most effective use of irony is evident in the *estribillo* where the *bongó,* personification of the *son,* mocks the hypocrites who deny the African aspect of their heritage; for those who consider themselves "superior" are attracted to its call, and by responding to the rhythms of this "primitive" instrument, they acknowledge the power of the African lineage. In essence, their actions belie their pose, an idea that is developed in the third solo stanza in the contrast between "insultarme-no de corazón" and "me escupa en público-cuando a solas me besó . . ."

In the last stanza, incremental repetition is utilized to create a sense of the mounting rhythms of the *bongó,* through which the poet appeals for solidarity with key words like "perdón" (pardon), "ajiaco" (a kind of Cuban stew), and "abajo-arriba." By sharing the same meal, music, and culture, Guillén seems to feel that the opposing terms of the social relationship can be reconciled. Furthermore, the "abajo-arriba" antithesis suggests that the most humble component will become the most esteemed. In short, the *bongó,* an African-based instrument that plays a mulatto music, occupies this honored position for it represents the synthesis of the two legacies.

The last aspect of folklore analysis according to the triadic scheme is context. While the immediate context of **"La canción del bongó"** is the collection of poems called **Sóngoro Cosongo,** the wider social situation in which the *son* functions often involves a cabaret setting. Therefore, all of the poems within the volume serve to create a festive mood. In addition, the occasion varies, running the gamut from a house party to a tavern gathering (*solar*) to an outdoor carnival, especially during a holiday season. In this manner Guillén captures the euphoric spirit of the cumbancha. (According to Ortiz, [in *Glosario de afronegrismos,* 1924] *cumbancha,* of African origin, comes from the Afro-Cuban term "*cumbé,*" which was an old *son* dance that the slaves performed during various carnival celebrations and which, in the old days, was associated with gaiety and good times.) Such a dionysiac, "devil-may-care" atmosphere prevailed in the Havana *solar* where the *son* was extremely popular during the period 1920-30.

Although the poems of **Sóngoro Cosongo** are primarily concerned with evoking the mood of the *solar,* **"La canción del bongó"** stands out because it is the only one to indicate Guillén's painfully increasing awareness of racial conflicts in Cuba. At issue here is the incongruity between myth and reality. On the one hand, the poet expresses the sentiment that Cuba is a mulatto nation, the child who resulted from the union of the West African and Euro-Hispanic civilizations in the New World. In this sense *mulatismo* implies racial harmony. On the other hand, the concept of *mestizaje,* traditionally advocated by writers, educators, politicians, and other guardians of Latin America's cultural heritage, has been questioned and found wanting in recent years by scholars such as Solaún, Kronus, Hoetink, Comas, and Jackson. According to Jackson,

[in *The Black Image in Latin American Literature,* 1976] *mestizaje* constitutes a kind of "ethnic lynching," or "the physical, spiritual, and cultural rape of black people." Therefore, racial-cultural amalgamation in Latin America, achieved through a process known as *blanqueamiento* (whitening), does not necessarily insure racial harmony since it is predicted upon the notion that white is superior.

Guillén is very conscious of the cleavage between myth and reality, as evinced both in his opening remarks to **Sóngoro Cosongo** and in various lines of **"La canción del bongó."** Moreover, this *son*-poem anticipates the poet's subsequent efforts to deepen and broaden his perspective of the problem by combining art with social protest. Thus, **"La canción del bongó"** contains the seeds of the *hombre-poeta,* or polemicist-lyricist, a stance that Guillén would first assume in the collection **West Indies Ltd.** (1934). By projecting the image of the *son* as the symbol of a racially and culturally integrated society, Guillén seeks to reconcile in literary form the fact of *mulatismo* with the myth of racial harmony in Latin America. Consequently, it is not amiss to assert that his voice is unique within the context of the Afro-Cuban movement of the 1930's in that it sincerely attempts to address itself to the literary implications of *mestizaje.*

Lorna V. Williams (essay date 1982)

SOURCE: "The Revolutionary Alternative," in *Self and Society in the Poetry of Nicolás Guillén,* The Johns Hopkins University Press, 1982, pp. 115-38.

[*In the following essay, Williams discusses Guillén's treatment of the Cuban Revolution in his poetry. Williams notes that although Guillén's poems reveal his commitment to the socialist cause, they also raise doubts about the revolution's extremism and Cuba's political isolation.*]

That the Cuban Revolution did not seek merely to transform the material conditions of man is well known. Ernesto (Che) Guevara's pronouncements on the need to create a "new man," as well as the debate regarding moral and material incentives in economic policy, are a clear indication that the revolutionary leadership not only undertook to restructure the socio-economic institutions of Cuban society, but also aimed at effecting [what Richard R. Fagan, in *The Transformation of Political Culture in Cuba* (1969) Called] a complete "transformation of political culture." Writers and intellectuals were expected to contribute to this project by endorsing revolutionary values in their work. Aware that a socialist consciousness could not be readily induced in a people long exposed to bourgeois modes of thought, the revolutionary government created a number of cultural organs—publishing houses, journals, literary prizes, and conferences—to provide writers with a forum for mediating between the repudiated points of reference and the desired moral order. To writers who feared that support by and for the Revolution automatically delimited their sphere of activity, Fidel Castro's dictum, "Within the Revolution, everything; against the Revolution, no rights at all," a position that was subsequently legitimized in the Constitution, was intended as a guarantee that official policy was not synonymous with restraints on artistic expression.

In Guillén's case, the expectation that his poetry would reflect a revolutionary posture was not perceived as a curtailment of his artistic freedom, since . . . Guillén had long advocated the socialist measures now being called into existence by the regime. It is therefore not surprising that he would choose to commemorate selected moments in recent Cuban history, such as the literacy campaign and the implementation of the programs for agrarian reform. But it is the poem, **"Tengo"** (I have), that best summarizes his attitude toward the realization of the object of his desire:

> Cuando me veo y toco
> yo, Juan sin Nada no más ayer,
> y hoy Juan con Todo,
> y hoy con todo,
> vuelvo los ojos, miro,
> me veo y toco
> y me pregunto cómo ha podido ser.

> [When I see and touch myself,
> I, John with Nothing only yesterday,
> and today John with Everything,
> and today with everything,
> I turn my eyes, I look,
> I see and touch myself
> and I wonder how it could have been.]

Here the persona reflects upon his instant transition from a state of destitution to one of proud ownership. However, for the speaking subject, ownership is less defined by an accumulation of tangible objects than by a radical change in self-perception, which results in an altered relationship between self and world. Indeed, the basis of self-interest is so fundamentally restated as to have established an equivalence between personal fortune and the national patrimony:

> Tengo, vamos a ver,
> tengo el gusto de andar por mi país,
> dueño de cuanto hay en él,
> mirando bien de cerca lo que antes
> no tuve ni podía tener.
> Zafra puedo decir,
> monte puedo decir,
> ciudad puedo decir,
> ejército decir,
> ya míos para siempre y tuyos, nuestros,

> [I have, let's see,
> I have the pleasure of walking around my country,
> master of all there is in it,
> looking very closely at what
> I did not and could not have before.
> Sugar crop, I can say,
> mountain, I can say,
> city, I can say,
> army say,
> now mine forever and yours, ours,]

Since the boundaries between self and other have become blurred, the satisfaction of basic individual needs is held in abeyance and appears almost as an afterthought in this catalog of recently acquired rights:

> Tengo, vamos a ver,
> que ya aprendí a leer,
> a contar,
> tengo que ya aprendí a escribir
> y a pensar
> y a reír.
> Tengo que ya tengo
> donde trabajar
> y ganar
> lo que me tengo que comer.
> Tengo, vamos a ver,
> tengo lo que tenía que tener.

> [I have, let's see,
> like I already learned to read,
> to count,
> I have, like I already learned to write
> and to think
> and to laugh.
> I have, like I now have
> a place to work
> and earn
> what I need to eat.
> I have, let's see,
> I have what I had to have.]

Even these objects of appropriation are not expressive of singularity, for if they signify the acquisition of properties hitherto unimaginable to the enunciating-I, they also point to a condition that he shares with an entire social class. The voice of the speaking subject therefore presents itself as a communal one, celebrating the end of necessity and announcing the possibility of harmonious relations in an ideal community, in which all obvious social differences are erased:

> Tengo, vamos a ver,
> tengo el gusto de ir
> yo, campesino, obrero, gente simple,
> tengo el gusto de ir
> (es un ejemplo)
> a un banco y hablar con el administrador,
> no en inglés,
> no en señor,
> sino decirle compañero como se dice en español.

> Tengo, vamos a ver,
> que siendo un negro
> nadie me puede detener
> a la puerta de un dancing o de un bar.
> O bien en la carpeta de un hotel
> gritarme que no hay pieza,
> una mínima pieza y no una pieza colosal,
> una pequeña pieza donde yo pueda descansar.

> [I have, let's see,
> I have the pleasure of going,
> I, a peasant, a worker, an ordinary person,
> I have the pleasure of going

(it's an example)
to a bank and speaking to the manager,
not in English,
not in Sir,
but calling him brother as one says in Spanish.

I have, let's see,
like being black
no one can stop me
at the door of a dance hall or a bar.
Or else in the lobby of a hotel
shout at me that there is no room,
a tiny room and not a great big room,
a small room where I can rest.]

It is interesting to note that the persona has taken no active part in bringing this state of affairs into being. In fact, in confessing his astonishment at "how it could have been," he demonstrates the aptness of one definition of the Cuban situation as an instance of "revolutionary paternalism." [Nelson P. Vald's, "Revolution and Institutionalization in Cuba," *Cuban Studies/Estudios Cubanos,* January and July, 1976.] Despite the note of inevitability on which the poem ends ("I have what I had to have"), the process of change to which it refers is anterior to the "when" of the opening lines, and consequently one is led to assume that it was the fulfillment of the character's needs that sparked his recognition that there had been a series of lacks in his life.

Be that as it may, the acquisition of certain elemental rights by the formerly dispossessed now causes the present to appear as a unique moment of plenitude. Marginality is believed to be transcended when one has access to all areas of the national territory and is able to apply the possessive adjective to its institutions. The political events that made this possible therefore come to be regarded as a privileged moment of origin for both man and society, since they are thought to have created a higher form of existence out of the nothingness and deprivations of yesterday.

The nature of the new departure is indicated by **"Puedes?"** (Can You?), where the virtues of a non-mercenary mode of interaction are affirmed. Through the dialogic structure of the poem, a neo-pastoral vision is expressed, in which the natural elements are shown to exist in and for themselves, as companions to man, rather than as resources to be exploited by him for profit:

    ¿Puedes venderme el aire que pasa entre tus dedos
    y te golpea la cara y te despeina?
    ¿Tal vez podrías venderme cinco pesos de viento,
    o más, quizás venderme una tormenta?
    ¿Acaso el aire fino
    me venderías, el aire
    (no todo) que recorre
    en tu jardín corolas y corolas,
    en tu jardín para los pájaros,
    diez pesos de aire fino?

        El aire gira y pasa
        en una mariposa.
        Nadie lo tiene, nadie.

    [Can you sell me the air that passes through your
       fingers
    and strikes your face and messes up your hair?
    Could you perhaps sell me five pesos' worth of
       wind,
    or better, maybe sell me a storm?
    Perhaps you could sell me
    some clean air, the air
    (not all of it) which runs through
    corollas and corollas in your garden,
    in your garden for the birds,
    ten pesos' worth of clean air?

        The air turns and passes
        on a butterfly.
        Nobody owns it, nobody.]

But the poem focuses on items of differential value; the air and the sky, which serve as the organizing principle for the first two stanzas, are not ordinarily salable commodities, as are water and land, around which the two final verses are ordered. However, the recurrence of key phrases, as in the refrain, "Nobody owns it (them), nobody," and the parallelism that informs the poem, are strategies that attempt to negate the opposition between both sets of elements and render them indistinguishable to the reader. Thus, the concept of private property is emptied of meaning, and money is revealed to be irrelevant and contingent, as the continuity between man and nature is restored, without the mediation of the market-place.

In this context, it is assumed that once the connection between price and value is severed, pleasurability returns to natural phenomena, which once again recover their autonomy. With the transitivity accorded by the poem to the natural world, property ceases to be an object of social division that pits man in a competitive struggle against his neighbor for monopolistic control of it. If anything, use of the land rather than its value as a term in a commercial system of exchange is stressed:

    La tierra tuya es mía.
    Todos los pies la pisan.
    Nadie la tiene, nadie.

    [Your land is mine.
    All feet tread it.
    Nobody owns it, nobody.]

An egalitarian social order is thereby posited as the highest good whereby the general well-being of all assumes primacy over individual economic success.

The underlying assumption of such a vision is a belief in the brotherhood of man. Thus, concern is expressed [in the poem **"El hambre"**] for people in other parts of the globe, where existential conditions militate against the achievement of a similar community of interests among men:

    Ésta es el hambre. Un animal
    todo colmillo y ojo.
    No se harta en una mesa.
    Nadie lo engaña ni distrae.

No se contenta
con un almuerzo o una cena.
Anuncia siempre sangre.
Ruge como león, aprieta como boa,
piensa como persona.

El ejemplar que aquí se ofrece
fue cazado en la India (suburbios de Bombay),
pero existe en estado más o menos salvaje
en otras muchas partes.

No acercarse.

[This is hunger. An animal
all fangs and eyes.
It does not get its fill at a table.
Nobody diverts it nor wards it off.
It is not content
with a lunch or a supper.
It always announces blood.
It roars like a lion, squeezes like a boa,
thinks like a person.

The specimen displayed here
was caught in India (slums of Bombay),
but it exists in a more or less wild state
in many other places.

Keep away.]

Through the metaphorical language of the poem, a graphic image of the dire consequences of human neglect is created. And, in a paraphrase of René Depestre, one could say that the implication here is that phenomena like hunger, which are brutal forces that undermine social harmony, have been controlled in Cuba through the efforts of the revolutionary government.

It is this perception of Cuba as a nation where problems that alienate man from his neighbor have been resolved that explains Cuba's presumed centrality to the struggle for social justice in the rest of the hemisphere. That Cuba has succeeded in altering the conditions of existence of its own population is not considered sufficient cause for celebration. The exemplary nature of the Cuban experience is believed to require recognition by the significant others in Latin America before the revolutionary gesture will have meaning. A familiar chronicle of ills—weak economies geared to the export of a single product in a fluctuating world market, rudimentary institutions unresponsive to the needs of the general population, a disenfranchised majority, social cleavages—facilitates the articulation of an alternative system of relationships. Cuba's recent experience seems to stand as a viable model for other Latin Americans to follow in acting on their world. But even as language aspires to maintain the illusion of a common cause with the sister republics of Latin America, once the attempt is made to ground the lessons of Cuba in the larger hemispheric context, conditions begin to lose their specificity and the likelihood of creating a new historical situation in Latin America becomes indeterminate. Thus, in **"Brasil-Copacabana,"** the anticipated revolutionary

moment loses its immediacy and remains suspended in a future eternally on the horizon:

Lo vi, en La Habana.
Lo vi, no lo soñé.
Palacios de antiguo mármol
para el que vivió sin zapatos.
Castillos donde el obrero reposa
sentado a la diestra de su obra.
El cigarral de la duquesa
para la hija de Juan, que está enferma.
La montaña y la playa y el vichy y el caviar
para los que antes no tenían donde estar.

¿Y aquí en Copacabana, aquí?
También lo vi.
Pues aunque todavía
es un sueño,
siento venir el día,
ha de llegar el día,
se oye rugir el día
con el viente nordeste de Pernambuco y de Bahía,
un día de sangre y pólvora bajo el sol brasileño.

[I saw it in Havana.
I saw it, it was no dream.

Palaces of ancient marble
for he who wore no shoes.
Castles where the worker rests
seated on the right side of his labor.
The orchard of the duchess
for John's daughter, who is ill.
The mountain and the beach and the vichy and the
    caviar
for those who had no place to stay before.

And here in Copacabana, here?
I saw it too.
Well even though
it is still a dream,
I feel the day coming,
the day must come,
one hears the day roaring
with the northeast wind from Pernambuco and
    Bahia,
a day of blood and gunpowder under the
    Brazilian sun.]

What is now a political reality in Havana is perceived as a utopian dream in Copacabana, and the chances of that dream being realized recede with each progressively more emphatic attempt to announce its imminence. The apocalyptic vision of the process of social change in Brazil simply emphasizes its removal to a dimension beyond human time.

No doubt the difficulty of envisaging the revolutionary future of Latin America in more concrete terms lies in the very fact that the future has yet to occur, and so, by definition, is not readily transposed into familiar categories. At the same time, while it is evident that the Revolution represents a moment of rupture in Cuban history, an effort is made to restore continuity by embedding the actions of the revolutionary vanguard in a previous moment of national liberation:

> Garra de los garroteros,
> uñas de yanquis ladrones
> de ingenios azucareros:
> la devolver los millones,
> que son para los obreros!
> La nube en rayo bajó,
> ay, Cuba, que yo lo vi;
> el águila se espantó,
> yo lo vi;
> la coyunda se rompió,
> yo lo vi;
> el pueblo canta, cantó,
> cantando está el pueblo así:
> —Vino Fidel y cumplió
> lo que prometió Martí.

> [Clutch of the loan sharks,
> nails of the Yankee robbers
> of sugar factories:
> to return the millions
> that go to the workers!
> The cloud descended in a lightning flash,
> oh, Cuba, for I saw it;
> the eagle got scared,
> I saw it;
> the yoke snapped,
> I saw it;
> the people sing, sang,
> the people are singing this:
> "Fidel came and fulfilled
> that which Martí promised."]

("**Se acabó**")

In view of Castro's redistributive policies, the appeal to Martí evidently goes beyond the ritual invocation of Martí's name by earlier leftist politicians, and therefore serves to legitimize the perception of the present as the fulfillment of an earlier prophecy.

Despite such attempts at minimizing the strangeness of recent events, there are some individuals to whom the disjuncture is all too apparent. Theirs is not the euphoria of the crowd, for they regard the new social arrangements as a threat to their personal well-being. For them, exile is preferable to continued existence under a regime from which they feel increasingly estranged. Although their departure is viewed by the revolutionary leadership as a blessing, in that it facilitates the process of political consolidation, to Guillén their emigration signifies their displacement to a metaphysical void, since it involves a decentering of culture without the possibility of creating a new system of reference. In Guillén's view, arrival in the United States represents a series of negations for Cubans, not the least of which is the inability to articulate their own sense of being:

> Tú, que partiste de Cuba,
> responde tú,

> ¿dónde hallarás verde y verde,
> azul y azul,
> palma y palma bajo el cielo?
> Responde tú.

> Tú, que tu lengua olvidaste,
> responde tú,
> y en lengua extraña masticas
> el güel y el yu,
> ¿cómo vivir puedes mudo?
> Responde tú.

> [You, who left Cuba,
> answer me,
> where will you find green and green,
> blue and blue,
> palm and palm under the sky?
> Answer me.

> You, who forgot your language,
> answer me,
> and in a strange tongue mumble
> (g)well and jou,
> how can you live in silence?
> Answer me.]

("**Responde tú**")

The Spanish of the exile is not regarded as a valid means of self-expression; it is seen, rather, as a symptom of his loss of coherence. Since the fatherland is considered to be the primary source of identity, it is assumed that departure from it leads to the superimposition of a false self on the authentic self, whose gestures toward meaning in the new environment result only in further self-estrangement. Arrival in the United States represents self-denial on another level, for it implies that Cubans have renounced their national heritage and identified with the enemies of the fatherland:

> Uno se siente más tranquilo
> con Maceo allá arriba,
> ardiendo en el gran sol de nuestra sangre,
> que con Weyler, vertiéndola a sablazos.
> [One feels more tranquil
> with Maceo on high,
> blazing in the big sun of our blood,
> than with Weyler, shedding it with strokes from his
>   saber.]

("**La herencia**")

The patriotic allusion, which links the Revolution with the Wars of Independence, causes emigration to appear as an act of betrayal. Moreover, it is suggested that in choosing to abandon the fatherland at a critical moment of its history, the exiles do more than simply impede the process of reconstruction by depriving the fatherland of their talents; they also express a refusal to participate in the national project of reappropriating an alienated heritage:

> Sin embargo, no sé qué penetrante,
> qué desasosegada
> lástima me aprieta el corazón, pensando

en tus remotos descendientes,
dormidos en su gran noche previa,
su gran noche nonata.
Porque algún día imprevisible,
aún no establecido, pero cierto,
van a verse acosados
por la pregunta necesaria.
Tal vez en la clase de historia
algún camarada.
Acaso en una fábrica. La novia
pudiera ser. En cualquier sitio, en fin,
donde se hable de este hoy
que será para entonces un portentoso ayer.
Sabrán lo que es la herencia que les dejas,
esta especie de sífilis
que ahora testas con tu fuga,

[Nevertheless, I can't explain what a deep,
what a disturbing
pity seizes my heart, when thinking
of your distant descendants,
asleep in their big predestined darkness,
their big, unnaturally born night.
For on some unforeseeable day,
not yet appointed, but certain,
they are going to find themselves harassed
by the necessary question.
Perhaps in history class
a friend.
Maybe in a factory. It could be
the fiancée. In short, any place
where they talk about this today
which will be by then an extraordinary yesterday.
They will learn of the heritage that you leave them,
this kind of syphilis
that you now bequeath with your flight,]

Absence from Cuba thus comes to appear as a willful form of self-mutilation in that it represents a renunciation of the national quest for wholeness. By rejecting the radiant center of Cuba for the dark night of the United States, the exiles condemn themselves and their descendants to a lifetime of incompleteness, of which their degraded speech is but a visible sign.

Nevertheless, if living in the United States is thought to establish a discontinuity in the consciousness and experience of all Cubans, it is considered to pose an even greater threat to the being of Afro-Cubans:

Un negro en Miami
no tiene casa donde vivir;
un negro en Miami
no tiene mesa donde comer;
un negro en Miami
no tiene cama donde dormir;
un negro en Miami
no tiene vaso donde beber,
si no es la casa,
si no es la mesa,
si no es la cama,
si no es el vaso
de un negro negro lo mismo que él.

[A black man in Miami
has no place to live;
a black man in Miami
has no place to eat;
a black man in Miami
has no place to sleep;
a black man in Miami
has no place to drink,
except in the house,
except at the table,
except in the bed,
except from the glass
of another black man as black as himself.]
                                    (**"¡Ay, qué tristeza que tengo!"**)

Presumably, it is the nature of race relations in the American South that circumscribes the existence of Afro-Cubans. What Guillén fails to point out, however, is that other Cubans also contribute to the difficulties experienced by Afro-Cubans in Miami. Yet, even as he calls into question the chances for survival of the Cuban self in exile, Guillén suggests that the process of adaptation will be less problematic for the bourgeoisie because their prerevolutionary lifestyle was so similar to the American way of life:

Y de repente, Miami. Como si dijéramos La Habana
que buscabas,
tu Habana fácil y despreocupada.
(Políticos baratos ¡que costaban tan caro!
Burdeles, juego, yanquis, mariguana.)
Magnífico.

[And suddenly, Miami. As if we said that you
    were looking
for Havana,
your easy and relaxed Havana.
(Cheap politicians, who cost so much!
Brothels, gambling, Yankees, marijuana.)
Fine.]
                                            (**"La herencia"**)

In the case of blacks, on the other hand, emigration is considered to result in a more definitive state of homelessness, since in Miami they are denied both the material and spiritual benefits that were made available to them in revolutionary Cuba:

Ay, qué tristeza que tengo,
ay, qué tristeza tan grande,
viendo correr a este negro
sin que lo persiga nadie.

Se asustó,
parece que se asustó,
de Cuba se fue, salió,
llegó a Miami
y allá en Miami se quedó.

. . . . .

—A Miami te fuiste un día,
    vendiste tu libertad,

tu vergüenza y tu alegría,
yo sé que te pesará!

[Oh, how sad I feel,
oh, what a great sadness,
on seeing this black man run
without anybody pursuing him.
He got scared,
it seems that he got scared,
he went away from Cuba, he left,
he arrived in Miami
and there in Miami he stayed.

. . . . .

                       "One day you went away to
Miami,

            you sold your freedom,
            your dignity and your joy,
            I know you will regret it!"]

                 ("¡Ay, qué tristeza que tengo!")

By indicating that fears about the course of events in Cuba are insufficient grounds to warrant the emigration of blacks to the United States, Guillén evidently subscribes to the popular view that blacks are the principal beneficiaries of the Revolution, and as such, are ill-advised to abandon the system that endowed them with "freedom, dignity, and joy." The persistence of a differential perception of blacks and whites, even in a revolutionary situation, has caused several black scholars to be skeptical of the egalitarian postures of Cuba's revolutionary government.

But, if one may borrow a phrase from Roberto Fernández Retamar [in *Essayo de otro mundo,* 1969], and define freedom as "consciously assuming the true condition of our history," then it appears from Guillén's poem, **"Vine en un barco negrero"** (I came on a Slave Ship), that to a certain extent, blacks in revolutionary Cuba are in a state of freedom. Unlike the protagonists of Guillén's early poems, who are generally dehumanized figures of fun, passive spectators of history, or entertainers of one sort or another, the persona of the poem is cast in a more heroic light by virtue of his association with exemplary figures from the past. The poem thus traces his constitution as a knowing subject as he progresses from being an object of manipulation by others: "me trajeron" (they brought me), to his arrival at a stage of greater awareness: "veo" (I see). Through his assumption of the experience of slave rebellions, the Wars of Independence, and the trade unionism of the 1940s, the character reflects a growing historical consciousness that is readily perceptible to the reader because of the dramatic structure of the poem. At the same time, the language that records the changes in his social condition also contains a psychological dimension. Thus, whereas the image of slavery is evoked by the phrase, "sudor como caramelo" (sweat like a caramel), a more dynamic register is chosen for portraying the struggle for Independence:

Pasó a caballo Maceo.
Yo en su séquito.

Largo el aullido del viento.
Alto el trueno.
Un fulgor de macheteros.
Yo con ellos.

[Maceo came on horseback.
I in his retinue.
Long the howl of the wind.
Loud the thunder.
A splendor of machete-wielders.
I with them.]

              ("Vine en un barco negrero. . . . ")

The more positive sense of self projected by the persona has caused one critic [Robert Marquez in the introduction to *Man-Making Words,* 1972] to assert that in the poem, Guillén expresses pride in "who he has been and who he is today." And indeed, in his willingness to treat slavery and Independence not as simply prehistorical phenomena, but as events whose course was affected by the intentional acts of Aponte and Maceo, Guillén does appear to take pride in "who he has been." Moreover, the statement, "Soy un negro" (I am a black man), seems to indicate a high degree of self-esteem. Yet, when the statement is situated in its context and regarded as a synthesized view of "who he is today," it fails to serve as an adequate comment on the contemporary situation, since the situation is perceived so schematically:

¡Oh Cuba! Mi voz entrego.
En ti creo.
Mía la tierra que beso.
Mío el cielo.

Libre estoy, vine de lejos.
Soy un negro.

[Oh Cuba! I submit my voice.
I believe in you.
Mine is the land that I kiss.
Mine the sky.

I am free, I came from afar.
I am a black man.]

Even while freedom is being extolled, the persona, who presumably embodies the idea of freedom, is not placed in a position in which to exercise his new-found freedom. At the same time, as if to indicate their superfluousness in the present, no modern equivalent of Aponte, Maceo or Menéndez appears.

And yet, it has been noted that many of Guillén's revolutionary poems tend to "focus on the situation of blacks in the United States" [Constance Sparrow de García-Barrio, "The Image of the Black Man in the Poetry of Nicolas Guillén," in Miriam DeCosta's *Blacks in Hispanic Literature,* 1977]. In fact, not only does Guillén express concern for the plight of the average black American, but he has also composed poetic tributes to Angela Davis and Martin Luther King. In Guillén's reluctance to portray contemporary Afro-Cubans in other than a conformist light, and in his writing of political activists in the United States, one perceives the well-known revolutionary contention that militancy is justified only in capitalist societies where private ownership of the means of production functions to maintain blacks in a subordinate position, as opposed to the situation in socialist societies, where militancy is unnecessary because all men have become brothers. Thus, as in the poem, **"K K K,"** racism appears to be a specifically American problem:

> Este cuadrúpedo procede
> de Joplin, Misurí.
> Carnicero.
> Aúlla largamente en la noche
> sin su dieta habitual de negro asado.
>
> Acabará por sucumbir.
> Un problema (*insoluble*) alimentarlo.
>
> [This quadruped comes from
> Joplin, Missouri.
> Butcher.
> He howls all night long
> without his steady diet of roasted blacks.
>
> He will end up by dying.
> An (*insoluble*) problem is feeding him.]

The note of optimism on which the poem ends derives from the assumption that racial equality has been achieved in Cuba through the measures adopted by the revolutionary government for institutionalizing equality. However, even if one chooses to ask, as does Carlos More [in *Prénce Africaine* 52 (1964)], whether there is a place for blacks in revolutionary Cuba, it should be stated that the political process that elicited poetic responses like Guillén's **"Cualquier tiempo pasado fue peor"** (All Past Time was Worse) reveals a public acknowledgement of the existence of racial discrimination in Cuba. In the words of Leslie Rout [in *The African Experience,* 1976], when this public acknowledgement is seen in the context of Spanish-American race relations, it constitutes in itself a revolutionary act.

Moreover, as Guillén indicates in the following epigram, racial inequality is embedded in the very fabric of the Spanish language:

> Pienso:
> ¡Qué raro
> que al tiro al blanco
> no le hayan puesto *tiro al negro!*
>
> [I think:
> How strange
> that they have not substituted
> *tiro al negro* for target shooting!]
>   (**"Epigramas"**)

"Negro" (black) cannot be readily substituted for "blanco" (white) without raising the specter of genocide. On the other hand, if the color component in the referential code of both terms is placed in parentheses, the attempt at transvaluation results in a loss of intelligibility.

The inquiry to which Guillén's epigram leads is not confined to the field of race relations, for the center/periphery dialectic also affects the area of international affairs. In everyday use of the idiom "tiro al blanco" (target shooting), the process by which "blanco" (white) becomes "target" remains concealed; similarly, in the following stanzas of the poem **"Problemas del subdesarrollo"** (Problems of Underdevelopment), the method by which particular states becomes inscribed in the center of the international community also remains hidden:

> Monsieur Dupont te llama inculto,
> porque ignoras cuál era el nieto
> preferido de Víctor Hugo.
>
> Herr Müller se ha puesto a gritar,
> porque no sabes el día
> (exacto) en que murió Bismarck.
>
> Tu amigo Mr. Smith,
> inglés o yanqui, yo no lo *sé,*
> se subleva cuando escribes *shell.*
> (Parece que ahorras una ele,
> y que además pronuncias *chel.*)
>
> [Monsieur Dupont calls you a savage,
> because you do not know which was Victor Hugo's
> favorite grandson.
>
> Herr Müller has started screaming,
> because you do not know the (exact) day
> when Bismarck died.
>
> Your friend, Mr. Smith,
> Englishman or American, I am not sure,
> has a fit when you write *shell.*
> (It seems that you leave off one l,
> and besides you pronounce it *chel.*)]

Since the causes of effects are erased, what becomes visible are results that are immobilized into absolute categories of value. In nations that are situated on the periphery of the global community, historicity withdraws from events that take place in the metropolis. Thus, when specific items of knowledge about France or Germany lose their signs of localization, they acquire the status of eternal truths. For the non-European, absence from the place where the activities of Bismarck acquire social significance, and the unidirectional flow of the information that he subsequently receives, emphasize his subordination to the dispensers of enlightenment. His dependence is further dramatized by the fact that he remains the same, even as they are differentiated one from the other. Nevertheless, as the encounter with Mr. Smith indicates, information from the metropolis is not poured into an empty cultural space. Competing phonetic systems simply objectify the existential condition of people in underdeveloped countries who must retain local allegiances even as they are obliged to participate in the affairs of the world at large.

It seems that for Guillén, centrality is simply a question of interchangeable linguistic signs. Hence he gives the following advice to his imaginary listener:

Bueno ¿y qué?
Cuando te toque a ti,
mándales decir cacarajícara,
y que dónde está el Aconcagua,
y que quién era Sucre,
y que en qué lugar de este planeta
murió Martí.

Un favor:
que te hablen siempre en español.

[Well, and so what?
When it's your turn,
order them to say cacarajícara,
and ask where is the Aconcagua,
and who was Sucre,
and in what part of this planet
did Martí die.

One favor:
have them always speak to you in Spanish.]

As the amended list of cultural phenomena reveals, what Guillén proposes is an insertion of Spanish-American references in the site previously occupied by Victor Hugo and company. Yet, except in the case of Martí, the list as it stands is merely a catalog of atemporal essences that give no indication of their human significance. National culture is here perceived as a predetermined repertoire of objects whose meaning is already an element of their structure, and thus no longer requires the mediation of active human agents to bring their social value into being. However, the degree of identification that the poem assumes with its implied audience suggests that interpretation is considered a less urgent task than the project of achieving cultural autonomy. But even if cultural ex-centricity is reflected in language, the "problems of underdevelopment" are not resolved by mere linguistic acts, for the phenomenon of cultural domination is only one dimension of a larger problem not readily visible in Guillén's text. Equally absent is the enabling mechanism that would bridge the gap between the present, when Monsieur Dupont exercises cultural initiative, and the anticipated moment "when it's your turn." In the face of the missing third term, the attempt to alter the existing asymmetrical arrangement in Spanish America's favor remains the expression of a desire, grounded on the verbal proposition, "mándales decir" (order them to say).

Undoubtedly, the desire to enter the mainstream of history was one of the causes of the Cuban Revolution. Yet, even as the revolutionary vanguard strove to assert their control over the course of events, they set in motion forces hostile to their definition of self-determination. Guillén's poems on the blockade, the Bay of Pigs incident, and the Missile Crisis record some of the obstacles faced by the Cuban leadership in the international sphere, while "Balada" (Ballad) indicates that the consolidation of power within Cuba itself has required the crushing of forces actively opposed to the regime. If the list of fallen heroes like Conrado Benítez and Camilo Cienfuegos serves as a convenient focus for expressions

of solidarity, it also emphasizes the high cost of revolutionary struggle.

While there is no doubt that Guillén supports the general principles of the Revolution, it is also clear that he is well aware of some of its limitations. In the following epigram, for example, he comments on the instant mobility achieved by those who chose to remain in Cuba and were thrust into positions of responsibility for which they were ill-prepared:

Maravillan
las cosas que hay en este mundo:
ese muchacho zurdo
dejó el abecedario
para enseñar filosofía.

[This is
indeed a strange world:
that left-handed kid
quit the alphabet
in order to teach philosophy.]

At the same time, there is also a recognition on Guillén's part of some of the more problematic aspects of the effort to build socialism in Cuba:

Está el tenor en éxtasis
contemplando al tenor
del espejo, que es el mismo tenor
en éxtasis
que contempla al tenor.
Sale a veces a pasear por el mundo
llevado de un bramante de seda,
aplaudido en dólares,
tinta de imprenta
y otras sustancias gananciales.
(*A quien el Zoo le molesta*
cantar por la comida
y no es muy generoso con sus arias.)
Milán Scala.
New York Metropolitan.
Ópera de París.

[The tenor is in ecstasy
beholding the tenor
in the mirror, who is the same tenor
in ecstasy
beholding the tenor.

Sometimes he travels around the world
led by a silk thread,
applauded in dollars,
printer's ink
and other profitable substances.
(*Here in the Zoo it bothers him*
to sing for his supper
and he is not very generous with his arias.)
Milan, La Scala.
The New York Metropolitan.
The Paris Opera.]

("**Tenor**")

The parenthetical comment by Guillén, the tour guide, brings into focus the lack of congruence between the collectivizing intentions of the regime and individual modes of behavior that frustrate the realization of those intentions. Guillén's satiric tone makes even more evident the fact that in an economy of scarcity, where artists are expected to be motivated by altruism, the willed separation between individual effort and personal reward often fails to produce the desired results. Instead of leading to a heightened sense of identification between tenor and society, the expectation that the tenor subordinate his talents to the needs of the community results in the disengagement of the artist from the very society he is supposed to serve. An exaggerated degree of self-centeredness is only part of the problem. A more fundamental issue is that for the tenor the locus of value is situated on the far side of the cage, where artistic success is measured in materialistic terms. Thus, restrictions on his mobility fail to make him a more contented and productive worker.

It was against such residual expressions of bourgeois egoism that the Revolutionary Offensive was launched in 1968. The logical result was a call for greater ideological purity. In the face of the mounting insistence on orthodoxy, Guillén's reaction was the poem, **"Digo que yo no soy un hombre puro"** (I say that I am not a pure man):

> Yo no voy a decirte que soy un hombre puro.
> entre otras cosas
> falta saber si es que lo puro existe.
> O si es, pongamos, necesario.
> O possible,
> O si sabe bien.

> [I am not going to tell you that I am a pure man.
> Among other things
> it is necessary to find out if purity exists.
> Or if it is, let's say, necessary.
> Or possible.
> Or if it tastes good.]

Guillén's critique was evidently motivated by a desire to see the revolutionary system function more effectively. He is careful to project his criticism from "within the Revolution" and not exceed its permissible limits by supporting such counterrevolutionary vices as homosexuality:

> Yo no te digo pues que soy un hombre puro,
> yo no te digo eso, sino todo lo contrario.
> Que amo (a las mujeres, naturalmente,
> pues mi amor puede decir su nombre),
> y me gusta comer carne de puerco con papas,
>
> . . . . .
>
> Soy impuro ¿qué quieres que te diga?
> Completamente impuro.
> Sin embargo,
> creo que hay muchas cosas puras en el mundo
> que no son más que pura mierda.
> [I am not telling you that I am a pure man,
> I am not saying that, but quite the opposite.

> That I love (women, naturally,
> since my love can voice her name),
> and I like to eat pork and potatoes,
>
> . . . . .
>
> I am impure, what do you want me to say?
> Completely impure.
> However,
> I believe there are many pure things in the world
> that are only pure shit.]

Perhaps part of the difficulty in establishing a socialist paradise in Cuba lies in the fact that socialism has yet to be presented in consistently positive terms. In other words, instead of being presented as a state to be striven *for,* socialism is often defined *against* a competing ideological system. Richard Fagen has already examined the predominance of negative images of the future during the early phases of the Revolution and pointed out the critical importance of "the enemy" for crystallizing popular enthusiasm in the revolutionary situation. Nevertheless, in Guillén's **"Unión Soviética"** (Soviet Union), the friend, so crucial for the survival of the revolutionary effort in Cuba, is virtually engulfed by the enemy, who is indeed the absent center of the text:

> Jámas he visto un trust soviético en mi patria.
> Ni un banco.
> Ni tampoco un ten cents.
> Ni un central.
> Ni una estación naval.
> Ni un tren.
> Nunca jamás hallé
> un campo de bananas
> donde al pasar leyera
> "Máslov and Company, S. en C.
> Plátanos al por mayor. Oficinas en Cuba:
> Maceo esquina con No-sé-qué."

> [I have never seen a Soviet trust in my country.
> Nor a bank.
> Nor a dime store either.
> Nor a sugar factory.
> Nor a naval station.
> Nor a train.
> I never passed by
> a banana field
> where it said:
> "Maslov and Company, Ltd.
> Wholesale bananas. Cuban Office:
> Corner of Maceo and Such-and-Such-A-Street."]

Admittedly, Cuba's proximity to the United States, and the degree of American involvement in Cuba before the Revolution, help to explain the continued perception of the United States as an overwhelming presence in revolutionary Cuba. Moreover, the geopolitical consequences of the Revolution cause the United States to play a silent but important role in the daily affairs of revolutionary Cuba. Thus, even when a positive reference is made to the Soviet Union in Guillén's poem, it appears in the form of a reply to a hypothetical question posed by the enemy:

En nuestro mar nunca encontré
piratas de Moscú.
(Hable, Caribe, usted.)
Ni de Moscú tampoco en mis claras bahías
ese ojo-radar superatento
las noches y los días
queriendo adivinar mi pensamiento.
Ni bloqueos.
Ni marines.
Ni lanchas para infiltrar espías.
¿Barcos soviéticos? Muy bien.
Son petroleros, mire usted.
Son pescadores, sí, señor.
Otros llevan azúcar, traen café
junto a fragantes ramos de esperanzas en flor.

[In our sea I never found
pirates from Moscow.
(Speak, Caribbean.)
Nor from Moscow in my clear bays
that superattentive radar-eye
night and day
wishing to guess my thoughts.
Nor blockades.
Nor marines.
Nor boats for infiltrating spies.
Soviet ships? Very well.
They are oil tankers, see.
They are fishing boats, yes, sir.
Others carry sugar, bring coffee
as well as fragrant branches of hope in flower.]

It is this explicitly committed stance in Guillén's revolutionary poems that has earned them a negative evaluation from critics like Lourdes Casal. Yet, poems like **"El cangrejo"** (Cancer) and **"Bomba atómica"** (Atomic Bomb) indicate that Guillén is concerned not only about the survival of the Cuban Revolution, but also about the fate of man and society in general. Moreover, while poems like **"Tengo"** (I have) and **"¿Puedes?"** (Can You?) express unqualified support for the utopian aims of the Revolution, **"Digo que yo no soy un hombre puro"** (I say that I am not a pure man) criticizes the Revolution's extremism, and **"Tenor"** raises doubts about the prospects for the birth of "the new socialist man" in a climate of political isolation. On the other hand, as Keith Ellis has observed [in "Cuban Literature and the Revolution," *The Canadian Forum* 48 (January 1969)], social poetry like Guillén's, which Lourdes Casal seeks to bracket and thereby preclude from serious consideration, has been a marked characteristic of Cuban literature in particular, and of Latin American literature in general, since their early beginnings. Consequently, Guillén's endorsement of the revolutionary belief in the perfectibility of man and society is simply another contribution to this poetic tradition.

Keith Ellis (essay date 1983)

SOURCE: "The Poetry," in *Cuba's Nicolás Guillén: Poetry and Ideology,* University of Toronto Press, 1983, pp. 147-61.

[*In the following excerpt, Ellis examines poems in* Tengo, *Guillén's first book after the Cuban Revolution.*]

La paloma de vuelo popular was published on 28 December 1958. The flight of [Cuban President Zaldívar Y] Batista from Cuba in the early hours of 1 January 1959 marked the triumph of Fidel Castro's rebel army. Guillén returned to Cuba on 23 January 1959 and was given a welcome the size and warmth of which suggested that he was popularly regarded as one of the heroes of the revolutionary struggle. He immediately undertook a variety of new tasks on behalf of the revolution. The popular poetry readings he had given in the late thirties and forties during the course of usually unsuccessful political campaigns were repeated now as events of acknowledged national importance. At the same time, his administrative abilities were put to the service of helping to design a cultural policy for his country and, as was indicated earlier, of establishing the Union of Writers and Artists of Cuba. He resumed, too, his activities in journalism, and the diplomatic position of ambassadro-at-large was soon added to his duties. Along with all this activity, he continued to exercise his high artistic gifts, and published, in 1964, the collection *Tengo* (*'I Have'*).

The title itself, especially as it is elaborated in the title poem, reflects the satisfaction brought by the revolution. Yet while this satisfaction is expressed in several other poems of the collection, it would be erroneous to see *Tengo* as a book that is predominantly celebrative in tone. For Guillén's perception of the content that was now making its way to the surface of his society allowed him to use the word 'Tengo' not only to mean the realization of a long sought goal, but also to indicate a new sense of responsibility. What results, then, is a reaffirmation of revolutionary commitment from the new setting of a society that had made the decision to change its structure completely, to establish a new base. Thus in several poems, the preoccupation is with nurturing the revolution and defending it from the past and from a vast array of machinations. In others, those who died in its service are mourned. Beyond Cuba, there is a searching attack on racism in the United States, while solidarity is expressed with certain countries and people whose goals are viewed as admirable. The host of forms involved in their elaboration attest to Guillén's fecundity. The sixty-four poems of the collection are divided among an initial section of nineteen poems and three other sections: 'Sones, sonetos, baladas y canciones' ('*Sons,* Sonnets, Ballads and Songs') (eight poems), 'romancero' ('Collection of Ballads') (twenty-six poems) and 'Sátira' ('Satire') (eleven poems). In addition, there is the witty dramatic farce 'Floripondito,' Guillén's second contribution to the theatre genre. The poems of celebration are usually structured on a basis of antithesis, the significance of the revolution being emphasized by contrast with the past. The poem **'Canta el sinsonte en el Turquino'** (**'The Mockingbird Sings on Turquino Peak'**), for instance, provides a wide-ranging retrospective viewing of Cuban life, the poet's exile, and his return in a new dawn. From this vantage point, there is a wave of reiterated, happy goodbyes to U.S. personnel: to governors of Cuba between 1898 and 1909 (Leonard Wood,

Howard Taft, Charles Magoon), to the adviser on constitutional matters under Taft (Enoch Crowder), and to other prominent figures such as Charles Lynch and Richard Nixon. The promise of the new dawn is developed in the final section of the poem, which is preceded and followed by the salutation 'Buenos días, Fidel'; and 'buenos días' is the leitmotif of this section, greeting metonyms of a variety of aspects of Cuba's sovereignty. An impressive economy of usage results from all this due to the polyvalence of 'buenos días.' For example, the verse 'Palma, enterrada flecha, buenos días' ('Palm tree, buried arrow, good morning') recalls and integrates into the new life the 'Palma sola' of *El son entero,* making active the long-submerged potential for a decisive, vibrant Cuban presence. There is a vigorously etched image of Antonio Maceo:

> Buenos días, perfil de medalla, violento barbudo
> de bronce, vengativo machete en la diestra.

> Good morning, medal profile, bearded violent one
> of bronze, vengeful machete in his right hand.

The title of the poem appears in its penultimate line—the mockingbird singing on the highest peak of the Sierra Maestra, El Turquino—crowning the suggestion of triumph. A mood of exaltation is conveyed by the *sones* **'Soy como un árbol florido'** (**'I Am Like a Tree in Bloom'**), in which *paronomasia* is developed with variations of the word 'flor,' and **'Se acabó'** (**'It is over'**) in which the lines

> Te lo prometió Martí
> y Fidel te lo cumplió

> Martí promised it to you
> and Fidel delivered it to you

serve as an *estribillo.* The power of these verses rests on the conveyance in them of history and poetry. Chiasmus plays a strong linking role here, allowing the juxtaposition through enjambment of the two great Cuban leaders 'Martí y Fidel' in this summation of their historical roles with the Cuban people.

Fidel Castro is also a central presence in the series of five historical *romances,* the verse form of the ancient Spanish epics, used here to convey the epic events in the early life of the struggle to establish the revolution. The first of these, **'Son más en una mazorca . . . (They Are More on a Corncob'**), dealing with the arrival on the Cuban coast of Fidel and the nucleus of his guerrilla force in the Granma to later establish themselves, after severe losses, in the Sierra Maestra, is rich in metaphor, metonymy, personification, and zeugma. The first three of these figures are continued prominently in the rest of the series. In the second, **'Tierra de azules montañas . . . (Land of Blue Mountains'**), the simile 'como espumoso torrente' ('like a foaming torrent'), appearing four times in the poem, is the key image in suggesting the swell of support for the guerrillas. The pre-Columbian name of Santo Domingo is used in the next poem, **'Hacia la esclava Quisqueya . . .'** (**'Towards the Slave Quisqueya'**), as the destination of

the fleeing Batista. The oxymoron 'jóvenes abuelos' ('young grandfathers') applied to the victorious guerrillas refers at once to their bearded visages and to the knowledge and experience they had acquired during their years of combat and study. Maceo and Martí are evoked metonymically by reference to San Pedro and Dos Ríos, the respective places of their deaths, and the image 'palmas baten los palmares' ('palm groves clap hands') is reminiscent of the action, in a different mood, of the agitated canes at the beginning of the **'Elegía a Jesús Menéndez.'** In **'Abril sus flores abría . . .'** (**'April was Opening its Flowers'**) the surreptitious and treacherous nature of the attack on the motherland at the Bay of Pigs (April 1961) is developed in the first part of the poem through usages like 'herir con fácil cuchillo / . . . el gran pecho de Girón' ('to wound with easy knife / . . . the great breast of Girón'). The firm response to this comes in the second part of the poem, where a profusion of verbs are structured in patterns that form incremental chiasmus, thereby underlining the idea of envelopment that is conveyed semantically:

> pero el pueblo los achica,
> los achica y los envuelve,
> los envuelve y los exprime
> y los exprime y los tuerce.

> but the people humble them,
> humble them and envelop them,
> envelop them and squeeze them
> and squeeze them and bend them.

In the last of these, **'Está el bisonte imperial . . .'** (**'The Imperial Bison is . . .'**), another antithesis is developed, this time between imperialism and the revolution, symbolized by a bison and a dove respectively. The frustrated aggressiveness of the bison conveyed in the images of the first part of the poem gives way to the lofty militancy of the dove, which is supported materially and spiritually by the people:

> los milicianos la visten
> de pólvora y de ternura
> y de hierro y de esperanza
> y de granito y de espuma.

> Militiamen clothe it [the revolution]
> with gunpowder and tenderness
> and with iron and with hope
> and with granite and with foam.

The confidence expressed in the permanence of the revolution, found elsewhere in the poem **'Nadie'** (**'Nobody'**), comes at the end of a series that shows a process of cause, leadership, struggle, popular commitment, and triumph. The poem celebrating this triumph from a popular perspective is the title poem of the collection, **'Tengo,'** in which a representative ordinary Cuban pays homage to the revolution by showing the contrast between the past and the present. The speaker's identity is thus protean, covering the range of economic and social statuses occupied by the heretofore suffering classes: 'yo, campesino, obrero, gente simple' ('I, a peasant, worker, simple person'). With this mobility he can attest to the variety of new freedoms, rights, and opportunities in what is now seen as an open, democratic society. Besides, there is the perception of the revolution as an open-ended developmental force that sponsors the growth and fulfilment of the people:

Tengo, vamos a ver,
que ya aprendí a leer,
a contar,
tengo que ya aprendí a escribir
y a pensar
y a reír.

I have, let's see,
I've already learned to read,
to count,
I've already learned to write
and to think
and to laugh.

Here, then, is another instance of Guillén's allying the concept of improvement to his view of the simple man. Closely linked to the idea of celebration is the idea of the defence of the revolution. This defence is undertaken in two principal ways: first, by retrospective viewings of the past in poems in which sarcasm and satire function conspicuously and, second, by exposing present dangers. The poem that most clearly spans celebration and defence is the *canción* **'Muchacha recién crecida'** (**'New Grown Girl'**) in which the 'paloma' as an object to be cherished is used as a symbol of the revolution. The retrospective views, carrying implicit warnings against the recrudescence of pre-revolutionary ills, and contained most prominently in the poems **'Allá lejos'** (**'Far Away'**) and **'Cualquier tiempo pasado fue peor'** (**'Any Past Time Was Worse'**). As the titles suggest, the reality that has been superseded by the revolution is represented in them as being spatially and temporally distant from the new reality. This pattern appears in concentrated and acerbic form in the poem **'Como quisimos'** (**'As We Desired'**), where the pattern in the first two quartets of three eleven-syllable lines and a final seven-syllable one yields in the final quartet to one eleven-syllable line and three seven-syllable ones, each with a marked caesura. This effects a slowing of pace to achieve affirmation precisely where the resolve to defend tenaciously the new status is being expressed. The poems **'Bonsal'** and **'Frente al Oxford'** (**'Facing the Oxford'**) provide examples of the kinds of resistance the revolution must combat. In the former poem, the duplicitous diplomatic advances that would steer the revolution from its course are exposed by a technique in which the U.S. ambassador is shown as an animal clothed in charm and as seeking talks with a persistence that seems indecent. In the latter, the whole background to the immediate affront—the stationing of the warship Oxford outside Havana harbour to monitor the effectiveness of the U.S.-inspired economic blockade of Cuba—is articulated with serene anger in a poem in which the speaker addresses a friendly foreigner. The ship is seen as the embodiment of a paradigm of evils that includes Ben Johnson, Charles Lynch, William Walker, the Truman of Hiroshima, Joe McCarthy, U.S. military aggressiveness and

economic exploitation. The poems **'¡Míster, no!'** and **'Como del cielo llovido . . .'** (**'As if Rained Down from Heaven'**) and the sonnets **'Abur, Don Pepe'** (**'So Long, Don Pepe'**) and **'Al mismo individuo'** (**'To the Same Individual'**) both dealing with the then Costa Rican president, José Figueres, form, together with **'Bonsal,'** a paradigm based on diplomatic intrigue against the revolution. Forming a paradigm with **'Frente al Oxford'** that involves aggressive military and economic acts are **'Son del bloqueo,'** (**'Blockade *Son*'**) **'Touring for Trujillo,' 'Marines U.S.A.,'** and **'(¡Oh, general en tu Pentágono!'** (**'Oh, General in Your Pentagon!'**).

There are also three poems in which the broad Latin-American problem of poverty and underdevelopment and approaches to them are considered. In **'Coplas americans'** (**'American Verses'**), a poem of studied simplicity, an intricate and appealing verse form is employed in which a five-syllable second line ending with a stressed syllable is in assonance with the final stressed eighth syllable of the fourth line of each quartet. This verse form serves to accent musically the intense presentation of the sad dependency of the Latin-American and Caribbean countries. The Alexandrine couplets of **'Crecen altas las flores'** (**'The Flowers Grow Tall'**) are presented by a speaker who establishes his knowledgeable authority by enumerating at the outset the eclectic components of his identity—as a thick-skinned alligator, as a Chinese, an Indian, a Soviet citizen, a black man, as one who understands the influence exerted by Charles Lynch and Jim Crow, and who knows in 1964 that the founder of McCarthyism, Joseph McCarthy (1908-1957) is not dead:

Murió McCarthy, dicen. (Yo mismo dije: 'Es cierto, murió McCarthy . . .') Pero lo cierto es que no ha muerto.

McCarthy is dead, they say. (I myself said: 'It is true, McCarthy is dead . . .') But the truth is that he is not dead.

With these credentials he sets out to attack the 'Alliance for Progress' with images that suggest the inherent incompatibility of U.S. interests and attitudes with Latin American ones. In the *letrilla* **'Las dos cartas'** (**'The Two Charters'**), two declarations concerning the future of Latin America with Cuba as the central preoccupation—the San José declaration of the Foreign Ministers of the Organization of American States of August 1960 and the Declaration of Havana made by Fidel Castro in September 1960—are considered. Yet another form of antithesis is revealed here by Guillén. Each stanza consists of two *redondillas* as questions and is followed by an answer that alternately names one or the other declaration. And since the judgments are diametrically opposed, the images to which **'Con la Carta de la Habana'** (**'With the Havana Charter'**) is answered suggest, both in their visual and auditive aspects, what is desirable. These images are also predominant in the poem since the first and last stanzas have the Havana Charter as their subject.

The fate of individual countries is examined in other poems: **'Panamá,'** where there is expectation of change; in the eleven-syllable tercets of **'A Chile'** (**'To Chile'**), which express sad farewell and solidarity; and in the *décimas* of **'A Colombia'** (**'To Colombia'**), where metonymy is used in the representation of this country of flowers: '¡Oh Colombia prisionera / orquídea puesta en un vaso!' ('Oh imprisoned Colombia / an orchid placed in a glass!'). With imperialism such a pressing concern, a view of relations with a big country that is not imperialistic is provided in the poem **'Unión Soviética'** (**'Soviet Union'**). Long anaphorical series beginning with 'Ni' are developed to indicate the absence of the curses of imperialism and racism in Soviet-Cuban relations. That a poet should speak of this is a matter that is raised within the poem itself, and it is soon realized that 'poet' here is invested with all the fine perception of social and political questions that has been noticed throughout the course of Guillén's poetry. Thus verses like the following are spoken with comprehensive authoritativeness:

En nuestro mar nunca encontré
piratas de Moscú.
(Hable, Caribe, usted.)
Ni de Moscú tampoco en mis claras bahías
ese ojo-radar superatento
las noches y los días
queriendo adivinar mi pensamiento.
Ni bloqueos.
Ni marines.
Ni lanchas para infiltrar espías.
¿Barcos soviéticos? Muy bien.
Son petroleros, mire usted.
Son pescadores, sí señor.
Otros llevan azúcar, traen, café
junto a fragantes ramos de esperanzas en flor.
Yo, poeta, lo digo.
Nunca de allá nos vino nada
sin que tuviera el suave gusto del pan amigo,
el sabor generoso de la voz camarada.

In our sea I have never found
pirates from Moscow.
(You can attest to that, Caribbean.)
Neither from Moscow is there in my limpid bays
that attentive radar-eye
night and day
trying to read my thoughts.
Nor blockades.
Nor marines.
Nor launches for infiltrating spies.
Soviet ships! Very well.
They are oil tankers, look!
They are fishing boats, yes, sir.
Others take away sugar and bring coffee
together with fragrant branches of flowering hopes.
I, a poet, say this:
Nothing has ever come to us from there
that did not have the smooth taste of friendly
   bread,
the generous flavour of the comradely voice.

The poems **'¿Puedes?'** (**'Can You?'**) and **'Tierra en la sierra y en el llano'** (**'Land in the Hills and on the Plain'**)

develop one of the principal tenets of the praised **'Carta de la Habana:'** that people should have access to land. In **'¿Puedes?'** as in 'las dos cartas' questions play a central role. They show the preposterousness, readily acknowledged, of the private appropriation of elements such as air, water, and sky. This prepares the way for insistent questioning about the final element, land, which must evoke the response that is valid in the other cases. The *son* **'Tierra en la sierra . . . '** (**'Land in the Hills'**), in celebrating from the point of view of the hitherto landless peasant and the agrarian reform of 1959, furthers the notion of the justness of land distribution. Nor is the topic of defections from Cuba overlooked. In both poems touching on this topic, **'Responde tú'** (**'You, Answer'**) and **'¡Ay qué tristeza que tengo!'** (**'Oh, How Sad I Am!'**), the concern shown is not a sudden one related only to immediate developments. It has to do with some long-standing issues raised in Guillén's poetry and prose, with the 'convivencia' ('living together') and 'connivencia' ('connivance') advocated, for example, in the closing lines of the **'Son número 6'**: 'De aquí no hay nadie que se separe' ('No one will leave us'), a sentiment that has, of course, a new dimension in the post-revolutionary society, as the poem **'Prólogo'** of *La rueda dentada* will show.

This topic has links with the treatment of the question of race in *Tengo.* In the poem **'Vine en un barco negrero'** (**'I Came in a Slave Ship'**), for instance, a line of struggle by blacks for a dignified existence is traced, while the yagruma tree with its two-toned leaves forms an enduring Cuban symbol, from the days of slavery to the present, from Aponte through Maceo and Menéndez to the poet who writes in the period of full liberation. This state, as shown in the poems **'Está bien'** (**'It's alright'**), **'Gobernador'** (**'Governor'**), **'Escolares'** (**'Schoolboys'**), and **'Un negro canta en Nueva York'** (**'A Black Man Sings in New York'**), still eludes blacks in the United States.

A keen sense of history is evident in the finely crafted sonnets to Mella and Che Guevara. The images of the first vividly convey the daring and tenacity of Cuba's first communist leader. There is here, too, the idea of time that allows the grafting of a better future on to a past that was in dire need of change. A parallel between San Martín and Martí on the one hand and Che Guevara and Fidel Castro on the other is the basis on which the sonnet **'Che Guevara'** is developed. The duality of firmness and gentle warmth that make them excellent guides is emphasized in the portraits of both Lenin and Martí. Lenin is at once 'tempestad y abrigo' ('storm and shelter'), while with Martí it is necessary to see beyond the voice that seems to be a sigh and hands that seem like shadows, that

Su voz
abre la piedra, y sus manos
parten el hierro.

His voice
breaks stone, and his hands
split iron.

Continuity in Guillén's poetry may be observed in his treatment, with new formal procedures, of certain other subjects with which he had dealt in earlier books, such as the soldier, nature, and death. In the poem **'Balada,'** the loss of two soldiers in a national effort, indicated by the metonym 'bandera' ('flag'), is the cause of the sadness of the 'paloma,' the symbol of the revolutionary spirit. Two different kinds of fighters with two opposing motives for fighting are presented in the two stanzas of **'Canción.'** The unreflecting, automatic soldier with an underdeveloped consciousness of the world and of the possibilities of military uses will die unremembered, while the battler against the banditry of soldiers will spawn an ineffaceable line of resisters.

Nature is subtly treated in two poems of the collection and in a way that is consistent with its treatment in other parts of Guillén's work. The poem **'Voy hasta Uján' ('I Am Going as Far as Uján')**, one of five dealing with China, is presented as a dialogue, which on the surface resolves the question as to whether the speaker should go to Shanghai, where he is inclined to go, or to Uján, the destination of his interlocutor. The speaker finally opts for Uján. The poem, though, treats the question of man's precedence over nature. Shanghai is presented in the garb of nature. It is at the mouth of the Yang-tse-kiang—the river on which the two are travelling—the confluence of river and sea that had so entertained the imagination of the speaker as he admired the cloudless sky. On the other hand, Uján is given no other identity in the poem than the fact that his friendly interlocutor is going there. By outgrowing his attraction to nature and putting man in the ascendancy, the speaker shows an attitude consistent with views established throughout Guillén's poetry. The inadequacies of nature in the face of man's inhumanity to man that were shown earlier in Guillén's **'Arte poética'** of *La paloma de vuelo popular* are demonstrated here in the Alexandrine sonnet addressed to the moon, **'Pascuas sangrientas de 1956' ('Bloody Christmas 1956')**, one of the two poems dealing with a brutal night-time slaughter of twenty-one civilian opponents of Batista by his soldiers. In the precise case of the moon, its inadequacies, coupled with doubts about the real basis of its prestige, were evident in Guillén's poetry as long ago as 1931, in his poem **'Elegía moderna del motivo cursi' ('Modern Elegy of the Motif of Affectation')**. The last four lines of the sonnet are:

Luna grande del trópico, alta sobre el palmar,

tú que despierta estabas aquella noche triste.
Luna fija y redonda, tú que todo lo viste,
no te puedes callar, ¡no te puedes callar!

Big tropical moon, high above the palm grove,

you were awake on that sad night.
Fixed and round moon, you who saw everything,
you must not be silent, you must not be silent!

The lines are complexity ironical, and they go beyond pathos to deep indignation. The big tropical moon appears here in anything but its stereotypic romantic role. It is the mute, insensate witness to a slaughter that has national reverberations, as is indicated by 'palmar,' and although it is a pathetic fallacy to expect it to speak, it is neverthe-

less the least likely of those who witnessed or participated in the atrocity to wish to withhold evidence against the criminals. Thus the moon bears a moral superiority to them; but ultimately, because it must remain frustratingly quiet, it is useless and irrelevant to a society that demands justice.

Death as a topic appears in the poems **'Camilo,' 'A Conrado Benítez'** and **'La sangre numerosa' ('The Numerous Blood')**. The first of these, considering the death of the revolutionary leader Camilo Cienfuegos, focuses, as did the poem **'Paul Eluard,'** on the abruptness of the disappearance. This for the speaker is a troubling characteristic, since it frustrates the materialist desire to understand the how and the why of his death; but ultimately Camilo's death is transcended by the permanence of his contribution. This kind of transcendence is evident, too, in the poem dedicated to Conrado Benítez, the young teacher who was hanged by counter-revolutionaries in his school in the remote Escambray region of Cuba as he worked in the literacy program in 1961. In this poem, it is shown clearly that the link between present and future is a part of a revolutionary identity, a notion from which the idea of the immortality of the revolutionary follows:

Maestro, amigo puro,
verde joven de rostro detenido,
quien te mató el presente
¿Cómo matar creyó que iba el futuro?
Fijas están las rosas de tu frente,
tu sangre es más profunda que el olvido.

Teacher, pure friend,
green youth with well-cared face,
whoever killed your present
how did he think he could kill your future?
Secure are the roses of your forehead,
your blood is more profound than oblivion.

This concept is developed powerfully in **'La sangre numerosa.'** The poem is dedicated to the militiaman Eduardo García who was mortally wounded on 15 April 1961 in one of the raids carried out by U.S. planes on Cuban military and civilian airports in preparation for the Bay of Pigs invasion. Before dying, he struggled to a wall and wrote with his blood the name 'Fidel.' This information is contained basically in the dedication that accompanies the poem, the text of which is:

Cuando con sangre escribe
FIDEL este soldado que por la Patria muere,
no digáis miserere:
esa sangre es el símbolo de la Patria que vive.

Cuando su voz en pena
lengua para expresarse parece que no halla,
no digáis que se calla,
pues en la pura lengua de la Patria resuena.

Cuando su cuerpo baja
exánime a la tierra que lo cubre ambiciosa,
no digáis que reposa,
pues por la Patria en pie resplandece y trabaja.

Ya nadie habrá que pueda
parar su corazón unido y repartido,
No digáis que se ha ido;
su sangre numerosa junto a la Patria queda.

When with his blood
this soldier who dies for the Fatherland writes
FIDEL, do not say miserere:
that blood is the symbol of the Fatherland that
    lives.

When in pain his voice
seems not to find language to express itself,
do not say that he is silent,
since he resounds in the pure language of the
    Fatherland.
When his body descends
lifeless to the earth that ambitiously covers him,
do not say that he is at rest,
since upright for the Fatherland he shines and
    works.

There is now no one who can
still his united and shared heart.
Do not say that he has gone:
his numerous blood nurtures the Fatherland.

Here again Guillén has discovered a metrical form that merges impeccably with the other aspects of his poem. The four stanzas are symmetrically constructed except for the absence of the anaphoric 'Cuando . . . ' in the final one. In each case the initial seven-syllable verse is in effect prolonged into the following Alexandrine by enjambment. Besides, caesura occurs precisely after the seventh syllable in the two Alexandrines in each of the four quartets, thus providing a measured rhythm. But these pauses are subordinated to the sustained, taut, rhythmic pattern in the initial twenty-one-syllable sense period of each stanza. This in turn results from a rising intonation in these sense periods that is due to the fact that they end strongly, usually in verbs, and in two exceptional cases, in adjectives. Both of these adjectives attain special strength: 'ambiciosa,' because of personification and 'repartido,' because of its paradoxical function. The rising intonation in all the twenty-one-syllable sense periods is begun in each case in the first, seven-syllable line, which also almost invariably ends in a verb. All these musical features contribute to the high solemnity, dignity, and power of the content. These characteristics of content are supplied semantically from the outset by such items as 'sangre,' 'FIDEL,' 'este soldado,' 'Patria,' and 'muere.' They are furthered by the use of the formal second-person plural 'digáis' and the *cultismo,* or learned word, 'miserere' in the third seven-syllable verse. In the fourth verse of the stanza, the metaphor with 'sangre' as its tenor provides a vehicle, 'símbolo de la Patria que vive,' that maintains with clarity the elevated level of expression. The contrast created by this vehicle with the second verse of the stanza, 'este soldado que por la Patria muere,' underlines the power brought to 'sangre' by its associations.

The pattern of adverbial clause containing an act or attitude of the soldier, followed by a precluded incorrect interpretation and then by the correct interpretation, which occupies the three punctuated segments of the first stanza, is continued in the next two stanzas. Continued, too, is the loftiness of tone, which is contributed in the second stanza in the formal sense by hyperbaton and in the ideological sense by the relaying of the voice of the soldier to that of the Fatherland. In the third stanza, the adjective 'ambiciosa' serves as an example of the kind of subtle complexity that abounds in Guillén's poetry. It modifies and personifies 'tierra.' At the same time, by its semantic value it points to a double inadequacy: it shows the futility with which the earth attempts to contain the heroic soldier and it mocks the idea of personification itself, making conspicuous the fact that 'tierra' cannot really be personified and is of a lower order than man. The full effect of this is to keep unsullied the image of the soldier, as the verb 'resplandece' of the last line of the stanza confirms. The denial of the notion that the soldier's legacy can be contained is made categorical and the possible agents of its suppression raised to the human level in the final stanza. The adjectives 'unido' and 'repartido' used in this stanza pose a paradox in their immediate context; the paradox is resolved by taking into account the identity that by now has been securely established between the exemplary soldier and the people. Thus 'unido' evokes the idea of the bond between the people as a whole and the soldier created by his sentiment and his courage ('corazón'), while 'repartido' suggests the idea of the diffusion among the people of these qualities; and 'sangre numerosa' affirms the broad, salutary effect of his example.

It is important to notice that the speaker is here addressing, with the authority of a firm and wise teacher, an audience made up of the people in general, the unspecified subject of 'digáis.' Since their attitudes and impressions, which he corrects, are already sympathetic ones that needed to be refocused and refined, their silent acquiescence may be assumed and in this raised state of consciousness they may be regarded as joining the paradigm formed by the soldier, FIDEL, and the Fatherland. Besides, owing largely to the special function of the anaphoric 'Cuando . . . ' in the poem, the elevating effect of the soldier's act must be perceived as a sustained one; for 'Cuando' is not used here in a future conditional sense. The images it introduces are events that have taken place, but the broad public has not actually witnessed them as they unfolded. The images can only be seen as replays in the popular imagination of each of these events. The idea of recurrence suggested in this contributes to giving sustained effect to the exemplary behaviour of the national hero. While there is no explicit antithesis to this lofty unanimity in the poem itself, in the light of the dedication that accompanies it—'To Eduardo García, the militiaman who wrote with his blood, upon dying machine gunned by Yankee aviation in April 1961, Fidel's name'—the forces that killed this soldier form the unstated antithesis. Thus two opposing silences, the non-representation of aggressive external force on the one hand and the silence of the determined, unified people on the other are operative in the poem, heightening its tension. With **'La sangre numerosa,'** Guillén has made of a historical event an enduring lesson and a permanent work of art.

Finally, a prayer, 'A la virgen de la Caridad' ('To the Virgin of Charity'), that demonstrates in yet another form our poet's ability to combine piquant humour and serious social commentary. In this *décima* (the form appropriate for dealing with such popular matters as Cuba's patron saint), the speaker, functioning as the voice of the poor, touches economically on such subjects as poverty, class privilege, and inequality and on the failure of the religious approach to remedy them:

> Virgen de la Caridad,
> que desde un peñón de cobre
> esperanza das al pobre
> y al rico seguridad.
> En tu criolla bondad,
> ¡oh madre!, siempre creí,
> por eso pido de ti
> que si esa bondad me alcanza
> des al rico la esperanza,
> la seguridad a mí.

> Virgin of Charity,
> who from your copper pedestal
> giveth hope to the poor
> and to the rich security.
> In your Creole kindness,
> Oh Mother! I have always believed,
> and so I beg of you
> that if that kindness extends to me
> give to the rich hope,
> and security to me.

Tengo, then, as befits its place in Guillén's first book of the post-revolutionary period, contributes a mood of celebration, new in its prominence, to his poetry. It combines this with several of the preoccupations that produce the ironic, satiric, sarcastic, and elegiac moods of his earlier poetry. But whether the mood be new or old, the formal means he employs in evoking it displays constant innovation. He adapts here traditional forms such as the *romance,* the *redondilla,* Alexandrine and eleven-syllable sonnets to new realities, adjusts his previous innovations such as the *son* to give them new possibilities, or creates new forms, all to accommodate his revolutionary insights into historical reality. The breadth of the collection is a measure of the enormous scope of Guillén's poetic powers.

Jean A. Purchas-Tulloch (essay date 1985-86)

SOURCE: "The Yoruban-Cuban Aesthetic, Nicolas Guillen's Poetic Expressions: A Paradigm," in *Current Bibliography on African Affairs,* Vol. 18, No. 4, 1985-86, pp. 301-7.

[*In the essay below, Purchas-Tulloch examines African folkloric, musical, and religious elements in Guillén's poetry.*]

The transplantation of the African slave to the Americas, and more specifically, Cuba, was to result in the offshoot of a folklore tradition prolific in African elements, forming an amalgam with the Cuban. Nicolas Guillen's Afro-Cuban grounding stems from this transplantation, and his work has been singled out here as a tribute to his fifty plus years of dedication to this field. His work, replete with Afro-Cuban folkloric elements, is representative of a twentieth-century Afro-centric trend in the arts.

The role of folklore in a provincial and rustic society is incomprehensible, illogical, and even obnoxious to many an outsider-onlooker. Black folklore has often been condemned by this sentence. Consequently, many strange notions have sprung up around this lore, assigning it to labels of "primitive," "exotic," "carnal," "banal," "purely sensuous," "crude," and so on. Yet, what is folklore? According to the Spanish critic, Ildefonso Pereda Valdes, in his work on the "dynamics of folklore" [*Dinamica del Folklore,* 1966], it is art created by a homogeneous group of people. By homogeneous we mean that this art is produced by a people linked ethnically, regionally, nationally, religiously, or occupationally, in other words, with a collective spirit, a unifying bond, an *esprit de corps.*

Within the realms of the Black Aesthetic this "body-spirit" manifested itself in the oral traditions passed down through the generations in the form of myths, legends, fables, superstitions, rituals, songs, rhymes, proverbs, riddles, games, and other forms of expression. This is an aesthetic of great structural-functional import, a dynamic and vibrant aesthetic, as it is constantly being created and recreated, as it is passed from mouth to ear, to mouth to ear. It is to Guillen's voicing of this rich folklore in his poetry, a genre which lends itself to orality, that we shall focus our attention.

The negro prototype is not alien or novel to Spanish literature; this character appeared in the works of Spanish writers as early as, and as celebrated as Cervantes, Quevedo, Lope de Vega, Lope de Rueda, Gongora, and others. The negro as simple buffoon, as apish, caricatured charlatan, has permeated the literature of various periods. However, in the later writings of Lope de Vega, one does notice a trend toward the "crude African" being displaced by nobles and kings of African descent, thus placing the African on a more dignified and elevated plane. Of writers of black and white origin, there evolved in the 1920s a whole new perspective of the negro in hispanic literature, and it is toward Guillen and this trend that we now turn.

Nicolas Guillen, a mulatto, was born in Camaguey, Cuba, in 1902. To his ancestry, his father, a writer/senator, and man of great political fame, and his grandfather, a carpenter/nature poet, one may attribute his early inheritance of "poetic genes." Guillen was also obviously influenced by the turbulent times through which he lived—the Batista/Castro battle was at its foment—his incarceration, and later freeing in 1936. His later writings reveal a vehement and militant "anti-anything" that smacks of the yanqui and imperialism. His earlier writings have strong folkloric overtones, which attempt to camouflage his less overtly manifested sociopolitical themes.

Here, in these earlier works Guillen appears to flirt with a kaleidoscope of tropical images, to reminisce with the African past, and to gaze in nostalgia at a remote future. Yet, as Guillen's writings mature, the warm azure seas, the verdure and fruitfulness of the palm, cane, melon, and the coconut, the flora and fauna of the Tropics, are but a backdrop to the passionate, pulsating of the drum, the rhumba and the son. And, though it is sometimes difficult to siphon off the African elements from the Spanish, this article will highlight those folkloric elements that are definitely African.

From the very opening lines of **"Son Number 6"** Guillen asserts his African ancestry, calling himself the "Yoruba of Cuba":

> I am a Yoruba man, I weep in Yoruba,
> in lucumi.
> Since I am a Cuban Yoruban,
> I want my Yoruban tears to rise up in Cuba;
> Let the happy Yoruban tears which I emit
> Flow out.
>
> . . . . .
>
> I am Congo, Mandinga, Carabali

In similar vein, in **"The Surname"** he baptizes himself: "Nicholás Yelofé," "Nicholás Bakongo," "Guillén Banguila," "Guillén Kumbá," and "Guillén Kongué," using his original names as first names, along with his new Afro-Cuban surnames. Guillen also reordains the Yoruba gods: Shango ↦ Changó, Eshu ↦ Echú, Obatala ↦ Obatalá, and Olorun ↦ Olorún. By asserting his African identity Guillen is demonstrating why he must, of necessity, write in a tone that reflects his Afro-Cubanness. He has undergone the process of acculturation, and it is this cultural conjugal relationship that he has experienced, which permeates his works.

The presence of certain linguistic elements is reminiscent of "black" speech, yet this is not exclusively so. These elements will therefore be mentioned merely in brief, laying greater stress on the narrative, musical, and religious elements, which have a more markedly African origin. Several morphological changes which are found in works as early as Gongora, Lope de Vega, and others, also find themselves represented in Guillen's poetry. Apocopation, aferesis, betacismo, seseo, yeismo, contractions and duplications, all manifest themselves in Guillen's works. These forms add to his creations a certain sonorous and musical tone, intrinsic to the dialect of the Afro-Cuban.

The *Jitanjafora* is due one's mention here as it is a form which occurs frequently in Guillen's poetry. Evoking an air of African resonance, it is significant not so much for its sense-impact as it is for its sensory impact. These words are therefore important not for their logical value, but for the emotions and sensations they evoke, and the repetitive impulses they emit, which hit the tympanic membrane like the throbbing pulsations of the drum. There is a cornucopia of these jitanjaforic words in **"Negro Song"** (cited in Spanish to retain this jitanjaforic effect):

> ¡Yambambo, yambambé!
> Repica el congo solongo
> repica el negro bien negro;
> congo solongo del Songo,
> baila yambó sobre un pie
> Mamatomba,
> serembe cuserembá
>
> . . . . .
>
> Acueme serembó
> aé;
>   yambó
>   aé

"Sensemayá," a jitanjaforically-titled poem (whose very sound casts a hypnotizing and mortifying spell upon the venomous snake, protecting the man who is killing it), is replete with other words of a jitanjaforic-magical quality. The repetition of "¡Mayombe (region in French Congo)-bombe-mayombé!" serves to create, along with "Sensemáya!," a desensitizing effect. The poem begins slowly and suavely, continues crescendoing to a rapid precipitation of "jitanjáforas," finally decrescendoing with the passing of the snake. This poem is perhaps where Guillen attains the zenith of his verbal musicality.

After a long day's work, scorched by the broiling sun, tattered by the whip, the slaves often retired to intermissions of storytelling and riddling. These interludes though seemingly for pure diversity, though offering merely a brief respite to an arduous day's toil, also served to alleviate and postpone the numerous and taxing problems besetting the slaves' perturbed mind and physically depressed body, to appease a sometimes angry spirit, and latently to pass on his traditions orally. Here, in what appeared to be a casual manner the slave was able to discuss recent happenings, sometimes within the camouflage of an animal story. These stories later found their counterparts in diverse parts of the African diaspora with protagonists as: Ti Malice (Haiti), Aunt Nancy (U.S.A.), Brer Anansi (Jamaica), and so on.

Narrative elements: stories, legends, proverbs, riddles, reminiscent of this oral tradition, are also present in Guillen. In **"Ballad of the Guije,"** he alludes to the legend of the evil spirit capable of enticing little children; in **"Sensemayá"** he recalls Congolese witchcraft; in **"Riddles"** he asks the reader to guess from different descriptions—the keys being: "the Negro," "hunger," "cane," "alms," and the last "Guillen himself."

The African is a celebrated symphony of sounds and rhythms, whether in Cuba, the Caribbean, Central America, South America, or the United States. Wherever the African has set foot he has left entrenched in the soils, footprints of his musical ingenuity. Music, therefore, forms an indispensable accessory to Guillen's poetry. This is evidenced in his numerous allusions to musical forms in the titles of several of his collections. *Motivos de Son* (1930), *Songoro Cosongo* (1931), *Cantos para Soldados y Sones para Turistas* (1937), *El Son Entero* (1947), *Tengo (Sones, Sonetos, Bala-*

das y Canciones) (1964); the poem **"Son No. 6"** which he dedicates more to his reaffirmation of his Yoruban origin than a descriptive exposition of the *son* itself.

The *Son,* to which Guillen so often alludes, is a dance, slow and graceful, danced in couples; it is everybody's dance, and, according to Guillen, it is never-ending. In movement it contrasts strikingly with the fast, frenzied, serpentine, sensuous motions of the rhumba. The former, originally liturgical and curative in function, was transformed into a type of popular song-dance upon being transported to Cuba by the slave. The latter is notorious for the frenetic, hallucinatory, rhythmic pitch which the dancer attains akin to a possession of the spirit; a possession which Guillen himself refers to as "madness of the lower regions of the pelvis." This dance maddens not only the participant, but also charges the anxieties of the "observer-now-participant."

In others of Guillen's poems his musical allusions are moreso in content than in form. The **"Ballad of the Two Grandfathers"** and **"Guije's Ballad"** are two examples of the ballad-poem manifested in his works. Though the ballad itself is inherently a musical composition for accompanying singing/dancing, and is of European origin, Guillen adopts this song-poem style in these two poems using African/Afro-Cuban themes in his narrative. The poem, **"Two Grandfathers,"** discusses the African/European ancestry of the Afro-Cuban who, like Guillen himself, has undergone the process of mullatoization. The "Guije" poem tells the story of a mother warning her child of this legendary evil spirit which is capable of luring her offspring away. This idea of a gnomic evil spirit is not peculiar to this folklore, as various forms of the "boogey man" appear in European as well as African literatures, yet the "coco" and "guije" are found in Afro-Cuban terminology, as the "tunda" is of Ecuador, the "patica" of Colombia, and the "quimbungo" of the Bantu peoples.

From the short narrative-type poem, a predilection of African literature, we move to the *Cancion,* which again is significant in the Afro-Cuban context, for the images it projects. The *cradle song* or *lullaby* as a song form, is important, yet not exclusive, to African literature. In this **"Song to Awaken a Little Black Child,"** we hear in its beginning, the soft cadences of a Creole mother attempting to awaken her little "negrito," crescendoing into strong satirical overtones. It is as if the little child is the passive Afro-Cuban whom Guillen is trying to awaken from his stupor, to awaken to an awareness of his cunning master lying in ambush. The "lullaby," **"Newborn Girl-Child,"** is really not a lullaby at all in terms of content, but like the previous poem, is a satirical awakening of the Afro-Cuban, inciting him to rise up against his adversary.

Afro-Cuban musical instruments also form an integral part of Guillen's poetry: the indispensable, deified drum-the *bongo* and *gongo* whose resonant voices reverberated across those distant waters from Africa to Cuba, the former finding its niche in the title of a poem **"Song of the Bongo"** (which invokes the participating spirits of both black and white), as well as in other references by Guillen.

The *maracas* is an Afro-Cuban instrument made of gourds (calabashes) with seeds or dried bird excreta inside, shaken to produce a metronomic rhythmic effect (to this maracas Guillen dedicates an entire poem). Yet again, like the poem about the bongo it is not descriptive of the supposed subject of the title. It is a satire on the tourist maracas that fawningly seeks the subscription of the yanqui dollar. Guillen contrasts this maracas to the "rootsy" maracas which totally ignores the yanqui. In Guillen's estimation this maracas is the epitome of Afro-Cuban rebelling expressed in its truest form. The *guiro* or half calabash, as Ortiz describes it in "Maracas," is native neither of Spain nor of Cuba, but of Africa. The *guitarratres,* a three-stringed guitar of Cuban origin is also mentioned by Guillen.

African religion, like African music and narrative also found its way across the mighty waters, giving us till this day our practices of Voodoo in Haiti, Obeah and the Lucumian Santeria in Cuba.

These latter, Naniguismo and Santeria, feature in Guillen's works. Naniguismo, an Afro-Cuban syncretistic religion, is synonymous to superstitition, magic and the satanic, and includes the Santería. This Santería came out of the presence of the Lucumi slaves (of Yoruban descent) in Cuba, and their contact with Spanish Catholicism. As a consequence of this syncretism, a colossal pantheon of gods whose ancestry was found in African gods and Catholic saints (*santos*) arose, hence—*santería,* and the expression, *con santo*—"possessed." Each god in the hierarchy had his own language, functions, magic and sacrifices. *Chango* was one of the most popular of the Lucumi gods—the god of thunder and of war, and of fire, and of the drum—the male counterpart of Santa Barbara.

Magico-religious ritual also surfaces in Guillen's **"Sensemayá"** where the totemic creature, the snake, is killed by this seance-like invocation. In his **"Ballad of the Guije"** the phantasmal and diabolic spirit, "siren" of little children, is described. Chango is also mentioned in this poem. Describing the horrendous death of her child the mother sings:

> The turbulent waters of the river
> are deep and contain the dead;
> turtle shells,
> heads of black children.
> At night the river stretches out its hands
> and scrapes the silence
> with its nails, nails
> that belong to a frenzied crocodile.
>
> . . . . .
>
> and strangles travellers

In the vibrance of the rhumba there is a message, in the resonance of the son there is a tale, in the pulsation of the drum there is a code—all tell of the African past. Guillen's poetry resounds with the rhumba and the son in kaleidoscopic symphony. The voice of the Yoruban-Cuban continues unsilenced, it is the voice of the anguish, fears, yearnings, tears, of a people of African descent, a voice whose repercussive melodies have been heard through over half a century of poetic expression.

Roberto Gonzáles Echevarría on the critical reception of Guillén's work:

The most advanced criticism on Nicolás Guillén has shown that he is not one poet but many. The monolithic Guillén, chiseled and shaped by official critics and bureaucrats into a monument called. The National Poet of Cuba, simply will not do any longer. We are in a phase in which Guillén's work, having all of its moral and political battles behind it, must test itself in the broader arena of modern poetry. Who but the most recalcitrant ideologues would deny that Guillén made manifest the dignity of Afro-Antillean culture through his poetry, or that he eloquently denounced the many injustices to which blacks were and still are subjected? Who but, again, the most recalcitrant and dull-minded ideologues would want to persist in heaping praise on his works for reasons that, though in some ways valid, are not related to their poetic worth? One often hears the name of Guillén alongside those of the major Spanish-American poets of this century (César Vallejo, Pablo Neruda, Octavio Paz, José Lezama Lima), but one is always left with the impression that his inclusion obeys more a desire to do justice to the marginal to whom he gave a voice than to the conviction that his works are of the highest order. Is Guillén merely an Afro-Cuban poet or simply a poet? Does Guillén need the rhetorical pedestal erected by the State, or can he stand on his own two feet as poet? I would not be writing this if I did not believe the latter. Guillén is a major writer as Afro-Antillean poet—Afro-Antilleanism being not merely a thematic with sociopolitical relevance but also part of a general poetic revision at the core of modern poetry written in the Spanish language.

Roberto Gonzáles Echevarría, in Callaloo, *Vol. 10, No. 2, Spring, 1987.*

Gustavo Pérez-Firmat (essay date 1987)

SOURCE: "Nicolás Guillén between the son and the Sonnet," in *Callaloo,* Vol. 10, No. 2, Spring, 1987, pp. 318-28.

[*In the essay below, Pérez-Firmat discusses Guillén's use of the* son *and sonnet forms, stating that Guillén imposed "poetic form on native rhythms" with the son and infused "traditional form with indigenous vitality" with the sonnet.*]

Nicolás Guillén, best-known as a composer of *sones,* has also favored the sonnet. Although the fame of the author of *Sóngoro cosongo* (1931) rests primarily on his innovative nativist verse, from his earliest poems Guillén has shown a special predilection for traditional poetic forms, and particularly for the sonnet. Indeed, almost half of the poems written before *Motivos de son* (1930) are sonnets. His first collection, *Cerebro y corazón,* completed in 1922 but not published until 1965, already contains twenty-two of these compositions. In Guillén's liter-ary career, the sonnet preceded the *son;* the mature *sonero* grew out of the juvenile sonneteer. Beginning with *Motivos de son,* sonnets appear less frequently in his work, but they never disappear altogether. One finds sonnets in *West Indies, Ltd.* (1934), in *Cantos para soldados y sones para turistas* (1937), in *Elegía a Jacques Roumain* (1948), in *La paloma de vuelo popular* (1958), in *Tengo* (1964), and in *Poemas de amor* (1964). In his recent poetry, Guillén has continued to resort to this form with some frequency; *La rueda dentada* (1972) includes eight sonnets, and there are sonnets also in *El diario que a diario* (1972) and *El corazón con que vivo* (1975).

In spite of Guillén's persistent use of the sonnet and other traditional forms, the critical consensus seems to be that Guillén's "learned" poetry is less significant than his vernacular verse. Ezequiel Martínez Estrada [in *La poesía afrocubana de Nicolás Guillén,* 1977], for one, does not find much interest in the Guillén of the sonnets:

El poeta conoce y maneja con maestría el verso regular; usa de la rima y escande como cualquier aventajado escolapio de la Poética Didascálica. Ha compuesto, a veces, intercalados con piezas vernáculas y aborígenes, impecables sonetos, silvas, romances, madrigales y hasta tercetos a la manera de Dante. No es ésa, naturalmente, la poesía que nos interesa de él, pues aunque de méritos artísticos incomparablemente más altos, carece de otros valores que no acierto a calificar mejor que con dos palabras griegas de expendio libre: *ethos y ethnos,* en que reside su fuerte personalidad humana y poética.

[The poet knows and handles with mastery regular verse forms; he uses rhyme and he scans like any bright student of Didascalic Poetry. At times he has composed, interspersed among his vernacular and aboriginal works, impeccable sonnets, *silvas,* madrigals and even tercets in the manner of Dante. But, obviously, this is not the poetry that interests us, since although it has incomparably higher artistic merits, it lacks other values that I can only describe with two Greek words: *ethos* and *ethnos,* where Guillén's strong human and poetic personality resides.]

In my view, however, the interest of these poems *fechos al itálico modo* lies precisely in their combination of *ethos* and *ethnos* with traditional forms like the sonnet or the madrigal. Guillén's sonnets and madrigals are worthy of attention because they mark the point of intersection between his "white" literary formation and his attempt to develop a vernacular literary idiom. Indeed, one could say that Guillén's project of creating a poetry with "Cuban color" (as he put it in the prologue to *Sóngoro cosongo*) finds its definitive challenge, and perhaps its consummate accomplishment, in genres like the sonnet and the madrigal. To write a mulatto madrigal or a *mestizo* sonnet is to transform, to transculturate, two of the "whitest" literary forms, two genres whose whiteness extends even to their conventional content, the stylized portrait of a limpid *donna de la mente.* Guillén's achievement, as we will see, is to add color, and even local color, to the pallid outlines of this conventional figure.

The Nicolás Guillén who will appear in these pages, therefore, is neither the social reformer nor the practitioner of onomatopoetic, incantatory verse. I am interested in a more elusive Guillén, one who does not quite fit the image of Cuba's "black Orpheus." I am interested in the poet who, alongside such poems as **"Sensemayá"** and **"Canto negro,"** composed sonnets and madrigals. Guillén's "white" verse, or the "white" strain in his vernacular verse, is undoubtedly the least studied aspect of his poetic production. Although a great deal has been said about his "mulatto" poetry, this discussion has generally drawn attention to the black ingredient in the mix. And yet, as Nancy Morejón has mentioned (not without some exaggeration perhaps), Guillén "is the most Spanish of Cuban poets" [*Nación y mestizaje en Nicolás Guillén,* 1982].

Guillén's use of the sonnet is not only persistent but varied. He has written sonnets in hendecasyllables, in alexandrines, and in free verse. At times he employs consonance (with varying rhyme schemes), at other times assonance. In the choice of subject matter there is also considerable diversity. His sonnets deal with a whole gamut of topics, from the political to the culinary. One memorable instance of the latter is a sonnet entitled **"Al poeta español Rafael Alberti, entregándole un jamón,"** which reaches heights of sybaritic indulgence worthy of Baltazar de Alcázar. It begins:

> Este chancho en jamón, casi ternera,
> anca descomunal, a verte vino
> y a darte su romántico tocino
> gloria de frigorífico y salmuera.
> Quiera Dios, quiera Dios, quiera Dios, quiera
> Dios, Rafael, que no nos falte el vino,
> pues para lubricar el intestino,
> cuando hay jamón, el vino es de primera.

> [This calf-sized pig, turned into a huge haunch of ham, came to see you and give you its romantic bacon, the glory of refrigerators and salts. May God, may God, may God, may God, Rafael, provide us with wine, since, when there's ham, the intestines need to be lubricated with a fine wine.]

As I have already indicated, Guillén's earliest sonnets appear in *Cerebro y corazón.* Nearly all of the poems in this volume demonstrate his debt to the poetry of the *modernistas,* making plain the young poet's apprenticeship in the works of Darío, Silva, Casal, Nervo, and other figures of the turn of the century. A typical example of this youthful poetry is a sonnet entitled **"Tú."**

> Eres alada, y vaporosa, y fina:
> hay algo en ti de ensueño o de quimera,
> como si el alma que te anima fuera
> la musa de Gutierre de Cetina.

> Tu piel es porcelana de la China;
> tus manos, rosas de la Primavera
> y hay en la gloria de tu voz ligera
> un ruiseñor que, cuando cantas, trina . . .

> Un torrente es tu loca cabellera,
> y tu cuerpo magnífico de ondina
> bambú flexible o tropical palmera . . .

> Y eres alada, y vaporosa, y fina
> como si el alma que te anima fuera
> la musa de Gutierre de Cetina.

> [You are winged, and vaporous, and refined: there's something dreamlike or chimeric about you, as if the soul that animated you were Gutierre de Cetina's muse. Your skin is Chinese porcelain; your hands are Spring roses; and in your glorious, light voice there's a nightingale that trills when you sing. . . . Your wild hair is a torrent; your magnificent, undine-like body is a flexible bamboo or a tropical palm. And you are winged, and vaporous, and refined, as if the soul that animated you were Gutierre de Cetina's muse.]

The author of **"Sensemayá"** is nowhere to be found in these vaporous and vapid verses. The one vernacular note is the passing reference to the "tropical palm," though even this insinuation of the poet's real-life environment is vitiated by being made of a woman with the body of a water-sprite, a creature that has never graced the fauna of Cuba. Rather than a flesh-and-blood woman, the lady of the poem is only a tissue of descriptive commonplaces that, as the references to Gutierre de Cetina attest, go back to Renaissance Petrarchism. More than a *mujer,* this lady is a *mujer-cita.* As the speaker himself recognizes, she is nothing but a chimera—an entity built from disparate scraps and thus lacking a distinct identity. Even though the sonnet begins as a straightforward definition ("Eres . . ."), with the adjectives that follow—" alada, y vaporosa, y fina"—it becomes clear that the woman's insubstantiality precludes further specification. In fact, all of this lady's attributes lead *away* from her: her skin comes from China; her hands belong to the Spring; her voice is like a nightingale; she has the body of a sprite; and her soul belongs to Gutierre de Cetina, her spiritual daddy. By the end of the enumeration, **"Tú"** has been emptied of any individualizing content, and the word itself is less a "personal" pronoun than an impersonal marker of Guillén's debt to a certain literary tradition and its attendant conception of woman. What Guillén "addresses" in this poem is simply a constellation of commonplaces.

Using **"Tú"** as a term of comparison, let me now take a look at the first sonnet of Guillén's mature work, **"El abuelo,"** which appeared in *West Indies, Ltd.* (1934).

> Esta mujer angélica de ojos septentrionales,
> que vive atenta al ritmo de su sangre europea,
> ignora que en lo hondo de ese ritmo golpea
> un negro el parche duro de roncos atabales.

> Bajo la línea escueta de su nariz aguda,
> la boca, en fino trazo, traza una raya breve,
> y no hay cuervo que manche la solitaria nieve
> de su carne, que fulge temblorosa y desnuda.

> ¡Ah, mi señora! Mírate las venas misteriosas;
> boga en el agua viva que allá dentro te fluye,
> y ve pasando lirios, nelumbios, lotos, rosas;

> Que ya verás, inquieta, junto a la fresca orilla,
> la dulce sombra oscura del abuelo que huye,
> el que rizó por siempre tu cabeza amarilla.

[This angelic lady with septentrional eyes, who lives attentive to the rhythm of her European blood, ignores that in the depths of that rhythm a black man beats the taut skin of hoarse drums. Beneath the outlines of her small nose, her mouth, with a delicate contour, traces a brief line, and there is no crow to stain the solitary snow of her skin, which glows tremulous and naked. Oh, my lady! Look into your mysterious veins; travel in the living waters that flow inside you; go by lilies, nelumbiums, lotuses, roses; and you will see, restless, next to the fresh shore, the sweet, dark shadow of your fleeing grandfather, the one who permanently curled your yellow head.]

There are significant affinities between this sonnet and the previous one. Both poems derive from the tradition of Petrarchan love poetry, a fact that shapes the appearance of the women as well as the manner of description. **"El abuelo"** begins by actually quoting this tradition, since "mujer angélica" is a transposition of *donna angelicata,* one of the epithets applied to the Lauras and Beatrices of Medieval and Renaissance poetry. This little lady is no less a *mujer-cita* than "tú." In addition, the description in both instances follows a downward path, from the head to the torso, as was prescribed by classical rhetoric. In **"El abuelo"** the descending trajectory generates a fairly detailed catalog of traits. The lady, perhaps, is naked before a mirror, and we watch as her glance inspects her physical charms, beginning with her light-colored eyes and ending with her limpid skin.

The tradition of Renaissance love poetry is also present in the subtle insinuation of the motif of vassaldom, an essential element in the thematics of courtly love. By addressing her as "mi señora," the speaker adopts the conventional posture of a lover subjugated by an indifferent mistress. These connections with the Petrarchan tradition are reinforced by the fact that **"El abuelo"** follows rather closely the structural format of the Italian sonnet, since it divides into two metrical and conceptual units (the two quartets and the sestet) separated by a *volta,* that is, a change or modulation in the line of argument. Here the *volta* is punctuated by the exclamation with which the first tercet begins: "¡Ah, mi señora!" Upon reaching this point, the sonnet "turns" in a number of directions: the speaker modulates from a description in the third person to a direct address, from "esta mujer" to "mi señora"; he abandons the catalog of physical charms in favor of a description of her state of mind; and he brings to an end the downward trajectory in order to peer into his lady's soul. Psychological intimacy replaces physical intimacy. The speaker proposes now to accompany the woman on a journey into the innermost recesses of her being, and the two verbs of sight which appear in the tercets, "mírate" and "verás," have to do less with physical sight than with spiritual vision. In the two quartets the description had gone from top to bottom; in the sestet the direction is not down but in, from the lady's skin to her soul, from her physique to her psyche.

This movement inward is accompanied by a retrospective glance, by a kind of flashback. Since by peering into her soul the speaker discovers his lady's ancestry, looking in

means looking back. Thus, the tercets are successively introspective and atavistic. They take us from the here and now of the lady's resplendent skin to the *illo tempore* of her place of origin. As we move from her boudoir to the African jungle, the modern world gives way to the colonial epoch. The poem as a whole shifts from inspection to introspection to retrospection: from the lady's snowlike skin to her heart of darkness to the dark shadow of her fugitive grandfather. We should recall that in the earlier sonnet there was also a movement away from the woman's immediate physical presence, but it only led into the rarefied realm of literary convention. Here the displacement takes us to very different surroundings and has a very different effect, for this is not a voyage of escape but of discovery, and even, as the reference to the slave trade suggests, of entrapment. This journey back to the source concludes in the last line of the poem, which suddenly redirects our gaze back to the body of the woman, to her "cabeza amarilla." We return to the woman's body, and specifically to her upper body, which had been the sonnet's point of departure.

The phrasing at the end suggests, however, a marked switch in focus. In the last line of the poem the speaker employs not the metaphorical language of amorous encomia, but the prosaic lexicon of impassive description. In **"Tú"** the "wild hair" of the woman had been compared, with typical hyperbole, to a torrent. At the end of **"El abuelo"** the hyperbolic torrents have been replaced by a "yellow head." One can summarize the argument of the poem by juxtaposing its opening words with its closing ones: "mujer angélica" and "cabeza amarilla." On one level, the two phrases are nearly synonymous, since angel ladies are always blond. But these two phrases reflect diverse ways of looking at the woman's blond hair. In one instance, idealization and hyperbole; in the other, sobriety and simplicity. As happens with numberless love sonnets, this poem recounts the transformation of the poet's lady, but in a direction contrary to the traditional one, for there is no idealization or sublimation. By the end of the poem the earth-angel of the opening lines has been transformed into a flesh-and-blood woman whose blood pounds to the beat of African drums. The subject of **"El abuelo"** is not blanching but coloration. Guillén adds color, Cuban color, to the *versos blancos* of the Petrarchan sonnet.

Another point of contact between **"Tú"** and **"El abuelo"** is their attention to genealogy. **"Tú"** may be seen as an exploration of the protagonist's genealogy, which goes back to Gutierre de Cetina, for it turns out that this winged lady ("alada, y vaporosa, y fina") has flown in from the Renaissance. In other words, Cetina is the "grandfather" of **"Tú."** By the same token, **"El abuelo,"** from the title on, makes evident its interest in the lady's ancestry, though here the regress leads back to a workhorse of a different color. A black slave now occupies the position assigned to Cetina in the other sonnet. But the claims that **"Tú"** makes for Cetina's influence on the lady are similar to the claims made on behalf of the black ancestor. In both instances the forebear infuses his descendant with vital breath; just as Cetina "animates" the protagonist of **"Tú,"** the black ancestor determines the very pulsations in the veins of his granddaughter, whose apparent whiteness is revealed as mere illusion, as a kind of *engaño de los ojos*. With his typical wit, Fernando Ortiz once remarked that there were Cubans so light-skinned that they could pass for white. He must have been thinking of someone like this angelic woman, mulatto in head and heart but white everywhere else. At any rate, the mixed heritage of the lady is crucial not only because it symbolizes Cuba's *mestizo* culture, but also because it marks the spot where Guillén deviates from the literary tradition that animates his own poem. The intrusion of that dark, fleeing shadow represents what one might term the "barbaric" moment in the poem, that is, the point at which Guillén has grafted foreign matter—be it lexical or, as in this case, racial—unto the European family tree. In **"Tú"** there is no question of barbarism, since this poem prolongs or perpetuates tradition in a pure, unproblematic way; but in **"El abuelo"** Guillén departs from his earlier sonnet as well as from its models by injecting into the poem a "barbaric" or foreign ancestry.

The transculturation of the angel-lady into a Cuban mulatto entails important alterations in the rest of the poem. One of the dogmas of formalist criticism is that changing one element in a system alters it as a whole. Something of this sort happens in **"El abuelo,"** where the transfiguration of the lady transfigures other elements as well. Foremost among these is the motif of vassaldom. Once it has been transferred from the never-never-land of courtly love to Cuban territory, this conventional gesture acquires a profoundly human dimension, since it can now be construed as a reference to the institution of slavery. What appeared initially as a deference to literary usage now becomes a reference to a deplorable historical reality. As a result, the speaker's exclamation, "¡Ah, mi señora!," acquires an unsuspected pathos. As by anamorphosis, the entire scene suddenly changes complexion: no longer does a suitor address a fickle lady, but a slave addresses his mistress. Seen from this perspective, **"El abuelo"** enacts one of the paradigmatic scenes in Cuban literature (and in Cuban history as well), the depiction of an interracial romance. Moreover, by relating the speaker of the poem to the grandfather, Guillén suggests that, if the suitor is being spurned, the reason lies perhaps in the lady's aversion to her own black background.

Another element that is altered by the lady's mixed ancestry has to do with the place of this poem in the tradition of the sonnet. As its name indicates, the sonnet was initially a musical form; a *sonnetto,* literally, is a brief song, or—to express it in terms closer to Guillén—a brief *son*. As the paranomasia suggests, the Cuban *son* and the Italian sonnet are distant relatives, for both are musical forms. The *son* is Cuba's native sonnet, and the sonnet is Italy's native *son*. In the first stanza the speaker states that in the depths of this woman one can hear the sound of African drums; but this percussive beating constitutes, of course, the most important antecedent of the Cuban *son*. Those drums are beating out the rhythms of an ancestral *son,* a chant whose echo is perhaps audible in the assonance of *hondo* and *ronco* in lines three and four. What the angel lady carries within her is the deep beat of

a *son*. What a sonnet carries within itself, also, are the vestigial echoes of a "sonnetto," a *son*. By referring to the lady's origins in musical terms Guillén has collapsed her genealogy with that of the sonnet. Just as the woman travels back to her African origins, the sonnet itself may be said to travel back to its acoustic origins.

The role of music in **"El abuelo"** makes it perfectly compatible with Guillén's "folkloric" poetry. In fact, this poem may be read as an Italianate version of the **"Canción del bongó."** Both poems make the same point: that all Cubans are mulatto, if not ethnically ("cueripardos"), then culturally ("almiprietos"). Therefore, all Cubans, regardless of social class, are susceptible to the call of the African drums.

> Esta es la canción del bongó:
> —Aquí el que más fino sea,
> responde, si llamo yo.

> [This is the song of the bongo drums: When I call, everybody here answers.]

The essential subject of **"El abuelo"** is the angel-lady's belated response to the sound of the bongo, represented in the sonnet by the atavistic *atabales*. In spite of superficial differences (and let us not forget that the theme of **"El abuelo"** is the deceptiveness of surfaces), **"Canción del bongó"** and **"El abuelo"** are cognate works—the sonnet is a "white" version of what the *son* renders in mulatto. In more general terms, it may be said that the *son* and the sonnet are the two opposite but mutually implicated poles of Guillén's poetry, the two terms in his Cuban counterpoint. In the case of the *son,* he needs to impose poetic form on native rhythms, to turn the beat of the bongo into a "song." In the case of the sonnet, he needs to infuse a traditional form with indigenous vitality, to highlight the "son" in the sonnet.

If we listen a little longer to what may now be called "el son de la dama," we will notice that the first stanza is not the only place in the poem where the distant *atabales* resound. The densest, most charged word in the poem is the adjective "inquieta" in the first line of the closing tercet:

> que ya verás, *inquieta,* junto a la fresca orilla
> la dulce sombra oscura del abuelo que huye,
> el que rizó por siempre tu cabeza amarilla.

> [. . . and you will see, *restless,* next to the fresh shore, the sweet, dark shadow of your fleeing grandfather, the one who permanently curled your yellow head.]

Marking the precise spot of the lady's anagnorisis and underscoring it with the choking sound of a plosive consonant, "inquieta" summarizes the poem's meaning, since it brings about the reunion of granddaughter and grandfather. At first glance "inquieta" seems to modify the "tú" implicit in "verás." The woman feels restless, perturbed, upon discovering that she is mulatto, and the adjective highlights her disquieting realization. But it is equally plausible to read "inquieta" as a description not of the woman but of her grandfather, the fleeting and fleeing shadow that moves across the last lines. The sense would now be: "que ya verás [la sombra] inquieta . . . del abuelo que huye." The lady is restless or troubled because of her impending realization; the grandfather is troubled or restless because of his flight from the slave traders. Separated by centuries and circumstances, granddaughter and grandfather join in a shared anxiety, albeit one with very different roots.

This second reading of *inquieta,* of course, supposes that the adjective is displaced, distanced from the noun it modifies. This hyperbatonic placement is not inconsistent with the poem's meaning. Hyperbaton names the separation of sentence parts that normally go together; it is a form of syntactical displacement, of grammatical dislocation. But displacement and dislocation are precisely what this poem is about. What does the poem describe if not the black grandfather's own dislocation, his enslavement and exile? The dislocated syntax functions as an analogue of his historical dislocation. Or, to reverse the analogy, exile itself is a sort of hyperbaton, an existential dislocation that shatters the concinnity of self and surroundings. Slavery disjoins the grandfather and his African home just as the hyperbaton disjoins adjective and noun.

"Inquieta," therefore, has an ambiguous referent, as it can apply both to the woman and to her grandfather. This ambiguity is a cypher of the poem's meaning, which is simply that the black slave and the white lady, in a profound sense, are indistinguishable. "Inquieta" joins the grandfather with his granddaughter, grammatically and affectively. From this arises a certain ironic parallelism between the lives of the two relatives: the granddaughter, like her ancestor, tries to escape; but that from which she flees is her grandfather. There is a double, failed flight in the sonnet: the grandfather attempts to flee from the slave trader but, as the lady's curls attest, he does not succeed; the girl attempts to avoid her black origins but, as the grandfather's shadow attests, she also does not succeed. If he is enslaved by a white man, she is "trapped" by her black ancestor.

The poem contains yet another foiled escape. Although in modern Spanish *inquieta* only means restless or perturbed, etymologically the word has an acoustic grounding, as is evidenced by *quieto*'s etymological doublet, *quedo. Quieto* goes back to *quietare,* to silence, to make quiet. In its phonic sense, *inquieto* means noisy, not silent. That is to say, the word resonates with the beating of the *atabales* of the opening stanza. "Inquieta" marries sound and sense, *son* and sense, sound and sonnet. Although the sonnet as a genre has all but forgotten its musical origins, in "**El abuelo**" these origins are noisily retrieved. Much like the poem's protagonist, the genre recalls its own ancestry. In a kind of metaleptic reversal, Guillén's transculturated sonnet is actually closer to the source, more "primitive" than its predecessors.

This means that *inquieta* not only links grandfather and daughter, but also makes explicit the figurative bond that unites them—the sound of the *atabales.* In this voluble word, the poem voices the acoustic conceit with which it began (the equation of the lady's negritude with the beating of the African drum). In order to ascertain Guillén's

revisionary use of the sonnet form in "**El abuelo,**" it is enough to remember that in "**Tú**" the "light voice" of the girl had been likened to a "nightingale that trills." By comparing the girl's voice to a nightingale's song, Guillén is still working with the commonplace metaphors of traditional love poetry. However, by substituting the percussive drums for the melodious nightingale, he is incorporating into this network of imagery an entirely uncommon place (Africa), a place foreign to the tradition of the sonnet as a whole but very much a part of this sonnet's historical background. Those African drums also mark the spot of Guillén's deviation from tradition, his "literary barbarism." In fact, the drums are "barbaric" in the genuine sense of the term, for the messages they send are surely incomprehensible to the girl. Like the girl's mulattoness, of which they are the phonic metaphor, the *atabales* bear loud witness to Guillén's daring, noisy intervention in the Western literary tradition.

My discussion of this poem demonstrates that Guillén's "learned" poems do not lack, as Martínez Estrada claimed, *ethos* and *ethnos.* "**El abuelo**" is an "ethnic" sonnet, as it were, and one could show that Guillén's use of other traditional forms is similarly innovative. Even when Guillén begins from a constellation of received attitudes and themes like the stylized portrait of an ethereal woman, he manages to give it a sound and sense all his own. A more accurate way of looking at Guillén's poetry, it seems to me, is contained in the following statement by Juan Marinello, which appeared in an early review of *West Indies, Ltd.* [in *Ensayos,* 1977]:

> Hay en el poeta de *West Indies* una milagrosa capacidad para insuflar su potencia natural en moldes de la mejor calidad tradicional. El perfecto maridaje entre el soplo primitivo y la expresión culta de viejas sabidurías es la clave del valor de estos poemas. Nunca, en nuestra lírica, la voz múltiple de la masa ha encontrado vestiduras como éstas, a un tiempo fieles y transformadoras.

> [The poet of *West Indies, Ltd.* has a miraculous capacity for wedding his natural potency to the finest traditional moulds. In the perfect marriage between primitive breath and old, learned forms of expression lies the key to the worth of these poems. Never before in our lyric poetry has the multiple voice of the people found vestments like these, at once faithful and transforming.]

Guillén's sonnet fits this description well, for it is both faithful and transforming, traditional and innovative—as if Gutierre de Cetina also played the *bongó.*

Ian Isidore Smart (essay date 1990)

SOURCE: "The Central Creative Conflict, *Mulatez,*" in *Nicolás Guillén: Popular Poet of the Caribbean,* University of Missouri Press, 1990, pp. 159-73.

[*In the following excerpt, Smart examines the synthesis of European and African cultural influences, or* mulatez, *in Guillén's poetry.*]

Mulatez is a cultural concept of direct artistic relevance, which involves an awakening to the full importance of the African cultural heritage. This new awareness engenders conflict in every cultural sphere, be it social, political, economic, or psychological—the inevitable conflict between Eurocentered and Afrocentered realities. In Guillén's view, the conflict of thesis and antithesis must be faced and resolved through the harmonious blending or synthesis of the opposing elements. In a real sense, there is conflict at the heart of Guillén's creativity; it is the very fount of that creativity. Without the tensions generated by the clash between Europe and Africa, Guillén's best and most characteristic work would have no emotional core.

The concept of *mulatez* finds direct expression in several of Guillén's poems. The most significant is, perhaps, the **"Balada de los dos abuelos."** This work, from the collection ***West Indies, Ltd,*** is written predominantly in octosyllabic lines, combined with five- and three-syllable lines. There appears to be no regular rhyme scheme, but an assonance in *e-o* imposes itself throughout the entire poem. Significantly, this is the assonance in the words *abuelo, negro* and *veo* (I see), the last word of the first line. By the same token, the assonance *a-o,* as in *blanco* (white), is also frequently employed. The stanzas are irregular in length. The poet is clearly not making any great effort to stay within the well-worked traditions of Hispanic verse. However, this poem is not a *son;* it is close to the innovative, somewhat rebellious, spirit of contemporary Hispanic poetry and, in this regard, looks more to the *abuelo blanco* than to the *abuelo negro.*

The *abuelos* are introduced as *sombras* (shadows) and then presented in a series of paired images that symbolize and characterize them. In the second strophe, "lanza con punta de hueso" (lance with a bone tip) and "tambor" (drum), associated with the *abuelo negro,* are paired with "Gorguera en el cuello ancho" (Ruff on a wide collar) and the "gris armadura" (gray armor), associated with the *abuelo blanco.* Then in the third stanza, "Africa de selvas húmedas" (Africa with its damp jungles) is contrasted with the "galeón ardiendo en oro" (galley ablaze with gold). Of the two *abuelos,* one is dying and the other is tired. One is associated with the sun and the other with the moon.

In the fourth stanza, the historical and geographical context of their confrontation is clarified further. The opening lines evoke images of ships, black people, sugarcane, the whip, and the slaveholder. Then the horrors of slavery are suggestively presented:

> Piedra de llanto y de sangre,
> venas y ojos entreabiertos,
> y madrugadas vacías,
> y atardeceres de ingenio,
> y una gran voz, fuerte voz
> despedazando el silencio.

> A stone of tears and blood,
> veins and eyes wide open,
> and early morning emptiness,
> and dusks at the sugar mill,

and a great voice, a loud voice
ripping the silence to shreds.

These images are based on the implied, in fact preconscious, complicity of the reader, who thereby enters into the creative process with the poet. This aspect of Guillén's creative technique is, of course, consistent with the major trends in nineteenth-century and contemporary Western art.

In the penultimate stanza, the *sombras* metamorphose into more material existence. They become individuals with names, Don Federico and Taita Facundo—the "Don" that immediately precedes the given name is the traditional Hispanic formula for showing respect, and "Taita" has the same force as "Uncle," in "Uncle Remus" or "Uncle Tom" for example. The last line of this penultimate stanza manifests the powerful force of poetic volition and effects the synthesis, the harmonious blending of Europe and Africa, in the stark "Yo los junto" (I join them). The counterpoint carried on throughout the poem thus attains its intellectual peak.

The rhythm of the final stanza intensifies, mostly through the repetition of the line "los dos del mismo tamaño" (the two of the same stature). The new urgency of the rhythm gives the impression of an erotic coupling that is resolved in the climactic two-syllable line "Cantan" (they sing) with which the poem concludes, peaking affectively. A most appropriate final stanza for this ballad, it reads:

> —Federico!
> ¡Facundo! Los dos se abrazan.
> Los dos suspiran. Los dos
> las fuertes cabezas alzan;
> los dos del mismo tamaño,
> bajo las estrellas altas;
> los dos del mismo tamaño,
> ansia negra y ansia blanca,
> los dos del mismo tamaño,
> gritan, sueñan, lloran, cantan.
> Sueñan, lloran, cantan.
> Lloran, cantan.
> ¡Cantan!

> —Federico!
> Facundo! The two embrace.
> The two sigh. The two
> raise their strong heads;
> the two of the same stature,
> under the far-off stars;
> the two of the same stature
> black and white, both longing,
> the two of the same stature,
> they shout, they dream, they cry, they sing.
> They dream, they cry, they sing.
> They cry, they sing.
> They sing!

The rhythmic pattern is, of course, the familiar one of the *son* poems, the most effective rhythm of the poet's repertoire and the artistic element that accounts for much of the beauty of this poem. The poem represents the realization of *mulatez,* speaking through technique as well as theme to the fundamental relationship, the partnership, between Europe and Africa, the two *abuelos.* The harmonious aesthetic union in both form and content effectively symbolizes the cultural union that is *mulatez.*

Many other poems directly address the concept of *mulatez.* In fact, the image of the shadowy *abuelo* is used in the poem **"El abuelo"** of the same book, *West Indies, Ltd.* It is an alexandrine sonnet with a twist, entirely worthy of the Caribbean master bard who was also the consummate smartman. The first line presents:

> Esta mujer angélica de ojos septentrionales,
> que vive atenta al ritmo de su sangre europea,
> ignora que en lo hondo de ese ritmo golpea
> un negro el parche duro de roncos atabales.

> This angelic woman with her northern eyes,
> who lives attentive only to the rhythm of her Eu-
>   ropean blood,
> in ignorance of the fact that deep within this
>   rhythm a black
> beats the coarse skins of raucous drums.

The shadowy element is essential to the thrust of the sonnet, for the punch line in the final tercet reads:

> que ya verás, inquieta, junto a la fresca orilla
> la dulce sombra oscura del abuelo que huye,
> el que rizó por siempre tu cabeza amarilla.

> One day you will see, to your chagrin, close to
>   the cool bank
> the sweet dark shadow of the fleeing grandfather,
> the one who put that permanent curl in your yel-
>   low hair.

The blonde female so proud of her European heritage is reminded by the poet, in his inimitably picaroon style, of the ubiquity of *mulatez.* These lines recall those of an earlier poem, **"La canción del bongo"** (The song of the bongo) from *Sóngoro cosongo:*

> siempre falta algún abuelo,
> cuando no sobra algún Don

> There's always either a grandfather missing,
> or some noble title slipped in.

Both poems depend for their effectiveness on the readers' understanding of, if not familiarity with, the whole question of race relations in Cuba—and, indeed, in the Americas in general. They could be written only by a poet honest enough to include into his poetic universe elements from both the thesis and the antithesis which create the synthesis that is Cuban culture.

The poem **"Dos niños"** (Two children), again from *West Indies, Ltd,* also explicitly addresses the question of the relationship between the sons of Europe and Africa in Cuba. In **"Poema con niños"** (A poem with children) from

El son entero, the poet presents in dramatic form a conflict among four children, one Jewish, one European, one Chinese, and one African. The mother of the Euro-Cuban child resolves the conflict by invoking the principle of *mulatez.* **"Son número 6"** (*Son* number 6), also from *El son entero,* begins with a resounding proclamation of the persona's African heritage:

> Yoruba soy, lloro en yoruba
>
> . . . . .
>
> Yoruba soy, soy lucumí,
> mandinga, congo, carabalí.
> I am Yoruba, I weep in Yoruba
>
> . . . . .
>
> I am Yoruba, I am *lucumi* [a Yoruba speaker]
> Mandingo, Congo, *carabali* [Ibo].

However, the theme of the racial blend that constitutes the Cuban ethos is also presented and, in fact, becomes paramount. The abiding image of the work is contained in the following lines from the central *son* portion of the poem:

> Estamos juntos desde muy lejos,
> jóvenes, viejos,
> negros y blancos, todo mezclado;
>
> We have been together for quite a long time,
> young, old,
> blacks and whites, all mixed together.

The Martinican critic Alfred Melon has been particularly struck with how often these, or remarkably similar, images turn up in Guillén poetry (he uses the term *obsession* in his analysis) [in *Recopilación de textos sobre Nicolás Guillén,* edited by Nancy Morejón]: "The constant juxtaposition in fraternal solidarity of blacks and whites, rather, their constant mixing, is perhaps Nicolás Guillén's greatest obsession, and it is not mere sentimentality for it bespeaks a constructive efficacy and force." Since the mulatto is biologically at the crossroads where Europe and Africa meet, his physical duality has frequently been accompanied by sociological and psychological dysfunction. His identity is frequently assailed in the most fundamental fashion by external pressures and, indeed, intense internal pressures too. [In a footnote, the critic adds: Carl N. Degler, *Neither Black nor White: Slavery and Race Relations in Brazil and the United States,* confirms my assertion. Although he is speaking principally of the Brazilian situation, it is clear that the Cuban situation could not have been very different. The situation in Trinidad and Tobago, my native country, has been similar in many ways to that described in Degler's book. It seems quite reasonable to assume that analogous patterns would have developed in countries as similar as Cuba, Trinidad, and Brazil, along with many others that have had similar historical experiences in the matter of race relations. Degler asserts poignantly, with more than adequate demonstration, "The lot of the mulatto in Brazil can be anxiety-producing. Not white, yet often wanting to be so, the mulatto nevertheless can be classed as a black at any time a room clerk or maitre d'hotel chooses to treat him as such. This, too, is the negative side of the mulatto escape hatch." There is evidence that at least some of this turmoil was experienced by Guillén, and it is borne out in his remark about being a "mulato bastante claro 'y de pelo.'"] Neither black nor white, the mulatto's metaphysical alienation is likely to give him a clearer insight into the primordial contradiction of the human condition. Guillén seems to have developed the potential of this difficult position. He avoided the pathological pitfalls of his own biological and sociological *mulatez,* and, by elaborating on its positive aspects and incorporating these into his active artistic and psychological life, he converted a potential nightmare into poetic inspiration. The artist often builds beauty out of his own psychoses and neuroses; however, in this case, the aesthetic profit appears to have been made only after the destructive *mulatez* was transformed into a positive force.

Melon, being a Marxist critic, is naturally partial to the idea of synthesis and sees Guillén as "el poeta de la síntesis" (the poet of synthesis), a view he defends with masterful arguments [in his "El poeta de la síntesis" in *Recopilacíon*]. He asserts, for example, that the poet's "synthesizing vocation" was already evident in his earliest works, and he cites the following lines from **"La balada azul":**

> Frente al mar, viendo las olas
> la quieta orilla besar,
> los dos muy juntos, muy juntos

> Facing the sea, seeing the waves
> kiss the still shore,
> the two of us together, close together.

Of course, the image of "los dos muy juntos" is natural in a love poem. However, Melon attaches special significance to it. He points out that it is repeated later in the same poem:

> al pie de la fuente clara
> juntos, muy juntos los dos.

> At the foot of the clear fountain
> together, the two of us close together.

He cites this as yet another example of "the obsession with pairs, the reiteration of the expressions *de dos en dos, los dos juntos, muy juntos,*" in Guillén's poetic work.

Samples of these recurring images of pairing and togetherness can be seen in the poems I analyzed previously in this chapter. Melon cites many other examples, especially in the poem **"No sé por qué piensas tú"** (I don't know why you think), from the collection *Cantos para soldados y sones para turistas,* which was first published in Mexico in 1937. Perhaps the most aesthetic example of Guillén's obsession with duality, this poem is a clever and moving play on "tú" (you) and "yo" (I). All the lines, except three, end with "tú" or "yo." The three exceptions act as the strong link, like two strong hands firmly clasped, uniting "tú" and "yo." Two exceptions come from the line "si

somos la misma cosa" (if we are the same thing), which is repeated to heighten its intensity, and the third exception is the only line in which the pivotal "juntos" is articulated, "juntos en la misma calle" (together in the same street).

Much of the effectiveness of the poem, and this is often the case with Guillén, comes from its simplicity. It begins:

> No sé por qué piensas tú,
> soldado, que te odio yo,
> si somos la misma cosa
> yo,
> tú.

> I don't know why you think
> soldier, that I hate you
> if we are the same thing
> I,
> you.

Written in 1937, the year Guillén joined the Communist party, the poem evokes deep emotions of revolutionary solidarity between the divided, and conquered, oppressed groups. It represents what Frantz Fanon called the Radicalization phase, when the native artist or intellectual participates in the real revolutionary struggle. Guillén tries to persuade the soldier, who is one of the Cuban people, to open his eyes, become aware of, and desist from his complicity in the brutal oppression of his brothers, a complicity that is a necessary, and indeed sufficient, condition for the colonial process. In the stanza quoted above, three octosyllabic lines are joined to the two one-syllable lines, "yo" and "tú," to take the strophe beyond the limits of the traditional, and very popular, romance form. The special structure is intimately bound to the content, with that impressive matching of form and content that always attends good art.

Building through the rhythmic interplay of "tú" and "yo," the final stanza comes to a climax:

> Ya nos veremos yo y tú
> juntos en la misma calle,
> hombro con hombro, tú y yo,
> sin odios ni yo ni tú,
> pero sabiendo tú y yo,
> a dónde vamos yo y tú . . .
> ¡No sé por qué piensas tú,
> soldado, que te odio yo!

> One day we'll meet, I and you,
> together on the same street,
> shoulder to shoulder, you and I,
> with no hatred either in me or in you,
> but knowing, you and I,
> where we're going, I and you . . .
> I don't know why you should think,
> soldier, that I hate you!

The obsession with pairing reaches its highest pitch of intensity in this last strophe, since not only are "tú" and "yo" matched by being the final words of the lines and hence the basis of the rhyme, but also, in most of the lines, they are actually joined as well: "tú y yo." The only line that does not enter into this pattern is the one that contains the very significant image "juntos." In fact, the sense of "juntos" is reaffirmed by the "misma" (same) that qualifies "calle," and so a double idea of unity is employed to bond "tú y yo."

. . . . .

Duality is at the core of reality. Guillén himself posited *mulatez,* an expression of duality and the creative dialogue between Africa and Europe, as the core of his art. . . . [It] is precisely this *mulatez* that links Guillén's art so closely to the Caribbean sensibility and culture, for this same duality is at the core of West Indianness or Caribbeanness. Every Caribbean artistic expression examined in these chapters—from the Cuban *son* to the kaiso from Trinidad and Tobago or the Colombian *vallenato*—results from some synthesis of African and European elements. For example, the particular process that produced the carnival in Trinidad and Tobago (with its accompanying kaiso) was seen to be a rich, complex synthesis uniting various European elements—Spanish, French, and English, in particular—with African culture, which was itself the end product of the synthesizing processes of New World slavery.

Anyone interested in forging, or merely exploring, a common Caribbean sensibility, in order to remedy the pernicious fragmentation imposed by the colonial experience, must, then, take the carnival kaiso from Trinidad and Tobago into very careful consideration. However, the *mulatez* at the core of Guillén's poetry is, in fact, synthesis enough—it provides an area of cultural communality within the fragmented Caribbean. It is interesting that, although this region is populated overwhelmingly by African-ancestored peoples, the fragmentation is found mostly in the European element, the most important element of diversity being the various European languages spoken in the area. The original African ethnic groups and their corresponding cultures quickly lost their functional specificities under the barbaric treatment meted out by the Europeans. However, the Africans' experience with the process of cultural synthesis will bear fruit in the Caribbean, through *mulatez,* as has already happened in Guillén's poetry. Thus, the creative dialogue, which generated this poetry by overcoming the stony silence imposed by Europe's cultural hegemony, must in time grow to fill the entire region with its rich cadences, to banish forever the hostile, self-serving, limitingly egocentric silences that once prevailed.

Edward J. Mullen (essay date 1992)

SOURCE: "Some Early Readings of *Motivos de son,*" in *Romance Quarterly,* Vol. 39, No. 2, May, 1992, pp. 221-30.

[*In the essay below, Mullen examines various critical interpretations of* Motivos de son *in order to show "the multiplicity of ways in which the same poem becomes a radically different object in the context of different critical approaches."*]

When Nicolás Guillén died on July 16, 1989, he left behind an enormous *obra,* much of which has gone unstudied. His work, which had celebrated Cuba's multiracial and ethnic mix, had garnered for him in recent years wide recognition in the Latin American community. There is little doubt, however, that of all that he wrote, his starkly realistic portraits of black urban life in Havana—*Motivos de son*—occupy a privileged place in his writings. Guillén's *Motivos de son* not only represents a clear rupture in a continuous tradition but shares a relationship with the Africanist poetics of òther black writers in the Caribbean and the United States, such as Jacques Roumain and Langston Hughes. In re-reading the criticism dealing with Guillén's *Motivos de son,* however, one is struck not only by the privileged place it occupies in his total *obra,* but by the array of readings produced by what in reality is not a book but eight brief poems.

If we assume that Guillén's *Motivos de son* constitute a *text* (irrespective of its physical format), I would argue that there exists a *critical* text which has to some degree shaped our contemporary apprehension of the original. Fredric Jameson's formulation [in *The Political Unconscious,* 1981] that "texts come before us as the already read; we apprehend them through sedimented layers of previous interpretation," seems to take on additional meaning when we think of it in relation to the chain of critical reaction to *Motivos de son.* By and large due to the scholarship carried out during the last decade by Angel Augier, Nancy Morejón, María Luisa Antuña, Lorna V. Williams, Keith Ellis, and Richard Jackson, it is now possible to reconstruct the original conditions which shaped the earliest critical response to Guillén's *Motivos de son,* and thus provide the contemporary reader with clues as to how the text was first read.

The purpose of this essay, then, will be to examine *Motivos de son* in the context of its interpretative tradition, in an effort not so much to retrieve an original meaning but to show how a text can be consecutively rewritten through a series of critical readings. The examples of the early critical interpretations of this book will show the multiplicity of ways in which the same poem becomes a radically different object in the context of different critical approaches.

A reading of the critical text which envelops *Motivos de son* can also serve as a point of departure to correct previous errors of fact about the book as well as to obtain a telling look at the development of Afro-Cubanism, albeit on a very reduced scale.

Before one can enter into a productive discussion of the critical interplay which has produced the various readings of *Motivos de son,* some discussion of its first context of production is essential. It is helpful to restate that the "text" under discussion was first published on April 20, 1930, not in book form but in the Havana newspaper, *Diario de la Marina.* The poems appeared in a subsection of the Sunday literary page directed by Gustavo Urrutia called Ideales de una Raza, which had been founded on April 28, 1928. Urrutia, one of the earliest spokesmen for black rights on the island, played a role somewhat analogous to that which W. E. B. Du Bois and Charles S. Johnson have assumed in the advancement of civil rights for Afro-Americans. He founded this section by directly approaching the editor of the paper, José (Pepín) Rivero. The paper, founded in 1832, was one of the most conservative pro-slavery, pro-Spanish periodicals in the country, and the accession of Rivero to Urrutia's request is an index of the growing economic impact of the middle-class black readership for which it was intended. It is important to bear in mind that in spite of the existence of a large number of exclusively black periodicals, the general prestige and wide circulation of the *Diario de la Marina* allowed Ideales de una Raza to play a role similar to that of the black newspapers in the United States, such as the *Pittsburgh Courier* and the *Baltimore Afro-American.*

Ideales de una Raza was *not* a Sunday supplement (i.e., a physically separate page) but rather a page intercalated in the general literary section between *Literatura* (canonical texts) and *Cinematografía* (popular culture). Its location is a telling statement vis-à-vis its perceived status as an object of consumption. The eight *Motivos,* dedicated to José Antonio Fernández de Castro, were printed in the center of the page in three columns: **"Negro bembón," "Mi chiquita,"** and **"Búcate plata"** (left of center), **"Sigue," "Ayer me dijeron Negro"** (center), and **"Tú no sabe inglé," "Si tú supiera,"** and **"Mulata"** (right of center). The physical arrangement is further framed by a cubist drawing of a black drum player by Karreño that provides an important subtext. It illuminates Guillén's words by referring to an entire tradition of visual art which at once explains the implicit reference to dance. At the same time it presents the poems that follow as related but independent artifacts capable of expressing via a totally different system the same ideas, images, and feelings. Also of considerable importance is the framing effect of the articles by Gustavo Urrutia ("Incidencia y reflexión") and Lino D'Ou ("Espigando en la inquietud") which stand both in physical (located on facing columns) and generic (they are prose) juxtaposition to the freer poetic forms which form the visual center of the page. Urrutia's comments on the paradox of Cuba's legal system, which acts to marginate the black population, and Lino D'Ou's review of Juan Marinello's *Sobre la inquietud cubana* both function as a sort of ideological dictionary offering the readers of Guillén's poems information about the historical, economic, and intellectual position of Cuba's black population.

In sum, the first appearance of *Motivos de son* took the form of an inserted text within the frame of a larger discourse on the black condition in a Havana newspaper. Because of the printed form in which it appeared (i.e., the essentially disposable nature of newsprint), it would have undoubtedly passed into oblivion if it were not for a series of progressive re-editions of the somewhat slightly altered versions of the same *text* in the following order: (1) a printing in booklet form ostensibly for purposes of copyright protection by the author; (2) reproductions of the poems in early reviews; (3) the inclusion of the *Motivos* as a subsection of Guillén's first edition of *Sóngoro cosongo,* published in 1931; (4) the printing of the majority of

the *Motivos* in influential period anthologies of black poetry by Emilio Ballagas, Ramón Guirao, and Ildefonso Pereda Valdés, (5) the sound recording of some of the *Motivos* by Emilio Grenet and Rita Montaner; and (6) finally, the inclusion of these texts in Guillén's *Son entero: Suma poética 1929-1946* (Buenos Aires: Pleamar, 1946) and *Antología mayor* (La Habana: Instituto Cubano del Libro, 1969).

In spite of the tendency by Formalist and Postmodernist critics to diminish the role of the author as a valid commentator on his own work, there is little doubt that the first context in which a work is viewed by many readers and critics is the bio-autobiographical dimension. As Edward Said reminds us, the words "author" and "authority" both derive from the Latin *author,* which connotes ownership. Thus, in spite of its relationship to putative fact which may be tenuous, the commentary (both direct and indirect) made by an author about the genesis, value, or meaning of his own work may shape future readings of his or her written text.

Guillén's personal commentary on his own work serves not only to highlight the essentially problematic relationship between an author and his or her text, but more importantly, helps readers to apprehend, not so much the meaning per se, but the essentially dynamic nature of his written texts. Guillén's personal commentary can be broadly subdivided as follows: (1) a series of five essays published in the *Diario de la Marina* largely connected to the issue of race, which prefigure the publication of the *Motivos* via the establishment of an authorial contract between Guillén and his theoretical audience, (2) interviews in which Guillén responds to direct questions concerning the book's sources and reception of the book and (3) three essays in which Guillén directly comments on *Motivos de son.*

In reference to the Guillén essays in the *Diario de la Marina,* critics such as Angel Augier, J. A. George Irish, and Roberto Márquez have all been emphatic in stressing the interrelationships between poetry and prose. Augier wrote [in the prologue to *Prosa de prisa,* Vol. 1]: "Con su artículo *El camino de Harlem*-aparecido en la edición del 21 de abril de 1929—emprendió Guillén su colaboración regular en "Ideales de una Raza," y hay que advertir una relación directa de esta prosa resuelta en artículos, crónicas, entrevistas reportajes, con la obra poética que inauguran los *Motivos de son* y que se consolida hacia nuevas etapas con *Sóngoro cosongo.* Son artículos polémicos que establecen los derechos y valores de la población negra cubana, y que ya plantean la necesidad de la integración efectiva como única solución a un grave problema históricia de la nacionalidad."

Likewise, Irish views Guillén's essays [in "Nicolás Guillén's Position on Race," *Revista Interamericana* 7 (1976)] as the intellectual matrix from which he was to shape his poetic (imaginative) projections of the lives of Cuba's black population: "The earliest phase of his prose manifests a basic preoccupation with race and racial attitudes in Cuba and therefore related directly to the poems of the early thirties—*Motivos de son* (1930) and *Sóngoro cosongo* (1931)." In short, it is clear that Guillén, to use the critical formulation of James Olney, consciously and unconsciously chose as his metaphor the black condition in Cuba wherein his poetic persona became the embodiment of the ordinary, marginated black Cuban, and that this metaphor shaped both formally and thematically his creative endeavors.

The second division of Guillén's personal critical text, based as it is on interviews, allows the reader/critic to extrapolate from Guillén's direct commentary on his own work and formulate yet another elaboration of similar materials. Thus, from Nancy Morejón's very useful "Conversación con Nicolás Guillén," we learn that Guillén still displays a marked ambivalence towards the *Motivos*. When Morejón asked how the public received *Motivos,* Guillén replied: "De este no vale la pena hablar, porque Augier lo hace extensamente en su libro. Pero fue un gran escándolo; un escándolo que dura todavía. . . ." With reference to the question of direct influence, Guillén suggested that while all writers are inspired by a previous intellectual and cultural canon, this material gains new meaning as it is filtered through the imaginative fiction of the next originator: "Hay que ser bastante estúpido para pensar que salimos de la nada. No recuerdo quién, pero sé que se ha dicho que en el arte como en la vida siempre somos padres e hijos de alguien. La influencia más señalada en los *Motivos* (al menos para mí) es la del Sexteto Habanero y el Trío Matamoros. . . ."

The third aspect of this personal text is more problematic, since it relates to his views of both the creative process per se, as well as of the inherent value of literary texts. Guillén spoke to the issue of the critical reception of *Motivos de son* in three basic essays: "Sones y soneros," "Presencia en el Lyceum," and "Charla en el Lyceum." It should be noted that only the first was written to be a printed text while the latter two were originally given as lectures to the Sociedad Femenina Lyceum in Havana.

"Sones y soneros" was a reply to Ramón Vasconcelos's negative review of *Motivos de son,* which had been published in *El País* on July 6, 1930. In this essay, Guillén stresses the tentative nature of materials, the limited size of the first edition ("tan limitada, que no llegó a los cien ejemplares") and perhaps most importantly, that in spite of their simplistic appearance, the *Motivos* were the result of a deliberate but difficult process of conscious artistic creation: "Aunque a Vasconcelos le han parecido muy fáciles, a mí me costaron muchísimo trabajo, porque pretendí comunicarles una ingenuidad de técnica que nunca he tenido y una frescura de motivación que les era necesaria. A pesar del tiempo que esa tarea me ganó, ni la ingenuidad no la frescura han sido tantas que disimulen el origen de los poemas. Y yo sí quería hacer algo verdaderamente sencillo, verdaderamente fácil, verdaderamente popular. Algo que fuera como el son de los que protestaron contra el son. ¿Usted no conoce ese cuento, Vasconcelos? ¿Si? Y el lector también, ¿no es eso? Pues de todos modos voy a referirlo."

Some two years after the original publication of the *Motivos* and the subsequent appearance of *Sóngoro cosongo,* Guillén again returned to the question of genesis and

meaning of *Motivos,* but through the more suggestive vehicle of the public lecture. Here, he distanced himself esthetically from his subject, choosing to articulate his perceptions through the voice of a double, an alter ego embodied in a fictionalized secretary. *Motivos de son* are here not treated in relation to the polemic of high art vs. folk art, but rather as projections of a growing view of art as social praxis. Thus, the racial question is subsumed under a broader notion of *mulatez* (i.e., both racial and spiritual homogeneity): "Estos pequeños poemas recogen los menudos conflictos de la masa, y cada uno trata de ser un cuadro breve, enérgico y veraz del alma negra, enraizada profundamente en el alma de Cuba. El poeta cuidó de ajustarlos al ritmo del son en forma tal, que a veces dictan al compositor el movimiento que les conviene." As a logical corollary of his argument, the early *Motivos* gain value in the eyes of Guillén, then, as components of a progression, a sequence of texts of which the *Motivos* form a substratum and the value of which is contingent on their relationship to the more socially valid poems of *Sóngoro cosongo.* Of *Motivos* he wrote: "Publicó un folleto, con lo cual nuestra disputa quedó tablas. Aquellos poemas eran ciertamente una interesante novedad, pero que había que moler con vigor para extraerle el zumo íntimo. En ese camino, *La canción del bongó* recoge acentos máspuros."

In a talk given some fifteen years later to Lyceum Lawn Tennis Club del Vedado, a sort of *Historia de mis libros,* Guillén spoke of the creation of the *Motivos de son* in radically different terms. Its genesis, he said, was linked to "una experiencia onírica de la que nunca he hablado en público." He recounts hearing the words *negro bembón* repeated rhythmically to him in his sleep, which led to a spontaneous act of creativity: "Escribí, escribí todo el día, consciente del hallazgo. A la tarde ya tenía un puñado de poemas—ocho o diez—que titulé de una manera general *Motivos de son.*" Guillén's confession, which stands in marked contrast to his earlier Apollonian formulation (i.e., poet as classic maker), seems reflective of Jungian thesis of the *poeta vates* and may have helped to shape later critical commentary, which depicted these early poems as comic and folkloric, a formulation repeated by critics such as José Luis Varela, Cintio Vitier, Eugenio Florit, and Roberto Fernández Retamar, among others. Guillén's commentary on his own work not only provides important information about the publishing history of *Motivos de son,* but suggests parallels between the poet's own apprehension of his work and the critical text generated by a group of theoretically more objective, professional critics.

Given both the extension as well as the thematic diffusion of the critical reaction to *Motivos de son* (a series of comments which spans some fifty years), the most productive way to make sense of a vast, ever-shifting critical text is to graph significant changes on the critical continuum as these changes appear creating suggestive disruptions or breaks with the earlier pattern of responses.

When *Motivos de son* was first published (i.e., both in newsprint and book form), the reaction to it was by and large favorable. This critical reaction took the form of letters to Guillén by personal friends such as Emilio Ballagas, Langston Hughes, and Alfonso Hernández Cata, formal reviews in literary magazines, and informal commentary intercalated in more generalized essays. Three early reactions deserve special commentary, since they have an emblematic relationship to the critical text as a whole: Ramón Vasconcelos's "Motivos de son," Gustavo Urrutia's "La conferencia de Guillén," and Fernando Ortiz's "*Motivos de son* por Nicolás Guillén con glosas por Fernando Ortiz."

Vasconcelos's review of *Motivos* [in *Diario de la Marina*, 15 June 1930] (he was specifically reviewing the printed booklet sent to him by Guillén) is an excellent summary of all that which educated white Cubans would find objectionable in them. Vasconcelos had praise for the appeal of the poems to the sensuous and primitive ("Son el producto espontáneo de la tierra natal, todo atavismo, sensualidad y sol a plomo"). But he objected to the influence of North American black poetry, to Guillén's appropriation of forms of popular culture ("La musa, callejera, fácil, vulgar y desconyuntada"). Most significantly, he criticized Guillén's greater concern with what it meant to be black and with specific polemics ("El son no necesita ser un medio de protesta social,"), rather than with universal revelation and art.

While Vasconcelos's review has been traditionally cited as a paradigm of "La metalidad y los valores neocoloniales de la época", it was not a document which stood in critical isolation. It was not only the white intelligentsia who were offended by the book, but, in a case which clearly parallels the critical reception in the United States of Langston Hughes's *Fine Clothes to the Jew* (1927), a number of conservative black intellectuals clearly felt uncomfortable with what they perceived to be a negative image of blacks projected in the collection. In fact, in one case, Guillén was accused of imposing "literary discrimination." Guillén challenged these assumptions in a talk given to the conservative black society, El Club Atenas, which, in turn, was summarized by Gustavo Urrutia in the *Diario de la Marina*. The reservations held by the *Ateneístas* parallel almost exactly the ideological position held by the senior black American scholar, Allison Davis, who in 1928 had articulated his position from the pages of *The Crisis,* in an essay called "Our Negro Intellectuals":

> Our writers started almost ten years ago to capitalize on the sensational and sordid in Negro life, notably in Harlem, by making it appear that Negro life is distinctive for its flaming "color," its crude and primitive emotion. This facile acceptance of the old, romantic delusion of "racial literatures," which goes back beyond Taine all the way to Mme. de Stael, was a convenient mold for the energies of writers who had no tradition to guide them in treating Negro themes. What was more to the point, it interested the sophisticated reading public, at the height of the "jazz age" following the war, because it seemed to bring fresh and primitive forces to a jaded age.

Approximately a month after the appearance of Ramón Vasconcelos's review, Fernando Ortiz published a long review essay [in *Archives del Folklore Cubano* 5, July-Sept., 1930] relating to the publication of the *Motivos,* in which he reprinted the poems themselves and excerpts from the major critical reactions to them, including the observations of Vasconcelos, M. Sire Valenciano, and Gustavo Urrutia.

Although Ortiz's introductory comments are brief, they serve as a frame for the entire essay and shape to some extent its meaning. Fernando Ortiz was at the time of the publication of the *Motivos* the senior Cuban scholar actively engaged in the formation of a national folk esthetic and his unqualified endorsement of Guillén's work cannot be overestimated. Although nurtured in high art, Ortiz, through his ethnographic investigations into Cuba's black heritage (*Los negros brujos,* 1906; *Los negros esclavos,* 1917), had developed a deep affinity for folk art and saw Guillén's early poems as perfect exemplifications of his embryonic theory of transculturation. Ortiz's formulation adopts two fundamental and complementary positions: (1) Guillén's poetry, while not conforming technically to current definitions of folklore, was reflective of an unconscious feeling of primitive sensuousness inherent in Cuba's black and mulatto population and (2) that the value of Guillén's verse appears to rest less in its meaning or technical beauty than significance as a first stage in the development of a genuine national literature. In terms not dissimilar from Ralph Waldo Emerson's Harvard declaration of American literary independence from Britain, Van Wyck Brooks's enunciations in *America's Coming of Age,* or Carl Van Doren's speech "The Younger Generation of Negro Writers," Ortiz declared: "Estos versos de Guillén reflejan un momento de la poesía popular con que nuestro pueblo traduce sus sentimientos más espontáneos, extravasándolos de los moldes cursis y vulgarotes de la vieja y presuntuosa cacharrería. Por eso vienen a estos ARCHIVOS." Given his privileged position in Cuban literary circles, Ortiz's efforts to give respectability and substance to the criticism of Afro-Cuban poetry would have a continuing importance in the shaping of the critical reaction to *Motivos de son.*

With the publication of *Sóngoro cosongo* in 1931, the critical debate over the revolutionary nature of Guillén's early poems was gradually subsumed into a discussion of this volume and his later collections of verse. Guillén's subsequent books of verse, in spite of their beauty and evocative power, were nonetheless far more conventional in theme and technique, closer to eurocentric cultural norms, and in many ways more easily interpreted. Much of the critical commentary written on Guillén's work during the 1940s, 1950s and 1960s seemed to bypass the problems posed by these eight powerful dialect poems. Recent critical studies, particularly those which have focussed on Guillén's relationship to the Africanist poetics of the 1920s and 1930s, as well as those critiques which share a predominantly sociohistorical perspective (I refer to Williams and Ellis in particular), have again resurrected the *Motivos de son* as objects of intense scrutiny.

A survey of the early critical reaction to the writings of Nicolás Guillén reveals that Guillén was engaged for much of his early career as a writer in a critical debate with his interpreters who spent much of their time dealing with issues other than the artistic worth of what he produced. His reputation as a writer was shaped for much of his career by critics belonging to the mass media (newspapers and magazines) who had great difficulty evaluating the work of a writer working so clearly out of the mainstream. Typical of the more debatable early critical reactions to his work was the obsession of some (Ramón Vasconcelos) in comparing him to the more universalist writers of the Hispanic tradition, and others (Fernando Ortiz) in viewing his work as purely an exemplification of African cultural transmissions. In this regard, the comments of Arnold Rampersad [in "The Universal and the Particular in Afro-American Poetry," *CLA Journal* 25 (Sept. 1981)] are particularly illuminating:

> As the history of black poetry demonstrates, to turn away from received notions of the universal is a radical and even sometimes a revolutionary act; the dissenting writer and critic risk the censure of those who claim to have created the universal, as well as those of their own group unable to confront the paradox between their abused social and material state and the advertised standards of the culture into which they have been indoctrinated. The work of the dissenter is dismissed either summarily or with condescensionit is often called "protest" literature and consigned to the literary attic. Neither literature nor literary criticism can flourish under such conditions.

In addition to the problems inherent in the formulation outlined by Rampersad, most readers and critics failed to note that Guillén in his *Motivos* was approaching his audience simultaneously through two complementary but distinct media (poetry and music), and that both the form of the poems and the nature of music stressed the performance aspect. Thus, these *Motivos de son* texts, at once festive, mocking, and somber, continue to be enigmasparts of a larger puzzle yet to be resolved.

FURTHER READING

Bibliographies

Kubayanda, Josaphat B. *The Poet's Africa: Africanness in the Poetry of Nicolás Guillén and Aimé Césaire.* New York: Greenwood Press, 1990, pp. 153-70.
    Primary and secondary bibliography of Guillén's works.

Kutzinski, Vera M. *Against the American Grain: Myth and History in William Carlos Williams, Jay Wright, and Nicolás Guillén.* Baltimore: The Johns Hopkins University Press, 1987, pp. 282-86.
    Lists works by Guillén published in Spanish, English translations, and critical studies.

Criticism

Callaloo 10, No. 2 (Spring 1987).
    Special issue devoted to Guillén. Includes a brief interview

with the poet and essays on such topics as Guillén's incorporation of the baroque into his verse and the relationship between Guillén's poetry and that of Puerto Rican poet Luis Palés Matos.

Chrisman, Robert. "Nicolás Guillén, Langston Hughes, and the Black American/Afro-Cuban Connection." *Michigan Quarterly Review* 33, No. 4 (Fall 1994): 807-20.
    Discusses Guillén's relationship with American poet Langston Hughes and each poet's influence in their respective countries.

Coulthard, G. R. *Race and Colour in Caribbean Literature.* London: Oxford University press, 1962, 152 p.
    Explores various treatments of the theme of race in Caribbean literature and includes discussion of Guillén's poetry.

Dathorne, O. R. "Afro-New World Movements: Harlem Renaissance, Negrista, and Négritude," in *Dark Ancestor: The Literature of the Black Man in the Caribbean,* pp. 172-209. Louisiana State University Press, 1981.
    Examines Guillén's place in the development of black Caribbean poetry. Dathorne states that Guillén's contributions were original and complex compared to his predecessors who emphasized Spanish influence in Cuba or presented simplified portraits of blacks.

Ellis, Keith. "Images of Sugar in English and Spanish Caribbean Poetry." *Ariel* 24, No. 1 (January 1993): 149-59.
    Discusses images of sugar cane in the works of such poets as Guillén, Nathaniel Weekes, A. N. Forde, and William S. Arthur. Ellis examines poems by Guillén, including "Cane" and "West Indies, Ltd.," and concludes that no writer explores sugar imagery with "greater range or depth" than Guillén.

Espinosa, Monica. "Nicolás Guillén's Poetry of Synthesis and Revolution." *Critica* 2, No. 2 (Fall 1990): 113-25.
    Maintains that although Guillén frankly addressed social, political, and economic difficulties in Cuba and advocated change, he also celebrated his Caribbean identity and Cuban culture.

Gonzáles-Cruz, Luis F. "Nature and the Black Reality in Three Caribbean Poets: A New Look at the Concept of *Négritude.*" *Perspectives on Contemporary Literature* 5 (1979): 138-46.
    Comparative analysis of negrism and négritude in the works of Guillén, Aimé Césaire, and Luis Palés Matos. Gonzáles-Cruz concludes that Césaire and Palés Matos present two different conceptions of the "black theme" while Guillén "represents the encounter and further unification of the white and black worlds."

Infante, G. Cabrera. "Nicolas Guillen: Poet and Partisan." *Review: Latin American Literature and Arts* 42 (January-June 1990): 31-3.
    Tribute to Guillén in which Infante provides a brief overview of Guillén's life and offers personal recollections of his friendship with the poet.

King, Lloyd. "Nicolás Guillén and Afrocubanismo," in *A Celebration of Black and African Writing,* edited Bruce

King and Kolawole Ogungbesan, pp. 30-45. Zaria, Nigeria: Ahmado Bello University Press, 1975.

Examines the social and political content of Guillén's poetry.

Márquez, Robert. Introduction to *¡Patria O Muerte! The Great Zoo and Other Poems,* by Nicolás Guillén, edited and translated by Robert Márquez, pp. 13-29. New York: Monthly Review Press, 1972.

Provides a thematic and stylistic overview of Guillén's career.

Márquez, Robert, and David Arthur McMurray. Introduction to *Man-Making Words: Selected Poems of Nicolás Guillén,* translated by Robert Márquez and David Arthur McMurray, pp. ix-xviii. Amherst: University of Massachusetts Press, 1972.

Considers Guillén's role in "the struggle between progress and reaction which continues to shape contemporary history."

Smart, Ian I. "Nicolás Guillén's *son* Poem: An African Contribution to Contemporary Caribbean Poetics." *CLA Journal* XXIII, No. 3 (March 1980): 352-63.

Examines Guillén's development of the *son* poem, a blending of "African cultural patterns and European scribal literary traditions," focusing in particular on the form's rhythm and humor.

————. "'Mulatez' and the Image of the Black 'mujer nueva' in Guillén's Poetry." *Kentucky Romance Quarterly* 29, No. 4 (1982): 379-90.

Discusses the presence of an idealized black female persona called the *mujer nueva* in Guillén's poetry.

Sparrow de García Barrio, Constance. "The Image of the Black Man in the Poetry of Nicolás Guillén," in *Blacks in Hispanic Literature: Critical Essays,* edited by Miriam DeCosta, pp. 105-13. Port Washington, N.Y.: Kennikat Press, 1977.

Discusses Guillén's depiction of black people in his poetry, maintaining that Guillén avoided stereotypes and "created black figures new to Spanish-American literature."

Spicer, Eloise Y. "The Blues and the *Son:* Reflections of Black Self Assertion in the Poetry of Langston Hughes and Nicolás Guillén: *Langston Hughes Review* III, No. 1 (Spring 1984): 1-12.

Evaluates several early poems from *Motivos de son,* comparing Guillén's development of the *son* to Hughes's poetic use of the blues musical form.

Turull, Antoni. "Nicolás Guillén: People's Poet." In *Cuba: The Second Decade,* edited by John Griffiths and Peter Griffiths. London: Writers and Readers Publishing Cooperative, 1979, pp. 214-22.

Provides an overview of Guillén's career.

White, Jeannette S., and Clement A. White. "Two Nations, One Vision. America's Langston Hughes and Cuba's Nicolas Guillén: Poetry of Affirmation: A Revision." *Langston Hughes Review* XII, No. 1 (Spring 1993): 42-50.

Argues that the relationship between Guillén and Langston Hughes needs to be reexamined. The critics conclude that "their poetry exudes a commonality which reminds us that their literery and personal relationship was not at all casual. . . . Their poetry shared an affirmative vision of and for Blacks."

Additional coverage of Guillén's life and career is contained in the following sources published by The Gale Group: *Black Literature Criticism,* Vol. 2; *Black Writers; Contemporary Authors,* Vols. 116, 125, 129 [obituary]; *Contemporary Literary Criticism,* Vols. 48, 79; *Hispanic Literature Criticism,* Vol. 1; and *Hispanic Writers.*

Homer

Circa Eighth Century B.C.

Greek poet.

INTRODUCTION

Homer's two epics, the *Iliad* and the *Odyssey*, have greatly influenced the style and content of Western literature and are considered two of the greatest literary artifacts of Western civilization. Taken together, the *Iliad* and the *Odyssey* display comic as well as tragic elements, and cover a broad range of themes that are still relevant today: war, religion, honor, betrayal, vengeance, and humanity's quest for immortality. Over the centuries, the poems have left an indelible imprint on the fields of literature, art, philosophy, and ethics. Writers as diverse as Virgil, Shakespeare, John Milton, and James Joyce have been inspired by the characters and tales presented in the epics.

Biographical Information

Almost nothing is known about Homer, but scholars hypothesize that he was an Ionian Greek (probably from the coast of Asia Minor or one of the adjacent islands), that he was born sometime before 700 B.C., and that he lived in approximately the latter half of the eighth century B.C. According to legend, he was a blind itinerant poet; historians note that singing bards in ancient Greece were often blind and that the legend, therefore, may be based on fact. It is also possible that Homer may have lost his sight only late in life or that his purported blindness was meant to mask his illiteracy. Biographies of Homer exist in the form of six early "lives" and assorted commentaries by ancient and Byzantine scholars, but the information they contain is considered unreliable and mostly mythical. Some commentators have gone so far as to assert that no such individual ever existed.

The paucity of information regarding Homer and his relation to the *Iliad* and the *Odyssey* has incited much scholarly inquiry and has brought together the efforts of experts in such fields as archeology, linguistics, art, and comparative literature. As a result of their research, three main theories regarding the composition of the poems have emerged: the analytic, the unitarian, and the oral folkepic. Until the publication of the Friedrich Adolph Wolf's *Prolegomena ad Homerum* in 1795, the notion that Homer was the author of the *Iliad* and the *Odyssey* was largely undisputed. However, citing certain inconsistencies and errors in the texts, Wolf asserted that the two works were not the compositions of one poet, but the products of many different authors at work on various traditional poems and stories. Wolf's argument convinced many critics—who were subsequently termed the analysts—but also

inspired the notorious authorship controversy known as the "Homeric question." Although Wolf's view prevailed throughout the nineteenth and early twentieth centuries, it was ultimately challenged by an opposing group of critics, the unitarians, whose primary spokesman was Andrew Lang. The unitarians insisted that a single individual of genius composed the Homeric epics, and they supported that claim by citing a unified sensibility, original style, and consistent use of themes and imagery in the poems.

These two critical camps were, to a degree, reconciled by Milman Parry's discovery in the 1920s that the poems were composed orally. Parry established that Homeric verse is formulaic by nature, relying on generic epithets (such as "wine-dark sea" and "rosy-fingered dawn"), repetition of stock lines and half-lines, and scenes and themes typical of traditional folk poetry. Comparing Homer's poetry with ancient oral epics from other cultures, Parry deduced that Homer was most likely a rhapsode, or itinerant professional reciter, who improvised stories to be sung at Greek festivals. As a public performer, Homer probably learned to weave together standard epic story threads and descriptions in order to sustain his narrative, and relied on mnemonic devices and phrases to fill the natural metrical units of poetic lines. Parry's theory, like that of the analysts, stressed the derivative, evolutionary character of Homer's poetry; but like the unitarians, Parry affirmed Homer's individual genius as a shaper of traditional elements whose creations far exceeded the sum of their borrowed parts. Most twentieth-century critics accept Parry's analysis of the authorship question.

Major Works

Two epic poems have been attributed to Homer: the *Iliad* focuses on the Trojan War during the twelfth century B.C., in particular the actions of the Greek or Achaean hero Achilles—a warrior who is both brave and headstrong; the *Odyssey* is set after the Greek victory in the Trojan War and recounts the adventures and long-delayed homecoming of the clever Greek hero Odysseus. Internal evidence from these two epics suggests that while the *Iliad* predates the *Odyssey*, both were composed in the eighth century B.C. in a dialect that was a mixture of Ionic and Aeolic Greek.

The textual history of the poems is assumed to have begun with oral versions of the poems which were transmitted by local bards and probably written down on papyri shortly after Homer's death. Once set down in writing, the poems most likely became the exclusive property of the *Homeridae*, or sons of Homer, a bardic guild whose members performed and preserved the poems. Scholars believe that in the second half of the sixth century B.C., they established a Commission of Editors of Homer to edit the text of the poems and remove any errors and interpolations that had accumulated in the process of transmission—thereby establishing a Canon of Homer. The first printed edition of Homer's poetry appeared in Europe in 1488 and remained in use until the seventeenth century. Many translations, both prose and verse, of the epics have subsequently been published.

Critical Reception

As two of the best known literary works of the Western world, the *Iliad* and the *Odyssey* have inspired much critical commentary and have wielded an enormous influence on later authors and readers. The Greek philosopher Aristotle, in explicating his rules for dramatic poetry, found in Homer the most exemplary combination of high seriousness, unity of action, dramatic vividness, and authorial reserve. In classical times, Homer's works formed the basis of any educational curriculum and therefore left an indelible imprint on the fields of literature, art, philosophy, and ethics. Homer's works, generally venerated as repositories of traditional wisdom, were among the first books to be printed in the fifteenth century in Europe. The vogue for restraint and correctness that characterized the critical thought of the sixteenth century led many scholars to reject Homer's works in favor of those of Virgil. However, Homer's preeminence as an epic poet was reestablished in the eighteenth century by the translations of Chapman and Pope and the essays in praise of Homer by Joseph Addison.

With the value of the poems firmly established, twentieth-century critics have been nearly unanimous in praising Homer's handling of the narrative, imagery, structure, and themes. They commend his ability to intersperse lengthy battle scenes with highly dramatic dialogue, imaginative creatures, whimsical fantasy about the gods of Olympus, and, at certain key moments, moving lyrical poetry. Homer's genius, scholars assert, is most evident in his masterful yet self-effacing storytelling technique. In a perfectly plain and direct manner, the narrator carries the action forward, examining the events in great detail and occasionally digressing from the main narrative, but always in such a manner that the tales seem completely natural. Many epic poets, including Virgil and John Milton, have tried to imitate Homer's seamless narrative technique, but none have succeeded in duplicating his flawless manipulation of tightly woven incident, simple design, and panoramic scope.

PRINCIPAL WORKS

Poetry

The Iliads of Homer (translated by George Chapman) 1611

The Odyssey (translated by George Chapman) 1615

The Iliad of Homer (translated by Alexander Pope) 1715-20

The Odyssey of Homer (translated by Alexander Pope) 1726

Homer's Iliad and Odyssey (translated by William Cowper) 1791

The Iliad of Homer (translated by William Cullen Bryant) 1870

The Odyssey of Homer (translated by William Cullen Bryant) 1871

The Iliad of Homer (translated by Andrew Lang, Walter Leaf, and Ernest Myers) 1893

The Anger of Achilles (translated by Robert Graves) 1959

The Odyssey of Homer (translated by Richard Lattimore) 1967

The Odyssey (translated by Albert Cook) 1974

The Iliad (translated by Robert Fitzgerald) 1992

The Odyssey (translated by Robert Fitzgerald) 1992

CRITICISM

John A. Scott   (essay date 1963)

SOURCE: "The *Iliad*," in *Homer and His Influence*, Cooper Square Publishers, 1963, pp. 41-53.

[*In the following essay, Scott describes the* Iliad *as a poem about wrath and warfare and focuses on quotations from the poem that display Homer's skill at evoking emotions and profound ideas.*]

The first word of the *Iliad* is "Wrath" which reveals at once the kernel of the poem, since the *Iliad* does not depend on the fate of Achilles, but solely on his wrath. There are no unanswered questions concerning this wrath, its origin, its course, or its results; but the death of Achilles, the return of Helen, the end of the war seem hardly nearer than when the poem began. The historical element in the *Iliad* is thus but slight, even if it does concern an actual war.

The speeches of the quarrel scene and of the embassy, the pleadings of Thetis with Zeus, the parting of Hector from Andromache, the making of the shield, the games, the father begging for the delivery of the corpse of his son are all poetic creations, unhampered by time or place.

Recent excavations made at Troy and geographical surveys in the Troad are of great value and prove that the poet chose a real city and an actual landscape for his setting, also that he was describing a civilization that had once existed, but, even granting all this, Homer has none the less given to "airy nothing a local habitation and a name."

A real Mt. Ida there must have been, but the scene thereon between Zeus and Hera is still mythical; genuine is the wall of Troy, but Helen's appearance at its summit and Hector's parting from Andromache are merely the creation of the poet's fancy.

Into the story of Achilles' anger the poet has woven most of the great human emotions and has endowed all his actors with an individuality that has never been surpassed. It is easier to enter into familiar companionship with the great Homeric creations than with Miltiades, Themistocles, Thucydides, or with most of the historical characters of Greece. We know Nestor better than we know even so famous a man as Pericles, in spite of Thucydides, Plutarch, and the comic poets.

The *Iliad* introduced to literature such outstanding figures as Agamemnon, Achilles, Hector, Paris, Priam, Diomede, Nestor, Odysseus, Helen, Hecuba, and Andromache. Each appears as a distinct personality and has ever since preserved the Homeric features.

A discussion of the plot and the great scenes of the *Iliad* would far transgress the limits set for this book, yet the poet's ability to set forth striking ideas in a few words may be illustrated by a series of brief quotations and running comments.

Nestor, a speaker whose talking pleased others and himself, is described as "a speaker from whose lips speech sweeter than honey flows." The conservative Odysseus put into a single sentence the slogan of autocracy: "A government by the many is not a good thing. Let there be one ruler, one king to whom Zeus has given dominion," and Helen's description of Agamemnon as "both a good king and a mighty warrior" has been the ideal of aspiring princes.

When Agamemnon saw that Menelaus had been shot, in violation of the truce, he exclaimed: "Not in vain are the

sacred oaths, the blood of lambs, and solemn compacts, for if Zeus does not show his power at first, he will in the end punish mightily the guilty with utter destruction."

Strife is described as "small at first but at last it strides with its feet on earth and head in heaven," an image which Virgil repeats but applies to Rumor (*Fama*). Nestor grieved that although he had years and experience he was without youth and vigor, then comforts himself by saying: "The gods have never yet given all things at the same time to any man." This has been repeated by Virgil in his famous phrase:

Non omnia possumus omnes.

Axylus is described as "a man who lived in a house by the side of the road and gave hospitality to all." This evidence of a sense for social service has been the subject of many an address or essay.

The words of Glaucus, "As is the race of leaves, so is the generation of men, the wind casts some leaves to the ground, others the flourishing forest brings forth when spring has come, so is the generation of men, one is born and another passes away." This has the honor of being the first quotation made by any ancient writer where the nativity of the poet of the *Iliad* was given. Simonides quotes it as by the man of Chios. Shelley was much impressed by these lines and incorporated them in one of his youthful poems.

This same Glaucus, in his enthusiasm at finding an ancestral friend in Diomede, exchanged his own armor of gold for Diomede's armor of bronze, the proverbial example of those who in a moment of excitement throw away on trifles their most precious possessions; and this is the Greek equivalent of "selling one's birthright for a mess of pottage."

Zeus boasted that he was so strong that he could draw up earth and sea, then suspend them in air, bound with a golden chain to a spur of Olympus. This "golden chain" or *aurea catena* was a prominent element in later philosophical theories of the universe.

Odysseus tried to arouse Achilles by saying: "There is no means for finding a cure when once the evil is done," but Achilles replied: "Cattle and sheep may be won back, tripods and horses be seized, but you cannot recover the human life that has once departed from the body."

Into the story of Achilles' anger the poet has woven most of the great human emotions and has endowed all his actors with an individuality that has never been surpassed.

—*John A. Scott*

Hector's reply to Polydamas, who had tried to check him in his victorious career because the omens of birds were unfavorable, is absolutely modern and is often regarded as the finest expression of patriotism ever spoken. "You bid me put my trust in broad-winged birds, but I refuse to follow them, I care not whether they move to left or right. One omen alone is best, to fight for native land." Professor Gildersleeve pronounced this last verse "the world's greatest verse of poetry." It is translated by Pope with a superb couplet:

> *Without a sign his sword the brave man draws,*
> *And asks no omen but his country's cause.*

This however misses the simple dignity of the original, since Homer used but six words. It seems to me that Chapman missed the tone absolutely in his: "One augury is given to order all men best of all: Fight for thy countrie's right." The Earl of Derby's rendering is nearly perfect:

> *The best of omens is our country's cause.*

On another occasion Hector inspired his men with the words: "It is glorious to die fighting for one's native land," and this has been repeated by Horace in the verse:

> *Dulce et decorum est pro patria mori,*

a motto which has been a favorite inscription on military monuments.

During the struggle for the body of Patroclus deep night spread over the field, when Ajax in anguish prayed that Zeus might slay him, if he only gave him light. This has been adapted by Longfellow:

> *The prayer of Ajax was for light;*
> *Through all that dark and desperate fight,*
> *The blackness of that noonday night,*
> *He asked but for the return of sight,*
>   *To see his foeman's face.*

When the warriors were preparing for battle down in the plain, the old men too feeble to fight sat on the walls "chirping like grasshoppers," as they discussed the merits of the different chieftains, or sat in silence while Helen pointed out and named for them Agamemnon, Odysseus, Ajax, and Idomeneus. Longfellow with wonderful aptness drew on this scene for his poem, *Morituri Salutamus,* delivered on the occasion of the fiftieth anniversary of his graduation from college:

> *As ancient Priam at the Scaean gate*
> *Sat on the walls of Troy in regal state*
> *With the old men, too old or weak to fight,*
> *Chirping like grasshoppers in their delight*
> *To see the embattled hosts, with spear and shield,*
> *Of Trojans and Achaians in the field;*
> *So from the snowy summits of our years*
> *We see you in the plain, as each appears,*
> *And question of you; asking, 'Who is he*
> *That towers above the others? Which may be*
> *Atreides, Menelaus, Odysseus,*
> *Ajax the great, or bold Idomeneus?'*

When the corpse of Patroclus came back to his tent Briseis uttered a dirge of bitter sorrow, grieving in his death, and all the women joined therein: "apparently weeping for Patroclus, but in truth each wept for her own sorrows."

When a laugh was forced from the angry Hera it is said that "She laughed with her lips but there was no joy in her face."

Andromache described the cup of charity which is doled out to orphans, as: "a drink which moistens the lips but does not reach to the palate."

When Hector challenged the best of the Greeks to meet him in single combat: "They all remained silent, ashamed to refuse but afraid to accept."

The aim of education was to make one "a speaker of words and a doer of deeds."

When Achilles mourned for Patroclus he said: "I shall never forget him, so long as I share the lot of the living, and if they forget the dead in Hades, even there will I remember my beloved companion."

Bellerophon carried to Lycia a secret order for his own death, a thing which suggested to Young in his *Night Thoughts*:

> *He whose blind thought futurity denies,*
> *Unconscious bears, Bellerophon! like thee*
> *His own indictment: he condemns himself.*

Zeus uttered the amazingly frank statement: "There is nothing more wretched than man, nothing of all the things which breathe and move on the face of the earth." This sentiment is very like the words of Achilles: "The gods have decreed that wretched mortals should live in sorrow, while they themselves are free from cares."

The following verses are much quoted and self-explanatory:

> Potent is the combined strength even of frail men.
> Sleep which is the brother of death.
> The purposes of great men are subject to change.
> Whoever obeys the gods, him they especially hear.
> When two go together, one thinks before the other.
> Good is the advice of a companion.
> War is impartial and slays the slayer.
> Zeus does not bring to pass all the purposes of
>   men.
> Even a wood-chopper accomplishes more by skill
>   than by strength.
> A fool can understand, when the thing is done.
> Whatever word you utter, just such a word you
>   will be obliged to hear.

The actors of the *Iliad,* excepting gods and priests, are all warriors or their dependents and the poem is drawn with a military setting, but the real greatness of that poem is in the portrayal of powerful human emotions rather than in military exploits.

No blood is shed in the first three books of the *Iliad* and there is no fighting in the last two. Strange as it may seem only a minor part of the poem is given to actual warfare, while most of the great scenes are without fighting.

Even those books which are most martial, such as the fifth, have long stretches in which no blood is shed.

The world has always been interested in wars and in warriors, so that many of the most famous names of history belong to military heroes. Homer wisely chose this absorbing theme as the background of his poem, but it is little more than the background, the setting. So great was his genius that he drew scenes of battle with such power and painted war with such faithfulness that a Napoleon was convinced that the *Iliad* was the work of an expert military tactician, but the poet's heart was elsewhere and it was far different qualities which he honored.

Patroclus was much the greatest Greek warrior to be slain in the action of the *Iliad.* When his body was in danger of falling into the hands of the foe, Menelaus urged the Greeks to the rescue with these words: "Let each one now remember the gentleness of poor Patroclus, for the knew how to be gentle to all." The fact that the companion of this great warrior should recall the gentleness and not the prowess of the fallen leader shows the sentiments of the poet. Homer was able so to stress the kindlier elements in the character of Hector as to win for him the appearance of greatness in spite of his repeated military failures.

Of all the Homeric similes but five are taken from warfare, and of the 665 tropes no more than fifteen are military.

There were other sources of fame than war, since the assembly was called "man-ennobling," and the council is referred to as "the place where men become very conspicuous." In the *Odyssey* a good speaker is said to be "preëminent among assembled men, and when he moves throughout the city the people gaze at him, as if he were a god." How different all this from the feelings of a real war-poet, Tyrtaeus, who said: "A man who possesses every excellence is nothing, if he be not mighty in war!"

The Homeric warriors were all men of might, but still they were men. Achilles could be wounded and he had no abnormal traits or powers, such as mark the heroes of most sagas. In the Indian epics the heroes uproot mountains and slay their foes by the thousands. The bow of Rama must be carried by five thousand men. In the Irish tales the hero has seven pupils in each eye, and in his anger flames stream from his mouth while a jet of blood higher than the mast of a ship shoots up from the top of his head. In these Irish epics men are slain by thousands through the might of a single arm. The exploits of Achilles, though great, are within the limits of the possible and they seem almost tame in comparison with the thrilling adventures of some of the decorated heroes of The World War.

Albert Cook   (essay date 1966)

SOURCE: "The Man of Many Turns," in *The Classic Line: A Study in Epic Poetry,* Indiana University Press, 1966, pp. 120-37.

[*In the following essay, Cook assesses the themes, settings, and tone of the* Odyssey, *maintaining that the poem is lighter in tone but equally as profound as the* Iliad.]

The epic poem is all-embracing; it is comprehensive, rather than encyclopedic, in character. It is their focus, more even than their lack of verse form, which deprives *Finnegans Wake* or *La Comédie Humaine* of an epic aura, and which almost gives one to *War and Peace.* The distinction, while elusive, is nicely illustrated by the contrast between the encyclopedic *Tesoro* of Dante's master Brunetto Latini and the comprehensiveness of the *Divina Commedia* itself.

The code that is to press the mortality of the hero, the verse style that is to sound the depths of his objectified feeling, though they must derive from tradition, cannot simply be received from it, even if the tradition be that of the man's earlier work.

An epic poem must find its embodiment in a wholly adequate fable. The test of adequacy is not to be found in some generality such as War, the subject of many long poems, or Wandering, the subject of many others. An epic adequacy, moreover, cannot be said to be guaranteed by the resonance of an archetypal plot. Poems with stories, short and long, in all conventions, draw as heavily on the archetypal situation as they do on the rhythmic emphasis of a meter—that is to say all but universally—and perhaps for related reasons. It may be said, in brief, that epic adequacy resides in some myth that can unify all the incidents of a given poem into a view of experience large enough to pose completeness for the life of the protagonist. The poet's great task of invention is finding the myth for his particular poem, a problem that Homer had to solve by centering on Achilles no less than Milton did by centering on Adam. Such adequacy may not be gained by merely choosing a subject which superficially resembles some other adequate myth. Each epic, to possess its own universality, must fully articulate the view it envisions on ground it wins for itself. It is the poet of *Beowulf* who makes his myth superior to that of the *Waltharius.* Looking at epic poems after the fact, we can remark on the aptness of the invention: if such aptness were completely bound up with generic laws, we would have more epic poems than we do. Getting the right myth and a "classic line" together at full pitch is one of the rarest of literary acts.

So Homer—if we may conceive of the same man moving on with the same traditional equipment from *Iliad* to *Odyssey*—did not repeat himself by selecting some similar myth. He did not go on to the Seven Against Thebes or some other war, as Apollonius superficially chose Jason because Odysseus had been done, as Statius and so many others opted for their own or another national myth of war, aping the *Iliad.* Nor did he handle his verse in quite the same way.

Homer managed the complexity of the *Iliad* by coordinating an entire society at war. This achievement was unique, and since it was, it could not serve him for a poem which presents a like complexity in the sequential experience of a single hero.

Achilles stands at the center of the *Iliad,* but his world measures him. Odysseus, however, measures his world as he moves through it. And it does not alter him; he remains the same from first to last, not only in the actual time span of the poem, but also, essentially, over the twenty years of his wanderings.

In his dominance of the action he resembles Beowulf, Roland, and the Cid. But their experience is also single, while Odysseus goes through varieties of experiences that intimately mirror his complexity while testing his mind and emotions. In its characteristically light and subtle way, the *Odyssey* exhibits a hero whose experience is internalized; whose psyche is plumbed. So the heroes of the best epic poems after Homer—Aeneas, Dante, Adam—resemble Odysseus more closely than they do Achilles. And Pound has taken Odysseus in *The Cantos* for the persona most fit to mirror his varieties of experience.

The actual fable *(logos)* of the *Odyssey* is short, as Aristotle points out [in the *Poetics*]. And yet the poem is complexly interwoven *(peplegmenon)*. This is because we have recognition *(anagnorisis)* throughout, he says, and this simple term serves as well as any other to describe Homer's mediation between his single hero and the hero's manifold experience.

The poem insists on this singleness, and this complexity, in its very first line:

> Tell me, Muse, about the man of many turns, who
> many. . .

Man, the first word. Complexity is named twice, in *polutropon,* "of many turns," and also in *polla,* "many."

Odysseus' situation deepens in time, and the situation of the poem deepens as it progresses; yet Odysseus' adequacy remains everywhere the same in all its aspects *(polutropos).* Only by a kind of alteration of the substance of the poem can we accept Cedric Whitman's reading of a developing self for Odysseus [in his *Homer and the Homeric Tradition,* 1958]. His wholeness appears from the beginning in the memory of friends and comrades about him, in the persistence of his return, in his adroitness at meeting the enigmas of societies so variable that beside them the forms of Proteus which Menelaus must master seem simple indeed.

Through all the "change" of the poem—the term is Whitman's—Odysseus, by intelligence and striving (as the opening tells us) copes consistently with minds and peoples:

> Tell me, Muse, about the man of many turns, who
> many
> Ways wandered when he had sacked Troy's holy
> citadel;
> He saw the cities of many men and he knew their
> thought.

The variations of scene in the *Odyssey* involve a progression from the young to the mature (Telemachus to Odysseus), from the old to the new (Ithaca to a Phaeacian present), from the single to the complex (Nestor to Menelaus; Calypso to and through Circe), from the hostile to the hospitable (Ciconians to Phaeacians), from the natural to the fantastic (Ciconians to Hades, to the Oxen of the Sun groaning on the roasting spits), from the known Troy far from home to the remote Phaeacia whence Odysseus may soon sail for Ithaca.

Underlying these progressions is the psyche of the hero, broad because we have narrow ones (Nestor, Telemachus) for comparison. And since everyone's experience is appropriate for his character, the experience becomes a figure of the extent and complexity and subtlety of his inner life.

Applying this principle of congruence between a man's self and his destiny to the smaller characters, to the other peoples, we may apply it *a fortiori* to Odysseus. In this principle lies the canon of unity for the whole poem. Character in the *Iliad* is a given affirmation of a man's stable situation. In the *Odyssey* the situation is in flux, which means not that character changes, but that the flux of situation itself is seen to rest obscurely on the predisposition of the person or persons involved, character as fate.

The heroes return from war on voyages that are revelatory to us of their very selves. The simple Nestor had a straight return, the proud Agamemnon a disastrous one. The subtle and elegant Menelaus, a slighter of the gods, finds a return which tests his subtlety. Prompted by a nymph, he must first grapple with Proteus' sleepy noon disguises on lonely Pharos; then sacrifice in Egypt to the gods. Far more various are the wanderings of Odysseus, and consequently far more famous is Odysseus himself. He is outstanding in all virtues (IV, 815: *pantoies aretesi kekasmenon*). And the fullness of his humanity is mirrored in his wanderings.

Telemachus, too, voyages to learn to become like his father, to overcome his excessive respect *(aidos, III, 24).* He already has too much of what Achilles had too little. As the disguised goddess of wisdom says to him:

> Few are the sons who are equal to their fathers;
> Most are worse, but few are better than their
> fathers.
> If you would not be a coward hereafter, and
> senseless,
> If the counsel of Odysseus has not forsaken you
> wholly,
> Your hope in that case is to bring these deeds to
> pass.
>
> (II, 276-280)

Telemachus passes over into his manhood; it is through him, as he moves into the present of the poem, that the narrative begins, evoking both memory and futurity in the longing for Odysseus, and also the dim sense that the father who has been gone so long may have come to his mortal end.

Telemachus, risking a voyage to learn the facts about his father, learns that no simple facts are forthcoming, because facts undergo the alteration of memory; the glorious Trojan war that Nestor tells about, in which he and Odysseus were equal counsellors, does not seem the exploit that subtle Helen and Menelaus remember, focusing as it does on the deceptions of the wooden horse.

How a man sees things depends on who he is; Intelligence is the presiding goddess. These gods are not objective, standing for the unknown-and-visible, as in the *Iliad.* They are clear in the *Odyssey,* and yet they too vary according to the observer, who is then himself objectively presented in the foreground of the poem. To Menelaus they are beings who must be propitiated. Nestor sees them as stubborn, Helen as capable of great favor, the Phaeacians as always benign. At the same time this particular people takes the gods with sophisticated familiarity and humor, laughing at Demodocus' tale about Ares and Aphrodite; adultery occasions mirth for them—the very evil that Penelope has been avoiding for twenty years.

Character is fate: who a man is also determines how far he goes, how widely he is tested, what sort of a home he has made his own. In this sense men get exactly what they deserve, a moral transparently presented at the very outset in Zeus' speech to Athene and the other gods:

> Well now, how mortal men do accuse the gods!
> They say evils come from us, yet they themselves
> By their own recklessness get pains beyond their
>   lot.

The Phaeacians are near to the gods; they dwell far away from other mortals, having been close to the challenging Cyclops. Their location and their way of life are taken altogether for a total character that compasses Odysseus at this stage, but does not absorb him.

Each man is closed in the world of his own perceptions, and so is each people. Each place visited is an episode for the variable Odysseus, as in a lesser way for his searching son. Nestor lives a simple life, his boys doing his work for him. It is a comfortable life, too; there are smooth stones before his palace. Beyond his imagination, overland from his territory, lies the elegant court of Menelaus, come upon characteristically in the midst of a wedding celebration. In that court there is a dominance of ceremoniousness all but total. But neither of Telemachus' hosts exhibits any trait so surprising as the near-supernaturalism of the Phaeacians, who also marry their cousins; or the out-and-out incest of the forever dining children of Aeolus.

Pain befalls man, but the gods have taken pain away from the Phaeacians. With pain, the gods have taken away the sort of wholeness exemplified, as always, by Odysseus, who lands naked and hungry on *their* shore just before finally going home. Nestor can face pain in nostalgia, but Menelaus can stand little pain. His "heart breaks," he tells us, when he learns from Proteus that he must sail the relatively little distance from Pharos to Egypt. And he has small patience for combat, as his words imply:

> quick is the glut of cold lamentation
>
>   (IV, 103)

Helen passes to her guests a drink with a nepenthe in it, to make the drinker so forget all his pain that:

> He would not shed a tear down his cheeks the
>   whole day long,
> Not if his mother and his father were both to die,
> Not if right in front of him his brother or his dear
>   son
> Were slaughtered with bronze, and he saw it with
>   his own eyes.
>
>   (IV, 224-7)

Through the formality of Helen and Menelaus there is felt a certain coldness. And to Odysseus the Phaeacians display a childish eagerness, for all their own elegance. Menelaus has the servants bathe Telemachus, a task Nestor assigned to his own daughter. Anxious about their cleanliness, Menelaus orders the bath as soon as they arrive; Nestor has had it done as a send-off. Such coldness, in this poem of heartfelt pain and joy, may evidence cruelty. Menelaus mentions casually that if Odysseus should care to settle nearby, he would gladly sack and depopulate a city for his old friend.

Each character, of place and society, becomes objectified in the comparing eye of the visitor; Telemachus, like his father, can compass the varieties by encountering them. Home is the norm, and Ithaca—unlike Aeaea or Ogygia or Phaeacia or Pylos or Argos—has no special features other than the chaos into which it has fallen.

Odysseus discovers himself on his way home. The wideness of the way, the wideness of the character destined for so much turning, becomes apparent by comparison with the briefer ways of others, and by the more circumscribed societies, each of which objectifies a whole moral attitude and destiny: a character (*ethos*) of the sort Aristotle asserted this poem to be woven from (*peplegmenon*).

Ithaca lacks the heightened felicity of Lacedaemon and Phaeacia, their ordered painlessness and easy delight. Subject to pain and chaos, it is the more rooted in the human variety known and sought by its absent overlord, and it stands waiting in memory, changing in reality, for his rearrival. When he does arrive, his reinstitution must be so deliberate as to take nearly half the poem. While Odysseus wanders, Ithaca stands in unseen relation to him, though from the beginning it is portrayed in its changed reality. Perpetually the poem holds his biased and unswaying nostalgia in a comparison, often unexpressed, between home and the place of sojourn. Explicitly he declares that Calypso surpasses Penelope in appearance and form, but such ideal excellence pales before the real rootedness of his mortality. Telemachus, in refusing Menelaus' gift of horses, admits that Ithaca affords poor pasturage; but he persists in his superlative praise of the island:

> In Ithaca there are no broad courses or any
> meadow;
> It has pasture for goats and is pleasanter than a
> horse pasture.
> But none of the islands that lie by the sea has
> good meadows
> Or a place for driving horses, and Ithaca surpasses
> them all.
>
> (IV, 605-8)

So he feels; and so does his father, enough to strain his ingenuity to return there.

This epic hero substitutes supple intelligence for the courage and prowess of the Cid, Beowulf, and Achilles. He follows not a code but the course of his own longing, an inner canon the poem sets out as equally to be trusted. Consistently, then, he does not gather all he knows in order to face the unknown. He acts on hunches (Lestrygonians) or social canniness (Phaeacia) or a surfaced feeling (Calypso) or luck (Circe) or improvised plan (Cyclops). In a sense there is nothing he can rely on as known, because he always copes with a wholly new situation in utter ignorance:

> For I have arrived here as a long suffering stranger
> From afar, from a distant land; so I know no one
> Of the men who conduct this city and its fields.
>
> (VII, 22-25)

He faces not the unknown but the new, not death but transience. Transience, itself a consequence of mortality and a kind of figure for it, replaces death in the imaginative vision of this epic. Longing for permanence drives the resourceful Odysseus round the changing seas and years.

Home itself changes, in the relentless metamorphosis of a third of a life-time. Permanence and change, satisfaction and longing, joy and pain, foresight and happenstance—these never get fixed in hard opposition because Odysseus moves too fast and copes too variously. His fable allows him to embody all these complexities without setting one stiffly against another; without overembroiling himself in any, and also without slighting the real difficulty or allure of a single one.

It is not death he must face. From the present time of the poem on, that risk is slight. In this epic, a life rounds itself out by return to an original mature circumstance that the very course of life has altered.

Change brings pain, and yet the joy of changelessness among the lotus eaters or the Phaeacians lacks the fullness of changeful life. Death may be taken as a fearful circumstance and at the same time as bland fact. The

death of his mother Anticleia is spoken of matter-of-factly in a salutation wishing joy.

In the seeming universality of transience, arrival seems forever debarred, and Odysseus comes back a second time to Aeolus, who will not help him; to Circe, who greets him with a warning. Back again he comes, also, to Scylla and Charybdis. Death lies as a test in the future. Though the hero's own death is vague and remote, he must risk it and pass its country in order to return. Odysseus can get back only by visiting the dead, all the way past the eternally shrouded Cimmerians. Even then it takes the escort of the Phaeacians, who are near to gods, to get him back. The Phaeacian vessel, moving like a star, unerringly and effortlessly swift, bears Odysseus in a sleep "most like to death" (XIII, 879-92) to the home he has not been able to sight for twenty years.

Homer managed the complexity of the *Iliad* by coordinating an entire society at war. This achievement was unique, and since it was, it could not serve him for a poem which presents a like complexity in the sequential experience of a single hero.

—*Albert Cook*

Odysseus has changed so much himself, and Ithaca has become so remote to him, that he does not know where he is when he wakes up there. Of the disguised Athene he asks a question at once obvious and profound: are the inhabitants hospitable or wild?

All is old, and all is new. If Odysseus did not recognize old elements in any new situation, he could not exercise his many wiles. If he did not have to confront the new, there would be less need for any wiles at all.

The need dwindles at the end, but it has not disappeared. At the end of his life he must undertake another journey across the sea and set up a tomb to Poseidon among men who do not know the sea.

Odysseus stands midway between the easier returners, achievers of a simpler permanence, Menelaus and Nestor, and those who have died on the return, the victims to change, Agamemnon and Ajax, not to mention all his own followers.

Permanence brings joy, transience pain. The living sustain a subtle balance between permanence and transience, and so between joy and pain. The sea is sparkling but treacherous; to the solitary Odysseus Ogygia is joyful for its unearthly beauty but painful for its not being home. Pain coalesces with joy, or else a life is shown to lack the epic wholeness: if pain becomes total, one is to die; if joy fully dominates, one enters the lifeless permanence of the

Lotus Eaters and the Phaeacians, whom Odysseus' long tale of suffering fills not with tears like his own but with a feeling of charm, the poem twice says (*kelethmos*: XI, 334; XIII, 2).

To return brings joy but causes pain. It is of the joy of return that Agamemnon speaks—he who least of all would have cause to remember that joy. Yet the pain of becoming reinstated in a changed home offsets, precedes, and intensifies, the joy of restitution.

In his coping, Odysseus works his way through contrarieties; pain and suffering he names at once when he is asked what his wanderings have brought. Joy can be as much a trial as pain; heartbroken with longing on Calypso's isle, he refuses her blissful immortality but enjoys her in the cave. He lives a year with Circe. The Lotus Eaters, the Phaeacians, and the Sirens all promise—the first could even fulfill—a painless existence wherein the pain might be obviated and even the longing be gone. But the fullness of life demands the wholeness of longing; and Odysseus, delighted and also pained, pushes on to his return. All the sufferings of wandering are told, after the tears of a delightful song, to the banqueting, hedonistic court of an Alcinoos who has already promised escort home. The habit of Ithaca counters the novelty of the strange delights, and yet habit too is the enemy of the remembered home: Odysseus stays seven years on Calypso's island.

Within its scheme of variety, this broad poem can vary the key of an alteration between joy and pain without changing its tone. Each episode has a different flavor of joy or pain. As Odysseus sails away from Cyclops, he gets exulting delight in exchange for teeth-gnashing despair. Aeolus occasions first impulsive gladness and then a resigned, fearful despondency. An ocean of moods for the longing hero is held in the single vision of the poem.

The poem sustains a sense of the hero's fine equanimity in transience and permanence, in sorrow and joy, by having placed him in a flexible situation where he transcends every person and every people he meets. The equanimity of the hero also enters the verse, for example in its descriptions of the visible world through which Odysseus moves.

A fine veil of poetry, simple and delectating, limns the changing landscapes, none so fully described as Ithaca, and all consequently more immediately redolent of an almost lyric singleness, a seemingly mythic signification. But the significance merely impresses in passing, and does not construct allegories. What are the Cimmerians at the bounds of the deep-flowing ocean, shrouded in darkness and cloud, who never see the beams of the sun or the starry heaven? They are far (Ithaca is nearness) and shrouded (the mists part often in the clarity of the Adriatic sun; Ithaca sees sun and starry heavens). They stand before the underworld, sharing some of its obscurity.

As Stella points out [in *Il Poema d'ulysse,* 1955], the fruits and trees of this landscape are described more realistically

than the fabulous vegetation found not only in the jewelled forests of Gilgamesh, but in such Greek legends as the Golden Apples of Hesperides. Yet as Max Treu says [in *Von Homer Zur Lyrik,* 1955], we cannot distinguish between fairytale and real in the landscape descriptions of the *Odyssey.* Its epithets are at once evocative and descriptive, far looser than those in the *Iliad*:

> The sun arose, leaving the *lovely* lake,
> Into the *much-bronze* heaven, where for immortals it shone,
> And for mortal men upon the *life-giving* earth.
>
> (III, 1-3)

All the grandeur of the *Iliad,* as Longinus says, but less intensity. *Polychalchon,* much-bronze, sets off no contrasts between "lovely" and "life-giving." The attributions are not faceted situationally, as they are in the *Iliad.* They merely rise to their seemingly haphazard descriptiveness, and their rightness seems to reside somewhat in a mythic resonance. The real and the fairy-tale are mingled in the memory of the recounting Odysseus and the perceptions of the poem's hearer. Against the joy of a given place stands the hero's own pain; against the beauty of life the hard risk of death, and the difficult, losing battle against time. At the end of all the easy hospitalities of Phaeacia, of the checked Circe, of Calypso, lies the difficult restitution in Ithaca. The transience of an arriver's longing, of the guest's contingency, clings to the poetry, for Odysseus' longing son as for himself:

> And they came to hollow Lacedaemon full of ravines.
>
> (IV, 1)

This is a new sight to Telemachus, a temporary one; his enjoyment of the visual loveliness, the presence of this poetic line in the narrative, is tinged with his fearful search for light about his father. Helen's nepenthe does not last for him, though it may for the Lacedaemonian court.

> They when they saw it
> Wondered at the house of the king nourished by Zeus;
> Like the beam of the sun it was or like the moon.
>
> (IV, 43-5)

But the sun goes down, the moon rises, and by day or night there is toil. Lacedaemon for the son, like Phaeacia or Ogygia for the father, is a delightful interlude, something unreal in the reality of life. A man who has a full life on his hands can see the loveliness, along with some of the unreality. His eyes enjoy the glitter, but his heart is in his mouth; the words catch the glitter, the rhythm moves wave on nostalgic wave in the total feeling of the poem.

The hexameter—lightly!—bears the burden of sadness, reiterating in its "disappointed" last foot the sorrow of the total fable. Poetry makes people weep in the *Odyssey,* even finally in the Phaeacian court. Odysseus himself weeps to hear of Troy, though he weeps behind his veil.

"The accents of the Homeric hexameter are the soft rustle of a leaf in the midday sun, the rhythm of *matter*"— Spengler's fine ear [in his *The Decline of the West,* 1928] has picked up the characteristic rhythm of the **Odyssey.** Not, I feel, of the **Iliad.** In both poems, of course, quantity determines the main rhythm, and not accent. Where Vergil patterns the subordinate accents, Homer lets them fall where they may. This randomness in the **Iliad** produces a surging afflatus, rather the way the free meter of the ballad does. In the **Odyssey,** I do not hear these free syllables as surging. The unaccounted accents play, as it were, over the surface of the statement, as the words themselves seem to do. In the **Iliad** the unaccounted accents do a more strenuous work, and yet are closer to prose in their lack of emphasis; in the **Odyssey** they twitch the veil of the poetry, rhythmically carrying a sense of the variety of life.

The poetry reveals its lightness in the very particularity of its designations; it touches lightly on literalness, and quite haphazardly. All is known, but the known is a mystery. Home remains the same, but time changes it. Take the line about the constellation Bear, "which they also call by the name Wagon":

> And it alone has no share in the washings of
> Ocean.
>
> (V, 275)

The statement conveys a literal piece of astronomical fact, but with a light resonance that lies in each word. "Oie," alone, echoes the aloneness of Odysseus. "Has no share," or "unfated" *(ammoros):* in the very negation lies a whole sense of fate, at once specific and general. The "washings" *(loetroi)* are carrying Odysseus too; he is caught in the wash of the ocean stream above which gleams the Bear. In its suggesting of analogy, though, the line is not metaphoric. It merely speaks of the natural world, the stars and the sea, in words that usually apply to man, and so it hints at a participation in a total situation which is not patterned but merely moves ahead in its predictable but incalculable alterations. This hint is absent from the line when it occurs in the **Iliad** merely to describe a point of Achilles' shield.

And the tone of the poem, the fine veil of what, for lack of a more delicate term, we may call irony—that tone veils all the actions and the landscapes. The hexameter carries that tone, forbidding, as it were, even the most dire incident from carrying a tragic cast. The elegiac becomes a delectated likeness. At the height of the grisly Cyclops episode, a joke: Odysseus is "no man." Homer may have got this joke from a folk-tale or not; it has the same effect in the poem, the consonant presentation of an exultant joy within a crushing sadness.

Through its tone of equanimity, the verse conveys pain and joy without setting one paradoxically off against the other, as the **Iliad** somewhat schematically sets the actuality of pain against the memory of joy. The veil of mystery covers everything in the **Odyssey;** yet everything also shows through the tonal veil. Deception comes up again

and again, the host of disguises and feints and subtle unmentioned calculations and adjustments which every character makes, and preeminently the resourceful Odysseus. Even gods deceive; right at the start in Book I they quickly hold their committee meeting about Odysseus, while his enemy Poseidon, the opposition, is conveniently far away among the Ethiopians.

For all the deceptions, clarity. For all the caprice, justice. For all the wanderings, return. Here the world is utterly clear and whole, and utterly mysterious. Its clarity is its mystery, the poetry is declaring. The same blue Aegean washes real and miraculous shores, and the real and the miraculous differ only in incidental, equally perceptible details, which the poetry proffers:

> On the hearth a big fire was burning, and the smell from afar
> Of cedar and easy-split pulp was exhaled to the island
> As it blazed. She within, singing in a lovely voice,
> Going to and fro at the loom, wove with a golden distaff.
> Wood was growing around the cave in abundance,
> Alder and black poplar and well-scented cypress,
> Where the birds with their long wings went to sleep,
> Horned owls and hawks and, with their long tongues,
> Salt water crows, who are busy with the things of the sea.
>
> (V, 59-67)

A superlative place, but with a quality finely perceptible as of itself; distinct from the superlative of Lacedaemon or Phaeacia or Aeaea. The cave, the trees, the birds, and later the springs and meadows, characterize the physical world of Calypso, which is at the same time her world of spirit, just as the deepness of Ithaca resides for the poetry, as for the naming Telemachus, in the very physical homeliness and roughness of the place.

Often we are given designations for the sea, wine-faced or grey, Protean as the numberless lands are different. Yet each is clear and whole unto itself, each capable of receiving at times the enumerative detail Auerbach claims is typical of the **Odyssey** generally.

Homer, however, is not so enumerative in his verse as Auerbach claims. The poet does tend to linger over detail of the narrative, as Auerbach follows Schiller in asserting; but not utterly for the sake of the detail. If we cannot read some other significance into the detail—the ritual use of Calypso's trees, for example—we cannot obliterate significance either. Certainly to assert that Homer tells "everything" would be to make him inarticulate. He must select, though more abundantly than the inspired author of *Genesis.*

Nor can it be said, with Auerbach [in his *Mimesis,* 1957], that the **Odyssey** has no "background," no hidden depths of motive. It is all foreground, to be sure, but a light irony holds all the detail. That light irony constitutes the background, the delicate and profound sense of success in transience, of unfinality in any terror, which renders the epic sense of life to the *Odyssey,* lightening the poetry and unifying the fable; so that the poem stands as something at once close to what we expect from a novel in its incident, and yet utterly different from a novel in its final bearing.

In all the alterings of circumstance, in all the pains, the hero's self remains wholly adequate in its adaptability (*polutropos*)—and without being defined. To take Odysseus' wanderings as deepening him, the way Cedric Whitman does, involves reading the significance of the places he visits as allegory or symbol. They do have the ring of archetype, and they do figure a total spiritual condition, each of them, mysteriously. Yet to read their significance as symbol or allegory is to pierce the veil of mystery. The depth is all on the surface, a sunlit mystery. No totality glides like a Moby Dick in the darkness beneath these waters. To interpret the surface of this poem metaphorically is to translate the surface as gaining significance from some depth; but the significances are all there on the surface, embodied simply in landscape and lightness of gesture.

Achilles develops and realizes his manhood. Odysseus moves ahead with his into time, changing only as he ages, while events at once tax and fortify him. He simply exists. No coordinated social world can deepen him; there is only the series of unpredictable surfaces, each complete and partial in itself, which he shows himself capable by meeting, and whole by transcending. Intelligence attends him from first to last, and the manifestation of Athene at his landing on Ithaca attests no special consideration, no final success, but only a momentary embodiment, as the world of his striving has actualized itself under his feet without his being aware of it.

When Odysseus speaks to himself, as he does after having set out from Ogygia, the soliloquy explores no motive but merely develops and estimates the incidence of misfortune. Once again, it is all on the surface: the depth inheres in the irony with which it is presented, an irony so slight as to seem transparent, vanishing at a breath.

The irony may at numerous moments emerge into event. Odysseus slights Calypso in his account to Arete, falsifies his contact with Nausicaa, and delicately implies a refusal of Alcinous' marriage offer by mentioning in the course of his narrative how he has often refused such offers elsewhere. Menelaus, who had to wander years because he had slighted the gods, gives Telemachus a libation bowl! So, the poem hints, he has learned his lesson. Athene sacrifices to her enemy Poseidon. But the events need not be ironic; they may be deadly serious, and irony is still conveyed in the uniform tone of the verse.

Without the *poetry,* the flexible Odyssean hexameter, the humor would be episodic, and so would the nostalgia. The variety of incident would then merely add up to a superficial romance of the picaresque with some fine detail and

occasional lyric moments, rather like the *Lusiads.* But in the *Odyssey* nostalgia comments on humor. Humor and nostalgia blend but do not fuse in the epic unity of this poem, lighter than the *Iliad,* but no less profound.

Suffering, even the dark terror of Cyclops or Odysseus' wholesale slaughter of the suitors, is kept serenely in vision, as it is not in even so equanimous a comedy as the *Tempest.* Only loosely can the *Odyssey* be called a comedy, or even a comic epic. It is an epic whose lightness compasses comic events, and also tragic; that allows of both tragic and comic events without inventing a whole philosophic relation for them (or a Dantesque justification) beyond the unitary tonal feeling of myth and verse.

C. M. Bowra   (essay date 1972)

SOURCE: "The Poetry of Action," in *Homer,* Duckworth, 1972, pp. 141-64.

[*In the following essay, Bowra explores the dramatic quality of the Homeric epics, maintaining that although it "arises from action, it often goes beyond it and touches on the character of the actors, their thoughts and their feelings as their words reveal them."*]

The *Iliad* and the *Odyssey* are preeminently poems of action. Their first purpose is to engage the hearers in what happens, to involve them imaginatively in it. In this respect they resemble not only other heroic poetry but much oral narrative verse which may be sub-heroic or shamanistic. Their main objective can be paralleled in ancient poems like *Gilgamesh* and in modern ones like the Kirghiz *Manas.* In such poems the thrill of action comes first but is attended by much else, notably by a concern for what human beings do and suffer and the many ways in which they face their challenges. In heroic poetry this is all-important because without it the mere account of violent behaviour would pall even for the most assiduous addict and lose much of its significance by its neglect of human feelings and considerations. In the Homeric poems the action is wonderfully varied, and though we know in general what is going to come next, we seldom know exactly how it will come. Surprise is never lacking and sharpens an endless range of effects.

Though the strong dramatic quality of the Homeric poems arises from action, it often goes beyond it and touches on the character of the actors, their thoughts and their feelings as their words reveal them. Speeches, even soliloquies, abound and add an element of drama, which is woven closely into the narrative and wins attention by its advance beyond mere action to the motives that prompt it. In this respect, there emerges what may be called a lyrical spirit, partly in dealing with nature whether directly in descriptions or indirectly in similes, and partly in presenting powerful emotions such as affection or grief. Both of these classes would, if expressed in the first person, inspire lyrical poems, but in Homer they are indispensable to the narrative and to its human rise and fall. Even contemplative poetry, which assumed an unashamedly didactic form with Hesiod and made possible the first outbreaks into philosophy, occurs in both poems in general considerations advanced by the characters. Odysseus' comments on the shameless demands of an empty belly have their counterpart at a much higher level in what Achilles says to Priam about the way in which the gods apportion good and bad to men. Such generalizations help the audience to understand what is happening, but through the mouths of the characters and not of the poet. They do not break the general objectivity of heroic narrative, but make the characters more real by giving their underlying views on human life. These thoughts arise from the action, and are less a comment on it than an actual part of it.

The heroic poet does not normally assert his own opinions or pass judgments on what happens. Perhaps he is not of sufficient social standing to lay down the law to an audience which may include the local rulers; perhaps the effort of heroic poetry to attain a self-contained life of its own excludes personal intrusions which interfere with the story. In either case the rule is generally followed. Homer reveals himself in the nature and quality of his creation; he does not attempt to guide our reactions to them. His independence from his work may be illustrated by a small point in which he allows himself a small comment on what happens. He often uses the word *nepios,* which means, in colloquial English, 'poor', with often some slight suggestion of 'silly'. It is applied to Patroclus when he asks Achilles to send him to battle, and there Homer explains that his request is really for death. Telemachus uses it of himself, with special reference to his boyhood when he did not know how to deal with the Suitors. In these cases we may discern understanding and compassion, and also perhaps in the use of the word for the companions of Odysseus when they court doom by eating the cattle of the Sun or linger disastrously in the land of the Ciconians. The word suggests that men sometimes act as children and pay for it. It is a small indication of what Homer feels for his characters, of his tenderness for them in their mistakes, but it is not a judgment, still less a condemnation. His characters stand in their own right and do what they do without Homer's comments.

This is not to say that he has not his preferences and distastes among them, but this emerges indirectly from his presentation of them. An obvious case is that of Thersites, who is introduced with no pretence of approval:

> Thersites alone railed at them, with uncontrolled speech;
> he knew in his mind many disorderly words, to speak
> at random and not in decency, to quarrel with the kings.
>
> (ii 212-14)

Something of the same contemptuous spirit appears in the account of the beggar Irus:

> Then came the public beggar, who went begging through
> the town of Ithaca; he excelled in his gluttonous belly,
> to eat and drink without ceasing. He had no strength
> or force, but in appearance he was very big to look at.
>
> (18.1-4)

We naturally assume that such cases illustrate the poet's personal dislike, but we must not rule out the possibility that in them he reflects the views of his noble patrons, who think poorly of such ill-born specimens. It is easy for the poet to agree with them, but at least the characters stand out clearly, even if it is with the clarity of contempt.

A similar objectivity is shown in the presentation of the background against which the actions take place. This must be real and convincing, especially when nature is in question. The Greeks never gave to nature that exclusive attention which later ages have given, nor did they find so much in her. They were not town-dwellers and did not seek a refuge in her, but took her for granted as the setting and the background of their busy lives. In the Homeric poems nature is treated handsomely in the similes and incidentally in the narrative. Twice in the *Odyssey* Homer indulges in what looks like description for description's sake. First there is the cave of Calypso, surrounded by trees of many kinds, mantled with a vine and haunted by sea-birds. Outside it are meadows watered by four streams, and the poet does not conceal his pleasure in it:

> There at that time even an immortal would wonder at
> seeing it and be delighted in his heart.
>
> (5.73-4)

The second case is the garden of Alcinous. It is four-square, surrounded by a wall, and rich in fruit-trees and vines. But it has a touch of the miraculous, since the trees and the vines bear fruit all the year round, and one crop follows another in unfailing succession. Each of these scenes serves a purpose. Calypso's cave sets the note for Odysseus' remote exile with a goddess on a lonely island. This is how an immortal nymph lives, but Odysseus does not find it enough and pines to escape and go home. The garden of Alcinous is part of his half-mythical existence. Though he and his Phaeacians are distinguishably human, he lives on the edge of the known world and is entitled to some alleviation of its restrictions.

Such full descriptions are rare and special, but the poems incidentally touch on landscape when it affects the narrative, and give it character and solidity. This is very much the case with the plain of Troy, which presents features that affect the action. Homer appeals to the visual imagination, and the desire for reality creates something clear and clean. This is especially true when something in the landscape has a special significance for the action. More care is taken, and striking results follow. When Achilles fights the river-god Scamander, he calls the fire-god Hephaestus to his succour, and the effects of devastating fire are aptly related:

> Elms, willows and tamarisks caught fire; and the lotus
> and rushes and galingale that grew in plenty about the
> beautiful banks of the river were burned. Troubled too
> were the eels and fishes that tumbled in the eddies, this
> way and that, in the beautiful streams, worn out by
> the breath of cunning Hephaestus.
>
> (xxi 350-5)

This is factual and true to reality. The unusual character of the action needs the precise details which give verisimilitude to it. This manner is not too different from the less dramatic and more unassuming account of Ithaca as Odysseus first sees it after being set ashore in his sleep by the Phaeacians. The harbour itself is like the modern Vathy, but the description would fit many Greek anchorages, and some of its phrases are used for the harbour of the Laestrygonians. What follows is more individual. At the head of the harbour is an olive-tree and the Cave of the Nymphs, which is carefully described, with its stone formations inside, its water-supply and its two entrances, one on the north for men, one on the south for the gods. This serves a real purpose. The treasures of Odysseus must be got out of the way while he deals with the Suitors, and there is much to be said for this unusual hiding-place.

The same selective objectivity can be applied to the works of men. We form our mental picture of Troy almost entirely from its epithets. The palace of Odysseus reveals its plan, never very clearly, when it matters for the story, notably when Penelope comes down from her quarters upstairs or Eumaeus gets out through a small door and a passage concealed in the wall. Nothing is very clear, but in general the palace seems to resemble the so-called Palace of Nestor at Ano Englianos. The small touch that the palace of Circe is made of polished stone increases its strangeness on a lonely island. On the other hand the splendour of the palace of Menelaus at Sparta impels him to explain that all this wealth was gathered on his travels, and so prepares the way for the story of them. The palace of Alcinous has walls of brass, a cornice of blue enamel, golden doors and a silver lintel, and gold and silver dogs on guard, made by Hephaestus. But this, like other things in Phaeacia, is just outside the familiar world and its very wealth prepares the way for the rich gifts which Odysseus is soon to receive from his hosts. Such descriptions were well calculated to suit their place in the story, but their comparative rarity stresses the way in which Homer gives first priority to actions and uses these subsidiary aids to provide background and perspective.

Artefacts, being essential to the action, provide more than decoration and excite professional attention. Though archers are rare in the *Iliad* and Odysseus leaves his great bow at home, the bow of Pandarus, which breaks the truce between the armies, is described at length. It is made from the horns of an ibex which he himself shot; they measure sixteen hands, and have been fitted together, polished and given a golden tip at the end. The members of the audience would know about archery and appreciate that this was indeed an unusual bow and that its very strangeness fits it for the dramatic purpose of breaking the truce. Even more unusual is the headgear made of boars' teeth on felt which Odysseus wears on night operations. It is described with care, and it seems to be something of an heirloom. In fact it is exactly like a type of Mycenaean helmet of which we have both models and remains, and is by any calculation a remarkable curiosity. We do not know whether Homer had heard of it or actually seen an example, but in either case he knew that was worthy of mention. The poet is a repository of knowledge of the past, and details like

this confirm his authority and the worth of his narrative. Perhaps something of the kind is true of the brooch of Odysseus, to which we have no close archaeological parallel, but the scene depicted on it, of a dog throttling a deer, looks like a Mycenaean subject, while the structure of the pins looks much later. The brooch fails as a means to identify the stranger who tells Penelope about it, but adds another clue to the identification of him. When Hera decks herself in her finest finery to allure Zeus and trick him into sleep, it is right that we should be told all about it, and we cannot but note with interest the robe fastened with golden clasps, the girdle with a hundred tassles, the earrings, each with a cluster of four drops, the headdress bright as the sun. All this has a place in Hera's stratagem and needs to be related.

Conversely, sometimes merely utilitarian objects may call for a detailed description if the audience is to envisage exactly what happens. This is the case with the waggon which is loaded with the ransom for Hector and driven by Priam himself. The account is precise, and special care is given to the way in which the yoke is fastened to the shaft of the waggon. The lead pair are mules, the wheel pair horses, and this may have been an intentional oddity, meant to illustrate how horses trained to chariots in war are less suitable than mules to draw a heavy waggon. We do not know why the fitting of the yoke receives such care. It must have been a fairly familiar action, and the words, being technical, would have no meaning unless they conformed to current usage. The care given may be due to a desire to make the episode absolutely convincing, especially since it is not what is expected in a heroic setting, and its oddity marks it out for special treatment.

In the Homeric poems the action is wonderfully varied, and though we know in general what is going to come next, we seldom know exactly how it will come. Surprise is never lacking and sharpens an endless range of effects.

—C. M. Bowra

Clearly unusual and calling for special care is the raft of Odysseus which he makes with his own hands. It is meant for him alone, and therefore it cannot be large, though it is in fact as wide as a ship of burden, though not necessarily as long. Odysseus makes it from twenty trees, alder, black poplar and fir, because they will float lightly, and this suggests that the craft is of no great size, especially as one tree would be needed for the mast, and part of another for the yard. He works with axe, adze and gimlets, and the timbers are well fastened together. It has a sort of deck, supported by props which protect the voyager from being drenched. It has also a mast and a yard, a rudder or steering oar, and a railing of wicker bulwarks to keep off the spray. Odysseus makes it in three days and even he could not construct a complete ship in that time; it is a raft which he hopes to sail and to steer. In fine weather he can sleep on it on a couch provided with rugs and cloaks by Calypso. This raft not only shows Odysseus' gift for skilled craftsmanship but has a special interest for its unique purpose, which is to carry a crew of one for a voyage of seventeen days. The careful account is worthy of the important occasion when Odysseus, after eight years with Calypso prepares to leave and travel alone over the unknown sea. He works with knowledge and precision, and it is not his technical fault that the raft fails to finish its journey.

Quite different from these solid, workaday descriptions is one notable long passage in which Homer gives a full account of the shield which Hephaestus makes for Achilles to take the place of that seized by Hector from the body of Patroclus. The shield is not something that the poet himself has seen. It is too elaborate, too costly, too accomplished, but we may speculate from what sources he invented it. Its technique of gold, silver, tin and blue enamel is not unlike that of the dagger-blades from the shaft-tombs at Mycenae. Some object, not necessarily on this enormous scale, may have survived into Homer's time and excited his wonder. Equally, even if all such objects had disappeared in the intervening centuries, they may have left memories in formulaic song. In the passage of years the accounts might lose something of accuracy, and of course each new bard could, if he wished, make his own improvements. The shield, with its concentric scenes of nature and human life, could only be a decorative object, quite unfit for use in battle, but that need not trouble Homer who profits from the loss of Achilles' armour to embark on a splendid piece of descriptive poetry. In battle the splendour of the new armour does not matter and is hardly mentioned. For the moment it is a rich flight of imagination and we take it as it comes. The shield is the handiwork of a god, suited to the half-divine hero Achilles, and in the broad range of the subjects depicted on it is a microcosm of life as Homer knew it. It gives him a chance to extend his scope beyond the battlefield and the doings of heroes into other less exalted but not less attractive fields. It is Homer's ideal work of art, what he thinks metal-work could be in the hands of a god, and it is noteworthy that six times he uses adjectives which convey much the same note of admiration, 'beautiful', 'lovely' and 'awaking desires'. These are applied to the scenes made by Hephaestus, not to any possible originals they may have copied in nature or human society. The shield is what art ought to be—a representation of things in a beautiful way. It gives delight, and is to this degree comparable to heroic song. Nor is it reckless to imagine that in conceiving this supreme work of art Homer tried to do for visual art what he himself did for words. Both arts transform reality, and in this their beauty lies.

The strength of the poetical tradition can be seen in the knowledge which the *Iliad* reveals of Troy and the Trojan plain. We have seen how apt the epithets for these are, but there is more to be considered than epithets. The *Iliad* has a good general grasp of Troy in its geographical setting, and from the top of Hisarlik we can identify most of the sites which Homer mentions. The Achaean camp

could be set to the north, where the coast takes a sharp turn eastwards, and the battlefield is between this and the city. At some distance to the west are the twin peaks of Samothrace, from which Poseidon watches the battle. To the east, and much closer, is Mount Ida, whence Zeus in his turn watches the battle, and from which wood is brought to make a pyre for Patroclus. Nearer home, to the east of Achaean camp and still identifiable, in the village of Keren Koi, is the high ground Callicolone, where the gods who favour Troy gather. On the plain itself is a slight elevation, which suits the place where the Trojans gather before an attack.

These small touches suggest some knowledge of the terrain, and this knowledge is at times used with dramatic effect. The large view from the top of Hisarlik confirms the ease with which Helen points out the Achaean leaders from the walls. When Achilles fights the river-god Scamander and Hephaestus comes to his rescue and burns all the vegetation.

> Burned were the elms and the willows and the tamarisks,
> and burned was the clover and the rushes and the
> galingale.

> (xxi 350-1)

This is the vegetation which still flourishes on Trojan river-banks. When Achilles pursues Hector three times round Troy, we might expect it to be a heroic prodigy, but in fact the distance is not great, nor the terrain very difficult. When Priam goes out at night to visit Achilles in the Achaean camp, he can travel easily in a wagon, for almost the whole journey is over level ground. When Achilles drags Hector's body behind this chariot round Troy, Andromache comes out of her house on to the walls by a tower and sees what is happening. These are but small points, but in them the physical setting adds something to the story. Once or twice it does so more unexpectedly. When Patroclus attempts to scale the walls of Troy, he tries three times and three times he fails:

> 'Three times Patroclus moved on to the angle of the
> lofty wall, and three times Apollo drove him away by
> force'.

> (xvi 702-3)

Now it happens that the lower part of the walls of Troy are at an angle which makes it not too difficult to climb them, but at the top of this were perpendicular battlements. Patroclus reaches the angle (literally 'elbow'), where these meet, and is pushed down. A batter of this kind is rare, and this looks like a genuine reminiscence. Again, Andromache tells Hector:

> 'Station the host by the wild fig-tree, where the city
> is most easily approached and the wall may be scaled'.

> (vi 433-4)

It happens that the excavations have revealed a weak spot in the western fortifications, and of this the passage may contain some echo.

Not everything in the Homeric scene of Troy can be substantiated, and one or two problems remain unsolved. First, the two rivers Scamander and Simois may be identified with the modern Mendere and In-tepe Asmak, but in the flat plain these rivers often change their courses and we have no assurance that their present position is what was known to Homer. On the whole his picture is clear. The two rivers flow, very roughly parallel, across the plain to the sea. But two points are difficult. First, it looks as if the battle swayed between the rivers without obstacle, and yet at one point we heard that the rivers join their streams. It does not much matter, but it may come from a time when the rivers had different courses, and the battle would not flow easily between them. Secondly, there are three places where there is a ford over Scamander. We might expect the ford to be a place to cross the river, but this seems to be used for watering horses and then passed on the flank—not impossible but curious. A similar difficulty arises with the hot and cold springs which Hector and Achilles pass in their race. The description is exact and convincing and looks like a real memory but though the Troad offers some natural hot springs, no springs like these have been discovered. Time may have changed them, or perhaps legend, knowing something not very accurately, has built up a picture. Yet neither with the springs nor with the rivers can we say that the *Iliad* is wrong. Such divagations as it presents from the present geography can be explained by the changes brought by time.

If we allow that much of the knowledge of Troy, such as that displayed by the epithets, is of ancient origin, it is always possible that the living poet has made his own contributions and may even have visited the site of Troy, which was beginning to revive in the eighth century with Greek colonists. For this there are certain not final, but at least favourable, arguments. First, the account of the landscape is remarkably consistent and creates no difficulties. A poet working only with traditional material might well make blunders, and his failure to do so suggests that he knows something of the subject. Secondly, the country and the city are used with great dramatic effect, whether in the ebb and flow of battle or the nocturnal journey of Priam or the appearance of characters on the city walls. Such use would come more readily with actual knowledge.

Ithaca, which is the scene for much of the *Odyssey,* presents a different case. Historically this small, rocky, and barren island had one great advantage. It stood off the western end of the Gulf of Corinth and commanded the sea-ways to and from the west. This may account for its place in legend. Nor need we doubt that Homer's Ithaca is in some sense the modern Thiaki or Ithaki, which has kept the name through the centuries. What we may doubt is how much the poet knew of it. Some at least of his story fits into the modern island. Odysseus is landed in the harbour of Phorcys, which corresponds to Vathy. His palace is some way from this and may be placed on the west of the island at Polis. The steading of Eumaeus fits the southern part of the island and the remote dwelling of Laertes the northern. The adjective 'under Neius' agrees with Mount Anoi. There is a recognizable fountain of Arethusa, and a small harbour of St Andrea on the south

coast, where Telemachus can land on his return from Pylos. Not quite so neat but still possible, if we allow for poetical transformation, is a cave near but not very near to Vathy, which will serve as the cave of the Nymphs, though it is not immediately by the harbour. Perhaps the island of Dhascalio, in the strait between Ithaca and Cefalonia, will do for the island of Asteris, behind which the Suitors lie in ambush. It may not matter that the modern island is much too small, since it may have been reduced by earthquakes. So far the Homeric Ithaca betrays some local knowledge, which got into the tradition, despite the remoteness of Ithaca from Ionia. We might even think that these details come from a time before the migrations eastward. But this is not the whole story. There are places where the *Odyssey* speaks of Ithaca in a way which does not suit the present island, still less the semi-island of Leucas, with which it has sometimes been identified. The chief of these is the account given by Odysseus himself to Alcinous:

> 'Itself it is low-lying, and lies, furthest out, in the sea towards the gloom, and the other islands are separate towards the east and the sun.'
>
> (9.25-6)

This contains three false statements. Ithaca is not low-lying, and we have no right to say that the word means 'near the shore', which anyhow it is not. It is not furthest out, even if we assume that the coast was thought to run east to west, which of course it does not. So far from the other islands being to the east and the sun, they are to the south, west and north. It looks as if while the tradition was still forming and new features were added, somebody who knew almost nothing about Ithaca added these lines to make it more convincing.

What counts most in the Homeric poems is action. It awakes the responses through which we judge the poetry. To the range of these responses there is almost no limit. There is almost no human reaction which Homer did not translate into a concrete poetical form. The one of which he is a little sparing is laughter. This is applied abundantly to the gods, who laugh at each other and whose merriment is presumably shared by the poet's audience, especially in such full-scale episodes as the Deception of Zeus or the song of Demodocus on the love of Ares and Aphrodite. Among men this is much rarer. It is true that there is gentle fun in the exchange of armour between Glaucus and Diomedes, where the generous impulse of Glaucus makes him give away his golden armour in exchange for the bronze armour of Diomedes, which is worth only a ninth of it. There are too outbursts of bitter laughter, as when the Achaeans laugh at the blow which Odysseus gives to Thersites with his sceptre or the frenzied laughter of the Suitors which Athene sends to them. But this is not humour, but derision and, as such, well fitted to the heroic temper in its wilder or angrier moods.

With this partial exception there is almost no human emotion which Homer does not present or which he does not arouse. His effect is the more powerful because it is direct, immediate and single. He may be compared first with other

practitioners of oral heroic song, and we mark the enormous difference of range between him and not merely the
author of the *Song of Roland* and the poets of the *Elder
Edda* but the authors of *Gilgamesh* and *Beowulf,* to say
nothing of Mongol or Tatar poets still or recently at work.
These other poets have indeed moments of concentrated
force and assertive power, but so has Homer; what they
have not got in his wonderful range which seems to cover
all human experience that is worth covering. Heroic poets
are not expected to do this; their job is rather to catch
certain high moments and concentrate on them. Homer has
an effortless grasp of most elementary human states, and
moves easily from one to another. Conversely, he may be
compared, in quite a different respect, with those poets,
writers of literary epic, who sought to imitate and rival and
improve him. Of these Virgil is first and foremost. Though
he knew that he could never really rival Homer in his own
field, he still tried to do something comparable, and attained at least a noble scope and dignity. He is hampered
by his own contorted, conflicting, uncertain emotions and
by his insecurity of belief and outlook. By trying to believe more than he did he succeeded in believing less, and
his vision of imperial Rome is much vaguer than Homer's
vivid sense of heroic manhood. Homer would not have
maintained his wonderful directness of approach if he had
not sung to a listening audience and felt himself bound to
make everything beautifully clear to it. Conversely, in exploiting a far wider range of themes than other heroic poets
he may have been helped by the wealth and antiquity of the
Greek poetical tradition which accumulated stories over a
long period, and reflected a generous taste for life because
it was almost the only fine art that flourished in the dark
ages after the collapse of the Mycenaean civilization. A
poet could take advantage of this and learn from it, but he
would not have gained much if he had not possessed to a
very high degree the imaginative insight and the creative
understanding which turn human emotions into poetry.

In depicting the emotions at work Homer makes his audience share them and enter into the spirit of his characters.
This happens so effortlessly that we hardly notice it, but
the ease is largely due to Homer's concentration on a
single mood and his subjection of everything to this.
Thus the quarrel between Agamemnon and Achilles in
Book i is a study in anger on both sides. Each hero is
dominated by it because he thinks that he has been wounded in his honour, Agamemnon by having to give up
Chryseis, Achilles by having Briseis taken from him. Anger
flares through the book and takes vivid forms, from rabid
abuse to thoughts of violence which come very near to
action. In the exchange of insults the two heroes are well
matched. We may not for the moment ask who has right
on his side, and it is not till later that we see the case of
Achilles. This is the authentic Homeric technique. The
simple, powerful emotions promote swift and overwhelming action. The high temper displayed by the two heroes
is self-destructive and leads to untold harm, but it can take
other, less deadly forms, and in any case it is essential to
the action on the battlefield, to the impetus which carries
Hector or Patroclus, Diomedes or Sarpedon, on his unre-
lenting course. It sets the tone for the fiercest events, and
everything follows naturally.

Just as in his construction of narrative Homer follows the
rule of 'one thing at a time', so this enforces on him a
simplification and indeed a simplicity of poetical effect.
Every episode has on the whole a single character, but once
it is finished we may expect something quite different. Once
his direction is set, he goes irresistibly ahead. So when Iris
tells Achilles to appear at the trench and dismay the Trojans, she does it after scenes of lamentation and grief, but
at this point Homer takes a new direction and the whole
passage is an astonishing display of what the mere appearance of Achilles can do. A fierce, heroic splendour shines
in every line, and it is right and proper that at the sight
twelve Trojan charioteers die of shock. So too, when Odysseus strings the bow, we are held in tense expectation,
but the whole situation moves forward with increasing excitement as he first shoots an arrow down the line of the
axes and then leaps upon the platform, throws off his rags,
and announces his new task of vengeance. The tone is
suddenly changed and then maintained for the new actions.

This concentration is applied to quite small matters, and
does much to integrate them into the main poem. For
instance in Book i the angry quarrel between Agamemnon
and Achilles is interrupted by a description of the voyage
in which Odysseus brings back Chryseis to her father. It
tells the successive stages of the voyage, the landing, the
welcome, the feast, and the departure. Each is factual and
precise and brief, and the whole episode breaks for a few
moments the violence of the quarrels behind it. It is quite
wrong to think it an interpolation; it fulfils a need, and
it does so by keeping its own quiet tone without a
mistake. Rather more exciting but equally well maintained
is the small episode in which Odysseus, drawing unknown near to the hut of Eumaeus, is attacked by the
dogs and fortunately rescued by the swineherd. It is a
sudden moment of excitement, admirably sustained, entirely true to Greek life, and an excellent introduction to
Eumaeus. The different elements are fused into a single
whole, which has a character different both from what
precedes and from what succeeds it.

The direct movement of narrative is enriched by Homer's
eye for the illuminating detail, the small touch which throws
a vivid light on what happens. Thersites, for instance, makes
only one appearance in the *Iliad,* but though it is short it
is important because he embodies unheroic, even anti-he-
roic qualities, and these are reflected in his appearance:

> He was the ugliest man who came to Troy. He was
> bandy-legged and lame in one foot. His shoulders were
> bent and met over his chest. Above, he had an egg-
> shaped head, and on it sprouted some scanty hairs.

(ii 216-19)

Such an appearance fits Thersites' character and behaviour and marks him out for contempt. Less obviously
brutal but no less telling is the introduction of Dolon:

> He had much gold and much bronze. He was ugly to
> look at but fast on his feet, and he was an only son,
> with five sisters.

(x 315-17)

This is nicely damaging and makes it easier to endure Dolon's death which soon follows. Such touches are unexpected and sometimes bizarre, but they are delightfully apt. A small but delightful touch comes from Menelaus when he tells how Helen walked round the Wooden Horse and addressed the Achaean leaders, imitating the voices of their wives. We can believe it of her, but it is told so simply that it takes a moment to see how illuminating it is. So too when a very unusual situation is in question, Homer makes sense of it by some deft stroke of insight. When Menelaus lies in wait for the sea-god Proteus, he and his companions hide by wrapping themselves in newly-flayed seal-skins:

> 'There would our lying-in-wait have been most horrible, for the deadly stink of the sea-bred seals wore us down terribly; for who would lie down to rest by a creature of the sea?'

>   (4.441-3)

Fortunately they are saved by the goddess putting ambrosia under their nostrils—but the point has been made, and illustrates the unusual nature of the adventure.

Such small touches may give a powerful reinforcement to some general effect which is intended. When Hector, takes advantage of a lull in the battle to go into Troy, he finds his wife Andromache on the walls. They exchange touching and beautiful words about the dark prospects that face them, and then Hector turns to his small child Astyanax:

> After speaking, Hector reached out his arms for his child; but the child shrank back crying to the bosom of his deep-girdled nurse, frightened helmet. His dear father and his lady mother laughed. Then shining hair plume, which he marked as it nodded terrible from the crest of the helmet. His dear father and his lady mother laughed. Then shining Hector took the helmet from his head, and set it, all glittering, on the ground.

>   (vi 466-73)

This changes the tone, which is beginning to reach a tragic temper, and introduces the warmth of a young family, but the one rises out of the other, since the child is the token of the love of Hector and Andromache. The common, human touch adds to the grandeur and nobility of the occasion. So too when Achilles has tied the dead Hector to his chariot and is already dragging him round Troy, Andromache does not yet know what is happening. She is busy with her embroidery, and then she gives orders to her slaves to heat the water for Hector's bath when he comes back from battle. She then hears the sound of wailing, rushes out and sees the worst. The small domestic touches mark the gap between the life of a woman and the life of a man, and their juxtaposition shows how closely interwoven they are. At a less tragic level but deeply touching is the dog Argos, who recognizes Odysseus after twenty years and then dies. He is the true and faithful servant who knows his master without any marks or signs, and suffers for his loyalty as he lies cast on the midden, neglected and full of ticks. These are an indication of his loyalty, and death is the right end at the right time.

Homer reveals himself in the nature and quality of his creation; he does not attempt to guide our reactions to them.

—*C. M. Bowra*

In these cases, and in many others like them, a detail adds something highly individual and yet illuminating, and such details are more effective when they strengthen some display of emotion or affection. They are as necessary to the heroic outlook as any kind of prowess, for they provide the hero with a solid background and bind his friends to him. The *Iliad,* like other heroic poems, has its examples of heroic friendship, not only in Achilles and Patroclus but on the Trojan side in Sarpedon and Glaucus. These friendships find their chief outlet in war, where each friend helps the other, and if either is in trouble he calls for the other's help. So Sarpedon reminds Glaucus that they receive great honours in their own homeland, which they do not deserve if they fail to rise to the present challenge; so let them take the risk and advance to battle. Later, when Sarpedon has been mortally wounded by Patroclus, he calls on his friend to look after his body and his armour after his death, and this Glaucus, with the help of the gods, does.

The affection between Achilles and Patroclus is more powerful and more tragic, since Achilles feels that he failed to save Patroclus. So long as Patroclus is alive Achilles treats him as an equal and shares his troubles with him. When Patroclus is deeply distressed by the disasters of the Achaeans, Achilles mocks him gently and compares him to a child running to its mother, but when he knows what the trouble is, he treats it seriously and not only lets Patroclus go to battle but lends him his own armour. The strength of his love for Patroclus is revealed when the latter is killed, and takes almost extravagant forms, so that Antilochus is afraid that Achilles will cut his throat from grief. Because Patroclus has been killed by Hector, Achilles is obsessed by a desire to kill Hector in return, but even this is not enough for him, and when he has killed Hector, his troubles are not finished.

These male affections are stronger and more demanding than affections between men and women. Since the woman is dependent on the man, she finds her fulfilment in him. Andromache's whole life is centred on Hector and their small child. Indeed they can hardly be otherwise; for her whole family has been killed by Achilles, and her husband takes their place:

> 'Hector, you are my father and my lady mother and my brother, and you are my sturdy husband.'

>   (vi 429-30)

In her love for him she foresees his death and knows that it means the end for herself and her child. Yet in this there is nothing mawkish. Andromache lives entirely for her duties as a wife and a mother, but she has her woman's honour which lies in her husband's prowess. She is still a very young woman, and her pathos is enhanced by it, but she is not pathetic in any cheap or commonplace way. She knows what the dangers are and she is ready to face them.

In this matter there is a great difference between Achilles and Hector. Even in battle it is noteworthy that while one of Hector's gifts is for rallying and inspiring his fellows, Achilles needs no support and fights alone. This reflects the great difference between their personal lives. Patroclus is deeply attached to Achilles, but hardly says so, and complains that he is not the son of Peleus and Thetis but of the sea and the rocks. Patroclus may even be said to die for Achilles in so far as his career in battle is caused by his shame at Achilles' abstention from it. But the ties between them are quite different from the steady, quiet devotion which bind Andromache and Hector. Nor is Thetis dependent on Achilles in any respect. She is deeply involved in his life, and feels his sorrows all the more because he is doomed to die young. This is about all the affection which Achilles inspires, and the contrast is complete with Hector, who is the mainstay not only of Andromache but of Priam, who sees in his death the end of Troy, of Hecuba, who loves him more than all her other children, and of Helen, who is deeply conscious of his kindness to her. In the scarcity of his human ties Achilles stands out more emphatically as a hero, while Hector is a little too human to be a hero of the highest class. Yet both are presented through the affections that they arouse in others or feel for them. It is not their only claim, but it is a background against which their other qualities show their worth. It is right that they should be pitted against each other, and each gains something by it.

In the study of Homeric affections Odysseus and Penelope have a special place. When we are introduced to them, they have been severed for twenty years, and after all this time Penelope cherishes his memory and breaks constantly into tears at the thought of him. She is convinced that he is dead, but such is her love for him that she clings to hope and trusts that every rumour of his survival may be true. She does not speak explicitly of her love for him. That is taken for granted, and yet, when he is at last restored to her, her inbred suspicion is strong and she hesitates before she accepts him. This is true to human nature, and after all he has been away for a very long time. On his side Odysseus is almost equally undemonstrative, but he reveals his true feelings to Calypso when, to no purpose, she hopes that he will stay with her, and he answers:

> 'Lady goddess, be not angry with me in this way; I too know very well that wise Penelope is inferior to you in looks and figure for the eyes to see; for she is a mortal woman, and you are immortal and free from old age. But even so I wish and hope all my days to go home and see the day of my return.'

> (5.215-20)

When at the end of a long story husband and wife are alone together they pick up an old intimacy and Penelope cannot take her arms off her husband. This decorous, lasting affection does not touch us very deeply, and we cannot but compare it with the love which Odysseus' mother, Anticlea, feels for him, and which we hear of when he calls up her ghost at the end of the world. He asks her what brought her death, and she answers:

> 'The far-seeing shooter of arrows did not come upon me in my chambers or kill me with her gentle shafts, nor did any sickness attack me, such as most often takes away life from the limbs with hideous wasting. But it was longing for you and for your ways, glorious Odysseus, and for your gentleness of heart, that took away life from my limbs.'

> (11.197-203)

This is the most direct and most powerful outburst of affection in Homer, and it illustrates how his concentration on a single mood gives a uniquely dramatic power.

When Homer has exploited a single mood or tone, he changes to another, and this too is done simply but conclusively. The most complex case is in Book ix when an embassy comes to Achilles to make amends for Agamemnon and to ask him to relent, but he refuses and they go away unsuccessful. Inside this main plan of failure Homer marks three stages and each makes a dramatic surprise. At 357 ff. Achilles announces that he will sail away on the morrow; at 618 ff. that he will sail away in the morning; at 650-3 that he will join battle when Hector reaches the ships of the Myrmidons. Though for the moment these amount to a refusal, in the long run they mark stages towards the still distant moment when Achilles will return to battle. The change is deftly and delicately presented, and each section has its own character. So too in the exploits of Patroclus there is a marked variation of tone and effect. In the first stage he carries all before him. Then Apollo opposes him, and the mood changes to uncertainty, doubt, and alarm, until finally Patroclus is wounded and disarmed and killed. The two phases are quite distinct; each has its own marked character, the first working through the thrills of a victorious progress, the second through a sense of forthcoming failure and defeat.

The emotions which Homer shows at work are those of living beings, human or divine or animal. In the last class are the horse of Achilles and the dog of Odysseus, both deeply concerned with their masters and each showing it in his own way, the horse by speaking in a human voice, the dog by wagging its tail and dying. The gods are close to us because they are like human beings. They are vastly more powerful and do what men cannot possibly do, but this somehow enhances their likeness and makes us treat them as we would men who are not doomed to die. They have distinct personalities and move in their own right. Each of the three goddesses, Athene, Hera and Aphrodite, is moved by proper pride, as heroes are, and pursues her enemies without qualm. But the gods are brought closer to men in other, more interesting ways. First, they have their human children. Aphrodite is the mother of Aeneas, and protects him in battle; Zeus is the father of Sarpedon and would protect him if it were possible. Though they themselves cannot really be hurt, the gods can be wounded in their affections when their children suffer. Secondly, the gods have their human attachment. We have seen how strong is Athene's for Odysseus, but in a different way Aphrodite's care for Paris is hardly less strong, though less friendly and intimate. Because he gave her the prize of beauty, she gives him Helen, and both saves him from death in the duel with Menelaus and consoles him by forcing Helen to do what he wishes. The affections of the gods do not touch us very deeply but make the gods more likeable. It is the other side of their hatreds, of the injured pride which compels them to maintain unceasing hostility to those who have in some sense dishonoured them. That is why Athene and Hera fight on the other side to Aphrodite, why Poseidon harries Odysseus for blinding Polyphemus and hates Troy because he was cheated by Laomedon.

By giving human traits to his gods and his animals Homer unifies his approach to his complex subject, and this attitude helps to explain his intention in composition. It is clear on all sides that he does not wish to instruct. His comments on the action are hardly ever his own, but are made by the characters on each other. Even if the Trojan War is due to the shamelessness of Paris in preferring Aphrodite to Hera and Athene, the poet does not actually condemn Paris; he merely reports why the gods acted as they did, and assumes that Paris was, as he is elsewhere, mad about women. Nor elsewhere does he condemn any action by one of his characters, or even praise one. Nor is it clear that he tells his tale to instil ideals of manhood and present models of it for imitation. He certainly holds these ideals and they give shape to his narrative, but he does not underline them or drive them home. In later times Homer was regarded as a teacher of the young, well versed in the right kinds of behaviour and able to give vivid instances of it, but this was simply a means to justify the study of him in schools. When Plato attacks him for his low view of the gods or his over-indulgence in the emotions, it was because these were accepted as norms of behaviour. But there is no reason to think that Homer himself created types of manhood for imitation or even as warnings. His personalities derive their being from his passionate interest in them, and this itself may well have been fostered by a tradition which rejoiced in the glorious doings of men. This is the central spring of his power and if incidentally he inspires or instructs, it is because he believes so strongly in the reality and worth of certain human qualities. No doubt he composes poetry because he must, and that is explanation enough.

In his poetry Homer wishes to give delight. This is the intention which he ascribes to his imaginary bards. Telemachus explains to Penelope that Phemius gives pleasure as his spirit moves him, and Alcinous speaks of Demodocus in similar words. Both ascribe this power to a god and so exalt it. When Homer invents a father for Phemius he calls him Terpiades, where the root *terp-* is that of the word 'delight'. This is a kind of enchantment. Penelope uses the word 'enchantments' of songs in general, and when Odysseus tells his own story, the audience is held 'by a spell.' Since the bard is inspired by a god, it is right that his song should have a magical power of holding his hearers. This

view presupposes a high level of style and outlook. Homer aims not at mere enjoyment, but at enjoyment of a lofty kind which comes from the gods and holds the attention of men. This view of poetry is by no means unique, but seems to be held quite often in circles where heroic song is honoured. The bards are so sure of the worth of their material and of their own ability to handle it that they can afford to present it without didactic or moralistic additions. It is later that the poet becomes a teacher, as he certainly did in Greece. Homer's impact is different, and all the stronger because he is concerned primarily with the vivid presentation of human beings. Moreover, since he presents them in action, he makes them living entities without any of the distortion introduced by abstraction and instruction.

Homer has his own view of the place of song in the world. This he states both in the *Iliad* and in the *Odyssey,* and though the words vary a little, and suggest that they are not strictly formulaic, the main substance is the same. In the *Iliad* Helen tells Hector that she and Paris are the cause of the troubles of Troy:

> 'Upon us Zeus set an evil doom, that afterwards we may be sung of by men to come.'
>
> (vi 357-8)

In the *Odyssey,* before Odysseus begins his long story, Alcinous, noticing his distress, on hearing a tale of Troy, says of this doom:

> 'The gods fashioned it, and they wove destruction for men that they might be a song for those in the future.'
>
> (8.579-80)

This is a clear and emphatic view, and not what we should expect to find in Homer or what in fact we find in other heroic poetry. It asserts the supremacy of art over human fortunes and justifies them because of the pleasure which songs about them will give. Whatever the social position or authority of the poet was, he had no doubt of the importance of his art, and he asserts this confidently through two important witnesses, Helen and Alcinous. Even though we argue that this belief is relevant to Helen's own case and helps her to endure her troubles, Alcinous is above the battle and offers consolation to the much-enduring Odysseus. No doubt Homer's own patrons were comforted by the thought that their doings would be remembered in song; Homer himself went further and saw in song a consolation and an explanation of the ills and sufferings of mankind. It commemorates them and transcends them, and raises them to an unperishing order of being.

Martin Mueller   (essay date 1984)

SOURCE: "Fighting in the *Iliad,*" in *The Iliad,* George Allen & Unwin, 1984, pp. 77-107.

[In the following excerpt, Mueller discusses ways in which individual warriors are represented fighting, dying or exulting over the bodies of their enemies in the Iliad.*]*

[My purpose in this essay] is to survey the representation of battle in the *Iliad,* moving from the components that make up the individual encounter to the devices by which larger narrative units are created from such encounters.". . . Here my chief aim is to classify phenomena and to convey a sense of their relative frequency. It is in the battle scenes that the modern reader is most likely to be wearied by the seemingly endless succession of virtually identical incidents and to experience the 'formulaic style' at its stereotyped worst. For this reason there is some virtue in sorting out the frequency of typical incidents and in establishing the degree of variation between closely related phenomena. As it turns out, the impression of endless repetition rests on a fairly small base, and many details of battle owe their 'typically Homeric' status not to repetition but to vividness of language, like the 'Homeric' laughter of the gods that arises only once in the *Iliad* (1.599).

There is no doubt that battle scenes, which amount to 5,500 lines or a good third of the *Iliad,* enjoy considerable autonomy in the poem. The poet and his audience like such scenes, and their periodic occurrence requires no greater motivation than bar-room brawls in a Western. But, although narrative control over the battle scenes is often relaxed, it is rarely absent, and it would be a great mistake to ignore specific narrative aims that guide the elaboration or deployment of particular motifs. Such questions as 'Why does this convention occur three times in this part of the poem?' often have an answer that points to the story of Achilles, Patroklos and Hektor. Often, but not always: a judicious reader must be alert to the function of detail without demanding the rigorous integration of every particular into the design of the poem. (In the following [essay] I am much indebted to Friedrich, 1956, and Fenik, 1968, whose books subsume much of the extensive literature on fighting in the *Iliad.*)

Warfare in the *Iliad* depends entirely on the strength and courage of the individual fighter. There is no room for strategy or cunning. There is not even much interest in skill. It is assumed that the warrior knows how to throw a spear or wield a sword, but special dexterity in the use or avoidance of a weapon is not a significant feature of the narrative. This attitude is Iliadic rather than Homeric or heroic. Cunning is highly regarded in the *Odyssey,* and in the *Iliad* there are occasional references to it. The shield of Achilles shows men gathered in an ambush and increasing their strength through cunning. Idomeneus praises the sang-froid Meriones would display in an ambush. Nestor likes to give orders and advice of a strategic kind; he also tells Antilochos how a good charioteer can use intelligence (*metis*) to compensate for inferior horses, and the dutiful son remembers the advice so well that he seeks to improve his position in the race by reckless cheating. On another occasion Nestor tells how in the old days Lykurgos killed Areïthoös 'by guile rather than force.' But, while the *Iliad* is clearly familiar with a world in which the outcome of contests turns on the unscrupulous use of intelligence and the ruthless exploitation of the opponent's weakness, the poem banishes both from its arena and presents a spectacle of war at once brutal and innocent: no ambush, no stratagem, no diversionary or dilatory

tactic qualifies the encounter of enemies in the field of battle. The bow is a marginal weapon in this world and does not become a major warrior. It is used by Pandaros, Paris and Teukros, but Odysseus, who gives a taste of his cunning in the wrestling match with Aias, left his bow at home when he sailed for Troy and like other major warriors fights with spear and sword. Only accident is allowed to qualify open force: some dozen warriors in the *Iliad* lose their lives because they stand in the path of a spear aimed at someone else. The trickery of the gods is a special case. The one part of the *Iliad* in which deception plays a major role, the Doloneia (Book 10), has been firmly established as a later addition to the epic.

The ethos of fighting is perfectly embodied in the words that precede Hektor's attack on Aias in their duel in Book 7:

> Yet great as you are I would not strike you by stealth, watching
> for my chance, but openly, so, if perhaps I might hit you.
>
> (7.242-3)

Fighting in this spirit not only despises guile and cowardice; it is also constrained by an implicit notion of fairness. The actual fighting in the *Iliad* does not always live up fully to that ideal; indeed, it is Hektor himself who runs away from Achilles and takes ruthless advantage of Patroklos' injury. How typical are these striking violations of the code?

The question of fairness arises wherever a warrior is taken by surprise. Leaving aside the few bow-shots and the spear-casts that hit someone else, such surprise is not very common. In the fourth book, Elephenor bends over a slain warrior to strip him. As he does so, his ribs are exposed and Agenor hits him. Similarly, Koön takes Agamemnon by surprise as he removes the armour of Iphidamas. These incidents reflect on the victim's lack of caution. On two occasions in Book 13 a Trojan warrior unsuccessfully attacks an Achaean only to be caught unawares by Meriones on his retreat. A more drastic instance of intervention by a third warrior occurs when Menelaos kills Dolops from behind as he is facing an attack by Meges. All three cases seem less than heroic and occur in a stretch of fighting distinguished by savagery of other kinds. None of these incidents, however, matches the ruthlessness of Hektor's killing of Patroklos. On three occasions a warrior kills an enemy whom he has previously disabled. But there is no other case of a warrior killing an enemy whom someone else has disabled.

If the death of Patroklos is the most serious violation of fairness, the duel of Hektor and Achilles provides the most glaring example of loss of courage. The Homeric warrior aims at inspiring in his opponent the uncontrollable fear that leads to flight (*phobos*). Instances of such panic are numerous, but they are typically a collective phenomenon. Individual flight is a much rarer and more qualified phenomenon. When Zeus turns the scales of battle in favour of the Trojans and the Achaeans run away, Diomedes is the only warrior to come to the help of the stranded Nestor. He calls on Odysseus as he runs past, but Odysseus does not hear him or does not listen (the text is ambiguous, 8.97). Odysseus, however, makes the fullest statement of the code of courage when, surrounded by Trojans, he refuses to yield in the face of overwhelming odds. Between these extremes, there are intermediate positions. Diomedes is afraid to yield lest Hektor accuse him of cowardice. It takes the advice of Nestor and three thunderbolts from Zeus to persuade him that retreat on this occasion is inevitable and not shameful. The hand of the god is generally a valid excuse for yielding. So Diomedes in Book 5 organises a retreat because Hektor is aided by a god. Zeus inspires Aias with fear, but even so his retreat is slow and reluctant. A warrior may without serious loss of face retreat from an enemy who is clearly superior. Thus Menelaos persuades himself that he may abandon the body of Patroklos when Hektor approaches, and Aeneas yields to Menelaos and Antilochos, but Diomedes scornfully rejects the advice to retreat before the joint attack of Aeneas and Pandaros, and events prove him right.

There are limits to Hektor's courage even before the encounter with Achilles. At the order of Zeus he avoids Agamemnon just as at the order of Apollo he avoids Achilles, although he breaks that command when he witnesses the death of his brother Polydoros. He also avoids Aias on his own initiative. When Patroklos routs the Trojans, Hektor at first resists the attacks of Aias by his skill at evasive action—the only time in the *Iliad* this skill is made much of—but then he, too, joins the rout. He teams up with Aeneas against Automedon in the hope of conquering the horses of Achilles, but he retreats in fear when the Aiantes come to the aid of Automedon. But neither his previous behaviour nor the other scenes of more or less honourable retreat are any precedent for his extraordinary loss of courage at the approach of Achilles. A warrior may persuade himself to stay (Odysseus) or to retreat (Menelaos), but only Hektor persuades himself to stay and fails to live up to his resolution. It is important to remember, however, that the poet sees Hektor's flight less as a failure of Hektor's courage than as a symptom of the overwhelming terror emanating from Achilles.

The unit of fighting is the individual encounter. The most salient feature of this unit is its brevity. In other forms of heroic poetry warriors demonstrate their prowess in protracted struggles with one or more opponents. Hours or days and many lines may pass before the decisive stroke, and the victor may suffer as many wounds as the vanquished. Not so in the *Iliad,* where the first blow disables the opponent, occasionally through injury, but mostly through death, which is always instantaneous.

Except for two occasions, the injured warrior has no power to strike back. Agamemnon and Odysseus withdraw from battle after killing the men who injure them. The other injured warriors do not return to battle until a god heals or strengthens them as happens to Diomedes, Aeneas, Glaukos and Hektor. The wounding of Menelaos by Pandaros does not occur in battle. Sometimes injuries are forgotten or trivial and healed by the surgeon. Sarpedon,

who suffers a serious thigh-wound on the first day, fights on the third day as if nothing had happened to him. Similarly, Teukros suffers what appears to be a disabling shoulder injury on the second day of fighting, but is all there again on the following day. It is hard to tell whether these cases are due to heroic resilience or to a lapse of memory, but the three Achaean leaders wounded in Book 11 hobble to the assembly on the following day.

Out of some 140 specified encounters only twenty involve more than one blow, and except for the duel of Hektor and Aias no encounter goes beyond a second exchange of blows. On three occasions, the victim is only disabled by the first blow, and it requires a second blow to kill him. The death of Patroklos at the hands of Apollo, Euphorbos and Hektor is an elaboration of these cases.

On two occasions, the warriors let go of their missiles simultaneously. On seven occasions, the aggressor misses the enemy or does not pierce his armour fatally and is killed or disabled in return. The victim is always a Trojan. We find this pattern with Pandaros and Diomedes, Ares and Diomedes/Athene, Euphorbos and Menelaos, Hektor and Aias. A slight variation occurs in the duel of Meges and Dolops. Meges is hit by Dolops, whose spear does not pierce. Meges, who has used his spear to kill another Trojan, hits Dolops with his sword. This stroke, however, is not fatal, and Dolops is killed by Menelaos, who comes up from behind and pierces his chest with his spear. Finally, in two closely related scenes, the Trojan aggressor injures an Achaean who retains enough strength to avenge himself on his aggressor but is then forced to leave the battle. This pattern is found in the wounding of Agamemnon and Odysseus in Book 11 by Koön and Sokos. Agamemnon is injured less seriously than Odysseus but, while he continues to fight for a while after Koön's death, the poet does not attribute any named slayings to him.

Only eight encounters go beyond a first exchange of blows—a telling indication of the narrator's preoccupation with the decisive moment. The first exchange always involves spears and has a variety of outcomes. Peneleos and Lykon miss one another. So do Sarpedon and Patroklos, but each of them hits another victim, the latter the charioteer of Sarpedon, the former the tracehorse of Patroklos. The outcome of the first exchange reflects the relative strengths of the combatants in the duels of Paris and Menelaos and Achilles and Aeneas. On both occasions, the Trojan fails to pierce the Achaean's shield. The Achaean does pierce the armour of his opponent, who somehow 'ducks' the spear. On four occasions it is the victor who misses on the first throw. Thus Agamemnon misses Iphidamas, Menelaos Peisandros, Achilles Asteropaios and Achilles Hektor. In each case the opponent hits but fails to pierce; the ambidextrous Asteropaios discharges two spears at once, one of which sticks in Achilles' shield whereas the other grazes his hand.

There is no standard procedure for the second exchange, although it usually involves a change from spear to sword. Menelaos attacks Paris with a sword, which breaks. He then pulls Paris by the strap of his helmet, but Aphrodite snaps the helmet strap. Agamemnon hits Iphidamas with his sword. The duels of Peisandros and Menelaos and Lykon and Peneleos are alike in that both involve a simultaneous exchange of blows in which the Trojan's blow fails. But Peisandros wields a battle-axe instead of a sword, the only warrior in the *Iliad* to do so. Sarpedon and Patroklos exchange spears in the second round. The former misses, the latter hits. Asteropaios, the man with two spears, has no sword. As he vainly tries to pull the spear of Achilles out of the ground, Achilles dispatches him with his sword. Achilles rushes at Aeneas with his sword, and Aeneas stands ready to throw a rock, but Poseidon puts an end to the encounter before the second exchange can take place. The most famous victim of Achilles can only be a victim of his spear: Hektor rushes at Achilles with his sword, but Achilles kills him with the spear that Athene returned to him after he missed on his first throw.

The longest fight in the *Iliad,* curiously enough, is the not entirely serious encounter of Hektor and Aias in Book 7. Their duel does not involve the characteristic change from spear to sword, but is based on the triple repetition of a throwing contest in which Aias comes out slightly ahead each time. When the warriors turn to their swords the heralds put an end to the fighting by pointing to the onset of night.

Battle narrative in the *Iliad* is dominated to the point of obsession by the decisive and disabling blow. Some 170 Trojan and fifty Achaean named warriors lose their lives in the *Iliad*; another dozen, evenly divided between the two sides, are injured. About eighty of these die in lists, two, three or four to a line, such as the following victims of Patroklos:

> Adrestos
> first, and after him Autonoös and Echeklos,
> Perimos, son of Megas, and Epistor, and
>   Melanippos,
> and after these Elasos, and Moulios, and Pylartes.

(16.694-6)

The remaining 140, only two dozen of them Achaeans, attract more of the poet's attention at the point of their death. The degree of attention varies enormously and observes a delicately graded hierarchy: Hektor, Patroklos and Sarpedon, but also Euphorbos, Iphidamas and Sokos, stand out against the many warriors about whom the poet tells us no more than their name, patronymic, and the nature of their invariably fatal injury. What unites the greatest and the least warriors is the experience of sudden and violent death.

The poet goes out of his way to introduce variety into his grim litany. Take the narrative stretch that describes a rout of the Trojans and shows six Achaean leaders each killing an opponent. Hodios falls off his chariot hit by Agamemnon's spear between the shoulders. Idomeneus hits Phaistos on the right shoulder as he mounts his chariot. Menelaos, like his brother, hits the fleeing Skamandrios between the shoulders. Meriones' spear pierces the right buttock and bladder of Phereklos. Meges hits Pedaios in

the back of the head, cutting through his teeth and tongue. Eurypylos rushes at Hypsenor with a sword and cuts off his arm. A similar stretch in the Patrokleia features wounds in the thigh, chest, hip, flank, shoulder, neck, shoulder, mouth, as well as a cut-off head.

Here are the victims of Achilles, the final list of slayings in the *Iliad*. Iphition is hit in the middle of the head, Demoleon on the temple. His helmet does not hold: the spear crashes through the bone and brain splatters on the inside of the helmet. Hippodamas is hit in the back, Polydoros in the navel: he falls holding his guts in his hands. The spear of Achilles hits Dryops in the neck and Demouchos in the knee. Laogonos and Dardanos are dispatched with spear and sword respectively, but their injuries are not specified. Tros vainly seeks to supplicate Achilles: a sword-stroke makes his liver slip out. The spear drives in at one ear of Moulion and out at the other. The sword plunges deep into the neck of Echeklos and is heated by his blood. Deukalion is hit in the elbow; unable to move, his head is cut off and flung away with the helmet. Marrow jets out of his spine. Rhigmos is hit in the abdomen, Areïthoös in the back.

This survey of some two dozen injuries from four killing scenes provides a fairly representative sample of injury and death in the *Iliad.* The upper body and the head are the most common targets for the spear, the neck and head for the sword. In any sequence of killings the poet will vary the injuries and the degree of detail. He may state the mere fact of death, or he may dwell in great detail on the circumstances of a particular slaying, but most commonly he will use a phrase that is specific without being very descriptive, such as 'on the right shoulder', 'through the chest', 'below the ear'. Against the background of ordinary killings some scenes stand out for their special precision, atrocity or extravagance. In our sample, the victims of Meriones and Meges in Book 5 as well as several of Achilles' victims fall in this category.

> There is no doubt that battle scenes, which amount to 5,500 lines or a good third of the *Iliad,* enjoy considerable autonomy in the poem. The poet and his audience like such scenes, and their periodic occurrence requires no greater motivation than barroom brawls in a Western.
>
> —*Martin Mueller*

These special injuries require separate attention because they have an effect quite disproportionate to their scarcity. Mention the *Iliad* in a conversation, and someone is likely to point to some particularly grisly injury as a typical instance of Homeric narrative. But such injuries are not nearly so pervasive as casual readers assume. Out of 140 specified injuries only thirty are remarkable in one way or another, and their description takes up a bare hundred lines. Far from being instances of epic battle-lust, these descriptions are associated with particular characters or situations, and they owe their prominence as much to strategic placement as to vividness of detail.

First a brief survey of the grisly scenes. A few injuries are remarkable less for their cruelty than for their attention to real or imagined anatomical detail. Thus Amphiklos is hit 'at the base of the leg where the muscle / of a man grows thickest so that on the spear head the sinew / was torn apart.' Ancient scholiasts wondered about this injury because it does not appear to be particularly lethal. Antilochos rushes at Thoön and 'shore away the entire vein / which runs all the way up the back till it reaches the neck'. For all its precision, the description defies human anatomy. The third example of what Friedrich has called fake realism occurs in Book 14 where Archelochos is hit 'at the joining place of head and neck, at the last / vertebra, and cut through both of the tendons.'

Much more important to the tone of the poem are scenes in which a head is either severed or smashed in a particularly brutal way. Three times, and in words that echo each other, the helmet shatters under the blow of a spear and is besplattered on the inside with brain. Idomeneus drives a spear through the mouth and into the brain of Erymas. The skull splits, teeth fall out, and the eye sockets fill with blood, which also wells up through nose and mouth. The helmet of Hippothoös cannot withstand the force of Aias' blow, 'and the brain ran from the wound along the spear by the eyehole, bleeding.' The spear of Diomedes drives through eye, nose and teeth of Pandaros before cutting off his tongue at the base. A whole line is given over to Pandaros' tongue, perhaps because he had been such a braggart in his life, but Pedaios and Koiranos suffer a similar fate. The realm of the probable is clearly left behind in two scenes where the violence of the blow forces the eyes out of their sockets so that they fall on the ground, the fate of Peisandros and Kebriones.

Decapitation occurs half a dozen times, sometimes as a form of mutilation. Aias Oileus cuts off the head of the dead Imbrios and throws it before Hektor's feet. Agamemnon chops off Koön's head over the body of his brother Iphidamas. When he hews off the arms and head of Hippolochos, killing and mutilation are both present. The same is true of one of the most grotesque scenes in the *Iliad*. Ilioneus is speared in the eye; as he falls backward, Peneleos cuts off his head and triumphantly lifts his spear, with the head stuck on it 'like a poppy.' The same Peneleos later severs the head of Lykon so that it dangles from the body by a mere piece of skin.

Abdominal injuries are not uncommon, but are usually not specified beyond such phrases as *kata laparen* ('in the flank'), *mesen kata gastera* or *neiairei en gastri* ('in the middle or lower belly'). Where the wound is elaborated, the poet dwells on the image of guts spilling out of the body. This happens to Peiros, and to three victims of Achilles. The gruesomest image, however, occurs in Book 17. On two occasions a spear misses and continues to quiver after it hits the ground. This image is varied in the

death of Aretos, whom Automedon, the charioteer of Patroklos, kills in revenge for his fallen comrade: the spear quivers in the entrails of the hapless victim.

Groin injuries occur four times. One of them is passed over in a phrase, the other three are remarkable for being the work of Meriones, a ruthless and somewhat sneaky warrior. The first injury is suffered by Phereklos, son of the man who built the ships for Paris' fateful voyage. An ancient scholiast interpreted the wound as poetic justice for the whoring of Paris. The other two occur in adjacent and similar passages in the aristeia of Idomeneus: a Trojan fails to pierce the armour of an Achaean; as he retreats, Meriones hits him in the groin 'where beyond all places / death in battle comes painfully to pitiful mortals.' The death spasms of the victims are compared to a twitching bull and a wriggling worm—unique images that make it clear that a sense of revulsion is intended and not the result of a more refined sensibility.

There remain three unique and bizarre scenes of death in the *Iliad*. Two of them involve charioteers. A straightforward version of a charioteer's death occurs after the death of Asios. His unnamed charioteer loses his wits, is hit in the stomach by Antilochos and falls off his chariot. In Book 5, Menelaos kills Pylaimenes, and once more it is Antilochos who kills the charioteer, but the motif of the fallen warrior is varied: his head is stuck in the deep sand, and the body remains standing for a while—an image that gains force from the contrast with typical closing phrases like 'he fell thunderously and his armour clattered about him'. In the other version, the motif of the charioteer's paralysis is varied. Patroklos kills the terrified Thestor by stabbing him in the jaw and then

> hooked and dragged him with the spear over the
>   rail, as a fisherman
> who sits out on the jut of a rock with line and
>   glittering
> bronze hook drags a fish, who is thus doomed, out
>   of the water.
> So he hauled him, mouth open to the bright spear,
>   out of the chariot,
> and shoved him over on his face, and as he fell the
>   life left him.
>
>   (16.406-10)

Finally, perhaps the most bizarre death of all, a second variation on the theme of the spear quivering in the ground. Paralysed by Poseidon, Alkathoös stands immobile as Idomeneus pierces his armour and drives the spear through his heart:

> He cried out then, a great cry, broken, the spear in
>   him,
> and fell, thunderously, and the spear in his heart
>   was stuck fast
> but the heart was panting still and beating to shake
>   the butt end
> of the spear. Then and there Ares the huge took
>   his life away from him.
>
>   (13.441-4)

169

With the exception of Koiranos, the victims of gruesome injuries are always Trojans, a reflection of the bias of the poet's narrative sources. Some interesting conclusions emerge from looking at the distribution of these injuries and at the identity of the killers. Twenty-eight of thirty injuries occur in Books 5, 13-14, and in the aristeias of Achilles, Agamemnon and Patroklos (including the fight over his body). The killers are either minor warriors or major warriors in extreme situations. The reasons for this distribution are not hard to find. Minor warriors are both distinguished and placed by their association with fanciful and cruel injuries. Meriones is the specialist in groin injuries; Peneleos acquires similar notoriety through the brutality of head wounds he inflicts. The cluster of unusual injuries in Books 13 and 14 has two reasons. We may distinguish in the *Iliad* between fights that sharply focus on a concrete object (the wall in Book 12, the ships in Book 15, the body of Patroklos in Book 17) and diffuse fighting scenes in which the general sense of battle yields to the individual encounter. Gruesome injuries are almost completely absent from the fighting scenes of the former type (except for the fighting over Patroklos), and they are clustered in the scenes of the latter type. The desire to make individual encounters more colourful and inevitably more brutal accounts for the frequency of unusual injuries in Book 5 and in Books 13 and 14, but it does not explain the much greater brutality of Books 13 and 14. Again the reason is not hard to find. The cruelty of Books 13 and 14 measures the changing nature of the war. The reminder of increasing brutality comes just before Patroklos re-enters the fighting. Patroklos, we recall, is singled out in the *Iliad* for his gentleness, and the brutality of his fate is a major theme of the poem. But, if Patroklos becomes a victim of war, he is also transformed by its rage: the fighting he leads is exceptionally bloody, and of the five unusual injuries it causes he himself is responsible for two.

It is hardly necessary to point out why cruel injuries are frequent in the aristeia of Achilles: his violence is a response to and further intensification of the brutality that has claimed Patroklos, but as with Patroklos it is at odds with his 'character': 'Achilles' unyielding harshness to both living and dead enemies is less the function of his nature than of his fate' (Friedrich).

Agamemnon is a different case. His cruelty manifests itself in the first scene of the *Iliad* when he rebuffs Chryses, and his bloody aristeia seems quite in character. On the other hand, Agamemnon as the leader of the expedition has the strongest sense of the wrong done by the Trojans. His killing of the suppliants Adrestos and Hippolochos is motivated by his sense of outrage. Thus even the Iliadic Agamemnon may not be cruel by nature, but we discover in his portrayal the theme of the brutalising force of a moral mission, which Aeschylus was to develop with magnificent thoroughness.

The preoccupation with the individual encounter and the decisive stroke of death appears in another Iliadic convention, the phrase, ranging in length from a half-line to three lines, by which the poet confirms the death of the victim.

These poetic death certificates appear roughly a hundred times and exhibit considerable variety.

Death appears as the loosener of limbs in a set of phrases of which *luse de guia* (X 6) is the commonest. Another set of phrases equates death with the literal fall of the warrior. *Doupesen de peson*, 'he fell with a thud' (X 12), occurs most frequently, its very sound echoing the fall of the warrior on the ground. Less onomatopoeic is a set of phrases that are derived from the verb *ereipein*, 'to fall', and specify the direction or origin of the fall, such as 'from the chariot', 'over his feet', or 'in the dust'. The phrases *keito tanustheis* (X 2) and *keito tatheis* (X 2), 'he lay stretched out', dwell on the result of the fall. After the death of Kebriones there is fighting over his body, and the poet returns to the body on the ground: *ho d'en strophalingi konies/keito megas megalosti lelasmenos hipposunaon* ('he lay in the whirling dust mightily in his might, his horsemanship all forgotten').

The falling phrases may stand by themselves but more commonly they are combined with others. The most famous of these combinations contrasts the thudding sound of the body with the clatter of its armour, imitating the contrast in its own phonetic structure: *doupesen te peson, arabese de teuche' ep'autoi*, 'he fell with a thud and his armour clattered about him' (X 6). Another phrase for the accompanying noise of the armour is *amphi de hoi brache teuchea poikila chalkoi*, 'his glittering armour clattered about him' (X 3), and a unique variant focuses on the noise of the helmet: *amphi de pelex smerdaleon konabese peri krotaphoisi pesontos*, 'the helmet crashed fearfully about the temples of the falling man'.

The sound can also be the death shout of the falling warrior, as in *gnux d' erip' oimoxas*, 'he fell backwards in the dust with a shout', and in the phrase that closes the falls of Asios and Sarpedon:

> *hos ho prosth' hippon kai diphrou keito tanustheis*
> *bebruchos, konios de dragmenos haimatoesses*
> So he lay there felled in front of his horses and
>   chariot,
> roaring, and clawed with his hands at the bloody
>   dust.
>
> (13.392-3 = 16.485-6)

A similar gesture of futility appears in the line *ho d'en konieisi peson hele gaian agostoi*, 'falling in the dust he clutched the earth with his hand' (X 5). Even more pathetic is the vision of the dying warrior stretching out his hands towards his comrades: *ho d'huptios en konieisi kappesen ampho cheire philois hetaroisi petassas*, 'he fell backward in the dust stretching out his hands towards his companions' (X 2).

The contrast of death and fertility occurs in a line that closes catalogue killings: *pantas epassuterous pelase chthoni pouluboteirei*, 'all these he felled to the bountiful earth in rapid succession' (X 3). Perhaps a similar association informs the line *keito tatheis, ek d'haima melan rhee, deue de gaian* ('he lay at length, and the black blood flowed, and the ground was soaked with it'). The most impressive of these closing phrases transform the absence of life into a dark and threatening presence. *Ton de skotos osse kalupse,* 'darkness covered his eyes' (X 11), is the commonest version of a theme on which the poet likes to play sombre variations: *thanatos de min amphekalupse,* 'death covered him all around'; *nephele de min amphekalupse kuane ,* 'a dark cloud covered him all around'; *stugeros d' ara min skotos heilen,* 'hateful darkness took him' (X 3); *ton de kat' osse/ellabe porphureos thanatos kai moira krataie,* 'the red death and destiny the powerful took hold of both his eyes'; *amphi de min thanatos chuto thumoraistes,* 'life rending death was poured about him'; *ton de kat' ophthalmon erebenne nux ekalupse,* 'baleful night covered him from the eyes down'.

In a few cases, this possession appears as a grim exchange: *oka de thumos o 'chet' apo meleon, stugeros d' ara min skotos heilen,* 'swiftly the spirit fled from the limbs but hateful darkness took him' (X 2); and *psuche de kat' outamenen oteilen essut' epigomene, ton de skotos osse kalupse,* 'life rushed from the wound, urged on, but darkness covered his eyes'.

The collective impact of these phrases is very powerful and shapes the representation of death as a sudden and violent disaster. The frequency and elaboration of such phrases in different parts of the narrative is random. In this they differ from the unusual injuries, which are highly context-bound. It is clear, however, that the poet avoids the use of the same phrase in successive scenes. Such repetition occurs twice with relatively colourless phrases, and the arresting line *ho d'en koni isi pes n hele gaian agost i,* 'falling in the dust he clutched the earth with his hands', occurs twice within the space of thirteen lines, possibly to underscore the tit-for-tat of slaying and counter-slaying. But a survey of scenes in which warriors are killed in quick succession shows the poet at pains to achieve variation. This is most apparent in the fifty-line stretch in Book 5, where six Trojans die, each with a different closing statement:

> He fell, thunderously, and his armour clattered
> upon him
>
> (5.42)

> He dropped from the chariot, and the hateful
> darkness took hold of him.
>
> (5.47)

> He dropped forward on his face and his armour
> clattered upon him.
>
> (5.58)

> He dropped, screaming, to his knees, and death was
> a mist about him.
>
> (5.68)

> and he dropped in the dust gripping in his teeth
> the cold bronze.
>
> (5.75)

> and the red death
> and destiny the powerful took hold of both eyes.
>
> (5.82-3)

The deaths of Patroklos and Hektor are so central to the poem that the poet invents a special elaborate death formula and stresses the interrelation of the two events through its use on those two occasions only:

> He spoke, and as he spoke the end of death closed
> in upon him,
> and the soul fluttering free of his limbs went down
> into Death's house mourning her destiny, leaving
> youth and manhood behind her.
>
> (16.855-7, 22.361-3)

Of the victims in the *Iliad* only Sarpedon, Patroklos and Hektor, and to a lesser degree Asios, Pandaros and Euphorbos, play any role prior to their death. The rest appear and disappear at the moment of their death and occupy the poet's attention for the space of a few lines only. Most of these victims might as well be nameless, but in some thirty cases the poet gives a sketch of the warrior's background and history. These little necrologues, consisting typically of three or four lines, are, like the similes, a master-stroke of Iliadic art. Through them the poet not only introduces variety into his narrative, but also the collective effect of these miniatures is to create a powerful image of the suffering of war and to extend the narrator's sympathy to Trojans and Achaeans alike.

Evidently the narrative has a strong Achaean bias. Achaeans are killed rarely; even in scenes of Trojan victory, the Achaeans win most of the individual fights, and Achaeans are spared cruel and undignified injuries. Despite the premiss that without Achilles the Achaeans are at the mercy of Hektor, no Achaean fighter of rank is defeated by Hektor, who in fact loses both to Aias and to Diomedes, does not confront Agamemnon, and is even denied the glory of killing Patroklos in open combat. It would have been possible for the poet to motivate this superiority of the Achaeans in moral terms and to attribute the defeat of the Trojans to a moral failing. Herodotus, who thought of his history as in some sense a continuation of the *Iliad,* interpreted the war of the Greeks and Persians as an east-west conflict, in which voluntary submission to law triumphs over the despotism of an oriental ruler. There are traces of such a conception in the *Iliad.* When the armies first clash, the order and silence of the Achaeans are contrasted with the noisy confusion of the Trojans and their allies. Such lack of control is easily related to great wealth and to the foolish passion of Paris that caused the war. Occasionally a Trojan death is seen as the consequence and punishment of wickedness. Thus Menelaos in a speech over the fallen Peisandros sees his victory as just retribution for Trojan licence. In two other cases the sketch of the victim's background sounds a similar theme. We hear of Phereklos that he was the son of Harmonides, who built the ships for Paris' fateful expedition. Peisandros and Hippolochos are the sons of Antimachos, who took bribes from Paris and prevented the return of Helen. Agamemnon, on listening to their supplication, remembers that their father proposed to kill Menelaos and Odysseus when they were on a diplomatic mission to Troy, and he proceeds to avenge the father's disgraceful deeds on the children.

Such moralising, however, is exceptional in the *Iliad.* The necrologue characteristically ignores the division of Achaean and Trojan and deals with the death of the warrior as a human event. Thus the pro-Achaean narrative bias of the poem generates its own counterpoint: the greater the successes of the Achaeans on the battlefield, the more the Trojan victims evoke the poet's sympathy. The poem's narrative bias leads to an unequal division of the poet's impartial sympathy: only seven victims with stories are Achaeans.

The narrator's impartial pity is established early and firmly. At the end of Book 4, the Aetolian Dioreus, an Achaean ally, and the Thracian Peiros, a Trojan ally, have both been killed. The poet takes leave of this part of the battle by dwelling on the common fate that unites them in death:

> So in the dust these two lay sprawled beside one
>   another,
> lords, the one of the Thracians, the other of the
>   bronze-armoured
> Epeians; and many others beside were killed all
>   about them.
>
> (4.536-8)

The simplest necrologues add to the name of the father that of the mother and dwell on the circumstances of birth or conception. One is tempted to call the effect pastoral because it turns on the nostalgic evocation of a natural habitat from an unnatural perspective. On three occasions the mother is a *numphe neis,* a water nymph whom the father encountered while tending his flocks or herds. Here is the story of Aisepos and Pedasos and their father Boukolion (the name means 'cowherd'):

> Aisepos and Pedasos, those whom the
>   naiad
> nymph Abarbare had borne to blameless Boukolion.
> Boukolion himself was the son of haughty
>   Laomedon,
> eldest born, but his mother conceived him in
>   darkness and secrecy.
> While shepherding his flocks he lay with the
>   nymph and loved her,
> and she conceiving bore him twin boys. But now
>   Mekistios'
> son unstrung the strength of these and the limbs in
>   their glory.
>
> (6.21-8)

Similar stories are told about Satnios and Iphition. The mother of Simoeisios was human, but not unlike a water nymph she gave birth to her son on the banks of Simoeis, while following the flocks of her parents. On other occasions the poet simply states the beauty of the mother or the wealth and status of the father.

Some of the biographical detail is anecdotal in character. Skamandrios, killed by Menelaos, was a favourite of Artemis, who taught him skill in hunting,

> Yet Artemis of the showering arrows could not
>   now help him,
> no, nor the long spearcasts in which he had been
>   pre-eminent.
>
> (5.53-4)

Pedaios was the bastard son of Antenor, whose wife treated him like one of her own children to please her husband. The three Achaean victims Medon, Lykophron and Epeigeus are exiles who left their home after killing a man. This is of course the fate of Patroklos as well, and it may not be random that the three vignettes occur shortly before or during the Patrokleia. Periphetes, a victim of Hektor, is described as a better man than his father Kopreus (Dung), whom Eurystheus sent on errands to Herakles. This is one of two occasions when a necrologue refers to the body of legend outside the poem. The other and rather obscure passage refers to the father of Atymnios and Maris as the man who reared the *amaimakete chimaira,* a monster of uncertain nature. In another case, the necrologue refers to an earlier event in the Trojan war: when Agamemnon slays Isos and Antiphos we learn that on a previous occasion Achilles captured them alive and freed them for ransom.

A motif that occurs three times in Book 13 and nowhere else involves a Trojan ally who is married to or a suitor of a Trojan princess. Imbrios married a bastard daughter of Priam and returned to Priam's house when war broke out. Othryoneus wooed Kassandra, the most beautiful of Priam's daughters, and boasted that he would drive off the Achaeans in return for her hand. Alkathoös was the son-in-law of Anchises

> and had married the eldest of his daughters,
>   Hippodameia,
> dear to the hearts of her father and the lady her
>   mother
> in the great house, since she surpassed all the girls
>   of her own age
> for beauty and accomplishments and wit; for which
>   reason
> the man married her who was the best in the wide
>   Troad.
>
> (13.429-33)

It is quite common in the *Iliad* for brothers to suffer death at the hands of one warrior, and three passages in which the poet looks at brothers united in death are particularly affecting. But the most memorable of the necrologues dwell on the grief of the survivors, the parents—more specifically the father—and the wife. They echo and universalise the suffering of Andromache, Priam and Peleus, and in so doing they establish a powerful thematic link between the major and minor characters of the *Iliad.* Simoeisios, the first warrior to be singled out for a necrologue, 'did not return his parents' care for him'. If in this instance the grief of the survivors is only implicit, it is very explicit in the story of the father of Xanthos and Thoön:

but Phainops was stricken in sorrowful old age
nor could breed another son to leave among his
    possessions.
There he killed these two and took away the dear
    life from them
both, leaving to their father lamentation and
    sorrowful
affliction, since he was not to welcome them home
    from the fighting
alive still; and remoter kinsmen shared his
    possessions.

                        (5.153-8)

Harpalion followed his father to war 'and did not come home again to the land of his fathers'; indeed, the grieving father walks behind the Paphlagonians who rescue the son's body. Ilioneus, we learn, is the only son of his wealthy father; Polydoros the youngest and favourite son of Priam, who vainly tried to keep him out of battle. In the case of Sokos, the figure of the grieving parents appears in Odysseus' speech of exultation. The motif also appears in the exchange of speeches between Euphorbos and Menelaos and is confirmed in the elaborate tree simile in which the dead Euphorbos is compared to a young tree, tended carefully by a man in a lonely place and suddenly torn up by a gust of wind.

Sometimes the father is a prophet. The soothsayer Merops vainly tried to prevent his sons from joining the war. Eurydamas, on the other hand, refused (or neglected) to interpret the dreams of his sons Abas and Polyides. Euchenor faces a dilemma not unlike that of Achilles: his father tells him that he must choose between a lingering sickness at home or death in battle. He chooses the latter and, curiously enough, dies at the hands of Paris, as Achilles later will.

The grieving wife appears in the story of Protesilaos, the first Achaean warrior to die at Troy, while his wife 'cheeks torn for grief, was left behind in Phylake / and a marriage half completed'. The theme is implicit in the finest and most elaborate of all necrologues, the story of Iphidamas. Brought up by his maternal grandfather, he married his daughter and went from his wedding straight to the war, where he was killed by Agamemnon:

So Iphidamas fell there and went into the brazen
    slumber,
unhappy, who came to help his own people, and
    left his young wife
a bride, and had known no delight from her yet,
    and given much for her.
First he had given a hundred oxen, then promised a
    thousand
head of goats and sheep, which were herded for
    him in abundance.

                        (11.241-5)

The impartial sympathy that the poet shows for the fallen warrior sharply contrasts with the savage partisanship the victors display on such occasions. But the gloating speeches are similar in function to the necrologues in that they keep the fallen warrior a little longer in the limelight. The distribution of gloating speeches relates them closely to grisly injuries. Of the sixteen instances, eight are found in Books 13 and 14, three in the Patrokleia, and four in the aristeia of Achilles. Only one such speech is found outside this complex of scenes. On two other occasions, Pandaros and Paris exult prematurely at the prospect of triumph over Diomedes. But Pandaros misses his target and Paris does not inflict a fatal wound.

The gloating speeches share with the necrologues the motif of the grieving survivor, but they vary it to reflect the hostile perspective of the speaker. The triumphant warrior dedicates the corpse to animals and imagines the survivors' mourning deepened by the lack of the body to care for. The motif occurs in Achilles' speeches to Lykaon and Hektor; Odysseus' words to the body of Sokos form an unusually sombre and restrained instance of the genre:

Sokos, son of wise Hippasos the breaker of
    horses,
death was too quick for you and ran you down,
    you could not
avoid it. Wretch, since now your father and your
    honoured mother
will not be able to close your eyes in death, but
    the tearing
birds will get you, with their wings close-beating
    about you.
If I die, the brilliant Achaians will bury me in
    honour.

                        (11.450-5)

The motif of burial is absent from the speech over the body of Ilioneus in which Peneleos contrasts two sets of survivors. The whole scene is worth quoting because it shows a single slaying elaborated by a grisly wound, a necrologue, a simile (short but striking) and a gloating speech, with the different components carefully interrelated. The death of Ilioneus brings to a close the string of brutal slayings in Books 13 and 14; its elaboration is in accordance with the climactic position it occupies:

               He then stabbed with the
    spear Ilioneus
the son of Phorbas the rich in sheepflocks, whom
    beyond all men
of the Trojans Hermes loved, and gave him
    possessions.
Ilioneus was the only child his mother had borne
    him.
This man Peneleos caught underneath the brow, at
    the bases
of the eye, and pushed the eyeball out, and the
    spear went clean through
the eye-socket and tendon of the neck, so that he
    went down
backward, reaching out both hands, but Peneleos
    drawing
his sharp sword hewed at the neck in the middle,
    and so dashed downward
the head, with helm upon it, and still the spear
    point stuck

in the eye socket. He lifted the head high like a
   poppy,
displayed it to the Trojans, and spoke vaunting
   over it:
'Trojans, tell haughty Ilioneus' beloved father
and mother, from me, that they can weep for him
   in their halls, since
neither shall the wife of Promachos, Alegenor's
son, take pride of delight in her dear lord's coming,
   on that day
when we sons of the Achaians come home from
   Troy in our vessels.'

                                    (14.489-505)

On four prominent occasions the gloating speeches display coarse and savage irony. Thus Idomeneus addresses
the body of Othryoneus, the boastful suitor of Kassandra,
and offers him one of Agamemnon's daughters if he would
join the Achaeans. After Idomeneus has killed Asios,
Deïphobos kills Hypsenor in return and boasts that he has
provided him with an escort on the way to Hades. Poulydamas goes one better on this conceit and boasts that his
spear will serve his victim as a walking-stick. It is significant that the gentle Patroklos at the height of his triumph
is tempted into such language. Here he is commenting on
the fall of Kebriones from his chariot:

   See now, what a light man this is, how agile an
      acrobat.
   If only he were somewhere on the sea, where the
      fish swarm,
   he could fill the hunger of many men, by diving for
      oysters;
   he could go overboard from a boat even in rough
      weather
   the way he somersaults so light to the ground from
      his chariot
   now. So, to be sure, in Troy also they have their
      acrobats.

                                    (16.745-50)

Twice the gloating speech turns into genealogical display.
More important to the structure of the poem is the preoc-
cupation of several speeches with the theme of revenge.
This theme links the speeches of Books 13 and 14 so that
in each book they form a tight cluster. Thus, in Book 13,
Deïphobos thinks of his killing of Hypsenor as revenge
for the death of Asios, but Idomeneus retaliates by killing
Alkathoös, and referring to his victories over Othryoneus,
Asios and Alkathoös he replies: 'Deïphobos, are we then
to call this a worthy bargain, / three men killed for one?'
In Book 14, Aias kills Archelochos in return for the slaying of Prothoenor by Poulydamas, whose boast he answers thus: 'Think over this Poulydamas, and answer me
truly. / Is not this man's death against Prothoenor's a
worthwhile / exchange?' The Trojan Akamas thereupon
kills Promachos and boasts that the Trojans are not alone
in suffering pain and misery. This prompts Peneleos to kill
Ilioneus and to compare the sufferings of his parents with
those of Promachos' wife in the passage quoted above.
The chain of retribution that is thematised in these exchanges clearly points forward to the major version of the

revenge triangle in the story of Patroklos, Hektor and Achilles. The theme recurs in the speech of Automedon over the
body of Aretos, whose death he sees as retribution, however inadequate, for the death of Patroklos. For the last
time, it appears in Achilles' words to the dying Hektor:

   Hektor, surely you thought as you killed Patroklos
      you would be
   safe, and since I was far away you thought nothing
      of me,
   o fool, for an avenger was left, far greater than he
      was,
   behind him and away by the hollow ships.

                                    (22.331-4)

Speeches of exultation form an important part of the aristeia
of Achilles and culminate in the words just quoted. The
first addressee is Iphition, for no other reason than that
he is his first victim. The victim's fate is briefly sum-
marised, but then Achilles lingers over the description of
his home in a manner that recalls the rhetoric of the unreal
with which he envisaged the life in Phthia to which he,
likewise, will not return:

   Lie there, Otrynteus' son, most terrifying of all
      men.
   Here is your death, but your generation was by the
      lake waters
   of Gyge, where is the allotted land of your fathers
   by fish-swarming Hyllos and the whirling waters of
      Hermos.

                                    (20.389-92)

The other speeches occur in the encounters with Lykaon,
Asteropaios and Hektor. Of these only the Asteropaios
scene stays within the convention of minor encounters. In
both the Lykaon and Hektor scenes the speech of exultation is part of a more complex pattern.

Paolo Vivante   (essay date 1985)

SOURCE: "Homer and the Reader," in *Homer,* Yale University Press, 1985, pp. 1-18.

[*In the following essay, Vivante offers a stylistic analysis
of Homer's epic verse, in particular, his use of recurrent
images, analogies, and epithets.*]

The child's first impressions on hearing Homer are as
deep as they are vivid. The wrath of Achilles conjured up
all at once; Achilles and Agamemnon standing out in
strife against each other; Chryses suddenly appearing
before the Achaeans to ransom his daughter; Chryses
rebuffed and walking in angry prayer along the shore;
Apollo listening and descending from Olympus—such
scenes, enacted as they are moment after moment, are
naturally impressive by virtue of their own strength.

How to explain the spell they cast upon a child's mind?
How to explain it quite apart from any preliminary learn-

ing? One reason for it is precisely that no preliminary learning is required. For these scenes are self-contained and self-explanatory. What they present comes to life through a power of its own. It is indeed the suddenness of realization which makes them so forcible.

Take the wrath of Achilles, the first thing mentioned in the *Iliad.* No need for any narrative detail. His wrath is immediately singled out because it is momentous, explosive by its very nature. Is it simply an overwhelming human emotion or, rather, a divine power? No matter. So bold and forthright is its presentation that it appears as an uncontroversial and central event in its own right, rising far above the incidental occasion. We wonder, but hardly question. Even before we learn the full story, this wrath inhabits our imagination. And in this we are at one with the child. The apprehended thing is as real as the apprehending mind is malleable, receptive, elastic.

Or take the appearance of Chryses, the starting point of the action in the *Iliad* (1.12ff.):

> he came to the Achaean swift
> ships to have his daughter released / and bearing an
>   infinite ransom
> holding the crown in his hands / the crown of far-
>   shooting Apollo
> over the golden sceptre, / and to all the Achaeans
>   he so prayed

Again the power of the bold, forthright stroke. There are no preliminaries. We are told nothing about the raid, the plunder, the occasion that saw a father bereft, a daughter dragged away. All the more majestic does the old man's figure appear against the silent background—as if the burden of experience were simply understood in the compelling visual significance of a suppliant human shape.

To appreciate this presentation more fully, let us give rein to that naive capacity to visualize even while we read or listen. For we touch here on something concrete and universally appealing, a plastic form in the expression. See, in this instance, how the god's name with its epithet and the mention of the divine emblems accrue to the man's presence, composing one encompassing image. Solidly implanted, he suddenly stands before us. Solidity and suddenness blend, giving the whole scene a compact quality. Chryses is not described first and dramatized later. No, the speech that follows is like an emanation of his presence. He is all at one with his function here and now; he hardly exists apart from what he does, says, and appears to be in the present instance. How could it be otherwise? you may ask. And yet this simplicity is the rarest thing. A poetic logic expunges all extraneous details, giving us the sense of an inevitable development.

The next moment sees Chryses withdrawing, rejected by Agamemnon:

> So he spoke. Suddenly feared / the old man and
>   obeyed his word

and in silence he walked / by the shore-of-the-wide-
    roaring-sea.
Then, as he moved away, / intense was the old
    man's prayer
to Apollo the king / whom-fair-tressed-Leto-gave-
    birth-to:
"Listen, o Silver-bow". . . .

A solitary man walking along the shore absorbed in fateful prayer—a picture both simple and pregnant, such as to impress the child and give pause to the scholar. Why is this so? The reason again lies in sudden compact imagery grasped at one stroke. The sea-smitten shore conspires all at once with the presence of the man and his emotion. Even as we follow him, Chryses blends with the space which the brief and yet ample cadence of the verse summons up in the resounding name of the sea.

These initial remarks could be applied in various ways to many passages throughout the poems. What is this quality that lies at the core of Homer's art? It is the capacity to let a thing become an image the moment it is mentioned; and by "image" I mean a thing rendered so as to be strongly fixed in the field of vision, both a presence in itself and an element in the narrative sequence. In Homer, to mention is to summon up, to realize. Such an image clings to the perceptive mind of the reader or listener. It has a power of attraction; and any apposition immediately leans upon it, becomes part of it, holding in check any comment or digression.

Why is it, for instance, that Andromache is so impressive when she meets Hector in *Il.* 6.394ff.? One reason is her mere presence on the ramparts of Troy and, along with it, the way she is presented as an image:

> There the bountiful wife / came face to face running
>   to meet him
> Andromache who was daughter / of Eetion-the-
>   great-hearted
> Eetion who once lived / under mount Placus-rich-
>   wooded
> in Hypoplacian Thebes / and on the Cilicians held
>   sway;
> his own daughter it was / now wedded to Hector-
>   bronze-armed;
> Hector there did she meet, / and with her was
>   walking the handmaid
> holding the child on her bosom, / the tender child,
>   but an infant,
> Hector's son the belovéd, / like to a beautiful star.

If we were to take the text literally or as mere narrative, we would hardly have any idea of how simple the means, how strong the effect. Andromache comes running, she is suddenly there; and verse after verse, her presence acquires substance through the names and epithets of father, city, country which, weighty as they are, still seem to quiver with the initial impact of her appearance. As if by a miracle, we have fullness of form without description. Any further detail would weaken the point of focus, within whose vital range the nurse and child take their place—

no narrative addition, but extension of the same movement, as in the encompassing rhythm of a sculptural group.

Or take Priam coming to Achilles in *Il.* 24.477ff.:

> Unnoticed by them did he enter / great Priam, and
> standing close by
> he laid hold of Achilles; / clasped his knees, kissed
> his hands
> dreadful murderous hands / that had slain many of
> his sons.
> And as when deep folly / comes upon one that at
> home has taken the life of a man / and to other
> people he comes
> into a rich great house, / amazement besets those
> who see him;
> thus was Achilles amazed / at the sight of Priam-
> the-godlike
> and amazed were they all, / and at one another
> they looked.

The passage makes explicit what is everywhere implicit in the poet's art: sudden and outright visualization. Not without reason does Priam enter unseen, an immediate, amazing presence heightened by the simile. The reader's wonder thus becomes that of the bystanders who suddenly see him and gaze at one another. Surprise, contemplation, nothing portentous or spectacular; simply an old man's appearance surrounded by unfathomable silence.

We may compare a passage from the *Odyssey* 1.328ff.:

> Up from her chamber did she / in her heart catch
> the song god-inspired
> she the daughter of Icarius, / Icarius' thoughtful
> Penelope;
> and by the lofty stairs / down she came from her
> room
> not alone but together / also two handmaids came
> with her.
> Then when among the suitors / she arrived, the-
> divine-among-women,
> she stood still by the pillar / the pillar of the-
> closely-built-roof,
> over in front of her cheeks / holding up the
> glistening veil;
> and with her, there, at each side / a careful
> handmaid stood by.
> Then breaking out in tears / she spoke to the singer
> divine.

This is our first meeting with Penelope in the *Odyssey*. Again, there is no wearisome introduction: the person's identity merges with the appearance itself. She is presented on the spur of the moment, on the last note of Phemius's music, no sooner mentioned than standing before us. Whatever details are given are not descriptive but touches in her materialization; for her approach, her stance, her holding the veil are hardly things intended to satisfy our curiosity or our taste for realism. What we have here is something of a more fundamental nature. Each detail both builds up Penelope's image and advances the action.

It is as if a progressive rhythm made her more and more palpable step by step. We have, in each instance, a moment that lingers in the suspense of the verse and does not pass without leaving a vital contour. What emerges is a growing sense of form. Even the handmaids on either side of her contribute to it, like figures at the extremities of a pediment.

Compare, in the same book (lines 102ff.), Athena's appearance in Ithaca:

> She went down from Olympus / down from its
> peaks with a leap;
> she stood in Ithaca's land / right there at
> Odysseus's portals,
> upon the courtyard's threshold: / and she held a
> spear in her hand
> resembling a guest in looks, / even Mentes king of
> the Taphians.

Again, the presentation is as simple as it is powerful: no account of Athena's flight from Olympus to Ithaca, no strange epiphany as she arrives, simply the purest motion and position. The Greek verbs have a striking effect. *To go, to leap, to stand*: it is as if the goddess were an instant embodiment of these acts, as if these simple acts acquire through her a portentous substance and quality. She thus naturally appears in human form, like Mentes, as she usually does when seen with Telemachus. Homer's anthropomorphism is true to his sense of form.

The image-making process continually tends to absorb the narrative. Thus the Penelope passage quoted above occurs elsewhere; so does the verse portraying Athena's leap; and, with slight variations, the verse portraying a man walking, like Chryses, by the sea. The narrative hardly affects these image-making positions or movements; on the contrary, it is the narrative (or the ebb and flow of circumstance) which is magnetically drawn around them.

Least of all can the Homeric poems be read with a voracious interest in plot and its dénouement. It is not so much a question of reading as of rereading, absorbing, becoming attuned. The reader may even find the literal content disappointing; but what will challenge his imagination, if he is at all sensitive, is the representation itself. For sheer variety of incidents or for fantastic and mythical events, he will turn with advantage elsewhere: here, the poetry lies in a fundamental way of being, of happening.

A way of being, of happening: this is what Homer's recurring imagery is all about. Why is it that by its recurrence it does not dull our senses but, rather, never ceases to delight us? How is it that Homer's poetry, qua poetry, is hardly conceivable without it? We here come to a crux of modern scholarship, its tantalizing effort to justify Homer's so-called formulas (or repeated phrases and sentences), which it regards as a Homeric peculiarity alien to modern taste and only to be appreciated as a form of "oral" compositional technique. What lies in question here is Homer's style. We must do justice to it. We must try to see how it is, not only *not* alien to modern taste, but how it satisfies that primordial instinct for form which is common to all poetry.

The response of the common reader, or even of the child, may be of interest to the critic on this point. How often we come across people who have a vague knowledge or memory of Homer but still remember with pleasure such phrases as "swift-footed Achilles," "rose-fingered Dawn," "resounding sea," "wingéd words," "long-shadowed spear." Why? These phrases are in the themselves memorable, haunting. And yet the reader would soon forget them did they not often recur in the poems, and at significant vantage-points. For they are not mannerisms or mere figures of speech: they arrest the transient image where verse and sense allow it, lifting it above the blunting literal meaning of the surrounding passage. The realization of images is thus generalized into a typical mode of expression. Form emerges, as it were, from below—from a sense of sheer existence surfacing above the shifting relations of the narrative.

Consider the simplest designation of things. In *Il.* 3.346-47, for instance: "First did Alexander send forth the long-shadowed-spear and he struck on Menelaus' all-even-shield." Spear and shield are given in Homeric form: their recurring shape makes them at once familiar and impressive. But no less recurrent is that "sending forth" and that "striking" of metal against metal. The epithets thus give sensuous evidence and weight to the moment; and such a moment so binds the thing to its intrinsic occasion that the narrative interest wanes and we might even forget who is striking whom, seeing nothing but the actuality of the event arrested in its form.

Compare "sailing with the well-benched ship over the wine-colored sea" (*Il.* 7.88), "we came with the dark, swift ship" (*Od.* 3.61), and "They steered the ships-that-are-curved-on-both-sides" (10.91). Would not the simple verb *to sail* do as well? Why is this sailing so richly expressed? The reason is that it is not taken for granted. Wherever an opening perspective allows it, we are made to see the ship image itself, a shape against the background of the sea.

The same applies to people. Why, for instance, "swift-footed Achilles so spoke"? Why an epithet for any hero speaking, rising, standing, or moving? Again, it is a question of sudden relief. The fleeting human occasion brings the hero's image to the forefront. How effective in this connection is the epithet "swift-footed"! The very fact that it has no pointed connection to anything else makes Achilles' image clear and strong in itself and by itself, utterly absorbed into the position and stance of the moment.

The reader of Homer can easily multiply such instances. Everything in the poems flashes brightly before it passes away; and yet everything also finds its place and moment by striving toward constant outline and rhythm. Occurrences become recurrences; and, through persisting association, the things so brought into play acquire an intrinsic function, take position and form, become as symbolic

of themselves as they are true to nature. Here is a self-consistent fullness upon the strength of which anything mentioned tends to appear as an inevitable image.

For the poet's treatment is never fastidiously graphic, realistic, minute. From the tangled mass of things and their occasions what stands out is anything that has contour or resonance. Thus the forward movement of a warrior conjures up that of a lion; his fall, that of a tree cut down by the foresters. Why is it that the similes strike up analogies to the human action throughout the world of nature? Not, certainly, for mere ornament or to provide a break in tense passages. Rather, the image-making force breaks through the bounds of a passage and gathers its own force, drawing the poetry toward a sense of form and away from narrative or description.

The world is thus both simplified and enriched with life—reduced, that is to say, to vantage-grounds that are scenes of action: windy Troy no less than rocky Ithaca. And this concentration is no less true of any focal point on Homer's large canvas—no less true of a throbbing heart than it is of sea-smitten shore. Hardly anything is mentioned that is not singled out and sharply exposed insofar as it crystallizes an act or a state of being. We have at one and the same time an object and a pulse of life.

If Homer's imagery deeply affects the reader, the reason is that it is solidly implanted in the perception of nature.

—Paolo Vivante

It is no wonder, then, that Homer's image-making sentences have a haunting effect, that even the casual reader remembers them over and above the specific subject matter. It is not really a question of vivid coloring. The reason goes much deeper. We touch, rather, upon ontological grounds. To read here is to tap the imaginative source of our understanding, to carry out in the realm of art that process which we have also carried out in actual life before our perceptions were jaded into notions taken for granted. "What is that?" asks a child, pointing to a train or a waterfall; and there is a vital urge to know in the question, a vital realization in the answer. He now recognizes things. They appear to him in the fresh evidence of their existence, taking their pertinent place in the field of vision. A word becomes a discovery. Rather than a display of fluid impressions, here form arises in all its aesthetic cogency, with delight in its definition, with wonder at its significance. And the spell persists until it is lost in a hackneyed order of things learned by rote. What then? Lost forever? No. Poetry—and art in general—come to remove, as Coleridge puts it, the "film of familiarity which blinds us to the truth and wonder of the world about us."

This poetic effect is eminently Homeric. A fresh sense of life and resilience is always brought home to us by letting the image of a thing come into view on the cadence of a verse that does no more than realize in rhythm a basic movement or position. The music and the imagery blend with the vocabulary. It is as if a new poetic language came into our ken. Here the "long-shadowed spear" finds its place as well as the "wing-stretching birds" or the "robe-trailing women" or the "taper-leaved olive-tree"—each thing singled out in its individuality and yet bearing the mark of a common touch.

This delight in images is increased by their recurrences and the kindred patterns of form they cast over existence. What ultimately comes into play is a sense of recognition, a primal urge to establish identities, what metaphysicians call "the principle of individuation." For nothing is dearer to the mind than to perceive, and perceive clearly, a faculty which Homer's imagery elicits on a large scale. The interest of finding the same Homeric phrase over and over again is no idle pleasure. We look for resemblances in whatever we see. It means finding our way through the multiplicity of things.

We undergo the same process on a more elementary level when we first learn our native language: words are deeply assimilated in that they seem to conspire with the order of nature. Homer leads us to abridge and intensify this process. His imagery gives us essential contours of the things or phenomena which we actually see in the world around us; and the recurrences of his image-making phrases suggest corresponding harmonies in existence itself. For Homer avoids what is merely peculiar, something that could be remembered only so long as the interest in it remains. Nothing is here merely "interesting." The apprehension of a shape, distinctive as it is, suggests an encompassing sense of form; and this sense of form evokes kindred objects the world over. Curiosities could not be so suggestive. If Homer's imagery deeply affects the reader, the reason is that it is solidly implanted in the perception of nature.

Modern scholarship has deterred the reader from taking Homer's expression at its face value. Between the poet and nature it has interposed the thick wall of what is called tradition or "traditional poetry": formulas, themes, conventions, and techniques that are usually taken for granted.

We must encourage the frightened reader to think for himself, to appreciate Homeric poetry by appealing directly to the truth of nature. Or, conversely, we may look at nature through Homeric eyes. For the poet's meaning must be given its full force. It does not merely consist in the designation of a literal fact or a statement that can be stripped of stylistic superfluities. The wording itself is most important. It implies a whole mode of perception and expression.

Indeed many of the "formulas" are most significant in this respect, particularly those recurring verses which arrest an event in the moment of its image-making realization. For example,

Il. 1.476, etc.

When the early-born one appeared / Dawn-with-her-fingers-of-rose

spells out the moment when the slanting rays of the rising sun actually *touch* into radiance anything exposed to their light. Those fingers express contact, that rose is sensuous freshness as well as color. Do we have here a goddess or simply a natural phenomenon? Both at the same time. The image contains the sense of what is occurring. Hence the felicity of the expression.

Od. 2.388, etc.

Then did the sun sink down / and enshadowed
    were all the streets

may remind us of Virgil's *maioresque cadunt altis de montibus umbrae,* "and longer the shadows fall down from the heights of the mountains." But Homer's verse is simpler and universally applicable, rendering no picturesque effect but evoking that imponderable moment when, in any place, things lose their edge as day yields to night.

Od. 13.79, cp. 2.398, etc.

Upon him did sleep / sweet sleep on the eye-lids fall

makes the moment palpable; for we realize the truth of experience at a most sensitive point, that soft pressure which "weighs the eye-lids down" (cp. Shakespeare, *Henry IV*, part 2, 3.1.6).

Od. 4.794, 18.189

There she sank back in sleep, / and all her joints
    were set loose

conveys the actual breathing-space between waking and sleep, the sweet abandon of a woman's body (cp. *Od.* 20.57, *Il.* 23.62).

Il. 17.695-96, etc.

Long was silence upon him, / wordless; the eyes
with tears were filled, / and checked was the
    flourishing voice.

Here is no cry, no gesture, no realistic touch fitted to the particular occasion. This silence is more eloquent, more broadly significant: we all know the moment of amazement or grief that defies all words.

Il 1.201, etc.

And at once speaking out / he addressed to her
    wingéd words.

The truth of this verse is borne home to us when our words come spontaneously, prompted suddenly by the passing occasion, taking flight.

Od. 9.67-69, cp. 5.292-94, 12.313-15

A wind he stirred, the North-wind, / Zeus-
    assembler-of-clouds
with wondrous blast, / and with fog did he
    encompass the earth at once and the sea, / down
    from the sky emerged night.

Further description would weaken the meaning. We know the sudden impact of a storm: a turning-point or a single touch all at once encompassing the elements. The god thus has a poetic function, bringing the various phenomena within the compass of the same power, so that any detailed account is left out of the picture.

Il. 1.481-82, *Od.* 2.427-28

Full blew the wind, / mid-sail, and the wave
round the bows darkly-seething / sang loud, as the
ship moved on.

Wind, sail, wave, sound make one instant vital impression. A boat passing with swelling sails will ever give us such an airy, joyous sense of movement.

What do all these instances have in common? If they induce us to look at things with Homeric eyes, in what way do they summon up an image of reality?

In the first place, they do not describe in detail, they do not explain, but let the object of representation simply be what it is before it passes away. We have an outline as clear as it is swift, no arbitrary development, emphasis, no exaggeration. Further, they do not merely report a happening, they do not merely mention a thing. Whatever is said must be given its rightful cadence, its proper ground and moment. Hence no flimsiness, but a natural fullness of representation.

In other words, and to put the matter positively, what we have is concrete realization. This means that an event is seen in its actuality: the doing, the taking place, the coming to fruition are implicit in the expression, quite apart from any narrative requirement. Thus "to utter wingéd words" is not the same as "to say": the very phrase makes us feel the actual achievement of the utterance—how a word suddenly exists, how it finds its moment to fly out to the hearer. If, on the other hand, I were to say, "the occasion immediately elicited these words from his lips," I would be explaining the situation and thus would lose the gracious moment of utterance. In the same way we may appreciate such phrases as "sleep fell on the eyelids" or "the rose-fingered Dawn appeared." Though they avoid any description of sleepiness or of early morning, they are not the same as "he fell asleep" or "it was daybreak." What we always find is an immediate sense of the occurrence itself—how it materializes, how it is verified instantly at a fine point of contact.

Things find here an intrinsic function that brings them to the fore; and, by the same token, functions appear unthinkable without a thing to give them body. Hence the vitality of this imagery. The "formulas" are no more than an ultimate flagrant example of Homeric concreteness. Strip any event of all accessories, strip it of all descriptive and casual details, yet maintain a sense of its emergence in the field of vision—what remains? Nothing but simplicity and fullness of outline. So in Homer, we find the constant striving toward form: in the battle scenes, for instance, the relentless clash and clang and fall; in the animal similes, the perpetual attack, pursuit, escape.

But why is this form so forceful? Because it never degenerates into stale mannerism, because it vibrates with life.

We have here a poetic measure that pervades the language. Quite apart from any particular imagery, it is found in the simplest instances. Any act or state appears reduced to the essentials of position and movement, and yet it is filled with its own intrinsic force. We are not told, as we are in an ordinary or easy-going narrative, that a man goes or stops somewhere: no, his going is presented as if it were a movement taking a body; his standing, as if it were a body finding its moment of rest, resistance, balance. The same effect is achieved in rendering, say, a wave or a rock. A thing always blends with the significance of its concrete position to which the surrounding action gives a dramatic relevance. The resulting image seems to be produced by the movement stilled within it or by the weight that holds it where it is.

The mere fact of standing or moving thus seems to have its own solemnity, so intimately is it fused with a body. "Who is that broad strong man conspicuous among the Argives, rising above them by his head and large shoulders?" Priam asks Helen (*Il.* 3.226ff.), and she replies, "That is Ajax-the-massive-one, wall to the Achaeans; and Idomeneus, like a god in the midst of the Cretans, stands out beyond; and around him the chiefs of the Cretans are gathered." Compare Odysseus's rendering of Ithaca (*Od.* 9.21): "Ithaca-seen-from-afar do I inhabit; in it a mountain, leaf-shaking Neritos, clear to the eye; and many islands around stand out very near one another, Dulichium and Same and wooded Zacynthus." The expressions are both plain and strong. The reason lies in the sharp sense of position, the sheer wonder of a body seen standing where it is, no matter whether it is the body of an island or a person (note that the verb *naietao,* "to inhabit," applies both to people and to places: places inhabit the earth just as people inhabit places). As a result, what we might take for granted is felt in its existential value. The islands, as well as the heroes, take position, form a constellation, creating their own space and opening up an airy perspective.

In the same light consider a simile (*Il.* 5.522ff.): "They stood like clouds which Zeus sets still upon the peaks of mountains in the windless air—steadfast as long as the Northwind is asleep." Again here is a strong sense of position. It gives life to the simile. That precarious stillness imparts to such disparate things as clouds and men an instant relevance; their shapes are rendered as being at one with a point of balance or a poise in existence. The similes seem to grow out of the very way the poet looks at the world.

Image-making moments whose truth is the ultimate reason both for their literal recurrences and for the broader analogies which they persistently suggest, moments as real in themselves as they are typical of what must inevitably happen or exist—these produce a mode of expression that is embedded in Homer's style. The style itself is thus part and parcel of the Homeric imagination; for it naturally brings out basic patterns in the flux of existence and, in so doing, is at one with Homer's tendency to humanize or naturalize whatever the subject matter affords. The reader who is seeking extraordinary things will be disappointed to find Homer restrained in this respect—disappointed, for instance, at the fact that Achilles in Homer is not at all invulnerable, not at all a portentous being. How could he be when he, as inevitably as anyone else, must launch his long-shadowed spear, must nimbly ply his feet and knees, must feel his heart sway with passion, must be shown as a recumbent figure crushed with grief?

Henry Staten   (essay date 1993)

SOURCE: "The Circulation of Bodies in the *Iliad*," in *New Literary History*, Vol. 24, No. 2, Spring, 1993, pp. 339-61.

[*In the following essay, Staten examines the feud between Achilles and Agamemnon in the* Iliad *and explores the socioeconomic importance of war booty, vengeance, and mourning in the poem.*]

"Appropriations tantamount to theft and rape": that is how Luce Irigaray characterizes the economy of capitalism [in *This Sex Which is Not One*, 1985], and especially its sexual economy, whose hidden essence is the essence of the whole. Women are commodities, exchange objects whose value is defined by the relationship between men, the subjects of exchange. Thus "economic organization is homosexual," and "woman exists only as an occasion for mediation, transaction, transition, transference, between man and his fellow man, indeed between man and himself."

The first part of Irigaray's thesis, that the appropriation of women is "tantamount to theft and rape," rips no interpretive veils from the *Iliad*, a narrative that unembarrassedly represents theft and rape as the modalities of appropriation. As concerns the commodification of women, too, what could be more brutally explicit than the scene in Book 23 in which a woman designated as worth four oxen is offered as *second* prize in a wrestling contest, the winner of which is to receive a tripod? Strictly speaking of course, neither woman nor tripod is a "commodity"; we are dealing here with what Louis Gernet [in *The Anthropology of Ancient Greece*, translated by John Hanilton and Blaise Nagy, 1981] calls "the substance of a noble commerce," "premonetary signs" whose function as bearers of value is rooted in the contests of a warrior nobility and not in the idea of profit. Thus the word for goods or possessions, *ktemata*, refers primarily to "things acquired as a result of war, the games, or gift-giving. The term never gives primary emphasis to the idea of commercial gain." But precisely for this reason, we seem to see here the perspicuous protoform of appropriation and commodification that capitalism will occult.

The second part of Irigaray's thesis, on the other hand, is not given in the manifest content of the *Iliad*—but it immediately hooks onto an element of that content. "Economic organization is homosexual," Irigaray argues, and thus physical homosexual relations between men are forbidden by society *"because they openly interpret the law according to which society operates."* Here we think not only of Achilleus and Patroklos, but also of the tantalizing fact that, even though the Greeks of the classical period

already interpreted this as a homosexual relationship (for example in Plato's *Symposium*), there is not a single unarguable reference to homosexuality in the entire *Iliad*. Even when the rape of Ganymede is mentioned, as it is twice, there is no hint that he was taken for erotic purposes. It may be, as K. J. Dover concludes [in *Greek Homosexuality*, 1978] that the Homeric poems simply antedate the efflorescence of Greek homosexuality; yet it is very striking how apt to the purposes of the fifth-century homoerotic imagination the Achilleus-Patroklos relationship proved. The argument concerning the relation between Achilleus and Patroklos has recently been updated by Thomas McCary [in *Childlike Achilles: Ontogeny and Phylogeny in The Iliad*, 1982], who argues that it instances, not covert or censured, but *incipient* homosexuality, Greek homosexuality in its chrysalis stage. And in that case, we could still pursue an analysis of this relationship along Irigarayan lines, looking to decode its connection with the economic law of this society. McCary, incidentally, is apparently uninfluenced by Irigaray, and yet his interpretation of the *Iliad* reads like an application of Irigaray's thesis that women matter only as objects of men's rivalry with each other. This suggests, if not that this is the truth of the *Iliad,* at least that the convergence of critical discourses of the present moment makes such a reading inevitable.

But there is an essential aspect of economics concerning which Irigaray and McCary say nothing. Appropriation and possession imply the possibility of *loss,* and sociolibidinal economics is incomplete without an account of the economic strategies for managing loss. Perhaps worse than merely incomplete. It may be that the problem of loss is the core problem of economics, that loss is not secondary to the operations of appropriation, possession, and exchange—an accident or misfortune that derails the smooth functioning of an integral system—but rather conditions the logic of the entire system, motivates it at the most fundamental level. Certainly the *Iliad* itself thematizes the problems of loss and mourning in the most explicit way. To a considerable extent, we need only be attentive to the articulation of the economy of loss that the *Iliad* already provides.

It would be difficult to overstate the thoroughness with which the question of equitable distribution of shares permeates archaic Greek thought and vocabulary, and especially the Homeric poems. The words for destiny or fate, *moira* and *aisa,* mean "share" or "portion" and are commonly used to mean both the ultimate portion of death and also the share of meat or booty that falls to an individual as his just desserts. *Daimon* (divine power, deity) appears to be derived from *daio,* a word which means "to divide" or in the middle voice "to distribute." The communal banquet, center of Iliadic social life, is called *dais,* a word also etymologically connected with *daio,* and the Homeric formulas connected with the *dais* emphasize the equitable distribution of shares of meat.

But, as Gregory Nagy points out [in *The Best of the Achaens,* 1979], the *dais* is repeatedly in poetic tradition the site of quarrels leading to feuds. The heroes are driven by an intense desire to secure their *moira* (rightful portion) and this jealous competitiveness continually threatens to break into open violence. It is of course at the *dais* (wedding feast) of Peleus and Thetis (parents of Achilleus) that the golden apple appears that causes the dispute among the goddesses that leads to the Trojan War.

The story of the judgment of Paris does not appear in the *Iliad,* but it is directly alluded to in Book 24, and, as Karl Reinhardt showed in a famous essay ["Das Parisurteil," in his *Tradition und Geist: Gesammelte Essays Zur Dichtung,* edited by Carl Becker, 1960], it is clearly present as the immediate background of a number of scenes in the *Iliad* involving Hera and Athena. The all-consuming rage against the Trojans of the two goddesses spurned by Paris has no other explanation than the "folly of Paris / who insulted the goddesses when they came to him in his courtyard / and favored her who supplied the lust that led to disaster." Since in any case the story of the judgment perspicuously represents the same system of tensions found in the *Iliad* it is worth pausing for a moment to consider it.

Whereas in the world of the *Iliad* we might be inclined to attribute the outbreak of conflict to the contingent condition of limited resources, the story of the apple of *Eris* (Discord) points to a deeper, structural analysis. The golden apple for which the goddesses strive is not taken from anyone but freely (and maliciously) *given* by Eris. It represents a *pure principle of disequilibrium* because its only value is in the disruptive distinction it marks and which it introduces into the society of the gods. Just as in Rousseau's fable, the introduction of a comparative judgment of better and worse is the fall from idyllic harmony. Aphrodite does not incur the wrath and enmity of Athena and Hera because she comes into possession of a golden apple which they crave, but because she is marked by a distinction whose positive value entails, and partly consists in, a diminution of their own value. And once the principle of disequilibrium begins to operate, it keeps generating new disequilibria: the Trojan War ensues as a direct consequence of the judgment of Paris, and the quarrel between Agamemnon and Achilleus as a consequence of the war. In case we might be tempted to think that Aphrodite's distinction as "most beautiful" is real or grounded in a positive content, the myth informs us that it is not because of her beauty that she receives the apple but because of what she promises Paris. The decision is thus made on "political" grounds rather than on the basis of any inherent merit, and Athena and Hera know it. Again, lest it should seem that Aphrodite cheats, both Athena and Hera make ulterior promises as well; Aphrodite's action conforms to the norm. It would be difficult to frame a more explicit representation of the arbitrariness of distinction than this story; yet once the meaning of the apple has been assigned, the distinction it confers is real and powerfully operative. Hera and Athena are as relentless in their anger at this loss of *tim* (honor) as is Achilleus at his; the *Iliad* is in fact the story of two parallel angers, that of the goddesses and that of the man.

Turning now to the beginning of the *Iliad* we can begin to analyze its more complex structure in relation to the perspicuous model provided by the judgment of Paris. The object at issue here is first Agamemnon's "prize," Chryseis, and then Achilleus's prize, Briseis. Even the close similarity of the names indicates the interchangeability of

the two women in the operative system of exchange; but, unlike the apple of Eris, the women are more than purely arbitrary markers of distinction. Agamemnon describes the virtues, physical and mental, of Chryseis and declares his intention to have her in his bed; Achilleus will later tell us he loved Briseis "from the heart" and Briseis herself will inform us that plans were afoot to make her Achilleus's wedded wife. Nevertheless, they also function as conventional, if not purely arbitrary, markers of distinction. Each woman has been assigned to her respective possessor by the Achaians acting as a collective authority, as his rightful prize from the booty taken by the army. This is, however, a special category of prize, one that goes beyond the ordinary *moira* (rightful portion) of the warrior. The term for this special kind of prize is *geras,* which Benveniste defines [in *Indo-European Language and Society,* translated by Elizabeth Palmer, 1973] as an "honorific portion" which is "over and above" the ordinary *moira;* Jean Lallot in his summary of Benveniste's chapter calls it an "honorific supplementary share." Thus the *geras* is a special or "supplementary" mark of distinction; this is why Achilleus takes it as such an injury to his *tim* when he is left without this special prize. Achilleus still possesses a large share of booty from his maraudings, as he admits in Book 9 when he says that in addition to the wealth he left at home, "from here there is more gold, and red bronze, / and fair-girdled women, and grey iron I will take back; / all that was allotted to me." Yet all of this cannot balance the loss of his "honorific supplementary share": "But my prize [*geras*]: he who gave it. . . has taken it back again / outrageously."

The women are in fact involved in a structure of "supplementation" in the Derridean sense of the word. They are extra, added on to the fullness of the warrior's *moira;* and yet they leave an unfillable gap in the plenum from which they turn out to be missing. Chryseis, Agamemnon's *geras,* although she is held by Agamemnon, is held *illegitimately;* she is the daughter of the priest of Apollo and therefore cannot be held against her father's will. There is a formal or magical boundary that excludes her from the circle of Agamemnon's possessions even while he holds her captive. There is thus a structural disequilibrium built into the situation with which the *Iliad* opens: the lack that causes this disequilibrium is one which is *incapable of being filled.* If Agamemnon gives up Chryseis, he, the paramount king and therefore the most to be distinguished by *geras,* would be in the anomalous and intolerable position of being the only one of the Achaians who would have no *geras.* As Achilleus points out, all the booty has been distributed and there exists no common store from which Agamemnon could have his loss made good. From this it follows that Agamemnon must take the *geras* of one of the other heroes, and that this in turn will necessarily leave a new and once again intolerable absence of *geras* for someone else.

Briseis thus becomes the equivalent of the apple of discord, the moveable marker of distinction which leaves a yawning absence of distinction in its wake, thus throwing social relations among the competitors into disequilibrium as a consequence of the envy and rancor that the loser feels toward the winner. If such disequilibrium is not regulated in some way, the resultant violence could rupture the entire social system. This is what threatens when Achilleus contemplates killing Agamemnon, a crime which would violate the most fundamental and thus divinely sanctioned of rules.

Therefore there exists a system of conventional equivalences according to which compensation or reparation may be made for injury suffered or loss incurred and in this way the vengeful anger of the injured party may be appeased. This system gives Agamemnon a publicly acknowledged and thus face-saving way of conciliating Achilleus; when Agamemnon realizes the disastrous nature of his affront to Achilleus he offers him an *apoina* (reparation) that is considered by the other Achaians, though not by Achilleus himself, more than adequate to make up for Achilleus's previous loss.

In this system, even the most extreme sort of injury, which could easily be felt as incommensurable with any compensation, the murder of close kin, is reparable by the paying of a material equivalent, *poine* (blood money). Blood money is the last brake on vendetta, the hinge between the functioning of lawful order and the outbreak of murderous violence, as is indicated in the allegory inscribed on Achilleus's shield. Two cities are pictured on the shield, a city at peace and a city at war. But within the peaceful city itself we move from the opening description of marriage festivals to a description of a tense judicial scene in which one man refuses to accept from another *poine* for a murder; this description mediates between the scene of marriage and the immediately following scene, in the second city, of open warfare. The crucial role of blood money is also made apparent by Aias in his appeal to Achilleus in Book 9, where Aias urges Achilleus to accept Agamemnon's propitiation by giving this most extreme example of the placability of disruptive violence: "And yet a man takes from his brother's slayer / the blood price, or the price for a child who was killed, and the guilty / one, when he has largely repaid, stays still in his country, / and the injured man's heart is curbed, and his pride, and his anger / when he has taken the price." Because there are compensatory equivalences, there are limits on violence, which is to say limits on the boundless augmentation of a particular kind of affect: anger, vengeful fury.

There is no clear line between community and noncommunity with respect to the problem of vengeful fury. On one hand, the violence that unleashes vengefulness infects even the innermost core of community, the kinship group. On the other hand, even between enemies equivalences are available that make exchange possible, and these exchanges palliate the absoluteness of war, introduce some limit to the eruption of absolute violence (ransoming of prisoners, gift-exchange among enemies, ritualized duals, restoration of things stolen). These exchanges function as the medium of a kind of "conversion" of affect, its transformation from one form into another (hostility into friendliness) or its "capturing" in objective social form (hostility captured or contained in a formal relation of friendliness). Ransom, reparation, and blood money are mediations between the subjective order and the political order. The subjective wound finds its symbolic equivalent and the

stream of affect is rechannelled in a way less destructive to culture.

The operation of various sorts of limits in the war between Trojans and Achaians has in fact created up to the moment that the *Iliad* opens a condition of *stalemate*: for nine years the war has remained undecidable. The gift-exchanges between Aias and Hektor, Glaukos and Diomedes, in the early part of the poem are reminders of this earlier stage of the war in which the enemies still recognize the option of "conversion" of hostility through symbolic exchange, thus still recognize some symbolic order that encompasses both sides and keeps the enmity of war from being total. We are also repeatedly reminded that taking prisoners in battle and holding them for ransom was formerly a common practice, but, as Robert Redfield points out [in *Nature and Culture in the Iliad,* 1975] in the *Iliad* even though ransom is offered in several instances, it is always refused and not one prisoner is taken for ransom.

The *Iliad* thus marks the breakdown of the condition of stalemate/equilibrium, and this breakdown takes the form of a breakdown in the circulation of equivalences. Agamemnon will not accept *apoina* (ransom; reparation) for Chryseis; Achilleus will not accept *apoina* for Agamemnon's insult to him, and later on he will not accept *apoina* for the body of Hektor. These three refusals are the pivotal points on which the plot of the *Iliad* turns.

What is at issue in the *Iliad* is thus *an accelerating crisis of equivalence* which is at least nominally set in motion by Agamemnon's refusal to accept the ransom offered by the priest of Apollo in exchange for his daughter Chryseis.

The system of conventional equivalences is central to the system of social order. If Agamemnon had accepted the value of the proffered *apoina* as proportional to his desire for the daughter and his frustration at losing her, he could have fulfilled his obligation to respect Apollo's priest while at least publicly maintaining the honorable stance that he had received a prize that adequately supplied the lack of the one he lost. In that case order would have been maintained and no quarrel with Achilleus would have ensued. If Achilleus, in turn, had been willing to accept Agamemnon's reparation as proportional to his pain at losing Briseis and the damage to his *tim* at being publicly humiliated, he could honorably have let go his anger and rejoined the Achaian host.

The crucial point is that ransom or reparation is only worth the injury it comes to make up for if the injured party agrees that it is, and this agreement is not in the *Iliad* easy to secure. It is in the interest of the group that such equivalence should be accepted, as we see from the way the other Achaians urge Agamemnon and Achilleus in their respective cases to accept ransom or reparation (*apoina*). But the injured party finds it more difficult than those not directly involved to feel that the reparation actually does measure up to the loss.

Achilleus's complaint against Agamemnon in Book 9 wavers between his claim that he loves Briseis as his *alokhos* (wife) and his claim that she is his *geras* (prize). Her role is structurally ambivalent: she functions on the level of both social and libidinal economy. And the laws of these two economies are partly in conflict. Insofar as she is more than a mere exchange object to Achilleus, her rape opens the question of irreparable loss; that is, the question of mourning. The full force of mourning will of course befall Achilleus as a consequence of the loss of Patroklos, not Briseis, but we shall see that there is no *opposition,* no either/or, between Achilleus's love for Patroklos and his or other men's love for women—for example, Hektor's for Andromache. Rather, the former lays bare a libidinal structure that also inhabits the latter. The remainder of this essay will be a demonstration of this thesis.

To be the cause of mourning, and most specifically of the mourning of women: this is the final resonance of the satisfaction of vengeance, of the reparation vengeance offers for one's own grief.

—Henry Staten

We recognize in the motif of the loss and return of Briseis that type of circulation of a symbolic object that functions at a meta-narrative level. Once we are alerted to the level of abstraction at which the poem represents the circulation of symbolic objects, we see that it articulates a continuous problematic of exchange, loss, and symbolic reparation, a problematic whose most prominent articulations are five types of refusal of reparation. We may schematize them thus: (1) refuse ransom, kill male captive (recurring instance); (2) refuse ransom, keep female captive who is *phile* (dear, well loved) (Agamemnon and Chryseis); (3) lose female captive who is *phile,* refuse conciliatory reparation (Achilleus and Briseis); (4) lose one's *philos* (loved one, kin), refuse conciliatory reparation (pictured on shield); (5) keep body of slain captive, refuse ransom for body (Achilleus and Hektor). It should be apparent that these situations form a transformational series in which the same basic themes are variously intertwined and a single complex problematic is elaborated. The crisis of equivalence that is set in motion by Agamemnon's refusal of ransom for Chryseis is finally resolved, at least for the purposes of poetic closure, by Achilleus's acceptance of ransom for Hektor's dead body. We may reconstruct the underlying logic of this series in terms of an initial situation involving possession of an object, one that is libidinally cathected (a woman or friend); followed by the loss of this object, against the will of the possessor and without compensation; after which compensation is required, either through vengeful aggression against a substitute object that comes into one's possession (the living or dead body of the enemy), or through the option that is so hard to come by in the *Iliad,* acceptance of *apoina* as conciliating reparation.

The Homeric warriors are supposed to be motivated by the pursuit of greater and greater *time.* Yet the action of the

Iliad is set in motion by a yawning insufficiency of booty such that someone, either Agamemnon or one of the other heroes, must necessarily be left at least temporarily without his honorific portion and thus without his proper share of *time.* This means that the *time* in question at the center of the poem must come belatedly, not as the positivity of the glory that a warrior pursues, but as compensation for a loss that he has previously endured. The forms of reparation, *apoina* and *poine,* participate in the preservation or restoration of *time* as a substitute or compensatory equivalent for what is properly a prize of honor, *moira* or *geras.* But as we pursue the logic of compensation we begin to suspect that reparation may participate in the essential constitution of that *time* which it supposedly comes to repair.

In one way it seems that to kill one's enemies, and to kill them as brutally as possible, humiliating them in the process, would be the fulfillment of the warrior's vocation, that the warrior would then be most himself. This is how he gains *tim* and subsequently the *kleos* (glory) of poetic renown; and this form of *time* seems to be the true warrior honor, beyond the apportionment of tributes and women. And yet the poem also portrays this *time* as vengeful in its essence, as the last desperate expedient upon which men fall back when the system of symbolic compensation and reparation fractures and fails.

The sociosexual humiliation Achilleus suffers hurls him, at least for the moment, entirely outside the system of conventional equivalences. The absolute incommensurability between his suffering and any possible restitution or reparation: this is what he declares in the crescendo of hyperbole with which he rejects Agamemnon's *apoina*:

> Not if he gave me ten times as much, and
> twenty times over as he possesses now, not if
> more should come to him from elsewhere, or gave
> all that is brought in to Orchomenos, all that is
> brought in to Thebes of Egypt, where the
> greatest possessions lie up in the houses, Thebes
> of the hundred gates, where through each of the
> gates two hundred fighting men come forth to
> war with the horses and chariots; not if he gave
> me gifts as many as the sand or the dust is, not
> even so would Agamemnon have his way with
> my spirit until he had made good to me all this
> heartrending insolence.
>
> (9.379-87)

Achilleus rejects the "conversion" of his vengefulness by the formal process of reparation; he wants what we could call a *raw equivalation,* "pain for pain, dishonor for dishonor" as Robert Fitzgerald freely, but I think accurately, translates the last line above.

Animals of course do not seek vengeance; vengeance is not "raw" in the sense that it could exist outside the context of language and culture. The very fact that vengeance is essentially a form of compensation or equivalence means that its conception involves a mental operation of a sophisticated order. Furthermore, the enjoyment of vengeance requires an acute perception of the subjectivity of the other, a sense of the reality and intensity of the suffering he or she experiences at our hands. If nevertheless I call venge-fulness the desire for a raw equivalation it is to mark its tendency to escape and undermine the system of conven-tional equivalences established by culture. "An eye for an eye" is already an attempt to limit vengefulness by a conventional definition; the **Iliad** suggests that what the unconstrained urge seeks as compensation for suffering undergone is not the formal equivalence of objects or body parts but the feeling that the other experiences with-in his or her interiority a suffering at least equal to what the avenger has suffered. But there is no way of measur-ing or setting a limit to this subjective sensation. As long as I am in the throes of suffering over an injury done me, the sensation of grievance is unbounded. If the entire substance of my being is convulsed by pain or grief over an injury or loss, if the loss can never be undone as such, only an equally unbounded and irremediable suffering on the part of the transgressor can count as a compensatory equivalent. Such suffering is what Achilleus attempts to exact from Agamemnon, and later from the Trojans.

Vengeance is here the attempt to find an equivalent for the incommensurable, reparation for the irreparable. It is, in other words, the last measure for *staunching the flow of mourning.* Thus Euphorbos says to Menelaos:

> you must now pay the penalty
> for my brother, whom you killed, and boast that
>   you did it,
> and made his wife a widow in the depth of a
>   young bride chamber
> and left to his parents the curse of lamentation and
>   sorrow.
> Yet I might stop the mourning of these unhappy
>   people
> if I could carry back to them your head.
>
> (17.34-39)

This logic of equivalence, according to which vengeance and mourning inflicted can compensate for and assuage mourning suffered, structures the entire **Iliad,** but is most insistently and nakedly visible in a sequence near the end of Book 14. Poulydamas, having killed a Greek, Prothoënor, "vaunted terribly over him" and "sorrow [*akhos*] came over the Argives at his vaunting," stirring the vengeful anger of Aias, who kills a Trojan. Aias then shouts at Poulydamas, "Is not this man's death. . . a worthwhile exchange [*anti. . . axios*]?" In response, "sorrow [*akhos*] fastened on the Tro-jans," and the Trojan Akamas kills Promachos, at which *akhos* once more comes over the Greeks, so that Peneleos kills Ilioneus and then vaunts:

> Trojans, tell haughty Ilioneus' beloved father
> and mother, from me, that they can weep for him
>   in their halls, since
> neither shall the wife of Promachos, Alegenor's
> son, take pride of delight at her dear lord's coming.
>
> (14.501-4)

This logic is carried to its limit in Achilleus's motivation, as he seeks to assuage his grief for his losses first by humiliating Agamemnon and then by the holocaust of

vengefulness in which he engages against the Trojans: measureless reparation for his measureless pain.

We learn from Achilleus that it is *life itself* for which *time* would come to compensate if it could. Achilleus, weeping like a baby beside the sea, says to Thetis:

> Since, my mother, you bore me to be a man with
>   a short life,
> therefore Zeus of the loud thunder on Olympos
>   should grant me
> honour [*time*] at least. But now he has given me
>   not even a little.
> Now the son of Atreus, powerful Agamemnon,
> has dishonoured me [*étimesan*], since he has taken
>   away my prize and keeps it.
>
> (1.352-56)

That he is "a man with a short life"—that is what grieves Achilleus so deeply and for which he feels he is owed compensation. But it is the definition of *men in general* that they are born to a short life. Achilleus's is particularly short, but no shorter than that of many other warriors in the **Iliad,** and the perspective of the immortal gods is always there to remind us that even the longest human life is pathetically short.

But even this limited recognition of *time* as having a value that might compensate for shortness of life is withdrawn by Book 9. Agamemnon's proffered gifts are truly vast. We should compare what is normally called "countless gifts" in the **Iliad** with what Agamemnon offers; all other instances are paltry by comparison. If the size of the reparation is proportionate to the *time* bestowed, this is an extraordinary *time* indeed. And yet for Achilleus now even an *infinite* amount of such reparation would mean nothing. Achilleus is no longer thinking or feeling within the system of cultural equivalences. He feels so aggrieved, he has nursed his resentment so assiduously, that he touches his own subjectivity in a profound new way. Whereas his *time* could earlier, so long as it remained intact, still mask his sense of the fleetingness of his own life, the violation of his *time* by Agamemnon makes him feel the full surge of automourning, of grief over his own death. And now he becomes conscious of the subjective essence of his own being as *psykhe,* the elusive breath of life that is incommensurable with any *time* that booty can bring:

> "For not
> worth the value [*antaxion*] of my life [*psykhe*] are
> all the possessions they fable were won for
> Ilion". . .
>
> Of possessions
> cattle and fat sheep are things to be had for the
> lifting, and tripods can be won, and the tawny
> high heads of horses, but a man's life [*psykhe*]
> cannot come back again, it cannot be lifted nor
> captured again by force once it has crossed the
> teeth's barrier.
>
> (9.401-49)

Achilleus does not mention *time* in these lines, but within the structure of distribution of booty that these lines presuppose, the same structure within which Briseis and his other honorific portions have been bestowed, booty must be allotted by the group after it has been taken, and embodies *time*.

The *psykhe* is here pictured by analogy with precious possessions, objects that may be wrested from the possession of someone else and made one's own, circulate from one owner to another, be lost, and then regained or at least compensated for. These are the objects in terms of which the conventional system of exchange and equivalence functions. The *psykhe* does not belong to this system; it is a precious object that will not circulate; once lost it is lost forever.

In the ***Iliad,*** compensation will always fail to catch up with the anteriority of loss, which reasserts itself at the end of the series of compensations. Culture declares the commensurability of loss with compensation or reparation, but culture also generates tensions that rupture the equivalences it proclaims, that reveal some final inadequacy in them to balance the loss they come to repair. I will take advantage of the ironically double sense of the term *moira* (rightful portion; fate, death) and call the logic of this regression *moiranomics*; opposing it to the official ideology of the warrior culture, its *oikonomics,* voiced by Aias, according to which no loss is uncompensatable and everything finds its equivalent, even the loss of one who is most near and dear. This is good sense, good management; the system of exchange and substitution must reach all the way into the interior of the *oikos* (household), for only then can it properly regulate the retaliatory violence that would otherwise shake the foundations of social order (for instance, in the regicide that Achilleus almost commits). But Achilleus, far from accepting a substitute or equivalent for Briseis, refuses to accept *Briseis herself* as reparation for herself; he reacts as though her loss were absolute, as though she were dead. (This is what Aias senses when he tells Achilleus that a man accepts reparation even for a dead son.)

We now see how it is that Briseis's structural location at the intersection of inside and outside, as both prize of honor and beloved wife, opens the possibility of Achilleus's break with the official ideology—a break which also reveals the inner dynamic of that ideology, the resentful urge for vengeance that is the unrestricted form of the demand for reparation, the insatiable maw that all material forms of *time* attempt to appease. Briseis, whom Achilleus loves, is at the same time part of Achilleus's *moira,* the supplementary part, the part that both is and is not part, the part that somehow escapes and leaves an unstaunchable wound, a wound which she herself, restored, cannot staunch. As such, she breaks open the system of circulating equivalences, hurls Achilleus into an aggrieved awareness of the ironic double meaning of *moira,* of the system of moiranomics that unfolds within oikonomia: "*Moira* is the same for the man who holds back, the same if he fights hard. / We are all held in a single *time,* the brave with the weaklings. / A man dies still if he has done

nothing, as one who has done much." This aggrieved awareness will in turn lead to the loss of Patroklos, and only then will Briseis return.

What we see in the ***Iliad*** is a chain of *desires for reparation for the suffering incurred in the foregoing loss of objects of desire,* such that each of these desires for reparation substitutes for the preceding and in its turn fails of satisfaction; or more precisely, the very attempt to obtain reparation leads to the next loss that in its turn calls for compensation. The case of Achilleus shows us that the pursuit of *time* is involvement in this chain, is in fact a culturally mediated expression of *ressentiment* against the world and other people for the deprivations it and they necessarily inflict upon even the most powerful, and fundamentally for the ultimate deprivation of death. This is the bitter irony in Achilleus's words to Lykaon in Book 21 as he refuses Lykaon's plea that Achilleus take him for ransom. Once he took the Trojans for ransom "in droves," Achilleus says, but no more; now that Patroklos has died, Achilleus sees that he too must die and pursues a different kind of compensation:

> So, friend, you die also. Why all this clamour about
> it?
> Patroklus also is dead, who was better by far than
> you are.
> Do you not see what a man I am, how huge, how
> splendid
> and born of a great father, and the mother who
> bore me immortal?
> Yet even I have also my death and my strong
> destiny [*moira*].
>
>   (21.106-10)
>
>   die all an evil death, till all of you
> pay for the death of Patroklos and the slaughter of
> the Achaians.
>
>   (21.133-34)

Nature itself, in the form of the river Skamandros, revolts against the gruesome extremity of Achilleus's vengeance that chokes Skamandros's water with corpses.

But there is a most refined delectation of vengeance beyond even that of killing the enemy, one that comes from the imaginative anticipation of the helpless abjection of mourning that one inflicts upon the wife and parents of the slain enemy. *To be the cause of mourning,* and most specifically of the mourning of women: this is the final resonance of the satisfaction of vengeance, of the reparation vengeance offers for one's own grief. Of course the women are in more obvious ways the final index of triumph over the enemy; as Nestor says, each Achaian must bed a Trojan wife in vengeance for Helen. But here is how at one point Achilleus describes the vengeance he intends for Patroklos: "Now I must win excellent glory, / and drive some one of the women of Troy, or some deepgirdled / Dardanian woman, lifting up to her soft cheeks both hands / to wipe away the close bursts of tears in her lamentations." Similarly, the cruder sensibility of Diomedes expresses itself in the boast that "if one is struck by me only a little,. . . that man's wife goes with cheeks torn in lamentation." Or the women of the enemy may be made to grieve for *one's own,* even while their countrymen are slaughtered. Achilleus thus makes this promise to the dead Patroklos:

> Before your shining pyre I shall behead twelve glorious
> children of the Trojans, for my anger over your slaying.
> Until then, you shall lie where you are in front of my armed ships
> and beside you women of Troy and deed-girdled Dardanian women
> shall sorrow for you night and day and shed tears for you.
>
> (18.336-40)

Foremost among these women is his prize of honor, Briseis, who, now at last restored to Achilleus, leads the mourning for Achilleus's greatest loss. The theft and rape of women by those two comrades comes in the end to this, that they might have a mourning chorus.

Achilleus weeps, and makes women weep, for himself and for his loss. To wreak vengeance means, finally, to be the cause of mourning, to transform the passive affect of grief into the active, compensatory pleasure of inflicting grief upon others and, most conclusively, upon the women. But grief tends to become generalized, for vengefully inflicted grief is no more than the reflection of the avenger's own. In the end, victim and avenger weep together, as Priam and Achilleus will do.

Beyond conventional equivalence, there is vengeance; but a man cannot avenge himself for the loss of his own life. He can, however, avenge the loss of his *philos* (one who is near and dear), and if the *philos* is a mirror of his own mortality, as Patroklos is of Achilleus's, then vengeance for the *philos*'s death would be a sort of vengeance for his own; and mourning for the *philos* would be mourning for himself. Gregory Nagy has shown how deeply woven into the language and traditional material of the *Iliad* is the theme of mourning. Even the name *Achilleus* appears to be derived from the word *akhos,* or "grief"; and Nagy offers a fascinating argument that Achilleus's epic glory in the *Iliad* is an extension into poetry of the institution of lamentation for him as represented in his hero-cult.

Nagy builds on Johannes Kakridis's demonstration [in *Homeric Researches,* 1949] that even though Achilleus's death and burial are not represented in the *Iliad,* in Book 18 where Thetis and the Nereids mourn the living Achilleus "Homer used as a model an older epic description of the prothesis of Achilles and his funeral." The existence of this model is known to us from references in the cyclic *Aethiopis* and the second Nekyia of the *Odyssey.* Kakridis points out that in the established form of the mourning ritual as we see it in the case of Patroklos and Hektor, one woman, the nearest kin to the dead man, leads the lamentation and a chorus wails in response. In Hektor's case,

his wife Andromache begins the *goos* (death-lament), which is then taken up in turn by his mother and his sister-in-law Helen. In the Greek camp, however, there are no kinswomen; "but custom exacts that [Patroklos] shall be mourned by women, and the place of his kinswoman is taken by Briseis and the other captive women." Similarly, Thetis begins the *goos* for Achilleus in Book 18 while her sister Nereids play the chorus to her lament. And when Thetis after the death of Patroklos takes the head of grief-struck Achilleus in her hands, she reproduces what Kakridis identifies as a ritual gesture of mourning. (This gesture is reproduced by Andromache and Hekuba with the corpse of Hektor and by Achilleus with that of Patroklos.) Kakridis thus demonstrates that although it is Patroklos who has died, it is Achilleus who is mourned.

But, as Nagy argues, "the Iliadic tradition requires Achilles to prefigure his dead self by staying alive, and the real ritual of a real funeral is reserved by the narrative for his surrogate Patroklos"; "the death of Patroklos is a function of his being the *therápon* of Achilles: this word *therápon* is a prehistoric Greek borrowing from the Anatolian languages". . . where it had meant 'ritual substitute'."

Patroklos is most intimate, most *philos* to Achilleus; he belongs to the inmost interiority of Achilleus's circle of propriety. They sleep in the same tent, and Achilleus had hoped that one day, when Achilleus was dead, Patroklos would take Achilleus's son Pyrrhos back to Phthia to see the domains of his father. When Achilleus retires to privacy from the forum where warriors appear for each other in order to win *time,* he retires in the company of Patroklos. *Time* is the modality of the manifestation of a warrior's selfhood before the group to which he belongs; the reality of *time* is public appearance, the self invested in its *time* is a self as seen by the group. It is of the essence of the giving of honorific shares, *moira* and *geras,* that these are public rituals; these are not possessions with an independent value that could be enjoyed in private, like the miser's gold. So, too, the loss of *geras* is feared as a public humiliation.

When Achilleus refuses Agamemnon's offer of reparation he is attempting to step outside the system of social valuations that makes his *time* a dependent and relative variable. In the end, of course, Achilleus is drawn back little by little into the matrix of social valuations, first by the appeals of Phoinix and Aias, then by that of Patroklos, but even then he is not fully reconciled to the sphere of mutuality. If the self is dependent upon its reflection in the eyes of others, he wishes at least that he could retreat to the *minimal sphere* of self-reflection. There is a very strong evocation of the exclusiveness of the dual relation between Achilleus and Patroklos, their tendency to form a dyad independent of the rest of the Achaians. Patroklos's ghost recalls that in life the two of them would "sit apart from our other / beloved companions and make our plans." And in a striking image, Achilleus expresses to Patroklos as Patroklos goes forth to battle the apocalyptic wish that "not one of all the Trojans could escape destruction, not one / of the Argives, but you and I could emerge from the slaughter / so that we two alone could break Troy's hallowed coronal." And Achilleus intends that he and Patroklos should be buried in the same grave mound. There must be *at least* one other human being who reflects his glory back to him; but ideally there should be *only* one other, and this one should be as close as possible to Achilleus himself, differed from him only far enough to provide his reflection. Achilleus would then be an autonomous totality, or as nearly so as a being can be who must split himself in two in order to feel himself as himself. In the immediate proximity to each other of these two *philoi* who are one self differed, there would be no opening for such woundings of the self-substance as even Achilleus cannot fend off so long as he subjects himself to the system of public valuations. Achilleus's *time* would circulate in a closed circuit between himself and the one who remains most proximate to him.

But precisely in proportion as Patroklos is *philos* to Achilleus, Achilleus is exposed to the possibility of another kind of loss, one more profound than the loss of prizes or honor, but which reveals the hidden essence of what those losses partly express and partly occult.

Mourning in the ***Iliad*** is represented as a structure of self-reflection in which the death of the other arouses auto-mourning in the onlooker. The mimetic stimulation of mourning culminates in the reconciliation scene between Priam and Achilleus in Book 24. "Take pity upon me / remembering your father," says Priam to Achilleus, and Achilleus sees in Priam's grief for dead Hektor the grief of Peleus for Achilleus's own expected death. Achilleus imagines his father weeping inconsolable tears for him, then weeps for his poor father weeping for him and in this way affects himself with the pathos of his own disappearance. Achilleus's grief for his own death thus arises here in a double reflection as he sees Peleus's grief reflected in Priam's and then in the mirror of Peleus's mirrored grief finds the magnified representation of his own grief for himself.

There is an earlier suggestion of the structure of self-reflection involved in Achilleus's spectation of Peleus's grief in Book 19, when Achilleus remarks that nothing could be worse suffering for him than the death of Patroklos, not even the death of Peleus, "who now, I think, in Phthia somewhere lets fall a soft tear / for bereavement of such a son, for me." Here Achilleus imagines the greatness of his father's bereavement as a function of his own greatness, the greatness of "such a son," and touches himself with the immensity of the pathos of his own disappearance through the greatness of bereavement that he imagines on the part of his father.

And now we see that this same movement of automourning shapes the otherwise apparently somewhat incoherent farewell of Hektor to Andromache in Book 6. After Hektor says that it is her pain to come that troubles him above all, when she is led away captive and becomes the servant of some Greek, he continues:

> and some day seeing you shedding tears a man will
>   say of you:
> "This is the wife of Hektor, who was ever the

bravest fighter
of the Trojans, breaker of horses, in the days when
    they fought about Ilion."
So will one speak of you; and for you it will be a
    fresh grief
to *be widowed of such a man* who could fight off
    the day of your slavery.
But may I be dead and the piled earth hide me
    under before I
hear you crying and know by this that they drag
    you captive.

> (6.459-65; italics added)

The apparent incoherence in Hektor's words is this: that Hektor is the stay of Ilium, the one upon whom it depends to keep the Trojan women from captivity, and that, *ex hypothesi,* if Andromache is made captive, Hektor will be dead. But in a moment of profound feeling Hektor projects himself as witness of a widowed Andromache who weeps for him dead, with a grief which he imagines in the shape most fulfilling to the desire to be mourned, a grief that springs always anew across the passage of time, at the reminder of what a man it was whom she has lost: "and for you it will be a fresh grief, / to be widowed of such a man." Of course this grief of the beloved is unbearable to contemplate, even though it has been contemplated, in the most vivid detail, and *must* be contemplated, because it would be even more unbearable to think that his death would inflict no indelible wound of loss, that the loss might quickly begin to heal. Hektor imagines the first unbearability and then flees from it: "may I be dead". . . before."

Hektor's words precisely anticipate Achilleus's fantasy of his father's grief: "To be widowed of such a man": *khetei toioud' andros;* "bereaved of such a son": *khetei toioud' huios.* Each imagines a scene from which he is missing and the pathos of this self-lack, and each imagines it in the same terms. The sense of the "such a —" is fully unfolded in Hektor's speech: the occasion of renewal of Andromache's grief is the speech, apparently imagined as overheard by her, that names Hektor's greatness as bravest or best of the Trojans (*hos aristeueske*) in battle. Hektor imagines, in other words, his *kleos* (fame, report of his glory) and his captive wife as memorials of this fame (not, as McCary suggests, of his shame), a fame parallel to that of Achilleus, who, as Nagy has shown, is consistently named by the ***Iliad*** as best (*aristos*) of the Achaeans. Again consistently with Nagy's studies, Hektor's *kleos* arouses unforgettable grief in the wife who will have lost him; but Hektor describes his own *kleos* precisely in order to imagine most vividly Andromache's grief over the loss of him, her grief as the ultimate resonance of his pathos of self-loss, a resonance that gives full affective value to the thought of this *kleos* which is the sonorous trace of his absent being (*kleos* comes from root *kluó:* "hear, hearken").

The economy of Hektor's self-affection here is thus not far from that of Achilleus's association of his desire to win "some excellent *kleos*" with the aim of making "some one of the women of Troy. . . to wipe away the close bursts of tears in her lamentations." Mourning as vengefully inflicted, mourning as unbearable and most necessary tribute from the beloved: there is no absolute boundary between the two. Hence the specific form of Achilleus's anger in Book 1. His wish as he withdraws is that his absence will wring the tribute of grief from the hearts of his *philoi*:

> some day longing for Achilleus will come [*pothe hixetai*] to the sons of the Achaians,
> all of them. Then although you be stricken with grief [*akhnumenos per*], you will be able
> to do nothing. . .
> And then you will eat out the heart within you
> in sorrow [*thumon amuseis khoomenos*], that you gave no *time* [*ouden etisas*] to the best of the Achaians.

(1.240-45; translation slightly modified)

The aesthetic representation of someone else's mourning is capable of stimulating the affect of mourning in the audience because mourning "itself" is already spectatorial and specular. This means that the separation between the affect of epic and that of cult is not as clear as Nagy suggests. Nagy writes that "the death of Achilles may have been unsuitable for the *kleos* of the Iliadic tradition partly *because the audience itself was involved* in his death. . . . The death of Achilles would be an *akhos* [grief]. . . to the community at large, in cult." But everything about the *Iliad* is constructed precisely in such a way that it involves the spectator in the scene of mourning it constitutes, to remind him/her that mourning always flows in an unbroken circuit between other and self. And Nagy himself actually blurs his own distinction between *kleos* and cult when he argues that Achilleus's epic is an "extension of the lamentation sung by the Muses over the hero's death."

Kleos (glory) is supposed to be the warrior's ultimate consolation or compensation for the *akhos* or *penthos* (grief) of his mortality. Nagy has argued that the concept of *kleos* has in fact an essential connection with poetry, that "*kleos* was the formal word which the Singer himself (*aoidos*) used to designate the songs which he sang in praise of the gods and men." But if Achilleus's own song, the *Iliad,* is an extension of the *threnos* of lamentation over his death, then if Achilleus could hear his own *kleos* sung it would bring him to tears. Something like this actually happens in the *Odyssey,* where Odysseus hears the singer Demodokos singing Odysseus's own *kleos,* and is overcome with grief; "we see from the evidence of epic itself," Nagy concludes, "that the *kleos* heard by its audience may be *akhos/penthos* for those involved in the actions it describes." Odysseus's grief is for his sufferings and those of his companions rather than for his own death; the genius of the *Iliad* is in the way it can, by means of the figure of Patroklos, represent Achilleus mourning his own death while he yet outlives it.

But in the *Iliad* mourners are predominantly, overwhelmingly, female. Aged fathers are prominent, too, among the mourners, but when we come to the great, concluding ritual scenes of mourning it is the women who take center stage—at least in two of these three scenes. First, Thetis

and the Nereids mourn Achilleus. Last, Andromache, Hekuba, and Helen mourn Hektor. In between, Achilleus mourns Patroklos. The place of the chief mourner is marked in each scene by the same gesture: Thetis holds Achilleus's head; Andromache holds Hektor's head; Achilleus holds Patroklos's head. As Plato disapprovingly recognized, Achilleus as mourner occupies a structural slot that is marked as a woman's. Mourning belongs preeminently to women, and a man when he mourns ceases to be a man. This is what Achilleus says to Patroklos at the beginning of Book 16, when Patroklos is overcome by grief at the sufferings of the Achaians. Achilleus tells him that he is "crying like some poor little girl" who wants to be comforted by her mother. But it is Achilleus who cries out to be comforted by his mother in Book 1, when it is himself he mourns, and whose cries bring her pityingly to him once again in Book 18 after the death of Patroklos.

Deeply inscribed in the tradition of epic poetry, Nagy shows, is the antithesis between deathless *kleos* and unforgettable woe; the former belongs to the triumphant, the latter to the losers. And yet *kleos* and grief turn out in the hands of the *Iliad* poet(s) to be intimately interwoven. How could it be otherwise once Achilleus must die young in order to gain his *kleos*? *Kleos* is *time* in the mode of *tele, time* at a distance, *tele-time*; in its essence it implies the absence of the one celebrated. Achilleus rejoices when he sings the *klea* of the other heroes but would have to weep if he heard his own. *Kleos* is structured according to the logic of moiranomics. On one hand, moiranomics is the logic of heroic masculinity as something that secures for itself an ever-expanding share of *time* and ultimately of *kleos.* But it is also the logic of reparation that is ultimately ineffectual for a loss that is always anterior and that reasserts itself at the end of the series of reparations. Thus it is a logic that will sooner or later feminize the hero, render him as powerless and grief-stricken as a bereaved mother or wife, and reduce him to tears in the face of his own death through the mirror of the death of those he loves, or of their grief for his.

Maria C. Pantelia   (essay date 1993)

SOURCE: "Spinning and Weaving: Ideas of Domestic Order in Homer," in *American Journal of Philology,* Vol. 114, No. 4, Summer, 1993, pp. 493-501.

[*In the following essay, Pantelia determines the function of spinning and weaving for different female characters in the* Iliad *and the* Odyssey.]

Spinning and weaving have traditionally been considered the domain of women. All evidence suggests that in antiquity the working of wool and the production of garments were primary occupations of women, who, regardless of their social status—be they slaves or queens—contributed through their handiwork to the self-sufficiency of their own households. In the Homeric poems all women, including queens and goddesses, are either specifically described or said to be involved in the spinning of wool or the creation of cloth on their looms. Their work symbolizes the normal order of life, in which women take care of their households while men defend the city.

Although modern scholarship has appropriately recognized the symbolic or metaphorical function of weaving in literature and in the Homeric poems in particular, no distinction has yet been made between weaving and spinning. Traditionally, spinning has been viewed either as another occupation of women or simply as part of the process of weaving. Despite their obvious connection—both spinning and weaving were performed by women and in a sequence, since weaving depends on the prior production of thread—the two activities do indeed represent different processes of creation. The ancient loom stood upright, and weavers walked to and fro, passing their bobbins through the threads of the warp. It is obvious that this kind of work required a certain amount of physical energy, which probably made weaving an occupation more suitable for younger women. Since looms were situated in the inner palace, weavers could isolate themselves and perform their art away from the public eye. On the other hand, the spinning of wool could easily be done by all women, regardless of age. Since it was portable and could be performed in a standing or a sitting position, it gave the spinner the flexibility to move around, and possibly engage in other tasks, such as the supervision of servants, in the case of queens. Furthermore, the art of weaving produces a fabric which often bears a design and has the potential for conveying a concrete message. In contrast, spinning produces only the thread, that is, the raw material which makes weaving possible and, most importantly, allows the weaver to speak and express herself through the specific artifact she produces on her loom.

My purpose here is to examine the various descriptions of weaving and spinning in Homer, in an effort to show that the poet exploits the differences between the two activities and uses them consistently, as he develops the individual portraits of his female characters.

There are twenty-two passages in Homer in which references to work at the loom occur, but only five female characters are actually depicted as weaving. Homer also uses the verb *hyphainein* metaphorically in several other passages to describe the intellectual process by which men "weave" words or wiles. Spinning is mentioned in several passages either as a separate activity or in conjunction with weaving, although only two women, Helen and Arete in the *Odyssey,* are actually presented as spinning wool. But let us begin with a brief discussion of the actual scenes where either spinning or weaving occur.

Helen's work at the loom in *Iliad* 3.125-28 marks her first appearance in literature and is, without doubt, the best known and most studied scene of weaving in Homer. When Iris comes to summon Helen to the Wall to witness the decisive duel between Menelaus and Paris, Helen is weaving "a great, double-folded purple web" on which she depicts scenes of the Trojans and the Achaeans fight-

ing for her sake. In the context of the *Iliad,* where her marital status and social identity are ambivalent, Helen finds relief and escape from her sad reality by depicting on her loom images which actually record history as she herself sees it. Men like Achilles find consolation in singing of the *klea andron.* Helen, as a woman, acquires a voice and identity, it may be argued, only through the creativity of her weaving. Like an epic poet who preserves through his song the glorious deeds of his heroes, Helen weaves on her loom the story of the war. Her web fulfills her need to overcome death by producing an artifact which will survive and "tell *her* story," her *kleos,* to all future generations.

Andromache's condition in the *Iliad* is in many ways similar to Helen's. Both women face an uncertain future and express themselves through the images they depict on their webs. Both are shown in the inner palace weaving purple double-folded robes. Andromache's web, however, is not *megas.* It may be artistically elaborate (*throna poikil'*) but it does not have the kind of social significance that the poet has bestowed upon the web of Helen. The subject matter of Andromache's web, although it is not specifically described, reflects her view of the world, for Andromache, unlike Helen, does not have a broader vision and purpose in life. Her role in her society and in the poem can only be defined in terms of her relationship with Hector. Consequently, her weaving does not have a social significance comparable to Helen's recording of history. It reflects merely the traditional idea of familial order which is based on the balance between two separate but nevertheless interdependent spheres, those of female domesticity and male politics, Andromache's loom acquires its function through this opposition. Once the balance is lost, the loom can no longer serve its intended purpose. Andromache's weaving, simultaneous with Hector's defense of Troy, expresses her hope that if she takes care of *her* duties, Hector's political and military success will also continue. As long as the war continues, Andromache's domestic and marital stability is being threatened. It is therefore significant that the poet pictures her weaving while she is waiting for Hector and, more importantly, at the very moment when she receives the news of his death. Without Hector, Andromache passes from a state of insecurity into a state of complete and irretrievable loss of identity. At that moment, symbolized by the dropping of her shuttle, the function of the loom, both actual and symbolic, comes to its end.

Andromache's role in the poem ends essentially with the death of Hector, but Helen's presence continues far beyond the end of the *Iliad.* It can be no coincidence that when we see Helen again in the *Odyssey* she is no longer weaving, but spinning wool with her golden spindle. In the postwar setting of the *Odyssey* Helen does not have to worry about her present or future status, since her identity as wife of Menelaus and queen of Sparta has been reestablished and a place for Menelaus and her in the Elysian Fields is assured. Secure in this position, Helen is now capable of benefiting others by redirecting her creativity towards other human beings. Instead of weaving, she now spins the thread which will empower other women, less fortunate than herself, to weave their stories and, in this way, to cope with their particular condition. Helen's new status is further symbolically epitomized in her gift of a robe to Telemachus, a robe which she had woven in times of uncertainty and will help preserve her *memory*. Penelope will keep it as a wedding gift for Telemachus. With this gift Helen offers Penelope some hope for the future, since this artifact is reminiscent not only of Helen's past, but also of the happy ending of her story and her return to her previous royal and divine status.

Penelope herself is also characterized through her weaving. In fact, she proves that she is Odysseus' worthy wife when she deceives the suitors by turning her actual weaving of Laertes' shroud into "a wile." In this case, the web becomes not only a symbol of the female sphere of influence and the traditional idea of familial order that Penelope seems to accept and represent in the poem, but also the very weapon which she uses in order to protect and maintain this kind of order by deceiving those who threaten it. It is significant that the design on Penelope's web is not described. Since her future with Odysseus has not yet been determined and will not be determined until Odysseus returns home, the subject matter of her weaving cannot take a specific shape. On the other hand, the purpose of her weaving is clear and indicative of her concern for the traditional social and familial order. Penelope's weaving of a shroud for Odysseus' father reflects her commitment to her husband's family and symbolizes her loyalty to the patrilinear order which she is determined to protect. However, when the "mature" Telemachus returns from his journey, ready to assume his responsibilities, Penelope is described as "spinning fine thread on her distaff." Shortly after that, Odysseus himself orders Penelope's maids to help their queen with her spinning, not her weaving. The poet seems to suggest by this that with Odysseus' return, Penelope—although she does not yet know it—no longer needs to worry about the preservation of order at Ithaca. The replacement of her weaving with spinning symbolizes the renewal of her marital stability and the transfer of power and responsibility from her hands back to Odysseus'.

The looms of Helen, Andromache, and Penelope are further connected through images of death and *kleos*. Penelope weaves a funerary cloth in an effort to maintain order and also to preserve Odysseus' position and fame. Andromache, who works into her loom images of life when she receives the news of Hector's death, imagines that the clothes she and other women have woven in the palace will be used at Hector's funeral, in his honor (*kleos*, 22.514). Interestingly enough, the robes used at Hector's funeral are described as "purple," like the web that Andromache had been weaving. As for Helen, her web depicts the struggles and death of the Greeks and the Trojans in order to make sure that the memory of the heroes and, therefore, their *kleos* will survive their deaths.

The production of textiles is not limited to mortal women. Circe and Calypso are also shown as weaving in **Odyssey** 5.61-62 and 10.220-23. The images the two goddesses depict on their webs are not described, except that Circe's web is said to be "delicate, exquisite, and dazzling." The fact that both goddesses are described as working at their looms when they are first introduced in the poem must have some significance. Calypso is weaving when Hermes tells her that she must let Odysseus go; Circe is weaving when Odysseus and his men arrive at her island. Although it may be said that gods do not necessarily experience human pain and anxieties, at least in the same way which mortals do, it is also clear that even goddesses like Circe and Calypso are not different from other female characters in the patriarchal setting of the Homeric poems. Their identity is defined and validated only through their relationships with male companions. Like their human counterparts, Circe and Calypso feel that their lives are incomplete without the presence of a man in their world (Odysseus in this case), a man whom ironically neither will be able to keep. In this sense, they use the creativity of their weaving to escape temporarily from their domestic instability. Their hopes and emotions are expressed through the images which they depict on their looms. But unlike mortal women, for whom the loom functions in part as a substitute for expression, Circe and Calypso are able to sing; in fact they are the only female characters in Homer who appear singing while they weave. Their singing points to and reinforces the connection between epic poetry and immortality. Just as the epic bard has the ability to confer immortality upon the subjects of his poetry by preserving them in the memory of future generations, goddesses like Circe and Calypso can also sing and promise their "hero" immortality. In this way, Circe and Calypso differ from Homer's mortal female characters. Through their weaving, however, they join all other Homeric women in their painful search for domestic harmony and order.

All five scenes mentioned above take place in situations characterized by a lack of domestic stability. Helen weaves while a war is being fought for her sake and is interrupted at the moment when her future is apparently about to be determined by the duel between her two husbands. Andromache weaves while Hector is fighting, and her work is interrupted by the news of his death. Penelope weaves Laertes' shroud and unravels it at night in order to maintain her domestic stability. Calypso weaves at the very moment when Hermes' arrival shatters her hope that Odysseus will stay with her forever. And Circe weaves when Odysseus first comes to her house. Like Calypso, she will fail to entice him to stay with her. Regardless of the differences we see in the purpose, the subject matter of the web, or even the character of the weaver, there is no doubt that all five women, mortal or immortal, see their weaving as an escape from a state of domestic disorder. Unable to speak or act with consequence, they seek refuge in the most private part of their homes, where they reproduce on their looms literally and symbolically the images of their hopes. In contrast, the women who finally achieve domestic stability in the **Odyssey**—Helen at Sparta as Menelaus' wife and queen, and Penelope in Ithaca after Odysseus' return—cease their weaving and are depicted as spinning once the circumstances around them have changed.

Besides Helen and Penelope, another powerful woman, Arete, is described as sitting beside the hearth, turning her "sea-purple yarn" on her distaff. Arete possesses unusual power and intelligence; she is honored and respected both by her people and by Alcinoos "as no other woman." It is quite apparent that Arete has never experienced any fear of disruption of either her political or her domestic stability. Alcinoos indeed relies on her intelligence and allows her to play an important role in her society by resolving disputes among the Phaeacians. Most importantly, as Nausicaa warns Odysseus at least twice, it is Arete's favor he has to win in order to receive help from the royal family. There is no doubt that the queen of Phaeacia deserves a place in the list of female Homeric characters such as Circe, Calypso, Helen, and Penelope, who, in Helene Foley's words, have "the special power to stop or transcend change in the sphere under their control."

Arete, Helen, and Penelope possess an understanding of life that other Homeric characters never achieve. Their power comes from their intelligence and their ability to see the true meaning of events. In the *Iliad* Helen understands the social role of history and the need to preserve present events for future generations. In the *Odyssey* she is able to recognize Telemachus, although she has never seen him before, and to relieve men's pain with her drugs. Penelope uses her intelligence, literally weaves her wiles, to protect her family order. Last but not least, Arete uses her excellent mind to assist her husband in maintaining social order in Phaeacia. Interestingly enough, these three women are not only the most powerful mortal female characters in Homer but also the only women associated with spinning. Arete is never shown weaving, and it is obvious that she has enjoyed a status of power and security since her marriage to Alcinoos. Helen and Penelope cease their weaving as soon as all threats to their domestic harmony have disappeared.

The life-giving or life-preserving function of thread is a well-known mythological theme. We know, for example, that the Fates spin the thread of man's life, and that Theseus finds his way out of the Minoan Labyrinth by using Ariadne's thread. The theme of the all-powerful woman/goddess who spins and helps the "hero" can be seen in other mythologies. The Navaho myth of the Two Warriors, in which the Spider Woman advises and protects the Twin Warriors with her magic charms, provides an interesting parallel. It could, therefore, be suggested that spinning and weaving carry different symbolic functions in the Homeric poems. More specifically, they signify the particular status of a female character. Women who feel uncertain about their future or identity, especially in regard to their marriage, use the creativity of their weaving as an escape from reality or as the means through which their identity will be preserved beyond the physical limitations of their mortal existence. On the other hand, women like Arete, Helen, and Penelope, especially in the later and established stages of their lives, do not have the need for such expression. Their identity and future have been determined. From a position of power and security, they are able to redirect their energies towards others by producing the thread, that is, the material other women may use in order to "weave" their own lives.

FURTHER READING

Bibliography

Combellack, F. M. "Contemporary Homeric Scholarship: Sound or Fury?" *The Classical Weekly* 49, Nos. 2, 3, and 4 (October 24; November 14; November 28, 1955): 17-26, 29-44, 45-55.

> Surveys Homeric scholarship up to 1955, examining the state of studies on such topics as orality, archeology, literary merit, sources transmission, and editions of the poems.

Criticism

Adkins, Arthur W. H. "Homer: Free Will and Compulsion." In *Merit and Responsibility: A Study in Greek Values*, pp. 10-29. Oxford: Oxford University Press, 1960.

> Examines the influence of the gods and of fate over the actions of the characters in Homer's epics.

Adorno, T. W. "Odysseus, or Mythos and Enlightenment." In *Homer: The "Odyssey,"* translated and edited by Albert Cook, pp. 428-36. New York: W. W. Norton and Company, 1974.

> Views the *Odyssey* as a struggle between fact and fantasy with the clever hero, Odysseus, striving for knowledge.

Allen, Thomas W. *Homer: The Origins and the Transmission.* London: Oxford University Press, 1924, 357 p.

> Overview of the origins, evolution, and transmission of Homeric poetry.

Bassett, Samuel Eliot. *The Poetry of Homer.* Berkeley: University of California Press, 1938, 273 p.

> Determines the importance of Homer's epics to Western literature and the effect of oral poetry upon an audience and analyzes the poetic devices employed in the *Iliad* and the *Odyssey*.

Bespaloff, Rachel. "The Comedy of the Gods." In *On the "Iliad,"* translated by Mary McCarthy, pp. 71-9. Washington, D. C.: Pantheon Books, 1947.

> Explores the comic irresponsibility of the gods in the *Iliad*, including their quarrels among themselves and their familiarity with human beings.

Burkert, Walter. "Homer's Anthropomorphism: Narrative and Ritual." In *New Perspectives in Early Greek Art*, edited by Diana Buitron-Oliver, pp. 81-91. Washington, D. C.: National Gallery of Art, 1991.

> Attempts to answer the questions: "Why are the gods of Homer so human, and why are the Greeks from an early date both so impressed by and so critical of them?"

Butler, Samuel. "The Humour of Homer." In *The Humour of Homer and Other Essays*, edited by R. A. Streatfeild, pp. 59-98. New York: Mitchell Kennerley, 1914.

Discusses Homer's comical treatment of gods and humans and argues that the *Iliad* and the *Odyssey* were composed by different people.

Camps, W. A. *An Introduction to Homer*. New York: Oxford University Press, 1980, 108 p.
    An overview of the poem which includes sections on historical background, characterization, performance, translation, and style.

Carpenter, Rhys. *Folktale, Fiction and Saga in the Homeric Epics*. Berkeley: University of California Press, 1946, 198 p.
    Analyzes the preponderance of fiction versus fact in oral epic poetry such as the *Iliad* and the *Odyssey*.

Coffey, Michael. "The Function of the Homeric Simile." *American Journal of Philology* 78, No. 2 (1957): 113-32.
    Provides a detailed analysis of the simile and its application in the two epics.

De Jong, Irene J. F. "The Subjective Style in Odysseus' Wanderings." *Classical Quarterly* 42, No. 1 (1992): 1-11.
    Contends that while the primary narrator of the *Odyssey* is objective in tone, the secondary narrator—Odysseus himself—employs "emotional and evaluative language."

Dilworth, Thomas. "The Fall of Troy and the Slaughter of the Suitors: Ultimate Symbolic Correspondence in the *Odyssey*." *Mosaic* 27, No. 2 (June 1994): 1-24.
    Maintains that the killing of the suitors in the *Odyssey* helped to assuage the guilt of the Greek public over the sacking of Troy.

Dodds, E. R. "Agamemnon's Apology." In *The Greeks and the Irrational*, pp. 1-27. Berkeley: University of California Press, 1951.
    Determines the nature and role of religious feeling in both of Homer's epic poems.

Greene, Thomas. *The Descent from Heaven: A Study in Epic Continuity*. New Haven: Yale University Press, 1963, 434 p.
    Traces the development of the European Renaissance epic from its origins in the *Iliad* and the *Odyssey*.

Griffin, Jasper. "The *Odyssey*." In *Homer*, pp. 46-76. Oxford: Oxford University Press, 1980.
    Offers a thematic and stylistic overview of Homer's epic, which Griffin describes as "the ultimate ancestor of the novel in Europe."

Havelock, Eric A. *The Greek Concept of Justice: From Its Shadow in Homer to Its Substance in Plato*. Cambridge: Harvard University Press, 1978, 382 p.
    Examines the relationship between the oral nature of the epics to the concepts of morality, ethics, and justice.

Heilbrun, Carolyn G. "What Was Penelope Unweaving?" In *Hamlet's Mother and Other Women*, pp. 103-11. New York: Columbia University Press, 1990.
    Explores the role of weaving in the *Odyssey*.

King, Katherine Callen. *Achilles: Paradigms of the War Hero from Homer to the Middle Ages*. Berkeley: University of California Press, 1987, 335 p.
    Assesses the characterization of Achilles in the *Iliad* and traces his appearance and transformation in later works of art and literature.

Lang, Mabel L. "Lineage-Boasting and the Road Not Taken." *Classical Quarterly* 44, No. 1 (1994): 1-6.
    Discusses the role of "lineage-boasting," or describing one's ancestry, in the *Iliad*.

Lord, Albert B. *The Singer of Tales*. Cambridge: Harvard University Press, 1960, 309 p.
    Defines the method and history of oral transmission of the two epics, and discusses their place within the long tradition of oral poetry.

Michalopoulos, Andre. *Homer*. New York: Twayne Publishers, 1966, 217 p.
    Provides a general overview of the *Iliad* and the *Odyssey*, as well as a selected bibliography.

Murnaghan, Sheila. "Maternity and Mortality in Homeric Poetry." *Classical Antiquity* 11, No. 2 (October 1992): 242-64.
    Examines the tendency in the Homeric epics to associate women with death.

Nagy, Gregory. "Homer and Comparative Mythology." In *Greek Mythology and Poetics*, pp. 7-17. Ithaca, NY: Cornell University Press, 1990.
    Determines the difference between myth and fiction in the poems, and discusses them within the traditions of Indo-European mythology and society.

Nilsson, Martin P. *Homer and Mycenae*. Philadelphia: University of Pennsylvania Press, 1933, 283 p.
    Explores the question of who authored the epic poems, and connects the characters, locations, and events in Homer's epics to the Mycenaean Age.

Parry, Milman. *The Making of Homeric Verse: The Collected Papers of Milman Parry*, edited by Adam Parry. Oxford: The Clarendon Press, 1971, 483 p.
    Collection of doctoral dissertations and published essays by the influential Homeric scholar.

Rabel, Robert J. "Agamemnon's *Iliad*." *Greek, Roman, and Byzantine Studies* 32, No. 2 (Summer 1991): 103-17.
    Analyzes the characterization of Agamemnon as it unfolds in the *Iliad*, and discusses the ways in which it affects the poem's structure.

Schein, Seth L. *The Mortal Hero: An Introduction to Homer's "Iliad."* Berkeley: University of California Press, 1984, 223 p.
    Provides a thematic analysis of Homer's epic.

Silk, M. S. *Homer: The "Iliad."* Cambridge: Cambridge University Press, 1987, 116 p.
    Book-length analysis of the epic.

Steiner, George, and Fagles, Robert, eds. *Homer: A Collection of Critical Essays*. Englewood Cliffs, NJ: Prentice-Hall, 1962, 178 p.

    Collection of anecdotes, poems, and essays by well-known authors and critics.

Vivante, Paolo. *Homer*. New Haven: Yale University Press, 1985, 218 p.

    Offers an stylistic and thematic overview of Homer's epics.

Willcock, M. M. *A Companion to the "Iliad."* Chicago: University of Chicago Press, 1976, 293 p.

    Provides an introductory survey of the action, characters, and themes of the epic, as well as explanatory appendices on transmission of the text, methods of warfare, and mythology.

Wright, John, ed. *Essays on the "Iliad."* Bloomington: Indiana University Press, 1978, 150 p.

    Collection of critical essays on Homer's epic.

Additional coverage of Homer's life and career is contained in the following sources published by The Gale Group: *Classical and Medieval Literary Criticism*, **Vol. 1, 16;** *DISCovering Authors; DISCovering Authors: British; DISCovering Authors: Canadian; DISCovering Authors: Most-studied Authors Module; DISCovering Authors: Poets Module;* **and** *World Literature Criticism Supplement.*

Garrett Hongo
1951-

(Full name Garrett Kaoru Hongo) American poet, editor, memoirist, and dramatist.

INTRODUCTION

An award-winning poet, Hongo is an important voice in post-World War II Asian American literature. Ethnic considerations are constant elements in his work, as he explores the experiences of Asian Americans in Anglo society and seeks to come to terms with his own identity in American culture. Delving into history and memory to express the bitterness of prejudice, Hongo frequently employs character studies and anecdotal first-person narratives to express his thoughts. Of his creative impulse he has stated: "My project as a poet has been motivated by a search for origins of various kinds, quests for ethnic and familial roots, cultural identity, and poetic inspiration, all ultimately somehow connected with my need for an active imaginative and spiritual life."

Biographical Information

Born in the village of Volcano, Hawaii, Hongo was raised on the North Shore of the island Oahu and later in Southern California, where his family moved when he was six. He attended a racially mixed high school in a working-class Los Angeles neighborhood, where he was exposed to the urban street life and cultural alienation that color his work. Hongo subsequently studied at Pomona College and graduated with honors in 1973. A fellowship enabled him to spend the following year in Japan writing. Upon returning from abroad, he enrolled in Japanese language and literature classes in a graduate program at the University of Michigan. While there, he won the university's Hopwood Poetry Prize. Prior to completing graduate studies, Hongo moved to Seattle, where he worked as poet-in-residence for the Seattle Arts Commission and founded a locally based theater group. His play, *Nisei Bar and Grill,* premiered in 1976, and two years later he co-authored a volume of poetry entitled *The Buddha Bandits Down Highway 99* together with fellow Asian American writers Alan Chong Lau and Lawson Fusao Inada. Hongo returned to graduate studies in 1978, this time at the University of California, Irvine. In 1980 he received his M.F.A. degree. That year Hongo also was selected one of four winners in the annual Discovery/ *The Nation* poetry contest and has since received numerous awards and fellowships. In the following two decades, he has taught at several universities, served as the poetry editor of *The Missouri Review,* and edited influential volumes of Asian American poetry and essays. Hongo is presently a professor at the University of Oregon.

Major Works

In *Yellow Light,* his first book-length volume of verse, Hongo presents images from his childhood and family life growing up in a multicultural Los Angeles neighborhood. Some of the poems are portraits of difficult lives, depicting dispossessed members of the underclass, or lonely, isolated individuals of foreign descent suffering oppression and discrimination in American society. In other cases Hongo has commented on trials endured by immigrants, including the forced internment of Japanese Americans during World War II and the anti-Japanese sentiment they suffer today. When the poet shows assimilation having been achieved, it is often at the cost of estrangement from cultural history. In more personal poems, Hongo explores the origin of his creativity and his need to express himself in verse. He also seeks connection with his Japanese heritage, but recognizes that he has been considerably shaped by American pop culture. In his second book of poetry, *The River of Heaven,* Hongo continues to combine personal memories with observations about individual lives and the significance of cultural bonds.

Critical Reception

Hongo has been praised for his powers of description and the depth of feeling conveyed by his verse. Commentators find that despite taking on subjects such as victimization and prejudice, he successfully avoids moralizing or sentimentality. Comparing Hongo's style to that of Walt Whitman, critics have noted that both poets celebrate their creative urge and the feeling that they are linked to their surroundings and history. Furthermore, Hongo frequently utilizes literary devices typical of Whitman's poetry, such as long, flowing lines, descriptive lists, and repetitive use of phrasing and word order. Diane Wakoski, in reviewing *Yellow Light,* highlighted perhaps the most important quality of Hongo's poetry when she called attention to the "enthusiasm" and "spirit of life" evident in his verse.

PRINCIPAL WORKS

Poetry

The Buddha Bandits Down Highway 99 [with Alan Chong
   Lau and Lawson Fusao Inada] (poetry) 1978
Yellow Light (poetry) 1982
The River of Heaven (poetry) 1988

Other Major Works

Nisei Bar and Grill (play) 1976
The Open Boat: Poems from Asian America [editor]
   (poetry collection) 1993
Under Western Eyes: Personal Essays from Asian America
   [editor] (essay collection) 1995
Volcano: A Memoir of Hawai'i (memoir) 1995

CRITICISM

Diane Wakoski (essay date 1984)

SOURCE: A review of *Yellow Light,* in *The American Book Review,* Vol. 6, No. 2, January-February 1984, pp. 4-5.

[*In the following, Wakoski lauds* Yellow Light *as "one of the most exciting books of poems I have read in recent years."*]

In the spring of 1963, Gilberto Sorrentino, primary book reviewer for *Kulchur* magazine, reviewed my second appearance in print, a book called, as a joke by its editor LeRoi Jones, *Four Young Lady Poets.* In his review, Sorrentino said,

> Diane Wakoski is the least interesting of the four poets presented. . . . Essentially, this is middle-class poetry . . . Miss Wakoski's poems are disguised in the

"modern" trappings but she is as superficial as Edward Albee, another middle-class product.

Of the three other poets, Carol Berge has gone on to become an interesting avant garde fiction writer; Rochelle Owens, an impressive avant garde playwright; and, until recently, Barbara Moraff had more or less disappeared from the literary world, to my knowledge not having published any books for the past 10 years. For better or worse, I have published 13 collections of poems, numerous small press "slim volumes," and a bit of writing on contemporary American poetry.

I have begun my review with this painful memory, never quite healed, to say that I vowed when reading that unthinking and condescending view of my work (though, I must say, I am a deep admirer of Albee's plays, but I am afraid that our work has little in common, not even middle-classness, for when Sorrentino was writing those lines he had obviously not investigated my life. I come from the lower classes, with virtually uneducated poverty-line parents) that I would never so thoughtlessly review young writers, first books, new work. The three books of poems I want to talk about here are very fine examples of poetry and authors whose work I am thankful to talk about. I would like to say things about Hongo, Luhrmann, and Williamson that I wish had been said about my early work, for I feel great affinities with all these poets, each so different but each working in the strength of "American grain."

It was not entirely gratuitous of me to quote Sorrentino's words about my early poems. For something he said as condemnation—"Middle-class"—is now, 20 years later, something we must reckon with as mainstream reality. And for better or worse, we have made a middle-class art in America, to serve I suppose, the first genuine middle-class country where, according to the authors of *Megatrends,* there are now more white collar workers than blue, and information is our new industry.

When we use words like "academic," "middle-class," and "bourgeois," as pejorative now, I think we all sound a little dated and out of touch. There *is* a new American poetry which comes out of comfortable orderly lives. It is written by the Kinnells, Staffords, Levertovs, Creeleys, Kumins, Rothenbergs, and even Ginsbergs. The "men in Brooks Brothers suits" are no longer the enemies. In fact, we live in a decade where it is hard to identify the enemy, though many of the predictions of Orwell's *1984* have come true. Self-destruction seems far more a hazard of our society than either a Big Brother or a Gestapo-style police.

It is to these problems that Tom Luhrmann addresses himself in *The Objects in the Garden.* Like most of us, Luhrmann is a member of the American middle-class who perceives inherent difficulty and pain in the comfortable, even beautiful way of life we have achieved. . . .

In contrast to *The Objects in the Garden,* Garrett Hongo's **Yellow Light** could originate in another world. And perhaps it does. Hongo is first generation American, with Japanese parents. Some part of his childhood was lived in Hawaii, and most of his poems are located in Southern California. This is a dull way to introduce what I think is one of the most exciting books of poems I have read in recent years. It was love at first reading, that had me walking through the midwestern streets of East Lansing, Michigan, dreaming of Southern California, thinking of Rexroth's poems, feeling the spice of crossing two cultures and having the riches of both. Hongo's language is more sensuous than Kinnell's or Levertov's or Lorca's, at his best. Not to slight those poets, all favorites of mine, but Hongo is astonishing. After reading **"Who Among You Knows The Essence of Garlic?"** I may give up writing food poems, for this one tops everything I have seen in my *Feastletters* search.

> Flukes of giant black mushrooms
> leap from their murky tubs
> and strangle the toes of young carrots.
>
> Broiling chickens ooze grease,
> yellow tears of fat collect
> and spatter in the smoking pot.
>
> Soft ripe pears, blushing
> on the kitchen window sill,
> kneel like plump women
> taking a long, luxurious shampoo,
> and invite you to bite their lips.
>
> Why not grab basketfuls of steaming noodles
> lush and slick as the hair of a fine lady,
> and squeeze?
>
> Two shrimps, big as Portuguese thumbs
> stew among cut guavas, red onions

etc.

It is an amazing piece of descriptive writing. But that is the least of Hongo's skills. He has written the best poem I have ever seen on the American treatment of native Japanese during the Second World War, because it is not really written about that subject, nor does it preach or editorialize in any way. It is a poem called **"Off from swing shift,"** which is about his father coming home from work and getting involved with his passion of gambling, in this case, the horse races. He ends the poem,

> There are whole cosmologies
> in a single handicap,
> a lifetime of two-dollar losing
> in one pick of the Daily Double.
>
> Maybe tonight is his night
> for winning, his night
> for beating the odds
> of going deaf from a shell
> at Anzio still echoing
> in the cave of his inner ear,
> his night for cashing in

> the blue chips of shrapnel still grinding
> at the thickening joints of his legs.
>
> But no one calls
> the horse's name, no one
> says Shackles, Rebate, or Pouring Rain.
> No one speaks a word.

It is true, when one has a rich ethnic background, full of unusual customs, interesting foods, a different language or perhaps even religion that there might be something richer in a person's life to write about. Perhaps Sorrentino's dismissal of the middle-class was a feeling that there could be nothing to write about in the uniform lives of the suburbs compared to the slums of big cities. Yet, John Updike has magnificently disproved that in his Rabbit series. The one difference I see between Hongo and Luhrmann's middle-classness, has nothing to do with richness of materials, for both have immense imagination and sensuous powers of description. No, the difference is that Luhrmann's poems are shadowed with a sense of impending crisis, both social and personal (because the social will affect us all), and Hongo's poetry simply is filled with a—what shall I call it—*joie de vivre? Elan?* Somehow there is no contemporary word, but there is an enthusiasm which simply cannot be suppressed. In a long poem, **"Cruising 99"** the reader can feel the spirit of life itself moving from rhythmic incantation to prophecy. But unlike Luhrmann's prophecy, Hongo's comes from the persona of a wayside palmist who tells him,

> Look at your hand now.
> You can see yourself dancing
> on the hell just above the wrist.
> You must be a happy man.
> You'll be born again and again,
> get to the threshold of Heaven,
> never enter but keep coming back,
> here, for fun, for friends,
> until this will be Paradise,
> and Paradise just an old resort
> the highway's passed by.
>
> Well have a nice trip.
> You'll make it yet.
> Says so right in that curvy line
> around the Mount of Venus,
> that thumbstump there,
> right where the long straight line
> cuts across like an interstate.

Contrast this with Lurhmann's lines in "Hurricane Weather,"

> The hurricane has come
> and overturned the Ferris wheel.
> It has covered the bugle with dust
> and set the rocking horse on fire.
> It has mated the ostrich and the rhino
> and made one of us think he's in Heaven.
>
> And no wonder words don't work.

Perhaps I love Luhrmann's poems for their sense of doom, just as I love Hongo's for their insouciance. What the truth of American poetry today is, is that both Hongo and Luhrmann came through middle-class college educations, Luhrmann at Sarah Lawrence and New College, Hongo at Pomona College; and both have MFA degrees in writing, from Columbia and UC, Irvine, respectively. And they have personal individual visions, not some stereotype we must label and reject as "middle-class."

George Uba   (essay date 1985)

SOURCE: A review of *Yellow Light,* in *The Journal of Ethnic Studies,* Vol. 12, No. 4, Winter, 1985, pp. 123-25.

[*In this review, Uba asserts that the "principal concerns" of* Yellow Light *are "the quest for a personal identity and the desire to build and retrieve a collective identity by sifting through the past."*]

A few years back a popular weekly newsmagazine ran an article on Japanese Americans, treating them as an American success story. The article was headlined—"Outwhiting the Whites." Garrett Kaoru Hongo's book of poetry, *Yellow Light,* demolishes the onesidedness of such headlines and grapples with the underlying problem toward which they unintentionally point: the problem of an ethnic group whose own identity remains ill-defined.

Not that Hongo merely trumpets the familiar tune of ethnic pride. Rather, he excels at balancing a passionate interest in ordinary working-class people performing ordinary activities, with a deep-felt concern over what they are often the unknowing victims of. In the title poem, **"Yellow Light,"** for instance, an unidentified Los Angeles woman returns with a load of groceries to her "neighborhood of Hawaiian apartments, / just starting to steam with cooking" but fails to observe the "war" being waged between the "dim squares" of kitchen light in the barrio and the "brilliant fluorescence" emanating from the wealthy Miracle Mile district. Neatly skirting both the sentimentality and the obvious partisanship that this scenario invites, Hongo concludes the poem without even a glimmer of awareness on the woman's part of the class conflict to which she seems heir, but instead with a riveting, ambiguous image of the yellow moon, at once minatory and transfiguring, that devours "everything in sight." In **"Off from Swing Shift,"** one of several fine poems written about his father, Hongo combines an incisive portrayal of a factory worker who, only within the safe confines of home, dares remove "the easy grin / saying he's lucky as they come," with a genuinely moving depiction of hope seasoned with despair, as the man, a Japanese American war veteran gradually growing deaf "from a shell / at Anzio," listens for the late race results on the radio.

The balance Hongo strikes between the individual's private experience and the larger cultural matrix of which the individual constitutes a part refers the reader to the principal concerns of the book as a whole: the quest for a

personal identity and the desire to build and retrieve a collective identity by sifting through the past. In his search for personal identity, Hongo not only jockeys back and forth through time but also through space, traveling from California to Japan and back again. In Japan he finds himself inescapably the outsider, reduced, at least at first, to writing "postcards" back home. But these **"Postcards for Bert Meyers"** are not filled with the banalities of the ordinary tourist; instead, they define both what has been lost and what has been retained in modern Japan's headlong rush for technological advance. At one point the poet is the bemused foreigner caught in the literal crush of rush hour commuters, able to recover his equilibrium only at the moment when the train stops "And lets out a small puff / Full of tiny Japanese people" (**"Yamanote Sen"**). At another point he is a lone human figure magically transformed in an urban landscape itself transformed by a sudden rain: "All around me / the ten thousand things / of the universe go slack / in the day's new lagoon, / and I seep out of myself like / water from the soaked earth . . ." (**"Alone in a Shower"**). Gradually, the poet achieves a harmony with that part of the Japanese past that remains alive to the mutual imagination of its descendants on both sides of the Pacific.

Throughout the book, Hongo's wit and humor leaven the more programmatic elements of his quest. In **"Crusing 99,"** even as he journeys toward the California town called Paradise, he playfully admits that he is inclined to allow his "mind to wander" and at one point even grumbles that the "Dodgers / haven't made it to Vero Beach." And in the marvelous, whacky tour de force, **"Who Among You Knows the Essence of Garlic,"** he savages the pretensions of foreigners by converting their interest in exotic foods into a weapon turned back upon them.

While Hongo's personal quest carries him afar, his attempt to build a collective identity leads him to concentrate wholly upon the Japanese experience in America. Except for the long, hortatory poem **"Stepchild,"** Hongo resists the twin temptations to script an Asian American history at a single stroke and to lash out at those elements of American culture that have worked to deprive Japanese Americans not only of their identity but, more insidiously, of their awareness of their need for one. Instead, he concentrates on individuals and on fragments of lives, and allows their interconnections steadily and silently to accumulate. Within this compass, Hongo ranges widely, from a memorable portrait of a hard-drinking plantation laborer in Hawaii named Kubota who "laughs and lights a cigarette, / breathes out a wreath of smoke / for his funeral, fifty years away" (**"Kubota"**) to an evocative description of a visit to the Nippon Kan in Seattle's Astor Hotel, where yellowing programs and an "open tray of greasepaint," lonely artifacts from a final stage performance in the fall of 1941, help lead to a surrealistic epiphany, a moment of total engagement within the past (**"On the Last Performance of *Musumé Dojoji* . . ."**). **"And Your Soul Shall Dance"** is a hymn to the artist and writer Wakako Yamauchi, who, as a child, yearns so intensely to escape the unpoetic confines of her environment, a "flat valley grooved with irrigation ditches," that when she enters the schoolyard her "classmates scatter like chickens, / shooed by the storm brooding" on her horizon.

Occasionally, Hongo slips. The poem **"Roots,"** which celebrates the links the poet has forged with his Japanese past and the self which has come into his possession, is overburdened finally by the weight of its message. Simply to affirm that there is "a signature to all things / the same as my own" is not enough when the reader expects to be shown that this is so. The long **"Crusing 99"** suffers from the opposite problem: despite its boisterous humor, it is never completely clear of purpose and ultimately grinds to a halt before a mystifying "scarecrow / made of tumbleweeds" and its own disconcerting mixture of poetic styles. And perhaps more poems on the war-time internment of the Japanese on the West Coast are in order too, given Hongo's avowed concern with curing the condition of "amnesia" within Japanese American culture. Nevertheless, this is an excellent volume of poetry, make no mistake. Hongo applies wit, intelligence, and craftsmanship to his serious theme as few others have been able to do. His book is certain to gain a privileged station in Asian American literature courses, as well as to fuel the continuing controversy over enlarging the American literary canon.

Phoebe Pettingill (essay date 1988)

SOURCE: "Voices of Democracy," in *The New Leader,* Vol. LXXI, No. 10, 13 June 1988, pp. 15-16.

[*In the following review, Pettingill maintains that the poems in* The River of Heaven *are Hongo's "elaborate ritual of atonement for leaving behind his culturally ambiguous background."*]

Each year the Academy of American Poets sponsors the publication of the Lamont Selection, a promising writer's second book of verse. The latest to appear is Garrett Hongo's *The River of Heaven.* The author, of Japanese descent, was born in Volcano, Hawaii. The exotic places he describes—seedy Chinatowns, Pacific ports with their international jumble of peoples and customs—might sound, in paraphrase, like backdrops for Mr. Moto or Charlie Chan. Yet they are really nothing like that: "I have no story to tell about lacquer shrines / or filial ashes, about a small brass bell, / and incense smoldering in jade bowls." Hongo's tale, in fact, concerns what it feels like to grow up as the child of unassimilated immigrants, to be soaked with values incompatible with those of one's ancestors, yet not fully accepted by the new culture.

Given Hongo's themes, it is understandable that his method has been powerfully shaped by the poetry of Philip Levine. The old saw that imitation is the sincerest form of flattery never seemed more applicable. Not that Hongo lacks a distinct voice. Rather, Levine's style has provided a vehicle for the disciple to release his own pent-up cries of cultural loss and longing, from the opening **"Nostalgic Catalogue"** of Hawaii's ethnic diversity to the oriental

simplicity of the book's final elegy for a victim of random street violence:

> Let the night sky cover him as he dies.
> Let the weaver girl cross the bridge of heaven
> and take up his cold hands

Hongo chooses his memorable images to illustrate the cruel paradox that those outside the mainstream must purchase success at the price of estrangement from their own peoples.

One of the most effective poems here tells of Hongo's experience as a student in a California high school, where he was put in "advanced placement, / segregated from the rest of the student body." He admirably evokes the intellectual ghetto the "AP" system can create, and the ambivalence of the mostly Japanese whiz kids in it toward the casual lives of those tracked for a more limited education. Looking back, Hongo realizes that his fellow students were all, in a sense, losers: "Free, white and twenty-one' is the formulaic. / Cynical and exclusive, it doesn't mean / 'Emancipation,' that freedman's word / signifying unlimited potential, an open road / like Whitman saw, a view from the prospect / of *Democratic Vistas,* a sense of magnificence / and of election." The punks disappeared into the small time criminal world of the West Coast's oriental slums, and even the bright students remained outside the Anglo establishment they had been ostensibly groomed to enter. "There are none of us elect. Jap or Sheenie / hawking rags in the New York streets, / nothing matters under corrosive skies, / the burdened light that bears down on us / with the tremulous weight of guilt and outrage."

Hongo's verses become an elaborate ritual of atonement for leaving behind his culturally ambiguous background. A pair of historical monologues narrate the tragedies of men trapped between two ways of life. "**Pinoy** at the **Coming World,**" based on a true account, tells of a sugar cane cutter who has risen to plantation bookkeeper. He sets himself above his former fellows, boasting of children "*born,* not smuggled here." This hubris is punctured when his offspring become victims of the 1919 flu pandemic. An equally sad story belongs to Jigoku, who declaims "on the glamor of Self-Hate." A Japanese-Hawaiian veteran of the Korean War, he returns to a life of gambling and pimping, then emigrates to Japan, hoping "to drift, guiltless, / on the aspic of Tokyo's squalid human sea." Instead, awash with homesickness, he fancies how his drowned corpse might be borne by the current back to "Hilo Bay, / fused in a posture of supplication / . . . as a fan is folded."

Do these two books [*The River of Heaven* and Philip Levine's *A Walk with Thomas Jefferson*] signal a loss of faith in Whitman's *Democratic Vistas*? I don't think so. Whitman never claimed that the melting pot had already dissolved every boundary of race or economic class. He *did* believe that "The United States themselves are essentially the greatest poem," continuously writing itself, resolving its failures along the way to an eventual apotheosis. What could be more truly democratic than to acknowledge shortcomings, while at the same time preserving faith in the Ideal? In this sense, Philip Levine and Garrett Hongo prove to be genuine descendants of Tom and Walt.

Robert Schultz (essay date 1989)

SOURCE: "Passionate Virtuosity," in *The Hudson Review,* Vol. XLII, No. 1, Spring, 1989, pp. 149-57.

[*In the review below of* River of Heaven, *Schultz admires Hongo's "rich vocabulary and undulant syntax," which "hold his stories of loss and remembrance in a secure, distinctive music."*]

Like [Philip] Levine, Garrett Hongo, in *The River of Heaven,* attends with care to those excluded from whatever the American Dream has become in the 1980s. In **"The Underworld,"** he recounts watching a movie—a slapstick comedy—in the old Orpheum in Los Angeles, and listening to the chatter and laughter of "the shimmering, mingled throngs of the poor" who take "a common pain or delight in, just once, / another's humiliation." Hongo has even dedicated a poem, **"Choir,"** to Levine, but here a difference between the two poets is apparent. Hongo, the younger poet, seems less alone, less embittered than Levine does in his newest book. The central moment of **"Choir"** is the poet's recollection of singing in his junior high hallways with a makeshift quartet: himself, "a black kid, a white one, and another Japanese." The "black kid" taught the group "Summertime," and "Together our voices made a sound none could make alone, / 'Harmonics,' Harold said, a tone from the choir itself. . . ." Such moments of connection, usually achieved through storytelling or music, buoy this poetry, lending it a sweetness even as it sings of indignity or loss.

The first part of Hongo's book is carefully structured to make explicit the way music and story can mitigate suffering. A poem, **"Mendocino Rose,"** is about driving through the countryside north of San Francisco, listening to a taped Hawaiian ballad and seeing the viney flower "overtaking all the ghost shacks and broken fences / crumbling with rot. . . ." he poem ends in a revelatory moment when the flower, the ballad, and the poet's own emotion fuse in his desire to make a music that can garland this landscape of decay:

> . . . the roses seemed everywhere around me then,
>   profuse and luxurious
> as the rain in its grey robes,
>   undulant processionals over the land,
> echoes, in snarls of extravagant color,
>   of the music
> and the collapsing shapes
>   they seemed to triumph over.

The fact is collapse; the response is a music that follows the contours of collapse but triumphs over it. Therefore, in the poems which immediately follow, the act of commemorating, of saving into music, is primary.

The music he finds, at its most effective, is Whitmanic. He uses the catalogue effectively, as in **"Nostalgic Catalogue,"** and parallel phrasing, as in *"O-Bon:* **Dance for the Dead,"** which builds to an impressive climax:

> I want the cold stone in my hand to pound the earth,
> I want the splash of cool or steaming water to wash my
>   feet,
> I want the dead beside me when I dance, to help me
> flesh the notes of my song, to tell me it's all right.

The poem is a high point in the collection, and it teaches us again that rhetoric and poetry are not best understood as opposing terms. By comparison, several poems in the final third of the book seem lax and prosey, the most extreme of these being **"96 Tears."** In most of his work, however, Hongo's rich vocabulary and undulant syntax hold his stories of loss and remembrance in a secure, distinctive music.

Garrett Hongo with Alice Evans (interview date 1992)

SOURCE: "A Vicious Kind of Tenderness: An Interview with Garrett Hongo," in *Poets & Writers Magazine,* Vol. 20, No. 5, September-October 1992, pp. 37-46.

[*In the following conversation, Hongo discusses the craft of writing and the role of his family history in his poetry.*]

[Alice Evans]: *At a craft workshop recently, you talked about how important it is for the individual to act as a witness to history. Witnessing appears to be a primary directive in your work. How would you describe the poet's role as historian, from both a broad view and a personal one?*

[Garrett Hongo]: As poets we need to portray the events of the world from our own point of view. We need to be attached to the events of the world in our own lives. Sometimes history passes us by and we don't know it. I believe that poets must speak as witnesses to historical events. I don't believe in [the official version of] American history; I believe in what we've witnessed as the travesties in American history.

I try to be faithful to the history of Japanese in America and write from it, and I've made it my responsibility to know everything that I can about it. It's like Czeslaw Milosz says about Lithuania: "If there is no singer there is no history." That's how I go into the world: if I don't write it, it's not going to get written, and I don't want people to stop that. I see that the person in my way who is causing me difficulty is also repressing the expression of the history of my people.

I have a lot of pride. It comes from my people, my whole family. I had a very proud grandfather and grandmother whose pride was taken away because of World War II. You don't forget it.

Tell me about your own history. What were the forces that produced an acclaimed poet? How did the doors open for you?

The reason I'm doing anything at all is because I'm an individual who is part of a corrective process in American history. I got educated because Governor Pat Brown funded a program for poor kids to study at the best universities in California. So I was given an academic scholarship to go to a very elite school, Pomona College. Because this education came from a political circumstance of opportunity and empowerment, it's not hard for me to believe the thing that I believe. And I never give a damn about making it.

You say you don't give a damn about making it, but you have made it. You've been very honored as a poet. What has that meant for you?

It's not a question of making it. It's a question of standing up and honoring a past which I feel was dishonored. It's on those principles that I carry myself forward.

Yes, I've been honored, and I'm happy for that, for complicated reasons, I suppose. One of the nice things about that is it gives me more opportunity to address my subjects. Honors, insofar as that's concerned, are very good. They endorse my projects and they give me the opportunity to address my subjects. They also are great medallions and great weapons in the fight to get that story told.

I wish my grandfather had been honored, but this country did not do that to him, so I do it.

Your poetry shows great depth of feeling, a characteristic I find unusual for a man.

Maybe it's a human characteristic. Most males are not human any more. I like that joke in the book *Little Big Man,* where the Cheyenne call themselves human beings and they call the other people ghosts—or the "white man." Maybe male culture—I don't want to offend anybody—but maybe people have forgotten how to be human beings.

My grandfather was not this way, my father was not this way, Hawaiians are not this way. We have a lot of *aloha*—spirit, love, trust. When I moved from Hawaii to Los Angeles there was no *aloha* in Los Angeles. Man, there was a lot of brutality. But it's good that I learned about that too, because you have to ward things off. Tenderness is a very underrated emotion. It's also much attacked and maligned. So I've made it my job to learn a vicious kind of tenderness.

Could you elaborate?

James Wright's tenderness I believe in. You know the poem, "To a Blossoming Pear Tree"—"the dark blood in my flesh drags me down with my brother"—that's the kind of tenderness I believe in. I love you because I know we're both going to die. I love you because everyone else

is trying to beat us up. "Flayed without hope, I held the man for nothing in my arms."

A lot of people were excited about having you come to teach at the University of Oregon. What kind of teacher are you? What do you emphasize and what ticks you off?

The kinds of things I might criticize a student for are a lack of commitment, a lack of concern for the reader, obscurity. I like things to be reasonably clear. I don't go in for a lot of verbal pyrotechnics, but there's always a Gerard Manley Hopkins out there, or a Hart Crane, or a Charles Wright. You've got to worship them.

I care a lot about self-knowledge, knowing what you're going to write about, knowing what you sing, knowing what you like to sing about, and helping the students connect with that.

I guess I'm still a Confucian. I believe that people are basically good, not basically bad. So I believe that if they learn to trust their nature, something good will emerge out of it, even if it's an angry nature. You know, people aren't angry for no reason, they're angry for a reason usually. And poetry is a loving craft, so even angry poems are in the service of some love.

You talked at the craft workshop about poetry being treated as an elite practice. You mentioned being turned off by literary aloofness, obscurity, a system of privileged meaning accessible only to those initiated into that system. What kind of emphasis do you put on technique?

Technique can show a commitment, technique can show energy. Technique shows you've invested. Also candor shows you've invested, you've invested in trust.

The thing I work to build first in the workshop is trust. Not only that the students trust me, but that they trust each other, because the thing that kills expression and creativity is a lack of trust, an environment of hostility. And the workshop's primary function to me is to give people a sense of a sympathetic yet creatively critical audience. That's the main job.

I've been in some very destructive workshop situations.

Well, it's easy to be destructive—to be critical and careless. It's harder to be critical and supportive. There are not too many people who have shown the ability to do that in our history. Some of my heroes are people who have been great teachers—Bruce Lee, Theodore roethke, Philip Levine. When I interviewed for this job, and people asked me why I wanted to do this, I said: because this is a self-assignment for me. I believe in the craft, I believe in the profession, I believe in the cause, and in my own mind I'm not going to be significant in terms of my people unless my work is shown to be valuable, in that it helps better the world. In the martial arts, as in anything, the final requirement of someone in the profession—in the art—is that they start a school that lives beyond their own life, that they help people find what is valuable in the art, that they inspire people not only to do well but to try to do well for others. And that's what's left for me to do yet. That's the reason I came here. It was an opportunity for me to test and extend myself, but also to contribute.

We have to increase the opportunity for people to have free voice, free expression, and that's what I hope for here.

Poetry—creative writing—is free speech. That's why Jesse Helms wants to shut us down. There are very strong forces in play right now that want to shut down the National Endowment for the Arts, because the understanding is that it is a forum for free speech in America. It really is.

I have a friend who's a legal scholar, in what they call critical legal studies. She did an article on poetry—particularly women's poetry—as an alternate system of jurisprudence to the law, and I think that's the reason why people are so upset by it. That's why poetry is so threatening and why it's practiced by so many people who are outside of economic and political power. Because it's our system of jurisprudence. Poetry is another judgment.

And speech with devotion to private moments of emotion also has a place in poetry as well as speech about unauthorized history. After all, that's what the Old Testament was about. And the New Testament. They're unauthorized histories.

Donald Barthelme said, "Do you think the Bible would have been written if people thought they were writing the Bible?" That's pretty good, I've got to say. Barthelme inspired me a lot, and his confidence that this could be done helped me. . . .

Let's talk a little about your writing habits now. Are you a disciplined writer, do you write every day?

I'm an actor as a writer. I prepare the character, you know, like Stanislavsky.

So the idea of the character dictates the poem?

Not really, no. The gut, the feeling, the emotional and narrative core of the book does.

I was talking to Barry Lopez and asked him how it was to work with a certain editor. He said "I don't know yet, I haven't shown her anything." He's been working on this book for two and a half years—three years almost—and said, "I don't know, I don't know this book very well yet." I said "huh?" and he kept talking: "the way I do things, I never show an editor anything until I get at least a complete draft done, and then I'll go over it line by line." He's still kind of putting the book together and doesn't know what kind of a book it is, what the personality of it is, what's going to go in it. He *lives* the book; he's preparing it.

That's the way I do it too, but I don't know what I'm doing. He knows what he's doing, For him it's a method. For me it's floundering.

It was great to hear him tell me that because when I write my book of poems I kind of run into the poetry, I run into the book. Like, I was writing and it didn't really come together, but I just kept living with this feeling of trying to capture the love, the *aloha* [a word of welcome], the commitment to democracy my father had, because I knew I didn't have what he had. So that was my *koan* [a prayer of meditation], that was my problem with **The River of Heaven.** And once I got it, once I felt "in the feeling," then the poems started to come, one by one, then more, then more and more and more and more.

Every time I extended myself I realized something new, and I pushed myself to the next level; the last poem I wrote for the book was **"The Pier,"** a long poem at the end of **The River of Heaven.** It's a democratic statement. My father had those beliefs. He's a Hawaiian Democrat.

He was active politically?

Every Hawaiian is active politically. You know, equal rights, enfranchisement for all peoples, and Go For Broke. And that's kind of, like, you talk that way, you think that way on the mainland—especially in Orange County at the "University of Apartheid"—you're ostracized, you're looked upon as some kind of dirty, rotten ethnic. So I wanted to do something that might blossom, because they're trying to take that belief away from me. It's like a religion. You kill the religion first and it's easy to have the people die.

I wanted to bring the religion back in me and there were certain fathers behind it also, not just my own flesh fathers, but William Butler Yeats and his great poem, "Among Schoolchildren," and William Wordsworth, in "The Immortality Ode." "Among Schoolchildren" is a model behind **"The Pier."** Instead of schoolchildren it's Cambodians and Vietnamese that I see. Those two poems are ghost poems behind **"The Pier."**

So I took on as much as I could, I took on my father's life and his democratic principles, and I wished to critique the oppressive ideology of white racism and to invoke the great fathers of mystic revelation and poetic power, William Butler Yeats and William Wordsworth—and I tried to put it together in **"The Pier."**

My working method is to let the meditation grow. I guess it's kind of Eastern, but it's also like Wordsworth. He walked all over the Wye Valley, meditating, ruminating, and he'd come back and then write the poem about it after his long walks. I don't have a craftsman-like, disciplined daily writing method.

The River of Heaven *came together at the MacDowell Colony in six weeks, I read somewhere.*

It wasn't only those six weeks, though they were crucial. MacDowell helped a lot and going to Hawaii helped a lot. Just before I was at MacDowell I was in Hawaii with my friend Edward Hirsch. I was running around, I was showing Hawaii to this person, who wanted to know me and my history and he appreciated it so much. It inspired me, his love for my people's way, it inspired me to share more of my heart through poetry with the rest of the world.

Tell me about the book you're working on now, **Volcano Journal.**

It's a book of retreat and return, meditation on going home to a home I never knew, which is this volcano. And coming back to it, to the history of my family, coming back to that culture, the biology, the *biota* [the animal and plant life of a particular region considered as a total ecological entity], the rainforest, the volcano itself. It's nonfiction, not like John McPhee, more like Thoreau.

When you read from that book the other night, you mentioned that you needed to experiment with form. Could you talk about that?

In writing this book, the poetic form needed to expand for me. What I found to be the form was the Japanese *nikki.* It's a travel diary, poetic prose. We have examples in American literature in *Moby Dick* and *Walden.* In that vein I write this book.

You were eight months old when your family left Volcano. What took you back there?

I was invited, when I was about 31, to give a couple of readings in the islands and was invited to give a reading in Volcano, where they have an art center.

What happened for you there?

I knew that that was it. I knew I had to go back. I knew I wasn't finished with it. I knew there was something. And I was true to it. I was true to that little insinuation, and it's made all the difference in my heart. It's made all the difference in the soul of my family. My boys love it, my wife, everything. So I didn't ignore my calling.

It seems that in Volcano you found yourself as a writer.

That's right. In geography and geology, you know, when lava comes out of the earth it's not magnetized, and the way they can map continental drift is by tracing the magnetic fields, because after the lava is emitted and solidifies, then it's magnetized, and it's magnetized according to our orientation to magnetic north. So there's something to that, the first time you come into the world. Many people are magnetized. You get your little stratigraphy, that kind of thing. I feel perfect there, I can't tell you. It's always a good day in Volcano.

I have a friend, Native American poet Ray Young Bear. When I met him I was nothing, I was completely shiftless. He had a feeling for his ancestors, he had a feeling for his tribe and his people, he knew where he stood, he walked with the grandfathers. I took that as a criticism of my own psyche and soul. When we were eighteen, I didn't have that. When I was eighteen, I was like the "stolen child." But I have that now. I walk with my grandfathers and have

absolutely complete confidence. I'm their grandson. It took me a lot longer than Ray, but I got there.

In **Yellow Light,** *you write about returning to Japan to find your family's name. Are you talking about your natal family?*

Everybody. I'm talking about those that the literature has forgotten, those that the culture has forgotten. It's important to me that we be remembered, that there be a literature for us, that we be sung about, that there be songs for the lives that my people have lived. That's why the poetry of Philip Levine inspired me so early—"Vivas for those who have failed," the names of the lost.

I said in an interview somewhere, sometime, part of the motivation behind my first book was to recuperate or reinscribe our name in the registry, the list of names in Japan, the list of names in Hawaii.

So not literally Hongo, but the lost names of all your people.

There's a serious pun in that, because my name means homeland. Hongo means homeland.

I was a little confused because there was some mention of changing names, or taking on a new name.

A lot of Japanese did that. Like people coming through Ellis Island, they just changed their names.

Tell me about the use of oral history in your poetry. You write very eloquently about people not directly connected to you.

You write the history of the tribe and you sing from sources. I used the Oral History Project of the Ethnic Studies Department at the University of Hawaii, God bless them. We need to be liberated, the love of oral history needs to be liberated, the love of our people needs to be liberated. We're a colonized place, culturally colonized.

This is our pride, this is our history, this is our identity. We're a colonial people. We're like the blacks in southern culture. I mean, politically we're a canceled culture. We're like the copper miners in Chile—there's no difference. We're like the students in Tiananmen.

So you're trying to reawaken. . . .

I'm not trying, I have to. It's a compulsion with me. I don't have a choice. If I'm going to be what my grandfather was, I have to do it this way. For me to be a person in my eyes, this is what I have to be.

Your mother's father is the one who was taken away?

That's right. It's like Indians say: you have ghosts, you have your *aumakua.* I have my *aumakua,* I have my guardian spirits.

Tell me more about your work habits. When you're in Eugene, are you able to write?

No—impossible.

That's what I thought. You need the open time that a Guggenheim provides; you need NEA [fellowships]. If you wanted to now, could you earn your living solely as a writer?

I could probably get an advance, but I don't know if I could live on it. I'm still learning to be a prose writer and still learning what kind of a prose writer I am. I'm enjoying the experience, finally.

I'd like to get back to your writing question. I like to write seven pages every day except weekends, which I like to spend with my family.

Sometimes I just get a page. I just get a bad page. I get a lot of pages that are real lousy but I've started working on a problem, or a theme, a beat, narrative or emotional, and the next pages are really . . . I just trash it and I find my way into the subject. I'm enjoying myself, so I write between a page and seven pages a day, single-spaced.

You work first thing in the morning?

Pretty much.

Your poetry is very songlike at times, it's very lush. You've described your style as narrative, Whitmanesque. You relate oral history, you talk about your roots, both family personal and family historical, and it seems to me you go all the way back to the universe itself. Your work has lots of references to the universe.

Thank you. I've looked down into the middle. You stand over a pond of lava boiling up, or you stand on the top of Mauna Kea and you look up at a star, it's impossible to think anything else.

Well, it's a very expansive view. A lot of poetry is focused only on the personal these days, only on the wounds the person has suffered. Yours branches out into the universe.

There are so many things to wither the soul, and poetry does the opposite. I won't let my poetry wither my soul, poetry has to enhance it. I don't believe in poetry as a discipline, or a narrow field, or an elite practice. I believe in poetry as empowerment. *Singing for Power,* you know, that great book by Ruth Underhill about the Papago Indian ceremonies. I mean, I like those ideas that poetry is like singing for power, trying to find, crying for your own vision. Every one of us finds it in our own way, if we're worth anything. But one of the things I like about being a poet, is that I get to do that. I don't always have it, but I get to do it every now and then. I like it.

I feel privileged to be able to do this. I feel very grateful to be able to do it. At the same time I feel proud. I've sacrificed. I haven't cared about cars, or career, or those

kinds of things. I've been caring for the singing. I mean, I've had great teachers—like Bert Meyers, like Charles Wright—great, scrupulous, ethical, dedicated artists who have helped me feel the right way, who have confirmed my intuition and instincts and who fostered my loyalties. I needed those teachers to help me along, I did, I did.

To help you find your song?

Yeah, particularly my man, Charles Wright.

What did he teach you?

To believe in my poetry, to let my poetry lead me into my life, not the other way around.

Who's helped you the most with craft?

Well, with the technique, I can help my own self. What I needed help with was to believe in my spirits and to confirm my impulses and to deepen them, and also to challenge me to be loyal to them.

C. K. Williams was the most instrumental. I brought a poem into class, the one about the woman on the bus, **"Stay With Me."** C. K. looked at me like this, he drilled me with his eyes. "This is the real thing," he said. "If you can write like this, I don't understand why you write all that other stuff." He was working on "Tar," a breakthrough poem for American literature. It's no wonder how passionate he was. He said, "I don't see why you waste your time, and what's more, I don't see why you're wasting *mine.*" The next week I wrote **"Yellow Light,"** then **"Off from Swing Shift."** All the poems in *Yellow Light* were written under C. K. Williams and Charles Wright.

C. K. taught me to write from a grander state than the mundane, to take the big thing and put all of it in the poem, not to divide it off into short story or essay. He confirmed me in my devotion to writing my own thing. He pounded me on top of my head until I got mad and charged. He motivated me. If it weren't for him I don't know if I would have had the guts. I can't slack off from that level of vision.

Mark Jarman (essay date 1996)

SOURCE: "The Volcano Inside," in *The Southern Review,* Vol. 32, No. 2, April, 1996, pp. 337-43.

[*In the review below, Jarman calls* Volcano *"a remarkable, profound, and haunting book."*]

> He must have come wanting little,
>   except to belong to the land,
> red volcanic soil loamed with ferns,
>   drenched in mists and the constant drizzle
> of 4,000 feet and the cloud-catch of Mauna Loa,
>   amphitheater for rain and sunshowers,

and to his own father as well . . .
            Garrett Hongo, **"Cloud-Catch"**

When the poet Garrett Hongo was six years old, his parents, both descended from Japanese immigrants and like himself natives of Hawai'i, left the islands and moved their family to Los Angeles. It was the late 1950s, for immigrants a time of great promise—a promise that American history has shown was not an illusion. The prospects were especially bright in Los Angeles, for even then that amazing incorporation of cities, spread over two vast, linked areas, the Los Angeles Basin and the San Fernando Valley, was a site of unique multiculturalism. Los Angeles included the second-largest Spanish-speaking population in North America (after Mexico City), and the second-largest Japanese population in the United States (after Honolulu). Hongo grew up within and surrounded by communities noted for their ethnicity. His high school in Gardena, a city with a predominantly Japanese population, represented the African, Asian, Anglo, and Hispanic peoples of greater Los Angeles, a rich flood that filled the grid sprawling between the San Gabriel Mountains and the Pacific Ocean.

It is clear from **Volcano, a Memoir of Hawai'i,** a remarkable, profound, and haunting book, that Hongo missed nothing of L.A.'s panorama of diversity. Yet from his perspective today, the move his parents made from Hawai'i to Southern California was a catastrophic act of deracination. Forced by family conflict to leave their home, the Hongos subjected themselves and their son to an experience of alienation that marked the father for tragedy, and the son for a crisis of identity. **Volcano** is not only a contribution to immigrant literature, that most American of forms, but it is an account of questing and returning, a search for the father's origins and a reenvisioning of the son, that borders on the Homeric.

Hongo's native place is the big island of Hawai'i, with its towering peak, Mauna Loa, and active volcanic craters. According to family lore he was born either in Hilo or behind the store his grandfather established and his parents operated at a little wayside named after the mileage marker on the road from Hilo—29 Miles Volcano. It is Volcano, which is more or less a country village, that Hongo considers his birthplace. His book recounts, in part, his numerous returns and extended visits there. The first time he returns, as a grown man with a wife and child, he is recognized by the local postman as his father's son. Albert Hongo ran his father's place, the Hongo Store (which still stands), only for a year after leaving the service, then took his family to Oahu. After a droll badinage about the senior Hongo, the postman, speaking Pidgin, asks the author "in that bemused and intimate, derisive way of island Japanese, 'So what? You come back for search your roots or somet'ing?'"

Hongo is indeed in search of his roots—and something else. In Hawai'i he connects with family—aunts, uncles, and the wives of his grandfather—who make him listen to their story of Eden and his family's particular fall from grace. His meetings are all revelations, but none can change his own story:

How can one derive a sense of self from something as lately invited into one's life as Volcano was for me? I was born there, but left it after only eight months. It was a mystery to me, and one for which I had no special curiosity until I was past thirty. Though my anxiety demanded that identity have its source in the unchanging—a place and attendant culture somehow "fixed" in the scheme of things, a thing easily characterized and identifiable—my thoughts ran otherwise, saying I belonged nowhere, that a shopping mall in Missouri or a trout stream in Oregon or a Hilo movie theater could explain me as well as the lava eddying out of the lake at the vent of Kupaianaha.

There is something that makes this book more than a search for roots, more than another immigrant memoir. Admittedly there is nothing in the facts of the story to distinguish it from other such quests. The something more is the passion of the writing. Hongo writes as if the island of Hawai'i, with its weather and geology, its birds and plants, could be translated from mute existence into speech. The following passage is typical of the intensity he brings to small but telling details. Here he describes the breeding habits of a Hawaiian club moss that favors the soil of volcanic vents.

The gametophytes ferret themselves into minute cracks in the lava, hidden away in the microgaps of basaltic rock where moisture collects from rainfall and where it condenses from the sulphurous vents of steam billowing from the cliffsides and cracked earth near Kilauea. Swain and maiden find both their underground nursery and their darkened bower within the scores of gaping fumaroles and sulphur banks along the rim of the summit caldera. They swarm into life inside the volcanic vents, sustained by heat from the volcano and hidden by its crevices, a Paolo and Francesca of biology, thrilled in innocence, embryos of sexual experience perpetually sequestered in the dark infernos of earth. It is their very immaturity, their primitive but abundant adolescence (the gametophytes grow in uncountable swarms), that produces offspring, those "adult" plants that are the sexless green *professori* greeting me, nodding under cool, gray robes of afternoon rain, sleeves full of hidden energy. For the club moss, it is its embryos that are the parents, giving birth to adults and not to children, its existence an evidence of life sent into a strange reversal of the conventional anthropomorphic narratives of maturity.

Everything Hongo evokes, even the busywork, as he calls it, of his naturalist notebook, resonates with his obsession: to give new birth to himself. At the same time, in the tradition of the travel book, the stranger gains intimate experience of a foreign place he or she may never visit except through the imagination of the surrogate traveler.

This extended work of prose, a memoir as its subtitle tells us, fleshes out many of the subjects treated in Hongo's collections of poetry, **Yellow Light** and **The River of Heaven***;* and in many ways **Volcano** is itself a poem. One might expect that the analogous poetic form would be the epic. Indeed, many of Hongo's references, many of the figures to which he compares himself and his quest for patrimony and *patria,* are from the Western epic tradition. But this book, in the guise of a nonfiction account of one man's search for and reclamation of his origins, also contains elements of the lyric poem. Wordsworth's *Prelude* might be an apt analogy, but Hongo's language has a lushness, derived from a love of the names, epithets, images, and metaphors of the natural world, that exceeds Wordsworth's. Here the presiding genius of the English lyric tradition is John Keats. Hongo's negative capability consists in the way he manages to let his Keatsian impulse keep company with Japanese and Hawaiian folk song and the haiku of Bash and Issa.

Yet *Volcano* is thoroughly modern, containing as it does a Joycean multiplicity of voices and allusions, formal language and slang, Pidgin English, Japanese, and Hawaiian, and references to Asian and Western myth. With Hongo as the Stephen Dedalus/Telemachus figure, and for Dublin both Hawai'i and Los Angeles, it does invite us to consider its story as a latter-day quest. It also has that modern sense that something more urgent than literature is intended, that by sheer force of imagination the author can remake himself, and that we are reading the record of that remaking. It is a postmodern book, too, because it is a postcolonial book, with all that means about the interpenetration of an imperial culture and an indigenous culture that must, by the work of the artist, reassert itself. The reassertion is problematic, especially for an artist who sees himself as part of a dispersed people, but this, too, is an element of the book's postcolonial character.

To accomplish his task, Hongo has made himself a student of a place. He has tried to sublimate the volcano inside him into the island of his study. He acknowledges implicitly that the volcano he describes in Hawai'i is an objective correlative, a metonymy for his own psychology. Viewing a video of himself reading his poetry to an audience in Los Angeles, he recognizes suppressed anger in the contradictions between his role as a teaching poet and the character he sees before him on the screen.

> I was nothing like the standard image of a college professor. I was nothing like the intellectuals who had educated me. I was working-class—like Chicano rockabillies from East L.A. or the *chang-a-lang* bad boys that made up all the bands that played the clubs along Hotel Street in Chinatown Honolulu. There was no imperturbable chill about me. I fussed. I raged a little. A sacrifice to my passion, I was caustic and daunting on the screen, combative and elemental. Like raw earth, I boiled in my own moods, swollen in a petty defiance, telling myself I mimicked nothing.

If he mimics anything it is the lava tubes that carry magma from Mauna Loa to the sea, breaking out in fumaroles and spatter cones along the way. He associates volcanoes with birth, yet the real analogy is his developed psyche. The idea or image of fire blossoming, flowering out of the inner earth, runs throughout the book, making it chthonic, truly. The imagination's work, to create a home, or as he says, "a land," finds its parallel in the geologic upheaval in which the earth's molten core becomes manifest through

lava, which in turn becomes a solid place where life is lived, plants flourish, and people make their homes.

Hongo contrasts the nostalgic but half-forgotten world of Hawai'i with the actual world of Los Angeles, where he grew up. When writing about Los Angeles, Hongo's style has a more acute angle, a leanness, as in this passage about his high school in Gardena:

> School was tepid, boring. We wanted cars, we wanted clothes, we wanted everything whites and blacks wanted to know about sex but were afraid to tell us. We "bee-essed" with the black kids in the school parking lot full of coastal fog before classes. We beat the white kids in math, in science, in typing. We ran track and elected cheerleaders. We *ruled,* we said. We were dumb, teeming with attitude and prejudice.

He associates the mainland with his early lessons about adaptation to language and custom, which included the discarding of his island memories. Most important, it is on the mainland that he learns about race and its most significant manifestation in the history of Japanese-Americans—their relocation during World War II. When he falls in love with a white girl in high school, he learns that she thinks of herself as Portuguese and that "white people were *always* something too." Both his racial group and hers resent their pairing, and each of them is punished violently. "Race," the teenage Hongo learns, "is an exclusion, a punishment, imposed by the group." When as an adult he learns about the relocation of mainland Japanese after Pearl Harbor (those in Hawai'i were treated to other indignities), he discovers that race can also be an exclusion, a punishment, imposed *on* the group. He is outraged, and aims his fury not only at this crime against humanity, but at the silence of the older generation of Japanese-Americans who never made an issue of it and never told him of the event.

Yet it is another kind of silence that shrouds his father's sad life—that of cultural dispossession. Though race and relocation are adjunct themes, the motive force for Hongo's Telemachean search is the mystery of his father's lost identity. In his father he sees a stunted artist who as a boy raised bonsai trees. He even refers to him as "a botanical Wallace Stevens of Honolulu." As an adult, a father and husband, Albert Hongo works in Los Angeles as a troubleshooter on the assembly line for an electronics firm, increasingly isolated by his deafness, his Pidgin English, his estrangement from his past. He works the swing shift to avoid the requirements of a social life, but endures a buildup of daily humiliations at his job. In his spare time he reads spiritualist and metaphysical texts (what his son calls "self-help"), plays the horses, and memorizes sports statistics. By the time of his early death, from heart failure, he has few if any friends and little connection with his family. Whoever he was has been lost. His gravesite in San Pedro is devoid of any sense that he was part of a society or a culture:

> If you stood at his marker and gazed toward the water,
> a steel suspension bridge between the mainland and the

naval shipyard at Terminal Island was usually visible through ocean vapors and the constant smog. His grave was near the curb of the road that wound through the hillside plots, and the mottling shade of a stand of eucalyptus trees swept his headstone at dusk. Nothing on it said he was a "local boy," that he raised *bonsai* on Wiliwili Street and shined shoes on McCully Street in Honolulu, that he was a son of Hawai'i who never came home.

Hongo searches for and finds the initiating event, perhaps the original sin, that led to his family's loss of their Hawaiian Eden, his father's fate, and what he calls his own "dispiritedness." He tells a complex emotional story of abandonment and betrayals, both petty and great. When he considers his reconnection with his native place, as he brings his wife and children there to visit, he sees it has taken "the better part of four generations" to absolve the sin that separated him from his land.

Garrett Hongo has attempted to write a book equal to the recreation of his identity. It includes a gorgeous plumbing of geologic depths, a naturalist's excitement about utterly new plants and animals, and a discoverer's enthusiasm for what was already there. But it also contains a bleak admission of the need for affection, some response from the making earth, which leads him on more than one occasion to desire a lethal unity with that earth. As he explores a fresh lava field, Hongo admits:

> It was still hot, giving off shimmers of heat, and I could feel the skin on my face prickle, the heels of my feet getting warm. I wasn't wearing shoes, just a thick pair of beach sandals. I wanted to *feel* that lava, would've gone barefoot over it if I could've.At one point he curls up in the sulfurous breath of a newly petrified wave of molten rock. He associates his rebirth with a physical assimilation of the island where he was born.

In his writing, both poetry and prose, Hongo has attempted to embody what he calls the "world of feeling and specificities among the vast and monolithic Other of race in America." If he has succeeded, as I think he has time and again, then his experience must become part of our experience. Surely this is different from the assumption of universality, one questioned by so much that makes up contemporary literature. And yet one of the most moving passages of *Volcano* is affecting because of the way it extends our universe as readers. Dreaming of his maternal grandfather, Kubota, on the night he died, Hongo sees him night-fishing on a beach in Oahu that he loved:

> "The moon is leaving, leaving," he sang in Japanese. "Take me deeper in the savage sea." He turned and crouched like an ice-racer then, leaning forward so that his unshaven face almost touched the light film of water. I could see the light stubble of beard like a fine gray ash covering the lower half of his face. I could see his gold-rimmed spectacles. He held a small wooden boat in his cupped hands and placed it lightly on the sea and pushed it away. One of his lanterns was on it and, written in small neat rows like a sutra scroll, it had been decorated with the silvery names of all our dead.

With lyric poetry like this, we have to feel—to be made to feel—what the poet feels. I think we do. We may not claim the dead whose names are inscribed on the sutra scroll, but we feel what it means to call them ours. In the end, *Volcano* is less an epic, the history of a people told in poetry, than a lyric, the yearning song of a soul, which might be the reader's, too. It is certainly one the reader will not soon forget, like amazing news, like news from home, coming from beyond rivers and mountains.

FURTHER READING

Hai-Jew, Shalin. Review of *Volcano*. *Northwest Asian Weekly* 14, No. 23 (9 June 1995): 15.
    Recounts Hongo's search for "personal peace" in his memoir.

Review of *Yellow Light*. *Los Angeles Times Book Review* (16 May 1992): 9.
    Praises the "full poetic arsenal" Hongo displays in this collection. "By discovering his family" in these poems, the critic observes, "the poet discovers himself. And through him, a vivid sense of the Japanese-American past and present emerges."

Moffett, Penelope. "Verses Chronicle Tales of Asian-Americans." *Los Angeles Times* (19 March 1987): V 1, 19.
    Biographical sketch and interview with Hongo.

Moyers, Bill. "Garrett Kaoru Hongo." In *The Language of Life: A Festival of Poets,* pp. 201-15. New York: Doubleday, 1995.
    Interview addressing the sources and inspiration for Hongo's works and the practice of poetry in modern America.

Oyama, Richard. "You Can Go Home Again: Writer and Poet Garrett Hongo Reclaims His Birthplace and Heritage in *Volcano: A Memoir of Hawaii*." *Asianweek* 17, No. 3 (8 September 1995): 13.
    Characterizes Hongo's memoir as "a beautiful song of place, history, and familial inheritance."

St. John, David. "Raised Voices in the Choir: A Review of 1982 Poetry Selections." *The Antioch Review* 41, No. 2 (Spring 1983): 231-44.
    Includes an assessment of *Yellow Light,* calling it "a beautifully written and extremely moving book."

Sato, Dan. "*Volcano*: A Poet's Record of His Search for His Roots." *International Examiner* 22, No. 10 (6 June 1995): 13.
    Mixed review of *Volcano* that admires Hongo's "fierce intelligence and showy, florid metaphorical language," but censures his occasional ponderousness and focus on minutia.

Tillinghast, Richard. Review of *Yellow Light*. *The Sewanee Review* XCI, No. 3 (Summer 1983): 478.
    Commends the "unusually wide range of moods,

subjects, and settings" displayed in Hongo's first collection.

Review of *Yellow Light. The Virginia Quarterly Review*

59, No. 1 (Winter 1983): 26.
Judges *Yellow Light* "a very uneven work" in which "some fine pieces of writing" are "[s]quirreled away among many seemingly pointless poems."

Additional coverage of Hongo's life and career is contained in the following sources published by The Gale Group: *Contemporary Authors,* **Vol. 133;** *Contemporary Authors Autobiography Series,* **Vol. 22;** *Dictionary of Literary Biography,* **Vol. 120; and** *EXPLORING Poetry.*

Alexis Saint-Léger Léger
1887-1975

(Full name Marie-Rene Auguste Alexis Saint-Léger Léger; also known by pseudonyms St.-John Perse, Alexis Léger, and Saintléger Léger) French West Indies–born French poet and essayist.

INTRODUCTION

Best known by the pseudonym St.-John Perse, Léger was a Nobel laureate whose verse reflected his perception that humanity is universally subject to alienation. Léger's focus on loneliness and solitude was tempered, however, by his acceptance of positive facets of existence. This latter position is demonstrated in his vivid descriptions of exotic landscapes and kinetic language praising the spiritual and physical aspects of life. Often prosaic in appearance, Léger's poetry is written in the free verse style of verset which, with its heavily cadenced, incantatory rhythms and reverential content, resembles portions of the Old Testament as well as the poetry of Walt Whitman and Paul Claudel.

Biographical Information

Léger was born on Saint-Léger-les-Feuilles, an island owned by his family in the French West Indies. As a child, Léger was exposed to the lush foliage and natural disasters—hurricanes, tidal waves, and earthquakes—indigenous to the tropics. Raised in Roman Catholicism, he became familiar with Hinduism through his childhood nurse. These elements provided him with a knowledge of botany, natural history, and diverse religions, all of which are amply displayed in his verse. Financial difficulties caused by a massive earthquake eventually forced Léger's family to sell the island and relocate to France. After an education encompassing medicine, philosopy, and literature, Léger embarked upon a career as a diplomat. As secretary of the French Embassy in Peking, China, he befriended Chinese philosophers and became familiar with Asian culture. His intellectual and professional development was influenced by the poet Paul Claudel, who acted as his mentor and advisor. Léger's esteemed government career climaxed when he was appointed Secretary-General of the French Foreign Ministry in 1932. Before this promotion, he had already published *Eloges* (1911) and *Anabase* (1924; *Anabasis*) but foreswore publishing future poems while in public service. Léger did continue to write, however, and reputedly amassed several volumes of manuscripts that were confiscated by Nazi soldiers in 1940. After refusing to cooperate with the collaborationist government in Vichy, he was stripped of his French citizenship. Léger fled France for England, and this traumatic exile is reflected in his later work. He settled in Washington, DC, and served as Fellow for the Library of Congress, consulting on French literature. With his French citizenship restored after the war, he returned to his native country in 1957 and received the Nobel Prize for Literature in 1960. Léger died in 1975.

Major Works

In many of the poems of *Eloges,* Leger evokes memories of his childhood and details life in the tropics through the use of sensuous and precise language. The poem sequence "Images à Crusoé" ("Pictures for Crusoe"), inspired by Daniel Defoe's prose work *Robinson Crusoe,* presents Crusoe as an emblem of solitude and loneliness. Similar themes pervade all of Léger's work. *Anabasis,* which is perhaps Léger's most celebrated composition, revolves around a nomadic tribe that explores and civilizes an arid, windy area similar to the Gobi Desert. Once the land is settled, a sense of longing provokes another excursion into the desert to repeat the process, and so illustrates the restless nature of humanity. The pieces in *Exil* recount the desperation of exile in images that are derived from contemporary and personal situations but are universally applicable. Léger claimed that he was redeemed from this bleakness through the inspiration and creation of poetry. *Vents* traces the destructive results of human knowledge on the development of modern civilization, as evidenced by the atomic explosion at Hiroshima. Léger's last major volumes, *Amers* and *Chronique,* focus on the affirmative qualities of life. Included in *Amers* are descriptions of erotic love, while

Chronique captures Léger meditating on his life's experiences and alluding freely to his previous works.

Critical Reception

Commentators have noted the rich imagery and complex style of Léger's verse, and some maintain that this style provided an almost hermetic quality that made it inaccessible to readers. Similarly, critics have complained that many of the words Léger employed are arcane, almost undefinable. Yet readers praise Léger's unusual uses of language that often result in innovative and unexpected phrasing. A standard approach Léger's work depends heavily on biographical interpretation, and commentators have traced his development as a poet from the early autobiographical subject matter to later work characterized by more impersonal language and generalized subjects. For Léger's exaltation of imagination and inclination toward antirealism, he is sometimes linked with the French Symbolist poets.

PRINCIPAL WORKS

Poetry

Éloges [as Saintléger Léger] 1911
Amitié du prince [*Friendship of the Prince*] 1924
Anabase [*Anabasis*] 1924
Exil [*Exile*] 1942
Pluies [*Rains*] 1944
Quatre Poèmes 1941-1944 [*Four Poems*] 1944
Vents [*Winds*] 1946
Amers [*Seamarks*] 1953
L'ordre des oixeaux [*Birds*] 1962
Oeuvres completes [*Complete Works*] 1972
Chant pour un équinoxe [*Song for an Equinox*] 1975

Other Major Works

A Selection of Works for an Understanding of World Affairs since 1914 [as Alexis Saintléger Léger] (essays) 1943
On Poetry (speech) 1961
Letters of St.-John Perse (letters) 1979

*Published as an expanded second edition in 1925 under the pseudonym St.-J Perse.

CRITICISM

Katherine Garrison Chapin (essay date 1952)

SOURCE: "Saint-John Perse: Notes on Some Poetic Contrasts," in *Sewanee Review,* Vol. LX, No. 1, Winter, 1952, pp. 65-81.

[*In the following essay, Chapin examines contradictory elements of Léger's poetry, describing them as the "aristocratic" and "primitive" aspects of his writing.*]

"O Poète, ô bilingue, homme assailli du dieu! homme parlant dans l'équivoque!"

Vents (II)

The poetry of Saint-John Perse, constantly becoming more available to American readers, is taking its place here in a peculiarly alien soil. This has little to do with the fact that he has elected to live among us for the last ten years, years stretched beyond the necessary exile imposed on an important diplomatic figure when his government took a role of compromise and cowardice to which he could not give his allegiance. The legend of the poet veiled and separated from the man of affairs continues to surround him. Under varying aspects this separation is at the basis of some of the significant conflicts and contrasts to be found throughout his work.

The austerity of this separateness and the hermetic quality of the poetry itself—as well as the long unrhymed strophe, the lack of syntax and the elliptical approach—have made it difficult for the general reader, and kept it a poetry for the few. But today it is receiving recognition long overdue with the publication of the French quarterly, *Les Cahiers de la Pleiade,* given over entirely to appreciation of Saint-John Perse. Here the elder writers, Gide, Claudel and Valery Larbaud, join younger critics and poets of many different schools and nationalities (English, Spanish, German, Italian, Swiss, American) to attest his significance. Such a tribute to a French poet during his lifetime is as rare as the criticism is interesting.

The American reader, who has become familiar with the influence of the French Symbolists on modern writing through Pound and Eliot, is finding in this epic poetry of Perse a stimulation and satisfaction far beyond his knowledge of the foreign tongue in which it is written. Almost impossible as it is to translate into poetry—the very metal of the French language relates to a distinctive table of values—the fine rhythmic English of T. S. Eliot's [translation of] *Anabase*; the translations of Louise Varese, and Denis Devlin, in bi-lingual editions respectively of *Éloges* and *Exil,* serve at least as introduction and guidance to the originals.

That this poetry has been translated into many other foreign tongues is a recognition of its vitality. Pierre Jean Jouve, the French poet, has suggested that Perse himself has the ambitious dream of creating a universal language of poetry. This, I think, is erroneous. The voice is French, in all its nuances, to be heard in its special richness of overtone, in its epic music, in its delicate inner rhyming, only by ears attuned to French. Yet its breadth and power extend beyond the frontiers of language. It is outside of time and space, having neither region nor era.

"Il n'est d'histoire que de l'âme, il n'est d'aisance que de l'âme."

The whole meaning of Perse will not be found within the confines of any one national literature, and he himself, with his declared hatred of "literary doctrine," will never be interested in elucidating it, in the fashion of some contemporary poets. I propose here to consider a few of the poetic conflicts and contradictions in his work, for the sidelights they may throw on an impressive body of poetry. These conflicts are, in themselves, creative, they are often the spark which sets off the fire. One might almost say, as in a primitive myth, they are the male and female principle in all things which join together to fructify. This deep vein of oppositeness—the strophe and antistrophe, the dramatic clashes of personality—exist in this poetry to a fecund use. The poet is both "un homme assailli du dieu," and "un homme parlant dans l'équivoque." These poems, in which we find opposed violence and wisdom, barbarity and serenity, chaos and a supreme spiritual order, take form and content from these vivid antagonisms of his own poetic personality.

Yeats has said: "I make out of the quarrel with my friends, rhetoric; out of the quarrel with myself, poetry." Perse's attitude to *rhétorique* is as austere as was Verlaine's to *éloquence*; but from these profound disagreements with his other self, what we shall call, for lack of better words, his aristocratic personality and his primitive personality, spring some of his most memorable poetry.

This contrast serves also to illuminate some of his remarkable uses of language, and the imaginative contradictions within his images. Much has been written of that language, the exotic and archaic words, the concrete names of strange trades and professions culled from distant parts of the world, belonging to French speech, but a speech seldom heard in poetry. Valery Larbaud, in his introduction to the Russian edition of *Anabase* (as early as 1926), thus records the impact of this strange tongue on contemporary French writers: "In his hands the language of French poetry is like some splendid thoroughbred he is riding; he uses its qualities but forces it to move at a gait new to it, and contrary to its habits." Perse does not use words in a foreign tongue, except an occasional American noun, and never the expressions or images from any literature, except the Bible as myth, or from history, or from what he calls the Great Books. But in the imaginative image, the image perhaps based on a real act or emotion, the startling twist, the unexpected, is, as it were, the sound of that other voice. "At the pitch of passion, at the peak of desire, the same gull on the wing." . . ."he who discovers one day the very perfume of his soul, in the planking of a new sail boat.". . ."Et il y avait aussi bien à redire à cette enseigne du bonheur, sur vos golfes trop bleus, comme le palmier d'or au fond des boîtes à cigares." Over and over again, the anastrophic voice speaks and the eye sees, the naked, impudent eye, never impressed by the accepted, the classic view, but, as in *Anabase,* with a quick, crude touch of the actual, "la ville jaune, casquée d'ombre, avec ses caleçons de filles aux fenêtres."

In *Éloges* he has immortalized some of the picture memories of his own childhood in Guadaloupe and the West Indies, where, as a very French product of French parents, he was born and spent the first twelve years of his life. Here as a child of a fresh, explorative nature, he was observant at once of vast aspects and definite details— "the sea like a sky," the "wounding of sugar cane at the mill", "the happy adventure of a million children rushing to the shore, wearing their eyelashes like umbels of flow-

ers." Seldom has the quality of childhood been more sensitively expressed than in the verse where he tells his nurse not to pull his hair, as she brushes it, ending with this description of his own preoccupations:

> je sortirai, car j'ai affaire: un insecte m'attend pour traiter. Je me fais joie
> du gros oeil à facettes: anguleux, imprévu, comme le fruit du cyprès.
> Ou bien j'ai une alliance aves les pierres veinées-bleu: etvous me laissez également,
> assis, dans l'amitié de mes genoux.

The two important strains of personality were evident in this poet from his earliest beginnings. Even the little boy sitting in the friendship of his knees was aware of existence on more than one level. He looked at the immediate world of his elders, listened to "things said in profile," and took his place within the formal pattern of a colonial homestead. The authoritative patrician, whom he saw in his father, surveying his plantation, directing and teaching his dependents, became symbolic, and the whole country of this childhood remembrance was an ordered hierarchy. He fitted into it, now from one side, now from the other, young and imperious, or the little savage who loved a horse, remembering with affection his mulatto nurse who smelt deliciously of castor bean, and the servitors in the tall wooden house whose names he did not know, but whose faces

> insonores, couleur de papaye et d'ennui, qui s'arrêtaient derrière nos chaises comme des astres morts.

He was impatient with the sick man who wished to stop the boat, fascinated by the dead fish-head which jeered, the Negro towering like a prophet about to shout into a conque, and the "yellow black-spotted-purple-at-the-base flowers that are used for the diarrhea of horned animals." The memory of the tropic islands and waters of *Éloges* is never the sentimental backward looking to a happier time. It represents a Garden of Eden of peculiar purity and vitality, a state of mind, a time of discovery of man and beast. The nostalgia for this land he framed into a series of short poem sketches called *Images à Crusoé.* Here the free adventurer and explorer is imprisoned in a city The evening descends in a "reek of men," and symbols of the parrot, his Man Friday, and his goatskin parasol return to mock him with their metamorphoses into their civilized degenerations.

Thus at the outset of Perse's poetic career the two deep and underlying contrasts make themselves felt—the man of authority and the impulsive, the natural man. The aristocratic thread of personality does not belong to any traditional point of view, or attach itself to any social or economic system. It is a spiritual nobility which assumes lineage of pure blood, in animals as among men. It implies strength and decision, freedom from waste mixtures; blood that is purified, ideas that are renewed by contact with the sources of life.

And alongside of this strain of classic restraint runs the other, the free, the uncivilized, the radical overthrower of ancient systems, the innovator, the lover of wild and empty places, "flagrants et nul," where life may start again, the man with bare head and empty hands, whose eyes are for the new day, the new forces stirring in the world, even if they should become forces which will overwhelm him.

It might be easy to exaggerate what this Antillian childhood planted in him. His love for it returns in images again and again. Paul Claudel speaks of him as belonging to the West, the land of the setting sun toward which turn a poet's desires. But the years in which he wandered among the islands in comparative freedom were counterbalanced later by the classical French education in town and university, including studies in both law and medicine, the contact of reality with men in military service, the development continually of the delights of botanist, anthropologist and geographer. Unlike the city bred Frenchman, he was always ready to travel, to wander, to explore any corner of the earth, preferably the parts where man had not set foot, but at least where man's life had not become so crystalized that the unexpected could not upset it.

This interest in the bizarre, which has been remarked by critics and called "exotic" by different names, and which finds expression in his impatience before certain usually accepted forms of art, springs from a conviction that the thing which is perfectly finished is dead. The form which is entirely harmonious and of its time, has expressed itself fully, can say no more, and Perse finds no incentive in contemplating the past. The past appears only as affecting the present and the future. Within these poems nothing is ever static. "I honor the living," he cries at the end of *Éloges.* He is essentially a poet of the verb, of action. The incongruous which he enumerates many times, the strange juxtapositions of dignity and impudence, the classical restraint yet barbaric interference, these things are not fossils, they carry the seeds of life, are still in flux, and express the moving and vital world wherein as poet he lives. He writes in *Vents* "et trois feuilles errantes autour d'un osselet de Reine morte mènent leur dernière ronde." For the moment the three leaves and the knuckle bone of the dead Queen, whether he imagined or saw them, expressed a point of silence and the futility of pride.

Into these strange poetic dialogues in which, as Roger Caillois has pointed out, the reader is never quite certain who speaks or who is listening, run continually these contrasting strains of personality. One protagonist is pictured clearly for us by those who establish his fame, in *L'Amitié du Prince,* an early poem, published shortly after *Éloges.* The discourse here is turned over to "men on journeys arguing the things of the spirit." It is they who tell of the Prince, "the man of thin nostrils among us. . . . Healer and Assessor and Enchanter . . . I have seen the sign on your forehead . . . you may be silent among us, if that is your pleasure, or decide to go alone. . . . We ask of you nothing but to be there." "Homme très simple parmi nous; le plus secret dans ses desseins; dur à soi-même . . . et fomentant au plus haut point de l'âme une grande querelle." What this soul's quarrel is we are not told. But almost at once that other personality, the barbaric, the man in touch with live and sentient things, comes into being. The Prince "seizes

by its nostrils an invisible quivering beast . . . and goes through the day that has the odor of entrails, and nourishes his clean thoughts on the whey of the morning." There are descriptions of the Prince with his aigrette, in his "mouchoir de tête," shaking dice and bones, covered with heavy gold. He is named no further, but the Narrator hastens to meet him saying that "friendship is welcome, like a gift of odorant leaves." This poem, part of a spiritual biography called "La Gloire des Rois," ends at each section with the cryptic refrain: "It is of the King that I speak, ornament of our vigils, honor of the sage without honor," and the poem takes on a quality of mystery.

It would be impossible to consider the poetry of Saint-John Perse even in a cursory way without giving place to his sense of mystery. It is present in every poem, and is at the basis of his conception of poetry itself.

In the early poems, as in *Éloges,* the interest in occult things is objective, and we read of the dreamer with dirty cheeks who comes slowly out of an old dream; of men and their daughters who chewed a certain herb. They are as fascinating to the young explorer as animals and boats. In *Anabase* we continually find the trappings of the magical, omens and rites—"sacrifices of colts on the tombs of children"—and in *Pluies* he says, "let him come and live on my roof among the signs and portents." He speaks of "Gods close by, bleeding gods" in *Poème à l'Etrangère,* and asks for the "favor of the god" on his poem, in *Vents.*

This evocation of the mystical is not a lip-service, a rhetorical expression. At the basis of his poetry is the acknowledgment of a mysterious power. There are things we shall never know, a veil which will never be withdrawn. We read of the enigma of the neant in *Exil,* and of the abyss in *Vents.* Mysterious is the "force occulte de ton chant" in *Exil,* the source of poetry.

This characteristic as poet is the expression of both personalities, the authoritative and the humble. Paul Valéry has said that "un homme qui n'a jamais tenté de se faire comme les dieux, c'est moins qu'un homme." Perse was a very young man when he wrote *Éloges* but already he had assumed one quality of the god, the mystery of silence, with no desire to be completely understood—"bouche close à jamais sur la feuille de l'âme." This is not always a proud or dominant silence, it may be concerned with humility, as in *Exil* where everything is strange, his own power strangest of all. This pervading sense of the unseen, the intangible, has nothing to do with a religious belief or fervor. Yet there is great reverence in it, wonder and reverence for life, for the multiple, changing aspects of life, and for the inexplicable essence of living.

Anabase, the poem which is essentially the expression of what we have called the aristocratic spirit, which is indeed "a song of strength for men," may also be read on another level as prophetic speech. Like the Sun, "who is unnamed but whose power is amongst us," the speaker represents the moving forces behind this anabasis. The title itself evokes a double meaning; a journey into the interior, a journey which goes on "les routes où s'en aillent les gens de toute race," but which is also a spiritual journey. We read of the cycles of men on earth, the founding of a city, the establishing of laws, always with the knowledge that "we shall not dwell forever in these yellow lands, our pleasance." Here also we find kings, ambassadors, and princes but they pass through the poem leaving less trace than the "Master of the Grain," the "Master of the Salt," and other conditions of men in their ways and manners, "the man with the flute," "the man with the falcon," "the man with the bees." The humble man takes over again and the face of the poem is toward the future, and a new "Terre arable du songe!"

It would be impossible to consider the poetry of Saint-John Perse even in a cursory way without giving place to his sense of mystery. It is present in every poem, and is at the basis of his conception of poetry itself.

—Katherine Garrison Chapin

After the publication of *Anabase* in 1924 there was silence for eighteen years from this poet who was living the double life of statesman and *Voyant,* and not publishing what he wrote. There were the years in China as a young diplomat with opportunities to sense the cross-currents flowing into and around a conventionalized and ancient culture, the other world quality of the "native city" of Peking where he lived, and his travels in the Gobi desert. There were the years in Europe and the experiences of dealing with important men and small men in that separate life of statecraft and diplomacy in France—the life from which he kept his *vie de l'esprit* hermetically sealed. Like the Stranger in *Anabase* he "lived naked under his tent" and did not come out. In the interval that one poem moved about Europe, translated into at least four foreign languages. Then came the abrupt ending of that life, when the war sent him to the United States and the Wanderer and Explorer became in fact the Exile. We do not know in what manner he would have spoken again, what different discoveries and prophecies would have filled the gap between *Anabase* (1924) and *Exil* (1942) if the consequences of the war had not intervened. All his unpublished work of those years was stolen and destroyed by the Nazis with German thoroughness, when they occupied Paris, and raided his apartment, for they ranked him high on their list of public enemies.

There have been exiled poets before in the history of the world's literature, and their severe upheavals have been expressed in new spiritual and poetic direction. We think of Isaiah's imperishable Lament by the Waters of Babylon, Dante's long inward journey, and the renewed lyrical vitality of Victor Hugo exiled in Guernsey. It did not matter if the imposed separation was as severe physically as mentally, or whether it covered much territory. For Dante, exiled from his beloved Florence, the journey to the Inferno was less difficult. But exile for each poet carried that sense of loss, the sense of being cut off from what was rightly his own. This has been true of Saint-John Perse even though, as poet,

exile has been his native air. He has been able to put the seal on one era or phase of his own life and start again, with a richness as of a fresh insemination, what might be called his "American decade." This does not imply in any way a change of allegiance or change of personality. The exile in a strange land can be more surely a creature of himself, of his own language and inheritance, of his own nourishing roots and background, than one who returns to take up a changed life in changed surroundings. But it is an act of will. There can be no regrets wasted over the "poèmes nés d'hier." Once their author was heard to say, to the condolences of a sympathizer, "perhaps after all it is a good thing, the page is wiped clean for a fresh start." Here the Prince speaks once more, the Prophet, uncertain of everything in the material future, yet sure of the fact that the lightning will lay bare to him again, "the bed of its immense designs."

Into *Anabase* the voice and figure of the Poet enters only on the side, in one or two beautiful images:

> And the earth in its winged seeds, like a poet in
> his thoughts, travels.

But when the Exile, facing the sea, on a lonely island, "comme l'ossuaire des saisons," looks into the complete emptiness of the future, it is as poet only, stripped of all human allegiance, concerned with the syntax of the lightning, with the errant force in the world which will draw song again from his lips, with the birth once more of a poem. He is Wanderer, Stranger, and Peregrine, he yearns to lie down "en tous lieux vains et fades où gît le gout de la grandeur." But the contrasting personality comes vividly to life in the free man with his hands "more naked than at birth," his Numidian soul, and his gift of prophecy, who will assemble on the wastes of exile a great poem "born of nothing, made of nothing," which nothing can destroy. He assumes a primal strength in his repudiation of the past, "le môt vain," and "les poèmes nés d'hier, ah! les poèmes nés un soir à la fourche de l'éclair, il en est comme de la cendre au lait des femmes, trace infime. . . ." In a long passage he describes other lives which were lonely and separated from their fellows by choice or occupation. Of these he says: "Ceux-la sont princes de l'exil, et n'ont que faire de mon chant."

This poem suggests the obscure essence of poetry: "O Prodigue sous le sel et l'écume de juin! Garde vivante parmi nous la force occulte de ton chant!". . . Yet even at the moment of spiritual aloofness the poet faces the necessity of living in the world and ends with the exhortation: "Et c'est l'heure, Ô Poète, de decliner ton nom, ta naissance, et ta race."

I have given this much space to a consideration of *Exil,* his first poem written in America, because it contains the keynote for those that follow. Under the new and deeper emotion it is interesting to find other contrasts and contradictions at work.

In *Poème à l'Ètrangère* (1942), poignant, though shorter and less far-reaching in its implications than the other poems, we are made conscious of the weight of nostalgia in the warm and muted "third summer of exile." We hear the voice of the poet apostrophizing the foreign lady, whose "green blood of the Castiles" beats in her temples. The poet walks "with my freeman's stride, without horde or tribe . . . and my bare forehead laurelled with phosphorescent bees." He expresses the quiet depth of his loneliness with a yearning for "ma chienne d'Europe, qui fut blanche et, plus que moi, poète."

Pluies (1943) is a poem of man's aspirations and failures. Its abstract ideas are expressed in concrete, colorful images—the sterility of man's intellectual life contrasted with the cleansing fertilizing power of the warm rains on the earth. It is written in three contrapuntal voices. One voice describes the rain, and the idea for a poem the poet will write, "L'Idée, plus nue qu'un glaive au jeu des factions"; a second is the poet's own, and a third, the critical personality, a new antagonist. This "Seigneur terrible de mon rire" sees the poem, "la rose obscène," as sentimentality, as fraud, even as self-pity, and the poet begs to be saved from "l'aveu, de l'acceuil et du chant."

Neiges (1944) speaks with an undertone of profound sadness, yet lifted into a song of reverence and praise. It celebrates the "first snows of absence," and in various shades of white—white fog, white mist, owls, mistletoe, white dahlias—evokes the image of an older woman whose high spiritual lineage is a "great *Ave* of grace on our path." Here the interesting contrasts are subtle differences between the spoken and the silent word.

The qualities of these first four poems written in America, *Exil, Pluies, Neiges* and *Poème à l'Etrangère,* are present in *Vents,* the last and so far the most ambitious. Claudel has said that it rises "au milieu de notre langue français tel qu'un Mont St. Michel," and Léon Paul Fargue, in a letter written just before his death, spoke of it as the opening of a new poetic country. Concerned as always with the "histoire de l'âme," he speaks with prophetic and incantatory voice, but in it there is also recognizable for once an actual path that men and their ideas have taken in history. The winds symbolize the great forces that sweep before them the migrations from east to west. It moves, as do all his poems, in space rather than time. The winds contain in themselves opposing qualities, are nourishing, refreshing, are breath and life; and are also destructive, the counsellors of violence. They buffet and cajole, sweep men onward toward the west to explore and to conquer, and finally bring them back. "Nous reviendrons un soir d'Automne, avec ce goût de lierre sur nos lèvres." No one must desert the men of his race, he says, lifting what André Breton has called a lance of St. George for his own people. "Et vous, hommes du nombre et de la masse, ne pesez pas les hommes de ma race. Ils ont vécu plus haut que vous dans les abîmes de l'opprobre."

Vents is the speech of philosopher, man of action, European man, but it also tells the spiritual travails of the poet. His final words, the strophe which André Gide quotes at the end of his preface to his *Anthologie de la Poesie Francaise* (Perse is the only living poet included in this notable collection) are worth quoting in full.

Quand la violence eut renouvelé le lit des hommes
  sur la terre,
Un très vieil arbre, à sec de feuilles, reprit le fil de
  ses maximes . . .
Et un autre arbre de haut rang montait déjà des
  grandes Indes souterraines,
Avec sa feuille magnétique et son chargement de
  fruits nouveaux.

It is characteristic that the end of his most important poem leaves us in a prophetic ambiguity. We are uncertain if the great tree is poetry, or language, or the symbol of man's spiritual growth. Perhaps it is all three. This ambiguity is rooted in the underlying conflicts which I have noted and enters into the construction of his own art. It is also found in his attitude to words.

It would be too long to chronicle all the salient things said by Perse about "the word." It is magic, it is a spark, a flash of lightning, a fall of dew. There is scarcely anything as pristine as the "éheance d'un mot pur." The word is often personified—"et mon coeur visité d'une étrange voyelle"—the very syllables of a word having potency: "à l'heure où les constellations labiles qui changent de vocable pour les hommes d'exil." A name has a special meaning but more powerful when it is unnamed. In *Anabase* he says: "Thus was the city founded and placed in the morning under the labials of a holy name." But the name is never given. This myth of the unnamed belongs to the essence of the poetic mystery, and carries over into all the poems, which are never given a designation of place. Poignant details of description—"busy lands with the locusts at noon," "bay leaves at morning all laden with gold lemons"—suggest the countries of *Anabase.* "La mer à la ronde roule son bruit de crânes sur les grèves" speaks in *Exil* of the shores of a sea. The country of *Neiges* is the north, across an ocean and out to great plains. The country of *Pluies* is in the south, where the rain takes hold of the city like the descending roots of the banyan tree. The continent of *Vents* is more clearly designated than the others. Who could misplace these images?

Hiver, bouclé comme un bison, . .
Hiver, au gout de skunk et de carabe et de fumée
  de bois de hickory . . .

Yet each of these regions is seen in a peculiar and imaginative light; they are unidentified, unnamed, yet belong vividly to this earth.

Perse contrasts the living word of language and the dead or written word of literature. The word, as language, has again a magic quality. Its personification and delineations are wide. Language in *Neiges* is a great country, and the poet desires to wander in it, among the oldest layers of speech, "ascending that pure unwritten delight where runs the ancient human phrase." *Unwritten* is the key word here. For to Perse language, the great tree of language we meet at the beginning of *Vents,* is never the written language of books, of learning, or erudition. It is never language put into order or form, especially the forms of literature.

There are two significant passages where he condemns the written word; one is in ***Pluies,*** where the Rains are exhorted to "wash from the heart of man . . . the most beautiful sentence, the most beautiful sequence . . . the well-turned phrase, the noble page. Wash, wash from the hearts of men their taste for roundelays and for elegies . . . wash the bedding of dream and the litter of knowledge." In this poem his contradictions meet head on, for in the end, the magic Rains he has invoked wash away his poem, "mon Poème, ô Pluies! qui ne sera pas écrit-"

The other passage is in ***Vents,*** where he condemns Books and Libraries, the "Basilica of the Book," "où sont les livres au sérail, où sont les livres dans leur niches . . . les livres tristes . . . Prêtres et prêtise."

This priesthood of the books, all that is stale or sterile in culture and knowledge, is antagonistic to the man to whom the excitement of words, the very breath of the new word is

> une fraîcheur d'haleine par le monde
> comme le souffle même de l'ésprit.

yet describing in ***Vents*** the sweep of the new lands, he can turn about, and say: "Toute la terre aux arbres, par là-bas, sur fond de vignes noires, comme un Bible d'ombre et de fraîcheur dans le déroulement des plus beaux textes de ce monde." To evoke a new country by the rhythm and beauty of the most ancient of writings is characteristic of the refreshing unexpectedness of this poet.

Throughout these pages I have traced the significant conflicts and contrasts in the writings of Perse, which spring from what for convenience I have called the "aristocratic" and the "primitive" poetic personalities, and indicated their development through brief surveys of the substance of his major poems. I have left till the end the memorable things he has said about the function of the poet, and poetry itself. Each poem builds into this picture and we are confronted by a richness of image piled on image, fresh, provocative—and enigmatic.

One must at once accept the impersonal quality of this poetry. His characterizations of speaker or listener are as ambiguous as they are evocative, Wanderer, Narrator, Stranger, Enchanter. When we meet the word Poet it may not refer to the writer of the particular poem which we happen to be reading. In ***Anabase*** the figure of the Poet strides through the poem and out again. In ***Pluies*** the voice of the Poet is only one in the antiphonal trio. ***Exil*** is concerned with the poet's realization of himself. ***Vents*** unfolds an important spiritual growth of the Poet in the development of the race of men, with its recurring urgency—"et vous avez si peu de temps pour naître à cet instant." Yet there are moments when he heaps scorn on the rhetorician, the poetaster: "je t'ai pesé, poète, et t'ai trouvé de peu de poids." He weighs the poet, and dismisses him, even as he does the "green locust of sophism" "Et toi, Poète, ô contumace et quatre fois relaps." What the relapses are we are not told.

Yet Perse has given us a new idea of what both the poem and the poet can be, an ideal of greatness. In revealing images he speaks of his own conviction that the source of poetry is the subconscious, the occult force, "au point sensible de mon front ou le poème s'établit." The poet is silent before this power, and yields to his inspiration: "he who enters the arena of his new creation, uplifted in his whole being and for three days no one may look upon his silence." The poet under different titles is Seer, Diviner, Magician; he is Prophet, one of those who blows with horns at the gates of the future. At his highest he too partakes of that division of personality. In his own person he speaks with two tongues.

"Ô Poète, Ô bilingue! . . . homme assaili du dieu, homme parlant dans l'équivoque." "Equivocal" in Perse's far-reaching overtones has not the questionable meaning which it has in English. The word is a key to an important quality of this poet. It concerns the duality of all things, the mysteries of language, and the poet's pursuit of the absolute, the ineffable, which may be captured only to be lost again, "the great delible poem." His poetry is part of that "other tongue," that "seule et longue phrase sans césure à jamais inintelligible," the long strophe which he has clothed in a symbolism that only to the eye of reason will be forever unintelligible.

Wallace Fowlie (essay date 1953)

SOURCE: "The Poetics of St.-John Perse," in *Poetry,* Vol. 82, No. 6, September, 1953, pp. 345-50.

[*In the following favorable review of* Vents, *Fowlie places Léger within the context of modern French poets as well as the tradition of Symbolism and Surrealism.*]

St.-John Perse revindicates, reactivates the ancient belief that each event in the history of man signifies something else. In this sense, the work of the poet is comparable to the work of the psychoanalyst who explores the meanings of things and at the end of the search illuminates them. Poetry is a combination of two languages: one, the words defined in dictionaries and used by the contemporaries of the poet, the vocabularies of the uneducated and the educated; and the other, the rhythm of language, the spell created by combinations of words. This second language is in reality the poet's effort to move beyond langauge, to reach the ineffable. Language itself may be for man his deepest spiritual experience. Beyond language extends the void, the unmeasured spaces inhabited by the winds of which Perse speaks in his poem. The meaning of the winds which blow over the face of the earth and disturb all perishable things is the subject matter of his poem. The opening words speak of the winds in quest, of oracles and maxims, and of the narrator who seeks for his poem the favor of a god.

St.-John Perse, as the contemporary poet, does not borrow from the traditional forms of poetry, but from the words of language itself and from the sentiment of vertigo felt by the poet on the brink of space, in the midst of limitless winds. As much as any man of any period, Alexis Léger has travelled along the highways of many lands and across the oceans of the world. The course of his poem is the meaning of such travels, the new style of grandeur he refers to, and the pure song about which there is no real knowledge. The weight of the words would seem to be the only force not dispersed by the winds. The words, riveted to the pages, are those signs, fixed forever, of things which move with the wind and die in it. "Ashes and squams of the spirit," he says. "Taste of asylum and casbah."

At the opening of the poem, other words, deeply imbedded in the text, appear almost synonymous with "winds": "dreams," for example, when joined with such an adjective as "favorable"; and "intoxicated," whereby "wine" is associated with the invasions of doctrine. Such words have the same power of describing circles around the earth. The poet who "is still with us" has once again spoken the words of a living man which recreate his world with some of its multiple meanings. He is the one taught to think something, and then within and through that something he thinks something else. Poetry, in such a work as **Winds,** reaffirms its power and its destiny to draw upon all forms of knowledge: psychoanalysis, history, phenomenology, autobiography. It is perhaps the one art of synthesis, able to show at moments of intense illumination the once complete form of our shattered world.

Certain poems, like the one under discussion, are able to be composed because man inhabits what Perse calls "the calcinated earth of dreams." We may be certain that whatever thought occurs to us, its depth and its originality will not at first be recognizable to us. The finite brief character of a human existence echoes depths which will never be sounded. No one thought remains for long what it seems to be at first. The poet is precisely the one who torments traditionally accepted words and things until they release some of their unsuspected meanings. In order to rise up once again into the world, such meanings had to take detours and even provoke ruses and deceptions.

Claudel in his essay on **Vents,** reprinted from *La Revue de Paris* of November 1949, in this elaborately prepared American edition, says that the second part of the poem evokes America, both the puritan melancholy of the north and the stagnant stupor of the south. Certain words in the text clearly justify this belief: Audubon, sumac, hanging moss, Columbus. The poem unfolds in wave after wave of images, almost as if they preceded the poet, because their very profusion might have paralyzed him. Their forms do not appear in the least contestable or corroded, and yet they proclaim the primacy of the obscure, the sulphurous, the pythic. The winds, in this section of the poem, carry with them the smell of fire. They may well establish an "ascetic rule."

The poet, the man "assailed by the god," speaks equivocally. He speaks with brilliance about the negative traits of his art. He knows what his method is not: an intellectual program, a will to please, a self-complacency not always communicable. What his method is, is too vast to define,

too close today to our manner of reading poetry. **Vents** of St.-John Perse, as well as *Les Illuminations* of Rimbaud, and to some extent *Les Fleurs du Mal* of Baudelaire, are among those modern works of poetry reflecting the complex degree of sensibility which man reached in the 19th century and continues to maintain in the 20th. Perse has taken his place beside the four or five major poets of modern France: Baudelaire, Mallarmé, Rimbaud, Valéry, Claudel. Like theirs, his work defies any facile nomenclature of romantic or classical. A major poetic work will always appear in excess of the literary school closest to it. Adherence to classicism seems to imply an emphasis on form, on the poet as demiurge and creator. Romanticism is revealed in the poet's passivity to the exterior world, to the cosmos of matter. Perse and the other poets whose tradition he continues represent extremes in their role of demiurge and in their trait of passivity to the cosmic forces. They are extraordinary technicians drawing upon all the known resources of their art, upon the most modern beliefs in ancient poetic wisdom, and upon the most ancient tenets still visible in symbolism and surrealism. Each in his own way strives for some balance between his inner psychic tensions and his virtuosity. But the balance reached has many degrees. The art of Valéry and that of a typical surrealist would represent extremes of this very balance.

Part Three of **Winds** evokes the history of the conquerors, their long itineraries, the new lands, the setting up of new trade. The poet too belongs to the race of discoverers: to the conquistadores, well-diggers, astrologers. In his acquisitions he seizes with similar boldness the goals of his search, of his humor and of his sorrow. Into a poem he puts the originality of his discovery as one puts the essence of flowers into a flask. After that is done, there are darker and often humiliating ways to follow in the transmission of the poem to publisher and from publisher to public. The Bollingen presentation of **Winds,** in large format and handsome typography reaches, as the poem does in its right, an extreme and a generosity calculated to make of this transmission an exemplary trade.

The general effect of the entire poem, and especially of the third section, where the wanderers are men with antennae, is one of constant movement through fear that all movement will cease. In the midst of the poem, it is impossible to believe that it will ever end. The poet is no longer the prisoner of his form; he is the prisoner of his poem which is limitless. Each stanza, as it moves ahead, acts as a detonator for the next. No one picture is allowed to remain static for fear that it might settle into a symbol with an established human relationship. This is no poem to be anthologized where it might testify to a moment in time and to the achievement of a literary school. It testifies only to itself, to the honor of men and their failure, to their torches held in the wind and extinguished, to the conjunction of their experiences. Even the form of the novel would attempt the imposing of greater limitations on such an inexhaustible subject matter. All the characters are phantoms in these winds, liberated, authentic phantoms whose power is never confused with any vulgar opportunism.

The wind is the element giving us life. It is in our lungs and in our mouth in capsules of emptiness, necessary for us whether we move over distances covered by a Drake or a crusader, or whether we remain in one corner of the planet and perish through excess of wisdom. Poems, in a destiny comparable to the winds, bear seed and fruit. A book is a series of separations, departures, returns, of changings of speed. The fourth section of **Winds** evokes not only the plateaux of the world and the aging roads of pilgrimages. It evokes as well the dilemma of man's ceaseless questioning and the equivocal mask of art placed over all interrogations. The poem here is less a novel or an epic than it is a cosmology. A cosmological novel, perhaps.

The poet's experience which made possible such a poem as **Winds** is beyond question irreplaceable and unique. But the poem is also the history of contemporary sensibility. The paradox is constructed around the subjective uniqueness of the poem and its universality. The rigorous methods employed in the writing of history will never succeed in providing the kind of history of modern man narrated in such a poem as **Winds.** Historians are quickly dated even if their subject matter never goes out of date. Poets take generations and even centuries to come into some kind of comprehensible focus, and their poems, more intense and penetrating than written history, combine with the future in order to bring it about.

The action of a literary school, such as symbolism or surrealism, tends to serve as the history of a moment and of a sensibility. The major poet is usually characterized by his separation from the school and from any historical approach. This was the case of Mallarmé and Rimbaud. It is the case today of Claudel and St.-John Perse. Exile and solitude are themes in the poetry of Perse and they appear to be the conditions of the present life of Alexis Léger. The major traits of his art tend to make it into a sacred text: elegance of circumlocution, unusual words, constant reference to celebrations and rituals, ambiguities arising from the juxtaposition of the cultivated and the elemental, the baroque and the bare.

No message is visible in **Winds,** but the poem is a remarkable statement of the poet's principal paradox. The poet is both separated from human activity and deeply involved in customs, beliefs, rites, relationships. He is both contemplator of what the world holds and participant in his social group and in his national life. The seriousness with which he considers life seems to come from this combination of homogeneity and isolation. The official attitude of the symbolists was aloofness. The official attitude of the surrealists was aggressiveness. St.-John Perse represents a more traditional, more central attitude of the poet. The precise word is difficult to choose, because on the whole this attitude is seldom felt today, but it would be perhaps solemnity or sacredness. It would be a word powerful enough to contain and harmonize the contradictions of man's fate as it appears to us within the limits of time and space.

Arthur J. Knodel (essay date 1955)

SOURCE: "The Imagery of Saint-John Perse's *Neiges*," in *PMLA,* Vol. LXX, No. 1, March, 1955, pp. 5-18.

[*In the following essay, Knodel offers a close reading of* Neiges *to demonstrate Léger's ability to convey "the most intimate of his feelings" through language that seems impersonal and objective.*]

The most significant studies to date of Saint-John Perse approach his work "extensively," keeping the poet's total output in the foreground. Commentary on individual poems is not entirely lacking, especially on *Anabase* and *Vents,* but nothing approaching exhaustive textual analysis of any one poem has yet been attempted. The present study has been undertaken in the belief that an intensive approach to a small segment of Perse's work may supplement and give sharper relief to the insights of more general studies and perhaps lead some readers more directly to the actual text of one of the unquestioned major poets of our time.

For the purpose of such a study *Neiges* offers several advantages. First, there are the purely mechanical ones: *Neiges* is neither too long nor too short, and it already exists in numerous editions. It is, moreover, quite exemplary of Perse's highly personal idiom. And, although it is acknowledged to be one of the poet's most beautiful pieces, *Neiges* has been relatively neglected. That fact alone would justify speaking of the poem at some length. But more important than all these advantages is one that will become more apparent as examination of the text proceeds. It stems from the fact that the subject-matter of *Neiges* is a human relationship felt and understood by almost all mankind, whereas most of the other long poems, from *Anabase* on, have subjects that can be formulated only in elaborate intellectual terms, and then frequently with great difficulty.

The analysis of *Neiges* will be made largely in terms of its imagery, for it is the imagery that forms the real armature of the poem; and prosody, syntax, and vocabulary tend to be functions of that imagery. This statement is not meant to imply that such is always the case or that Perse's prosody, syntax, and especially vocabulary are negligible or routinely traditional. Nothing could be further from the truth. All three merit separate studies. Here, however, the chief interest lies in presenting a single artistic unit in which, as I hope to show, the crucial principle of unity is the imagery.

Neiges is the fourth poem of the "American series," which began with *Exil* (1941), and in the Bollingen edition it bears the postscript: "New York, 1944." That indication facilitates comprehension of the poem, as does the dedication "A Françoise-Renée Saint-Léger Léger"—the poet's mother. The poem is divided into four sections: the first two of equal length, and the last two somewhat longer, but also of about equal length. The first section does no more than evoke the new-fallen and still-falling snow on the city of New York in the early morning hours. The second section extends this evocation from the immediately visible landscape westward until, in the poet's mind, the far western verge is reached—an extremity that reminds him of distances extending in the other direction, back to France whence he has come. The third section then openly speaks of the poet's aged mother, praying in captive France, and then returns to New York, where the poet lives in exile, inhabiting at the moment the corner room of some hotel or apartment house. The fourth section is a kind of "philological rhapsody" and constitutes one of the most curious passages in all Perse's poetry. In a striking way it fuses all the material of the three preceding sections, completing a very personal tribute of the poet to his mother. Such, then, are the bare essentials of the poem's content.

As to its form, like most of Perse's poems, *Neiges* has the typographic aspect of prose. Throughout his work the spacing of this "prose" varies greatly. In *Neiges* the disposition is relatively uniform, each of the poem's four sections being subdivided into a series of "prose-stanzas" of about equal length. These prose-stanzas are quite long and are essentially units of meaning rather than of rhythm. In *Neiges,* as in all the other poems, rhyme occurs, if at all, only incidentally and most irregularly, usually not in end-positions. The other sonorous devices favored by Perse— various alliterative and assonantal effects, anagrams and metatheses—though not over-abundant in *Neiges,* are all there. The syntax, too, with its frequent vocatives and its abundance of connectives (especially of introductory conjunctions: twenty-six of *Neiges*'s sixty-three sentences begin with "Et") is entirely typical of the ensemble of Perse's work.

That ensemble presents a surprising uniformity in tone and diction. Whole sentences from the *Images à Crusoë* (1904) could be quite successfully transposed and incorporated into the very recent *Amers.* The characteristic note was struck early and has been sustained ever since. That fact has tended to obscure the very real changes that Perse's work shows through the course of the years. The most obvious of these changes is that in subject-matter. The early poems celebrate the young poet's idyllic island childhood, are often frankly autobiographical, and have a definite locus in time and space. But already in some of the *Eloges* the subject-matter becomes more impersonal. Experiences are presented in a kind of void, cut off from the poet and generalized. Pure, detached sensation becomes the real subject-matter of many of these poems. This depersonalization then takes another form, becoming epic in *L'Amitié du Prince* and in *Anabase.* These poems are essentially straightforward narrative, in spite of their tightly compressed texture and symbolic overtones, and in spite of the shadowiness of the sages, princes, and military conquerors whose exploits are extolled. Coming to the American series, one still moves in an essentially epic world, but consecutive episodic portrayal of a single cultural group or tradition gives way to a bewildering telescoping of historical traditions, myths, human events, and natural phenomena; for the real subject-matter of these later poems is, crudely but briefly stated, a quest for human values within the framework of modern historical relativism. There are, however, two exceptions: *Poéme à l'étrangère* and *Neiges,* both of which are lyric effusions, albeit extremely discreet ones. *Poème à l'étrangère* is the intimate, elegiac counterpart to the epic aloofness of *Exil.*

Neiges, however, ties in with those early poems, especially *Pour fêter une enfance,* in which Perse speaks, even though with great reticence, of his family. This reversion to very early subject-matter will be seen to confer a special poignancy upon *Neiges.*

Quite as significant as the changes in subject, however, are those that one finds in the way Perse arranges his imagery. It is tempting to establish a one-to-one correlation between the two sorts of changes, thereby reinforcing the Flaubertian contention that there is only one way to express any one feeling, idea, or situation. Unfortunately, the data at hand are not so accommodating. There is considerable correlation between the changes in subject-matter and those in disposition of imagery, of course; but it is far from perfect. If it were, then the imagery of *Neiges* should be organized much as we find it in the very early poems. But such is patently *not* the case, for the configuration of imagery in *Neiges* is of a piece with that in the other American poems.

In the earlier poems one finds a radical suppression of transitional material, a procedure carried furthest in certain passages of *Anabase.* But beginning with *Exil,* the poems of the American series move in the opposite direction. Instead of ellipsis there is elaboration. Instead of juxtaposition there is a rhetorical concern for transition and exhaustive statement that sometimes lapses into mere wordiness (in parts of *Vents* and especially in *Amers*). The difference may be clarified by considering part of an early *éloge* (IV) alongside the opening lines of *Neiges*—both passages being concerned, though in entirely different contexts, with the act of awakening. Here is part of the *éloge.*

> Je m'éveille, songeant au fruit noir de l'Anibe dans
>   sa cupule verruqueuse et
> tronquée . . . Ah bien! les crabes ont dévoré tout
>   un arbre à fruits mous. Un
> autre est plein de cicatrices, ses fleurs poussaient,
>   succulentes, au tronc. Et un
> autre, on ne peut le toucher de la main, comme on
>   prend à témoin, sans qu'il
> pleuve aussitôt de ces mouches, couleurs! . . . Les
>   fourmis courent en deux sens.
> Des femmes rient toutes seules dans les abutilons. . . .

Here the immediate connection between the sequence of sentences and the isolated image which each sentence presents is not immediately apparent, and the cohesion of the imagery is obscurely felt long before one perceives the justification of its arrangement. The whole poem, of which about half is given, is certainly an expression of a sudden awakening of sexual desire. The aniba in its cupule—in form, a sort of tropical counterpart to the acorn—is at once vaguely phallic and mammary. Then suddenly the avidity of the land-crabs is mentioned, those fruit-eating migratory crabs of the tropics that can rapidly despoil a tree. The suggestion of sexual violence hardly requires pointing out. The image of flowery trunk that is now only a mass of scars becomes perfectly clear. And what better way of expressing primal itch and titillation than the rain of teeming flies and the scurrying of ants? The whole disjointed series is then focussed in the evocation of the laughing women (probably mulattoes, color of the fruit of the aniba) in the lush clumps of mallow-like abutilons. If anyone has any doubt as to the import of the whole poem, he has only to read the remainder, which is even more explicitly sexual than the portion quoted. But what is of interest here is not the sexual theme but the juxtaposed, disjointed arrangement of the imagery and syntactical units. In this *éloge* the same sort of arrangement of imagery is already achieved that one finds later in *Anabase,* where, however, the individual unconnected images of the opening sections are developed during the course of the whole long poem in a thematic, almost fugal, fashion.

But now consider the opening prose-stanza of *Neiges.*

> Et puis vinrent les neiges, les premières neiges de l'absence, sur les grands lés
>
> tissés du songe et du réel; et toute peine remise aux hommes de mémoire, il y eut
>
> une fraîcheur de linges à nos tempes. Et ce fut au matin, sous le sel gris de
>
> l'aube, un peu avant la sixième heure, comme en un havre de fortune, un lieu
>
> de grâce et de merci où licencier l'essaim des grandes odes du silence.

Here each sentence leads quite smoothly into the next, and each successive image is foreshadowed in the preceding one. Indeed, actual repetitive elaboration holds throughout. "Les neiges" alone will not do; "les premières neiges de l'absence" must be added. "Les grands lés" are elaborated into "une fraîcheur de linges à nos tempes." "Au matin" is not sufficiently precise; "le sel gris de l'aube" and "la sixième heure" reinforce it. And finally, "un havre de fortune" is expanded in "un lieu de grâce et de merci." Moreover, the description, far from being "set" once and for all in these lines, is elaborated throughout seven more prose-stanzas. Instead of concentration without transition, one finds a repetitive luxuriance that recalls the proliferation of tapestry-designs or a forest of frost-patterns on a windowpane. The technique is now decidedly extensive rather than intensive. And the imagery, instead of being merely juxtaposed, or stated and then developed thematically in a linear fashion, is made to converge around a central metaphor, like crystals forming on an axis. In fact, from *Exil* on, the dominant organization of the imagery in Perse's poems might be termed *centripetal.*

All this represents an over-simplification, of course; for it is not possible to parcel out each section of each poem and show that it is purely "juxtaposed," or purely "linear," or purely "centripetal." In fact, such a vast poem as *Vents* combines all three arrangements. But a shift to preponderantly centripetal organization is one of the marked characteristics of the American series, and nowhere is it to be found in a clearer form than in *Neiges.* There is in *Neiges* a piling-up of metaphor and simile which, in the hands of a lesser poet, would at best present a tiringly sumptuous chaos. But this profusion is ordered by the subordination in various ways of all the figures of speech to the central snow-image.

First there is the simple enriching of the snow-image itself; that is, every resource of figurative language is utilized to make the sight, feel, and sound of snow more vivid to the reader. Consider the lines that open the second prose-stanza of the first section: "Et toute la nuit, à notre insu, sous ce haut fait de plume, portant très haut vestige et charge d'âmes, les hautes villes de pierre ponce forées d'insectes lumineux n'avaient cessé de croître et d'exceller, dans l'oubli de leur poids." The feathery snow, "ce haut fait de plume," falls slowly down around the sky-scrapers of New York, wherein, all through the night, windows suddenly turn bright with electric light and then go dark once more, as if fireflies burrowed through the concrete that seems porous as pumice stone. The pumice stone, moreover, suggests the lightest of rocks, so that the sky-scrapers—concretizations of strange human aspirations—seem to lift themselves higher than usual. More specifically, slow-falling vertical snow, if watched intently, may seem to become immobile and imparts to the objects in the background an apparent rising movement, as if the objects were suddenly weightless. Perse's compounding of imagery to convey this special quality of windless snow around skyscrapers is magnificent.

> In *Neiges* Perse achieves the supreme *tour de force* in expressing the most intimate of his feelings in imagery that is precisely the reverse of intimate.
>
> —*Arthur J. Knodel*

It is surpassed in sumptuousness, however, in the lines that occur in the next prose-stanza: "Il neigeait, et voici, nous en dirons merveilles: l'aube muette dans sa plume, comme une grande chouette fabuleuse en proie aux souffles de l'esprit, enflait son corps de dahlia blanc." The snowflake-filled dawn becomes a white dahlia, which is itself first described in terms of a huge white owl whose feathers are ruffled by the winds of the spirit—this latter touch helping to convey the strange immateriality of the snowfall already hinted at in the preceding prose-stanza.

But even that will not suffice. The second section of the poem super-saturates the imagery, elaborating metaphors only incidentally stated in the first section. The "havre de fortune" mentioned in the poem's opening lines is now given an effective backdrop: "Je sais que des vaisseaux en peine dans tout ce naissain pâle poussent leur meuglement de bêtes sourdes contre la cécité des hommes et des dieux; et toute la misère du monde appelle le pilote au large des estuaires." The intertwining and reinforcement of images here are noteworthy. The comparison of desperately bellowing cattle to the foghorn-wailing ships is reinforced by the simple phrase "en peine"—which has far stronger overtones in French than the equivalent "in distress" has in English. And then, the blinding mist of snow is called "naissain pâle"—pale oyster-spat—a sea-image prefiguring the association in the next prose-stanza between the gleaming snow and mother-of-pearl: "De grandes nacres en crois-sance, de grandes nacres sans défaut méditent-elles leur réponse au plus profond des eaux?" And then, in the lines immediately following the evocation of the fog-bound, snow-filled estuary, there occurs a telescoping of images that involves two of those scientific names so dear to Perse: "Je sais qu'aux chutes des grands fleuves se nouent d'étranges alliances, entre le ciel et l'eau: de blanches noces de noc-tuelles, de blanches fêtes de phryganes." Why, other than for the obvious reason of alliterative binding, "noces de *noctuelles*" and "fêtes de *phryganes*"? Or, in more general terms, why is Perse so fond of recondite words taken from the natural sciences? There are various reasons for this fondness, and Perse's vocabulary—especially its scientific and technical terms—deserves a separate study. Let us cite, then, only those reasons immediately relevant. One is sim-ply a deep concern for accuracy. The "étranges alliances entre le ciel et l'eau" (such as the huge billows of mist that arise above Niagara Falls and which would, in overcast weather, seem to merge with clouds and falling snow) are underscored by the "fêtes de phryganes," for the phryga-nea are a family of caddis-flies, small insects with delicate net-veined wings that swarm and breed over water and whose larvae live in water. But surely another reason for employing these scientific terms is that most of them are really metaphors, drawn from Latin and Greek (albeit fre-quently from a rather bastard Latin and Greek). Perse, who is very much of a classical scholar, undoubtedly appre-hends the metaphor in scientific names much more quickly than most of his readers. But even at that, many scientific names easily betray at least some part of their metaphoric content. For example, there is a metaphor embedded in "noctuelles." The snow began to fall in the darkness of early morning and the noctuids include most of the dull-colored moths, and among them those that commonly fly at night. The connection with night is obviously underscored by the *noct*-stem in "noctuelles." But the more precise root—*noctua* L. 'night-owl'—which is not so likely to be generally recognized, is not without interest, for it ties in with the "grande chouette fabuleuse" that is one of the focal metaphors of the first section.

It may be legitimately objected that an extended use of such terms is pure pedantry and that it is absurd to expect an *honnête homme* to descend to such minutiae. But the objection is somewhat counteracted when one realizes that Perse's use of such terms is not simply a matter of gratuitous exhibitionism, but rather an integral part of his technique, and even, as I hope to show in a subsequent article, an integral part of his temperament and personality.

In the prose-stanza immediately following the "noctuelles" passage there occurs another rare word, but this time drawn from the crafts rather than from the natural sciences. The poet speaks of the vast defense plants of the Great Lakes regions, "où les chantiers illuminés toute la nuit tendent sur l'espalier du ciel une haute treille sidérale: mille lampes choyées des choses grèges de la neige . . . ." "Grège"—a loan-word derived from the *greggia* of *seta greggia*, at-testing the Italian origins of the silk industry in France—is a term applied exclusively to silk, "soie grège" being raw silk. But Perse has wrenched the word from its textile

setting and from it created a beautiful metaphor, under-scored by rhyme: "choses grèges de la neige." The En-glish translation has had to use the makeshift "raw-silk things of snow," but the unavoidable mention of silk in the English version spoils the discretion of the metaphor in French, where silk is implied but not named, since "grège"—unlike "raw"—can be applied only to silk. One need not labor the felicity of the comparison between freshly falling snow in the yellowish light of electric lamps and the purity, coolness, and peculiar texture of raw silk. And once more we have the developing of a hint from the first section where it is a question of "le premier affleure-ment de cette heure soyeuse."

One could go on line by line through the whole of the first two sections of the poem (and even in parts of the third and fourth, where, however, the interest shifts) showing how ingeniously metaphorical saturation is made to evoke the snowfall. But such imagery, for all its beauty, is essentially preparatory, filling in the concrete content of the focal snow image rather than bringing the reader directly in touch with the true subject-matter of the poem. This more difficult and essential task is done by relating various aspects of the snowfall to all the fragile and elusive aspects of the poet's filial affection. Thus, in the first line of the poem an essen-tial equation is posited: "Et puis vinrent les neiges, les premières neiges de l'absence .. . .." The sense of isolation that newfallen snow can bestow is familiar to anyone who has lived in a cold climate. And hence the separation of the poet from his mother is anticipated from the outset, later to be recalled in very similar, but significantly modified terms: "neiges prodigues de l'absence, neiges cruelles au cœur des femmes où s'épuise l'attente. . . ."

But the sense of isolation can also be delicious and sooth-ing, or, in the very phrase that follows the opening ones: "un havre de fortune, un lieu de grâce et de merci où licencier l'essaim des grandes odes du silence." The strange and almost embarrassing gentleness of snow (beautifully conveyed in the rhetorical question asked further on: "Et sur la hache du pionnier quelle inquiétante douceur a cette nuit posé la joue?")—that gentleness, combined with the feeling of seclusion, makes the moment propitious for the expression of the son's love, for: "il y a un si long temps que veille en moi cette affre de douceur." The purity of the "affre de douceur," as well as the "pureté de lignage,"—which is one of Perse's earliest and most important themes—is obviously suggested by the white purity of the snows. And so, all the imagery of the poem that is not merely purely descriptive of the snowfall, in some way that is usually fairly obvious, ties in with the main theme.

There are, however, two important clusters of imagery that would not seem to lend themselves readily to incorpora-tion into the focal snow-image. They are the recurrent ecclesiastical figures and the last section's philological metaphors. Perse's mother is a pious woman who is pre-sented in an attitude of prayer: "du fond de son grand âge [elle] lève à son Dieu sa face de douceur." And, since she must worship more or less secretly in her bomb-devastat-ed, captive land, references are made to crypts or cata-combs: "vos Eglises souterraines où la lampe est frugale et l'abeille est divine." But one recalls that, from the outset of the poems, there is the suggestion that a snow-isolated place is a "lieu de grâce et de merci"—like a church-crypt, for example, with the promise of resurrection as symbolized by the sacred bee. And towards the end of the third section the tie-in is even more explicit, where the poet speaks of how "un oiseau de cendre rose, qui fut de braise tout l'été, illumine soudain les cryptes de l'hiver," going on to compare the pink bird in the snow (perhaps a linnet) to "l'Oiseau du Phase aux Livres d'heures de l'An Mille"—the flamboyant bird of an illuminated Book of Hours, dating from around the troublous period of 1000 A.D. and seen by Perse in one of the many museums and libraries he has frequented. But even better, in one of the most beautiful synesthetic images of the poem, the snow-image and the ecclesiastical strain fuse: "Et comme un grand *Ave* de grâce sur nos pas chante tout bas le chant très pur de notre race," which becomes at the end of the poem: "et comme un grand *Ave* de grâce sur nos pas, la grande roseraie blanche de toutes neiges à la ronde."

But the real *tour de force* is the linking of philology and snow, which occurs in the last and climactic fourth section of the poem. There one finds Perse establishing an elaborate and ingenious comparison between certain philological problems and the specific problem of expressing his filial veneration. He has recourse to the concept of primitive parent-languages or *Ursprachen,* and the linguist's effort to reconstruct such an *Ursprache* is equated with the poetic problem of finding the purest, most unequivocal, most completely tactful expression of the "affre de douceur" (so pitifully but unavoidably watered down in the English "agony of sweetness") which the poet feels for his mother. This "affre" is indeed complex, for the poet is paying homage to the woman who bore and nurtured him, but likewise to the most perfect embodiment of the poet's pure lineage, and, by extension, of purity and selfless devotion in all things. In addition, he sees in her the widow who merges in his mind with widowed France, much of whose manpower was doing enforced labor in Germany or languishing in prison and concentration camp. And lastly, it must be admitted that there is in the poet's homage a strong element of resignation that might be stated in psychoanalytic terms as a regressive desire for maternal protection and the pre-natal safety of the womb—an aspect of his feeling that is beautifully expressed in the question: "Quelle flore nouvelle, en lieu plus libre, nous absout de la fleur et du fruit?" as well as in the sentences immediately following the question. But beyond that is an even more all-embracing symbol; and the poet's veneration comes to appear as the most quintessential of human emotions, as a sort of *Urgefühl* that, indeed, can be expressed only by an *Ursprache.* That is why his intention is stated in the terms: "voici que j'ai dessein d'errer parmi les plus vieilles couches du langage, parmi les plus hautes tranches phonétiques . . . ." Perse's wanderings among these strata may not always stand the close scrutiny of modern linguistics. For example, if, by a "langue très entière et très parcimonieuse" Perse means—as one would immediately surmise—a highly "synthetic" language, then the illustrative example appears somewhat irrelevant: "très entière et très parcimonieuse, comme ces langues dravidi-

ennes qui n'eurent pas de mots distincts pour 'hier' et pour 'demain' . . . ." Perhaps Perse wanted to underscore the idea of timelessness which would be indicated by an indifference to certain time distinctions. But the lack of linguistic representation for such distinctions would have little to do with the "entirety" or highly "synthetic" quality of a language. It might indicate either a real lexical lack or, more likely, the fundamental indifference to chronology characteristic of the Indian cultures which employed various Dravidian dialects.

Perse is safer when he goes on to tell us to follow him towards "ce pur délice sans graphie où court l'antique phrase humaine"—for the various *Ursprachen* are indeed artificial reconstructions, sets of starred forms for which no graphs are extant. And thus, no one will cavil when Perse goes on to say: "nous nous mouvons parmi de claires élisions, des résidus d'anciens préfixes ayant perdu leur initiale . . . ." For it is indeed by moving about among residual vestiges that the linguist does gain some partial access to the "pur délice sans graphie" of, let us say, primitive Indo-European. But the poet wishes to go even further: "devançant les beaux travaux de linguistique, nous nous frayons nos voies nouvelles jusqu'à ces locutions inouïes, où l'aspiration recule au delà des voyelles et la modulation du souffle se propage, au gré de telles labiales misonores, en quête de pures finales vocaliques." "In-ouïes" is the right word, for vowels that are *followed* by aspiration and *semi*-vocalization of labials present linguistic anomalies.

But where, one asks, do the snows come in? In the passage preceding this philological rhapsody the poet tells of those men who go farther and farther from the river mouth, upstream, until they come to the mountain freshets and then beyond that to the glaciers, and finally to the névé at the glacier's head, where "ils sont gagnés soudain de cet éclat sévère où toute langue perd ses armes. Ainsi l'homme mi-nu sur l'Océan des neiges, rompant soudain l'immense libation, poursuit un singulier dessein où les mots n'ont plus prise . . . ." So the mountaineer goes higher and higher, up the slopes of some unimaginable linguistic Everest, where the landscape is only snow—snow and ice. Or the skier climbs to the snowy eminence whence he can leap fabulously through space. And a few lines further on, the snowfields are quite appropriately equated with the unsullied white page: "cette page où plus rien ne s'inscrit . . . ." as the last words of the poem say. And thus, magnificently, the whole linguistic section, the very climax of the poem, is subordinated to the central snow-image.

In one of his early poems Perse speaks of "gentle things"—"choses douces": "douces comme la honte, qui tremble sur les lèvres, des choses dites de profil . . . ." In *Neiges* the problem was to find a method at once so unequivocal and so oblique that the poet could express without embarrassment the "affre de douceur" of all he felt towards his mother. There can be no doubt that Perse has here succeeded in solving the problem; for the elaboration of the basic snow-image serves as a perfect vehicle for his "grande ode du silence" which moves inevitably, as he tells his mother, towards "ce langage sans paroles dont vous avez l'usage."

This highly centripetal organization of imagery may not seem quite so successful in the other long poems of the American series; but the imperfection may there be more apparent than real, for in those poems the second member of the key-metaphor, which would constitute the real subject-matter of the poem, is far more complex and exclusively intellectual than the mother-son relationship celebrated in *Neiges*. The first, or figurative, member of the focal images of the other poems is frequently indicated by the title: *Pluies, Vents, Amers,* while in *Exil* the sandy beach is the focal image. But the true subject of each of these poems proceeds from the one essential concern that I have already tried to summarize (with, alas, unavoidable pedantry) as "a quest for human values within the framework of modern historical relativism." When we become more familiar with Perse's intellectual preoccupations through continued persual of all his works and with the help of his best commentators, we shall perhaps come to recognize that the centripetal arrangement of imagery is quite as successful in the other poems as in *Neiges.*

However, there is one important aspect of the imagery of *Neiges* that is common to all of Perse's poetry, from the earliest to the most recent, and that is its open-air or outdoor quality. In *Neiges,* to express the most intimate and spiritualized of relationships, Perse evokes immense vistas: snow as it falls upon the wide American continent, men as they travel into glacial fastnesses, ships as they move through fog that seems almost continuous with sky and sea. The quality may be best emphasized by contrast with a poet who, strangely, is echoed in *Neiges.* In spite of the outdoor setting of *L'Après-midi d'un faune* and of various other of Mallarmé's poems, Mallarmé seems to find his natural locus chiefly in closed interiors or when treating of the bibelots and art-objects that grace such interiors—one thinks of Hérodiade's sumptuous chambers, of the lonely drawing-room of the "ptyx" sonnet, of the various "Eventails" and the vase of "Surgi de la croupe." It is as if the external world—and especially its most brutal manifestation, the outdoors—must be shut out so that Mallarmé's hopeless pursuit of a pure poetic Absolute may not be diverted.

In Perse the movement is in precisely the opposite direction. Interiors are seldom described, and when they are, they become continuous with their outer surroundings. The plantation-house of the early *Pour fêter une enfance* is merely part of the garden-isle; the palaces and other buildings of *Anabase* are viewed from the outside, from terraces, public squares, or streets; the house of *Exil* is "une maison de verre" with its doors open upon the dunes, into which the poet promptly escapes. And in *Neiges* the corner room of a New York apartment-hotel is merely a vantage-point from which the poet embraces the snow-covered city and river. Even more strikingly, a typical indoor setting may be strangely exteriorized, as in that extraordinary evocation in *Vents* of the Library of Congress in terms of sedimentary concretions, of great geological processes—a passage that ends with a ritual aëration

in which the great halls are "restored" to the wide outside world. In *Neiges* Perse achieves the supreme *tour de force* in expressing the most intimate of his feelings in imagery that is precisely the reverse of intimate. In short, *Neiges,* for all its delicate subjective lyricism, in no way abandons Perse's characteristic idiom, which here reveals unexpected flexibility and a wealth of unsuspected possibilities.

Byron Colt (essay date 1960)

SOURCE: "St.-John Perse," in *Modern Language Quarterly,* Vol. XXI, No. 3, September, 1960, pp. 235-38.

[*In the following essay, Colt discusses the influence of Friedrich Nietzsche's philosophy on Léger's work.*]

Appraisals of St.-John Perse, the French poet, by American critics leave one with the double impression of their high estimation of the man and their inability to come to grips with his work. For example, the reviews of *Amers,* Perse's latest work, give clear evidence that the poetry has eluded the commentators in a surprising way. When we are not being told that "in the world of *Seamarks* the sea is central," we read that "the pseudonym of the poet, after the Roman Persius, is as *vague and evocative as his poetry*" (italics mine) or that Perse "creates absolute metaphors whose effectiveness owes little to reference. Such images as 'the white bitches of disaster capped with gold' offer little hold for exegesis."

These comments are indeed intersting. For many of us, the more we read Perse, the more convinced we become of the relentless precision of his work and the concreteness of the metaphors which, in contradistinction to surrealist practice, are always rooted in reality, if only we probe far enough. If the origin of some of the metaphors still escapes us, it is probably because our imaginations fail to take the leap that the poet originally made or that we did not see one evening an agitated ocean under a light which illumined the "absolute metaphor" cited above by the critic.

But such cavils aside, it seems curious that Perse's antecedents have not been more thoroughly explored. Amos Wilder, who devotes a chapter to the work of Perse, says that "the poems are written in a kind of Dionysiac free verse." He then gives a two-page quotation from *Exil* ("Toujours il y eut cette clameur . . . ." and following strophes) and ends with the comment: "Whatever else there be in these lines there is at least a magnificent communication of the ceaseless procession and tumult of the breakers about the shores of the world." It is time, then, to ask ourselves why Perse's effect in our day has been so great.

The figure of the Prince, one that recurs throughout the work of Perse, seems to have a special importance in the aristocratic world of his poetry. The characteristics of this symbolical personage are given most fully in *Amitié d'un Prince,* published in France in the same year as *Anabase.* We gather from the description that the Prince is a thin man with delicate nostrils, unused to association with men, dissident, secret in his plans, hard with himself, clear thinking, liking women and solitude. Have we not encountered a similar figure in literature before? The particularity and humor in this portrait (in the final part of the poem the Prince plays at dice on the threshold of his house, his head covered with a kerchief) remind us of the characterization of the aristocratic Zarathustra; but we will not concern ourselves here with this figure in the pseudo-Jacobean of the English translation. Instead, we will take a sentence from another work by Nietzsche, a sentence that will illumine not only the nature of the Prince, but the bias of the narrator of these poems.

> The noble man honours in himself the powerful one, him also who has power over himself, who knows how to speak and how to keep silence, who takes pleasure in subjecting himself to severity and hardness, and has reverence for all that is severe and hard. *(Beyond Good and Evil)*

"Who knows how to speak and how to keep silence"—this characteristic of the noble nature Perse stresses often in his work, even as he has embodied it in his life. There was a lapse of thirteen years between his first and second books, seventeen years between his second book and the publication of the poem *Exil* in America. In his work, which has been a sustained affirmation of life, Perse seems always to have been guided by the Nietzschean idea that "It is the powerful who *know* how to honour" *(Beyond Good and Evil)*. Its lack of pity is clear already in *Éloges* in the adumbration of the egotistical and visionary colonial childhood. This same quality is celebrated in *Anabase* in a way which makes us think of Nietzsche's comment on the aristocratic races "who have left the idea 'Barbarian' on all the tracks in which they have marched; nay, a consciousness of this very barbarianism, and even a pride in it, manifests itself even in their highest civilisation" *(Genealogy of Morals)*.

Having said this, we can suggest why Perse has had such an appeal for our own period. At a time when European poets, like Breton, were engaged in incantations against the age in which they lived (which boiled down to Rimbaud's "en querellant les apparences du monde"), Perse had gone beyond the age. When men like Prevent and Brecht were swallowing all the bitter poisons of their time, Perse had already rid his system of them, using the great antidotes of solitude and isolation. And the perspective to which he had now come reminds us forcibly of that held by the German philosopher. For Perse, as indeed for Nietzsche, gaining this perspective demanded a kind of spiritual reversion.

The man of Perse's own nationality and tradition who most clearly illustrates this problem is Rimbaud. Not so much the theorist of symbolism as its legend, he is far more important to our purposes than is the quiet *maître* of the Rue de Rome, who held meetings in his apartment, for from Rimbaud sprang the two currents of the third-generation symbolist movement that have no relationship with literary Parisianism. What Rimbaud was searching for in his work is suggested by a phrase from the poem *Angoisse* in the *Illuminations*: "Que des accidents de féerie scientifique et des mouvements de fraternité sociale soient cheris comme restitution progressive de la franchise première . . . ?" This "first franchise" of childhood continued to elude Rimbaud throughout the poetic phase of his life.

Three principal elements inform the *Illuminations*: the vision of childhood, the possibility of love, and the power both of inspiration and of the written word. It is the first that satisfied Rimbaud most completely, and it is the first that is the most satisfying to his readers. *Déluge* and the five parts of *Enfance* deal with the power of early apprehension and its loss. The rest of the poems show the attempts either to find a substitute for it or to atomize the world which caused it to vanish. Instead of asking about scientific magic or social fraternity, Rimbaud might have written: "What advance in poetic virtuosity, what new development in love, will give me back this vision?" The answer: neither.

When Rimbaud sought a reason for this loss (in poems like *Les Premières communions* and above all in *Une Saison en enfer*), he found it in the Christian religion in which he had been reared. The chapter "L'Impossible" in *Une Saison* shows how urgently Rimbaud tried to see his way around or behind Christ, who had cut man off from nature by declaring the single path to salvation. It was the discovery of the East and the Hellenic world that in this life men could walk and think like gods. It was the discovery of Christianity that the divine life could never be realized on this earth. Rimbaud tried and failed to find this knowledge once again, even as Nietzsche had for a time found it and as had Thoreau. But if one could not find it and did not have an established faith, one was reduced to living "en nous amusant, en revant amours monstres et univers fantastiques, en nous plaignant et en querellant les apparences du monde . . .". But for Rimbaud, his poetry had to come from faith or from "the primitive father land," "la sagesse de l'Orient." He would not under any other circumstances "entertain" himself by writing.

We know which of the above alternatives was most frequently adopted by the symbolist poets, just as among the English pre-Raphaelites. The movement was for many a new anti-materialism, with Catholicism at the end of the road. These conversions often strike us as being weak, somewhat decadent affairs. But there was one man who explicitly owed his conversion to Rimbaud for whom this was not true. Paul Claudel represents the greatest example of the first of these historical alternatives. And the greatest example of the other is Perse, who found his way around the Christian religion to the spiritual homeland which Nietzsche reached in his maturity. If we were to make a crude analogy, we might say that Perse was the Nietzsche to Claudel's Wagner, bearing in mind the latter's flamboyant drama with all the stops pulled out and the severe, epic lyricism of the former with its ring of "new tablets." The comparison still holds in Claudel's influence on the early Perse, which Gide in his correspondence with Claudel called "violent." But our main point here is that Perse's special success puts him in a relation to his forerunner that has gone undiscussed, except in the matter of technique, while that of Claudel with the same man has been widely examined.

Hölderlin has an interesting phrase, paralleling a sentence of Nietzsche quoted above, to the effect that poetry is produced when man is passing out of nature into civilization and out of civilization into nature. This *état sauvage* was one that Rimbaud could never find. It is the very atmosphere of Thoreau's *Journals.* It is also present in **Anabase,** which is a true "up-going" to the sources of the spirit "out of civilization into nature." It is the work of a mind that would applaud the sentence of Pericles on Greek civilization: "Our audacity has forced a way over every land and sea, rearing everywhere imperishable memorials of itself for *good* and *evil*" (*Genealogy of Morals*). We would not hesitate to place this poem beside the work of a man like Ernst Jünger, who was writing at the same time in Germany. And for a glimpse of how this state of mind regarded the political power movements of the period, we have Jünger's *Auf den Marmorklippen* to guide us.

It does not matter for the sake of our argument whether the German philosopher was a conscious influence on the French poet; similar states of mind can have different births if the time is right. But undoubtedly there is voiced in the last two works of Perse, **Vents** and **Amers,** the same cry that we find in *Genealogy of Morals*:

> a glimpse of a man that justifies the existence of man, a glimpse of an incarnate human happiness that realises and redeems, for the sake of which one may hold fast to *the belief in man.* . . . The sight of man now fatigues.

And having said this, we have explained why Perse fascinates his time. His work is a necessary development, and the result of a destiny rather than of the aesthetic impulse which Rimbaud disdained. And have we suggested the answer to the puzzle of the commentators' vagueness? Is it because they are trying to praise a work with whose direction they are not in sympathy? The narrator of these great poems is, like Zarathustra, preëminently "the man without nausea." This characteristic is so increasingly rare in our time that, when we see it, we spontaneously tend to praise it without realizing what the spirit must experience and accept in order to reach this altitude. "He who can breathe in the air of my writings knows that it is the air of the heights, that it is bracing. A man must be formed for it . . ." (*Ecce Homo*). He must be formed for it if he intends to live there, not if he is only on an alpine excursion.

C. E. Nelson (essay date 1962)

SOURCE: "Saint-John Perse: A Way to Begin," in *Books Abroad,* Vol. 36, No. 4, Autumn, 1962, pp. 375-78.

[*In the following essay, Nelson provides a stylistic analysis of "Poème: pour M. Valery Larbaud."*]

More so than in most poetry, structure is the problem for the reader of St.-John Perse, for contrary to our usual expectations of poetry, a poem by Perse generally offers few direct references to the world outside the poem. That is, in Perse there are few points of reference within the poem which, by their simultaneous pointing to the general world of experience and the unique world of the poem, guide the reader to the poet's meaning. Thus, his images do not so much help us to understand the poem as the poem helps us to understand the images. This is the reason that while in much poetry we can go from the parts to the whole, in Perse we must generally go from the whole to the parts. And the whole, in Perse, is the structure of the poem.

The purpose of this essay is to examine a relatively unknown short poem of Perse. And unfortunately, what has just been said may appear to be given the lie by what is to follow. However, **"Poème: pour M. Valery Larbaud"** (*Les Cahiers de la Pléiade,* X [Été-Antomne 1950], though it does involve certain external referents, is, finally, typical of Perse:

> Servante, l'homme bâille, J'appelle!
> Voici des pence pour Haendel, voici nos livres pour le Fleuve.
> Et il y eut un jour qu'on appela Dimanche—ennui solaire des Empires dans toutes glaces de nos chambres.
> On dit que les coucous fréquentent aux jardins d'hôtels,
> On dit que les oiseaux de mer, par-dessus les Comtés, jusqu'aux jardins des villes . . .
> Et l'étranger lit les gazettes sous un vieil arbre de Judée:
> On lui remet deux lettres
> Qu'il ne lit.
> ". . . Roses, rosemaries, marigold leaves and daisies . . ." Vous arrosez les roses avec du thé,
> Car il y eut un jour qu'on appela Dimanche et, pardessus les villes à cantiques et les lawns,
> De ces grands ciels à houppes comme on en vit à Santa-Fé.
> Allez et nous servez, qui sommes vieux comme l'insecte sur ce monde,
> Allez et nous laissez à nos façons de vivre qui sont telles, sur toutes rives de ce monde . . .
> Et l'étranger inscrit un nom, et ce n'est point le sien; inscrit la ville qu'il habite, et il n'est point de ville qu'il habite
> ". . . roses, rosemaries, marigold leaves and daisies. . . ."
> Un peu avant le gong du soir et la saison d'un souffle dans les tentes,
> Mon coeur est plein d'une science,
> Mon coeur est plein d'extravagance, et danse, comme la fille de Lady J . . . en souliers de soie d'or, et nue, entres ses glaces, au son des clefs de malles par le monde et des orchestres mis en serre sur toutes rives de l'Empire.
> Bonheur à naître sous l'écaille et toutes roses de l'Empire! De quelles pures Zambézies nous souvient-il au soir? . . . un peu avant le gong du soir et la saison d'un souffle dans les toiles,
> quand le soleil fait son miel du corps des femmes dans les chambres, et c'est bonheur à naître aux percées d'Isthmes, sur toutes routes de l'Empire,

et les vaisseux pleins de voyelles et d'incestes,
aux fifres des cristaux d'Europe, vont sur la mer
déserte. . . .
Servante! l'homme bâille. J'appelle!
Ouvrez les portes sur le fleuve! toutes choses dites
à la mer
Et pour ce soir encore, c'est fort bein—mais
demain, ô ma fille, nous verrons à changer
Ce grand parfum irrespirable de l'année.

"Poème" is primarily an occasional piece, and thus it does have built-in referents. The initiate will realize that Valery Larbaud was known, among other things, for the creation of Barnabooth, a discouragingly wealthy South American who is massively bored, and who spends his time traveling from sensation to sensation. Also he will realize that this poem is personal in tone and that it uses a Barnabooth-like personage to objectify the *private* meaning of the poem. Nevertheless, to examine the poem with this in mind gives us surprisingly little help in understanding it, and we may conclude that it is, perhaps, most profitable to forego the *private* context when we are in search of *public* meaning.

The theme of **"Poème"** is ennui. This ennui has two aspects: sitting still, and movement to other places to sit still. Also, though it is objectified in one personage, ennui is developed in terms of a whole civilization. The "plot" of the poem has five stages—roughly, one in each section. First, the main character, the Tired One, is identified in terms of external environment; next, his personality within that environment is emphasized. Third, he focuses on sensuality as episode in ennui, which, fourth, leads him to the idea of travel as release. Last, he decides to move on, tomorrow. All five of these stages are set in a context of imagery that stresses the dull comings and goings and movements of the world. Beginning then with this idea of the whole structure, we may go on to more specific considerations.

The most essential mystery of Perse's structure is point of view. First the reader must be aware that the poem will present a complex system of *personae* which represent different points of view and which serve as masks for an impersonal "narrator." Second, he must realize that these persons are constantly appearing and disappearing, sometimes abruptly, sometimes fluidly, and that at other times the narrator will step forth to speak unmasked. On occasion Perse will, by some device of punctuation or syntax, or even by bold statement, inform the audience of the transition. More often however, he will not.

In the first two lines, in the simplest way, Perse presents two voices: the main character, Barnabooth if you wish, but, more generally, the Tired One; and the narrator:

Servante, l'homme bâille. J'appelle!
Voici des pence pour Haendel, voici nos livres
pour le Fleuve.

The Tired One is allowed the action of speech, the narrator is merely shown behind the poem in "l'homme bâille."

Then, a third mask, an editorial observer who is in the action of the poem (as the narrator is not) speaks in 11.3-7:

Et il y eut un jour qu'on appela Dimanche—ennui
solaire des Empires dans toutes glaces de nos
chambres.
On dit que les coucous fréquentent aux jardins
d'hôtels,
On dit que les oiseaux de mer, par-dessus les
Comtés, jusqu'aux jardins des villes. . . .

The nature of the observer is quite ambiguous. We are not told who or what he is, or why he speaks; this is common in Perse. We cannot be certain whether he is here a third party or is an interior monologue of the Tired One—though later in the poem this is certainly what he becomes. We do know, however, that he is separate from the Tired One who speaks aloud, to other personages of the poem, and who takes letters and reads newspapers. Also, though the observer speaks to the Tired One, he is never spoken to or answered. Finally, the observer uses a number of apparent or "pseudo" references which are, however, actually fictional specifics. That is, the "Comtés," like the "Fleuve" in the second line, and "la fille de Lady J .. .." are to be taken as references to the world of the poem. The observer, by invoking fictional specifics, outlines the structure of the bored civilization that makes up this world. Revealing parallels for them, even in the work of Valery Larbaud, are not to be sought.

Following the observer the impersonal narrator reappears in l. 8:

Et l'étranger lit les gazettes sous un vieil arbre de
Judée:
On lui remet deux lettres
Qu'il ne lit.

Thus at the end of the first section of the poem we have three views of the Tired One and his milieu. The action begins with the Tired One's own speech, continues as he listens to the observer's remarks, then fades as he turns his attention to inactivity and is passively described by the narrator. This shifting of *personae,* functioning in the same way, continues throughout the poem.

Another aspect of Perse's technique, the attributive epithet, is nicely illustrated in the first section of **"Poème."** For example take "Et l'étranger lit les gazettes." At first glance this may seem to be a simple matter; that is, the stranger as stranger—he who has just arrived and who is unknown among known people. However, this figure is not nominative; it is attributive. The "étranger," here the Tired One, is the exceptional man—exceptional because, for whatever reason, he can find no roots. Such epithets, which can be finally understood in the context of each poem, continually appear in Perse.

But to return to the problem of point of view, it should be noticed that the structure of the shifting *personae* operates within a structure of shifting geographical reference. As elsewhere, the apparent reference to specifics is a fictional specificity. Images of "Santa-Fé," "toutes rives de ce monde," "pures Zambézies," "percées d'Isthmes," etc., backed up by mention of "oiseaux de mer," "clefs de malles," and snatches of English, add up to a wide world in which no destination can be found by the Tired One.

Using all of these devices, the poem goes on to its climax in the final three lines where the heretofore concrete figure of the "servante," may be discovered to be the spirit, or mind, or consciousness of the "étranger." This particular servant-soul, whose habitat is perpetual Sunday, is shown to be as unsatisfactory as its setting. At the end of a pageant of reminiscence and fantasy, the last lines of the poem seal the structure into fixity—there is no moral progress evident; there is only a vision of the past and the bored confirmation of that vision for the future. He who is in many ways "vieux comme l'insecte sur ce monde" says:

> Ouvrez les portes sur le fleuve! toutes choses dites
>   à la mer!
> Et pour ce soir encore, c'est fort bien—mais
>   demain,
> ô ma fille, nous verrons à changer
> Ce grand parfum irrespirable de l'année.

The Tired One, caught among his thoughts between tea-time and the evening on the Sunday afternoon of the soul in the provincial towns of the mind, once more rediscovers his boredom; he projects himself in fantasies of travel that would lead him away from the decadent sensualities and the glassed-in culture, the sealed-in-mirrors environment in which he is caught—the "fifres des cristaux d'Europe." Coming back to himself, he ends as he began: he yawns and commands that all things be told to the sea. He can only dream of movement.

As already emphasized, the structure of the shifting point of view, a structure that is actually founded on a constant narrator who changes masks and perspectives, is the basic difficulty of Perse's poetry. Also, when one can make his compromise with the apparent specificity of his reference, and the actual specificity of his theme, Perse's poetry will, in an amazingly explosive manner, spring into focus.

Arthur J. Knodel (essay date 1964)

SOURCE: "Towards an Understanding of *Anabase*," in *PMLA,* Vol. LXXIX, No. 3, June, 1964, pp. 329-43.

[*In the following excerpt, Knodel explores the function of anonymity in* Anabase.]

Anabase was the first of Saint-John Perse's poems to be widely translated into other languages, as well as the first to receive widespread critical attention. Yet, despite several recent attempts at detailed exegesis, the poem remains baffling in many of its details and even in some of its more general implications. Close scrutiny of the text of the poem is, of course, the most natural and legitimate way of coming to grips with its meaning, but the more recent commen-taries on *Anabase* too often prove that close textual examination alone is not an adequate safeguard against runaway interpretation. The present study, therefore, seeks to supplement close scrutiny of the text with references to other of Saint-John Perse's writings, especially to certain of his pronouncements on the nature of poetry in general and, most particularly, to his declaration of intent in writing *Anabase.*

That declaration is found in the text of an interview granted to the journalist Pierre Mazars immediately after Saint-John Perse was awarded the Nobel Prize for literature. [In *Le Figaro littéraire,* November 5, 1960, the] poet is quoted as saying:

> *Anabase* a pour objet le poème de la solitude dans l'action. Aussi bien l'action parmi les hommes que l'action de l'esprit envers autrui comme envers soimême. J'ai voulu rassembler la synthèse non pas passive mais active de la ressource humaine. Mais on ne traite pas de thèmes psychologiques par des moyens abstraits. Il a fallu 'illustrer': c'est le poème le plus chargé de concret; aussi on y a vu de l'orientalisme.

This passage is most un-Persean in its fuzziness and inelegance. Mazars was undoubtedly reporting from notes that had to be taken down very hastily. But even though we see in a glass darkly, what does come through is of great interest. The poem, we learn, is meant to convey the loneliness of action or, to put it in the more concrete terms Saint-John Perse constantly seeks, the loneliness of the man of action. As anyone who has read *Anabase* knows, its protagonist is the man of action par excellence—a military conqueror and empire-builder. (We shall refer to him simply as the "Leader.") In his dual military and political role, the Leader is a focal image for "la resource humaine"—that reservoir of human potentialities to be "actively" illustrated in the poem.

A specific personage in a specific historical setting is certainly the most obvious "illustration" of such a theme. Saint-John Perse, however, has avoided this obvious choice. Chronologically, all one can say of *Anabase* is that it belongs to any period within a span of history extending from the post-Alexandrian era at the far end up to the pre-industrial epochs of more recent date, for the Leader speaks of "grandes histoires seleucides" (Canto viii), referring to the inheritors of the Asiatic portion of Alexander's empire, and he moves among peoples who have writing, metallurgy, banking, and a complex social organization but still lack mechanization. The Leader himself, who is both narrator and protagonist, does not closely resemble any of the famous empire-builders of history. He is nameless and even faceless. The more one becomes familiar with the poem, the more does the Leader become an astonishingly live and real presence. Yet we know him *only from within.* And though he reveals to us his inmost thoughts and urges, he is most reticent about his biography. We know nothing of his appearance, his manners, or his habits, let alone his ancestry and origins.

The action of *Anabase* is somewhat more clearly defined geographically than it is chronologically, though even here the limits are blurred. There are actually no clear-cut place-references for any of the episodes of the poem, but the few place-names that do occur, all quite incidentally, are all Asiatic, with one easily assimilable exception. But if the hero is anonymous and the chronology so vague, why should there be even this approximate localization of the poem somewhere in Asia? I think the reason is that Asia, from very early times, has been a continent over which, in spite of staggering geographical barriers, the tides of conquest and migration have repeatedly flowed and ebbed. It is the continent into which Alexander and the Roman conquerors penetrated deeply, the continent from which Cyrus, Attila, Genghis Khan, Tamerlane, and Baber sprang. It is the heartland where Occident and Orient, arctic and tropical peoples have coexisted and clashed since time immemorial. Nowhere else has "la ressource humaine" been so uninterruptedly at work.

The Asiatic fusion is, moreover, well suited for throwing into relief what, for want of a better term, I shall call "historical simultaneity." When we consider *all* the peoples on the face of the earth today, from the most populous and far-flung ethnic groups to the most isolated and vestigial tribes, we are confronted with every level of development, sclerosis, and decay. Stages in human development that we think of as belonging irrevocably to the distant past are found to be very much alive. This historical simultaneity, this projection of the past into the present, is very real, and Saint-John Perse has an acute awareness of it, especially evident in *Exil* and *Vents,* but already present in *Anabase.*

The simultaneity presented in *Anabase* does, however, omit the recent mechanized phases of human history. This omission, I think, is intentional, for the poet wishes to place man against the background of the more elemental forces that are always present but that mechanization tends to obscure. He is quoted by Mazars as saying of his travels in Mongolia: "On a dit que je parcourais le désert avec des préoccupations d'érudition ou d'archéologie. Ce qui m'attirait là-bas, c'était seulement un mode de vie animale et de nature, qui touche aux choses éternelles, comme toujours le désert!" It is this preoccupation that underlies *Anabase,* and it was upon his return to Peiping after a trip into the Gobi that Saint-John Perse is said to have composed the poem.

The poem is made up of an opening and a closing *chanson* and ten intervening sections (which we shall refer to as "cantos"), which constitute the narrative proper. The entire text is recited by the Leader himself. The Opening Song merits close scrutiny, for it establishes the poem's dominant tone and hints at all the main themes of the subsequent narrative. Reciprocally, passages occurring in the narrative will frequently illuminate items in the Opening Song.

That Song is divided into three paragraph-like sections ("strophes"). The first and third of these begin with a statement concerning the birth of a colt: "Il naissait un poulain sous les feuilles de bronze" and "Il naquit un poulain sous les feuilles de bronze"—the only difference

being the shift in tense from imperfect to past definite. At the outset the birth is still in process; by the beginning of the last strophe the colt has been successfully foaled. On reading the rest of *Anabase,* it becomes immediately clear that we are concerned with a group of horse-nomads. (The camel is mentioned in Canto vii, but only in a metaphorical context.) The epic thus begins with the birth of the animal that is the very key to this nomadic people's mode of life. The successful foaling of a colt augurs well for the Leader's growing resolve.

That resolve takes shape gradually as the Opening Song unfolds. The narrator says: "Un homme mit des baies amères dans nos mains. Étranger. Qui passait."—a shadowy but important figure who becomes, in the second strophe: "Etranger. Qui riait." And then in the third: "Un homme mit ces baies amères dans nos mains. Etranger. Qui passait."—lines that are reinforced by the words that occur toward the end of the same strophe: "et l'Etranger à ses façons par les chemins de toute la terre!" This wanderer over the roads of the world puts berries in the hands of the Leader, who has tasted them and found them bitter. Bitterness provokes thirst, in short, arouses a desire. The berries have been brought by the Stranger from a land through which he has passed and about which he has spoken, for the nomad Leader says: "Et voici qu'il est bruit d'autres provinces à mon gré." And the second strophe states: "Car le Soleil entre au Lion et l'Etranger a mis son doigt dans la bouche des morts. Etranger. Qui riait. Et nous parle d'une herbe." It is high summer, late in July, to be precise, for the sun is entering the sign of Leo. In the northern hemisphere it is a period of great heat, and frequently a time of drought and pestilence. Either pestilence, drought, or both seem to have hit the distant province, for the Stranger has seen the dead exposed there and has put his finger in their mouths, perhaps to determine the possible causes of death. Things may not be going well out there, and the Stranger laughs provocatively and goes on to speak of a kind of grass, the staff of life for a nomad people. These far-off and perhaps vulnerable grasslands are a growing temptation to the nomad Leader, all the more so in that his own tribe seems to have reached a plateau of material well-being. This well-being is concretely symbolized in the Leader's salutation to his daughter, indicated by quotation-marks that make the salutation a kind of aside. The first strophe ends: "Je vous salue, ma fille, sous le plus grand des arbres de l'année!'" and the third, "'Je vous salue, ma fille, sous la plus belle robe de l'année'." The largest tree at the height of summer and the most beautiful robe of the year. The nomad princess is an embodiment of a plenitude that is also a culmination. But there is a peculiar variant of the line in the second strophe, where it reads: "'Mon âme, grande fille, vous aviez vos façons qui ne sont pas les nôtres'." Some connection between his daughter and his own soul is posited by the Leader. She has been his very soul up to this moment, but now the Leader turns to something more fundamental, his own ways, those that drive him on to vaster exploits. The passage immediately preceding this address to his soul reads: "Qu'il est d'aisance dans nos voies! que la trompette m'est délice et la plume savante au scandale de l'aile!" The unhampered mobility of nomad life, the exhilaration of battle to which the trumpet calls—these are the Leader's true ways. The feather perfectly aligned in the soaring wing is for him a keen delight. Ease and perfection of movement and the attendant suggestion of migration are beautifully condensed in this "plume savante au scandale de l'aile!"

In the second strophe the Leader exclaims: "Ah! tant de souffles aux provinces!" This ties in with the "bruits d'autres provinces à mon gré" in the first. These winds from the far provinces shake the bronze leaves of "le plus grand des arbres de l'année." For in the last strophe we are told, "Et voici d'un grand bruit dans un arbre de bronze." This repeated use of the qualifier "bronze" in the Opening Song, and always in connection with a tree, illustrates a favorite device of Saint-John Perse. The recurrence of "bronze" makes quite clear that the tree under which the colt is foaled and the one rustling in the winds, as well as "le plus grand des arbres de l'année," are all the same tree. The epithet evokes leaves that have a metallic luster, as many leaves do, especially in bright sunlight. But bronze likewise makes one think of weapons, especially spearheads in this instance, because of the connection with leaves. (Compare the botanist's designation of a certain leaf-shape as "lanceolate.") So there is a faint suggestion of battle. This exploiting of connotative meanings is a device that Saint-John Perse shares with many poets and uses extensively in the "jeu, très allusif et mystérieux [. . . .] à la limite du saisissable," which, he says, constitutes the kind of poetry he is seeking to write.

Another device in this "very allusive and mysterious play" is the enrichment during the course of the narrative of hints that are merely thrown out, though significantly isolated, in the Opening Song. In the last strophe we find: "Bitume et roses, don du chant! Tonnerre et flûtes dans les chambres!" These isolated sub-stantives reinforce the already-stated theme of ease and well-being. But they go even further. Later in the poem there are other references to bitumen. It is connected with the dead, for it was used in embalming corpses as far back as the early Egyptian dynasties. Roses, cultivated as opposed to wild, have funereal overtones in *Anabase.* The well-being verges on boredom and stagnation. The vaguely ominous thunder mingles with the fluting and song. Well-being becomes stifling; it is time to heed the Stranger, to renew contact with the mainsprings of human restlessness. This combination of "cross-referencing" and thematic development of imagery is . . . one of the main devices that help convert a highly condensed narrative into a poem of vast proportions and endless resonance.

The main lines of the narrative, however, are quite simple. The first five cantos are an account of the actual work of constructing and organizing a great port on an estuary. Thereafter, restlessness grows, leading to the *anabasis* proper, which is described in Cantos viii, ix, and x. But what actually goes on within each canto is not always obvious, for the main narrative employs a technique that is only slightly less elliptical and concentrated than the Opening and Closing Songs. T. S. Eliot clearly sensed this difficulty when he translated *Anabase* into English, and in the preface to his translation he gives a series of "canto-

headings," which were first thought up by Lucien Fabre, whose 1924 review of *Anabase* still remains the best introduction to the poem. . . .

[Although I am not] in complete agreement with any one commentator about all details, I have more often corroborated and expanded previous analysis—especially the earlier ones—than contradicted them. There is, however, a view expressed in the later exegeses that I find quite untenable. This is the view that the military expedition, which gives *Anabase* its title, is a symbolic dramatization of two "deeper" parallel themes, one having to do with mankind's spiritual struggle upward through the ages, the other having to do with the problem of poetic expression or the role of the poet in society. I find no evidence of either the "human progress" or the "poetic" theme in *Anabase.* The historical awareness manifest in the poem is obvious. But this consciousness of historical forces never constitutes a separate theme and never takes on the slightest character of an epic of human progress. Indeed, the ever-present sense of what I have called historical simultaneity emphasizes the constant recurrence of the past in the present rather than any upward pageant of human progress. There is even less reason to treat *Anabase* as a poem about the creative act or the role of the poet in society. The protagonist does recite his own chronicle, but nowhere is he concerned with his role as a poet. And even less is there any hint of the Leader (or the author) establishing an analogy between the drama of migration and conquest and the *agon* of the poet struggling with his subject-matter or with society.

The chronicle of empire-building is an admirable vehicle for the development of what Saint-John Perse himself has declared to be the main concern of the poem: "la solitude dans l'action" and "la synthèse, non pas passive, mais active de la ressource humaine." To treat the poem as the symbolical dramatization of separate but parallel themes nowhere made explicit in the poem is to make of it a three-level allegory. And to do that is to run counter to the very spirit of this poetry. Saint-John Perse has explained, fascinatingly and at length, that his poetry seeks above all to communicate human experience with maximum concreteness. He even goes so far as to say that poetry is not really poetry "qu'à condition de s'intègrer elle-même, vivante, à son objet vivant: de s'y incorporer pleinement et s'y confondre, substantiellement." And of *Anabase* in particular he went on to say: "Mais on ne traite pas de thèmes psychologiques par des moyens abstraits. Il a fallu 'illustrer'; c'est le poème le plus chargé de concret."

This brings us back to one of the apparent paradoxes of *Anabase.* Since Saint-John Perse was determined to "illustrate" his theme concretely, why did he make his Leader so anonymous and his geography and chronology so vague? Curiously enough, I think he did this in the interest of concreteness. Had his Leader been recognizably Alexander or Genghis or Baber, then the preconceived image of the historical personage would have interposed itself between the reader and the live presence the poem seeks to create. The history-book figure of Alexander is already somewhat typed, somewhat abstract. Similarly, if the poem were rooted in a given locale at a given period, then such notions as we might have, let us say, of medieval Persia would intrude themselves between us and the brute phenomena of the poem and pigeon-hole them in a pre-established framework. It must be reiterated that the synthesis Saint-John Perse creates is made up of individual phenomena all of which are taken from reality and are never fanciful. But the poet seeks to make us experience these phenomena in all their fresh immediacy; so they are presented with a minimum of orientational materials.

The method is not without risks. If the suppression of orientational materials obliges the reader to work too hard to find the guiding thread, bewilderment is likely to obscure the impact of immediacy, and the reader will become distracted and bored. It is natural to ask whether *Anabase* avoids this pitfall. The poem is admittedly difficult and highly condensed. [In the preface] T. S. Eliot himself wrote, "I was not convinced of Mr. Perse's imaginative order until I had read the poem five or six times." The strangeness of the poem's idiom, however, is greatly diminished when one is familiar with the rest of Saint-John Perse's work, especially the earlier poems and the vast later poem, *Vents*. But even if the reader knows little of the other works, the extraordinary *tone* of *Anabase* helps the sensitive reader to surmount the sometimes bafflingly cursive shorthand of the poem. Fabre, once more, puts the matter most neatly. After quoting the first lines of the Opening Song, he comments:

> Celui qui ne comprend pas une chose d'une telle beauté est-il digne qu'on la lui explique? Peut-être, pourtant, s'il en sent confusément la grandeur; s'il est saisi par le *ton* magnifique du héros de l'*Anabase*. L'étrangeté vient de la solennité avec laquelle le héros nous rapporte ces faits simples—et qui prouve leur importance à ses yeux. . . . J'ai honte d'insister, et il va sans dire qu'à tout lecteur sensible à la poésie la glose est inutile; il découvre avec délice, à chaque mot, sans réfléchir. La vertu toute puissante du *ton* et des vocables y suffit.

There are other poems by Saint-John Perse that one may prefer to *Anabase* and that are less stenographic. But *Anabase* is a haunting poem that is perhaps unique in French literature—as Larbaud and Von Hofmannsthal and Eliot and MacLeish all explicitly declare, and as Rilke evidently thought, since, just before his death, he had started work on a German translation of the poem. This list of names is significant. All are poets, and some, supremely gifted ones. Perhaps *Anabase* is essentially a poem for other poets. But not exclusively; for it speaks to us non-poets as well, if we will just lend an attentive ear.

Mechthild Cranston (essay date 1966)

SOURCE: "'L'Activité du Songe' in the Poetry of Saint-John Perse," in *Forum for Modern Language Studies,* Vol. II, No. 4, October, 1966, pp. 356-67.

[*In the following essay, Cranston examines the role of the sea, violence, and dreams in Léger's poetry.*]

Mer de la transe et du délit;
Mer de la fête et de l'éclat;
et Mer aussi de l'action!

                                                          (*Amers*)

Like every true poet, Saint-John Perse is forever singing but one song. For the Guadeloupean poet, this song is the song of the sea. The oneness of Perse's poetry lies in the double nature of that sea: sea of childhood, innocence and peace, but also of temptation and war. Two main principles can be derived from this ambiguity: that of violence, which rules in the world of action, and that of acquiescence, governing the sphere of dreams. These mutually oppose each other and are, by turns, opposed by death and, possibly, *ennui*. The interplay of these two principles can be observed even in Perse's earliest works. It is, surely, the mainspring of *Anabase,* where the opposition is perhaps momentarily resolved.

In the *Images à Crusoé* (1904), activity governs "la ville", while to the "Ile natale" belong silence, indolence and dream. But from these early dreams there already breaks forth a cry:

> Le pan de mur est en face, pour conjurer le cerele
>   de ton rêve.
> Mais l'image pousse son cri
>   [All references are to the latest edition of the
>   *Œuvres poétiques* in 2 vols. (Gallimard, 1960).]

This cry comes from the city to tear the dreamer away from memories of his island home. The word "cri" reappears in **"Le Perroquet"**, where it also breaks the circle of a dream:

> . . . Tu regardes l'œil rond sous le pollen gâté de la
> paupière; tu regardes le deuxième cercle comme un
> anneau de sève morte. Et la plume malade trempe dans
> l'eau de fiente.
>   O misère! Souffle ta lampe. L'oiseau pousse son cri.

The parrot comes in the night of dreams which, however, he soils with his eyelid of putrid pollen and his sick feather trailing in the "eau de fiente". His cry thus has overtones of sickness and death. These are better defined in **"L'Arc"**: the sound of a snapping interrupts the dream before the hearth:

> c'est ton arc, à son clou, qui éclate. Et il s'ouvre tout
> au long de sa fibre secrète, comme la gousse morte aux
> mains de l'arbre guerrier.

This choice of the "warrior-tree" is of interest here, as it links to the premonition of death the foreboding of war. Death also comes to the purple seed that did not sprout ("La Graine"). For Perse, "violet" has (besides its common association with things royal) a connotation of violence. But whatever interpretation we give to it here, we are left with an impression of insufficiency in the dream-world of Crusoé, so easily disturbed by cries of death.

As the *Images* come to a close, the poet seems to long for the alternative of action. In the night of "long rains" rolls a storm, a call for departure welcomed by the dreamer torn from distorted visions of harmony and peace:

> L'éblouissement perdu,
>
> . . . . .
>
> tu promenais un doigt usé entre les prophéties, puis le regard fixé au large, tu attendais l'instant du départ, le lever du grand vent qui te descellerait d'un coup, comme un typhon, divisant les nuées devant l'attente de tes yeux.

The wind, element of force (and even violence) opposes the rain of dreams. Watchful waiting seems to augur the sudden act: "Le vent se lève! . . . Il faut tenter de vivre!"

That act, however, does not come about—at least, not in *Éloges* which celebrates the sea of festivals and childhood dreams. **"Written on the Door"** is the poet's satisfaction with his sedentary island life, where contemplation in "sweetness and light" is his only activity. And indeed, in the plenitude of his island life, there is little need for exertion.

Soon, however, there comes a hint at something lacking in the poet's dream world, "le blanc royaume où j'ai mené peut-être un corps sans ombre". His existence is shadowless. The simple declarative statement (later repeated as: "J'ai fait ce songe, il nous a consumés sans reliques") gathers emotive strength from the remembrance of death which follows: "O mes plus grandes fleurs voraces, parmi la feuille rouge, à dévorer tous mes plus beaux insectes verts". Green, we remember, is Perse's favourite colour, the colour of childhood and dream. The red connotes, once again, force and violence. The death of green insects is then linked, in memory, to the death of a "very young sister". There follows the reminder that "il ne fallait pas tuer l'oiseau-mouche". There is in this juxtaposition of human impotence (indolence, perhaps?) and the omnipotence of death an ironic poignancy crying for vengeance. And so, as the "song" ends,

> Les fleurs s'achevaient en des cris de perruches.

"Perruche" suggests both parakeet and sail and thus takes us back to Robinson's dying parrot, while it forecasts atonement in the rising sail.

The idea of hurt is repeated in the "blessures des cannes au moulin", which cast their shadow upon the "règnes et confins de lueurs" of the following poem. There also, in the feverish sky, is a renewed call to action, unheeded by the weeping child. The cycle of "Pour fêter une Enfance" closes on the "faces insonores, couleur de papaye et d'ennui, qui s'arrêtaient derrière nos chaises comme des astres morts". To the challenge of death is thus further added the danger of "ennui". And *ennui* in Perse is not an offspring of *Les Fleurs du Mal*. It is rooted, rather, in the Christian (and Dantesque) *acedia*, sin of the "anime triste di coloro / Che visser sanza infamia e sanza lodo. . ." [*Inferno*].

The "Dreamer" awakens in the *Éloges* proper from an old dream "tout rayé de violences, de ruses et d'éclats", and in *Éloge* iii, the child dreaming by the shore has the first clear vision of the duplicity of the sea in the man that walks "les chemins de la mer frauduleuse", fraudulent because it holds false promises of both man's strength and childish dreams.

"Nos bêtes sont bondées d'un cri" (iv), but "bonder" will not turn into "bondir". The reminiscence of death which follows here opposes not dreams, but the promise of action in the unborn cry, and we return to the silent "solitudes molles du matin" (v) to which the sea, colour of innocence and milk, chants the guileful creed of acquiescence: "Il n'est que de céder . . . ."

In the next poem, however, "l'enfance adorable du jour" makes way for "une aisance du souffle / et l'enfance agressive du jour. . ." The word "souffle" is, for Perse, a near synonym of "vent", thus, besides the *creator spiritus,* a sign of all activity, whether spiritual or physical, potential or actual.

In *Éloge* vi there is, furthermore, a first sign of shame:

> c'est le matin, ce sont des choses douces qui supplient, comme la haine de chanter,
>   douces comme la honte, qui tremble sur les lèvres, des choses dites de profil . . .

While we do not know what these "things said in profile" are, we know that they must be of the world of dreams. Upon them there is a shame that is sweet, but of that sweetness hatred is born. This is the revelation that comes to the child who, "full of health", will tell the sick man of the "sources beneath the sea":

> Et voici qu'il me hait.
>
> (vii)

The word is strong (almost un-Persian) and produces the desired effect when indolence, "ennui" and dream are momentarily swept aside by the impatient sail:

> Oh! finissez! Si vous parlez encore d'atterrir, j'aime mieux vous le dire je me jetterai là sous vos yeux.

Here is a first note of haste which, of course, belongs to the wind and the active world. The child, however, soon sinks back into indolence, indifference even, and the leitmotiv of dreams reappears: "Céder!"

Silence follows upon "le mot sec" (synonym of the earlier "cri"). The poem ends in the twofold temptation (of security or risk) of the sail:

> et la présence de la voile, grande âme malaisée, la voile étrange,
> là, et chaleureuse révélée, comme la présence d'une joue . . . O bouffées!

The warmth of the sail, likened to that of a cheek, suggests a mother's protectiveness, "la sécurité du royaume".

And yet the sail is strange, restless and uneasy, and this restlessness rises in gusts of wind.

Éloges xii and xiii again show the child calm and unconcerned in the face of death. Still, he is as yet innocent insofar as he is not yet capable of clearly seeing the incongruity of his dreams in the light of the active world. Guilt sets in, however, in *Éloge* xiv where, wilfully, the Dreamer has withdrawn his feet:

> Voici d'un ciel de paille où lancer, ô lancer! à
> tour de bras la torche!
> Pour moi, j'ai retiré mes pieds . . .

The fire and the verb "lancer" (like the earlier "jeter") obviously signify action, perhaps even war:

> . . . et le Songeur est couché là, et il tient au
> plafond son œil d'or qui guerroie . . .

He now clearly hears the call to action; his golden eye is bent upon war, yet the Dreamer does not rise from dream. Even when the threat of death is made incarnate in the man "envahi par le goût de tuer (qui) se met en marche vers le Château d'Eau avec trois billes de poison" the child, calm and unconcerned, chants his indolent refrain:

> Pour moi, j'ai retiré mes pieds.

The Dreamer openly takes his place among "Questi seiagurati, ehe mai non fur vivi".

Éloge xvi restates the problem of choice in the image of the swimmer, who has "une jambe en eau tiède, l'autre dans un courant frais". The warm water is of the rain, while over the cool current there blows the wind, "le plus frais de l'année". And with this wind the island green grows blue, the cause seems won for the unfurling wind until, suddenly, the wind itself comes to rest "au sein du vieillard".

The temptation of flight (first proposed by the wind, the "perruches" and the sail) returns in *Éloge* xvii, where the child, almost untouchable in his pride, "veut qu'on le peigne sur le pas de la porte". The verb "haïr" comes back and descends upon those whose realism breaks through the dream-world of the child. For the power of dreams (scaled upon the *green* sky) is stronger than the reality of birds in their flight:

> Ne tirez pas si loin sur mes cheveux,

and in the word "loin" are echoes of wind and sail.

Like the *Images à Crusoé, Éloges* ends in the equivocal:

> Je sortirai, car j'ai affaire: un insecte m'attend pour
> traiter . . .
> Ou bien j'ai une alliance avec les pierres veinées-
> bleu . . .

"Traiter" and "alliance" are taken from the world of politics and commerce. They announce *Anabase*. The insect also belongs to the winds, but the blue-veined stone must stand for stability, purity and peace. The final lines, however (among the most beautiful in Perse) seal the pact of dreams:

> . . . et vous me laissez également, assis, dans
> l'amitié de mes genoux.

In the **"Récitation à l'Éloge d'une Reine"** (1907) and *Amitié du Prince* (1924), Queen and Prince are but human forms of rain and wind. The former, image of the "fertile woman", is described as "tiède" (attribute, we remember, of the rain), "parfaitement grasse", immobile and secure. The Prince is "maigre" and "flairé d'abeilles". He speaks of haste and bids the Narrator take the road of adventure. But the night of closed eyelids opposes the vigilance of day: "Il n'est plus question d'agir ni de compter, mais la faiblesse gagne les membres du plus fort".

"Histoire du Régent" (which originally figured among the *Éloges*) is the first poem to speak of an accomplished act:

> Tu as vaineu! tu as vaineu!

It speaks of the blade, of the flight of birds and of cripples jeering. It speaks of contempt for men of good will. Whatever the battle fought here, it ended in the victory of kings over prophets. Yet, ironically, these kings themselves take the position of the dreamer, as they lie down in the delight of "white bones bathing in pure wine".

> El mundo, con ser el mundo, en la mano de una
> niña cabe.
>
> [Rafael Alberti]

This, in essence, is the Song of the **"Présomptif".** And he goes on to sing of the unquiet soul; of the Horseman and of haste; of smoke that rises (and is carried by the winds) and of the shrinking honour of the House. He sings of *Anabase*:

> Tous les chemins du monde nous mangent dans la
> main!

Why then, it may be asked, does a "Lullaby", written some twenty years after both the **"Chanson du Présomptif"** and *Anabase* stand between the two poems? The only obvious answer seems to lie in the song's restatement of the question Prufrock asked:

> Dérangerez-vous l'ordre et le rang?

A last hesitation precedes the affirmation of war as the Horseman prepares to set out in conquest of his shadow.

Anabase opens on a song, but that song is of war. There "bronze leaves" are over the birth of a colt and *bitter* (the word recurs in Perse as a sign of violence) bay is in the Stranger's hand. He speaks of "souffles" and of distant lands, of history and conquest. The sea, once seat of silent wonder, now rolls on "comme une présomption de l'esprit" banishing memory and dream: "Aux ides pures du matin que savons-nous du songe, notre aînesse?" But "ennui" rises against the futility of action in "l'éternité qui bâille sur les sables".

"Le vent se lève" (again we think of Valéry) dispelling sadness and sloth, and although "le doute s'élève sur la réalité des choses", the city is founded (iv). Commerce flourishes in the freshness of laughter and white skies. But the ships come to a halt in the "deadwater where floats a dead ass". When action is thus shown impotent as acquiescence in the face of death, the temptation of dreams revisits the Conqueror ("cousues d'aiguilles nos paupières! louée l'attente sous nos cils . . . ."). Mistrustful ("la nuit donne son lait, qu'on y prenne bien garde . . . .") he wants to turn away: "Je m'élèverai dans mes pensées contre l'activité du songe". But as the colt puts its chin into the hand of the yet innocent child (we recall the wind coming to rest "au sein du vieillard"), the Stranger chooses, not without an awareness of guilt, the ways of solitude and silence.

"Canto" vi then opens on the reaffirmation of force. "Un chant de force pour les hommes" is published over the seas; habits of violence and fury rage at the countries "*infestés* de bien-être". Treaties and alliances replace solitude, and the colt born to the army is born under a sign of war. But night and sea again drown "la fureur du jour", for the sea rusts the swords of the warrior, and

> . . . le pouvoir s'exile chaque soir
>
> . . . . .
>
> et les vents calmes hébergeaient au fond des golfes
> désertiques.

The Conqueror's assertion of violence (like his drifting into dreams) engenders a feeling of guilt:

> . . ."Je vous parle, mon âme!—mon âme tout
> enténébrée d'un parfum de cheval!"
>
> (vii)

Then the soul darkened at dawn by the symbol of war seeks rest in memory and the peace of noon. While man sinks into dream, mountains "march in silence over the pale incandescence of the plain"

> et s'agenouillent à la fin, dans la fumée des songes,
> là où les peuples s'abolissent aux poudres mortes de
> la terre.

Into this world of calm, however, there falls the shadow of a great bird, being of ambiguity, tempter of the active world.

Canto viii resumes the "marches of the spirit . . . and the earth (is) given over to explanations. . ." Yet even "le grand principe de violence" is shrouded in leaves of grass, and the warrior returns in dream "dans un grand pays d'herbages sans mémoire". His thoughts stray once more to sensuous pleasures (ix). Once more his dreams seem suspect ("Ouvre ma bouche dans la lumière . . . et si l'on trouve faute en moi, que je sois congédié"), but he does not now admit to guilt, for he has seen beyond the war of activity and dream, and he foretells

> les temps d'une grande faveur et la félicité du soir sur
> nos paupières périssables . . .

In the simplicity of this vision the poet seems to have resolved the problem of acquiescence versus force in his acceptance of death. For death now is seen not as the avenger of indolence or war, but as the companion of dream, and the eternal happiness of evening is written upon "perishable" eyelids.

Anabase x returns, fittingly, with the songs of childhood. The "grand chapeau dont on séduit le bord" recalls the "chapeau en moelle de sureau" of **"Écrit sur la Porte"**. The celebration of all things green takes us back to the *Éloges.* After haste and war, the colt comes to rest on the tomb of a child. Order is restored to the country and honour to all men. And the men of all occupations are now subordinated to him who has none ("bien mieux, celui qui ne fait rien"); the "Cavalier" yields to the "Conteur", to the genealogist who has seen "each thing in its shadow and the virtue of its age"; to the dreamer, who has won— and overcome—his shadow.

> Terre arable du songe! Qui parle de bâtir?

The unequivocal song of earth falls back into the enigma of the sea, and "calm of mind all passion spent" the poet resumes—gladly and without guilt—"l'activité du songe".

The "war-song" which opened *Anabase* then returns, modulated into a song of peace. The horse has halted. The bronze-leaves have burst into "feuilles vivantes". Doves have risen from the "seandale de l'aile". The "pure" dream of dawn has effaced the "uneasy" dreams of night; "une chose très douce" has sprung from the bitter bay:

> Et paix à ceux, s'ils vont mourir, qui n'ont point
> vu ce jour.

Small wonder, then, that in the very confusion of *Exil* (1942) Saint-John Perse should sing poems of peace. He has known the futility of lightning and wind, war and sail. From the shores of the Atlantic the poet returns in memory to the island sea and takes up once more the leitmotiv of acquiescence: "La simple chose, la simple chose que voilà, la simple chose d'être là, dans l'écoulement du jour".

However, when "ennui" and sadness try again to invade the realm of peace, the dreamer turns once more to the alternative of action: "L'éclair m'ouvre le lit de plus vastes desseins" (vii). And this cycle, like *Crusoé* and *Éloges,* also ends in the equivocal:

> Et c'est l'heure, ô Poète, de décliner ton nom,
> ta naissance, et ta race.

While the comparison with Turoldus is interesting, we do not need it to explain the enigma here proposed by the verb *décliner*: Will the immigrant simply state his name? Will he state it simply? Will he choose the name of conqueror or poet? Will he sing of humility or pride; will he choose action or dream? *Which* name will he "inhabit"?

The answer will come in *Pluies,* where salvation is found in acceptance of all things, and the man of pure heart is the man "sans refus".

Although not free from hesitation, the cycle of *Pluics* (1943) sings, in essence, the affirmation of the new dream, washed of temptation and the guilt of both indolence and war: "Qu'il est de fraudes consumées sous nos plus hautes migrations" (ii). The warm rains will drown the cries of parakeet and sail; they will cleanse the fraudulent sea. They will efface history and reinstate man in the memory of a new childhood, free from the temptations of lightning and storm: "La ruche encore est au verger, l'enfance aux fourches du vieil arbre, et l'échelle interdite aux beaux veuvages de l'éclair".

Like every true poet, Saint-John Perse is forever singing but one song. For the Guadeloupean poet, this song is the song of the sea.

—Mechthild Cranston

The rains fall upon dream and reality alike, and they are rains not of vengeance, but ablution. They wash the "sad, sweet" faces of the violent, "car leurs voies sont étroites et leurs demeures incertaines" (vii). They wash the merely beautiful, they wash the eloquent (Verlaine's precept is stated simply); they must cleanse "la literie du songe" with "la litière du savoir" (vii), and peace will be to the man reconciled to his "instance humaine". This word in Perse rings with all its etymological overtones of *stare*— "to remain standing," "to remain still" and even, as we remember the temptation of the sail, "to be at anchor". Thus the rains are asked to reinstate man in his "condition humaine" and to grant to the momentariness of his life the permanence of peace.

But *Pluies* closes with a foreboding of *Vents*:

Seigneur terrible de mon rire, vous porterez ce soir l'esclandre en plus haut lieu.

. . . Car telles sont vos délices, Seigneur, au seuil aride du poème.

In the word "esclandre" echoes the warsong of *Anabase* ("le seandale de l'aile"). The "seuil *aride* du poème" hints at the insufficiency of the theme chosen by the rains.

Neiges (1944) then comes with a double mission. Like the rain, it washes the stains of action: "Et sur la hache du pionnier quelle inquiétante douceur a cette unit posé la joue?" (ii). But at the same time, it blocks the road to dream. In their very sweetness the snows are bitter. In their very whiteness they efface the traces which would lead to the purity of man: "Neiges cruelles qui nous ravissent la trace de nos pas" (ii). Here the poet, thinking of

his mother, does not seek the traces of history or conquest, but those of the "Paradis Terrestre" of his island as he knew it before the revelation of guilt.

Now the poet cannot sing, for the "foreign lady", "un chant du soir à la mesure de (son) mal" (*Poème à l'Étrangère,* ii), for his thoughts are bent on war: "Le front nu, lauré d'abeilles de phosphore" (we think of the Prince) he will walk "au bas du ciel très vaste d'acier vert". He thinks of the leaves of bronze and his mind is opened to the winds. His dog now a greater poet than he.

Vents (1946), counterpart of *Pluies,* is a song of action and force. The winds rise against "le goût de paille" (i), colour of death. (Cf. *Vents* iv: "L'emphase immense de la mort comme un grand arbre jaune"). They speak of haste and forgetting: "Enchante-moi, promesse, jusqu'à l'oubli du songe d'être né" (i: 3). They celebrate the "déracinement" imposed by the snows: "les îles pétries d'herbage . . . qu'elles s'en aillent" (i: 4). They are the enemies of dream: "Ceux qui songeaient les songes dans les chambres se sont couchés hier soir de l'autre côté du siècle, face aux lunes adverses" (i: 6). But the death of dreams does not result in the desired purity: "Ivre, plus ivre, disais-tu, de renier l'ivresse" i: 6). And the winds' "red torch of awakening" (ii: 5—again "red" stands for violence) cannot lighten the shadow of the palm (ii: 5).

The New World is composed of men of action, banished from a world of dream. But it is these very men who beg:

"Ah! qu'on nous laisse, négligeables, à notre peu de hâte"

To the long "chant de force", *Vents* iii: 3-6 sing their countertones of peace. There is a return to festivity and to the calm of noon. "Le savoir et l'éclair s'enveniment au pire scandale de l'histoire" (iii: 3). Man will be renewed not in action, but in dream (iii: 6). Man and the poet will patiently walk "sur les chemins de la tristesse" and "aux chantiers de l'erreur" (iii: 4). On the highway of conquerors will march "les grands aventuriers de l'âme" (iii: 5), and upon the man "infesté du songe" will descend the cry that delivers (iii: 6). The winds suddenly are quiet (iv), and man comes to rest in his "instance humaine": "Mais quoi! n'est-il rien d'autre, n'est-il rien d'autre que d'humain?" (iv: 1). He recognizes the *vanitas vanitatum* of all his quests:

Et qu'il fut vain, toujours, entre vos douces phrases familières, d'épier au très lointain des choses ce grondement, toujours, de grandes eaux en marche vers quelque Zambézie! . . .

(iv: 1)

But the vengeance of the wind is upon him: "Le vent est ivre d'un principe amer" (iv: 3—we think of the "bitter bay"). "Nous en avions assez de ces genoux trop calmes" the final line of *Éloges* comes to mind). "The warmth and weakness" of the esthete will be blown over by the angry wind.

The storm, however, is silenced again. Man will turn eastward, and the hour of his departure will be an hour of dream. This time, moreover, he will not be alone in his struggle against the temptation of violence. For he has found love, not only in the sensuous realm of Queens, but in the perishable alliance of all mortals:

> Amour, aviez-vous done raison contre les monstres de nos fables?

The reign of force thus ushers in the reign of love.

Amers (1957), the poet's longest song, sings the sea of alliance and love, victorious over death. It is a song sung "dans les fougères encore de l'enfance et le déroulement des crosses de la mort", written upon the "tender page of light" against the "nuit sans tain des choses". The guiltless victory of *Anabase* returns:

> Et vous, qu'êtes-vous done, ô Sages! pour nous réprimander, ô Sages! Si la fortune de mer nourrit encore, en sa saison, un grand poème hors de raison, m'en refuserez-vous l'accès? Terre de ma seigneurerie, et que j'y entre, moi! n'ayant nulle honte à mon plaisir
>
> . . . .

The cry of a bird is heard again ("Strophe") but is drowned in the chorus of "Tragédiennes" who sing the repudiation of "ennui" and the defeat of death:

> Oui, ce fut un long temps d'attente et de sécheresse, où la mort nous guettait à toutes chutes de l'écrit. Et l'ennui fut si grand, parmi nos toiles peintes, l' eœurement en nous si grand, derrière nos masques, de toute l'œuvre célébrée.
>
> ("Strophe")

These masks they cast away, keeping but the "anneau d'or", sign of alliance with the sea that forged them. They revisit in memory a place of birth which, cleansed of all personal remembrance, attains the purity of the archetype:

> Il nous est souvenu du lieu natal où nous n'avons naissance, il nous est souvenu du lieu royal où nous n'avons séance.

In quest of a new "legitimacy" (the child's search for his shadow), they follow "la mer de l'écume", the sea of dreams. They are, however, not free from the temptations that were upon the child, for they, too, are afraid of the wind that rises upon the water: "Mais vous, qu'alliez-vous craindre du message?" They have known the temptation of war:

> Il est, dans la cassure des choses, un singulier mordant, comme au tesson du glaive ce goût d'argile sèche et de poterie de fer, qui tentera toujours la lèvre du mieux-né.

But the storm now will not debase the dream, for the "Tragédiennes" have won the acceptance of *Pluies*:

> Amitié! amitié à toutes celles que nous fûmes . . .

They know that the hour of undefiled beauty will come in the warmth of evening. They know that they have pledged their alliance to the best of men: "Et l'homme de mer est dans nos songes. Meilleur des hommes, viens et prends!" They know, moreover, the mortality of man and the immortality of his shadow (and their alliance): "Tu vois ton ombre, sur l'eau mûre, quitte enfin de son âge".

> Étroits sont les vaisseaux . . .

But the certainty of that knowledge is not won without a struggle. There is, even in the song of love, a note of uneasiness:

"Qui rêve l'épée nue couchée dans les eaux claires n'a point banni du conte les flambeaux et les larmes". The remembrance of Tristan rings true. The perfect circle of the sea "cède au ciseau ses cubes, ses trièdres". Death's chariot appears drawn by "ses chevaux de parade". At dawn the green island-fish grows blue; the "white otters of childhood" appear, but in the brightness of day the unquiet dreams of night seek expression. The eagle-face of the Lover once more watches over the rising of a wind: "L'intrigue est sur le front de mer", and the alliance of love is broken. A crowd seizes upon the Lovers' dream. But in the Beloved there is forgiveness:

> Et toi, cœur d'homme non cruel, veuille le Ciel aussi t'absoudre de ta force".

Only then does the Lover come to acknowledge the omnipotence of love: "J'en atteste la mort qui d'amour seul s'offense" and is, at last, reconciled to his mortality:

> "Gardez" disait l'homme du conte, "gardez ô Nymphe non mortelle, votre offre d'immortalité. Votre île n'est pas mienne où l'arbre ne s'effeuille; ni votre couche ne m'émeut, où l'homme n'affronte son destin." Plutôt la couche des humains, honorée de la mort!

Thus, in the last analysis, the struggle between activity and dream, violence and peace is but Perse's metaphor for the great theme of every great singer's song: the struggle between life and death. For Perse, at least, that struggle ends in the victory of life which embraces both dream and death.

> . . . Aber dieses
> *ein*Mal gewesen zu sein, wenn auch nur *ein* Mal:
> *irdisch* gewesen zu sein, scheint nicht widerrufbar.
> [Rilke, *Duineser Elegien:* Die Neunte Elegie.]

In the voluntary renunciation of the green island of his childhood, the poet has rejoined the childhood of the world in its primeval unity and peace. In this world, reality is but the Creator's dream (freed from guilt, shame and fear), and dream the only reality:

> Pour nous la mer invétérée du songe, dit réel, et ses grandes voies d'empire portant au loin l'alliance.

The duplicity of that sea has thus been resolved in an alliance of love, in acceptance of the "univalence" of the world that encompasses activity and dream, life and death.

Nous qui mourrons peut-être un jour disons l'homme
immortel au foyer de l'instant.

("Dédicace")

I do not know—in any language—a more beautiful affirmation of the oneness of life.

Kathleen Raine (essay date 1967)

SOURCE: "St.-John Perse: Poet of the Marvellous," in
Encounter, Vol. XXIX, No. 4, October, 1967, pp. 51-61.

[*In the following essay, Raine explores the defining characteristics of Léger's verse.*]

In conversation the author of the poems published under
the pseudonym St.-John Perse once said to me what a pity
it was that whereas up to the beginning of the last war
English and French poets knew one another's work as a
matter of course, this was no longer so. The context of St.-
John Perse's poetry is by no means limited by the language in which he writes. His earliest master was Conrad,
whom as a young man he knew intimately, and who introduced him also to W. H. Hudson and his writings; one of
his earliest poems (**Images à Crusoé**) is an evocation of
Defoe's hero by a poet whose boyhood was lived in the
tropical archipelago of the Antilles. He was associated, in
the period between the two world wars, with the Ameri-
can-born Duchess of Sermoneta, Marguerite Caetani, in
the editing of the magazine *Commerce;* as was also Paul
Valéry. His latest—and finest—work has been written in
America, in whose natural features and majestic scale he
has found the correspondence of his characteristic themes.
Alexis St.-Léger Léger, one-time Permanent Secretary of
the French Foreign Office, has lived in the United States
ever since the destruction of the Third Republic; at which
time he lost, with everything else he then possessed (including the manuscripts of several unpublished poems),
his French citizenship; he has now once again a house in
France, but (though no longer as an exile) continues to
reside in America, where his work is known and better
understood by poets of the New World and the heirs of
Walt Whitman than it is in England.

Like most of my generation I read **Anabase** because it was
translated by T. S. Eliot, in 1930. Even in this early poem
(first published in 1924) and indeed in the earlier **Eloges,**
his inimitable style ("Innumerable the image, and the metre
prodigal") was already formed. But I remember being puzzled where to fit this poet into the picture my generation
was at that time building up of what modern poetry was
and should be. Surrealism was easy to understand, being
little more than avant-gardism as such; Joyce and Proust
had obvious contemporary points of reference; but its
very originality made the **Anabase** seem the more strange.
Its theme—the setting-out of a nomadic prince on an
expedition of conquest—was in no obvious way related to
contemporary experience although the images (exotic in
the style of Gauguin) were, as such, pleasurable. The great
sweep of the rhythm had no obvious similarity (other than

not being confined within any traditional metrical form) with
the Free Verse of Pound or Eliot; (it is in fact nearer to
Rimbaud and Claudel). It was not clear what affinity such
poetry had with Eliot's own theory and practice as a poet;
nor do I even now know the answer to that question.

Twenty years were to pass between the first publication of
Anabase and the appearance of **Exil, Poème à l'Etrangère,
Pluies,** and **Neiges** in 1942. These poems were written in the
United States, and in France first published on the presses
of the *Résistance,* without the name of the author. During
the intervening years the diplomat had kept "his brother
the poet" in abeyance. We shall never know (unless those
lost manuscripts should be recovered) how St.-John Perse
developed from the author of the romantic epic **Anabase**
into the poet of **Exil** and the greater poem of exile, **Vents**
(written in the United States in 1945 and published in
1946). With these poems, the poet and the times moved
into conjunction; what had formerly been a personal voice
became a voice of the age. If **Vents** is his greatest poem
this is surely so in part because the vision of these "very
great winds over all the faces of this world" (*"de très
grands vents sur toutes faces de ce monde," **Vents,*** I)
whose storm tore down the edifice of European civilisation and carried the poet into the New World was experienced so immediately by "his brother the prince," Alexis
Léger; as Dante, Milton, Byron and Yeats, whether as
rulers or as exiles, played their part in and shared the
suffering of their cities. No more than these is he a political poet; but like them, political concern and knowledge
is part of the structure of his thought, giving authority to
his prophetic speech. There is no longer, in 1945, any
question of how St.-John Perse's poetry relates to the
contemporary experience: the migrant tribe is ourselves,
the country we must leave, our own past, and western
civilisation; whether as conquerors or exiles—and there is
little difference—we must set forth again into that future
open alike to all.

All to be done again. All to be told again.
And the scything glance to be swept across all
man's heritage.

*Tout à reprendre. Tout à redire. Et la faux
du regard sur tout l'avoir menée!*

[**Vents**]

The state of exile, in many cases physical, but above all
spiritual exile, is the typical condition of poet and prince
alike in the new dark age of barbarism and the reversal of
the natural hierarchies with all their values; the state to be
explored.

Claudel, writing of **Vents,** pointed out that whereas the
Odyssey is an epic of home-coming, **Vents,** an epic description of the fall of the civilisation whose beginnings
Homer scarcely saw, is a poem of setting-out; as that
other epic, *Finnegans Wake,* ends, like the *Götterdäm-
merung,* with a purification by re-immersion in the source.
But for Perse, this purification, re-immersion, and setting-
out is not cyclic, but at every moment to be enacted as life
moves always into its future.

He chooses for his symbols those freely-moving elements which traverse and unite all times and spaces—seas, winds, birds, the perpetual setting-out of migrant swarms, flocks, human tribes; an "open" poetry in which all spaces and times coexist in a single present. No theme could be more true to one of the as yet unformulated experiences of this time. The scope of his poetry is coterminous with the earth in its single and continuous space-time.

The English reader may be alarmed by the initial difficulty of a poetry whose vocabulary is full of unfamiliar words, many of them not to be found in a dictionary, which in any case tells us little. The writings of Darwin, the paintings of Audubon, or a text-book on boat-building could tell us more, an acquaintance with the things themselves more still. Knowing that his translator Eliot was interested in words and read largely in the *Oxford Dictionary,* I asked if this was a meeting-point between the poet and his translator. But this was not so, he said; for Eliot's interest in words was literary and philological, whereas his own vocabulary comes from his knowledge of many skills, his travels in many places, his knowledge of plants and their products and uses, the flora and fauna of many coasts, the ethnography of outer Mongolia; of whatever mankind has made or valued; objects rather than myths, all that can be handled rather than what has been thought. His interests are not primarily literary, less still academic; a man of wide experience, he is able to create those astonishing syntheses and analogies which could occur only to a man of trained sensibility and many kinds of exact knowledge. Only if "exotic" and "tropical" are synonymous can even his early imagery be so described; but in so far as the word implies a certain artificiality (as in Beardsley) this is not so. Those immense random samples of the wonders of the world (*"La terre enfante des merveilles"*), miraculous drafts from that thalassic fecundity are all taken from the real, and the accessible. Modern mankind inhabits, as did no former generation, the earth as a whole, whose flora and fauna with all the regions they inhabit, have for the first time become a book open to all.

All the land of trees, out there, its background of black vines, like a Bible of shadow and freshness in the unrolling of this world's most beautiful texts. . . . The land in its long lines, on its longest strophes, running, from sea to sea, to loftiest scriptures. . . . And this great winter prose that is, to the Old World's flocks, the wolf-lore of the New World. . . . Those flights of insects going off in clouds to lose themselves at sea, like fragments of sacred texts, like the tatters of errant prophecies and the recitations of genealogists and psalmists. . . .

Toute la terre aux arbres, par là-bas, sur fond de vignes noires, comme une Bible d'ombre et de fraîcheur dans le déroulement des plus beaux textes de ce monde. . . . Et la terre à longs traits, sur ses plus longues laisses, courant, de mer à mer, à de plus hautes écritures. . . . Et ces grandes proses hivernales, qui sont aux laines du Vieux Monde la louveterie du Nouveau Monde. . . . Ces vols d'insectes par nuées qui s'en

allaient se perdre au large comme des morceaux de textes saints, comme des lambeaux de prophétieserrantes et des récitations de généalogistes, de psalmistes. . . .

[*Vents* II. 1-4]

Our generation has become intellectually, but not imaginatively, habituated to the retrospect of natural evolution, to the new spacious simultaneity of the relativity of time and place. In reading the poetry of St.-John Perse we experience this new freedom, familiar to the scientist, which poetry has been slow to enter. Plato called the world a happy and immortal animal, one immortal joy sweeping through its myriads of component lives; and all Perse's poems are (as one is entitled) praises, *éloges,* of this "moving image of eternity." His prodigality of image both illustrates and suggests an infinitely various and inexhaustible fecundity.

When we come to examine those "marvels" which are ever before the eyes of the poet, we recognise, with some astonishment, that they are such as are everywhere present but generally unheeded; the moon "thin as the ergot on a white rose" (the English translator—Hugh Chisholm—has missed the beauty of this comparison of the misty moon with the familiar fungoid blight to which white roses are particularly subject); or, from one of his earliest poems, ***Images à Crusoé,***

Hear the hollow creatures rattling in their shells—
Against a bit of green sky a sudden puff of smoke
is the tangled flight of mosquitoes . . . and other
gentle creatures, listening to the evening, sing a song
purer than their announcing of the rains: the swallowing of two pearls swelling their yellow gullets.

*Entends claquer les bêtes creuses danseurscoques—
Il y a sur un morceau de ciel vert une fumée hâtive qui
est le vol emmêlé des moustiques. . . . Et d'autres bêtes
qui sont douces, attentives au soir, chantent un chant
plus pur que l'annonce des pluies: c'est la déglutition
de deux perles gonflant leur gosier jaune. . . .*

[*Elogies*]

You can hear and see the like on any shore or by any pond where the frogs make their continuous music. The exotic strangeness of some images (the "two pearls" in the frog's gullet, or "Anhinga, the bird, fabled water-turkey, whose existence is no fable . . . it is enough for me that he lives") (*"Et l'Oiseau Anhinga, la dinde d'eau des fables, dont l'existence n'est point fable . . . et c'est assez pour moi qu'il vive—"*) is diffused upon all, reminding us that common and rare alike participate in the same marvel of existence, the *magia.* This world which seems remote and unreal to poets and their readers is one in which any naturalist would feel at home; the world of the scientists which often seems infinitely more poetic than the dull round of poets and their readers, who notice, as a rule, very little, and have lost the habit of regarding knowledge of many kinds—or of any kind—as the material of poetry.

At my first meeting with the poet, I listened with enchantment while he spoke of the wildest shores and deserts of the world (his conversation is like his poems, rich in marvels) and I asked if living in Georgetown he did not miss such things. He pointed to the sky where two vultures were wheeling, and spoke of W. H. Hudson who had studied dispersal of tropical plants and insects brought ashore at English sea-ports, and those fungi which thrive on the paste used for bill-sticking; for St.-John Perse the great cities are themselves only another wave-crest raised by the ocean of inexhaustible life. The "marvels," purified from all commonplace associations and the unreal values utility assigns, are, in his poetry, revealed in their absolute nature.

If at first sight the vocabulary of St.-John Perse seems difficult, his themes exotic, there is an underlying simplicity about this poetry of "the many," "the ten-thousand creatures." Its amplitude is tremendous but it is not as Joyce, semantically, or, as Eliot, in historical and literary allusiveness, or, as Yeats, in metaphysical and mythological import, complex poetry at all. That may well be part of its difficulty for readers more attuned to a trivial complexity than to a simple grandeur. It is "nature-poetry," that genre so dear to the English; but upon a scale which surpasses our national expectations: it is to the "nature-poetry" of the post-Wordsworthians as the ocean to a village pond.

In one of his very few prose statements [*On Poetry,* 1961] the poet defined certain attributes of poetry which are presumably those he would wish us to find in his own work. Poetry and science, he said, are alike ways of exploring an "original night" in itself unknowable.

> If poetry is not itself, as some have claimed, "reality absolute," it is poetry which shows the strongest passion for, and the keenest apprehension of it, to that extreme limit of complicity where reality seems to shape itself within the poem.

> By means of analogical and symbolic thinking, by means of the far-reaching light of the mediating image and its play of correspondences, by way of a thousand chains of reactions and unusual associations, by virtue also of a language through which is transmitted the very rhythm of Being, the poet clothes himself in a surreality to which the scientist cannot aspire. Is there, for man, any dialectic more compelling, or capable of engaging him more fully? When the philosophers themselves abandon the threshold of the metaphysical, it falls to the poet to take the place of the metaphysician; and at such times it is poetry and not philosophy which is revealed as the true "daughter of wonder," to use the phrase of the ancient philosopher who most mistrusted her.

> *Car si la poésie n'est pas, comme on l'a dit, "le réel absolu," elle en est bien la plus proche convoitise et la plus proche appréhension, à cette limite extrême de complicité où le réel dans le poème semble s'informer lui-même.*

> *Par la pensée analogique et symbolique, par l'illumination lointaine de l'image médiatrice, et par le jeu de ses correspondances, sur mille chaînes de réactions et*

> *d'associations étrangères, par la grâce enfin d'un langage où se transmet le mouvement même de l'Etre, le poète s'investit d'une surréalité qui ne peut être celle de la science. Est-il chez l'homme plus saisissante dialectique et qui de l'homme engage plus? Lorsque les philosophes eux-mêmes désertent le seuil métaphysique, il advient au poète de relever là le métaphysicien; et c'est la poésie alors, non la philosophie, qui se révèle la vraie "fille de l'étonnement," selon l'expression du philosophe antique à qui elle fut le plus suspecte.*

Claudel wrote of the eyes of the poet as "two round holes which I am tempted to refer to as magnets." My own first impression of the poet—whose appearance for the rest is correct and somewhat retiring—was of those eyes, as of a man enchanted by what he contemplates. St.-John Perse's poetry has been described (by Gaëtan Picon) as "a magic positivism and pragmatism"; it is true that a materialist might (disregarding his own confessed concern with the metaphysical) so read it; but his "marvels" are more akin to *maya* than to matter, and suggest Conrad's "a man that is born falls into a dream like a man who falls into the sea," or (from the preface to *The Shadow Line*)—

> All my moral intellectual being is punctuated by an invincible conviction that whatever falls under the dominion of our senses must be in nature and, however exceptional, cannot differ in its essence from all the other effects of the visible and tangible world of which we are a self-conscious part. The world of the living contains enough marvels and mysteries acting upon our emotions and intelligence in ways so inexplicable that it would almost justify the conception of life as an enchanted state.

For St.-John Perse it is true, as Blake claimed for himself, that "I see everything I paint In This World." Blake also said that "to the Eyes of the Man of Imagination, Nature is Imagination itself"; and that the world perceived by the senses is the fourth region of consciousness, externalised by the illusory philosophy of materialism: "although it appears without, it is within, in your imagination." In the poetry of Perse, the sensible world is restored as a region of the imagination; for the content of his imagination is "nature" itself.

The unbounded nature of the poet's theme, free in time as it is uncircumscribed by space, determines the prodigality of his metre. Accustomed as we are to minimal vision, our attention solicited by, and for, the pathological, the criminal, the immature, the uneducated, the ignorant and the unskilled of all sorts presenting the articulations of ignorance as communications of knowledge and achievements of art, we have all but lost the capacity for the total response his poetry demands. The "self-expression" of the individual (always more or less handicapped in one or more of the above ways) has no place in his art. Claudel called him "a Mont St. Michel immensely accentuated in an ebbing tide"; and if this mountain is generally unnoticed in post-war England this may well be because, by standards designed for measuring mole-hills, mountains are unperceived. Yet his unbounded vision of "the visible and tangible world of which we are a self-conscious part" is a liberation offered to whoever is willing to entrust himself to the great open sea (*"le mouvement même de l'Etre"*) of the poetry of Perse.

Our generation has become intellectually, but not imaginatively, habituated to the retrospect of natural evolution, to the new spacious simultaneity of the relativity of time and place. In reading the poetry of St.-John Perse we experience this new freedom, familiar to the scientist, which poetry has been slow to enter.

—*Kathleen Raine*

As against the continuous and relentless attrition, the dwindling of knowledge, the coarsening of sensibility, the abdication in thought, feeling and conduct of even the conception of the best, tacitly demanded and too often accorded in defence to the all-too-common man, St.-John Perse summons to an expansion of consciousness, to a total realisation of being. He speaks as the "free man of high caste," reminding those who are determined to forget how great are the demands made by the aristocratic view of man, which alone protects and fosters the highest human potentialities: knowledge, and the freedom to translate knowledge and imagination into action (the prince) and into art (the poet, who is "brother" to the prince). For Perse, as for Plato, and Manu, the superiority of the "man of high caste" lies not in his status but in his quality of being; his superior knowledge and freedom of action. Whether as acknowledged leader, or as exile from a fallen civilisation, "the superior man" remains such by virtue of what he is. The prince-poet has given himself totally to the fullest attainable human experience, accepting those hard terms upon which alone freedom of act and of thought are given. We are again reminded of Conrad, whose heroes also are "free men of high caste," and of his phrase about "the unknown disciples of the self-imposed task." Sex and the dead, Yeats somewhere said, are the only matters serious enough to engage the thoughts of an ageing poet; and erotic love and death are the frontiers which bound the world of St.-John Perse's prince-poet: mortal, we are possessed by, but cannot possess, the immortal life which the sexual mystery confers, and death takes away; no other limits can impede the freedom of act and thought of whoever fears neither the loss of life nor of possessions; courage, magnanimity and wisdom—the aristocratic virtues—are the fruits of this proud detachment. The plebeian whine comes from those (of whatever social class, since caste and class are not coterminous) who have not looked at life and death. The sense of immortality is lost precisely when we seek to bind it to ourselves. *"Il faut que vous mettez la tête dans la gueule du lion"* was the memorable advice the poet once gave me; for such is the condition accorded by reality itself, that lion's-mouth ever open before us.

One same wave throughout the world, one
same wave since Troy
    Rolls its haunch towards us. On a far-off open
sea this gust was long ago impressed.

*Une même vague par le monde, une même
vague depuis Troie/Roule sa hanche jusqu'à
nous. Au très grand large loin de nous fut im-
primé jadis ce souffle.*

[*Amers* IX.]

The sea, ancient and universal symbol of material flux, impressed by the "breath of life," in the beginning is an image from Genesis acceptable alike to Platonist and evolutionist.

M. Léger admitted a certain affinity with the thought of Teilhard de Chardin, at the same time denying indebtedness and withholding that kind and degree of admiration for the Jesuit to be found in "certain Paris salons." Such ideas, he said, had long been in the air. Yet both are discernibly of the same generation, and the vision common to both lends to the modern experience of nature an amplitude, spaciousness and purity to be found in no living or recent English writer known to me. (It is characteristic that after disclaiming any indebtedness to Teilhard he added: "But for one thing I admire him: his Order offered him freedom from his vows of obedience, in all honour; and he refused." The admiration of the poet, like the action of the Jesuit, was that of the "free man of high caste.")

"One law of harmony governs the whole world of things." The amplitude of that harmony, of the free-flowing "wave throughout the world" characterises the cadences of the verse of St.-John Perse; for verse it is (so he insists) though of very long lines, and in no way to be confused with prose-poetry; or, in England, with the cadenced poetic prose of David Jones. (Readers of Proust will remember that the two maids at Balbec were incredulous when Marcel, reading—was it?—*Eloges,* told them that this was "poetry.") It is difficult to attune a foreign ear, not to the sweep of the larger pattern, but to the very subtle internal cross-patterns (again like waves, whose regularity of rhythm breaks down into such variety) of rhythm, assonance, even internal rhyme. The ruling pattern is liturgical, with returning phrases which, as in an Introit psalm, define and continually reaffirm the theme.

One same wave throughout the world, one
same wave reaching to us, in the very great
distance of the world and of its age . . . and such
a surge, from all sides, that rises and finds its
way up into us. . . .
*Une même vague par le monde, une même
vague jusqu'à nous, au très lointain du monde et
de son âge . . . et tant de houle, et de partout,
qui monte et fraye jusqu'en nous. . . .*

One same wave throughout the world, one
same wave our course. . . . Narrow the measure,
narrow the caesura, which breaks the woman's
body at the middle like an ancient metre. . . .

*Une même vague par le monde, une même
vague notre course. . . . Etroite la mesure, étroite
la césure, qui rompt en son milieu le corps de
femme comme le metre antique. . . .*

[Amers IX]

One same wave throughout the world, one
same wave among us, raising, rolling the hydra
enamoured of its force. . . . And from the divine
heel, that very strong pulsation, which rules
everywhere. . . . Love and the sea of the same
bed, love and the sea in the same bed. . . .

*Une même vague par le monde, une même
vague parmi nous, haussant, roulant l'hydre
amoureuse de sa force. . . . Et du talon divin,
cette pulsation très forte, et qui tout gagne. . . .
Amour et mer de même lit, amour et mer au
même lit. . . .*

[Amers IX]

One same wave throughout the world, one
same wave throughout the city. . . . Lovers, the
sea follows us! Death is not! The gods hail us
in the port. . . .

*. . . Une même vague par le monde, une même
vague par la ville. . . . Amants, la mer nous suit!
La mort n'est point! Les dieux nous hèlent à
l'escale. . . .*

[Amers IX]

In **Vents** (the *"très grands vents sur toutes faces de ce
monde," "sur toutes pistes de ce monde"*) recurring themes
are *"S'en aller! S'en aller! Parole de vivant!"* and *"Parole du Prodigue"*; *"Eâ, dieu de l'abîme"*; *"Et le poète
aussi est avec nous"*; *"O vous, que refraîchit l'orage."*
(St.-John Perse makes ridiculous the timid fear of the orator's vocative.) No two poems are alike, nor their imagery
interchangeable. A superficial reader of Perse will be impressed by the consistency of his inimitable style, his
"breath," but a closer reading reveals the architectural
unity of theme, imagery and even metre within each.

Concluding his analysis of **Vents**, Claudel (after quoting
long sections of particularly magnificent evocations of
that spacious cosmology of Perse's world) exclaims, "We
are a long way from Marcel Proust." Guadeloupe with its
swarms of green insects and boats with white sails on
tropical seas may be a long way from Combray with its
lilacs and its hawthorn, the nomadic horde and the anonymous exile from the Boulevard St. Germain. St.-John Perse
is himself by no means a Proustian; yet certain themes
belong to the period to which both have given expression.
Both are impressionists, imaginatively recreating the "minute
particulars" of the sensible world; above all both are concerned with palingenesia, the restoration of all things to
their primal perfection, the state of Paradise: Proust by the
emancipation of memory from the bondage of time; St.-
John Perse by the freedom and simultaneity of all existence within nature's long present and single now. For
Proust, the element in which all is freed from time is mind

itself, the only paradise the paradise we have lost, for only
when twice-born in memory do things enter upon this
timeless and immortal contemporaneity. For St.-John Perse
all in nature is immortal and contemporaneous in so far as
the many participate in the one. Like Proust, too, the poet
places the supreme value not in the qualities of things but
in their mere existence. In a passage in *Jean Santeuil* (a
hundred others may be found, but I happened to be reading the lesser book) the narrator, sitting in the kitchen of
the family house at Etreuilles (Combray) is speechlessly
happy as the cook stirs her pans on the open fire and
takes his damp shoes to dry them:

> At such moments the sound of the cook's voice, saying
> "I should just think those shoes of yours *are* wet!" is
> pleasant in your ears, because it is something that
> *exists,* as, too, the sight of the old chemist standing by
> his window, absorbed in the concoction of some mixture
> and brightly illumined by the lamp, is also full of
> charm because he *is.*

> *Dans ces moments le bruit de la voix de la cuisinière
> disant: "Ce qu'elles étaient mouillées, tout de même,
> vos chaussures," vous impressionne agréablement
> parce que le bruit de voix c'est une chose qui est,
> comme par la fenêtre le vieux pharmacien absorbé
> dans un mélange et vivement éclairé par la lampe vous
> charme aussi parce qu'il est.*

If this be existentialism both Proust and Perse are existen-
tialists in the existential not in the theoretical sense: for
both the marvel of *"les merveilles"* is that *they are.*

But if Claudel's phrase is intended to praise the poet at
the expense of the novelist, admirers of both may well see
in the passage quoted an element entirely absent from the
writings of St.-John Perse—the human as such. The poet
stops short, in his account of man, precisely with what is
(in terms of all the higher religions) precisely human in
man, his individual being. The gods whom he invokes are
the old pantheistic gods, *"Eâ, dieu de l'abîme," "mer de
Baal, mer de Mammon,"* Dionysus with the rigging of his
ship entwined with vines; the many-armed, skull-adorned
fertility goddess of southern India; nor does he shrink
from those more barbaric Mexican deities to whom blood
sacrifice was made, from a sense (so I remember the poet
saying) of the inexhaustible abundance of life. Some might
see in this re-immersion of man in the pre-human a post-
Christian vision (if we may so describe a mode of apprehending life which Teilhard's Alpha and Omega perhaps
insufficiently consecrate) essentially nihilistic. Upon the
charge of nihilism this most life-praising of poets must be
acquitted; even though (as Edwin Muir said also of D. H.
Lawrence) the "life" he praises is "not human life as such."
It is, however, a "divine" life, not some mechanistic nihil.
But the creator of the Baron de Charlus is within the
Christian tradition, the poet of **Amers** outside it.

Erotic love (and **Amers** is the most splendid poem known
to me upon that theme) celebrates the re-immersion of man
and woman, in the act of love, in the "one same wave" of
the immortal and indivisible life of the cosmos: "In the

divine promiscuity and man's depravation in the gods" (*"Dans la promiscuité divine et la dépravation de l'homme chez les dieux. . . ."*) who here represent the immortal cosmic life. For the poet man is but the crest of the advancing wave of nature; the life and the joy in which he participates is impersonal: "In the destructive element, immerse"—such, following Conrad (whose Stein was quoting his Goethe), is the invitation of his poetry.

Individual woman is but an aspect of that "universal bride," the fecund sea of life:

> Towards you, the universal bride in the midst of the congregating waters, towards you, the licentious bride in the abundance of her springs and at the high flood-tide of her maturity, all earth itself streaming descends the gorges of love.

> *Vers toi l'Epouse universelle au sein de la congrégation des eaux, vers toi, l'Epouse licencieuse dans l'abondance de ses sources et le haut flux de sa maturité, toute la terre elle-même ruisselante descend les gorges de l'amour.*

A long way—Claudel might have said—from the vision of Dante; yet it is a sacred poem. Having in *Vents* said all he (and through him the former diplomat) wished to say of our *"rendez-vous avec la fin d'un âge,"* the poet like some modern Antony who has risen out of his own defeat, divests himself of the prince and becomes the lover. There is in Perse's erotic poem some of that dazzling quality of the barge of Cleopatra, as she, mediating the goddess Isis herself, advances to meet her lover (worthy, in the eyes of her love, to be set at "Jove's side" and attended by the page Eros). (His imagery is at all times of truly Shakespearean fertility.) In Perse's poem woman is herself the ship in which the lover puts to sea upon the occasion of existence, carried by that "one same wave" in the act of love, obscene and sacred, in which every mortal creature participates, in the *hieros gamos* with *"l'Epouse éternelle."*

We may reflect, in passing, how little, for all the current obsession with "sex," has been written on this theme, in English, which, beside *Amers,* does not seem vulgar and trivial. Is it an after-image of Protestant puritanism that in place of the erotic, in Anglo-Saxon countries, has left only the pornographic?

The sea as symbol of material existence and its flux is age-old and universal—Hebraic, Neoplatonic, Hermetic, Vedantic; and woman as the *foederis arca* who in her body bears immortal life over those dangerous waves where Odysseus sailed among marvels and perils. But in the poetry of Perse it is the existential reality rather than the symbolic analogies on other planes of the real, which are made apparent. The wave of the sea that with "such a surge . . . rises and finds its way up into us" might be (like the hot heart of the bird in *Oiseaux* whose burning is its life) the *"simple fait biologique"*; for the salinity of blood biologists relate to the salinity of the sea where all organic life originated;

> The Sea, woven in us, to the last weaving of its tangled deeps, the Sea, in us weaving its great hours of light and its great trails of darkness.

> *La Mer, en nous tissée, jusqu'à ses ronceraies d'abîme, la Mer, en nous tissant ses grandes heures de lumière et ses grandes pistes de ténèbres. . . .*

Neither of St.-John Perse's two subsequent poems is on the same scale, or so magnificent, as *Vents* and *Amers. Chronique* (1960) is on the theme of age; and the approach to death is still a setting-forth, an *éloge. Oiseaux* (1966) illustrated by four lithographs by Georges Braque, a collaboration in which the poem existed first, is the poet's definition and exploration of the relation of art to nature, nature to consciousness. Classical, economical ("laconic") in contrast with the superb prodigality and amplitude of *Amers,* this poem is not an essay in criticism but itself exemplifies what it explores in an existential identity of thought and expression, comparable with the identity, in nature, of existence and being, form and life.

> Man has rejoined the innocence of the wild creature, and the bird painted in the hunter's eye has become the hunter himself in the eye of the creature, as it does in Eskimo art. Wild thing and hunter together cross the ford of a fourth dimension. From the difficulty of being to the ease of loving they move in step at last, two real beings who form a pair.

> *L'homme a rejoint l'innocence de la bête, et l'oiseau peint dans l'oeil du chasseur devient le chasseur même dans l'oeil de la bête, comme il advient dans l'art des Eskimos. Bête et chasseur passent ensemble le gué d'une quatrième dimension. De la difficulté d'être à l'aisance d'aimer vont enfin, du même pas, deux étres vrai , appariés.*

> [*Oiseaux*]

Of inner and outer worlds the bird (a symbol especially apt perhaps because of all creatures the bird is the most free to move in all elements and to "lose its shadow") is the unifying image. In the immediacy of primitive art, related rather to the skills of the hunter than to aesthetics, the poet finds the very point at which, in the transition from sky to eye, the image passes from nature into art; and as for Proust memories are alone freed from the restrictions of time and place, so for St.-John Perse whatever enters art enters the paradisal state of coexistence and unity; while at the same time art is itself but another region of nature. In this superb image we see what the *ars poetica* can achieve by means of the "mediating image and its play of correspondences, by way of a thousand chains of reactions and unusual associations" without being symbolic. Again we may think of Proust, whose rejection of "realism" was not on metaphysical grounds, but because it is in the nature of sensations to evoke those thousand associations. It is these alone, their resonances and evocations, which enrich and give meaning to the sensations which occasion them. Or again,

> At the hypnotic point of an immense eye inhabited by the painter, like the very eye of a cyclone in its course—all things referred to their distant causes and all fires crossing—there is unity at last re-knitted and diversity reconciled. After such and so long a consummation of flight, behold the great round of birds painted on the zodiacal wheel and the gathering of an entire family of wings in the yellow wind, like one vast propeller in quest of its blades.

> *Au point d'hypnose d'un oeil immense habité par le peintre, comme l'oeil même du cyclone en course—toutes choses rapportées à leurs causes lointaines et tous feux se croisant—c'est l'unité enfin renouée et le divers réconcilié. Après telle et si longue consommation du vol, c'est la grande ronde d'oiseaux peints sur la roue zodiacale, et la rassemblement d'une famille entière d'ailes dans le vent jaune, comme une seule et vaste hélice en quête de ses pales.*

> [*Oiseaux,* XI.]

In entering consciousness, multiplicity enters the state of unity.

None of the poet's translators is in all ways excellent; Eliot's knowledge of French seems the most perfect; his polished renderings are faultless, linguistically, though his own dignified and processional *lento* at times slows down Perse's "rhythm of Being itself." Sometimes he misses the naked simplicity of St.-John Perse's images, as in the sedate 17th-century "earth is brought to bed of wonders" for *"la terre enfante des merveilles"*; Eliot's own practice as a poet is to evoke literary overtones and to call up the past echoed in every word and image; whereas St.-John Perse's images all alike seem to belong to a "nature" which has no past, no history, in which fossil, ephemerid, or modern city alike belong to the one here and now. His language is without echoes or penumbra. Hugh Chisholm's *Vents* seems to me best to catch the rhythm of the original, while Wallace Fowlie's *Amers* fails to do so. Denis Devlin's *Exil* is perhaps (after Eliot) the most poetic. Robert Fitzgerald (whose knowledge of French seems less good than any of these) does nevertheless (as in the above quotations from *Oiseaux*) capture the poet's absolutely modern quality, places his work in the present of the 1960s and not of the 1920s. It is not for an English reader to discuss the many untranslatable aspects of his style; every language places on reality itself different contours; even simple nouns are untranslatable; but the "play of correspondences" of his "mediating image" is generally not semantic, and is therefore not greatly weakened in translation. As in (to take another example from *Oiseaux*):

> The more they fly, the more wholly they come to the delight of being: birds of the longest day and the longest resolve, with brows like newborn infants or the dolphins of old fables.

> *Plus qu'ils ne volent, ils viennent à part entière au délice de l'être: oiseaux du plus long jour et du plus long propos, avec leurs fronts de nouveau-nés ou de dauphins des fables. . . .*

> [*Oiseaux,* X.]

The complexity here is not verbal, yet the internal so-to-say valencies of the figure are as firmly established as the forces which hold together a molecule. The "long day" of the birds who follow the sun; the strength of the instinct which urges the migrant on is implicit in the "brows like new-born infants," doubly apt from the projecting rounded form of the bird's head, and the implication of a perpetual setting-forth, the creature at every moment new-born into the future. The beautiful modulation to the brow of the dolphin (bulbous also) and the swiftest-travelling creature of another element is introduced like a change of key in music. The poet (a man of the sea) has doubtless seen many dolphins in the water; but the deliberate evocation here of the dolphin of art ("old fables") brings in the legend of Arion and the dolphin as the vehicle of the poet, and of poetry itself; so that the bird with its *"longue propos"* (and we are here reminded that Braque's birds belong not to nature but to art) becomes also the vehicle of imagination and its "long purpose." None of this is stated yet all is implicit in the configuration of the image. Such poetry is, in Shelley's full sense, "the language of the imagination," expressing essences and relations entirely qualitative.

St.-John Perse's existentialism (if such it is) might seem opposed to the symbolist tradition which (under whatever name) stems from some form of Platonism. Neither poetic practice can be detached from that view of the nature of things in which it is grounded. The symbol presumes multiple planes of being linked both by cause and by analogy; without understanding of this metaphysical ground, symbolist poetry becomes meaningless. In Perse's existentialist use of the image a metaphysical ground is no less implicit, by his own confession. No less than the poetry of Yeats his work must remain opaque to vulgar positivism, for he too uses the term "divine," though for him divinity is existentially implicit. Perhaps the two apparently opposite modes may be compared to different phases of waves; at their point of intersection we have the existential image; at the limit of their amplitude, the analogies and resonances of the symbol. And like the symbolists, St.-John Perse not only assumes but affirms and uses as the instrument of his art the law of harmony which subsists in and unifies the cosmos; his universe is neither arbitrary nor indeterminate; and is governed by that symmetry, unity and accord in which Plotinus discovers the essence of "the beautiful."

The symbol is, besides, itself rooted in nature, and in that reading of the great Bible of the world which precedes all written books, those remote copies of the intrinsic meanings of things. I was myself dramatically reminded of this when in the summer of 1966 I saw flying over the Temple of Aesculapius at Epidaurus (of all places) an eagle with a writhing serpent in its beak. This symbol, first used as a metaphor by Homer, has accompanied European poetry and symbolic thought throughout its history, gathering on its way symbolic associations profound and various. The alchemists made of eagle and serpent figures of their mythology; Ovid, Spenser, Blake and Shelley have in turn clothed the image in literary form and symbolic connotations. But seeing the thing itself (as if a piece of writing in the sky torn loose from all these books) I thought of St.-John Perse; whose poetry re-immerses all our used images in "that original night" of Orphism, contemporaneous with every period of history and every moment of life, and gives back to us a world at every moment newly created.

Wallace Fowlie (essay date 1967)

SOURCE: "Saint-John Perse's Quest," in *Climate of Violence: The French Literary Tradition from Baudelaire to the Present,* Macmillan, 1967, pp. 87-101.

[*In the following essay, Fowlie provides a thematic and stylistic analysis of* Amers.]

Abruptly, with the announcement in the late fall of 1960 that Saint-John Perse had been awarded the Nobel Prize for literature, the work of a relatively obscure poet became a public concern. The work itself had been previously scrutinized and studied only by that small public that is devoted to the cause of poetry and aware of the poetic ambitions of our age, although to a wider public the name of Saint-John Perse was known, as were the few biographical details that have been rehearsed so often in print: the birth of Alexis Léger on a coral island near Guadeloupe in 1887, his education in France, his choice of the diplomatic service in 1914, his sojourn of seven years in China, his high post at the Quai d'Orsay in the Ministry of Foreign Affairs, his refusal to work for the Vichy government, and his arrival in the United States in 1940, where he lived for seventeen years, before returning to France.

With the honor of the Nobel Prize, which in a sense was the world's recognition of Saint-John Perse, the wide international public that follows literary matters, asked, with perfect justice, Why this man? Why a poet? Why a French poet so soon after the award to Albert Camus? Why this particular poetic work? Does it bear a relationship to that cause of man associated with the Swedish Academy awards?

From his earliest poems, those published under the title *Eloges* in 1910, through *Anabase* of 1924 (translated by T. S. Eliot in 1930), and *Exil,* published in French in *Poetry Magazine* (Chicago) in 1942, and *Amers* (*Seamarks*), published in 1957 and *Oiseaux* of 1963, Saint-John Perse has continued to describe and analyze the condition of man in our time, the fate of man at this moment in history. His poetry has always had a singular effect in France. Yet no poetic work exists alone. The poetry of Saint-John Perse has affiliations with certain formal rhetorical aspects of Claudel's work, and with poetic theories of Mallarmé. However, and this is the miracle of every major poet, the work of Saint-John Perse is unique and incomparable.

Such a historical event as the Nobel Prize announcement indicated the need and the duty to reassess the function of poetry, to increase our understanding of the very notion of poetry. A great art comes from a precise moment in history, reflects it and testifies to it, and at the same time surpasses its historical moment. The virtue of transcendence has to inhabit every major work of art. The actual poetic work of Saint-John Perse is quite limited in its proportions, but it stands, in its modest totality, as a work that contains the full mystery of poetic form and utterance. It testifies to the mystery of poetic rhythm: the sheer weight and force of words, their resonance and their meaning. It is music, beyond a doubt, and it is more than music. It is an effort to rediscover the lost language of man.

When news of the Nobel Prize award reached M. Léger in his home in Giens, in southern France, his first statement expressed his satisfaction that it was poetry that was being honored. The award represented for him an act of confidence in the belief that a single line of poetry has the power to arouse awareness of the deepest problems of man, of the most difficult and persistent of his problems.

Poetry today is jealous and watchful of its secret. But this experience of jealousy and watchfulness is not new in the history of poetry. It is the ritual secrecy associated with early Orphic poetry. It is comparable to the youthful ambitions and pride of the French Renaissance poets, and to the esoteric theories of the symbolists. The poets today, as heirs of the oldest of poetic traditions, are fervently aware of the intangibility of their art, of the constant need to use disguises in the composing of their poems.

Why is this? Poetry has always been a protest. It has never been, in its great instances, a mere inoffensive diversion or entertainment. Poetry is that language out of harmony with social language. The poetic act is a testimonial to the insufficiency, first, of the poet himself, and then of all mankind. Poetry is always the compensation for some kind of distress. Saint-John Perse knows, as all his ancestors among the French poets knew, that man is made to live at peace with nature, that the first function of man is to establish a peaceful relationship between himself and the entire universe. The poetic act testifies both to the immediacy of this belief and to its imperfect, sometimes tragically imperfect, realizations.

And this is why, despite varying poetic theories and emphases throughout the centuries, poetry has always been a token for the future, a pledge and a sign for the future of man. Such a pledge is as audible in the poetry of the German Goethe, of the American Whitman, of the French Rimbaud, as it is in the work of Saint-John Perse.

It is well known that his early diplomatic career, had he persued it, would have led him to one of the highest positions in the French government. But he chose the secret destiny of the poet. And even in this vocation, he has always refused to be the professional man of letters. The chronicle of his real life is in his work. It is a personal work, in the deepest sense, and yet it has no trace of the confession. He is both seer and visionary, both the man who has seen what the world is and the man who sees what the world may become. The poet is invulnerable. He is the man who reconstitutes himself after every blow, after very assault. Out of his private destiny, he is constantly formulating a protest. Poetry is the revelation of this man perpetually rehabilitated from the shocks and the clashes of his destiny.

The actual poetic work of Saint-John Perse is quite limited in its proportions, but it stands, in its modest totality, as a work that contains the full mystery of poetic form and utterance.

—Wallace Fowlie

In the same way, poetic theory is constantly being broken down, metamorphosed and annulled. For each poem, the theory demands reconstruction. In *Anabase,* in *Vents,* in *Amers,* the poet sought to express the wholeness of man, the integral forces of his life and his memory. Even more than that, he sought to project man ahead into the uncharted and the new, into a future that was impatient to live. It is not sufficient in the case of Saint-John Perse to say that rhythm and image constitute the essence of poetry. This definition applies, however, provided it is supported by the axiom that poetry is a creative impulse, a manifestation of human energy.

The many elements that compose a poem are not decomposable. This commonplace is admirably illustrated in the strong *verset* of Saint-John Perse where the form is one with the idea. There is no distance between the subject matter of the line and its expression, no distance between the periphery and the center, between the technique and the spirit. The miracle of poetry lies in this unique relationship, this fusion of art and its subject matter.

There is a dramatic movement everywhere in these poems where man, in his historical and natural environment, is playing the role of his existence. This sense of drama and the high nobility of the poet's language provoke from time to time a comparison with Racine. And yet the differences between the poetry of Racine and that of Saint-John Perse help to define the art of the twentieth-century poet.
In the tragedies of Racine, the universe is summarized and ennobled in the human figure. There is no sense of the world around the figure, and no sense of his past and his future. The human figure, the protagonist, is in the epic poems of Saint-John Perse: the conqueror in *Anabase,* the exiled poet in *Exil,* the lover in *Amers.* Whereas the Racinian protagonist has in his poetic utterances the elevation and the simplicity of his solitude in the world, the protagonist of the twentieth-century poems has the elevation and the nobility in his speech which are comparable to Racine's, and he also has the denseness and the richness of his memories of time and the natural world. The actors of Greek drama, the conquerors of the Renaissance, modern man in exile because of his wars, are the poet's

protagonist portrayed in his dramatic intercourse with the world: with the deserts and seaports and oceans, with the erosions of time, with the abiding hope of the future.

This poet's work relates the secular and the spiritual efforts of man to see himself as a part of the natural world, to tame the hostile powers of the world, to worship the endlessly renewed beauty of the world, to conjugate his ambitions and dreams with the changes and modifications of time. One of his constant preoccupations is the will to approve of all the past attainments of man, and to magnify the work of man today as the heir of the past, as the only voice that can speak of the past and remember its accomplishments. This became especially clear in his last long work, *Amers,* a massive ceremonial poem that revealed an extraordinary sensibility to historic man.

The manner of *Amers* is a fuller development of the manner characteristic of the earlier poems. It involves all the diverse activities of man and states them in successive gestures. The world of this poetry has the freshness of a new creation. It is total and totally present. Whatever legendary elements remain are actualized in this poetry which is always praise, as the title of the first volume, *Eloges,* revealed.

Man's fate, throughout history, has always been a drama of violence. Conquest has almost always signified war and destruction. Even the spread of religious faiths has aroused hate and led to massacre. *Amers* is a poem that moves far beyond the violence of man's history in order to exalt the drama of his fate which is looked upon as a *march,* the march of all humanity. Saint-John Perse himself, in a very brief statement about his poem, calls it the march toward the sea (*la marche vers la mer*). The word sea (*la mer*) is in the title of seamarks (*amers*), those signs on the land, both natural and man-made, which guide navigators as they approach the coastline. Around the sea the action of the poem will take place.

The sea is both the real sea and a symbol. It is real, as the source of life, and it is symbolic as being the mirror reflecting the destiny of man. The march toward the sea is an image for the quest, for man's eternal search for some experience with the absolute. But this search, as it continues in *Amers,* is exaltation. Man, as the poet sees him, man in his role of poet, in fact, is exalted in his vocation of power and in his desire to know the absolute, to approach the divine. The image of power comes to him from the sea, and from the endless power of words. Covered with foam, the sea resembles a prophetess speaking the most secret, the most enigmatic words of the poet:

> *La Mer elle-même tout écume, comme Sibylle en fleurs sur sa chaise de fer . . .*

> (The Sea itself all foam, like a Sibyl in flower on her iron chair . . .)

From the opening passages, we realize that this poem will contain all the images of man's dreams (of this poet's dreams) and of his thoughts. Such matters have to be seen, have to be reflected. The vastness of the sea, and its eternity, will allow this. The poem has very little temporal sense. It is composed at some distance from our time, from the specific history and problems of our time. The characters referred to in the poem are dignitaries and leaders: Tetrarchs, Patricians, Prophets, City founders, Magicians, Conquerors. Greatness is being celebrated throughout the work, because by greatness, man moves beyond violence. At the very beginning, the poet is careful to tell us that the poem sings not of the sea itself but of the reign of the sea in man:

> *Et de la Mer elle-même il ne sera question, mais de son règne au coeur de l'homme.*

> (And of the Sea itself it will not be question, but of its reign in the heart of man.)

At every point this greatness is allied with poetry, with the poem that is being written and that celebrates greatness.

Thus the poetic adventure is on the same level as conquest, as the march to the sea. To reach a lofty permanence, man will have to merge with all the great forces in the world, both the spiritual and physical forces. He has to engage in complicity with them and with the sea. Man has to know both the culture of the past and the power of the elements. But the elemental forces in nature and the basic drives in man are expressions of violence. By understanding them and using them and celebrating them, the violence is diminished. *Amers* is the poem of victory over violence.

One of the key words of the work is *alliance,* which is precisely the concept named in opposition to violence. It occurs for the first time in the fifth section of the *Invocation* where the poet says he had nursed for a long time a taste for his poem:

> *mêlant à mes propos du jour toute cette alliance, au loin, d'un grand éclat de mer . . .*

> (mingling in my daily talk all that alliance, afar, of a great flash of sea . . .)

This word announces the fundamental unity of the world. The extensive knowledge of this poet permits him to celebrate the alliance of elemental forces with all the aspects of culture: history, geography, natural sciences, linguistics, religions, technology, ethnology, drama, symbolism, and finally, the greatest of all alliances, that of man with the sea.

In his Stockholm address, given on the occasion of the Nobel Prize award, Saint-John Perse used the word "surreality" in defining the poet's role, and pointed out that it is unlike the surreality of science. The order discovered by the poet is not an apparent order, a superficial order, but a profound, secretive cohesion. *Le poète s'investit d'une surréalité qui ne peut être celle de la Science.* The sought-after unity of the poetic work is first to be seen in the fundamental unity of creation. A religious thinker would say: in the oneness of God, in the oneness of his creation. Thus the poet favors a union which he calls alliance. In his practice of poetry, the poet has to use figures of rhetoric: metaphor, antithesis, simile. These are all means of discovering alliances. In the Stockholm text, Saint-John Perse calls the thought of the poet and his art, analogical and symbolic. An image is a mediator. It throws its light far out into the obscurity of man's thought, and by the reactions it creates, by the associations it calls up, by its correspondences (as Baudelaire would say), it transmits life and movement, within its own means, which are far different from the means of science.

Throughout the centuries, civilization has made a constant effort to remove men from the great forces of nature, to protect them from the violence of nature and natural forces. The work of Saint-John Perse seems to be consecrated to pointing out a way to reconcile man with nature, and hence with himself. In *Anabase,* of 1924, man is seen confronting the burning of the desert sands; in *Vents,* of 1946, man confronts the violence of the winds, as he confronts the violence of the sea in *Amers,* of 1957. The poet is determined to reestablish contact with the elements. Not only in *Eloges* of 1910, but in all the subsequent poems, he praises the sky and sea, the earth and the winds, the snow and the rains. These are not fearful elemental forces, but forces loved by the poet.

All of creation speaks to this poet, and he speaks to it in the *verset* he uses in the writing of his poetry, and which, in *Exil,* he calls a long sentence forever unintelligible:

> *la longue phrase à jamais inintelligible.*

Unintelligible, surely not in the usual dogmatic sense of the word, but in the sense of irreducible to the usual processes of the intelligence. The learned words Saint-John Perse uses, and the technical words (*mots de métier*), are always charged with additional meanings.

What do the four sections of *Amers* represent in their thematic structure? The task of defining them is far from easy because of their richness and complexity.

I. *Invocation* is the poem's prologue. In it we see man turning to the sea, for a sense of freedom, for a liberation. The sea is at all times alive. It is constantly recreating itself. The sea is thus the great force in nature that will guide the poet and inspire him in the creation of his poem. In the six brief parts of *Invocation,* the sea is a festival (*la grande chose fériée*), a celebration which intoxicates the poet. From the very beginning of the poem, and throughout the long work, it is difficult to distinguish the sea from the poem. The singer is born out of what he sings. The sea reigns in his heart, and since it is the sea of every age, the poet is able to live in closeness with every age. In the beginning was the water. The sea is the source of our dreams. Such is the closeness between the sea and the poet, that he is the singer docile to the poem which is being born. The sea is wisdom, power, presence. Out of the sea will come all life and the poem itself.

II. *Strophe* is the body of the poem and is composed of nine parts. It is "strophe" in the ancient sense of movement and rhythm, of poetic speech which is action and which is different from the speech of prose. Part 1 is the introduction to the site of the poem's action: the cities bordering on the sea. They represent the chorus moving around the altar. The scene is a hemicycle of coastal cities. The eight sections following the introduction are each dominated by different actors, by different celebrants we might say, because the unfolding of the poem is at all times liturgical.

In part 2, the master of stars and navigation speaks words of the sea. He is called the Dark One. (*Ils m'ont appelé l'Obscur.*) The tragediennes appear in part 3, and we see them hastening to the shores. They have come to reenact the drama of man, the drama of everything that is human, on the stone around the sea, and in full sight of the sea. The Patrician Women of part 4 are not actresses, but they too in their role of creatures of the earth, wish to come to the sea. The single woman of part 5, called "poetess," is language. She is the one by whom all things that are consumed close to the sea will be remembered. In part 6, another girl appears, a girl prophet among the poets. She speaks the prophecies that are too profound for an easy understanding. Then, in part 7, all the girls from the countryside leave their childhood and go toward the sea. These are the daughters, ready for love, the girls ready to assume their role as living women. Part 8 is a brief interlude between the coming of the girls to the sea, and the final part concerning the lovers. A Stranger appears, coming from the sea. He comes mysteriously, as if to consecrate the evening of love which is celebrated in the long part 9: **Etroits sont les vaisseaux** (**Narrow are the vessels**), composed in seven sections. This love song: part dialogue, part speech in unison, and part speech by the woman, describes a night of love. We witness the approach of the lovers, their union and ecstasy, and their repose after love. The poem is built on the alliance of the sea and love. The night of love is the sea night, and the passion of this love is total in its freedom and power and joy. In his own brief analysis of the themes of **Amers,** Saint-John Perse calls *Strophe* the hemicycle of marine cities (part 1) and eight figurations, evoked in their alliance with the sea.

III. *Choeur,* which opens with the solemn line,

> *Mer de Baal, Mer de Mammon—Mer de tout âge et de tout nom*

> (Sea of Baal, Sea of Mammon—Sea of every age and every name),

is a unified, somewhat abstract poem, a homage to the sea. It is a single lyric movement of exaltation, in which the people, the celebrant or the reciter, and the city itself, are united in their approach to the sea, in their desire to honor the sea. The sea is apostrophized as the measure of being. In making this identification, the poet is the leader of the chorus. His poem here is a sacred recitative.

IV. *Dédicace,* a brief page, is the conclusion of the long work, and the restitution of the poet to his normal life of man. In his role of poet he has sung of those forces that are beyond man, and he had now at last earned this

moment of restitution, which is destitution, because he divests himself of his gold in honor of the sea,

> *se dévêt de son or en l'honneur de la Mer.*

The poet has brought his work to its dual culmination: the full expression of his faith in man and his allegiance to the sea.

The opening passage of *Strophe,* the first two sections of *Des Villes Hautes s'éclairaient,* reveals the fundamental violence which the poet intends to transcend in his poem. The tall cities themselves bordering the sea, *des villes hautes,* are seamarks (*amers*). When they flame in the sun, they are visible to the mariner far out at sea, *in the golden salts of the open sea* (*dans les sels d'or du large*). The cities are characterized by their sea walls and ramps, by the stone concepts of their design. They stand between the sea and the land, a frontier architecture. Are they hostile countries, the sea and the land? The subject of the poem is precise here. They would be hostile, if the sea were a natural force feared by man, over which he has no control. Is man hiding behind the walls he has built? Are these fortifications destined to protect him against the sea? Are the jagged rocks lining the sea a natural protection for the men on land? Do the tall cities with their ramparts represent an age-old struggle of man against the elements? Deliberately, specifically, the poet announces the intention of his poem: to reveal or to bring about an alliance between the men on land and the sea that surrounds the land. A gold marriage ring is to be forged by the poet:

> *Trouve ton or, Poète, pour l'anneau d'alliance.*

The passage opens on a bustling port scene. Port officers are in conference, and they are likened to frontier guards. It is this dangerous word frontier which implies hostility, that has to be changed. The people are crowded along the seawalls where they are waiting for Plenipotentiaries of the high sea, hoping that the alliance will be offered. Thus the words frontier and alliance are opposed. There seems to be a delay in the arrival, a delay perhaps caused by an erroneous reading of signs, such as the moon and the tides. Nature is not at fault, but man's incapacity to read nature and comprehend its signs.

The will to reach an alliance comes from the people. They are praying to both the sea and the land to bring about an exchange. Work carried on in a harbor, concerns necessarily both the land and the sea. *Travaux mixtes des ports.* The sea is apostrophized by the people as mediatrix: *Mer mitoyenne,* and the land is called the land of Abel (*Terre d'Abel*). It is the earth loved and tilled by the second son whose sacrifice will be fruitful. In their prayer,

> *Nous vous prions, Mer mitoyenne, et vous, Terre d'Abel,*

the people reason out why the alliance must be made, why the marriage ring must be forged, and the alloys formed for the bells that will ring in the pilot lanes,

*et tes alliages pour les cloches, aux avenues de
pilotage.*

The reason is everywhere: in the sea breeze that comes to
every door in the city, and the sea itself which is at the
end of every street. The breeze from the sea, and the sea,
are in the bits of wisdom by which the people live, and in
the earliest form of their laws by means of which they live
at peace with one another.

*C'est brise de mer dans nos maximes et la
naissance de nos lois . . .*

The very air they breathe is from the sea. The water they
need for themselves and for their work, is held on hire in
their shelters, and this water is in secret alliance with the
sea water.

The last three lines of the passage are a brilliant transcription of this indispensable alliance which the people understand secretly and which the poet is able to expose. On
the outer harbor is an escutcheon of a winged beast,
chosen by the ancestors of these people. This very symbol of *bête ailée* represents an alliance of beast and bird,
of land and sea. The pierhead (*musoir*) has a male ring
(*anneau mâle*) to which boats can be attached. The words
recall a horse or beast whose muzzle is pierced by a ring.
This figurative horse, the *bête ailée* attached to the pierhead, with its ring, is conceived of by the poet as dreaming of distant relays (*lointains relais*) "where foam flies
from other manes" (*où fument d'autres encolures*). The
fabulous horse (Pegasus) passing in flight over the sea, is
witness to the joining of the elements.

Everything in the passage seems associated with the need
to unite, to reunite. The men of the port cities are priests
of commerce (*Prêtres du Commerce*) and commerce always suggests sinister insinuations of war. The male element of commerce and conquest signifies closeness to
the land. But the sea, more powerful and more enduring
than the land, is female. A woman's body, a Patrician
Woman, is the highest luxury. Yes, the sea is female in its
fluidity and grace. The Patrician Woman will pacify. Just
preceeding the final image of the winged beast is a line
describing the sea in an image that is feminine and at the
same time evocative of the creation of poetry. Spasmod-
ically the sea unfolds its answers, golden answers in the
sun, "in great luminous phrases" (*par grandes phrases
lumineuses*). The waves of the sea are thus compared to
the assembling of words in a poem. A poem is a creation
that transcends the mere sound of words. It is a force of
alliance, of a reuniting in which the human being (the
creature) finds his place in the universe (creation).

In his speech at Stockholm, Saint-John Perse emphasized
the power of this adventure called poetry and claimed it
is not inferior to the great dramatic adventures of science.
The title word *amers,* in its most eloquent meaning, has
nothing about it that is "bitter." It should not evoke the
meaning of the familiar French adjective. Rather than on
bitterness, the poem is built on hopefulness, on enthusi-

asm and optimism. The course of the mariner can be guided by the seamarks (*les amers*). The poet's purpose is to
consecrate the alliance between man and the creation, and
he needs the seamarks to show that the alliance takes
place when the land recognizes its relationship of vassal
to the sea. If the sea is female in its self-perpetuation and
fluidity and spasmodic undulations, the poem is male. It is
the ring in the muzzle of the beast, it is the force that will
direct and lead and explain. The end of the alliance is unity
when man is integrated with the creation.

This is Saint-John Perse's answer to the violence in the
world. The image of *relay,* used in the metaphor of the
winged horse, is a way of demonstrating the continuing
forces of life. Poetry itself is a kind of *relay*: it picks up
and sustains the element of the divine, when religious
belief weakens, and when mythologies no longer function
as explanations for disasters and catastrophes.

When Saint-John Perse speaks of the "sea of every age
and every name," at the beginning of *Choeur,* and of the
long time he had been nursing a taste for this poem of the
sea, in *Invocation,* he may well have been thinking of the
long history of the sea in poetry, of the power the sea
possesses to call up the poet and create him. The Homeric
voyage might have been in his mind. At the beginning of
Etroits sont les vaisseaux, he evokes magnificently the
unity of history and time with the words:

*. . . Une même vague par le monde, une même
vague depuis Troie*
Roule sa hanche jusqu'à nous.

. . . One same wave throughout the world, one
same wave since Troy
Rolls its haunch toward us.

The sea was important in the medieval voyage of Tristan
and the quest voyages for the Holy Grail. And more immediately, many French poets of the nineteenth and twentieth centuries had sung of the sea: Victor Hugo in *Oceano
Nox*; Baudelaire whose *Voyage* alludes to the adventure
of Ulysses and the voyage taken by the imagination of a
child as he pores over maps and prints; Arthur Rimbaud,
whose *Bateau Ivre* is, in a way, an answer to Baudelaire's
question, *Dites, qu'avez-vous vu?*; Lautréamont, whose
sea violence is matched by the sadism of Maldoror; Cor-
bière, the Breton poet, inspired by the sea and who chose
the name of Tristan for himself; Valéry, the Mediterranean
poet who found in the sea, contemplated from his cemetery at Sète, an incitement to life; Claudel, who like Saint-
John Perse, frequently crossed the oceans of the world, in
diplomatic missions and who analyzed the religious meaning of water in his ode *L'Esprit et l'Eau.*

In *Amers,* the sea has reminiscences of all of these uses
of the sea metaphor. With no trace of metaphysical tor-
ment, it is celebrated as that place of meeting where all the
paths taken by men in every age will converge. It is the
goal of the march of mankind. It is the one image and the
one reality able to sustain all the themes and unite them:
the reality of the sea, the limitless power of life that is best

transcribed by the sea, the eternity of man in his continuous action, the personal themes of man's solitude and freedom and love, and finally the poet's creation: the image of the poem. In its ceremonial walk around the sea, the movement of the chorus is compared to the circuit of the strophe. Whatever the Reciter says is in honor of the sea. The sea itself is comparable to the web of poetry (*l'immense trame prosodique*). The endlessness of poetry is the nameless prolixity of the sea:

> *. . . mer innombrable du récit, ô mer prolixité sans nom!*

Passage after passage, especially in *Choeur,* evokes the violence of the sea in its relationship to the history of man:

> *ô Mer violence du Barbare* (O Sea violence of the Barbarian)
>
> *Mer agressive de nos Marches* (aggressive Sea of our Marches)
>
> *Mer de violence, et de mer ivre, parmi tes grandes roses de bitume* (Sea of violence, Sea drunk with sea, in the midst of your large roses of bitumen).

All fables and incarnations of history are in the sea and in the lofty ode of the poet's homage. The *Chorus* sings of alliances and progressions. In the love-song of *Strophe,* the most personal, the most intimate experience of man's nature is related in terms of the sea. At the moment of union, the lovers obey the sea's rhythm without fully understanding it. The lover, when she speaks, identifies herself with the sea. She is both woman and sea, and the night of love is a sea night. It is difficult to keep in mind that during the violence of passion and during the long moment of appeasement after passion, the poet himself, in the power of his language, is recreating the sea and recreating his lover. From the beginning to the end of *Amers,* the sea is the sign of the poet's irrepressible need to create.

The usual dimensions of poetry, in length, in meter, in theme, are surpassed in *Amers,* because the vastness of the sea is reflected in it. The enumerations are not mere lists or proliferations. They are in the poem because man in the poem is the figuration and the witness of the history of the earth. He is both a single secret presence on the earth, and an ensemble of all wars and revolutions, of the endless surging of mankind, of the choral celebration of mankind—a solitary man who finds himself in the midst of life and desirous of understanding it. Man, facing the sea, is a power that has to be spent. He is a potentiality, or a vital tension that refuses the concept of tragedy. His fate is not death, but a merging with the continuous life of the universe. His love song has no trace of narcissism, no trace of facile sentimentality. He raises the image of love to the hyberbolic level of a cosmic force. In the experience of love, when man is usually centered upon himself, he is, in *Amers,* seeking to identify himself with the vastness and the prolixity of the sea.

Although the fury of violence is at times the subject of this sea-poem, the fury is controlled by a poetics fully conscious of its method. At all times, the Reciter is serene. The sea he celebrates is the sea of language. The seamarks are those signs that regulate chaos, because they are the instruments of man's knowledge. As it is sung, the poem reveals the coherence of life. The experiences behind the poet are often the violence of nature and the violence of man's life in nature, but the poem is the celebration of the mysteries of this violence. No matter what its subject, language has the dignity of ritual. The poetic act is solemnity articulated.

Roger Little (essay date 1970)

SOURCE: "Language as Imagery in Saint-John Perse," in *Forum for Modern Language Studies,* Vol. VI, No. 2, April, 1970, pp. 127-39.

[*In the following essay, Little discusses the function of language in Léger's poetry.*]

There are two obvious ways in which Perse reveals his attachment to language. The first shows in his technical mastery and his sensitivity to philology, the second in his extensive use of language itself as an image. Not only is language likened to things; things are also likened to language. The various manifestations of language become images in their own right, so creating the curious situation in which the tool becomes an integral part of the end product.

The process is essentially one of the materialisation of language by association with concrete phenomena and a consequent etherealisation of those phenomena through that association. A simple example will serve to make this clearer. Perse mentions in *Eril,* VI, "le Dépôt des Phares, où gisent les fables, les lanternes". The linking of items lying together makes the lanterns somehow less real and the temptation to translate *fables* as "yarns" almost irresistible, so material do the sailor's tales seem to have become. Similarly, addressing the Stranger, Perse assimilates into terms of finance the notion of the foreign language he speaks:

> tu ne franchiras point le seuil des Lloyds, où ta parole n'a point
> eours et ton or est sans titre . . .
>
> (*Exil,* VI)

Through the parallelism of phrasing, *parole* is given the value of *or.* By the simple insertion of a word apparently out of context, Perse both arrests our attention and indicates the importance he attaches to language. So the Prince is "vêtu de (ses) sentences" (*Amitié du Prince,* I); horsemen wonder: "lèverons-nous le fouet sur les mots hongres du bonheur?" (*Anabase,* VIII).

Working from this principle, one finds both eondensed and extended examples, revealing as ever Perse's fascination for language and keenness of observation. Even in the early poems the interest is present, if muted. In *Éloges,* V, the swabbing of the deck before dawn leaves a film of water mirroring the sky, and so giving an account of it:

> Le pont lavé, avant le jour, d'une eau pareille en
> songe au mélange de l'aube, fait une belle relation
> du ciel.

For Crusoe, "le silence multipliera l'exelamation des astres solitaires" (*Images à Crusoé: La Ville*), showing a link between language and outer space which is to bear further fruit. From the most sophisticated forms of linguistic arrangements in poetry to the mere shape of a letter on a page, words are grist to the mill of imagery:

> Étroite la mesure, étroite la césure, qui rompt en son
> milieu le corps de femme comme le mètre antique.
>
> (*Amers, Strophe*, IX, 3—2)

This needs no explanation, but the following complex image includes an assumption of familiarity with uncial script and a purely visual reaction to illuminated capitals:

> Au pur vélin rayé d'une amorce divine, vous
> nous direz, ô Pluies! quelle langue nouvelle
> sollicitait pour vous la grande onciale de feu vert.
>
> (*Pluies,* IV)

Another visual image is far simpler:

> l'Oiseau Anhinga (. . .) apposera-t-il ce soir
> l'absurde paraphe de son col?
>
> (*Vents,* II, 4)

Here the similarity of shape between the Water-Turkey or Snake-bird's neck and the flourish added to a written word is evident.

The dimensions of time and space find echoes in linguistic imagery appropriate to their importance. The opening section of *Vents,* for example, ends with two illuminating paragraphs in this connection. After linking a historical notion with the image of a tree, both the past century and the wintry tree hollow and rattling before the great winds, Perse retains the tree and switches the historical notion to the genealogical tree of language. One is prepared very subtly for this shift, the word *désinence* meaning specifically a flexional ending:

> Car tout un siècle s'ébruitait dans la sécheresse
> de sa paille, parmi d'étranges désinences (. . .)
> Comme un grand arbre tressaillant dans ses
> crécelles de bois mort (. . .).
>   (. . .)
> Et ne voilà-t-il pas déjà toute ma page elle-même
> bruissante,
>   Comme ce grand arbre de magie sous sa pouillerie
> d'hiver: vain de son lot d'icônes, de fétiches,
>   Berçant dépouilles et spectres de locustes;
> léguant, liant au vent du ciel filiales d'ailes et
> d'essaims, lais et relais du plus haut verbe—
>   Ha! très grand arbre du langage peuplé 'oracles,

de maximes et murmurant murmure d'aveugle-né
dans les quinconces du savoir . . .

> (*Vents,* I, 1)

The very word *lais* is brilliantly chosen and placed. As the plural of *lai* it may be seen as the poetic form dating from the Middle Ages. As a singular it means the same as *baliveau*, a staddle, or single tree chosen to be left standing when the undergrowth and other saplings are cleared from around it. To translate *lais et relais* as "tide-marks" as Chisholm does [in *Winds,* 1961] betrays a strange insensitivity to the image-structure, which here brings the ideas of tree and language deftly together in a single word.

Space suggests another extended simile in *Oiseaux,* 8. The closing line of the preceding section seems to trigger off the parallel:

> C'est une poésie d'action qui s'est engagée là.

Poetry and action combine in the bird, the pure epitome of both; the phrase in part 13, "Laconisme de l'aile!" expresses the relation most succinctly. After a full description of the perfect muscular adaptation for flight and of the functioning of the bird's dynamics, Perse naturally turns to the bird as poetry. The description does not share the density of texture of the poems (*Oiseaux* being a *méditation poétique* and not a fully-fledged poem), but the point is made all the more lucidly:

> Dans la maturité d'un texte immense en voie
> toujours de formation, ils ont mûri comme des
> fruits, ou mieux comme des mots: à même la sève
> et la substance originelle. Et bien sont-ils comme
> des mots sous leur charge magique: noyaux de
> force et d'action, foyers d'éclairs et d'émissions,
> portant au loin l'initiative et la prémonition.
>
> (*Oiseaux,* 8)

Perse's attitude to language here shows a recognition of the power of ambiguity in an individual word, a historical sense of linguistic development, and an understanding of the widespread power of words. The apparently casual *ou mieux* introduces the obviously pre-ordained central simile of the section:

> Sur la page blanche aux marges infinies, l'espace qu'ils
> mesurent n'est plus qu'ineantation. Ils sont, comme dans
> le mètre, quantités syllabiques. Et procédant, comme les
> mots, de lointaine ascendance, ils perdent, comme les mots,
> leur sens à la limite de la félieité.

Space is a text, a Mallarméan blank page with infinite margins, and the "fowl that may fly above the earth in the open firmament of heaven" of the Genesis account of creation imprint themselves upon it. In the beginning, too, was the Word, but the link between bird and word is by no means restricted to Christian texts. The dove descends in other forms to other intermediaries:

> A l'aventure poétique ils eurent part jadis, avec
> l'augure et l'aruspice. Et les voici, vocables

assujettis au même enchaînement, pour l'exercice
au loin d'une divination nouvelle . . . Au soir
d'antiques civilisations, c'est un oiseau de bois,
les bras en eroix saisis par l'officiant, qui tient
le rôle du seribe dans l'écriture médiumnique,
comme aux mains du sourcier ou du géomaneïen.

(ibid.)

Words, like birds, are media for divination. Where the
effigy of a bird once played its part in primitive ritual, we
now use words. And the suggestion that words are mate-
rialised remains. A thing may be sophisticated into a verbal
formula, but that formula in turn becomes an object in itself.
But a form of mediation between man and the unknown is
necessary, and so language has a basic and universal
function:

Oiseaux, nés d'une inflexion première pour la
plus longue intonation . . . Ils sont, comme les
mots, portés du rythme universel; ils s'inserivent
d'eux-mêmes, et comme d'affinité, dans la plus
large strophe errante que l'on ait jamais vue se
dérouler au monde.

(ibid.)

The immensity of space moving through the immensity
of time is regularly seen by Perse in terms of language. It
is almost as if he used the metaphor of language when at
a loss for a comparison with the vast elements and forces
of this world. For him language is in itself a cosmic force
in terms of which land, sea and stars become more comprehensible:

Pour l'oiseau (. . .) quel privilège déjà, sur la
page du eiel, d'être à soi-même l'arc et la flèche
du vol! le thème et le propos!

(*Oiseaux,* 5)

And not only for the bird, since the page of the sky, open
for all to read, changes its mood as often as a narrative:

Les constellations labiles (. . .) changent de
vocable pour les hommes d'exil.

(*Exil,* IV)

At night the stars seem to run a paper-chase across the sky,
and the poet standing alone sees them as Princes distributing
leaflets like a meteor-shower scattering its particles:

Que j'aille seul avec les souffles de la nuit, parmi
les Princes pamphlétaires, parmi les chutes de
Biélides! . . .

(*Anabase,* V)

The very approach of night may also be seen in terms of
language; day elides into night, a cosmic *lapsus:*

soir de grand erg, et très grand orbe, où les
premières élisions du jour nous furent telles que
défaillances du langage.

(*Chronique,* 1)

By day, the sky's moods are similarly recorded:

ton ciel est pareil à la colère poétique,

(*Vents,* II, 3)

and again, reducing from simile to metaphor,

Syntaxe de l'éclair! ô pur langage de l'exil!

(*Exil,* VII)

The gaze is borne on wings arching like eyelashes into the
vast unknown:

. . . Pétrels, nos cils, au creux de la vision
d'orage, épelez-vous lettre nouvelle dans les
grands textes épars où fume l'indicible?

(*Vents,* IV, 4)

Petrels are sea-birds, and Perse a man of the sea, but land
enjoys similar treatment in his language of language. But
again, land is seen as continents, as vast spaces between
oceans, and man stands gazing over its expanses, "inter-
prétant la feuille noire et les arborescences du silence dans
de plus vastes syllabaires." Before him, he sees

Toute la terre nubile et forte, au pas de
l'Étranger, ouvrant sa fable de grandeur aux
songes et fastes d'un autre âge,
Et la terre à longs traits, sur ses plus longues
laisses, courant, de mer en mer, à de plus hautes
écritures, dans le déroulement lointain des plus
beaux textes de ce monde.

(*Vents,* II, 1)

The starting-point of the extensive discussion of the *Ur-
sprache* in **Neiges,** IV, is the terrestrial phenomenon of a
sea of snow. A complex series of ideas combine to suggest
the need to find the source of rivers formed from melting
snows, the source of life and that of language: those who
are prepared to search, "remontant les fleuves vers leur
source",

sont gagnés soudain de cet éclat sévère où toute
langue perd ses armes.

The verbs of the following sentence would normally apply
to a river; here they are transferred to aspects of language
to continue the image:

remontons ce pur délice sans graphic où court
l'antique phrase humaine.

Such a transference is not in itself unusual; it is, after all,
part of a poet's stock-in-trade. But what is less usual is the
linguistic imagery involved and the extension it assumes.

On another occasion other features of winter are evoked
as the wind wanders

sur toute cette grande chronique d'armes par là-bas
Et ces grandes proses hivernales.

(*Vents,* II, 2)

Winter's *chroniques* and *proses* are created from its *mots de fer,* an indication of the season's and of language's physical force:

> Hiver, Hiver, (. . .)
> Enseigne-nous le mot de fer, et le silence du savoir.
>
> (ibid.)

Speech, here, is iron, and silence golden.

The margins of the earth and sea likewise attrack Perse's attention in this as in so many other respects. "La erépitation du sel" of *Exil,* II, is echoed and enlarged upon in the following line from *Amers:*

> Tu es l'exclamation du sel et la divination du sel, lorsque la mer au loin s'est retirée sur ses tables poreuses.
>
> (*Amers, Strophe,* IX, 3—2)

The miniature explosions and sputterings as the tide ebbs from the shore are not a language but ejaculations suggestive of language. On the beach again, "parmi les sables très mobiles", other feet tread on closely observed stones:

> Et de la paume du pied nu sur ces macérations nocturnes (. . .) nous suivons là ce pur langage modelé: relief d'empreintes méningées, proéminences saintes aux lobes de l'enfance embryonnaire . . .
>
> (*Amers, Strophe,* VI)

What lies to seaward? Ships sailing from sheltered water out to sea are

> tout un propos de toiles vives adonnées au délice du large.
>
> (*Anabase,* VI)

One sees,

> sur la haute page tendue du ciel et de la mer, ces longs convois de nefs sous voiles qui doublent soudain la pointe des Caps.
>
> (*Amers, Strophe,* III)

The wind fills their sails, accompanied by the

> chant des hautes narrations du large.
>
> (*Vents,* I, 3)

The poet in exile watches from the shore, and sees

> la fraîcheur courant aux crêtes du langage, l'éeume encore aux lèvres du poème.
>
> (*Pluies,* VIII)

Out to sea, too, go migrating birds and insects, and two passages in *Vents* depict scattering pages as living creatures. Firstly, the poet evokes

> la Ville basse vers la mer dans un émoi de feuilles blanches: libelles et mouettes de même vol.
>
> (*Vents,* I, 6)

To give due credit, Chisholm successfully retains the ambiguity by writing of "a flutter of white leaves: leaflets and sea-mews in the same flight". Secondly, Perse shows pages scattering through the forces of history as well as those of the wind when he evokes

> Ces vols d'insectes par nuées qui s'en allaient se perdre au large comme des morceaux de textes saints, comme des lambeaux de prophéties errantes et des récitations de généalogistes, de psalmistes . . .
>
> (*Vents,* II, 4)

Such a line showing the migrating swarm of fragmented manuscripts may reasonably introduce the study of a highly original connection in Perse between language and the bee.

The image of the bee, its habits and attributes, recurs in Perse's poetry, and often it presents a puzzle which can in part be solved by seeing the history of the image in his writings. The poet's highly individual approach to symbol and image necessarily creates problems of interpretation and at times risks closing the poetry to the reader in an apparently private world. As this is not wilful obscurantism, some threads of imagery are at hand to help us through the labyrinth of language.

By assembling the various references in Perse's work to the bee, a pattern emerges showing that beyond the insect standing simply for itself, a *Ding an sich,* it is associated in the poet's mind with purposeful migration on the one side and sagacity and language as functions of human intelligence on the other. The first of these is a natural extension of the bee's habit of swarming; the second derives from its remarkable organisation within the hive, the strictly ordered hierarchy of its society, and the creative nature of its principal activities. The greater credit given to the bee rather than, say, to the ant, is ultimately fortuitous: honey was the sugar of the ancients, the ambrosia of the gods in the land of Mount Hymettus, and so brought the bee community into the anthropocentric scheme. Among others, Aristotle, Virgil and Pliny the Elder wrote at considerable length and in considerable detail of bees and their habits. Where their observations were less than scientific, they allowed the bee an area of mythology which it enjoyed across much of the world.

Perse's use of the bee as an image owes little to Virgil's *Georgic* or Maeterlinck's *Vie des abeilles.* His reading only serves to support his powers of observation which he uses in this case to express his fascination with language. Reference is first made to bees in *Amitié du Prince,* and they are immediately associated with the Prince's oriental wisdom:

> Tel sous le signe de son front, les cils hantés d'ombrages immortels et la barbe poudrée d'un pollen de sagesse, Prince flairé d'abeilles sur sa chaise d'un bois violet très odorant, il veille.
>
> (*Amitié du Prince,* II)

Swarming bees seek a shady place to settle, and the Prince, who provides the cool of a tree's shade to travellers (ibid.,

III), has the *ombrages immortels* which attract the bees. They are also present for a reason made valid by the poetry alone. The Prince's greying beard is dusted with the pollen of wisdom. The link is continued in a later line:

> Et comme celui, sur son chemin, qui trouve un arbre à ruches a droit à la propriété du miel, je recueillerai le fruit de ta sagesse.
>
> (ibid., IV)

So, towards the end of the poem, the reader is completely open to the suggested association between bees emerging in the evening and the baring of foreheads behind which dreams will be dreamed and thoughts given shape.

> Les abeilles quittent les cavernes à la recherche des plus hauts arbres dans la lumière. Nos fronts sont mis à découvert.
>
> (ibid., IV)

It would clearly be wrong to attempt to force each reference to the bee into a single mould. Each poem has preoccupations within the texture of its imagery which mean a shift of emphasis or a development of any given aspect. So if *Amitié du Prince* is the expression of a confrontation of a western man with an archetypal and proverbial eastern leader, where the bee is linked with sagacity, *Anabase* has the insect serve other ends:

> Je sais (. . .) les essaims du silence aux ruches de lumière.
>
> (*Anabase,* VII)

The general sense of space, with silence and the yellow light that pervades the poem, is enhanced in two ways. Firstly, just as the *criquets à midi* (ibid., II) heighten by contrast the effect of silence, so here does the swarm of bees. Secondly, the coupling of the aural with the visual has its synaesthesia extended into movement by the suggestion of the bees' migration. The pure quest undertaken by the leader and the poet is shared by the bees.

An additional note of purity is suggested by the woman offered to the stranger by way of hospitality:

> Ouvre ma bouche dans la lumière, ainsi qu'un lieu de miel entre
> les roches, et si l'on trouve faute en moi, que je sois congédiée.
>
> (ibid., IX)

This is not merely the offer of a dental inspection which one might normally reserve for an animal. It also serves to link the mouth with the wild hive, and so language with the bee. Such a connection is to be made more explicit in later poems, with variations on the theme of the honied tongue. *Le meil de l'euphuisme* (*Pluies,* VII) is certainly the most direct and commonplace, but the banal notion takes on the richest extensions through Perse's expansive technique.

In the *Exil* tetralogy, for instance, occur echoes of earlier usage and new applications. The poet himself, his brow

wreathed in inspiration reminiscent of the Prince's wisdom, has

> le front nu, lauré d'abeilles de phosphore.
>
> (*Poème à l'Étrangère,* III)

He stands ready to unleash his words like bees, making the surrounding silence meaningful: in exile he has found

> un lieu de grâce et de merci où licencier l'essaim des grandes odes du silence.
>
> (*Neiges,* I)

And to underline the fact that neither exile nor war dates from yesterday, again he uses the image of the swarm:

> Et cette histoire n'est pas nouvelle que le Vieux Monde essaime à tous les siècles, comme un rouge pollen.
>
> (*Poème à l'Étrangère,* III)

Small wonder, then, if at this stage it is considered quite legitimate to call the bee divine:

> Et qui done vous mènera, dans ce plus grand veuvage, à vos Églises souterraines où la lampe est frugale, et l'abeille, divine?
>
> (*Neiges,* III)

There seems no need to read this specifically as Candlemas, or to recall the bee-gods of ancient mythologies. Without any disrespect, this is the word made flesh. It can of course have various manifestations, and with the image basically agreed Perse may write:

> Dressez, dressez (. . .) les hauts ruchers de l'imposture,
>
> (*Pluies,* V)

or of

> l'éclair de partout essaimant ses présages.
>
> (*Amers, Strophe,* IX, 4-2)

Vents serves both to confirm the association of the bee with language and to reintroduce after the relatively—and understandably so in the circumstances—static *Exil* tetralogy the idea of migration. Early in the poem the link is recalled when the winds

> éveillaient pour nous (. . .) comme nymphes en nymphose parmi les rites d'abeillage (. . .) les écritures nouvelles.
>
> (*Vents,* I, 3)

But nothing could be more direct than the following phrase, reminding us now of both the Prince and the poet in earlier works:

> l'abeille du langage est sur leur front.
>
> (*Vents,* IV, 4)

The notion expands into the following comparison made with the *Voyageur:*

> comme au rucher de sa parole, parmi le peuple de ses mots, l'homme de langage aux prises avec l'embûche de son dieu.
>
> (ibid., II, 4)

The poet, the *homme de langage,* is both worker and traveller, like the bee, and creates from raw materials in the highly developed and sophisticated organisation of the hive of words. For the bee, if not for man, the production of honey is a mere function, complex but natural. So poetry for the poet. And just as the hive is left by the Queen to migrate to form a new community, so once a poem is completed, the poet must move on to the next. If the honey is appreciated, so much the better, but this remains irrelevant to its production. The poet constantly seeks "le monde où frayait une abeille nouvelle" (ibid., IV, 6), and greets "l'heure (. . .) où sur les routes méconnues l'essaim des songes vrais ou faux s'en va encore" (ibid., IV, 4).

A number of other references in *Vents* recall the link of the bee with migration:

> Elles (i.e. les grandes forces du vent) s'annexaient en cours de route (. . .) l'abeille sauvage du désert et les migrations d'insectes sur les mers.
>
> (ibid., I, 3)

> Des essaims passent en sifflant, affranchis de la ruche.
>
> (ibid., II, 4)

The winds themselves, symbolic of both cleansing and creation, share the bee's migratory urge:

> les vents tièdes essaiment.
>
> (ibid., II, 3)

Even the theme of *Amers* is anticipated by the mention of

> La teneur à son comble des grands essaims sauvages de l'amour.
>
> (ibid., I, 7)

The great epic of love and the sea pursues the pattern as before, though naturally the context enlists other notions to link the image with the sea. Thus the immensity of the ocean puts man's efforts into their due proportion, and we read of

> les essaims fugaces de l'esprit sur la continuité des eaux.
>
> (*Amres, Strophe,* V)

Just as the image was appropriated by the winds, so it is by the sea, "pressant, haussant l'essaim des jeunes vagues" (ibid., IX, 6-2), and again:

> Nous (. . .) te parasiterons, ruche des dieux, ô mille et mille chambres de l'écume où se

consume le délit.

> (ibid., *Chœur,* 2)

But the main themes are continued. First that of migration:

> (Ainsi j'ai vu un jour, entre les îles, l'ardente migration d'abeilles, et qui croisait la route du navire, attacher un instant à la haute mâture l'essaim farouche d'une âme très nombreuse, en quête de son lieu . . .)
>
> (ibid., *Strophe,* IX, 6-2)

and secondly, within a page, that of intellectual activity:

> pour nous, ô face très prodigue, l'immense ruche du futur, plus riche d'alvéoles que les falaises trouées d'idoles du Désert.
>
> (eod. loc.)

One reference in *Amers* reflects a literary source among the classics, though so thoroughly assimilated as to escape notice:

> O mon amour au goût de mer, que d'autres paissent loin de mer l'eglogue au fond des vallons clos—menthes, mélisse et mélilot, tiédeurs d'alysse et d'origan—et l'un y parle d'abeillage et l'autre y traite d'agnelage, et la brebis feutrée baise la terre au bas des murs de pollen noir.
>
> (ibid., *Strophe,* IX, 2-2)

Shepherds and bee-keepers have their inland occupations, very different from those of a man of the sea, as different, one might say, as Virgil's *Georgics* from the *Aeneid*. The latter part of the third *Georgic* is devoted to the rearing of sheep and the fourth of course to bee-keeping. Is it then mere coincidence to find here the word *églogue,* the title of another of Virgil's books? Perse may well say, with Valéry: "Rien pour moi dans *les Géorgiques*", and claim the sea as his element, but a book is not rejected without its first being read. So the detailed naming of plants includes two which, while fully satisfying the demands of alliteration, are also noted suppliers of highly-esteemed brands of nectar: *mélisse et mélilot*. The first, melissa balm, is suggested by Virgil as a means to attract a swarm to a shady place near water. The second, melilot or sweet clover, heads the list of "des plantes dont les organes fournissent aux abeilles des sues particulièrement riches en substances propres à donner de la cire". Yet such elucidation seems unnecessary in a passage so mellifluous and moving.

"L'abeille du langage" seems therefore fully established as an extended image with numerous applications in Perse's work. It does not occur often, and yet by gradual accretion of meaning assumes the qualities of richness and complexity peculiar to Perse. One cannot blame him, particularly as *Vents* was written in exile, for attributing at that time the inspiration of the bee to the French language alone, for showing the one side of his outlook which is—according to one's point of view—specifically patriotic or chauvinistic. Language is a poet's weapon, and his moth-er-tongue can have no rivals:

> —Et vous, hommes du nombre et de la masse,
> ne pesez pas les hommes de ma race. Ils ont
> vécu plus haut que vous dans les abîmes de
> l'opprobre.
>
>   Ils sont l'épine à votre chair; la pointe même
> au glaive de l'esprit. L'abeille du langage est sur
> leur front,
>
>   Et sur la lourde phrase humaine, pétrie de tant
> d'idiomes, ils sont seuls à manier la fronde de
> l'accent.
>
> (*Vents,* IV, 4)

As Claudel wrote [in *La Messe là-bas,* 1957]: "L'abeille (. . .) a le sentiment (. . .) de l'hexagone."

Perse's deep feeling for his mother-tongue made exile that much harder to bear. Between the North American continent and the hexagon of France lie some three thousand miles of ocean which for many reasons would draw and hold his attention. In spite of the separation, he persists in his view of the world and its history as a unity, and at the opening of *Exil,* III, sees the wave of poetic inspiration running across the world both geographically and historically. However trite the phrase "wave of inspiration" may be, Perse rescues it from banality by complex additions to the image pattern and by a use of words which warrants and rewards the closest attention.

> . . . Toujours il y eut cette clameur . . .

At the outset one is unsure of the sense and implications, but these are gradually revealed by association in turn with:

> Cette grande chose sourde par le monde . . .
> Cette chose errante par le monde . . .
> la même vague . . .
> ce très haut ressac au comble de l'accès . . .
> la même plainte sans mesure . . .

The link is withheld but ultimately quite clear. The mutations which the rest of the imagery undergoes, weaving a developing pattern upon this loom of sea and language, trace a history of movement and creation from suggestions of Old Testament times and Rome to the gull sweeping across the poet's field of vision, centralising and crystallising his image.

The link between the sea and the imagery of language takes on its fullest extension in *Amers.* If already in *Vents* Perse can write that the sea "m'est alliance et grâce, et circonlocution" (*Vents,* IV, 2), this sea which surrounds him with its language understandably speaks more clearly and subtly in the longer poem in praise of the sea.

The image lasts from the very first paragraph of *Amers* to the end of the Chorus. Indeed, by extending the image to that of the drama which is so important to the poem it lasts from the first page to the very last line of all. From the start we see:

> La Mer en fête sur ses marches comme une ode
> de pierre: (. . .) la Mer elle-même notre veille,
> comme une promulgation divine.
>
> (*Amers, Invocation,* I)

The sea's association at its edges with rocky shores lends it the lapidary quality of a finely chiselled ode, the ode which is the poem *Amers* itself. As a piece of ceremonial conceived in the Greek fashion, it assumes the qualities of sacred ritual. After the divine promulgation has been read, and consequently the relationship between the sea, the poem, and the ritual established. Perse is free to indulge in such a passing reference as the following, where the very attention to detail indicates the completeness of the link between sea and language:

> La Mer! (. . .) dans l'ébullition sacrée de ses
> voyelles.
>
> (*Amers, Invocation,* 3)

It is perhaps going too far to see in *ébullition,* as well as its root word *bulle* ("bubble") the homonym *bulle* ("bull", of the papal variety), but the context nonetheless invites the idea, which although philologically unwarranted is poetically justifiable.

The sea shortly returns as language after a few pages:

> Par grands soulèvements d'humeur et grandes
> intumescences du langage, par grands reliefs
> d'images et versants d'ombres lumineuses, courant
> à ses splendeurs massives d'un très beau style
> pérodique, (. . .)
>
>   La Mer mouvante et qui chemine au glissement
> de ses grands muscles errants . . .
>
> (*Amers, Invocation,* 6)

The physical force of language is seen, its muscularity and even violence noted, again in all things like the sea. The "Mer vivante du plus grand texte", now fully established as an image in the poem, may be used to express the same dialogue with inspiration which figured in *Exil,* III. The Tragédiennes invoke for the poet as well as for themselves the great sea-swell style of poetry that Perse has made his own:

> Ah! qu'un grand style encore nous surprenne, en
> nos années d'usure, qui nous vienne de mer et de
> plus loin nous vienne, (. . .) et qu'un plus
> large souffle en nous se lève, qui nous soit
> comme la mer elle-même et son grand souffle
> d'étrangère!
>
> (*Amers, Strophe,* III)

The sea is an exemplar for the poet, teaching him order and movement, rhythm and patience.

> De plus grand mètre à nos frontières, il n'en
> est point qu'on sache. Enseigne-nous, Puissance!
> le vers majeur du plus grand ordre, disnous le ton
> du plus grand art, Mer exemplaire du plus grand
> texte! le mode majeur enseigne-nous, et la mesure
> enfin nous soit donnée (. . .)! . . . Au

mouvement des eaux princières, qui renouera pour
nous la grande phrase prise au peuple?

                                                        (ibid.)

The sea has long been an inspiration for poets, but it has
not before been presented as an *example* of language in
this way. After a passage transparently evoking the poet
himself—"nous viendra-t-il de mer ou bien des Iles?"—
another splendid conjunction of sea and language is
presented:

>   Textuelle, la Mer
>   S'ouvre nouvelle sur ses grands livres de pierre.

                                                        (ibid.)

One recalls the "ode de pierre" of the opening page, and
notes the lapidary form the sea assumes as it imprints
itself on the rocks. The internal rhymes of this sentence
support the rhythmic idea of waves lapping on the shore,
curling over like turning pages. Here, as ever, Perse's
interest is with the creation of the text and its development—the sea—rather than with the book produced—
the rock. His contempt for books as dead museums contrasts sharply with his passion for linguistic creativity.

The living language of the sea "change de dialecte à
toutes portes des Empires" (*Amers, Strophe,* IV), a highly
expressive way of indicating the ocean's changing face
which as a sailor Perse would know intimately. But beneath the diversity lies the unity—"unité recouvrée sous
la diversité" (*Oiseaux,* 4)—a unity shown clearly in the following passage where the image of woven cloth undergoes
several transformations before appearing finally as a *trame*—
both "weft" and "plot"—for the sea's ritual utterings:

>   . . . Innombrable l'image, et le mètre, prodigue.
>   (. . .)
>   Le Récitant fait face encore à l'étendue des
>   Eaux. Il voit, immensément, la Mer aux mille
>   fronces.
>   Comme la tunique infiniment plissée du dieu
>   aux mains des filles de sanctuaires,
>   Ou, sur les pentes d'herbe pauvre, aux mains
>   des filles de pêcheurs, l'ample filet de mer de la
>   communauté.
>   Et maille à maille se répète l'immense trame
>   prosodique—la Mer elle-même, sur sa page,
>   comme un récitatif sacré.

                                            (*Amers, Chœur,* 3)

The modulations from the puckering of the sea's face to that
of a ceremonial robe, to that of a fishing-net being untangled
and mended and so back to the sea with its ceremonious
network of waves are both intricate and simple to follow.

Greater complexity is to be found in the final metaphor in
this category occuring in *Amers.* Language itself contains
unsatisfactory elements: the notion that words can be a
barrier to communication as well, paradoxically, as being
our principal and subtlest means of communication is familiar. Ultimately, Perse praises

>   Non point l'écrit, mais la chose même, prise en

son vif et dans son tout.

                                                    (*Vents,* III, 6)

So towards the end of the Chorus of *Amers,* poet, language and sea become utterly bound up together, so
completely fused as to defy differentiation. The words
have become the objects they designate, and the poet is
indistinguishable from his text and from the sea in which
he and it are bathed.

>   Nous t'invoquons enfin toi-même, hors de la
>   strophe du Poète. Qu'il n'y ait plus pour nous,
>   entre la foule et toi, l'éclat insoutenable du
>   langage:
>   ". . . Ah! nous avions des mots pour toi et
>   nous n'avions assez de mots,
>   Et voici que l'amour nous confond à l'objet
>   même de ces mots,
>   Et mots pour nous ils ne sont plus, n'étant
>   plus signes ni parures,
>   Mais la chose même qu'ils figurent et la chose
>   même qu'ils paraient;
>   Ou mieux, te récitant toi-même, le récit, voici
>   que nous te devenons toi-même, le récit,
>   Et toi-même sommes-nous, qui nous étais
>   l'Inconciliable: le texte même et sa substance et
>   son mouvement de mer,
>   Et la grande robe prosodique dont nous nous
>   revêtons. . ."

                                            (*Amers, Choeur,* 4)

Mechthild Cranston (essay date 1978)

SOURCE: "Voice and Vision, Cry and Gesture: The Birds
of Saint-John Perse," in *Symposium,* Vol. XXXII, No. 2,
Summer, 1978, pp. 103-13.

[*In the following essay, Cranston asserts that birds are
"the overarching theme of Léger's œuvre."*]

The Saint-John Foundation, organized in 1976, placed its
inaugural exhibit in Aix-en-Provence under the heading,
"Les Oiseaux et l'Œuvre de Saint-John Perse," a title at
once appropriate and surprising. While Perse's "cult of
movement" has received much scholarly attention, this
theme has generally been linked not to the flight of birds,
but to the interplay of cosmic phenomena as seen in
Pluies (1943), *Neiges* (1944), and *Vents* (1944), or to the
long marches across land and sea sung from *Anabase*
(1924) to *Amers* (1957). These are, by common consensus,
the milestones on Perse's way.

The 1962 "méditation poétique" that came to be known as
Oiseaux (1963), on the other hand, met with reservations
in accounts such as Victor Brombert's [in *The Hudson
Review,* Autumn, 1966] and Arthur Knodel's [*Saint-John
Perse,* 1966] discussion. The *Oiseaux* texts, though his
last major work, are not generally considered Perse's best.
[In *Saint-John Perse,* 1973] Roger Little assigns to the
collection a limited value when he concludes: "The text

has the great virtue, however, of revealing much of Perse's mature poetics just because it does not have the density of texture of the poems. For some readers, therefore, it might provide access to the more intensely poetic works."

It is not my purpose here to analyse the merits or defects of the *Oiseaux* texts, but rather to show how birds do indeed form the overarching theme of Perse's *œuvre*. From one of his earliest meditations, **"Pour fêter des oiseaux"** (which became **"Cohorte,"** 1907), to *L'Ordre des Oiseaux,* the 1962 collaboration with Braque later called *Oiseaux,* the avian order is at the center of the Persean universe, where birds serve as the mediators between earth and sky, allowing us to accede to the poet's view of language, and being: "A mi-hauteur entre ciel et mer, entre un amont et un aval d'éternité, se frayant route d'éternité, ils sont nos médiateurs, et tendent de tout l'être à l'étendue de l'être."

"Cohorte," communicated, in part, to Gide in 1910 (via Jacques Rivière), but withdrawn, in proof stage, from the *Nouvelle Revue Française,* was reproduced in full only in the 1972 Pléiade edition of the *Œuvres complètes,* where it occupies nearly seven pages. Although Perse's view of the early text was generally unfavorable, **"Cohorte"** is important to us not only because fragments of it pass directly into *L'Ordre des Oiseaux,* but also because it introduces the reader to the indispensable primogenitor of Perse's avian order. Dismissing all literary ancestors (indicated by the Albatross: "Il est d'usage de citer l'Albatros. Nous n'avons point d'égard pour celui-là," the poem celebrates the *Innommé* come from an island "étrangère à tout nom" and sustaining on an "aile immuable" the "arrogance souveraine du vol sous l'immobilité du geste." The bird is, at once, nameless, and identified as the bird-vessel, the "Frégate-Aigle" (that reappears in *Chronique,* where it is named with the Southern Cross), spanning time and space in a country where "l'aube est durée et l'espace, contrée . . .". As he passes, his flight is perceived as a "vibration étrange" answered by a cry, "ce cri, ce cri de tous: 'Il nous a vus!'" The poem ends in the migration of the bird (most members of the *Oiseaux* order will be migratory birds) and the "migration des mots" mutually made manifest in sound.

Several things stand out and are worth noting in the portrayal of Perse's first master-bird. Among them are his refusal—despite the specificity of a name—of realistic representation as of symbolic significance; the identification of the bird and vessel as mediators between the elements, between animal and man, nature (bird) and culture (boat); the perception of the bird's flight as something close to stillness in motion, and the interception of that stillness in the sound of a cry, which may furnish the key to the Persean aviary, as it displaces the early Verlainian *sanglot* (restricted to the *Éloges* series) and moves into the silent speech of gesture.

When Saint-John Perse returns to "fêter des oiseaux," more than half a century after **"Cohorte,"** in *L'Ordre des Oiseaux,* his rejection of all literary models becomes more radical and more explicit. The albatross is now identified as the tortured bird of Baudelaire. With Pindar's eagle, the cranes of Mal-

doror, and the great white bird of Arthur Gordon Pym, he makes way for the *Ur-Vogel,* the Bracchus Avis Avis, the bird reduced—or elevated—to the nakedness of the scientific archetype, neither sign nor symbol, "mais la chose même dans son fait et sa fatalité—chose vive, en tout cas, et prise au vif de son tissu natal" (*Oiseaux*).

One of the most memorable of Perse's feathered friends is an early bird, **"Le Perroquet,"** of the *Images à Crusoé,* 1904. A sorry creature at first sight—and certainly less elegant than the innumerable nightingales and swallows of lyric poetry—this parrot has, nevertheless, a certain mysterious attraction for Robinson and his audience. Set into the dark of night, the bird is said to have been given by a stammering sailor to an old woman who sold it into captivity. Exiled, like Robinson-Saint-Leger, in the sordid city dwelling, the bird's feather is caught in excrement, its eyelids are heavy with pollen gone bad, its eyes ringed with dead sap, its voice echoing, perhaps, the cry of the stammering sailor (modulated, many years later, into the plain-chant of that other exile, the "mouette sur son aile . . . ralliant les stances de l'exil" (*Exil* [1941]).

Le Perroquet

C'est un autre.
  Un marin bègue l'avait donné à la vieille femme qui l'a vendu. Il est sur le palier près de la lucarne, là où s'emmêle au noir la brume sale du jour couleur de venelles.
  D'un double cri, la nuit, il te salue, Crusoé, quand, remontant des fosses de la cour, tu pousses la porte du couloir et élèves devant toi l'astre précaire de ta lampe. Il tourne sa tête pour tourner son regard. Homme à la lampe! que lui veux-tu? . . . Tu regardres l'œil rond sous le pollen gâté de la paupière; tu regardes le deuxième cercle comme un anneau de sève morte. Et la plume malade trempe dans l'eau de fiente.
  O misère! Souffle ta lampe. L'oiseau pousse son cri.

(Images à Crusoé)

Despite the minute description of the bird's physical appearance, the parrot's most haunting attribute is its cry. "D'un double cri, il te salue, Crusoé." The verb *crier,* a near homonym of *créer,* is at the heart of Saint-John Perse's creation, where it carries—along with the word *siffler*—the burden of original speech, "ce pur délice sans graphie où court l'antique phrase humaine." *Crier* and *créer* are the modes of action that, in *Amers,* counter the threat of death: "Faut-il crier? faut-il créer?—Qui donc nous crée en cet instant? Et contre la mort elle-même n'est-il que de créer?"

Earlier the speaker of **"Cohorte"** exclaimed: "Nommer, créer! Qui donc en nous créait, criant le nom nouveau?" Commenting on the poem, Alexis Saint-Leger wrote to Valery Larbaud, in 1911: "Je n'ai jamais aimé nommer que pour la joie, très enfantine ou archaïque, de me croire créateur du nom. Pensez avec moi à toute l'extrême différence qu'il y a entre le 'mot' et le 'nom.' Je me souviens d'un long poème sur des Oiseaux de mer . . . qui m'eût paru le fait d'un maniaque ou d'un cuistre en ornithologie, si la plu-part de ces oiseaux n'avaient reçu de moi, sans imposture, le baptême de leur nom."

We had the words, but Shelley named the skylark, as Stevens named the blackbird, Mallarmé the swan, Chateaubriand the thrush, Char the *loriot,* Alexis Saint-Leger the parrot, and Saint-John Perse the *oriole.* The birds of the early **"Cohorte"** may be real birds, but far from receiving their life from any outer reality, their existence is conascent with the voice that names them and the cry that spells their name. In his last published text, **"Sécheresse,"** the poet writes: "Et moi, dit l'Appelé, j'ai pris mes armes entre les mains: torches levées à tous les antres, et que s'éclaire en moi toute l'aire du possible! Je tiens pour consonance de base ce cri lointain de ma naissance."

The identification made public in the controversy sparked by Maurice Saillet and Roger Caillois over the identity of birds like the Annaô may be of interest to literary historians, but is, ultimately, less important to our understanding of the bird than the naming achieved in the poem that contains the bird (or the bird that contains the poem). In the cry of the Annaô—that runs the scale from the alpha to the omega of its name—the bird is created, regardless of any prior dictionary existence. Likewise, the "Oiseau Anhinga, la dinde d'eau des fables, dont l'existence n'est point fable, dont la présence m'est délice et ravissement de vivre" *(Vents)* is, as Christian Doumet reminds us [in *Les Thèmes aériens dans l'œuvre de Saint-John Perse,* 1976], *désémantisé* into a pure *signifiant,* the truly "proper" name that precedes the common noun (subject to linguistic classification). Not only literary ancestors, but creatures of fable, history and science as well are eliminated from the poet's aviary, where the bird literally—yet outside the realm of letters—inhabits its name.

The birds of **"Cohorte"** have a dual habitat, echoed in the dual cry of Robinson's parrot. Evoked in the magnificence of those names given to them by "les Doctes," men of letters and of science, the "Phaeton Ethéré," the "Anchise" and the "Frégate-Aigle" hold fable, myth, and history in the span of their wings consigned to the stillness of the word inscribed in space and time. That stillness is, however, also the state of death. The true name—the name that does not kill by designation—must remain internal, *innommé,* unspoken except in the very act of self-presencing that is at once origin and end, the alpha and omega.

> Ah ça! nous direz-vous le vrai de votre appellation?
> parcelles vives arrachées au tout de l'Innommé. . . .
>
> Et l'aile qui battait en nous, et s'affolait pour nous
> aux toiles de la tente (le fou de Dieu soit avec
> nous!) ne nous laissait de cesse ni patience que
> nous n'eussions trouvé le nom nouveau!
>
> ("**Cohorte**")

In the impossibility of *proper* naming, the poet reaches the frontiers of language, and of his poem. How can the name be spoken—and, *a fortiori,* written—without reference to that which is exterior, and therefore, expropriated?

Though it reduces the dual articulation of language (into sounds and into words) by eliminating the trajectory of words, even the cry still moves into air where sounds, however pure, mark a trace. Even the body that vibrates re-sounds.

Lévi-Strauss and Derrida have reminded us that one never names. One classifies the self or the other ("C'est un autre") within a system of differences already circumscribed. Every *nom propre* must, of necessity, always already be a *non-propre.* If naming is to be pure self-presencing, only the being-to-be-named can speak its name (an apparent contradiction), only the image—which yet images or imagines nothing—can "pousser son cri." That originary image without imitation or representation, conceived in traditional terms, can, however, only be reserved to the $\acute{\epsilon}\iota\kappa\omega\nu$ or God himself. And it is only in relation to such an originary image that man can turn the cry into the $\nu\epsilon\upsilon\mu\hat{\alpha}$ or the Augustinian jubilation: "For to whom is such a jubilation suitable, unless to an ineffable Being? and how can we celebrate this ineffable Being, since we cannot be silent, or find any thing in our transports which can express them, unless unarticulated sounds?"

> Le cri! le cri perçant du dieu! qu'il nous
> saisisse en pleine foule, non dans les chambres,
> Et par la foule propagé qu'il soit en nous
> répercuté jusqu'aux limites de la perception

cries the speaker of *Vents,* and in *Amers* the poet announces "ce cri de l'homme à la limite de l'humain." In metaphysical terms, the "original cry" must be perceived as God's voice which, passing into prayer and jubilation among the "peuple d'élus," returns the ineffable to the silence of its self-made image.

The eye can see farther than the ear can hear. The "limites de la perception" and the "limite de l'humain" are reached not in voice (name, word, sound), but in vision, or better, in gesture which prefigures both voice and vision in the aphasic articulation of movement suspended. Sound as "pure" (i.e., unheard) extension is held in the tension of arms and hands inscribing in space the signifier unsevered from the self, signifying nothing. While allowing—through distancing—the minimal differentiation of meaning, the gesture, returning forever to itself, is the originary self-presencing of being that annuls re-presentation. In the gesture, the hierarchical *pré-séance* of the pecking (and world) order takes its place in the undifferentiated *hic et nunc* of an interior order, the *céans* of the *Innommé:* "Mais trêve à toutes préséances et place au Maître du céans!" (**"Cohorte"**).

In Perse's early work, that interior space, the place of the poem, is generally disputed by two alternative modes of being: voice and vision, cry and gesture, mutually exclusive. In **"Le Perroquet,"** the gesture that raised the lamp silenced the bird. The light extinguished called forth the cry in the first recorded association of *souffle* and *cri*: "Souffle ta lampe. L'oiseau pousse son cri." Speech did not operate within vision, but re- (or dis-) placed that which it named. Conversely, the spatial and visual spelled the death of discourse. The prayer sustaining the nameless bird in the "arrogance souveraine du vol" was hidden and caught, like the word (*arrogance-rogare*) in the silence of an immobile gesture. As the bird emits the vibration that turns "le cri aux lèvres" into the cry of recognition ("Il nous a vus"), the *Innommé* takes flight. . . .

Recognition of the other articulated in voice opened the difference between pleasure and desire where a poem like **"Le Perroquet"** ("C'est un autre") was inscribed. As the *Innommé* moves from "son plus long plaisir" of pure auto-affection to the "souffle du désir," the desire of the "terrible délice" turns the docile tail into a "tige de fer," the feather into the pen, and flight into poem. Traveling on the road to (of) language, the bird's tail, "très fourchue," no longer trails in its own excrement, but inscribes in the "sûr clivage" of exterior space the "faille du chemin" of difference.

Voice and vision separate at the crossroads of *Vergegenwärtigung* and *Vorstellung,* as the figures of the festival, brought out into the open and drawn together around the celebration of the sea and the ἐπιφᾳνής of the *Innommé,* are driven back into the house of language, where they become the *figurants* of discontinuous space and time. Resuming functionary and representative positions, "le monde . . . aux terrasses" divides once more into master and servant, man and beast, "la maison du Gouverneur, . . . les femmes blanches, les prélats, les amiraux en toile blanche, le factionnaire casqué de blanc, les domestiques en surah blanc et l'enfant maître d'un poney pie, taché de rouge et blanc" (**"Cohorte"**). Casting off the festival garments of pure transparency (all were dressed in white!), the figures at the bridge pass over into meaning. The *Innommé,* breaking once more into all the designated names ("Frégate-Aigle," "Frégata Magnificens") not proper to itself, flies from the "terrible délice" of recognition back into the unknown.

The "pollen gâté" found on the eyelids of Robinson's parrot bears fruit in the dissemination of sound. The blind eye listens. The migration of the bird and the migration of words consecrate the (seasonal) differentiations that clear the space for sacrifice and prayer: "ah! tout l'afflux de tes légions, ah! tout l'afflux de ta saison, et la beauté, soudain, du mot: 'cohorte'! . . . (**"Cohorte"**), the cohort of angels. The cry, whether animal or human, is clearly associated in the work of Saint-John Perse with the "peuple d'élus" named in **"Cohorte,"** The word *crier* evokes for the poet not only its near homonym, *créer,* but also the rhyme word, *prier,* The two are expressly linked in *Amers,* where, addressing the sea, the poet asks: "Faut-il crier? faut-il prier? . . . Tu vas, tu vas, l'Immense et Vaine, et fais la roue toi-même au seuil d'une autre immensité." The birds of prey are birds of prayer also, and of praise. The woman's cupped hand held against the flame and lifted towards the seagull of *Vents,* and Robinson's face offered to the night "comme une paume renversée" (*Images à Crusoé*) gesture towards the originary image.

Knodel rightly places *Oiseaux* among the "Votive Poems" (a category that all of Perse's works may share). For René Galand [in *Saint-John Perse,* 1972] the gull forever on its wing embodies "the divine power in pursuit of the poet's

soul." Far from a witticism, the Bracchus Avis Avis of *L'Ordre des Oiseaux* seems the final solemn transfiguration of the threefold *Ave* sung in *Neiges,* where "comme un grand *Ave* de grâce sur nos pas chante tout bas le chant très pur de notre race," and the purity of snow is traced, like the bird's, to the pure lineage of a "création première" (*Oiseaux*). In the very nakedness of its scientific reduction, the bird of Braque hovers on the angel wings of the Annunciation.

Sacred bees and prophetic eagles fly through much of Perse's work, making holy noises in the echo-chambers of our literary memories. But the cry of the *Ur-Vogel* (which comprehends both parrot and frigate-bird, the animal and the human, the natural and the cultural order) must at last be intercepted at the more rudimentary level of an *Ur-Sprache* both prior and posterior to any constituted language or religion, sacrament or sacrifice.

To the group *crier-créer-prier* belongs the earlier mentioned *siffler,* and who would dare whistle in church? And yet the poet, asked to compose a song of consolation for the Foreign Lady who, like him, lives in exile, is heard whistling to his "peuple d'incrédules" (*Poème à l'Étrangère* [1942]) that recall the earlier "peuple d'élus" of **"Cohorte."** And the poet of *Amers* entreats his Beloved, and the sea: "Et toi, l'Amante, pour ton Dieu, tu siffles encore ton sifflement d'orfraie. Et toi, l'Amante, sur ton souffle, tu t'arqueras encore pour l'enfantement du cri—jusqu'à cette émission très douce, prends-y garde, et cette voyelle infime, où s'engage le dieu . . .".

The *sifflement* of the Beloved is identified with breath itself, the *souffle* or *creator spiritus* that inhabits man (woman), the elements, and the bird, engendering, at last, God himself in the lowly or minute vowel, the "mute" *e* of the "Amante" and the *orfraie* or the *effraie* of the same poem: "l'esprit sacré s'éveille aux nids d'effraies." That mute vowel would become sound, made *grave* in the unnamed mother and sea (*mère-mer*) swelling in the "enfantement du cri."

And yet, the "mot pur" (*Exil,*) and the "nom pur," the "sifflement si pur" of *Anabase* and the "sifflement qui dure" of **"Cohorte,"** "le plus pur vocable" of *Neiges* and the "voyelle infime"—which is, surely, also the "voyelle infinie"—cannot be rendered in sound, just as the "real" bird cannot move on the stillness of the wing, and the bird designated in space cannot inhabit its name. That is, of course, the predicament of poets at least from Mallarmé to Saint-John Perse. Even the "langage sans paroles" (*ibid.*) of whistling and crying produces a melody.

While the early poems marked the *écart* between vision and voice, the mature work of Saint-John Perse restores the mythic unity via "the phonetic confiscation of the hand" achieved in the interiorization of both gesture and cry. The transition is effected visually by the hand of man made wing and the heart that takes flight in the votive offering of *Chronique* (1959): "Nous élevons à bout de bras, sur le plat de nos mains, comme couvée d'ailes naissantes, ce cœur enténébré de l'homme où fut l'avide, et fut l'ardent, et tant d'amour irrévélé. . .". The phonic juncture is achieved in the apostrophe to the Foreign Lady, addressed as: "Ô grande par le coeur et par le cri de votre race!" (*Poème à l'Etrangère*). *Cœur* and *cri*, once caught in the dark *Images à Crusoé*, are brought into that interior light where stammering turns into jubilation, and the cry is answered "par illumination du cœur" (*Vents*). The poem resolves the conflict of presence and representation in the inexorable wing of "Sécheresse" that beats from within the earth, out of the burden of its own prefixes, into the consciousness of the heart and its own being: "Écoute, ô cœur fidèle, ce battement sous terre d'une aile inexorable." Whatever its metaphysical overtones, the Persean cry is, at the end (as at the beginning), an act as purely physical as gesture itself, as elemental as the "frôlement de cils" (*Neiges*), the beating of the heart, or the rhythmic repetitions of respiration.

Probably no bird of the Persean order rises from the page like the creature of dawn conceived by the poet in exile, in the first snows of a New York winter (*Neiges,* 1944). Here a fabulous owl—a bird of prayer and of praise, not of fable or ill omen—sings the *laudes* of early dawn not in words, but in the very contraction and expansion of its body, vibrating to the sound of a "pure" name (Dahl) made flower (dahlia):

> Et ce fut au matin, . . . un peu avant la sixième
> heure, comme en un havre de fortune, un lieu de
> grâce et de merci où licencier l'essaim des grandes
> odes du silence.
>
> . . . . .
>
> Il neigeait, et voici, nous en dirons merveilles:
> l'aube muette dans sa plume, comme une grande
> chouette fabuleuse en proie aux souffles de
> l'esprit, enflait son corps de dahlia blanc. Et de
> tous les côtés il nous était prodige et fête.
>
> (*Neiges*)

Who would name the bird at once owl and dahlia that silently officiates at the celebration of a *grande heure,* singing odes without sound in the elemental gesture of respiration? Neither bird nor flower, but dawn itself, hovering, like the *Innommé,* on a silent wing, this fable-creature (yet of no fable) speaks the ineffable language of the invisible image in the total transparency of its *fête.* Like Husserl's "ideal" voice, or the voice of silence, the bird of Saint-John Perse "se réduit phénoménologiquement lui-même, transforme en pure diaphanéité l'opacité mondaine de son corps. Cet effacement du corps sensible et de son extériorité est *pour la conscience* la forme même de la présence immédiate du signifié."

The words at last refuse to pay tribute to the language that would use them, and devour—like insects—the "feuille" that would hold them in place: "Et les mots au langage refusent leur tribut: mots sans office et sans alliance, qui dévorent, à même, la feuille vaste du langage comme feuille verte de mûrier, avec une voracité d'insectes, de chenilles . . . " ("Sécheresse"). The blinding whiteness of the image effaces the black lines tracing its contours on the page.

The bird becomes the scribe of its own incantation, tracing the originary image in the words without meaning:

> Sur la page blanche aux marges infinies, l'espace
> qu'ils mesurent n'est plus qu'incantation. Ils
> sont, comme dans le mètre, quantités syllabiques.
> Et procédant, comme les mots, leur sens à la
> limite de la félicité.
>   A l'aventure poétique ils eurent part jadis, avec
> l'augure et l'aruspice. Et les voici, vocables
> assujettis au même enchaînement, pour l'exercise
> au loin d'une divination nouvelle. . . . Au soir
> d'antiques civilisations, c'est un oiseau de bois,
> les bras en croix saisis par l'officiant, qui tient
> le rôle du scribe dans l'écriture médiumnique,
> comme aux mains du sourcier ou du géomancien.
>
> (*Oiseaux*)

In its final "transfiguration," the bird is a "geste écouté" living in the space of the *contrée* . . . and the *in illo tempore* (the "aube . . . durée") that precede the constitution of both things and names. The final gesture is an erasure, the final cry, the voice suspended in the opening of a flower, in the arching of lungs or lips, the swelling of the sea. The final movement is the interior (in-) articulation of cry and gesture rejoicing in the sovereign self-presence that, God-like, suffices unto itself, inhabiting the space and time of its self-made image and self-given name, as unmediated vision and voice, unseen and never spoken.

From the flowers which end "en des cris de perruches" (*Pour fêter une enfance*) to the bird breathing within the body of the flower, from the "image [qui] pousse son cri" to the cry muted in image, the Persean order, like the anabasis, moves inward, where the bird preys, at last, upon itself ("en proie aux souffles de l'esprit," . . .), set free from encyclopedia and myth, history and invention, into the *marges* of its own being, praying its *proper* name. From the nameless bird of **"Cohorte"** to the unnamable creature of dawn, the birds of Saint-John Perse migrate to a region where they, like words, lose their meaning, the final name being blessed, like the tree dedicated by Perse to Gide, with the joy of signifying nothing. "Et de tous côtés il nous était prodige et fête."

Peter Baker (essay date 1991)

SOURCE: "The Sexuation of Poetic Language in Saint-John Perse's *Anabase,*" in *Obdurate Brilliance: Exteriority and the Modern Long Poem,* University of Florida Press, 1991, pp. 30-40.

[In the following essay, Baker examines Anabase *from a feminine perspective.]*

A serious meditation on sexual difference serves to motivate the disposition of the text of *Anabase,* both in its specific language and its overall strategies of representation. Beginning with specific uses of language means re-examining the often-remarked strangeness of the language Perse employs to describe objects in the natural world. Analysis of this "semiotics of the natural world" in *Anabase* shows that the descriptive register of objects in nature and gender-marked human traits intermingle in figural strategies that defy traditional tenor/vehicle distinctions. The traditional inner/outer distinction drawn between "man" and nature is refigured in the register of sexual differences. Like the human/natural difference, sexual difference is both nonassimilable and nonoppositional and serves to place in question the logical oppositions of rational discourse through figural means. The figural, following Jean-François Lyotard, operates a "renversement" whereby what is thought to be outer reverses the logical categories of the inner. This approach to poetic language necessarily goes against the traditional interpretation of *Anabase* in terms of Perse's "imaginaire." The traditional view claims the central character of the poem to be a version of the poet's alter ego and, in one specific instance, discusses the voyager's encounters with women and other images of femininity as revealing the inner workings of Perse's psyche. Perse's own remarks seem to legitimate this approach; he says, for instance, that the poem's title has a strictly etymological sense of "a journey to the interior," with a willed ambiguity between the geographical and spiritual senses of that phrase. According to the interpretation advanced here, Perse's journey to the interior in *Anabase* discovers an *exteriority,* or nonassimilable sexual difference, that is central to the representation of the foundations of human society.

The overall structure and progression of the poem *Anabase,* with its ten "Chants" and opening and closing "Chansons," have always been viewed as referring to a voyage undertaken by a character representing the poet's alter ego. The Stranger, or Voyager, as he is alternately called in the text, sets out on a voyage to the interior, presumably involving discovery, conquest, and settlement. In fact, were it not for the schema developed by T. S. Eliot proposing this structure, few readers would perceive a narrative structure this organized. Instead, the reader is instantly immersed in a strange and unsettling mixture of high diction and startling images. Apparent from the outset is that the protagonist is not only an outsider but also someone who is viewed from the outside, "Étranger. Qui passait [Stranger. Who passed]" ("Chanson," verset 1). And one senses further from the concrete imagery employed that his voyage will be somehow sensitive to the profound differences of other cultures. The analysis of sexuation of poetic language that follows will focus on two Chants (II and IX) where the confrontation with this charged alterity is most heightened.

If *Anabase* as a whole and particularly Chant II have always been considered obscure and of difficult access for the reader, as [Mireille] Sacotte rightly states, they have also received high quality critical attention, which facilitates the subsequent critic's task. The difficulty of movement in the logical progression from verset to verset stems from what Eliot called the "logic of the imagination." But perhaps even more strange and disturbing on first impression is the interpenetration of natural and gender-

marked human attributes in the images. Into an imaginative space that is already constructed according to a powerful suspension of historical, geographical, and literary standards of reference, Perse introduces a language that questions human/natural and interpersonal boundaries usually taken for granted.

Chant II opens with a series of images that disorient the reader by shifting place and tone in a way radically different from Chant I (Sacotte). The most unsettling instances are those in parentheses in versets three and four:

> Nous enjambons la Robe de la Reine, toute en dentelle avec deux bandes de couleur bise (ah! que l'acide corps de femme sait tacher une robe à l'endroit de l'aisselle!).
> Nous enjambons la robe de Sa fille, toute en dentelle avec deux bandes de couleur vive (ah! que la langue de lézard sait cueillir les fourmis à l'endroit de l'aisselle!).

> We step over the gown of the Queen, all of lace with two grey stripes (and how well the acid body of a woman can stain a gown at the armpit).
> We step over the gown of the Queen's daughter, all of lace with two bright stripes (and how well the lizard's tongue can catch ants at the armpit).

In the overall strange and unsettling world of Perse's poems, these are certainly two of the strongest moments of confrontation with alterity. Surely, no other interpretation could account for the presence here of such poetic force. As [Jacques] Geninasca has observed: "Everything happens here as if woman were considered in the same way as a natural species." The whole of *Anabase* constructs a world in which women and the natural world are described in communicating semantic registers. This phenomenon may be examined more closely through attention to linguistic features in the text. (This linguistic phenomenon should not be confused with the mythological assimilation of the earth to female figures or deities. Perse's break from the myth-thinking will become clearer in the analysis of the status of enunciation in the poem.)

The dress of the Queen and that of her daughter already echo the usage of dress (*robe*) in the opening "Chanson" (presented here with the similar passage from the first verset as well): "Je vous salue, ma fille, sous le plus grand des arbres de l'année [Hail, daughter! under the most considerable of the trees of the year]" (verset 1); "Je vous salue, ma fille, sous la plus belle robe de l'année [Hail, daughter! robed in the loveliest dress of the year]" (verset 3; trans. modified). This prior "substitution" in Roger Caillois's terms, already introduces a sort of equivalence between *robe* and *arbre*. The mention of "fille" also echoes the previous usage, although with the difference that the Voyager in the initial "Chanson" says "ma fille." In fact, the word "fille" (daughter/girl) occurs at least a dozen times in the poem, and fully half of these occurrences are linked with possessive adjectives. These girl/daughters are figurally linked with mules and undergarments in Chant IV, perfumed in Chant VI, and at the end of Chant IX, "les filles urinaient en écartant la toile de leur robe [the girls urinated by holding aside their print gowns]" (133; trans. modified).

What are we to make of the action of the voice who says, "Nous enjambons [We step over]"? In the strict sense, the action is that of stepping over first the dress of the Queen and then that of her daughter. The images of washing (versets 2 and 7) and of clothes hung out to dry lead one to assume that the Queen and her daughter are not in their clothes. However, if they were wearing their clothing, the action of the verb "enjamber" would carry a strong sexual connotation, "bestriding" the women as one would bestride a horse. Whether in connection with the verb or through a metonymic association with the dresses, the following verset poses the hypothesis: "Et peut-être le jour ne s'écoule-t-il point qu'un même homme n'ait brûlé pour une femme et pour sa fille [And perhaps the day does not pass but the same man may burn with desire for a woman and for her daughter]" (verset 5). The imagery of this passage is sexually charged and would tend to legitimate the examination of the poem on the basis of the poet's desire or unconscious.

In fact several critical readings interpret the following verset as a sexual image: "Rire savant des morts, qu'on nous pèle ces fruits! [Knowing laugh of the dead, let this fruit be peeled for us]" (verset 6). While both Sacotte and Geninasca reject this overly fixed interpretation, Geninasca allows for the idea to be present in the passage. In effect, the verb *cueillir* (pick, gather) and the adjective *acide* (acid) that are first used to describe the body of the woman and the lizard's tongue suggest together the semantic category /fruit/ and thus introduce the interpenetration of the semantic categories of woman and fruit even before the verset in question.

In the two versets in question, the area of the dress and/ or woman is the *aisselle*, or armpit, itself a potentially sexually charged image. The verb used for the act of staining is *savoir*. "Sait tacher" causes Geninasca to invoke "a knowledge of the somatic essence of women"; but the actual staining itself is caused implicitly by the woman's bodily fluids. A strict feminist interpretation, following the lead of [Luce] Irigaray's work on the imagery of fluids and femininity (*Ce sexe*), could find consistent evidence for these associations in Perse's work, particularly in **Anabase.**

All of the foregoing remarks point to the difficulty of any unitary explanation for the parenthetical versets in Perse's poem. The "acide corps de femme [acid body of a woman]" and the lizard's tongue seeking out ants in the woman's armpit are surely images that evoke associations which defy our ability to fix exactly in discursive terms their value or precise significance. One would be tempted to invoke the fashionable notion of "indeterminacy" and say that the poetic text generates but does not control possible interpretations.

Two formal principles of analysis may aid us to investigate more fully this apparently unresolvable ambiguity of the text: the study of cumulative structuring repetition and the status of enunciation. Recent linguistic analysis has heightened our appreciation of the structures of repetition in Perse's work. On the basis of the previous remarks on the repetition of *fille(s)*—and a parallel enumeration could be made for *femme(s)*—it may already be sensed that a linguistically oriented analysis might lead to rather standard conclusions. For this reason, it is crucial to examine the status of enunciation, particularly as it comes to the fore in Chant IX, as a means of deepening our reflections on the representation of sexual difference.

Previous discussions of Perse's "imaginaire" have tended to privilege the interiority of the speaker of the text, often to the extent of equating the speaker with the poet himself. Generally speaking, this same privileging of interiority informs most Perse scholarship and corresponds to the view expressed by Roger Little [in *Saint-John Perse,* 1973] that there is "a depth of sincerity to the poems to which the reader's latent Romanticism responds." Little also states that in **Anabase** "we are aware that this is an *interior* monologue, that beyond the concrete imagery lies a psychological and spiritual realm to be explored." My view is rather that Perse is one of the least Romantic of modern poets and there is no realm "beyond the concrete imagery," that the vision of the inner in Perse's universe is exactly a vision of the outer.

Following the semantic analysis of the language of Chant II, I would argue that it represents a version of what Irigaray calls the "sexuation of discourse." The meditation on difference in this text appears to charge the very language used in a way that cannot be reduced to logical oppositions. Furthermore, the strategy of the figural is to reverse the arrangement of mental/imaginary space. In this paradoxical reversal, the "sincere," or what can be isolated from the text and assented to, represents the inner; the imaged, or figure that cannot be reduced to its content, menaces the space of logical or even emotional understanding from the outside.

In this way, the lizard licking the ants from the woman's armpit threatens not only logical but also emotive contexts. Like the mysterious additional "jambe de gauche [left leg]" in Rimbaud's "Antique," this unaccustomed, impossible image forces us to question the status of who is speaking. For the traditional approach to Perse's "imaginaire," this basic question of who is speaking becomes something of a scandal. The customary position is to identify the discursive stance as an *interior* monologue and the parts of the text that are surrounded by quotation marks as a *still further inner* form of expression. Even Sacotte's excellent analysis stumbles over this question in relation to Chant IX, recognizing that a woman is speaking, but preferring to see one woman where there are probably several, in order to salvage a view of Perse's "imaginaire." It is likely that there are several women who speak in Chant IX; the one who sleeps with the stranger (verset 11) is unlikely to be the one who says in the following *laisse* that she does not know what his ways are with women. The reversal in the status of the speaker in this pivotal section of the poem allows for unassimilable difference to be figured through the voices of women who describe the stranger from a position of *exteriority*.

Moreover, Chant IX is framed by an exterior view of the young women in question. Going toward the West, the speaker suddenly announces: "Jeunes femmes! et la nature d'un pays s'en trouve toute parfumée [Young women! and the nature of a land is all scented therewith]" (verset 3). The four passages which follow are spoken by at least two different women, as my subsequent analysis will show. At the end of the Chant, the speaker returns to the exterior view of the women in question:

> et debout sur la tranche éclatante du jour, au seuil d'un grand pays plus chaste que la mort,
>   les filles urinaient en écartant la toile peinte de leur robe.

> and erect on the shining edge of day, on the threshold of a great land made more chaste than death,
>   the girls urinated by holding aside their print gowns.

(versets 22-23; trans. modified)

The same interpenetration of natural and gender-marked human description that dominates in Chant II is operative in these frame passages, always with the insistence on death and the strange physical details that assimilate the women figures to the status of natural phenomena.

If this exterior view of the women—and thus by implication the speaker/poet's imaginative processes—were all we had, there would be no questioning Sacotte's analysis: "One can deduce the process of the imagination: the poet, disturbed by an interior fecundity, involuntary, passive, over which the man is not master and which his imaginary tendency always carries toward prompt abortions, dreams of a woman's body without mystery, almost transparent like the network of veins beneath the skin, and of an exterior fecundity, visible and also dominated by him" (my trans.). This is a perceptive, even brilliant, deduction of what must have been the poet's inner psychology. But, of course, the nature of the question posed determines the kind of answer that can be given. And if the question is not to interrogate the author's supposed inner state, but rather the disposition of the text at hand, then a different approach is necessary. An examination of what the *jeunes filles* (young women) themselves say indicates that the very status of the women as speakers necessarily works against an "inner" view of the poet's psyche.

From the first words of the first speech, "Je t'annonce [I tell you]" (verset 4; my trans.), repeated at the beginning of each subsequent speech, a relational structure is engaged. The speaker, a woman ("our women's bodies"), addresses the Voyager as "tu," implying either an established intimacy or the cultural difference of a language that does not recognize polite forms of address. In addition to expressing a stance toward the male Voyager, she goes on to express a stance toward herself as one of a class of women:

> mais le plaisir au flanc des femmes se compose, et dans nos corps de femmes il y a comme un ferment de raisin noir, et de répit avec nous-mêmes il n'en est point.

> but the pleasure forms itself within our flanks, and in our women's bodies there is a ferment of black grape, and we have no respite with ourselves.

(verset 7; trans. modified)

Other than verset 5 in Chant II where it is speculated that perhaps a man is unable to spend a day without burning for both mother and daughter, this is the first mention of physical pleasure. Is it purely accidental that the speaker is a woman? Is it merely a strategy by a male poet to find expression for his desire? These questions do not begin to do justice to the complexity of a vision based on a profound respect for alterity. One might rather ask: what poet (male or female) has posed the question of the woman's body, "nos corps de femmes," in such strange and compelling terms? Both inner and outer—a fermentation of black grapes and a lack of respite among themselves—such is the view presented through the first woman's words.

The second *laisse* complicates the enunciative structure by posing a question (as well as the uncertainty whether this is the same young woman or another who speaks):

> Ceux qui savent les sources sont avec nous dans cet exil; ceux qui savent les sources nous diront-ils au soir
>   sous quelles mains pressant la vigne de nos flancs
>   nos corps s'emplissent d'une salive? (Et la femme s'est couchée avec l'homme dans l'herbe; elle se lève, met ordre aux lignes de son corps, et le criquet s'envole sur son aile bleue.)

> Those who know the springs are with us in this exile; those who know the springs will they tell us at evening
>   beneath what hands pressing the vine of our flanks
>   our bodies are filled with saliva? (And the woman has slept with the man in the grass; she rises, arranges the lines of her body, and the cricket takes flight on its blue wing.)

(versets 9-11; trans. modified)

"Ceux qui savent les sources [Those who know the springs]" are presumably the older persons, invoked in the previous *laisse*, "qui vieillissent dans l'usage et le soin du silence [who grow old in the custom and the care of silence]." The speaker wants to know if they will reveal the secret of the men (presumably) who press her and the others' flanks, causing them to fill with saliva. The continuity of imagery is striking, from the vine image that recalls the previous passage, to the saliva image that recalls the theme of liquids and the woman's body (Irigaray). Certainly, there is an implied physical union in the parenthetical phrase, "the long-awaited union" as Sacotte puts it, but the representation participates in the same mystery of difference (male/female; human/natural) that dominates the image sequences in the poem. They sleep together in the grass. The woman rises. The cricket flies away on its blue wing. Can we really say that some kind of system of opposition, whether male/female, amazon/queen (Sacotte), serves to organize the logic of these associations? Rather, what strikes us is the force of these images that call for a meditation, probably unresolvable, on the very nature of these differences. Not rational explanation, but wonder; not empty amazement, but rather a profoundly unsettling experience that challenges the very system of oppositions that organizes our mental and social structures.

The speaker of the third passage must be different from the speaker of the second, or else the woman who sleeps with the Stranger is not the one who speaks in versets 8-11. Here the representation of difference as exteriority reaches its apex:

> Mais l'Etranger vit sous sa tente, honoré de laitages, de fruits. On lui apporte de l'eau fraîche
>
>   pour y laver sa bouche, son visage et son sexe.
>   On lui mène à la nuit de grandes femmes brehaignes (ha! plus nocturnes dans le jour!) Et peut-être aussi de moi tirera-t-il son plaisir. (Je ne sais quelles sont ses façons d'être avec les femmes.)

> But the Stranger dwells in his tent, honoured with gifts of dairy produce and fruit. He is offered fresh water
>
>   to wash therewith his mouth, his face and his sex.
>   At night he is brought tall barren woman (more nocturnal in the day!) And perhaps of me also will be have his pleasure. (I know not what are his ways with women.)

>   (versets 13-15)

The series of differences is both extended and deepened in this passage. The *je/tu* (I/thou) structure of enunciation is complicated by the description of the Stranger in the third person. (Does this mean that he wasn't the one being addressed all along?) The meditation on the otherness of woman is extended by the image of the barren women brought to his tent, with the adjective *brehaigne* (barren), one that normally describes horses. The Stranger is brought fruit and milk products on the same level as he is brought the women. These are all concurrent images with those previously examined, showing women as an extension of the natural world.

The strange reversal that traverses this passage is the Stranger being described in both physical terms and in terms of pleasure by the women themselves. Despite all the images of women in the poem to this point, there has been nothing quite so direct as verset 14 where the Stranger washes his mouth, face, and sexual organ (or perhaps it is the women who do the washing, as is traditional in some cultures). While this is certainly not shocking and the

tone is flat, the impact is undoubtedly greater as a result. And the woman then goes on to wonder whether the Stranger will take his pleasure with her, thus negating the possibility of there being a single woman who both speaks all the versets in Chant IX and also sleeps with the Stranger. This musing is followed by the now familiar parenthetical expression wherein the speaker states that she does not know his ways with women (echoing the difference of *façons,* or customs, implied in the opening "Chanson," verset 2). Cultural difference, sexual difference, and difference of class or social role—all these differences are at once brought to the fore. The language throughout this sequence has barely been figural at all, thus establishing difference itself as the dominant figure, a difference that figures a radical exteriority at the center of this journey to the interior.

The final passage returns to the figure-image of the woman as part of the world of nature as well as to a direct address to a "tu," presumably the Stranger. Among the images in this beautiful and moving passage are ones that rhyme with those already examined:

> et compagnon de l'angle de tombeau, tu me verras longtemps muette sous l'arbre-fille de mes veines . . . Un lit d'instances sous la tente, l'étoile verte dans la cruche, et que je sois sous ta puissance! nulle servante sous la tente que la cruche d'eau fraîche! (Je sais sortir avant le jour sans éveiller l'étoile verte, le criquet sur le seuil et l'aboiement des chiens de toute la terre.)

> and companion of the grave-corner, you shall see me for long time unspeaking under virgin Branches of my veins. . . . A bed of entreaties under the tent, the green star in the cruse, and may I be under your dominion! no serving-maid under the tent but the cruse of cool water! (I have ways to depart before day without wakening the green star, the cricket on the threshold and the baying of the dogs of the whole world.)

>   (verset 19)

Sacotte elegantly explains the image of the veins like an "arbre-fille" (*lit.,* tree-daughter) as those that the Stranger sees beneath a transparent skin. Yet *arbre* and *fille* are also the two interchangeable words from the opening "Chanson" and hence participate in the woman-as-part-of-nature structure. But even that assertion would be an oversimplification of what operates here as much at the level of language itself, a striking instance of what seems from this perspective to be sexuation of poetic language.

The startling reversal thus uncovered at this turning point in **Anabase** is the substitution of the other's view for what we had expected to be an inner experience. Instead of the *interiority* we expect from poetry, we are presented with a radical *exteriority*. The male protagonist is not given as an "object" for study, but rather the view of *difference itself* is presented, using a form of enunciation in which that difference is a central figure. Outside the bounds of logical thought, this nonoppositional difference upsets conventional order and threatens the foundations of logical discourse. The way is prepared by the language of the poem, its strange insistence on the radical alterity of women and the positing of a commonality between woman and nature. To establish that reversal and then use the voices of these women to describe the male protagonist *from the outside*—such is Perse's project, a wager placed against the odds of a society that probably could not accept its message and remain the same.

This theory of difference operates as a figure of the postmodern. None of the traditional guiding ideas (*métarécits,* Lyotard) of culture can assimilate this presentation of difference and use it to achieve ends to which the social network would readily assent. As feminist discourse haunts the margins of the paternal order, threatening to disrupt its neat oppositional systems, so Perse's text is deliberately marginal with respect to the poetic practice representing the "great ideas" of Western civilization. It has always been assumed that Alexis Leger chose the pseudonym Saint-John Perse to protect the dignity and independence of his diplomatic career. Perhaps the choice of a pseudonym also served to protect the long-term development of a poetic project that seriously challenges the societal structures within which Leger the diplomat had no choice but to work.

FURTHER READING

Criticism

Ashton, Dore. "St.-John Perse's Guadeloupe." *The Kenyon Review* XXIII, No. 3 (Summer 1961): 520-26.
Provides a biographical approach to Legér's work.

Carmody, Francis J. "Saint-John Perse and Several Oriental Sources." *Comparative Literature Studies* II, No. 2 (1965): 125-51.
Discusses various influences on *Anabase, Exil* and *Vents.*

Cocking, J. M. "The Migrant Muse: Saint-John Perse (1887-1975)." *Encounter* XLVI, No. 3 (March 1976): 62-8.
Surveys Léger's life and work.

Fowlie, Wallace. "A Note on St.-John Perse." *Poetry* 74, No. 6 (September 1949): 343-48.
Discusses the major themes of *Exile and Other Poems.*

Galan, René. *Saint-John Perse.* New York: Twayne Publishers, 1972, 172 p.
Full-length critical study of Léger's work.

Knodel, Arthur. *Saint-John Perse: A Study of His Poetry.* Edinburgh: Edinburgh University Press, 1966, 214 p.
Thematic and stylistic analysis of Léger's work.

Little, Roger. *Saint-John Perse.* London: The Athlone Press, 1973, 139 p.
Provides a critical assessment of Léger's work.

MacLeish, Archibald. "St. John Perse: 1949." In *Continuing Journey,* pp. 313-17. Boston: Houghton Mifflin Company, 1968.
Places Léger's poetry within the context of other modern poets.

Martz, Louis L. "*Paradise Lost*: Princes of Exile." *ELH* 36 (1969): 232-49.
Compares Léger's poetry with that of the seventeenth-century English poet John Milton.

Paz, Octavio. "St.-John Perse: Poet as Historian." *The Nation* 192, No. 24 (17 June 1961): 522.
Praises the treatment of history in Léger's *Chronique,* asserting that his poetry "should be read as an exercise in spiritual intrepidity."

Price, John D. "Man, Women and the Problem of Suffering in Saint-John Perse." *The Modern Language Review* 72, No. 3 (July 1977): 555-64.
Examines the function of male-female interaction in Léger's poetry.

Weinberg, Bernard. "Saint-John Perse: *Anabase.*" In *The Limits of Symbolism: Studies of Five Modern French Poets,* pp. 365-419. Chicago: The University of Chicago Press, 1966.
Offers a thorough thematic and structural analysis of Léger's poem *Anabase.*

Additional coverage of Léger's life and career is contained in the following sources published by The Gale Group: *Contemporary Literary Criticism,* Vol. 11; and *DISCovering Authors: Poets Module.*

Vachel Lindsay
1879-1931

(Full name Nicholas Vachel Lindsay) American poet and essayist.

INTRODUCTION

Lindsay was a popular American poet of the early twentieth century who celebrated small-town Midwestern populism in strongly rhythmic poetry designed to be chanted aloud. He is widely known for his often-anthologized poems "General William Booth Enters into Heaven" and "The Congo," which are notable for their vividness, vigor, and popularity with lecture audiences. While these poems secured recognition for Lindsay during his lifetime and typify the characteristics with which the poet's work is associated, their reception imposed limitations on his career, as audiences and critics concentrated on his exuberant showmanship and neglected his deep concern for beauty and democracy.

Biographical Information

Lindsay was born in Springfield, Illinois. In 1897 he attended Hiram College, a small sectarian school in Ohio, and studied medicine. Showing little aptitude for medical studies, he abandoned his medical education and in 1901, enrolled at the Art Institute in Chicago. In 1903 he left Chicago and enrolled at the New York School of Art to study painting. Encouraged to pursue his love of poetry, Lindsay took his verses to the New York streets in 1905, distributing copies of his poems among merchants and passersby for a nominal sum. He then tramped across the country, offering a sheet of his verses in exchange for bed and board. In 1912 he met Harriet Monroe, the founder of the periodical, *Poetry*. She published his poem, "General William Booth Enters into Heaven," garnering favorable critical attention for Lindsay's verse.

Lindsay spent the rest of his career touring professionally as a dramatic poet, giving lively readings that employed audience participation. Although he grew tired of the exhausting schedule, he needed the income. He married in 1924, at the age of forty-five, and had two children. However, during the 1920s his popularity waned as the country turned toward more cosmopolitan interests. In the last years of his life, Lindsay experienced crushing debts, deteriorating health, and periods of irrational rage and paranoia. In 1931, Lindsay poisoned himself.

Major Works

Lindsay's first major work, *General William Booth Enters into Heaven, and Other Poems*, and another collection *The Congo, and Other Poems*, are characterized by their attempts to reach a less educated and less culturally so-

phisticated audience than that addressed by Lindsay's contemporaries. He insisted that poetry is most effective when recited, and many of his selections were accompanied by marginal notations governing the specific volume and tone of voice to be used. It had also occurred to him, in observing the overwhelming popularity of vaudeville, that certain of its elements might be employed to capture an audience's attention. Lindsay devised verse he dubbed "poem games," that required the participation of an audience as well as specific players. The fervent rhythms of Lindsay's poetry are based on those of the Protestant camp meeting. Imbued with faith in the inherent goodness and efficacy of common people united in a democratic cause, his poems encourage the continued efforts of people to better and beautify their lives and environment. His poetic portraits of American heroes embellished history with his own imaginative additions to arouse the ambition of his readers to live up to the nation's heritage; his widely anthologized "Abraham Lincoln Walks at Midnight," for instance, departs from a staid representation or rigid documentary style to present a great leader who cannot rest peacefully because of worldwide strife and injustice. Many of his works also extol nature and a life lived close to the soil, and nearly all affirm God's immanence.

Critical Reception

When Lindsay's poem, "General William Booth Enters into Heaven," appeared in *Poetry* in 1912, it was well received by readers and critics alike. In fact, his first three collections earned him praise as the "people's poet," but critics also caricatured Lindsay as a vagabond shouting his poetry to the clouds and stars as he strode across the Midwestern plains. He enjoyed moderate success for several years, but by the early 1920s, his popularity began to wane. Disparagement of his work became widespread. Although some critics denigrate his ideals and unsophisticated style, many agree that his best efforts are found in his verses commemorating America's heroes. Although Lindsay's work is no longer widely read, most commentators find his contribution to American poetry valuable because of his colorful depiction of American themes and his attempt to address sectors of society ignored by other artists.

PRINCIPAL WORKS

Poetry

Rhymes to Be Traded for Bread 1912
General William Booth Enters into Heaven, and Other Poems 1913
Adventures While Preaching the Gospel of Beauty 1914
The Congo, and Other Poems 1914
A Handy Guide for Beggars 1916
The Chinese Nightingale, and Other Poems 1917
The Golden Whales of California 1920
Collected Poems 1923
Johnny Appleseed, and Other Poems 1928
Selected Poems of Vachel Lindsay 1963
Springfield Town Is Butterfly Town, and Other Poems for Children 1969

Other Major Works

The Art of the Moving Picture (criticism) 1915
Letters of Vachel Lindsay (letters) 1979

CRITICISM

Louis Untermeyer (essay date 1923)

SOURCE: "Vachel Lindsay," in *American Poetry Since 1900*, Henry Holt and Company, 1923, pp. 88-112.

[*In the following essay, Untermeyer, a poet and editor, derides the jingoistic and burlesque qualities of Lindsay's verse.*]

Two impulses dominate *The Golden Whales of California* (The Macmillan Company, 1920); two tendencies that are almost opposed in mood and treatment. Sometimes the Jerusalem theme is uppermost; sometimes the jazz orches- trations drown everything else. Frequently, in the more successful pieces, there is a ragtime blend of both. But a half-ethical, half-æsthetic indecision, an inability to choose between what most delights Lindsay and what his hearers prefer is the outstanding effect—and defect—of this collection. Lindsay, the grotesque entertainer, he of the moaning saxophone and the squawking clarinet, is continually disturbing—and being disturbed by—Lindsay the mystic, the cross-roads missionary.

Had Lindsay been let alone, he would undoubtedly have developed the romantically religious strain so pronounced in his earliest pamphlets—the strain that was amplified in *General Booth Enters into Heaven* and extended in that *tour de force* of spiritual syncopation, **"The Congo."** But, with the sweeping success of the latter poem, a new element began to exert a potent influence on Lindsay's subsequent work: the element of popularity which, beginning by smiling on the astonished poet, immediately made fresh demands of him. Audiences called for more drums and brassier cymbals. And Lindsay complied. The surge and gusto of **"The Congo,"** the uncanny power of **"Simon Legree,"** the basic dignity of **"John Brown"** were forgotten and only their loudest, most sensational, lowest-common-denominator qualities retained. Result: **"The Daniel Jazz,"** **"The Blacksmith's Serenade,"** **"The Apple Blossom Snow Blues,"** **"Davy Jones' Door-Bell,"** **"A Doll's Arabian Nights."** Undeniably light-hearted and humorous some of these are; their incongruities and release of animal spirits are contagious, particularly when the audience helps to make them a communal performance. But Lindsay is beginning to step over the delicate line that separates buoyance (and even boisterousness) from burlesque. He continues to broaden his effects, to over-emphasize his tympanic tricks; he begins to depend too much on the stuffed trumpet and a freak battery of percussion. Lindsay, at least this phase of him, is the chief exponent of a movement that might be called (if the chauvinists will permit an umlaut) an American *Uberbrett'l*. But, pandering to a cruder response, what (in **"The Santa Fé Trail," "The Congo," "King Solomon"**) was dedicated to the shrine of a Higher Vaudeville, is now offered on the platform of a lower cabaret.

> "His sweetheart and his mother were Christian and
>   meek.
> They washed and ironed for Darius every week.
> One Thursday he met them at the door:—
> Paid them as usual, but acted sore.
>
> "He said:—'Your Daniel is a dead little pigeon.
> He's a good hard worker, but he talks religion.'
> And he showed them Daniel in the Lion's cage.
> Daniel standing quietly, the lions in a rage. . . .
>
> "Thus roared the lions:—
> 'We want Daniel, Daniel, Daniel,
> We want Daniel, Daniel, Daniel.
> Grrrrrrrrrrrrrrrrrrrrr
> Grrrrrrrrrrrrrrrrrrrrrr.'"

It is too easy a laugh to be proud of. And in the delightful Rhymed Scenario dedicated to Mae Marsh, the whimsy and delicate colors of Lindsay's pattern are broken by the raucous refrain. Romance yields to tinsel; the gaudy rhythms, the lit run-way and the entire New York Winter Garden chorus are summoned by lines like:

> *Oh, quivering lights,*
> *Arabian Nights!*
> *Bagdad!*
> *Bagdad!*

Politically, Lindsay is even less compelling. He has a score of confident though contradictory ideals, a hundred factional idols. Experience does not make Lindsay more critical; he never seems to lose an illusion. On the contrary, he assimilates new slogans, new causes, new enthusiasms with an incredible appetite and an iron digestion. There is something sublime about a nature that can celebrate, with blithe impartiality and equal vigor, John L. Sullivan, Prohibition, Theodore Roosevelt, William Jennings Bryan, Kerensky, Mary Pickford, localism, Americanism, Internationalism, Campbellism. On one page Lindsay exhorts us to Sew the Flags Together, an inspiring appeal which is preceded by the crude and pompously jingoistic information that

> . . . now old Andrew Jackson fights
> To set the sad, big world to rights.
> He joints the British and the French.
> He cheers up the Italian trench.
> He's making Democrats of these,
> And freedom's sons of Japanese.
> His hobby-horse will gallop on
> Till all the infernal Huns are gone.

And (in **"Shantung"**) there is, in three lines, a significant and astonishing assemblage:

> *In the light of the maxims of Chesterfield, Mencius,*
> *Wilson, Roosevelt, Tolstoy, Trotzky,*
> *Franklin or Nietzsche, how great was Confucius?*

This undeviating catholicity proves nothing so much as the fact that Lindsay is not, as he fondly believes, a politically-minded person, a reconstructive philosopher. In his ready admiration, he is a radiant, undiscriminating emotionalist; even when he thinks he thinks, it is strong feeling that impels him. It is this very lack of intellectual *finesse* that makes his religious rhymes so obviously robust. **"John Brown,"** one of our finest interpretations of native folk-lore and possibly the noblest poem Lindsay has achieved, is full of a reverent sonority. So is that strange tract, **"A Rhymed Address to All Renegade Campbellites Exhorting Them to Return."** And the first of the Campbell trilogy, entitled **"My Fathers Came from Kentucky,"** is even more surprisingly successful.

It is only when one pauses to synthesize Lindsay's attitude to life, that one is struck by his amazing distrust of it. Life and (with even greater emphasis) passion are never accepted by him as conditions through which the ordinary world passes. They are, on the contrary, the wildest and most dangerous traps to snare the soul. In the earlier **"The Firemen's Ball,"** life is compared to a burning building,

roaring with the flames of lust. The fire-obsession persists. Here in one of his most recent poems, Lindsay returns to the fantasy:

> The door has a bolt.
> The window a grate.
> O friend, we are trapped
> In the factory, Fate!

"The flames pierce the ceiling; the brands heap the floor"—and what can save us? anxiously inquires the poet of his sweetheart. And it is love, of all things—The Fire-Laddie, Love—which is to extinguish the fire and rescue them from life! It is a queer mixture of fascination and fear that keeps Lindsay dreaming of a spotless and almost sexless love. His emotions are not so much Buddhistic as determinedly innocent; the great sin is not growing wicked but growing up. In that naïve echo of childhood **"For All Who Ever Sent Lace Valentines,"** Lindsay expresses this phase in another guise:

> "The lion of loving,
> The terrible lion,
> Woke in the two
> Long before they could wed.
> The world said: 'Child hearts,
> You must keep till the summer.
> It is not allowed
> That your hearts should be red.'"

And Lindsay concludes:

> "Were I god of the village
> My servants should mate them.
> Were I priest of the church
> I would set them apart.
> If the wide state were mine
> It should live for such darlings,
> And hedge with all shelter
> The child-wedded heart."

"The child-wedded heart." It is, in spite of a frequent violence of manner, the apotheosis of this poet. Is it unnatural that such a genuinely ascetic and childhood-yearning spirit should overcompensate by flying from the extremes of hushed intimacies and whispered dream-stuff to the limits of brassy declamations? This very backward-turning hunger drives Lindsay to his best achievements. He shines brightest not in the rôle of prophet, politician, or jazz-conductor but in the far more homely part of country chronicler, the reminiscent collector of the strange *minutia* that compose the background of ruralism. It is the inspired reporter that, after a turgid beginning, builds so powerful a climax in **"Bryan, Bryan, Bryan, Bryan"** (that amazing compound of mid-western vigor and American Esperanto) or turns (in **"John L. Sullivan, the Strong Boy of Boston"**) an almanac of 1889 into a humorous panorama. In 1923, The Macmillan Company brought out a ***Collected Poems*** which contains all of Lindsay's previous work, with a valuable preface and several new poems. One of these added pieces illustrates the difficulties in which Lindsay's natural extravagance frequently lands him. **"Lit-**

any of The Heroes" is epical in conception, muddled and monotonous in execution. It is a rhymed list of twenty-four famous characters of history, closing with—I quote Lindsay's own estimate of his incredible *finale*—"Socrates and Woodrow Wilson as the two men who point to the future!" And yet it is this very catholicity, this uncritical exuberance that impels the best of his galloping meters. It is the whimsical buoyancy, the side-spring, the happy appraisals which prevent Lindsay the missionary from completely converting Lindsay the minstrel.

Clement Wood (essay date 1925)

SOURCE: "Vachel Lindsay: Jazz and the Poet," in *Poets of America,* E. P. Dutton & Company, 1925, pp. 229-45.

[*In the following essay, Wood traces the thematic and stylistic development of Lindsay's poetry.*]

The Norman came upon the Anglo-Saxon in one of his frequent moods of penitential groveling, of somber abasement before a Fate breathing blackly. The Norman came with a song on his lips, a laugh in his heart:

> The time will come when caste will fall,
>   And lofty kings be slain with laughter.

The time has been, too; and the Gargantuan mirth of the Channel conquerors drove the bleak deities of their Teutonic cousins to worm into a serf's low lot for long low years. But the worm bored inward: and there have been periodic reappearances of his depressing philosophy and his cerement living. America has been ridden with these ticking borers since Plymouth Rock echoed hollowly to the first iron step. Today we are in the throes of one of the typical Puritanic miasmas, attested by a contagion of movements and prohibitions whose apparent ultimate aim is to abolish laughter and song forever. But this is an old wives' tale in the diverging history of the English peoples: the same somber mood spoke, beside healthier tongues, in serf rebellions, in Roundhead triumphs, in much of the eighteenth-century thinking. It was phrased with succinct perfection in the simple words of Rev. Nicholas Carter to his daughter Elizabeth, a translator of Epictetus:

> You seem extremely found of her (Mrs. Rowe's) writings. I have seen some that have in them a tincture of enthusiasm. 'Tis proper to caution you not to read them with too much pleasure. Enthusiasm grows upon us insensibly.

That morbid son of a Methodist god, Charles Wesley, muttered aloud:

> The reproach of Christ I am willing to bear; but not the reproach of enthusiasm.

With the romantics came a rebirth of enthusiasm and gusto; but these were in time thinned by the Victorians into at the end a passable semblance of Wesleyan gloom. Gloom is a lean road to truth, winding through shriveled,

harassed November landscapes; there are spring roads, and the Normans knew one of them. Vachel Lindsay has taken his reforming text from the purifiers in heart; but his utterance at his best is the yea-yawp of the glittering overseas conquerors.

On November 10, 1879, the poet was born in Springfield, Illinois. He graduated from the Springfield High School, attended Hiram College for three years, and studied at the Art Institute in Chicago and the New York School of Art. He has never married, and has devoted his life to preaching a long sermon on localized beauty. He has lectured for Y. M. C. A.'s and Anti-Saloon Leagues; he has been on odd evangelical tramping trips, from Illinois to New Mexico, through the industrial East, and as far south as Florida—peddling his rhymes for transient bed and board, and exhorting for his "Gospel of Beauty." He has published four or five volumes of verse, a study of the motion pictures, two whimsical narratives of his wanderings, and many pamphlets and dodgers. He is still living in Springfield, with occasional chanting trips as near as the next village or as far as London. One of his rules of the road indicates his unique conception of tramping: "Be neat, deliberate, chaste, and civil." Most of his brothers of the road are stumped by the very first of these. It is good advice, and therefore anathema to the insuppressive perverse in man.

One of his preoccupations is reshaping his native Springfield toward beauty. His advice to me, given years ago, is characteristic of his lifelong attitude; it was given with energetic gravity: "There are two things you ought to do: go back and stay in Birmingham, Alabama; and join the Salvation Army." His gospel is a mystic patchwork, containing such obvious enthusiasms as "Bad Taste Is Moblaw; Good Public Taste Is Democracy." He has wandered the New World to impress upon each man he met the supreme importance of abiding at one's own hearthside: a fantastic blend G. K. Chesterton has seductively elaborated on several occasions. The practice has been foreshadowed by a greater teacher, who might have said that a man must lose his home to find it. Vachel Lindsay has wandered from Charing Cross to Macon, Georgia, from the Congo to Heaven, from the Hills of Han to Simon Legree's carefree hell: he has found himself at home in all of them.

His virtue is the discovery of the thumping beauty in usual things; his vice, a pathetic lack of discrimination which made him at least once prefer his treacly verses to Mary Pickford to the orotund splendor of **"The Congo."** In **"The Kallyope Yell,"** published in 1913, he commenced with a yawp—as American as P. T. Barnum, and as unlike Whitman as "Tam o' Shanter" differs from "Blow, winds, and crack your cheeks!" It is music, as the best of Lindsay is: the voice, the author might explain, should simulate the metallic liquidity of the steam piano in rendering it:

> I am the Kallyope, Kallyope, Kallyope,
> Tooting hope, tooting hope, tooting hope, tooting
>   hope; . . .

SHRIEKING of the better years.
Prophet-singers will arise,
Prophets coming after me,
Sing my song in softer guise,
With more delicate surprise;
I am but the pioneer
Voice of the Democracy;
I am the gutter-dream,
I am the golden dream,
Singing science, singing steam.
I will blow the proud folk down,
(Listen to the lion roar!)
I am the Kallyope, Kallyope, Kallyope,
Tooting hope, tooting hope, tooting hope, tooting
   hope,
Willy willy willy wah HOO!
Hoot toot, hoot toot, hoot toot, hoot toot,
Whoop whoop, whoop whoop,
Whoop whoop, whoop whoop,
Willy willy willy wah HOO!
Sizz. . . .
Fizz. . . .

"General William Booth Enters Into Heaven," title poem
of his first volume, which appeared the same year, was a
new note in American poetry, and a queerly successful one:

Booth led boldly with his big bass drum—
(Are you washed in the blood of the Lamb?)
The Saints smiled gravely, and they said: "He's
   come."
(Are you washed in the blood of the Lamb?)
Walking lepers followed, rank on rank,
Lurching bravos from the ditches dank,
Drabs from the alleyways and drug fiends pale—
Minds still passion-ridden, soul-powers frail:—
Vermin-eaten saints with mouldy breath,
Unwashed legions with the ways of Death—
(Are you washed in the blood of the Lamb?)

They suffered a Heaven-change:

The banjos rattled and the tambourines
Jing-jing-jingled in the hands of Queens.

And when Booth halted by the curb for prayer
He saw his Master thro' the flag-filled air.
Christ came gently with a robe and crown
For Booth the soldier, while the throng knelt down.
He saw King Jesus. They were face to face,
And he knelt a-weeping in that holy place.
Are you washed in the blood of the Lamb?

His is not "that reconciliation of faith and science, this
discovery of a father near at hand within the inexorable law
of evolution . . . (that) we call the Victorian compromise,"
as Paul Elmer More sharply phrased it; his is a simpler faith:

Within their gutters, drunkards dream of Hell.
I say my prayers by my white bed tonight,
With the arms of God about me, with the angels
   singing,

singing,
Until the grayness of my soul grows white.

How many poets have said, or could say, that second line
in sincerity? He phrases his belief definitely in this volume:

God has great estates beyond the line,
Green farms for all, and meat and corn and wine.

There is no more vision here than in a Methodist bishop;
but it is saturated with sincerity. He brings God into direct
human affairs, as in **"Why I Voted the Socialist Ticket"**:

Come, let us vote against our human nature,
Crying to God in all the polling places
To heal our everlasting sinfulness
And make us sages with transfigured faces.

Anglo-Saxon Puritanism, of course, is always "against our
human nature"; it sees in man an everlasting sinfulness;
and the odd remedy, this juvenile conception of Socialism,
will turn the voters into "sages with transfigured faces."
This is an unexpected vision of Marx, Lenin, Trotzky. We
find in anything what we look for: some find in a running
brook good fishing; some, books; some, a mirror for God;
some, a reflection of the stellar universe, as fenced by
Einstein and rigidified by Ouspensky. If we can smile at this
Lindsay, we can at least applaud the forthright vehemence
of "To the United States Senate," on the seating of Lorimer:

And must the Senator from Illinois
Be this squat thing, with blinking, half-closed eyes?
This brazen gutter idol, reared to power
Upon a leering pyramid of lies? . . .

Too many weary men shed honest tears,
Ground by machines that give the Senate ease.
Too many little babes with bleeding hands
Have heaped the fruits of empire on your knees.

And swine within the Senate in this day,
When all the smothering by-streets weep and wail,
When wisdom breaks the hearts of her best sons;
When kingly men, voting for truth, may fail:—

These are a portent and a call to arms.

But portents do not arouse the blind; and calls to arms fall
lightly on deaf ears and asses' ears.

In *The Congo* (1914), the poet reached the peak of his
singing. Some time before, G. K. Chesterton, one of the two
or three most important poets across the water, had set to
deathless music the martial crusade of "Lepanto":

Dim drums throbbing in the hills half heard,
Where only on a nameless throne a crownless
   prince has stirred,
Where, risen from a doubtful seat and half attained
   stall,
The last knight of Europe takes weapons from the
   wall,

The last and lingering troubadour to whom the bird
    has sung,
That once went singing southward when all the
    world was young.
In that enormous silence, tiny and unafraid,
Comes up along a winding road the noise of the
    Crusade.
Strong gongs groaning as the guns boom far,
Don John of Austria is going to the war,
Stiff flags straining in the night-blasts cold,
In the gloom black-purple, in the glint old-gold,
Torchlight crimson on the copper kettle-drums,
Then the tuckets, then the trumpets, then the
    cannon, and he comes,
Don John laughing in the brave beard curled,
Spurning of his stirrups like the thrones of all the world,
Holding his head up for a flag of all the free.
Love-light of Spain—hurrah!
Death-light of Africa!
Don John of Austria
Is riding to the sea.

It was this music, called to the poet's attention by a
literary friend, which came to a new native birth in that
vigorous baritone solo, *The Congo*:

Fat black bucks in a wine-barrel room,
Barrel-house kings, with feet unstable,
Sagged and reeled and pounded on the table,
Pounded on the table,
Beat an empty barrel with the handle of a broom,
Hard as they were able,
Boom, boom, BOOM,
With a silk umbrella and the handle of a broom,
Boomlay, boomlay, boomlay, BOOM.
THEN I had religion, THEN I had a vision,
I could not turn from their revel in derision.
THEN I SAW THE CONGO, CREEPING
    THROUGH THE BLACK,
CUTTING THROUGH THE FOREST WITH A
    GOLDEN TRACK.
Then along that riverbank
A thousand miles
Tattooed cannibals danced in files;
Then I heard the boom of the blood-lust song
And a thigh-bone beating on a tin-pan gong.
And "BLOOD" screamed the whistles and the fifes
    of the warriors,
"BLOOD" screamed the skull-faced, lean witch-
    doctors,
"Whirl ye the deadly voo-doo rattle,
Harry the uplands,
Steal all the cattle,
Rattle-rattle, rattle-rattle,
Bing,
Boomlay, boomlay, boomlay, BOOM."
A roaring, epic, ragtime tune
From the mouth of the Congo
To the Mountains of the Moon.

Lindsay has a tune for all of this, too; and the repetitions
and roars, meaningless on eye reading, fit, when rightly
rendered, into a large scheme of song. The mood progress-

es through an idyl of Congo joys to a more serious vein
of Negro sermonizing, which brought about "a land transfigured, . . . a new creation." "The Congo" is indeed a
singing wind sweeping through the American nation.

**Lindsay had from the start a burly,
swaggering man-music, at times as softly
sweet as bells heard over the hill, at times
as enormous as the rumbling thunder
deafening in the bell-tower.**

—Clement Wood

The second poem in this book, **"The Santa-Fé Trail,"** is
as successful, and is more innately American in theme.
There is a deeper faithfulness to today in making a symphony out of a road humming with motor cars, than in
repeating the more familiar music of savage jungle and
Chinese tapestry. As a soft counter-chorus to the raucous
roar of the motors comes the song of the bird, the Rachel-
Jane, and this typical flight of whimsey:

I want live things in their pride to remain.
I would not kill one grasshopper vain
Though he eats a hole in my shirt like a door.
I let him out, give him one chance more.
Perhaps, while he gnaws my hat in his whim,
Grasshopper lyrics occur to him.

At the same time, a more careful craftsman would have
avoided the displacement in the first line, the inversion in
the second. The third of these chants, **"The Firemen's
Ball,"** is a Buddhistic moral tag appended to a booming
fire-engine tune; it is Buddha, of course, as seen by the
eyes of Springfield, Illinois. Awkward as this blend is, it is
hardly a foretaste of the Sunday-school side-show that
follows. There are charming moon whimseys, **"The Spice
Tree"** being especially magical. With shrewd effect comes
the satire of **"What the Moon Saw," "Factory Windows are
Always Broken,"** and this rounded **"The Leaden-Eyed"**:

Let not young souls be smothered out before
They do quaint deeds and fully flaunt their pride.
It is the world's one crime its babes grow dull,
Its poor are ox-like, limp and leaden-eyed.
Not that they starve, but starve so dreamlessly,
Not that they sow, but that they seldom reap,
Not that they serve, but have no gods to serve,
Not that they die, but that they die like sheep.

This is strong in its music, wide in its vision. But the
remainder of the volume is tasteless bon-bons, or sober
moralizing to the hillocked tune of:

Oh, thrice-painted dancer, vaudeville dancer,
Sad in your spangles, with soul all astrain,
I know a dancer, *I* know a dancer
Whose laughter and weeping are spiritual gain.

Admirers of the worthwhile in Lindsay's singing felt that he could not go much lower than this. The next volume revealed how wrong they were. **"The Chinese Nightingale,"** which opens the book, is an exquisite chant, lighter and lovelier than any sustained poem preceding it. **"Here's to the Mice"** is sharp satire; **"The Broncho that Would Not Be Broken of Dancing"** is effective; **"Simon Legree,"** especially, of the Booker Washington Trilogy, is a strong negro study; there is a hint of excellence in a few other chants. But page after page declaims on:

> When Bryan speaks, the wigwam shakes.
> The corporation magnate quakes.
> The pre-convention plot is smashed.
> The valiant pleb full-armed awakes.

> When Bryan speaks, the sky is ours,
> The wheat, the forests, and the flowers.
> And who is here to say us nay?
> Fled are the ancient tyrant powers.

Few things as unintentionally funny as **"The Bankrupt Peace Maker"** have ever been emitted by a poet of any standing:

> Then he pulled out the nails. He shouted "Come in."
> To heal me there stepped in a lady of sin.

This deferential description is reminiscent of wash-and similar "ladies."

> Her hand was in mine. We walked in the sun.
> She said: "Now forget them, the Saxon and Hun.
> You are dreary and aged and silly and weak.
> Let us smell the sweet groves. Let the summertime
>   speak."

The Puritan conception of evil, it may be noted, is to smell the sweet groves and let the summertime speak.

> We walked to the river. We swam there in state.
> I was a serpent. She was my mate.

His sentence structure at times is as elaborate as page three of the modern First Reader. "This is a boy. That is a girl. Does the boy like the girl? You said it!"

> I forgot in the marsh, as I tumbled about,
> That trial in my room, when I did not hold out.
> Since I was a serpent, my mate seemed to me
> As a mermaiden seems to a fisher at sea,
> Or a whiskey-soaked girl to a whiskey-soaked king.

"This, My Song, is Made for Kerensky" is an appalling philippic, almost as funny:

> The soldiers of the Lord may be squeaky when
>   they rally,
> The soldiers of the Lord are a queer little army,
> But the soldiers of the Lord, before the year is
>   through,
> Will gather the whole nation, recruit all creation,
> To smite the hosts abhorred, and all the heavens

> renew—
> Enforcing with the bayonet the thing the ages
>   each—
> Free speech!
> Free speech!

> Down with the Prussians, and all their works,
> Down with the Turks.
> Down with every army that fights against the soap-
>   box,
> The Pericles, Socrates, Diogenes soap-box,
> The old Elijah, Jeremiah, John-the-Baptist soap-box,
> The Rousseau, Mirabeau, Danton soap-box,
> The Karl Marx, Henry George, Woodrow Wilson
>   soap-box.
> We will make the wide earth safe for the soap-box.

And so it stage-thunders on; while the land to whom it was addressed set about renewing the heavens by means of free speech; for a start jailing Eugene V. Debs and other enthusiasts of "the Karl Marx, Henry George, Woodrow Wilson soapbox." Perhaps the low song mark of the volume is **"The Drunkard's Funeral"**—although other verses belligerently dispute this reverse accolade:

> That fellow in the coffin led a life most foul,
> A fierce defender of the red bar-tender,
> At the church he would rail,
> At the preacher he would howl.
> He planted every deviltry to see it grow.
> He wasted half his income on the lewd and low.
> He would trade engender for the red bar-tender,
> He would homage render to the red bar-tender,
> And in ultimate surrender to the red bar-tender
> He died of the tremens, as crazy as a loon . . .

> > "The moral,
> > The conclusion,
> > The verdict now you know:
> > 'The saloon must go,
> > The saloon,
> > The saloon,
> > The saloon,
> > Must go.'"

The saloon went; this verse remains. After this, we could expect anything.

"The Golden Whales of California," which came next, has all of the vices, and nary a virtue, unless perhaps one or two lost lines of beauty:

> My heart is a kicking horse
> Shod with Kentucky steel.

With this might be mentioned the congruous phantasmagoria of **"A Doll's 'Arabian Nights,'"** and the characteristic **"Another Word on the Scientific Aspiration."** Of course, this is remote from poetry; but it is at least intelligible cleverness of no basement order. It is high above the rest of the book. The title poem has lines of this sort:

Goshawfuls are Burbanked with the grizzly bears.
At midnight their children come clanking up the
    stairs.
They wriggle up the canyons,
Nose into the caves,
And swallow the papooses and the Indian braves.
The trees climb so high the crows are dizzy
Flying to their nests at the top.
While the jazz-birds screech, and storm the brazen
    beach,
And the sea-stars turn flip-flop.

"Kalamazoo" is perilously close to drivel; "John L. Sullivan, the Strong Boy of Boston" contains a nice catalog of the fads of 1889, but cannot be stretched into poetry. "Bryan, Bryan, Bryan, Bryan" is as poetic as its title, with lyric touches like:

Oh the long horns from Texas,
The jay hawks from Kansas,
The plop-eyed bungaroo and giant giassicus,
The varmint, chipmunk, bugaboo . . .
The rakaboor, the hellangone,
The whangdoodle, batfowl and pig

—named among the other supporters of Bryan.

Election night at midnight:
Boy Bryan's defeat.
Defeat of western silver.
Defeat of the wheat.
Victory of letterfiles
And plutocrats in miles
With dollar signs upon their coats,
Diamond watchchains on their vests
And spats on their feet.

By the time we have read this far, we are frankly surprised that the watchchains were not on the feet, the spats on their vests. There is an unexpected note of stately music in the conclusion of this. Then there is "The Daniel Jazz," with lines as mildly amusing as:

His sweetheart and his mother were Christian and
    meek.
They washed and ironed for Darius every week.
He said: "Your Daniel is a dead little pigeon.
He's a good hard worker, but he talks religion."

One of the least objectionable lines of the poem is:

Grrrrrrrrrrrrrrrrrrrrrrrrrrrrr.

The poet tried to write a serious tribute to Joyce Kilmer, a young American singer who died in the war: this is his opening:

I hear a thousand chimes,
I hear ten thousand chimes,
I hear a million chimes
In heaven.
I see a thousand bells,

I see ten thousand bells
I see a million bells
In heaven.

There is much else as depressing, in a less mathematical way.

Here we have the gradual degradation of a great gift. Lindsay had from the start a burly, swaggering man-music, at times as softly sweet as bells heard over a hill, at times as enormous as the rumbling thunder deafening in the bell-tower. He had a homelier music than "Lepanto," a blazing rainbow of colors, a gaiety like "Tam o' Shanter," a vivid primitive pictorial sense. If his equipment had stopped with these, he could hardly have abased his singing to its present state. One thing more he had: a Sunday-school conscience; one thing he lacked: discrimination. Much of the early singing was vigorous, gusty poetry: the later notes are mere robot roars—the metallic yawps of a Frankinstein's monster.

Something may be said concerning the causes of this downward progression. "The Congo" and its fellow chants were great, not because they brushed jazz, but because they were poetry. The few sharp social satires were effective because they were sharp authentic satires, not because they dealt with phases of reform. It is quite conceivable that Lindsay, a popular platform reader, has faced many audiences who admired the first group for their quality of noisy syncopation; it is unquestionable that he has in himself a persistent audience which admires the satires because they voice a moral judgment. Syncopation for a method, reform for a theme, became his practice. Worst of all, he read in certain eyes that he was expected to be a cheap vaudevillian, a slapstick minstrel entertainer. They guffawed at the blare and the jitney comedy; and these are all he gives today, except for an occasional soapbox sermon. It is a painful thing for a deep admirer of the genuine music of Lindsay:

There, where the wild ghost-gods had wailed
A million boats of the angels sailed,
With oars of silver, and prows of blue,
And silken pennants that the sun shone through.

And now I hear, as I sit all alone
In the dusk, by another big Santa-Fe stone,
The souls of the tall corn gathering around,
And the gay little souls of the grass in the ground.

"Who shall end my dream's confusion.
Life is a loom, weaving illusion . . .
I remember, I remember
There were ghostly veils and laces . . .
In the shadowy bowery places . . .
With lovers' ardent faces
Bending to one another,
Speaking each his part.
They infinitely echo
In the red cave of my heart . . .
'Sweetheart, sweetheart, sweetheart,'
They said to one another.
They spoke, I think, of perils past.

They spoke, I think, of peace at last.
One thing I remember:
Spring came on forever,
Spring came on forever,"
Said the Chinese nightingale.

We have rarely encountered a strain in all modern poetry as haunting and enduringly beautiful as these lines, as delivered by the poet himself. And now we must grit our teeth against this stone for bread:

Then Hanna to the rescue, . . .
Invading misers' cellars,
Tin-cans, socks,
Melting down the rocks,
Pouring out the long green to a million workers,
Spondulix by the mountain-load, to stop each new
    tornado,
And beat the cheapskate, blatherskite,
Populistic, anarchistic.
Deacon—desperado.

Grrrrrrrrrrrrrrrrrrrrrrrrrrrrrrrr!—It is a wrenching thing to turn from the poetry above, to the poetic poverty that has succeeded it. The later things are amusing, as Happy Hooligan was amusing, as Billy Sunday is amusing. To this Lindsay has descended: a petty destination, for him whose goal was "the mystery the beggars win."

Vachel Lindsay's position in our poetry is established by the early chants and lyrics. A kindly future can do him no greater service than to supply the discrimination he lacks; to elide the drivel he has uttered; and to preserve the golden residue of his genuine music.

Gorham B. Munson (essay date 1928)

SOURCE: "Vachel Lindsay, Child-Errant," in *Destinations: A Canvas of American Literature Since 1900,* J. H. Sears & Company, 1928, pp. 67-74.

[*In the following essay, Munson deems Lindsay's poetry trivial and ineffective.*]

Vachel Lindsay has a program for an American renaissance and he writes poetry. Since his poetry is the direct answer to his program, I shall begin with his scheme for transfiguring the United States.

The basis of his plan is localism. Our small cities and towns and agrarian communities are to be awakened and inspired to create their own arts and crafts. Democracy is to be beautiful and Beauty is to be democratic and the Church is to clasp hands with both. The neighborhood spirit serving God and Art and Democracy is the force that shall create a rebirth for which the metropolis is sterile. And the method? Lindsay is doer as well as dreamer. He has experimented as a tramp troubadour, exchanging broadsheet rhymes for bread and lodging in Florida, Georgia, the Carolinas, in New Jersey and Pennsylvania, in Illinois,

Missouri and Kansas. He has lectured, read and exhorted in hundreds of auditoriums. He has shown his drawings and published his books of verse and prose, including one on the moving picture as a democratic medium capable of becoming a transforming art for "prophet-wizards." In his home city, Springfield, Illinois, he has performed special missionary work.

Quite apart from the merits or feasibility of his program, one cannot ridicule the earnestness, the energy, the effort expended by Lindsay in his endeavor to actualize his dream. The effort at least is admirable, however deficient in understanding of the engineering technic for a renaissance or of the true nature of a renaissance Lindsay happens to be.

To my mind, it is a bad fallacy to expect as Vachel Lindsay and many others do that a renaissance will come *from below up.* On the contrary, we should look for it to come *from above down.* To clarify these crude expressions, let us admit that we distinguish various levels of social and individual manifestation, such as barbarism, civilization, and culture. Let us then translate these terms into psychological meanings and we discover that barbarism is expressive chiefly of instinctive life, civilization glorifies the expansive emotions (Rousseauism in philosophy, romanticism in literature, Freudism in psychology, and both imperialism and democracy in politics), and culture approximates a balance and a harmony by adding the intellect as measurer to man's practical and emotional life. In addition, there are shadowy records of states of society and of individuals that have surpassed culture to reach an expression of *all* of man's psychological powers—a level that we might call conscious culture, meaning that those who have participated in it have been fully conscious of an intelligible world order.

Therefore, if we agree in making conscious culture our Mt. Everest of human development, we can draw a line from it down through successive contractions of psychological power until we strike the faint ideas, the rudimentary emotions and the physical skill of the savage. No one has faith that the Australian bushman or the negritos in the Philippines will give the impulses toward cultural florescence, but nevertheless very many do talk about such impulses rising from the soil or the proletariat or, as Vachel Lindsay does, from the neighborly villager, which is to believe that a renaissance comes from below up.

History instructs us otherwise. The forming and regenerating impulse appears to come from a leader of great personal development and his band of specially trained followers. Thus it was in the case of Buddha and his Brotherhood, of Pythagoras and his Institute at Crotona, of Jesus and his Disciples, and—less clearly—of the Florentine scholars who discovered Plato and Greek thought in general. Here we have, in each case, the tapping of a source for a renaissance that lies above the level of that which is to be reborn; here we have the generative impulse coming from above down.

Lindsay is right in his feeling against the metropolis, for the modern metropolis represents cosmopolitanism or the transfusion and exchange of cultural impulses and influences *on the same level.* But it seems to me that he reacts blindly when he places his hopes on the communal feeling of our agrarian population.

According to history, the emphasis ought to be placed on individual perfection. The problem of creating an American renaissance is as concrete as this: the development to a high pitch of understanding and power of twelve individuals. Place these in an undecided and chaotic mass and you have an incomparable leaven. In other words, it is a matter of leadership and standards, both of which Vachel Lindsay totally ignores.

Yet owing to circumstances Lindsay is himself a sort of leader. He has an audience but the singular thing is that he has no followers. Nevertheless, we need to examine him qua leader even though he marches without recruits and munches ginger snaps to retain his courage.

Vachel Lindsay is the unmythical "average American" articulating himself in the media of letters and visual art. He is essentially a small town man. He is a Campbellite. He is a prohibitionist and for years crusaded for the Anti-Saloon League: that is, he is a reformer seeking to improve, not to revolutionize, a given situation. He is a patriot reverencing Andrew Jackson, Abraham Lincoln, Governor Altgeld and Theodore Roosevelt and confident of the future splendor of his country. He is humanitarian to a mild degree, romantic in his love of the sentimentally picturesque, and democratic in the Kansan sense. Finally, he has gusto, humor, and an optimistic outlook that covers all his behavior.

What could be more "average American" than Lindsay's appeal to our architects to take hold of the motion picture and use it as propaganda for making the United States an enormous permanent World's Fair?

But instead of becoming a crossroads preacher, Lindsay entered upon the writing of poetry. No one has ever claimed that his poetry was *great* and to-day there is some question even among those who once committed themselves as admirers whether it is good poetry. Indeed, all regret that a large proportion of his poems is flat and platitudinous, brilliant neither in wording or form, and suspiciously subject to echolalia.

If the reader will make a comparison between Poe and Lindsay, he will have performed the one operation necessary for a judgment of Lindsay's poetry. Poe's intellectual power and musical finesse made the epithet—"jingleman"—ludicrously inappropriate when bestowed upon him. But to Lindsay, lacking intellectual power and musical finesse, the term sticks like a burr to wool. Compare only two poems: the overrated **"Chinese Nightingale"** with *"The Raven,"* and the qualitative difference in workmanship and conception is inescapable.

Granted that occasionally Lindsay is entertaining, but both he and we want more than entertainment in his work. We both desire profundity, intensity and imagination. But is there anything profound in the **"Litany of Heroes"** which chants among others of Amenophis Fourth, Alexander the Great, St. Paul, Dante, Darwin, Woodrow Wilson and Socrates? Is there not something decidedly shallow in the mind that can celebrate all these on the same level? And the **"Congo"**—it is vivacious and thumping, but can it be called intense? As for imagination, **"The Chinese Nightingale"** has been called delicately imaginative, but to this critic it appears simply fanciful and picturesque.

Lindsay's achievement in verse almost simmers down to the introduction of those novelties which he now refers to rather slightingly: namely, the booming oratorical chant, the jazz-beat poems, the **"Kallyope Yell"** based on a University of Kansas cheer. These have the artistic virtue of producing new effects, but they have the inherent defect of not being able to develop. What can be done in their direction more than Lindsay has accomplished?

In a word or two, Vachel Lindsay's poetry is mainly an agent for voicing his yearnings and wishes with intervals for preachment or fancies or buffoonery.

Henry W. Wells (essay date 1943)

SOURCE: "Romanticism and the Frontier," in *The American Way of Poetry,* Russell & Russell, 1964, pp. 122-34.

[*In the following essay, originally published in 1943, Wells regards Lindsay as a quintessentially American poet.*]

The country has produced no one more distinctively American than Vachel Lindsay. One cannot think of him without the Middle Western background, with its amazingly dynamic and uncritical spirit of fifty years ago. He was even more unusual as a man than as a poet and more gifted in the acting or reciting of his verses than in the writing of them. In addition to being a poet, he was a painter, propagandist, mystic, eccentric saint, and Middle Western revivalist in the newly discovered religion of beauty. In a society fond of fantastic and exaggerated conduct, he become fantastic and extravagant in the extreme. Although he first attained fame about 1912, better than any other poet of his generation he bridged the gulf between the Old West and the New, between the pioneering era and the sophisticated movement in modern Chicago. The pioneer spirit suffered, to be sure, a great dilution in Lindsay's romantic consciousness. Yet a strong retrospective element made itself felt upon his character. His imagination was colored by family traditions that carried him back to Lincoln and the Civil War days, to the early history of his ancestors in Kentucky and the South and even to a semi-mythical ancestor among the Spanish conquistadors. He had a strong if sentimental affection for American schoolboy history from Washington and Jefferson to Jackson. All his life he lived, as he was born, under the shadow of the Lincoln legend. American popular mythology, from Pocahontas to Johnny Appleseed, captured his romantic fancy. Ghosts of Indians and buffaloes haunted his dreams. John Brown and Simon Legree lived closer to him than his real friends. He passionately loved stories about Mark Twain and Edwin Booth. As he himself admitted, he never grew up, which meant substantially that his mind stopped developing when he was a high-school boy of sixteen during the great Bryan year of 1896. His memory even wandered affectionately back to the still more epic year of 1889, "when John L. Sullivan, the strong boy of Boston, fought seventy-five red rounds with Jake Kilrain." This fondness for retrospection by no means signifies, of course, that he closed his eyes to the present, but only that his imagination embraced a viewpoint formed more in the century of his birth than in that of his death.

The formula for considering his work is a simple one. Most truly American or native to the West are the few poems in which he depicts life directly and simply, with a maximum of impersonal, straightforward imagery and a minimum of egoism or romantic sentiment. Still valuable in interpreting the sentimental spirit actually rampant in the West of about 1900, but somewhat diluted with literary sophistication, are the greater number of pieces by which he is widely known. And, finally, of a small interest either as literature or as a record of Western life is a still larger number of poems of trifling sentiment or pathological idealism. Lindsay's art, to give instances, ranges from lyrics such as **"Kansas,"** a frank, honest, and impersonal picture of harvest time in the great prairie state, through romantic politics such as **"Bryan, Bryan, Bryan, Bryan"** and purer Coleridgian fantasies like **"The Chinese Nightingale,"** to his well-forgotten pieces on Cleopatra Queen of Egypt or on behalf of the Anti-Saloon League of America. A youthful and Western America prompted his greatness, a decadent romanticism very nearly effected his undoing. The story progresses through poems reporting the obvious and external features of Western landscape and society and those reflecting the genuine emotional tremors of the Western people to the sterile fantasies of Lindsay's own romantic madness. The only proper concern of posterity is with his evocation of American life.

A few stanzas from **"Kansas"** disclose his sincere grasp of the Midwestern scene and its people, the endless fields of grain and the rough labor summoned by the harvesting:

Oh, I have walked in Kansas
Through many a harvest field,
And piled the sheaves of glory there
And down the wild rows reeled:

Each sheaf a little yellow sun,
A heap of hot-rayed gold;
Each binder like Creation's hand
To mould suns, as of old. . . .

And we felt free in Kansas
From any sort of fear,
For thirty thousand tramps like us
There harvest every year. . . .

We sang in burning Kansas
The songs of Sabbath-school,

The "Day Star" flashing in the East,
The "Vale of Eden" cool. . . .

We feasted high in Kansas
And had much milk and meat.
The tables groaned to give us power
Wherewith to save the wheat.

I loved to watch the windmills spin
And watch the big moon rise.
I dreamed and dreamed with lids half-shut,
The moonlight in my eyes.

For all men dream in Kansas
By noonday and by night,
By sunrise yellow, red and wild
And moonrise wild and white.

Here is abundant strength with an elemental feeling for the dynamics of nature worthy of Van Gogh.

Such impersonal and unaffected writing is occasionally found in other of Lindsay's work. It invigorates such a lyric as **"Factory Windows Are Always Broken,"** with its proletarian bias, and **"The Raft,"** a sensitive tribute to the creator of Huckleberry Finn. He proves that he cast a keen eye about him by his verses on the electric signs of Broadway and on the billboards defacing the bayside drive at Biloxi on the Gulf of Mexico. His account of Negro festivities in the section of **"The Congo"** entitled "Their Irrepressible High Spirits" has much sound objectivity and verisimilitude. The enumeration of the incoherent events in America of 1889, the poem called **"John L. Sullivan, the Strong Boy of Boston,"** reads like a poetically inspired sociological document. With unusual dignity and restraint he writes on the legend that Edwin Booth first performed *Hamlet* in a primitive theatre in old San Francisco. The most remarkable instance of his fine objectivity curiously superimposed upon a delicate allegory appears, however, in **"The Broncho That Would Not Be Broken."** This poem Lindsay describes as a "Souvenir of Great Bend, Kansas." Its forty lines consist solely of a detailed description of the broncho and its fate. So considered the poem remains both matter of fact and highly moving. In addition there is the more or less hidden Rousseauistic meaning: mankind in general or Lindsay in particular is such a colt, tamed and killed by a mindless and cruel civilization.

Much of **"The Santa Fé Trail"** comes remarkably close to the American soil and people. The evocation of a Western atmosphere heavy with dust and sunlight, electrified by wind and heat, the sense for the boundless plain and the over-reaching sky—all are rich in local coloring. With his lyrical intensity Lindsay achieves what other poets of the prairie states such as Paul Engle or painters such as Thomas Benton have never quite equaled. One of the most brilliant and thoroughly American aspects of the poem is its picture of the interminable line of cheap automobiles, the clatter of their loosely fitting parts, and the varied cacophony of their horns.

"Simon Legree," one of his most vivid folk lyrics, stands midway between his more objective and his more subjective or romantic pieces. The imagery makes it abundantly clear that the poet is thinking not of Mrs. Stowe's novel but of one of the most remarkable episodes of theatrical history, the vogue of *Uncle Tom's Cabin* in its dramatic form which for over fifty years swept the United States as a folk ritual. In so far as Lindsay gives an amazingly lively account of the performance, he remains the inspired objective poet. Of course the entire episode is itself an instance of folk romanticism.

Other of Lindsay's poems are more distinguished for depicting the spirit or sentiment of American life than its outward appearances. Such poems inevitably shared to some extent the romantic tradition as altered in its passage across the Atlantic and the Alleghenies. Their historical and poetic validity rests on the emotionalism native a generation or two ago to the Middle Western States, due largely to subliterary and sociological conditions. Lindsay captures the soul of a youthful and romantic people.

By far the most remarkable of these poems is **"Bryan, Bryan, Bryan, Bryan."** This is no artificial vaporing but a recollection, twenty-three years afterwards, written by Lindsay at the height of his powers when he was a visitor at the Guanella Ranch at Empire, Colorado, in August, 1919. What Lindsay so vividly recalled was Bryan's visit to Springfield, Illinois, the boy's home town when he was himself a high-school boy of sixteen. Lindsay, the eternal child, always loved a party, whether on the occasion of his birthday, a Christmas, a Thanks-giving, a Fourth of July, a circus, or an election eve. Indeed one feels that art for him was itself essentially a party and a festival, so that a backwoods performance of *Hamlet* was not essentially unlike a roast-turkey picnic. Throughout his life he remained tremendously sensitive to the excitement of any celebration. The reception of Bryan in Springfield was probably the wildest and most ecstatic party Lindsay ever beheld. Here was the last great American orator of the old school since Andrew Jackson and the first great political embodiment of the new American West. Lindsay worshiped Lincoln, but always wished that the great president might somehow have been a Democrat instead of a Republican. Bryan answered his every need. The reception in Springfield was actually one of unusual fervor even for the prairie states, for at that time Altgeld, Illinois' remarkable governor, the implacable foe of Cleveland and Bryan's most effective champion, was at the state capital. Lindsay's poem is the perfect expression of what he calls "the ultimate fantastics of the far western slope." We see the long lines of queer farm wagons from surrounding villages, the frantic torchlight procession, and the frenzied reception accorded to the great speaker. It is democracy's proudest hour. Lindsay attained so deep an excitement that his art by no means deserted him when his "cheapskate, blatherskite, populistic, anarchistic Deacon-desperado" left Springfield. His theatrical sense enabled him to bring fine contrast and movement into essentially lyrical poems. Here the reader follows the dramatic sweep of events—the apparent triumph of Bryan's cause throughout the summer, the slow pressure, during the autumn, of the anti-Bryan forces with their enormous wealth mustering in the East, the final defeat on election day and the

passing of the excitement into a dream cherished throughout the years. Lindsay's poem is aesthetically sound as it is thoroughly American. The bold irregularity of meter, rhythm, line, and rhyme, the impromptu style and spontaneous high spirits perfectly wed its meaning and form. Like a thunderous undertone we hear the half-triumphant, half-ominous refrain of political crowds shouting "Bryan, Bryan, Bryan, Bryan!"

Although this ode surpasses in explicitness all his other poems expressing the acutely sentimental temperament of the Western states, other pieces less strongly focused epitomize the region's extravagant, boastful, and optimistic soul. **"The Golden Whales of California"** voices the exuberance of body and spirit characterizing that epic state. It celebrates the San Francisco which arose in thoughtless magnificence from dust and ashes of earthquake and fire. With fantastic extremes of panegyric and bitterness it commemorates a city which has betrayed its ideal. The poem effects a conjunction between the spirits of Paul Bunyan and Saint Francis of Assisi.

A more sustained work of equally exuberant temper, **"The Kallyope Yell,"** has for its double nucleus the famous football cheer of the University of Kansas and Lindsay's life-long boyish ecstasy at the circus. Although he many times attempted to enlarge upon the theme, as in **"Every Soul Is a Circus,"** he merely diluted its meaning, unwittingly accentuating the shallowness of the romantic philosophy and clouding the depths of the childlike veracity. Lindsay's democratic feelings at the circus are much more important to us than his reflections regarding the universe. **"The Kallyope Yell"** is a dashing tribute to the glamor of the circus as it relieved the monotony of life on the Western plains. Lindsay will not have the word "Calliope" pronounced in four syllables in classical fashion, with reference to the Muse, but in Western fashion, with three syllables, with reference to the prodigious marriage of music and steam which stood at the heart of all provincial circus entertainments a generation or two ago:

> Music of the mob am I,
> Circus day's tremendous cry. . . .
> Born of mobs, born of steam,
> Listen to my golden dream. . . .
> I will blow the proud folk low,
> Humanize the dour and slow,
> I will shake the proud folk down,
> (Listen to the lion roar!)
> Popcorn crowds shall rule the town—
> Willy willy willy wah Hoo!
> Steam shall work melodiously,
> Brotherhood increase,
> You'll see the world and all its holds
> For fifty cents apiece.

With a quirk of thought scarcely thinkable outside the western United States, Lindsay finds an equation between the child's joy at the great culminating act of the circus, the glittering Roman chariot race accompanied by a fortissimo on the steam **"Kallyope,"** and the pure joy of life in Utopia or the Earthly Paradise:

I am but the pioneer,
Voice of the Democracy;
I am the gutter dream,
I am the golden dream,
Singing science, singing steam. . . .
I am the Kallyope.

Lindsay also drew effectively from his native vein when he worked in materials of America's almost legendary past, the dim, half-romantic realm of the Indians, Pocahontas, Johnny Appleseed, and the buffaloes. Unfortunately he was in these instances writing of thoroughly mental experiences; Johnny Appleseed and the wild buffalo herds were to him dreams rising like vapor from the soil of his homeland. Hence in these poems the dilution of romance grows increasingly marked. Like Hart Crane, he intellectualizes Pocahontas into a symbol for the poetical and spiritual autonomy of America. Johnny Appleseed he sees through a tender haze of idealization. In **"The Ghosts of the Buffaloes"** he imagines the Indians and the buffaloes sweeping across the midnight sky to vanish in the west. Inspiring the lines is the sense of the passage of time peculiar to the Western mind, itself fed outwardly on the march of vast clouds across unbroken horizons and on the trek of races across a continent, which left scarcely more traces of their passing than the clouds. These poems are American in more than subject matter or poetical technique. The basic temper of their imagination springs from a spacious land with silences broken only by winds and rains.

Expressive of the most exotic phase of American life are Lindsay's poems inspired by the American Negro. With his inexhaustible fund of Western whimsy and exuberance he naturally appreciated the lighter aspects of the Negro heart. His fine sense for the dramatic lyric appears in his juxtaposition of this Negro high jinks with the Negro religion. But unfortunately he understood their humor better than their faith. The deeper qualities of the Negro religion, which have produced their finest spirituals, lay beyond him. The contrast in this instance between his art and theirs accentuates his frequent theatrical shallowness and their quiet sincerity. The highest success in art depends upon a spiritual veracity and an aesthetic discipline which were beyond the grasp of the glittering, oratorical, and external culture of the young and as yet superficial mind of the American West. Negro religion in America, though commonly found in a Baptist or a Methodist dress, is grounded upon primitive religious instincts which exile, slavery, and distress have been unable to destroy. The defect in Lindsay is not alone one of religion. It undermines his whole character, moral, intellectual, and aesthetic. Want of a steady and intense sincerity vitiates most of the lines of **"The Congo,"** like Poe's *"Bells"* a marvelous poem for spectacular recitation but an indifferent work when soberly judged by the standards of true poetry. In **"John Brown"** he comes closest to an understanding of the grave religious feeling which endeared the stories of the Bible to the Negro heart. With a typically bold and effective stroke of fancy, true to the exotic imagination of the New World, he transfers John Brown to Palestine, painting him as brother to Abraham and the Old Testament patriarchs.

Thus Lindsay has left a considerable body of verse which sincerely expresses the American soul. With only a few exceptions, all his notable poems point in this direction, while his still larger volume of verse dominated either by personal eccentricity or romantic literary convention contains little remarkable. It is true that at times he composes fairly conventional romantic verse which, if we give no undue attention to its subject matter, has virtually no national or regional quality. For an almost sophisticated self-analysis of his romantic philosophy one turns to his surprising poem, **"I Know All This When Gipsy Fiddles Cry,"** a worthy epilogue to Whitman's *"Passage to India"* and to the fascination which the Far East held for the American transcendentalists. His well-known **"Abraham Lincoln Walks at Midnight,"** a patriotic lyric written during the war of 1914-1918, is merely in a faintly Arnoldian style. Similarly the perfectly competent lines entitled **"Niagara,"** contrasting the vanities of the citizens of Buffalo with the sublimity of the great falls, might have been written in the East as well as in the West and by an Englishman as well as by an American. His **"Chinese Nightingale"** is an American equivalent of *"Kubla Khan."*

Lindsay's frequent offenses against standard literary taste are due quite as often to prevalent weaknesses in the American spirit as to his own eccentricities. His fantastic efforts to preach the political and artistic millennium in his home town of Springfield contributed as little of lasting importance to literature as to life. To the occasional prudishness of the Y.M.C.A. he adds the unconscious and therefore sentimental lubricity of the American moving pictures. Both his lyrics and his pictures frequently betray a low ebb of American taste. His entire tragic life, as recounted by his friend and fellow poet from Illinois, Edgar Lee Masters, affords, indeed, a fascinating study in cultural sociology.

He assimilated both the best and the worst in the spirit of the American states of approximately the year 1900 or earlier, from Kentucky and Tennessee across the prairies and the mountains to the western ocean. Lindsay is a regional poet distinguished as spokesman for the youthful mind in the outposts of advancing democracy. Despite the raw and undigested quality of much of his work, by virtue of his sympathy with the folk mind he has made a definite if only a minor contribution to American literature. Among Western poets themselves he obviously stands with the most genuinely American in art and imagination. Though others, as Masters, Neihardt, and Engle, have dealt even more assiduously than he with a regional subject matter, they have usually followed conservative artistic patterns of European origin and failed to develop genuinely American forms, as did the ingenious and fearless author of **"The Congo"** and **"The Kallyope Yell."** The rich voice of the erratic artist upon the phonograph in the readings or chantings of his poetical whimsies perpetuates as no other medium the spirit and accent of a distinct phase of American life.

Babette Deutsch (essay date 1952)

SOURCE: "Farewell, Romance," in *Poetry In Our Time,* Columbia University Press, 1956, pp. 28-54.

[*In the following essay, originally published in 1952, Deutsch categorizes Lindsay as a poet in the Romantic tradition.*]

A native of Springfield, Illinois, Lindsay was insistently aware of his heritage. His feeling for the town, half sentimental, half visionary, as a kind of New Jerusalem, is a permanent element in his verse. Among other peculiarly American traditions of his childhood was the fanfare of the torchlight parades at election time, and the memory of them, like that of the visits of returned missionaries, keeps breaking out in his exuberant stanzas. His work is a curious medley of strong local patriotism and the enthusiasm of a young evangelist, seeking utterance in the mysterious music of which, as Lindsay early discovered, Poe was the master. All this indicates no kinship with the British sailor poet, yet Lindsay's verse is suffused with the proselytizing faith of the Quaker lady who rouses the soul of Saul Kane in [John] Masefield's "Everlasting Mercy," and the same poem has passages instinct with the sense of outrage that cries out in Lindsay's lines on the stunted bodies and starved minds of the slum children. The poetry of both men shows a quickness of sympathy half obscured by an oversimplification of social and psychological problems, and of aesthetic problems as well.

Lindsay was apt to identify the evils of our civilization with the brute machine, and to some degree with the Republican party. A few passages in his work, for all their naïveté, kindle with indignation at the forces that sap the idealism of youth and the manhood of the poor. "Not that they starve, but starve so dreamlessly," he says in **"The Leaden-Eyed."** His juniors were to say the same things more penetratingly but with no deeper feeling. There is an ironical fidelity to fact in his **"Factory Window Song"** with its reiterated "Factory windows are always broken." There is not the sharpness of a later generation of poets who had seen more than factory windows broken.

The rules that Lindsay laid down for himself when he tramped across the country, literally trading his rhymes for bread with small townspeople and farmers, are curiously like the duties enjoined on the members of a workers' collective outlined by a much lonelier evangelist who wrote his poetry in the form of prose parables: Franz Kafka. Lindsay had something of the religiosity of Kafka but not his profundity. Nor did his conscience extend to his art. His work is marred by the facile phrase, the stereotyped metaphor, the tendency to inflation that marks the sentimentalist.

His ethical bias tended to put a curb on his fantasy, but it was less hampering to his lyrical impulse. His stanzas are rich in gay sound patterns and have a novel, riotous freedom of rhythm suggestive of the revivalist's shout and the college yell. The poet had an ear for the popular song, the counting-out rhyme, and the "train-caller in a union depot" as well as for the old hymn tunes. Thus, **"John L. Sullivan, the Strong Boy of Boston"** introduces, along with the mockingbird singing in the lane, the shrill voices of the pavements chanting, "East side, west side, all around the town," "Ring-around-a-rosie," and "London

Bridge is falling down." Lindsay's music ranges from the rousing drum beat of

> Booth led boldly with his big bass-drum—
> (Are you washed in the blood of the Lamb?)

and the thousand-throated whisper of **"The Kallyope Yell"** to the plangent sweetness of **"The Chinese Nightingale."** The skillful use of the pause is especially noticeable in the pieces that Lindsay called Negro sermons, such as the half-humorous, half-solemn stanzas on **"How Samson Bore Away the Gates of Gaza."** His performance, like Masefield's, betrays a simplicity of thought and feeling. This may have helped him to enlarge the audience for his chosen art.

Lindsay, too, wanted a public made up of ordinary people, the people whom he met casually as he tramped from one state to another, preaching his Gospel of Beauty, speaking for a "new localism." He found a slightly more sophisticated audience which enjoyed his showmanship but failed to respond as he had dreamed to the civic ardor that inspired it. Like the man who wrote it, Lindsay's verse was the battleground of a zeal to reform the world and a delight in pure art. The struggle invalidates most of his poems, including the one that first brought him recognition: **"General William Booth Enters Into Heaven."** This, the earliest of his works to require instrumental accompaniment, moves to the thrumming of banjos, the calling of flutes, the jingling of tambourines, the hard throb of drums. But though Lindsay scored the poem as though thus seeking to enhance the sense of valor or tenderness or exaltation that a given stanza was to convey, he insisted that "poetry is first and last for the inner ear."

His own favorite among his long poems was neither the hymn to General Booth nor the resonant **"Congo,"** which, though absurdly subtitled "A Study of the Negro Race," is more obviously a study in vowel and consonantal harmonies. He may have preferred **"The Chinese Nightingale"** above his other poems because it satisfied his hunger for melody and color. The poem sets a Chinese laundryman bowed over his ironing board in the midst of "dragon-mountains" and "rainbow-junks," and the great clock on his wall, the railroad yard beyond his door are less loud than the sound of temple gongs and "the howl of the silver seas." The poem has the flaws that Lindsay's work never escapes, but the shadowy visions that float upon the words as upon the smoke of burning joss sticks, the musical cadences, have a lasting enchantment.

> "One thing I remember:
> Spring came on forever,
> Spring came on forever,"
> Said the Chinese Nightingale.

An insatiable romanticism of the kind that was to show itself again in the verse of Stephen Benét and Paul Engle, allowed Lindsay to gild the American past with the wonder of legend and to exalt popular heroes from presidents to prize fighters and movie stars. His starved imagination, attaching itself to the raw America of the Midwest, led him toward the same rootless fantasy that shaped the Wizard of Oz and that is shown up in Walt Disney's versions of folk tale. His verse is apt to veil the actualities of American life in an eager optimism. Yet the giants to whom it pays tribute include, along with the orthodox representatives of the native tradition, the forgotten eagle, Governor John P. Altgeld, who had dared to reopen the Haymarket case and pardon the three remaining victims of that notorious affair.

In **"General William Booth,"** as elsewhere, Lindsay seems trying to recall, together with the glamour of the bonfires and brasses of the political parades of his boyhood, the image of a renewed democracy which floated like a banner above them for the dreamy eyes of a boy. In his efforts to produce a kind of communal poetry, using words snatched from the street, using chants in which the audience might freely join, he was working to retrieve something of that lost glory.

However naïvely and inadequately, he was seeking to express with the same religious fervor a vision of America kindred to that which trembles and gleams and sings in the ambitious structure of Hart Crane's *The Bridge.* The gulf between the achievement of the two poets is enormous. It may be glimpsed in their treatment of an identical subject, the half-mythical figure of the woman whom Lindsay called "Our Mother Pocahontas" and whom Crane addressed as "Princess." Crane identified her with the American continent. Both poets saw her as a kind of primitive Demeter, a native Corn-Goddess. Lindsay was incapable of Crane's imaginative flights, telescopic imagery, and heavily loaded diction. Yet he remains unique in his generation for having anticipated Crane's dream, and he was among the first American poets to find their materials in their native background, to give currency to the native songs, and to employ, if not without a measure of awkward archaisms, the American language.

Albert Edmund Trombly (essay date 1962)

SOURCE: "The Unforgetting of Vachel Lindsay," in *Southwest Review,* Vol. XL VII, No. 4, Autumn, 1962, pp. 294-302.

[In the following essay, Trombly provides a thematic and stylistic overview of Lindsay's work.]

During the early 1920's Vachel Lindsay was undoubtedly the most widely known and popular of contemporary American poets. Tens of thousands of people in the United States, Canada, and England had heard him recite his poems and had applauded lustily. Although he was only fifty-two when he died, he lived to see health and creative powers fail him, his popularity wane, his kind of poetry superseded by another. Now, a generation later, it may be well to reappraise his contribution.

Lindsay was already thirty-three years old when, in 1912, he wrote **"General William Booth Enters into Heaven,"** the poem that won him a hearing and launched him on his

colorful and brief career. At that moment he had been writing verse for some fifteen years, although from 1900 to 1908 he had given his time and thought primarily to the study of drawing and painting. A few of his earlier poems—the airy and delightful **"Queen of Bubbles,"** the stately **"On the Building of Springfield,"** and the profoundly moving elegy on Governor Altgeld, **"The Eagle That Is Forgotten"**—were capital; but they gave no intimation of what was to come. So when the Booth poem appeared in the January, 1913, number of *Poetry: A Magazine of Verse,* it was enthusiastically and widely acclaimed. Here was something strangely new, vigorous, alive, something that people knew at a first reading to be as authentic as it was extraordinary.

The title is explicit: we witness Christ's reception in heaven of the man who made responsive and responsible men and women of society's misfits and outcasts and got them, if not a place in the sun, at least an entering wedge. We are caught up by the initial verse and swept along to the last. A first and indelible impression is of the poem's wholehearted sincerity. This makes it one of the most compelling of Lindsay's poems and will make it one of the most durable. Sincerity apart, it owes its power to its freshness, to its sharply stressed rhythm, to the chorus-like use it makes of a verse borrowed from a Salvation Army song, and to its childlike and effective blending of the earthly and the spiritual. The heaven it reveals—a glorified courthouse square—is just such a heaven as we fancy the lowly folk it receives might imagine it to be.

Instructions for the rendition of the poem say that it is "to be sung to the tune of 'The Blood of the Lamb' with indicated instrument"; and for each stanza there are further instructions as to which of the instruments—bass drum, banjos, flutes, tambourines—are to be used. Obviously Lindsay neither intended nor expected that his reader should hire a band whenever he was moved to read the poem; rather was he suggesting a sort of accompaniment the reader might imagine as he went along. And this is essentially true of instructions for the reading of later poems.

The poem's popularity, as well as the poet's, was greatly increased as soon as he began to recite it in public. His platform manner was easy, informal, ingratiating, his voice resonant and flexible; and his audience found him an irresistible entertainer. This aspect of his success revealed possibilities that he was quick to exploit. People would listen to poetry, if it was intelligible enough to be enjoyable, and if the poet, in presenting it, could and would bridge the gap which so often separated reader from audience. So, making the most of his gifts and of the response they evoked, he went about developing his themes accordingly.

Some of his poems, beginning with **"General Booth,"** suggest motion pictures; and there can be no doubt that his own development was influenced by that of this new art. He even wrote a poem, **"A Doll's Arabian Nights,"** which he subtitled "A Rhymed Scenario for Mae Marsh, when she acts in the new many-colored films." The world of his restless and essentially pictorial imagination was a continuously unwinding reel of people and things in motion; and his poems are the glimpses of it that he re-created verbally. They more nearly resemble such pictures as he would have producers make (in his *The Art of the Moving Picture*) than those they do make.

During his lifetime **"The Congo"** was the most popular of his poems. He recited it countless times; and long after he himself had grown deathly weary of it, his audiences continued to clamor for it. What they never realized—and it would have made little difference if they had—was that they were carried away by the recitation rather than by the poem. Of this Lindsay was well aware. Yet the fault was largely his, for in reciting the poem, he could never resist the temptation to overdo the part. An analogous situation is a commonplace of the concert hall where, as so frequently happens, the performer's bravura means more to the audience than does the music. He knows what is expected of him and gives it.

"General Booth" and **"The Congo"** have much in common. Both treat of a group or a people redeemed, the one from the squalor of slums, the other from savagery. Both make use of alliteration, of staccato rhythm, of sharp contrasts of loud and soft, of visual, kinetic, and auditory imagery, and of chorus-like parts. Lindsay had learned much from the writing of **"General Booth,"** as **"The Congo"** shows; for the latter is more consecutive, more tightly jointed, more fluent. Inevitably we respond physically to both poems, for their initial appeal is to our senses; but **"General Booth"** moves us spiritually. The poet's admiration and reverence for his hero, his sympathy with the unfortunate, these we feel and share; but in **"The Congo"** he fails to persuade us that his sympathies are fully engaged, and consequently neither are ours.

As we have seen, Lindsay was late in getting under way; but once launched, he went far and fast, too fast. **"General Booth"** was written in 1912, **"The Congo"** in 1913, and among the poems of 1914 were **"The Santa Fe Trail"** and **"The Chinese Nightingale."** For the theme of the former he returned to the tramping tour he had made through Illinois, Missouri, Kansas, and Colorado in the summer of 1912 and later recorded so engagingly in the leisurely prose of *Adventures While Preaching the Gospel of Beauty.* The poem is the re-creation in fact and fancy of a day on the trail: the poet's feelings and reflections, the sights and sounds he saw and heard as he tramped along. Again we have contrasts of loud and soft, harsh and sweet, and a chorus-like part in the song of the Rachel-Jane (changing imperceptibly in the closing verses of the poem to the whispered song of the prairie fairies) which redeems the day from utter desecration by the shriek of automobile horns and the roar of freight trains. In calling the poem a "humoresque" Lindsay was implying, no doubt, that it had no other intent than to be fanciful and pleasing. This it assuredly accomplishes; and it affords us a charming sketch of the poet, afoot in the heart of agricultural America, trading his rhymes, drawings, and Gospel of Beauty for bread and a night's lodging.

The metrical pattern is essentially that of **"General Booth"** and **"The Congo"**: an irregularly stressed anapestic tetrameter. In the passage,

> *I am a tramp by the long trail's border,*
> *Given to squalor, rags and disorder.*
> *I nap and amble and yawn and look,*
> *Write fool-thoughts in my grubby book . . .*

the poet seems to be stressing the verses to the beat of his stride as he tramps along. Walking was a passion, a necessity with him. He had already tramped over a fair portion of the United States; and in this particular poem he was on the road again. So it may not be unreasonable to suppose that the rhythm of this compelling physical activity had so entered his blood and brain that, given a propitious opening like this one, it surged up spontaneously and determined the rhythm of his verses. Quite possibly the same phenomenon was responsible, at least in part, for the rhythm of **"General Booth."**

Lindsay characterized **"The Chinese Nightingale"** as "a song in Chinese tapestries"; and these were probably the pictures and feelings evoked by his study of Chinese art, thought, history, and fairy tales, and by reports of relatives then living in China. What he did with these images when—as a result, in all probability, of a profoundly stirring experience—he got them into focus, was to create a most extraordinary love song.

The scene is laid in San Francisco's Chinatown. Deep in the night when the city "sleeps as the dead," Chang, the laundryman, is still busily ironing. Questioned as to why this should be,

> *"I will tell you a secret," Chang replied;*
> *"My breast with vision is satisfied,*
> *And I see green trees and fluttering wings,*
> *And my deathless bird from Shanghai sings."*

With a bit of magic he stirs to life the josh standing in a corner of the room, conjures up a nightingale and the lady he had loved in his former incarnations, then resumes his ironing and from that moment on seems oblivious to all else, although it is clear from the verses quoted above that nothing of what goes on is lost on him.

Now the lady sings to him, calling up phases and incidents of the life they had shared and asking whether he remembers them. It is the nightingale, the "soul of Chang," which answers; and the burden of its song is

> *One thing I remember:*
> *Spring came on forever . . .*

After all the ages and changes, the one significant thing that Chang remembers of all he has experienced is the great love that made his life an eternal spring. And because he remembers it, that spring still blossoms even here in this humble quarter of an alien city, far from the land that was once his domain, and transfigures him and his existence as it did long ago.

Nothing that Lindsay had done thus far seems so spontaneous; yet it is obvious that the poem was meticulously planned and executed. Even in the descriptions of splendor there is an uncommon economy of expression; and the verse is firmly controlled throughout. The entire poem is musical; and the final section, beginning "Then sang the bird, so strangely gay," where what is said and the manner of saying become that unity which is poetry, is surely one of the finest passages of lyrical utterance in all our poetry and comes as close to being purely music as verbal expression can come without losing its identity.

The passing of the old West, of Indian and buffalo, has been a source of inspiration to painters, sculptors, story tellers, and poets; and in **"The Ghosts of the Buffaloes"** we have Lindsay's midnight vision of it. To a galloping rhythm "tide upon tide" of Indians come rushing by, riding all manner of strange mounts—bears, elk, deer, eagles, longhorns, broncos—symbolic, perhaps, of the affinity of the Indians and the beasts of plain and forest. We feel the earth shake beneath us, shudder at the wild cries we hear, and spellbound watch the weird cavalcade disappear in the western sky. It is followed by

> *Buffaloes, buffaloes, thousands abreast,*
>
> . . . . .
>
> *Cows with their calves, bulls big and vain,*
> *Goring the laggards, shaking the mane,*
> *Stamping flint feet, flashing moon eyes . . .*

and they too go thundering by and vanish in the west.

Here, as often, Lindsay introduces, among his loud and robust passages, snatches of delicate song; and these rather than the loud passages may actually voice the burden of the whole. The exquisite song of the wind in the chimney sighs not only for the passing of an era, but likewise for the passing of all things that are mortal.

> *Dream, boy, dream,*
> *If you anywise can.*
> *To dream is the work*
> *Of beast or man.*
> *Life is the west-going dream-storms' breath,*
> *Life is a dream, the sigh of the skies,*
> *The breath of the stars, that nod on their*
>   *pillows*
> *With their golden hair mussed over their eyes.*

Some ten of twelve years later Lindsay returned to the passing of the old West, this time in the muted tones of a brief and exquisite elegy, **"The Flower-Fed Buffaloes."**

In **"John Brown"** it may surprise us to find the uncompromising abolitionist in an Old Testament setting; but on reflection we realize that his "God-inspired" fanaticism seems to justify it, and we feel no incongruity. The sharp etching of Brown in the final stanza, surely one of the most persuasive "portraits" of him, is unforgettable.

The metrical pattern is fresh and apt: brisk, three-stress verses in the first five stanzas, and two-stress, slow-footed verses in the last. The repetition of the *-ine* rhyme in the first three stanzas, echoed in the fifth, is incantatory and prepares us for a strange land and a strange personage. In truth, the poem suggests a vision, a sudden and distinct awareness of something not of our immediate world, yet not wholly unlike it; and we are reminded of Blake's visions.

> **Lindsay's platform manner was easy, informal, ingratiating, his voice resonant and flexible; and his audience found him an irresistible entertainer. This aspect of his success revealed possibilities that he was quick to exploit.**
>
> *—Albert Edmund Trombly*

For the rendition of the poem, Lindsay supplied these directions: "To be sung by a leader and chorus, the leader singing the body of the poem, while the chorus interrupts with the Question." In practice, he himself was the leader, his audience the chorus. He began each stanza with "I've been to Palestine"; the audience (now become chorus) asked, "What did you see in Palestine?" and in the remainder of the stanza he answered the question. This illustrates how Lindsay, by sharing the performance with his hearers, made them feel at one with him and thereby enjoy the poem doubly.

Among Lindsay's heroes were men who had played important roles in our political life: Jefferson, Andrew Jackson, Lincoln, Theodore Roosevelt, Wilson, and Bryan. What he admired above all else in the last-named was the orator, as he shows clearly in **"Bryan, Bryan, Bryan, Bryan."** But the poem is much more than praise of Bryan. It is a realistic and vivid re-creation of the excitement, the hubbub, the contesting forces and issues, the farce and tragedy of a presidential campaign, specifically the campaign of 1896 as the sixteen-year-old boy witnessed it and as the man recalled it and still thrilled to it twenty-three years later.

Although Bryan was at his best in this campaign, his abilities fell far short of his ambition and of the hopes he raised among his followers. Even Lindsay realized this in time, as he shows in the closing verses of his poem where he speaks of Bryan as if he were dead, when, in fact, he was still living—at least in the flesh. But this does not detract from the merits of the poem which is fully alive, well organized, advancing inexorably as a tragedy, written in language ranging from slang to the most elevated utterance, and in rhythms that vary from those of speech to those of elegy. And the concluding stanzas toll a knell not only for the participants in the campaign of 1896, but also for all men who loom large for a time, seem too vital ever to die, and yet inevitably disappear.

I believe that at the time it was written, this poem fell on deaf ears because of the low estate into which Bryan's reputation had sunk. It was to sink still lower. But readers of a later generation, in whom the name Bryan will arouse no feelings of antipathy and ridicule, may reckon the poem as unique of its kind and among Lindsay's best.

"The Trial of the Dead Cleopatra" was written in 1923 and included two years later in the revised edition of the *Collected Poems.* It is the longest of Lindsay's poems, running to more than five hundred lines, and one of the best organized and best written. It falters momentarily in the closing verses, which have no relation to the rest and are purely *postiche.* The unrhymed and basically five-stress iambics, the closest Lindsay comes to traditional blank verse, are a medium that he handles easily and well.

The narrative tells of the long struggle of Cleopatra's soul with Set, the prosecutor, who would condemn it to obliteration, and of its final justification. It may remind the reader of medieval tales of angel and devil contending for the soul of a dying Christian. While the idea that after death man's soul must stand such a trial as Lindsay pictures here is derived from ancient Egyptian religious belief, this particular trial is original with the poet. And romantic hero-worshiper that he was, he accepted the tradition of Cleopatra's irresistible fascination, treated her sympathetically, and saw her vindicated.

What he evoked, charged with his own admiration, and made live again in the hero of his **"Old, Old, Old, Old Andrew Jackson"** was the violent, opinionated, arbitrary, domineering individual, the people's champion who rode roughshod over gentility, wealth, and privilege; and rarely, if ever, did he write anything so high-spirited as is this dithyramb.

It has been said of Jackson that he was more popular when he left the White House than when he entered it; and it is a wave of this still vital popularity that Lindsay transmits to us. And how graphically and picturesquely does he set off his hero with an epithet, a phrase, or a few verses:

> *Old buffalo knee-deep in the weeds*

. . . . .

> *The old, old raven*
> *Lean as a bone*

. . . . .

> *And he thinks of Van Buren and all such men,*
> *Then stands up and laughs,*
> *And laughs again.*
> *For he thinks what all lions think of all jackals*

. . . . .

> *Some men are born saddled and bridled to be*
>   *ridden,*
> *Others born booted and spurred to ride.*

> *I sing the song*
> *Of Andrew Jackson*
> *Born*
> *Booted and spurred to ride!*

The movement of the poem is anapestic, well suited to portray the hard-riding Jackson; and the emotional intensity of the utterance determines the varying length of the verses. So admirably sustained throughout as to seem almost effortless, this poem marks a high point in the development of Lindsay's lyrical gift.

There are others of the longer poems which may be no less significant than those I have discussed: **"The Kallyope Yell"** ringing with the carefree merriment of circus day and re-creating its atmosphere far more successfully than the longer and more ambitious **"Every Soul Is a Circus,"** written years later; **"Shantung, Or the Empire of China Is Crumbling Down,"** a tribute to the empire that outlasted civilizations, nations, conquerors, and dynasties because of the vitality of its culture; **"In Praise of Johnny Appleseed,"** diffuse, yet alive with enthusiasm for the kindly soul who sowed the wilderness with appleseeds in the hope that they might produce fruit-bearing trees for the generations that would follow him (as Lindsay himself was sowing the seeds of his Gospel of Beauty in the wilderness of our materialism); **"King Solomon and the Queen of Sheba,"** which, although it still reads well, gives no idea of the spell it cast when Lindsay chanted it; **"I Know All This When Gipsy Fiddles Cry,"** a successful experiment in unrhymed iambic pentameter where the poet, responsive to the music of the gypsy fiddlers, sees in his mind's eye the whole story of these strange people unroll before him and feels that when they have roamed over the entire earth, "picking the brains and pockets of mankind," they, like other wanderers, will return to their original home, and that he, likewise a wanderer, will follow their example; **"Virginia,"** the wistful song of the sons of the great state who, as they migrated westward, taking their way of life and their pride with them, never forgot through generation after generation that they were Virginians and Virginia was their true home; and **"The Virginians Are Coming Again,"** the last of Lindsay's longer and more serious poems, lilting to the hoofbeats of the cavalcade, strident in its denunciation of the Babbitts, and joyfully confident that the Virginians will sweep them off the face of the earth.

I have called attention to some excellent short poems written by Lindsay before 1912; and during the following fifteen years or so he wrote many more. With the outbreak of World War I, he, who hated violence and believed that differences between individuals, groups, and nations could and should be resolved without it, found utterance for his feeling in several poems. As during the Civil War Lincoln had spent sleepless nights pacing his room in meditation and prayer, so in **"Abraham Lincoln Walks at Midnight"** he appears walking the streets of Springfield by night, unable to sleep even in his grave because men are making war again. In the pathos and economy of this evocation Lindsay has sketched one of the most moving of Lincoln "portraits." Others of his war poems are shrill with vituperation; and in **"The Unpardonable Sin"** he flays the self-styled Christians who deny Christ by justifying, supporting, and waging war, and have the blasphemous effrontery to pretend that they do it in His name. Equally forceful, but imploring rather than strident, and inspired by the Sermon on the Mount, is **"Where Is the Real Non-Resistant,"** in which the poet pleads for the truly Christian spirit, the complete surrender of the self to Christ, apostle of charity and peace. The devotional tone of this poem is not unusual in Lindsay's work; and in the brief lyrics **"The Sun Says His Prayers"** and **"Look You, I'll Go Pray"** it springs from the sincerity of the feeling and the simple adequacy of the expression.

Some of the most successful of Lindsay's shorter poems were those he wrote about or for children: **"The Lame Boy and the Fairy," "The Potatoes' Dance," "The King of Yellow Butterflies,"** the fanciful and delightful **"Moon Poems," "A Dirge for a Righteous Kitten," "Two Old Crows,"** and **"The Calico Cat."** Two of these and many others he calls "poem games," verses that groups of children might interpret for their own enjoyment in dance and play measures. The poetry, he might have said, was not necessarily in the verses, but in what the children did with them.

Youth always appealed to Lindsay; his favorite audiences were high-school and college students. In **"The Leaden-Eyed"** he pleads,

Let not young souls be smothered out before
They do quaint deeds and fully flaunt their
     pride

and in **"These Are the Young"** he exclaims,

This is a chosen people,
This is a separate race,
Speaking an alien tongue—
These are the darlings of my heart,
These are the young.

For the best of his love poems—always excepting **"The Chinese Nightingale,"** which stands alone—one must turn to those written at the time of his marriage. He had known the daydreams of romantic love, and now in his middle forties he had attained the maturity that could make him say,

Only boys keep their cheeks dry.
Only boys are afraid to cry.
Men thank God for tears,
Alone with the memory of their dead,
Alone with lost years.

Thus ripened he wrote **"The Angel Sons," "The Hour of Fate,"** and what is perhaps the finest of these later love poems, **"The Writhing, Imperfect Earth."**

Dear love, if you and I had perfect love,
No doubt we could not face the imperfect
     earth.
We have a little, struggling, deathless love,
Struggling up through the writhing, imperfect earth.

It was generally in his longer poems that Lindsay introduced his original metrical patterns. In his shorter ones he tended to resort to traditional verse and stanza, although in the work that followed the *Collected Poems* he experimented with freer measures, as in this brief poem which he called **"The Whirlwind"**:

Said the Red Indian
Medicine-Man to his son:—
When you take your bride
Be a bull of power.
Be an eagle
Flying over red-eagle,
A whirlwind
Going up a flower.

Milton, Poe, and possibly Swinburne were the poets Lindsay read most assiduously; yet there is little trace of them or of other poets in his mature work. Obviously the poem **"To Eve, Man's Dream of Wifehood As Described by Milton"** was suggested by the reading of *Paradise Lost;* and in **"The Firemen's Ball,"** as in a few lines of **"The Chinese Nightingale,"** there may be an echo of Poe's "The Bells." But there can be no question of Lindsay's originality. His best creations are unlike anything else in our literature. He evolved a medium well suited to his gifts, used and thereby encouraged the serious use of popular language, and favored American themes; for, as he said, his life's quest was the soul of America. At a time when our poetry had fallen very low, he poured life, enthusiasm, purpose into it, made it an oral art again, taught the public to listen to it, and by reciting his poems throughout the land and through many years, prepared the way for poets coming after him. His Gospel of Beauty, implicit in such poems as **"On the Building of Springfield,"** has probably been far more fruitful than we suspect; and his advocacy of a universal church may have some relation to our interest in that problem today.

Lindsay himself was largely responsible for the decline in his popularity. Deficient in critical judgment, he published too much, too hurriedly; and by padding his books with trivial improvisations and prentice work that should have been destroyed long before, he alienated readers and made them doubtful of even his best work. None of his books is free of shoddy; and the *Collected Poems* (revised edition), weighted with virtually all the inferior material of the earlier books, adds some of its own, and is further marred by slovenly proofreading. He published four more books of verse, yet a slender volume could hold all they contain that is worthy of him. And such a volume would have been better for his reputation.

Readers had always been the lesser part of his audience; and by 1925 there is reason to believe that their numbers were dwindling. The appearance of new fashions in poetry may have been partly responsible, but only partly; for some of his contemporaries continued to write as they had always written and to flourish. His listeners, far more numerous than his readers, remained fairly constant to the end; but when, in 1931, death stilled the voice with which they identified his poetry, it dispersed the audience and left the poems stranded and scattered. So, after long neglect, it may be time that we return to them and gather together those we find still animate and young.

Hoxie Neale Fairchild (essay date 1962)

SOURCE: "Overtly Romantic Modernists," in *Religious trends in English Poetry, Volume V: 1880-1920,* Columbia University Press, 1962, pp. 486-536.

[*In the following excerpt, Fairchild examines religious aspects of Lindsay's poetry.*]

Another Chicago School reviver of the spirit—not, in this case, of the art—of Walt Whitman was the folk-minstrel and missionary of democratic "beauty," (Nicholas) Vachel Lindsay. Though between 1912 and about 1916 he was regarded in this country as one of the leading "new poets," he was an innovator only in his attempt to get poetry out of "unpoetic" subjects and to make himself the mouthpiece of the latent creativity of the American farmer and small-townsman. He had a considerable natural talent, a big tender heart, no taste, and no brains. He was too proud of the fact that he had never grown up. Even more than Sandburg he was torn between his realism and his sentimentalism. And while Sandburg was usually at peace with himself, Lindsay "remained . . . the victim of an inner chaos. [Van Wyck Brooks, *The Confident Years, 1885-1915*]. He had both too much and too little education for his aims: his desire to seem rustic and popular and his desire to seem "cultured" were mutually destructive. So few of his poems possess intrinsic literary merit apart from the familiar anthology pieces—**"General William Booth Enters into Heaven," "The Congo,"** and **"The Chinese Nightingale"** (deservedly his favorite)—that we shall consider him only as an illustration of a particular aspect of spiritual pathology. Henry Wells [in *New Poets From Old*] has already found in Lindsay "a perfect example of a Protestant fashioning his own God and his own saints" and of the close relation between romanticism and nonconformist enthusiasm. As manifested in England, this historical nexus has figured prominently in my own studies. In Chapter VIII of the present volume, Robinson and to some extent Frost have reminded us that it is also deeply imbedded in American poetry. Sandburg illustrates the same process, although his Swedish background introduces a differentiating factor.

Lindsay's case, however, is more strikingly clear. In New England and the more sophisticated parts of the Middle Atlantic States, the Puritan tradition has now become so completely submerged that the modern romantic of those regions, unless he possesses some historical knowledge, is usually unaware of his deeply buried seventeenth-century roots. But even today, when rural and urban cultures have been considerably homogenized, those roots are very close to the surface, and often emerge above it, in the Southern "Bible Belt," in the Midwest, and in the

agricultural sections of the prairie states. This situation was even more characteristic of the years when Lindsay, born in 1879, was growing up in Springfield, Illinois. Lincoln's mainly rural-minded little city looked west and south toward the Bible-reading farms and villages; but it was also beginning to look north toward Chicago, where the expansive energies of the Protestant ethos had already assumed their modern secularized forms. And in the great exhibition of 1893 Chicago, no longer content with the rôle of hog-butcher, began to amalgamate the spirit of the Midwest with the trends which had shaped the intellectual and imaginative life of the whole modern world. In the state of Illinois between 1880 and 1910 the main phases of spiritual history from the seventeenth century to the twentieth existed almost simultaneously.

In the preface to his *Collected Poems* of 1923, characteristically called **"Adventures While Singing These Songs,"** Lindsay describes his parents as devout Campbellites: that is, they belonged to a rigidly Calvinistic denomination founded in 1809 by the brothers Thomas and Alexander Campbell as an American version of the super-orthodox splinter groups which in Scotland had revolted against what they regarded as the excessive latitudinarianism of the Established Kirk. "Disciples of Christ" is the official title of this still active sect, but its members often refer to themselves simply as "Christians." Here I am concerned with it only in relation to Lindsay's early environment. It was, he recalls, by no means "enthusiastic" in the theological sense: "Our precise, pedantic, frigidly logical Campbellite scholars . . . were the enemies of all the religious ecstatics of their time, and I still resent being called a Methodist." But Lindsay goes on to qualify this description. The Campbellites "breathed fire, but they thought in granite. Scotch heads. Red Indian and Kentucky blood." A potentially explosive mixture. We may be sure that Lindsay preferred the fire and blood; his admiration for cold granite was never more than theoretical. But although he came to feel that a more warmly revivalistic sectarianism was in closer accord with the spirit of the American folk, as a boy he was a faithful Campbellite. A sister became a missionary in China, and for several years he dreamed of following in her footsteps. From 1905 to 1909 he was a Y.M.C.A. lecturer, and in a broader sense he was a missionary all his life.

As an adult he cared very little about precise theological doctrines, whether Campbellite or Methodist or Holy Roller. Throughout his career, nevertheless, many poems bear witness to the impact of evangelical Protestantism as a way of living, feeling, and imagining. In **"Two Easter Stanzas"** on the death of a beloved woman he relies upon "the hope of the Resurrection" and a loving God's mercy at the Day of Judgment. Religion is a factor in his views on current affairs. A wartime poem answers the question, **"Who Is the Real Non-Resistant?"**, by saying that the only genuine pacifist is he who has made a complete self-surrender to the Prince of Peace. Lindsay offers a penitential explanation of **"Why I Voted the Socialist Ticket:"**

I am unjust, but I can strive for justice.
My life's unkind, but I can vote for kindness.

. . . . .

Come let us vote against our human nature,
Crying to God in all the polling places
To heal our everlasting sinfulness
And make us sages with transfigured faces.

Less narrowly topical themes give his imagination more
scope. In **"General Booth"** he not only apprehends but
quite movingly communicates the authentic devotion to
Christ which underlies what more fastidious and often
more cold-hearted Christians condemn as the "bad taste"
of the Salvation Army.

Of course he is a strong advocate of foreign missions:

This is our faith tremendous,—
Our wild hope, who shall scorn,—
That in the name of Jesus
The world shall be reborn!

We too easily forget that *The Congo* is not a mere piece
of verbal ragtime about "fat black bucks in a wine-barrel
room." The subtitle describes it not only as "A Study of
the Negro Race" but as "a memorial to Ray Eldred, a
Disciple missionary of the Congo River." The theme of the
last section is "The Hope of Their Religion," a hope revealed as the Christian hope when, to the tune of "Hark,
ten thousand harps and voices,"

the twelve Apostles, from their thrones on high,
Thrilled all the forest with their heavenly cry:—
"Mumbo-Jumbo will die in the jungle;
Never again will he hoo-doo you."

Among Protestants of the hinterlands an Eleventh Com-
mandment claimed, as it claims even today, a status almost equal to that of the original Ten: "Thou shalt consume no manner of alcoholic beverage." Lindsay wrote
such poems as **"The Drunkard's Funeral"** in 1909 and
1910 while officially employed by the Anti-Saloon League
as a fieldworker and lecturer. In **"King Arthur's Men Have
Come Again"** he struggles to raise his duties to a literary
level:

King Arthur's men have come again.
They challenge everywhere
The foes of Christ's Eternal Church.
Her incense crowns the air.

In the subsequent stanzas the knights of Total Abstinence successively become "Cromwell's men" and "Lincoln's men." Lindsay would not object to calling them
also "Bryan's men." Though parts of the *Idylls* are decidedly sensual, and Tennyson himself dearly loved his bottle
of port, the allusion to Arthur does not conflict with
Lindsay's principles. **"On Reading Omar Khayyam"** is a
different matter. The author informs us that it was written
"During an anti-saloon campaign, in central Illinois." Disapproving of Omar-FitzGerald's glorification of wine, woman, and song, especially the wine, he shook off the sweet
corruption; but for a short time

The ways of the world seemed good,
And the glory of heaven dim.

Disguised as "culture," the Serpent had slithered into the
dry Eden of Nonconformity.

It is ironic that the Campbellite granite should have been
softened first of all by a parental influence. Like so many
naively aspiring Midwesterners, his physician father and
his ex-schoolma'am mother believed that literature and the
fine arts, cultivated in a properly reverent spirit, were
conducive to the moral and even to the religious "uplift"
of the American people. They had met while traveling in
Europe, where their similarly moralistic responses to the
world's masterpieces suggested that they were made for
each other. They sent their son to Hiram College—not a
deeply sophisticated institution, but the Tempter can exploit even the slenderest opportunities. They did not discourage Vachel from studying art in New York, and they
were probably gratified when he took to the road, not now
as an agent of the Y.M.C.A. or the Anti-Saloon League,
but as an independent lecturer on "'The Nature of Gothic'
. . . approving all Ruskin said."

The influence of Ruskin soon mingled with that of Blake,
Shelley, Thoreau, Whitman, and the later Tolstoy. From
about 1910 onward, increasing familiarity with the British
romantic tradition accelerated, within his own mind, that
broadening, loosening, subjectivizing trend which was steadily but more slowly affecting the Evangelicalism of his original environment. To the end of his days he was often
willing to use the pious language of his boyhood. He felt,
on the whole quite correctly, that it was the indigenous
preromantic myth-language of the America which he aspired to represent as minstrel and prophet. But the actual
beliefs of his maturity were very different from those of his
early youth. Old Alexander Campbell would be puzzled by
a poem which hails him as "The great high priest of the
Spring" and by one which places the district school on an
equal footing with the church as an agency of making

the whole wide village gleam
A strangely carved celestial gem,
Eternal in the beauty-light,
The Artist's town of Bethlehem.

The restive Disciple wrote three friendly **"Poems Speaking of Buddha," "A Rhyme for All Zionists"** and four
flagrant expressions of the sentimental Popery which is
often cultivated by romanticized Protestants who want
something more or less religious to feel romantic about.
Eventually, Lindsay predicts, America

Shall make one shining, universal church,
Where all Faiths kneel, as brothers, in one place.

Springfield would some day become the New Jerusalem of a
partly Western-Utopian, partly Comtian religion of humanity.

These broad views enable him to cultivate stock romantic
attitudes which bear no necessary connection with the
ethos of the Midwest. In **"The Jingo and the Minstrel,"**

the minstrel's "Argument for the Maintenance of Peace and Goodwill with the Japanese People" is that Japan, with her samurai and bushido and the like, is so delightfully chivalric. Her true spiritual name is Avalon. The author of **"The Drunkard's Funeral"** becomes at last the author of **"The Drunkards in the Street."** They are so "great of heart and gay" that they restore to "the cautious Pharisee" his lost awareness of God's joyous omnipresence. Lindsay similarly admires gypsies for their wild free pride and their sense of the magical. In **"I Heard Emmanuel Singing,"** a vague, soft Evangelicalism is used for an expression of the familiar "God is the greatest poet" theme. A more overtly romantic view of the glorious doom of the poet as rebellious demigod is set forth in **"The Last Song of Lucifer."** The headnote will suffice:

In the following narrative, Lucifer is not Satan, King of Evil. . . . Lucifer is here taken as a character appearing much later, the first singing creature weary of established ways in music, moved with the lust of wandering. He finds the open road between the stars too lonely. He wanders to the kingdom of Satan, there to sing a song that so moves demons and angels that he is, at its climax, momentary emperor of Hell and Heaven, and the flame kindled by the tears of the demons devastates the golden streets. Therefore it is best for the established order of things that this wanderer shall be cursed with eternal silence and death. But since then there has been music in every temptation, in every demon voice.

Lucifer-Lindsay cannot feel disheartened while there is a moon to gaze upon:

The full moon is the Shield of Faith:
  As long as it shall rise,
I know that Mystery comes again,
  That Wonder never dies.

But in another poem even the moon is not quite good enough:

My Sweetheart is the TRUTH BEYOND THE
  MOON,
And never have I been in love with Woman,
Always aspiring to be set in tune
With one who is invisible, inhuman.

          . . . . .

I have a lonely goal beyond the moon;
Ay, beyond Heaven and Hell, I have a goal!

Such yearnings are an old story to students of nineteenth-century British poetry. They frequently debilitate Lindsay's efforts to reveal the subliterary romanticism of the American folk through exploitation of its indigenous mythology. Even his beloved Springfield, where **"Abraham Lincoln Walks at Midnight,"** can relapse into the self-conscious literariness of **"Springfield Magical"**:

In this, the City of my Discontent,
Sometimes there comes a whisper from the grass,
"Romance, Romance—is here. No Hindu town
Is quite so strange. No Citadel of Brass
By Sinbad found, held half such love and hate.

Lindsay is at least a better poet when he finds fresher, more distinctively American ways of being a bad one. No British writer would think of using **"The Kallyope Yell"** to symbolize his own romantic faith through that of his nation. I quote most of the final stanza:

I am the Kallyope, Kallyope, Kallyope,
Tooting hope, tooting hope, tooting hope, tooting
  hope;
Shaking window-pane and door
With a crashing cosmic tune,
With the war-cry of the spheres,

     . . . . .

SHRIEKING of the better years.
Prophet-singers will arise,
Prophets coming after me,
Sing my song in softer guise,
With more delicate surprise;
I am but the pioneer
Voice of the Democracy;
I am the gutter dream,
I am the golden dream,
Singing science, singing steam.

       . . . . .

I am the Kallyope, Kallyope, Kallyope,
Tooting hope, tooting hope, tooting hope, tooting
  hope,
Willy willy willy wah HOO!
Hoot toot, hoot toot, hoot toot, hoot toot,
Whoop whoop, whoop whoop,
Whoop whoop, whoop whoop,
Willy willy willy wah HOO!
Sizz . . .
Fizz . . .

But at last there was no more hope to toot, and in 1931 Lindsay committed suicide.

John T. Flanagan (essay date 1967)

SOURCE: "Vachel Lindsay: An Appraisal," in *Essays on American Literature in Honor of Jay B. Hubbell*, edited by Clarence Gohdes, Duke University Press, 1967, pp. 273-81.

[*In the following essay, Flanagan, an American educator and critic, urges a reappraisal of Lindsay's poetry.*]

There can be no question that the reputation of Vachel Lindsay has declined sharply since the days when he won fame as a bardic poet and recited **"The Congo"** to thousands of tense listeners. When Norman Foerster published the first edition of his popular anthology *American Poetry and Prose* in 1925, he naturally included Lindsay and selected six poems to represent one of the freshest American talents since Poe. A quarter of a century later, F. O. Matthiessen in *The Oxford Book of American Verse* allotted Lindsay twenty-one pages and chose to include six poems. But in 1965 the situation was quite different. In their anthology entitled *American Poetry,* Gay Wilson Allen, Walter B. Rideout, and James K. Robinson resurrected Frederick Tuckerman, gave space to H.D., and allocated forty pages to many obscure and untested poets such as Robert Creeley and Wendell Berry, but failed to include a single poem by Vachel Lindsay. The nadir of Lindsay's fame has certainly been reached when a collection of American verse running in excess of twelve hundred pages completely omits his work.

This abrupt shift in critical esteem of a poet who once enjoyed international recognition can hardly be unexpected. In an age of abrasive sound, of deliberate harshness and shock, Lindsay's often musical lines seem to find small appeal. In an age of intellectual poetry when thought seems to transcend form or is even consciously muddy in the hope that it will impress readers as profound, Lindsay's ideas seem vague and naïve. In an age of dissidence and revolt, when nonconformity in both action and thought becomes freakish, Lindsay's romanticism is jejune. In an age of ringing asseveration of civil rights and human dignities, Lindsay's patriotism seems parochial, a pallid imitation of Whitman's grander sympathies which is clearly out of joint with the times. Even Lindsay's symbolism, his frequent use of the butterfly and the spider, of the rose and the lotus, appears obvious and commonplace at a time when symbols are extremely complex and personal.

Contemporary poets have their causes and are sometimes annoyingly insistent in pleading them. It is not only the hirsute folksingers who argue in verse for Marxist proletarianism or desegregationism. But Lindsay also had causes for which he crusaded—temperance, a mild agrarianism, municipal beautification, the replacement of the Mammon-soul of avarice in public life with the spirit of beauty. The trouble is that in comparison these goals seem naïve and elusive. Today's partisans of a militant church will hardly be much impressed by the dream of a world religion in which Springfield, Illinois, would become the site of a great cathedral open to all and adorned by statues of Gautama Buddha, St. Francis of Assisi, and Johnny Appleseed. The Village Improvement Parade, symbols and lines from which decorate the end pages of Lindsay's *Collected Poems,* seems as ineffectual and pointless now as the miscellany of sketches and proclamations which once filled his "annual" periodical, the *Village Magazine.* Lindsay was unquestionably sincere, but many of his esoteric visions carried little conviction to his readers. As he once wrote in his journal, "I scarcely think one thought a year, and visions come in cataracts."

Indeed a chief factor accounting for Lindsay's decline in popularity is the illusionary character of much of his thinking. He had a rich and colorful imagination but virtually no sense of logic. Stephen Graham, the English writer who accompanied Lindsay on a hiking trip through the Rockies, observed that his companion "loves oratory more than reason, and impulse more than thought." Edgar Lee Masters, his first important biographer and an acquaintance of the poet, expressed it differently; according to him, Lindsay's religion made him "myopic to reality." It should be

remembered that the poet's mother, a dominant personality and an orthodox Campbellite, often thought of her son as a great Christian cartoonist. Egyptian hieroglyphics, first garnered from a close study of Rawlinson's history of Egypt, adorn his drawings, and the Orient was never far from his fancy. His sister Olive had married a medical missionary and had lived for some time in China; by sending him pictures of the Kamakura Buddha and other sculptures she provided another channel of images for the poet. Lindsay's interest in the graphic arts, his reading in art periodicals, his vicarious experience of exotic countries— all inflamed his imagination without giving substance or firmness to his own work. As Masters pointed out, Lindsay with all his interest in drawing was never able to sketch the human face.

Any appraisal of Lindsay must of necessity take into account his deep nationalism. He was proud of being an American and once wrote in **"Doctor Mohawk"**: "The soul of the U.S.A.: that is my lifequest." It pleased him to think of an Indian strain somewhere in his remote lineage and to remember that his mother could possibly claim some Spanish blood. Even greater than his profound Americanism was his pride in his Southern ancestry. "No drop of my blood from north / Of Mason and Dixon's line," he wrote in his tribute to Alexander Campbell. His **"Litany of the Heroes"** introduces Lincoln and in the final stanza equates Woodrow Wilson and Socrates as martyrs to a cause, the one figuratively and the other literally drinking a cup of hemlock. A late poem, entitled **"The Virginians Are Coming Again,"** utilizing the title as a refrain, pours scorn on the Babbitts of the world he knew with their avarice and their rackets and cites Washington, Jefferson, and Lee as exemplars of a different code. The statue of Old Andrew Jackson striding his charger and bearing a sword "so long he dragged it on the ground" became a symbol to the poet of native power and glory.

Lincoln of course received his sincerest accolade and in Springfield, Illinois, Lincoln's town, Lindsay was born and died. The poet visualized the tall gaunt figure, still wearing his shawl and his top hat, pacing restlessly near the old court house, unable to sleep because the world was sick. For Lincoln the poet retained a lasting devotion. But Lindsay found American heroes elsewhere and often in strange locations. He imagined himself on a mining camp street in California listening to Edwin Booth as the actor enunciated a "whispering silvery line" which he was resolved to speak aright. He praised Governor Altgeld of Illinois, savior of the Chicago anarchists, as "the eagle that is forgotten." He could celebrate John L. Sullivan, the strong boy of Boston, who "fought seventy-five red rounds with Jake Kilrain." William Jennings Bryan, of course, won his admiration, and in the poem with the quadruplicate title he praised the "gigantic troubadour" who "scourged the elephant plutocrats / With barbed wire from the Platte." Bryan's defeat for the presidency Lindsay saw as a plot engineered by Mark Hanna in which Western democracy collapsed before the onslaught of Wall Street and State Street.

And always Johnny Appleseed fixed his attention, the gentle Swedenborgian horticulturist who came down the

Ohio River with a cargo of tracts and apple seeds determined to distribute both along the frontier. Johnny Appleseed was the man who "ran with the rabbit and slept with the stream" and who as a knotted and gnarled septuagenarian still planted trees in the clearings of Ohio and Indiana. Once Lindsay even imagined his saintly pomologist as praying on Going-to-the-Sun Mountain in Glacier Park surrounded by a flood of dark rich apples.

For a time Lindsay was the victim of his own success. Harriet Monroe printed his early poems in *Poetry: A Magazine of Verse;* and H. L. Mencken some of his later ones in the *American Mercury.* But he won his fame on the recital platform, in a thousand churches, schools, auditoriums, lecture halls—declaiming, shouting, whispering as his lines ebbed and flowed, providing his own acoustical accompaniment, his own clarion and tympani. Inevitably the spell faded and the fountain dried up. Lindsay could and did write better verse than **"The Congo"** but audiences demanded **"The Congo"** just as concert-goers demanded the C sharp minor "Prelude" from Rachmaninov. In a letter to his friend Lawrence Conrad he referred to the poems on General Booth and the Congo with positive disgust. "I have *had* to recite those two poems and those only, since 1913, till I have nearly cracked up the back." Lindsay lost his touch even when he tried to write in the same vein. Later poems like **"The Trial of the Dead Cleopatra"** reveal both the poet's orientalism and his lush fancy but lack the magic of **"The Chinese Nightingale."** In the late 1920's, as many letters confirm, Lindsay grew physically tired and emotionally frustrated. Also, according to the latest biographical dicta, he was a victim of epilepsy. It is small wonder that he eventually chose the path trod earlier by Hart Crane and later by Ernest Hemingway, becoming one of the three great American literary suicides of the twentieth century.

Early in his life, perhaps when he was peddling **"The Cup of Paint"** and **"We Who Are Playing"** along New York's Broadway, selling his poetic leaflets for two cents, Lindsay resolved to write brassy, stentorian verse, verse suitable for oral delivery and immediately challenging to his audiences. He even devised a label for it, the "higher vaudeville." Generations of listeners became familiar with these fortissimo poems, rich in alliteration, heavy of accent, full of spondaic feet and emphatic caesuras. Transposed to the printed page, they carried elaborate stage directions. **"John Brown"** he envisaged as a classical antiphony, with a leader and a chorus alternating, the leader providing the substance of the poem, the chorus or audience interrupting with leading questions: *"What did you see in Palestine?"* **"Daniel"** was intended to combine touches of "Dixie" and "Alexander's Ragtime Band." **"The Santa-Fé Trail"** was to be sung or read at times with great speed, preferably in a rolling bass, the interpreter was advised to utter the resonant place names of the second section like a union depot train-caller, but to enunciate the synonyms for auto horns with a "snapping explosiveness" and finally to end with "a languorous whisper." Carl Van Doren pointed out years ago many of the ingredients of Lindsay's poetic style: the revival

hymn, the sailor's chantey, the military march, the Negro cake-walk, even fragments of patriotic songs. The result of this mélange, as seen conspicuously in **"The Congo,"** **"General William Booth Enters into Heaven,"** and **"The Santa-Fé Trail,"** became Lindsay's trademark and one of the most distinctive achievements in the whole range of American poetry. Even in the booming verses so familiar to audiences there are memorable phrases or lines, but chiefly they linger in the memory because of their stridency.

What readers and critics of Lindsay's work often overlook today is the poet's gentler side, his attention to little things, his softness, his tender romanticism, which led Masters to term **"The Beggar's Valentine"** one of the "most moving love poems in the language." The subject matter of these briefer poems is in itself revealing. Lindsay could write about mice, turtles, snails, crickets, toads, grasshoppers, crows, butterflies, and meadowlarks. The dandelion as well as the rose and the lotus appealed to him, and memories of long hours of toil in the wheat fields under a blazing sun could not erase the pleasure in being in the open air, as a reading of **"Kansas"** will confirm. Some of the larger mammals also attracted his attention, the buffalo of the prairies and the golden whales of California, although inevitably these creatures became symbolic. He remembered the experience of watching hands on a Western ranch attempting to discipline a young horse, and he later transmuted this experience into **"The Broncho That Would Not Be Broken."** These poems are brief, whimsical, sometimes wryly humorous, though in general humor was not Lindsay's forte. There is probably no better example of the poet's delicate touch than **"What the Rattlesnake Said"**:

> The moon's a little prairie-dog,
> He shivers through the night.
> He sits upon his hill and cries
> For fear that *I* will bite.

Here the sly anthropomorphism, the simple language, the use of the familiar ballad stanza in an unpretentious lyric—all suggest Lindsay's deftness.

As a love poet Lindsay was generally less successful. He seemed unable to get away from triteness and conventional hyperbole. Early poems to unknown inamoratas are hardly memorable. **"With a Rose, to Brunhilde"** was addressed to Olivia Roberts, a Springfield neighbor and writer who attracted him briefly. Sara Teasdale, to whom he dedicated his *Collected Poems,* was his Gloriana, but although he exaggerated her physical qualities (her "burning golden eyes" and her "snowy throat"), his romantic admiration for her never achieved impressive form. Briefly he thought that a girl he had met while he was teaching at Gulf Park Junior College in Mississippi, Elizabeth Wills, was his Dulcinea, but although he compared her to a bird's wing which "spreads above my sky," his devotion was not transformed into imperishable verse and his offer of marriage was spurned. After his marriage in 1925 to Elizabeth Conner he published a number of love poems, collected in *The Candle in the Cabin* and suffused with a romantic color, but this "weaving together of script and singing," as the subtitle has it, is not particularly successful. Most of the poems reflect the Glacier Park scenes which the couple viewed on their honeymoon, and even the landscape descriptions are curiously subdued and flat.

The subjects which moved Lindsay most deeply were places and people intimately associated with his own early life, or subjects with which he could achieve a family and almost a racial intimacy. **"The Proud Farmer,"** a quietly impressive tribute to his maternal grandfather E. S. Frazee which in tone and workmanship reminds one of Masters's tribute to his own grandmother, "Lucinda Matlock," is genuine and devoted. The Hoosier preacher-farmer who read by night and built his world by day left an indelible mark on both his daughter and his grandson and became the subject of one of Lindsay's best elegies. **"Dr. Mohawk,"** the account of a half-mythical figure who is both the poet's putative aboriginal ancestor and his physician father, suggests the son's fear of and respect for his parent and Dr. Lindsay's understandable bewilderment at the occasional behavior of his gifted son. **"Billboards and Galleons,"** inscribed to Stephen Graham, is a fantasy inspired by his days at Biloxi and contains the reference to Don Ivan, his Spanish ancestor, whom Lindsay conceived as a friend of Columbus and a guest of Queen Isabella.

Lindsay's natal town of Springfield, even though he spent many years away from it, always cast a spell on him. His hope for the future of the community was unrealistic but genuine. "A city is not builded in a day," he declared and added that a great city need not be large; neither Athens nor Florence achieved immensity. What was needed most was "many Lincoln-hearted men." He certainly envisaged the Village Improvement Parade as taking place in Springfield and hoped that farm boys, builders, craftsmen, marchers of all kinds carrying banners inscribed with slogans would bring about a municipal revolution. But even though the slogans might win approval ("Bad public taste is mob law—good public taste is democracy"), the parade in Springfield or anywhere else never got started. To his chagrin Springfield remained the city of his discontent.

Of a different nature were the tributes paid to public figures, the well-known encomiums to Jackson, Lincoln, Altgeld, Bryan, Alexander Campbell, Governor Bob Taylor of Tennessee, sincere if not always highly perceptive, terse characterizations which seized upon familiar details and phrased them memorably. Lindsay attempted no career judgment but sought rather a brief illumination, a vision of light or a brilliant profile, and often achieved more than pages of expository prose could do.

Some of his most striking effects occur in poems less familiar than **"The Congo"** or **"The Santa-Fé Trail"** although he employed identical methods. **"Simon Legree— A Negro Sermon,"** the first part of the Booker T. Washington trilogy, is a fanciful account of a meeting between the ignominious overseer and the Devil in Hell where each tries to outdo the other in viciousness. Legree's puffed-out cheeks which were a fish-belly white in color probably owe something to Mark Twain's description of Huck's father but are not necessarily less vivid because of the

similarity, and the picture we are given of the overseer gambling, eating, and drinking with the Devil on his wide green throne is one of Lindsay's magnificent achievements. Equally vivid is **"The Ghost of the Buffaloes"** with its extraordinary picture of the animals stampeding madly,

> Stamping flint feet, flashing moon eyes,
> Pompous and owlish, shaggy and wise.

One remembers, too, the parade of fabulous animals invoked in **"Bryan, Bryan, Bryan, Bryan,"** the bungaroo and giassicus, the rakaboor and hellangone, all mixed up with prairie dog and horned toad and longhorn. In a very different key is the poem **"I Know All This When Gipsy Fiddles Cry"** in which his own experiences on the open road, begging and tramping in a way that Whitman never did, breed a sympathy in him for those wanderers who for centuries have been itinerant without losing their identity or their interest.

The critics have not always been kind to Lindsay, although he has had his defenders. Conrad Aiken, writing in *Scepticisms* in 1919, was willing to credit the poet with originality but objected to the orotund style, the echolalia, the banalities. He also found fault with Lindsay for being overly topical, thus denying him the very virtue celebrated by others of making use of the American scene in a frank and unhackneyed manner. Aiken gave Lindsay small chance for survival unless he abandoned the traits which inhere basically in the higher vaudeville. Llewellyn Jones was less harsh, but he also preferred the quieter poems. Yet he felt that some of Lindsay's tributes might well be grouped together into a kind of American hagiography. T. K. Whipple in *Spokesmen* asserted categorically that Lindsay was the author of *six* poems, the chosen six including of course all the famous bravura pieces plus **"The Chinese Nightingale."** Writing in 1928, only three years before the poet's death, Whipple could say, "His achievement has not yet been commensurate with his possibilities." Stephen Graham in a kind of obituary letter alluded to Lindsay's bitter disillusionment in love and to his deliberating grief at the time his mother died; he also termed Lindsay the greatest American poet of his age. Willard Thorp wrote in the *Literary History of the United States* that the twenty or so of Lindsay's poems which the poet's audiences clamored to hear over and over again "are as exciting as when they were first declaimed." William Rose Benét was convinced that Lindsay's best work would be read with admiration by posterity at the very time that he as the editor of an important literary periodical was constrained to refuse the poet's latest productions.

Ludwig Lewisohn, William Marion Reedy, and Carl Van Doren all thought highly of Lindsay's gifts although none was willing to deny obvious imperfections. In *Many Minds* Van Doren pointed out Lindsay's limited range but praised him for his free use of the American language, for his willingness to introduce a new idiom into poetic practice. Edgar Lee Masters cited nine poems as being among the poet's best, added another twenty as being significant, and concluded that collectively these poems constituted "the most considerable body of imaginative lyricism that any American has produced." To offset this enthusiasm one might allude to Allen Tate's cautious assertion that Lindsay's early poems had an original rhythm but that his use of language was undistinguished and his poetic subjects on the whole rather dull. Horace Gregory and Marya Zaturenska in their *History of American Poetry* quote liberally and approvingly from Lindsay, although they discourage anyone from reading through the **Collected Poems** and feel that some of the verse would not have been allowed to stand if Lindsay himself had been a more reliable self-critic. It is interesting that they found **"I Heard Immanuel Singing"**—a poem which Lindsay himself treasured—a valuable and interesting American spiritual.

In one of the last poems of the late Theodore Roethke, entitled "Supper with Lindsay," the author imagined Lindsay stepping into his chamber carrying the moon under his arm and deluging the furniture with a flood of creamy light. The two poets ate a meal of homely food together—corn bread, cold roast beef, and ice cream—until the lunar glow began to fade. With that change Lindsay decided that the feast was over and rose to depart, asking as he did so to be remembered to William Carlos Williams and Robert Frost. Of the three names Lindsay's in his time was the best known, as celebrated as a platform performer and declaimer as the Russian poet Andrei Voznesensky is today. Lindsay's verse has earned him a permanent place in American literature, and future anthologists who deny him that place will reflect only their own myopic vision.

Ann Massa (essay date 1968)

SOURCE: "The Artistic Conscience of Vachel Lindsay," in *Journal of American Studies,* Vol. 2, No. 2, October, 1968, pp. 239-52.

[*In the following excerpt, Massa, author of* Vachel Lindsay: Fieldworker for the American Dream, *explores the relationship between Lindsay's artistic awareness and his social conscience.*]

Lindsay was convinced of the existence of a national *malaise*; and it was this conviction which diverted his artistic conscience into social channels. He was worried about amorality, conspicuous consumption, and urban eyesores. He was horrified by the perversion of electoral processes at city level, and by scandals at Federal Government level. Darwinistic indifference to social and financial inequalities appalled him; so did the jungle that awaited immigrants. Dedicated materialism was gaining adherence, while traditional standards of religion and morality, to which he subscribed, were slipping.

He determined to stir up awareness of these alarming tendencies; and in the *War Bulletins* of 1909 (his privately printed monthly journal, which only ran to five issues) and in **'The Golden Whales of California'** . . . he fulminated against the almighty dollar. To counteract American 'deviationism' he put together his gospel of (oecumencial) Religion, (moral) Beauty, and (socialist) Equality; and

through a series of poems on American history and myth—**"Our Mother Pocahontas"**, **"In Praise of Johnny Appleseed"**, **"Old, Old, Old Andrew Jackson"**, **"Abraham Lincoln Walks at Midnight"**, **"Bryan, Bryan, Bryan, Bryan"**, **"The Eagle That Is Forgotten"** (John Peter Altgeld), and **"Roosevelt"**—he tried to establish an American entity. It is in such social contexts that the bulk of Lindsay's writings become comprehensible. . . .

Lindsay moved in the theological milieu of the reform impulse of the first two decades of the twentieth century. He had points of contact with the political theories of Herbert Croly, the economic panaceas of Henry George, the Social Gospel of Walter Rauschenbusch, and the muckraking activities of Henry Demarest Lloyd. But his diagnosis of the national *malaise* was too grim for him to affiliate himself with men whose vision of a root evil, and whose advocacy of one-stroke remedies—the readjustment of constitutional checks and balances, a Single Tax, the municipal ownership of utilities, trustbusting—sprang from basic confidence in a just off-course, easily righted America. Lindsay was not so sanguine. He considered America's problems were as much the formidable problems of mentality as the soluble ones of institutional defects. For him the American Dream had become 'a middle-class aspiration built on a bog of toil-sodden minds'.

In the 1920s his brand of pessimistic realism made him an even more alien figure. 'Arm yourself against the worst so that disappointment in humanity is impossible' he had noted in his diary; and he had too few expectations to be disillusioned by the 1914-18 war, or by the Peace of Versailles (in his eyes it was a step forward that the idea of international government had been given top-level airing). As an internationalist he found it hard to condone American isolationism and crudely domestic Presidential criteria; as a conscientious practitioner of the kind of Christian morality that was preached in the Mid-west bible belt he could not come to terms with the decade's frenetic relaxation of taboos and its cultivation of materialism for its own sake.

But it was not solely in his capacity as an American citizen that Lindsay took it upon himself to criticize and protest; if the national need arose, the artist, as an individual with exceptional talents of perception and expression, had a duty to practise remedial art. Lindsay thus had a writer's concern with style and form; but the nature of his concern was idiosyncratic. He believed that a writer's duty was not to himself, but to his audience, which should be all-class and nation-wide. His artistic conscience told him to put matter and mass appeal before self-expression and aesthetics. Form was to follow the function of social utility.

In 1915 in *The Art of the Moving Picture,* and again in the 1922 edition, Lindsay hailed the motion picture as the most important artistic event of his lifetime. Not only could it lure people in for entertainment, and proceed to please whilst insidiously educating; it was an art form, with an art form's power to regenerate and refine. He tried to imitate it by making his writing a deceptive art for the people.

This stance was as extreme as art for art's sake, and as open to disputation. The logic of Lindsay's theory placed severe limitations on subtleties of construction and vocabulary; obliqueness was at a premium when the common man was the envisaged audience. For, while Lindsay believed in a dormant equality of taste, the American masses he was writing for were at the stage when 'they love best neither the words that explain, nor the fancies that are fine, nor the voice that is articulate with well-chosen speech'. They only responded to emotional, raucous modes of expression, and 'words must be chosen accordingly'.

It could be argued that Lindsay's disregard for traditional refinements of style, and for the Imagist experiments of the New Poetry, was less revolutionary and independent than it seemed. One of his talents was for the production of large, generous, rumbustious verse, which flowed along in spite of its imperfections, and without a great deal of stylistic reworking. A poet of emotion rather than one of intellectual discipline, he had a voracious appetite for recitation, both professionally (from 1913 to 1931) and in his leisure time at home. His conscientious response to duty, in fact, came easily, fulfilled his dramatic dimension, and involved genuine pleasure.

But talent and enjoyment did not guide his conscience; on the contrary, he almost failed to make the connexion. The national literary circuit acclaimed the choruses in **"The Congo"** of 'Boomlay, boomlay, boomlay, Boom', and 'Mumbo-Jumbo will hoo-doo you'; but Lindsay wondered whether he was writing poetry. After all, he admitted, 'one composes it not by listening to the inner voice and following the gleam, but pounding the table and looking out of the window at electric signs'. Even a prize from *Poetry* in 1913 for **"General William Booth . . . "** did not still his doubts; it took the approval of William Butler Yeats to do that.

Lindsay and Yeats met at a dinner party given by Harriet Monroe for Yeats in Chicago in March 1914. Lindsay's recitation of **"The Congo"** was the sensation of the evening, and impressed Yeats. In after-dinner conversation with Lindsay he preached the virtues of folk-culture, and told Lindsay that all that survived in America of the much-to-be-desired 'primitive singing of poetry' and the Greek lyric chant was American vaudeville and Vachel Lindsay. The *imprimatur* reconciled Lindsay to his achievement; a man whose artistic conscience was avowedly a social conscience was bound to develop what he came to call 'The Higher Vaudeville'. . . .

To emphasize that his aim was more serious than vaudeville's, and to counteract its slapstick and revue connotations, Lindsay coined the phrase 'The Higher Vaudeville' to describe the poems he wrote in 'a sort of ragtime manner that deceives them [the American masses] into thinking they are at the vaudeville'. In spite of the rag-time manner he was 'trying to keep it to an art': it was a refined vaudeville, which sprang from his sensitive, critical response to American society, and his awareness of 'democracy [which] is itself a paradox'. Any beauty the Higher Vaudeville might describe or create was as paradoxical as democracy. . . .

One might usefully coin a . . . term, Higher Chautauqua, to convey what Lindsay was trying to achieve in the Higher Vaudeville, and throughout his writings. The Chautauqua movement (1875-*c*. 1925), which carried on the popular educational traditions of the lyceums with correspondence courses and tours of eminent speakers ranging from Phineas Taylor Barnum to William Rainey Harper, was a uniquely effective way of communicating with the adult population. Chautauqua's aim was mass morality and mass education, McGuffey-style; and Chautauqua's realistic and successful technique was to insert entertainments—minstrels, opera singers, circus acts—among its educational items, or even to disguise education as entertainment. . . .

The Higher Vaudeville coincided with the pre-war heyday of Imagism, a movement which reflected precisely that dedication to form for form's sake, to the intrinsic worth of beautifully constructed, but comparatively unread and unheard poems, which Lindsay opposed. He scornfully called the imagists 'the Aesthetic Aristocracy', who 'were singing on an island to one another while the people perish'. Ezra Pound, *imagiste,* spoke for this school when he gleefully noted in July 1918 about the fourth volume of *The Little Review:* 'The response has been oligarchic; the plain man, in his gum overshoes, with his touching belief in W. J. Bryan, is not with us.' In the September issue, Lindsay was stung into an equally exaggerated, but telling response: 'I write for the good-hearted People of the Great Pure Republic.

He might be writing for the people; but was he reaching them? Lindsay found himself in a quandary. He had the message—but had he found the medium? Higher Vaudeville recitations brought in a large audience, and reached a new set of hearers (and sometimes readers): the American *bourgeoisie*. But Lindsay gradually realized that audiences enjoyed and remembered **'The Kallyope Yell,'** for instance, because that poem revived memories of steam and circus, and not because he had made the calliope an image of bathetic democracy in the lines

> I am but the poineer
> Voice of the Democracy;
> I am the gutter dream
> I am the golden dream
> Singing science, singing steam. . . .

As well as becoming dissatisfied with audience responses, Lindsay came to feel the difficulty of tying the Higher Vaudeville, a natural 'fun' medium, to serious topics; and he began to think of other media and other audiences. He was learning the hard way what Albert McLean noted about vaudeville, that 'cause and effect relationships were completely bypassed, the question of ultimate ends was never raised, and the problem of higher values could be submerged in waves of pathos and humor'. But up to 1920 he continued to operate within the limitations of his audiences; the acclaim he received from 1913 to 1920, however narrowly based, was exhilarating, and must have seemed to him to augur well for the popularization of his ideas through literature. However, in 1920 the tide swung against him. The Higher Vaudeville was no longer a novelty, and his unfashionable artistic conscience would not allow him to project universal dilemmas in personal terms, as Hemingway and Fitzgerald did so successfully. And in 1920 his message in its most studied form, *The Golden Book of Springfield,* flopped. Ironically, its failure was partly due to the logic of Higher Chautauqua. Lindsay was still orienting himself to an all-class audience, and tempered his discussion of social and political trends with a linking fantasy-cum-story. The end-product was an incongruous mixture of the sane and the silly, which irritated serious readers, and bored the rest. Stylistically, the sentiment and rhetoric which he could control in poetry ran away with him in prose. Digressions and exaggerations spilled over one another. But what uncomfortably persistent critique would have been acceptable in 1920, except Mencken's unique brand? Lindsay had picked the wrong moment to be preoccupied with what Americans ought to be: hedonism was about to set in. Today, the sombre fascination of Lindsay's perceptions redeems the book; an ironic reversal of the stylistic success of the Higher Vaudeville. In neither case was the medium the message.

Lindsay hung on to his belief in equality of taste; but he concluded that mass potential was more deeply buried than he had imagined, and mass crassness more deeply rooted. He decided to concentrate on élite audiences, who might read his books, and respond to his schemes: on teachers, students, journalists, businessmen and local dignitaries. Higher Chautauqua techniques were not applicable to these audiences; and he approached them differently. He prepared the ground by sending out a circular letter, 'The kind of visit I like to make'. The letter adjured journalists to teach his verses 'by running them in the newspaper with paraphrases and local applications by the editor'; and made it clear that Lindsay expected the English teachers to have his books 'in the school library or the public library the month beforehand. I mean nothing whatever to an audience unfamiliar with my work . . . I want every member of my audience to have at least some knowledge of these books. When he lectured on one particular book, 'Dear reader, either bring the book or stay away!' . . . At one time he made the half-serious suggestion that only those who could pass an examination on his books should be admitted to his recital/lectures.

Lindsay's attitude to his audience was barely recognizable as that of a creative writer seeking a hearing. He had come to think of himself as a teacher, and of his writings as textbooks. He had obviously become irritated and impatient, for he believed, however mistakenly, that he was offering a vital service to a public which would not avail itself of the service. An element of compensatory, personal arrogance was involved; but so was a generic, artistic arrogance. . . .

To his contemporaries Lindsay's work seemed stagnant and retrospective, though in content, if not in style, it was naggingly valid. In one sense, however, he was an anachronism: he was a precursor and practitioner of present-day 'pop art'. He affirmed that popular taste—'the human soul in action'—was a neo-artistic perception; and he, as an artist, by acts of will, representation and reproduction,

made this perception total art. Mass consensus had made Mary Pickford a folk-culture queen; and Lindsay repeatedly celebrated her national visual impact in a way comparable to Andy Warhol's statement-painting 'Marilyn Monroe', which consists of repeated rows of her face. The American collage of popcorn and yellow cabs, 'Arrow-collar heroes' and the Star Spangled Banner preoccupied him as realistically and sentimentally as it does many pop artists. And, just as pop artists let others finish their creations, and have them mass-produced, Lindsay, with the same mixture of arrogance and humility, urged other people to adapt and rewrite his work—though he was too far ahead of his times to be taken at his word.

Lindsay diverged from the main stream of pop art in that his aim was propaganda; pop artists tend to draw the line at comment. He was as much concerned to create as to accept popular culture, and he was interested in new media for the specific purposes of uplifting and educating the masses. Yet his enthusiastic support of the motion picture bears comparison with the pop-art theory of the interchangeability of words and pictures, and the communication potential of a nationally recognized alphabet of images. 'Edison is the new Gutenberg. He has invented the new printing', Lindsay wrote; and he went so far as to try his own hand at a new word/picture art which he called 'hieroglyphics': an entirely public art, an easily identified currency of national symbols. His nearest approximation of a successful hieroglyphic was the drawing of a lotus/rose . . . to celebrate the East/West symbolism of the Panama Canal; a pacific symbolism that would have found one American dissenter in T. R.! Motion pictures were hieroglyphics of a more complex sort. They were sculpture-in-motion, painting-in-motion, architecture-in-motion and furniture-in-motion; they were the American people in its envisaged likeness; they were the pop artist's multievocative images.

H. L. Mencken wrote of Lindsay's career that 'the yokels welcomed him, not because they were interested in his poetry, but because it struck them as an amazing and perhaps even a fascinatingly obscene thing for a sane man to go about the country on such bizarre and undemocratic business'. As usual, Mencken had a point amidst his hyperbole. Lindsay was implying not only mass deprivation, but temporary mass inferiority. He thus showed a certain lack of tact; and also, in failing to follow up the implications of the theory his conscience made him formulate, a lack of rationality. For instance, was abstract art necessarily selfish art? Did social insight always accompany creative ability? Was equality of taste desirable? Could any writer, without being an ideological weather-vane, consistently appeal to mass audiences which changed their tastes and *mores* in less than a generation?

Lindsay's failure to answer, perhaps even to pose, such questions made him react irrationally to his popularity with an audience which licked off the sugar coating, but left the rest of the pill. He had wanted to be like William Jennings Bryan—but resented being gaped at like a 'Bryan sensation' or 'like Tagore in his nightgown'. He felt he was being 'speculated in like pork'—but wasn't he himself pushing a commodity—his gospel and his urban blue-print—and making certain assumptions about the market? He was paying the penalty of his illogic; he was reacting with heart rather than mind. But his confusion and irate-ness were measures of his ambitious, earnest socioartistic conscience; and they were telling comments on his orga-nization of himself as a writer.

John C. Ward (essay date 1985)

SOURCE: "The Background of Lindsay's 'The Chinese Nightingale'," in *Western Illinois Regional Studies,* Vol. 8, No. 1, Spring, 1985, pp. 70-80.

[*In the following essay, Ward examines the autobiograph-ical elements of "The Chinese Nightingale."*]

Imagine Vachel Lindsay sitting upstairs in his family home in Springfield, Illinois as sounds of the summer of 1914 floated through the open window, musing over a draft of **"The Chinese Nightingale."** How could he conjure up, with any accuracy, the fabulous and unknown world of China? What resources did Lindsay draw on to create the grace, delicacy, and awareness of Chinese culture we find in this poem? Critics have assumed that the shadowy other world of the Orient was a mystery to the sheltered midwest-ern poet, that the details of the poem were bits of fantasy woven into the fabric of a dream vision, uninformed by actual experience. Appraising Lindsay's career in the *South-ern Review* [September, 1936] W. R. Moses dismissed the poem, both for its stylistic lapses and its shallowness:

> **"The Chinese Nightingale,"** now, written chiefly in the headlong iambic with sprinkled anapests and more or less irregular line-length and rhyme scheme that seem to distinguish all of Lindsay's 'best' poems, depends pretty largely, like all the 'best' poems, upon its vigor, without which it would appear sprawling and sentimental. Sentimental to a degree it is anyhow, but not troublesomely so, on the contrary characterized by a good deal of what seems genuine sentiment. The familiar line, 'Spring came on forever,' is broadly appealing. Let me remark, however, that it is hard to believe the poem has anything peculiarly Chinese about it except a little external paraphernalia. It seems the result of an interest used because of the romantic flavor that could be infused into it by the poet without really mastering it.

This critical view, collected in a recent edition of essays by John Flanagan, remains current, uncorrected by subse-quent analysis. While the poem is often admired, Lindsay is assumed to know little, and care less, for the actuality of distant China. On the contrary, Lindsay knew a surpris-ing amount about the world, and tried his best to evoke the true quality, the essential "otherness," of ancient and modern China.

Today, while the great chanting pieces which made him famous in the second decade of the twentieth century are virtually unknown, **"The Chinese Nightingale"** is still familiar to some academic readers. In the past twenty years, talking about American poetry and Vachel Lindsay with colleagues teaching high school or college English, I have discovered that **"The Chinese Nightingale"** re-mains attractive and useful to many teachers of poetry. Does its attractiveness only prove that we select poems if they extend traditions, in this case the tradition of "night-ingale" poems, from Milton through Coleridge and Keats to Yeats and T.S. Eliot, all dealing with despair and love, sleep and dreams? In this line, to be sure, comparisons come readily to mind, and Lindsay's lines seem neither eccentric nor obscure. Perhaps the poem's success also demonstrates our interest in Lindsay's life experience: both Eleanor Ruggles [in *The West-Going Heart: A Life of Vachel Lindsay,* 1959] and Mark Harris [in *Selected Poems of Vachel Lindsay,* 1963] note that Lindsay, while in New York trading rhymes for bread, entered a Chinese laundry and tried to interest the Chinese man ironing there in the dream poetry Lindsay was composing. However, the fact that this visit took place in 1905, nine years before the poem was composed in 1914, gives us some room to speculate. We should consider the sequence of events and experiences that informed the composition of this poem, that gave it its tone and character.

In my view the character of **"The Chinese Nightingale"** does not depend primarily on the "nightingale" tradition, nor was Lindsay's experience in the Chinese laundry in 1905 crucial, although it may have prompted the idea of the setting. In fact, as Lindsay was tramping those New York streets, his sister and brother-in-law were planning a move to China, a move about which only Lindsay in the family knew. By providing some information about that move and what Lindsay was learning from the distant world of China in the years just before he wrote the poem, I wish to give his insights some deserved authority, to credit him with a transformation of personal experience, and thus to correct the impression that the poem merely either comments on a particular personal episode, or re-sponds to a famous series of lyric poems.

In the autumn of 1905 Lindsay's sister Olive and her husband Paul Wakefield sailed for China on a medical missionary appointment. The following summer Lindsay himself set sail with his sister Joy and his parents for a trip through Europe. Often seen primarily as a midwestern poet, informed and limited by his life in Springfield, Illi-nois, and dedicated to the language and landscape of that region, Lindsay and his family constantly reached beyond their midwestern setting to ancient or distant cultures. In his mid-twenties Lindsay returned to the United State full of the images of European art and history, prepared to receive and assimilate the images of Asian and Chinese culture which his sister and brother-in-law were beginning to send to him.

In the ten years preceding the publication of **"The Chi-nese Nightingale"** Lindsay had had plenty of opportunity to learn about the fascinating and complex world of China. Lindsay received letters steadily from Olive and Paul through 1906-08, describing their experiences and urging him to visit. In 1908-1910, by now "old China hands," Dr. and Mrs. Wakefield returned to Springfield on sick leave and lived in the family home with Lindsay and his aging parents, detailing their China work and tempting the post with the images and artifacts of a splendidly unfamiliar world. Fascinated for years by the imagery of the Orient, both the near east and the far east, Lindsay began work on designs and poems linking east and west, first among these **"The Lotus and the Rose"** printed as a broadside in 1912 and then in the volume *General William Booth* in 1913. This volume was dedicated "to Dr. Arthur Paul Wakefield and Olive Lindsay Wakefield. Missionaries in China." Significantly, he yielded the ninth in a series of ten lectures he was giving at the Springfield YMCA to a "mystery" speaker, introduced on the night of the lecture as Dr. Wakefield, to address the topic of Chinese culture, advertised with the title "The Chinese Genius and the Chinese Laundry," its decorative flyer emblazoned with the design of a dragon rampant. The date of this address was December 9, 1908; here Lindsay was deferring to his brother-in-law on a topic that was increasingly interesting him.

When the Wakefields returned to China in 1910, Lindsay asked for their daughter's Chinese embroidered baby shoes, one of which he carried in his pocket for years as a talisman, a continuing reminder of his family's Chinese experience. In a letter in which he refused an invitation to China in 1912 ("Cannot at present accept. In the first place I haven't any money and little prospect of any.") he closes with a postscript: "Get The Rose and the Lotus printed in an English-speaking newspaper out there. No charge. And get it translated into Chinese for a Chinese speaking paper. Merely a suggestion in passing." Lindsay was trying to reach an audience in China before he had one in the United States.

His parents were so involved with the Wakefields' work in China and so devoted to international travel and self-education that, at their advanced ages, they went out for a tour, departing in May 1914 and returning in November 1914. Thus four people who were precious to Lindsay were in China the year he composed **"The Chinese Nightingale."** The process of this composition is described in part by Eleanor Ruggles, who divines the relationship between the princess in the poem and Sara Teasdale, to whom the poem, the volume (*The Chinese Nightingale*) and the *Collected Poems* (1923) are all dedicated. Lindsay's mother, anticipating a wedding, brought back a "magnificent Manchu coat of blue and rose satin" from her trip to China, but the coat was not to be worn by Lindsay's bride until 1925, when he gave it to Elizabeth Conner after their wedding.

The poem repeatedly speaks of "sorrow and love;" did he suspect that his love for Sara Teasdale would not end happily? Was he fully aware of the cultural contrasts presented in the view of China he was deriving from his family? A review of the poem will provide some answers, and may correct the impression that the poet was dreamy, escapist and self-indulgent, intoxicated by a new love and the fame that he was, at thirty-five, experiencing for the first time.

The hallmarks of the poem are controlled contrasts and self-effacement. Lindsay mutes his midwestern, jazzy and didac-

tic voice in order to allow another world to speak, a world of figures and visions he was just coming to understand. In an early letter to his brother-in-law in China he wrote;

> On my dresser is the picture of the Kamakura Buddha Olive sent. It is a great consoler, especially the message on the back. And on the other side of the dresser is the Buddha after his forty day's fast—from a Gandhara sculpture. These two pictures mean a heap to me somehow. They may not supply me with religion—they at least help me in my philosophy. I could write a book about either of them, as works of art—or as counselors . . . I have never been more serene and cheerful in my young life than of late. I have attained a sort of Nirvana,. . . . It is a strange feeling of assurance. The Buddha may not help me to this mood—it may merely express the mood, but it is a great satisfaction for that reason. . . . But when the Buddha is before me—all Asia is before me—and it is a sort of link with you.

It is this sense of self, peaceful and serene, that he associated with China and its images, and which he tried to embody in **"The Chinese Nightingale."** As in the letter, objects in the poem speak volumes or "express the mood," while human observers are mute or barely speak. Chang, the laundryman, begins the ritual that transforms the drab workplace into a magic cave of illusion, but is mechanical, restrained, stony-faced ("While Chang, with a countenance carved of stone, / Ironed and ironed, all alone."), while the joss on the shelf, like the Buddha on Lindsay's dresser in his Springfield home, and the dog in its arms stir and create their visions of nightingale and princess. Neither bird nor lady appeared before the rituals of lighting firecracker and burning of joss-stick, but now, stimulated by the narrator's question and the laundryman's action, they express the history and mood of the Orient.

In awe of the magnificance of Chinese culture which he had been glimpsing in earlier reading and through the letters from China, as well as through the articles on China which his parents had been mailing to him to type and submit to the *Illinois State Register,* Lindsay as individual recedes in the poem, yielding the bulk of the narrative to the princess who urges Chang to remember their heroic and romantic past. That past is defined by graceful commerce ("sold our grain in the peacock town"), ceremony ("drank our tea in China beneath the sacred spice-trees"), and artful industry (copied deep books and we carved in jade, / and wove blue silks in the mulberry shade . . ."), as contrasted to the violent European world, which as Lindsay was composing his poem was already engaged in a savage and exhausting war. Lindsay surely feared, in the fall of 1914, the conventional western process of civilization and progress fueled by conflict, and saw the alternative in the flowering springs of China which the princess recalls. The harbor town of Shanghai ("Built on the edge of sea-sands brown") was the entry point for most western visitors bound for the Chinese interior: Lindsay's family had entered there, and had described those flowering springs.

As the princess continues her appealing narrative, she recalls the "palace of heart-red stone," bringing to the mind's eye the rosy-red-walled palaces in the imperial Forbidden City of Peking, which Lindsay's parents had seen and described. Its spacious and gracious courtyards were perfect for the "fete and carnival" which Lindsay visualizes taking place there; its palace roofs crest and descend in "dragon-peak" style and detail. Dr. Lindsay's travel postcards included many from Peking: photographs of the imperial buildings show dragons on walls, dragons sculpted, and dragons on the peaks of the palace roofs, protecting the buildings and their dwellers. Lindsay had been asking repeatedly for material and advice from his parents as they traveled, and some of their responses were creeping into the poem:

> I am still struggling with The Ghosts of the Buffaloes and the Chinese Nightingale. You may be able to offer me suggestions on the Nightingale when you return. Still it makes some progress. . . . And I am beginning to feel happy about it.

> My principal anxiety at present is the Chinese Nightingale. I read it to most everyone in Springfield, but it is still in a half-baked condition. I recopy it once or twice every day. You will get home just in time to suggest little touches of nature and scenery, and fix up the Botony and Zoology.

It is indeed possible to find Lindsay's most personal concerns in the details of the poem, as Ruggles has suggested, but he is careful with these references. Although he was writing to Sara Teasdale almost daily throughout the period in which the poem was being composed, he did not ask her for as much advice as he did for other poems in progress in this period, an indication that for him **"The Chinese Nightingale"** was genuinely inspired by sources abroad. In several letters (all in the Beinecke Library's collection at Yale University), he informed her of his progress, but did not seek advice until the poem was virtually complete. He called Sara "my princess' in these letters, but the princess of the poem does not respond with the words of love that Lindsay wished to hear from his "Sara-phim." Finally, in October 1914 he sent her an elaborate draft of the poem and asked for "a list of corrections." What she suggested we cannot know since on her engagement to Ernest Filsinger that fall, Lindsay destroyed all her letters to him. But we may surmise that her response was more curt than Lindsay would have wished; he complained steadily throughout their exchanges of her reluctance to respond or elaborate.

Two small details from that draft of October 1914 (also at the Beinecke Library) suggest Teasdale's importance to Lindsay, and at the same time underline the tension between his love for her and his desire to be true to the vision of China he was trying to render authentically. First, in the draft written before his parents returned with the blue Manchu coat they thought would be a wedding gift for Sara, the silks in the shade are "white," whereas they are finally "blue." Second, in the earlier draft the lady was not "arch, and knowing and glowing" "she was laughing and gay." Both changes remind us that Lindsay was subtly incorporating elements of his personal experience

in the final version of the poem. If Lindsay had been writing a love poem to Sara Teasdale, he accepted the facts of her distance from him in its final version, and let his love, like other personal considerations, blend into the ornate patterns of the Chinese world. The princess is always articulate, caring and insightful; Chang the lover is always respectful, distant, honest and self-controlled; the visitor, a version of Lindsay, at the San Francisco laundry is virtually silent.

If the dimly remembered scene on the streets of New York, when Lindsay tried to peddle his verse in the laundry, is evoked here, it is transmuted in these respectful lines. The belligerent and proud joss (a term meaning idol or figure, derived from early European visitors' words for god, *deus*) speaks incomplete rhymes, with heavy emphases in broken lines, and contrasts sharply with the graceful, fluid and regularly rhymed lines of the lady. China's history of strife among war lords and pirate predators is suggested by the joss's assertions and style, but this unhappy record gives way to the music and textures of enduring beauty detailed by the princess. When the narrator tempts Chang to seek oblivion in sleep, recalling Keats' option early in his "nightingale" ode, Chang responds that a peculiarly Chinese vision of beauty consoles him, beauty which endures and outlasts ambition, chauvinism, even love. Finally, the joss and lady fade as this nightingale sings its muted song of dim but deeply echoing recollection. Given the repeated charge to remember ("Dare you forget" and "do you dream" and "do you remember") Chang's final accomplishments may seem meager ("I vaguely know" and "One thing I remember"), but the chaotic present does not manage to drive the vision of beauty from the minds of Chang or the narrator.

Currently indicated with charges of brassy tone, chauvinism, missionary zeal, or midwestern parochialism, Lindsay proves his objectivity and self-discipline to the perceptive reader with his precise, melodic portrait of a distant world in "The Chinese Nightingale."

—John C. Ward

However, the reader of the poem can, in effect, end Chang's "dream's confusion" for we collect the elements of Chinese culture and history to produce a whole. "Palace gate" and "heroes of old" and "lovers' ardent faces" are the closing images of the nightingale's song, and all are elaborated earlier in the poem. As Yeats later would in "Lapis Lazuli," Lindsay has delicately conveyed the past in the present objectified by the Chinese artisan. Both poets trusted the message implicit in the artifact, joss or stone, the suggestion that art transforms all that dread, that spring will come on for ever. Yeats, who heard Lindsay read at a banquet gathering of poets in Chicago on March 1, 1914 and admired his work (the episode is fully recounted in Ruggles' biography, Chapter 37), must have read **"The Chinese Nightingale"** when it appeared early the next year, and may have recalled it when he later composed his "Byzantium" poems.

If it is, by now, difficult to think of Lindsay's poems without reference to Keats or Yeats, we need not regret the association to the "nightingale" tradition, as at first we might have done. The association is, of course, an honorable one, as Edgar Lee Masters' estimate of Lindsay's poem demonstrates:

> Lindsay thought that **"The Chinese Nightingale"** was his best poem, and perhaps of his long poems it is the most finished, the most coherent and balanced to the end. To study it is to note the Lindsay vigor putting the first foot down hard as he did in the Booth poem. Its music may not be so delicate as that of "Kubla Khan," or the "Ancient Mariner," but it is more original. Coleridge took accents from the ballads to be found in Percy's "Reliques"; and he transsubstantiated some of the harmonies of the English odes of an earlier day than his. But where will the intonations of Lindsay's poem he [sic] found except in his own voice? Nowhere else are the variations so musically rung on sorrow and love, glory and love, and love and creation as eternal. Life is a loom weaving an illusion, bringing dreams that are good, and dreams like those of the "Ancient Mariner," and dreams of romantic lost loves cushioned upon the velvet violet lining of a study chair, where a black raven has perched on a white bust of the goddess of classic Athens. All is fresh and miraculous with the setting of Lindsay's poem. Its message is not out of any Christian sophistry, namely that "he prayeth best who loveth best"; the small gray bird on the joss carols that love and creation are eternal. The Chinaman Chang declares that his breast with vision is satisfied. True it is that Buddha is Lindsay's highest god, not Christ. In this poem Lindsay touched hands with the young Keats who saw the truth is beauty and beauty touch, and he left Coleridge behind. Listening to the small gray bird sing "like a long unwinding silk cocoon,: he turned away from the bird that croaked, "nevermore," for love and creation are eternal. [*Vachel Lindsay: A Poet in America*, 1935]

Carefully constructed, accurate in its cultural references, sensitive to the changing voices of its various speakers, and neither didactic nor intensely personal, **"The Chinese Nightingale"** may differ from much of Lindsay's poetry. But a reconsideration of Lindsay and his place in American letters must start with a review of his best work, work which in style and subject matter extends the reach of American poetry. Dennis Camp's complete edition of his poetry makes such a review possible, and readers need to be encouraged to seek poems that sing as sweetly as the final lines of the **"Chinese Nightingale"** do:

> I remember, I remember
> There were ghostly veils and laces . . .
> In the shadowy bowery places . . .
> With lovers' ardent faces
> Bending to one another,
> Speaking each his part.
> That infinitely echo
> In the red cave of my heart.

> 'Sweetheart, sweetheart, sweetheart,'
> They said to one another.
> They spoke, I think, of perils past.
> They spoke, I think, of peace at last.
> One thing I remember;
> Spring came on forever,
> Spring came on forever,
> Said the Chinese nightingale.

Currently indicated with charges of brassy tone, chauvinism, missionary zeal, or midwestern parochialism, Lindsay proves his objectivity and self-discipline to the perceptive reader with his precise, melodic portrait of a distant world in **"The Chinese Nightingale."**

Stanley Wertheim (essay date 1988)

SOURCE: "Vachel Lindsay's American Dream," in *Columbia Library Columns*, Vol. XXXVII, No. 3, May, 1988, pp. 13-24.

[*In the following essay, Wertheim discusses the social and historical context of Lindsay's major poems.*]

When Vachel Lindsay ended his life by drinking a bottle of Lysol on the evening of December 4, 1931, in the same house in which he had been born, he was bankrupt, depressed, and ill. His literary reputation had entered an eclipse from which it would never fully emerge, and the lifelong vision of seeing his native city of Springfield, Illinois transformed into an American utopia was no nearer to realization than when he first began to preach the "Gospel of Beauty." Even at the height of his transitory fame, only a handful of poems—those set pieces which still survive in anthologies: **"The Eagle That Is Forgotten," "General William Booth Enters into Heaven," "The Congo," "Abraham Lincoln Walks at Midnight," "Bryan, Bryan, Bryan, Bryan,"** and **"The Santa-Fé Trail"**— were regularly read or recited. The rest of his diverse literary output, including nine books of poetry (and an incomplete *Collected Poems* in 1923), five prose works, numerous articles and short stories, and much privately-published ephemera, fell stillborn from the press, or more properly, since Lindsay was an avid and flamboyant reciter of his writings, fell upon deaf ears.

Lindsay's democratic, expansive, and overtly moralistic poetry stands midway in an American bardic tradition which reaches backward to Emerson and Whitman and had an evanescent revival in the 1950s with Charles Olson and Allen Ginsberg. In this poetic mode, assertion takes precedence over suggestion and nuance, and the understatement and irony inherent in the best modern poetry are almost entirely absent. Form is subordinated to social utility, and mass appeal is more important than aesthetics. Lindsay had an idiosyncratic concern with style, but he believed that the poet's first duty was to his readers or his audience, which should be nationwide and comprise all classes. His perspective was instrumentalist and didactic, and his primary goal was not artistic achievement but social amelioration. In an era of introspective poets such as T.S. Eliot and Wallace Stevens, centered upon intellectual values, personal identity, and survival, Lindsay strove to create a public poetry, popular not in the debased connotation of that term but in the sense of a mass culture of high quality which would be available to everyone. Like Hart Crane and William Carlos Williams, Lindsay deplored the deracination of his literary contemporaries and advocated concentration upon the American scene and the American heritage. While he believed that Whitman's involuted style could only appeal to the sophisticated, he empathized with Whitman's celebration of American historical events, places, occupations, and people. "The New Localism," as expressed in Lindsay's *Adventures While Preaching the Gospel of Beauty* (1914), an account of his walking tour into the West in 1912, stresses that:

> The things most worth while are one's own hearth and neighborhood. We should make our own home and neighborhood the most democratic, the most beautiful and the holiest in the world. The children now growing up. . . . should find their talent and nurse it industriously. They should believe in every possible application of art-theory to the thoughts of the Declaration of Independence and Lincoln's Gettysburg Address. They should, if led by the spirit, wander over the whole nation in search of the secret of democratic beauty with their hearts at the same time filled to overflowing with the righteousness of God. Then they should come back to their own hearth and neighborhood and gather a little circle of their own sort of workers about them and strive to make the neighborhood and home more beautiful and democratic and holy with their special art.

Intrinsic to ethnocentric poetry is the eulogizing of national heroes. An undiscriminating patriotism caused Lindsay in his **"Litany of the Heroes,"** to equate Emerson, Lincoln, Wilson, and Theodore Roosevelt with such figures as Moses, Confucius, Saint Paul, Dante, and Shakespeare as avatars of the spirit which defies mutability. Another mythical idealization, and the subject of eight of Lindsay's poems, was Johnny Appleseed, the nickname of John Chapman (1774-1847), a nomadic Swedenborgian horticulturist who came down the Ohio River with a cargo of tracts and apple seeds which he distributed along the frontier. For Lindsay, Johnny Appleseed embodied the highest aspirations of Manifest Destiny; he was a gentle, almost saintly figure, "the nearest to Buddha and St. Francis and Tolstoy of all West-going pioneers," Lindsay wrote in his diary. "He is the West-going heart, never returning, yet with civilization always near enough to keep his heart tender for mankind. My God is the God of Johnny Appleseed, and some day I shall find Him."

Like Edgar Lee Masters and Carl Sandburg, who also grew up in west-central Illinois in the twilight of the pioneer era, Lindsay was haunted by the brooding presence of Abraham Lincoln, who practiced law in Springfield from 1836 to 1860 and is buried there. Lincoln had often visited the house in which Lindsay lived, and as a child Lindsay played in the Lincoln home. Lindsay's Lincoln is more a legendary neighbor representing the highest development of the common man than an historical person. Of all Lindsay's writings on Lincoln, the most compelling is **"Abra-ham Lincoln Walks at Midnight,"** which first appeared in *The Congo and Other Poems* (1914) shortly after the outbreak of war in Europe. Lindsay imagines Lincoln returned to life, walking the streets of Springfield unable to sleep because of the war, reminiscent for him of the great internecine slaughter over which he unwillingly presided, and fearful that another disaster is about to be visited upon the hapless common man: "Too many peasants fight, they know not why, / Too many homesteads in black terror weep." Lincoln the idealist waits for "a spirit dawn" that will bring "long peace to Cornland, Alp and Sea."

Another "Lincoln-hearted man" admired by Masters and Sandburg as well as Lindsay was William Jennings Bryan. In his poem with the quadruplicate title, **"Bryan, Bryan, Bryan, Bryan,"** Lindsay describes Bryan's visit to Springfield during the Presidential campaign of 1896 in which the agrarian states west of the Mississippi, generally aligned with the Democrats, supported inflation based upon the unlimited coinage of silver, while the East under the Republican banner was committed to a policy based upon the gold standard. Lindsay conceived of the issues in simple oppositional terms—East versus West, gold versus silver, the plutocrat versus the common man. When Bryan came to Springfield, almost all the residents of the town and the neighboring farm hamlets turned out to see and hear him:

> And the town was all one spreading wing of
>   bunting, plumes, and sunshine,
> Every rag and flag, and Bryan picture sold,
> When the rigs in many a dust line
> Jammed our streets at noon,
> And joined the wild parade against the power of gold.

The enthusiasm aroused by Bryan's simplistic economic theories and the power of his oratory was dispelled by the election victory of William McKinley, whose campaign had been adroitly managed by the Cleveland capitalist Mark Hanna. Lindsay's disillusionment was not ultimate since his aspirations were not narrowly political. His great Americans, Lincoln, Bryan, and John Peter Altgeld, personified hopes and dreams. Their idealism gave promise of a grander if more vague ultimate reality than would have been realized by the triumph of their mundane national goals. Bryan's mythical dimensions transcended defeat. He remained

> The one American Poet who could sing outdoors,
> He brought in tides of wonder, of unprecedented
>   splendor,
> Wild roses from the plains, that made hearts tender,
> All the funny circus silks
> Of politics unfurled,
> Bartlett pears of romance that were honey at the
>   cores,
> And torchlights down the street, to the end of the
>   world.

Altgeld, Governor of Illinois from 1892 through 1896, had been Lindsay's next-door neighbor. Lindsay's house overlooked the Governor's mansion, and he often saw Altgeld, whom he identified with Lincoln and Bryan as a simple and compassionate man who suffered greatly for his defense of the underdog. In 1893 Altgeld pardoned the foreign-born "anarchists" who had been convicted of causing disruptions which resulted in the death of policemen during the Chicago Haymarket Riot of 1886. The next year he publicly condemned Grover Cleveland's dispatch of Federal troops to Chicago to crush the Pullman strike. For these acts and for his lifelong advocacy of humanitarian causes, Altgeld was vilified as a radical and a subversive alien (he was born in Germany). After his death in 1902 he was praised perfunctorily by those in high places but quickly forgotten. Altgeld's career was both inspirational and disillusioning for Lindsay. "He was my last idol," Lindsay, in a letter now in the Allan Nevins Papers, wrote to Brand Whitlock who had been Altgeld's secretary, "After that I grew up." Lindsay's tribute to Altgeld, **"The Eagle That Is Forgotten,"** with its reflective and somber refrains, remains one of the finest American elegies:

> Sleep softly. . . . eagle forgotten. . . . under the
>   stone,
> Time has its way with you there and the clay has
>   its own.
> Sleep on, O brave-hearted, O wise man, that
>   kindled the flame—
> To live in mankind is far more than to live in a
>   name,
> To live in mankind, far, far more . . . than to live in
>   a name.

The qualities Lindsay extolled in his American heroes, personal charisma tempered by humanitarianism and a passion for justice, reveal the essentially limited and anachronistic nature of his vision. These are the virtues of prairie lawyers who represent a Jeffersonian ideal, the development of an agrarian civilization. Lindsay's conception of progress centered upon the apotheosis of the Illinois village. **"On the Building of Springfield,"** the third of three poems grouped under the title of "The Gospel of Beauty," stresses that small towns might become the nuclei of a burgeoning American culture, "remembering / that little Athens was the Muses' home, / That Oxford rules the heart of London still, / That Florence gave the Renaissance to Rome." In some of the most dramatic of the illustrations which Lindsay drew to accompany his poems, huge censers swung by invisible angels waft perfume over the roofs of Springfield, Lincoln's tomb, and the Illinois State Capitol. Springfield is accorded the potential of a Bethlehem:

> Some city on the breast of Illinois
> No wiser and no better at the start
> By faith shall rise redeemed, by faith shall rise
> Bearing the western glory in her heart.
>
> The genius of the Maple, Elm and Oak,
> The secret hidden in each grain of corn,
> The glory that the prairie angels sing
> At night when sons of Life and Love are born. . . .

Lindsay was not averse to celebrating the artifacts of industrialization. In **"The Kallyope Yell"** he bathetically

exhorted readers to "Hail, all hail the popcorn stand," and he composed **"A Rhyme about an Electrical Advertising Sign"** which depicted America's most garish urban environment in terms of beauty and promise:

> The signs in the street and the signs in the skies
> Shall make a new Zodiac, guiding the wise,
> And Broadway make one with that marvellous stair
> That is climbed by the rainbow-clad spirits of
>   prayer.

Yet, unlike Hart Crane in "The Bridge," Lindsay's deep agrarian and populist sympathies made it impossible for him to contrive an untragic myth of progress out of the achievements of the machine age. He was appalled by the development of industrial slums in American cities and a debased working class. "Factory windows are always broken," he noted sadly. "Other windows are let alone. / No one throws through the chapel-window / The bitter, snarling, derisive stone." One of his most Blakean lyrics, **"The Leaden-Eyed,"** deplores the growing use of child labor in factories and sounds an uncharacteristically discouraged and monitory note:

> Let not young souls be smothered out before
> They do quaint deeds and fully flaunt their pride.
> It is the world's one crime its babes grow dull,
> Its poor are ox-like, limp and leaden-eyed.
> Not that they starve, but starve so dreamlessly,
> Not that they sow, but that they seldom reap,
> Not that they serve, but have no gods to serve,
> Not that they die, but that they die like sheep.

While adverse valuations of America's material progress are not uncommon in Lindsay's poetry, ultimately the bardic voice of affirmation prevails. Despite his fears of an unintelligent submission to mechanization and its consequences for the ideal of an egalitarian society, Lindsay did not reject industrialization entirely but sought to sanctify it through a vague conception of social evolution in which the secular and materialistic Midwestern cities would in some indefinite manner transform themselves into spiritually enlightened and democratic communities. He was averse to ideologies and uncommitted to any specific program of social reform, and he made no sustained effort to provide a political context for his deep-rooted egalitarianism. Nominally, he identified as a socialist and in 1908 voted for Eugene Debs, against, as he acknowledged in **"Why I Voted the Socialist Ticket,"** his natural inclinations:

> I am unjust, but I can strive for justice.
> My life's unkind, but I can vote for kindness.
> I, the unloving, say life should be lovely.
> I, that am blind, cry out against my blindness.

Lindsay's confidence in the progress-affirming myth of American materialism and the evolution of a democratic society gradually gave way to despair with the onset of the Depression, and this to some extent was responsible for his suicide in 1931 as well as that of Hart Crane in 1932. But for Lindsay as for Crane, personal disillusionment was more destructive than the common tragedy. For the vast, mundane public whose adulation he craved, Lindsay had become a very visible poet. He was more seen than read, and between 1913 and 1930 become a one-man vaudeville show which played to audiences that totalled well over a million people. For them he built up a recitation ritual which mixed the histrionic and the exquisite, the humorous and the sentimental. To emphasize that his visionary chant poetry was more serious than vaudeville and to counteract its slapstick and revue connotations, Lindsay coined the term "The Higher Vaudeville" to describe both the poems he wrote in a ragtime manner and his technique of delivering them. At Lindsay's performances the audience clamored for readings of **"General William Booth Enters into Heaven"** and **"The Congo"** until he grew weary of them, and gradually he came to feel that the quiet poetry which embodied his deeply felt social and religious themes was despised and neglected.

"General William Booth Enters into Heaven," when first published in Harriet Monroe's *Poetry: A Magazine of Verse* in January, 1913, helped to establish the reputation of both its author and the magazine. Lindsay in his walking tours across America had at times slept in Salvation Army shelters, and he identified with the outcast and submerged population that Booth was committed to saving physically and morally. The poem, with its cinematic effects, jazz rhythms, and electric sense of urgency, conveys Lindsay's evangelical purposes with the background evocation of Salvation Army bass drums, banjos, and tambourines:

> Booth led boldly with his big bass drum—
> (Are you washed in the blood of the Lamb?)
> The Saints smiled gravely and they said: "He's
>   come."
> (Are you washed in the blood of the Lamb?)
> Walking lepers followed, rank on rank,
> Lurching bravos from the ditches dank,
> Drabs from the alleyways and drug fiends pale—
> Minds still passion-ridden, soul-powers frail:—
> Vermin-eaten saints with moldy breath,
> Unwashed legions with the ways of Death—
> (Are you washed in the blood of the Lamb?)

More than **"General William Booth,"** Lindsay's recitations of **"The Congo"** especially captivated his audiences as he rocked on the balls of his feet, his voice strident, alternately shouting and whispering, "With a boomlay, boomlay, boomlay, BOOM. / THEN I SAW THE CONGO, CREEPING THROUGH THE BLACK, / CUTTING THROUGH THE FOREST WITH A GOLDEN TRACK." The source of the image was a passage from Conrad's *Heart of Darkness* describing Marlow's fascination with a river on the map of Africa, "a mighty big river . . . resembling an immense snake uncoiled," but Lindsay's immediate inspiration was the Black American subculture. His intent was to portray a primitive people encumbered by the sinister superstitions of their African background but endowed with the capacity for joy and a gift for expressing it and ultimately redeemed through religious faith. The poem, with its references to "Fat black bucks" and "Wild crap shooters," was easily misunder-

stood. Some considered it deprecatory, and Lindsay, who often expressed his belief in racial equality, found himself in the anomalous position of clashing with W. E. B. Dubois. Nevertheless, listeners continued to be transported by the swaying rhythms of **"The Congo,"** and William Butler Yeats, before whom Lindsay declaimed the poem at a banquet in Chicago on March 1, 1914, praised its strange beauty.

Despite their originality and power, set pieces with signature lines such as **"General William Booth"** and **"The Congo"** depended for their success upon Lindsay's transient ability to declaim them on the lecture platform. As the 1920s faded into the Depression, Lindsay's ebullience and optimism seemed increasingly jejune and his patriotism provincial. His Jeffersonian model for American society became more the America of the past than the country in which he lived. Lindsay felt increasingly rejected, and his creative ability declined. In the half century since his death, he has been given only perfunctory attention by the critical establishment. Today, the scratchy recordings of his recitals seem merely quaint, and we must read him with a certain effort of the historical imagination. What endures is a number of fine lyrics, an original and inimitable use of the vernacular in poetry, a gallery of larger-than-life American heroes, and an Edenic view of America itself, which, while antipodal to our conflict-ridden reality, serves to remind us of the enduring quality of the American dream.

FURTHER READING

Biography

Massa, Ann. *Vachel Lindsay: Fieldworker for the American Dream.* Bloomington: Indiana University Press, 1970, 310p.
    Surveys Lindsay's Life and work. Massa includes a primary and secondary bibliography.

Masters, Edgar Lee. *Vachel Lindsay: A Poet in America.* New York: Charles Scribner's Sons, 1935, 392 p.
    Biography that includes lengthy excerpts from Lindsay's journals and offers insights into the poet's life and career.

Ruggles, Eleanor. *The West-Going Heart: A Life of Vachel Lindsay.* New York: W. W. Norton & Company, 1959, 448 p.
    Biographical and critical study of Lindsay.

Criticism

Diggory, Terence. "Natural Speech: The Nineteen-Tens." In *Yeats & American Poetry: The Tradition of the Self,* pp. 59-86. Princeton: Princeton University Press, 1983.
    Examines the influence of W. B. Yeats on Lindsay's work.

Enkvist, Nils Erik. "The Folk Elements in Vachel Lindsay's Poetry." *English Studies* 32, Nos. 1-6 (1951): 241-49.
    Examine's the sources and treatment of American

folklore, Negro history, and American Indian legend in Lindsay's work.

Gray, Paul H. "Performance and the Bardic Ambition of Vachel Lindsay." Text and Performance Quarterly 9, No. 3 (July 1989): 216-23.

Explores Lindsay's public presentations of his work.

Hallwas, John E. and Reader, Dennis J., eds. *The Vision of This Land, Studies of Vachel Lindsay, Edgar Lee Masters, and Carl Sandburg*. Macomb, Ill.: Western Illinois University, 1976, 129p.

Includes essays by Dennis Q. McInery, Marc Chenetier, and William White that reassess the poet's place in American literature.

Mencken, H.L. "Vachel Lindsay: The True Voice fo Middle America." *The Courier* II, No. 4 (December 1962): 13-16.

Proclaims Lindsay a representative voice of America and the only poet since Walt Whitman to display any notable originality.

Monroe, Harriet. "Vachel Lindsay." In *Poets & Their Art*, pp. 21-8. New York: MacMillan, 1932.

Favorable assessment of Lindsay's poetry, praising his wisdom, humor, and insight.

Ward, John. "Walking to Wagon Mound: Composing Booth." Western Humanities Review XXXX, No. 3 (Autumn 1986): 230-43.

Discusses the compostition of "General William Booth Enters into Heaven" and its relation to "The Gospel of Beauty."

Additional coverage of Lindsay's life and career is contained in the folowing sources published by The Gale Group: *Twentieth Century Literary Criticism*, Vol. 17; *DISCovering Authors*; *DISCovering Authors: Canadian*; *DISCovering Authors: Most-Studied Authors Module*; *DISCovering Authors: Poets Module*; *World Literature Criticism, 1500 to the Present*; *Contemporary Authors*, Vols. 114, 135; *Concise Dictionary of American Literary Biography*; *Dictionary of Literary Biography*, Vol. 54; and *Something About the Author*, Vol. 40.

Elinor Wylie
1885-1928

(Full name Elinor Morton Hoyt Wylie Benét) American poet, novelist, short story writer, and essayist.

INTRODUCTION

In her lifetime, Wylie garnered notoriety for her unconventional private life and acclaim for her poems and novels. She was considered one of the most distinguished American poets of the 1920s. Though her literary career lasted only eight years, she was recognized as an extremely adept, accomplished author. Wylie's poetry is marked by a lively inventiveness, a subtle treatment of emotion, and a detached sensibility that Louis Untermeyer has described as "a passion frozen at its source."

Biographical Information

Wylie was born in Somerville, New Jersey, the oldest child of parents well-known in society and public affairs. In 1905 she met and married Phillip Hichborn, with whom she had a son. After five years of a difficult marriage, Wylie left Hichborn and her son to live with a married lawyer, Horace Wylie. After being ostracized by their families and friends and mistreated in the press, the couple moved to England, where the poet published her first collection, *Incidental Numbers* (1912). They returned to the United States in 1916 after Hichborn committed suicide and Horace Wylie's wife agreed to a divorce; these events permitted the poet's second marriage in 1917. At the same time, friends such as John Dos Passos, John Peale Bishop, and Edmund Wilson convinced her to seriously pursue a writing career. In November, 1919, Wylie sent some poems to *Poetry* despite her fears that her work was not "modern enough." But Harriet Monroe, *Poetry*'s editor, allayed Wylie's concerns, publishing four poems and asking for more. Wylie left her second husband and moved to New York in 1921. Nine years after *Incidental Numbers*, Wylie published *Nets to Catch the Wind*, a poetry collection which she considered her first significant book. It was followed in quick succession by three volumes of verse and four novels, several of which won high praise from America's most influential critics. One of these critics, William Rose Benét, became Wylie's third husband in 1923. In 1926, Wylie separated from Benét though they remained married, living together occasionally. During the last year of her life, she became romantically involved with Henry de Clifford Woodhouse, the husband of a friend. The relationship inspired the love sonnets in her last book. On the evening of December 16, 1928, during a visit with Benét, she completed the drafts for her last work, *Angels and Earthly Creatures*, and then suffered a fatal stroke.

Major Works

Wylie anonymously published her first book of verse, *Incidental Numbers* (1912), a small collection composed between 1902 and 1911. Though she did not find these poems worthy of inclusion in her subsequent volumes, they contain some of the themes she would continue to explore—magic, love, entrapment and isolation—and reveal her indebtedness to the poets of the aesthetic movement. Wylie kept this collection secret, claiming in a 1919 letter to Harriet Monroe, "I have never published anything—never tried to, until the last few weeks." Wylie was greatly influenced by the works of Percy Shelley, though this was not the only influence on her work. Some aspects of her verse, in particular her wit and subtlety of thought, were in the tradition of the seventeenth-century metaphysical poets, especially John Donne. In what most critics regard as her best works, *Nets to Catch the Wind* (1921) and *Black Armour* (1923), Wylie dramatically portrays the disparities between the individual's aspirations and the limited satisfactions offered by life. Though *Trivial Breath* (1928) and *Angels and Earthly Creatures* (1928) contain some of Wylie's most ambitious poems, including the sonnet sequence "One Person," they also suggest that the poet abandoned the themes and convictions of her earlier work in pursuit of the cult of the beautiful. There is a sense in these works that the gifted individual requires beauty, refinement, and variety, while the world offers commonness, coarseness, and vulgarity.

Critical Reception

The peak of Wylie's literary reputation was reached early in her career. It has been suggested that part of the reason Wylie's contemporaries praised her work so effusively was because they were under the spell of her physical beauty and social charm. Her poems were considered intellectually brilliant, and she was compared to such masters as T. S. Eliot. Subsequent criticism has been scanty and less favorable. However, new works examining Wylie indicate a reawakening of critical appreciation for her, and the inclusion of her poetry in recently published anthologies confirms a continuing interest her works. *Incidental Numbers*, though often characterized as immature and undisciplined, has been well regarded by critics for its expression of Wylie's major themes and as a promise of its author's later development. The poems in *Nets to Catch the Wind* and *Black Armour* have been the subjects of several critical explications which have focused on their precise structural aspects and imagery. In these collections, particularly in such poems as "The Eagle and the Mole" and "Velvet Shoes," Wylie achieves what has been characterized as a genuine and consistent style altogether free from affectation. It has been asserted that these poems demonstrate her exceptional skill in handling the materials of her ornamental and illusory "crystal world." In her later verse, however, Wylie's perceptions have been assessed as less coherent, and her language redundant, highly conventional, even trite in content and idiom. Critics discussing Wylie's later works have tended to explore the relationship between Wylie's emotional life and her work.

PRINCIPAL WORKS

Poetry

Incidental Numbers 1912
Nets to Catch the Wind 1921
Black Armour 1923
Angels and Earthly Creatures: A Sequence of Sonnets 1928
Trivial Breath 1928
†*Collected Poems of Elinor Wylie* 1932
†*Last Poems of Elinor Wylie* 1943

Other Major Works

Jennifer Lorn: A Sedate Extravaganza (novel) 1923
The Venetian Glass Nephew (novel) 1925

The Orphan Angel (novel) 1926; also published as *Mortal Image* 1927
Mr. Hodge and Mr. Hazard (novel) 1928
Collected Prose of Elinor Wylie (novels, short stories, and essays) 1933

*Published anonymously.

†Published posthumously.

CRITICISM

Edna St. Vincent Millay (review date 1922)

SOURCE: "Elinor Wylie's Poems," in *The New York Post,* January 28, 1922, p. 379.

[*In the following excerpt from a review of* Nets to Catch the Wind, *Millay describes Wylie as a poet of abundant talent and excellent taste.*]

The publication recently of Elinor Wylie's *Nets to Catch the Wind* is an event in the life of every poet and every lover of poetry. The book is an important one. It is important in itself, as containing some excellent and distinguished work; and it is important because it is the first book of its author, and thus marks the opening of yet another door by which beauty may enter to the world.

The material from which these poems is made is not the usual material. They are not about love, not about death, not about war, not about nature, not about God, not exclusively Elinor Wylie. They are not pourings forth. There is not a groan or a shout contained between the covers. They are carefully and skilfully executed works of art, done by a person to whom the creation of loveliness and not the expression of a personality through the medium of ink and paper is the major consideration.

One places this book, for some reason, alongside the poems of Ralph Hodgson. It contains no "Eve," no "Bull," no "Song of Honour." It is a small book of small poems, made, one would say, for the most part, out of moods and fancies, rather than out of emotions and convictions. Yet to say that Mrs. Wylie has not written a sustained and lofty poem seems as irrelevant as to say that she has not been to Taormina. One is convinced that she could go there, should she set her heart on it.

Nets to Catch the Wind begins badly. The opening poem is perhaps the worst poem in the book. It is called **"Beauty."** Of its twelve lines the first two are commonplace, the entire second stanza is awkward and dull, and the beginning of the last stanza is commonplace. Then, like a sword from ambush, into the sleepy consciousness of the strolling reader bites the sharp, cold wonder of the final phrase,

> Enshrine her and she dies, who had
> The hard heart of a child. . . .

It is with beating heart, as the old chronicles have it, that the reader, shaken by this first encounter, fares onward into the book, prepared for anything. . . .

[The second poem, **"The Eagle and the Mole,"**] must surely delight—and this whether or not they subscribe to its philosophy—all who admire the clean-lined and uncompromising in art. . . .

The third poem is called **"Madman's Song."** Which is another way of telling us that it is the Song of any Poet in his Right Mind. It is gracefully done, but even as it is being read is forgotten, in the rich memories of Yeats which it evokes. It is difficult to write nowadays of "silver horns," "golden pillows," and "the milk-white hounds of the moon" without finding one's-self outvoiced by one's overtones.

The book contains eight sonnets. Of these the four grouped under the title **"Wild Peaches"** are, except for **"Atavism,"** the most successful. The second and fourth of this group are especially fine, although the octave of the third—or rather the septave; it is a thirteen-line sonnet—is charming. The sonnet to **"Nancy"** is trivial and too palpably a stalk to upbear the blossom of its last line. **"Blood Feud"** is almost worthless. It is an attempt to retell a story which in the original was perhaps impressive, but which the present narrator has failed to make even interesting. It contains lines of purely statistical importance which have nothing to do with poetry, such as "He'd killed a score of foemen in the past," a line which might better be a marginal note. . . .

In order to get the full substance of Mrs. Wylie's poems one should learn them by heart. And the fact that they are easy to learn by heart speaks well for their weight and vigor and for the artistic integrity of their craftsman. Obviously the poems which are difficult to learn by heart are those poems which might as well have been written in some other way, which are too thin for their form, and have been fattened in the flesh but not in the spirit of them, whose authors have contented themselves with the time-tried figure and the approximate word. Such poems slip through the mind of the reader as they slipped through the fingers of the writer. And more often than not the author himself cannot quote them from memory. . . . [But a poem such as Mrs. Wylie's **"Escape"**] will not easily be erased or partially blotted even from the mind whereon they once have inscribed their peculiar quality.

There are other poems which I should like to quote if there were space here in which to do so: **"Water Sleep," "Village Mystery," "The Crooked Stick," "The Tortoise in Eternity,"** marred by the word "scornful" in the last line; **"The Fairy Goldsmith,"** pretty and unimportant, made by the word "monstrous" in the last stanza, a word which bulges and snores in its context like a sleeping giant; the gay and delightful **"Prinkin' Leddie,"** with her "ermine hood like the hat o' a miller," and her "cramoisie mantle that cam' frae Paris"; **"Fire and Sleet and Candlelight,"** with its interesting occasional internal rhyme, its ascetic paucity of figure, its impersonality as of a chorus of fates;

"Bronze Trumpets and Sea Water," twelve splendid lines which give the lie to their own thesis; and the delicate and exquisite **"Velvet Shoes,"** a poem seemingly not printed but sighed upon the paper like breath upon glass, the poem with which the book should have ended.

But if the little of Mrs. Wylie's work which I have been able to cite in this appreciation of it does not convey to the reader the conviction that she is a distinctive poet and that her book is necessary to him it would be useless to continue. . . .

There are poems in the book which are not excellent; such poems appear in every book. The author of *Nets to Catch the Wind* has the fine equipment of intelligence, skill, discrimination reserve, and the full powers of sorcery.

Malcolm Cowley (review date 1923)

SOURCE: "The Owl and the Nightingale," in *The Dial,* Vol. 74, June, 1923, pp. 624-26.

[*In the following review of* Black Armour, *Cowley praises Wylie's ability to combine "intellect and emotion" and compares her poetry to that of T. S. Eliot.*]

Fantasy is the quality of an agile mind working freely, as if in a vacuum. It consists in the unexpected combination of ideas and images so as to create a world apart from the world, governed by a more arbitrary logic. The poems of Elinor Wylie, at any rate the best of them, have fantasy. They share the quality with T. S. Eliot, and reading *Black Armour* for the first time one is reminded of him forcibly.

But of which Eliot . . . the question is legitimate; he is never quite the same; he changes his style to keep pace with the continued development of his ideas. An author who depends on the sole resources of his own temperament (take Sherwood Anderson for example) is perfectly consistent with his own temperament; he changes rarely. There is an opposite type, that of Apollinaire or Picasso: intellectual artists, perfectly conscious, who gather information wherever they can find it and imitate anybody except themselves. They move from one theory to another, emitting disciples like sparks as they pass through each stage: the disciples have separate relations to the master and are usually one another's enemies. Eliot is an artist, a master, of this type.

As in the case of Picasso, where Pink and Blue and Classical eras are distinguished, one can name the eras of Eliot: for example the period of the early realistic poems, the Prufrock stage, the quatrains about Sweeney, Gerontion, The Waste Land. Each era has a separate influence whose history can be traced; *Black Armour* belongs in great part to the history of the quatrains. Remembering Burbank in Venice one reads:

> Castilian facing Lucifer,
> Juan does not remove his cap;

Unswaddled infantile to her
His soul lies kicking in her lap.
While she, transported by the wind
Mercutio has clasped and kissed . . .
Like quicksilver, her absent mind
Evades them both, and is not missed.

In these two stanzas her qualities are evident. A poem by Elinor Wylie is the quick notation of a guess, a situation, a metaphor; it contains a bit of drama, rarely a narrative, often a character drawn briefly, but not hastily. Her metre is like Eliot's; her images have a similar air of being jumbled together, with deliberation; her vocabulary, though not the same, is parallel and includes strange words, words out of history and science, words used for their own sake, but exactly, with a parade of erudition which is justified in the fact. Alarums rhymes with bar-rooms and sentient with bent; Apeneck Sweeney nods his maculate head in approval.

But the resemblance to Eliot is more on the surface than beneath, and when Miss Wylie uses the same dictionary and the same metrics she uses them to her own purpose. She has a personality which is in many ways his opposite. He is afraid of intimate emotions, hides them politely, holds them at arm's length when he wishes to describe them; she is both emotional and intimate, as if her subject were a penny world to eat with Pippit behind the screen.

She writes in a medium which Eliot never attempted: magazine verse. Literature takes curious forms and magazine verse is one of them. It is bound by conventions as rigid, perhaps, as those of Racinian tragedy or the Noh drama; the perspective of a century will be needed to appreciate how they are narrow. Magazine verse must fill the bottom of a page, agreeably. It is limited to certain subjects treated with a certain degree of lyricism; to emotions neither too personal nor impersonal and to a few stanzas in a minor tradition. Apparently these conventions should prevent the writing of even passable verse, but talent thrives on conventions. Miss Wylie is talented.

She writes genuine poetry while observing even the minor conventions of her medium. For example it is the general consent that human bodies are composed of breast, hands, head. *Black Armour* is in five sections to cover them: breastplate, gauntlet, helmet, beaver (Beaver Up!) and plumes. The legs are left unprotected through delicacy, or they are lacking. And nevertheless *Black Armour* gives no sense of being incomplete; within limitations it is unexcelled. The verse is hard and bright as a piece of machinery; there are no loose screws about it; metres are varied with astonishing skill. Miss Wylie is a craftsman who cannot be praised too highly, but her real achievement is to write magazine verse which is not repulsive to the intelligence. I doubt whether any one else has done as much.

Only, you form such a high opinion of her talents that you expect too much of them, saying to yourself: The last poem was agreeable, but the next will be a masterpiece . . . or surely the one after. At the end of the book you are left still unsatisfied, still expecting another something which will come, perhaps, in a future volume. The feeling is not disagreeable. Sometimes you wish she would write in other conventions, more ambitious, complete anatomically, giving more scope to her notations of character and her dramatic power. As it is, she never lacks charm and only at her worst is she cute.

Apparently her greatest virtue should be the fact that she combines, in wise proportions, intellect with emotion. It is a defect instead, perhaps her gravest, for although she combines them in a book she has fused them perfectly in no single poem. She has emotion and fantasy by turns. She thinks in one poem and thinks well; feels in one poem and feels strongly; allows thought and feeling to be separate. She is the Owl and the lyric Nightingale at sea in a beautiful pea-green boat; during the honeymoon they write verses dedicated to each other, but obviously by two authors.

It is the Owl who is more modern. . . . There is a group of phenomena in contemporary letters, which, if taken together, are the elements of a movement perhaps important enough to be compared with the classicism of the seventeenth century or the romanticism of the nineteenth. Different aspects of the movement have been referred to as cubist, neo-classical, abstract, fantastic, but the one term which includes all its tendencies is Intellectualism. The decade, perhaps the century will be intellectualist. . . . Miss Wylie, with her double personality, is half in the movement and half outside of it. In a way this is a judgement, for although it is no virtue to be modern, none to be conservative, there is a difficult virtue in extremes.

Anna Hempstead Branch (review date 1928)

SOURCE: "Fiery Essences," in *The Saturday Review of Literature,* Vol. V, No. 13, October 20, 1928, p. 267.

[*In the following excerpt, Branch offers a complimentary review of* Trivial Breath, *emphasizing Wylie's intellect and the vivacity of her poems.*]

It is a very great pleasure indeed, to be able to record in this review a sincere admiration of Elinor Wylie's new book, *Trivial Breath.* Her music, practically unfailing, ranges from the gossamer delicacy of **"Desolation is a Delicate Thing"** to the hard athletic vigor of **"The Innocents"** and **"Minotaur."** With all her lightness, gaiety, and elegance of diction, her often worldly, and often-sophisticated accent, such as we find in a wholly delightful poem **"Miranda's Supper,"** she is also capable of rugged energy and the abrupt vigorous intonation of an old Puritan hymn.

Her thought runs rather apart from the current mood of the day. She gives us, from her heart, sensitive and lovely and loving portrayals of the perceptions of a fine intellect. Elinor Wylie seems to be instinctively reserved in regard to revelations of emotions as such and we think there is something fine and proud in her unwillingness to be betrayed into an expression of "feelings" unless "feelings" are absolutely necessary. Whatever the subject may be, there is no doubt that these poems spring from high clear sources of intellect and emotion.

After all, it makes very little difference whether poetry is hard or soft, cold or hot, emotional or intellectual, as long as it is poetry. If it is poetry, real poetry, there is just one thing to do and that is, to be grateful to the gods—and in this book there is so much real poetry!

Elinor Wylie's verse is polished. Courtly, well groomed, finished—but beneath the larger movement of her poetry as a whole is a fine pulsation of high blooded life like the rippling movement under the skin of a spirited horse. Her verse is essentially well-bred—I mean by this that her values are not episodic, but are constant and a quality of being. Within the elegance there often burns a white-hot intensity of spirit, within the light movement is seriousness, and behind the finish is an actual beauty of contour delightful to all lovers of shape. There is no mistaking the vitality of that fine-poem called **"The Innocents"** or the volcanic energy of a poem with a few fierce splendid stanzas called **"Minotaur."**

> From flesh refined to glass
> A god goes desert-ward
> Upon a spotted pard
> Between an ox and ass.

This poem with its abrupt definite impact is a veritable arrow head of song-its brazen wedge carved with the head of the esoteric bull.

One must be prepared in Elinor Wylie's poetry to meet and to enjoy a certain temperamental gaiety and occasional bursts of high spirits.

In **"Malediction Upon Myself"** it is evident that the author is enjoying herself intensely. This poem, which celebrates the excellence of Holy Beauty, wherever and however unexpectedly beauty may occur, and which defines the curse which falls upon one who denies the Holiness, is ornately served, but far more appalling than any similar malediction ever uttered by Jonathan Edwards in whose school of theology Elinor Wylie certainly seems versed. Her satisfaction in the awful results which she calls down upon traitors to loveliness is not more artistic than is Jonathan Edward's more austere enjoyment of his own description of a spider suspended by a thread over red hot coals. After all, something very like all this does really happen-in time-to the betrayers of beauty. . . .

"Address to My Soul" is a reticent, but very real contribution to philosophic reflection upon the spirit. It reminds one of Virgil's "Animula vagula" and has in it a fresher vision than many a poem that says more in a more imitative manner.

"To a Book" is an extraordinary achievement. It reveals that lightness of touch and gaiety of spirit which Elinor Wylie carries with her into the world of pure thought and is destined to last because it is the perfect expression of the well-night inexpressible-a perfection which unlike that in **"True Vine"** is not likely to tarnish. This poem is one of the poet's best, for it shows her fine gift for revealing the inner luminous life of abstract ideas, their fiery essences, their living energies.

"Dedication" is a singularly beautiful poem on an exquisite subject-a child learning to read.

> Profuse and fabulous appeared the page
> On which your youngest lessons were emblazoned,
> Enchantments that unlock a crystal cage
> An alphabet with astral fires seasoned.

That is a classic statement in regard to one of the great events of childhood. In fact the lines describe one of the most profound reactions the spirit knows, its reactions to literature-which is one of the manifestations of life itself and just as much an act of nature as a waterfall or a forest. This remarkable poem will live as long as children learn to read and mothers watch them. **"True Vine"** is a piece of mature wisdom gravely and exquisitely sung and **"Last Supper,"** has the same fine sensitiveness and self restraint:

> So short a time remains to taste
> The ivory pulp, the seven pips.
> My heart is happy without haste
> With revelation at its lips.
>
> So calm a beauty shapes the core,
> So grave a blossom frames the stem.
> In this last minute and no more
> My eyes alone shall eat of them.

This poem with its high-minded perception of the dignity of abstinence, the finer colors, the subtler flavors of relinquishment, reminds one of the hero of one of Vernon Lee's essays—"the things he abstained from were all exquisite."

Donald Davidson (review date 1929)

SOURCE: "Elinor Wylie," in *The Spyglass, Views and Reviews, 1924-1930,* Vanderbilt University Press, 1963, pp. 115-17.

[*In the following review, originally published in the "Critics Almanac" of* The Spyglass, *Davidson considers* Angels and Earthly Creatures *to be Wylie's best book of poetry and praises her use of traditional sonnet forms.*]

The day before she died, it happened that Elinor Wylie was arranging for publication a book of poems. This book now appears under the title *Angels and Earthly Creatures.* Everywhere it reads as if she had the taste of death already on her tongue, so that one is moved to wonder whether Elinor Wylie did not, like Shelley, foresee her fate. However that may be, there is little doubt that *Angels and Earthly Creatures* is her best book of poetry. It is more or less free from the finical toyings with words for their own sakes that had seemed at times to threaten her poetic art with decadence. This book has a sincere force, a humanity (if still shot through with fantasy and a tentative mysticism), and an open fervor that her poetry did not always have in the past. I am forced to confess myself a false prophet, for I remember that I once remarked that

Elinor Wylie, if she had lived to be a centenarian, would have made no material advance in poetry.

What transformed her art, we can only speculate. Some of the poems seem to be highly autobiographical, and suggest a new, passionate experience that gave a fresh stimulus to poetic creation. Another thing is that her style, instead of becoming more modern and experimental, is more definitely shaped into traditional modes, flavoring strongly of the seventeenth century metaphysical poets and the Elizabethans—a tendency that her work had already shown.

There is even a little of Milton in the fine **"Hymn to Earth." "This Corruptible"** with its dialogue between Mind, Heart, Body and Spirit, reflects the method of John Donne and his followers. And the central feature of the whole book, a sonnet sequence entitled **"One Person,"** fully illustrates the Elizabethan manner.

These sonnets are written in the "Italian" form, but with the idiom of Shakespeare. They celebrate the love of a woman for a man (reversing the conventional situation of the sixteenth century sonneteers), and are probably very strong examples of the turn that amorous poetry will take, now that women are writing more and more of it. They have a tenderness both fierce and sorrowful. Their mood is one of utter surrender, self-abasement, and idealistic worship. It is little short of startling, too, to find in them the exact manner, even to language and stock conventions, of the sixteenth century sonnet cycles: the compliments of the beloved, the dissection of the lover's intimate feelings, the half-veiled hints of the details of an "affair," the brooding over mortality, the elaborate conceits centered around mythological and chivalric lore-all are here, of course somewhat transformed by Elinor Wylie's characteristic style.

Phrases like "Time, who sucks the honey of our days"; "Had enriched my sight"; "To memorize the pure appointed task" are all Elizabethan. In its air of self-depreciation, in the very cadence and accent of the words, this sonnet is Elizabethan:

The little beauty that I was allowed-
The lips new-cut and coloured by my sire,
The polished hair, the eyes' perceptive fire-
Has never been enough to make me proud:
For I have moved companioned by a cloud,
And lived indifferent to the blood's desire
Of temporal loveliness in vain attire:
My flesh was but a fresh-embroidered shroud.

Now do I grow indignant at the fate
Which made me so imperfect to compare
With your degree of noble and of fair;
Our elements are the farthest skies apart;
And I enjoin you, ere it is too late,
To stamp your superscription on my heart.
["Sonnet V"]

In a previous Romantic revival, poets went back, as Elinor Wylie did, to the fountains of inspiration of the sixteenth and seventeenth centuries. *Angels and Earthly Creatures*

is another mark of the steady movement of our poetry toward refreshing itself from an old tradition.

The question of Elinor Wylie's greatness or non-greatness need hardly be discussed. It will finally settle itself. But we can observe that in a distinguished volume like this the satisfaction with the almost perfect art will outweigh the melancholy uneasiness that one feels over a somewhat fragmentary career, or the suspicion that one has of an attitude that is part pose and part an intense yet uncertain striving for some kind of human salvation. I should be loath to join with those who have adopted canonical enthusiasms and have spoken with bated breath of "Saint Elinor." A firm estimate of her work would probably show that it lacks the final touch that sets major above minor. Possibly Elinor Wylie was not a great enough person to be a really great poet. No matter—we can hardly ask for a better artistic performance than *Angels and Earthly Creatures.* Slight though its compass is, it will be for many tastes the book of poems of the year.

M.D.Z. [Morton Dauwen Zabel] (review date 1932)

SOURCE: "The Pattern of the Atmosphere," in *Poetry: A Magazine of Verse,* Vol. XI, No. V, August 1932, pp. 273-82.

[*In the following excerpt from a review of* The Collected Poems of Elinor Wylie, *Zabel faults Wylie's work, assessing it as repetitive and ineffectively ornate.*]

Mrs. Elinor Wylie was a poet of late development but of enviable successes. By the testimony of every acquaintance, the graces exhibited in her verse are corroborated in her actual life. An agile wit was the factor which propelled her from charm to charm in her choice of materials: from historic themes of the most ingenious fragility and inaccessibility, to familiar encounters rendered desirable by the humor and elegance of imagination she brought to them. Thus seventeenth-century Venice had no riches to strike envy in the heart of a pioneer farmer on the Chesapeake: for each of them she conjured an experience of equal splendor. There was a prodigality in her verbal invention which certainly stemmed from something deeper than museum catalogues or encyclopedias; if we are to praise phonetic dexterity in Byron and Browning, we must praise it in her. The pictorial and impressionistic efforts of the 'nineties wilt feebly in comparison with the brittle imagery of her designs. In the tradition of *Émaux et Camées* she is, on first acquaintance at least, an austere and distinguished disciple. Of that style in contemporary art which shifts from tenet to tenet under the name of "classicism," she is undoubtedly a notable exemplar, and students of modern poetry will be grateful to Mr. Benét for issuing her **Collected Poems,** with many hitherto inaccessible additions (but a somewhat unfortunate *Foreword*), and in a distinguished format. To anyone acquainted with her work since its first appearance, however, and who re-reads poems now quite familiar, this gratitude is tempered by two inescapable convictions: that throughout her work Mrs. Wylie never crossed the line that separates her from poets of her own admiration, like Donne, Waller, and Landor, or from Emily Brontë and Miss Dickinson; and that from the beginning she mistook virtuosity for convictions, and that it betrayed her in the end.

It is a principle of any usage that the energy of forms is exhaustible, and that overuse depletes it. Mrs. Wylie aimed at concreteness. She did not favor the practice of certain of her more philosophic contemporaries who have brought to the humiliation of parody the terms of their favorite themes: *time, mind, despair, change, heart, silence.* Like Miss Sitwell's, her mind operated best under the spur of allegory, and thus her pages spill with meteors, moonstones, goblins, knights, fairy goldsmiths, mandrakes, blackamoors, and saints; with filigree, mistletoe, snowflakes, wasp-nests, stalactites, bronze, goldfish, silver, moonbeams, *marbre, onyx,* and *émail* upon which a labor no longer rebellious was required for fashioning and shaping. Tray after tray of choice images is heaped before the enchanted banquet, a banquet at all events enchanted when this connoisseurship in exquisite miracles and jewels followed a decade of gusty eloquence in various national and partisan literary causes. For her American contemporaries Mrs. Wylie's service resembled that of Rossetti for his generation, of Gautier for his coterie, of the first (but latterly impoverished) imagists for their pioneer readers. Mrs. Wylie has had her imitators, for whom she cannot be held responsible. Yet among them must be counted herself, if we are to count as imitation a duplication of effects which is unjustified by something new to say. There is never, in her work, the slightest difficulty in understanding her meaning—when a meaning is present. In **"Address to My Soul"** there is perhaps material for a quatrain; it has been expanded into eight:

> Fear not, pathetic flame;
> Your sustenance is doubt:
> Glassed in translucent dream
> They cannot snuff you out.
>
> Wear water, or a mask
> Of unapparent cloud;
> Be brave and never ask
> A more defunctive shroud.
>
> The universal points
> Are shrunk into a flower;
> Between its delicate joints
> Chaos keeps no power.

Of ear-pleasure there is a share here, but it requires little inquiry into the content of these statements, or into the mere possibility of a single entity's being capable of sustaining these sleight-of-hand changes in identification (*flame-water-cloud-shroud-flower-chaos*), to reveal the almost complete emptiness of the entire performance.

Excess of verbal symbols is, however, a sin that requires indulgence in Spenser, Shelley, and Swinburne. In itself it is not the worst offense against a creative endowment. But inevitably it endangers the judgment itself, and the reserves of honesty and authority over which the judg-

ment discriminates. Mrs. Wylie celebrated the value of life at its richest, and for her the Puritan instinct disclosed richness in fundamental aspects of simple experience which, however she may have lived apart from them, won her envy and praise. The integrity of human faculties was her single clue to the accessibility of this rich and final experience. Her poems progressively enlarge upon this theme: **"Wild Peaches," "Velvet Shoes," "True Vine," "Innocent Landscape," "Havre de Grace," "One Person," "Hymn to Earth," "This Corruptible," "Nonsense Rhyme," "Indentured."** These are her most ambitious poems; her actual successes lie among the fanciful morsels of her own delight, but there the success was easy. It is in the effort toward philosophy that she invites greater sympathy. Like too many of her contemporaries, however, her praise of integrity is not accompanied by a sufficient respect for it. This could be traced in several details; one of them is her exploitation of the erotic. Mr. Tate has recently referred (*The Symposium,* April, 1932) to the subtle interfusion of the erotic in Emily Dickinson, its unsuspected but essential reinforcement of her symbols, and its relevance to the emotional capacities of a mind which required no mysterious lover for realization. Instinct with a sense of realism, her images at once shock and survive in the mind, and the motivation of them seldom errs through sensational emphasis. Miss Dickinson did not write, in a traditional sense, love poetry, whereas Mrs. Wylie did. Here the amatory element is forthright, and thus open to the dangers of having its mysterious and esthetic energy immediately reduced. In **"One Person"** the philosophic theme is involved in a great deal of traditional literary rhetoric; in only three sonnets it merges with the available symbolism—particularly in *VIII*; in most of the others a species of rhetorical forcing is applied, with the result that an exhaustion sets into the lines, reduces their ability to communicate, and finally escapes by the slightest subterfuge from rendering the intended poignance of the conclusion banal. What distresses one here, as in **"Fatal Interview,"** is that a strenuously urgent and heroic enthusiasm has been reduced to a perilous relationship with the spurious by reason of over-lavish *pastiche* and by redundant ornamentation, although Mrs. Wylie has been wise enough to curb her design to eighteen sonnets. And there remains the conviction that the celebrated clairvoyance of modern love poetry does not discredit the finest achievements in this line among the Victorians—the ten or twelve masterpieces among *The Sonnets from the Portuguese,* or the extraordinary power of that singular and almost unrivalled poem, *Modern Love.*

Pastiche was, indeed, the threat that dogged Mrs. Wylie, like a number of her conspicuous contemporaries, from the beginning. In the sense that one ascribes a grasp of the past to Bridges, Pound, and Eliot, she hardly knew the past at all. Her imitative phrases soon took on the hollow quality of mere baroque excrescence, and resulted in the dispiriting fables which she tolerated in most of her ballads. Folklore was the past she tried to transfix; she also toyed with late Renaissance romances, with artificial epochs such as furnished her with material for her novels, and with the seventeenth-century metaphysical mysteries. With none did she stay long enough to make them her own, although where so much purely meretricious writing succeeds in the market, it is doubtless reprehensible to charge with defection from seriousness the author of *The Venetian Glass Nephew, Jennifer Lorn,* and her various narrative poems. The point is that Mrs. Wylie earnestly sued for an exceptional dignity in her work, and even gave frequent promise of it. Superficially she was a master of her technique: she brought it to yield all that she exacted of it. She did not, however, exact the purposes we look for in significant poetry. She hardly surpassed Miss Lowell in what she had to say, although from the start she was removed by mere fastidious choice from the technical chaos and mental dissipation into which Miss Lowell steadily drifted. Of verbal exercises Mrs. Wylie, in **"Minotaur,"** confessed her fatigue. Of the trumpery of specious feeling and faith, she wrote a malediction in **"Innocent Landscape."** For her art she hoped more than a "pattern of the atmosphere." She did not achieve it, but she lived to provide a volume of divertissements among which are the half-dozen poems that confess a consciousness of esthetic responsibility and ambition which she did not live to fulfil. They do not place her among the exceptional talents of her time, but it is to them, and not to personal testimonials, that the reader of poetry must go for her quality. With any understanding of the genuine sources of modern creative authority he will discern her shortcomings without wishing to sacrifice the pleasure, which, at their best, her wit and dexterity provide.

Allen Tate (review date 1932)

SOURCE: "Elinor Wylie's Poetry," in *The New Republic,* Vol. LXXII, No. 927, Sept. 7, 1932, p. 107.

[*In the following review of* Collected Poems of Elinor Wylie, *Tate acknowledges Wylie's technical skills but suggests that her poetry lacks distinguishing features that would establish her as a stylistically great poet.*]

This collection [the ***Collected Poems*** (1932)] of the verse of Elinor Wylie contains her four volumes exactly as they first appeared and, in addition, forty-seven poems that were not printed in her books. Of these, twenty appear in print for the first time. The book is handsomely bound and beautifully printed, and the editing has been done with great propriety by the poet's husband, Mr. William Rose Benét. Mr. Benét's task was difficult; one is grateful for the restraint and simplicity of his brief memoir, and for the lack on his part of any attempt at criticism.

Although Mrs. Wylie died four years ago—in 1928—and the air of faction that inevitably surrounds a famous poet has lifted, it is still difficult to judge her work. She was both facile and versatile. Her first volume, the book of verse ***Nets to Catch the Wind,*** appeared in 1921, when she was thirty-four; in the seven years to 1928 she issued three more volumes of poems and four novels. All this work is uneven, and it is hard to select the best of it just because, from first to last, her technical competence permitted her to absorb so many of the literary and moral

influences of her time. And I think this same technical mastery kept her, at moments, from ever quite knowing what was her own impulse and what she had assimilated.

It is this feature of her work that explains her brilliant moments and in the end her lack of style: style is that evenness of tone, and permanence of reference for all perceptions, which comes from a mind that, though it may avoid fixed opinions, has nevertheless a single way of taking hold of its material. And this Mrs. Wylie never had. The poet who could write, in **"Hymn to Earth,"**

> A wingless creature heavier than air
> He is rejected of its quintessence;
> Coming and going hence,
> In the twin minutes of his birth and death,
> He may inhale his breath,
> As breath relinquish heaven's atmosphere,
> Yet in it have no share,
> Nor can survive therein
> Where its outer edge is filtered pure and thin:
> It doth but lend its crystal to his lungs
> For his early crying, and his final songs.

—the same poet could write:

> O love, how utterly am I bereaved
> By Time, who sucks the honey of our days,
> Sets sickle to our Aprils, and betrays
> To killing winter all the sun achieved! . . .

One of the defects of Mrs. Wylie's work is that the worst poems have much of the superficial merit of the best. The worst have invariably a metrical finish, a technical form, a verbal completness, that remains hollow inside; the poet did not define her own relation to the material. This is a problem for the poet at all times, but it is now peculiarly the modern problem, and one feels that Mrs. Wylie might have written more solidly in some other age, when the difficulty of self-definition was not so great.

Harriet Monroe (essay date 1932)

SOURCE: "Elinor Wylie," in *Poets & Their Art,* Macmillan, 1932, pp. 106-13.

[*Monroe was a famous poet and the editor of* Poetry: A Magazine of Verse. *In the following excerpt, she praises Wylie's poetic skills and ability to capture the essence of passion and spirit in her poems.*]

Though Elinor Wylie died at forty-two, in a sense her work was complete, was finished. She had perfected her style and delivered her message. Death merely rounded the circle, gave her career a wholeness, a symmetry, as when a thorough-bred racer wins a trophy at the goal which was his starting-point a few minutes before.

Her first poems, like the racer's first paces, were of an instinctive yet trained precision; there was no fumbling or halting, never a stumble or a false step. To be sure, she began later than most poets, never discovering her literary gift until she was well past thirty and disciplined by a tragic experience of life. Still, waiting beyond youth for one's debut in any art does not imply adequate practice in technique—a late beginning tends to make the first steps slow and painful. Not so, however, in Elinor Wylie's case; the four poems printed in 1921 in *Poetry,* which she called her "first acceptor," showed her a master of her tools, capable of artistry which admitted no compromise. She never surpassed the muted music of **"Velvet Shoes,"** and in **"Fire and Sleet and Candle-light"** she traced what became a favorite rhythmic pattern:

> For this you've striven
>   Daring, to fail;
> Your sky is riven
>   Like a tearing veil.
>
> For this you've wasted
>   Wings of your youth;
> Divined, and tasted
>   Bitter springs of truth.
>
>   . . . . .
>
> Your race is ended-
>   See, it is run:
> Nothing is mended
>   Under the sun.
>
> Straight as an arrow
>   You fall to a sleep
> Not too narrow
>   And not too deep.

Here we have at once that exactness of method—the true word, the balanced line, the close rhyme-scheme, in short, the skill and polish—which characterize all her work. We have also the personal significance—her own friendships, loves, joys, agonies implied but never stated, suggested but never sentimentalized. **"Atavism,"** in this earliest group, may be a literal confession of her own feelings; yet, reading it, one gets no facts, but merely a kind of aura surrounding a distinguished human spirit, an aura defending her against mysteries beyond.

The contents of her first three small books of verse are just one hundred poems, most of them very brief, two or three of about fifty lines, and one of nearly two hundred. What she seems to say in the sharp intensity of these poems is the fragility of life in its well-nigh intolerable beauty, and she says it with a sparkle of rich many-colored glazes, like eighteenth-century French porcelains. Her art, indeed, allies itself with the eighteenth century, not so much with the poetry of that period as with those other arts, at once hard as jewels and supremely delicate, which must pass through fire to earn perfection. Like them, she protected emotion with an armor of artificiality, she glazed it with shining colors. And like those rigid old porcelains, so enduring in their fragility, her poems would seem to be protected by their quality, as faultless exhibits from our multi-varied century set up for future generations to wonder at.

It would be interesting to trace the emotional motive in such art. In a picture like Millet's *Angelus,* in lyrics like Sara Teasdale's, the emotional motive is stated in the simplest terms of beauty. But one may be deeply stirred also by a Watteau picnic, or by such a poem as **"A Strange Story,"** even though the emotion here is corseted and veiled and embroidered in all the artificialities of a super-subtle civilization. Not that Elinor Wylie is a Watteau—she is too much a creature of her own time to use his particular kind of elaborately costumed images; but she sees life, as he did, encumbered with all the paraphernalia of civilization, and she goes further than he did in finding it almost overwhelmed under the load. . . .

To return to the poems, which, as her most important work, should alone engage us. I have quoted half of a poem from her first book, with its short lines and staccato rhythm. This pattern delighted her to the end for purposes more or less satiric; we find her using it in **"Peregrine,"** the longest poem in her second book, *Black Armor,* and doubling it into the tetrameter lines of **"Miranda's Supper"** in *Trivial Breath.* The swift steps of the measure accept happily that intricate play of highly original rhymes in which she delighted; she tosses them like a juggler his balls, and catches them dangerously at the end of a line as they seem about to escape her handling. They are clever, witty, miraculously effective; but more than that, they are robust, muscular—they carry the light texture of these poems with authority and power.

But these quick-stepping staccato rhythms were merely the lighter resource of her skilful art. From the first he used the sonnet form now and then, **"Atavism"** being her earliest sonnet, winning from it slow sweeping rhythms. And one of the most beautiful poems in *Trival Breath* **"Desolation is a Delicate Thing,"** trails still slower cadences in lines of variable length. Each new volume shows increased technical expertness, a new delight in fitting her ideas and emotions to the exact forms that reveal them most effectively, and the rhythms that accept most musically her highly figurative language.

Angels and Earthly Creatures, the posthumous book of forty poems which she had arranged just before her sudden death, gives evidence that her art fed and grew to the end upon an ever-enriching spiritual experience. The nineteen sonnets which open the volume form one of the memorable love—sequences of a language supreme in such confessional records of human passion. But even here Elinor Wylie preserves her reticence, speaks proudly from behind a luminous veil of figurative denial:

> Although these words are false, none shall prevail
> To prove them in translation less than true,
> Or overthrow their dignity, or undo
> The faith implicit in a fabulous tale.

Through the richly colored texture of these sonnets one discerns that they are dedicated to a lover of mythical range in tragic power:

The shadow of its light is only this:
That all your beauty is the work of wars
Between the upper and the nether stars;
Its symmetry is perfect and severe
Because the barbarous force of agonies
Broke it, and mended it, and made it clear.

And the sequence as a whole expresses the age-old womanly tribute to masculine strength, the feminine feeling of deprecation in giving to the partnership merely its more fragile and decorative elements. One might quote almost any sonnet to prove this worshipful posture . . .

Besides this sequence, other poems in this book are done on a large scale—they give one a sense of size and mastery in the contemplation and artistic expression of love and death, the two universal elements of the human problem which enthralled her heart and imagination as if with a premonitory warning. Toward the end of her life she seemed to breathe

the honey breath
Issuing from the jaws of death.

The splendid **"Hymn to Earth"** and **"This Corruptible"** celebrate the triumph of death. Almost she begins to accept the ultimate dissolution in a high spirit of reconciliation.

Life for Elinor Wylie was not a simple affair of obvious choices; it was a conflict between, not spirit and flesh, but spirit and intellect. In the **"Song in Black Armor,"** she says wistfully:

When I am dead, or sleeping
Without any pain,
My soul will stop creeping
Through my jewelled brain.

Her jewelled brain defied the claims of the flesh and challenged the claims of the spirit; it dramatized and adorned the hazards of life:

In coldest crucibles of pain
Her shrinking flesh was fired,
And smoothed into a finer grain
To make it more desired.

She could not accept the obvious happiness or the common woe; thought crept in to torture her emotions and temper her art. It gave to her nature a spiral twist and spring, and to her poetry the hard keenness of knowledge. For her there was no peace, except perhaps in another world. But she loved this world of search and strife; in **"Last Supper"** we find her ecstatic over the beauty of it, even while she tastes the pomegranate of Proserpine, and feels in her mouth the seven seeds of death. . . .

It may be proper to close this brief study with a sentence or two from the last letter I received from this poet of high desires and deep despairs. This letter, which was sent from England six weeks before her death in grateful acknowledgment of the Levinson Prize, ends with a ref-

erence to her convalescence after the accident of the previous summer:

Being unable to write novels, I wrote some forty poems of a certain merit. So do you really think it was an "unfortunate accident," or are you not convinced for the thousandth time of an astonishing beauty and strangeness of life?

The beauty and strangeness of life—these she felt intensely and expressed to the limit of her power, like all poets who, in the brief years accorded to them, struggle to give utterance to the inexpressible.

William Rose Benét (essay date 1934)

SOURCE: *The Prose and Poetry of Elinor Wylie,* Wheaton College Press, 1934, 24 p.

[*In the following excerpt from the Annie Talbot Cole Lecture of Wheaton College, Benét describes his late wife as a "great poet," possessed of a natural talent and love of the English language.*]

I contend that [Elinor Wylie] was a great prose writer because she was a great poet. What then is a poet such as she? Such poets have puzzled fine minds through the ages for definition of the quality of their work. For one thing, she was born to welcome the most intensely arduous mental labour in passionate exploration of the utmost resources of the English language in order to express every finest shade of thought and feeling that she experienced. She was abnormally sensitive to the powers latent in language. She had an altogether unusual intuition for the exact word, and had assimilated a large vocabulary. She was unusually erudite, and had her life led her in another direction, might have been a great scholar. And because of these gifts of hers she was greatly humble before the English language. You may recall the "Dedication" to her next but last book of poems that bears the gently ironical title, *Trivial Breath.* That dedication is a fervent tribute to the English language, one she read before the Phi Beta Kappa chapter of Columbia University, and one of the few occasional poems I know that has real poetic fire. It is a sequence of four sonnets. In it she bestows upon our great heritage of the English tongue what she chooses to call "the dull mortal homage of the mind." her fidelity was ever to "early wells of English undefiled." And this is noteworthy in a day when a number of gifted people are calling the English language into question as insufficient in resource for the expression of the extreme subtlety of their thoughts and feelings. For the processes of Elinor Wylie's intuition and reason were the most subtle I have ever known; and she found the finest use of English sufficient, and more than sufficient, for her purposes.

Elinor Wylie wrote with extraordinary precision; but it was a precision that never for a moment sacrificed the incalculable turn of phrase, the spontaneously felicitous expression, that intuitive visitation of words that seems to us who have it not as a gift from the gods. Her subconsciousness was constantly preoccupied with the shape, look, colour, and sound of words; just as the rhythms of poetry were matters to her of second nature, and her sometimes intricate interior rhyming, art concealed by art, in the same kind. The rhythms of her prose, when she came to them, were distilled from the assimilation of an eclectic reading extensive even in childhood. And if, as Emily Dickinson says, "The soul selects its own society," Elinor's mind from the beginning selected its own society and instinctively chose the type of mind and manner of expression germane to her nature. Most Catholic in her relish for good writing of every description, she yet was sure of her own particular province from the beginning.

I have said that the most important thing about Elinor Wylie's prose was that she was a poet. To put it in another way, her prose exhibited the same unusual care in the use of words and had the same stylistic virtue that her poetry possessed. This is true up to a point. . . .

Elinor's poetry was often deeply ironic or delicately ironic or fantastic, but it is rarely satirical. . . .

She leaves an imperishable name and the work of a dedicated artist. She leaves to those who loved her a guiding and luminous presence. She demonstrated what one woman's striving and courageous spirit and indomitable mind can accomplish in a few years in a bewildering world, where life may take strange turnings, but where one's purpose in life can finally be found and mastered. Now her work speaks for her to future generations, and speaks with the incorruptible accent that was all her own.

Alfred Kreymborg (essay date 1934)

SOURCE: "Women as Humans, as Lovers, as Artists," in *A History of American Poetry: Our Singing Strength,* Tudor Publishing Company, 1934, pp. 438-65.

[*In the following excerpt from his book of historical criticism, Kreymborg discusses the pessimism in some of Wylie's poems.*]

The despair and disillusionment setting in after the World War found its most tragic voice abroad in T. S. Eliot. On this side the Atlantic, it found a feminine counterpart in the marvelous brain of Elinor Wylie. Her work was not a direct reaction to the aftermath, but was raised on the private life of an aristocratic nature in no wise akin with the mob or democracy. Among the new aristocracy of intellects rearing ivory towers out of independent domiciles, Eliot was the prince, Elinor Wylie the princess. Each has had a long line of retainers and imitators. The despair of the woman was a positive thing; it was composed, not of self-pity, but of heroic acceptance. A proud person does not trouble himself with improving or reforming life. If he is an esthete, he evades humanity and fashions replicas of himself in beautiful stones, songs, poems. Fairly soon, the esthete turns to a consideration and adoration of death. He turns mystic and

metaphysician, studies the dark, attempts communication with angels and demons, interprets all things in the light of the grave and beyond. Life and the world are imperfect; there is nothing to do but study the microcosm, see it unflinchingly, perfect it supremely, shape one's transitory days into an art for art's sake, an art in league not with mortality, but immortality. Metaphysicians rear their systems on a species of insanity with an extraordinarily brilliant logic no sane man can answer. And these esthetic mystics support their mad reasoning with a magnificent range of cultures out of the past—out of dead mystics strangely reborn in the present. The gorgeous cultural equipment of Elinor Wylie was based on such metaphysicians as Webster, Donne, Blake-and latterly, Eliot. To these she added her own spirit and an intellectual equipment comparable, according to Mary Colum, with the visionary sainthood of "Theresa, and Catherine, and Hildegarde."

I have heard that William Rose Benét was reading the death scene of Mrs. Browning when his wife was mortally stricken with paralysis. A day or two before her death, she had arranged her last collection of poems, *Angels And Earthly Creatures,* and taken it to her publishers. In the course of seven swift years, she had finished four volumes of verse and four of prose. Then the mad flame sank. Her poetry books are *Nets To Catch The Wind, Black Armour, Trivial Breath* and the posthumous volume. *Nets To Catch The Wind* is an unusual first volume that owes its power to the maturity of the woman behind it. It contains a number of lyrics and ballads unique in their hard clarity. The opening poem declares that Beauty has "the hard heart of a child." Then comes the didactic ballad, **"The Eagle And The Mole,"** in which we are told to

Avoid the reeking herd,
Shun the polluted flock,
Live like that stoic bird,
The eagle of the rock.

Here are the leading notes of Elinor Wylie: the aristocratic scorn, the penetrating language, the adoration of symbolical animals, the concern with "disembodied bones," the perfect craftsmanship. As a craftsman, she has few peers and no superiors in our poetry. **"Madman's Song,"** a hunting song inspired by the "milk-white hounds of the moon," the Blakean **"Lion And The Lamb," "Winter Sleep,"** with its hatred of a world "wicked and cross and old," **"Escape,"** with its longing for "a little house" where "you may grope for me in vain," **"A Proud Lady,"** with its refrain that the world, "with hard finger tips" has "chiseled and curled" the "inscrutable lips"—these are lyric diaries of a spirit determined to live apart and carve its own life and art. **"The Tortoise In Eternity,"** bearing "the rainbow bubble earth square on my sorrowful back," is Elinor Wylie in person. But she is not completely blind to her surroundings. **"A Crowded Trolley Car"** is a work of imaginative realism in which the passengers are seen, "hanging by the hands," as if swinging from rope, the while their

Glances strike and glare,
Fingers tangle, Bluebeard's wives
Dangle by the hair.

The lyric concludes:

> One man stands as free men stand,
> As if his soul might be
> Brave, unbroken; see his hand
> Nailed to an oaken tree.

Proverbial feminine softness is absent here. And the title of the second volume, **Black Armour,** is hardly feminine. Neither is the book masculine, except for the incisive intellectual power of its bold images. Indeed, most of Elinor Wylie's poetry is epicene. At times, she rages against the "carnal mesh," or wearies of her "mischievous brain," her body a battleground of cruel, opposing forces. In **"Prophecy,"** there is a further longing for a woodland hut where at the last, the wind may "set his mouth against a crack and blow the candle out." And in **"Song,"** a further hope that

> My soul will stop creeping
> Through my jewelled brain . . .

and a reaching out to "dumb faces and the dusty ground." Though she is "weary forever and ever of being brave," bravery continues. One is not amazed that the swaggering ballad, **"Peregrine,"** was composed by her. This "liar and bragger" who "had no friend"

> Except a dagger
> And a candle-end,

and who fondles "nature's breast, not woman," is "a good fighter, but a bad friend," "a good hater, but a bad lover." Again one pays homage to the masterly versification: the firm hard line and original rhymes-rhymes sometimes strained for originality. Fortunately, there are contradictions in the work of Elinor Wylie. Just as one pronounces finalities about her nature, one finds she is not heartless, not inhuman, not epicene—but a woman, lonely, though proud. In a superb lyric, she renounces a former comparison with the eagle:

> I was, being human, born alone;
> I am, being woman, hard beset;
> I live by squeezing from a stone
> The little nourishment I get.

And the patrician personality asks no charity. The "impressive" hand "preserves a shape too utterly its own." **"Fable"** is a ballad full of devastating images of a white raven "dipping her beak" in the blood of a knight. The ballad is Poesque in its piling of the grotesque on the horrible, and is not unrelated to Keats' "La Belle Dame Sans Merci." **"Castilian"** is a brilliant portrait of the portrait-painter, Velasquez. It vies with Browning's portraits of artists and escapes the optimistic smudges of an ultimate Victorian moral. **"Sequence"** is a poem in six austere, rather vague stanzas. Though love is not referred to concretely, one receives an impression that something has gone to its grave, and possibly a man or two.

> And I am barren in a barren land,
> But who so breaks me, I shall pierce his hand.

Here is none of Miss [Edna] Millay's farewell flippancy. Though Elinor Wylie is equally self-centred in the same situation, it is clear to her that the man must "go his way, in agony and sweat, because he could not pity nor forget." The penultimate stanza is a triumph in proud self-revelation:

> For various questions which I shall not ask,
> And various answers which I cannot hear,
> I have contrived a substituted task
> To prove my body is devoid of fear;
> To prove my spirit's elemental blood
> Is pure, courageous, and uniform,
> I shall submerge my body in the mud,
> I shall submit my spirit to the storm;
> I shall bend down my bosom to the snake,
> As to an infant for its father's sake.

"Trivial Breath" opens with a Dedication to the English language—"that conduit whose veins are threaded with pellucid truth!" And to this tongue she devoted herself from infancy: "The woman never wandered in vile devotion to a lesser prince." As Elinor Wylie was an inveterate reader of classical English, so her development as an artist grew more and more literary, less and less concrete. Her last two books are subtler esthetic productions than the first two, and still farther removed from ordinary existence. Fine-spun abstractions thread an exquisite tapestry, a more-than-human, less-than-human design. Dreaming "no ill of Death," the artist concerns herself with metaphysical ghosts, with extinction of the body and the trumpeting of dust. But the balladist continues to expound powerful chants in **"Peter And John," "The Innocents," "A Strange Story," "The Puritan's Ballad," "As I Went Down By Havre De Grace."** **"A Strange Story"** and **"Malediction Upon Myself"** are tributes to the London which became the capital of her wandering spirit during the later years. **"A Strange Story"** owes its charm to a traditional play on names of places: old quarters in which the poet assumes she has died: Berners Street, Houndsditch, Holborn, Marleybone, Lincoln's Inn, Bloomsbury. The heroic mood pervades **"Unwilling Admission," "False Prophet," "Hospes Comesque Corporis," "Address To My Soul," "Last Supper," "Lament For Glasgerion."** The soul remains securely serene in the midst of planetary wars.

> Five-petalled flame, be cold:
> Be firm, dissolving star:
> Accept the stricter mould
> That makes you singular.

Here is the didactic note of the older metaphysicians, reborn in Elinor Wylie, reborn again in her disciples. Nor does the head droop in the face of advancing time:

> The vanishing dust of my heart is proud
> To watch me wither and grow old.

The final volume, most of which was written in England, has a surprising return to the feminine: the clearest revelation of the woman the poet ever revealed. But the metaphysical note persists: reaches its deepest, most abstract, most poignant and beautiful tones. The slender book is divided into four groups: a sequence of nineteen sonnets to **"One Person," "Elements And Angels," "Earthly Creatures," "Elegies And Epistles."** The earthly creatures have an unearthly, English air. The ballad of **"Robin Hood's Heart"** is a disguised ballad; so are **"The Mountaineer's Ballad"** and **"Hughie At The Inn."** The valiant Hughie combating enemies, seen and unseen, is Elinor Wylie. **"Bread Alone"** is a perfect lyric, in which the woman humbles herself because of a heart that "is not great."

> Ah, poor machine, and faithful,
> That limps without a wing!
> My love, be never wrathful
> With this imperfect thing.

The sonnet sequence is a confession of love, adoration and faith in an Englishman, and the prefatory sonnet a proud prophecy:

> The ashes of this error shall exhale
> Essential verity, and two by two
> Lovers devout and loyal shall renew
> The legend, and refuse to let it fail.

That this love should have come just before death, and be most clearly revealed, is a characteristic coda to a life lived intensely and fearlessly. And now the lover, not the woman, becomes the symbolical eagle, and the woman a "hound for faithfulness." Pride, scorn and the ego have grown humble:

> Now do I grow indignant at the fate
> Which made me so imperfect to compare
> With your degree of noble and of fair;
> Our elements are the farthest skies apart;
> And I enjoin you, ere it is too late,
> To stamp your superscription on my heart.

The "Platonic mind" gives way "to those sharp ecstasies the pulses give." Even so, "both soul and body are unfit to apprehend this miracle, my lord!" Deepest of all is the will not to hurt:

> What voice can my invention find to say
> So soft, precise, and scrupulous a word
> You shall not take it for another sword?

Elsewhere she asks him for strength to "set me where I bear a little more than I can bear." No matter what the outcome, she lives triumphant and will die the same,

> Upon the fringes of this continent,
> This map of Paradise, this scrap of earth
> Whereon you burn like flame upon a hearth.

Such metaphysical poems as **"Chimæra Sleeping," "Absent Thee From Felicity Awhile," "O Virtuous Light," "Hymn To Earth," "This Corruptible,"** are probably the finest ever written by Elinor Wylie. **"O Virtuous Light"** hovers on the verge of insanity. "Where the slow miracles of thought take shape through patience into grace"—

> This light begotten of itself
> Is not a light by which to live!

The body—heart, brain and spirit—must be translated into clay. For epitaph, we need not go beyond the poet herself: the woman-artist so intimate with death and the death in living:

> Farewell, sweet dust; I was never a miser:
> Once, for a minute, I made you mine:
> Now you are gone, I am none the wiser
> But the leaves of the willow are bright as wine.

Horace Gregory and Marya Zaturenska (essay date 1946)

SOURCE: "Elinor Wylie and Léonie Adams: The Poetry of Feminine Sensibility," in *A History of American Poetry, 1900-1940,* Harcourt, Brace and Company, 1946, pp. 282-99.

[*In the following excerpt from their critical collection, the authors compare Wylie's style to that of other female writers including Edith Wharton, suggesting that Wylie's final sonnets were influenced by Wharton's novel* The House of Mirth.]

Elinor Wylie, who was born September 7, 1885, and died in New York December 16, 1928, was not a precocious poet, and her publications, like the brilliant, public events of her career, were timed with art; she appeared before her readers as the finished artist, correct and polished. Her second book, *Nets to Catch the Wind,* 1921, was published when Mrs. Wylie was in her thirties and its appearance quickly established her reputation. (In 1912 her first book of poems, *Incidental Numbers,* a private edition of sixty copies with the author's name withheld from the title page, was printed in London.) Unlike Edna St. Vincent Millay, Mrs. Wylie did not choose to conduct her education in public: refinement and fastidiousness were among the chief characteristics of the legend built around her name and among her chief literary influences were Lionel Johnson, Walter Savage Landor, and Thomas Love Peacock, all writers who combined the imaginative warmth of the Romantic Movement with the decorum, the restraint, the rhetorical elegance of the eighteenth century. It has been said that she had been influenced by the poetry of W. B. Yeats, but if this is true, her work reflected Yeats's poetry whenever it seemed to be most notably influenced by his early friend and contemporary, Lionel Johnson. From John Donne, she, like many young writers of the 1920's, acquired subject matter and "metaphysical" attitudes, rather than the qualities of his vigorous intellect, the depth of his insight, and his masculinity. From Shelley (whom she romanticized all her life and seemed to have loved for the wrong reasons, always loving rather than understanding him) the chief influence came through his letters with their boyish mixture of eighteenth-century diction and Romantic sensibility. In fact it might be said of her lifelong passion for Shelley that, unlike Amy Lowell's patient, humble, almost maternal devotion to Keats's memory, hers was a passion of self-identity. She re-created Shelley in her own image, and with this vision before her as she sat down to write, she half convinced herself that she *was* Shelley, writing the poems that he would have written—if he had been a beautiful woman and a poet, living as she lived, and writing in the 1920's. She also wrote as if to please the minds of Walter Savage Landor and Thomas Love Peacock—and if Landor's personal relationship to Shelley may be reduced to a bowing acquaintance on the streets of Pisa, and if Peacock's memoirs revealed the young poet in the light of half cynical, half affectionate regard, these men were the most fastidious and (in an intellectual and esthetic sense) the most respectable of Shelley's friends and contemporaries.

No woman (especially in the 1920's—and Edna St. Vincent Millay shows only too well the dangers of that period) could have chosen finer models than Peacock and Landor, for both were men of the world, men of wit and intellect, and what is even more important, both were fastidious and brilliant writers. There is considerable evidence that Elinor Wylie took their virtues to heart and in so doing avoided the pitfalls and temptations of many women writers. As early as 1854, a Mr. George Bethune, who edited a popular anthology containing the best selections he could find of all the Englishwomen writing poetry, from the Duchess of Newcastle to Elizabeth Barrett Browning, and who had made a wide study of his subject, wrote sadly:

> The prominent fault of female poetical writers is an unwillingness to use the pruning knife and the pumicestone. They write from impulse and as rapidly as they think. The strange faculty, which women have, of reaching conclusions (and, in the main, safe conclusions) without the slow process of reasoning through which men have to pass; the strong moral instincts with which their nature is endowed, far above that of the other sex; their keen and discerning sensibility to the tender, the beautiful and luxuriant render them adverse to critical restraint.

If one puts aside the comments on the strong moral instincts of women (since in the 1920's many who had them were careful to disguise them or to call them something else), Elinor Wylie was almost completely free of these particular defects in Mr. Bethune's female Muse. Because it lacked these flaws, her work was a memorable example to her immediate contemporaries; it set a standard and a taste whose influence should not be underestimated, and even today, one rediscovers the imprint of its mark upon the verse written by her followers. Such an influence (for she, like Miss Millay, became headmistress of a literary school) is often the direct result of a powerful or attractive personality—and the personality with which Elinor Wylie faced the world was so passionately self-obsessed, sharp, and self-penetrating that it took on (like all transfigurations of true love) an almost impersonal air. It was as though she had seen her face in the mirror and found it so compelling and beautiful that the self-image was reflected everywhere. Even in her portrait of a painter (and it would be Velásquez!) there is a double image of a beautiful and arrogant woman, disguised as a painter leaning from his studio window, and a Castilian gentleman walking down the street. The emotion in the scene is completely self-absorbed and completely feminine:

> He burnt the rags in the fireplace
> And leaned from the window high;
> He said, "I like that gentleman's face
> Who wears his cap awry."
>
> This is the gentleman, there he stands,
> Castilian, sombre-caped,
> With arrogant eyes, and narrow hands
> Miraculously shaped.
>
> **"Castilian"**

If Elinor Wylie's self-absorption may be defined in terms of what the eighteenth century called a "ruling passion," like all overwhelming and consuming emotions it carried with it the conviction of having an importance beyond the mere reflection in a glass; and she conveyed her "passion" with all the art her skill could master. To this day we have unconsciously amusing parodies of her style, poems that speak of proud boys running in the wind, poems of equally proud, fastidious, well-dressed, good-looking women who yearn to possess the "hard heart of a child," to own things that contain the qualities of quicksilver and of crystal—but it is the attitude and not the essence that her imitators have caught—and she, like many a good artist before her, cannot be held responsible for all the inept vanities and empty gestures of the school which followed her. Carl Van Doren defined one of her more valuable characteristics when he said, "She respected the passions and she respected mind and manners," and this form of respect—in her case, self-respect-was as rare twenty-five years ago as it is today, and those who have it are seldom shoddy craftsmen.

Her novels were, as H. Lüdeke, a Dutch commentator, wrote, limited to "a dream world, a dream-perfume distilled from literature," a world which was perhaps best achieved and created in the early poetry of Edith Sitwell. Too many literary fancies and vanities employed Elinor Wylie's moments as she composed her prose romances. But where was the form into which the essence of her personality could find hope of an endurance beyond the moment of creation? what form could contain the perishable mood, the willful mannerism? what air could keep the grass green in that artful, seemingly artificial, world, could keep the strange, metallic, blown-glass flowers blooming? The answer may be found in her poetry.

Her posthumously published ***Collected Poems*** containing her four books of poems between the covers of a single volume appeared in 1932. The book was edited by her husband, William Rose Benét, and his preface, unlike most pieces written on such occasions (one has only to remember the ghoulish figure of J. Middleton Murry over the remains of Katherine Mansfield) is an excellent tribute to Mrs. Wylie's memory, informal, light in texture, and yet sustained by dignity. The span of Elinor Wylie's professional writing lasted for the comparatively short space of seven or eight years—and in fashion or out, her poems have retained all that a brief moment in prose letters had to say.

The external world that Elinor Wylie's poetry reflected in the public mind was of Washington, D. C., and New York society in which Mrs. Wylie had been a conspicuous figure, and probably the most innocent betrayal of the milieu was in a story of her life written by her sister, Nancy Hoyt, *The Portrait of an Unknown Lady* (1935). There, the buying of an expensive pair of silver slippers, or a gown to be worn at a literary soirée, or the acquisition of a Shelley autograph were placed on the same level as the writing of a fine poem or the last scene of an unhappy love affair. The poet herself cannot be blamed for the revelations contained in a biography, but if one reads another record of the period by one of the most intelligent members of a group that moved in the same literary orbit, one is again struck by Nancy Hoyt's artless accuracy: for Edmund Wilson's *I Thought of Daisy* re-creates the same moral climate and confusion of values—and will no doubt cause a future historian of our time, of our literary life and its morals and manners, the same amusement and distress.

Elinor Wylie (unlike many of her friends and imitators) was born into a scene of social activity that Henry James or Edith Wharton or Amy Lowell of Sevenells would have understood, and here, one may truly add, "that she lived as she wrote and wrote as she lived." Rarely in literary history have a personality and the actual details of living been so completely unified. "Elinor was accustomed to reading the best books, wearing the nicest tea-gowns, and living the most quiet of quiet lives"—wrote Nancy Hoyt, but again one must add that the "quiet life" had almost come to an end the moment Elinor Wylie became a literary figure of some consequence. She displayed her aloofness to large and admiring groups of what were then known quaintly as "sophisticates" in New York literary society, and her beauty, her temperament, her romantic domestic history had already preceded her. She appeared at Poetry Society dinners attired with a *chic* until then unknown to literary ladies, or walked into poetry recitals of the MacDowell Colony Club reading badly in a shrill voice that was said to have resembled Shelley's— but dressed to perfection, looking, as Carl Van Doren remarked, "like the white queen of a white country," and she entertained at her apartment in New York's 9th Street in an exquisitely furnished room, "dominated by its memorable silver mirror." Her poems, as each slim volume appeared, furthered the atmosphere of glamour surrounding her name to an increasing public, and her novels, which made solid sums of money and were published in an amazingly rapid progression, sustained the legend of the hand that wrote:

> O, she is neither good nor bad,
> But innocent and wild!
>
> ["Beauty"]

and

> Five-petalled flame, be cold:
> Be firm, dissolving star:
> Accept the stricter mould
> That makes you singular.
>
> "Address to My Soul"

Among those with whom she had lived before her marriage to William Rose Benét in 1923, her devotion to poetry was singular enough, but the sense of doom that was so mem-

orably expressed in the concluding sonnet of her posthumously published *Angels and Earthly Creatures* (1929) had its analogy to one of the closing scenes in Edith Wharton's masterpiece, *The House of Mirth,* that novel of fashionable New York society whose heroine, Lily Bart, lived within the same moral and social environment that Mrs. Wylie had inhabited. And though Mrs. Wylie's character and temperament were as clearly self-realized as Lily Bart's were vague and immature, their sensibilities were of like depth and quality; and Elinor Wylie was as fine an artist in the writing of her sonnets as Edith Wharton was a true mistress of her art in writing prose. The analogy is one in which premonitions of disaster are also of like depth and quality; and the very details of dress, their emotional importance to Lily Bart, created an atmosphere which was far better suited to express the sense of loss that was conveyed in the sonnets of *Angels and Earthly Creatures* than any recital of biographical facts and their relationship to Elinor Wylie's poetry:

> The remaining dresses, though they had lost their freshness, still kept the long unerring lines, the sweep and amplitude of the great artist's stroke, and as she spread them out on the bed the scenes in which they had been worn rose vividly before her. An association lurked in every fold: each fall of lace and gleam of embroidery was like a letter in the record of her past. She was startled to find how the atmosphere of her old life enveloped her. But, after all, it was the life she had been made for: every dawning tendency in her had been carefully directed toward it, all her interests and activities had been taught to centre around it. She was like some rare flower grown for exhibition, a flower from which every bud had been nipped except the crowning blossom of her beauty.

> Last of all, she drew forth from the bottom of her trunk a heap of white drapery which fell shapelessly across her arm. It was the Reynolds dress she had worn in the Bry *tableaux.* It had been impossible for her to give it away, but she had never seen it since that night, and the long flexible folds, as she shook them out, gave forth an odour of violets which came to her like a breath from the flower-edged fountain where she had stood. . . . She put back the dresses one by one, laying away with each some gleam of light, some note of laughter, some stray waft from the rosy shores of pleasure. She was still in a state of highly-wrought impressionability, and every hint of the past sent a lingering tremor along her nerves.

The note that Edith Wharton touched so clearly was elegiac, and in the concluding paragraphs of her novel, the appropriately brief scene after Lily Bart's death, one has a glimpse of the same moment that Elinor Wylie felt so surely before her own untimely death. Lily Bart's lover had come to her rooms.

> It was this moment of love, this fleeting victory over themselves, which had kept them from atrophy and extinction; which, in her, had reached out to him in every struggle against the influence of her surroundings, and in him, had kept alive the faith that now drew him penitent and reconciled to her side.

He knelt by the bed and bent over her, draining their last moment to its lees; and in the silence there passed between them the word which made all clear.

And this last scene was re-enacted in the last eight lines of her last sonnet, a sonnet of sixteen lines, for which she had a precedent in Meredith's sixteen-line sonnets in his sequence, *Modern Love:*

> And let us creep into the smallest room
> That any hunted exile has desired
> For him and for his love when he was tired;
> And sleep oblivious of any doom
> Which is beyond our reason to conceive;
> And so forget to weep, forget to grieve,
> And wake, and touch each other's hands, and turn
> Upon a bed of juniper and fern.

Throughout her later work there is a quality not common to lyric poetry that moves as easily as hers and that quality is best described in terms of poetic intelligence and wit. Her intelligence was of a sort that implied the uses of self-conscious art: hers was the expression of a larger movement toward conscious artistry in poetry, a movement which at its best includes such diverse figures as Conrad Aiken and T. S. Eliot and the later William Butler Yeats. And since formality was among the laws by which she lived, the sonnet became the means by which her world of bright objects, chamber music, and self-identified emotions took fire, and in her last sonnet sequence discovered its most fortunate and enduring form.

Nor after one has praised her sonnets, should one fail to mention once again her gifts for re-creating verbal music, her sharp and clearly discerning ear. Many of Elinor Wylie's shorter lyrics bear testimony to this feeling for music and it is one of the reasons why her poems were often reread and are still read with pleasure. One of the most subtle and technically adroit of her later poems—which contains her characteristic music at its best and which illustrates her art in reiterating her major theme-is **"Chimaera Sleeping."**. . .

To all who wrote in her genre during the first half of the 1920's in America (and the list would include those novelists whose accomplishments brought to transitory life the dreams and aspirations of the forgotten Donald Evans), Elinor Wylie's poetry became the very personification of their art; their intentions were endowed with a brittle, and yet unmistakable, distinction, and their desires were cast into a form that is most likely to endure.

James G. Southworth (essay date 1954)

SOURCE: "Elinor Wylie: 1825-1928," in *More Modern American Poets,* Basil Blackwell, 1954, pp. 35-40.

[*In the following excerpt from his collection of critical essays, Southworth faults Wylie's poetry, suggesting that it lacks the necessary quality that would enable it to maintain the status of exceptional literature over time.*]

Miss Elinor Wylie has been favoured with a good "press" and she has often been spoken of as one of America's great women poets. . . . [Although] I can admire some fifteen of her poems, I do not think Time will continue to do what her late husband and his and her friends with ready access to the public's ear were so able to do for her. The poems on which her reputation will rest are early as well as late, serious, humorous, and ironic, and are confined to no one subject. Taken in order from her *Collected Poems,* they are "Velvet Shoes," "Let No Charitable Hope," "Cold-Blooded Creatures," "Love Song," "The little beauty that I was allowed," "I have believed that I prefer to live," "Little Elegy," "Pretty Words," "Viennese Waltz," "Golden Bough," and "A Tear for Cressid." Not all of these are of the same quality and I think none of them ranks with the truly great lyrics in our heritage of English literature. . . .

[Miss Wylie] has a tendency to over-emphasize her state. . . . Particularly is she apt to overstress her ability to make a synthesis out of refractory materials and to over-estimate the precision of her mind.

Death is important in her poetry, particularly as a release of the soul from the prison of the body, a release often intimately bound up with love. But it is her treatment of love that will most appeal to the majority of her readers. Her approach is what Mr. [John Crowe] Ransom calls the "heart's desire" approach, and it reaches its greatest intensity in the sonnet sequence from Section One of *Angels and Earthly Creatures,* known as **"One Person."** Although the reader will not question the intensity of the emotion, he may well question the artistry with which she expresses that emotion. At no time is the precision of her mind more open to question than in her treatment of details. Extravagance and confusion are often present. . . . Personally, I have always found it difficult to understand why lovers could not be friends, but Miss Wylie, being extremely feminine in her whole approach to life, believes that it is impossible, and is explicit on the subject on several occasions. Her love poems, in spite of their imperfections (or because of them) will appeal to the same readers as does Elizabeth Barrett Browning's "How do I love thee," for which I have never greatly cared.

Certain weaknesses of Miss Wylie are obvious; others call for attention. Quite obvious, for example, is the fact that she is incapable of sustained flight. In **"Miranda's Supper,"** she not only fails with the poem as a whole, but the rhyme word often dictates the thought and some of the rhymes are inexcusable. Even in a shorter poem, such as **"Wild Peaches,"** the thought is often dictated by the rhyme rather than the reverse, as, quite obviously, it should be. Bad rhymes occur frequently throughout her poetry. At times Miss Wylie's rhythms, never anything but traditional, are too facile, as in **"Silver Filigree"** and some of her ocrosyllabics, always a dangerous measure.

My greatest quarrel is with the details of many of the poems. As pleasant as is **"Velvet Shoes,"** for example, I find **"White as a white cow's milk"** a little silly. I never thought the whiteness of the cow affected the colour of the milk. In **"Sequence,"** which I confess I find confusing in general, I think her statement that a man might find her skeleton and bury it to "circumvent the wolf" attributes to the wolf an interest in dry bones that he probably does not possess. Were these . . . isolated cases, I should not call attention to them, but such weaknesses flaw poem after poem.

It would be unfair to Miss Wylie, however, not to make some amends. . . . [**"Little Elegy"**] and **"Velvet Shoes"** will certainly be long remembered. In these two the rhythms are more distinctively her own. Elsewhere the music is strongly derivative. There are obvious echoes of Shakespeare. Shelley, and Keats, with an occasional echo of A. E. Housman and Emily Dickinson. Because her rhythms exact no effort from the reader before her music can be enjoyed—it being obvious rather than subtle and delicately modulated—she must pay the penalty of being sooner passed by. Max Friedlander, the great art critic, has remarked that a truly great work will repel before it begins to attract. . . . Miss Wylie's poetry begins by attracting.

Babette Deutsch (essay date 1956)

SOURCE: "The Ghostly Member," in *Poetry in Our Time,* Columbia University Press, 1956, pp. 220-53.

[*In the following excerpt from her collection of critical essays, Deutsch discusses Wylie's metaphysical style in comparison to traditional metaphysical poets.*]

Working closely within the tradition, Mrs. Wylie had the craftsman's concern for phrasing, and for the particular qualities of words. Her poem, **"Bronze Trumpets and Sea Water—On Turning Latin into English,"** is eloquent of this. She never indulged in the verbal sport of Edith Sitwell and Wallace Stevens, nor rose to their imaginative power. She cherished her nouns and adjectives as she did such ornaments of life as rich stuffs, fine china, tooled volumes, gardens, jewels. If her verse displays the conceits of seventeenth-century poetry and sometimes approaches its passionate intellectualism, it can also breathe the cool elegance of the eighteenth century, and is relatively free of a Shelleyan vagueness. Mrs. Wylie's devotion to that arch-romantic never fooled her into believing that he was her proper model. By the same token, though as homesick as Miss Sitwell for the dignities and beauties of an irrecoverable age, she rejected that poet's means of recapturing them.

One may gauge the distance between these two by examining such a piece as **"Miranda's Supper,"** the account of a Virginian lady's recovery of the treasures she had buried at the coming of the Northern invader, and contrasting it with Miss Sitwell's treatment of similar themes. Mrs. Wylie's couplets have the sparkle of the silver, the delicate colors of the porcelain, and something of the precious quality of the heirlooms they describe. Miss Sitwell's lyrics hover elegiacally about "a land, austere and elegant" and

with a longer, nobler history than Miranda's. She introduces us to its gardens and its castle, which "seemed an arabesque in music," and achieves effects more magical than Mrs. Wylie's smooth numbers produce; but abruptly she breaks the spell. The rhythms become jerky because in working out her abstract designs she ignores the larger pattern of the melodic line, or she presents superimposed images like the lines of a blurred palimpsest. Sometimes she obtrudes a flat statement such as "When we were young, how beautiful life seemed!"—a gaucheness from which Mrs. Wylie was saved by her habit of ironic self-contemplation, though it also prevented her from plunging as deep or soaring as far as this like-minded poet.

Mrs. Wylie's early lyrics sang of Love the lamblike and the leonine in the pure tones of the *Songs of Innocence,* and with something of the fierce insight of the *Songs of Experience.* But here was clearly no masculine voice. It was as feminine as that of a previous traveler who went companioned by the single hound of her own identity. These alliances are natural. Inasmuch as Blake was in rebellion against his century, he was in sympathy with those earlier poets who had lived not in time but in Eternity. Emily Dickinson, as much a heretic in her generation as Blake in his, was their true descendant. Her poetry exhibits a nice mixture of wit and intensity. Elinor Wylie shared her belief that

> The Myrrhs and Mochas of the mind
> Are its Iniquity,

and that

> Much madness is divinest sense
> To a discerning eye,

as strongly as she shared the conviction that every human soul is its own "indestructible estate." Both women, like Blake before them, were at home in the company of the physician who had once felt through all his fleshly dress "Bright shootes of everlastingnesse," and the shoemaker's child for whom "something infinite behind everything appeared: which talked with [his] expectation and moved [his] desire."

Elinor Wylie used familiar forms, the carefully wrought lyric, the ballad, the ode, producing, among other things, a sonnet sequence that celebrates a tragic passion as memorably as any similar performance in our time. Characteristically, while the tone of the sequence is gravely romantic, the introductory sonnet is threaded with a sad irony. Having played variations on the theme of loyalty and betrayal in love, it concludes:

> These words are true, although at intervals
> The unfaithful clay contrive to make them false.

This ironic note as much as the employment of subtle conceits show her allegiance to John Donne. Such a lyric as **"O Virtuous Light,"** desperately acknowledging the mystic's danger, and the austere **"Birthday Sonnet,"** composed most fittingly the day before her death, the many poems pointed with self-mockery, amplify the evidence of her tutelage by that inquisitorial lover and passionate penitent. Her verse gives us a spirit coolly studying its own wounds.

That she was a metaphysical poet in the wider as well as in the narrower sense of the term is proven by several lyrics, notably by the one entitled **"This Corruptible."** The cadences are as full of small surprises as a sixteenth-century melody, the language is deliberately archaic, and the argument one of perennial interest to mortal men, for here the Mind, the Heart, and the Soul discourse upon the dissolution of the body with deceiving urbanity and deep feeling. The Mind is scornful of the Body's claims to anything more than food and rest. The Heart, weary of this "fustian cloak," would gladly put it off for "embroidered archangelic plumage." But the Spirit, wiser than both, addresses the Body with a half-wry tenderness:

> O lodging for the night!
> O house of my delight!

and pleads with it to endure yet another day. It is the Body, the unlucky slave, unkindly used by these whom it serves, that will in the end escape

> In some enchanting shape
> Or be dissolved to elemental nothing.

Those others, Mind and Heart and Spirit, are forever captive to themselves, whereas the Body is bound to be released, its substance transformed, its shape quite altered. The poem concludes, compassionately and chillingly:

> "'Tis you who are the ghost,
> Disintegrated, lost;
> The burden shed; the dead who need not bear it;
> O grain of God in power,
> Endure another hour!
> It is but for an hour," said the Spirit.

The poets grouped together here have been able to write of spirit without embarrassment. The suspicion that attaches to the word is felt least by those who can answer the altering seasons, whether of nature or of the personal life, with something of the religious exaltation communicated by the devotional poets of the seventeenth century, an emotion tempered, for some, with critical audacity and psychological penetration. Whatever their period, however individual their voices, such writers fasten their attention upon the mystery of being, and especially upon that which chiefly bears witness to it, the imaginative faculty. They are the victims and the devotees of an awareness which, as in the poem just cited, recognizes its own limitations. And they are sufficiently appreciative of the miracles open to "the chief inlets of soul in this age," as Blake called the five senses, to keep from being trapped by a mysticism that denies the flesh, along with the world and the devil. The harmony that they feel, however darkly, to be governing the universe allows them to believe with him that "Eternity is in love with the productions of time."

Thomas A. Gray (essay date 1963)

SOURCE: "Elinor Wylie: The Puritan Marrow and the Silver Filigree," in *Arizona Quarterly,* Vol. 19, No. 4, Winter, 1963, pp. 343-57.

[In the following, Gray analyzes Wylie's ability to combine Imagistic techniques and Romantic themes.]

It should be obvious that quite as much banality, raw emotion, crudity of image, and bathos can be produced by Imagists as by anyone else. While often avoiding the vices of the color-mongers and jade-purveyors, [John Gould] Fletcher and [Amy] Lowell fall into equally nauseating practices. But this is not surprising where the poet's emphasis is on the purely physical, where he scrupulously divests his poetry of idea to present "things in their thinginess." In order to be fresh and original the Imagist poet must either search for new things—of which there will eventually be a limited number—or describe old things in a new way, both of which practices will lead him further and further toward the grotesque, the merely picturesque, or the banal.

Elinor Wylie avoids most of this in her best poems: the raw emotion of [Edna St. Vincent] Millay, the banality of Lowell, the bathos of Lowell and Millay, and the crudity of John Gould Fletcher. The precise control of emotion through carefully selected image and figure is the most admirable trait of her poetry. This careful control, however, does not diminish the impact of the emotion; it concentrates and distills it to an intense potency. A poem like **"Fable"** seems not a personal creation but a myth, whose emotional content has been constantly deepened and enriched but refined and clarified through several generations. The poem has all the restraint which gives the old ballads their telling emotional intensity. . . .

Only the next to the last stanza is at all open to question: "Insensate" and "cruel" break the chill tone of detachment which characterizes the rest of the stanzas. Aside from this, little of Wylie's own feeling is expressed overtly. Yet, it is implicit in the way she describes the knight. He has a "lean and carven head," "great gold eyes"; his beard is "ravelled up / In stiff and webby skeins"; he has a broad skull. These few details are sufficient to show that the knight lying dead is somehow nobler than others of his class, and that his fate has been hard and possibly unjust. This feeling is intensified by the description of the raven dipping her beak in blood and sipping the knight's brains. Had the raven been black the sense of outrage would still be strong, but making the raven white and having her fly to "God's house" to drink "the virtuous air" gives the poem an intense irony. This is no longer mere desecration of a noble form by a carrion bird, but a hint at cosmic outrage in which God is involved. Yet none of this is given directly; there is no coercion of the feelings. The emotion is carried only by the simple and spare image of the raven and the fallen knight.

Few of Elinor Wylie's poems have the compression and intensity of **"Fable,"** but others show the same care to avoid direct statement of emotion, and an excess of sentiment. **"Death and the Maiden,"** with its hard, bright tone of irony, exerts a stiff control over the hardest of all subjects to write about without sentimentality and cries of self-pity: one's own death.

> Fair youth with the rose at your lips,
> A riddle is hid in your eyes;
> Discard conversational quips,
> Give over elaborate disguise.
>
> The rose's funereal breath
> Confirms my intuitive fears;
> To prove your devotion, Sir Death,
> Avaunt for a dozen of years.
>
> But do not forget to array
> Your terror in juvenile charms;
> I shall deeply regret my delay
> If I sleep in a skeleton's arms.

The personification of death as a young man with a rose at his lips, conventionally figuring forth love, is in itself an irony. But the development of this figure is even more an irony. "I can see through your disguise, death; but play your role for a little longer, and mind you when you come at last don't leave your disguise behind. I am not fooled by your disguise, but I prefer it to your usual form." The use of images and figures that suggest love, to describe death not only prevents sentimentality, but refines the emotion: death is both welcome and unwelcome. Elinor Wylie communicates an emotion which is at the root of all self-pity without a trace of sentimentality.

Equal with death in its power to elicit the too conscious sigh and the too obvious tear is the lover absent from his love. But Elinor Wylie is able to trim the usual vague emotion of love into precise poetic statement. She is aware, in Sonnet VII of **"One Person,"** that while a lover should pay no attention to "the syntax of things," a poet must.

> Would I might make subliminal my flesh
> And so contrive a gentle atmosphere
> To comfort you because I am not there;
> Or else incorporate and carve afresh
> A lady, from the chilly heaven and clear
> Which flows around you like a stream of air,
> To warm and wind you in her body's mesh.
>
> So would I cherish you a loving twice;
> Once in a mist made matter; once again
> In my true substance made ethereal:
> And yet I cannot succour you at all
> Whose letter cries, "my hands are cold as ice."
> The while I kiss the colder air in vain.

Both the point of view and the details of the poem work to prevent coercion of the reader's emotions. The commonest center of attention in a love poem is the self; the speaker concentrates narcissistically on describing his own undefined feelings. In this poem the narrator concentrates on the absent person, her response to the situation con-

trolled and modified by the response of the absent one. Through the images of "gentle atmosphere" and the carved lady, both extensions of the speaker of the poem, the intensity of the speaker's desire to be with the absent one is made clear. Thus the emotion is refined both through point of view and through images until it becomes precise and accurate statement.

But the best example of Wylie's care to avoid raw emotion and sentimentality is Sonnet XVIII of **"One Person."** The subject is again a common one: two lovers spurn the world and take refuge in their own relationship. The first octave gives a picture of the world to be spurned, and the reasons for spurning it.

> Let us leave talking of angelic hosts
> Of nebulae, and lunar hemispheres,
> And what the days, and what the Uranian years
> Shall offer us when you and I are ghosts;
> Forget the festivals and pentecosts
> Of metaphysics, and the lesser fears
> Confound us, and seal up our eyes and ears
> Like little rivers locked below the frosts.
>
> And let us creep into the smallest room
> That any hunted exile has desired
> For him and for his love when he was tired;
> And sleep oblivious to any doom
> Which is beyond our reason to conceive;
> And so forget to weep, forget to grieve,
> And wake, and touch each other's hands and turn
> Upon a bed of juniper and fern.

Instead of raving, "The world is too much with us," Elinor Wylie defines that world and its specific negative effects on human beings. The first octave presents cosmic dimensions of space and time (. . . angelic hosts / Of nebulae and lunar hemispheres / And what the days, and what the Uranian years / Shall offer us . . ."). Through these images and figures the vastness of the macrocosm is defined. But besides the unfathomable universe itself is the complexity given it by human efforts to understand it: "Forget the festivals and pentecosts / Of metaphysics . . . ," for the abstractions invented by men are just as meaningless as the vast tracts of space and time. Then there are the ordinary everyday complexities. Even if one is able to forget the sheer size of the infinite and the obscurities of man's abstract world, the petty, ordinary events of life will block one's perceptions, blind the senses to the things they were fashioned to record: ". . . the lesser fears / Confound us, and seal up our eyes and ears / Like little rivers locked below the frost." Some defense is required against the too wide, the too vague, the too complex, and the too mysterious.

The second octave presents the defense, the refuge, from the world revealed in the first octave. The contrast is immediately obvious in the figure of ". . . smallest room / That any hunted exile has desired. . . ." The limited size of this world is still further defined and emphasized by the figure of ". . . sleep oblivious to any doom / Which is beyond our reason to conceive. . . ." Let the world be only as large as our understanding of it extends, and that will be large enough for our limited, human purposes. The last two lines, which take the poem out of the sonnet class, show what is possible under these "cozier skies." Some appreciation of things on a human, sensuous level is possible. The senses are not "locked below the frost." None of this is forced directly on the reader; no preaching or whining occurs, though the idea and the emotion are conveyed strongly by ". . . touch each other's hands and turn / Upon a bed of juniper and fern." The odor, the sensation of touch, the sound is only very delicately suggested by the images of the last two lines. Elinor Wylie only very lightly touches the keys of the reader's response.

But those added lines: it seems reasonable to believe that when Wylie began the poem she intended to write a standard Italian sonnet, but found that she could not do all she wanted to in fourteen lines. Not just the last two lines, but the last four lines are involved in the problem. Having committed herself, in the first octave, to a description of the frightening immensity of the extrahuman world and the "lesser fears," Wylie was bound to present somewhere in the poem the results of contemplation of the "too much." Having committed herself to defining the smaller, more habitable human world, she had to come to "beyond our reason to conceive." She discharges both commitments with the lines: "Which is beyond our reason to conceive; / And so forget to weep, forget to grieve . . ." Weeping and grieving are the inevitable results of becoming preoccupied with the ultimate or the infinite. Happiness and fulfillment are possible only in a more limited, more humanly scaled world. But this last is not conveyed by lines 13 and 14, though lines 7 and 8 commit the poet to do this. ". . . seal up our eyes and ears . . . ," one of the effects of the too large world, must be balanced by an opposite effect of the smaller world described in the second octave. This is the reason for "And wake, and touch each other's hands, and turn / Upon a bed of juniper and fern." The poem demands the last two lines, and Elinor Wylie is enough of a poet to realize it. She is not only in control of emotion in this poem; she has a tight control over technical details.

But she does not always hold the emotion under such perfect control. Sonnet VIII of **"One Person,"** though technically a sonnet, stands in shocking contrast to Sonnet VII and Sonnet XVIII. . . .

The poem is a strange mixture of raw emotion and poetic clichés combined with some really effective figures of speech. "Sets sickle to our Aprils" (echoing at least two of Shakespeare's sonnets) and ". . . what the clock and what the season says / Is rumour neither valued nor believed. . . ." are good poetry, as is ". . . together / We grow beyond vagaries of the weather / And make a summer of our mingled breaths. . . ." But even these do not redeem the first two lines or the cliché-ridden lines 9 and 10. The poem has damning weakness and surprising strength, but neither is characteristic of Elinor Wylie's best poetry. The weakness is not characteristic because it could be that of any poet. The strength is not characteristic because it is that of her mentor in the sonnet, Shakespeare.

Her unique strength is her ability to shape and carve a figure until it fits the exact curve and line of idea or emotion or evokes precisely the mood or quality of a scene. In **"Velvet Shoes,"** her best imagistic poem, this refining of image is toward the ever more diminutive and delicate, and is carried out within the poem itself. . . .

The development of the poem is not continuous. Stanzas 1 and 3 mainly concern the softness underfoot. Stanzas 2 and 4 concern the softness of the wool, silk, and velvet. It is within these units that the refinement of image and figure occurs. For example, "white snow" of stanza 1 becomes "white down," "silver fleece" and "softer than these." "Shod in silk" and "in wool" that is "white as a white cow's milk" and "More beautiful / Than the breast of a gull" are distilled into "velvet shoes." But there is not only refinement of visual images. "With footsteps quiet and slow" of the first stanza becomes "Silence will fall like dews / On white silence below."

Another of Wylie's imagistic poems [**"Unfinished Portrait"**], though not so well known, nor so perfect, contains the same gradual refinement of image and figure, though its effect is not purely imagistic. It objectifies an idea and an emotion. . . .

Though almost all the lines are phrased in the negative, there is still a movement toward refinement of all the figures used: from "cage you in enamel," to "gold and silver trickery," to "blood of meteors"; to "lantern like a shell," to "jewelled arabesques," to the ultimate refinement of "Water, or light, or air that's stained by both." **"Unfinished Portrait"** is one of Elinor Wylie's best poems, second only to **"Velvet Shoes"** in the skillful refining of its images and figures.

In **"Velvet Shoes"** and **"Unfinished Portrait"** this refining is carried out with virtuoso skill, but in **"Nancy"** it degenerates into mere prettiness and effeminate daintiness. The same refining process that produces the unique effects of **"Velvet Shoes"** produces only nausea in the poem called **"Nancy."** Elinor Wylie's characteristic weakness grows out of her characteristic strength. . . .

There is something in this cuteness that I hate. It wouldn't be so bad if the bird were not "pretty" or the squirrel "little." It is easy to imagine this being soulfully read at the local tea and literary society meeting, and hearing all the "quaints," "dears," "cutes," and "absolutely darlings" that would gush. "Needlepoint of ice" is good, but not with "intenser than." This verges on coercion. Then the stock expressions: the rose with the sharp spines was pretty well stripped four hundred years ago. The same is true of the diamond and fire metaphors. "Pierces like a star" is sufficiently vague to have been copied from Swinburne. But the last line goes to the limit of both the "pretty" and the trite. To have put in sugar and spice at this point is past comment, but, having started with pretty birds and little squirrels, it is a logical way to conclude.

"The Fairy Goldsmith" is in the same class of "pretty" poems. While it is not marred by clichés, it is perhaps even more precious than **"Nancy."** Again the refining of images is carried to an extreme, and in the process the amber, jade, lacquer idiom of the most slanteyed of the Imagists is dragged in. . . .

In this poem the "prettiness" exists for its own sake. Having begun a catalog of the daintiest images she could invent, Wylie can end it only through the trite mechanism of fairyland and quicksilver dust. It is a good children's poem. The only really successful attempt at the refinement, within a poem, of image and figure is **"Velvet Shoes,"** whose success is due largely to the simplicity and economy of the images. More representative of Elinor Wylie's success with the refinement of image and figure is **"August."** In this poem, refined and muted images are contrasted with gross and heavy images. The characteristic subduing of color and sound, reduction of size and refining of shape do not exist for their own sake. Working in contrast with the images of grossness in the octave, the carefully refined images of the sestet carry an idea. All of Wylie's poetry is free from the blatancy of John Gould Fletcher's; more than that, poem after poem reveals an absolute aversion for the gross and the heavy. Where such images appear they are counterbalanced by their opposites:

Why should this Negro insolently stride
Down the red noonday on such noiseless feet?
Piled in his barrow, tawnier than wheat,
Lie heaps of smouldering daisies, sombre-eyed,
Their copper petals shrivelled up with pride,
Hot with a superfluity of heat,
Like a great brazier borne along the street
By captive leopards, black and burning pied.

Are there no water lilies, smooth as cream,
With long stems dripping crystal? Are there none
Like those white lilies, luminous and cool,
Plucked from some hemlock-darkened northern
    stream
By fair-haired swimmers, diving where the sun
Scarce warms the surface of the deepest pool?

The octave presents images and figures of extreme heat, gaudily intense color, grossly obtrusive action. "Red noonday," "smouldering daisies," "copper petals," "like a great brazier," "leopards, black and burning pied" all evoke the "superfluity of heat." "Negro," "red noonday," "daisies sombre-eyed," suggest intense, bold primary colors. "Insolently stride" and "shrivelled up with pride," even without the obvious rhyme link, work together to make the action bold and uninhibited, so much so as to be obtrusive. The general evocation of the whole is torried color, heat, and emotion.

In the sestet the contrast is almost too obvious. Opposed to the torrid colors of the daisies "Hot with a superfluity of heat" are water lilies, "luminous and cool." Opposed to the Negro insolently striding down the red noonday are the "fair-haired swimmers." Instead of daisies with copper petals "shrivelled up with pride," there are water lilies "smooth as cream / With long stems dripping crystal." The red noonday is set in contrast to "hemlock-darkened" waters. The insolent, purposeful strides of the Negro are

countered by the fair-haired swimmers' play in the deep pools of the hemlockdarkened water. The general impression is of faint color or no color, coolness, and relaxation. Particularly effective in conveying this last characteristic is the contrast between the shrivelled petals of the daisies and the long, languid stems of the water lilies. The poem would be outstanding if it were only a study in contrasting imagery. But the rhetorical form ("Why should this Negro insolently stride . . . ?" and "Are there no water lilies . . . ?") makes obvious a strong preference for the one sensuous world over the other. And while it is plausible that the contrast between the two worlds merely emphasizes a reaction to extreme heat, employment of "insolently stride" and "shrivelled up with pride" in the context of all the other details hints at a wider reaction—to intensity generally.

Through refinement of image and figure Wylie's best poems gain precision to objectify, define, and control emotion. The best example of this is **"Fable,"** where the refinement results in the simple, stark, but highly suggestive, scene of the dead knight and the preying raven. Because of such refinement Wylie's poetry is relatively free of gross and crude imagery, though the process of refinement, when carried too far, results in a lavishness of the diminutive and dainty that can only be called precious. In this respect **"Velvet Shoes"** and **"The Fairy Goldsmith"** are opposite in their effects. In **"August"** Wylie finds a use for the refined image and figure, and, at the same time, a means of controlling the refining process. In this poem the movement toward refinement is controlled by the demands of the antithesis between the two sensuous worlds. In **"The Fairy Goldsmith"** no such demands are present, and the images might, had the poet so decided, have run on indefinitely. There was no idea except to create ever finer, more delicately fragile pictures. This is one way of avoiding blatancy and banality, but the poet does so at the cost of preciousness. However the Imagists might try to minimize idea, their best poems owe their excellence not entirely to clarity and precision of image but to the coherence of their images, for coherence is possible only if an informing idea is followed. **"Velvet Shoes"** represents the limit of what can be done through refinement of image alone. In no other poem is the result half so effective. Fletcher, in seeking the ever brighter, more overpoweringly sensuous image, and Elinor Wylie, in seeking the ever more muted, more delicately sensuous image, are driven against opposite walls. Generally, Elinor Wylie was able to avoid the descriptive clichés of Imagism through refinement of image, but the trite words are there: the jade, the amber, the crystal.

Most of Elinor Wylie's poems exist in a purely imaginative world, a world "more wonderful than probable." Special limitations in this world give the imagery of a poem like **"Velvet Shoes"** its peculiar effectiveness, but the same limitations give that of **"The Fairy Goldsmith"** its extreme preciosity. Avoiding the banality of Amy Lowell's trowel-and-flowerpot poetry, Elinor Wylie carries things "off to lady land." In such a land extensive refinement of picture leads to quite as much grotesqueness as Fletcher's lavishness of color. **"Velvet Shoes"** has a more realistic setting than **"The Fairy Goldsmith,"** and it is as if the setting exerted a control over the potentially precious refinement. In both poems, however, one characteristic is common. Though they begin at different points, each describes a world that never was. **"Velvet Shose"** has a strong foundation in the actual, but Wylie's imagery transforms it into a kind of "lady land." **"The Fairy Goldsmith"** begins and ends in a fairyland, where everything is so delicate that "in your monstrous day / They will crumble away / Into quicksilver dust." Since ultra-refinement of image (which, more often than not, gives a poem an unearthly quality) and emphasis on fable-like subjects and fable-like methods are the most obvious characteristics of Elinor Wylie's poetry, it appears that, under the cloak of some Imagist practices, she has a strong bent toward the romantic. The term Imagist/Romantic might seem fanciful, but it seems the most nearly correct for Elinor Wylie.

Celeste Turner Wright (essay date 1966)

SOURCE: "Elinor Wylie: The Glass Chimera and the Minotaur," in *Twentieth Century Literature,* Vol. 12, No. 1, April, 1966, pp. 15-26.

[In the following excerpt Wright groups Wylie's poems by their imagery and links the images to Wylie's personality.]

The poet-novelist Elinor Wylie (1885-1928) shows a marked preference for certain imagery: she loves figurines and other beautiful objects made from gems, porcelain, ivory, Venetian glass, and especially crystal, her symbol of purity. Her fondness for these treasures has affected—perhaps distorted—not only her literary reputation, but the world's image of her personality.

The essay **"Jewelled Bindings"** (1923) states her artistic credo in terms of this predilection. She likens most contemporary poets, including herself, to "careful lapidaries," all busy inlaying their work with moonstones and blue chalcedonies; they work "in metal and glass, in substances hard and brittle." For a minor poet, she reasons, this tendency is preferable to being "soft and opulently luscious." She and her confreres, cultivating "a small clean technique," contrive each poem like a musical snuff-box: two or three polished stanzas make "a small jewelled receptacle" for a gilded bird. "Our work," she adds, "is notoriously brittle, and I have no fear that its forms will ever imprison an authentic genius." If she dared suspect that her own bird was a live eagle or a nightingale, she would let him out of the snuff-box.

A writer, like any other person, is accepted largely upon his own estimate of himself. With **"Jewelled Bindings"** before him, a critic might be disposed to see Elinor Wylie as "a hard, jewel-like nature, [which] reflected the world coldly and glitteringly," as if all were "snow and ice, metallic and gleaming"; her artistry as "a sword, intricately carved, magnificently polished, and terribly effective"; her woman's form as cold, though within it "burned a high, proud heart, and a rebellious spirit beat itself into concentrated and exquisitely finished poetry." This account of

her, drawing somewhat upon Louis Untermeyer's *Modern American Poetry* (1925), appeared in a widely adopted textbook, *Contemporary American Literature* (1929), by John Matthews Manly and Edith Rickert. Subsequent critics have tended to use the same adjectives.

But even a reader without preconceptions will soon see for himself that the novel *Jennifer Lorn* (1923) resembles a curio cabinet, affording glimpses of amethyst rings, purple porphyry flowers, pale green porcelain sherbet cups, a sandalwood screen set with mother-of-pearl. These and similar displays are appropriate to a tale of high life in eighteenth-century England, India, and Persia. Carl Van Vechten, in his preface, rightly called the details "fascinating, . . . staggering in their implications of the [author's] knowledge of her selected period and milieu." He was constitutionally disposed to excuse any novelist for emphasizing background and decoration.

Conceivably, Elinor Wylie drew some of her inspiration from *Peter Whiffle,* which her friend Van Vechten had published the year before. Both novels display charm, wit, irony, and a polished style. To the whimsical Peter, life seems an exciting collection of objects; he says that all the "great writers" (such as Oscar Wilde) use "catalogues, catalogues, catalogues." Peter wants to assemble three hundred pages of lists. He delights especially in jewels— amethysts, emeralds, jade, chalcedony, red jasper—and in stories about them, for example that Pope Paul II died of a chill caught by loading his aged fingers with rings.

The author of *Peter Whiffle* may have shown Elinor Wylie the books of Edgar Saltus, a prolific, now almost forgotten American writer of the 1880's and 1890's. *The Merry-Go-Round* (1918), a book of Van Vechten's criticism, includes a chapter on Saltus, whose *Imperial Purple* (1893) brings decadent Rome to life much as *Jennifer Lorn* recaptures eighteenth-century England and India. Like Saltus, Elinor Wylie enjoyed fantasies about unicorns, chimaeras, and centaurs. Like him she strove for "jewelled workmanship," though she would have seen the absurdity of his affirming that in "literature only three things count, style, style polished, style repolished." Like him she described rich ornaments, rich furnishings. But whereas he marvels at the rich people who wiped their hands, "wetted in a golden bowl, in the curly hair of a tiny serving boy," she would have satirized those parvenus with all the joy of a Petronius Arbiter. . . .

In her early verses, the images we have been tracing are conspicuous. **"To Aphrodite, with a Talisman,"** published in 1923, concerns a "graven" amethyst charm. Marianne Moore had already composed "A Talisman" regarding "a scarab of the sea," the gull that some ancient Greek had carved from lapis lazuli. The two poems, though not alike, both reflect the influence of the Imagists, especially H. D. One sees that influence also in **"Gifts at Meeting (From the Greek),"** where Elinor Wylie mentions "cups of lapis" among a score of other delights, some of which (such as "cream, new crudded") are not gemlike; she has many other catalogues of this kind. She loves treasures with an historical connotation. **"King's Ransom"** is a chain of riddles about pearls—for example, the pearl dissolving "within the deep Egyptian flagon" (Cleopatra's carouse to Antony), or the pearl that Cellini might use "to set an eyeball for a falcon." Relishing the unexpected, she lists "crusty cherry pies" along with "the nine Visigoth crowns in the Cluny Museum"—this in **"Parting Gift,"** a meditation upon the joys she would like to give her beloved.

A gem may be central to one of her poems. **"The Madwoman's Miracle"** involves the sapphire rings that lie buried with a girl. In **"Fabulous Ballad"** a lady, mistaken for the Virgin Mary, gives "a delicate celestial chain of sapphires" to a half-crazed gypsy, who has lost some ordinary blue beads. When the lady's husband (rather like Godiva's or the Hungarian Saint Elizabeth's) deplores this openhandedness, she refers him to I Corinthians on charity.

So fond was Elinor Wylie of jewels, her poem **"The Fairy Goldsmith"** turns cherries to "black onyx," spring raindrops to a turquoise chain, the notes of a lute to a "filigree frost." Even her women become jewels, like the "mother-of-pearl" maiden in the same poem, or the heroine of **"Miranda's Supper, 1866,"** whose eyes are "agate." This last comparison has a psychological bearing, for the poet's own eyes had been described in the same way. A noted beauty, she often wrote of herself in terms of an artistic creation. **"To a Lady's Countenance"** describes her own facial contours as "a whim of the glass-blower," and her "little lips" as "uncut, uncarved," made of a clay "delicate and cold." According to her photographs and the testimony of her sister, Nancy Hoyt, Elinor Wylie had a tiny mouth. In **"A Proud Lady"** the lips have been "sweetly chiseled." In the sonnets to **"One Person"** they are "new-cut and coloured," and she thinks of *carving* a living replica of herself, to solace the absent lover. **"Self-Portrait"** compares Elinor Wylie to a crystal lens, an intaglio, or a flint that is "finer-grained than snow."

One reason for fancying herself inanimate may have been the amazing whiteness of her skin; she is said to have looked "like a white queen of a white country." As a girl she had rhymed about keeping her hands whiter than the angels', for the sake of her betrothal ring. This adolescent "song" appeared in her first volume, *Incidental Numbers* (1912), which she later repudiated; but she continued to be fully conscious of her own beauty. At forty-two, in the tenth sonnet to **"One Person,"** she expresses the fear that her hand, although "white as porcelain," may not be gentle enough for her wounded lover. An English friend, Edith Olivier, in a preface to the *Last Poems* (1943), remembers especially that "the hand which rested on the banister was white, like a hand seen under water." The poet may have heard the same compliment before that meeting: **"Spring Pastoral"** (1921) pictures a girl's long, white fingers as steeped in water till the rosy nails have become pearly. She loved coolness; and new acquaintances sometimes described her manner as lacking in warmth. If she seemed reserved, the reason may well have been the humiliation she had long endured. At twenty-four, after five years of an unhappy marriage, she had run away with Horace Wylie, a married man much older than herself. Living quietly in England, under an assumed name, they were still acutely aware of being an embarrassment to their families. Cast out of the Social Register, an aristocrat like Elinor Wylie might well need to erect a facade of coldness. But after she and Horace were able to marry and returned to America, she made countless literary friends; Carl Van Vechten recalls that her conversation was "very lively" and that he saw in her books "the beautiful essence of her nature."

Judging from one of her poems, she longed to be freed from hardness, liberated from marble: **"Sleeping Beauty,"** published after her death, shows a strong man carving the "living rock" and releasing, not the angel that Michelangelo is said to have set free, but "a lady like a lioness." This is Elinor Wylie, for her friends compared her bronze hair to a lion's mane, and she identifies herself with lions in several poems—**"Pity Me," "Unfinished Ballad,"** and **"A Proud Lady."** The image of herself as sculptor's work recalls her way of comparing her characters to dolls. She admired the miniature in art: at the British Museum her principal reading matter was the labels on the Tanagra figurines (or so she assures the readers of her essay **"The Pearl Diver"**). **"The Ivory Statuette"** (one of her *Last Poems*) praises such a figure, six inches tall, above the Winged Victory of Samothrace.

She perceived her own habit of diminishing (in poetry and fiction) the stature of any man she loved—witness her fantasy about shaping Mr. Hazard, that "little image of an idealist," out of clay; and the whimsy about Shelley, in **"A Birthday Cake for Lionel,"** playing the "favorite doll" of two little girls. A light poem, **"The Broken Man,"** informs her beloved that at seven years of age she adored, prophetically, his double—a Chelsea figurine. Often damaged, often mended with a rivet, the white porcelain figure gradually became "a gentleman of steel," with "the iron even entering" his soul—a forecast of the adult lover's history. This fancy recalls *The Rivet in Grandfather's Neck,* a novel that James Branch Cabell reissued in 1922; but Elinor may, like her friend, have borrowed directly from Andersen's fairytale about figurines—the Chimney Sweep, his love the Shepherdess, and the tyrannical grandsire, whom a rivet finally prevented from nodding to an odious suitor. The second sonnet to **"One Person"** addresses a lover whose beauty has been broken, and mended, and "made clear." **"The Doll"**—again, a bit of light verse-speaks of molding a tiny man out of almond paste, enameling him, and keeping him in a crystal box. To this legend the poet prefixes a revealing quotation from George Meredith:

> For woman's manly god must not exceed
> Proportions of the natural nursing size.

She needed no "analyst" to tell her that her fancied transformation of men into figurines implies a certain timidity regarding sex. She felt that her last and greatest lover (whose name she confided to Carl Van Doren) matured her and rendered her, for the first time, capable of passion. A sonnet to **"One Person"** repudiates the concept of herself as his mother; instead, she now feels like Eve confronting Adam:

> Torn from your body, furbished from your rib,
> I am the daughter of your skeleton,

Born of your bitter and excessive pain;
I shall not dream you are my child again.

This man is the lover whose beauty had been broken, and mended, and "made clear."

When her characters are becoming purified, the process is like subjecting the body to a furnace, a knife, or a sculptor's chisel. The lady in **"Epitaph"** passes through "coldest crucibles of pain," which leaves her lips clearer than glass, carves her beauty, and fires her "shrinking flesh" into a finer texture. (One thinks of Rosalba, changed into Sèvres porcelain.) Elinor Wylie knew what it was to endure physical suffering: she often had migraine headaches, the result of incredibly high blood pressure.

In **"Spring Pastoral"** her brows long for the touch of a girl's cold fingers, which have been dabbling in a spring. Water, one of her favorite images, here represents a surcease of pain. Mr. Hazard cools his fevered wrists in the river; and so, in the poem **"A Courtesy,"** does Elinor Wylie, comforting herself for the loss of love. A variant of this image—in her poem **"Beware!"**—warns a pianist against plunging the wrists, not merely the fingertips, into a stream of music. **"August,"** a sonnet blazing with images of a hot day, pictures—for relief—some white water-lilies, taken from a shaded northern stream.

The "crystal" that drips from those lily-stems symbolizes purity, of course; and so does a bottle of the "crystal element," hidden among white roses, which an innocent lover presents to Jennifer Lorn. (The cruel Gerald grinds those roses underfoot.) An ideal gift for Shelley in **"A Birthday Cake for Lionel"** is said to be "crystal gallons of spring water," and the same poet (Shiloh) in *The Orphan Angel* is teased for always talking about "crystal springs."

Ice and snow are favorite images related to water; and they have added much to the impression that Elinor Wylie inhabits a cold and glittering world. Loving New England in the winter, she wrote **"Silver Filigree"** in praise of icicles. **"Farewell, Sweet Dust,"** pictures her lost lover as feathering the snowflakes or sparkling in ice:

Who wouldn't be glad to find a splinter
That once was you, in the frozen grass?

No poem of hers has been oftener anthologized than **"Velvet Shoes,"** wherein she wanders through a snowy world. Snowflakes, a "crystal dust," are compared to the vanishing of a sorrow (this time in **"Desolation Is a Delicate Thing"**). To the Cardinal in *The Venetian Glass Nephew,* spilt drops of snow-water represent "beauty's evanescence." In part, therefore, snow indicates the poet's realization that all beauty must be transitory. She worried, even more than most women, about growing old. It was probably fortunate, as Carl Van Doren reflected, that she died as early as forty-three, her face still lovely, serene, and proud.

Crystal and ice and snowflakes are all colorless. In one of her songs, **"It Is My Thoughts That Color My Soul,"** Elinor Wylie disdains her thoughts as "a rainbow nuisance" (a phrase which would have delighted Emily Dickinson). After death the soul, no longer creeping through the "jewelled brain," will flow clear and quiet, like "a river of air." **"Address to the Soul"** describes a pure integral form that is "glassed in a translucent dream"; rightfully it should wear water. **"Unfinished Portrait,"** instead of depicting her beloved in the favorite "jewelled arabesques," leaves him as "an uncaptured element"—water, or light, or air. Weaving Shelley **"A Red Carpet,"** a tribute in sonnets, Elinor Wylie humbly describes it as mere patchwork, unfit for him to walk upon, because it is barbarously "stained by mortality's vermilion," the scarlet of her veins.

Included in her philosophy of purity was at first a sense that the skeleton is the cleanest portion of man. **"Full Moon"** laments that she cannot tear from her ribs the "carnal mesh"; the "clean bones" long to become ivory. One thinks of King Lear, tearing off his garments, those mere "lendings," and wiping his hand because it "smells of mortality." **"Sequence"** predicts that a kindly lover, mourning after her death, will see her skeleton as a "filigree of pearl." **"The Eagle and the Mole"** counsels the wise to commune underground with the "disembodied bones."

Elinor Wylie's idealization of crystal beauty, and her love of the exotic, are well represented by a late poem, **"Chimaera Sleeping,"** wherein the Chimaera is no monster, but a "lovely thing" of glass, lying in a thicket. Through its body and even through the "blank crystal" of its brain, the poet beholds the leaf and the flower. Here is that "foreknown and holy ghost, / Beauty's pure pathetic shape." She uses the word *pathetic*: the brain is blank and the body has been left hollow because the life of "fiery gold" has departed, like a serpent out of its "winter skin." The spirit of beauty, ever elusive, has fled once more; and the poet, weeping, must continue to pursue it.

This, one of the poems that Elinor Wylie arranged for a volume immediately before her death, may intimate a dissatisfaction with the brittle treasures that had once delighted her. The sonnets to **"One Person"** describe a great change in her own nature:

The glass of heaven was split, and by that token
I knew the bubble of my heart had broken;
The cool and chaste, the iridescent sphere . . .

Her heart, a microcosm, has been shattered by love. The bursting of that heart, a cool bubble filled (she says) with a vernal essence, an innocence, represents the end of her coldness, and the coming of a mature love. The symbol was more apt than she knew, for the violence of her emotions, during the final year or two of her life, may have brought on the several strokes that destroyed her.

As early as *Jennifer Lorn,* Elinor Wylie had sensed the dangers of an excessive refinement; a fastidious nature cannot endure much stress. A priest in that novel compares the young prince to a glass tube, through which the strong fluid of life is being piped: whereas such tubes of azure or sapphire glass may burst like a bubble, an old earthen pipe like himself can drink voraciously of life. Similarly **"True Vine,"** a poem published in 1928, warns against the "wild fastidious hope" which will disappear swiftly (like the elusive spirit of Beauty in the Chimaera poem). The first stanza presents the traditional images, but with disapproval:

> The virgin silver shield no longer burnished,
> The pearly fruit with ruin for its center.

We are advised to seek, not the perfection that will tarnish, but a living emblem, the True Vine, that flourishes even where the soil is "corrupt and faulty." This vine is

> the obdurate and savage lovely,
> Whose roots are set profoundly upon trouble.
> This flower grows so fiercely and so bravely
> It does not even know that it is noble.

The leaves of this plant have drunk the skies and have nourished the earth. The connotation is religious, of course: the True Vine in the Bible represents Christ. But the image, a direct contrast to Elinor Wylie's former favorites, represents a whole new philosophy, her acceptance of the actual, the human.

In **"Minotaur"** (contemporary with **"True Vine"**) a god, "from flesh refined to glass," rides into the desert on a "pard," the animal identified with Shelley in **"Adonais"** and also in Elinor Wylie's ninth sonnet to **"One Person"**:

> A subtle spirit has my path attended,
> In likeness not a lion but a pard.

If we would retain this god, "this burning vistant," our own flesh must become of "fiercer grain" than at present. **"Minotaur"** warns us in the same manner as **"True Vine"**:

> Distrust the exquisite,
> The sharpened silver nerve,
> The lacquered, nacred curve
> Wherein a moon is lit.

Relinquishing the "over-fine," Elinor Wylie urges us to study those "black, lava-encrusted coins" that are stamped with the "heavy brow and limb" of the Minotaur, a bull-man copper-throated like a trumpet:

> Gaze ever and at length
> Upon the carven head,
> Devouring it as bread
> To thrive upon its strength.

Again the intensity seems religious; the words suggest a sacramental meal. As Untermeyer has observed, the contemplation of the minotaur would not be easy or natural for Elinor Wylie; she was too patrician. Still, she advised it.

According to **"Minotaur,"** the flesh at last survives "because it is not pure." In one of her last poems, a poetic

debate entitled **"This Corruptible,"** the Heart and the Mind scorn the Body as clay, "a grosser stuff," but the Spirit comforts that "poor companion," pointing out that all flesh is grass and can therefore become "a grain of God in power"— the wheaten Bread of the Eucharist.

In a literary period when restraint and craftsmanship are not generally regarded as virtues, many readers may fail to catch the emotion lying just beneath the surface of Elinor Wylie's poems. Even her earliest lyrics—for example **"Sanctuary,"** or **"Prophecy,"** or **"Epitaph"**—convey, without histrionics, a powerful feeling. For the later work, such as the fervent sonnets to **"One Person,"** the cold words *jewelled* and *glittering* are even less appropriate. Anthologists are beginning to realize that Elinor Wylie wrote something besides the snow-poem **"Velvet Shoes"**; they are now reprinting **"Hymn to Earth,"** strophes that one would call "sublime" if that word were not out of fashion. The Hymn celebrates, not sapphires or figurines, but the four elements: fire, "secret at the core" of the universe and of life; earth, where man plows the furrow and sows himself for seed; a little sea water, to make his tears; and the air, lending its crystal to his lungs. Aside from that mention of crystal, the Hymn contains no trace of the once-beloved imagery. Instead of beauty-worship, it expresses sympathy for man's weakness, confidence in his worth, and a willingness to share his lot.

At its best, Elinor Wyle's genius was a live eagle or a nightingale, not a small gilded toy to be kept in a snuffbox. A "hard, jewel-like nature," which "reflected the world coldly and glitteringly," did not write this stanza from **"Let No Charitable Hope"**:

> I was, being human, born alone;
> I am, being woman, hard beset;
> I live by squeezing from a stone
> The little nourishment I get.

Emily Stipes Watts (essay date 1977)

SOURCE: "1900-1945: A Rose Is a Rose with Thorns," in *The Poetry Of American Women from 1632 to 1945,* University of Texas Press, 1977, pp. 149-76.

[*In the following excerpt from her book of feminist criticism, Watts compares Wylie to other female poets, including Edna St. Vincent Millay and Elizabeth Barrett Browning.*]

Millay and Wylie were good friends, and their poetry is often considered together as "female Lyrist," apparently a new twentieth-century category of poetry which has been conceived especially for women poets such as Millay, Wylie, [Sara] Teasdale, [Lizette] Reese, and others. . . . Actually, the term *Lyrist* itself is a catchall and condescending critical term which is a development from the concept of "female poetry" of the nineteenth century. Moreover, the generalization which this term demands is wrong. Sara Teasdale is not Lizette Woodworth Reese is not Elinor Wylie is certainly not Edna St. Vincent Millay.

Actually, of all these women, Wylie does most closely resemble the "Lyrist" poet as that term is defined: she did wish to produce small, neat, meticulous poems; she did use traditional meters; and her images are often not essential to the poem. With influence from Shelley, her style is poetically between those of Teasdale and Millay. Poems such as **"Pity Me"** and **"Let No Charitable Hope"** are reminiscent of Teasdale's poetry of withdrawal; **"Where, O, Where?"** and **"Enchanter's Handmaiden"** suggest the independent and vigorous poetry of expansion of Millay and Dickinson. One of her most interesting poems is **"Letter to V——,"** addressed to Millay—a listing of their theological and hence for them essentially personal differences. In certain of her ballads and her self-conscious thrust toward a more general humanism, Wylie also resembles Guiney, who was writing her best poetry when Wylie was a teenager. . . .

Wylie did not understand the dynamic power of words (in the way, for example, Dickinson did), but she is sensitive to their sound and connotative qualities, as is evident in **"Pretty Words."** She mixes an emotional softness, as in **"Bread Alone,"** with types of poems which critics like to term "masculine," such as **"Peregrine."** At times, as in **"Heroics,"** she believes that the world is a wasteland, but she is also able to accept the truth of simple, optimistic morality (**"The Lion and the Lamb"**) and, in other poems, is willing to assert that the reality of the world is certain and "lovely," even though it is "a thin gold mask" (**"Sunset on the Spire"**). In poems such as **"Nancy"** and **"Francie's Fingers,"** there are traces of nursery rhymes in her verse. She asserts her individuality, her sense of self-value in **"Unfinished Portrait"** and **"False Prophet"**; offers a gift from a "sorceress" to the familiar female mythological figure in **"To Aphrodite, with a Talisman"**; and honors other women, as, for example, in **"On a Singing Girl"** and **"To Claudia Homonoea."** As she grew older, she came to love London; and, as in **"One Person,"** her poems began to resemble those of Elizabeth Barrett Browning.

Stanley Olson (essay date 1979)

SOURCE: *Elinor Wylie: A Life Apart, a Biography,* Dial Press, 1979, 376 p.

[*Olson is a biographer whose work includes studies of John Singer Sargent. In the following excerpt from his biography of Wylie, Olson provides information about Wylie's life as it informs the themes of her major books of poetry.*]

Unlike Lord Byron and Lytton Strachey, Elinor did not wake up one October morning in 1921 to find herself famous. The recognition she received for *Nets to Catch the Wind* was of a more somber variety, and very long in coming. . . . When critics opened [the book], they found a great deal to arrest them. The most captivating things were the certainty and the angular emotions of the poems. Phrases like Louis Untermeyer's "sparkle without burning," "frigid ecstasy," "passion frozen at its source," became critics and reader's leitmotifs in describing her

work. She seemed capable of combining stunning craftsmanship with ethereal sentiments. She was a nimble, yet sure, technician of almost orgiastic images, which she destroyed as decisively as she built them up. Her ability to convey lushness through austerity was startling. All the confidence that was absent in her life was distilled on the page. . . .

[Most of the poems that make up *Black Armour*] were published in periodicals beforehand. Like her headaches, [Elinor's] poetry offers an index to her feelings. While the letters reveal a certain degree of childlike absurdity, since she was playing up to Bill [Benét] and indulging in a degree of arrogance, her poems uncover a darker, almost fatalistic submission. There she descended into the emotions that in life she tried so hard to hide, and even then she was not direct. She abstracted her emotions, moving from reality to myth, and so giving them dignity. Her imagery reversed night and day. She turned standard symbolism around, equating daylight with fantasy and night with harsh reality. Truth unfolded in blackness, while fantasy thrived in full light. This extraordinary reversal had its root in nothing more complicated than her chronic fear of her own feelings. . . .

Trivial Breath, taken as a whole, was a tidying-up exercise. After disposing of the burden of Shelley, Elinor moved straight on to herself as the main subject matter for her poems. The material in these poems is entirely different from that encountered in her first two books: the Elinor here has grown weary of paradox, distrustful of striking imagery, and indeed, disdainful of her own excessive frigidity. Less antagonistic, less brittle, less harsh, she seems finally to have crossed over into the region of more human feelings—a journey she had been making steadily in her poetry since 1923, but had only recently achieved in her novels. She appeared to retire from the battle waged heroically with herself. The transition was swift and undramatic, but it is difficult to read the collection of poetry in any light other than autobiographical. The relationship with Bill is lightly touched upon in **"Peter and John,"** . . . and her visit to the Powyses (where she stayed in a nearby cottage that had been owned by a man who had recently drowned) is celebrated in **"The Coast Guard's Cottage."** Rather than looking back, the sonnets that open the third section of the book hint at the **"One Person"** sonnets that signaled her farewell. Other poems, like **"'As I Went Down by Havre de Grace . . .'"**—which sings a *ritornello* on her entire life, looking far back to her father's grave at Forty Fort, Pennsylvania—and **"A Strange Song,"** stand among the finest she ever wrote. The bitterness of her poetry six years before has been sweetened, not by greater strength or mere cleverness, but by resignation. The current of transition is strong in these poems.

Elinor's **"One Person"** sonnets are, perhaps, her finest achievement. They are her testimony to the power of her emotions, distilled and purified. It is appropriate that she should have chosen the form of Petrarch, which was so suited to and famous for love. The love in these poems is not a private love, not a variety of confession, but an abstracted one, free of the protection of subjectivity. And although her expression is clear throughout, she does not ignore the pain that affection arouses; she does not, as she had done in her actual relationship with [Cliff] Woodhouse, misinterpret, overbalance, or spill into excess. The nineteen sonnets are paced with strength, energy and undeniable feeling, sustained as a group by shifting through the complexities and vicissitudes of love. And the confidence that had been born in doubt is impressive.

Judith Farr (essay date 1983)

SOURCE: "Debut as Aesthete," in *The Life and Art of Elinor Wylie,* Louisiana State University Press, 1983, pp. 58-83.

[*In the following excerpt from her full-length critical study of Wylie's poetry and prose, Farr analyzes poems from* Incidental Numbers *and* Nets to Catch the Wind.]

Incidental Numbers, a small collection of verses composed between 1902 and 1911, was Elinor Wylie's first book of poems. Privately printed in England, in an edition of only about sixty copies, the book's pale blue binding and navy lettering imitated an edition of Blake's *Songs of Innocence.* Copies were presented as gifts to Elinor's family and acquaintances. Her mother paid the publication costs. When *Incidental Numbers* appeared, Elinor was twenty-seven years old and living out of wedlock with Horace Wylie in Burley, England. The scandal created by her elopement had cost her her social position in America; her former friends were "convinced that she was done for, socially, and . . . that she had not the courage to form herself into a writer or painter." The slender volume was testimony to the author's determination to discipline her energies despite the ambiguity and turmoil of her life.

The poetic style is experimental, and there is no single poem worthy of inclusion in Elinor Wylie's second volume, *Nets to Catch the Wind.* Nevertheless, there are continuities between *Incidental Numbers* and her later work. The poems exhibit the interest in technical refinement—metrical variations, inventive rhyming patterns, subtle changes of measure or sound within apparently simple poetic frames—developed in her later volumes. Its themes—magic and enchantment, distress in love, the beauties of nocturnal landscape or of the pastoral in general, pleasure in certain colors, particularly white and silver—consistently reappear later. Even the book's title, *Incidental,* suggesting the author's diffidence (and a nuance of the proud self-deprecation also evident, for example, in *Trivial Breath*), and *Numbers,* directing attention to the poems as exercises in verbal music, establishes a discreet and formal note typical of the later poems.

The volume is eclectic. Both the prose and the poetry of Elinor Wylie always exhibit influences, even borrowings. Most of these are deliberately courted or included for artistic purposes and subsumed into her own style. In *Incidental Numbers,* however, rather than the mature Wylie's characteristic voice, one hears the voice of a poet who has herself heard several voices.

Despite Wylie's lifelong interest in Shelley, his poetry does not instruct her juvenilia. Despite her conscious femininity she does not take significant lessons from such women poets as Emily Dickinson, Christina Rossetti, or Emily Brontë. (Rossetti's melodious quatrains may have appealed to her, but *Incidental Numbers,* for all its visual qualities, shows none of Rossetti's anguish or Gothic power). Wylie's early poems reflect knowledge of male poets fashionable when she was a girl and doubtless appreciated by Horace Wylie. They were the same poets read by Eliot, Stevens, Pound, and everyone else who began to think about writing poetry in the early 1900s: the poets of the Aesthetic movement.

Wylie's **"The Fairy,"** for instance, which is typical of the collection, exhibits that affection for folklore common to some early poems of Yeats and de la Mare as well as a lush yet artificial and visionary landscape and a concern with traditional metrics and intricate rhyming patterns that these poets, in their youth, shared with the Aesthete Ernest Dowson.

"The Fairy" is the song of a sprite separated from his adventurous and "magical kin." Hearing their wild singing through long nights in valleys mortals love for their safety, he vows someday to escape his enclosure and to join his fellows:

> The folk of the valleys
>   They are not my kin,
> They walk in cool alleys
>   Green gardens within,
> Through closes of roses
>   And orchards within.
>
> Their feet are submitted
>   To pathways secure,
> My footsteps have flitted
>   From lure to bright lure
> Of rillsides' and hillsides'
>   More perilous lure.
>
>   . . . . .
>
> Some midnight when mortals
>   Are sleeping I'll win
> My way past the portals
>   Of cloud to my kin,
> And meet them, and greet them—
>   My magical kin.
> On the moon-whitened meadows,
>   That look to the sky
> Like silvery shadows,
>   We'll dance, they and I,
> With laughter, hereafter,
>   Forever and aye.

"The Fairy" is a slight poem, and it is musical. Its theme of escape prefigures later Wylie poems in which the speaker sets herself apart from the human world. But it is chiefly interesting because its rhyme patterns, ghostly pastoral, and diction call to mind the work of Dowson and Yeats. Dowson's "Beata Solitudo" describes a "silent valley"

Where all the voices
Of humankind
Are left behind.

Although the poem's persona does not crave merry company, his imaginary land "where pale stars shine" has much in common with the fairy's. And Wylie's landscape composed of white heather, moonlight, and silver shadows and of green gardens with "closes of roses" recalls the moonlit landscape of Dowson's *The Pierrot of the Minute,* the twilit aura of his love lyrics in "Amor Profanus," and the stayed, artificial greenery of "Coronal." Dowson, too, habitually used "closes of roses"—in "Sapientia Lunae," in "The Garden of Shadow," in "You Would Have Understood Me, Had You Waited," and in "Vitae summa brevis spem nos vetat incohare longam" (They are not long, the weeping and the laughter). It is, of course, an inevitable rhyme; George Herbert rhymes "closes" with "roses" in "Vertue." But the presence in Wylie's **"Fairy"** of many trappings reminiscent of Dowson—not only the wistful pose of alienation but the setting, theatrically lit in silver, and the languorous language—suggests that his verse served her as one of several models in this early period.

Another model was the early verse of Yeats, whose poems she seems to have known well. *Nets to Catch the Wind* borrows occasional images from Yeats, and Wylie's review of his autobiographical prose shows pronounced interest in his life. (In the only critical review she ever wrote, Edna St. Vincent Millay, later a close friend, scolded Wylie for the abject Yeatsianism of **"Madman's Song."**) Yeats's poem "The Stolen Child," published in *The Crossways* volume of 1889 which Wylie had probably read by 1909 when she was writing **"The Fairy,"** presents a situation similar to that of her poem. In it a "human child" escapes to the realm of faerie, leaving behind a world "full of weeping" but also of comforting pleasures—a kettle on a hob, calves on warm hillsides, the "oatmeal-chest"—akin to the mortal attractions of Wylie's poem with its "cool alleys," "green gardens," and "pathways secure." Yeats's fairy speaker attracts the child with a description of wild dances under the moon that resembles Wylie's:

Where the wave of moonlight glosses
The dim grey sands with light,
Far off by furthest Rosses
We foot it all the night,
Weaving olden dances,
Mingling hands and mingling glances
Till the moon has taken flight.

Yeats's vague moonlit landscape is akin to Wylie's "moon-whitened meadows" and fairies that move "like silvery shadows." Each poem depicts human life as unfavorable to transport or happiness and the escapist delights of the fairy world as worth striving for.

"The Fairy"'s theme of alienation from the actual is found, too, in the poetry of Walter de la Mare, who became a friend of Wylie's and shared her interest in porcelain, silver, and small objects. In his first book, *Songs of Child-*

hood (1902), he created a haunted world of reverie and enchantment, a world of pale moonlight where both trees and people are spectral. The poem "The Fairies Dancing" in that volume depicts "fairies in a ring" who "Sing as they tripped a lilting round / Soft as the moon on wavering wing." The poem's speaker watches day rise, the fairies' "beauty" lie "as a mist," and their singing grow faint under the roar of sunlight. The landscape, waking him "from moonlit dreams," seems somehow diminished, despoiled of the radiance of magic.

If de la Mare's attraction to a gentle landscape, to dream states, and to ideas of sterile perfection or uncanny glamour invites comparison to Elinor Wylie's preoccupation with them in *Incidental Numbers,* so also does his fascination with whiteness. The use of the word *white* to create an aura of romantic mystery and an obsession with the conceit of whiteness, seen to represent many states from purity of soul or form to neurosis, were characteristic of the Aesthetic movement, described by Holbrook Jackson in *The Eighteen Nineties.* In *Incidental Numbers* Elinor Wylie demonstrates this Aesthetic interest in the idea of white and its more lustrous counterpart, silver; she retained that interest throughout her writing career. Dorothy Parker remarked in *The New Yorker* (March 21, 1928), only a few months before Wylie's death, "It is impossible, I think, to write of [her] or her work without somewhere using the word 'silver.' It is her word, made for her." **"Birches"** and other poems in *Incidental Numbers* which describe trees like sylphs "slim in their silver white / Nothing defaces," glimmering "pale in the ardent light," "slender in shining white" present an ideal of Aesthetic perfection founded—as in many poems of Dowson, Johnson, Arthur Symons, Yeats, or in the paintings of the Aesthete James McNeill Whistler—on the conceit of luminous whiteness.

Although her later volumes make the relation of Elinor Wylie to the Aesthetes more imperative, *Incidental Numbers* reveals a sensibility that instinctively chose themes and language reminiscent of theirs. Poems like **"Eve in Heaven,"** which honors the carnal experience of Eve above the innocence of the Virgin Mary; **"To Paolo and Francesca in Purgatory,"** which values passion, not purity; **"The Knight Fallen on Evil Days,"** a tribute to learning, Satan, and solitary endeavor recall the iconoclasm of the Aesthetes; their interest in religion, scholarship, and legend; their whimsy; and their absorption in their craft. Carl Van Doren [in *Three Worlds*] is correct in saying that Elinor Wylie was not a precocious poet. *Incidental Numbers* marks the debut of a promising amateur whereas *Nets to Catch the Wind,* published ten years later in 1921, is the work of a much more assured writer with a more complex and developed imagination. Nonetheless, *Incidental Numbers* contains distinct Aesthetic patterns of vision and technique that characterized Elinor Wylie's art throughout her career.

By 1921, Elinor Hichborn, then thirty-six had at last become the legal wife of Horace Wylie. She had suffered a great deal and was shortly to renounce the husband for whose love she had suffered. Whether her bookish seclusion with the literate Wylie had helped her to shape an artistic vision and whether the pain of censure and isolation had hurt her into real poetry, the verse that appeared in *Nets to Catch the Wind* had the technical finish promised by her juvenilia but an intellectual and emotional content that could not have been predicted from it. She appeared on the literary firmament, said the Boston *Transcript* (November 30, 1921), with "amazing suddenness." *Nets to Catch the Wind,* her first professional book, won the Julia Ellsworth Ford prize for the best collection of poems published in 1921, the year Edna Millay brought out *Second April,* Marianne Moore, *Poems,* and H.D., *Hymen.* Edmund Wilson declared that *Nets to Catch the Wind* was not the work of a tyro. Its "style" and "accuracy" "never misse[d]; its colors [were] always right—two qualities exceedingly rare in contemporary American verse."

The title of *Nets to Catch the Wind,* borrowed from a play of John Webster's [*The Devil's Law Case*], draws attention to the idea of art. Wylie's poems were, like fine-spun nets, to trap the wind, identified with reality or, in the Romantic context of Wylie's favorite poets, with the wind, imagination. Babette Deutsch called the volume "almost one uninterrupted cry to escape"; and certainly the quest for escape from a hostile, ugly, or commonplace world is the subject of many poems. Yet the subject is variously viewed and treated with complacency, alarm, rejection, sublimation. The reader realizes that what hurt the woman, the "Proud Lady" of the poem that identifies Wylie as the victim of society's "finger of hate" (*Collected Poems,* 32), helped turn the poet to the craft of verse. It is art which begins to suggest itself in *Nets to Catch the Wind* as a mainstay for the author.

Three basic themes are presented in the volume: the scornful indignities suffered by the poet-speaker at the hands of a malicious and stupid world; her need to escape the world either by pastoral withdrawal, sleep, or death; and the attractions of a private universe of beautiful sights and objects which so stimulate the persona's imagination that she is able to conquer the world by art.

"Beauty," the first lyric in the volume, expresses the latter theme, its placement in the book implying its dominance. It is a significant poem not only for its technical proficiency—its internal variations show Wylie's skill with quatrains—but because, like others in the volume, it assumes attitudes toward art and its relation to the life of feeling which are Aesthetic:

> Say not of Beauty she is good,
> Or aught but beautiful,
> Or sleek to doves' wings of the wood
> Her wild wings of of a gull.
>
> Call her not wicked; that word's touch
> Consumes her like a curse;
> But love her not too much, too much,
> For that is even worse.
>
> O, she is neither good nor bad,
> But innocent and wild!
>
> Enshrine her and she dies, who had
> The hard heart of a child.

Beauty, the spirit informing art, is commendable not for those qualities of goodness, generosity, or civility praised in the moral order but for absoluteness and independence. Like Ariel, whom W. H. Auden represents in *The Sea and the Mirror* as an "unfeeling god," Beauty has the "hard heart of a child" and is to be valued for wildness and for her hostility to confinement and idealization alike. Elinor Wylie's Beauty, like Oscar Wilde's in the Preface to *The Picture of Dorian Gray* or Whistler's in the "Ten O'Clock Lecture," is "neither good nor bad." When Wilde wrote, "They are the elect to whom beautiful things mean only Beauty," he expressed the sentiment of Wylie's opening lines. When Whistler mocked the idea of "Beauty . . . confounded with virtue" and claimed that art is "selfishly occupied with [its] own perfection only," he defended the superiority of the creative spirit to partisan claim. Beauty to Elinor Wylie, as to Wilde and Whistler, is its own reason for being; it may not be expected to serve ethical values. Wylie's warning, "love her not too much," however, is significant in light of the poems and prose works she later wrote, many of which teach the enchantment of aesthetic objects and of art yet deplore excessive Aestheticism.

The second poem in *Nets to Catch the Wind,* **"The Eagle and the Mole,"** unites the themes of pain and escapism prominent in the volume. Widely anthologized, it earned the respect of William Butler Yeats, who told Dorothy Wellesley that it was his "sole excitement" in an otherwise bleak period. It might have been expected to capture his fancy, for its Blakean and Wordsworthian echoes and its conformity to the hermetic and escapist spirit of *Childe Harold, III,* support a Neo-Romantic attack on society and a preference for proud aloofness and dependency on nature that also inform many of Yeats's poems. The lyric is hortatory, an example of the economic emphasis Wylie managed well:

> Avoid the reeking herd,
> Shun the polluted flock,
> Live like that stoic bird,
> The eagle of the rock.
>
> The huddled warmth of crowds
> Begets and fosters hate;
> He keeps, above the clouds,
> His cliff inviolate.
>
> . . . . .
>
> If you would keep your soul
> From spotted sight or sound,
> Live like the velvet mole;
> Go burrow underground.
>
> And there hold intercourse
> With roots of trees and stones,
> With rivers at their source,
> And disembodied bones.

The poem rejects the contamination of society in favor of secretive contact with the private world of imagination nourished by nature. Its choice of alternatives recalls that of Thel's motto in Blake's *Book of Thel,* a poem which treats the problem of art and reality: "Does the Eagle know what is in the pit? / Or wilt thou go ask the Mole?" The contempt directed at the "reeking herd," "the polluted flock," "the huddled warmth of crowds" which "begets and fosters hate" recalls Childe Harold's conviction that he was "the most unfit / Of men to herd with Man," whose mindless constraints translated him from "a wild-born falcon . . . / To whom the boundless air alone were home" into "a thing / Restless and worn." Wylie recommends the eagle's life, akin to the falcon's. It is a solitary bird, sharp of sight, spectacular in daring, a Romantic metaphor of superb achievement. Yet, Wylie says, not everyone is strong enough to reach its sphere. Some, to avoid "spotted sight or sound," secular distractions that cheapen an artist's gift, must sequester themselves from society in a humbler way. They must "live like the velvet mole; / Go burrow underground." With this requisite detachment, they may then attain to that productive union with nature Wordsworth attributes to Lucy in "A slumber did my spirit seal." For in that elegy, the dead girl, withdrawn from life, finds a more enduring life:

> No motion has she now, no force;
>   She neither hears nor sees;
> Rolled round in earth's diurnal course,
>   With rocks, and stones, and trees.

Wylie's choice of "trees" and "stones" recalls Wordsworth's, and perhaps his use of "force" and "course" unconsciously suggested itself in her "intercourse" and "source." Her poem, like many Romantic and Neo-Romantic poems, recommends a personal disengagement that results in superior artistic engagement. Emblematic of her own experience in which attraction to a life of scintillation was matched and corrected by commitment to a life of thought, the poem synthesizes the proud passion for isolation that appears elsewhere in *Nets to Catch the Wind*.

"Madman's Song," which immediately follows, for example, enjoins

> Better to see your cheek grown hollow,
> Better to see your temple worn,
> Than to forget to follow, follow,
> After the sound of a silver horn.

However Yeatsian the image of the "silver horn" may be, the advice and antitheses of "Madman's Song" are characteristic of Elinor Wylie. She, who so respected the allure of physical beauty, placed it second to the lure of art. It was better to grow old in the "hunt" for ideal form than "to sleep with your head on a golden pillow": better to be "sallow" and gray early than to abandon the imagination's quest "after the milk-white hounds of the moon." If such advice was a "madman's," counter to that offered by a society interested in the cosmetic and comfortable, it was also Dionysian, hence practical for an artist.

"The Falcon," a later poem in *Nets to Catch the Wind*, poses similar antitheses: the life of the imitative crowd versus the adventurous one of the imaginative artist. Two voices speak, the first wondering and troubled; the sec-

ond, assertive and explanatory: the two selves, perhaps, of the poet. This poem declares that it is possible to domesticate imagination by the effort of craft and the gift of love. And, though she is a falcon—relative of the fierce eagle—she may be wooed with "a chain of silver twist," "a little hood of scarlet wool": small, exquisite offerings that recall the Aesthetic preoccupation with small objects, a preoccupation Elinor Wylie shared. In "Sunset on the Spire," a poem of seclusion and rapturous involvement with an image of aspiration that suggests the imaginative life, Elinor Wylie clarifies her commitment to art and her conviction that she is an artist. In that poem, food, drink, lover, and friend exist for her in the particularly dramatic, efflorescent moment in which sunset lights a spire. A description of the marriage of nature and artifice—the spire upward-tending like her eagle or falcon—the poem reveals the devotion to art, particularly decorative art ("thin gold mask"), for which she would become famous. Poems like these suggest that *Nets to Catch the Wind* is not a simple "cry to escape" but an effort to embrace a finer life than the ordinary offers. Other poems in the volume clearly describe that world which makes escape appealing or necessary.

"The Church-Bell," for instance, characterizes the mob of men as unable to tolerate a call to self-esteem, valor, or joy. Feet pounding monotonously, their market-carts rumbling, they ignore the bell which has "gone mad" from their indifference, and when its exhortation to freedom of mind becomes too loud and sweet, they tear "its living tongue / Out by the very root" (16-17).

"The Church-Bell" describes spiritual impoverishment in a country setting. In "A Crowded Trolley Car," the setting is urban, but the cowardice and villainy of humanity remain the same. With a use of synecdoche that contrives a nearly surrealistic vision, the poem defines trolley riders in terms of apparently disembodied hands and glances. One rider hangs from his strap like a hanged man. Others resemble Bluebeard's murdered wives, dangling by their hair. In a process of association that grows increasingly nightmarish, the riders become an "Orchard of the strangest fruits / Hanging from the skies." Insensitive, hateful to one another, they are reduced to brutishness by fear; and they repay courage and integrity with death. For the images of murder reach their fulfillment in the last quatrain of the poem in which the hand of Christ is nailed to the cross.

Nets to Catch the Wind finds various antidotes to the pain of living in a hostile world. "Bells in the Rain" contemplates the way in which nature, in this case sleep, heals those whom the world afflicts, "a live man's bloody head." The sleep of the dead, a "deep peace," is contrasted with the "tender[er]" peace afforded to the dreaming living to whom sleep on a rainy evening comes like the rain in "bells of glass / Thinned by the wind, and lightly blown." Droplets of rain, compared to frail glass, and moments of respite from the tortures of life come together in an imagery of artifice that demonstrates Elinor Wylie's Aesthetic response to experience. As the ordered and perishable object—glass, crystal, porcelain—occurred to Théophile Gautier or Oscar Wilde as examples of the beautiful or hopeful, so did they to Wylie. For her in life as in metaphor, the well-wrought artifact implied a tranquility and comeliness to which human nature aspired with difficulty. In **"Bells in the Rain,"** the answer to grief is semi-inanition, depicted in the static shapeliness of artifice.

"Winter Sleep," "Escape," "Sanctuary," and others propose avoidance of a world inimical, particularly to artists, but do so ambivalently. The "little house" (modest counterpart of Yeats "small cabin" in Innisfree) built by the speaker of **"Escape"** is related to the deadly "sanctuary" which ultimately denies life to the poet-speaker. In the contradictions of her treatment of the theme of withdrawal from the world, Wylie discloses the effects of a sympathetic reading of Yeats.

She handles the theme best in **"Wild Peaches."** This series of four related, capable sonnets entertains the romantic quest for escape, then rises into acceptance of the world's harshness, symbolically expressed, as elsewhere in the volume, by resignation to the idea of winter.

In the first three sonnets, the speaker and her companion decide, "When the world turns completely upside down," to "emigrate to the Eastern Shore / Aboard a riverboat from Baltimore." In fact, theirs is a retreat to the American past Elinor Wylie would describe in *The Orphan Angel*; for one wears a "coonskin cap" and the other "a gown / Homespun, dyed butternut's dark gold colour." The companion has a "lotus-eating ancestor" to whose euphoria the speaker relates their own: "We'll swim in milk and honey till we drown." Capacious, their images painterly and vivid, the first sonnets concentrate on benign seasons:

> The months between the cherries and the peaches
> Are brimming cornucopias which spill
> Fruits red and purple, sombre-bloomed and black;
> Then, down rich fields and frosty river beaches
> We'll trample bright persimmons, while you kill
> Bronze partridge, speckled quail, and canvasback.

In response to such revelry of feeling and sensuousness of theme, however, the speaker in the concluding sonnet bursts forth in distaste of lush escapism. The companion does not appear in this last sonnet. The speaker, no longer accommodating, defends an asceticism of the inner heart, and the lines are resolute, lively with conviction, even as those of the earlier sonnets seem leisurely and playful.

> Down to the Puritan marrow of my bones
> There's something in this richness that I hate.
> I love the look, austere, immaculate,
> Of landscapes drawn in pearly monotones.
>
> There's something in my very blood that owns
> Bare hills, cold silver on a sky of slate,
> A thread of water, churned to milky spate
> Streaming through slanted pastures fenced with stones.
>
> I love those skies, thin blue or snowy gray,
> Those fields sparse-planted, rendering meagre sheaves;

> That spring, briefer than apple-blossom's breath,
> Summer, so much too beautiful to stay,
> Swift autumn, like a bonfire of leaves,
> And sleepy winter, like the sleep of death.

The landscape at last elected in **"Wild Peaches"** resembles that of New England, "drawn in pearly monotones"; it is symbolic of an earnest life in which effort and hardship earn a beauty that is more poignant because it is spare and short-lived. In the earlier sonnets of the sequence, the speaker had envisioned a dream life of ease and plenty wherein "the squirrels in their silver fur will fall / Like falling leaves, like fruit, before [the] shot." Coddled by this imaginary nature lavish with strawberries, chestnuts, cider, and plums, she had promised in the octave of the third sonnet, "We shall live well—we shall live very well." Living well, however, is redefined in the last sonnet. There the speaker, declaring herself a "Puritan," abandons idyllic for Spartan pleasures. Now, "thin blue or snowy gray" skies, "bare hills," "meagre sheaves," "a thread of water" (compared with the "ocean swell" of the third sonnet) offer a parsimonious yet more valuable context in which to understand the significance of time and existence. The sestet of the sonnet hastens toward conclusion and the word "death" with a speedy propriety that suggests the brevity of life, like the brevity of spring and summer in New England. The poem entices biographical comment, and one is reminded by the line "There's something in this richness that I hate" of the Elinor Wylie who, however "thriftless of gold and prodigal of love," prided herself on the "strict ascetic habit of control / That industry ha[d] woven for [her] soul": on a life ultimately committed to the labor of art.

These essential alternatives—the prospect of escape through death or solitude or the wiser choice of triumphing over a hostile world by valor and by art—repeat themselves consistently in *Nets to Catch the Wind*. The latter alternative assumes higher importance and does so increasingly in Elinor Wylie's later volumes of verse. Yet the former theme, continually qualified, is never abandoned.

Several poems in *Nets to Catch the Wind* characterize the form of art to which Wylie's personae turn for satisfaction. One lyric, **"The Fairy Goldsmith,"** delights in a litany of rare and special objects wrought with magic craft, objects to which the real world is enemy. The poem attempts a tour de force of the decorative imagination, musically celebrating the charm of artifacts that imitate nature but are in their plasticity more formal and (ironically) in their whimsicality less durable than her products.

"The Fairy Goldsmith" offers "wonderful things" to the admiring observer, all of them miniature, "carven and cut / In intricate ways." Yet though he is aware of their perfection as artifacts, he concedes their uselessness in a real world.

> Touch them and take them,
> But do not break them!
>   Beneath your hand
> They will wither like foam
> If you carry them home
>   Out of fairy-land.

O, they never can last
Though you hide them fast
    From moth and from rust;
In your monstrous day
They will crumble away
    Into quicksilver dust.

Cherries made of onyx; buds of jade; gilded bees in "amber drops / Which look like honey" but are artificial, not natural; a girl wrought of mother-of-pearl: in each case, jewels crafted by the goldsmith substitute for the living reality. The transitory hence appealing natural phenomena, frost and rain (and sounds: "frail notes lost / From a fairy lute"), are translated into filigree and a chain of turquoises.

The goldsmith's bubble is made of opal. But the glamour of these artifacts is restricted to the world of imagination for in the "monstrous day" of real life they would "crumble away," their loveliness a function of fragility and precious wit.

"The Fairy Goldsmith," a small paradigm of the conceits of *The Venetian Glass Nephew,* reveals that devotion to gems, to colors sensuous or austere, to delicate and intricate small objects found in the literature of the Aesthetes. The charms of the exquisite—all the more charming because they cannot easily survive in the crude arena of ordinary life—are drawn with desire here as they are, for instance, in Wilde's *Picture of Dorian Gray.* In her review of Yeats's autobiographical prose, Elinor Wylie spoke of the "tragedy of [Wilde's] ruin" and appeared to have thought about Wilde—if, as she confessed, ungenerously—for some time ["Path of the Chameleon," in *Collected Prose*]. Humorous passages in her novels recall his wit; opulently perfumed phrases in the novels and in some poems evoke his exoticism; and she is of course concerned, like Wilde, with the relationship between life and art. In the gem catalog of *Dorian Gray*—itself, perhaps, influenced by the tortoise episode in Huysmans' *A Rebours*—there appears a fascination with jewels similar to that of "The Fairy Goldsmith" with "the olive-green chrysoberyl that turns red by lamplight, the cymophane with its wire-like line of silver, the pistachio-coloured peridot, rose-pink and wine-yellow topazes, carbuncles of fiery scarlet with tremulous four-rayed stars, flame-red cinnamon-stones. . . . the red-gold of the sunstone, and the moonstone's pearly whiteness, and the broken rainbow of the milky opal."

In Elinor Wylie's poem, objects fashioned from the onyx, chrysoprase, jade (Wilde with his passion for green liked jade, speaking in *Dorian* of vegetables of "jade-green"), pearl, and ivory that decorate the prose of Wilde's novel appear together. The same relation between nature and artifice is also sustained. Wilde's ivy has "green lacquer leaves"; the Goldsmith's "lacquer" is like the "scarlet skin" of an ivory apple. Both ivy and apple are valuable, perversely, because they are not made of natural fibers but cased in hard, glossy veneer. The appeal in such conceits is to a permanence (and strangeness) which artistic objects, unlike nature, can offer. Yet nature's "monstrous day" is there at the end to make the arbitrariness of artifice apparent.

In the Wylie Archive in the Beinecke Library there is a winsome, unpublished poem of Elinor Wylie called "What Did You Buy?" The imagery of this poem resembles that of "The Fairy Goldsmith." But it poses against artifacts, or natural phenomena seen momentarily as static, livelier images that belong to the hapless world. Like "The Fairy Goldsmith," the poem exhibits Elinor Wylie's preoccupation with the distinction between nature and artifice. . . .

At the left side of the manuscript page, the poets are identified (in a hand that could be Benét's) who would choose the items Wylie enumerates: Ralph Hodgson, the "blue doves and cinnamon bees"; Siegfried Sassoon, the "glitter of Picture-Show"; Robert Graves, the "prettiest Country Toys"; Vachel Lindsay, the "kicking Kentucky horse"; John Masefield, the "ship with sails of cramoisie" which, in the use of the arcane word for crimson, is typical of Wylie. What is interesting in the poem is the conflict between the expectation of the speaker that the listeners will buy objects like "sea-green slippers" or jade earrings and their choice of "thrushes' tunes" or "a . . . Golden Whale." At the last, an unidentified poetic voice declares, "I have bought honeydew and milk." It is that voice which defines Elinor Wylie's understanding of what was primarily important to the poetic mind.

Still, as she was to demonstrate in the often Wildean fancies of Gerald Ponyard in *Jennifer Lorn* or in the fable of *The Venetian Glass Nephew* with its parallels to *Dorian Gray,* the Aesthetic predilection for old brocades, green bronzes, lacquer-work, and carved ivories; the Aesthetic attraction to uncommon words and historic subjects; the interest in achieving "literary expression of that which is most ineffable, and in form the vaguest and most fleeting outlines" [Holbrook Jackson, *The Eighteen Nineties*] were instinctively her own. The most frequently anthologized poem from *Nets to Catch the Wind* is "Velvet Shoes." It is one of Elinor Wylie's virtuoso pieces, uniting that rapt, nearly hermetic elegance of vision and subtlety of technique for which she is known. More than many of her poems it bespeaks her gift. Yet its absorption in the idea of white may be found in the poetry of the Aesthetes. Louis Untermeyer impressionistically called it "perhaps the whitest poem ever written."

A controlled lyric, written in fours followed by threes which slow and solemnify its movement, the poem ["Velvet Shoes"] proposes a dignified progress through a dreaming and unreal landscape. The walkers are ceremoniously and inappropriately dressed for winter; but the snow which their rich shoes barely touch is not genuine but illusory. The suggestion in the first line, "Let us walk in the white snow," becomes intention in the last, "We shall walk in the snow." The intervening lines provide winsome images of peace and harmony that intensify and make resolute the speaker's mood. The poem celebrates certain aspects of landscape under fresh snow. But its deeper theme is whiteness itself with its synaesthetic correlative, silence. It is an excursion into an atmosphere of artifice chosen to describe one manifestation of nature. "Silk," "wool," "veils of white lace," "silver fleece," "white down," "velvet shoes": all are materials that suggest a costly and fine remove from discordant life. Natural elements that appear in the poem: "a white cow's milk," "the breast of a gull," "dews," accord with the concepts of colorlessness, soundlessness, and softness fused together in the conceit, *white.*

Here again, as in certain poems of *Incidental Numbers,* are echoes of that literature of whiteness remarked by Holbrook Jackson. In poems of Francis Thompson, Ernest Dowson, Lionel Johnson, Oscar Wilde, Arthur Symons, the early Yeats, and others, Jackson traces an obsession with the idea of whiteness (usually as an emblem of innocence) that found utterance in Aesthetic allusions to silver, moonlight, starlight, ivory, alabaster, and marble. He quotes from Richard Le Gallienne's "White Soul" in *Prose Fancies;* Le Gallienne explains that, in order to praise a girl's virginal innocence, he must use "snow-white words, lily-white words, words of ivory and pearl, words of silver and alabaster, words white as hawthorn and daisy, words white as morning milk, words 'whiter than Venus' doves, and softer than the down beneath their wings.'" Elinor Wylie, who declared, "I love words opalescent, cool, and pearly," and who described "lazy words" as "white cattle under trees" (*Collected Poems*), was also given to envisioning implicit character in words; and in **"Velvet Shoes"** she describes an event innocent of complication in language that recalls Le Gallienne's. His "white as morning milk" is similar to her "white as a white cow's milk"; gulls occur to her instead of doves; but both are white.

What appeals to the author of **"Velvet Shoes,"** as well as to Le Gallienne and other poets of the 1890s who wrote of "white silence" (Thompson) or "cloisters" "touched with white" (Johnson) or virginity's "swoon of whiteness" (Symons), is an immaculateness of experience. The white snow, Wylie says, is like "white silence." Those who tread upon it do so in no spirit of disturbance. The town is still; the snow is new-fallen, virgin; it elicits in the walkers an emotion of sensuous tranquillity. Jackson's hypothesis that, for the sophisticated Aesthete, whiteness was a symbol of perfection that is also "frankly sensuous" is supportable in Wylie's poem. For it describes a moment of pure sensuousness—stepping on silver fleece in velvet shoes—which, like the "fleeting outlines" of experience recorded by many Aesthetes, is more effective because it is transitory.

Elinor Wylie, once described by Carl Van Doren as looking like the "white queen of a white country," "white-faced in white satin," and who liked to be told she resembled "iced chalk," preserved throughout her life a fondness for white and silver dresses and, in art, for images of white, silver, crystal, and glass which helps to define the Aesthetic quality of her imagination. There were psychological reasons for her attraction to Aestheticism and to these images as, doubtless, there were for her preferences in dress and for the iconography of her novels.

Sandra M. Gilbert and Susan Gubar have written persuasively in *The Madwoman in the Attic* about the psychological significance of the wearing of white clothes by women, particularly women artists and in the nineteenth century. White gowns, alternately (and sometimes comprehensively) symbolizing purity/frigidity and vulnerability/magical power, appeared in literature and on the living bodies of those who read and wrote it as indications of a deep-seated response to art and life. Wylie's choice of white or silver dresses (some by Paul Poiret and beaded like armor) probably reflected her desire to advertise sexual aloofness because she had been punished for sexual ardor. Some of her attraction to the conceit *white* in life and in art must have come from a yearning to establish her own virginity. Gilbert and Gubar's psychological theses lend themselves to the interpretation of other aspects of Wylie's work: its fascination with women who attempt "the killing of oneself into an art object" and its preoccupation with thinness, glass, and her own image, all of which they regard as functions of the female artist's self-protective response to social animus. Louis Untermeyer remarked upon the "congealed brilliance" of *Nets to Catch the Wind*; he and others sometimes connected the coldness of Wylie's poetic landscape with what they inferred to be the coldness of her heart. Others realized that her obsession with whiteness was also related to her desire to associate the temper of her poems and the topography of her life. These attitudes were, of course, Aesthetic and related her to the Aesthetes, her early tutors.

The subjects and execution of many poems in *Nets to Catch the Wind* imply a design for writing verse identifiable with that of the Aesthetes. The plan Théophile Gautier devised for *Emaux et comées* (the title *Enamels and Cameos* suggests the affinity of his art with Wylie's) includes dicta respected by the English Aesthetes who were Gautier's disciples, dicta sustained in many successful poems of Elinor Wylie. Gautier, disapproving what he thought the sloppy self-indulgence of the Romanticism of Victor Hugo, determined to celebrate art above nature, poetic form above feeling, the miniature and rare above the grand or ordinary. In *Emaux et camées,* he would "treat . . . tiny subjects in a severely formal way . . . like working on gold or copper surfaces with brilliant enamels, or using a graver's wheel on precious stones, agate, cornelian or onyx." Elinor Wylie, who spoke of herself and her contemporaries as "enchanted by a midas-touch or a colder silver madness into workers in metal and glass, in substances hard and brittle, in crisp and sharp-edged forms" (*Collected Prose*), was both to practice this method and to argue its limitations. Convinced that Romantic art was greater in its spiritual aspiration than her own, she translated her formal preoccupation, her passion for "porcelain above humanity," into parables of warning.

Still, in the plan of Gautier as in his poems, there is a temper of mind which Elinor Wylie shared. Writers Elinor Wylie respected were influenced by Gautier's famous poem "L'Art" in which a statue or *médaille austère* outlasts cities and emperors; his "Fantaisies d'hiver" wherein old marbles, snow, and the idea of love unite in one image of still plasticity; and his worship of various images of whiteness in poems like "Symphonie en blanc majeur" in which the woman playing ivory piano keys resembles moonlight on ice, her white breast hiding "frozen secrets." For whether or not she read Gautier, she admired his disciple Austin Dobson's *Proverbs in Porcelain* and the verse of

Lionel Johnson from which she took the title of *Black Armour.*

To **"The Fairy Goldsmith"** and **"Velvet Shoes"** should be added another lyric that helps define the imagination of Elinor Wylie. **"Silver Filigree,"** one of the first poems she ever published (in *Poetry,* April, 1921), consists of four rhymed quatrains and captures a brief moment in which nature is an artificer. . . .

The speaker's interest in the icicles is earned by their decorative quality (they are "wreath[ed]" "in festoon"), their fragility and impermanence, their origin, being "made of the moon," in an ethereal world. The poem rehearses the subtle stages by which they "pass" "into crystal" from paper-thin transparencies shed by the pale moon with restrained fire. It is that moment when, having "smok[ed] a little," they freeze into "brittle / And delicate glass," the moment of alteration from a life of animation into one of artifaction that is significant. When not yet formed, the icicles "sway . . . to our breathing," responsive to the life of nature. Once frozen, they achieve the perfection of form and are "sharp-pointed flower[s]," nature hardened into design. Yet the design is fleeting, lasting "an hour," hence precious.

In **"Silver Filigree,"** Wylie shows characteristic attraction to that intense form of white, "silver," and the "filigree" of decoration that also interested the Aesthetes. The poem is not really about icicles but about the shapes they make. If it is contrasted with Coleridge's description in "Frost at Midnight," for example, of "silent icicles / Quietly shining to the quiet Moon," a difference is seen. Coleridge, depicting a soundless landscape under snow, summarizes its silence in the icicles' noiseless shimmer: they are indeed shapes, "h[u]ng up" by the "secret ministry of frost"; but it is their steadfast quietude that interests him. To Elinor Wylie, icicles become "brittle / And delicate glass." She is moved by their resemblance to artifacts and by the distinction between their formality— "Each a sharp-pointed flower"—and nature's fluidity—"the blue cave of night." Furthermore, her observation of one aspect of a wintry scene does not lead her, like Coleridge, to meditate on human concerns. Instead, her poem concentrates on the visual. Its quatrians are carefully carved, like the icicles, their subject.

When reading **"Velvet Shoes," "The Fairy Goldsmith,"** or **"Silver Filigree,"** one is reminded of a pronouncement of the Aesthetic painter James McNeill Whistler: "Art should be independent of all claptrap—and should stand alone and appeal to the artistic sense of eye or ear, without confounding this with emotions entirely foreign to it, as devotion, pity, love, patriotism and the like. All these have no kind of concern with it, and that is why I insist on calling my works "'arrangements' and 'harmonies.'" Whistler's was a typical defense of "art for art's sake" and a reaction against the Ruskinian expectation that art should inculcate moral values. Furthermore, his statement, insisting as it does on the visual and formal qualities of artifacts, may be more easily made by the graphic than by the poetic artist. Nevertheless, the Aesthetes as a group at-

tempted a celebration of beauty in design and of the emotional response which that beauty, apart from the spiritual significances it suggested, might provoke. None of Whistler's "arrangements," certainly not his most famous *Arrangement in Gray and Black No. 1,* fails to count on complex human responses to the solitary human form, to rivers at twilight or groups of figures placed together because of mysterious but fraught relationship. Still, their titles call primary attention to the disposition of forms and the tonal harmonies of Whistler's canvases. Similarly, the titles of Elinor Wylie's poems often emphasize their poetic design: **"Sea Lullaby," "Song," "Little Sonnet,"** within a pearly landscape reminiscent of Corot. It appears, too, in the sonnet **"August,"** which studies the distinction between heat and cold in a masterly series of images. The dark, "noiseless" figure of **"August"**'s Negro in the "red noonday," bearing black-eyed daisies whose copper petals "smoulder" like the sun and seem a "brazier" of burning light, flashes on the eye in the sonnet's octave, relating warm colors to heat and heat to pride and to death: the daisies are "shrivelled." Posed against it is the cry of the sestet for coolness, reserve, and the northern clime, here seen as comfortable and always preferred by Elinor Wylie.

In **"August,"** as in many other poems, she employs figurative speech to suggest aspects of design that comment on life. The burned petals that are brazierlike; the birds of **"Winter Sleep"** like "bubbles of glass"; the strap-hangers in **"A Crowded Trolley Car"** who seem an "orchard of the strangest fruits / Hanging from the skies" are viewed in a figurative mode that is painterly yet depicts objects, often artifacts, to make a conceptual point.

The last poem in *Nets to Catch the Wind* is called **"Valentine."** Its title is gently ironic since the poem declares that the speaker's heart "shall swing" / "Too high, too high to pluck" and the lines promise conservation of feeling rather than its expenditure. Here again, in clean accents and cool cadence, are two of the prominent themes of this volume: the need for dignified retreat from a world too often predatory and at the same time a sense of the cost of such retreat. The poet resolves that the heart shall be "A fruit no bee shall suck / No wasp shall sting." Still, in the second quatrain, she recognizes what must be the defeat of all who eschew engagement and suffering. The heart, "on some night of cold," will "fall to ground," for no one living, least of all a **"Proud Lady"** like herself, sensitive to public censure, can achieve sanctuary. In that instant, the speaker will protect her heart—her self—as she can:

> In apple-leaves of gold
> I'll wrap it round.
>
> And I shall seal it up
> With spice and salt,
> In a carven silver cup,
> In a deep vault.

Gold apple-leaves and the "carven silver cup" suggest the comforting power of aesthetic objects, her private universe, to which this speaker turns from the natural and hostile world. The comfort is fatal, however, "spice," "salt," and "vault" the accoutrements of death. But the poem ends in paradox. The buried heart must be eaten—the speaker must take responsibility for her choice—before she can herself die. It might be expected to be bitter gall:

> But I shall keep it sweet
> By some strange art;
> Wild honey I shall eat
> When I eat my heart.
>
> O honey cool and chaste
> As clover's breath!
> Sweet Heaven I shall taste
> Before my death.

The heart preserved from natural discord in an atmosphere of elegant artifice will nonetheless achieve a wild sweetness. This poem, blazoning as it does Elinor Wylie's early sense of her own difference and destiny, proclaims as well what was to her a boon: the loveliness of the world of fine things which could substitute for faithless humanity. This final poem, like others in *Nets to Catch the Wind,* asserts her Aesthetic commitment with an eloquence that did not discount the dangers of its position: dangers increasingly understood as her art matured.

Hyatt H. Waggoner (essay date 1984)

SOURCE: "Elinor Wylie," in *American Poets,* Louisiana State University Press, 1984, pp. 459-64.

[*Waggoner is a scholar noted for his studies of Nathaniel Hawthorne and Ralph Waldo Emerson. In the following excerpt he discusses Emersonian aspects of Wylie's poetry.*]

Expressing very similar attitudes, developing often the same themes, in a style derived, like Teasdale's, from the English Romantics, particularly from Shelley, Elinor Wylie created more poems that are still good to read. The several best of them, especially **"Wild Peaches"** and **"Innocent Landscape,"** are very good. Wylie's spirit was tougher than [Sara] Teasdale's had been before *Strange Victory,* and her mind clearer.

But what we are likely to notice first, as we read through her collected poems, is the similarity of the two. Among poets less gifted than the major figures of the age, the number of possible reactions to "the modern temper" was severely limited. Thus Wylie, echoing Teasdale, writes often of the advantages of a cold mind and of the heart's strategies of survival with a minimum of sustenance. In her best-known poem, **"Let No Charitable Hope,"** she writes, "I live by squeezing from a stone / The little nourishment I get." She is preoccupied always with erecting defenses against both "love's violence" and the knowledge of impending doom. Hearing continuously "the end of everything" approaching with a sound "insane, insistent," she seeks out ways to "be fugitive awhile from tears" and finds one of them in listening to a **"Viennese Waltz"**:

> Now falling, falling, feather after feather,
> The music spreads a softness on the ground;
> Now for an instant we are held together
> Hidden within a swinging mist of sound.

So sad have the strains of a gay waltz become to ears attuned to "Doomsday" sounds. "Malicious verity" has touched everything, even Beauty and Love.

Often, reading poems like **"Viennese Waltz,"** we wish for the astringencies of Marianne Moore or the intellectual firmness of [Emily] Dickinson. This is a reaction especially hard to avoid when the poet attempts affirmations of self-sufficiency after the example of [Ralph Waldo] Emerson and Shelley. **"Address to My Soul"** begins,

> My soul, be not disturbed
> By planetary war;
> Remain securely orbed
> In this contracted star.
> Fear not, pathetic flame;
> Your sustenance is doubt:
> Glassed in translucent dream
> They cannot snuff you out.

"They" floats freely in the sentence, not needing to be attached to anything; readers of the period knew well enough who the enemies of the soul were. The "chaos" and "void" and "dissolving star" mentioned later in the poem were understood before being named as the reasons why the soul must try to "be brave." And the poem's concluding advice to the soul could also be anticipated: "Five-petalled flame, be cold."

Shelley has been drawn upon here to help Wylie make her affirmation ("Life, like a dome of many-colored glass, stains the white radiance of eternity"), and Emerson, with his confidence in the "singular" soul's ability to move through its "predestined arc." (One wonders why the poet never acknowledged her debt to Emerson as she did that to Shelley, calling herself once "a woman by an archangel befriended," with Shelley in the angelic role; and on another occasion spreading **"A Red Carpet for Shelley."**) But the use made of both older poets is ultimately superficial. Something has been borrowed from the superstructure of their vision, but the foundations have been omitted—both the pantheism suggested by Shelley's "white radiance of eternity," and Emerson's faith in the Soul, and in growth, in process.

Sometimes Wylie's debt to Emerson is more specific than that to Shelley. When it is, her way of contracting his meaning becomes, unfortunately, even clearer. **"Beauty,"** for instance, draws from both "Each and All" and "The Rhodora," but what it omits from Emerson's poems and what it adds to them makes apparent the thinness of Wylie's romanticism. Emerson had said that "Beauty is its own excuse for being," which becomes Wylie's initial injunction, "Say not of Beauty she is good, / Or aught but beautiful." Emerson had warned that the bride would diminish from "fairy" to "gentle wife" when caged in marriage, as a "bird from the woodlands" would cease to sing in captivity.

Wylie expressed this by saying that beauty must be left "innocent and wild": "Enshrine her and she dies."

What she has omitted is the Emersonian vision that gives his maxims their meaning. He had concluded "The Rhodora" by saying that "The selfsame Power that brought me there brought you," which is to say, both flower and observer are directly related to, and derive their meaning from, the Over-Soul, and from this relationship get their relationship to each other. In "Each and All," he had discovered the organic unity of being which made futile all efforts to separate truth and beauty for the purpose of analysis. The speaker "yielded" himself "to the perfect whole," secure in the faith that nature was "Full of light and of deity." The beauty of every concrete aspect of being derives from, and is symbolic of, unconditioned Being. Thus it is that beauty needs no practical ("humanistic") justification, that it cannot be analyzed or controlled, that it disappears when separated, and that it can only be intuited in submission to the "perfect Whole." These are some of the meanings underlying and giving shape to Emerson's two poems.

Naturally enough, such Transcendental faith was impossible for Wylie. When she borrowed from Emerson, she could not borrow *this*. But to paraphrase Emerson's conclusions without supplying any substitute for the rejected religious vision on which they ultimately rested was to diminish the Transcendental to the merely sentimental.

Wylie's other borrowings from Emerson are similar. In **"The Eagle and the Mole"** she sounds very Emersonian, though she is probably also remembering Blake, when she counsels the soul to "Avoid the reeking herd" and "The huddled warmth of crowds," but what the eagle will gain, except possibly blindness, when he "stares into the sun," or what the mole will discover in his "intercourse / With roots of trees and stones, / With rivers at their source," the poem does not say or in any way suggest. Similarly, in **"Let No Charitable Hope,"** the poet who lives, as she puts it, by squeezing her nourishment from a stone, says she looks on time without fear as

> In masks outrageous and austere
> The years go by in single file.

The metaphor is adapted from Emerson's "Days," in which the days march by the speaker "single in an endless file," but there is no relation in *meaning* between Emerson's poem and Wylie's.

It is hardly surprising, therefore, that her best poems are those in which she seems most remote from either Emerson or Shelley. Her sense of man's plight in a meaningless universe was her own, not borrowed and not wished for. From it came the "mind of winter" poems that are generally her best. **"Innocent Landscape,"** for instance, notes that though the "reverential" trees look "like saints," yet

> Here is no virtue; here is nothing blessèd
> Save this foredoomed suspension of the end;
> Faith is the blossom, but the fruit is cursèd;
> Go hence, for it is useless to pretend.

"Wild Peaches" is her finest poem. In it she manages to make the familiar "mind of winter" theme seem fresh and compelling. For one thing, the personal approach, with its "I" and "we," suits her talent better than the bardic tone of her more openly "philosophic" poems. The poem means more than her other poems partly because it seems not to be *trying* to say so much, merely to be saying "I hate," and "I love"; and partly because its texture is richer than is common in her work. The poem consists of four sonnets so closely linked that in effect they are stanzas in a single poem. The first three describe a kind of return to an unfallen Eden on "the Eastern Shore" reached by "a riverboat from Baltimore":

> We'll live among wild peach trees, miles from town,
> You'll wear a coonskin cap, and I a gown
> Homespun, dyed butternut's dark gold colour.

There the two will "swim in milk and honey," and find "All seasons sweet, but Autumn best of all"; there the squirrels will fall to the hunter "like fruit" and the "autumn frosts will lie upon the grass / Like bloom on grapes." The spring in that mild climate will begin "before the winter's over," and with it the months that are like "brimming cornucopias" spilling out their gifts of nature's richness.

The poem succeeds as well as it does partly because the picture in the first three stanzas of a friendly and fruitful earth is so concrete. We see and smell and taste lovely things until the senses are cloyed and we are ready for the last stanza's renunciation, its turn to the bareness and whiteness of a real winter:

> Down to the Puritan marrow of my bones
> There's something in this richness that I hate.
> I love the look, austere, immaculate,
> Of landscapes drawn in pearly monotones.
> There's something in my very blood that owns
> Bare hills, cold silver on a sky of slate,
> A thread of water, churned to milky spate
> Streaming through slanted pastures fenced with stones.

The reason—never stated, fortunately—for the speaker's preference for the bare winter New England landscape to the friendlier Eastern Shore of Maryland is that it is more "real." Innocence has been lost for good, and nature as a whole is *not* friendly, however fertile Maryland soil may be. The "Puritan" sensibility responds to severity. Looking at the seasons of man's life, it sees that spring is "briefer than apple-blossom's breath" and summer is "much too beautiful to stay." Its own seasons are

> Swift autumn, like a bonfire of leaves,
> And sleepy winter, like the sleep of death.

Sara Teasdale had not yet written so well as this, and Elinor Wylie, who died young in 1928, would not again. Edna St. Vincent Millay, the youngest of the three, would come close to it only at the very beginning of her career, but for a while in the 1920's and 1930's she was more famous than either of the others.

FURTHER READING

Biography

Clark, Emily. "Elinor Wylie." In *Innocence Abroad*, pp.167-86. New York, London: Alfred A. Knopf, 1931.
>   An account of Wylie's first trip to Virginia, during which she met James Branch Cabell, and of her frequent trips to England.

Colum, Mary M. "Elinor Wylie" and "Death of Elinor Wylie." In *Life and the Dream*, pp. 334-45, pp. 358-67. Garden City, NY: Doubleday & Company, 1947.
>   Personal descriptions of the friendly acquaintance between Colum and Wylie and recollections of their last meeting, which took place days before Wylie's death.

Hoyt, Nancy. *Elinor Wylie: The Portrait of an Unknown Lady*. New York: Bobbs-Merrill, 1935, 203 p.
>   Anecdotal biography by the poet's sister that describes concerns of fashion in as much detail as Wylie's literary accomplishments.

Untermeyer, Louis. "Bill and Nefertiti." In *From Another World*, pp. 229-53. New York: Harcourt, Brace and Company, 1939.
>   Personal recollection reconstructing the relationship between Wylie and William Rose Benét, discussing their first meeting, eventual friendship, and love.

Van Doren, Carl. "Elinor Wylie." In *Carl Van Doren*, pp. 66-90. New York: Viking Press, 1945.
>   Tribute to Wylie by her friend and editor. Van Doren discusses the "legend" surrounding Wylie's life upon her reception in New York and the literary world.

Criticism

Brenner, Rica. "Elinor Wylie." In *Poets of Our Time*, pp. 313-53. Harcourt, Brace and Company, 1941.
>   Details the interplay between Wylie's personal life and her career as a poet.

Brooks, Cleanth. "Poets and Laureates." *Southern Review (1936-1937)*, Vol. II, pp. 391-98. Baton Rouge: Louisiana State University Press, 1965.
>   Compares Wylie's poetry to that of Helen Cornelius.

Cluck, Julia. "Elinor Wylie's Shelley Obsession." *PMLA* LVI, (1941): 841-60.
>   Points out allusions to Shelley in Wylie's poetry.

Colum, Mary M. "O Virtuous Light." *The Saturday Review* V, No. 44 (25 May 1929): 1043-44.
>   Complimentary review of Wylie's *Angels and Earthly Creatures* emphasizing its intellectual appeal.

Ducharme, Edward. "Again, Evasion of the Text." *The English Record* XXI, No. 1 (October 1970): 108-12.
>   Explication of Wylie's poem "The Eagle and the Mole."

Farr, Judith. "Elinor Wylie, Edna St. Vincent Millay, and the Elizabethan Sonnet Tradition." In *Poetic Traditions of the English Renaissance*, pp. 287-305. New Haven and London: Yale University Press, 1982.
>   Compares Wylie's "One Person" sonnets with the work of Millay, William Shakespeare, Thomas Nash, and John Donne.

Gray, Thomas. *Elinor Wylie*. New York: Twayne Publishers, 1969, 171 p.
>   First book-length analysis of Wylie's poetry and the influences upon it. Includes a brief annotated bibliography of secondary sources.

Hoagwood, Thomas Allan [Terence]. "Wylie's 'Beauty.'" *The Explicator* 43, No. 1 (Fall 1984): 53-5.
>   Close reading of Wylie's poem "Beauty."

Hoagwood, Terence Allan. "Wylie's 'The Crooked Stick.'" *The Explicator* 44, No. 3 (Spring 1986): 53-5.
>   Close reading of Wylie's poem "The Crooked Stick."

Hoffman, Charles. "Invasion of the Text." *The English Record* XXI, No. 1 (October 1970): 103-07.
>   Response to Edward Ducharme's explication of Wylie's poem "The Eagle and the Mole." Hoffman suggests that the poem does not require close reading to be appreciated.

Kelly, Edward H. "'The Eagle and the Mole': The Affective Fallacy Revisited." *The English Record* XXI, No. 1 (October 1970): 57-9.
>   Answer to Edward Ducharme's and Charles Hoffman's analyses of Wylie's poem. Kelly offers a symbolic reading and makes comparisons to Wylie's poem, "Sanctuary."

Lowell, Amy. "Two Generations of American Poetry." *New Republic* (5 December 1923): 1-3.
>   Historical perspective of Wylie's poetry.

Lüdeke, H. "Venetian Glass: The Poetry and Prose of Elinor Wylie." *English Studies* XX, No. 6 (December 1938): 241-50.
>   Suggests that while Wylie's poetry is stylistically sophisticated, it lacks depth of feeling, especially in comparison to the poetry of Elizabeth Barrett Browning.

MacLeish, Archibald. Review of *Black Armour*. *The New Republic* XXXVIII, No. 470, Part II (5 December 1923):16-18.
>   Complimentary review of Wylie's aesthetic talents.

Perrine, Laurence. "Wylie's 'Velvet Shoes.'" *The Explicator* XIII, No. 3 (December 1954): Item 17.
>   Analyzes the imagery in "Velvet Shoes."

Raiziss, Sona. "Macleish—Wylie—Crane." In *The Metaphysical Passion: Seven Modern American Poets and the Seventeenth-Century Tradition*, pp. 212-41. Westport, Conn.: Greenwood Press, 1952.
>   Briefly compares Wylie's poetry to that of Emily Dickinson, John Donne, and William Blake.

Saul, George Brandon. "'Icy Song': The Verse of Elinor Wylie." *Bulletin of the New York Public Library* 69, No. 9 (November 1965): 618-22.

> Brief overview of Wylie's poetry that examines her ballads, lyrics, and metaphysical style.

Sergeant, Elizabeth Shepley. "Elinor Wylie." In *Fire Under the Andes: A Group of North American Portraits,* pp.107-21. New York, London: Alfred A. Knopf, 1927.

> A biographical and critical study that presents an imaginative portrait of Wylie's life and her development as a writer.

Wertenbaker, Jr., Thomas J. "Into the Poet's Shoes." *The English Journal* LIII, No. 5 (May 1964): 370-72.

> Analyzes Wylie's poem "Velvet Shoes," comparing it to the work of Robert Frost.

Zabel, Morton Dauwen. "The Mechanism of Sensibility," *Poetry* XXXIV (June 1929): 150-55.

> Describes the ways in which Wylie's poetry is metaphysical.

Additional coverage of Wylie's life and career is contained in the following sources published by The Gale Group: *Contemporary Authors*, Vol. 105; *Dictionary of Literary Biography*, Vols. 9 and 45; and *Twentieth-Century Literary Criticism*, Vol. 8.

Poetry Criticism
INDEXES

Literary Criticism Series
Cumulative Author Index

Cumulative Nationality Index

Cumulative Title Index

How to Use This Index

The main references

Calvino, Italo
1923–1985 .... CLC 5, 8, 11, 22, 33, 39,
73; SSC 3

list all author entries in the following Gale Literary Criticism series:

BLC = *Black Literature Criticism*
CLC = *Contemporary Literary Criticism*
CLR = *Children's Literature Review*
CMLC = *Classical and Medieval Literature Criticism*
DA = *DISCovering Authors*
DAB = *DISCovering Authors: British*
DAC = *DISCovering Authors: Canadian*
DAM = *DISCovering Authors: Modules*
  DRAM: *Dramatists Module;* *MST*: *Most-Studied Authors Module;*
  MULT: *Multicultural Authors Module;* *NOV*: *Novelists Module;*
  POET: *Poets Module;* *POP*: *Popular Fiction and Genre Authors Module*
DC = *Drama Criticism*
HLC = *Hispanic Literature Criticism*
LC = *Literature Criticism from 1400 to 1800*
NCLC = *Nineteenth-Century Literature Criticism*
PC = *Poetry Criticism*
SSC = *Short Story Criticism*
TCLC = *Twentieth-Century Literary Criticism*
WLC = *World Literature Criticism, 1500 to the Present*

The cross-references

See also CANR 23; CA 85-88;
obituary CA116

list all author entries in the following Gale biographical and literary sources:

AAYA = *Authors & Artists for Young Adults*
AITN = *Authors in the News*
BEST = *Bestsellers*
BW = *Black Writers*
CA = *Contemporary Authors*
CAAS = *Contemporary Authors Autobiography Series*
CABS = *Contemporary Authors Bibliographical Series*
CANR = *Contemporary Authors New Revision Series*
CAP = *Contemporary Authors Permanent Series*
CDALB = *Concise Dictionary of American Literary Biography*
CDBLB = *Concise Dictionary of British Literary Biography*
DLB = *Dictionary of Literary Biography*
DLBD = *Dictionary of Literary Biography Documentary Series*
DLBY = *Dictionary of Literary Biography Yearbook*
HW = *Hispanic Writers*
JRDA = *Junior DISCovering Authors*
MAICYA = *Major Authors and Illustrators for Children and Young Adults*
MTCW = *Major 20th-Century Writers*
NNAL = *Native North American Literature*
SAAS = *Something about the Author Autobiography Series*
SATA = *Something about the Author*
YABC = *Yesterday's Authors of Books for Children*

Literary Criticism Series
Cumulative Author Index

Aldiss, Brian W(ilson) 1925-... **CLC 5, 14, 40;**
DAM NOV
See also CA 5-8R; CAAS 2; CANR 5, 28, 64;
DLB 14; MTCW; SATA 34

Alegria, Claribel 1924-...**CLC 75; DAM MULT**
See also CA 131; CAAS 15; CANR 66; DLB
145; HW

Alegria, Fernando 1918- .... **CLC 57**
See also CA 9-12R; CANR 5, 32; HW

Aleichem, Sholom .... **TCLC 1, 35**
See also Rabinovitch, Sholem

Aleixandre, Vicente 1898-1984 ..... **CLC 9, 36;**
DAM POET; PC 15
See also CA 85-88; 114; CANR 26; DLB 108;
HW; MTCW

Alepoudelis, Odysseus
See Elytis, Odysseus

Aleshkovsky, Joseph 1929-
See Aleshkovsky, Yuz
See also CA 121; 128

Aleshkovsky, Yuz .... **CLC 44**
See also Aleshkovsky, Joseph

Alexander, Lloyd (Chudley) 1924- ..... **CLC 35**
See also AAYA 1; CA 1-4R; CANR 1, 24, 38,
55; CLR 1, 5, 48; DLB 52; JRDA; MAICYA;
MTCW; SAAS 19; SATA 3, 49, 81

Alexander, Samuel 1859-1938 .... **TCLC 77**

Alexie, Sherman (Joseph, Jr.) 1966-...**CLC 96;**
DAM MULT
See also CA 138; CANR 65; DLB 175; NNAL

Alfau, Felipe 1902- .... **CLC 66**
See also CA 137

Alger, Horatio, Jr. 1832-1899 .... **NCLC 8**
See also DLB 42; SATA 16

Algren, Nelson 1909-1981 .... **CLC 4, 10, 33**
See also CA 13-16R; 103; CANR 20, 61;
CDALB 1941-1968; DLB 9; DLBY 81, 82;
MTCW

Ali, Ahmed 1910- .... **CLC 69**
See also CA 25-28R; CANR 15, 34

Alighieri, Dante
See Dante

Allan, John B.
See Westlake, Donald E(dwin)

Allan, Sidney
See Hartmann, Sadakichi

Allan, Sydney
See Hartmann, Sadakichi

Allen, Edward 1948-........................**CLC 59**

Allen, Paula Gunn 1939- ...... **CLC 84; DAM**
MULT
See also CA 112; 143; CANR 63; DLB 175; NNAL

Allen, Roland
See Ayckbourn, Alan

Allen, Sarah A.
See Hopkins, Pauline Elizabeth

Allen, Sidney H.
See Hartmann, Sadakichi

Allen, Woody 1935- .. **CLC 16, 52; DAM POP**
See also AAYA 10; CA 33-36R; CANR 27, 38,
63; DLB 44; MTCW

Allende, Isabel 1942- ... **CLC 39, 57, 97; DAM**
MULT, NOV; HLC; WLCS
See also AAYA 18; CA 125; 130; CANR 51; DLB
145; HW; INT 130; MTCW

Alleyn, Ellen
See Rossetti, Christina (Georgina)

Allingham, Margery (Louise) 1904-1966
CLC 19
See also CA 5-8R; 25-28R; CANR 4, 58; DLB
77; MTCW

Allingham, William 1824-1889 .... **NCLC 25**
See also DLB 35

Allison, Dorothy E. 1949- .... **CLC 78**
See also CA 140; CANR 66

Allston, Washington 1779-1843 .... **NCLC 2**
See also DLB 1

Almedingen, E. M. ....**CLC 12**
See also Almedingen, Martha Edith von
See also SATA 3

Almedingen, Martha Edith von 1898-1971
See Almedingen, E. M.
See also CA 1-4R; CANR 1

Almqvist, Carl Jonas Love 1793-1866
NCLC 42

Alonso, Damaso 1898-1990 .... **CLC 14**
See also CA 110; 131; 130; DLB 108; HW

Alov
See Gogol, Nikolai (Vasilyevich)

Alta 1942-..**CLC 19**
See also CA 57-60

Alter, Robert B(ernard) 1935- .... **CLC 34**
See also CA 49-52; CANR 1, 47

Alther, Lisa 1944- ....**CLC 7, 41**
See also CA 65-68; CANR 12, 30, 51; MTCW

Althusser, L.
See Althusser, Louis

Althusser, Louis 1918-1990 .... **CLC 106**
See also CA 131; 132

Altman, Robert 1925- ....**CLC 16**
See also CA 73-76; CANR 43

Alvarez, A(lfred) 1929- .... **CLC 5, 13**
See also CA 1-4R; CANR 3, 33, 63; DLB 14, 40

Alvarez, Alejandro Rodriguez 1903-1965
See Casona, Alejandro
See also CA 131; 93-96; HW

Alvarez, Julia 1950- ....**CLC 93**
See also AAYA 25; CA 147; CANR 69

Alvaro, Corrado 1896-1956 .... **TCLC 60**
See also CA 163

Amado, Jorge 1912-.. **CLC 13, 40, 106; DAM**
MULT, NOV; HLC
See also CA 77-80; CANR 35; DLB 113; MTCW

Ambler, Eric 1909- ....**CLC 4, 6, 9**
See also CA 9-12R; CANR 7, 38; DLB 77;
MTCW

Amichai, Yehuda 1924- ....**CLC 9, 22, 57**
See also CA 85-88; CANR 46, 60; MTCW

Amichai, Yehudah
See Amichai, Yehuda

Amiel, Henri Frederic 1821-1881 ..... **NCLC 4**

Amis, Kingsley (William) 1922-1995...**CLC 1,**
2, 3, 5, 8, 13, 40, 44; DA; DAB; DAC;
DAM MST, NOV
See also AITN 2; CA 9-12R; 150; CANR 8, 28,
54; CDBLB 1945-1960; DLB 15, 27, 100,
139; DLBY 96; INT CANR-8; MTCW

Amis, Martin (Louis) 1949-...**CLC 4, 9, 38, 62,**
101
See also BEST 90:3; CA 65-68; CANR 8, 27,
54; DLB 14, 194; INT CANR-27

Ammons, A(rchie) R(andolph) 1926-...**C L C**
2, 3, 5, 8, 9, 25, 57, 108; DAM POET; PC 16
See also AITN 1; CA 9-12R; CANR 6, 36, 51;
DLB 5, 165; MTCW

Amo, Tauraatua i
See Adams, Henry (Brooks)

Anand, Mulk Raj 1905-..**CLC 23, 93; DAM NOV**
See also CA 65-68; CANR 32, 64; MTCW

Anatol
See Schnitzler, Arthur

Anaximander c. 610B.C.-c. 546B.C....**CMLC 22**

Anaya, Rudolfo A(lfonso) 1937- .... **CLC 23;**
DAM MULT, NOV; HLC
See also AAYA 20; CA 45-48; CAAS 4; CANR
1, 32, 51; DLB 82; HW 1; MTCW

Andersen, Hans Christian 1805-1875
NCLC 7; DA; DAB; DAC; DAM MST,
POP; SSC 6; WLC
See also CLR 6; MAICYA; YABC 1

Anderson, C. Farley
See Mencken, H(enry) L(ouis); Nathan, George
Jean

Anderson, Jessica (Margaret) Queale 1916-
CLC 37
See also CA 9-12R; CANR 4, 62

Anderson, Jon (Victor) 1940- ... **CLC 9; DAM**
POET
See also CA 25-28R; CANR 20

Anderson, Lindsay (Gordon) 1923-1994...**CLC**
20
See also CA 125; 128; 146

Anderson, Maxwell 1888-1959 ..... **TCLC 2;**
DAM DRAM
See also CA 105; 152; DLB 7

Anderson, Poul (William) 1926- ....**CLC 15**
See also AAYA 5; CA 1-4R; CAAS 2; CANR 2,
15, 34, 64; DLB 8; INT CANR-15; MTCW;
SATA 90; SATA-Brief 39

Anderson, Robert (Woodruff) 1917-...**CLC 23;**
DAM DRAM
See also AITN 1; CA 21-24R; CANR 32; DLB 7

Anderson, Sherwood 1876-1941...**TCLC 1, 10,**
24; DA; DAB; DAC; DAM MST, NOV; SSC
1; WLC
See also CA 104; 121; CANR 61; CDALB 1917-
1929; DLB 4, 9, 86; DLBD 1; MTCW

Andier, Pierre
See Desnos, Robert

Andouard
See Giraudoux, (Hippolyte) Jean

Andrade, Carlos Drummond de .... **CLC 18**
See also Drummond de Andrade, Carlos

Andrade, Mario de 1893-1945 .... **TCLC 43**

Andreae, Johann V(alentin) 1586-1654...**LC 32**
See also DLB 164

Andreas-Salome, Lou 1861-1937 .... **TCLC 56**
See also DLB 66

Andress, Lesley
See Sanders, Lawrence

Andrewes, Lancelot 1555-1626 ....**LC 5**
See also DLB 151, 172

Andrews, Cicily Fairfield
See West, Rebecca

Andrews, Elton V.
See Pohl, Frederik

Andreyev, Leonid (Nikolaevich) 1871-1919
TCLC 3
See also CA 104

Andric, Ivo 1892-1975 ....**CLC 8**
See also CA 81-84; 57-60; CANR 43, 60; DLB
147; MTCW

Androvar
See Prado (Calvo), Pedro

Angelique, Pierre
See Bataille, Georges

Angell, Roger 1920- ....**CLC 26**
See also CA 57-60; CANR 13, 44; DLB 171, 185

Angelou, Maya 1928- .. **CLC 12, 35, 64, 77;**
BLC 1; DA; DAB; DAC; DAM MST,
MULT, POET, POP; WLCS
See also AAYA 7, 20; BW 2; CA 65-68; CANR
19, 42, 65; DLB 38; MTCW; SATA 49

Anna Comnena 1083-1153 ....**CMLC 25**

Annensky, Innokenty (Fyodorovich) 1856-1909
TCLC 14
See also CA 110; 155

Annunzio, Gabriele d'
See D'Annunzio, Gabriele

August, John
See De Voto, Bernard (Augustine)
Augustine, St. 354-430 .... **CMLC 6; DAB**
Aurelius
See Bourne, Randolph S(illiman)
Aurobindo, Sri
See Ghose, Aurabinda
Austen, Jane 1775-1817...**NCLC 1, 13, 19, 33, 51; DA; DAB; DAC; DAM MST, NOV; WLC**
See also AAYA 19; CDBLB 1789-1832; DLB 116
Auster, Paul 1947- .... **CLC 47**
See also CA 69-72; CANR 23, 52
Austin, Frank
See Faust, Frederick (Schiller)
Austin, Mary (Hunter) 1868-1934 .. **TCLC 25**
See also CA 109; DLB 9, 78
Autran Dourado, Waldomiro
See Dourado, (Waldomiro Freitas) Autran
Averroes 1126-1198 .... **CMLC 7**
See also DLB 115
Avicenna 980-1037 .... **CMLC 16**
See also DLB 115
Avison, Margaret 1918- ..**CLC 2, 4, 97; DAC; DAM POET**
See also CA 17-20R; DLB 53; MTCW
Axton, David
See Koontz, Dean R(ay)
Ayckbourn, Alan 1939-...**CLC 5, 8, 18, 33, 74; DAB; DAM DRAM**
See also CA 21-24R; CANR 31, 59; DLB 13; MTCW
Aydy, Catherine
See Tennant, Emma (Christina)
Ayme, Marcel (Andre) 1902-1967 ...... **CLC 11**
See also CA 89-92; CANR 67; CLR 25; DLB 72; SATA 91
Ayrton, Michael 1921-1975 .... **CLC 7**
See also CA 5-8R; 61-64; CANR 9, 21
Azorin .... **CLC 11**
See also Martinez Ruiz, Jose
Azuela, Mariano 1873-1952 .. **TCLC 3; DAM MULT; HLC**
See also CA 104; 131; HW; MTCW
Baastad, Babbis Friis
See Friis-Baastad, Babbis Ellinor
Bab
See Gilbert, W(illiam) S(chwenck)
Babbis, Eleanor
See Friis-Baastad, Babbis Ellinor
Babel, Isaac
See Babel, Isaac (Emmanuilovich)
Babel, Isaak (Emmanuilovich) 1894-1941(?) **TCLC 2, 13; SSC 16**
See also CA 104; 155
Babits, Mihaly 1883-1941 .... **TCLC 14**
See also CA 114
Babur 1483-1530 .... **LC 18**
Bacchelli, Riccardo 1891-1985 .... **CLC 19**
See also CA 29-32R; 117
Bach, Richard (David) 1936- .. **CLC 14; DAM NOV, POP**
See also AITN 1; BEST 89:2; CA 9-12R; CANR 18; MTCW; SATA 13
Bachman, Richard
See King, Stephen (Edwin)
Bachmann, Ingeborg 1926-1973 .... **CLC 69**
See also CA 93-96; 45-48; CANR 69; DLB 85
Bacon, Francis 1561-1626 .... **LC 18, 32**
See also CDBLB Before 1660; DLB 151
Bacon, Roger 1214(?)-1292 .... **CMLC 14**
See also DLB 115
Bacovia, George .... **TCLC 24**
See also Vasiliu, Gheorghe

Badanes, Jerome 1937- .... **CLC 59**
Bagehot, Walter 1826-1877 .... **NCLC 10**
See also DLB 55
Bagnold, Enid 1889-1981 .... **CLC 25; DAM DRAM**
See also CA 5-8R; 103; CANR 5, 40; DLB 13, 160, 191; MAICYA; SATA 1, 25
Bagritsky, Eduard 1895-1934 .... **TCLC 60**
Bagrjana, Elisaveta
See Belcheva, Elisaveta
Bagryana, Elisaveta .... **CLC 10**
See also Belcheva, Elisaveta
See also DLB 147
Bailey, Paul 1937- .... **CLC 45**
See also CA 21-24R; CANR 16, 62; DLB 14
Baillie, Joanna 1762-1851 .... **NCLC 71**
See also DLB 93
Bainbridge, Beryl (Margaret) 1933-...**CLC 4, 5, 8, 10, 14, 18, 22, 62; DAM NOV**
See also CA 21-24R; CANR 24, 55; DLB 14; MTCW
Baker, Elliott 1922- .... **CLC 8**
See also CA 45-48; CANR 2, 63
Baker, Jean H. .... **TCLC 3, 10**
See also Russell, George William
Baker, Nicholson 1957- .. **CLC 61; DAM POP**
See also CA 135; CANR 63
Baker, Ray Stannard 1870-1946 ..... **TCLC 47**
See also CA 118
Baker, Russell (Wayne) 1925- .... **CLC 31**
See also BEST 89:4; CA 57-60; CANR 11, 41, 59; MTCW
Bakhtin, M.
See Bakhtin, Mikhail Mikhailovich
Bakhtin, M. M.
See Bakhtin, Mikhail Mikhailovich
Bakhtin, Mikhail
See Bakhtin, Mikhail Mikhailovich
Bakhtin, Mikhail Mikhailovich 1895-1975 **CLC 83**
See also CA 128; 113
Bakshi, Ralph 1938(?)- .... **CLC 26**
See also CA 112; 138
Bakunin, Mikhail (Alexandrovich) 1814-1876 **NCLC 25, 58**
Baldwin, James (Arthur) 1924-1987...**CLC 1, 2, 3, 4, 5, 8, 13, 15, 17, 42, 50, 67, 90; BLC 1; DA; DAB; DAC; DAM MST, MULT, NOV, POP; DC 1; SSC 10; WLC**
See also AAYA 4; BW 1; CA 1-4R; 124; CABS 1; CANR 3, 24; CDALB 1941-1968; DLB 2, 7, 33; DLBY 87; MTCW; SATA 9; SATA-Obit 54
Ballard, J(ames) G(raham) 1930-...**CLC 3, 6, 14, 36; DAM NOV, POP; SSC 1**
See also AAYA 3; CA 5-8R; CANR 15, 39, 65; DLB 14; MTCW; SATA 93
Balmont, Konstantin (Dmitriyevich) 1867-1943 **TCLC 11**
See also CA 109; 155
Balzac, Honore de 1799-1850...**NCLC 5, 35, 53; DA; DAB; DAC; DAM MST, NOV; SSC 5; WLC**
See also DLB 119
Bambara, Toni Cade 1939-1995...**CLC 19, 88; BLC 1; DA; DAC; DAM MST, MULT; WLCS**
See also AAYA 5; BW 2; CA 29-32R; 150; CANR 24, 49; DLB 38; MTCW
Bamdad, A.
See Shamlu, Ahmad
Banat, D. R.
See Bradbury, Ray (Douglas)

Bancroft, Laura
See Baum, L(yman) Frank
Banim, John 1798-1842 .... **NCLC 13**
See also DLB 116, 158, 159
Banim, Michael 1796-1874 .... **NCLC 13**
See also DLB 158, 159
Banjo, The
See Paterson, A(ndrew) B(arton)
Banks, Iain
See Banks, Iain M(enzies)
Banks, Iain M(enzies) 1954- .... **CLC 34**
See also CA 123; 128; CANR 61; DLB 194; INT 128
Banks, Lynne Reid .... **CLC 23**
See also Reid Banks, Lynne
See also AAYA 6
Banks, Russell 1940- .... **CLC 37, 72**
See also CA 65-68; CAAS 15; CANR 19, 52; DLB 130
Banville, John 1945-.......................... **CLC 46**
See also CA 117; 128; DLB 14; INT 128
Banville, Theodore (Faullain) de 1832-1891 **NCLC 9**
Baraka, Amiri 1934-...**CLC 1, 2, 3, 5, 10, 14, 33; BLC 1; DA; DAC; DAM MST, MULT, POET, POP; DC 6; PC 4; WLCS**
See also Jones, LeRoi
See also BW 2; CA 21-24R; CABS 3; CANR 27, 38, 61; CDALB 1941-1968; DLB 5, 7, 16, 38; DLBD 8; MTCW
Barbauld, Anna Laetitia 1743-1825...**NCLC 50**
See also DLB 107, 109, 142, 158
Barbellion, W. N. P. .... **TCLC 24**
See also Cummings, Bruce F(rederick)
Barbera, Jack (Vincent) 1945- .... **CLC 44**
See also CA 110; CANR 45
Barbey d'Aurevilly, Jules Amedee 1808-1889 **NCLC 1; SSC 17**
See also DLB 119
Barbusse, Henri 1873-1935 .... **TCLC 5**
See also CA 105; 154; DLB 65
Barclay, Bill
See Moorcock, Michael (John)
Barclay, William Ewert
See Moorcock, Michael (John)
Barea, Arturo 1897-1957 .... **TCLC 14**
See also CA 111
Barfoot, Joan 1946- .... **CLC 18**
See also CA 105
Baring, Maurice 1874-1945 .... **TCLC 8**
See also CA 105; DLB 34
Barker, Clive 1952- .... **CLC 52; DAM POP**
See also AAYA 10; BEST 90:3; CA 121; 129; INT 129; MTCW
Barker, George Granville 1913-1991 .. **CLC 8, 48; DAM POET**
See also CA 9-12R; 135; CANR 7, 38; DLB 20; MTCW
Barker, Harley Granville
See Granville-Barker, Harley
See also DLB 10
Barker, Howard 1946- .... **CLC 37**
See also CA 102; DLB 13
Barker, Pat(ricia) 1943- .... **CLC 32, 94**
See also CA 117; 122; CANR 50; INT 122
Barlow, Joel 1754-1812 .... **NCLC 23**
See also DLB 37
Barnard, Mary (Ethel) 1909- .... **CLC 48**
See also CA 21-22; CAP 2
Barnes, Djuna 1892-1982...**CLC 3, 4, 8, 11, 29; SSC 3**
See also CA 9-12R; 107; CANR 16, 55; DLB 4, 9, 45; MTCW

Bellin, Edward J.
See Kuttner, Henry
Belloc, (Joseph) Hilaire (Pierre Sebastien Rene Swanton) 1870-1953...TCLC 7, 18; DAM POET
See also CA 106; 152; DLB 19, 100, 141, 174; YABC 1
Belloc, Joseph Peter Rene Hilaire
See Belloc, (Joseph) Hilaire (Pierre Sebastien Rene Swanton)
Belloc, Joseph Pierre Hilaire
See Belloc, (Joseph) Hilaire (Pierre Sebastien Rene Swanton)
Belloc, M. A.
See Lowndes, Marie Adelaide (Belloc)
Bellow, Saul 1915-...CLC 1, 2, 3, 6, 8, 10, 13, 15, 25, 33, 34, 63, 79; DA; DAB; DAC; DAM MST, NOV, POP; SSC 14; WLC
See also AITN 2; BEST 89:3; CA 5-8R; CABS 1; CANR 29, 53; CDALB 1941-1968; DLB 2, 28; DLBD 3; DLBY 82; MTCW
Belser, Reimond Karel Maria de 1929-
See Ruyslinck, Ward
See also CA 152
Bely, Andrey .... TCLC 7; PC 11
See also Bugayev, Boris Nikolayevich
Belyi, Andrei
See Bugayev, Boris Nikolayevich
Benary, Margot
See Benary-Isbert, Margot
Benary-Isbert, Margot 1889-1979 ..... CLC 12
See also CA 5-8R; 89-92; CANR 4; CLR 12; MAICYA; SATA 2; SATA-Obit 21
Benavente (y Martinez), Jacinto 1866-1954 TCLC 3; DAM DRAM, MULT
See also CA 106; 131; HW; MTCW
Benchley, Peter (Bradford) 1940- .. CLC 4, 8; DAM NOV, POP
See also AAYA 14; AITN 2; CA 17-20R; CANR 12, 35, 66; MTCW; SATA 3, 89
Benchley, Robert (Charles) 1889-1945...TCLC 1, 55
See also CA 105; 153; DLB 11
Benda, Julien 1867-1956 .... TCLC 60
See also CA 120; 154
Benedict, Ruth (Fulton) 1887-1948...TCLC 60
See also CA 158
Benedict, Saint c. 480-c. 547 .... CMLC 29
Benedikt, Michael 1935- .... CLC 4, 14
See also CA 13-16R; CANR 7; DLB 5
Benet, Juan 1927- .... CLC 28
See also CA 143
Benet, Stephen Vincent 1898-1943 .. TCLC 7; DAM POET; SSC 10
See also CA 104; 152; DLB 4, 48, 102; DLBY 97; YABC 1
Benet, William Rose 1886-1950 ..... TCLC 28; DAM POET
See also CA 118; 152; DLB 45
Benford, Gregory (Albert) 1941- .... CLC 52
See also CA 69-72; CAAS 27; CANR 12, 24, 49; DLBY 82
Bengtsson, Frans (Gunnar) 1894-1954...TCLC 48
Benjamin, David
See Slavitt, David R(ytman)
Benjamin, Lois
See Gould, Lois
Benjamin, Walter 1892-1940 .... TCLC 39
See also CA 164
Benn, Gottfried 1886-1956 .... TCLC 3
See also CA 106; 153; DLB 56

Bennett, Alan 1934-...CLC 45, 77; DAB; DAM MST
See also CA 103; CANR 35, 55; MTCW
Bennett, (Enoch) Arnold 1867-1931...TCLC 5, 20
See also CA 106; 155; CDBLB 1890-1914; DLB 10, 34, 98, 135
Bennett, Elizabeth
See Mitchell, Margaret (Munnerlyn)
Bennett, George Harold 1930-
See Bennett, Hal
See also BW 1; CA 97-100
Bennett, Hal .... CLC 5
See also Bennett, George Harold
See also DLB 33
Bennett, Jay 1912- .... CLC 35
See also AAYA 10; CA 69-72; CANR 11, 42; JRDA; SAAS 4; SATA 41, 87; SATA-Brief 27
Bennett, Louise (Simone) 1919-....CLC 28; BLC 1; DAM MULT
See also BW 2; CA 151; DLB 117
Benson, E(dward) F(rederic) 1867-1940 TCLC 27
See also CA 114; 157; DLB 135, 153
Benson, Jackson J. 1930- .... CLC 34
See also CA 25-28R; DLB 111
Benson, Sally 1900-1972 .... CLC 17
See also CA 19-20; 37-40R; CAP 1; SATA 1, 35; SATA-Obit 27
Benson, Stella 1892-1933 .... TCLC 17
See also CA 117; 155; DLB 36, 162
Bentham, Jeremy 1748-1832 .... NCLC 38
See also DLB 107, 158
Bentley, E(dmund) C(lerihew) 1875-1956 TCLC 12
See also CA 108; DLB 70
Bentley, Eric (Russell) 1916- .... CLC 24
See also CA 5-8R; CANR 6, 67; INT CANR-6
Beranger, Pierre Jean de 1780-1857..NCLC 34
Berdyaev, Nicolas
See Berdyaev, Nikolai (Aleksandrovich)
Berdyaev, Nikolai (Aleksandrovich) 1874-1948 TCLC 67
See also CA 120; 157
Berdyayev, Nikolai (Aleksandrovich)
See Berdyaev, Nikolai (Aleksandrovich)
Berendt, John (Lawrence) 1939-........ CLC 86
See also CA 146
Beresford, J(ohn) D(avys) 1873-1947..TCLC 81
See also CA 112; 155; DLB 162, 178, 197
Bergelson, David 1884-1952 .... TCLC 81
Berger, Colonel
See Malraux, (Georges-)Andre
Berger, John (Peter) 1926- .... CLC 2, 19
See also CA 81-84; CANR 51; DLB 14
Berger, Melvin H. 1927- .... CLC 12
See also CA 5-8R; CANR 4; CLR 32; SAAS 2; SATA 5, 88
Berger, Thomas (Louis) 1924-...CLC 3, 5, 8, 11, 18, 38; DAM NOV
See also CA 1-4R; CANR 5, 28, 51; DLB 2; DLBY 80; INT CANR-28; MTCW
Bergman, (Ernst) Ingmar 1918- ..CLC 16, 72
See also CA 81-84; CANR 33
Bergson, Henri(-Louis) 1859-1941 . TCLC 32
See also CA 164
Bergstein, Eleanor 1938- .... CLC 4
See also CA 53-56; CANR 5
Berkoff, Steven 1937- .... CLC 56
See also CA 104
Bermant, Chaim (Icyk) 1929- .... CLC 40
See also CA 57-60; CANR 6, 31, 57

Bern, Victoria
See Fisher, M(ary) F(rances) K(ennedy)
Bernanos, (Paul Louis) Georges 1888-1948 TCLC 3
See also CA 104; 130; DLB 72
Bernard, April 1956- .... CLC 59
See also CA 131
Berne, Victoria
See Fisher, M(ary) F(rances) K(ennedy)
Bernhard, Thomas 1931-1989 .. CLC 3, 32, 61
See also CA 85-88; 127; CANR 32, 57; DLB 85, 124; MTCW
Bernhardt, Sarah (Henriette Rosine) 1844-1923 TCLC 75
See also CA 157
Berriault, Gina 1926- ... CLC 54, 109; SSC 30
See also CA 116; 129; CANR 66; DLB 130
Berrigan, Daniel 1921- .... CLC 4
See also CA 33-36R; CAAS 1; CANR 11, 43; DLB 5
Berrigan, Edmund Joseph Michael, Jr. 1934-1983
See Berrigan, Ted
See also CA 61-64; 110; CANR 14
Berrigan, Ted .... CLC 37
See also Berrigan, Edmund Joseph Michael, Jr.
See also DLB 5, 169
Berry, Charles Edward Anderson 1931-
See Berry, Chuck
See also CA 115
Berry, Chuck .... CLC 17
See also Berry, Charles Edward Anderson
Berry, Jonas
See Ashbery, John (Lawrence)
Berry, Wendell (Erdman) 1934-...CLC 4, 6, 8, 27, 46; DAM POET
See also AITN 1; CA 73-76; CANR 50; DLB 5, 6
Berryman, John 1914-1972...CLC 1, 2, 3, 4, 6, 8, 10, 13, 25, 62; DAM POET
See also CA 13-16; 33-36R; CABS 2; CANR 35; CAP 1; CDALB 1941-1968; DLB 48; MTCW
Bertolucci, Bernardo 1940- .... CLC 16
See also CA 106
Berton, Pierre (Francis De Marigny) 1920- CLC 104
See also CA 1-4R; CANR 2, 56; DLB 68
Bertrand, Aloysius 1807-1841 .... NCLC 31
Bertran de Born c. 1140-1215 .... CMLC 5
Beruni, al 973-1048(?) .... CMLC 28
Besant, Annie (Wood) 1847-1933 ...... TCLC 9
See also CA 105
Bessie, Alvah 1904-1985 .... CLC 23
See also CA 5-8R; 116; CANR 2; DLB 26
Bethlen, T. D.
See Silverberg, Robert
Beti, Mongo .... CLC 27; BLC 1; DAM MULT
See also Biyidi, Alexandre
Betjeman, John 1906-1984...CLC 2, 6, 10, 34, 43; DAB; DAM MST, POET
See also CA 9-12R; 112; CANR 33, 56; CDBLB 1945-1960; DLB 20; DLBY 84; MTCW
Bettelheim, Bruno 1903-1990............. CLC 79
See also CA 81-84; 131; CANR 23, 61; MTCW
Betti, Ugo 1892-1953 .... TCLC 5
See also CA 104; 155
Betts, Doris (Waugh) 1932- .... CLC 3, 6, 28
See also CA 13-16R; CANR 9, 66; DLBY 82; INT CANR-9
Bevan, Alistair
See Roberts, Keith (John Kingston)
Bey, Pilaff
See Douglas, (George) Norman

Campbell, (Ignatius) Roy (Dunnachie) 1901-1957 .... **TCLC 5**
See also CA 104; 155; DLB 20

Campbell, Thomas 1777-1844 .... **NCLC 19**
See also DLB 93; 144

Campbell, Wilfred .... **TCLC 9**
See also Campbell, William

Campbell, William 1858(?)-1918
See Campbell, Wilfred
See also CA 106; DLB 92

Campion, Jane .... **CLC 95**
See also CA 138

Campos, Alvaro de
See Pessoa, Fernando (Antonio Nogueira)

Camus, Albert 1913-1960...**CLC 1, 2, 4, 9, 11, 14, 32, 63, 69; DA; DAB; DAC; DAM DRAM, MST, NOV; DC 2; SSC 9; WLC**
See also CA 89-92; DLB 72; MTCW

Canby, Vincent 1924- .... **CLC 13**
See also CA 81-84

Cancale
See Desnos, Robert

Canetti, Elias 1905-1994... **CLC 3, 14, 25, 75, 86**
See also CA 21-24R; 146; CANR 23, 61; DLB 85, 124; MTCW

Canin, Ethan 1960- .... **CLC 55**
See also CA 131; 135

Cannon, Curt
See Hunter, Evan

Cao, Lan 1961- .... **CLC 109**
See also CA 165

Cape, Judith
See Page, P(atricia) K(athleen)

Capek, Karel 1890-1938 ... **TCLC 6, 37; DA; DAB; DAC; DAM DRAM, MST, NOV; DC 1; WLC**
See also CA 104; 140

Capote, Truman 1924-1984... **CLC 1, 3, 8, 13, 19, 34, 38, 58; DA; DAB; DAC; DAM MST, NOV, POP; SSC 2; WLC**
See also CA 5-8R; 113; CANR 18, 62; CDALB 1941-1968; DLB 2, 185; DLBY 80, 84; MTCW; SATA 91

Capra, Frank 1897-1991 .... **CLC 16**
See also CA 61-64; 135

Caputo, Philip 1941- .... **CLC 32**
See also CA 73-76; CANR 40

Caragiale, Ion Luca 1852-1912 .... **TCLC 76**
See also CA 157

Card, Orson Scott 1951- .... **CLC 44, 47, 50; DAM POP**
See also AAYA 11; CA 102; CANR 27, 47; INT CANR-27; MTCW; SATA 83

Cardenal, Ernesto 1925- ...... **CLC 31; DAM MULT, POET; HLC; PC 22**
See also CA 49-52; CANR 2, 32, 66; HW; MTCW

Cardozo, Benjamin N(athan) 1870-1938 **TCLC 65**
See also CA 117; 164

Carducci, Giosue (Alessandro Giuseppe) 1835-1907 .... **TCLC 32**
See also CA 163

Carew, Thomas 1595(?)-1640 .... **LC 13**
See also DLB 126

Carey, Ernestine Gilbreth 1908- .... **CLC 17**
See also CA 5-8R; SATA 2

Carey, Peter 1943- ....**CLC 40, 55, 96**
See also CA 123; 127; CANR 53; INT 127; MTCW; SATA 94

Carleton, William 1794-1869 .... **NCLC 3**
See also DLB 159

Carlisle, Henry (Coffin) 1926- .... **CLC 33**
See also CA 13-16R; CANR 15

Carlsen, Chris
See Holdstock, Robert P.

Carlson, Ron(ald F.) 1947- .... **CLC 54**
See also CA 105; CANR 27

Carlyle, Thomas 1795-1881 ....**NCLC 70; DA; DAB; DAC; DAM MST**
See also CDBLB 1789-1832; DLB 55; 144

Carman, (William) Bliss 1861-1929...**TCLC 7; DAC**
See also CA 104; 152; DLB 92

Carnegie, Dale 1888-1955 .... **TCLC 53**

Carossa, Hans 1878-1956 .... **TCLC 48**
See also DLB 66

Carpenter, Don(ald Richard) 1931-1995...**CLC 41**
See also CA 45-48; 149; CANR 1

Carpentier (y Valmont), Alejo 1904-1980 **CLC 8, 11, 38, 110; DAM MULT; HLC**
See also CA 65-68; 97-100; CANR 11; DLB 113; HW

Carr, Caleb 1955(?)- .... **CLC 86**
See also CA 147

Carr, Emily 1871-1945 .... **TCLC 32**
See also CA 159; DLB 68

Carr, John Dickson 1906-1977 .... **CLC 3**
See also Fairbairn, Roger
See also CA 49-52; 69-72; CANR 3, 33, 60; MTCW

Carr, Philippa
See Hibbert, Eleanor Alice Burford

Carr, Virginia Spencer 1929- .... **CLC 34**
See also CA 61-64; DLB 111

Carrere, Emmanuel 1957- .... **CLC 89**

Carrier, Roch 1937- .... **CLC 13, 78; DAC; DAM MST**
See also CA 130; CANR 61; DLB 53

Carroll, James P. 1943(?)- .... **CLC 38**
See also CA 81-84

Carroll, Jim 1951- .... **CLC 35**
See also AAYA 17; CA 45-48; CANR 42

Carroll, Lewis ....**NCLC 2, 53; PC 18; WLC**
See also Dodgson, Charles Lutwidge
See also CDBLB 1832-1890; CLR 2, 18; DLB 18, 163, 178; JRDA

Carroll, Paul Vincent 1900-1968 .... **CLC 10**
See also CA 9-12R; 25-28R; DLB 10

Carruth, Hayden 1921-...**CLC 4, 7, 10, 18, 84; PC 10**
See also CA 9-12R; CANR 4, 38, 59; DLB 5, 165; INT CANR-4; MTCW; SATA 47

Carson, Rachel Louise 1907-1964 ... **CLC 71; DAM POP**
See also CA 77-80; CANR 35; MTCW; SATA 23

Carter, Angela (Olive) 1940-1992...**CLC 5, 41, 76; SSC 13**
See also CA 53-56; 136; CANR 12, 36, 61; DLB 14; MTCW; SATA 66; SATA-Obit 70

Carter, Nick
See Smith, Martin Cruz

Carver, Raymond 1938-1988...**CLC 22, 36, 53, 55; DAM NOV; SSC 8**
See also CA 33-36R; 126; CANR 17, 34, 61; DLB 130; DLBY 84, 88; MTCW

Cary, Elizabeth, Lady Falkland 1585-1639 **LC 30**

Cary, (Arthur) Joyce (Lunel) 1888-1957 **TCLC 1, 29**
See also CA 104; 164; CDBLB 1914-1945; DLB 15, 100

Casanova de Seingalt, Giovanni Jacopo 1725-1798 .... **LC 13**

Casares, Adolfo Bioy
See Bioy Casares, Adolfo

Casely-Hayford, J(oseph) E(phraim) 1866-1930 **TCLC 24; BLC 1; DAM MULT**
See also BW 2; CA 123; 152

Casey, John (Dudley) 1939- .... **CLC 59**
See also BEST 90:2; CA 69-72; CANR 23

Casey, Michael 1947- .... **CLC 2**
See also CA 65-68; DLB 5

Casey, Patrick
See Thurman, Wallace (Henry)

Casey, Warren (Peter) 1935-1988 ...... **CLC 12**
See also CA 101; 127; INT 101

Casona, Alejandro .... **CLC 49**
See also Alvarez, Alejandro Rodriguez

Cassavetes, John 1929-1989 .... **CLC 20**
See also CA 85-88; 127

Cassian, Nina 1924- .... **PC 17**

Cassill, R(onald) V(erlin) 1919- ..... **CLC 4, 23**
See also CA 9-12R; CAAS 1; CANR 7, 45; DLB 6

Cassirer, Ernst 1874-1945 .... **TCLC 61**
See also CA 157

Cassity, (Allen) Turner 1929- .... **CLC 6, 42**
See also CA 17-20R; CAAS 8; CANR 11; DLB 105

Castaneda, Carlos 1931(?)- .... **CLC 12**
See also CA 25-28R; CANR 32, 66; HW; MTCW

Castedo, Elena 1937- .... **CLC 65**
See also CA 132

Castedo-Ellerman, Elena
See Castedo, Elena

Castellanos, Rosario 1925-1974 ..... **CLC 66; DAM MULT; HLC**
See also CA 131; 53-56; CANR 58; DLB 113; HW

Castelvetro, Lodovico 1505-1571 .... **LC 12**

Castiglione, Baldassare 1478-1529 ...... **LC 12**

Castle, Robert
See Hamilton, Edmond

Castro, Guillen de 1569-1631 .... **LC 19**

Castro, Rosalia de 1837-1885 .....**NCLC 3; DAM MULT**

Cather, Willa
See Cather, Willa Sibert

Cather, Willa Sibert 1873-1947...**TCLC 1, 11, 31; DA; DAB; DAC; DAM MST, NOV; SSC 2; WLC**
See also AAYA 24; CA 104; 128; CDALB 1865-1917; DLB 9, 54, 78; DLBD 1; MTCW; SATA 30

Catherine, Saint 1347-1380 .... **CMLC 27**

Cato, Marcus Porcius 234B.C.-149B.C. **CMLC 21**

Catton, (Charles) Bruce 1899-1978 ... **CLC 35**
See also AITN 1; CA 5-8R; 81-84; CANR 7; DLB 17; SATA 2; SATA-Obit 24

Catullus c. 84B.C.-c. 54B.C. .... **CMLC 18**

Cauldwell, Frank
See King, Francis (Henry)

Caunitz, William J. 1933-1996 .... **CLC 34**
See also BEST 89:3; CA 125; 130; 152; INT 130

Causley, Charles (Stanley) 1917- .... **CLC 7**
See also CA 9-12R; CANR 5, 35; CLR 30; DLB 27; MTCW; SATA 3, 66

Caute, (John) David 1936- .....**CLC 29; DAM NOV**
See also CA 1-4R; CAAS 4; CANR 1, 33, 64; DLB 14

Cavafy, C(onstantine) P(eter) 1863-1933 **TCLC 2, 7; DAM POET**
See also Kavafis, Konstantinos Petrou
See also CA 148

Cavallo, Evelyn
  See Spark, Muriel (Sarah)
Cavanna, Betty .... **CLC 12**
  See also Harrison, Elizabeth Cavanna
  See also JRDA; MAICYA; SAAS 4; SATA 1, 30
Cavendish, Margaret Lucas 1623-1673...**LC 30**
  See also DLB 131
Caxton, William 1421(?)-1491(?) .... **LC 17**
  See also DLB 170
Cayer, D. M.
  See Duffy, Maureen
Cayrol, Jean 1911- .... **CLC 11**
  See also CA 89-92; DLB 83
Cela, Camilo Jose 1916-.... **CLC 4, 13, 59;**
  DAM MULT; HLC
  See also BEST 90:2; CA 21-24R; CAAS 10;
  CANR 21, 32; DLBY 89; HW; MTCW
Celan, Paul .... **CLC 10, 19, 53, 82; PC 10**
  See also Antschel, Paul
  See also DLB 69
Celine, Louis-Ferdinand. .**CLC 1, 3, 4, 7, 9, 15, 47**
  See also Destouches, Louis-Ferdinand
  See also DLB 72
Cellini, Benvenuto 1500-1571 .... **LC 7**
Cendrars, Blaise 1887-1961 .... **CLC 18, 106**
  See also Sauser-Hall, Frederic
Cernuda (y Bidon), Luis 1902-1963 . **CLC 54;**
  DAM POET
  See also CA 131; 89-92; DLB 134; HW
Cervantes (Saavedra), Miguel de 1547-1616
  LC 6, 23; DA; DAB; DAC; DAM MST,
  NOV; SSC 12; WLC
Cesaire, Aime (Fernand) 1913- ... **CLC 19, 32,**
  112; BLC 1; DAM MULT, POET
  See also BW 2; CA 65-68; CANR 24, 43; MTCW
Chabon, Michael 1963- .... **CLC 55**
  See also CA 139; CANR 57
Chabrol, Claude 1930- .... **CLC 16**
  See also CA 110
Challans, Mary 1905-1983
  See Renault, Mary
  See also CA 81-84; 111; SATA 23; SATA-Obit 36
Challis, George
  See Faust, Frederick (Schiller)
Chambers, Aidan 1934- .... **CLC 35**
  See also CA 25-28R; CANR 12, 31, 58; JRDA;
  MAICYA; SAAS 12; SATA 1, 69
Chambers, James 1948-
  See Cliff, Jimmy
  See also CA 124
Chambers, Jessie
  See Lawrence, D(avid) H(erbert Richards)
Chambers, Robert W(illiam) 1865-1933
  TCLC 41
  See also CA 165
Chandler, Raymond (Thornton) 1888-1959
  TCLC 1, 7; SSC 23
  See also AAYA 25; CA 104; 129; CANR 60;
  CDALB 1929-1941; DLBD 6; MTCW
Chang, Eileen 1920-1995 .... **SSC 28**
  See also CA 166
Chang, Jung 1952- .... **CLC 71**
  See also CA 142
Chang Ai-Ling
  See Chang, Eileen
Channing, William Ellery 1780-1842..**NCLC 17**
  See also DLB 1, 59
Chaplin, Charles Spencer 1889-1977...**CLC 16**
  See also Chaplin, Charlie
  See also CA 81-84; 73-76
Chaplin, Charlie
  See Chaplin, Charles Spencer
  See also DLB 44

Chapman, George 1559(?)-1634 ...... **LC 22;**
  DAM DRAM
  See also DLB 62, 121
Chapman, Graham 1941-1989 .... **CLC 21**
  See also Monty Python
  See also CA 116; 129; CANR 35
Chapman, John Jay 1862-1933 .... **TCLC 7**
  See also CA 104
Chapman, Lee
  See Bradley, Marion Zimmer
Chapman, Walker
  See Silverberg, Robert
Chappell, Fred (Davis) 1936- .... **CLC 40, 78**
  See also CA 5-8R; CAAS 4; CANR 8, 33, 67;
  DLB 6, 105
Char, Rene(-Emile) 1907-1988...**CLC 9, 11, 14,**
  55; DAM POET
  See also CA 13-16R; 124; CANR 32; MTCW
Charby, Jay
  See Ellison, Harlan (Jay)
Chardin, Pierre Teilhard de
  See Teilhard de Chardin, (Marie Joseph) Pierre
Charles I 1600-1649 .... **LC 13**
Charriere, Isabelle de 1740-1805 .... **NCLC 66**
Charyn, Jerome 1937- .... **CLC 5, 8, 18**
  See also CA 5-8R; CAAS 1; CANR 7, 61; DLBY
  83; MTCW
Chase, Mary (Coyle) 1907-1981 .... **DC 1**
  See also CA 77-80; 105; SATA 17; SATA-Obit 29
Chase, Mary Ellen 1887-1973 .... **CLC 2**
  See also CA 13-16; 41-44R; CAP 1; SATA 10
Chase, Nicholas
  See Hyde, Anthony
Chateaubriand, Francois Rene de 1768-1848
  NCLC 3
  See also DLB 119
Chatterje, Sarat Chandra 1876-1936(?)
  See Chatterji, Saratchandra
  See also CA 109
Chatterji, Bankim Chandra 1838-1894
  NCLC 19
Chatterji, Saratchandra .... **TCLC 13**
  See also Chatterje, Sarat Chandra
Chatterton, Thomas 1752-1770 .... **LC 3; DAM**
  POET
  See also DLB 109
Chatwin, (Charles) Bruce 1940-1989...**CLC 28,**
  57, 59; DAM POP
  See also AAYA 4; BEST 90:1; CA 85-88; 127;
  DLB 194
Chaucer, Daniel
  See Ford, Ford Madox
Chaucer, Geoffrey 1340(?)-1400...**LC 17; DA;**
  DAB; DAC; DAM MST, POET; PC 19;
  WLCS
  See also CDBLB Before 1660; DLB 146
Chaviaras, Strates 1935-
  See Haviaras, Stratis
  See also CA 105
Chayefsky, Paddy .... **CLC 23**
  See also Chayefsky, Sidney
  See also DLB 7, 44; DLBY 81
Chayefsky, Sidney 1923-1981
  See Chayefsky, Paddy
  See also CA 9-12R; 104; CANR 18; DAM DRAM
Chedid, Andree 1920- .... **CLC 47**
  See also CA 145
Cheever, John 1912-1982...**CLC 3, 7, 8, 11,**
  15, 25, 64; DA; DAB; DAC; DAM MST,
  NOV, POP; SSC 1; WLC
  See also CA 5-8R; 106; CABS 1; CANR 5, 27;
  CDALB 1941-1968; DLB 2, 102; DLBY 80,
  82; INT CANR-5; MTCW

Cheever, Susan 1943- .... **CLC 18, 48**
  See also CA 103; CANR 27, 51; DLBY 82; INT
  CANR-27
Chekhonte, Antosha
  See Chekhov, Anton (Pavlovich)
Chekhov, Anton (Pavlovich) 1860-1904
  TCLC 3, 10, 31, 55; DA; DAB; DAC;
  DAM DRAM, MST; DC 9; SSC 2, 28;
  WLC
  See also CA 104; 124; SATA 90
Chernyshevsky, Nikolay Gavrilovich 1828-1889
  NCLC 1
Cherry, Carolyn Janice 1942-
  See Cherryh, C. J.
  See also CA 65-68; CANR 10
Cherryh, C. J. .... **CLC 35**
  See also Cherry, Carolyn Janice
  See also AAYA 24; DLBY 80; SATA 93
Chesnutt, Charles W(addell) 1858-1932
  TCLC 5, 39; BLC 1; DAM MULT; SSC 7
  See also BW 1; CA 106; 125; DLB 12, 50, 78;
  MTCW
Chester, Alfred 1929(?)-1971 .... **CLC 49**
  See also CA 33-36R; DLB 130
Chesterton, G(ilbert) K(eith) 1874-1936
  TCLC 1, 6, 64; DAM NOV, POET; SSC 1
  See also CA 104; 132; CDBLB 1914-1945; DLB
  10, 19, 34, 70, 98, 149, 178; MTCW; SATA
  27
Chiang, Pin-chin 1904-1986
  See Ding Ling
  See also CA 118
Ch'ien Chung-shu 1910- .... **CLC 22**
  See also CA 130; MTCW
Child, L. Maria
  See Child, Lydia Maria
Child, Lydia Maria 1802-1880 .... **NCLC 6**
  See also DLB 1, 74; SATA 67
Child, Mrs.
  See Child, Lydia Maria
Child, Philip 1898-1978 .... **CLC 19, 68**
  See also CA 13-14; CAP 1; SATA 47
Childers, (Robert) Erskine 1870-1922
  TCLC 65
  See also CA 113; 153; DLB 70
Childress, Alice 1920-1994...**CLC 12, 15, 86,**
  96; BLC 1; DAM DRAM, MULT, NOV;
  DC 4
  See also AAYA 8; BW 2; CA 45-48; 146; CANR
  3, 27, 50; CLR 14; DLB 7, 38; JRDA;
  MAICYA; MTCW; SATA 7, 48, 81
Chin, Frank (Chew, Jr.) 1940- .... **DC 7**
  See also CA 33-36R; DAM MULT
Chislett, (Margaret) Anne 1943- .... **CLC 34**
  See also CA 151
Chitty, Thomas Willes 1926- .... **CLC 11**
  See also Hinde, Thomas
  See also CA 5-8R
Chivers, Thomas Holley 1809-1858...**NCLC 49**
  See also DLB 3
Chomette, Rene Lucien 1898-1981
  See Clair, Rene
  See also CA 103
Chopin, Kate .. TCLC 5, 14; DA; DAB; SSC 8;
  WLCS
  See also Chopin, Katherine
  See also CDALB 1865-1917; DLB 12, 78
Chopin, Katherine 1851-1904
  See Chopin, Kate
  See also CA 104; 122; DAC; DAM MST, NOV
Chretien de Troyes c. 12th cent. -.... **CMLC 10**
Christie
  See Ichikawa, Kon

Cowper, William 1731-1800 .. **NCLC 8; DAM POET**
See also DLB 104, 109
Cox, William Trevor 1928- .... **CLC 9, 14, 71; DAM NOV**
See also Trevor, William
See also CA 9-12R; CANR 4, 37, 55; DLB 14; INT CANR-37; MTCW
Coyne, P. J.
See Masters, Hilary
Cozzens, James Gould 1903-1978...**CLC 1, 4, 11, 92**
See also CA 9-12R; 81-84; CANR 19; CDALB 1941-1968; DLB 9; DLBD 2; DLBY 84, 97; MTCW
Crabbe, George 1754-1832 .... **NCLC 26**
See also DLB 93
Craddock, Charles Egbert
See Murfree, Mary Noailles
Craig, A. A.
See Anderson, Poul (William)
Craik, Dinah Maria (Mulock) 1826-1887 **NCLC 38**
See also DLB 35, 163; MAICYA; SATA 34
Cram, Ralph Adams 1863-1942 ...... **TCLC 45**
See also CA 160
Crane, (Harold) Hart 1899-1932...**TCLC 2, 5, 80; DA; DAB; DAC; DAM MST, POET; PC 3; WLC**
See also CA 104; 127; CDALB 1917-1929; DLB 4, 48; MTCW
Crane, R(onald) S(almon) 1886-1967...**CLC 27**
See also CA 85-88; DLB 63
Crane, Stephen (Townley) 1871-1900...**TCLC 11, 17, 32; DA; DAB; DAC; DAM MST, NOV, POET; SSC 7; WLC**
See also AAYA 21; CA 109; 140; CDALB 1865-1917; DLB 12, 54, 78; YABC 2
Crase, Douglas 1944- .... **CLC 58**
See also CA 106
Crashaw, Richard 1612(?)-1649 .... **LC 24**
See also DLB 126
Craven, Margaret 1901-1980 .. **CLC 17; DAC**
See also CA 103
Crawford, F(rancis) Marion 1854-1909 **TCLC 10**
See also CA 107; DLB 71
Crawford, Isabella Valancy 1850-1887 **NCLC 12**
See also DLB 92
Crayon, Geoffrey
See Irving, Washington
Creasey, John 1908-1973 .... **CLC 11**
See also CA 5-8R; 41-44R; CANR 8, 59; DLB 77; MTCW
Crebillon, Claude Prosper Jolyot de (fils) 1707-1777 .... **LC 28**
Credo
See Creasey, John
Credo, Alvaro J. de
See Prado (Calvo), Pedro
Creeley, Robert (White) 1926-...**CLC 1, 2, 4, 8, 11, 15, 36, 78; DAM POET**
See also CA 1-4R; CAAS 10; CANR 23, 43; DLB 5, 16, 169; MTCW
Crews, Harry (Eugene) 1935- .. **CLC 6, 23, 49**
See also AITN 1; CA 25-28R; CANR 20, 57; DLB 6, 143, 185; MTCW
Crichton, (John) Michael 1942-...**CLC 2, 6, 54, 90; DAM NOV, POP**
See also AAYA 10; AITN 2; CA 25-28R; CANR 13, 40, 54; DLBY 81; INT CANR-13; JRDA; MTCW; SATA 9, 88

Crispin, Edmund .... **CLC 22**
See also Montgomery, (Robert) Bruce
See also DLB 87
Cristofer, Michael 1945(?)- .... **CLC 28; DAM DRAM**
See also CA 110; 152; DLB 7
Croce, Benedetto 1866-1952 .... **TCLC 37**
See also CA 120; 155
Crockett, David 1786-1836 .... **NCLC 8**
See also DLB 3, 11
Crockett, Davy
See Crockett, David
Crofts, Freeman Wills 1879-1957 ... **TCLC 55**
See also CA 115; DLB 77
Croker, John Wilson 1780-1857 ...... **NCLC 10**
See also DLB 110
Crommelynck, Fernand 1885-1970 ... **CLC 75**
See also CA 89-92
Cromwell, Oliver 1599-1658 .... **LC 43**
Cronin, A(rchibald) J(oseph) 1896-1981...**CLC 32**
See also CA 1-4R; 102; CANR 5; DLB 191; SATA 47; SATA-Obit 25
Cross, Amanda
See Heilbrun, Carolyn G(old)
Crothers, Rachel 1878(?)-1958 .... **TCLC 19**
See also CA 113; DLB 7
Croves, Hal
See Traven, B.
Crow Dog, Mary (Ellen) (?)- .... **CLC 93**
See also Brave Bird, Mary
See also CA 154
Crowfield, Christopher
See Stowe, Harriet (Elizabeth) Beecher
Crowley, Aleister .... **TCLC 7**
See also Crowley, Edward Alexander
Crowley, Edward Alexander 1875-1947
See Crowley, Aleister
See also CA 104
Crowley, John 1942- .... **CLC 57**
See also CA 61-64; CANR 43; DLBY 82; SATA 65
Crud
See Crumb, R(obert)
Crumarums
See Crumb, R(obert)
Crumb, R(obert) 1943- .... **CLC 17**
See also CA 106
Crumbum
See Crumb, R(obert)
Crumski
See Crumb, R(obert)
Crum the Bum
See Crumb, R(obert)
Crunk
See Crumb, R(obert)
Crustt
See Crumb, R(obert)
Cryer, Gretchen (Kiger) 1935- .... **CLC 21**
See also CA 114; 123
Csath, Geza 1887-1919 .... **TCLC 13**
See also CA 111
Cudlip, David 1933- .... **CLC 34**
Cullen, Countee 1903-1946 ... **TCLC 4, 37; BLC 1; DA; DAC; DAM MST, MULT, POET; PC 20; WLCS**
See also BW 1; CA 108; 124; CDALB 1917-1929; DLB 4, 48, 51; MTCW; SATA 18
Cum, R.
See Crumb, R(obert)
Cummings, Bruce F(rederick) 1889-1919
See Barbellion, W. N. P.
See also CA 123

Cummings, E(dward) E(stlin) 1894-1962 **CLC 1, 3, 8, 12, 15, 68; DA; DAB; DAC; DAM MST, POET; PC 5; WLC 2**
See also CA 73-76; CANR 31; CDALB 1929-1941; DLB 4, 48; MTCW
Cunha, Euclides (Rodrigues Pimenta) da 1866-1909 .... **TCLC 24**
See also CA 123
Cunningham, E. V.
See Fast, Howard (Melvin)
Cunningham, J(ames) V(incent) 1911-1985 **CLC 3, 31**
See also CA 1-4R; 115; CANR 1; DLB 5
Cunningham, Julia (Woolfolk) 1916-...**CLC 12**
See also CA 9-12R; CANR 4, 19, 36; JRDA; MAICYA; SAAS 2; SATA 1, 26
Cunningham, Michael 1952- .... **CLC 34**
See also CA 136
Cunninghame Graham, R(obert) B(ontine) 1852-1936 .... **TCLC 19**
See also Graham, R(obert) B(ontine) Cunninghame
See also CA 119; DLB 98
Currie, Ellen 19(?)- .... **CLC 44**
Curtin, Philip
See Lowndes, Marie Adelaide (Belloc)
Curtis, Price
See Ellison, Harlan (Jay)
Cutrate, Joe
See Spiegelman, Art
Cynewulf c. 770-c. 840 .... **CMLC 23**
Czaczkes, Shmuel Yosef
See Agnon, S(hmuel) Y(osef Halevi)
Dabrowska, Maria (Szumska) 1889-1965 **CLC 15**
See also CA 106
Dabydeen, David 1955- .... **CLC 34**
See also BW 1; CA 125; CANR 56
Dacey, Philip 1939- .... **CLC 51**
See also CA 37-40R; CAAS 17; CANR 14, 32, 64; DLB 105
Dagerman, Stig (Halvard) 1923-1954 **TCLC 17**
See also CA 117; 155
Dahl, Roald 1916-1990 ..... **CLC 1, 6, 18, 79; DAB; DAC; DAM MST, NOV, POP**
See also AAYA 15; CA 1-4R; 133; CANR 6, 32, 37, 62; CLR 1, 7, 41; DLB 139; JRDA; MAICYA; MTCW; SATA 1, 26, 73; SATA-Obit 65
Dahlberg, Edward 1900-1977 .... **CLC 1, 7, 14**
See also CA 9-12R; 69-72; CANR 31, 62; DLB 48; MTCW
Daitch, Susan 1954- .... **CLC 103**
See also CA 161
Dale, Colin .... **TCLC 18**
See also Lawrence, T(homas) E(dward)
Dale, George E.
See Asimov, Isaac
Daly, Elizabeth 1878-1967 .... **CLC 52**
See also CA 23-24; 25-28R; CANR 60; CAP 2
Daly, Maureen 1921- .... **CLC 17**
See also AAYA 5; CANR 37; JRDA; MAICYA; SAAS 1; SATA 2
Damas, Leon-Gontran 1912-1978 ...... **CLC 84**
See also BW 1; CA 125; 73-76
Dana, Richard Henry Sr. 1787-1879 **NCLC 53**
Daniel, Samuel 1562(?)-1619 .... **LC 24**
See also DLB 62
Daniels, Brett
See Adler, Renata

Dannay, Frederic 1905-1982 .. **CLC 11; DAM POP**
See also Queen, Ellery
See also CA 1-4R; 107; CANR 1, 39; DLB 137; MTCW

D'Annunzio, Gabriele 1863-1938...**TCLC 6, 40**
See also CA 104; 155

Danois, N. le
See Gourmont, Remy (-Marie-Charles) de

Dante 1265-1321 .... **CMLC 3, 18; DA; DAB; DAC; DAM MST, POET; PC 21; WLCS**

d'Antibes, Germain
See Simenon, Georges (Jacques Christian)

Danticat, Edwidge 1969- .... **CLC 94**
See also CA 152

Danvers, Dennis 1947- .... **CLC 70**

Danziger, Paula 1944- .... **CLC 21**
See also AAYA 4; CA 112; 115; CANR 37; CLR 20; JRDA; MAICYA; SATA 36, 63; SATA-Brief 30

Dario, Ruben 1867-1916 .... **TCLC 4; DAM MULT; HLC; PC 15**
See also CA 131; HW; MTCW

Darley, George 1795-1846 .... **NCLC 2**
See also DLB 96

Darrow, Clarence (Seward) 1857-1938 **TCLC 81**
See also CA 164

Darwin, Charles 1809-1882 .... **NCLC 57**
See also DLB 57, 166

Daryush, Elizabeth 1887-1977 .... **CLC 6, 19**
See also CA 49-52; CANR 3; DLB 20

Dasgupta, Surendranath 1887-1952...**TCLC 81**
See also CA 157

Dashwood, Edmee Elizabeth Monica de la Pasture 1890-1943
See Delafield, E. M.
See also CA 119; 154

Daudet, (Louis Marie) Alphonse 1840-1897 **NCLC 1**
See also DLB 123

Daumal, Rene 1908-1944 .... **TCLC 14**
See also CA 114

Davenport, Guy (Mattison, Jr.) 1927-...**CLC 6, 14, 38; SSC 16**
See also CA 33-36R; CANR 23; DLB 130

Davidson, Avram 1923-
See Queen, Ellery
See also CA 101; CANR 26; DLB 8

Davidson, Donald (Grady) 1893-1968...**CLC 2, 13, 19**
See also CA 5-8R; 25-28R; CANR 4; DLB 45

Davidson, Hugh
See Hamilton, Edmond

Davidson, John 1857-1909 .... **TCLC 24**
See also CA 118; DLB 19

Davidson, Sara 1943- .... **CLC 9**
See also CA 81-84; CANR 44, 68; DLB 185

Davie, Donald (Alfred) 1922-1995...**CLC 5, 8, 10, 31**
See also CA 1-4R; 149; CAAS 3; CANR 1, 44; DLB 27; MTCW

Davies, Ray(mond Douglas) 1944- ..... **CLC 21**
See also CA 116; 146

Davies, Rhys 1901-1978 .... **CLC 23**
See also CA 9-12R; 81-84; CANR 4; DLB 139, 191

Davies, (William) Robertson 1913-1995 **CLC 2, 7, 13, 25, 42, 75, 91; DA; DAB; DAC; DAM MST, NOV, POP; WLC**
See also BEST 89:2; CA 33-36R; 150; CANR 17, 42; DLB 68; INT CANR-17; MTCW

Davies, W(illiam) H(enry) 1871-1940...**TCLC 5**
See also CA 104; DLB 19, 174

Davies, Walter C.
See Kornbluth, C(yril) M.

Davis, Angela (Yvonne) 1944-...**CLC 77; DAM MULT**
See also BW 2; CA 57-60; CANR 10

Davis, B. Lynch
See Bioy Casares, Adolfo; Borges, Jorge Luis

Davis, Harold Lenoir 1896-1960 .... **CLC 49**
See also CA 89-92; DLB 9

Davis, Rebecca (Blaine) Harding 1831-1910 **TCLC 6**
See also CA 104; DLB 74

Davis, Richard Harding 1864-1916...**TCLC 24**
See also CA 114; DLB 12, 23, 78, 79, 189; DLBD 13

Davison, Frank Dalby 1893-1970 .... **CLC 15**
See also CA 116

Davison, Lawrence H.
See Lawrence, D(avid) H(erbert Richards)

Davison, Peter (Hubert) 1928- .... **CLC 28**
See also CA 9-12R; CAAS 4; CANR 3, 43; DLB 5

Davys, Mary 1674-1732 .... **LC 1**
See also DLB 39

Dawson, Fielding 1930- .... **CLC 6**
See also CA 85-88; DLB 130

Dawson, Peter
See Faust, Frederick (Schiller)

Day, Clarence (Shepard, Jr.) 1874-1935 **TCLC 25**
See also CA 108; DLB 11

Day, Thomas 1748-1789 .... **LC 1**
See also DLB 39; YABC 1

Day Lewis, C(ecil) 1904-1972 ... **CLC 1, 6, 10; DAM POET; PC 11**
See also Blake, Nicholas
See also CA 13-16; 33-36R; CANR 34; CAP 1; DLB 15, 20; MTCW

Dazai Osamu 1909-1948 .... **TCLC 11**
See also Tsushima, Shuji
See also CA 164; DLB 182

de Andrade, Carlos Drummond
See Drummond de Andrade, Carlos

Deane, Norman
See Creasey, John

de Beauvoir, Simone (Lucie Ernestine Marie Bertrand)
See Beauvoir, Simone (Lucie Ernestine Marie Bertrand) de

de Beer, P.
See Bosman, Herman Charles

de Brissac, Malcolm
See Dickinson, Peter (Malcolm)

de Chardin, Pierre Teilhard
See Teilhard de Chardin, (Marie Joseph) Pierre

Dee, John 1527-1608 .... **LC 20**

Deer, Sandra 1940- .... **CLC 45**

De Ferrari, Gabriella 1941- .... **CLC 65**
See also CA 146

Defoe, Daniel 1660(?)-1731...**LC 1; DA; DAB; DAC; DAM MST, NOV; WLC**
See also CDBLB 1660-1789; DLB 39, 95, 101; JRDA; MAICYA; SATA 22

de Gourmont, Remy(-Marie-Charles)
See Gourmont, Remy (-Marie-Charles) de

de Hartog, Jan 1914- .... **CLC 19**
See also CA 1-4R; CANR 1

de Hostos, E. M.
See Hostos (y Bonilla), Eugenio Maria de

de Hostos, Eugenio M.
See Hostos (y Bonilla), Eugenio Maria de

Deighton, Len .... **CLC 4, 7, 22, 46**
See also Deighton, Leonard Cyril
See also AAYA 6; BEST 89:2; CDBLB 1960 to Present; DLB 87

Deighton, Leonard Cyril 1929-
See Deighton, Len
See also CA 9-12R; CANR 19, 33, 68; DAM NOV, POP; MTCW

Dekker, Thomas 1572(?)-1632 ... **LC 22; DAM DRAM**
See also CDBLB Before 1660; DLB 62, 172

Delafield, E. M. 1890-1943 .... **TCLC 61**
See also Dashwood, Edmee Elizabeth Monica de la Pasture
See also DLB 34

de la Mare, Walter (John) 1873-1956 **TCLC 4, 53; DAB; DAC; DAM MST, POET; SSC 14; WLC**
See also CA 163; CDBLB 1914-1945; CLR 23; DLB 162; SATA 16

Delaney, Franey
See O'Hara, John (Henry)

Delaney, Shelagh 1939-...**CLC 29; DAM DRAM**
See also CA 17-20R; CANR 30, 67; CDBLB 1960 to Present; DLB 13; MTCW

Delany, Mary (Granville Pendarves) 1700-1788 **LC 12**

Delany, Samuel R(ay, Jr.) 1942- . **CLC 8, 14, 38; BLC 1; DAM MULT**
See also AAYA 24; BW 2; CA 81-84; CANR 27, 43; DLB 8, 33; MTCW

De La Ramee, (Marie) Louise 1839-1908
See Ouida
See also SATA 20

de la Roche, Mazo 1879-1961 .... **CLC 14**
See also CA 85-88; CANR 30; DLB 68; SATA 64

De La Salle, Innocent
See Hartmann, Sadakichi

Delbanco, Nicholas (Franklin) 1942-...**CLC 6, 13**
See also CA 17-20R; CAAS 2; CANR 29, 55; DLB 6

del Castillo, Michel 1933- .... **CLC 38**
See also CA 109

Deledda, Grazia (Cosima) 1875(?)-1936 **TCLC 23**
See also CA 123

Delibes, Miguel .... **CLC 8, 18**
See also Delibes Setien, Miguel

Delibes Setien, Miguel 1920-
See Delibes, Miguel
See also CA 45-48; CANR 1, 32; HW; MTCW

DeLillo, Don 1936-...**CLC 8, 10, 13, 27, 39, 54, 76; DAM NOV, POP**
See also BEST 89:1; CA 81-84; CANR 21; DLB 6, 173; MTCW

de Lisser, H. G.
See De Lisser, H(erbert) G(eorge)
See also DLB 117

De Lisser, H(erbert) G(eorge) 1878-1944 **TCLC 12**
See also de Lisser, H. G.
See also BW 2; CA 109; 152

Deloney, Thomas (?)-1600 .... **LC 41**
See also DLB 167

Deloria, Vine (Victor), Jr. 1933- ...... **CLC 21; DAM MULT**
See also CA 53-56; CANR 5, 20, 48; DLB 175; MTCW; NNAL; SATA 21

Del Vecchio, John M(ichael) 1947- .... **CLC 29**
See also CA 110; DLBD 9

de Man, Paul (Adolph Michel) 1919-1983 **CLC 55**
See also CA 128; 111; CANR 61; DLB 67; MTCW

De Marinis, Rick 1934- .... **CLC 54**
See also CA 57-60; CAAS 24; CANR 9, 25, 50

Donnell, David 1939(?)- .... **CLC 34**
Donoghue, P. S.
    See Hunt, E(verette) Howard, (Jr.)
Donoso (Yanez), Jose 1924-1996...**CLC 4, 8,**
    11, 32, 99; DAM MULT; HLC
    See also CA 81-84; 155; CANR 32; DLB 113;
    HW; MTCW
Donovan, John 1928-1992 .... **CLC 35**
    See also AAYA 20; CA 97-100; 137; CLR 3;
    MAICYA; SATA 72; SATA-Brief 29
Don Roberto
    See Cunninghame Graham, R(obert) B(ontine)
Doolittle, Hilda 1886-1961...**CLC 3, 8, 14, 31,**
    34, 73; DA; DAC; DAM MST, POET; PC
    5; WLC
    See also H. D.
    See also CA 97-100; CANR 35; DLB 4, 45;
    MTCW
Dorfman, Ariel 1942- .... **CLC 48, 77; DAM**
    MULT; HLC
    See also CA 124; 130; CANR 67; HW; INT 130
Dorn, Edward (Merton) 1929- ..... **CLC 10, 18**
    See also CA 93-96; CANR 42; DLB 5; INT 93-
    96
Dorris, Michael (Anthony) 1945-1997 .... **C L C**
    109; DAM MULT, NOV
    See also AAYA 20; BEST 90:1; CA 102; 157;
    CANR 19, 46; DLB 175; NNAL; SATA 75;
    SATA-Obit 94
Dorris, Michael A.
    See Dorris, Michael (Anthony)
Dorsan, Luc
    See Simenon, Georges (Jacques Christian)
Dorsange, Jean
    See Simenon, Georges (Jacques Christian)
Dos Passos, John (Roderigo) 1896-1970
    CLC 1, 4, 8, 11, 15, 25, 34, 82; DA; DAB;
    DAC; DAM MST, NOV; WLC
    See also CA 1-4R; 29-32R; CANR 3; CDALB
    1929-1941; DLB 4, 9; DLBD 1, 15; DLBY
    96; MTCW
Dossage, Jean
    See Simenon, Georges (Jacques Christian)
Dostoevsky, Fedor Mikhailovich 1821-1881
    NCLC 2, 7, 21, 33, 43; DA; DAB; DAC;
    DAM MST, NOV; SSC 2; WLC
Doughty, Charles M(ontagu) 1843-1926
    TCLC 27
    See also CA 115; DLB 19, 57, 174
Douglas, Ellen .... **CLC 73**
    See also Haxton, Josephine Ayres; Williamson,
    Ellen Douglas
Douglas, Gavin 1475(?)-1522 .... **LC 20**
    See also DLB 132
Douglas, George
    See Brown, George Douglas
Douglas, Keith (Castellain) 1920-1944
    TCLC 40
    See also CA 160; DLB 27
Douglas, Leonard
    See Bradbury, Ray (Douglas)
Douglas, Michael
    See Crichton, (John) Michael
Douglas, (George) Norman 1868-1952
    TCLC 68
    See also CA 119; 157; DLB 34, 195
Douglas, William
    See Brown, George Douglas
Douglass, Frederick 1817(?)-1895 ..**NCLC 7,**
    55; BLC 1; DA; DAC; DAM MST, MULT;
    WLC
    See also CDALB 1640-1865; DLB 1, 43, 50, 79;
    SATA 29

Dourado, (Waldomiro Freitas) Autran 1926-
    CLC 23, 60
    See also CA 25-28R; CANR 34
Dourado, Waldomiro Autran
    See Dourado, (Waldomiro Freitas) Autran
Dove, Rita (Frances) 1952- ...... **CLC 50, 81;**
    BLCS; DAM MULT, POET; PC 6
    See also BW 2; CA 109; CAAS 19; CANR 27,
    42, 68; DLB 120
Doveglion
    See Villa, Jose Garcia
Dowell, Coleman 1925-1985 .... **CLC 60**
    See also CA 25-28R; 117; CANR 10; DLB 130
Dowson, Ernest (Christopher) 1867-1900
    TCLC 4
    See also CA 105; 150; DLB 19, 135
Doyle, A. Conan
    See Doyle, Arthur Conan
Doyle, Arthur Conan 1859-1930... **TCLC 7;**
    DA; DAB; DAC; DAM MST, NOV; SSC 12;
    WLC
    See also AAYA 14; CA 104; 122; CDBLB 1890-
    1914; DLB 18, 70, 156, 178; MTCW; SATA 24
Doyle, Conan
    See Doyle, Arthur Conan
Doyle, John
    See Graves, Robert (von Ranke)
Doyle, Roddy 1958(?)- .... **CLC 81**
    See also AAYA 14; CA 143; DLB 194
Doyle, Sir A. Conan
    See Doyle, Arthur Conan
Doyle, Sir Arthur Conan
    See Doyle, Arthur Conan
Dr. A
    See Asimov, Isaac; Silverstein, Alvin
Drabble, Margaret 1939-...**CLC 2, 3, 5, 8, 10,**
    22, 53; DAB; DAC; DAM MST, NOV, POP
    See also CA 13-16R; CANR 18, 35, 63; CDBLB
    1960 to Present; DLB 14, 155; MTCW; SATA
    48
Drapier, M. B.
    See Swift, Jonathan
Drayham, James
    See Mencken, H(enry) L(ouis)
Drayton, Michael 1563-1631 ......**LC 8; DAM**
    POET
    See also DLB 121
Dreadstone, Carl
    See Campbell, (John) Ramsey
Dreiser, Theodore (Herman Albert) 1871-1945
    TCLC 10, 18, 35, 83; DA; DAC; DAM MST,
    NOV; SSC 30; WLC
    See also CA 106; 132; CDALB 1865-1917; DLB
    9, 12, 102, 137; DLBD 1; MTCW
Drexler, Rosalyn 1926- .... **CLC 2, 6**
    See also CA 81-84; CANR 68
Dreyer, Carl Theodor 1889-1968 .... **CLC 16**
    See also CA 116
Drieu la Rochelle, Pierre(-Eugene) 1893-1945
    TCLC 21
    See also CA 117; DLB 72
Drinkwater, John 1882-1937 .... **TCLC 57**
    See also CA 109; 149; DLB 10, 19, 149
Drop Shot
    See Cable, George Washington
Droste-Hulshoff, Annette Freiin von 1797-1848
    NCLC 3
    See also DLB 133
Drummond, Walter
    See Silverberg, Robert
Drummond, William Henry 1854-1907
    TCLC 25
    See also CA 160; DLB 92

Drummond de Andrade, Carlos 1902-1987
    CLC 18
    See also Andrade, Carlos Drummond de
    See also CA 132; 123
Drury, Allen (Stuart) 1918- .... **CLC 37**
    See also CA 57-60; CANR 18, 52; INT CANR-
    18
Dryden, John 1631-1700 .... **LC 3, 21; DA;**
    DAB; DAC; DAM DRAM, MST, POET;
    DC 3; WLC
    See also CDBLB 1660-1789; DLB 80, 101, 131
Duberman, Martin (Bauml) 1930- .... **CLC 8**
    See also CA 1-4R; CANR 2, 63
Dubie, Norman (Evans) 1945- .... **CLC 36**
    See also CA 69-72; CANR 12; DLB 120
Du Bois, W(illiam) E(dward) B(urghardt) 1868-
    1963 ... **CLC 1, 2, 13, 64, 96; BLC 1; DA;**
    DAC; DAM MST, MULT, NOV; WLC
    See also BW 1; CA 85-88; CANR 34; CDALB
    1865-1917; DLB 47, 50, 91; MTCW; SATA
    42
Dubus, Andre 1936- . **CLC 13, 36, 97; SSC 15**
    See also CA 21-24R; CANR 17; DLB 130; INT
    CANR-17
Duca Minimo
    See D'Annunzio, Gabriele
Ducharme, Rejean 1941- .... **CLC 74**
    See also CA 165; DLB 60
Duclos, Charles Pinot 1704-1772 .... **LC 1**
Dudek, Louis 1918- .... **CLC 11, 19**
    See also CA 45-48; CAAS 14; CANR 1; DLB
    88
Duerrenmatt, Friedrich 1921-1990...**CLC 1,**
    4, 8, 11, 15, 43, 102; DAM DRAM
    See also CA 17-20R; CANR 33; DLB 69, 124;
    MTCW
Duffy, Bruce (?)- .... **CLC 50**
Duffy, Maureen 1933- .... **CLC 37**
    See also CA 25-28R; CANR 33, 68; DLB 14;
    MTCW
Dugan, Alan 1923- .... **CLC 2, 6**
    See also CA 81-84; DLB 5
du Gard, Roger Martin
    See Martin du Gard, Roger
Duhamel, Georges 1884-1966 .... **CLC 8**
    See also CA 81-84; 25-28R; CANR 35; DLB 65;
    MTCW
Dujardin, Edouard (Emile Louis) 1861-1949
    TCLC 13
    See also CA 109; DLB 123
Dulles, John Foster 1888-1959 .... **TCLC 72**
    See also CA 115; 149
Dumas, Alexandre (Davy de la Pailleterie) 1802-
    1870 .. **NCLC 11; DA; DAB; DAC; DAM**
    MST, NOV; WLC
    See also DLB 119, 192; SATA 18
Dumas (fils), Alexandre 1824-1895...**N C L C**
    71; DC 1
    See also AAYA 22; DLB 192
Dumas, Claudine
    See Malzberg, Barry N(athaniel)
Dumas, Henry L. 1934-1968...........**CLC 6, 62**
    See also BW 1; CA 85-88; DLB 41
du Maurier, Daphne 1907-1989...**CLC 6, 11,**
    59; DAB; DAC; DAM MST, POP; SSC
    18
    See also CA 5-8R; 128; CANR 6, 55; DLB 191;
    MTCW; SATA 27; SATA-Obit 60
Dunbar, Paul Laurence 1872-1906...**TCLC 2,**
    12; BLC 1; DA; DAC; DAM MST, MULT,
    POET; PC 5; SSC 8; WLC
    See also BW 1; CA 104; 124; CDALB 1865-
    1917; DLB 50, 54, 78; SATA 34

Falco, Gian
  See Papini, Giovanni
Falconer, James
  See Kirkup, James
Falconer, Kenneth
  See Kornbluth, C(yril) M.
Falkland, Samuel
  See Heijermans, Herman
Fallaci, Oriana 1930- .... **CLC 11, 110**
  See also CA 77-80; CANR 15, 58; MTCW
Faludy, George 1913- .... **CLC 42**
  See also CA 21-24R
Faludy, Gyoergy
  See Faludy, George
Fanon, Frantz 1925-1961 ..... **CLC 74; BLC 2;**
  DAM MULT
  See also BW 1; CA 116; 89-92
Fanshawe, Ann 1625-1680 .... **LC 11**
Fante, John (Thomas) 1911-1983 .... **CLC 60**
  See also CA 69-72; 109; CANR 23; DLB 130;
  DLBY 83
Farah, Nuruddin 1945- .... **CLC 53; BLC 2;**
  DAM MULT
  See also BW 2; CA 106; DLB 125
Fargue, Leon-Paul 1876(?)-1947 .... **TCLC 11**
  See also CA 109
Farigoule, Louis
  See Romains, Jules
Farina, Richard 1936(?)-1966 .... **CLC 9**
  See also CA 81-84; 25-28R
Farley, Walter (Lorimer) 1915-1989...**CLC 17**
  See also CA 17-20R; CANR 8, 29; DLB 22;
  JRDA; MAICYA; SATA 2, 43
Farmer, Philip Jose 1918- .... **CLC 1, 19**
  See also CA 1-4R; CANR 4, 35; DLB 8; MTCW;
  SATA 93
Farquhar, George 1677-1707 .... **LC 21; DAM**
  DRAM
  See also DLB 84
Farrell, J(ames) G(ordon) 1935-1979 .. **CLC 6**
  See also CA 73-76; 89-92; CANR 36; DLB 14;
  MTCW
Farrell, James T(homas) 1904-1979...**CLC 1, 4,**
  8, 11, 66; SSC 28
  See also CA 5-8R; 89-92; CANR 9, 61; DLB 4,
  9, 86; DLBD 2; MTCW
Farren, Richard J.
  See Betjeman, John
Farren, Richard M.
  See Betjeman, John
Fassbinder, Rainer Werner 1946-1982..**CLC 20**
  See also CA 93-96; 106; CANR 31
Fast, Howard (Melvin) 1914-...**CLC 23; DAM**
  NOV
  See also AAYA 16; CA 1-4R; CAAS 18; CANR
  1, 33, 54; DLB 9; INT CANR-33; SATA 7
Faulcon, Robert
  See Holdstock, Robert P.
Faulkner, William (Cuthbert) 1897-1962
  CLC 1, 3, 6, 8, 9, 11, 14, 18, 28, 52, 68; DA;
  DAB; DAC; DAM MST, NOV; SSC 1; WLC
  See also AAYA 7; CA 81-84; CANR 33; CDALB
  1929-1941; DLB 9, 11, 44, 102; DLBD 2;
  DLBY 86, 97; MTCW
Fauset, Jessie Redmon 1884(?)-1961...**CLC 19,**
  54; BLC 2; DAM MULT
  See also BW 1; CA 109; DLB 51
Faust, Frederick (Schiller) 1892-1944(?)**TCLC**
  49; DAM POP
  See also CA 108; 152
Faust, Irvin 1924- .... **CLC 8**
  See also CA 33-36R; CANR 28, 67; DLB 2, 28;
  DLBY 80

Fawkes, Guy
  See Benchley, Robert (Charles)
Fearing, Kenneth (Flexner) 1902-1961...**CLC 51**
  See also CA 93-96; CANR 59; DLB 9
Fecamps, Elise
  See Creasey, John
Federman, Raymond 1928- .... **CLC 6, 47**
  See also CA 17-20R; CAAS 8; CANR 10, 43;
  DLBY 80
Federspiel, J(uerg) F. 1931- .... **CLC 42**
  See also CA 146
Feiffer, Jules (Ralph) 1929- ..... **CLC 2, 8, 64;**
  DAM DRAM
  See also AAYA 3; CA 17-20R; CANR 30, 59;
  DLB 7, 44; INT CANR-30; MTCW; SATA 8,
  61
Feige, Hermann Albert Otto Maximilian
  See Traven, B.
Feinberg, David B. 1956-1994 .... **CLC 59**
  See also CA 135; 147
Feinstein, Elaine 1930- .... **CLC 36**
  See also CA 69-72; CAAS 1; CANR 31, 68; DLB
  14, 40; MTCW
Feldman, Irving (Mordecai) 1928- ...... **CLC 7**
  See also CA 1-4R; CANR 1; DLB 169
Felix-Tchicaya, Gerald
  See Tchicaya, Gerald Felix
Fellini, Federico 1920-1993 .... **CLC 16, 85**
  See also CA 65-68; 143; CANR 33
Felsen, Henry Gregor 1916- .... **CLC 17**
  See also CA 1-4R; CANR 1; SAAS 2; SATA 1
Fenno, Jack
  See Calisher, Hortense
Fenton, James Martin 1949- .... **CLC 32**
  See also CA 102; DLB 40
Ferber, Edna 1887-1968 .... **CLC 18, 93**
  See also AITN 1; CA 5-8R; 25-28R; CANR 68;
  DLB 9, 28, 86; MTCW; SATA 7
Ferguson, Helen
  See Kavan, Anna
Ferguson, Samuel 1810-1886 .... **NCLC 33**
  See also DLB 32
Fergusson, Robert 1750-1774 .... **LC 29**
  See also DLB 109
Ferling, Lawrence
  See Ferlinghetti, Lawrence (Monsanto)
Ferlinghetti, Lawrence (Monsanto) 1919(?)-
  CLC 2, 6, 10, 27, 111; DAM POET; PC 1
  See also CA 5-8R; CANR 3, 41; CDALB 1941-
  1968; DLB 5, 16; MTCW
Fernandez, Vicente Garcia Huidobro
  See Huidobro Fernandez, Vicente Garcia
Ferrer, Gabriel (Francisco Victor) Miro
  See Miro (Ferrer), Gabriel (Francisco Victor)
Ferrier, Susan (Edmonstone) 1782-1854
  NCLC 8
  See also DLB 116
Ferrigno, Robert 1948(?)- .... **CLC 65**
  See also CA 140
Ferron, Jacques 1921-1985 ..... **CLC 94; DAC**
  See also CA 117; 129; DLB 60
Feuchtwanger, Lion 1884-1958 .... **TCLC 3**
  See also CA 104; DLB 66
Feuillet, Octave 1821-1890 .... **NCLC 45**
  See also DLB 192
Feydeau, Georges (Leon Jules Marie) 1862-1921
  TCLC 22; DAM DRAM
  See also CA 113; 152; DLB 192
Fichte, Johann Gottlieb 1762-1814...**NCLC 62**
  See also DLB 90
Ficino, Marsilio 1433-1499 .... **LC 12**
Fiedeler, Hans
  See Doeblin, Alfred

Fiedler, Leslie A(aron) 1917- .... **CLC 4, 13, 24**
  See also CA 9-12R; CANR 7, 63; DLB 28, 67;
  MTCW
Field, Andrew 1938- .... **CLC 44**
  See also CA 97-100; CANR 25
Field, Eugene 1850-1895 .... **NCLC 3**
  See also DLB 23, 42, 140; DLBD 13; MAICYA;
  SATA 16
Field, Gans T.
  See Wellman, Manly Wade
Field, Michael 1915-1971 .... **TCLC 43**
  See also CA 29-32R
Field, Peter
  See Hobson, Laura Z(ametkin)
Fielding, Henry 1707-1754 .. **LC 1; DA; DAB;**
  DAC; DAM DRAM, MST, NOV; WLC
  See also CDBLB 1660-1789; DLB 39, 84, 101
Fielding, Sarah 1710-1768 .... **LC 1, 44**
  See also DLB 39
Fields, W. C. 1880-1946 .... **TCLC 80**
  See also DLB 44
Fierstein, Harvey (Forbes) 1954- ..... **CLC 33;**
  DAM DRAM, POP
  See also CA 123; 129
Figes, Eva 1932- .... **CLC 31**
  See also CA 53-56; CANR 4, 44; DLB 14
Finch, Anne 1661-1720 .... **LC 3; PC 21**
  See also DLB 95
Finch, Robert (Duer Claydon) 1900-...**CLC 18**
  See also CA 57-60; CANR 9, 24, 49; DLB 88
Findley, Timothy 1930- .. **CLC 27, 102; DAC;**
  DAM MST
  See also CA 25-28R; CANR 12, 42, 69; DLB 53
Fink, William
  See Mencken, H(enry) L(ouis)
Firbank, Louis 1942-
  See Reed, Lou
  See also CA 117
Firbank, (Arthur Annesley) Ronald 1886-1926
  TCLC 1
  See also CA 104; DLB 36
Fisher, M(ary) F(rances) K(ennedy) 1908-1992
  CLC 76, 87
  See also CA 77-80; 138; CANR 44
Fisher, Roy 1930-............................... **CLC 25**
  See also CA 81-84; CAAS 10; CANR 16; DLB
  40
Fisher, Rudolph 1897-1934 ..... **TCLC 11;**
  BLC 2; DAM MULT; SSC 25
  See also BW 1; CA 107; 124; DLB 51, 102
Fisher, Vardis (Alvero) 1895-1968 .... **CLC 7**
  See also CA 5-8R; 25-28R; CANR 68; DLB 9
Fiske, Tarleton
  See Bloch, Robert (Albert)
Fitch, Clarke
  See Sinclair, Upton (Beall)
Fitch, John IV
  See Cormier, Robert (Edmund)
Fitzgerald, Captain Hugh
  See Baum, L(yman) Frank
FitzGerald, Edward 1809-1883 .... **NCLC 9**
  See also DLB 32
Fitzgerald, F(rancis) Scott (Key) 1896-1940
  TCLC 1, 6, 14, 28, 55; DA; DAB; DAC;
  DAM MST, NOV; SSC 6, 31; WLC
  See also AAYA 24; AITN 1; CA 110; 123;
  CDALB 1917-1929; DLB 4, 9, 86; DLBD 1,
  15, 16; DLBY 81, 96; MTCW
Fitzgerald, Penelope 1916- ..... **CLC 19, 51, 61**
  See also CA 85-88; CAAS 10; CANR 56; DLB
  14, 194
Fitzgerald, Robert (Stuart) 1910-1985...**CLC 39**
  See also CA 1-4R; 114; CANR 1; DLBY 80

French, Marilyn 1929-..... **CLC 10, 18, 60;
DAM DRAM, NOV, POP**
See also CA 69-72; CANR 3, 31; INT CANR-31; MTCW

French, Paul
See Asimov, Isaac

Freneau, Philip Morin 1752-1832 ..... **NCLC 1**
See also DLB 37, 43

Freud, Sigmund 1856-1939 .... **TCLC 52**
See also CA 115; 133; CANR 69; MTCW

Friedan, Betty (Naomi) 1921-............. **CLC 74**
See also CA 65-68; CANR 18, 45; MTCW

Friedlander, Saul 1932-...................... **CLC 90**
See also CA 117; 130

Friedman, B(ernard) H(arper) 1926-..**CLC 7**
See also CA 1-4R; CANR 3, 48

Friedman, Bruce Jay 1930-........ **CLC 3, 5, 56**
See also CA 9-12R; CANR 25, 52; DLB 2, 28; INT CANR-25

Friel, Brian 1929-........... **CLC 5, 42, 59; DC 8**
See also CA 21-24R; CANR 33, 69; DLB 13; MTCW

Friis-Baastad, Babbis Ellinor 1921-1970
CLC 12
See also CA 17-20R; 134; SATA 7

Frisch, Max (Rudolf) 1911-1991...**CLC 3, 9, 14, 18, 32, 44; DAM DRAM, NOV**
See also CA 85-88; 134; CANR 32; DLB 69, 124; MTCW

Fromentin, Eugene (Samuel Auguste) 1820-1876
NCLC 10
See also DLB 123

Frost, Frederick
See Faust, Frederick (Schiller)

Frost, Robert (Lee) 1874-1963...**CLC 1, 3, 4, 9, 10, 13, 15, 26, 34, 44; DA; DAB; DAC; DAM MST, POET; PC 1; WLC**
See also AAYA 21; CA 89-92; CANR 33; CDALB 1917-1929; DLB 54; DLBD 7; MTCW; SATA 14

Froude, James Anthony 1818-1894
NCLC 43
See also DLB 18, 57, 144

Froy, Herald
See Waterhouse, Keith (Spencer)

Fry, Christopher 1907-... **CLC 2, 10, 14; DAM DRAM**
See also CA 17-20R; CAAS 23; CANR 9, 30; DLB 13; MTCW; SATA 66

Frye, (Herman) Northrop 1912-1991 ..**CLC 24, 70**
See also CA 5-8R; 133; CANR 8, 37; DLB 67, 68; MTCW

Fuchs, Daniel 1909-1993 .... **CLC 8, 22**
See also CA 81-84; 142; CAAS 5; CANR 40; DLB 9, 26, 28; DLBY 93

Fuchs, Daniel 1934-............................ **CLC 34**
See also CA 37-40R; CANR 14, 48

Fuentes, Carlos 1928-... **CLC 3, 8, 10, 13, 22, 41, 60, 113; DA; DAB; DAC; DAM MST, MULT, NOV; HLC; SSC 24; WLC**
See also AAYA 4; AITN 2; CA 69-72; CANR 10, 32, 68; DLB 113; HW; MTCW

Fuentes, Gregorio Lopez y
See Lopez y Fuentes, Gregorio

Fugard, (Harold) Athol 1932-...**CLC 5, 9, 14, 25, 40, 80; DAM DRAM; DC 3**
See also AAYA 17; CA 85-88; CANR 32, 54; MTCW

Fugard, Sheila 1932- .... **CLC 48**
See also CA 125

Fuller, Charles (H., Jr.) 1939- ... **CLC 25; BLC 2; DAM DRAM, MULT; DC 1**
See also BW 2; CA 108; 112; DLB 38; INT 112; MTCW

Fuller, John (Leopold) 1937-.............. **CLC 62**
See also CA 21-24R; CANR 9, 44; DLB 40

Fuller, Margaret .... **NCLC 5, 50**
See also Ossoli, Sarah Margaret (Fuller marchesa d')

Fuller, Roy (Broadbent) 1912-1991 **CLC 4, 28**
See also CA 5-8R; 135; CAAS 10; CANR 53; DLB 15, 20; SATA 87

Fulton, Alice 1952- .... **CLC 52**
See also CA 116; CANR 57; DLB 193

Furphy, Joseph 1843-1912 .... **TCLC 25**
See also CA 163

Fussell, Paul 1924-.............................. **CLC 74**
See also BEST 90:1; CA 17-20R; CANR 8, 21, 35, 69; INT CANR-21; MTCW

Futabatei, Shimei 1864-1909 .... **TCLC 44**
See also CA 162; DLB 180

Futrelle, Jacques 1875-1912 .... **TCLC 19**
See also CA 113; 155

Gaboriau, Emile 1835-1873 .... **NCLC 14**

Gadda, Carlo Emilio 1893-1973 .... **CLC 11**
See also CA 89-92; DLB 177

Gaddis, William 1922-...**CLC 1, 3, 6, 8, 10, 19, 43, 86**
See also CA 17-20R; CANR 21, 48; DLB 2; MTCW

Gage, Walter
See Inge, William (Motter)

Gaines, Ernest J(ames) 1933-...**CLC 3, 11, 18, 86; BLC 2; DAM MULT**
See also AAYA 18; AITN 1; BW 2; CA 9-12R; CANR 6, 24, 42; CDALB 1968-1988; DLB 2, 33, 152; DLBY 80; MTCW; SATA 86

Gaitskill, Mary 1954- .... **CLC 69**
See also CA 128; CANR 61

Galdos, Benito Perez
See Perez Galdos, Benito

Gale, Zona 1874-1938 .... **TCLC 7; DAM DRAM**
See also CA 105; 153; DLB 9, 78

Galeano, Eduardo (Hughes) 1940-..... **CLC 72**
See also CA 29-32R; CANR 13, 32; HW

Galiano, Juan Valera y Alcala
See Valera y Alcala-Galiano, Juan

Galilei, Galileo 1546-1642 .... **LC 45**

Gallagher, Tess 1943- ...... **CLC 18, 63; DAM POET; PC 9**
See also CA 106; DLB 120

Gallant, Mavis 1922- ... **CLC 7, 18, 38; DAC; DAM MST; SSC 5**
See also CA 69-72; CANR 29, 69; DLB 53; MTCW

Gallant, Roy A(rthur) 1924- .... **CLC 17**
See also CA 5-8R; CANR 4, 29, 54; CLR 30; MAICYA; SATA 4, 68

Gallico, Paul (William) 1897-1976 .... **CLC 2**
See also AITN 1; CA 5-8R; 69-72; CANR 23; DLB 9, 171; MAICYA; SATA 13

Gallo, Max Louis 1932- .... **CLC 95**
See also CA 85-88

Gallois, Lucien
See Desnos, Robert

Gallup, Ralph
See Whitemore, Hugh (John)

Galsworthy, John 1867-1933 ... **TCLC 1, 45; DA; DAB; DAC; DAM DRAM, MST, NOV; SSC 22; WLC 2**
See also CA 104; 141; CDBLB 1890-1914; DLB 10, 34, 98, 162; DLBD 16

Galt, John 1779-1839 .... **NCLC 1**
See also DLB 99, 116, 159

Galvin, James 1951- .... **CLC 38**
See also CA 108; CANR 26

Gamboa, Federico 1864-1939 .... **TCLC 36**

Gandhi, M. K.
See Gandhi, Mohandas Karamchand

Gandhi, Mahatma
See Gandhi, Mohandas Karamchand

Gandhi, Mohandas Karamchand 1869-1948
TCLC 59; DAM MULT
See also CA 121; 132; MTCW

Gann, Ernest Kellogg 1910-1991 .... **CLC 23**
See also AITN 1; CA 1-4R; 136; CANR 1

Garcia, Cristina 1958- .... **CLC 76**
See also CA 141

Garcia Lorca, Federico 1898-1936...**TCLC 1, 7, 49; DA; DAB; DAC; DAM DRAM, MST, MULT, POET; DC 2; HLC; PC 3; WLC**
See also CA 104; 131; DLB 108; HW; MTCW

Garcia Marquez, Gabriel (Jose) 1928-...**CLC 2, 3, 8, 10, 15, 27, 47, 55, 68; DA; DAB; DAC; DAM MST, MULT, NOV, POP; HLC; SSC 8; WLC**
See also AAYA 3; BEST 89:1, 90:4; CA 33-36R; CANR 10, 28, 50; DLB 113; HW; MTCW

Gard, Janice
See Latham, Jean Lee

Gard, Roger Martin du
See Martin du Gard, Roger

Gardam, Jane 1928- .... **CLC 43**
See also CA 49-52; CANR 2, 18, 33, 54; CLR 12; DLB 14, 161; MAICYA; MTCW; SAAS 9; SATA 39, 76; SATA-Brief 28

Gardner, Herb(ert) 1934- .... **CLC 44**
See also CA 149

Gardner, John (Champlin), Jr. 1933-1982
CLC 2, 3, 5, 7, 8, 10, 18, 28, 34; DAM NOV, POP; SSC 7
See also AITN 1; CA 65-68; 107; CANR 33; DLB 2; DLBY 82; MTCW; SATA 40; SATA-Obit 31

Gardner, John (Edmund) 1926- ..... **CLC 30; DAM POP**
See also CA 103; CANR 15, 69; MTCW

Gardner, Miriam
See Bradley, Marion Zimmer

Gardner, Noel
See Kuttner, Henry

Gardons, S. S.
See Snodgrass, W(illiam) D(e Witt)

Garfield, Leon 1921-1996 .... **CLC 12**
See also AAYA 8; CA 17-20R; 152; CANR 38, 41; CLR 21; DLB 161; JRDA; MAICYA; SATA 1, 32, 76; SATA-Obit 90

Garland, (Hannibal) Hamlin 1860-1940
TCLC 3; SSC 18
See also CA 104; DLB 12, 71, 78, 186

Garneau, (Hector de) Saint-Denys 1912-1943
TCLC 13
See also CA 111; DLB 88

Garner, Alan 1934- .... **CLC 17; DAB; DAM POP**
See also AAYA 18; CA 73-76; CANR 15, 64; CLR 20; DLB 161; MAICYA; MTCW; SATA 18, 69

Garner, Hugh 1913-1979 .... **CLC 13**
See also CA 69-72; CANR 31; DLB 68

Garnett, David 1892-1981 .... **CLC 3**
See also CA 5-8R; 103; CANR 17; DLB 34

Garos, Stephanie
See Katz, Steve

Gloag, Julian 1930- .... **CLC 40**
See also AITN 1; CA 65-68; CANR 10
Glowacki, Aleksander
See Prus, Boleslaw
Gluck, Louise (Elisabeth) 1943-...**CLC 7, 22,
44, 81; DAM POET; PC 16**
See also CA 33-36R; CANR 40, 69; DLB 5
Glyn, Elinor 1864-1943 .... **TCLC 72**
See also DLB 153
Gobineau, Joseph Arthur (Comte) de 1816-1882
NCLC 17
See also DLB 123
Godard, Jean-Luc 1930- .... **CLC 20**
See also CA 93-96
Godden, (Margaret) Rumer 1907-..... **CLC 53**
See also AAYA 6; CA 5-8R; CANR 4, 27, 36,
55; CLR 20; DLB 161; MAICYA; SAAS 12;
SATA 3, 36
Godoy Alcayaga, Lucila 1889-1957
See Mistral, Gabriela
See also BW 2; CA 104; 131; DAM MULT; HW;
MTCW
Godwin, Gail (Kathleen) 1937-...**CLC 5, 8,
22, 31, 69; DAM POP**
See also CA 29-32R; CANR 15, 43, 69; DLB 6;
INT CANR-15; MTCW
Godwin, William 1756-1836 .... **NCLC 14**
See also CDBLB 1789-1832; DLB 39, 104, 142,
158, 163
Goebbels, Josef
See Goebbels, (Paul) Joseph
Goebbels, (Paul) Joseph 1897-1945...**T C L C
68**
See also CA 115; 148
Goebbels, Joseph Paul
See Goebbels, (Paul) Joseph
Goethe, Johann Wolfgang von 1749-1832
**NCLC 4, 22, 34; DA; DAB; DAC; DAM
DRAM, MST, POET; PC 5; WLC 3**
See also DLB 94
Gogarty, Oliver St. John 1878-1957...**TCLC 15**
See also CA 109; 150; DLB 15, 19
Gogol, Nikolai (Vasilyevich) 1809-1852
**NCLC 5, 15, 31; DA; DAB; DAC; DAM
DRAM, MST; DC 1; SSC 4, 29; WLC**
See also DLB 198
Goines, Donald 1937(?)-1974**CLC 80; BLC 2;
DAM MULT; POP**
See also AITN 1; BW 1; CA 124; 114; DLB 33
Gold, Herbert 1924- .... **CLC 4, 7, 14, 42**
See also CA 9-12R; CANR 17, 45; DLB 2;
DLBY 81
Goldbarth, Albert 1948- .... **CLC 5, 38**
See also CA 53-56; CANR 6, 40; DLB 120
Goldberg, Anatol 1910-1982 .... **CLC 34**
See also CA 131; 117
Goldemberg, Isaac 1945- .... **CLC 52**
See also CA 69-72; CAAS 12; CANR 11, 32;
HW
Golding, William (Gerald) 1911-1993
**CLC 1, 2, 3, 8, 10, 17, 27, 58, 81; DA; DAB;
DAC; DAM MST, NOV; WLC**
See also AAYA 5; CA 5-8R; 141; CANR 13, 33,
54; CDBLB 1945-1960; DLB 15, 100;
MTCW
Goldman, Emma 1869-1940 .... **TCLC 13**
See also CA 110; 150
Goldman, Francisco 1954- .... **CLC 76**
See also CA 162
Goldman, William (W.) 1931- .... **CLC 1, 48**
See also CA 9-12R; CANR 29, 69; DLB 44
Goldmann, Lucien 1913-1970 .... **CLC 24**
See also CA 25-28; CAP 2

Goldoni, Carlo 1707-1793 .... **LC 4; DAM
DRAM**
Goldsberry, Steven 1949- .... **CLC 34**
See also CA 131
Goldsmith, Oliver 1728-1774 ...... **LC 2; DA;
DAB; DAC; DAM DRAM, MST, NOV,
POET; DC 8; WLC**
See also CDBLB 1660-1789; DLB 39, 89, 104,
109, 142; SATA 26
Goldsmith, Peter
See Priestley, J(ohn) B(oynton)
Gombrowicz, Witold 1904-1969...**CLC 4, 7, 11,
49; DAM DRAM**
See also CA 19-20; 25-28R; CAP 2
Gomez de la Serna, Ramon 1888-1963...**CLC 9**
See also CA 153; 116; HW
Goncharov, Ivan Alexandrovich 1812-1891
NCLC 1, 63
Goncourt, Edmond (Louis Antoine Huot) de
1822-1896 .... **NCLC 7**
See also DLB 123
Goncourt, Jules (Alfred Huot) de 1830-1870
NCLC 7
See also DLB 123
Gontier, Fernande 19(?)- .... **CLC 50**
Gonzalez Martinez, Enrique 1871-1952
TCLC 72
See also CA 166; HW
Goodman, Paul 1911-1972 .... **CLC 1, 2, 4, 7**
See also CA 19-20; 37-40R; CANR 34; CAP 2;
DLB 130; MTCW
Gordimer, Nadine 1923-...**CLC 3, 5, 7, 10, 18,
33, 51, 70; DA; DAB; DAC; DAM MST,
NOV; SSC 17; WLCS**
See also CA 5-8R; CANR 3, 28, 56; INT CANR-
28; MTCW
Gordon, Adam Lindsay 1833-1870...**NCLC 21**
Gordon, Caroline 1895-1981... **CLC 6, 13, 29,
83; SSC 15**
See also CA 11-12; 103; CANR 36; CAP 1; DLB
4, 9, 102; DLBY 81; MTCW
Gordon, Charles William 1860-1937
See Connor, Ralph
See also CA 109
Gordon, Mary (Catherine) 1949-...**CLC 13, 22**
See also CA 102; CANR 44; DLB 6; DLBY 81;
INT 102; MTCW
Gordon, N. J.
See Bosman, Herman Charles
Gordon, Sol 1923- .... **CLC 26**
See also CA 53-56; CANR 4; SATA 11
Gordone, Charles 1925-1995...**CLC 1, 4; DAM
DRAM; DC 8**
See also BW 1; CA 93-96; 150; CANR 55; DLB
7; INT 93-96; MTCW
Gore, Catherine 1800-1861 .... **NCLC 65**
See also DLB 116
Gorenko, Anna Andreevna
See Akhmatova, Anna
Gorky, Maxim 1868-1936 .. **TCLC 8; DAB;
SSC 28; WLC**
See also Peshkov, Alexei Maximovich
Goryan, Sirak
See Saroyan, William
Gosse, Edmund (William) 1849-1928
TCLC 28
See also CA 117; DLB 57, 144, 184
Gotlieb, Phyllis Fay (Bloom) 1926- .... **CLC 18**
See also CA 13-16R; CANR 7; DLB 88
Gottesman, S. D.
See Kornbluth, C(yril) M.; Pohl, Frederik
Gottfried von Strassburg fl. c. 1210-..**CMLC 10**
See also DLB 138

Gould, Lois .... **CLC 4, 10**
See also CA 77-80; CANR 29; MTCW
Gourmont, Remy (-Marie-Charles) de 1858-
1915 .... **TCLC 17**
See also CA 109; 150
Govier, Katherine 1948- .... **CLC 51**
See also CA 101; CANR 18, 40
Goyen, (Charles) William 1915-1983**CLC 5, 8,
14, 40**
See also AITN 2; CA 5-8R; 110; CANR 6; DLB
2; DLBY 83; INT CANR-6
Goytisolo, Juan 1931- ... **CLC 5, 10, 23; DAM
MULT; HLC**
See also CA 85-88; CANR 32, 61; HW; MTCW
Gozzano, Guido 1883-1916 .... **PC 10**
See also CA 154; DLB 114
Gozzi, (Conte) Carlo 1720-1806 ...... **NCLC 23**
Grabbe, Christian Dietrich 1801-1836..**NCLC 2**
See also DLB 133
Grace, Patricia 1937- .... **CLC 56**
Gracian y Morales, Baltasar 1601-1658...**LC 15**
Gracq, Julien .... **CLC 11, 48**
See also Poirier, Louis
See also DLB 83
Grade, Chaim 1910-1982 .... **CLC 10**
See also CA 93-96; 107
Graduate of Oxford, A
See Ruskin, John
Grafton, Garth
See Duncan, Sara Jeannette
Graham, John
See Phillips, David Graham
Graham, Jorie 1951- .... **CLC 48**
See also CA 111; CANR 63; DLB 120
Graham, R(obert) B(ontine) Cunninghame
See Cunninghame Graham, R(obert) B(ontine)
See also DLB 98, 135, 174
Graham, Robert
See Haldeman, Joe (William)
Graham, Tom
See Lewis, (Harry) Sinclair
Graham, W(illiam) S(ydney) 1918-1986
CLC 29
See also CA 73-76; 118; DLB 20
Graham, Winston (Mawdsley) 1910-...**CLC 23**
See also CA 49-52; CANR 2, 22, 45, 66; DLB
77
Grahame, Kenneth 1859-1932 .... **TCLC 64;
DAB**
See also CA 108; 136; CLR 5; DLB 34, 141, 178;
MAICYA; YABC 1
Grant, Skeeter
See Spiegelman, Art
Granville-Barker, Harley 1877-1946...**TCLC
2; DAM DRAM**
See also Barker, Harley Granville
See also CA 104
Grass, Guenter (Wilhelm) 1927-...**CLC 1, 2,
4, 6, 11, 15, 22, 32, 49, 88; DA; DAB;
DAC; DAM MST, NOV; WLC**
See also CA 13-16R; CANR 20; DLB 75, 124;
MTCW
Gratton, Thomas
See Hulme, T(homas) E(rnest)
Grau, Shirley Ann 1929- .... **CLC 4, 9; SSC 15**
See also CA 89-92; CANR 22, 69; DLB 2; INT
CANR-22; MTCW
Gravel, Fern
See Hall, James Norman
Graver, Elizabeth 1964- .... **CLC 70**
See also CA 135
Graves, Richard Perceval 1945- .... **CLC 44**
See also CA 65-68; CANR 9, 26, 51

Hellenhofferu, Vojtech Kapristian z
  See Hasek, Jaroslav (Matej Frantisek)
Heller, Joseph 1923-...**CLC 1, 3, 5, 8, 11, 36, 63; DA; DAB; DAC; DAM MST, NOV, POP; WLC**
  See also AAYA 24; AITN 1; CA 5-8R; CABS 1; CANR 8, 42, 66; DLB 2, 28; DLBY 80; INT CANR-8; MTCW
Hellman, Lillian (Florence) 1906-1984...**CLC 2, 4, 8, 14, 18, 34, 44, 52; DAM DRAM; DC 1**
  See also AITN 1, 2; CA 13-16R; 112; CANR 33; DLB 7; DLBY 84; MTCW
Helprin, Mark 1947- .... **CLC 7, 10, 22, 32; DAM NOV, POP**
  See also CA 81-84; CANR 47, 64; DLBY 85; MTCW
Helvetius, Claude-Adrien 1715-1771 ... **LC 26**
Helyar, Jane Penelope Josephine 1933-
  See Poole, Josephine
  See also CA 21-24R; CANR 10, 26; SATA 82
Hemans, Felicia 1793-1835 .... **NCLC 71**
  See also DLB 96
Hemingway, Ernest (Miller) 1899-1961...**CLC 1, 3, 6, 8, 10, 13, 19, 30, 34, 39, 41, 44, 50, 61, 80; DA; DAB; DAC; DAM MST, NOV; SSC 25; WLC**
  See also AAYA 19; CA 77-80; CANR 34; CDALB 1917-1929; DLB 4, 9, 102; DLBD 1, 15, 16; DLBY 81, 87, 96; MTCW
Hempel, Amy 1951- .... **CLC 39**
  See also CA 118; 137
Henderson, F. C.
  See Mencken, H(enry) L(ouis)
Henderson, Sylvia
  See Ashton-Warner, Sylvia (Constance)
Henderson, Zenna (Chlarson) 1917-1983... **S S C 29**
  See also CA 1-4R; 133; CANR 1; DLB 8; SATA 5
Henley, Beth .... **CLC 23; DC 6**
  See also Henley, Elizabeth Becker
  See also CABS 3; DLBY 86
Henley, Elizabeth Becker 1952-
  See Henley, Beth
  See also CA 107; CANR 32; DAM DRAM, MST; MTCW
Henley, William Ernest 1849-1903 ... **TCLC 8**
  See also CA 105; DLB 19
Hennissart, Martha
  See Lathen, Emma
  See also CA 85-88; CANR 64
Henry, O. .... **TCLC 1, 19; SSC 5; WLC**
  See also Porter, William Sydney
Henry, Patrick 1736-1799 .... **LC 25**
Henryson, Robert 1430(?)-1506(?) ...... **LC 20**
  See also DLB 146
Henry VIII 1491-1547 .... **LC 10**
Henschke, Alfred
  See Klabund
Hentoff, Nat(han Irving) 1925- .... **CLC 26**
  See also AAYA 4; CA 1-4R; CAAS 6; CANR 5, 25; CLR 1, 52; INT CANR-25; JRDA; MAICYA; SATA 42, 69; SATA-Brief 27
Heppenstall, (John) Rayner 1911-1981... **C L C 10**
  See also CA 1-4R; 103; CANR 29
Heraclitus c. 540B.C.-c. 450B.C. .... **CMLC 22**
  See also DLB 176
Herbert, Frank (Patrick) 1920-1986 **CLC 12, 23, 35, 44, 85; DAM POP**
  See also AAYA 21; CA 53-56; 118; CANR 5, 43; DLB 8; INT CANR-5; MTCW; SATA 9, 37; SATA-Obit 47

Herbert, George 1593-1633 .... **LC 24; DAB; DAM POET; PC 4**
  See also CDBLB Before 1660; DLB 126
Herbert, Zbigniew 1924- .... **CLC 9, 43; DAM POET**
  See also CA 89-92; CANR 36; MTCW
Herbst, Josephine (Frey) 1897-1969...**CLC 34**
  See also CA 5-8R; 25-28R; DLB 9
Hergesheimer, Joseph 1880-1954 ... **TCLC 11**
  See also CA 109; DLB 102, 9
Herlihy, James Leo 1927-1993 .... **CLC 6**
  See also CA 1-4R; 143; CANR 2
Hermogenes fl. c. 175- .... **CMLC 6**
Hernandez, Jose 1834-1886 .... **NCLC 17**
Herodotus c. 484B.C.-429B.C. .... **CMLC 17**
  See also DLB 176
Herrick, Robert 1591-1674 ..... **LC 13; DA; DAB; DAC; DAM MST, POP; PC 9**
  See also DLB 126
Herring, Guiles
  See Somerville, Edith
Herriot, James 1916-1995 .... **CLC 12; DAM POP**
  See also Wight, James Alfred
  See also AAYA 1; CA 148; CANR 40; SATA 86
Herrmann, Dorothy 1941- .... **CLC 44**
  See also CA 107
Herrmann, Taffy
  See Herrmann, Dorothy
Hersey, John (Richard) 1914-1993... **CLC 1, 2, 7, 9, 40, 81, 97; DAM POP**
  See also CA 17-20R; 140; CANR 33; DLB 6, 185; MTCW; SATA 25; SATA-Obit 76
Herzen, Aleksandr Ivanovich 1812-1870 **NCLC 10, 61**
Herzl, Theodor 1860-1904 .... **TCLC 36**
Herzog, Werner 1942- .... **CLC 16**
  See also CA 89-92
Hesiod c. 8th cent. B.C.- .... **CMLC 5**
  See also DLB 176
Hesse, Hermann 1877-1962...**CLC 1, 2, 3, 6, 11, 17, 25, 69; DA; DAB; DAC; DAM MST, NOV; SSC 9; WLC**
  See also CA 17-18; CAP 2; DLB 66; MTCW; SATA 50
Hewes, Cady
  See De Voto, Bernard (Augustine)
Heyen, William 1940- .... **CLC 13, 18**
  See also CA 33-36R; CAAS 9; DLB 5
Heyerdahl, Thor 1914- .... **CLC 26**
  See also CA 5-8R; CANR 5, 22, 66; MTCW; SATA 2, 52
Heym, Georg (Theodor Franz Arthur) 1887-1912 .... **TCLC 9**
  See also CA 106
Heym, Stefan 1913- .... **CLC 41**
  See also CA 9-12R; CANR 4; DLB 69
Heyse, Paul (Johann Ludwig von) 1830-1914 **TCLC 8**
  See also CA 104; DLB 129
Heyward, (Edwin) DuBose 1885-1940 **TCLC 59**
  See also CA 108; 157; DLB 7, 9, 45; SATA 21
Hibbert, Eleanor Alice Burford 1906-1993 **CLC 7; DAM POP**
  See also BEST 90:4; CA 17-20R; 140; CANR 9, 28, 59; SATA 2; SATA-Obit 74
Hichens, Robert (Smythe) 1864-1950 ...**TCLC 64**
  See also CA 162; DLB 153
Higgins, George V(incent) 1939-...**CLC 4, 7, 10, 18**
  See also CA 77-80; CAAS 5; CANR 17, 51; DLB 2; DLBY 81; INT CANR-17; MTCW

Higginson, Thomas Wentworth 1823-1911 **TCLC 36**
  See also CA 162; DLB 1, 64
Highet, Helen
  See MacInnes, Helen (Clark)
Highsmith, (Mary) Patricia 1921-1995...**CLC 2, 4, 14, 42, 102; DAM NOV, POP**
  See also CA 1-4R; 147; CANR 1, 20, 48, 62; MTCW
Highwater, Jamake (Mamake) 1942(?)-...**CLC 12**
  See also AAYA 7; CA 65-68; CAAS 7; CANR 10, 34; CLR 17; DLB 52; DLBY 85; JRDA; MAICYA; SATA 32, 69; SATA-Brief 30
Highway, Tomson 1951-..... **CLC 92; DAC; DAM MULT**
  See also CA 151; NNAL
Higuchi, Ichiyo 1872-1896 .... **NCLC 49**
Hijuelos, Oscar 1951- .... **CLC 65; DAM MULT, POP; HLC**
  See also AAYA 25; BEST 90:1; CA 123; CANR 50; DLB 145; HW
Hikmet, Nazim 1902(?)-1963 .... **CLC 40**
  See also CA 141; 93-96
Hildegard von Bingen 1098-1179 .. **CMLC 20**
  See also DLB 148
Hildesheimer, Wolfgang 1916-1991 ... **CLC 49**
  See also CA 101; 135; DLB 69, 124
Hill, Geoffrey (William) 1932-...**CLC 5, 8, 18, 45; DAM POET**
  See also CA 81-84; CANR 21; CDBLB 1960 to Present; DLB 40; MTCW
Hill, George Roy 1921- .... **CLC 26**
  See also CA 110; 122
Hill, John
  See Koontz, Dean R(ay)
Hill, Susan (Elizabeth) 1942- ..... **CLC 4, 113; DAB; DAM MST, NOV**
  See also CA 33-36R; CANR 29, 69; DLB 14, 139; MTCW
Hillerman, Tony 1925- ... **CLC 62; DAM POP**
  See also AAYA 6; BEST 89:1; CA 29-32R; CANR 21, 42, 65; SATA 6
Hillesum, Etty 1914-1943 .... **TCLC 49**
  See also CA 137
Hilliard, Noel (Harvey) 1929- .... **CLC 15**
  See also CA 9-12R; CANR 7, 69
Hillis, Rick 1956- .... **CLC 66**
  See also CA 134
Hilton, James 1900-1954 .... **TCLC 21**
  See also CA 108; DLB 34, 77; SATA 34
Himes, Chester (Bomar) 1909-1984... **C L C 2, 4, 7, 18, 58, 108; BLC 2; DAM MULT**
  See also BW 2; CA 25-28R; 114; CANR 22; DLB 2, 76, 143; MTCW
Hinde, Thomas .... **CLC 6, 11**
  See also Chitty, Thomas Willes
Hindin, Nathan
  See Bloch, Robert (Albert)
Hine, (William) Daryl 1936- .... **CLC 15**
  See also CA 1-4R; CAAS 15; CANR 1, 20; DLB 60
Hinkson, Katharine Tynan
  See Tynan, Katharine
Hinton, S(usan) E(loise) 1950- ..**CLC 30, 111; DA; DAB; DAC; DAM MST, NOV**
  See also AAYA 2; CA 81-84; CANR 32, 62; CLR 3, 23; JRDA; MAICYA; MTCW; SATA 19, 58
Hippius, Zinaida .... **TCLC 9**
  See also Gippius, Zinaida (Nikolayevna)
Hiraoka, Kimitake 1925-1970
  See Mishima, Yukio
  See also CA 97-100; 29-32R; DAM DRAM; MTCW

Hirsch, E(ric) D(onald), Jr. 1928- ...... **CLC 79**
See also CA 25-28R; CANR 27, 51; DLB 67;
INT CANR-27; MTCW
Hirsch, Edward 1950- .... **CLC 31, 50**
See also CA 104; CANR 20, 42; DLB 120
Hitchcock, Alfred (Joseph) 1899-1980...**CLC 16**
See also AAYA 22; CA 159; 97-100; SATA 27;
SATA-Obit 24
Hitler, Adolf 1889-1945 .... **TCLC 53**
See also CA 117; 147
Hoagland, Edward 1932- .... **CLC 28**
See also CA 1-4R; CANR 2, 31, 57; DLB 6;
SATA 51
Hoban, Russell (Conwell) 1925- ... **CLC 7, 25;
DAM NOV**
See also CA 5-8R; CANR 23, 37, 66; CLR 3;
DLB 52; MAICYA; MTCW; SATA 1, 40, 78
Hobbes, Thomas 1588-1679 .... **LC 36**
See also DLB 151
Hobbs, Perry
See Blackmur, R(ichard) P(almer)
Hobson, Laura Z(ametkin) 1900-1986...**CLC 7, 25**
See also CA 17-20R; 118; CANR 55; DLB 28;
SATA 52
Hochhuth, Rolf 1931-.... **CLC 4, 11, 18; DAM DRAM**
See also CA 5-8R; CANR 33; DLB 124; MTCW
Hochman, Sandra 1936- .... **CLC 3, 8**
See also CA 5-8R; DLB 5
Hochwaelder, Fritz 1911-1986...**CLC 36; DAM DRAM**
See also CA 29-32R; 120; CANR 42; MTCW
Hochwalder, Fritz
See Hochwaelder, Fritz
Hocking, Mary (Eunice) 1921- .... **CLC 13**
See also CA 101; CANR 18, 40
Hodgins, Jack 1938- .... **CLC 23**
See also CA 93-96; DLB 60
Hodgson, William Hope 1877(?)-1918...**TCLC 13**
See also CA 111; 164; DLB 70, 153, 156, 178
Hoeg, Peter 1957- .... **CLC 95**
See also CA 151
Hoffman, Alice 1952- .... **CLC 51; DAM NOV**
See also CA 77-80; CANR 34, 66; MTCW
Hoffman, Daniel (Gerard) 1923-...**CLC 6, 13, 23**
See also CA 1-4R; CANR 4; DLB 5
Hoffman, Stanley 1944- .... **CLC 5**
See also CA 77-80
Hoffman, William M(oses) 1939- .... **CLC 40**
See also CA 57-60; CANR 11
Hoffmann, E(rnst) T(heodor) A(madeus) 1776-1822 .... **NCLC 2; SSC 13**
See also DLB 90; SATA 27
Hofmann, Gert 1931- .... **CLC 54**
See also CA 128
Hofmannsthal, Hugo von 1874-1929 .. **TCLC 11; DAM DRAM; DC 4**
See also CA 106; 153; DLB 81, 118
Hogan, Linda 1947-.... **CLC 73; DAM MULT**
See also CA 120; CANR 45, 69; DLB 175;
NNAL
Hogarth, Charles
See Creasey, John
Hogarth, Emmett
See Polonsky, Abraham (Lincoln)
Hogg, James 1770-1835 .... **NCLC 4**
See also DLB 93, 116, 159
Holbach, Paul Henri Thiry Baron 1723-1789 **LC 14**

Holberg, Ludvig 1684-1754 .... **LC 6**
Holden, Ursula 1921- .... **CLC 18**
See also CA 101; CAAS 8; CANR 22
Holderlin, (Johann Christian) Friedrich 1770-1843...**NCLC 16; PC 4**
Holdstock, Robert
See Holdstock, Robert P.
Holdstock, Robert P. 1948- .... **CLC 39**
See also CA 131
Holland, Isabelle 1920- .... **CLC 21**
See also AAYA 11; CA 21-24R; CANR 10, 25,
47; JRDA; MAICYA; SATA 8, 70
Holland, Marcus
See Caldwell, (Janet Miriam) Taylor (Holland)
Hollander, John 1929- .... **CLC 2, 5, 8, 14**
See also CA 1-4R; CANR 1, 52; DLB 5; SATA
13
Hollander, Paul
See Silverberg, Robert
Holleran, Andrew 1943(?)- .... **CLC 38**
See also CA 144
Hollinghurst, Alan 1954- .... **CLC 55, 91**
See also CA 114
Hollis, Jim
See Summers, Hollis (Spurgeon, Jr.)
Holly, Buddy 1936-1959 .... **TCLC 65**
Holmes, Gordon
See Shiel, M(atthew) P(hipps)
Holmes, John
See Souster, (Holmes) Raymond
Holmes, John Clellon 1926-1988 .... **CLC 56**
See also CA 9-12R; 125; CANR 4; DLB 16
Holmes, Oliver Wendell, Jr. 1841-1935 **TCLC 77**
See also CA 114
Holmes, Oliver Wendell 1809-1894...**NCLC 14**
See also CDALB 1640-1865; DLB 1, 189; SATA
34
Holmes, Raymond
See Souster, (Holmes) Raymond
Holt, Victoria
See Hibbert, Eleanor Alice Burford
Holub, Miroslav 1923- .... **CLC 4**
See also CA 21-24R; CANR 10
Homer c. 8th cent. B.C.- .... **CMLC 1, 16; DA; DAB; DAC; DAM MST, POET; PC 23; WLCS**
See also DLB 176
Hongo, Garrett Kaoru 1951- .... **PC 23**
See also CA 133; CAAS 22; DLB 120
Honig, Edwin 1919-............................ **CLC 33**
See also CA 5-8R; CAAS 8; CANR 4, 45; DLB
5
Hood, Hugh (John Blagdon) 1928-...**CLC 15, 28**
See also CA 49-52; CAAS 17; CANR 1, 33; DLB
53
Hood, Thomas 1799-1845 .... **NCLC 16**
See also DLB 96
Hooker, (Peter) Jeremy 1941- .... **CLC 43**
See also CA 77-80; CANR 22; DLB 40
hooks, bell .... **CLC 94; BLCS**
See also Watkins, Gloria
Hope, A(lec) D(erwent) 1907-......... **CLC 3, 51**
See also CA 21-24R; CANR 33; MTCW
Hope, Anthony 1863-1933 .... **TCLC 83**
See also CA 157; DLB 153, 156
Hope, Brian
See Creasey, John
Hope, Christopher (David Tully) 1944-...**CLC 52**
See also CA 106; CANR 47; SATA 62

Hopkins, Gerard Manley 1844-1889 ..**NCLC 17; DA; DAB; DAC; DAM MST, POET; PC 15; WLC**
See also CDBLB 1890-1914; DLB 35, 57
Hopkins, John (Richard) 1931- .... **CLC 4**
See also CA 85-88
Hopkins, Pauline Elizabeth 1859-1930 **TCLC 28; BLC 2; DAM MULT**
See also BW 2; CA 141; DLB 50
Hopkinson, Francis 1737-1791 .... **LC 25**
See also DLB 31
Hopley-Woolrich, Cornell George 1903-1968
See Woolrich, Cornell
See also CA 13-14; CANR 58; CAP 1
Horatio
See Proust, (Valentin-Louis-George-Eugene-) Marcel
Horgan, Paul (George Vincent O'Shaughnessy) 1903-1995 .... **CLC 9, 53; DAM NOV**
See also CA 13-16R; 147; CANR 9, 35; DLB
102; DLBY 85; INT CANR-9; MTCW; SATA
13; SATA-Obit 84
Horn, Peter
See Kuttner, Henry
Hornem, Horace Esq.
See Byron, George Gordon (Noel)
Horney, Karen (Clementine Theodore Danielsen) 1885-1952 .... **TCLC 71**
See also CA 114; 165
Hornung, E(rnest) W(illiam) 1866-1921 **TCLC 59**
See also CA 108; 160; DLB 70
Horovitz, Israel (Arthur) 1939- ..... **CLC 56; DAM DRAM**
See also CA 33-36R; CANR 46, 59; DLB 7
Horvath, Odon von
See Horvath, Oedoen von
See also DLB 85, 124
Horvath, Oedoen von 1901-1938 .... **TCLC 45**
See also Horvath, Odon von
See also CA 118
Horwitz, Julius 1920-1986 .... **CLC 14**
See also CA 9-12R; 119; CANR 12
Hospital, Janette Turner 1942- .... **CLC 42**
See also CA 108; CANR 48
Hostos, E. M. de
See Hostos (y Bonilla), Eugenio Maria de
Hostos, Eugenio M. de
See Hostos (y Bonilla), Eugenio Maria de
Hostos, Eugenio Maria
See Hostos (y Bonilla), Eugenio Maria de
Hostos (y Bonilla), Eugenio Maria de 1839-1903 **TCLC 24**
See also CA 123; 131; HW
Houdini
See Lovecraft, H(oward) P(hillips)
Hougan, Carolyn 1943- .... **CLC 34**
See also CA 139
Household, Geoffrey (Edward West) 1900-1988 **CLC 11**
See also CA 77-80; 126; CANR 58; DLB 87;
SATA 14; SATA-Obit 59
Housman, A(lfred) E(dward) 1859-1936 **TCLC 1, 10; DA; DAB; DAC; DAM MST, POET; PC 2; WLCS**
See also CA 104; 125; DLB 19; MTCW
Housman, Laurence 1865-1959 .... **TCLC 7**
See also CA 106; 155; DLB 10; SATA 25
Howard, Elizabeth Jane 1923- .... **CLC 7, 29**
See also CA 5-8R; CANR 8, 62
Howard, Maureen 1930-......... **CLC 5, 14, 46**
See also CA 53-56; CANR 31; DLBY 83; INT
CANR-31; MTCW

Kastel, Warren
See Silverberg, Robert
Kataev, Evgeny Petrovich 1903-1942
See Petrov, Evgeny
See also CA 120
Kataphusin
See Ruskin, John
Katz, Steve 1935- .... **CLC 47**
See also CA 25-28R; CAAS 14, 64; CANR 12;
DLBY 83
Kauffman, Janet 1945- .... **CLC 42**
See also CA 117; CANR 43; DLBY 86
Kaufman, Bob (Garnell) 1925-1986 ..**CLC 49**
See also BW 1; CA 41-44R; 118; CANR 22; DLB
16, 41
Kaufman, George S. 1889-1961 ..... **CLC 38;**
DAM DRAM
See also CA 108; 93-96; DLB 7; INT 108
Kaufman, Sue .... **CLC 3, 8**
See also Barondess, Sue K(aufman)
Kavafis, Konstantinos Petrou 1863-1933
See Cavafy, C(onstantine) P(eter)
See also CA 104
Kavan, Anna 1901-1968 .... **CLC 5, 13, 82**
See also CA 5-8R; CANR 6, 57; MTCW
Kavanagh, Dan
See Barnes, Julian (Patrick)
Kavanagh, Patrick (Joseph) 1904-1967...**CLC**
22
See also CA 123; 25-28R; DLB 15, 20; MTCW
Kawabata, Yasunari 1899-1972... **CLC 2, 5,**
9, 18, 107; DAM MULT; SSC 17
See also CA 93-96; 33-36R; DLB 180
Kaye, M(ary) M(argaret) 1909- .... **CLC 28**
See also CA 89-92; CANR 24, 60; MTCW; SATA
62
Kaye, Mollie
See Kaye, M(ary) M(argaret)
Kaye-Smith, Sheila 1887-1956 .... **TCLC 20**
See also CA 118; DLB 36
Kaymor, Patrice Maguilene
See Senghor, Leopold Sedar
Kazan, Elia 1909- .... **CLC 6, 16, 63**
See also CA 21-24R; CANR 32
Kazantzakis, Nikos 1883(?)-1957...**TCLC 2, 5,**
33
See also CA 105; 132; MTCW
Kazin, Alfred 1915- .... **CLC 34, 38**
See also CA 1-4R; CAAS 7; CANR 1, 45; DLB 67
Keane, Mary Nesta (Skrine) 1904-1996
See Keane, Molly
See also CA 108; 114; 151
Keane, Molly .... **CLC 31**
See also Keane, Mary Nesta (Skrine)
See also INT 114
Keates, Jonathan 1946(?)- .... **CLC 34**
See also CA 163
Keaton, Buster 1895-1966 .... **CLC 20**
Keats, John 1795-1821 .. **NCLC 8; DA; DAB;**
DAC; DAM MST, POET; PC 1; WLC
See also CDBLB 1789-1832; DLB 96, 110
Keene, Donald 1922- .... **CLC 34**
See also CA 1-4R; CANR 5
Keillor, Garrison .... **CLC 40**
See also Keillor, Gary (Edward)
See also AAYA 2; BEST 89:3; DLBY 87; SATA
58
Keillor, Gary (Edward) 1942-
See Keillor, Garrison
See also CA 111; 117; CANR 36, 59; DAM POP;
MTCW
Keith, Michael
See Hubbard, L(afayette) Ron(ald)

Keller, Gottfried 1819-1890...**NCLC 2; SSC 26**
See also DLB 129
Keller, Nora Okja .... **CLC 109**
Kellerman, Jonathan 1949- ...**CLC 44; DAM**
POP
See also BEST 90:1; CA 106; CANR 29, 51; INT
CANR-29
Kelley, William Melvin 1937- .... **CLC 22**
See also BW 1; CA 77-80; CANR 27; DLB 33
Kellogg, Marjorie 1922- .... **CLC 2**
See also CA 81-84
Kellow, Kathleen
See Hibbert, Eleanor Alice Burford
Kelly, M(ilton) T(erry) 1947- .... **CLC 55**
See also CA 97-100; CAAS 22; CANR 19, 43
Kelman, James 1946- .... **CLC 58, 86**
See also CA 148; DLB 194
Kemal, Yashar 1923- .... **CLC 14, 29**
See also CA 89-92; CANR 44
Kemble, Fanny 1809-1893 .... **NCLC 18**
See also DLB 32
Kemelman, Harry 1908-1996 .... **CLC 2**
See also AITN 1; CA 9-12R; 155; CANR 6; DLB
28
Kempe, Margery 1373(?)-1440(?) .... **LC 6**
See also DLB 146
Kempis, Thomas a 1380-1471 .... **LC 11**
Kendall, Henry 1839-1882 .... **NCLC 12**
Keneally, Thomas (Michael) 1935-...**CLC 5, 8,**
10, 14, 19, 27, 43; DAM NOV
See also CA 85-88; CANR 10, 50; MTCW
Kennedy, Adrienne (Lita) 1931- .... **CLC 66;**
BLC 2; DAM MULT; DC 5
See also BW 2; CA 103; CAAS 20; CABS 3;
CANR 26, 53; DLB 38
Kennedy, John Pendleton 1795-1870...**NCLC 2**
See also DLB 3
Kennedy, Joseph Charles 1929-
See Kennedy, X. J.
See also CA 1-4R; CANR 4, 30, 40; SATA 14,
86
Kennedy, William 1928-.... **CLC 6, 28, 34, 53;**
DAM NOV
See also AAYA 1; CA 85-88; CANR 14, 31; DLB
143; DLBY 85; INT CANR-31; MTCW;
SATA 57
Kennedy, X. J. .... **CLC 8, 42**
See also Kennedy, Joseph Charles
See also CAAS 9; CLR 27; DLB 5; SAAS 22
Kenny, Maurice (Francis) 1929- ..... **CLC 87;**
DAM MULT
See also CA 144; CAAS 22; DLB 175; NNAL
Kent, Kelvin
See Kuttner, Henry
Kenton, Maxwell
See Southern, Terry
Kenyon, Robert O.
See Kuttner, Henry
Kepler, Johannes 1571-1630 .... **LC 45**
Kerouac, Jack .... **CLC 1, 2, 3, 5, 14, 29, 61**
See also Kerouac, Jean-Louis Lebris de
See also AAYA 25; CDALB 1941-1968; DLB 2,
16; DLBD 3; DLBY 95
Kerouac, Jean-Louis Lebris de 1922-1969
See Kerouac, Jack
See also AITN 1; CA 5-8R; 25-28R; CANR 26,
54; DA; DAB; DAC; DAM MST, NOV,
POET, POP; MTCW; WLC
Kerr, Jean 1923- .... **CLC 22**
See also CA 5-8R; CANR 7; INT CANR-7
Kerr, M. E. .... **CLC 12, 35**
See also Meaker, Marijane (Agnes)
See also AAYA 2, 23; CLR 29; SAAS 1

Kerr, Robert .... **CLC 55**
Kerrigan, (Thomas) Anthony 1918-...**CLC 4, 6**
See also CA 49-52; CAAS 11; CANR 4
Kerry, Lois
See Duncan, Lois
Kesey, Ken (Elton) 1935-...**CLC 1, 3, 6, 11, 46,**
64; DA; DAB; DAC; DAM MST, NOV,
POP; WLC
See also AAYA 25; CA 1-4R; CANR 22, 38, 66;
CDALB 1968-1988; DLB 2, 16; MTCW;
SATA 66
Kesselring, Joseph (Otto) 1902-1967...**CLC 45;**
DAM DRAM, MST
See also CA 150
Kessler, Jascha (Frederick) 1929- .... **CLC 4**
See also CA 17-20R; CANR 8, 48
Kettelkamp, Larry (Dale) 1933-...........**CLC 12**
See also CA 29-32R; CANR 16; SAAS 3; SATA 2
Key, Ellen 1849-1926 .... **TCLC 65**
Keyber, Conny
See Fielding, Henry
Keyes, Daniel 1927- .... **CLC 80; DA; DAC;**
DAM MST, NOV
See also AAYA 23; CA 17-20R; CANR 10, 26,
54; SATA 37
Keynes, John Maynard 1883-1946...**TCLC 64**
See also CA 114; 162, 163; DLBD 10
Khanshendel, Chiron
See Rose, Wendy
Khayyam, Omar 1048-1131...**CMLC 11; DAM**
POET; PC 8
Kherdian, David 1931- .... **CLC 6, 9**
See also CA 21-24R; CAAS 2; CANR 39; CLR
24; JRDA; MAICYA; SATA 16, 74
Khlebnikov, Velimir .... **TCLC 20**
See also Khlebnikov, Viktor Vladimirovich
Khlebnikov, Viktor Vladimirovich 1885-1922
See Khlebnikov, Velimir
See also CA 117
Khodasevich, Vladislav (Felitsianovich) 1886-
1939 .... **TCLC 15**
See also CA 115
Kielland, Alexander Lange 1849-1906...**TCLC 5**
See also CA 104
Kiely, Benedict 1919- .... **CLC 23, 43**
See also CA 1-4R; CANR 2; DLB 15
Kienzle, William X(avier) 1928- ..... **CLC 25;**
DAM POP
See also CA 93-96; CAAS 1; CANR 9, 31, 59;
INT CANR-31; MTCW
Kierkegaard, Soren 1813-1855 .... **NCLC 34**
Killens, John Oliver 1916-1987 .... **CLC 10**
See also BW 2; CA 77-80; 123; CAAS 2; CANR
26; DLB 33
Killigrew, Anne 1660-1685 .... **LC 4**
See also DLB 131
Kim
See Simenon, Georges (Jacques Christian)
Kincaid, Jamaica 1949-.. **CLC 43, 68; BLC 2;**
DAM MULT, NOV
See also AAYA 13; BW 2; CA 125; CANR 47,
59; DLB 157
King, Francis (Henry) 1923- .... **CLC 8, 53;**
DAM NOV
See also CA 1-4R; CANR 1, 33; DLB 15, 139;
MTCW
King, Kennedy
See Brown, George Douglas
King, Martin Luther, Jr. 1929-1968...**CLC 83;**
BLC 2; DA; DAB; DAC; DAM MST,
MULT; WLCS
See also BW 2; CA 25-28; CANR 27, 44; CAP
2; MTCW; SATA 14

King, Stephen (Edwin) 1947-...**CLC 12, 26, 37, 61, 113; DAM NOV, POP; SSC 17**
See also AAYA 1, 17; BEST 90:1; CA 61-64; CANR 1, 30, 52; DLB 143; DLBY 80; JRDA; MTCW; SATA 9, 55

King, Steve
See King, Stephen (Edwin)

King, Thomas 1943- ..... **CLC 89; DAC; DAM MULT**
See also CA 144; DLB 175; NNAL; SATA 96

Kingman, Lee .... **CLC 17**
See also Natti, (Mary) Lee
See also SAAS 3; SATA 1, 67

Kingsley, Charles 1819-1875 .... **NCLC 35**
See also DLB 21, 32, 163, 190; YABC 2

Kingsley, Sidney 1906-1995 .... **CLC 44**
See also CA 85-88; 147; DLB 7

Kingsolver, Barbara 1955- ..... **CLC 55, 81; DAM POP**
See also AAYA 15; CA 129; 134; CANR 60; INT 134

Kingston, Maxine (Ting Ting) Hong 1940-
CLC 12, 19, 58; DAM MULT, NOV; WLCS
See also AAYA 8; CA 69-72; CANR 13, 38; DLB 173; DLBY 80; INT CANR-13; MTCW; SATA 53

Kinnell, Galway 1927- ... **CLC 1, 2, 3, 5, 13, 29**
See also CA 9-12R; CANR 10, 34, 66; DLB 5; DLBY 87; INT CANR-34; MTCW

Kinsella, Thomas 1928- .... **CLC 4, 19**
See also CA 17-20R; CANR 15; DLB 27; MTCW

Kinsella, W(illiam) P(atrick) 1935-...**CLC 27, 43; DAC; DAM NOV, POP**
See also AAYA 7; CA 97-100; CAAS 7; CANR 21, 35, 66; INT CANR-21; MTCW

Kipling, (Joseph) Rudyard 1865-1936...**TCLC 8, 17; DA; DAB; DAC; DAM MST, POET; PC 3; SSC 5; WLC**
See also CA 105; 120; CANR 33; CDBLB 1890-1914; CLR 39; DLB 19, 34, 141, 156; MAICYA; MTCW; YABC 2

Kirkup, James 1918- .... **CLC 1**
See also CA 1-4R; CAAS 4; CANR 2; DLB 27; SATA 12

Kirkwood, James 1930(?)-1989 .... **CLC 9**
See also AITN 2; CA 1-4R; 128; CANR 6, 40

Kirshner, Sidney
See Kingsley, Sidney

Kis, Danilo 1935-1989 .... **CLC 57**
See also CA 109; 118; 129; CANR 61; DLB 181; MTCW

Kivi, Aleksis 1834-1872 .... **NCLC 30**

Kizer, Carolyn (Ashley) 1925-...**CLC 15, 39, 80; DAM POET**
See also CA 65-68; CAAS 5; CANR 24; DLB 5, 169

Klabund 1890-1928 .... **TCLC 44**
See also CA 162; DLB 66

Klappert, Peter 1942- .... **CLC 57**
See also CA 33-36R; DLB 5

Klein, A(braham) M(oses) 1909-1972...**C L C 19; DAB; DAC; DAM MST**
See also CA 101; 37-40R; DLB 68

Klein, Norma 1938-1989 .... **CLC 30**
See also AAYA 2; CA 41-44R; 128; CANR 15, 37; CLR 2, 19; INT CANR-15; JRDA; MAICYA; SAAS 1; SATA 7, 57

Klein, T(heodore) E(ibon) D(onald) 1947-
CLC 34
See also CA 119; CANR 44

Kleist, Heinrich von 1777-1811. **NCLC 2, 37; DAM DRAM; SSC 22**
See also DLB 90

Klima, Ivan 1931- .... **CLC 56; DAM NOV**
See also CA 25-28R; CANR 17, 50

Klimentov, Andrei Platonovich 1899-1951
See Platonov, Andrei
See also CA 108

Klinger, Friedrich Maximilian von 1752-1831
NCLC 1
See also DLB 94

Klingsor the Magician
See Hartmann, Sadakichi

Klopstock, Friedrich Gottlieb 1724-1803
NCLC 11
See also DLB 97

Knapp, Caroline 1959- .... **CLC 99**
See also CA 154

Knebel, Fletcher 1911-1993 .... **CLC 14**
See also AITN 1; CA 1-4R; 140; CAAS 3; CANR 1, 36; SATA 36; SATA-Obit 75

Knickerbocker, Diedrich
See Irving, Washington

Knight, Etheridge 1931-1991...**CLC 40; BLC 2; DAM POET; PC 14**
See also BW 1; CA 21-24R; 133; CANR 23; DLB 41

Knight, Sarah Kemble 1666-1727 .... **LC 7**
See also DLB 24, 200

Knister, Raymond 1899-1932 .... **TCLC 56**
See also DLB 68

Knowles, John 1926- ... **CLC 1, 4, 10, 26; DA; DAC; DAM MST, NOV**
See also AAYA 10; CA 17-20R; CANR 40; CDALB 1968-1988; DLB 6; MTCW; SATA 8, 89

Knox, Calvin M.
See Silverberg, Robert

Knox, John c. 1505-1572 .... **LC 37**
See also DLB 132

Knye, Cassandra
See Disch, Thomas M(ichael)

Koch, C(hristopher) J(ohn) 1932- ..... **CLC 42**
See also CA 127

Koch, Christopher
See Koch, C(hristopher) J(ohn)

Koch, Kenneth 1925- .... **CLC 5, 8, 44; DAM POET**
See also CA 1-4R; CANR 6, 36, 57; DLB 5; INT CANR-36; SATA 65

Kochanowski, Jan 1530-1584 .... **LC 10**

Kock, Charles Paul de 1794-1871 ... **NCLC 16**

Koda Shigeyuki 1867-1947
See Rohan, Koda
See also CA 121

Koestler, Arthur 1905-1983...**CLC 1, 3, 6, 8, 15, 33**
See also CA 1-4R; 109; CANR 1, 33; CDBLB 1945-1960; DLBY 83; MTCW

Kogawa, Joy Nozomi 1935- .... **CLC 78; DAC; DAM MST, MULT**
See also CA 101; CANR 19, 62

Kohout, Pavel 1928- .... **CLC 13**
See also CA 45-48; CANR 3

Koizumi, Yakumo
See Hearn, (Patricio) Lafcadio (Tessima Carlos)

Kolmar, Gertrud 1894-1943 .... **TCLC 40**

Komunyakaa, Yusef 1947-...**CLC 86, 94; BLCS**
See also CA 147; DLB 120

Konrad, George
See Konrad, Gyoergy

Konrad, Gyoergy 1933- .... **CLC 4, 10, 73**
See also CA 85-88

Konwicki, Tadeusz 1926- .... **CLC 8, 28, 54**
See also CA 101; CAAS 9; CANR 39, 59; MTCW

Koontz, Dean R(ay) 1945- .....**CLC 78; DAM NOV, POP**
See also AAYA 9; BEST 89:3, 90:2; CA 108; CANR 19, 36, 52; MTCW; SATA 92

Kopernik, Mikolaj
See Copernicus, Nicolaus

Kopit, Arthur (Lee) 1937- ... **CLC 1, 18, 33; DAM DRAM**
See also AITN 1; CA 81-84; CABS 3; DLB 7; MTCW

Kops, Bernard 1926- .... **CLC 4**
See also CA 5-8R; DLB 13

Kornbluth, C(yril) M. 1923-1958 ..... **TCLC 8**
See also CA 105; 160; DLB 8

Korolenko, V. G.
See Korolenko, Vladimir Galaktionovich

Korolenko, Vladimir
See Korolenko, Vladimir Galaktionovich

Korolenko, Vladimir G.
See Korolenko, Vladimir Galaktionovich

Korolenko, Vladimir Galaktionovich 1853-1921
TCLC 22
See also CA 121

Korzybski, Alfred (Habdank Skarbek) 1879-1950 .... **TCLC 61**
See also CA 123; 160

Kosinski, Jerzy (Nikodem) 1933-1991...**C L C 1, 2, 3, 6, 10, 15, 53, 70; DAM NOV**
See also CA 17-20R; 134; CANR 9, 46; DLB 2; DLBY 82; MTCW

Kostelanetz, Richard (Cory) 1940- .... **CLC 28**
See also CA 13-16R; CAAS 8; CANR 38

Kostrowitzki, Wilhelm Apollinaris de 1880-1918
See Apollinaire, Guillaume
See also CA 104

Kotlowitz, Robert 1924- .... **CLC 4**
See also CA 33-36R; CANR 36

Kotzebue, August (Friedrich Ferdinand) von 1761-1819 .... **NCLC 25**
See also DLB 94

Kotzwinkle, William 1938-........**CLC 5, 14, 35**
See also CA 45-48; CANR 3, 44; CLR 6; DLB 173; MAICYA; SATA 24, 70

Kowna, Stancy
See Szymborska, Wislawa

Kozol, Jonathan 1936- .... **CLC 17**
See also CA 61-64; CANR 16, 45

Kozoll, Michael 1940(?)- .... **CLC 35**

Kramer, Kathryn 19(?)- .... **CLC 34**

Kramer, Larry 1935-...**CLC 42; DAM POP; DC 8**
See also CA 124; 126; CANR 60

Krasicki, Ignacy 1735-1801 .... **NCLC 8**

Krasinski, Zygmunt 1812-1859 .... **NCLC 4**

Kraus, Karl 1874-1936 .... **TCLC 5**
See also CA 104; DLB 118

Kreve (Mickevicius), Vincas 1882-1954
TCLC 27

Kristeva, Julia 1941- .... **CLC 77**
See also CA 154

Kristofferson, Kris 1936- .... **CLC 26**
See also CA 104

Krizanc, John 1956- .... **CLC 57**

Krleza, Miroslav 1893-1981 .... **CLC 8**
See also CA 97-100; 105; CANR 50; DLB 147

Kroetsch, Robert 1927- ..... **CLC 5, 23, 57; DAC; DAM POET**
See also CA 17-20R; CANR 8, 38; DLB 53; MTCW

Kroetz, Franz
See Kroetz, Franz Xaver

Kroetz, Franz Xaver 1946- .... **CLC 41**
See also CA 130**

Lyre, Pinchbeck
See Sassoon, Siegfried (Lorraine)
Lytle, Andrew (Nelson) 1902-1995 ..... **CLC 22**
See also CA 9-12R; 150; DLB 6; DLBY 95
Lyttelton, George 1709-1773 .... **LC 10**
Maas, Peter 1929- .... **CLC 29**
See also CA 93-96; INT 93-96
Macaulay, Rose 1881-1958 .... **TCLC 7, 44**
See also CA 104; DLB 36
Macaulay, Thomas Babington 1800-1859
NCLC 42
See also CDBLB 1832-1890; DLB 32, 55
MacBeth, George (Mann) 1932-1992...**CLC 2,
5, 9**
See also CA 25-28R; 136; CANR 61, 66; DLB
40; MTCW; SATA 4; SATA-Obit 70
MacCaig, Norman (Alexander) 1910-...**C L C
36; DAB; DAM POET**
See also CA 9-12R; CANR 3, 34; DLB 27
MacCarthy, (Sir Charles Otto) Desmond 1877-
1952 .... **TCLC 36**
MacDiarmid, Hugh...**CLC 2, 4, 11, 19, 63; PC 9**
See also Grieve, C(hristopher) M(urray)
See also CDBLB 1945-1960; DLB 20
MacDonald, Anson
See Heinlein, Robert A(nson)
Macdonald, Cynthia 1928- .... **CLC 13, 19**
See also CA 49-52; CANR 4, 44; DLB 105
MacDonald, George 1824-1905 .... **TCLC 9**
See also CA 106; 137; DLB 18, 163, 178;
MAICYA; SATA 33
Macdonald, John
See Millar, Kenneth
MacDonald, John D(ann) 1916-1986...**CLC 3,
27, 44; DAM NOV, POP**
See also CA 1-4R; 121; CANR 1, 19, 60; DLB
8; DLBY 86; MTCW
Macdonald, John Ross
See Millar, Kenneth
Macdonald, Ross .... **CLC 1, 2, 3, 14, 34, 41**
See also Millar, Kenneth
See also DLBD 6
MacDougal, John
See Blish, James (Benjamin)
MacEwen, Gwendolyn (Margaret) 1941-1987
CLC 13, 55
See also CA 9-12R; 124; CANR 7, 22; DLB 53;
SATA 50; SATA-Obit 55
Macha, Karel Hynek 1810-1846 ..... **NCLC 46**
Machado (y Ruiz), Antonio 1875-1939
TCLC 3
See also CA 104; DLB 108
Machado de Assis, Joaquim Maria 1839-1908
TCLC 10; BLC 2; SSC 24
See also CA 107; 153
Machen, Arthur .... **TCLC 4; SSC 20**
See also Jones, Arthur Llewellyn
See also DLB 36, 156, 178
Machiavelli, Niccolo 1469-1527 . **LC 8, 36;
DA; DAB; DAC; DAM MST; WLCS**
MacInnes, Colin 1914-1976........... **CLC 4, 23**
See also CA 69-72; 65-68; CANR 21; DLB 14;
MTCW
MacInnes, Helen (Clark) 1907-1985...**CLC 27,
39; DAM POP**
See also CA 1-4R; 117; CANR 1, 28, 58; DLB
87; MTCW; SATA 22; SATA-Obit 44
Mackay, Mary 1855-1924
See Corelli, Marie
See also CA 118
Mackenzie, Compton (Edward Montague) 1883-
1972 .... **CLC 18**
See also CA 21-22; 37-40R; CAP 2; DLB 34, 100

Mackenzie, Henry 1745-1831 .... **NCLC 41**
See also DLB 39
Mackintosh, Elizabeth 1896(?)-1952
See Tey, Josephine
See also CA 110
MacLaren, James
See Grieve, C(hristopher) M(urray)
Mac Laverty, Bernard 1942- .... **CLC 31**
See also CA 116; 118; CANR 43; INT 118
MacLean, Alistair (Stuart) 1922(?)-1987
CLC 3, 13, 50, 63; DAM POP
See also CA 57-60; 121; CANR 28, 61; MTCW;
SATA 23; SATA-Obit 50
Maclean, Norman (Fitzroy) 1902-1990 ..**C L C
78; DAM POP; SSC 13**
See also CA 102; 132; CANR 49
MacLeish, Archibald 1892-1982...**CLC 3, 8,
14, 68; DAM POET**
See also CA 9-12R; 106; CANR 33, 63; DLB 4,
7, 45; DLBY 82; MTCW
MacLennan, (John) Hugh 1907-1990...**CLC 2,
14, 92; DAC; DAM MST**
See also CA 5-8R; 142; CANR 33; DLB 68;
MTCW
MacLeod, Alistair 1936- .... **CLC 56; DAC;
DAM MST**
See also CA 123; DLB 60
Macleod, Fiona
See Sharp, William
MacNeice, (Frederick) Louis 1907-1963...**CLC
1, 4, 10, 53; DAB; DAM POET**
See also CA 85-88; CANR 61; DLB 10, 20;
MTCW
MacNeill, Dand
See Fraser, George MacDonald
Macpherson, James 1736-1796 .... **LC 29**
See also Ossian
See also DLB 109
Macpherson, (Jean) Jay 1931- .... **CLC 14**
See also CA 5-8R; DLB 53
MacShane, Frank 1927- .... **CLC 39**
See also CA 9-12R; CANR 3, 33; DLB 111
Macumber, Mari
See Sandoz, Mari(e Susette)
Madach, Imre 1823-1864 .... **NCLC 19**
Madden, (Jerry) David 1933- .... **CLC 5, 15**
See also CA 1-4R; CAAS 3; CANR 4, 45; DLB
6; MTCW
Maddern, Al(an)
See Ellison, Harlan (Jay)
Madhubuti, Haki R. 1942- .... **CLC 6, 73;
BLC 2; DAM MULT, POET; PC 5**
See also Lee, Don L.
See also BW 2; CA 73-76; CANR 24, 51; DLB
5, 41; DLBD 8
Maepenn, Hugh
See Kuttner, Henry
Maepenn, K. H.
See Kuttner, Henry
Maeterlinck, Maurice 1862-1949..... **TCLC 3;
DAM DRAM**
See also CA 104; 136; DLB 192; SATA 66
Maginn, William 1794-1842 .... **NCLC 8**
See also DLB 110, 159
Mahapatra, Jayanta 1928- .... **CLC 33; DAM
MULT**
See also CA 73-76; CAAS 9; CANR 15, 33, 66
Mahfouz, Naguib (Abdel Aziz Al-Sabilgi)
1911(?)-
See Mahfuz, Najib
See also BEST 89:2; CA 128; CANR 55; DAM
NOV; MTCW

Mahfuz, Najib .... **CLC 52, 55**
See also Mahfouz, Naguib (Abdel Aziz Al-
Sabilgi)
See also DLBY 88
Mahon, Derek 1941- .... **CLC 27**
See also CA 113; 128; DLB 40
Mailer, Norman 1923-...**CLC 1, 2, 3, 4, 5, 8,
11, 14, 28, 39, 74, 111; DA; DAB; DAC;
DAM MST, NOV, POP**
See also AITN 2; CA 9-12R; CABS 1; CANR
28; CDALB 1968-1988; DLB 2, 16, 28, 185;
DLBD 3; DLBY 80, 83; MTCW
Maillet, Antonine 1929- .... **CLC 54; DAC**
See also CA 115; 120; CANR 46; DLB 60; INT
120
Mais, Roger 1905-1955 .... **TCLC 8**
See also BW 1; CA 105; 124; DLB 125; MTCW
Maistre, Joseph de 1753-1821 .... **NCLC 37**
Maitland, Frederic 1850-1906 .... **TCLC 65**
Maitland, Sara (Louise) 1950-............ **CLC 49**
See also CA 69-72; CANR 13, 59
Major, Clarence 1936-...**CLC 3, 19, 48; BLC
2; DAM MULT**
See also BW 2; CA 21-24R; CAAS 6; CANR
13, 25, 53; DLB 33
Major, Kevin (Gerald) 1949- ... **CLC 26; DAC**
See also AAYA 16; CA 97-100; CANR 21, 38;
CLR 11; DLB 60; INT CANR-21; JRDA;
MAICYA; SATA 32, 82
Maki, James
See Ozu, Yasujiro
Malabaila, Damiano
See Levi, Primo
Malamud, Bernard 1914-1986...**CLC 1, 2, 3, 5,
8, 9, 11, 18, 27, 44, 78, 85; DA; DAB; DAC;
DAM MST, NOV, POP; SSC 15; WLC**
See also AAYA 16; CA 5-8R; 118; CABS 1;
CANR 28, 62; CDALB 1941-1968; DLB 2,
28, 152; DLBY 80, 86; MTCW
Malan, Herman
See Bosman, Herman Charles; Bosman, Herman
Charles
Malaparte, Curzio 1898-1957 .... **TCLC 52**
Malcolm, Dan
See Silverberg, Robert
Malcolm X .... **CLC 82; BLC 2; WLCS**
See also Little, Malcolm
Malherbe, Francois de 1555-1628 .... **LC 5**
Mallarme, Stephane 1842-1898 ..**NCLC 4,
41; DAM POET; PC 4**
Mallet-Joris, Francoise 1930- .... **CLC 11**
See also CA 65-68; CANR 17; DLB 83
Malley, Ern
See McAuley, James Phillip
Mallowan, Agatha Christie
See Christie, Agatha (Mary Clarissa)
Maloff, Saul 1922- .... **CLC 5**
See also CA 33-36R
Malone, Louis
See MacNeice, (Frederick) Louis
Malone, Michael (Christopher) 1942-..**CLC 43**
See also CA 77-80; CANR 14, 32, 57
Malory, (Sir) Thomas 1410(?)-1471(?). **L C
11; DA; DAB; DAC; DAM MST; WLCS**
See also CDBLB Before 1660; DLB 146; SATA
59; SATA-Brief 33
Malouf, (George Joseph) David 1934- ..**C L C
28, 86**
See also CA 124; CANR 50
Malraux, (Georges-)Andre 1901-1976...**CLC 1,
4, 9, 13, 15, 57; DAM NOV**
See also CA 21-22; 69-72; CANR 34, 58; CAP
2; DLB 72; MTCW

McLoughlin, R. B.
See Mencken, H(enry) L(ouis)
McLuhan, (Herbert) Marshall 1911-1980**CLC 37, 83**
See also CA 9-12R; 102; CANR 12, 34, 61; DLB 88; INT CANR-12; MTCW
McMillan, Terry (L.) 1951- **CLC 50, 61, 112; BLCS; DAM MULT, NOV, POP**
See also AAYA 21; BW 2; CA 140; CANR 60
McMurtry, Larry (Jeff) 1936-**CLC 2, 3, 7, 11, 27, 44; DAM NOV, POP**
See also AAYA 15; AITN 2; BEST 89:2; CA 5-8R; CANR 19, 43, 64; CDALB 1968-1988; DLB 2, 143; DLBY 80, 87; MTCW
McNally, T. M. 1961- ....**CLC 82**
McNally, Terrence 1939-**CLC 4, 7, 41, 91; DAM DRAM**
See also CA 45-48; CANR 2, 56; DLB 7
McNamer, Deirdre 1950- ....**CLC 70**
McNeile, Herman Cyril 1888-1937
See Sapper
See also DLB 77
McNickle, (William) D'Arcy 1904-1977 . **C L C 89; DAM MULT**
See also CA 9-12R; 85-88; CANR 5, 45; DLB 175; NNAL; SATA-Obit 22
McPhee, John (Angus) 1931- ....**CLC 36**
See also BEST 90:1; CA 65-68; CANR 20, 46, 64, 69; DLB 185; MTCW
McPherson, James Alan 1943- ... **CLC 19, 77; BLCS**
See also BW 1; CA 25-28R; CAAS 17; CANR 24; DLB 38; MTCW
McPherson, William (Alexander) 1933- . **C L C 34**
See also CA 69-72; CANR 28; INT CANR-28
Mead, Margaret 1901-1978 ....**CLC 37**
See also AITN 1; CA 1-4R; 81-84; CANR 4; MTCW; SATA-Obit 20
Meaker, Marijane (Agnes) 1927-
See Kerr, M. E.
See also CA 107; CANR 37, 63; INT 107; JRDA; MAICYA; MTCW; SATA 20, 61
Medoff, Mark (Howard) 1940- .... **CLC 6, 23; DAM DRAM**
See also AITN 1; CA 53-56; CANR 5; DLB 7; INT CANR-5
Medvedev, P. N.
See Bakhtin, Mikhail Mikhailovich
Meged, Aharon
See Megged, Aharon
Meged, Aron
See Megged, Aharon
Megged, Aharon 1920- ....**CLC 9**
See also CA 49-52; CAAS 13; CANR 1
Mehta, Ved (Parkash) 1934- ....**CLC 37**
See also CA 1-4R; CANR 2, 23, 69; MTCW
Melanter
See Blackmore, R(ichard) D(oddridge)
Melies, Georges 1861-1938 ....**TCLC 81**
Melikow, Loris
See Hofmannsthal, Hugo von
Melmoth, Sebastian
See Wilde, Oscar (Fingal O'Flahertie Wills)
Meltzer, Milton 1915- ....**CLC 26**
See also AAYA 8; CA 13-16R; CANR 38; CLR 13; DLB 61; JRDA; MAICYA; SAAS 1; SATA 1, 50, 80
Melville, Herman 1819-1891 **NCLC 3, 12, 29, 45, 49; DA; DAB; DAC; DAM MST, NOV; SSC 1, 17; WLC**
See also AAYA 25; CDALB 1640-1865; DLB 3, 74; SATA 59

Menander c. 342B.C.-c. 292B.C. ......**CMLC 9; DAM DRAM; DC 3**
See also DLB 176
Mencken, H(enry) L(ouis) 1880-1956...**TCLC 13**
See also CA 105; 125; CDALB 1917-1929; DLB 11, 29, 63, 137; MTCW
Mendelsohn, Jane 1965(?)- ....**CLC 99**
See also CA 154
Mercer, David 1928-1980 ....**CLC 5; DAM DRAM**
See also CA 9-12R; 102; CANR 23; DLB 13; MTCW
Merchant, Paul
See Ellison, Harlan (Jay)
Meredith, George 1828-1909 ... **TCLC 17, 43; DAM POET**
See also CA 117; 153; CDBLB 1832-1890; DLB 18, 35, 57, 159
Meredith, William (Morris) 1919-...**CLC 4, 13, 22, 55; DAM POET**
See also CA 9-12R; CAAS 14; CANR 6, 40; DLB 5
Merezhkovsky, Dmitry Sergeyevich 1865-1941 **TCLC 29**
Merimee, Prosper 1803-1870 ... **NCLC 6, 65; SSC 7**
See also DLB 119, 192
Merkin, Daphne 1954- ....**CLC 44**
See also CA 123
Merlin, Arthur
See Blish, James (Benjamin)
Merrill, James (Ingram) 1926-1995...**CLC 2, 3, 6, 8, 13, 18, 34, 91; DAM POET**
See also CA 13-16R; 147; CANR 10, 49, 63; DLB 5, 165; DLBY 85; INT CANR-10; MTCW
Merriman, Alex
See Silverberg, Robert
Merriman, Brian 1747-1805 ....**NCLC 70**
Merritt, E. B.
See Waddington, Miriam
Merton, Thomas 1915-1968...**CLC 1, 3, 11, 34, 83; PC 10**
See also CA 5-8R; 25-28R; CANR 22, 53; DLB 48; DLBY 81; MTCW
Merwin, W(illiam) S(tanley) 1927-...**CLC 1, 2, 3, 5, 8, 13, 18, 45, 88; DAM POET**
See also CA 13-16R; CANR 15, 51; DLB 5, 169; INT CANR-15; MTCW
Metcalf, John 1938- ....**CLC 37**
See also CA 113; DLB 60
Metcalf, Suzanne
See Baum, L(yman) Frank
Mew, Charlotte (Mary) 1870-1928 ... **TCLC 8**
See also CA 105; DLB 19, 135
Mewshaw, Michael 1943- ....**CLC 9**
See also CA 53-56; CANR 7, 47; DLBY 80
Meyer, June
See Jordan, June
Meyer, Lynn
See Slavitt, David R(ytman)
Meyer-Meyrink, Gustav 1868-1932
See Meyrink, Gustav
See also CA 117
Meyers, Jeffrey 1939- ....**CLC 39**
See also CA 73-76; CANR 54; DLB 111
Meynell, Alice (Christina Gertrude Thompson) 1847-1922 ....**TCLC 6**
See also CA 104; DLB 19, 98
Meyrink, Gustav ....**TCLC 21**
See also Meyer-Meyrink, Gustav
See also DLB 81

Michaels, Leonard 1933-...**CLC 6, 25; SSC 16**
See also CA 61-64; CANR 21, 62; DLB 130; MTCW
Michaux, Henri 1899-1984 ....**CLC 8, 19**
See also CA 85-88; 114
Micheaux, Oscar 1884-1951 ....**TCLC 76**
See also DLB 50
Michelangelo 1475-1564 ....**LC 12**
Michelet, Jules 1798-1874 ....**NCLC 31**
Michener, James A(lbert) 1907(?)-1997 **CLC 1, 5, 11, 29, 60, 109; DAM NOV, POP**
See also AITN 1; BEST 90:1; CA 5-8R; 161; CANR 21, 45, 68; DLB 6; MTCW
Mickiewicz, Adam 1798-1855 ....**NCLC 3**
Middleton, Christopher 1926- ....**CLC 13**
See also CA 13-16R; CANR 29, 54; DLB 40
Middleton, Richard (Barham) 1882-1911 **TCLC 56**
See also DLB 156
Middleton, Stanley 1919- ....**CLC 7, 38**
See also CA 25-28R; CAAS 23; CANR 21, 46; DLB 14
Middleton, Thomas 1580-1627 . **LC 33; DAM DRAM, MST; DC 5**
See also DLB 58
Migueis, Jose Rodrigues 1901- ....**CLC 10**
Mikszath, Kalman 1847-1910 ....**TCLC 31**
Miles, Jack ....**CLC 100**
Miles, Josephine (Louise) 1911-1985...**CLC 1, 2, 14, 34, 39; DAM POET**
See also CA 1-4R; 116; CANR 2, 55; DLB 48
Militant
See Sandburg, Carl (August)
Mill, John Stuart 1806-1873 ..... **NCLC 11, 58**
See also CDBLB 1832-1890; DLB 55, 190
Millar, Kenneth 1915-1983 ....**CLC 14; DAM POP**
See also Macdonald, Ross
See also CA 9-12R; 110; CANR 16, 63; DLB 2; DLBD 6; DLBY 83; MTCW
Millay, E. Vincent
See Millay, Edna St. Vincent
Millay, Edna St. Vincent 1892-1950...**TCLC 4, 49; DA; DAB; DAC; DAM MST, POET; PC 6; WLCS**
See also CA 104; 130; CDALB 1917-1929; DLB 45; MTCW
Miller, Arthur 1915-...**CLC 1, 2, 6, 10, 15, 26, 47, 78; DA; DAB; DAC; DAM DRAM, MST; DC 1; WLC**
See also AAYA 15; AITN 1; CA 1-4R; CABS 3; CANR 2, 30, 54; CDALB 1941-1968; DLB 7; MTCW
Miller, Henry (Valentine) 1891-1980...**CLC 1, 2, 4, 9, 14, 43, 84; DA; DAB; DAC; DAM MST, NOV; WLC**
See also CA 9-12R; 97-100; CANR 33, 64; CDALB 1929-1941; DLB 4, 9; DLBY 80; MTCW
Miller, Jason 1939(?)- ....**CLC 2**
See also AITN 1; CA 73-76; DLB 7
Miller, Sue 1943- ....**CLC 44; DAM POP**
See also BEST 90:3; CA 139; CANR 59; DLB 143
Miller, Walter M(ichael, Jr.) 1923-...**CLC 4, 30**
See also CA 85-88; DLB 8
Millett, Kate 1934- ....**CLC 67**
See also AITN 1; CA 73-76; CANR 32, 53; MTCW
Millhauser, Steven (Lewis) 1943-...**CLC 21, 54, 109**
See also CA 110; 111; CANR 63; DLB 2; INT 111

Millin, Sarah Gertrude 1889-1968 ..... **CLC 49**
See also CA 102; 93-96

Milne, A(lan) A(lexander) 1882-1956
TCLC 6; DAB; DAC; DAM MST
See also CA 104; 133; CLR 1, 26; DLB 10, 77,
100, 160; MAICYA; MTCW; YABC 1

Milner, Ron(ald) 1938- .... **CLC 56; BLC 3;**
DAM MULT
See also AITN 1; BW 1; CA 73-76; CANR 24;
DLB 38; MTCW

Milnes, Richard Monckton 1809-1885...**NCLC**
61
See also DLB 32, 184

Milosz, Czeslaw 1911-...**CLC 5, 11, 22, 31,**
56, 82; DAM MST, POET; PC 8; WLCS
See also CA 81-84; CANR 23, 51; MTCW

Milton, John 1608-1674 ..... **LC 9, 43; DA;**
DAB; DAC; DAM MST, POET; PC 19;
WLC
See also CDBLB 1660-1789; DLB 131, 151

Min, Anchee 1957- ....**CLC 86**
See also CA 146

Minehaha, Cornelius
See Wedekind, (Benjamin) Frank(lin)

Miner, Valerie 1947-...........................**CLC 40**
See also CA 97-100; CANR 59

Minimo, Duca
See D'Annunzio, Gabriele

Minot, Susan 1956- ....**CLC 44**
See also CA 134

Minus, Ed 1938- ....**CLC 39**

Miranda, Javier
See Bioy Casares, Adolfo

Mirbeau, Octave 1848-1917 .... **TCLC 55**
See also DLB 123, 192

Miro (Ferrer), Gabriel (Francisco Victor) 1879-
1930 .... **TCLC 5**
See also CA 104

Mishima, Yukio 1925-1970 .... **DC 1; SSC 4**
See also Hiraoka, Kimitake
See also DLB 182

Mistral, Frederic 1830-1914 .... **TCLC 51**
See also CA 122

Mistral, Gabriela .... **TCLC 2; HLC**
See also Godoy Alcayaga, Lucila

Mistry, Rohinton 1952-............. **CLC 71; DAC**
See also CA 141

Mitchell, Clyde
See Ellison, Harlan (Jay); Silverberg, Robert

Mitchell, James Leslie 1901-1935
See Gibbon, Lewis Grassic
See also CA 104; DLB 15

Mitchell, Joni 1943- ....**CLC 12**
See also CA 112

Mitchell, Joseph (Quincy) 1908-1996...**CLC 98**
See also CA 77-80; 152; CANR 69; DLB 185;
DLBY 96

Mitchell, Margaret (Munnerlyn) 1900-1949
TCLC 11; DAM NOV, POP
See also AAYA 23; CA 109; 125; CANR 55; DLB
9; MTCW

Mitchell, Peggy
See Mitchell, Margaret (Munnerlyn)

Mitchell, S(ilas) Weir 1829-1914 ..... **TCLC 36**
See also CA 165

Mitchell, W(illiam) O(rmond) 1914-1998
CLC 25; DAC; DAM MST
See also CA 77-80; 165; CANR 15, 43; DLB 88

Mitchell, William 1879-1936 .... **TCLC 81**

Mitford, Mary Russell 1787-1855 .... **NCLC 4**
See also DLB 110, 116

Mitford, Nancy 1904-1973 .... **CLC 44**
See also CA 9-12R; DLB 191

Miyamoto, Yuriko 1899-1951 .... **TCLC 37**
See also DLB 180

Miyazawa, Kenji 1896-1933 .... **TCLC 76**
See also CA 157

Mizoguchi, Kenji 1898-1956 .... **TCLC 72**

Mo, Timothy (Peter) 1950(?)- .... **CLC 46**
See also CA 117; DLB 194; MTCW

Modarressi, Taghi (M.) 1931- .... **CLC 44**
See also CA 121; 134; INT 134

Modiano, Patrick (Jean) 1945-........... **CLC 18**
See also CA 85-88; CANR 17, 40; DLB 83

Moerck, Paal
See Roelvaag, O(le) E(dvart)

Mofolo, Thomas (Mokopu) 1875(?)-1948
TCLC 22; BLC 3; DAM MULT
See also CA 121; 153

Mohr, Nicholasa 1938- .... **CLC 12; DAM**
MULT; HLC
See also AAYA 8; CA 49-52; CANR 1, 32, 64;
CLR 22; DLB 145; HW; JRDA; SAAS 8;
SATA 8, 97

Mojtabai, A(nn) G(race) 1938-... **CLC 5, 9,**
15, 29
See also CA 85-88

Moliere 1622-1673 .. **LC 28; DA; DAB; DAC;**
DAM DRAM, MST; WLC

Molin, Charles
See Mayne, William (James Carter)

Molnar, Ferenc 1878-1952 .. **TCLC 20; DAM**
DRAM
See also CA 109; 153

Momaday, N(avarre) Scott 1934-...**CLC 2, 19,**
85, 95; DA; DAB; DAC; DAM MST,
MULT, NOV, POP; WLCS
See also AAYA 11; CA 25-28R; CANR 14, 34,
68; DLB 143, 175; INT CANR-14; MTCW;
NNAL; SATA 48; SATA-Brief 30

Monette, Paul 1945-1995 .... **CLC 82**
See also CA 139; 147

Monroe, Harriet 1860-1936 .... **TCLC 12**
See also CA 109; DLB 54, 91

Monroe, Lyle
See Heinlein, Robert A(nson)

Montagu, Elizabeth 1917- .... **NCLC 7**
See also CA 9-12R

Montagu, Mary (Pierrepont) Wortley 1689-1762
LC 9; PC 16
See also DLB 95, 101

Montagu, W. H.
See Coleridge, Samuel Taylor

Montague, John (Patrick) 1929- ..**CLC 13, 46**
See also CA 9-12R; CANR 9, 69; DLB 40;
MTCW

Montaigne, Michel (Eyquem) de 1533-1592
LC 8; DA; DAB; DAC; DAM MST; WLC

Montale, Eugenio 1896-1981...**CLC 7, 9, 18;**
PC 13
See also CA 17-20R; 104; CANR 30; DLB 114;
MTCW

Montesquieu, Charles-Louis de Secondat 1689-
1755 ....**LC 7**

Montgomery, (Robert) Bruce 1921-1978
See Crispin, Edmund
See also CA 104

Montgomery, L(ucy) M(aud) 1874-1942
TCLC 51; DAC; DAM MST
See also AAYA 12; CA 108; 137; CLR 8; DLB
92; DLBD 14; JRDA; MAICYA; YABC 1

Montgomery, Marion H., Jr. 1925-...... **CLC 7**
See also AITN 1; CA 1-4R; CANR 3, 48; DLB
6

Montgomery, Max
See Davenport, Guy (Mattison, Jr.)

Montherlant, Henry (Milon) de 1896-1972
CLC 8, 19; DAM DRAM
See also CA 85-88; 37-40R; DLB 72; MTCW

Monty Python
See Chapman, Graham; Cleese, John (Marwood);
Gilliam, Terry (Vance); Idle, Eric; Jones,
Terence Graham Parry; Palin, Michael (Edward)
See also AAYA 7

Moodie, Susanna (Strickland) 1803-1885
NCLC 14
See also DLB 99

Mooney, Edward 1951-
See Mooney, Ted
See also CA 130

Mooney, Ted ....**CLC 25**
See also Mooney, Edward

Moorcock, Michael (John) 1939-...**CLC 5, 27,**
58
See also CA 45-48; CAAS 5; CANR 2, 17, 38,
64; DLB 14; MTCW; SATA 93

Moore, Brian 1921-...**CLC 1, 3, 5, 7, 8, 19, 32,**
90; DAB; DAC; DAM MST
See also CA 1-4R; CANR 1, 25, 42, 63; MTCW

Moore, Edward
See Muir, Edwin

Moore, George Augustus 1852-1933...**TCLC 7;**
SSC 19
See also CA 104; DLB 10, 18, 57, 135

Moore, Lorrie ....**CLC 39, 45, 68**
See also Moore, Marie Lorena

Moore, Marianne (Craig) 1887-1972...**CLC 1,**
2, 4, 8, 10, 13, 19, 47; DA; DAB; DAC; DAM
MST, POET; PC 4; WLCS
See also CA 1-4R; 33-36R; CANR 3, 61; CDALB
1929-1941; DLB 45; DLBD 7; MTCW; SATA
20

Moore, Marie Lorena 1957-
See Moore, Lorrie
See also CA 116; CANR 39

Moore, Thomas 1779-1852 .... **NCLC 6**
See also DLB 96, 144

Morand, Paul 1888-1976 ..... **CLC 41; SSC 22**
See also CA 69-72; DLB 65

Morante, Elsa 1918-1985................**CLC 8, 47**
See also CA 85-88; 117; CANR 35; DLB 177;
MTCW

Moravia, Alberto 1907-1990...**CLC 2, 7, 11, 27,**
46; SSC 26
See also Pincherle, Alberto
See also DLB 177

More, Hannah 1745-1833 .... **NCLC 27**
See also DLB 107, 109, 116, 158

More, Henry 1614-1687 ....**LC 9**
See also DLB 126

More, Sir Thomas 1478-1535 .... **LC 10, 32**

Moreas, Jean ....**TCLC 18**
See also Papadiamantopoulos, Johannes

Morgan, Berry 1919- ....**CLC 6**
See also CA 49-52; DLB 6

Morgan, Claire
See Highsmith, (Mary) Patricia

Morgan, Edwin (George) 1920- ....**CLC 31**
See also CA 5-8R; CANR 3, 43; DLB 27

Morgan, (George) Frederick 1922- ... **CLC 23**
See also CA 17-20R; CANR 21

Morgan, Harriet
See Mencken, H(enry) L(ouis)

Morgan, Jane
See Cooper, James Fenimore

Morgan, Janet 1945-...........................**CLC 39**
See also CA 65-68

Morgan, Lady 1776(?)-1859 .... **NCLC 29**
See also DLB 116, 158

Osborne, John (James) 1929-1994... **CLC 1, 2, 5, 11, 45; DA; DAB; DAC; DAM DRAM, MST; WLC**
    See also CA 13-16R; 147; CANR 21, 56; CDBLB 1945-1960; DLB 13; MTCW
Osborne, Lawrence 1958- .... **CLC 50**
Oshima, Nagisa 1932- .... **CLC 20**
    See also CA 116; 121
Oskison, John Milton 1874-1947 ... **TCLC 35; DAM MULT**
    See also CA 144; DLB 175; NNAL
Ossian c. 3rd cent. - .... **CMLC 28**
    See also Macpherson, James
Ossoli, Sarah Margaret (Fuller marchesa d') 1810-1850
    See Fuller, Margaret
    See also SATA 25
Ostrovsky, Alexander 1823-1886... **NCLC 30, 57**
Otero, Blas de 1916-1979 .... **CLC 11**
    See also CA 89-92; DLB 134
Otto, Whitney 1955- .... **CLC 70**
    See also CA 140
Ouida .... **TCLC 43**
    See also De La Ramee, (Marie) Louise
    See also DLB 18, 156
Ousmane, Sembene 1923- ..... **CLC 66; BLC 3**
    See also BW 1; CA 117; 125; MTCW
Ovid 43B.C.-18(?)...**CMLC 7; DAM POET; PC 2**
Owen, Hugh
    See Faust, Frederick (Schiller)
Owen, Wilfred (Edward Salter) 1893-1918 **TCLC 5, 27; DA; DAB; DAC; DAM MST, POET; PC 19; WLC**
    See also CA 104; 141; CDBLB 1914-1945; DLB 20
Owens, Rochelle 1936- .... **CLC 8**
    See also CA 17-20R; CAAS 2; CANR 39
Oz, Amos 1939-.... **CLC 5, 8, 11, 27, 33, 54; DAM NOV**
    See also CA 53-56; CANR 27, 47, 65; MTCW
Ozick, Cynthia 1928-...**CLC 3, 7, 28, 62; DAM NOV, POP; SSC 15**
    See also BEST 90:1; CA 17-20R; CANR 23, 58; DLB 28, 152; DLBY 82; INT CANR-23; MTCW
Ozu, Yasujiro 1903-1963 .... **CLC 16**
    See also CA 112
Pacheco, C.
    See Pessoa, Fernando (Antonio Nogueira)
Pa Chin...**CLC 18**
    See also Li Fei-kan
Pack, Robert 1929-.............................**CLC 13**
    See also CA 1-4R; CANR 3, 44; DLB 5
Padgett, Lewis
    See Kuttner, Henry
Padilla (Lorenzo), Heberto 1932- ...... **CLC 38**
    See also AITN 1; CA 123; 131; HW
Page, Jimmy 1944- .... **CLC 12**
Page, Louise 1955- .... **CLC 40**
    See also CA 140
Page, P(atricia) K(athleen) 1916-...**CLC 7, 18; DAC; DAM MST; PC 12**
    See also CA 53-56; CANR 4, 22, 65; DLB 68; MTCW
Page, Thomas Nelson 1853-1922 .... **SSC 23**
    See also CA 118; DLB 12, 78; DLBD 13
Pagels, Elaine Hiesey 1943- .... **CLC 104**
    See also CA 45-48; CANR 2, 24, 51
Paget, Violet 1856-1935
    See Lee, Vernon
    See also CA 104; 166

Paget-Lowe, Henry
    See Lovecraft, H(oward) P(hillips)
Paglia, Camille (Anna) 1947- .... **CLC 68**
    See also CA 140
Paige, Richard
    See Koontz, Dean R(ay)
Paine, Thomas 1737-1809 .... **NCLC 62**
    See also CDALB 1640-1865; DLB 31, 43, 73, 158
Pakenham, Antonia
    See Fraser, (Lady) Antonia (Pakenham)
Palamas, Kostes 1859-1943 .... **TCLC 5**
    See also CA 105
Palazzeschi, Aldo 1885-1974 .... **CLC 11**
    See also CA 89-92; 53-56; DLB 114
Paley, Grace 1922-...**CLC 4, 6, 37; DAM POP; SSC 8**
    See also CA 25-28R; CANR 13, 46; DLB 28; INT CANR-13; MTCW
Palin, Michael (Edward) 1943- .... **CLC 21**
    See also Monty Python
    See also CA 107; CANR 35; SATA 67
Palliser, Charles 1947- .... **CLC 65**
    See also CA 136
Palma, Ricardo 1833-1919 .... **TCLC 29**
Pancake, Breece Dexter 1952-1979
    See Pancake, Breece D'J
    See also CA 123; 109
Pancake, Breece D'J .... **CLC 29**
    See also Pancake, Breece Dexter
    See also DLB 130
Panko, Rudy
    See Gogol, Nikolai (Vasilyevich)
Papadiamantis, Alexandros 1851-1911...**TCLC 29**
Papadiamantopoulos, Johannes 1856-1910
    See Moreas, Jean
    See also CA 117
Papini, Giovanni 1881-1956 .... **TCLC 22**
    See also CA 121
Paracelsus 1493-1541 .... **LC 14**
    See also DLB 179
Parasol, Peter
    See Stevens, Wallace
Pardo Bazán, Emilia 1851-1921 .... **SSC 30**
Pareto, Vilfredo 1848-1923 .... **TCLC 69**
Parfenie, Maria
    See Codrescu, Andrei
Parini, Jay (Lee) 1948-....................... **CLC 54**
    See also CA 97-100; CAAS 16; CANR 32
Park, Jordan
    See Kornbluth, C(yril) M.; Pohl, Frederik
Park, Robert E(zra) 1864-1944 .... **TCLC 73**
    See also CA 122; 165
Parker, Bert
    See Ellison, Harlan (Jay)
Parker, Dorothy (Rothschild) 1893-1967 **CLC 15, 68; DAM POET; SSC 2**
    See also CA 19-20; 25-28R; CAP 2; DLB 11, 45, 86; MTCW
Parker, Robert B(rown) 1932-...**CLC 27; DAM NOV, POP**
    See also BEST 89:4; CA 49-52; CANR 1, 26, 52; INT CANR-26; MTCW
Parkin, Frank 1940- .... **CLC 43**
    See also CA 147
Parkman, Francis, Jr. 1823-1893 .... **NCLC 12**
    See also DLB 1, 30, 186
Parks, Gordon (Alexander Buchanan) 1912- **CLC 1, 16; BLC 3; DAM MULT**
    See also AITN 2; BW 2; CA 41-44R; CANR 26, 66; DLB 33; SATA 8
Parmenides c. 515B.C.-c. 450B.C. .. **CMLC 22**
    See also DLB 176

Parnell, Thomas 1679-1718 .... **LC 3**
    See also DLB 94
Parra, Nicanor 1914- ...... **CLC 2, 102; DAM MULT; HLC**
    See also CA 85-88; CANR 32; HW; MTCW
Parrish, Mary Frances
    See Fisher, M(ary) F(rances) K(ennedy)
Parson
    See Coleridge, Samuel Taylor
Parson Lot
    See Kingsley, Charles
Partridge, Anthony
    See Oppenheim, E(dward) Phillips
Pascal, Blaise 1623-1662 .... **LC 35**
Pascoli, Giovanni 1855-1912 .... **TCLC 45**
Pasolini, Pier Paolo 1922-1975.. **CLC 20, 37, 106; PC 17**
    See also CA 93-96; 61-64; CANR 63; DLB 128, 177; MTCW
Pasquini
    See Silone, Ignazio
Pastan, Linda (Olenik) 1932-.. **CLC 27; DAM POET**
    See also CA 61-64; CANR 18, 40, 61; DLB 5
Pasternak, Boris (Leonidovich) 1890-1960 **CLC 7, 10, 18, 63; DA; DAB; DAC; DAM MST, NOV, POET; PC 6; SSC 31; WLC**
    See also CA 127; 116; MTCW
Patchen, Kenneth 1911-1972 .... **CLC 1, 2, 18; DAM POET**
    See also CA 1-4R; 33-36R; CANR 3, 35; DLB 16, 48; MTCW
Pater, Walter (Horatio) 1839-1894 ... **NCLC 7**
    See also CDBLB 1832-1890; DLB 57, 156
Paterson, A(ndrew) B(arton) 1864-1941 **TCLC 32**
    See also CA 155; SATA 97
Paterson, Katherine (Womeldorf) 1932-...**CLC 12, 30**
    See also AAYA 1; CA 21-24R; CANR 28, 59; CLR 7, 50; DLB 52; JRDA; MAICYA; MTCW; SATA 13, 53, 92
Patmore, Coventry Kersey Dighton 1823-1896 **NCLC 9**
    See also DLB 35, 98
Paton, Alan (Stewart) 1903-1988...**CLC 4, 10, 25, 55, 106; DA; DAB; DAC; DAM MST, NOV; WLC**
    See also CA 13-16; 125; CANR 22; CAP 1; MTCW; SATA 11; SATA-Obit 56
Paton Walsh, Gillian 1937-
    See Walsh, Jill Paton
    See also CANR 38; JRDA; MAICYA; SAAS 3; SATA 4, 72
Patton, George S. 1885-1945 .... **TCLC 79**
Paulding, James Kirke 1778-1860 .... **NCLC 2**
    See also DLB 3, 59, 74
Paulin, Thomas Neilson 1949-
    See Paulin, Tom
    See also CA 123; 128
Paulin, Tom .... **CLC 37**
    See also Paulin, Thomas Neilson
    See also DLB 40
Paustovsky, Konstantin (Georgievich) 1892-1968 .... **CLC 40**
    See also CA 93-96; 25-28R
Pavese, Cesare 1908-1950 ..**TCLC 3; PC 13; SSC 19**
    See also CA 104; DLB 128, 177
Pavic, Milorad 1929-........................... **CLC 60**
    See also CA 136; DLB 181
Payne, Alan
    See Jakes, John (William)

Pixerecourt, (Rene Charles) Guilbert de 1773-1844 .... **NCLC 39**
See also DLB 192
Plaatje, Sol(omon) T(shekisho) 1876-1932 **TCLC 73; BLCS**
See also BW 2; CA 141
Plaidy, Jean
See Hibbert, Eleanor Alice Burford
Planche, James Robinson 1796-1880...**NCLC 42**
Plant, Robert 1948- .... **CLC 12**
Plante, David (Robert) 1940- . **CLC 7, 23, 38; DAM NOV**
See also CA 37-40R; CANR 12, 36, 58; DLBY 83; INT CANR-12; MTCW
Plath, Sylvia 1932-1963...**CLC 1, 2, 3, 5, 9, 11, 14, 17, 50, 51, 62, 111; DA; DAB; DAC; DAM MST, POET; PC 1; WLC**
See also AAYA 13; CA 19-20; CANR 34; CAP 2; CDALB 1941-1968; DLB 5, 6, 152; MTCW; SATA 96
Plato 428(?)B.C.-348(?)B.C. .... **CMLC 8; DA; DAB; DAC; DAM MST; WLCS**
See also DLB 176
Platonov, Andrei .... **TCLC 14**
See also Klimentov, Andrei Platonovich
Platt, Kin 1911-................................. **CLC 26**
See also AAYA 11; CA 17-20R; CANR 11; JRDA; SAAS 17; SATA 21, 86
Plautus c. 251B.C.-184B.C. .. **CMLC 24; DC 6**
Plick et Plock
See Simenon, Georges (Jacques Christian)
Plimpton, George (Ames) 1927- .... **CLC 36**
See also AITN 1; CA 21-24R; CANR 32; DLB 185; MTCW; SATA 10
Pliny the Elder c. 23-79 .... **CMLC 23**
Plomer, William Charles Franklin 1903-1973 **CLC 4, 8**
See also CA 21-22; CANR 34; CAP 2; DLB 20, 162, 191; MTCW; SATA 24
Plowman, Piers
See Kavanagh, Patrick (Joseph)
Plum, J.
See Wodehouse, P(elham) G(renville)
Plumly, Stanley (Ross) 1939- .... **CLC 33**
See also CA 108; 110; DLB 5, 193; INT 110
Plumpe, Friedrich Wilhelm 1888-1931...**TCLC 53**
See also CA 112
Po Chu-i 772-846 .... **CMLC 24**
Poe, Edgar Allan 1809-1849...**NCLC 1, 16, 55; DA; DAB; DAC; DAM MST, POET; PC 1; SSC 1, 22; WLC**
See also AAYA 14; CDALB 1640-1865; DLB 3, 59, 73, 74; SATA 23
Poet of Titchfield Street, The
See Pound, Ezra (Weston Loomis)
Pohl, Frederick 1919- .... **CLC 18; SSC 25**
See also AAYA 24; CA 61-64; CAAS 1; CANR 11, 37; DLB 8; INT CANR-11; MTCW; SATA 24
Poirier, Louis 1910-
See Gracq, Julien
See also CA 122; 126
Poitier, Sidney 1927- .... **CLC 26**
See also BW 1; CA 117
Polanski, Roman 1933- .... **CLC 16**
See also CA 77-80
Poliakoff, Stephen 1952- .... **CLC 38**
See also CA 106; DLB 13
Police, The
See Copeland, Stewart (Armstrong); Summers, Andrew James; Sumner, Gordon Matthew
Polidori, John William 1795-1821 ..**NCLC 51**
See also DLB 116

Pollitt, Katha 1949- .... **CLC 28**
See also CA 120; 122; CANR 66; MTCW
Pollock, (Mary) Sharon 1936-...**CLC 50; DAC; DAM DRAM, MST**
See also CA 141; DLB 60
Polo, Marco 1254-1324 .... **CMLC 15**
Polonsky, Abraham (Lincoln) 1910-**CLC 92**
See also CA 104; DLB 26; INT 104
Polybius c. 200B.C.-c. 118B.C. .... **CMLC 17**
See also DLB 176
Pomerance, Bernard 1940-..... **CLC 13; DAM DRAM**
See also CA 101; CANR 49
Ponge, Francis (Jean Gaston Alfred) 1899-1988 **CLC 6, 18; DAM POET**
See also CA 85-88; 126; CANR 40
Pontoppidan, Henrik 1857-1943 ..... **TCLC 29**
Poole, Josephine .... **CLC 17**
See also Helyar, Jane Penelope Josephine
See also SAAS 2; SATA 5
Popa, Vasko 1922-1991 .... **CLC 19**
See also CA 112; 148; DLB 181
Pope, Alexander 1688-1744...**LC 3; DA; DAB; DAC; DAM MST, POET; WLC**
See also CDBLB 1660-1789; DLB 95, 101
Porter, Connie (Rose) 1959(?)- .... **CLC 70**
See also BW 2; CA 142; SATA 81
Porter, Gene(va Grace) Stratton 1863(?)-1924 **TCLC 21**
See also CA 112
Porter, Katherine Anne 1890-1980...**CLC 1, 3, 7, 10, 13, 15, 27, 101; DA; DAB; DAC; DAM MST, NOV; SSC 4, 31**
See also AITN 2; CA 1-4R; 101; CANR 1, 65; DLB 4, 9, 102; DLBD 12; DLBY 80; MTCW; SATA 39; SATA-Obit 23
Porter, Peter (Neville Frederick) 1929-...**C L C 5, 13, 33**
See also CA 85-88; DLB 40
Porter, William Sydney 1862-1910
See Henry, O.
See also CA 104; 131; CDALB 1865-1917; DA; DAB; DAC; DAM MST; DLB 12, 78, 79; MTCW; YABC 2
Portillo (y Pacheco), Jose Lopez
See Lopez Portillo (y Pacheco), Jose
Post, Melville Davisson 1869-1930 . **TCLC 39**
See also CA 110
Potok, Chaim 1929- .... **CLC 2, 7, 14, 26, 112; DAM NOV**
See also AAYA 15; AITN 1, 2; CA 17-20R; CANR 19, 35, 64; DLB 28, 152; INT CANR-19; MTCW; SATA 33
Potter, (Helen) Beatrix 1866-1943
See Webb, (Martha) Beatrice (Potter)
See also MAICYA
Potter, Dennis (Christopher George) 1935-1994 **CLC 58, 86**
See also CA 107; 145; CANR 33, 61; MTCW
Pound, Ezra (Weston Loomis) 1885-1972 **CLC 1, 2, 3, 4, 5, 7, 10, 13, 18, 34, 48, 50, 112; DA; DAB; DAC; DAM MST, POET; PC 4; WLC**
See also CA 5-8R; 37-40R; CANR 40; CDALB 1917-1929; DLB 4, 45, 63; DLBD 15; MTCW
Povod, Reinaldo 1959-1994 .... **CLC 44**
See also CA 136; 146
Powell, Adam Clayton, Jr. 1908-1972...**C L C 89; BLC 3; DAM MULT**
See also BW 1; CA 102; 33-36R

Powell, Anthony (Dymoke) 1905-...**CLC 1, 3, 7, 9, 10, 31**
See also CA 1-4R; CANR 1, 32, 62; CDBLB 1945-1960; DLB 15; MTCW
Powell, Dawn 1897-1965 .... **CLC 66**
See also CA 5-8R; DLBY 97
Powell, Padgett 1952- .... **CLC 34**
See also CA 126; CANR 63
Power, Susan 1961- .... **CLC 91**
Powers, J(ames) F(arl) 1917-...**CLC 1, 4, 8, 57; SSC 4**
See also CA 1-4R; CANR 2, 61; DLB 130; MTCW
Powers, John J(ames) 1945-
See Powers, John R.
See also CA 69-72
Powers, John R. .... **CLC 66**
See also Powers, John J(ames)
Powers, Richard (S.) 1957- .... **CLC 93**
See also CA 148
Pownall, David 1938- .... **CLC 10**
See also CA 89-92; CAAS 18; CANR 49; DLB 14
Powys, John Cowper 1872-1963...**CLC 7, 9, 15, 46**
See also CA 85-88; DLB 15; MTCW
Powys, T(heodore) F(rancis) 1875-1953 **TCLC 9**
See also CA 106; DLB 36, 162
Prado (Calvo), Pedro 1886-1952 ..... **TCLC 75**
See also CA 131; HW
Prager, Emily 1952- .... **CLC 56**
Pratt, E(dwin) J(ohn) 1883(?)-1964 . **CLC 19; DAC; DAM POET**
See also CA 141; 93-96; DLB 92
Premchand .... **TCLC 21**
See also Srivastava, Dhanpat Rai
Preussler, Otfried 1923- .... **CLC 17**
See also CA 77-80; SATA 24
Prevert, Jacques (Henri Marie) 1900-1977 **CLC 15**
See also CA 77-80; 69-72; CANR 29, 61; MTCW; SATA-Obit 30
Prevost, Abbe (Antoine Francois) 1697-1763 **LC 1**
Price, (Edward) Reynolds 1933-...**CLC 3, 6, 13, 43, 50, 63; DAM NOV; SSC 22**
See also CA 1-4R; CANR 1, 37, 57; DLB 2; INT CANR-37
Price, Richard 1949- .... **CLC 6, 12**
See also CA 49-52; CANR 3; DLBY 81
Prichard, Katharine Susannah 1883-1969 **CLC 46**
See also CA 11-12; CANR 33; CAP 1; MTCW; SATA 66
Priestley, J(ohn) B(oynton) 1894-1984...**CLC 2, 5, 9, 34; DAM DRAM, NOV**
See also CA 9-12R; 113; CANR 33; CDBLB 1914-1945; DLB 10, 34, 77, 100, 139; DLBY 84; MTCW
Prince 1958(?)- .... **CLC 35**
Prince, F(rank) T(empleton) 1912- .... **CLC 22**
See also CA 101; CANR 43; DLB 20
Prince Kropotkin
See Kropotkin, Peter (Alekseevich)
Prior, Matthew 1664-1721 .... **LC 4**
See also DLB 95
Prishvin, Mikhail 1873-1954 .... **TCLC 75**
Pritchard, William H(arrison) 1932-...**CLC 34**
See also CA 65-68; CANR 23; DLB 111
Pritchett, V(ictor) S(awdon) 1900-1997...**C L C 5, 13, 15, 41; DAM NOV; SSC 14**
See also CA 61-64; 157; CANR 31, 63; DLB 15, 139; MTCW

Rimbaud, (Jean Nicolas) Arthur 1854-1891
    NCLC 4, 35; DA; DAB; DAC; DAM MST,
    POET; PC 3; WLC
Rinehart, Mary Roberts 1876-1958...**TCLC 52**
    See also CA 108; 166
Ringmaster, The
    See Mencken, H(enry) L(ouis)
Ringwood, Gwen(dolyn Margaret) Pharis 1910-
    1984 .... **CLC 48**
    See also CA 148; 112; DLB 88
Rio, Michel 19(?)- .... **CLC 43**
Ritsos, Giannes
    See Ritsos, Yannis
Ritsos, Yannis 1909-1990 .... **CLC 6, 13, 31**
    See also CA 77-80; 133; CANR 39, 61; MTCW
Ritter, Erika 1948(?)- .... **CLC 52**
Rivera, Jose Eustasio 1889-1928 .... **TCLC 35**
    See also CA 162; HW
Rivers, Conrad Kent 1933-1968 .... **CLC 1**
    See also BW 1; CA 85-88; DLB 41
Rivers, Elfrida
    See Bradley, Marion Zimmer
Riverside, John
    See Heinlein, Robert A(nson)
Rizal, Jose 1861-1896 .... **NCLC 27**
Roa Bastos, Augusto (Antonio) 1917-...**C L C**
    45; DAM MULT; HLC
    See also CA 131; DLB 113; HW
Robbe-Grillet, Alain 1922-...**CLC 1, 2, 4, 6,**
    8, 10, 14, 43
    See also CA 9-12R; CANR 33, 65; DLB 83;
    MTCW
Robbins, Harold 1916-1997.....**CLC 5; DAM**
    NOV
    See also CA 73-76; 162; CANR 26, 54; MTCW
Robbins, Thomas Eugene 1936-
    See Robbins, Tom
    See also CA 81-84; CANR 29, 59; DAM NOV,
    POP; MTCW
Robbins, Tom .... **CLC 9, 32, 64**
    See also Robbins, Thomas Eugene
    See also BEST 90:3; DLBY 80
Robbins, Trina 1938- .... **CLC 21**
    See also CA 128
Roberts, Charles G(eorge) D(ouglas) 1860-1943
    TCLC 8
    See also CA 105; CLR 33; DLB 92; SATA 88;
    SATA-Brief 29
Roberts, Elizabeth Madox 1886-1941...**TCLC**
    68
    See also CA 111; 166; DLB 9, 54, 102; SATA
    33; SATA-Brief 27
Roberts, Kate 1891-1985 .... **CLC 15**
    See also CA 107; 116
Roberts, Keith (John Kingston) 1935-...**CLC 14**
    See also CA 25-28R; CANR 46
Roberts, Kenneth (Lewis) 1885-1957... **T C L C**
    23
    See also CA 109; DLB 9
Roberts, Michele (B.) 1949- .... **CLC 48**
    See also CA 115; CANR 58
Robertson, Ellis
    See Ellison, Harlan (Jay); Silverberg, Robert
Robertson, Thomas William 1829-1871
    NCLC 35; DAM DRAM
Robeson, Kenneth
    See Dent, Lester
Robinson, Edwin Arlington 1869-1935...**TCLC**
    5; DA; DAC; DAM MST, POET; PC 1
    See also CA 104; 133; CDALB 1865-1917; DLB
    54; MTCW
Robinson, Henry Crabb 1775-1867...**NCLC 15**
    See also DLB 107

Robinson, Jill 1936- .... **CLC 10**
    See also CA 102; INT 102
Robinson, Kim Stanley 1952- .... **CLC 34**
    See also CA 126
Robinson, Lloyd
    See Silverberg, Robert
Robinson, Marilynne 1944- .... **CLC 25**
    See also CA 116
Robinson, Smokey .... **CLC 21**
    See also Robinson, William, Jr.
Robinson, William, Jr. 1940-
    See Robinson, Smokey
    See also CA 116
Robison, Mary 1949- .... **CLC 42, 98**
    See also CA 113; 116; DLB 130; INT 116
Rod, Edouard 1857-1910 .... **TCLC 52**
Roddenberry, Eugene Wesley 1921-1991
    See Roddenberry, Gene
    See also CA 110; 135; CANR 37; SATA 45;
    SATA-Obit 69
Roddenberry, Gene ....**CLC 17**
    See also Roddenberry, Eugene Wesley
    See also AAYA 5; SATA-Obit 69
Rodgers, Mary 1931- .... **CLC 12**
    See also CA 49-52; CANR 8, 55; CLR 20; INT
    CANR-8; JRDA; MAICYA; SATA 8
Rodgers, W(illiam) R(obert) 1909-1969...**C L C**
    7
    See also CA 85-88; DLB 20
Rodman, Eric
    See Silverberg, Robert
Rodman, Howard 1920(?)-1985 .... **CLC 65**
    See also CA 118
Rodman, Maia
    See Wojciechowska, Maia (Teresa)
Rodriguez, Claudio 1934- .... **CLC 10**
    See also DLB 134
Roelvaag, O(le) E(dvart) 1876-1931...**TCLC 17**
    See also CA 117; DLB 9
Roethke, Theodore (Huebner) 1908-1963
    CLC 1, 3, 8, 11, 19, 46, 101; DAM POET;
    PC 15
    See also CA 81-84; CABS 2; CDALB 1941-
    1968; DLB 5; MTCW
Rogers, Samuel 1763-1855 .... **NCLC 69**
    See also DLB 93
Rogers, Thomas Hunton 1927- .... **CLC 57**
    See also CA 89-92; INT 89-92
Rogers, Will(iam Penn Adair) 1879-1935
    TCLC 8, 71; DAM MULT
    See also CA 105; 144; DLB 11; NNAL
Rogin, Gilbert 1929- .... **CLC 18**
    See also CA 65-68; CANR 15
Rohan, Koda .... **TCLC 22**
    See also Koda Shigeyuki
Rohlfs, Anna Katharine Green
    See Green, Anna Katharine
Rohmer, Eric .... **CLC 16**
    See also Scherer, Jean-Marie Maurice
Rohmer, Sax .... **TCLC 28**
    See also Ward, Arthur Henry Sarsfield
    See also DLB 70
Roiphe, Anne (Richardson) 1935-.... **CLC 3, 9**
    See also CA 89-92; CANR 45; DLBY 80; INT
    89-92
Rojas, Fernando de 1465-1541 .... **LC 23**
Rolfe, Frederick (William Serafino Austin Lewis
    Mary) 1860-1913 .... **TCLC 12**
    See also CA 107; DLB 34, 156
Rolland, Romain 1866-1944 .... **TCLC 23**
    See also CA 118; DLB 65
Rolle, Richard c. 1300-c. 1349 .... **CMLC 21**
    See also DLB 146

Rolvaag, O(le) E(dvart)
    See Roelvaag, O(le) E(dvart)
Romain Arnaud, Saint
    See Aragon, Louis
Romains, Jules 1885-1972 .... **CLC 7**
    See also CA 85-88; CANR 34; DLB 65; MTCW
Romero, Jose Ruben 1890-1952 ..... **TCLC 14**
    See also CA 114; 131; HW
Ronsard, Pierre de 1524-1585 .... **LC 6; PC 11**
Rooke, Leon 1934- ... **CLC 25, 34; DAM POP**
    See also CA 25-28R; CANR 23, 53
Roosevelt, Theodore 1858-1919 ...... **TCLC 69**
    See also CA 115; DLB 47, 186
Roper, William 1498-1578 .... **LC 10**
Roquelaure, A. N.
    See Rice, Anne
Rosa, Joao Guimaraes 1908-1967 ...... **CLC 23**
    See also CA 89-92; DLB 113
Rose, Wendy 1948-...**CLC 85; DAM MULT;**
    PC 13
    See also CA 53-56; CANR 5, 51; DLB 175;
    NNAL; SATA 12
Rosen, R. D.
    See Rosen, Richard (Dean)
Rosen, Richard (Dean) 1949- .... **CLC 39**
    See also CA 77-80; CANR 62; INT CANR-30
Rosenberg, Isaac 1890-1918 .... **TCLC 12**
    See also CA 107; DLB 20
Rosenblatt, Joe .... **CLC 15**
    See also Rosenblatt, Joseph
Rosenblatt, Joseph 1933-
    See Rosenblatt, Joe
    See also CA 89-92; INT 89-92
Rosenfeld, Samuel
    See Tzara, Tristan
Rosenstock, Sami
    See Tzara, Tristan
Rosenstock, Samuel
    See Tzara, Tristan
Rosenthal, M(acha) L(ouis) 1917-1996...**C L C**
    28
    See also CA 1-4R; 152; CAAS 6; CANR 4, 51;
    DLB 5; SATA 59
Ross, Barnaby
    See Dannay, Frederic
Ross, Bernard L.
    See Follett, Ken(neth Martin)
Ross, J. H.
    See Lawrence, T(homas) E(dward)
Ross, Martin
    See Martin, Violet Florence
    See also DLB 135
Ross, (James) Sinclair 1908- ..**CLC 13; DAC;**
    DAM MST; SSC 24
    See also CA 73-76; DLB 88
Rossetti, Christina (Georgina) 1830-1894
    NCLC 2, 50, 66; DA; DAB; DAC; DAM
    MST, POET; PC 7; WLC
    See also DLB 35, 163; MAICYA; SATA 20
Rossetti, Dante Gabriel 1828-1882 . **NCLC 4;**
    DA; DAB; DAC; DAM MST, POET; WLC
    See also CDBLB 1832-1890; DLB 35
Rossner, Judith (Perelman) 1935-...**CLC 6, 9, 29**
    See also AITN 2; BEST 90:3; CA 17-20R;
    CANR 18, 51; DLB 6; INT CANR-18;
    MTCW
Rostand, Edmond (Eugene Alexis) 1868-1918
    TCLC 6, 37; DA; DAB; DAC; DAM
    DRAM, MST
    See also CA 104; 126; DLB 192; MTCW
Roth, Henry 1906-1995 ...... **CLC 2, 6, 11, 104**
    See also CA 11-12; 149; CANR 38, 63; CAP 1;
    DLB 28; MTCW

Shelley, Mary Wollstonecraft (Godwin) 1797-
1851 ... **NCLC 14, 59; DA; DAB; DAC;
DAM MST, NOV; WLC**
See also AAYA 20; CDBLB 1789-1832; DLB
110, 116, 159, 178; SATA 29
Shelley, Percy Bysshe 1792-1822 ... **NCLC 18;
DA; DAB; DAC; DAM MST, POET; PC 14;
WLC**
See also CDBLB 1789-1832; DLB 96, 110, 158
Shepard, Jim 1956- .... **CLC 36**
See also CA 137; CANR 59; SATA 90
Shepard, Lucius 1947- .... **CLC 34**
See also CA 128; 141
Shepard, Sam 1943-...**CLC 4, 6, 17, 34, 41, 44;
DAM DRAM; DC 5**
See also AAYA 1; CA 69-72; CABS 3; CANR
22; DLB 7; MTCW
Shepherd, Michael
See Ludlum, Robert
Sherburne, Zoa (Morin) 1912- .... **CLC 30**
See also AAYA 13; CA 1-4R; CANR 3, 37;
MAICYA; SAAS 18; SATA 3
Sheridan, Frances 1724-1766 .... **LC 7**
See also DLB 39, 84
Sheridan, Richard Brinsley 1751-1816
**NCLC 5; DA; DAB; DAC; DAM DRAM,
MST; DC 1; WLC**
See also CDBLB 1660-1789; DLB 89
Sherman, Jonathan Marc .... **CLC 55**
Sherman, Martin 1941(?)- .... **CLC 19**
See also CA 116; 123
Sherwin, Judith Johnson 1936- ...... **CLC 7, 15**
See also CA 25-28R; CANR 34
Sherwood, Frances 1940- .... **CLC 81**
See also CA 146
Sherwood, Robert E(mmet) 1896-1955 **T C L C
3; DAM DRAM**
See also CA 104; 153; DLB 7, 26
Shestov, Lev 1866-1938 .... **TCLC 56**
Shevchenko, Taras 1814-1861 .... **NCLC 54**
Shiel, M(atthew) P(hipps) 1865-1947...**TCLC 8**
See also Holmes, Gordon
See also CA 106; 160; DLB 153
Shields, Carol 1935- .... **CLC 91, 113; DAC**
See also CA 81-84; CANR 51
Shields, David 1956- .... **CLC 97**
See also CA 124; CANR 48
Shiga, Naoya 1883-1971 .... **CLC 33; SSC 23**
See also CA 101; 33-36R; DLB 180
Shilts, Randy 1951-1994 .... **CLC 85**
See also AAYA 19; CA 115; 127; 144; CANR
45; INT 127
Shimazaki, Haruki 1872-1943
See Shimazaki Toson
See also CA 105; 134
Shimazaki Toson 1872-1943 .... **TCLC 5**
See also Shimazaki, Haruki
See also DLB 180
Sholokhov, Mikhail (Aleksandrovich) 1905-1984
CLC 7, 15
See also CA 101; 112; MTCW; SATA-Obit 36
Shone, Patric
See Hanley, James
Shreve, Susan Richards 1939- .... **CLC 23**
See also CA 49-52; CAAS 5; CANR 5, 38, 69;
MAICYA; SATA 46, 95; SATA-Brief 41
Shue, Larry 1946-1985...**CLC 52; DAM DRAM**
See also CA 145; 117
Shu-Jen, Chou 1881-1936
See Lu Hsun
See also CA 104
Shulman, Alix Kates 1932- .... **CLC 2, 10**
See also CA 29-32R; CANR 43; SATA 7

Shuster, Joe 1914- .... **CLC 21**
Shute, Nevil .... **CLC 30**
See also Norway, Nevil Shute
Shuttle, Penelope (Diane) 1947- .... **CLC 7**
See also CA 93-96; CANR 39; DLB 14, 40
Sidney, Mary 1561-1621 .... **LC 19, 39**
Sidney, Sir Philip 1554-1586.. **LC 19, 39; DA;
DAB; DAC; DAM MST, POET**
See also CDBLB Before 1660; DLB 167
Siegel, Jerome 1914-1996 .... **CLC 21**
See also CA 116; 151
Siegel, Jerry
See Siegel, Jerome
Sienkiewicz, Henryk (Adam Alexander Pius)
1846-1916 .... **TCLC 3**
See also CA 104; 134
Sierra, Gregorio Martinez
See Martinez Sierra, Gregorio
Sierra, Maria (de la O'LeJarraga) Martinez
See Martinez Sierra, Maria (de la O'LeJarraga)
Sigal, Clancy 1926- .... **CLC 7**
See also CA 1-4R
Sigourney, Lydia Howard (Huntley) 1791-1865
NCLC 21
See also DLB 1, 42, 73
Siguenza y Gongora, Carlos de 1645-1700
LC 8
Sigurjonsson, Johann 1880-1919 .... **TCLC 27**
Sikelianos, Angelos 1884-1951 .... **TCLC 39**
Silkin, Jon 1930- .... **CLC 2, 6, 43**
See also CA 5-8R; CAAS 5; DLB 27
Silko, Leslie (Marmon) 1948-.. **CLC 23, 74;
DA; DAC; DAM MST, MULT, POP;
WLCS**
See also AAYA 14; CA 115; 122; CANR 45, 65;
DLB 143, 175; NNAL
Sillanpaa, Frans Eemil 1888-1964 ..... **CLC 19**
See also CA 129; 93-96; MTCW
Sillitoe, Alan 1928- ...... **CLC 1, 3, 6, 10, 19, 57**
See also AITN 1; CA 9-12R; CAAS 2; CANR 8,
26, 55; CDBLB 1960 to Present; DLB 14, 139;
MTCW; SATA 61
Silone, Ignazio 1900-1978 .... **CLC 4**
See also CA 25-28; 81-84; CANR 34; CAP 2;
MTCW
Silver, Joan Micklin 1935- .... **CLC 20**
See also CA 114; 121; INT 121
Silver, Nicholas
See Faust, Frederick (Schiller)
Silverberg, Robert 1935-...**CLC 7; DAM POP**
See also AAYA 24; CA 1-4R; CAAS 3; CANR 1,
20, 36; DLB 8; INT CANR-20; MAICYA;
MTCW; SATA 13, 91
Silverstein, Alvin 1933- .... **CLC 17**
See also CA 49-52; CANR 2; CLR 25; JRDA;
MAICYA; SATA 8, 69
Silverstein, Virginia B(arbara Opshelor) 1937-
CLC 17
See also CA 49-52; CANR 2; CLR 25; JRDA;
MAICYA; SATA 8, 69
Sim, Georges
See Simenon, Georges (Jacques Christian)
Simak, Clifford D(onald) 1904-1988..**CLC 1, 55**
See also CA 1-4R; 125; CANR 1, 35; DLB 8;
MTCW; SATA-Obit 56
Simenon, Georges (Jacques Christian) 1903-
1989 ... **CLC 1, 2, 3, 8, 18, 47; DAM POP**
See also CA 85-88; 129; CANR 35; DLB 72;
DLBY 89; MTCW
Simic, Charles 1938- ... **CLC 6, 9, 22, 49, 68;
DAM POET**
See also CA 29-32R; CAAS 4; CANR 12, 33,
52, 61; DLB 105

Simmel, Georg 1858-1918 .... **TCLC 64**
See also CA 157
Simmons, Charles (Paul) 1924- .... **CLC 57**
See also CA 89-92; INT 89-92
Simmons, Dan 1948- ...... **CLC 44; DAM POP**
See also AAYA 16; CA 138; CANR 53
Simmons, James (Stewart Alexander) 1933-
CLC 43
See also CA 105; CAAS 21; DLB 40
Simms, William Gilmore 1806-1870...**NCLC 3**
See also DLB 3, 30, 59, 73
Simon, Carly 1945-............................. **CLC 26**
See also CA 105
Simon, Claude 1913-1984 ... **CLC 4, 9, 15, 39;
DAM NOV**
See also CA 89-92; CANR 33; DLB 83; MTCW
Simon, (Marvin) Neil 1927-...**CLC 6, 11, 31, 39,
70; DAM DRAM**
See also AITN 1; CA 21-24R; CANR 26, 54;
DLB 7; MTCW
Simon, Paul (Frederick) 1941(?)- .... **CLC 17**
See also CA 116; 153
Simonon, Paul 1956(?)- .... **CLC 30**
Simpson, Harriette
See Arnow, Harriette (Louisa) Simpson
Simpson, Louis (Aston Marantz) 1923-
CLC 4, 7, 9, 32; DAM POET
See also CA 1-4R; CAAS 4; CANR 1, 61; DLB
5; MTCW
Simpson, Mona (Elizabeth) 1957- ...... **CLC 44**
See also CA 122; 135; CANR 68
Simpson, N(orman) F(rederick) 1919-..**CLC 29**
See also CA 13-16R; DLB 13
Sinclair, Andrew (Annandale) 1935-..**CLC 2, 14**
See also CA 9-12R; CAAS 5; CANR 14, 38; DLB
14; MTCW
Sinclair, Emil
See Hesse, Hermann
Sinclair, Iain 1943- .... **CLC 76**
See also CA 132
Sinclair, Iain MacGregor
See Sinclair, Iain
Sinclair, Irene
See Griffith, D(avid Lewelyn) W(ark)
Sinclair, Mary Amelia St. Clair 1865(?)-1946
See Sinclair, May
See also CA 104
Sinclair, May 1863-1946 .... **TCLC 3, 11**
See also Sinclair, Mary Amelia St. Clair
See also CA 166; DLB 36, 135
Sinclair, Roy
See Griffith, D(avid Lewelyn) W(ark)
Sinclair, Upton (Beall) 1878-1968..**CLC 1, 11,
15, 63; DA; DAB; DAC; DAM MST,
NOV; WLC**
See also CA 5-8R; 25-28R; CANR 7; CDALB 1929-
1941; DLB 9; INT CANR-7; MTCW; SATA 9
Singer, Isaac
See Singer, Isaac Bashevis
Singer, Isaac Bashevis 1904-1991...**CLC 1, 3,
6, 9, 11, 15, 23, 38, 69, 111; DA; DAB;
DAC; DAM MST, NOV; SSC 3; WLC**
See also AITN 1, 2; CA 1-4R; 134; CANR 1, 39;
CDALB 1941-1968; CLR 1; DLB 6, 28, 52;
DLBY 91; JRDA; MAICYA; MTCW; SATA
3, 27; SATA-Obit 68
Singer, Israel Joshua 1893-1944 ..... **TCLC 33**
Singh, Khushwant 1915- .... **CLC 11**
See also CA 9-12R; CAAS 9; CANR 6
Singleton, Ann
See Benedict, Ruth (Fulton)
Sinjohn, John
See Galsworthy, John

Spacks, Barry (Bernard) 1931- .... **CLC 14**
  See also CA 154; CANR 33; DLB 105
Spanidou, Irini 1946- .... **CLC 44**
Spark, Muriel (Sarah) 1918-...**CLC 2, 3, 5, 8, 13, 18, 40, 94; DAB; DAC; DAM MST, NOV; SSC 10**
  See also CA 5-8R; CANR 12, 36; CDBLB 1945-1960; DLB 15, 139; INT CANR-12; MTCW
Spaulding, Douglas
  See Bradbury, Ray (Douglas)
Spaulding, Leonard
  See Bradbury, Ray (Douglas)
Spence, J. A. D.
  See Eliot, T(homas) S(tearns)
Spencer, Elizabeth 1921- .... **CLC 22**
  See also CA 13-16R; CANR 32, 65; DLB 6; MTCW; SATA 14
Spencer, Leonard G.
  See Silverberg, Robert
Spencer, Scott 1945- .... **CLC 30**
  See also CA 113; CANR 51; DLBY 86
Spender, Stephen (Harold) 1909-1995...**C L C 1, 2, 5, 10, 41, 91; DAM POET**
  See also CA 9-12R; 149; CANR 31, 54; CDBLB 1945-1960; DLB 20; MTCW
Spengler, Oswald (Arnold Gottfried) 1880-1936 **TCLC 25**
  See also CA 118
Spenser, Edmund 1552(?)-1599...**LC 5, 39; DA; DAB; DAC; DAM MST, POET; PC 8; WLC**
  See also CDBLB Before 1660; DLB 167
Spicer, Jack 1925-1965...**CLC 8, 18, 72; DAM POET**
  See also CA 85-88; DLB 5, 16, 193
Spiegelman, Art 1948- .... **CLC 76**
  See also AAYA 10; CA 125; CANR 41, 55
Spielberg, Peter 1929-.......................... **CLC 6**
  See also CA 5-8R; CANR 4, 48; DLBY 81
Spielberg, Steven 1947- .... **CLC 20**
  See also AAYA 8, 24; CA 77-80; CANR 32; SATA 32
Spillane, Frank Morrison 1918-
  See Spillane, Mickey
  See also CA 25-28R; CANR 28, 63; MTCW; SATA 66
Spillane, Mickey .... **CLC 3, 13**
  See also Spillane, Frank Morrison
Spinoza, Benedictus de 1632-1677 .... **LC 9**
Spinrad, Norman (Richard) 1940- ..... **CLC 46**
  See also CA 37-40R; CAAS 19; CANR 20; DLB 8; INT CANR-20
Spitteler, Carl (Friedrich Georg) 1845-1924 **TCLC 12**
  See also CA 109; DLB 129
Spivack, Kathleen (Romola Drucker) 1938- **CLC 6**
  See also CA 49-52
Spoto, Donald 1941- .... **CLC 39**
  See also CA 65-68; CANR 11, 57
Springsteen, Bruce (F.) 1949- .... **CLC 17**
  See also CA 111
Spurling, Hilary 1940- .... **CLC 34**
  See also CA 104; CANR 25, 52
Spyker, John Howland
  See Elman, Richard (Martin)
Squires, (James) Radcliffe 1917-1993...**CLC 51**
  See also CA 1-4R; 140; CANR 6, 21
Srivastava, Dhanpat Rai 1880(?)-1936
  See Premchand
  See also CA 118
Stacy, Donald
  See Pohl, Frederik

Stael, Germaine de 1766-1817
  See Stael-Holstein, Anne Louise Germaine Necker Baronn
  See also DLB 119
Stael-Holstein, Anne Louise Germaine Necker Baronn 1766-1817 .... **NCLC 3**
  See also Stael, Germaine de
  See also DLB 192
Stafford, Jean 1915-1979...**CLC 4, 7, 19, 68; SSC 26**
  See also CA 1-4R; 85-88; CANR 3, 65; DLB 2, 173; MTCW; SATA-Obit 22
Stafford, William (Edgar) 1914-1993...**CLC 4, 7, 29; DAM POET**
  See also CA 5-8R; 142; CAAS 3; CANR 5, 22; DLB 5; INT CANR-22
Stagnelius, Eric Johan 1793-1823 ... **NCLC 61**
Staines, Trevor
  See Brunner, John (Kilian Houston)
Stairs, Gordon
  See Austin, Mary (Hunter)
Stannard, Martin 1947- .... **CLC 44**
  See also CA 142; DLB 155
Stanton, Elizabeth Cady 1815-1902...**TCLC 73**
  See also DLB 79
Stanton, Maura 1946- .... **CLC 9**
  See also CA 89-92; CANR 15; DLB 120
Stanton, Schuyler
  See Baum, L(yman) Frank
Stapledon, (William) Olaf 1886-1950 **TCLC 22**
  See also CA 111; 162; DLB 15
Starbuck, George (Edwin) 1931-1996...**C L C 53; DAM POET**
  See also CA 21-24R; 153; CANR 23
Stark, Richard
  See Westlake, Donald E(dwin)
Staunton, Schuyler
  See Baum, L(yman) Frank
Stead, Christina (Ellen) 1902-1983... **C L C 2, 5, 8, 32, 80**
  See also CA 13-16R; 109; CANR 33, 40; MTCW
Stead, William Thomas 1849-1912 . **TCLC 48**
Steele, Richard 1672-1729 .... **LC 18**
  See also CDBLB 1660-1789; DLB 84, 101
Steele, Timothy (Reid) 1948- .... **CLC 45**
  See also CA 93-96; CANR 16, 50; DLB 120
Steffens, (Joseph) Lincoln 1866-1936 **TCLC 20**
  See also CA 117
Stegner, Wallace (Earle) 1909-1993...**CLC 9, 49, 81; DAM NOV; SSC 27**
  See also AITN 1; BEST 90:3; CA 1-4R; 141; CAAS 9; CANR 1, 21, 46; DLB 9; DLBY 93; MTCW
Stein, Gertrude 1874-1946...**TCLC 1, 6, 28, 48; DA; DAB; DAC; DAM MST, NOV, POET; PC 18; WLC**
  See also CA 104; 132; CDALB 1917-1929; DLB 4, 54, 86; DLBD 15; MTCW
Steinbeck, John (Ernst) 1902-1968...**CLC 1, 5, 9, 13, 21, 34, 45, 75; DA; DAB; DAC; DAM DRAM, MST, NOV; SSC 11; WLC**
  See also AAYA 12; CA 1-4R; 25-28R; CANR 1, 35; CDALB 1929-1941; DLB 7, 9; DLBD 2; MTCW; SATA 9
Steinem, Gloria 1934- .... **CLC 63**
  See also CA 53-56; CANR 28, 51; MTCW
Steiner, George 1929-.... **CLC 24; DAM NOV**
  See also CA 73-76; CANR 31, 67; DLB 67; MTCW; SATA 62
Steiner, K. Leslie
  See Delany, Samuel R(ay, Jr.)

Steiner, Rudolf 1861-1925 .... **TCLC 13**
  See also CA 107
Stendhal 1783-1842...**NCLC 23, 46; DA; DAB; DAC; DAM MST, NOV; SSC 27; WLC**
  See also DLB 119
Stephen, Adeline Virginia
  See Woolf, (Adeline) Virginia
Stephen, SirLeslie 1832-1904 .... **TCLC 23**
  See also CA 123; DLB 57, 144, 190
Stephen, Sir Leslie
  See Stephen, SirLeslie
Stephen, Virginia
  See Woolf, (Adeline) Virginia
Stephens, James 1882(?)-1950 .... **TCLC 4**
  See also CA 104; DLB 19, 153, 162
Stephens, Reed
  See Donaldson, Stephen R.
Steptoe, Lydia
  See Barnes, Djuna
Sterchi, Beat 1949- .... **CLC 65**
Sterling, Brett
  See Bradbury, Ray (Douglas); Hamilton, Edmond
Sterling, Bruce 1954- .... **CLC 72**
  See also CA 119; CANR 44
Sterling, George 1869-1926 .... **TCLC 20**
  See also CA 117; 165; DLB 54
Stern, Gerald 1925- .... **CLC 40, 100**
  See also CA 81-84; CANR 28; DLB 105
Stern, Richard (Gustave) 1928- ..... **CLC 4, 39**
  See also CA 1-4R; CANR 1, 25, 52; DLBY 87; INT CANR-25
Sternberg, Josef von 1894-1969 .... **CLC 20**
  See also CA 81-84
Sterne, Laurence 1713-1768 ...... **LC 2; DA; DAB; DAC; DAM MST, NOV; WLC**
  See also CDBLB 1660-1789; DLB 39
Sternheim, (William Adolf) Carl 1878-1942 **TCLC 8**
  See also CA 105; DLB 56, 118
Stevens, Mark 1951- .... **CLC 34**
  See also CA 122
Stevens, Wallace 1879-1955...**TCLC 3, 12, 45; DA; DAB; DAC; DAM MST, POET; PC 6; WLC**
  See also CA 104; 124; CDALB 1929-1941; DLB 54; MTCW
Stevenson, Anne (Katharine) 1933-...**CLC 7, 33**
  See also CA 17-20R; CAAS 9; CANR 9, 33; DLB 40; MTCW
Stevenson, Robert Louis (Balfour) 1850-1894 **NCLC 5, 14, 63; DA; DAB; DAC; DAM MST, NOV; SSC 11; WLC**
  See also AAYA 24; CDBLB 1890-1914; CLR 10, 11; DLB 18, 57, 141, 156, 174; DLBD 13; JRDA; MAICYA; YABC 2
Stewart, J(ohn) I(nnes) M(ackintosh) 1906-1994 **CLC 7, 14, 32**
  See also CA 85-88; 147; CAAS 3; CANR 47; MTCW
Stewart, Mary (Florence Elinor) 1916-..**CLC 7, 35; DAB**
  See also CA 1-4R; CANR 1, 59; SATA 12
Stewart, Mary Rainbow
  See Stewart, Mary (Florence Elinor)
Stifle, June
  See Campbell, Maria
Stifter, Adalbert 1805-1868...**NCLC 41; SSC 28**
  See also DLB 133
Still, James 1906- .... **CLC 49**
  See also CA 65-68; CAAS 17; CANR 10, 26; DLB 9; SATA 29
Sting
  See Sumner, Gordon Matthew

Syruc, J.
See Milosz, Czeslaw
Szirtes, George 1948- .... **CLC 46**
See also CA 109; CANR 27, 61
Szymborska, Wislawa 1923- .... **CLC 99**
See also CA 154; DLBY 96
T. O., Nik
See Annensky, Innokenty (Fyodorovich)
Tabori, George 1914- .... **CLC 19**
See also CA 49-52; CANR 4, 69
Tagore, Rabindranath 1861-1941 .. **TCLC 3, 53; DAM DRAM, POET; PC 8**
See also CA 104; 120; MTCW
Taine, Hippolyte Adolphe 1828-1893..**NCLC 15**
Talese, Gay 1932- .... **CLC 37**
See also AITN 1; CA 1-4R; CANR 9, 58; DLB 185; INT CANR-9; MTCW
Tallent, Elizabeth (Ann) 1954- .... **CLC 45**
See also CA 117; DLB 130
Tally, Ted 1952- .... **CLC 42**
See also CA 120; 124; INT 124
Tamayo y Baus, Manuel 1829-1898 .. **NCLC 1**
Tammsaare, A(nton) H(ansen) 1878-1940
TCLC 27
See also CA 164
Tam'si, Tchicaya U
See Tchicaya, Gerald Felix
Tan, Amy (Ruth) 1952- .... **CLC 59; DAM MULT, NOV, POP**
See also AAYA 9; BEST 89:3; CA 136; CANR 54; DLB 173; SATA 75
Tandem, Felix
See Spitteler, Carl (Friedrich Georg)
Tanizaki, Jun'ichiro 1886-1965 . **CLC 8, 14, 28; SSC 21**
See also CA 93-96; 25-28R; DLB 180
Tanner, William
See Amis, Kingsley (William)
Tao Lao
See Storni, Alfonsina
Tarassoff, Lev
See Troyat, Henri
Tarbell, Ida M(inerva) 1857-1944 ... **TCLC 40**
See also CA 122; DLB 47
Tarkington, (Newton) Booth 1869-1946
TCLC 9
See also CA 110; 143; DLB 9, 102; SATA 17
Tarkovsky, Andrei (Arsenyevich) 1932-1986
CLC 75
See also CA 127
Tartt, Donna 1964(?)- .... **CLC 76**
See also CA 142
Tasso, Torquato 1544-1595 .... **LC 5**
Tate, (John Orley) Allen 1899-1979...**CLC 2, 4, 6, 9, 11, 14, 24**
See also CA 5-8R; 85-88; CANR 32; DLB 4, 45, 63; MTCW
Tate, Ellalice
See Hibbert, Eleanor Alice Burford
Tate, James (Vincent) 1943- .... **CLC 2, 6, 25**
See also CA 21-24R; CANR 29, 57; DLB 5, 169
Tavel, Ronald 1940- .... **CLC 6**
See also CA 21-24R; CANR 33
Taylor, C(ecil) P(hilip) 1929-1981 ...... **CLC 27**
See also CA 25-28R; 105; CANR 47
Taylor, Edward 1642(?)-1729 ..... **LC 11; DA; DAB; DAC; DAM MST, POET**
See also DLB 24
Taylor, Eleanor Ross 1920- .... **CLC 5**
See also CA 81-84
Taylor, Elizabeth 1912-1975 .... **CLC 2, 4, 29**
See also CA 13-16R; CANR 9; DLB 139; MTCW; SATA 13

Taylor, Frederick Winslow 1856-1915...**T C L C 76**
Taylor, Henry (Splawn) 1942- .... **CLC 44**
See also CA 33-36R; CAAS 7; CANR 31; DLB 5
Taylor, Kamala (Purnaiya) 1924-
See Markandaya, Kamala
See also CA 77-80
Taylor, Mildred D. .... **CLC 21**
See also AAYA 10; BW 1; CA 85-88; CANR 25; CLR 9; DLB 52; JRDA; MAICYA; SAAS 5; SATA 15, 70
Taylor, Peter (Hillsman) 1917-1994...**CLC 1, 4, 18, 37, 44, 50, 71; SSC 10**
See also CA 13-16R; 147; CANR 9, 50; DLBY 81, 94; INT CANR-9; MTCW
Taylor, Robert Lewis 1912- .... **CLC 14**
See also CA 1-4R; CANR 3, 64; SATA 10
Tchekhov, Anton
See Chekhov, Anton (Pavlovich)
Tchicaya, Gerald Felix 1931-1988 .... **CLC 101**
See also CA 129; 125
Tchicaya U Tam'si
See Tchicaya, Gerald Felix
Teasdale, Sara 1884-1933 .... **TCLC 4**
See also CA 104; 163; DLB 45; SATA 32
Tegner, Esaias 1782-1846 .... **NCLC 2**
Teilhard de Chardin, (Marie Joseph) Pierre 1881-1955 .... **TCLC 9**
See also CA 105
Temple, Ann
See Mortimer, Penelope (Ruth)
Tennant, Emma (Christina) 1937-...**CLC 13, 52**
See also CA 65-68; CAAS 9; CANR 10, 38, 59; DLB 14
Tenneshaw, S. M.
See Silverberg, Robert
Tennyson, Alfred 1809-1892 ... **NCLC 30, 65; DA; DAB; DAC; DAM MST, POET; PC 6; WLC**
See also CDBLB 1832-1890; DLB 32
Teran, Lisa St. Aubin de .... **CLC 36**
See also St. Aubin de Teran, Lisa
Terence 195(?)B.C.-159B.C....**CMLC 14; DC 7**
Teresa de Jesus, St. 1515-1582 .... **LC 18**
Terkel, Louis 1912-
See Terkel, Studs
See also CA 57-60; CANR 18, 45, 67; MTCW
Terkel, Studs .... **CLC 38**
See also Terkel, Louis
See also AITN 1
Terry, C. V.
See Slaughter, Frank G(ill)
Terry, Megan 1932- .... **CLC 19**
See also CA 77-80; CABS 3; CANR 43; DLB 7
Tertullian c. 155-c. 245 .... **CMLC 29**
Tertz, Abram
See Sinyavsky, Andrei (Donatevich)
Tesich, Steve 1943(?)-1996 .... **CLC 40, 69**
See also CA 105; 152; DLBY 83
Teternikov, Fyodor Kuzmich 1863-1927
See Sologub, Fyodor
See also CA 104
Tevis, Walter 1928-1984 .... **CLC 42**
See also CA 113
Tey, Josephine .... **TCLC 14**
See also Mackintosh, Elizabeth
See also DLB 77
Thackeray, William Makepeace 1811-1863 **NCLC 5, 14, 22, 43; DA; DAB; DAC; DAM MST, NOV; WLC**
See also CDBLB 1832-1890; DLB 21, 55, 159, 163; SATA 23

Thakura, Ravindranatha
See Tagore, Rabindranath
Tharoor, Shashi 1956- .... **CLC 70**
See also CA 141
Thelwell, Michael Miles 1939- .... **CLC 22**
See also BW 2; CA 101
Theobald, Lewis, Jr.
See Lovecraft, H(oward) P(hillips)
Theodorescu, Ion N. 1880-1967
See Arghezi, Tudor
See also CA 116
Theriault, Yves 1915-1983 .... **CLC 79; DAC; DAM MST**
See also CA 102; DLB 88
Theroux, Alexander (Louis) 1939-...**CLC 2, 25**
See also CA 85-88; CANR 20, 63
Theroux, Paul (Edward) 1941-...**CLC 5, 8, 11, 15, 28, 46; DAM POP**
See also BEST 89:4; CA 33-36R; CANR 20, 45; DLB 2; MTCW; SATA 44
Thesen, Sharon 1946- .... **CLC 56**
See also CA 163
Thevenin, Denis
See Duhamel, Georges
Thibault, Jacques Anatole Francois 1844-1924
See France, Anatole
See also CA 106; 127; DAM NOV; MTCW
Thiele, Colin (Milton) 1920- .... **CLC 17**
See also CA 29-32R; CANR 12, 28, 53; CLR 27; MAICYA; SAAS 2; SATA 14, 72
Thomas, Audrey (Callahan) 1935-...**CLC 7, 13, 37, 107; SSC 20**
See also AITN 2; CA 21-24R; CAAS 19; CANR 36, 58; DLB 60; MTCW
Thomas, D(onald) M(ichael) 1935- . **CLC 13, 22, 31**
See also CA 61-64; CAAS 11; CANR 17, 45; CDBLB 1960 to Present; DLB 40; INT CANR-17; MTCW
Thomas, Dylan (Marlais) 1914-1953... **T C L C 1, 8, 45; DA; DAB; DAC; DAM DRAM, MST, POET; PC 2; SSC 3; WLC**
See also CA 104; 120; CANR 65; CDBLB 1945-1960; DLB 13, 20, 139; MTCW; SATA 60
Thomas, (Philip) Edward 1878-1917 .. **T C L C 10; DAM POET**
See also CA 106; 153; DLB 19
Thomas, Joyce Carol 1938- .... **CLC 35**
See also AAYA 12; BW 2; CA 113; 116; CANR 48; CLR 19; DLB 33; INT 116; JRDA; MAICYA; MTCW; SAAS 7; SATA 40, 78
Thomas, Lewis 1913-1993 .... **CLC 35**
See also CA 85-88; 143; CANR 38, 60; MTCW
Thomas, Paul
See Mann, (Paul) Thomas
Thomas, Piri 1928- .... **CLC 17**
See also CA 73-76; HW
Thomas, R(onald) S(tuart) 1913-...**CLC 6, 13, 48; DAB; DAM POET**
See also CA 89-92; CAAS 4; CANR 30; CDBLB 1960 to Present; DLB 27; MTCW
Thomas, Ross (Elmore) 1926-1995 .... **CLC 39**
See also CA 33-36R; 150; CANR 22, 63
Thompson, Francis Clegg
See Mencken, H(enry) L(ouis)
Thompson, Francis Joseph 1859-1907
TCLC 4
See also CA 104; CDBLB 1890-1914; DLB 19
Thompson, Hunter S(tockton) 1939-...**CLC 9, 17, 40, 104; DAM POP**
See also BEST 89:1; CA 17-20R; CANR 23, 46; DLB 185; MTCW

Thompson, James Myers
See Thompson, Jim (Myers)
Thompson, Jim (Myers) 1906-1977(?)...**C L C 69**
See also CA 140
Thompson, Judith ....**CLC 39**
Thomson, James 1700-1748 .... **LC 16, 29, 40; DAM POET**
See also DLB 95
Thomson, James 1834-1882 ..... **NCLC 18; DAM POET**
See also DLB 35
Thoreau, Henry David 1817-1862...**NCLC 7, 21, 61; DA; DAB; DAC; DAM MST; WLC**
See also CDALB 1640-1865; DLB 1
Thornton, Hall
See Silverberg, Robert
Thucydides c. 455B.C.-399B.C. ...... **CMLC 17**
See also DLB 176
Thurber, James (Grover) 1894-1961...**CLC 5, 11, 25; DA; DAB; DAC; DAM DRAM, MST, NOV; SSC 1**
See also CA 73-76; CANR 17, 39; CDALB 1929-1941; DLB 4, 11, 22, 102; MAICYA; MTCW; SATA 13
Thurman, Wallace (Henry) 1902-1934...**TCLC 6; BLC 3; DAM MULT**
See also BW 1; CA 104; 124; DLB 51
Ticheburn, Cheviot
See Ainsworth, William Harrison
Tieck, (Johann) Ludwig 1773-1853...**NCLC 5, 46; SSC 31**
See also DLB 90
Tiger, Derry
See Ellison, Harlan (Jay)
Tilghman, Christopher 1948(?)- ....**CLC 65**
See also CA 159
Tillinghast, Richard (Williford) 1940-...**C L C 29**
See also CA 29-32R; CAAS 23; CANR 26, 51
Timrod, Henry 1828-1867 ....**NCLC 25**
See also DLB 3
Tindall, Gillian (Elizabeth) 1938- ....**CLC 7**
See also CA 21-24R; CANR 11, 65
Tiptree, James, Jr. ....**CLC 48, 50**
See also Sheldon, Alice Hastings Bradley
See also DLB 8
Titmarsh, Michael Angelo
See Thackeray, William Makepeace
Tocqueville, Alexis (Charles Henri Maurice Clerel Comte) 1805-1859 .... **NCLC 7, 63**
Tolkien, J(ohn) R(onald) R(euel) 1892-1973
CLC 1, 2, 3, 8, 12, 38; DA; DAB; DAC; DAM MST, NOV, POP; WLC
See also AAYA 10; AITN 1; CA 17-18; 45-48; CANR 36; CAP 2; CDBLB 1914-1945; DLB 15, 160; JRDA; MAICYA; MTCW; SATA 2, 32; SATA-Obit 24
Toller, Ernst 1893-1939 ....**TCLC 10**
See also CA 107; DLB 124
Tolson, M. B.
See Tolson, Melvin B(eaunorus)
Tolson, Melvin B(eaunorus) 1898(?)-1966
CLC 36, 105; BLC 3; DAM MULT, POET
See also BW 1; CA 124; 89-92; DLB 48, 76
Tolstoi, Aleksei Nikolaevich
See Tolstoy, Alexey Nikolaevich
Tolstoy, Alexey Nikolaevich 1882-1945...**TCLC 18**
See also CA 107; 158
Tolstoy, Count Leo
See Tolstoy, Leo (Nikolaevich)

Tolstoy, Leo (Nikolaevich) 1828-1910
TCLC 4, 11, 17, 28, 44, 79; DA; DAB; DAC; DAM MST, NOV; SSC 9, 30; WLC
See also CA 104; 123; SATA 26
Tomasi di Lampedusa, Giuseppe 1896-1957
See Lampedusa, Giuseppe (Tomasi) di
See also CA 111
Tomlin, Lily ....**CLC 17**
See also Tomlin, Mary Jean
Tomlin, Mary Jean 1939(?)-
See Tomlin, Lily
See also CA 117
Tomlinson, (Alfred) Charles 1927-...**CLC 2, 4, 6, 13, 45; DAM POET; PC 17**
See also CA 5-8R; CANR 33; DLB 40
Tomlinson, H(enry) M(ajor) 1873-1958
TCLC 71
See also CA 118; 161; DLB 36, 100, 195
Tonson, Jacob
See Bennett, (Enoch) Arnold
Toole, John Kennedy 1937-1969 ..**CLC 19, 64**
See also CA 104; DLBY 81
Toomer, Jean 1894-1967 .. **CLC 1, 4, 13, 22; BLC 3; DAM MULT; PC 7; SSC 1; WLCS**
See also BW 1; CA 85-88; CDALB 1917-1929; DLB 45, 51; MTCW
Torley, Luke
See Blish, James (Benjamin)
Tornimparte, Alessandra
See Ginzburg, Natalia
Torre, Raoul della
See Mencken, H(enry) L(ouis)
Torrey, E(dwin) Fuller 1937- ....**CLC 34**
See also CA 119
Torsvan, Ben Traven
See Traven, B.
Torsvan, Benno Traven
See Traven, B.
Torsvan, Berick Traven
See Traven, B.
Torsvan, Berwick Traven
See Traven, B.
Torsvan, Bruno Traven
See Traven, B.
Torsvan, Traven
See Traven, B.
Tournier, Michel (Edouard) 1924-...**CLC 6, 23, 36, 95**
See also CA 49-52; CANR 3, 36; DLB 83; MTCW; SATA 23
Tournimparte, Alessandra
See Ginzburg, Natalia
Towers, Ivar
See Kornbluth, C(yril) M.
Towne, Robert (Burton) 1936(?)- ....**CLC 87**
See also CA 108; DLB 44
Townsend, Sue ....**CLC 61**
See also Townsend, Susan Elaine
See also SATA 55, 93; SATA-Brief 48
Townsend, Susan Elaine 1946-
See Townsend, Sue
See also CA 119; 127; CANR 65; DAB; DAC; DAM MST
Townshend, Peter (Dennis Blandford) 1945-
CLC 17, 42
See also CA 107
Tozzi, Federigo 1883-1920 ....**TCLC 31**
See also CA 160
Traill, Catharine Parr 1802-1899 ... **NCLC 31**
See also DLB 99
Trakl, Georg 1887-1914 .... **TCLC 5; PC 20**
See also CA 104; 165

Transtroemer, Tomas (Goesta) 1931-...**CLC 52, 65; DAM POET**
See also CA 117; 129; CAAS 17
Transtromer, Tomas Gosta
See Transtroemer, Tomas (Goesta)
Traven, B. (?)-1969 ....**CLC 8, 11**
See also CA 19-20; 25-28R; CAP 2; DLB 9, 56; MTCW
Treitel, Jonathan 1959- ....**CLC 70**
Tremain, Rose 1943- ....**CLC 42**
See also CA 97-100; CANR 44; DLB 14
Tremblay, Michel 1942-...**CLC 29, 102; DAC; DAM MST**
See also CA 116; 128; DLB 60; MTCW
Trevanian ....**CLC 29**
See also Whitaker, Rod(ney)
Trevor, Glen
See Hilton, James
Trevor, William 1928- . **CLC 7, 9, 14, 25, 71; SSC 21**
See also Cox, William Trevor
See also DLB 14, 139
Trifonov, Yuri (Valentinovich) 1925-1981
CLC 45
See also CA 126; 103; MTCW
Trilling, Lionel 1905-1975 .... **CLC 9, 11, 24**
See also CA 9-12R; 61-64; CANR 10; DLB 28, 63; INT CANR-10; MTCW
Trimball, W. H.
See Mencken, H(enry) L(ouis)
Tristan
See Gomez de la Serna, Ramon
Tristram
See Housman, A(lfred) E(dward)
Trogdon, William (Lewis) 1939-
See Heat-Moon, William Least
See also CA 115; 119; CANR 47; INT 119
Trollope, Anthony 1815-1882 ... **NCLC 6, 33; DA; DAB; DAC; DAM MST, NOV; SSC 28; WLC**
See also CDBLB 1832-1890; DLB 21, 57, 159; SATA 22
Trollope, Frances 1779-1863 ....**NCLC 30**
See also DLB 21, 166
Trotsky, Leon 1879-1940 ....**TCLC 22**
See also CA 118
Trotter (Cockburn), Catharine 1679-1749
LC 8
See also DLB 84
Trout, Kilgore
See Farmer, Philip Jose
Trow, George W. S. 1943- ....**CLC 52**
See also CA 126
Troyat, Henri 1911- ....**CLC 23**
See also CA 45-48; CANR 2, 33, 67; MTCW
Trudeau, G(arretson) B(eekman) 1948-
See Trudeau, Garry B.
See also CA 81-84; CANR 31; SATA 35
Trudeau, Garry B. ....**CLC 12**
See also Trudeau, G(arretson) B(eekman)
See also AAYA 10; AITN 2
Truffaut, Francois 1932-1984 ....**CLC 20, 101**
See also CA 81-84; 113; CANR 34
Trumbo, Dalton 1905-1976 ....**CLC 19**
See also CA 21-24R; 69-72; CANR 10; DLB 26
Trumbull, John 1750-1831 ....**NCLC 30**
See also DLB 31
Trundlett, Helen B.
See Eliot, T(homas) S(tearns)
Tryon, Thomas 1926-1991 .. **CLC 3, 11; DAM POP**
See also AITN 1; CA 29-32R; 135; CANR 32; MTCW

Tryon, Tom
See Tryon, Thomas
Ts'ao Hsueh-ch'in 1715(?)-1763 ....LC 1
Tsushima, Shuji 1909-1948
See Dazai Osamu
See also CA 107
Tsvetaeva (Efron), Marina (Ivanovna) 1892-1941 .... **TCLC 7, 35; PC 14**
See also CA 104; 128; MTCW
Tuck, Lily 1938- .... **CLC 70**
See also CA 139
Tu Fu 712-770 .... **PC 9**
See also DAM MULT
Tunis, John R(oberts) 1889-1975 .... **CLC 12**
See also CA 61-64; CANR 62; DLB 22, 171; JRDA; MAICYA; SATA 37; SATA-Brief 30
Tuohy, Frank .... **CLC 37**
See also Tuohy, John Francis
See also DLB 14, 139
Tuohy, John Francis 1925-
See Tuohy, Frank
See also CA 5-8R; CANR 3, 47
Turco, Lewis (Putnam) 1934- .... **CLC 11, 63**
See also CA 13-16R; CAAS 22; CANR 24, 51; DLBY 84
Turgenev, Ivan 1818-1883 .... **NCLC 21; DA; DAB; DAC; DAM MST, NOV; DC 7; SSC 7; WLC**
Turgot, Anne-Robert-Jacques 1727-1781 .**L C 26**
Turner, Frederick 1943- .... **CLC 48**
See also CA 73-76; CAAS 10; CANR 12, 30, 56; DLB 40
Tutu, Desmond M(pilo) 1931- .... **CLC 80; BLC 3; DAM MULT**
See also BW 1; CA 125; CANR 67
Tutuola, Amos 1920-1997 ... **CLC 5, 14, 29; BLC 3; DAM MULT**
See also BW 2; CA 9-12R; 159; CANR 27, 66; DLB 125; MTCW
Twain, Mark . **TCLC 6, 12, 19, 36, 48, 59; SSC 6, 26; WLC**
See also Clemens, Samuel Langhorne
See also AAYA 20; DLB 11, 12, 23, 64, 74
Tyler, Anne 1941- .. **CLC 7, 11, 18, 28, 44, 59, 103; DAM NOV, POP**
See also AAYA 18; BEST 89:1; CA 9-12R; CANR 11, 33, 53; DLB 6, 143; DLBY 82; MTCW; SATA 7, 90
Tyler, Royall 1757-1826 .... **NCLC 3**
See also DLB 37
Tynan, Katharine 1861-1931 .... **TCLC 3**
See also CA 104; DLB 153
Tyutchev, Fyodor 1803-1873 .... **NCLC 34**
Tzara, Tristan 1896-1963 ...... **CLC 47; DAM POET**
See also CA 153; 89-92
Uhry, Alfred 1936-**CLC 55; DAM DRAM, POP**
See also CA 127; 133; INT 133
Ulf, Haerved
See Strindberg, (Johan) August
Ulf, Harved
See Strindberg, (Johan) August
Ulibarri, Sabine R(eyes) 1919- ...... **CLC 83; DAM MULT**
See also CA 131; DLB 82; HW
Unamuno (y Jugo), Miguel de 1864-1936 **TCLC 2, 9; DAM MULT, NOV; HLC; SSC 11**
See also CA 104; 131; DLB 108; HW; MTCW
Undercliffe, Errol
See Campbell, (John) Ramsey

Underwood, Miles
See Glassco, John
Undset, Sigrid 1882-1949 ...... **TCLC 3; DA; DAB; DAC; DAM MST, NOV; WLC**
See also CA 104; 129; MTCW
Ungaretti, Giuseppe 1888-1970...**CLC 7, 11, 15**
See also CA 19-20; 25-28R; CAP 2; DLB 114
Unger, Douglas 1952- .... **CLC 34**
See also CA 130
Unsworth, Barry (Forster) 1930- .... **CLC 76**
See also CA 25-28R; CANR 30, 54; DLB 194
Updike, John (Hoyer) 1932-...**CLC 1, 2, 3, 5, 7, 9, 13, 15, 23, 34, 43, 70; DA; DAB; DAC; DAM MST, NOV, POET, POP; SSC 13, 27; WLC**
See also CA 1-4R; CABS 1; CANR 4, 33, 51; CDALB 1968-1988; DLB 2, 5, 143; DLBD 3; DLBY 80, 82, 97; MTCW
Upshaw, Margaret Mitchell
See Mitchell, Margaret (Munnerlyn)
Upton, Mark
See Sanders, Lawrence
Urdang, Constance (Henriette) 1922-...**CLC 47**
See also CA 21-24R; CANR 9, 24
Uriel, Henry
See Faust, Frederick (Schiller)
Uris, Leon (Marcus) 1924- . **CLC 7, 32; DAM NOV, POP**
See also AITN 1, 2; BEST 89:2; CA 1-4R; CANR 1, 40, 65; MTCW; SATA 49
Urmuz
See Codrescu, Andrei
Urquhart, Jane 1949- .... **CLC 90; DAC**
See also CA 113; CANR 32, 68
Ustinov, Peter (Alexander) 1921- .... **CLC 1**
See also AITN 1; CA 13-16R; CANR 25, 51; DLB 13
U Tam'si, Gerald Felix Tchicaya
See Tchicaya, Gerald Felix
U Tam'si, Tchicaya
See Tchicaya, Gerald Felix
Vachss, Andrew (Henry) 1942- .... **CLC 106**
See also CA 118; CANR 44
Vachss, Andrew H.
See Vachss, Andrew (Henry)
Vaculik, Ludvik 1926- .... **CLC 7**
See also CA 53-56
Vaihinger, Hans 1852-1933 .... **TCLC 71**
See also CA 116; 166
Valdez, Luis (Miguel) 1940- .... **CLC 84; DAM MULT; HLC**
See also CA 101; CANR 32; DLB 122; HW
Valenzuela, Luisa 1938- .. **CLC 31, 104; DAM MULT; SSC 14**
See also CA 101; CANR 32, 65; DLB 113; HW
Valera y Alcala-Galiano, Juan 1824-1905 **TCLC 10**
See also CA 106
Valery, (Ambroise) Paul (Toussaint Jules) 1871-1945 ..... **TCLC 4, 15; DAM POET; PC 9**
See also CA 104; 122; MTCW
Valle-Inclan, Ramon (Maria) del 1866-1936 **TCLC 5; DAM MULT; HLC**
See also CA 106; 153; DLB 134
Vallejo, Antonio Buero
See Buero Vallejo, Antonio
Vallejo, Cesar (Abraham) 1892-1938...**TCLC 3, 56; DAM MULT; HLC**
See also CA 105; 153; HW
Vallette, Marguerite Eymery
See Rachilde
Valle Y Pena, Ramon del
See Valle-Inclan, Ramon (Maria) del

Van Ash, Cay 1918- .... **CLC 34**
Vanbrugh, Sir John 1664-1726 ..... **LC 21; DAM DRAM**
See also DLB 80
Van Campen, Karl
See Campbell, John W(ood, Jr.)
Vance, Gerald
See Silverberg, Robert
Vance, Jack .... **CLC 35**
See also Kuttner, Henry; Vance, John Holbrook
See also DLB 8
Vance, John Holbrook 1916-
See Queen, Ellery; Vance, Jack
See also CA 29-32R; CANR 17, 65; MTCW
Van Den Bogarde, Derek Jules Gaspard Ulric Niven 1921-
See Bogarde, Dirk
See also CA 77-80
Vandenburgh, Jane .... **CLC 59**
Vanderhaeghe, Guy 1951- .... **CLC 41**
See also CA 113
van der Post, Laurens (Jan) 1906-1996..**CLC 5**
See also CA 5-8R; 155; CANR 35
van de Wetering, Janwillem 1931- ..... **CLC 47**
See also CA 49-52; CANR 4, 62
Van Dine, S. S. .... **TCLC 23**
See also Wright, Willard Huntington
Van Doren, Carl (Clinton) 1885-1950 **TCLC 18**
See also CA 111
Van Doren, Mark 1894-1972 .... **CLC 6, 10**
See also CA 1-4R; 37-40R; CANR 3; DLB 45; MTCW
Van Druten, John (William) 1901-1957 **TCLC 2**
See also CA 104; 161; DLB 10
Van Duyn, Mona (Jane) 1921- .. **CLC 3, 7, 63; DAM POET**
See also CA 9-12R; CANR 7, 38, 60; DLB 5
Van Dyne, Edith
See Baum, L(yman) Frank
van Itallie, Jean-Claude 1936- .... **CLC 3**
See also CA 45-48; CAAS 2; CANR 1, 48; DLB 7
van Ostaijen, Paul 1896-1928 .... **TCLC 33**
See also CA 163
Van Peebles, Melvin 1932- .. **CLC 2, 20; DAM MULT**
See also BW 2; CA 85-88; CANR 27, 67
Vansittart, Peter 1920- .... **CLC 42**
See also CA 1-4R; CANR 3, 49
Van Vechten, Carl 1880-1964 .... **CLC 33**
See also CA 89-92; DLB 4, 9, 51
Van Vogt, A(lfred) E(lton) 1912- .... **CLC 1**
See also CA 21-24R; CANR 28; DLB 8; SATA 14
Varda, Agnes 1928- .... **CLC 16**
See also CA 116; 122
Vargas Llosa, (Jorge) Mario (Pedro) 1936- **CLC 3, 6, 9, 10, 15, 31, 42, 85; DA; DAB; DAC; DAM MST, MULT, NOV; HLC**
See also CA 73-76; CANR 18, 32, 42, 67; DLB 145; HW; MTCW
Vasiliu, Gheorghe 1881-1957
See Bacovia, George
See also CA 123
Vassa, Gustavus
See Equiano, Olaudah
Vassilikos, Vassilis 1933- .... **CLC 4, 8**
See also CA 81-84
Vaughan, Henry 1621-1695 .... **LC 27**
See also DLB 131
Vaughn, Stephanie .... **CLC 62**

Vazov, Ivan (Minchov) 1850-1921 .. **TCLC 25**
See also CA 121; DLB 147

Veblen, Thorstein B(unde) 1857-1929 **TCLC 31**
See also CA 115; 165

Vega, Lope de 1562-1635 .... **LC 23**

Venison, Alfred
See Pound, Ezra (Weston Loomis)

Verdi, Marie de
See Mencken, H(enry) L(ouis)

Verdu, Matilde
See Cela, Camilo Jose

Verga, Giovanni (Carmelo) 1840-1922...**TCLC 3; SSC 21**
See also CA 104; 123

Vergil 70B.C.-19B.C. ... **CMLC 9; DA; DAB; DAC; DAM MST, POET; PC 12; WLCS**

Verhaeren, Emile (Adolphe Gustave) 1855-1916 **TCLC 12**
See also CA 109

Verlaine, Paul (Marie) 1844-1896...**NCLC 2, 51; DAM POET; PC 2**

Verne, Jules (Gabriel) 1828-1905...**TCLC 6, 52**
See also AAYA 16; CA 110; 131; DLB 123; JRDA; MAICYA; SATA 21

Very, Jones 1813-1880 .... **NCLC 9**
See also DLB 1

Vesaas, Tarjei 1897-1970 .... **CLC 48**
See also CA 29-32R

Vialis, Gaston
See Simenon, Georges (Jacques Christian)

Vian, Boris 1920-1959 .... **TCLC 9**
See also CA 106; 164; DLB 72

Viaud, (Louis Marie) Julien 1850-1923
See Loti, Pierre
See also CA 107

Vicar, Henry
See Felsen, Henry Gregor

Vicker, Angus
See Felsen, Henry Gregor

Vidal, Gore 1925-...**CLC 2, 4, 6, 8, 10, 22, 33, 72; DAM NOV, POP**
See also AITN 1; BEST 90:2; CA 5-8R; CANR 13, 45, 65; DLB 6, 152; INT CANR-13; MTCW

Viereck, Peter (Robert Edwin) 1916-... **CLC 4**
See also CA 1-4R; CANR 1, 47; DLB 5

Vigny, Alfred (Victor) de 1797-1863...**NCLC 7; DAM POET**
See also DLB 119, 192

Vilakazi, Benedict Wallet 1906-1947
TCLC 37

Villa, Jose Garcia 1904-1997 .... **PC 22**
See also CA 25-28R; CANR 12

Villaurrutia, Xavier 1903-1950 .... **TCLC 80**
See also HW

Villiers de l'Isle Adam, Jean Marie Mathias Philippe Auguste, Comte de 1838-1889
NCLC 3; SSC 14
See also DLB 123

Villon, Francois 1431-1463(?) .... **PC 13**

Vinci, Leonardo da 1452-1519 .... **LC 12**

Vine, Barbara .... **CLC 50**
See also Rendell, Ruth (Barbara)
See also BEST 90:4

Vinge, Joan D(ennison) 1948-... **CLC 30; SSC 24**
See also CA 93-96; SATA 36

Violis, G.
See Simenon, Georges (Jacques Christian)

Virgil
See Vergil

Visconti, Luchino 1906-1976 .... **CLC 16**
See also CA 81-84; 65-68; CANR 39

Vittorini, Elio 1908-1966 .... **CLC 6, 9, 14**
See also CA 133; 25-28R

Vizenor, Gerald Robert 1934- ...... **CLC 103; DAM MULT**
See also CA 13-16R; CAAS 22; CANR 5, 21, 44, 67; DLB 175; NNAL

Vizinczey, Stephen 1933-..................... **CLC 40**
See also CA 128; INT 128

Vliet, R(ussell) G(ordon) 1929-1984 .. **CLC 22**
See also CA 37-40R; 112; CANR 18

Vogau, Boris Andreyevich 1894-1937(?)
See Pilnyak, Boris
See also CA 123

Vogel, Paula A(nne) 1951- .... **CLC 76**
See also CA 108

Voigt, Cynthia 1942- .... **CLC 30**
See also AAYA 3; CA 106; CANR 18, 37, 40; CLR 13,48; INT CANR-18; JRDA; MAICYA; SATA 48, 79; SATA-Brief 33

Voigt, Ellen Bryant 1943- .... **CLC 54**
See also CA 69-72; CANR 11, 29, 55; DLB 120

Voinovich, Vladimir (Nikolaevich) 1932- **CLC 10, 49**
See also CA 81-84; CAAS 12; CANR 33, 67; MTCW

Vollmann, William T. 1959- .... **CLC 89; DAM NOV, POP**
See also CA 134; CANR 67

Voloshinov, V. N.
See Bakhtin, Mikhail Mikhailovich

Voltaire 1694-1778 .. **LC 14; DA; DAB; DAC; DAM DRAM, MST; SSC 12; WLC**

von Daeniken, Erich 1935- .... **CLC 30**
See also AITN 1; CA 37-40R; CANR 17, 44

von Daniken, Erich
See von Daeniken, Erich

von Heidenstam, (Carl Gustaf) Verner
See Heidenstam, (Carl Gustaf) Verner von

von Heyse, Paul (Johann Ludwig)
See Heyse, Paul (Johann Ludwig von)

von Hofmannsthal, Hugo
See Hofmannsthal, Hugo von

von Horvath, Odon
See Horvath, Oedoen von

von Horvath, Oedoen
See Horvath, Oedoen von

von Liliencron, (Friedrich Adolf Axel) Detlev
See Liliencron, (Friedrich Adolf Axel) Detlev von

Vonnegut, Kurt, Jr. 1922-...**CLC 1, 2, 3, 4, 5, 8, 12, 22, 40, 60, 111; DA; DAB; DAC; DAM MST, NOV, POP; SSC 8; WLC**
See also AAYA 6; AITN 1; BEST 90:4; CA 1-4R; CANR 1, 25, 49; CDALB 1968-1988; DLB 2, 8, 152; DLBD 3; DLBY 80; MTCW

Von Rachen, Kurt
See Hubbard, L(afayette) Ron(ald)

von Rezzori (d'Arezzo), Gregor
See Rezzori (d'Arezzo), Gregor von

von Sternberg, Josef
See Sternberg, Josef von

Vorster, Gordon 1924- .... **CLC 34**
See also CA 133

Vosce, Trudie
See Ozick, Cynthia

Voznesensky, Andrei (Andreievich) 1933-
CLC 1, 15, 57; DAM POET
See also CA 89-92; CANR 37; MTCW

Waddington, Miriam 1917- .... **CLC 28**
See also CA 21-24R; CANR 12, 30; DLB 68

Wagman, Fredrica 1937-..................... **CLC 7**
See also CA 97-100; INT 97-100

Wagner, Linda W.
See Wagner-Martin, Linda (C.)

Wagner, Linda Welshimer
See Wagner-Martin, Linda (C.)

Wagner, Richard 1813-1883 .... **NCLC 9**
See also DLB 129

Wagner-Martin, Linda (C.) 1936- ...... **CLC 50**
See also CA 159

Wagoner, David (Russell) 1926-...**CLC 3, 5, 15**
See also CA 1-4R; CAAS 3; CANR 2; DLB 5; SATA 14

Wah, Fred(erick James) 1939- .... **CLC 44**
See also CA 107; 141; DLB 60

Wahloo, Per 1926-1975 .... **CLC 7**
See also CA 61-64

Wahloo, Peter
See Wahloo, Per

Wain, John (Barrington) 1925-1994 .. **CLC 2, 11, 15, 46**
See also CA 5-8R; 145; CAAS 4; CANR 23, 54; CDBLB 1960 to Present; DLB 15, 27, 139, 155; MTCW

Wajda, Andrzej 1926- .... **CLC 16**
See also CA 102

Wakefield, Dan 1932- .... **CLC 7**
See also CA 21-24R; CAAS 7

Wakoski, Diane 1937-... **CLC 2, 4, 7, 9, 11, 40; DAM POET; PC 15**
See also CA 13-16R; CAAS 1; CANR 9, 60; DLB 5; INT CANR-9

Wakoski-Sherbell, Diane
See Wakoski, Diane

Walcott, Derek (Alton) 1930-...**CLC 2, 4, 9, 14, 25, 42, 67, 76; BLC 3; DAB; DAC; DAM MST, MULT, POET; DC 7**
See also BW 2; CA 89-92; CANR 26, 47; DLB 117; DLBY 81; MTCW

Waldman, Anne (Lesley) 1945- .... **CLC 7**
See also CA 37-40R; CAAS 17; CANR 34, 69; DLB 16

Waldo, E. Hunter
See Sturgeon, Theodore (Hamilton)

Waldo, Edward Hamilton
See Sturgeon, Theodore (Hamilton)

Walker, Alice (Malsenior) 1944-...**CLC 5, 6, 9, 19, 27, 46, 58, 103; BLC 3; DA; DAB; DAC; DAM MST, MULT, NOV, POET, POP; SSC 5; WLCS**
See also AAYA 3; BEST 89:4; BW 2; CA 37-40R; CANR 9, 27, 49, 66; CDALB 1968-1988; DLB 6, 33, 143; INT CANR-27; MTCW; SATA 31

Walker, David Harry 1911-1992 .... **CLC 14**
See also CA 1-4R; 137; CANR 1; SATA 8; SATA-Obit 71

Walker, Edward Joseph 1934-
See Walker, Ted
See also CA 21-24R; CANR 12, 28, 53

Walker, George F. 1947- ... **CLC 44, 61; DAB; DAC; DAM MST**
See also CA 103; CANR 21, 43, 59; DLB 60

Walker, Joseph A. 1935-.........**CLC 19; DAM DRAM, MST**
See also BW 1; CA 89-92; CANR 26; DLB 38

Walker, Margaret (Abigail) 1915-.. **CLC 1, 6; BLC; DAM MULT; PC 20**
See also BW 2; CA 73-76; CANR 26, 54; DLB 76, 152; MTCW

Walker, Ted .... **CLC 13**
See also Walker, Edward Joseph
See also DLB 40

Wallace, David Foster 1962-.............. **CLC 50**
See also CA 132; CANR 59

Wallace, Dexter
See Masters, Edgar Lee

Wallace, (Richard Horatio) Edgar 1875-1932
  TCLC 57
    See also CA 115; DLB 70
Wallace, Irving 1916-1990 .. **CLC 7, 13; DAM NOV, POP**
    See also AITN 1; CA 1-4R; 132; CAAS 1; CANR 1, 27; INT CANR-27; MTCW
Wallant, Edward Lewis 1926-1962...**CLC 5, 10**
    See also CA 1-4R; CANR 22; DLB 2, 28, 143; MTCW
Walley, Byron
    See Card, Orson Scott
Walpole, Horace 1717-1797 .... **LC 2**
    See also DLB 39, 104
Walpole, Hugh (Seymour) 1884-1941...**TCLC 5**
    See also CA 104; 165; DLB 34
Walser, Martin 1927- .... **CLC 27**
    See also CA 57-60; CANR 8, 46; DLB 75, 124
Walser, Robert 1878-1956...**TCLC 18; SSC 20**
    See also CA 118; 165; DLB 66
Walsh, Jill Paton .... **CLC 35**
    See also Paton Walsh, Gillian
    See also AAYA 11; CLR 2; DLB 161; SAAS 3
Walter, Villiam Christian
    See Andersen, Hans Christian
Wambaugh, Joseph (Aloysius, Jr.) 1937-...**CLC 3, 18; DAM NOV, POP**
    See also AITN 1; BEST 89:3; CA 33-36R; CANR 42, 65; DLB 6; DLBY 83; MTCW
Wang Wei 699(?)-761(?) .... **PC 18**
Ward, Arthur Henry Sarsfield 1883-1959
    See Rohmer, Sax
    See also CA 108
Ward, Douglas Turner 1930- .... **CLC 19**
    See also BW 1; CA 81-84; CANR 27; DLB 7, 38
Ward, Mary Augusta
    See Ward, Mrs. Humphry
Ward, Mrs. Humphry 1851-1920.... **TCLC 55**
    See also DLB 18
Ward, Peter
    See Faust, Frederick (Schiller)
Warhol, Andy 1928(?)-1987 .... **CLC 20**
    See also AAYA 12; BEST 89:4; CA 89-92; 121; CANR 34
Warner, Francis (Robert le Plastrier) 1937-
  CLC 14
    See also CA 53-56; CANR 11
Warner, Marina 1946- .... **CLC 59**
    See also CA 65-68; CANR 21, 55; DLB 194
Warner, Rex (Ernest) 1905-1986 .... **CLC 45**
    See also CA 89-92; 119; DLB 15
Warner, Susan (Bogert) 1819-1885...**NCLC 31**
    See also DLB 3, 42
Warner, Sylvia (Constance) Ashton
    See Ashton-Warner, Sylvia (Constance)
Warner, Sylvia Townsend 1893-1978 .. **CLC 7, 19; SSC 23**
    See also CA 61-64; 77-80; CANR 16, 60; DLB 34, 139; MTCW
Warren, Mercy Otis 1728-1814 ...... **NCLC 13**
    See also DLB 31, 200
Warren, Robert Penn 1905-1989...**CLC 1, 4, 6, 8, 10, 13, 18, 39, 53, 59; DA; DAB; DAC; DAM MST, NOV, POET; SSC 4; WLC**
    See also AITN 1; CA 13-16R; 129; CANR 10, 47; CDALB 1968-1988; DLB 2, 48, 152; DLBY 80, 89; INT CANR-10; MTCW; SATA 46; SATA-Obit 63
Warshofsky, Isaac
    See Singer, Isaac Bashevis
Warton, Thomas 1728-1790 ...... **LC 15; DAM POET**
    See also DLB 104, 109

Waruk, Kona
    See Harris, (Theodore) Wilson
Warung, Price 1855-1911 .... **TCLC 45**
Warwick, Jarvis
    See Garner, Hugh
Washington, Alex
    See Harris, Mark
Washington, Booker T(aliaferro) 1856-1915
  TCLC 10; BLC 3; DAM MULT
    See also BW 1; CA 114; 125; SATA 28
Washington, George 1732-1799 .... **LC 25**
    See also DLB 31
Wassermann, (Karl) Jakob 1873-1934
  TCLC 6
    See also CA 104; DLB 66
Wasserstein, Wendy 1950- .... **CLC 32, 59, 90; DAM DRAM; DC 4**
    See also CA 121; 129; CABS 3; CANR 53; INT 129; SATA 94
Waterhouse, Keith (Spencer) 1929-...**CLC 47**
    See also CA 5-8R; CANR 38, 67; DLB 13, 15; MTCW
Waters, Frank (Joseph) 1902-1995 .... **CLC 88**
    See also CA 5-8R; 149; CAAS 13; CANR 3, 18, 63; DLBY 86
Waters, Roger 1944- .... **CLC 35**
Watkins, Frances Ellen
    See Harper, Frances Ellen Watkins
Watkins, Gerrold
    See Malzberg, Barry N(athaniel)
Watkins, Gloria 1955(?)-
    See hooks, bell
    See also BW 2; CA 143
Watkins, Paul 1964- .... **CLC 55**
    See also CA 132; CANR 62
Watkins, Vernon Phillips 1906-1967 .. **CLC 43**
    See also CA 9-10; 25-28R; CAP 1; DLB 20
Watson, Irving S.
    See Mencken, H(enry) L(ouis)
Watson, John H.
    See Farmer, Philip Jose
Watson, Richard F.
    See Silverberg, Robert
Waugh, Auberon (Alexander) 1939- .... **CLC 7**
    See also CA 45-48; CANR 6, 22; DLB 14, 194
Waugh, Evelyn (Arthur St. John) 1903-1966
  CLC 1, 3, 8, 13, 19, 27, 44, 107; DA; DAB; DAC; DAM MST, NOV, POP; WLC
    See also CA 85-88; 25-28R; CANR 22; CDBLB 1914-1945; DLB 15, 162, 195; MTCW
Waugh, Harriet 1944- .... **CLC 6**
    See also CA 85-88; CANR 22
Ways, C. R.
    See Blount, Roy (Alton), Jr.
Waystaff, Simon
    See Swift, Jonathan
Webb, (Martha) Beatrice (Potter) 1858-1943
  TCLC 22
    See also Potter, (Helen) Beatrix
    See also CA 117
Webb, Charles (Richard) 1939- .... **CLC 7**
    See also CA 25-28R
Webb, James H(enry), Jr. 1946- .... **CLC 22**
    See also CA 81-84
Webb, Mary (Gladys Meredith) 1881-1927
  TCLC 24
    See also CA 123; DLB 34
Webb, Mrs. Sidney
    See Webb, (Martha) Beatrice (Potter)
Webb, Phyllis 1927- .... **CLC 18**
    See also CA 104; CANR 23; DLB 53
Webb, Sidney (James) 1859-1947 ... **TCLC 22**
    See also CA 117; 163; DLB 190

Webber, Andrew Lloyd .... **CLC 21**
    See also Lloyd Webber, Andrew
Weber, Lenora Mattingly 1895-1971...**CLC 12**
    See also CA 19-20; 29-32R; CAP 1; SATA 2; SATA-Obit 26
Weber, Max 1864-1920 .... **TCLC 69**
    See also CA 109
Webster, John 1579(?)-1634(?).... **LC 33; DA; DAB; DAC; DAM DRAM, MST; DC 2; WLC**
    See also CDBLB Before 1660; DLB 58
Webster, Noah 1758-1843 .... **NCLC 30**
Wedekind, (Benjamin) Frank(lin) 1864-1918
  TCLC 7; DAM DRAM
    See also CA 104; 153; DLB 118
Weidman, Jerome 1913- .... **CLC 7**
    See also AITN 2; CA 1-4R; CANR 1; DLB 28
Weil, Simone (Adolphine) 1909-1943
  TCLC 23
    See also CA 117; 159
Weinstein, Nathan
    See West, Nathanael
Weinstein, Nathan von Wallenstein
    See West, Nathanael
Weir, Peter (Lindsay) 1944- .... **CLC 20**
    See also CA 113; 123
Weiss, Peter (Ulrich) 1916-1982 .. **CLC 3, 15, 51; DAM DRAM**
    See also CA 45-48; 106; CANR 3; DLB 69, 124
Weiss, Theodore (Russell) 1916-...**CLC 3, 8, 14**
    See also CA 9-12R; CAAS 2; CANR 46; DLB 5
Welch, (Maurice) Denton 1915-1948..**TCLC 22**
    See also CA 121; 148
Welch, James 1940- .... **CLC 6, 14, 52; DAM MULT, POP**
    See also CA 85-88; CANR 42, 66; DLB 175; NNAL
Weldon, Fay 1931-... **CLC 6, 9, 11, 19, 36, 59; DAM POP**
    See also CA 21-24R; CANR 16, 46, 63; CDBLB 1960 to Present; DLB 14, 194; INT CANR-16; MTCW
Wellek, Rene 1903-1995 .... **CLC 28**
    See also CA 5-8R; 150; CAAS 7; CANR 8; DLB 63; INT CANR-8
Weller, Michael 1942- .... **CLC 10, 53**
    See also CA 85-88
Weller, Paul 1958- .... **CLC 26**
Wellershoff, Dieter 1925- .... **CLC 46**
    See also CA 89-92; CANR 16, 37
Welles, (George) Orson 1915-1985...**CLC 20, 80**
    See also CA 93-96; 117
Wellman, John McDowell 1945-
    See Wellman, Mac
    See also CA 166
Wellman, Mac 1945- .... **CLC 65**
    See also Wellman, John McDowell; Wellman, John McDowell
Wellman, Manly Wade 1903-1986 ..... **CLC 49**
    See also CA 1-4R; 118; CANR 6, 16, 44; SATA 6; SATA-Obit 47
Wells, Carolyn 1869(?)-1942 .... **TCLC 35**
    See also CA 113; DLB 11
Wells, H(erbert) G(eorge) 1866-1946
  TCLC 6, 12, 19; DA; DAB; DAC; DAM MST, NOV; SSC 6; WLC
    See also AAYA 18; CA 110; 121; CDBLB 1914-1945; DLB 34, 70, 156, 178; MTCW; SATA 20
Wells, Rosemary 1943- .... **CLC 12**
    See also AAYA 13; CA 85-88; CANR 48; CLR 16; MAICYA; SAAS 1; SATA 18, 69

Welty, Eudora 1909-...**CLC 1, 2, 5, 14, 22, 33, 105; DA; DAB; DAC; DAM MST, NOV; SSC 1, 27; WLC**
See also CA 9-12R; CABS 1; CANR 32, 65; CDALB 1941-1968; DLB 2, 102, 143; DLBD 12; DLBY 87; MTCW
Wen I-to 1899-1946 .... **TCLC 28**
Wentworth, Robert
See Hamilton, Edmond
Werfel, Franz (Viktor) 1890-1945 ..... **TCLC 8**
See also CA 104; 161; DLB 81, 124
Wergeland, Henrik Arnold 1808-1845
NCLC 5
Wersba, Barbara 1932- .... **CLC 30**
See also AAYA 2; CA 29-32R; CANR 16, 38; CLR 3; DLB 52; JRDA; MAICYA; SAAS 2; SATA 1, 58
Wertmueller, Lina 1928- .... **CLC 16**
See also CA 97-100; CANR 39
Wescott, Glenway 1901-1987 .... **CLC 13**
See also CA 13-16R; 121; CANR 23; DLB 4, 9, 102
Wesker, Arnold 1932-.... **CLC 3, 5, 42; DAB; DAM DRAM**
See also CA 1-4R; CAAS 7; CANR 1, 33; CDBLB 1960 to Present; DLB 13; MTCW
Wesley, Richard (Errol) 1945- .... **CLC 7**
See also BW 1; CA 57-60; CANR 27; DLB 38
Wessel, Johan Herman 1742-1785 .... **LC 7**
West, Anthony (Panther) 1914-1987 .. **CLC 50**
See also CA 45-48; 124; CANR 3, 19; DLB 15
West, C. P.
See Wodehouse, P(elham) G(renville)
West, (Mary) Jessamyn 1902-1984...**CLC 7, 17**
See also CA 9-12R; 112; CANR 27; DLB 6; DLBY 84; MTCW; SATA-Obit 37
West, Morris L(anglo) 1916- .... **CLC 6, 33**
See also CA 5-8R; CANR 24, 49, 64; MTCW
West, Nathanael 1903-1940 .. **TCLC 1, 14, 44; SSC 16**
See also CA 104; 125; CDALB 1929-1941; DLB 4, 9, 28; MTCW
West, Owen
See Koontz, Dean R(ay)
West, Paul 1930- .... **CLC 7, 14, 96**
See also CA 13-16R; CAAS 7; CANR 22, 53; DLB 14; INT CANR-22
West, Rebecca 1892-1983 ..... **CLC 7, 9, 31, 50**
See also CA 5-8R; 109; CANR 19; DLB 36; DLBY 83; MTCW
Westall, Robert (Atkinson) 1929-1993
CLC 17
See also AAYA 12; CA 69-72; 141; CANR 18, 68; CLR 13; JRDA; MAICYA; SAAS 2; SATA 23, 69; SATA-Obit 75
Westlake, Donald E(dwin) 1933- .. **CLC 7, 33; DAM POP**
See also CA 17-20R; CAAS 13; CANR 16, 44, 65; INT CANR-16
Westmacott, Mary
See Christie, Agatha (Mary Clarissa)
Weston, Allen
See Norton, Andre
Wetcheek, J. L.
See Feuchtwanger, Lion
Wetering, Janwillem van de
See van de Wetering, Janwillem
Wetherald, Agnes Ethelwyn 1857-1940
TCLC 81
See also DLB 99
Wetherell, Elizabeth
See Warner, Susan (Bogert)
Whale, James 1889-1957 .... **TCLC 63**

Whalen, Philip 1923- .... **CLC 6, 29**
See also CA 9-12R; CANR 5, 39; DLB 16
Wharton, Edith (Newbold Jones) 1862-1937
TCLC 3, 9, 27, 53; DA; DAB; DAC; DAM MST, NOV; SSC 6; WLC
See also AAYA 25; CA 104; 132; CDALB 1865-1917; DLB 4, 9, 12, 78, 189; DLBD 13; MTCW
Wharton, James
See Mencken, H(enry) L(ouis)
Wharton, William (a pseudonym) .. **CLC 18, 37**
See also CA 93-96; DLBY 80; INT 93-96
Wheatley (Peters), Phillis 1754(?)-1784...**LC 3; BLC 3; DA; DAC; DAM MST, MULT, POET; PC 3; WLC**
See also CDALB 1640-1865; DLB 31, 50
Wheelock, John Hall 1886-1978 .... **CLC 14**
See also CA 13-16R; 77-80; CANR 14; DLB 45
White, E(lwyn) B(rooks) 1899-1985...**CLC 10, 34, 39; DAM POP**
See also AITN 2; CA 13-16R; 116; CANR 16, 37; CLR 1, 21; DLB 11, 22; MAICYA; MTCW; SATA 2, 29; SATA-Obit 44
White, Edmund (Valentine III) 1940-...**CLC 27, 110; DAM POP**
See also AAYA 7; CA 45-48; CANR 3, 19, 36, 62; MTCW
White, Patrick (Victor Martindale) 1912-1990
CLC 3, 4, 5, 7, 9, 18, 65, 69
See also CA 81-84; 132; CANR 43; MTCW
White, Phyllis Dorothy James 1920-
See James, P. D.
See also CA 21-24R; CANR 17, 43, 65; DAM POP; MTCW
White, T(erence) H(anbury) 1906-1964
CLC 30
See also AAYA 22; CA 73-76; CANR 37; DLB 160; JRDA; MAICYA; SATA 12
White, Terence de Vere 1912-1994 .... **CLC 49**
See also CA 49-52; 145; CANR 3
White, Walter F(rancis) 1893-1955...**TCLC 15**
See also White, Walter
See also BW 1; CA 115; 124; DLB 51
White, William Hale 1831-1913
See Rutherford, Mark
See also CA 121
Whitehead, E(dward) A(nthony) 1933-...**CLC 5**
See also CA 65-68; CANR 58
Whitemore, Hugh (John) 1936- .... **CLC 37**
See also CA 132; INT 132
Whitman, Sarah Helen (Power) 1803-1878
NCLC 19
See also DLB 1
Whitman, Walt(er) 1819-1892 .. **NCLC 4, 31; DA; DAB; DAC; DAM MST, POET; PC 3; WLC**
See also CDALB 1640-1865; DLB 3, 64; SATA 20
Whitney, Phyllis A(yame) 1903- ..... **CLC 42; DAM POP**
See also AITN 2; BEST 90:3; CA 1-4R; CANR 3, 25, 38, 60; JRDA; MAICYA; SATA 1, 30
Whittemore, (Edward) Reed (Jr.) 1919-
CLC 4
See also CA 9-12R; CAAS 8; CANR 4; DLB 5
Whittier, John Greenleaf 1807-1892...**NCLC 8, 59**
See also DLB 1
Whittlebot, Hernia
See Coward, Noel (Peirce)
Wicker, Thomas Grey 1926-
See Wicker, Tom
See also CA 65-68; CANR 21, 46

Wicker, Tom .... **CLC 7**
See also Wicker, Thomas Grey
Wideman, John Edgar 1941-...**CLC 5, 34, 36, 67; BLC 3; DAM MULT**
See also BW 2; CA 85-88; CANR 14, 42, 67; DLB 33, 143
Wiebe, Rudy (Henry) 1934-.... **CLC 6, 11, 14; DAC; DAM MST**
See also CA 37-40R; CANR 42, 67; DLB 60
Wieland, Christoph Martin 1733-1813
NCLC 17
See also DLB 97
Wiene, Robert 1881-1938 .... **TCLC 56**
Wieners, John 1934- .... **CLC 7**
See also CA 13-16R; DLB 16
Wiesel, Elie(zer) 1928-...**CLC 3, 5, 11, 37; DA; DAB; DAC; DAM MST, NOV; WLCS 2**
See also AAYA 7; AITN 1; CA 5-8R; CAAS 4; CANR 8, 40, 65; DLB 83; DLBY 87; INT CANR-8; MTCW; SATA 56
Wiggins, Marianne 1947- .... **CLC 57**
See also BEST 89:3; CA 130; CANR 60
Wight, James Alfred 1916-1995
See Herriot, James
See also CA 77-80; SATA 55; SATA-Brief 44
Wilbur, Richard (Purdy) 1921-...**CLC 3, 6, 9, 14, 53, 110; DA; DAB; DAC; DAM MST, POET**
See also CA 1-4R; CABS 2; CANR 2, 29; DLB 5, 169; INT CANR-29; MTCW; SATA 9
Wild, Peter 1940- .... **CLC 14**
See also CA 37-40R; DLB 5
Wilde, Oscar (Fingal O'Flahertie Wills) 1854(?)-1900 ... **TCLC 1, 8, 23, 41; DA; DAB; DAC; DAM DRAM, MST, NOV; SSC 11; WLC**
See also CA 104; 119; CDBLB 1890-1914; DLB 10, 19, 34, 57, 141, 156, 190; SATA 24
Wilder, Billy .... **CLC 20**
See also Wilder, Samuel
See also DLB 26
Wilder, Samuel 1906-
See Wilder, Billy
See also CA 89-92
Wilder, Thornton (Niven) 1897-1975... **C L C 1, 5, 6, 10, 15, 35, 82; DA; DAB; DAC; DAM DRAM, MST, NOV; DC 1; WLC**
See also AITN 2; CA 13-16R; 61-64; CANR 40; DLB 4, 7, 9; DLBY 97; MTCW
Wilding, Michael 1942- .... **CLC 73**
See also CA 104; CANR 24, 49
Wiley, Richard 1944- .... **CLC 44**
See also CA 121; 129
Wilhelm, Kate .... **CLC 7**
See also Wilhelm, Katie Gertrude
See also AAYA 20; CAAS 5; DLB 8; INT CANR-17
Wilhelm, Katie Gertrude 1928-
See Wilhelm, Kate
See also CA 37-40R; CANR 17, 36, 60; MTCW
Wilkins, Mary
See Freeman, Mary Eleanor Wilkins
Willard, Nancy 1936- .... **CLC 7, 37**
See also CA 89-92; CANR 10, 39, 68; CLR 5; DLB 5, 52; MAICYA; MTCW; SATA 37, 71; SATA-Brief 30
Williams, C(harles) K(enneth) 1936-...**CLC 33, 56; DAM POET**
See also CA 37-40R; CAAS 26; CANR 57; DLB 5
Williams, Charles
See Collier, James L(incoln)
Williams, Charles (Walter Stansby) 1886-1945
TCLC 1, 11
See also CA 104; 163; DLB 100, 153

Williams, (George) Emlyn 1905-1987...**C L C 15; DAM DRAM**
See also CA 104; 123; CANR 36; DLB 10, 77; MTCW

Williams, Hank 1923-1953 .... **TCLC 81**

Williams, Hugo 1942- .... **CLC 42**
See also CA 17-20R; CANR 45; DLB 40

Williams, J. Walker
See Wodehouse, P(elham) G(renville)

Williams, John A(lfred) 1925- .... **CLC 5, 13; BLC 3; DAM MULT**
See also BW 2; CA 53-56; CAAS 3; CANR 6, 26, 51; DLB 2, 33; INT CANR-6

Williams, Jonathan (Chamberlain) 1929-
CLC 13
See also CA 9-12R; CAAS 12; CANR 8; DLB 5

Williams, Joy 1944- .... **CLC 31**
See also CA 41-44R; CANR 22, 48

Williams, Norman 1952- .... **CLC 39**
See also CA 118

Williams, Sherley Anne 1944- .... **CLC 89; BLC 3; DAM MULT, POET**
See also BW 2; CA 73-76; CANR 25; DLB 41; INT CANR-25; SATA 78

Williams, Shirley
See Williams, Sherley Anne

Williams, Tennessee 1911-1983...**CLC 1, 2, 5, 7, 8, 11, 15, 19, 30, 39, 45, 71, 111; DA; DAB; DAC; DAM DRAM, MST; DC 4; WLC**
See also AITN 1, 2; CA 5-8R; 108; CABS 3; CANR 31; CDALB 1941-1968; DLB 7; DLBD 4; DLBY 83; MTCW

Williams, Thomas (Alonzo) 1926-1990**CLC 14**
See also CA 1-4R; 132; CANR 2

Williams, William C.
See Williams, William Carlos

Williams, William Carlos 1883-1963... **CLC 1, 2, 5, 9, 13, 22, 42, 67; DA; DAB; DAC; DAM MST, POET; PC 7; SSC 31**
See also CA 89-92; CANR 34; CDALB 1917-1929; DLB 4, 16, 54, 86; MTCW

Williamson, David (Keith) 1942- .... **CLC 56**
See also CA 103; CANR 41

Williamson, Ellen Douglas 1905-1984
See Douglas, Ellen
See also CA 17-20R; 114; CANR 39

Williamson, Jack .... **CLC 29**
See also Williamson, John Stewart
See also CAAS 8; DLB 8

Williamson, John Stewart 1908-
See Williamson, Jack
See also CA 17-20R; CANR 23

Willie, Frederick
See Lovecraft, H(oward) P(hillips)

Willingham, Calder (Baynard, Jr.) 1922-1995
CLC 5, 51
See also CA 5-8R; 147; CANR 3; DLB 2, 44; MTCW

Willis, Charles
See Clarke, Arthur C(harles)

Willy
See Colette, (Sidonie-Gabrielle)

Willy, Colette
See Colette, (Sidonie-Gabrielle)

Wilson, A(ndrew) N(orman) 1950- ..... **CLC 33**
See also CA 112; 122; DLB 14, 155, 194

Wilson, Angus (Frank Johnstone) 1913-1991
CLC 2, 3, 5, 25, 34; SSC 21
See also CA 5-8R; 134; CANR 21; DLB 15, 139, 155; MTCW

Wilson, August 1945-...**CLC 39, 50, 63; BLC 3; DA; DAB; DAC; DAM DRAM, MST, MULT; DC 2; WLCS**
See also AAYA 16; BW 2; CA 115; 122; CANR 42, 54; MTCW

Wilson, Brian 1942- .... **CLC 12**

Wilson, Colin 1931- .... **CLC 3, 14**
See also CA 1-4R; CAAS 5; CANR 1, 22, 33; DLB 14, 194; MTCW

Wilson, Dirk
See Pohl, Frederik

Wilson, Edmund 1895-1972...**CLC 1, 2, 3, 8, 24**
See also CA 1-4R; 37-40R; CANR 1, 46; DLB 63; MTCW

Wilson, Ethel Davis (Bryant) 1888(?)-1980
CLC 13; DAC; DAM POET
See also CA 102; DLB 68; MTCW

Wilson, John 1785-1854 .... **NCLC 5**

Wilson, John (Anthony) Burgess 1917-1993
See Burgess, Anthony
See also CA 1-4R; 143; CANR 2, 46; DAC; DAM NOV; MTCW

Wilson, Lanford 1937-... **CLC 7, 14, 36; DAM DRAM**
See also CA 17-20R; CABS 3; CANR 45; DLB 7

Wilson, Robert M. 1944- .... **CLC 7, 9**
See also CA 49-52; CANR 2, 41; MTCW

Wilson, Robert McLiam 1964- .... **CLC 59**
See also CA 132

Wilson, Sloan 1920- .... **CLC 32**
See also CA 1-4R; CANR 1, 44

Wilson, Snoo 1948- .... **CLC 33**
See also CA 69-72

Wilson, William S(mith) 1932- .... **CLC 49**
See also CA 81-84

Wilson, (Thomas) Woodrow 1856-1924
TCLC 79
See also CA 166; DLB 47

Winchilsea, Anne (Kingsmill) Finch Counte 1661-1720
See Finch, Anne

Windham, Basil
See Wodehouse, P(elham) G(renville)

Wingrove, David (John) 1954- .... **CLC 68**
See also CA 133

Wintergreen, Jane
See Duncan, Sara Jeannette

Winters, Janet Lewis .... **CLC 41**
See also Lewis, Janet
See also DLBY 87

Winters, (Arthur) Yvor 1900-1968...**CLC 4, 8, 32**
See also CA 11-12; 25-28R; CAP 1; DLB 48; MTCW

Winterson, Jeanette 1959- ... **CLC 64; DAM POP**
See also CA 136; CANR 58

Winthrop, John 1588-1649 .... **LC 31**
See also DLB 24, 30

Wiseman, Frederick 1930- .... **CLC 20**
See also CA 159

Wister, Owen 1860-1938 .... **TCLC 21**
See also CA 108; 162; DLB 9, 78, 186; SATA 62

Witkacy
See Witkiewicz, Stanislaw Ignacy

Witkiewicz, Stanislaw Ignacy 1885-1939
TCLC 8
See also CA 105; 162

Wittgenstein, Ludwig (Josef Johann) 1889-1951
TCLC 59
See also CA 113; 164

Wittig, Monique 1935(?)- .... **CLC 22**
See also CA 116; 135; DLB 83

Wittlin, Jozef 1896-1976 .... **CLC 25**
See also CA 49-52; 65-68; CANR 3

Wodehouse, P(elham) G(renville) 1881-1975
CLC 1, 2, 5, 10, 22; DAB; DAC; DAM NOV; SSC 2
See also AITN 2; CA 45-48; 57-60; CANR 3, 33; CDBLB 1914-1945; DLB 34, 162; MTCW; SATA 22

Woiwode, L.
See Woiwode, Larry (Alfred)

Woiwode, Larry (Alfred) 1941- ...... **CLC 6, 10**
See also CA 73-76; CANR 16; DLB 6; INT CANR-16

Wojciechowska, Maia (Teresa) 1927-...**CLC 26**
See also AAYA 8; CA 9-12R; CANR 4, 41; CLR 1; JRDA; MAICYA; SAAS 1; SATA 1, 28, 83

Wolf, Christa 1929- .... **CLC 14, 29, 58**
See also CA 85-88; CANR 45; DLB 75; MTCW

Wolfe, Gene (Rodman) 1931-...**CLC 25; DAM POP**
See also CA 57-60; CAAS 9; CANR 6, 32, 60; DLB 8

Wolfe, George C. 1954- .... **CLC 49; BLCS**
See also CA 149

Wolfe, Thomas (Clayton) 1900-1938...**TCLC 4, 13, 29, 61; DA; DAB; DAC; DAM MST, NOV; WLC**
See also CA 104; 132; CDALB 1929-1941; DLB 9, 102; DLBD 2, 16; DLBY 85, 97; MTCW

Wolfe, Thomas Kennerly, Jr. 1931-
See Wolfe, Tom
See also CA 13-16R; CANR 9, 33; DAM POP; DLB 185; INT CANR-9; MTCW

Wolfe, Tom .... **CLC 1, 2, 9, 15, 35, 51**
See also Wolfe, Thomas Kennerly, Jr.
See also AAYA 8; AITN 2; BEST 89:1; DLB 152

Wolff, Geoffrey (Ansell) 1937- .... **CLC 41**
See also CA 29-32R; CANR 29, 43

Wolff, Sonia
See Levitin, Sonia (Wolff)

Wolff, Tobias (Jonathan Ansell) 1945- .. **C L C 39, 64**
See also AAYA 16; BEST 90:2; CA 114; 117; CAAS 22; CANR 54; DLB 130; INT 117

Wolfram von Eschenbach c. 1170-c. 1220
CMLC 5
See also DLB 138

Wolitzer, Hilma 1930- .... **CLC 17**
See also CA 65-68; CANR 18, 40; INT CANR-18; SATA 31

Wollstonecraft, Mary 1759-1797 .... **LC 5**
See also CDBLB 1789-1832; DLB 39, 104, 158

Wonder, Stevie .... **CLC 12**
See also Morris, Steveland Judkins

Wong, Jade Snow 1922- .... **CLC 17**
See also CA 109

Woodberry, George Edward 1855-1930
TCLC 73
See also CA 165; DLB 71, 103

Woodcott, Keith
See Brunner, John (Kilian Houston)

Woodruff, Robert W.
See Mencken, H(enry) L(ouis)

Woolf, (Adeline) Virginia 1882-1941... **T C L C 1, 5, 20, 43, 56; DA; DAB; DAC; DAM MST, NOV; SSC 7; WLC**
See also CA 104; 130; CANR 64; CDBLB 1914-1945; DLB 36, 100, 162; DLBD 10; MTCW

Woolf, Virginia Adeline
See Woolf, (Adeline) Virginia

Poetry Criticism
Cumulative Nationality Index

AMERICAN
Ammons, A(rchie) R(andolph) 16
Auden, W(ystan) H(ugh) 1
Baraka, Amiri 4
Bishop, Elizabeth 3
Bogan, Louise 12
Bradstreet, Anne 10
Brodsky, Joseph 9
Brooks, Gwendolyn 7
Bryant, William Cullen 20
Bukowski, Charles 18
Carruth, Hayden 10
Clampitt, Amy 19
Clifton, (Thelma) Lucille 17
Crane, (Harold) Hart 3
Cullen, Countee 20
Cummings, E(dward) E(stlin) 5
Dickinson, Emily (Elizabeth) 1
Doolittle, Hilda 5
Dove, Rita (Frances) 6
Dunbar, Paul Laurence 5
Duncan, Robert (Edward) 2
Eliot, T(homas) S(tearns) 5
Emerson, Ralph Waldo 18
Ferlinghetti, Lawrence (Monsanto) 1
Forche, Carolyn (Louise) 10
Frost, Robert (Lee) 1
Gallagher, Tess 9
Ginsberg, Allen 4
Giovanni, Nikki 19
Gluck, Louise (Elisabeth) 16
Hammon, Jupiter 16
Harper, Frances Ellen Watkins 21
Hass, Robert 16
Hayden, Robert E(arl) 6
H. D. 5
Hongo, Garrett Kaoru 23
Hughes, (James) Langston 1
Jeffers, (John) Robinson 17
Knight, Etheridge 14
Kumin, Maxine (Winokur) 15
Kunitz, Stanley (Jasspon) 19
Levertov, Denise 11
Levine, Philip 22
Lindsay, (Nicholas) Vachel 23
Lorde, Audre (Geraldine) 12
Lowell, Amy 13
Lowell, Robert (Traill Spence Jr.) 3
Loy, Mina 16
Madhubuti, Haki R. 5
Masters, Edgar Lee 1
McKay, Claude 2
Merton, Thomas 10
Millay, Edna St. Vincent 6
Moore, Marianne (Craig) 4
Nash, (Frediric) Ogden 21
Olds, Sharon 22
Olson, Charles (John) 19
Ortiz, Simon J(oseph) 17
Plath, Sylvia 1

Poe, Edgar Allan 1
Pound, Ezra (Weston Loomis) 4
Rexroth, Kenneth 20
Rich, Adrienne (Cecile) 5
Robinson, Edwin Arlington 1
Roethke, Theodore (Huebner) 15
Rose, Wendy 13
Rukeyser, Muriel 12
Sanchez, Sonia 9
Sandburg, Carl (August) 2
Schwartz, Delmore (David) 8
Sexton, Anne (Harvey) 2
Snyder, Gary (Sherman) 21
Song, Cathy 21
Stein, Gertrude 18
Stevens, Wallace 6
Swenson, May 14
Toomer, Jean 7
Wakoski, Diane 15
Walker, Margaret (Abigail) 20
Wheatley (Peters), Phillis 3
Whitman, Walt(er) 3
Williams, William Carlos 7
Wylie, Elinor (Morton Hoyt) 23
Zukofsky, Louis 11

ARGENTINIAN
Borges, Jorge Luis 22

AUSTRALIAN
Wright, Judith (Arandell) 14

AUSTRIAN
Trakl, Georg 20

CANADIAN
Atwood, Margaret (Eleanor) 8
Bissett, Bill 14
Page, P(atricia) K(athleen) 12

CHILEAN
Neruda, Pablo 4

CHINESE
Li Ho 13
Tu Fu 9
Wang Wei 18

CUBAN
Guillen, Nicolas (Cristobal) 23

ENGLISH
Arnold, Matthew 5
Auden, W(ystan) H(ugh) 1
Behn, Aphra 13
Blake, William 12
Bradstreet, Anne 10
Bronte, Emily (Jane) 8
Browning, Elizabeth Barrett 6
Browning, Robert 2
Byron, George Gordon (Noel) 16
Carroll, Lewis 18
Chaucer, Geoffrey 19
Clare, John 23

Coleridge, Samuel Taylor 11
Day Lewis, C(ecil) 11
Donne, John 1
Eliot, George 20
Eliot, T(homas) S(tearns) 5
Graves, Robert (von Ranke) 6
Gray, Thomas 2
Hardy, Thomas 8
Herbert, George 4
Herrick, Robert 9
Hopkins, Gerard Manley 15
Housman, A(lfred) E(dward) 2
Hughes, Ted 7
Jonson, Ben(jamin) 17
Keats, John 1
Kipling, (Joseph) Rudyard 3
Larkin, Philip (Arthur) 21
Levertov, Denise 11
Loy, Mina 16
Marvell, Andrew 10
Milton, John 19
Montagu, Mary (Pierrepont) Wortley 16
Owen, Wilfred (Edward Salter) 19
Page, P(atricia) K(athleen) 12
Rossetti, Christina (Georgina) 7
Sassoon, Siegfried (Lorraine) 12
Shelley, Percy Bysshe 14
Sitwell, Dame Edith 3
Smart, Christopher 13
Smith, Stevie 12
Spenser, Edmund 8
Swift, Jonathan 9
Tennyson, Alfred 6
Tomlinson, (Alfred) Charles 17
Wordsworth, William 4

FILIPINO
Villa, Jose Garcia 22

FRENCH
Apollinaire, Guillaume 7
Baudelaire, Charles 1
Breton, Andre 15
Gautier, Theophile 18
Hugo, Victor (Marie) 17
Laforgue, Jules 14
Lamartine, Alphonse (Marie Louis Prat) de 16
Leger, (Marie-Rene Auguste) Alexis Saint-Leger 23
Mallarme, Stephane 4
Marie de France 22
Merton, Thomas 10
Nerval, Gerard de 13
Rimbaud, (Jean Nicolas) Arthur 3
Ronsard, Pierre de 11
Valery, (Ambroise) Paul (Toussaint Jules) 9
Verlaine, Paul (Marie) 2
Villon, Francois 13

GERMAN
Bukowski, Charles 18
Goethe, Johann Wolfgang von 5
Holderlin, (Johann Christian) Friedrich 4
Rilke, Rainer Maria 2

PC Cumulative Title Index

Title Index

"At the National Black Assembly" (Baraka) 4:28, 38
"At the Piano" (Hardy) 8:93
"At the Tourist Centre in Boston" (Atwood) 8:5, 23
At the Very Edge of the Sea (Akhmatova) See *U samovo morya*
"At The-Place-of-Sadness" (Gallagher) 9:64
"At This Point" (Montale) See "A questo punto"
"At Waking" (Hardy) 8:104
"At Welsh's Tomb" (Wakoski) 15:353
Atarashiki yokujo (Hagiwara Sakutaro) 18:175
"Atavism" (Wylie) 23:301, 307
"Atavismo" (Pavese) 13:209, 214
Atemwende (*Breath-Turning*) (Celan) 10:96-7, 105, 110
"AThe Miracle" (Bukowski) 18:5
"Atherton's Gambit" (Robinson) 1:466
"Atlanta in Camden Town" (Carroll) 18:46
Atlanta Offering Poems (Harper) 21:189
"The Atlantic" (Tomlinson) 17:333
"Atlantic City Waiter" (Cullen) 20:52, 64
"Atlantic Oil" (Pavese) 13:223
"Atlantis" (Crane) 3:90, 97, 106, 110-11
"An Atlas of the Difficult World" (Rich) 5:398
An Atlas of the Difficult World: Poems, 1988-1991 (Rich) 5:398-99
"Attack" (Sassoon) 12:266, 283-84, 286
"An Attempt at a Room" (Tsvetaeva) See "Popytka komnaty"
"An Attempt at Jealousy" (Tsvetaeva) See "Popytka revnosti"
"Attention, Attention" (Baraka) 4:24
"The Attic Which Is Desire" (Williams) 7:351, 399
"Attis" (Tennyson) 6:363
"Atys, the Land of Biscay" (Housman) 2:179, 181
"Au caberet-vert" ("At the Caberet-Vert") (Rimbaud) 3:283
"Au Clair de la lune" (MacDiarmid) 9:191
"Au Comte d'Orsay" (Lamartine) 16:267
"Au lecteur" ("Hypocrite lecteur"; "To the Reader") (Baudelaire) 1:46, 57, 67, 70
"Au platane" (Valery) 9:365, 394-96
"Au Rossignol" (Lamartine) 16:280
"Au Roy" (Ronsard) See "Discours au Roy"
"Au Salon" (Pound) 4:364
"Aubade" (Gluck) 16:133
"Aubade" (Larkin) 21:259
"Aubade" (Lowell) 13:93
"Aubade" (Sitwell) 3:297
"Aubade" (Smith) 12:331
"Aubade: Harlem" (Merton) 10:340
"Aubade: Lake Erie" (Merton) 10:333, 340, 350
"Aubade--The Annunciation" (Merton) 10:339
"Aube" (Rimbaud) 3:261-62, 264
"L'aube spirituelle" (Baudelaire) 1:56, 63
"Audley Court" (Tennyson) 6:365
"Auf dem See" ("On the Lake") (Goethe) 5:255
"Auguries of Innocence" (Blake) 12:35-6
"Augurios" (Paz) 1:361
"August" (Rich) 5:371
"August" (Wylie) 23:319, 322, 332
"August 22, 1939" (Rexroth) 20:195
"August First" (Carruth) 10:91
"An August Midnight" (Hardy) 8:112
"August Night" (Swenson) 14:266, 284
"August on Sourdough, A Visit from Dick

Brewer" (Snyder) 21:288
"August Was Foggy" (Snyder) 21:288
Aujourd'hui (Hugo) 17:80
"Aul Bastundzi" (Lermontov) 18:300
"The Auld Farmer's New Year Morning Salutation" (Burns) See "The Auld Farmer's New Year Morning Salutation"
"The Auld Farmer's New Year's Day Address to His Auld Mare Maggie" (Burns) 6:78
"Auld Lang Syne" (Burns) 6:59, 75, 98-9
"AÚN" (Dario) 15:98
Aún (Neruda) 4:289
"Aunt Chloe's Politics" (Harper) 21:200, 202, 213
"La aurora" ("Dawn") (Garcia Lorca) 3:141
"Aurora Borealis" (Dove) 6:110
Aurora Leigh (Browning) 6:2, 6-7, 10-13, 21-3, 25-6, 31-2, 34-8, 40, 44, 46
"The Auroras of Autumn" (Roethke) 15:280
"The Auroras of Autumn" (Stevens) 6:338
Auroras of Autumn (Stevens) 6:303, 335
"Aurore" (Valery) 9:356, 363, 365, 367-68, 371, 394, 396
"Aus einer Sturmnacht" (Rilke) 2:277
"Ausencia" (Borges) 22:94
Ausgewahlte gedichte (Celan) 10:102
"Aussi bien que les cigales" (Apollinaire) 7:18, 22
"Aussöhnung" (Goethe) 5:250-51
"The Author to her Book" (Bradstreet) 10:7, 18, 27, 34
"The Author upon Himself" (Swift) 9:295-96, 304, 306, 308-09
"The Author's Earnest Cry and Prayer" (Burns) 6:78-9
"The Author's Manner of Living" (Swift) 9:295
"Autobiography" (Ferlinghetti) 1:177-80, 183-84, 187
Autobiography (Zukofsky) 11:365
"Autochthon" (Masters) 1:333
"Automne" (Apollinaire) 7:42
"L'automne" ("The Autumn") (Lamartine) 16:277, 290, 298, 301
"Automne malade" (Apollinaire) 7:39, 42-3
"Autopsicografia" ("Autopsychography") (Pessoa) 20:172
"The Autopsy" (Elytis) 21:123
"Autopsychography" (Pessoa) See "Autopsicografia"
"Autre complainte de Lord Pierrot" (Laforgue) 14:81, 97
Autre complainte de Lord Pierrot (Laforgue) 14:62, 88
"Autre complainte de l'orgue de barbarie" (Laforgue) 14:81, 98
Autrefois (Hugo) 17:80
"The Autumn" (Lamartine) See "L'automne"
"Autumn" (Lowell) 13:97
"Autumn" (Neruda) See "Otoño"
"Autumn" (Pasternak) 6:266
"Autumn" (Smith) 12:345
"Autumn" (Tomlinson) 17:339
"Autumn Cellars" (Montale) 13:149-50
"Autumn Equinox" (Rich) 5:351-52, 393
"Autumn Forest" (Pasternak) 6:267
"Autumn Gold: New England Fall" (Ginsberg) 4:54
"Autumn in California" (Rexroth) 20:194,

214
"Autumn Lament" (Mallarme) See "Plainte d'automne"
"Autumn Meditation" (Wang Wei) 18:343
"Autumn Sequence" (Rich) 5:363, 382
"Autumn Song" (Dario) See "Canción otoñal"
"Autumnal" ("Fall") (Dario) 15:117
Autumnal Leaves (Hugo) 17:44
"Aux Chrétiens" (Lamartine) 16:280
"Aux ruines de Montfort-L'Amaury" (Hugo) 17:89
"Avant-dernier mot" (Laforgue) 14:95
"Avarice" (Herbert) 4:102, 130
"Ave Imperatrix!" (Kipling) 3:190
"Ave Maria" (Crane) 3:84, 86
"Avenel Gray" (Robinson) See "Mortmain"
"Avenue of Limes" (Pasternak) 6:267
"The Avenue of Poplars" (Williams) 7:382
"Avisos" (Pessoa) 20:162
"Avondale" (Smith) 12:352
"Avondall" (Smith) 12:352
Avon's Harvest (Robinson) 1:465-66, 468-69
"Avtobus" ("Omnibus") (Tsvetaeva) 14:325, 327
Awake in th Red Desert (Bissett) 14:12, 14, 18-19
"Awakening of the Waterfall" (Tagore) See "Nirjharer svapnabhanga"
"Away, Melancholy" (Smith) 12:333
"Awe and Devastation of Solomos" (Elytis) 21:135
"Awful Music" (Merton) 10:337
The Awful Rowing Toward God (Sexton) 2:360, 367-68, 371-73
"The Awthorn" (Clare) 23:46-7
"Axe Handles" (Snyder) 21:308
Axe Handles (Snyder) 21:299-302, 307-10, 320
"The Ax-Helve" (Frost) 1:215
The Axion Esti (*Worthy It Is*) (Elytis) 21:118, 120-30, 133
"Ay qué tristeza que tengo!" (Guillen) 23:119-20, 127
"Ayer me dijeron negro" ("Yesterday I Was Called Nigger") (Guillen) 23:142
"Ayíasma" (Ekeloef) 23:64
"Aylmer's Field" (Tennyson) 6:362
"Aymerillot" (Hugo) 17:58
Ázma iroikó ke pénthimo yia ton haméno anthipolohaghó tis Alvanías (*Heroic and Elegiac Song for the Lost Second Lieutenant of the Alb nian Campaign*) (Elytis) 21:115, 120, 124, 127-29
"Azrail" (Lermontov) 18:300
Azul (*Blue*) (Dario) 15:78, 86-7, 91-2, 94-6, 102-03, 105-07, 115, 117-18, 120
"L'azur" ("The Azure") (Mallarme) 4:199-200, 208, 213
"The Azure" (Mallarme) See "L'azur"
"Azure and Gold" (Lowell) 13:60
"The Babe" (Olson) 19:319-20
"Babocka" ("The Butterfly") (Brodsky) 9:29
"The Baby" (Nash) 21:278
"Baby" (Sexton) 2:367
"Baby Picture" (Sexton) 2:370
"Baby V" (Levine) See "Baby Villon"
"Baby Villon" ("Baby V") (Levine) 22:213
"Babylon Revisited" (Baraka) 4:18
"The Bacchae" (H. D.) 5:305

Title Index

und Wein") (Holderlin)   **4**:146-51, 161, 166, 169, 171, 176
"Brother and Sister" (Eliot)   **20**:102, 124
"Brother and Sisters" (Wright)   **14**:336, 340, 351
"Brother, Do Not Give Your Life" (Yosano Akiko)
    See "Kimi Shinitamô koto nakare"
"The Brothers" (Wordsworth)   **4**:374, 380, 381, 393, 402, 414
The Brothers Highwaymen (Pushkin)
    See *Bratya Razboiniki*
Brothers, I Loved You All: Poems, 1969-1977 (Carruth)   **10**:69-70, 72-3, 91
"Brought from Beyond" (Clampitt)   **19**:102
"A Brown" (Stein)   **18**:3312
"Brown Boy to Brown Girl" (Cullen)   **20**:64
"A Brown Girl Dead" (Cullen)   **20**:55, 62
"The Brown Menace or Poem to the Survival of Roaches" (Lorde)   **12**:154-55, 158
"Brown River, Smile" (Toomer)   **7**:324
"Browning resuelve ser poeta" (Borges)   **22**:98
"Brown's Descent" (Frost)   **1**:195
"Bruce's Address" (Burns)   **6**:55
"A Bruised Reed Shall He Not Break" (Rossetti)   **7**:290; **50**:314
"Bryan, Bryan, Bryan, Bryan" (Lindsay)   **23**:265, 270, 273-74, 279, 287-88, 294-95
"Bubba" (Sanchez)   **9**:240
Buch der Bilder (*Book of Pictures*) (Rilke)   **2**:266-67
"The Buck in the Snow" (Millay)   **6**:238
The Buck in the Snow, and Other Poems (Millay)   **6**:213-14
Buckthorn (Akhmatova)
    See *Podorozhnik*
Bucolic Comedies (Sitwell)   **3**:293, 302-04, 307-08, 319, 322
"Bucolics" (Auden)   **1**:23
Bucolics (Vergil)
    See *Georgics*
"The Buddhist Painter Prepares to Paint" (Carruth)   **10**:89
"The Buds Now Stretch" (Roethke)   **15**:288
"Buenos Aires" (Lowell)   **3**:214
"La bufera" ("The Storm") (Montale)   **13**:113, 131
La bufera e altro (*The Storm and Other Things*; *The Storm and Other Things*) (Montale)   **13**:103-04, 107, 113-14, 117-18, 122, 125, 131-33, 141, 148-49, 156, 160, 165-67
"Buffalo Bill's Defunct" (Cummings)   **5**:93
"Le buffet" (Rimbaud)   **3**:271, 283
"The Bugler-Boy" (Hopkins)   **15**:138
"The Bugler's First Communion" (Hopkins)   **15**:136, 144
"Build Soil: A Political Pastoral" (Frost)   **1**:196, 199, 203, 217
"Builder Kachina" (Rose)   **13**:236-37
"The Building" (Larkin)   **21**:255
"The Building of the Trophy" (Rose)   **13**:235
"The Bull" (Wright)   **14**:333, 359
"The Bull Moses" (Hughes)   **7**:131, 140, 158
"Bull Song" (Atwood)   **8**:25
"Bullfrog" (Hughes)   **7**:165
"Bullocky" (Wright)   **14**:336, 340, 345, 349, 351, 357, 360, 368
"Bumming" (McKay)   **2**:226
"The Bunch of Grapes" (Herbert)   **4**:123, 125
"The Burden" (Kipling)   **3**:183
"A Burden" (Rossetti)   **7**:286

"Burden" (Tagore)
    See "Bhar"
"The Burghers" (Hardy)   **8**:99
"The Burglar of Babylon" (Bishop)   **3**:48, 56
"The Burial-place" (Bryant)   **20**:3
"The Buried Life" (Arnold)   **5**:37-8, 41-5, 47, 49-50, 59, 64
"The Burly Fading One" (Hayden)   **6**:196
"Burn and burn and burn" (Bukowski)   **18**:24
"Burned" (Levine)   **22**:220-21, 227-28, 232
"The Burning Child" (Clampitt)   **19**:83
Burning in Water Drowning in Flame: Selected Poems 1955-1973 (Bukowski)   **18**:21
"The Burning of Paper Instead of Children" (Rich)   **5**:371, 393-95
"Burning Oneself Out" (Rich)   **5**:360
"The Burning Passion" (MacDiarmid)   **9**:153
"Burning River" (Ortiz)   **17**:233
"Burning the Christmas Greens" (Williams)   **7**:360
"Burning the Tomato Worms" (Forche)   **10**:132, 134, 142
"Burnt Lands" (Pavese)   **13**:205
"Burnt Norton" (Eliot)   **5**:164, 166-68, 171, 174, 177-85, 201, 210
"The Burnt-Out Spa" (Plath)   **1**:389
"Bury Me In a Free Land" (Harper)   **21**:185, 187, 190, 192
"A Bus along St. Clair: December" (Atwood)   **8**:40
"Búscate plata" ("Git Dough"; "Go and Look for Bread"; "Go Get Money") (Guillen)   **23**:142
"The Buses Headed for Scranton" (Nash)   **21**:271
"The Bush Garden" (Atwood)   **8**:38-9
"Busie old foole" (Donne)
    See "The Sunne Rising"
"The Business Man of Alicante" (Levine)   **22**:213
"But Born" (Aleixandre)   **15**:5
"But He Was Cool; or, He Even Stopped for Green Lights" (Madhubuti)   **5**:329, 341
"But We've the May" (Cummings)
    See "Song"
"`Butch' Weldy" (Masters)   **1**:324
Butterflies (Gozzano)
    See *Le farfalle*
"The Butterfly" (Brodsky)
    See "Babocka"
"The Butterfly" (Giovanni)   **19**:112
"Butterfly Piece" (Hayden)   **6**:194, 198
"Butterflyweed" (Ammons)   **16**:4
"by 3/6/51" (Olson)   **19**:316
By Avon River (H. D.)   **5**:302
"By God I Want above Fourteenth" (Cummings)   **5**:94
"By Lamplight" (Kunitz)   **19**:171
"By Night When Others Soundly Slept" (Bradstreet)   **10**:62
"By Rugged Ways" (Dunbar)   **5**:131
By the Earth's Corpse (Hardy)   **8**:121
"By the Fireside" (Browning)   **2**:76, 78-9, 88
"By the Hoof of the Wild Goat" (Kipling)   **3**:186
"By the Lake" (Sitwell)   **3**:325
"By the Road" (Williams)   **7**:382-83
By the Seashore (Akhmatova)
    See *U samovo morya*
"By The Stream" (Dunbar)   **5**:127
"By the Waters of Babylon" (Celan)
    See "An den Wassern Babels"
"By Wauchopeside" (MacDiarmid)   **9**:197, 199

"By-pass" (Wright)   **14**:373
"Bypassing Rue Descartes" (Milosz)   **8**:200
"Byzantium" (Yeats)   **20**:308, 310, 316, 327, 334-35
"a C." (Montale)   **13**:138
"Ca' the Yowes to the Knowes" (Burns)   **6**:76
"Cabala" (Swenson)   **14**:288
"Cabaret" (Hughes)   **1**:237
"Cabaret Girl Dies on Welfare Island" (Hughes)   **1**:247
"A Cabin in the Clearing" (Frost)   **1**:212
"A Cabin Tale" (Dunbar)   **5**:120
Cables to Rage (Lorde)   **12**:140
"Cables to Rage, or I've Been Talking on This Street Corner a Hell of a Long Time" (Lorde)   **12**:155
"Cables to the Ace" (Merton)   **10**:337
Cables to the Ace; or, Familiar Liturgies of Misunderstanding (Merton)   **10**:338, 345, 348, 351, 354
"Caboose Thoughts" (Sandburg)   **2**:302
"Cabra" (Joyce)   **22**:149
"Le cacot" (Lamartine)   **16**:284
"Cadenus and Vanessa" (Swift)   **9**:253-55, 296
"A Cadenza" (Clampitt)   **19**:102
"Cadenza" (Hughes)   **7**:159
"Caerulei Oculi" (Gautier)   **18**:125
Caesar's Gate (Duncan)   **2**:101
"Café" (Milosz)   **8**:175
"Café at Rapallo" (Montale)   **13**:148
"Cafe du neant" (Loy)   **16**:312-13, 328
"Café Tableau" (Swenson)   **14**:275
A Cage of Spines (Swenson)   **14**:247-48, 252, 260, 277, 284
Cain (Byron)   **16**:86, 88, 90, 103-05, 108, 111
"Cake" (Stein)   **18**:322
The Calender (Spenser)
    See *The Shepheardes Calender: Conteyning Twelve Æglogues Proportionable to the Twelve Monethes*
"Caliban upon Setebos" (Browning)   **2**:58-9, 88, 95
"The Calico Cat" (Lindsay)   **23**:281
"The California Water Plan" (Snyder)   **21**:291
Californians (Jeffers)   **17**:134-35, 138
"The Call" (Herbert)   **4**:130
"Call" (Lorde)   **12**:139, 141
"Call Me Back Again" (Tagore)
    See "Ebar phirao more"
"The Call of the Wild" (Snyder)   **21**:292-93, 297
Call Yourself Alive? (Cassian)   **17**:4, 6, 13
"Las Calles" (Borges)   **22**:68
"Callie Ford" (Brooks)   **7**:62, 69
Calligrammes (Apollinaire)   **7**:3, 9-10, 12, 35-6, 42, 44, 46, 48-9
"A Calling" (Kumin)   **15**:210
"Calliope" (H. D.)   **5**:304
"Callow Captain" (Graves)   **6**:133
"The Calls" (Owen)   **19**:336
"The Calm" (Donne)   **1**:122
"The Calm" (Gallagher)   **9**:58
"Calming Kali" (Clifton)   **17**:24
"Calmly We Walk Through This April's Day" (Schwartz)   **8**:305-06
"Calverley's" (Robinson)   **1**:466
"Calypso" (H. D.)   **5**:306
"The Cambridge Ladies Who Live in Furnished Souls" (Cummings)   **5**:94
"Cambridge, Spring 1937" (Schwartz)   **8**:301
"The Camel" (Nash)   **21**:278
"Camelia" (Tagore)   **8**:417
"Camilo" (Guillen)   **23**:128

See "Elegy Written in a Country Church-
    yard"
"Churning Day" (Heaney) **18**:186
"The Chute" (Olds) **22**:319-22
La chute d'un ange (*The Fall of an Angel*)
    (Lamartine) **16**:263, 265, 269-70, 285-
    87, 293-94, 296-97
"Chuva Oblíqua" ("The Slanting Rain") (Pessoa)
    20:151, 165
"Ciant da li ciampanis" (Pasolini) **17**:256,
    265
"Ciants di muart" (Pasolini) **17**:256
"The Cicadas" (Wright) **14**:346
"Ciel brouillé" (Baudelaire) **1**:61, 66
La cifra (Borges) **22**:95, 97, 99
"Un cigare allume que Fume" (Apollinaire)
    See "Paysage"
"Cigola la carrucola del pozzo" (Montale)
    13:164
"Le cimetière marin" (Bishop) **3**:46
"Le cimetière marin" ("The Graveyard by the
    Sea") (Valery) **9**:348, 351-52, 355, 358,
    361, 363-80, 382, 384, 387, 389-93, 395-
    96, 398
The Circassian (Lermontov)
    See *The Circassian*
The Circassian Boy (Lermontov)
    See *The Novice*
"Circe's Power" (Gluck) **16**:171
The Circle Game (Atwood) **8**:3, 12, 15, 18,
    26-8
"Circles in th Sun" (Bissett) **14**:8, 19, 33
"The Circuit of Apollo" (Finch) **21**:162, 168
"A Circular Play" (Stein) **18**:347
"Circulation of the Song" (Duncan) **2**:127
"Circumjack Cencrastus" (MacDiarmid) **9**:157
"Circumstance" (Lowell) **13**:94
"The Circus Animals' Desertion" (Yeats)
    20:307, 311, 313, 327, 332, 336
"Cirque d'hiver" (Bishop) **3**:37
"El cisne" (Dario) **15**:113
"Los cisnes" ("The Swans") (Dario) **15**:115
"The Cited" (Garcia Lorca)
    See "Romance del emplazado"
"Cities and Thrones and Powers" (Kipling)
    3:183
"Citizen Cain" (Baraka) **4**:17, 24
"Città in campagna" ("City in the Country")
    (Pavese) **13**:227
"The City" (Blok) **21**:24
"The City" (Nash) **21**:272
"The City" (Pasternak)
    See "Gorod"
"The City Asleep" (Wright) **14**:362
"A City Dead House" (Whitman) **3**:379
"City in the Country" (Pavese)
    See "Città in campagna"
"The City in the Sea" (Poe) **1**:426, 431, 434,
    438, 443-45
"The City Limits" (Ammons) **16**:11, 23, 37,
    46
"City Midnight Junk Strains for Frank O'Hara"
    (Ginsberg) **4**:47
"City of Monuments" (Rukeyser) **12**:230
"The City of the Dead" (Gibran) **9**:73
"The City Planners" (Atwood) **8**:13
"City Psalm" (Rukeyser) **12**:221
"City Trees" (Millay) **6**:207
"City Walk-Up, Winter 1969" (Forche)
    10:141, 144, 147, 157-58
"City without a Name" (Milosz) **8**:194-95
"City without Walls" (Auden) **1**:20
"The City's Love" (McKay) **2**:211

"Ciudad" (Borges) **22**:94
"Ciudad sin sueño" ("Brooklyn Bridge Noc-
    turne"; "Unsleeping City (Brooklyn Bridge
    Nocturne)") (Garcia Lorca) **3**:139-40
"Ciudad viva, ciudad muerta" (Aleixandre)
    15:35
"Ciudades" (Cardenal)
    See "Las ciudades perdidas"
"Las ciudades perdidas" ("Ciudades"; "The Los
    Cities") (Cardenal) **22**:126-28, 132
"Civil Rights Poem" (Baraka) **4**:11, 19
"Clad All in Brown" (Swift) **9**:256-57
"The Claim" (Browning) **6**:14
"Clair de lune" ("Moonlight") (Apollinaire)
    7:45-6
"Clair de lune" ("Moonlight") (Verlaine)
    2:413, 420, 429
Claire de terre (Breton) **15**:51-2
"Claribel" (Tennyson) **6**:358-60, 365
"Clasping of Hands" (Herbert) **4**:130
"Class" (Tomlinson) **17**:320
"Class Struggle" (Baraka) **4**:30, 38
"Class Struggle in Music" (Baraka) **4**:40
"The Class Will Come to Order" (Kunitz)
    19:150
"Claud Antle" (Masters) **1**:334
"El clavicordio de la abuela" ("Grandmother's
    Clavichord") (Dario) **15**:80
"Clay" (Baraka) **4**:30
"clay and morning star" (Clifton) **17**:29
"Cleaning Day" (Wright) **14**:356
"Cleaning the Candelabrum" (Sassoon) **12**:248,
    259
"Clean,like,iodoform,between,the,tall" (Villa)
    22:356-57
"Clear Autumn" (Rexroth) **20**:209
"Clear, with Light Variable Winds" (Lowell)
    13:94
"Clearances" (Heaney) **18**:228-29, 232, 238
"Cleared" (Kipling) **3**:167
"The Clearing" (Baraka) **4**:5, 15
"Cleon" (Browning) **2**:36, 82, 95
"Cleopomop y Heliodemo" (Dario) **15**:81
"The Clepsydras of the Unknown" (Elytis)
    21:119
"Clerk's Tale" (Chaucer) **19**:13, 29, 54-60
"The Cliff" (Lermontov) **18**:297
"Cliff Klingenhagen" (Robinson) **1**:467, 486
"Clifford Ridell" (Masters) **1**:344-46
"The Climate of Thought" (Graves) **6**:139,
    143
"Climbing a Mountain" (Hagiwara Sakutaro)
    177
"Climbing Alone All Day" (Rexroth) **20**:193
"Climbing Milestone Mountain" (Rexroth)
    20:203
"Climbing Pien-chüeh Temple" (Wang Wei)
    18:371
"Climbing to the Monastery of Perception"
    (Wang Wei) **18**:384
"The Clinging Vine" (Robinson) **1**:468
"The Clipped Stater" (Graves) **6**:128, 137
"A Cloak" (Levertov) **11**:176, 194
"La cloche fêlée" ("The Cracked Bell")
    (Baudelaire) **1**:65
"A Clock in the Square" (Rich) **5**:352
"The Clock of Tomorrow" (Apollinaire)
    See "L'lorloge de demain"
"The Clock Stopped" (Dickinson) **1**:108
"The Clod and the Pebble" (Blake) **12**:7
"Clorinda and Damon" (Marvell) **10**:268, 271
"Closed for Good" (Frost) **1**:213
"Close-Up" (Ammons) **16**:24

"Clothes" (Sexton) **2**:367
"The Cloud" (Shelley) **14**:167, 171, 196, 207,
    212
"Cloud" (Toomer) **7**:338
"Cloud-Catch" (Hongo) **23**:204
The Cloud-Messenger (Kalidasa)
    See *Meghaduta*
"Clouds" (Levine) **22**:214, 219, 222
"Clouds" (Tomlinson) **17**:312
The Clouds (Williams) **7**:370
"Clover" (Dario)
    See "Trébol"
"The Clown Chastized" (Mallarme)
    See "Le pitre châtié"
Clown's Houses (Sitwell) **3**:290, 294, 301-02
Cluster of Songs (Tagore)
    See *Gitali*
Cluster of Songs (Tagore)
    See *Gitali*
"Coal" (Lorde) **12**:153
Coal (Lorde) **12**:142, 148
"The Coal Picker" (Lowell) **13**:84
"The Coast" (Hass) **16**:196
"The Coast Guard's Cottage" (Wylie) **23**:324
"Coast of Trees" (Ammons) **16**:45, 62
A Coast of Trees (Ammons) **16**:31, 45, 62
"The Coastwise Lights" (Kipling) **3**:162
"A Coat" (Yeats) **20**:320
"The Coats" (Gallagher) **9**:60
"Cobwebs" (Rossetti) **7**:278
"The Cock and the Fox" (Chaucer)
    See "Nun's Priest's Tale"
"The Cocked Hat" (Masters) **1**:325-26, 328-
    29, 342
"Cockerel" (Hagiwara Sakutaro) **18**:173
"The Cocks" (Pasternak) **6**:253
"Coconut Palm" (Tagore)
    See "Narikel"
"Cocotte" (Gozzano) **10**:178
"Coda" (Ekeloef) **23**:76, 86
"The Code" (Frost) **1**:195, 208, 226
"A Code of Morals" (Kipling) **3**:190
"Coeur, couronne et miroir" ("Heart, Crown
    and Mirror") (Apollinaire) **7**:32-6
"La coeur volé" ("The Tortured Heart")
    (Rimbaud) **3**:270
"Cohorte" (Perse) **23**:254-57
Coins and Coffins (Wakoski) **15**:338, 344,
    356, 369
"Cold" (Cassian) **17**:12, 15
"Cold in the Earth" (Bronte)
    See "Remembrance"
"Cold Iron" (Kipling) **3**:171
"Cold-Blooded Creatures" (Wylie) **23**:314
"Colin Clout" (Spenser)
    See *Colin Clouts Come Home Againe*
Colin Clouts Come Home Againe ("Colin
    Clout") (Spenser) **8**:336, 367, 387, 396
"The Coliseum" (Poe) **1**:439
"The Collar" (Herbert) **4**:102-03, 112-13,
    130-31
"The Collar" (Herrick) **9**:141
Collected Earlier Poems (Williams) **7**:367-
    69, 374-75, 378, 382, 387-88, 392-94,
    406-07, 409
Collected Early Poems (Pound) **4**:355
The Collected Greed, Parts 1-13 (Wakoski)
    15:356
Collected Later Poems (Williams) **7**:370, 375
*The Collected Longer Poems of Kenneth
    Rexroth* (Rexroth) **20**:197, 202, 204,
    209-10, 214
Collected Lyrics (Millay) **6**:227

Title Index

Title Index

"The Dying Queen" (Harper) **21**:198

"The Dying Swan" (Tennyson) **6**:359, 389-91

"The Dykes" (Kipling) **3**:182

The Dynasts: A Drama of the Napoleonic Wars (Hardy) **8**:79-81, 85-7, 95-6, 104, 108, 111, 121-22

The Dynasty of Raghu (Kalidasa)
  See *Raghuvamsa*

"Dytiscus" (MacDiarmid) **9**:157, 183

"Dzhulio" (Lermontov) **18**:300

"E. P. Ode Pour L'Election de son Sepulchre" (Pound) **4**:319

"Each and All" (Emerson) **18**:84, 94-96, 98-101, 107

"Each Bird Walking" (Gallagher) **9**:44

"Each Day of Summer" (Swenson) **14**:276

"Each of You" (Lorde) **12**:154

"Eagle" (Kunitz) **19**:147

"The Eagle and the Mole" (Wylie) **23**:301, 309, 322, 327, 334

"Eagle Confin'd in a College Court" (Smart) **13**:341

Eagle or Sun? (Paz) **1**:354, 359

"The Eagle That Is Forgotten" (Lindsay) **23**:277, 288, 294, 296

"Early Chronology" (Sassoon) **12**:245

"Early Evening Quarrel" (Hughes) **1**:247

"Early Lynching" (Sandburg) **2**:330

"Early March" (Sassoon) **12**:254, 259

"An Early Martyr" (Williams) **7**:353, 368

An Early Martyr, and Other Poems (Williams) **7**:350, 399, 402

"Early Morning: Cape Cod" (Swenson) **14**:276

"The Early Morning Light" (Schwartz) **8**:294

Early Poems (Crane) **3**:90-1

Early Poems, 1935-1955 (Paz) **1**:373, 375

Early Verse of Rudyard Kipling, 1877-99: Unpublished, Uncollected, and Rarely Collected Poems (Kipling) **3**:193

"The Earrings" (Montale)
  See "Gli orecchini"

"Ears in the Turrets Hear" (Thomas) **2**:379

"Earth" (Bryant) **20**:4, 17, 19, 35, 47

"The Earth" (Sexton) **2**:372, 374

"Earth" (Toomer) **7**:333

"Earth Again" (Milosz) **8**:209

The Earth Gods (Gibran) **9**:71, 75, 80

"The Earth in Snow" (Blok) **21**:4-5

"The Earth is Called Juan" (Neruda)
  See "La tierra se llama Juan"

"the Earth Lantern" (Bissett) **14**:7

"Earth Psalm" (Levertov) **11**:170

"Earth Your Dancing Place" (Swenson) **14**:283

Earthlight (Breton) **15**:73-4

"Earthly Creatures" (Wylie) **23**:311

The Earth-Owl and Other Moon-People (Hughes) **7**:120

"Earth's Answer" (Blake) **12**:7, 35, 44

"Earth's Bubbles" (Blok) **21**:14, 24, 31

"Earth's Children Cleave to Earth" (Bryant) **20**:16

"Earth-Song" (Emerson) **18**:79, 88

"Earthy Anecdote" (Stevens) **6**:294

"East Coker" (Eliot) **5**:164, 167-69, 171, 179-82, 198, 210

"East Coker" (Roethke) **15**:279

"East of Suez" (Kipling) **3**:179

"East of the Sun West of the Moon" (Wakoski) **15**:348

"East River" (Swenson) **14**:254

East Slope (Paz)
  See *Ladera este*

"The East that is Now Pale, the East that is Now Silent" (Bely)
  See "Vostok pobledneuskii, vostok onemesvshii"

"East, West, North, and South of a Man" (Lowell) **13**:87

East Wind (Lowell) **13**:76, 84-5

"Eastbourne" (Montale) **13**:106, 109, 120-21, 128-29, 148, 152

"An East-End Curate" (Hardy) **8**:101

"Easter" (Herbert) **4**:100, 120

"Easter" (Studwell)
  See "Easter: Wahiawa, 1959"

"Easter 1916" (Yeats) **20**:311, 313-14, 323, 325, 327, 349

Easter Day (Browning) **2**:32, 45, 71-2, 75

"Easter Eve 1945" (Rukeyser) **12**:225

"Easter Hymn" (Housman) **2**:184

"Easter Moon and Owl" (Wright) **14**:373, 375

"Easter Morning" (Ammons) **16**:30-2, 46, 63-4

"Easter: Wahiawa, 1959" ("Easter"; "Waialua") (Song) **21**:331, 335, 338, 340, 342-43, 350

"Easter Wings" (Herbert) **4**:114, 120, 130

Eastern Lyrics (Hugo)
  See *Les orientales*

Eastern Slope (Paz)
  See *Ladera este*

"Eastern War Time" (Rich) **5**:398

"Eastport to Block Island" (Rich) **5**:352

"Eating Fire" (Atwood) **8**:27-8

"Ebar phirao more" ("Call Me Back Again") (Tagore) **8**:409

"Ébauche d'un serpent" ("Le serpent"; "Silhouette of a Serpent") (Valery) **9**:352-53, 365-67, 371, 374, 384, 387, 390, 394-99

Ebb and Flow (Ishikawa) **10**:212-13, 215

"Ecce Puer" (Joyce) **22**:140-41, 147-48, 151-52

Ecclesiastical Sketches (*Ecclesiastical Sonnets*) (Wordsworth) **4**:399

Ecclesiastical Sonnets (Wordsworth)
  See *Ecclesiastical Sketches*

"Echo" (Lorde) **12**:155

"Echo" (Rossetti) **7**:280-81

"Echo" (Tagore)
  See "Pratidhyani"

"Echoes" (Carroll) **18**:46

"The Echoing Green" (Blake) **12**:7

"L'eclatante victoire de Saarebrück" ("The Sinking Ship") (Rimbaud) **3**:283

"L'eclatante victorie de Sarrebruck" (Rimbaud) **3**:283

"El eclipse" (Jimenez) **7**:200

"Eclogue" (Ronsard) **11**:262

"Eclogue" (Stevens) **6**:333

"Eclogue 4" ("Messianic Eclogue") (Vergil) **12**:363, 370, 372, 382-85, 392

"Eclogue 6" (Vergil) **12**:365, 371

"Eclogue 10" (Vergil) **12**:370-71

"Eclogue IV: Winter" ("Ekloga 4-aya: Zimnyaya") (Brodsky) **9**:22, 28-9

"An Eclogue, or Pastorall between Endymion Porter and Lycidas Herrick" (Herrick) **9**:86

"Eclogue V: Summer" (Brodsky) **9**:21, 28

"Eclogues" (Herrick) **9**:89

Eclogues (Petrarch) **8**:246

Eclogues (Vergil) **12**:365, 370-72, 375, 383, 388

"Ecologue" (Ginsberg) **4**:54, 82, 85, 89

"Economia de Tahuantinsuyo" ("The Economy of Tahuantinsuyo") (Cardenal) **22**:127-28, 132

"The Economy of Tahuantinsuyo"
  See "Economia de Tahuantinsuyo"

"Ecoutez la chanson bien douce" (Verlaine) **2**:416

"Écrit sur la Porte" (1)" (Perse) **23**:231

"Les Écrits s'en vont" (Breton) **15**:51

"The Ecstasy" (Carruth) **10**:71

"The Ecstasy" (Donne)
  See "The Exstasie"

"Eddi's Service" (Kipling) **3**:183

"Eden" (Tomlinson) **17**:342, 354

"Eden" (Wright) **14**:336, 341

"The Edge" (Gluck) **16**:125, 153

"Edge" (Plath) **1**:391, 393, 397

"Edge of Love" (Aleixandre) **15**:19, 23

"Edgehill Fight" (Kipling) **3**:183

"Edina, Scotia's Darling Seat!" (Burns) **6**:74

"Edinstvennye dni" ("Unequalled Days") (Pasternak) **6**:286

"Editorial Impressions" (Sassoon) **12**:268

"Edmonton, thy cemetery . . ." (Smith) **12**:293, 300

"Education" (Madhubuti) **5**:338

"Education a Failure" (Williams) **7**:370

"Education and Government" (Gray)
  See "Essay on the Alliance of Education and Government"

"Edward Gray" (Tennyson) **6**:358

"Edward III" (Blake)
  See "King Edward the Third"

"The Eel" (Montale)
  See "L'anguilla"

"Eel" (Rukeyser) **12**:211

"The Eemis Stane" (MacDiarmid) **9**:158, 187

"eet me alive" (Bissett) **14**:34

"The Effect" (Sassoon) **12**:285

"The Effectual Marriage" (Loy) **16**:333

Efterlämnade dikter (Ekeloef) **23**:78

"The Egg" (Gluck) **16**:125, 138-39

"The Egg and the Machine" (Frost) **1**:203

"Egg-Head" (Hughes) **7**:116, 118, 135, 140, 161

"Eggs" (Hagiwara Sakutaro) **18**:168

"Eggs" (Olds) **22**:311, 338

"Eggs and Nestlings" (Wright) **14**:348

"Ego Tripping" (Giovanni) **19**:118, 123, 141

"The Egoist" (Neruda)
  See "El egoísta"

"El egoísta" ("The Egoist"; "The Selfish One") (Neruda) **4**:290

Egorushka (Tsvetaeva) **14**:326-27

Ego-Tripping and Other Poems for Young People (Giovanni) **19**:123, 136

"Egy ev" ("One year") (Illyes) **16**:239

"The Eichmann Trial" (Levertov)
  See "During the Eichmann Trial"

"VIII" (Joyce) **22**:144-45, 153, 167, 170, 173

"8 Ahau" (Cardenal) **22**:
  See "Katun 8 Ahau"

"Eight Drinking Immortals" (Tu Fu) **9**:330

"Eight Laments" (Tu Fu) **9**:333-38, 341-42

"Eight Observations on the Nature of Eternity" (Tomlinson) **17**:328

"Eight O'Clock" (Housman) **2**:162, 164, 169, 182

"XVIII" (Joyce) **22**:145, 165, 167, 169

18 Poems (Thomas) **2**:378, 382, 384

"1887" (Housman) **2**:192, 194

"1805" (Graves) **6**:152

"The Eighth Crusade" (Masters) **1**:330

285-6, 288, 296, 298, 307-10
"The Eve of St. John" (Scott)   13:269
"The Eve of St. Mark" (Keats)   1:279, 304
"Eve Scolds" (Wright)   14:373, 375
"Eve Sings" (Wright)   14:373
"Eve to her Daughter" (Wright)   14:356
"Evelyn Hope" (Browning)   2:38
"Evelyn Ray" (Lowell)   13:66, 91
"Even" (Burns)   6:50
"Even If All Desires Things Moments Be" (Cummings)   5:95
"The Even Sea" (Swenson)   14:249, 263
"Even Song" (Herbert)   4:133
"Evening" (Merton)   10:340
"Evening" (Trakl)
   See "Der Abend"
"Evening" (Wheatley)
   See "An Hymn to the Evening"
Evening (Akhmatova)
   See *Vecher*
Evening Album (Tsvetaeva)
   See *Vecherny albom*
"The Evening Bell" (Ishikawa)
   See "Yube no kane"
"Evening Dance of the Grey Flies" (Page)   12:190
Evening Dance of the Grey Flies (Page)   12:181, 198-99
"Evening Fantasy" (Holderlin)   4:140
"Evening in the Sanitarium" (Bogan)   12:92, 99-101, 107, 121
"Evening of the Visitation" (Merton)   10:339
"The Evening Sea" (Ishikawa)
   See "Yube no umi"
"Evening Song" (Toomer)   7:320
Evening Songs (Tagore)
   See *Sandhya sangit*
"Evening Star" (Bogan)   12:98, 100
"Evening Star" (Poe)   1:448
"The Evening That Love Enticed You Down into the Ballroom" (Ronsard)
   See "Le soir qu'amour vous fist en la salle descendre"
An Evening Thought: Salvation by Christ with Penetential Cries (Hammon)   16:176-79, 183-87
"Evening Twilight" (Baudelaire)
   See "Le crépuscule du soir"
"An Evening Under Newly Cleared Skies" (Wang Wei)   18:369
"Evening Voluntary" (Wordsworth)   4:408
"The Event" (Dove)   6:110, 112, 114
"The Everlasting Gospel" (Blake)   12:31
"The Everlasting Voices" (Yeats)   20:309
"Everness" (Borges)   22:89
"Every Blessed Day" (Levine)   22:221
"Every Lovely Limb's a Desolation" (Smith)   12:314
"Every Soul Is a Circus" (Lindsay)   23:274, 280
"Every Traveler Has One Vermont Poem" (Lorde)   12:138
Everyone Sang (Sassoon)   12:280, 284, 289
"Everything Came True" (Pasternak)   6:266
"eve's version" (Clifton)   17:29, 36
Evgeni Onegin (Pushkin)
   See *Yevgeny Onegin*
"The Evil" (Rimbaud)
   See "Le mal"
"Eviradnus" (Hugo)   17:59, 61
"Evolution" (Swenson)   14:247, 251, 255, 275, 283-84, 286
"Evolutionary Poem No. 1" (Knight)   14:42

"Evolutionary Poem No. 2" (Knight)   14:42
"Evolution-Sustenance-Dissolution" (Tagore)
   See "Srishti-sthiti-pralaya"
"The Evolver" (Baraka)   4:24
"evry whun at 2 oclock" (Bissett)   14:33
"Ex ponto" (Ekeloef)   23:76
"Ex vermibus" (MacDiarmid)   9:190
"Exactly what is unexact" (Villa)   22:354
"The Exam" (Olds)   22:324
"Examination at the Womb-Door" (Hughes)   7:159
"Examination of the Hero in a Time of War" (Stevens)   6:318
"An Excellent New Ballad; or, The True English Dean to Be Hang'd for a Rape" (Swift)   9:267
"The Excesses of God" (Jeffers)   17:132
"The Exchange" (Swenson)   14:255, 288
"Exchanging Hats" (Bishop)   3:64
Exclamations: Music of the Soul (Nishiwaki)   15:237
"The Excrement Poem" (Kumin)   15:207
The Excursion, Being a Portion of "The Recluse" (Prospectus to the Excursion) (Wordsworth)   4:377-78, 383, 392, 397-99, 402-03, 405-09
"Excuse" (Arnold)
   See "Urania"
"Execration upon Vulcan" (Jonson)
   See "Execration upon Vulcan"
"Exhortation" (Bogan)   12:122
Exil (Exile and Other Poems) (Perse)   23:209, 211, 213-14, 216-18, 221-22, 231, 234, 240-42, 246, 248-50, 252, 254, 256
Exile and Other Poems (Perse)
   See *Exil*
"The Exile's Return" (Lowell)   3:200, 202, 234
"The Exit" (Elytis)   21:134
"Exit, Pursued by a Bear" (Nash)   21:271
"Exmoor" (Clampitt)   19:81, 88
"The Exorcism" (Roethke)   274, 278
"The Expatriate" (Forche)   10:138, 141, 144, 156
"The Expatriates" (Sexton)   2:359
"An Expedient-Leonardo da Vinci's-and a Query" (Moore)   4:242
"Experience Is the Angled Road" (Dickinson)   1:111
"L'Expiation" (Hugo)   17:79-80
"The Expiration" ("So, so breake off this last lamenting kisse") (Donne)   1:130
"Explaining a Few Things" (Neruda)
   See "Explico algunas cosas"
"The Explanation" (Kipling)   3:183
"Explanation" (Pasternak)   6:266
"Explanation and Apology, Twenty Years After" (Carruth)   10:78
"Explico algunas cosas" ("Explaining a Few Things"; "I Explain a Few Things") (Neruda)   4:297, 310-11
"The Explorers" (Atwood)   8:13
"The Explorers" (Rich)   5:362
"Expostulation and Reply" (Wordsworth)   4:419
"An Expostulation with Inigo Jones" (Jonson)   17:181-82
"Exposure" (Heaney)   18:194, 205
"Exposure" (Owen)   19:327, 332, 334
"Express" (Sandburg)   2:340
"Expression" (Clare)   23:44
"Expressions of Sea Level" (Ammons)   16:29, 42, 46; **108**:22

Expressions of Sea Level (Ammons)   16:4-5, 20, 27, 53
"The Exstasie" ("The Ecstasy") (Donne)   1:126, 128, 130, 135, 147, 152
"Extase" (Hugo)   17:91
"Extempore Effusion upon the Death of James Hogg" (Wordsworth)   4:402
"Extracts from Addresses to the Academy of Fine Ideas" (Stevens)   6:314
Extracts from an Opera (Keats)   1:311
"Un extraño" (Gallagher)   9:66
Extravagario (Book of Vagaries) (Neruda)   4:290
"Extremes and Moderations" (Ammons)   16:10-11, 18, 23, 28, 47-9
Exultations (Pound)   4:317
"Eye and Tooth" (Lowell)   3:215
"The Eyeglasses" (Williams)   7:381-83
"The Eye-Mote" (Plath)   1:389
"Eyes and Tears" (Marvell)   10:270-71
Eyes at the Back of Our Heads (Levertov)
   See *With Eyes at the Back of Our Heads*
"The Eyes of the Poor" (Baudelaire)
   See "Les yeux des pauvres"
"Ezekiel Saw the Wheel" (Montale)   13:109, 129, 165
"Ezerskij" (Pushkin)   10:391, 394
"Fable" (Cassian)   17:13
"Fable" (Emerson)   18:103-4
"A Fable" (Gluck)   16:161
"Fable" (Wylie)   23:310, 316, 319
"Fable of the Cock and the Fox" (Chaucer)
   See "Nun's Priest's Tale"
"The Fable of the Fragile Butterfly" (Wakoski)   15:333
The Fables (Esope) (Marie de France)   22:287-88
Fables (Smart)   13:341
"The Fabulists, 1914-1918" (Kipling)   3:172
"Fabulous Ballard" (Wylie)   23:321
Façade (Sitwell)   3:294, 303, 306, 319, 322, 325, 328
"The Face" (Levine)   22:224
"Face" (Toomer)   7:310, 333
"Face and Image" (Tomlinson)   17:348
"Face behind the Pane (An Old Man's Gaze)" (Aleixandre)
   See "Rostro tras el cristal (Mirada del viejo)"
"Face Lift" (Plath)   1:394
"Faces" (Whitman)   3:397
"Facing" (Swenson)   14:284, 286
"Facing the Oxford" (Guillen)
   See "Frente al Oxford"
"Fackelzug" ("Torch Procession") (Celan)   10:127
The Fact of a Doorframe: Poems Selected and New, 1950-1984 (Rich)   5:388-89
"Facteur Cheval" ("Postman Cheval") (Breton)   15:50
"Factory Windows Are Always Broken" (Lindsay)   23:268, 273, 276
"Facts" (Levine)   22:221
"Facts" (Snyder)   21:295-97
"Faded Leaves" (Arnold)   5:13
Fadensonnen (Thread-Suns) (Celan)   10:96, 98
The Faerie Queene, Disposed into Twelve Bookes Fashioning XII Morall Vertues (Spenser)   8:323-25, 327-28, 330, 332-34, 337, 339, 341-47, 349-50, 354, 360-61, 363, 365, 369, 371-72, 374-78, 380-82, 384-85, 388-93, 395-97
"Fafnir and the Knights" (Smith)   12:302, 329
"The Failed Spirit" (Smith)   12:333

Title Index

Title Index

Dies in the Fog, 1816") (Neruda) **4**:295
"Miranda's Supper" (Wylie) **23**:302, 307, 314-15, 321
"Miriam's Song" (Harper) **21**:194-95
"Mirror Image" (Gluck) **16**:162-63
"The Mirror in the Roadway" (Tomlinson) **17**:334
"The Mirror in the Woods" (Rexroth) **20**:181
"The Mirror in Which Two Are Seen as One" (Rich) **5**:368
"The Mirrors" (Williams) **7**:370
Miscellaneous Poems (Harper) **21**:185
Miscellaneous Poems (Marvell) **10**:257, 277, 311
Miscellanies (Swift) **9**:251, 253, 255, 275
A Miscellany of New Poems (Behn) **13**:7
Miscellany Poems on Several Occasions, Written by a Lady, 1713 (Finch) **21**:140, 148, 161, 163-64, 172-73
"Mise en Scene" (Lowell) **13**:96
"Miserie" (Herbert) **4**:108, 121
"Misery" (Hughes) **1**:328
"The Misfit" (Day Lewis) **11**:147
"Misgiving" (Frost) **1**:195
"Miss B—2 (Clare) **23**:25
"Miss Drake Proceeds to Supper" (Plath) **1**:398-99
"Miss Gee" (Auden) **1**:30
"Miss Rosie" (Clifton) **17**:32-33
"Mississippi Levee" (Hughes) **1**:256
"Mississippi Mother" (Brooks) **7**:96
"the missyun" (Bissett) **14**:24, 34
"Míster no!" (Guillen) **23**:126
"Mithridates" (Emerson) **18**:71
"Mito" ("Myth") (Pavese) **13**:210, 228-29
Mock Beggar Hall (Graves) **6**:127-28
"Mock Confessional" (Ferlinghetti) **1**:187
"Mock Orange" (Gluck) **16**:145, 164
Mockingbird, Wish Me Luck (Bukowski) **18**:19
"Models" (Clampitt) **19**:99
"Modern Elegy of the Motif of Affectation" (Guillen)
　　See "Modern Elegy of the Motif of Affectation"
Modern Fable Poems (Nishiwaki)
　　See *Kindai no Guwa*
"Modern Love" (Keats) **1**:311
"Modern Poetry Is Prose (But It Is Saying Plenty)" (Ferlinghetti) **1**:182-83
"A Modern Sappho" (Arnold) **5**:12
"Modes of Being" (Levertov) **11**:197-98
"A Modest Proposal" (Hughes) **7**:118
"Modulations for a Solo Voice" (Levertov) **11**:209
A Moelna Elegy (Ekelof)
　　See *En Mölna-elegi*
"Moesta et Errabunda" (Baudelaire) **1**:70
Mohn und Gedächtnes (*Poppy and Memory*) (Celan) **10**:95
Moi, Tituba, sorciére, noire de Salem (*I, Tituba, Sorceress, Black Woman of Salem*) (Conde)
"Molitva" ("A Prayer") (Tsvetaeva) **14**:312
"Molitvy" (Lermontov) **18**:303
"Molly Means" (Walker) **20**:291-92
En Mölna-elegi ("Elegy"; *A Moelna Elegy*) (Ekeloef) **23**:50-8, 62-3, 77-87
Molodets (*The Champion*) (Tsvetaeva) **14**:313, 325-26
"The Moment Cleary" (Kursh) **15**:179
"Moment of Eternity" (MacDiarmid) **9**:193
"Moments of Glory" (Jeffers) **17**:141
"Mon Dieu m'a dit" (Verlaine) **2**:415
"Mon Enfance" (Hugo) **17**:75

"Monadnoc" (Emerson) **18**:71, 74, 102-3, 111
"Monarchs" (Olds) **22**:307
"Monax" ("The Monk") (Pushkin) **10**:407
"Monday: Roxana; or The Drawing-room" (Montagu) **16**:338, 348
La moneda de hierro (Borges) **22**:96-7
"Monet's 'Waterlilies'" (Hayden) **6**:183, 195
"Money Goes Upstream" (Snyder) **21**:300
"Money, Honey, Money" (Walker) **20**:294
"Mongo" (Lermontov) **18**:281
"La monja gitana" ("The Gypsy Nun") (Garcia Lorca) **3**:132
"La monja y el ruiseñor" (Dario) **15**:107-08
"The Monk" (Pushkin)
　　See "Monax"
"The Monkeys" (Moore) **4**:270
The Monkey's Cloak (Matsuo Basho)
　　See *Sarumino*
The Monkey's Raincoat (Matsuo Basho)
　　See *Sarumino*
"Monk's Tale" (Chaucer) **19**:13, 42, 45, 56, 63
"The Monk's Walk" (Dunbar) **5**:121, 137-38, 141
"Monna Innominata" (Rossetti) **7**:271, 275, 280-1
"Le monocle de mon oncle" (Stevens) **6**:292, 295, 303, 327
"Monody" (Zukofsky) **11**:368
"Monody on the Death of Chatterton" (Coleridge) **11**:49, 52
The Monogram (Elytis) **21**:123
"Monotone" (Sandburg) **2**:303
"Mont Blanc" (Shelley) **14**:206, 211-12, 217, 241
Montage of a Dream Deferred (Hughes) **1**:244-45, 247-48, 251, 253, 258, 261, 263, 265-68, 270
"The Montain Village of Bastundzhi" (Lermontov)
　　See "The Montain Village of Bastundzhi"
"A Month among Children" (Montale)
　　See "Un mese fra i bambini"
"The Months: A Pageant" (Rossetti) **7**:280
"Montparnasse" (Apollinaire) **7**:34
La Montre; or, The Lover's Watch (*The Lovers Watch*) (Behn) **13**:3
Une montre sentimentale (Nishiwaki) **15**:237
"The Monument" (Bishop) **3**:37, 41-3, 48-9, 72
"Monument" (Pushkin)
　　See "Pamjatnik"
"Monument Mountain" (Bryant) **20**:14, 29, 47
"Monument of Love" (Jimenez) **7**:184
"Mood" (Cullen) **20**:63, 75
"The moon" (Borges)
　　See "La luna"
"The Moon" (Carruth) **10**:71
Moon Across The Way
　　See *Luna de enfrente*
Moon across the Way (Borges)
　　See *Luna de enfrente*
"Moon and Insect Panorama: Love Poem" (Garcia Lorca) **3**:141
"The Moon and the Yew Tree" (Plath) **1**:390, 409
"The Moon Being the Number 19" (Wakoski) **15**:364
Moon Crossing Bridge (Gallagher) **9**:62-5
"The Moon Explodes in Autumn as a Milkweed Pod" (Wakoski) **15**:364

"The Moon Has a Complicated Geography" (Wakoski) **15**:364
"The Moon in Your Hands" (H. D.) **5**:275
"The Moon Is the Number Eighteen" (Olson) **19**:293-94, 321
"Moon Poems" (Lindsay) **23**:281
"Moon Tiger" (Levertov) **11**:177
"Moonlight" (Apollinaire)
　　See "Clair de lune"
"Moonlight" (Verlaine)
　　See "Clair de lune"
"Moonlight and Jellyfish" (Hagiwara Sakutaro) **18**:168
"Moonlight Night" (Tu Fu) **9**:321
"Moonlight Night: Carmel" (Hughes) **1**:240
"Moonrise" (Plath) **1**:406
"Moonrise" (Sappho) **5**:416
"Moon-Set" (Carruth) **10**:85
"Moonset Glouster" (Olson) **19**:322-23
"Moonstruck" (MacDiarmid) **9**:160
The Moor of Peter the Great (Pushkin)
　　See *Arap Petra Velikogo*
"Moortown" (Hughes) **7**:162
Moortown (Hughes) **7**:157-58, 162-63, 165, 171
"The Moose" (Bishop) **3**:58-60, 73, 75
"The Moose Wallow" (Hayden) **6**:194-95
Moral Tales (Laforgue)
　　See *Moralités légendaires*
"Morale" (Gautier) **18**:158
Moralités légendaires (*Moral Tales*; *Six Moral Tales from Jules Laforgue*) (Laforgue) **14**:70
"Morality" (Arnold) **5**:42
"Un morceau en forme de poire" (Wakoski) **15**:372
"More" (Stein) **18**:319, 330
"More Clues" (Rukeyser) **12**:225
"More Foreign Cities" (Tomlinson) **17**:318
More Poems (Housman) **2**:167, 171-74, 176, 182-83, 188
More Poems, 1961 (Graves) **6**:154-56
More Poems to Solve (Swenson) **14**:276
"More Than a Fool's Song" (Cullen) **20**:57
"Mori no michi" (" Forest Path") (Ishikawa) **10**:213
"Mori no omoide" ("Memories of the Forest") (Ishikawa) **10**:212-13
"Moriturus" (Millay) **6**:236
"Morning" (Gluck) **16**:152
"Morning" (Wheatley)
　　See "An Hymn to the Morning"
"Morning" (Williams) **7**:352
"Morning After" (Hughes) **1**:256
"The Morning Baking" (Forche) **10**:142
"The Morning Bell" (Ishikawa)
　　See "Akatsuki no kane"
"Morning Exercises" (Cassian) **17**:11
"Morning Express" (Sassoon) **12**:275
"A Morning Imagination of Russia" (Williams) **7**:350
"Morning, Noon, and Night" (Page) **12**:173
"A Morning Ride" (Kipling) **3**:194
"Morning Song" (Plath) **1**:390
Morning Songs (Tagore)
　　See *Prabhat sangit*
"The Morning Star" (Pavese)
　　See "Lo steddazzu"
"Morning, the Horizon" (Ortiz) **17**:245
"Morning-Land" (Sassoon) **12**:240
"Mors" (Hugo) **17**:83
"Morskaya tsarevna" (Lermontov) **18**:292
"La Mort dans la vie" (Gautier) **18**:131, 155

Title Index

Title Index

"Three Meditations" (Levertov) **11**:169

"Three Modes of History and Culture" (Baraka) **4**:16

"Three Moments in Paris" (Loy) **16**:312, 327-28

"Three Movements and a Coda" (Baraka) **4**:9, 19, 24

"Three Nuns" (Rossetti) **7**:277

"Three old men" (Illyes)
  See "Harom oreg"

"Three Palm-Trees" (Lermontov) **18**:268, 293
  See "Tri palmy"

Three Poems under a Flag of Convenience (Elytis) **21**:131

"Three Postcards from the Monastery" (Merton) **10**:332

"Three Songs" (Crane) **3**:106

The Three Taverns (Robinson) **1**:465-66, 468

"Three Things" (Yeats) **20**:328

"Three Times in Love" (Graves) **6**:172

"Three Times the Truth" (Elytis) **21**:123

"Three Travellers Watch a Sunrise" (Stevens) **6**:295

"Three United States Sonnets" (Cummings) **5**:94

"Three White Vases" (Swenson) **14**:273

"Threes" (Atwood) **8**:21

"Three-year-old" (Tagore)
  See "Tritiya"

"Threnody" (Emerson) **18**:69, 81, 84, 86, 90, 102-3, 112-3

"Threnody for a Brown Girl" (Cullen) **20**:57-58, 62, 66

Thrones, 96-109 de los cantares (Pound) **4**:337-38, 352, 353, 357

"Through Corralitos under Rolls of Cloud" (Rich) **5**:401

"Through Nightmare" (Graves) **6**:137, 173

"Through the Looking Glass" (Ferlinghetti) **1**:173

"Through the Smoke Hole" (Snyder) **21**:292

"Throughout Our Lands" (Milosz) **8**:187, 194, 214

"Throw Away Thy Rod" ("Discipline") (Herbert) **4**:103, 121

A Throw of the Dice Never Will Abolish Chance (Mallarme)
  See *Un coup de dés jamais n'abolira le hasard*

A Throw of the Dice Will Never Abolish Chance (Mallarme)
  See *Un coup de dés jamais n'abolira le hasard*

"Thrushes" (Hughes) **7**:119, 169

"Thrushes" (Sassoon) **12**:253

"Thrust and Riposte" (Montale)
  See "Botta e riposta"

"Thunder Can Break" (Okigbo)
  See "Come Thunder"

"Thunder in Tuscany" (Tomlinson) **17**:349-50

"Thunder, Momentarily Instantaneous" (Pasternak) **6**:251

"A Thunder-Storm" (Dickinson) **1**:79

"The Thunderstorm" (Trakl)
  See "Das Gewitter"

"Thursday" (Millay) **6**:208, 211

"Thursday: The Bassette Table: Smilinda, Cardelia" (Montagu) **16**:338, 349

"Thurso's Landing" (Jeffers) **17**:141-42

Thurso's Landing, and Other Poems (Jeffers) **17**:122, 124-25, 135, 142

"Thyrsis" (Arnold) **5**:7-8, 18-19, 21, 23-4, 33, 36, 45, 47, 52, 55-6

Ti Jean l'horizon (*Between Two Worlds*) (Schwarz-Bart)

"The Tide at Long Point" (Swenson) **14**:247, 249

"Tierra de azules montañas" (Guillen) **23**:125

"Tierra en la sierra" (Guillen) **23**:127

"Tierra en la sierra y en el llano" (Guillen) **23**:127

"La tierra se llama Juan" ("The Earth is Called Juan") (Neruda) **4**:294

"The Tiger" (Blake)
  See "The Tyger"

"Till de folkhemske" (Ekeloef) **23**:76

"Tilly" (Joyce) **22**:

"Tilting Sail" (Hass) **16**:251

"Timbuctoo" (Tennyson) **6**:358, 389, 407-08, 413, 415-18

"Time Does Not Bring Relief" (Millay) **6**:205

"Time Goes By" (Pavese)
  See "Il tempo passa"

"Time Is the Mercy of Eternity" (Rexroth) **20**:181, 208-09, 216-18

"Time Lapse with Tulips" (Gallagher) **9**:37

"Time of Disturbance" (Jeffers) **17**:141

"Time Spirals" (Rexroth) **20**:195, 217-18

"A Time to Dance" (Day Lewis) **11**:126

A Time to Dance and Other Poems (Day Lewis) **11**:126-27, 129

"Time to Kill in Gallup" (Ortiz) **17**:240

"Times at Bellosguardo" (Montale) **13**:147, 152

"Time's Dedication" ("Dedication in Time") (Schwartz) **8**:305, 307, 314

Time's Laughingstocks and Other Verses (Hardy) **8**:93, 123

"Times Passes" (Pavese)
  See "Il tempo passa"

"Time's Revenges" (Browning) **2**:33

"Times Square Water Music" (Clampitt) **19**:81, 88

"The Times Table" (Frost) **1**:205

"Time-Travel" (Olds) **22**:322

"Tin Wedding Whistle" (Nash) **21**:268

"Tinder" (Heaney) **18**:202

"Tintern Abbey" (Wordsworth)
  See "Lines Composed a Few Miles Above Tintern Abbey"

"Tiresias" (Tennyson) **6**:361

Tiriel (Blake) **12**:61

"Tirzey Potter" (Masters) **1**:338

"'Tis April and the morning love" (Clare) **23**:23

"Tishina" ("Stillness") (Pasternak) **6**:286

"Tithonus" (Tennyson) **6**:366, 411

"Title Divine Is Mine the Wife without the Sign" (Dickinson) **1**:93

"Titmouse" (Emerson) **18**:79, 103-4, 113

"To—" (Owen) **19**:352

"To— — —" (Poe) **1**:436, 445

"To a Babe Smiling in Her Sleep" (Harper) **21**:197

"To a Book" (Wylie) **23**:303

"To a Brown Boy" (Cullen) **20**:52, 62

"To a Brown Girl" (Cullen) **20**:52, 62

"To a Captious Critic" (Dunbar) **5**:125, 127, 135

"To a Child Dancing in the Wind" (Yeats) **20**:338

"To a Clergyman on the Death of His Lady" (Wheatley) **3**:357

"To a Common Prostitute" (Whitman) **3**:416

"To a Contemporary Bunkshooter" (Sandburg) **2**:317, 330

"To a Contemporary Bunk-Shooter" (Sandburg) **2**:317, 330

"to a dark moses" (Clifton) **17**:34

"To a Dreamer" (Pushkin) **10**:407

"To a Fellow Scribbler" (Finch) **21**:168

"To a Fish Head Found on the Beach Near Malaga" (Levine) **22**:215

"To a Friend" (Arnold) **5**:12, 49

"To a Friend" (Herrick) **9**:90

"To a Friend" (Yeats) **20**:321

"To a Friend and Fellow-Poet" (MacDiarmid) **9**:183-84

"To a Friend Whose Work Has Come to Triumph" (Sexton) **2**:370

"To a Fringed Gentian" (Bryant) **20**:12, 45

"To a Gentleman on His Voyage to Great Britain for the Recovery of His Health" (Wheatley) **3**:358

"To a Gipsy Child by the Sea-shore" (Arnold) **5**:38, 49-50

"To a Giraffe" (Moore) **4**:242-43

"To a Highland Girl" (Wordsworth) **4**:404

"To a Husband" (Lowell) **13**:74

"To a Jealous Cat" (Sanchez) **9**:223, 232

"To a Lady and Her Children, On the Death of Her Son and Their Brother" (Wheatley) **3**:363

"To a Lady on Her Remarkable Preservation in an Hurricane in North Carolina" (Wheatley) **3**:354

"To a Lady on the Death of Three Relations" (Wheatley) **3**:343, 348

"To a Lady's Countenance" (Wylie) **23**:321

"To a Louse, on Seeing One on a Lady's Bonnet at Church" ("Address to a Louse") (Burns) **6**:65, 79

"To a lovely woman" (Lermontov) **18**:303

"To a Mountain Daisy, on Turning One Down with the Plough in April, 1786" (Burns) **6**:50, 74

"To a Mouse, on Turning Her Up in Her Nest with the Plough, November, 1785" (Burns) **6**:50, 65, 74, 80, 96

"To a Passing Woman" (Baudelaire)
  See "A une passante"

"To a Poet" (Jimenez) **7**:183

"To a Poet" (McKay) **2**:206

"To a Poor Old Woman" (Williams) **7**:390, 399

"To a Portrait" (Lermontov) **18**:297

"To a Portrait in a Gallery" (Page) **12**:168

"To a Republican Friend" (Arnold) **5**:49

"To a Shade" (Yeats) **20**:348

"To a Solitary Disciple" (Williams) **7**:357, 378

"To a Strategist" (Moore) **4**:266

"To a Waterfowl" (Bryant) **20**:5-6, 14, 18, 35, 42

"To a Winter Squirrel" (Brooks) **7**:82

"To a Wreath of Snow" (Bronte) **8**:67, 73

"To a Young Actress" (Pushkin) **10**:407

"To A Young Friend" (Burns)
  See "Epistle to a Young Friend"

"To a Young Girl" (Millay) **6**:217

"To a Young Girl" (Yeats) **20**:330

"To Adversity" (Gray)
  See "Ode to Adversity"

"To Alchymists" (Jonson) **17**:197

"To Alexander" (Pushkin)
  See "Aleksandru"

"To Alexis, in Answer to His Poem against Fruition" (Behn) **13**:26

"To All Brothers" (Sanchez) 9:224, 232
"To All Brothers: From All Sisters" (Sanchez) 9:221
"To All Gentleness" (Williams) 7:354
"To All Sisters" (Sanchez) 9:224, 231-32
"To Amintas, upon Reading the Lives of Some of the Romans" (Behn) 13:32
"To an Ancient" (Frost) 1:200
"To an Athlete Dying Young" (Housman) 2:180, 183, 185, 191-94, 198, 201
"To an Old Philosopher in Rome" (Stevens) 6:304, 324, 328
"To Another Housewife" (Wright) 14:356
"To Anthea" (Herrick) 9:145
"To Anthea Lying in Bed" (Herrick) 9:137
"To Anthea, Who May Command Him Any Thing" (Herrick) 9:102
"To Any Dead Officer Who Left School for the Army in 1914" (Sassoon) 12:268, 277
"To Aphrodite, with a Talisman" (Wylie) 23:320, 324
"To Autumn" (Gluck) 16:142, 149
"To Autumn" (Keats) 1:298-302, 314-15
"To Autumn" (Keats)
  See "Ode to Autumn"
"To Bargain Toboggan To-Woo!" (Nash) 21:265
"To Be a Jew in the Twentieth Century" (Rukeyser) 12:234
"To Be Carved on a Stone at Thoor Ballylee" (Yeats) 20:346, 348
"To Be in Love" (Brooks) 7:81-2
"To Be Liked by You Would Be a Calamity" (Moore) 4:250
"To Be Quicker for Black Political Prisoners" (Madhubuti) 5:330, 346
"To Be Sung on the Water" (Bogan) 12:90, 124
To Bedlam and Part Way Back (Sexton) 2:345-47, 349-50, 353, 355, 357-58, 360, 363, 367
"To Bennie" (McKay) 2:221
"To Blk/Record/Buyers" (Sanchez) 9:209, 217
"To Blossoms" (Herrick) 9:145
"To Bring the Dead to Life" (Graves) 6:143
"To Camden" (Jonson)
  See "To Camden"
"To Carl Sandburg" (Lowell) 13:67
"To Carry the Child" (Smith) 12:320
"To Cedars" (Herrick) 9:91
"To Celia" (Jonson) 17:170, 196
"To Certain Critics" (Cullen) 20:66, 83
"To Chaadaev" (Pushkin)
  See "Chaadayevu"
"To Change in a Good Way" (Ortiz) 17:234
"To Charis" (Jonson)
  See "To Charis"
To . . . Christopher Duke of Albemarle (Behn) 13:8
"To Chuck" (Sanchez) 9:224, 233
To Circumjack Cencrastus (MacDiarmid) 9:151-53, 158, 171, 175-77, 197
"To Clarendon Hills and H.A.H." (McKay) 2:222
"To Claudia Homonoea" (Wylie) 23:324
"To Cole, the Painter, Departing For Europe" (Bryant) 20:34, 44-5
"To Columbus" (Dario)
  See "A Colón"
"To Conclude" (Montale) 13:146
"To Confirm a Thing" (Swenson) 14:247,

252, 278
"To Constantia Singing" (Shelley) 14:177
"To Countess Rostopchina" (Lermontov) 18:297
"To Daddy" (Lowell) 3:226
"To Daffadills" ("Fair Daffodils") (Herrick) 9:101
"To Damon. To Inquire of Him If He Cou'd Tell Me by the Style, Who Writ Me a Copy of Verses That Came to Me in an Unknown Hand" (Behn) 13:30-1
"To Daphnie and Virginia" (Williams) 7:360, 363, 392
"To Dean Swift" (Swift) 9:295
"To Death" (Finch) 21:179-80
"To Deism" (Wheatley) 3:354
"To Delmore Schwartz" (Lowell) 3:219, 222
"To Desire" (Behn) 13:24
"To Dianeme" (Herrick) 9:145
"To Dispel My Grief" (Tu Fu) 9:326
"To *** Do not think I deserve regret" (Lermontov) 18:301, 304
"To Doctor Alabaster" (Herrick) 9:142
"To Don at Salaam" (Brooks) 7:84, 92
To Dream of A Butterfly (Hagiwara Sakutaro)
  See *To Dream of A Butterfly*
"To Earthward" (Frost) 1:197
"To Electra" (Herrick) 9:94
"To Elizabeth Ward Perkins" (Lowell) 13:90
"To Elsie" (Williams) 7:382, 384, 411
"To E.M.E." (McKay) 2:223
"To Endymion" (Cullen) 20:67, 86
"To Enemies" (Bely) 11:24
"To Enter That Rhythm Where the Self is Lost" (Rukeyser) 12:227
"To Eros" (Owen) 19:352
"To Ethelinda" ("Ethelinda") (Smart) 13:331, 347
"To Eve Man's Dream of Wifehood As Described by Milton" (Lindsay) 23:281
"To Evoke Posterity" (Graves) 6:143, 152
"To Fausta" (Arnold) 5:49
"To Find God" (Herrick) 9:109
"To Fine Lady Would-bee" (Jonson) 17:197
"To Flowers" (Herrick) 9:102
"To Flush My Dog" (Browning) 6:6-7
"To Ford Madox Ford in Heaven" (Williams) 7:370
"To France" (Cullen) 20:66
"To Galich" (Pushkin) 10:407
"To George Sand: A Recognition" (Browning) 6:26
"To Gerhardt" (Olson) 19:307
"To God" (Herrick) 9:94-5, 109, 118
"To God, His Good Will" (Herrick) 9:118
"To God, on His Sicknesse" (Herrick) 9:144
"To Gurdjieff Dying" (Toomer) 7:338
"To Hafiz of Shiraz" (Wright) 14:356, 366
"To Have Done Nothing" (Williams) 7:383, 389, 410
"To Heaven" (Jonson)
  See "To Heaven"
"To Helen" (Poe) 1:420, 424, 426, 428, 431, 438-39, 441, 443-45, 447
"To Help" (Stein) 18:313
"To Her" (Pushkin) 10:408-09
"To Her Father with Some Verses" (Bradstreet) 10:27, 35
"To Her Most Honoured Father Thomas Dudley" (Bradstreet) 10:2
"To His Book" (Herrick) 9:106, 109
"To His Closet-Gods" (Herrick) 9:88

"To His Coy Mistress" ("The Coy Mistress") (Marvell) 10:259, 265, 269, 271, 273-74, 277-79, 281-82, 290-94, 297, 304, 310-11, 313
"To His Excellency General George Washington" (Wheatley) 3:337, 341
"To His Father" (Jeffers) 17:131
"To His Friend on the Untuneable Times" (Herrick) 9:89
"To His Girles" (Herrick) 9:107
"To His Girles Who Would Have Him Sportfull" (Herrick) 9:107
"To His Honor the Lieutenant Governor on the Death of His Lady" (Wheatley) 3:340
"To His Mistresses" (Herrick) 9:128, 146
"To His Paternall Countrey" (Herrick) 9:108
"To His Savior, a Child; a Present, by a Child" (Herrick) 9:120, 143
"To His Saviour, the New Yeers Gift" (Herrick) 9:95
"To His Saviours Sepulcher: His Devotion" (Herrick) 9:122
"To His Watch" (Hopkins) 15:167
"To Homer" (Keats) 1:279, 314
"To Imagination" (Bronte) 8:54
"To Imagination" (Wheatley)
  See "On Imagination"
"To Insure Survival" (Ortiz) 17:225
"To Ireland in the Coming Times" (Yeats) 20:324, 347, 353
"To Ivor Gurney" (Tomlinson) 17:354-55
"to joan" (Clifton) 17:18
"To John Goldie, August 1785" (Burns) 6:70, 78
"To John Keats, Poet: At Spring Time" (Cullen) 20:62, 66, 86
"To Jos: Lo: Bishop of Exeter" (Herrick) 9:146
"To Joseph Sadzik" (Milosz)
  See "Do Jozefa Sadzika"
"To Juan at the Winter Solstice" (Graves) 6:137, 144, 146, 168, 171-72
"To Julia" (Herrick) 9:128, 143
"To Julia, in Her Dawne, or Day-breake" (Herrick) 9:143
"To Julia, the Flaminica Dialis, or Queen-Priest" (Herrick) 9:143
"To . . . K. Charles" (Jonson)
  See "To . . . K. Charles"
"To K. Charles . . . 1629" (Jonson)
  See "To K. Charles . . . 1629"
"To Keorapetse Kgositsile (Willie)" ("Willie") (Brooks) 7:83, 92, 105
"To Kevin O'Leary Wherever He Is" (Levertov) 11:189
"To King James"
  See "To King James"
"To Lady Crew, upon the Death of Her Child" (Herrick)
  See "To the Lady Crew, upon the Death of Her Child"
"To Laurels" (Herrick) 9:127
"To Licinius" (Pushkin)
  See "K Liciniju"
"To Live Merrily, and to Trust to Good Verses" (Herrick) 9:96, 103-05, 107, 114
"To Lord Byron" (Keats) 1:313
"To Lord Harley, on His Marriage" (Swift) 9:254
"To Lose the Earth" (Sexton) 2:363
"To Louise" (Dunbar) 5:121
"To Love" (Aleixandre) 15:19, 21
"To Lucia at Birth" (Graves) 6:137
"To Lucy, Countesse of Bedford, with Mr.

with the Moorhens") (Montale) **13**:112

"Voeu à Phebus" (Ronsard) **11**:256

"The Voice" (Arnold) **5**:49

"A Voice" (Atwood) **8**:14

"The Voice" (Hardy) **8**:88, 117-18, 135

"The Voice" (Levine) **22**:225

"The Voice" (Roethke) **15**:275

"Voice Arriving with the Coots" (Montale) **13**:146, 149

"The Voice as a Girl" (Snyder) **21**:289

"Voice Coming with the Moorhens" (Montale)
  See "Voce giunta con le folaghe"

"A Voice from a Chorus" (Blok) **21**:15

"Voice from the Tomb" (Smith) **12**:349

"The Voice of Rock" (Ginsberg) **4**:55

"The Voice of the Ancient Bard" (Blake) **12**:7

Voice of the Forest (Tagore)
  See *Banabani*

"Voice of the Past" (Bely)
  See "Golos proshlogo"

"The Voice of the People" (Holderlin)
  See "Stimme des Volks"

"Voices about the Princess Anemone" (Smith) **12**:298, 348-49

"Voices from Kansas" (Kumin) **15**:215

"Voices under the Ground" (Ekeloef) **23**:71, 73, 75

"Voicy le temps, Hurault, qui joyeux nous convie" (Ronsard) **11**:250

"Void in Law" (Browning) **6**:28, 32

"Void Only" (Rexroth) **20**:221

"La Voix" ("The Preferred Voice") (Baudelaire) **1**:73

Les Voix intérieures (Hugo) **17**:42, 45, 52, 63, 74, 76, 80, 83, 91-92, 96-97

Volcano a Memoir of Hawai< grave>i (Hongo) **23**:204-206

"An vollen Büschelzweigen" (Goethe) **5**:247

"Vollmondnacht" (Goethe) **5**:247

"Vol'nost': Oda" ("Liberty"; "Ode to Freedom"; "Ode to Liberty") (Pushkin) **10**:408-09

Volshebny fonar (*The Magic Lantern*) (Tsvetaeva) **14**:318

Volume Two (Villa) **22**:347, 353

"Voluntaries" (Emerson) **18**:76-77, 88, 113

"La volupté" (Baudelaire) **1**:71

"Von diesen Stauden" (Celan) **10**:122

Von Schwelle zu Schwelle (*From Threshold to Threshold*) (Celan) **10**:95, 121

"Vooruzhennyi zren'em uzkikh os" ("Armed with the vision of narrow wasps") (Mandelstam) **14**:154

"Voracities and Verities Sometimes Are Interacting" (Moore) **4**:261

"Vorobyev Hills" (Pasternak) **6**:251-54

Voronezh Notebooks (Mandelstam) **14**:123, 149-50

"Vorstadt im Föhn" (Trakl) **20**:261

"Vospominanie v Tsarskom Sele" (*Recollections of Tsarskoe-Selo*; "Remembrance in Tsarskoe Selo"; "Reminiscences at Tsarskoe Selo") (Pushkin) **10**:409, 421

"Vostok pobledneuskii, vostok onemesvshii" ("The East that is Now Pale, the East that is Now Silent") (Bely) **11**:32

"A Vow" (Ginsberg) **4**:56

"The Vow" (Lowell) **13**:86-7

"Vowels 2" (Baraka) **4**:24

"vowl man" (Bissett) **14**:15

"Voy hasta Uján" (Guillen) **23**:128

"Le voyage" (Baudelaire) **1**:50, 60, 70, 73-4

"The Voyage" (Jonson) **17**:207

"Le voyage à Cythère" ("Voyage to Cythera") (Baudelaire) **1**:65, 72-3

"Le Voyage de Tours, ou les amoureus Thoinet et Perrot" (Ronsard) **11**:260-61, 264

"The Voyage of Maeldune" (Tennyson) **6**:359, 369

"Voyage to Cythera" (Baudelaire)
  See "Le voyage à Cythère"

Voyage to the Island of Love (Behn)
  See *Poems upon Several Occasions, with a Voyage to the Island of Love*

"Voyagers" (Page) **12**:199

"Voyages" (Clampitt) **19**:91

"Voyages" (Crane) **3**:90, 97, 104

Voyages: A Homage to John Keats (Clampitt) **19**:87

"Voyages II" (Crane) **3**:80, 83, 96, 102

"Voyages III" (Crane) **3**:83

"Voyages IV" (Crane) **3**:83

"Voyages V" (Crane) **3**:83

"Le voyageur" ("The Traveler") (Apollinaire) **7**:48

"Les Voyelles" (Rimbaud) **3**:249, 268, 274

"Vozdushnyi korabl" (Lermontov) **18**:291

Vozmezdie (*Retaliation*; *Retribution*) (Blok) **21**:10, 17, 25-6, 39, 44

Vozvrat: Tretiia simfoniia (*The Return*; *The Third Symphony*) (Bely) **11**:3, 8-9, 14-17, 22

"Le vrai de la chose" (Laforgue) **14**:76

"Vriksha-ropan" ("Tree Planting") (Tagore) **8**:416

"Vriksha-vandana" ("Homage to the Tree") (Tagore) **8**:416

Vrindaban (*I Am in the Unstable Hour*) (Paz) **1**:361-63

"Vse Povtoryayv pervyi stikh" ("I Keep repeating the first line") (Tsvetaeva) **14**:329

"Vstrecha" ("A Meeting") (Pasternak) **6**:280

"Vsye eto bylo bylo bylo" (Blok) **21**:15

Vtoraia simfoniia: Dramaticheskaia (*The Second Symphony*; *Simfonija (2-aja)*) (Bely) **11**:3-4, 8-11, 13-16, 21, 27, 33

Vtoraya kniga (*A Second Book*; *Tristia*) (Mandelstam) **14**:106, 113-18, 121-22, 129, 135, 141, 150, 153, 155

"Vue" (Valery) **9**:392

"Vuelta" ("Return") (Paz) **1**:370-72, 374

Vuelta (*Return*) (Paz) **1**:370-71, 374, 376

"La vuelta a America" (Cardenal) **22**:110

"La vuelta a Buenos Aires" (Borges) **22**:94

"Vuelta de paseo" ("Back from a Walk") (Garcia Lorca) **3**:139

VV (Cummings)
  See *ViVa*

"Vykhozhu odin ja na dorogu" (Lermontov) **18**:303

Vyorsty I (*Mileposts I*; *Versts*; *Versty I*) (Tsvetaeva) **14**:310, 318

Vyorsty II (*Mileposts II*; *Versty II*) (Tsvetaeva) **14**:322

"Vysokaya bolesn" ("The High Malady") (Pasternak) **6**:265

"Vystrel" ("The Shot") (Pushkin) **10**:414

"W. S. Landor" (Moore) **4**:242, 259

"Wadin' in de Crick" (Dunbar) **5**:144

"Wading at Wellfleet" (Bishop) **3**:49, 57

"Waga Uta" ("My Songs") (Yosano Akiko) **11**:302, 306

"The Wagoner" (Pavese) **13**:205

"Waialua" (Song)
  See "Easter: Wahiawa, 1959"

"The Waiting" (Olds) **22**:330, 332, 334, 337, 340

"Waiting" (Wright) **14**:341

"Waiting by the Gate" (Bryant) **20**:8

"Waiting for Breakfast" (Larkin) **21**:226-27

"Waiting for *It*" (Swenson) **14**:263

Waiting for the King of Spain (Wakoski) **15**:366

"The Waiting Head" (Sexton) **2**:350

"Waiting Inland" (Kumin) **15**:208

"Wake-Up Niggers" (Madhubuti) **5**:329, 338

"The Waking" (Roethke) **15**:278, 286

"Waking an Angel" (Levine) **22**:213

"Waking in the Blue" (Lowell) **3**:209, 221

"Waking in the Dark" (Rich) **5**:370, 392, 395

The Waking: Poems, 1933-1953 (Roethke) **15**:249, 261, 263, 282, 284, 309

"Waking this Morning" (Rukeyser) **12**:230

"Waldeinsamkeit" (Emerson) **18**:76, 88

"Wales Visitation" (Ginsberg) **4**:74, 93-4

"The Walk" (Hardy) **8**:93

"A Walk in Late Summer" (Roethke) **15**:274

"A Walk with Tom Jefferson" (Levine) **22**:225-27

"Walking Down Park" (Giovanni) **19**:140-41, 143

"Walking in Paris" (Sexton) **2**:363

"Walking in the Blue" (Sexton) **2**:350

"The Walking Man of Rodin" (Sandburg) **2**:334

"Walking on the Prayerstick" (Rose) **13**:233

"The Wall" (Brooks) **7**:82

"The Wall" (Montale) **13**:148

"Walls" (Hughes) **7**:149

The Walls Do Not Fall (H. D.) **5**:272, 274-76, 293-95, 307, 309, 312, 314-15

"The Walrus and the Carpenter" (Carroll) **18**:51-52

"Walt Whitman" (Whitman) **3**:414

"Walter Bradford" (Brooks) **7**:92

"The Waltz" (Aleixandre) **15**:8, 14

"The Waltzer in the House" (Kunitz) **19**:155

"The Wanderer" (Pushkin) **10**:409

"The Wanderer" (Smith) **12**:326, 349-50, 354

"The Wanderer" (Williams) **7**:374, 382, 394

"The Wanderer's Song" (Hagiwara Sakutaro) **18**:183
  See "Hyohakusha no uta"

"The Wandering Jew" (Robinson) **1**:487

"The Wanderings of Cain" (Coleridge) **11**:89, 91

"The Wanderings of Oisin" (Yeats) **20**:353

The Wanderings of Oisin, and Other Poems (Yeats) **20**:298, 302, 344, 346

"Wanderschaft" (Trakl) **20**:241

Wang Stream Collection (Wang Wei) **18**:367, 370, 385

"Wang-ch`uan Garland" (Wang Wei) **18**:374

"The Want" (Olds) **22**:321, 325-26, 340

"Wanting to Die" (Sexton) **2**:364

"Wants" (Larkin) **21**:227, 242, 252

"War" (Levine) **22**:218

"The War Against the Trees" (Kunitz) **19**:175

War All the Time: Poems, 1981-1984 (Bukowski) **18**:15, 18-19

"War Pictures" (Lowell) **13**:76

War Trilogy (H. D.)
  See *Trilogy*

"The Ward" (Rukeyser) **12**:225

"Waring" (Browning) **2**:26

"A Warm Place to Shit" (Bissett) **14**:10

"Warning" (Hughes) **1**:252

"Warning to Children" (Graves) **6**:139, 143-44, 150

"A Warning to Those Who Live on Moun-

what poetiks (Bissett) **14**:15
"What Shall I Give My Children?" (Brooks) **7**:76
"What? So Soon" (Hughes) **1**:266
"What Stillness Round a God" (Rilke) **2**:275
"What the Bird with the Human Head Knew" (Sexton) **2**:372
"What the Light Was Like" (Clampitt) **19**:102
What the Light Was Like (Clampitt) **19**:85-7, 90-1, 93
"What the Moon Saw" (Lindsay) **23**:268
"What the Rattlesnake Said" (Lindsay) **23**:286
"What the Women Said" (Bogan) **12**:110
"What Then?" (Yeats) **20**:342
"What This Mode of Motion Said" (Ammons) **16**:20
"What Virginia Said" (Tomlinson) **17**:353
"What We Come To Know" (Ortiz) **17**:246
"what we dew if thrs anything" (Bissett) **14**:33
"What Were They Like?" (Levertov) **11**:176
What Work Is (Levine) **22**:220-21, 227-28, 231-32
"What Would Tennessee Williams Have Said" (Wakoski) **15**:368
"Whatever Happened?" (Larkin) **21**:235-36
"Whatever You Say Say Nothing" (Heaney) **18**:189, 205
"Whatever You Wish, Lord" (Jimenez) **7**:184
"WHATS HAPPNING OZONE CUM BACK WE STILL LOV YU" (Bissett) **14**:32
"What's Meant by Here" (Snyder) **21**:300
What's O'Clock (Lowell) **13**:66, 76, 84-5, 91, 93-4, 97-8
"What's That" (Sexton) **2**:359
"Whe' Fe Do?" (McKay) **2**:222-23
"Wheat-in-the-Ear" (Lowell) **13**:96
"The Wheel" (Hayden) **6**:194-95
"The Wheel of Being II" (Carruth) **10**:71
"The Wheel Revolves" (Rexroth) **20**:195
"Wheesht, Wheesht, My Foolish Heart" (MacDiarmid) **9**:156, 160
"When All My Five and Country Senses See" (Thomas) **2**:392
"When Black Is a Color Because It Follows a Grey Day" (Wakoski) **15**:348
"When Coldness Wraps This Suffering Clay" (Byron) **16**:89
"When de Co'n Pone's Hot" (Dunbar) **5**:117, 122
"When Death Came April Twelve 1945" (Sandburg) **2**:333
"When First I Saw" (Burns) **6**:78
"When from Afar" (Holderlin) **4**:174, 178
"When God Lets My Body Be" (Cummings) **5**:99
"When Guilford Good" (Burns) **6**:78
"When Hair Falls Off and Eyes Blur and" (Cummings) **5**:105
"When He Would Have His Verses Read" (Herrick) **9**:87, 96, 102, 109, 139, 145
"When I Buy Pictures" (Moore) **4**:251, 266
"When I consider how my light is spent" (Milton)
    See "When I consider how my light is spent"
"When I Die" (Brooks) **7**:68
"When I Die" (Giovanni) **19**:113
"When I Have Fears That I May Cease to Be" (Keats) **1**:314
"When I Nap" (Giovanni) **19**:112
"When I Roved a Young Highlander" (Byron) **16**:86
"When I Set Out for Lyonesse" (Hardy) **8**:92, 112, 115

"When I Was One-and-Twenty" (Housman) **2**:161, 192
"When I Watch the Living Meet" (Housman) **2**:184
"When in the Gloomiest of Capitals" (Akhmatova)
    See "Kogda v mrachneyshey iz stolits"
"When Jemmy First Began to Love" (Behn)
    See "Song to a Scotish Tune (When Jemmy First Began to Love)"
"When Lilacs Last in the Dooryard Bloom'd" (Whitman) **3**:378, 382, 396-97, 410, 418-19, 422
"When Lilacs Last in the Dooryard Bloomed" (Whitman) **3**:378, 382, 396-97, 410, 418-19, 422
"When Malindy Sings" (Dunbar) **5**:117, 119-21, 134, 146
"When Mrs. Martin's Booker T." (Brooks) **7**:67, 69
"When Once the Twilight Locks No Longer" (Thomas) **2**:402
"When Rain Whom Fear" (Cummings) **5**:105
"When Serpents bargain for the Right to Squirm" (Cummings) **5**:90, 107
"When Sir Beelzebub" (Sitwell) **3**:303
"When Smoke Stood Up from Ludlow" (Housman) **2**:184
"When Summer's End Is Nighing" (Housman) **2**:165, 181
"When the Dead Ask My Father about Me" (Olds) **22**:323, 326
"When the Lamp Is Shattered" (Shelley) **14**:177, 207
"When the Light Falls" (Kunitz) **19**:151, 155
"When the Shy Star" (Joyce)
    See "IV"
When the Skies Clear (Pasternak)
    See *Kogda razglyaetsya*
"When the Yellowing Fields Billow" (Lermontov) **18**:281
"When They Have Lost" (Day Lewis) **11**:144
"When Under the Icy Eaves" (Masters) **1**:328
"When Unto Nights of Autumn Do Complain" (Cummings) **5**:104
"When We with Sappho" (Rexroth) **20**:203, 216
"When We'll Worship Jesus" (Baraka) **4**:29, 39
"When You Are Old" (Yeats) **20**:355
"When You Lie Down, the Sea Stands Up" (Swenson) **14**:261
"When You Speak to Me" (Gallagher) **9**:36
"When You've Forgotten Sunday" (Brooks) **7**:53, 68
"Where Are the War Poets?" (Day Lewis) **11**:131
"Where can I go, now it's January?" (Mandelstam)
    See "Kuda mne det'sia v etom Ianvare?"
"Where Is the Real Non-Resistant?" (Lindsay) **23**:281
"Where Knock Is Open Wide" (Roethke) **15**:251, 261, 272, 275-76, 278, 298, 300
"Where, O Where?" (Wylie) **23**:324
"Where Shall the Lover Rest" (Scott) **13**:304
"Where, Tall Girl, Is Your Gypsy Babe" (Akhmatova)
    See "Gde, vysokaya, tvoy tsyganyonok"
"Where the Hell Would Chopin Be?" (Bukowski) **18**:4
"Where the Picnic Was" (Hardy) **8**:136
"Where the Rainbow Ends" (Lowell) **3**:200,

207
"Where the Tennis Court Was" (Montale)
    See "Dov'era il tennis"
"Where There's a Will There's Velleity" (Nash) **21**:265
"Where They So Fondly Go" (Bukowski) **18**:5
"Where We Live Now" (Levine) **22**:214
"Where's Agnes?" (Browning) **6**:24
"Where's the Poker" (Smart) **13**:348
"Whether on Ida's Shady Brow" (Blake) **12**:11
"Which, Being Interpreted, Is as May Be, or, Otherwise" (Lowell) **13**:91
"While Drawing in a Churchyard" (Hardy) **8**:120-21
"While Sitting in the Tuileries and Facing the Slanting Sun" (Swenson) **14**:261, 285
"While the Record Plays" (Illyes) **16**:249, 251
"whilst waiting for" (Bissett) **14**:32
"Whip the World" (MacDiarmid) **9**:187
Whipperginny (Graves) **6**:127-28, 131
"The Whipping" (Hayden) **6**:194-96
"The Whirlwind" (Lindsay) **23**:281
"Whiskers, A Philosophical Ode" (Pushkin) **10**:407
"whispered to lucifer" (Clifton) **17**:30
"Whispers of Heavenly Death" (Whitman) **3**:378
"Whistle and I'll Come tae Ye, My Lad" (Burns)
    See "Whistle and I'll Come tae Ye, My Lad"
"Whistle and I'll Come tae Ye, My Lad" ("Whistle and I'll Come tae Ye, My Lad") (Burns) **6**:59
"The Whistle Cockade" (Burns) **6**:82
Whistles and Whistling (Ishikawa)
    See *Yobuko to kuchibue*
"Whistling Sam" (Dunbar) **5**:122, 146
"White and Green" (Lowell) **13**:60, 69
"White and Violet" (Jimenez) **7**:183
"White Arrow" (Toomer) **7**:336
White Buildings (Crane) **3**:81, 84, 87, 90
"The White City" (McKay) **2**:211
The White Doe of Rylstone; or, The Fate of the Nortons (Wordsworth) **4**:394, 402, 407
"White Dwarf" (Ammons) **16**:45
White Flock (Akhmatova)
    See *Belaya staya*
"White Horses" (Kipling) **3**:183
"The White House" (McKay) **2**:210, 221, 229
"White Lady" (Clifton) **17**:28
"The White Lilies" (Gluck) **16**:170-71
"The White Man's Burden" (Kipling) **3**:192
"White Night" (Wright) **14**:372
"The White Porch" (Song) **21**:331-32, 334, 338, 340-41, 350
"White Shoulders" (Sandburg) **2**:303
"White Shroud" (Ginsberg) **4**:86, 90
White Shroud (Ginsberg) **4**:86-7, 89-90
"The White Snake" (Sexton) **2**:365
"The White Thought" (Smith) **12**:292, 341, 354
"The White Troops" (Brooks) **7**:73
"THe White Van" (Tomlinson) **17**:333
"White Wines" (Stein) **18**:341
The White-Haired Revolver (Breton)
    See *Le revolver á cheveux blancs*
"The White-Tailed Hornet" (Frost) **1**:221
"The Whitsun Weddings" (Larkin) **21**:228, 230, 238-39, 255
The Whitsun Weddings (Larkin) **21**:224, 227-28, 230, 233, 235, 240, 244, 253, 255, 259

Title Index